MW01167011

COMPUTER CRIME
LAW

By

Orin S. Kerr
Associate Professor
George Washington University Law School

AMERICAN CASEBOOK SERIES®

Mat # 40098894

American Casebook Series and West Group are trademarks registered in the U.S. Patent and Trademark Office.
© 2006 Thomson/West
     610 Opperman Drive
     P.O. Box 64526
     St. Paul, MN 55164–0526
     1–800–328–9352
Printed in the United States of America

ISBN–13: 978–0–314–14400–3
ISBN–10: 0–314–14400–5

TEXT IS PRINTED ON 10% POST CONSUMER RECYCLED PAPER

To my father, the original Professor Kerr

*

Preface

This book is designed to fill a gap in the modern law school curriculum. Traditional course offerings in criminal law and procedure largely ignore computer crimes. This was understandable a few years ago, when computer crime law was an esoteric specialty. Today, however, computer crime law is emerging as an important area of criminal law practice. A growing number of prosecutors and defense attorneys find themselves working with legal questions unique to digital crimes. The existing curriculum does not cover these topics, except perhaps for brief mention in a "cyberlaw" survey course. This book attempts to correct that situation by offering comprehensive coverage of the new field, assembled together in one place for the first time.

The materials are organized around three questions. First, what conduct involving a computer is prohibited by the criminal law? Second, what legal rules govern the collection of digital evidence in criminal investigations? Third, what powers do state, national, and foreign governments have to investigate and prosecute computer crimes? The first question looks at the substantive law of computer crimes, and is addressed in Chapters 2, 3, and 4. The second question examines the law of criminal procedure for digital evidence, and is covered in Chapters 5 and 6. The third question considers the role of jurisdiction and sovereignty in a world of global online crime, and is addressed in Chapters 7 and 8.

Although the materials are intended primarily for classroom use, my hope is that they will reach a broader audience. First, the materials should be helpful to criminal law practitioners. Computer crime law lacks a treatise that summarizes the field and explains how the pieces fit together. In light of that, I have made special efforts to explain basic doctrine in a way that practitioners should find useful. The law remains complex and sometimes uncertain, and this book makes no effort to pretend otherwise. At the same time, I hope these materials will serve as a reference work for prosecutors and defense attorneys in need of a primer on existing law.

The book also should be a useful resource for scholars. Computer crime law is new and evolving, and many issues remain open. Surprisingly little has been written about the major issues in the field. My hope is that the framework introduced in this book will help encourage and direct future scholarly efforts. To that end, the extensive commentary in these materials attempts both to review existing scholarship and to ask important questions for scholars to answer.

The materials in this book are best suited for classroom use in a one-semester course offered to upper-level law students, either as a three-credit class or a two-credit seminar. I assume that readers have some experience with basic criminal law, such as a first-year law school survey course. On the other hand, I do not assume that readers are familiar with the law of criminal procedure. In addition, I assume that readers have no special background with computers. Students with advanced knowledge of computers or criminal procedure will have a slight advantage understanding a few concepts, but the advantages on the whole are modest. In any event, no such background is assumed or required.

This project began with materials assembled for a computer crime seminar in the Fall 2000 semester, and I have many people to thank for their help during the six-year road to publication. Mark Eckenwiler, Erica Hashimoto, Mike Levy, Paul Ohm, Rick Salgado, and Peter Winn provided feedback on drafts and chapters. GW Law students Noah Falk '05, Kemp Brinson '04, and Tejbir Singh '03 collected materials during in the early stages of the project. In the last year, a small army of GW Law students helped me with formatting, citechecking, and editing: David Luden (who did a great deal of the work), Melissa Colangelo, Mark Knights, Sharmili Hazra, David Kim, Jennifer Best, Adam Schwartz, Erika Ban, Adele Ho, Alejandra Perez, Merel Berling, Claire Ogilvie, and Matt Benz. Dean Fred Lawrence provided resources and welcome encouragement. Finally, I am particularily grateful to my former colleagues at the Computer Crime and Intellectual Property Section (CCIPS) of the United States Department of Justice. This book covers issues I first encountered as an attorney at CCIPS from 1998 to 2001, and I could not have written it without the benefit of many illuminating discussions at CCIPS during that period. I am especially indebted to my friend Mark Eckenwiler, who patiently answered countless questions when I was new to the field.

To improve the readability of the materials, I have taken the liberty of removing citations, deleting unrelated portions of opinions, and otherwise streamlining the cases without necessarily indicating that the original material has been altered. Readers in need of greater precision should always consult the original sources.

ORIN KERR
WASHINGTON, DC

September 2006

Acknowledgments

Excerpts from the following books and articles appear with the kind of permission of the copyright holders.

Aldrich, Richard W., How Do You Know You Are at War in the Information Age?, 22 Hous. J. Int'l L. 223 (2000). Copyright © 2000 by the Houston Journal of International Law. Reprinted by permission.

Bellia, Patricia L., Defending Cyberproperty, 79 N.Y.U. L. Rev. 2164 (2004). Copyright © 2004 by New York University Law Review. Reprinted by permission.

Bellia, Patricia L., Surveillance Law Through Cyberlaw's Lens, 72 Geo. Wash. L. Rev. 1375 (2004). Copyright © 2004 by The George Washington Law Review. Reprinted by permission.

Berg, Terrence, WWW.WILDWEST.GOV: The Impact of the Internet on State Power to Enforce the Law, B.Y.U. L. Rev. 1305 (2000). Copyright © 2000 Brigham Young University Law Review. Reprinted by permission.

Brenner, Susan W., Need for Reciprocal Enforcement of Warrants and Subpoenas in Cybercrime Cases, 37 Prosecutor 29 (2003). Copyright © 2003 by the author. Reprinted by permission.

Brenner, Susan W. and Frederiksen, Barbara A., Computer Searches And Seizures: Some Unresolved Issues, 8 Mich. Telecomm. & Tech. L. Rev. 39 (2001–2002). Copyright © 2002 by Michigan Telecommunications and Technology Law Review. Reprinted with permission.

Demetriou, Christina; Silke, Andrew; A Criminological Internet "Sting": Experimental Evidence of Illegal and Deviant Visits to a Website Trap, 43 Brit. J. Criminology 213 (2003). Copyright © 2003 by Oxford University Press. Reprinted by permission.

Freiwald, Susan, Online Surveillance: Remembering the Lessons of the Wiretap Act, 56 Ala. L. Rev. 9 (2004). Copyright © 2004 by the author. Reprinted by permission.

Freiwald, Susan, Uncertain Privacy: Communication Attributes After the Digital Telephone Act, 69 S. Cal. L. Rev. 949 (1996). Copyright © 1996 by the author. Reprinted by permission.

Moohr, Geraldine Szott, The Problematic Role of Criminal Law in Regulating Use of Information: The Case of the Economic Espionage Act, 80 N.C. L. Rev. 853 (2003). Copyright © 2003 by North Carolina Law Review. Reprinted by permission.

Howell, Beryl A., Real World Problems of Virtual Crime, 7 Yale J. L. & Tech. 103 (2004–2005). Copyright © 2005 by the author. Reprinted by permission.

Ingraham, Donald G., On Charging Computer Crime, 2 Computer/L.J. 429 (1980). Copyright © 1980 by John Marshall Journal of Computer & Information Law. Reprinted by permission.

Katyal, Neal Kumar, Criminal Law In Cyberspace, 149 U. Penn. L. Rev. 1003 (2001). Copyright © 2001 by University of Pennsylvania Law Review. Reprinted by permission.

Keller, Bruce P., The Game's The Same: Why Gambling in Cyberspace Violates Federal Law, 108 Yale L.J. 1569 (1999). Copyright © 1999 by the Yale Law Journal. Reprinted by permission of The Yale Law Journal Company from The Yale Law Journal, Vol. 108, pages 1569–1609.

Kerr, Orin, Cybercrime's Scope: Interpreting "Access" and "Authorization" in Computer Misuse Statutes, 79 N.Y.U. L. Rev. 1596 (2003). Copyright © 2003 by New York University Law Review.

Loren, Lydia Pallas, Digitization, Commodification, Criminalization: The Evolution of Criminal Copyright Infringement and the Importance of the Willfulness Requirement, 77 Wash. U. L.Q. 835 (1999). Copyright © 1999 by Washington University Law Quarterly. Reprinted by permission.

McPhie, David, Almost Private: Pen Registers, Packet Sniffers, and Privacy at the Margin, Stan. Tech. L. Rev. 1 (2005). Copyright © 2005 by the Stanford Technology Law Review. Reprinted by permission.

Meese, Edwin, Big Brother on the Beat: The Expanding Federalization of Crime, 1 Tex. Rev. L. & Politics 1 (1997). Copyright © 1997 by Texas Review of Law and Politics. Reprinted by permission.

Mulligan, Deirdre K., Reasonable Expectations in Electronic Communications: A Critical Perspective on the Electronic Communications Privacy Act, 72 Geo. Wash. L. Rev. 1557 (2004). Copyright © 2004 by The George Washington Law Review. Reprinted by permission.

Olivenbaum, Joseph M., Ctrl-Alt-Delete: Rethinking Federal Computer Crime Legislation, 27 Seton Hall L. Rev. 574 (1997).

Parker, Donn B., Fighting Computer Crime (1983). Copyright © 1983 by Simon & Schuster, Inc. Reprinted by permission.

Perritt, Henry H., Jr., Jurisdiction in Cyberspace, 41 Vill. L. Rev. 1 (1996). Reprinted by permission.

Podgor, Ellen S., International Computer Fraud: A Paradigm for Limiting National Jurisdiction, 35 U.C. Davis L. Rev. 267 (2002). Copyright © 2002 by University of California at Davis Law Review. Reprinted by permission.

Rasch, Mark, Ashcroft's Global Internet Power-Grab, available at http://online.securityfocus.com/Columnists/39 (Nov. 25, 2001). Copyright © 2001 by the author. Reprinted by permission.

Robinson, Paul H. and Darley, John M., The Role of Deterrence in the Fromulation of Criminal Law Rules: At Its Worst When Doing Its Best, 91 Geo. L.J. 949 (2003). Copyright © 2003 by Georgetown Law Journal. Reprinted by permission of the publisher, Georgetown Law Journal (2003.

Rychlak, Ronald J., Legal Problems with On-Line Gambling, Engage: The Journal of the Federalist Society's Practice Groups Volume 6, Issue 1 (2005). Copyright © 2005 by the Federalist Society. Reprinted by permission from The Federalist Society.

Salgado, Richard P., Fourth Amendment Search and the Power of the Hash, 119 Harv. L. Rev. F. 38 (2006), available at http://www.harvardlawreview.org/forum/issues/119/dec05/salgado.pdf. Copyright © 2006 reprinted by permission of the Harvard Law Review Association and William S. Hein Company from The Harvard Law Review, Vol. 119, pages 42–43.

Savage, Jr., Joseph F.; Martel, Matthew A.; and Zwillinger, Marc J., Conflicting Views of the Economic Espionage Act, Criminal Justice 10 (Fall 2000). Copyright © 2000 by Criminal Justice. Reprinted by permission.

Shah, Monica R., Note, The Case for a Statutory Suppression Remedy to Regulate Illegal Private Party Searches in Cyberspace, 105 Colum. L. Rev. 250 (2005). Copyright © 2005 by Columbia Law Review. Reprinted by permission.

Smith, Bruce, Hacking, Poaching, and Counterattacking: Digital Counterstrikes and the Contours of Self-Help, 1 J.L. Econ. & Pol'y 171 (2005). Copyright © 2005 by the Journal of Law, Economics and Policy. Reprinted by permission.

Solove, Daniel J., Digital Dossiers and the Dissipation of Fourth Amendment Privacy, 75 Southern California Law Review 1083 (2002). Copyright © 2002 by Southern California Law Review. Reprinted with the permission of the Southern California Law Review.

Solove, Daniel J., Reconstructing Electronic Surveillance Law, 72 Geo. Wash. L. Rev. 1264 (2004). Copyright © 2004 by The George Washington Law Review. Reprinted by permission.

Stevenson, Dru, Entrapment by Numbers, 16 U. Fla. J. L. & Pub. Pol'y 1 (2005). Copyright © 2005 by University of Florida Journal of Law and Public Policy. Reprinted by permission.

Sullum, Jacob, Abetting Betting: Is Talking about Online Gambling Illegal?, Reason Online, April 9, 2004. Copyright © 2004 by Creators. Reprinted by permission.

Sussmann, Michael A., The Critical Challenges From International High-Tech and Computer-Related Crime at the Millennium, 9 Duke J. Comp. & Int'l L. 451 (1999). Copyright © 1999 by the author. Reprinted by permission.

Volokh, Eugene, Obscenity Crackdown (What Will the Next Step Be?, Cato Institute TechKnowledge, available at http:/www cato.org/tech/tk/040412-tk.html. (Issue #78 – April 12, 2004). Copyright © 2004 by Cato Institute. Reprinted by permission.

Walker, Kent, Federal Criminal Remedies for the Theft of Intellectual Property, 16 Hastings Comm. & Ent. L. J. 681 (1994). Copyright © 1994 by University of California, Hastings College of the Law. Reprinted from the Hastings Communications and Entertainment Law Journal, Volume 16, Number 4, 1994, 681, by permission.

Walters, Lawrence G., and DeWitt, Clyde, Obscenity in the Digital Age: The Re-evaluation of Community Standards, 10 NEXUS 59 (2005). Copyright © 2005 by NEXUS: A Journal of Opinion. Reprinted by permission.

Winick, Raphael, Searches and Seizures of Computers and Computer Data, 8 Harv. J.L. & Tech. 75 (1994). Copyright © 1994 by the Harvard Journal of Law & Technology. Reprinted by permission.

Zagaris, Bruce, Uncle Sam Extends Reach for Evidence Worldwide, 15 Crim. Just. 4 (2001). Copyright © 2001 by Criminal Justice. Reprinted by permission.

Summary of Contents

Table of Contents

Table of Cases

The principal cases are in bold type. Cases cited or discussed in the text are roman type. References are to pages. Cases cited in principal cases and within other quoted materials are not included.

Table of Statutes

*

Table of Authorities

References are to Pages

*

COMPUTER CRIME LAW

*

Chapter 1

INTRODUCTION

What is a computer crime? What topics are covered in a course on computer crime law? And what makes computer crimes different from other types of crimes?

These are three good questions, and this short introductory chapter will provide a few answers. The chapter begins with a brief overview of the field of computer crime law, as well as the coverage of this book. It then offers a hypothetical that introduces the basic differences between the law of traditional physical crimes and the law of modern computer crimes.

A. OVERVIEW OF COMPUTER CRIME LAW

There are two reasons to label criminal conduct a computer crime. First, an individual might use a computer to engage in criminal activity. Second, the evidence needed to prove a criminal case might be stored in computerized form. The law governing use of a computer to commit a crime is *substantive* computer crime law, because it concerns the scope of substantive conduct that has been criminalized. The law governing the collection of computerized evidence is *procedural* computer crime law, because it concerns the legal procedures investigators can use to collect digital evidence in criminal investigations.

Substantive computer crime law divides into two basic categories: computer misuse crimes and traditional crimes. Computer misuse crimes are a new type of criminal offense involving intentional interference with the proper functioning of computers. Examples include hacking offenses, virus crimes, and denial-of-service attacks. These offenses punish interference with the intended operation of computers, either by exceeding a user's privileges (as in the case of a hacking crime) or by denying privileges to others (as in the case of a denial-of-service attack).

As the label implies, traditional crimes are traditional criminal offenses facilitated by computers. These are information crimes with obvious physical-world counterparts. Examples include Internet fraud

1

schemes, online threats, distributing digital images of child pornography, and theft of trade secrets over the Internet.

Much like substantive computer crime law, procedural computer crime law consists of two relatively discrete topics. The first topic is the Fourth Amendment, which prohibits unreasonable searches and seizures. In the physical world, the Fourth Amendment creates constitutional limits on where the police can go and what evidence the police can collect in criminal investigations. Procedural computer crime law considers how the Fourth Amendment applies in the case of digital evidence collection. For example, when is retrieving evidence from a computer a "search"? When is it a "seizure"? When is the search or seizure "reasonable"?

The second area of procedural computer crime law is statutory privacy law. Traditional criminal procedure is primarily constitutional law, but much of the law regulating digital evidence collection derives from three privacy statutes: the Wiretap Act, the Pen Register statute, and the Stored Communications Act. As a practical matter, the divide between statutory and constitutional law often tracks the divide between evidence collection from stand-alone computers and computer networks. The law governing computer network surveillance is primarily statutory, and the law regulating retrieval of evidence from stand-alone computers is predominantly constitutional.

Jurisdictional disputes provide the third area of inquiry in computer crime cases. Traditional crimes usually are local. The defendant, the victim, and the evidence often are in the same place, and the charges tend to brought under state criminal codes wherever the offense occurred. Computer crimes present a very different dynamic. A defendant in one place may connect to a computer in a second place and launch an attack against a computer located in a third place. The victim, the defendant, and the evidence are located in different places—maybe different states, or even different countries. As a result, the law must define for each sovereign what kinds of conduct outside its borders can and should be criminalized, as well as what procedures regulate extraterritorial evidence collection. The global nature of Internet surveillance and terrorism investigations also creates jurisdictional friction between two competing legal regimes, the law of criminal investigations and the law of national security investigations.

The organization of this book tracks these three basic questions. Chapters 2, 3, and 4 address the substantive law of computer crimes; Chapters 5 and 6 cover procedural law; and Chapters 7 and 8 explore jurisdictional issues. In an investigation, the three questions typically present themselves in the reverse order from their order in the book. After a crime has occurred, the first issues are jurisdictional: What agency has jurisdiction over the offense, as well as the ability to collect evidence to prove it in court? The next issues are procedural: What rules must law enforcement officials follow to collect evidence and identify the suspect? The final questions are substantive: What crimes have been committed that the government can charge in court and try to prove beyond a reasonable doubt?

The three questions of computer crime law are really variations on a single theme, and that theme explains why it makes sense to study computer crime law in a separate course. Criminal law and procedure are both highly sensitive to facts, and the facts of computer crimes tend to be different from the facts of equivalent physical crimes. The shift from physical crimes to digital crimes changes the facts of how and where crimes are committed as well as how and where evidence is collected. When the facts change, the law must change with it. Old laws must adapt and new laws must emerge to restore the function of preexisting law.

Of course, the broad policy goals of criminal law and procedure are timeless. Criminal law identifies public conduct that is harmful and culpable, and criminal procedure articulates reasonable limits on police powers. So in a broad sense, nothing is new. But implementing those policy goals with legal rules depends on the facts, and the facts of digital crimes consistently challenge the assumptions of existing substantive, procedural, and jurisdictional laws. We can begin with the old legal rules, but after a while it becomes clear that some of the old rules need to bend and others need replacement. Computer crime law is the search for and study of new answers to timeless questions of criminal law when the facts switch from a physical environment to a digital environment.

B. COMPARING PHYSICAL CRIMES AND COMPUTER CRIMES

Consider the following two hypotheticals. The first is a traditional physical crime; the second is a roughly analogous computer crime. What if anything changes when we switch from the first example to the second example?

Physical Crime

Fred Felony is a resident of Phoenix, Arizona. Fred finds himself low on cash one day, and he decides to rob a jewelry store in downtown Phoenix. Fred drives to the store and parks his car on the street in front of the store. He walks in to the store and browses for a few minutes until the other customers depart.

After the customers leave, Fred pulls out a gun and runs over to the clerk working at the store that day. "This is a stick-up!" he yells to the clerk. "Give me some gold and no one will get hurt!" The clerk is extremely frightened that she will be shot, and she nervously opens one of the cabinets and hands Fred a collection of gold jewelry. Fred grabs the jewelry and stuffs it into a bag he is carrying. He runs out of the store, jumps into his getaway car, and speeds away.

After Fred leaves, the clerk immediately calls the store manager. She reports that the robber took jewelry with a retail value of about $5,000. The clerk is shaken up by the robbery, as well. Over the next month, she takes two weeks of sick leave to recuperate from her traumatic experience. She also has occasional nightmares of being victimized again.

Fred returns home with the loot and hides the jewelry in a closet for safekeeping. After a week, he visits a local Phoenix pawn shop and sells the jewelry for $800 in cash.

Computer Crime

This time, Fred Felony decides to commit his crime using a computer. Fred decides that he will steal credit cards remotely instead of stealing gold jewelry in person. His new target: An e-commerce company located in Los Angeles, California.

Fred logs on to the Internet from his home in Phoenix using an account he holds with a large Internet service provider (ISP) located in Dulles, Virginia. Although Fred's ultimate goal is to hack into the e-commerce site in Los Angeles, he first loops his attack through an intermediary computer to disguise his tracks. Starting from his Virginia ISP, Fred hacks into a computer in Ottawa, Canada, run by the Canadian tourism bureau. With access to the Canadian computer established, Fred targets the server of the e-commerce site in Los Angeles.

After several tries, Fred eventually guesses the master password correctly and logs in to the server hosted by the Los Angeles e-commerce site. He locates a file containing five hundred credit card numbers and downloads it to his computer at home. Later that day, Fred visits an Internet relay chat room occasionally used to arrange the sale of stolen credit card numbers. He sells the numbers for $800 to a user who goes by the handle "Boris11." Boris11 wires the $800 directly to an online bank account Fred controls. Fred does not know where Boris11 is located, but Boris11's English is quite poor. Fred suspects that Boris11 lives somewhere in Eastern Europe.

The next morning, an employee at the e-commerce site in Los Angeles realizes that the company has been victimized and that the credit card file has been accessed. The company spends $50,000 upgrading its computer security to ensure that no such attacks are successful again. It then notifies its customers and their banks that the breach occurred. Although the banks put a hold on all five hundred accounts, they are too late. By the time the accounts are frozen, an unknown individual in Moscow runs up a tab of $40,000 on several of the stolen accounts.

Notes and Questions

1. *Substantive law.* Compare the physical crime and the computer crime from the standpoint of substantive law. What crimes did Fred commit when he entered the jewelry store with a gun and ordered the store clerk to hand over the jewelry? How serious are those crimes? What harms did Fred cause? Why should the law deter such activity, and why was it morally culpable?

Now turn to the computer crime. How was Fred's conduct different in the second hypothetical? What harms did Fred cause when he committed the computer crime? Why should the law deter such activity, and why was it morally culpable? Did Fred actually "steal" anything, and does it matter? Is the computer crime fundamentally the same as the physical crime, or is it different?

Does punishing the computer crime require new laws, or are the traditional laws applicable in the case of the physical crime also sufficient to punish the computer crime? Which offense should be punished more severely: the physical crime or the computer crime? What punishment is appropriate for each?

2. *Procedural law.* Now compare the two crimes from the perspective of investigatory procedure. Imagine that you are a police officer in Phoenix, Arizona, and you are called to the jewelry store to investigate the crime just hours after it occurred. You want to collect evidence, identify a suspect, and prove your case beyond a reasonable doubt in court. What evidence can you collect, and how do you collect it? Who do you interview? What questions do you ask? What kind of evidence are you likely to find? How would you plan to investigate the case and prove it beyond a reasonable doubt in court?

Again, switch to the computer crime. Now imagine that you are a Los Angeles police officer called by the e-commerce company after they discover that they have been hacked and the file accessed without permission. What evidence do you collect, and how do you collect it? Who do you interview? What questions do you ask? What kind of evidence are you likely to find? How might you plan to investigate the case and trace the crime back to the wrongdoer?

What legal rules should regulate the steps you would take to investigate the physical crime? What rules should regulate the steps needed to investigate the computer crime? Are they the same or are they different?

3. As you ponder these questions, it may help to know a little bit about how computer intrusion investigations generally work. Most investigations follow two basic steps: tracing communications over the Internet back to their source, and then recovering and analyzing the computer used in the offense.

Investigators attempt to track communications to their source by collecting network logs. Computer networks normally are run by a system administrator, or "sysadmin" for short, who is responsible for keeping the computer running and for troubleshooting difficulties. System administrators ordinarily set their computers to generate records known as logs that record how the network was used. For example, a server might be configured to record the incoming Internet Protocol (IP) addresses and times of every attempt to log in to an account on the server. (IP addresses are numerical addresses that are akin to Internet phone numbers. Every user connected to the Internet is assigned an IP address, and the address is used to send information to the user.) In the case of an e-commerce site, it's a good bet that the network system administrator will have configured the network to generate access logs that recorded the time, IP address, and any other relevant information about each login into the network.

To trace back the crime, the investigators normally must go step by step, hop by hop, tracing the chain of communications from server to server. This is true because the IP addresses stored in a log only record the most immediate hop back in the chain of communications. If the e-commerce site in Los Angeles kept logs of the intrusion, those logs will show the attack coming from the Canadian tourism bureau in Ottawa, not Fred in Phoenix. At each stage investigators must try to collect evidence of the prior hop until they trace the attack back to the wrongdoer.

Most computer hacking investigations end with the seizure and subsequent search of the suspect's personal computer. The reason is simple: Because there are no eyewitnesses to most computer crimes, proving a case beyond a reasonable doubt usually requires direct evidence. The discovery of stolen files or other evidence on a suspect's personal computer can provide powerful evidence that the computer owner was responsible for the offense (and if no such evidence exists, can help exonerate the suspect). Personal computers often keep very detailed records of how and when they have been used, and those records can provide very powerful evidence in court.

What legal rules should regulate these steps of computer crime investigations? Should investigators need a search warrant or other authorization to collect logs from system administrators? Should they need a warrant or other authorization to search the suspect's computer for evidence? What rules should govern the search of the computer?

4. *Jurisdictional issues.* Finally, let's compare the physical crime and the computer crime from the standpoint of jurisdiction. What agency should investigate the jewelry store robbery? Where is the evidence of the crime located? If Fred is caught and prosecuted, what court will bring charges? Is the physical crime a case for state or federal investigators?

Now consider the computer crime. You are a Los Angeles police officer called to investigate the crime, and the system administrator tells you that his logs indicate the attack came from Ottawa, Canada. Does the Los Angeles Police Department have any powers to collect evidence in Canada? For that matter, if you can trace the attack back to the ISP in Virginia, do you have authority to collect evidence in Virginia? Imagine you decide to pass up the case to the Federal Bureau of Investigation field office in Los Angeles. Can they collect evidence in Canada? How can they obtain the records needed to trace the crime?

Imagine the FBI successfully traces the attack through the Canadian site and the Virginia ISP back to Fred Felony's home in Arizona. Can Fred Felony be charged with a violation of California law? Arizona law? Federal law? Should he be prosecuted in Phoenix? Los Angeles? What if the Canadian authorities want to bring Fred Felony to Ottawa to face charges for hacking into the Canadian tourism bureau site. Can Fred be extradited to Canada? If the Canadian authorities request the FBI's assistance in gathering evidence to charge Fred Felony in Canada, does the FBI have an obligation to provide that assistance?

5. *The road ahead.* Keep these questions in mind as you study the chapters ahead. The materials will start with substantive law, turn next to procedural law, and finish with jurisdictional issues. By the end of the book, you will be able to answer all of these questions for any computer-related crime.

Chapter 2

COMPUTER MISUSE CRIMES

———

Computer misuse crimes are offenses involving interference with the proper functioning of computers. Every computer is programmed to perform a particular set of functions for a particular set of users. Interfering with those functions can be a culpable act that causes significant harm.

Computer misuse can occur in two distinct ways. First, a user might exceed his privileges on a computer. For example, a person might hack into a remote network and view confidential files he is not supposed to see. Second, a person might deny others their privileges to use a computer. For example, a person might launch a denial-of-service attack that incapacitates a target network. Legitimate users will try to use the network but find that they cannot. These two types of computer misuse are distinct, but represent two sides of the same coin. In the first, the user exceeds his own privileges; in the second, the user denies privileges to others.

This chapter explores the law of computer misuse. It begins with a policy question: Should computer misuse be a crime, and if so, when? The materials then consider whether traditional criminal laws can address computer misuse, or whether new statutes are needed. The remaining parts of the chapter study the three most common types of computer misuse statutes: unauthorized access statutes, computer fraud statutes, and computer damage statutes.

A.   WHY PUNISH COMPUTER MISUSE?

Every first-year law student learns that there are two major reasons why wrongful acts are punished. The first reason is utilitarian. Utilitarians believe that punishment should be imposed because it can decrease the amount of crime in the future. For example, criminal punishment can deter harmful conduct: the prospect of punishment can encourage a person not to commit a criminal act. Punishment also can prevent crime by incapacitating or rehabilitating a defendant. *See generally* Herbert L. Packer, The Limits of the Criminal Sanction 39–61 (1968).

The second goal of criminal punishment is retribution. Retributivists believe that punishment should be imposed to ensure that individuals receive their just deserts. Some retributivists believe that punishment reflects society's revenge against the wrongdoer; from this perspective, punishment is an "eye for an eye." Others contend that punishment restores the moral order by denying the wrongdoer's claim to superiority. The common theme of retributive approaches to punishment is that they look back at the wrongfulness of the defendant's act rather than look forward at the effect punishment will have on future criminal activity.

Do these theories justify punishment for computer misuse? Consider the following two problems.

Problem 1

Bryan Smith is a 17 year-old high school senior living in Lincoln, Nebraska. His father is a small businessman, and his mother teaches second grade at a local public school. Bryan gets good grades, especially in math and science, and he hopes to attend college next fall at either Georgia Tech or MIT to study computer science.

Bryan first started playing with computers at the age of 13 when his parents purchased a home PC. At first, Bryan spent most of his time online sending e-mails and instant messages and web surfing, but he eventually developed an interest in computer programming. He learned the rudiments of the popular UNIX operating system, and began visiting chat rooms devoted to computer programming and Internet security.

In the last year, Bryan's interests in programming led him to experiment with computer hacking. Using the hacker pseudonym "KillerBee," Bryan started using prepared programs known as "scripts" to test the security of different sites on the Internet. He would usually test the site for obvious security flaws, and if the site had such a flaw, he would try to gain access to its central server. Once inside the network, he would take a quick look around, and then send a message from KillerBee to the network's system administrator explaining that he had broken in to the network using a widely known vulnerability and that the system administrator needed to pay better attention to network security. On occasion, in an effort to impress his girlfriend, Bryan would try to replace the site's web page with a large picture of a skull and a message saying "This Site Has Been Hacked by Killerbee! Sarah Is #1!" So far, Bryan has successfully placed this message on about a half-dozen websites, including those of a community college in Bangor, Maine; the Alabama Public Service Commission; and a small e-commerce company based in Miami, Florida.

Although Bryan realizes that the siteowners probably don't appreciate his activities, Bryan believes that his hacking is justifiable. Bryan reasons that his harmless pranks will encourage negligent system administrators to spend the time and money they will need to defend their sites against more malicious attacks. In less altruistic moments, Bryan will also admit that "KillerBee" thinks hacking is lots of fun: acting the part of a fearless online adventurer provides a much-needed escape from the tedium and stress of high school. Bryan also expects that as his hacking skills advance, he may some day be able to obtain work as an Internet security consultant. He figures that hacking today will develop the computer skills he will need in the future to help make the Internet safer (and to be paid handsomely for it).

Unsurprisingly, the network system administrators who are responsible for maintaining security at the computers targeted by KillerBee have a different take on Bryan's conduct. From their perspective, Killer-Bee's hacking is a nuisance, and an expensive nuisance at that. For example, in response to his activities, the e-commerce company hired security consultants who charged the company $50,000 just to review the contents of the company's servers, confirm that KillerBee had not done any other damage, and patch the vulnerability that had allowed Killer-Bee to break in. The company also suffered from lost business when the site was down for a few hours, and took a public relations hit among their vendors from being offline. Several of KillerBee's targets also concluded that they had to spend thousands of dollars to improve their security: two of them invested over $30,000 each in security products and testing to thwart hackers in the future.

Problem 2

Sarah Jones works as a network system administrator at a community hospital in Washington, D.C. Sarah's job, which she has held for two years, is to maintain the hospital's computer network. The hospital relies heavily on the network, using it to store and process patient medical records, employee records, supply records, and all of the hospital's financial records. As the system administrator, Sarah has "root" access to the network. This means that Sarah has a master account that allows her to access and modify any file within the network.

One afternoon while at work, Sarah decides to help out her friend Beth. Beth recently started a company that provides direct advertising for pharmaceutical companies. Beth's company targets individual patients in need of medical care and sends them advertisements for pharmaceutical products that relate to their medical problems. Sarah figures that she can help Beth by acquiring the names and mailing addresses of some of the hospital's patients, along with a short description of their medical conditions, and sending them on to Beth.

Sarah logs on to the network by entering her username, "sjones," and her password, "freekevin." She then bypasses the usual warning banner that appears on her monitor. The banner states: "WARNING: This network is authorized for official use only." Sarah accesses the portion of the computer where patient medical records are stored. Sarah starts scanning through the records for names and addresses. When she realizes that it will take several hours to obtain the names and addresses manually, she creates an automated program that scans the network's servers and looks for key words that signal patient medical records. Sarah designs the program to collect the records automatically and e-mail the file directly to Beth. Sarah also installs a surveillance tool called a "sniffer" that will read any new medical record as it is entered into the network and automatically e-mail it to Beth.

Beth is quite surprised when she accesses her e-mail the next day and finds a file from Sarah containing thousands of patient records. The records include patient names, addresses, and medical diagnoses along with lists of currently prescribed medications. Uncertain of the ethics and legality of using the list, Beth calls Sarah and asks her not to send any additional records. Sarah apologizes, and explains that she was only trying to help Beth with her new company. Beth decides to keep her copy of the list just in case she needs it, although she feels confident that she will never use or share it.

Notes and Questions

1. Should Bryan Smith's conduct be a crime? Should Sarah Jones's conduct be a crime? What punishment is appropriate for Bryan Smith? For Sarah Jones?

2. *The Hacker Ethic.* In the early days of computers in the late 1950s and early 1960s, a culture developed among some users that encouraged creative experimentation. In his book *Hackers*, Steven Levy focuses on the members of a student club at the Massachusetts Institute of Technology called the Tech Model Railroad Club. Members spent a great deal of time working on an early computer called the TX–0, and developed a number of principles that later coalesced into the "Hacker Ethic."

The Hacker Ethic reflects an open and free approach to using and exploring computers. One principle is that "access to computers—and anything which might teach you something about the way the world works—should be unlimited and total." Another related principle teaches that "all information should be free." The basic idea is that any computer user should have a right to tinker with and improve any computer, and that rules governing access should not be followed. *See* Steven Levy, Hackers 24–28 (1984). The term "hackers" was originally used in this sense to refer to skilled and enthusiastic computer programmers with a deep understanding of how computers work. Over time, however, the term has become synonymous with those who commit acts of unauthorized access to computers. *See* Pekka Himanen, The Hacker Ethic, at vii–ix (2001).

Does the hacker ethic help answer when computer misuse should be criminalized? Consider the argument that misuse consistent with the hacker ethic can help improve security. Hackers can identify security flaws and create patches, or inform others that the flaws exist. In addition, a teenager who becomes skilled at exploiting today's computers may become tomorrow's computer security professional tasked with protecting important networks. If hackers need to explore computers to improve them, should the law ensure that such exploration is possible? Is the notion that hacking is a form of "misuse" itself misguided?

Alternatively, is the hacker ethic a juvenile mythology that simply attempts to excuse harmful activity? Consider the teaching that "information should be free." Do you think that the medical records viewed by Sarah Jones should be free? Should we approve of her effort to share the records with her friend Beth as an attempt to "free" the medical records? Can the hacker ethic coexist with widely-held beliefs in the value of privacy?

3. *Responsibility for the consequences of poor computer security.* Every computer network is run by a system administrator who is tasked with keeping the network operating smoothly, responding to problems, setting up new accounts, and performing other routine network maintenance tasks. System administrators are usually the first to notice and respond to network intrusions. Consider this imaginary (but representative) exchange of views between a hacker and a system administrator:

> **Hacker:** System administrators should blame themselves if their networks are vulnerable. Many system administrators pay little or no attention to security, and their negligence is the true cause of most of the financial losses that result from so-called "computer crime." Hackers raise the level of network security by testing networks, offering solutions to existing vulnerabilities, and making sure that security remains a priority. Taking steps to understand a network shouldn't be a crime. Instead, it should be recognized as a public service.

> **System Administrator:** Your argument blames the victim for being victimized. We don't blame homeowners when their houses are burglarized just because they left weak locks on their front doors; instead, we blame the burglars. Also, it's hard to see why we should thank hackers for forcing us to spend money on network security, given that it is the hackers themselves we are trying to keep out. Here's an analogy: people who live in high-crime neighborhoods may have several locks on their doors and steel bars on their windows, but they don't thank the local burglars for encouraging them to raise the level of security in their homes. All hacking without the target's consent should be criminalized.

> **Hacker:** You're missing the point. Unlike homes, computers are inherently open. Any computer attached to the Internet can be accessed by millions of people around the world at any moment. The question is not *whether* a computer will be compromised, but rather *when* and *how*. In this environment, network operators should be responsible for network security, and should recognize that hackers play a vital role in helping system administrators secure their networks against the *real* criminals.

> **System Administrator:** No, you're the one who is missing the point. This is my network, and you don't have a right to break in to it. If you want to help me by exposing my network's vulnerabilities, you can just ask me for permission. If I think you can help me, I will let you try to hack in. But that's for me to decide, not you.

> **Hacker:** You are mired in the old way of thinking. Computers are different, and the law needs to recognize that.

Who has the stronger argument? If you think the hacker's argument is stronger, does it follow that "state and federal governments should immediately decriminalize all forms of non-malicious hacking?" Michael Lee, et. al.,

Comment, *Electronic Commerce, Hackers, and the Search for Legitimacy: A Regulatory Proposal*, 14 Berkeley Tech. L.J. 839, 882 (1999). If so, how would you articulate the difference between malicious hacking and non-malicious hacking?

4. *Financial loss from computer misuse.* Estimates of the losses caused by computer crime suggest that they are quite high. One FBI estimate put the cost of computer crimes in 2004 at about $400 billion. *See* McAfee Virtual Technology Report 5 (2005). Even individual computer misuse crimes can be quite costly. For example, the "I Love You" virus that spread around the world in 2000 has been estimated to have caused as much as $10 billion in loss. *See* Patricia L. Bellia, *Chasing Bits Across Borders*, 2001 U. Chi. Legal F. 35, 36. In 2005, 700 computer security practitioners responding to a joint CSI/FBI survey collectively reported about $130 million in losses arising from computer misuse crimes in the previous year. *See* 2005 CSI/FBI Computer Crime and Security Survey (2005).

The figures are impressive. But are they accurate? Most estimates of loss tend to be fairly rough, as they are derived primarily from anecdotal evidence and extrapolation. Further, the estimates generally rely on businesses and companies to self-report how much loss they suffered from a computer crime. Skeptics of high loss figures point to the institutional incentives of those who make such estimates. For example, some estimates are produced by consulting firms that offer a range of products and services to potential victims of computer misuse. Other estimates are produced by law enforcement agencies that may then use these figures to argue for larger budgets to address computer-related crime. *See* Elinor Abreu, *Net Crime Does Pay—For Cops*, The Industry Standard, Feb. 21, 2000. In light of these concerns, do you trust the loss figures reported in such studies?

If you were tasked with designing a survey to estimate the losses caused by computer crime, how would you do it? Is it possible to measure accurately the loss caused by computer crimes?

5. *Culpability and intent to profit.* Some hackers abide by the hacker ethic, and hack for the intellectual excitement or the thrill. Others hack for profit. Some attempt to hack into e-commerce sites to collect credit card numbers that can be sold later in anonymous Internet chat rooms. Others gain unauthorized access to distribute spam anonymously for a fee, or to look for an advantage over business competitors. According to some reports, Russian organized crime groups are actively involved in computer hacking. The Russian mafia hires hackers both to steal credit card numbers and to break into victim sites and demand expensive "consulting fees" in exchange for not doing significant damage. Others are hired to break into computers and find trade secrets that can be sold to competitors or outsiders. *See, e.g.,* Laura Lorek, *Russian Mafia Net Threat*, Eweek.com, July 16, 2001.

Does computer misuse deserve greater punishment when undertaken for profit? On one hand, perhaps computer misuse combined with a profit motive is likely to be more harmful because intent to profit generally suggests a lack of concern for other possible harms or the likelihood the conduct will be repeated. On the other hand, some of the harms caused by computer misuse are unintentional byproducts of otherwise intentional activity. The harm may have no direct link to the intent to profit. For example, imagine a person hacks into a computer for profit, and accidentally causes a great deal of damage to the server. Is that hacking really more culpable by virtue of the intent to profit?

6. *Insiders vs. outsiders.* Should "insiders" to a computer system (that is, those with accounts and certain access rights) be treated differently than "outsiders" to the system (who have no access rights, or only very limited access rights)? Compare the conduct of Fred Smith from Problem 1 with that of Sarah Jones from Problem 2. Did Sarah Jones really misuse the hospital's computers? Unlike Smith, Jones did not have to "break in" to the network: her account gave her root access, which entitled her to look at any file in the system. Is Sarah Jones's interference with the hospital computer different from Fred Smith's interference with the computer he hacked? In what way? Does it matter that Smith broke in to the computer while Jones did not?

Consider the effect of the hospital policy stating that the network was "authorized for official use only." Is using a network for unauthorized purposes as culpable as breaking in to that network? Does it matter whether the restriction on network use is reasonable or unreasonable? Imagine that an ISP's Terms of Service state that subscribers are not authorized to access the ISP to engage in conduct that "may be considered offensive." A user accesses the ISP and uses the ISP to send an offensive e-mail. Has that user engaged in computer misuse? Should the user be held criminally liable for violating the ISP's Terms of Service?

B. PROPERTY CRIMES AS A RESPONSE TO COMPUTER MISUSE

Assuming computer misuse should be criminalized, at least in some circumstances, the next question becomes *how* to criminalize it. Does the problem of computer misuse require new criminal laws? Or can traditional criminal laws handle these new crimes? This section considers whether traditional property crime laws can address the problem of computer misuse, or, alternatively, whether computer misuse requires the passage of new laws.

The enormous potential harms of computer misuse first became apparent in the early 1970s.[a] At that time, no legislature had enacted a computer crime statute. When prosecutors considered bringing criminal charges for computer misuse, they naturally turned to existing property crime laws, such as laws prohibiting trespass, burglary, and theft. The fit proved a poor one, however. In the case of trespass and burglary, the scope of existing laws plainly did not extend to computer misuse. In the case of theft, the law could be stretched to apply, but required judicial sleight of hand and resort to an unpredictable legal fiction.

Consider the crimes of trespass and burglary, both predominantly state offenses. Trespass crimes generally punish knowing entrance or presence on another person's property despite notice that the property

a. This material is adapted from Orin S. Kerr, *Cybercrime's Scope: Interpreting "Access" and "Authorization" in Computer Misuse Statutes*, 78 N.Y.U. L. Rev. 1596, 1605–10 (2003).

owner forbids it. At common law, burglary prohibited "breaking and entering" into a building without authorization and with the intent to commit a crime therein. Modern statutes tend to focus more on entering a building or occupied structure without license or privilege, combined with intent to commit a crime inside. Like trespass crimes, burglary focuses on the entry onto property without permission. Unlike trespass, however, burglary requires the intent to commit a crime, and usually carries relatively stiff criminal penalties.

At first blush, trespass and burglary law may appear to provide a logical starting point for applying property crimes to punish and deter computer misuse. It has been noted widely that many acts of computer misuse resemble trespasses. A user can exceed her privileges on a computer much like a trespasser can exceed her privileges on physical land. Computer hacking, for example, is akin to a trespass in cyberspace. Similarly, a hacker may break into a computer with intent to do mischief much like a burglar might break into a house with the same intent.

Despite the common principles, it seems that criminal trespass and burglary statutes have never been used to prosecute computer misuse. The primary reason is that both trespass and burglary statutes remain closely tied to the physical world rather than a virtual one. For example, trespass statutes generally require that part of the defendant's person pass the line of the threshold of the property trespassed. The same goes for burglary offenses. Criminal trespass and burglary statutes focus narrowly on presence of a human body on physical land, not interference with property rights more generally. This limited scope makes it difficult to apply trespass or burglary statutes to computer misuse; because the user does not physically enter the target computer, the existing statutes do not apply. Indeed, it appears that no criminal prosecution has ever used burglary or general criminal trespass statutes to prosecute computer misuse.

In contrast with burglary and trespass, the crime of theft has been used to prosecute computer misuse. Theft crimes consist of a family of related offenses, including larceny, embezzlement, conversion, fraud, and false pretenses. Today, most states have consolidated these various crimes into a single theft statute, which prohibits larceny, embezzlement, and false pretenses together. Federal theft crimes are more limited in scope, reflecting the constitutional limits of federal criminal law. The mail fraud and wire fraud statutes are the broadest federal theft offenses; they prohibit many interstate fraudulent schemes to obtain property. These statutes make it illegal to send an interstate wire, radio, or television communication, or to place a stolen item in the U.S. mail or with an interstate mail carrier, to help further a fraudulent scheme designed to obtain money or property.

Efforts to prosecute computer misuse as theft crimes generally follow a fairly simple rationale. By upsetting intended privileges relating to a computer, the thinking goes, the defendant committed a theft—the taking of property belonging to another. This rationale may seem plausible at first blush, but it creates serious difficulties defining a property interest and then identifying when that property has been taken. Theft statutes presume the existence of an identifiable piece of property, some clearly-defined "thing," that when taken deprives the owner of its bounty. We can understand this easily in the case of tangible property. For example, if someone steals my bicycle, it is easy to identify the property stolen (the bicycle) and to tell whether or not I have been deprived of it (either I have the bicycle or I don't).

In the case of computer misuse, however, identifying a property interest and then concluding that it was taken can require considerable creativity.

UNITED STATES v. SEIDLITZ

United States Court of Appeals for the Fourth Circuit, 1978.
589 F.2d 152.

FIELD, Senior Circuit Judge.

Bertram Seidlitz appeals from his conviction on two counts of fraud by wire in violation of 18 U.S.C. § 1343.[1] As grounds for reversal, he urges that * * * the prosecution failed to establish certain material elements of the crime. Although advanced in a somewhat novel factual context, we find appellant's contentions to be without merit.

On January 1, 1975, defendant Seidlitz assumed the position of Deputy Project Director for Optimum Systems, Inc. (OSI), a computer service company which was under contract to install, maintain, and operate a computer facility at Rockville, Maryland, for use by the Federal Energy Administration (FEA). Under the arrangement between OSI and FEA, persons working for FEA in various parts of the country could use key boards at communications terminals in their offices to send instructions over telephone circuits to the large computers in Rockville, and the computers' responses would be returned and reflected on a CRT (cathode ray tube) terminal which is a typewriter-like device with a keyboard and display screen similar to a television screen upon which the information is displayed as it is sent and received.[2] Mr. Seidlitz helped to prepare the

---

1. The federal wire fraud statute, 18 U.S.C. § 1343, provides:

Whoever, having devised or intending to devise any scheme or artifice to defraud, or for obtaining money or property by means of false or fraudulent pretenses, representations, or promises, transmits or causes to be transmitted by means of wire, radio, or television communication in interstate or foreign commerce, any writings, signs, signals, pictures, or sounds for the purpose of executing such scheme or artifice, shall be fined not more than $1,000 or imprisoned not more than five years, or both.

2. A remote user would dial on an ordinary telephone one of the several unpublished telephone numbers to which OSI subscribed and which were assigned to the computers. He would then connect the telephone to his terminal so that messages could be relayed between the terminal and the computers in the form of signals traveling over the telephone line. Because any of a number of commercially available terminal units could accomplish such a link to the computers, the user, as a security precaution, had to enter on his terminal keyboard a special access code before he would be permitted full use of the system. The code contained, among other things, the

software which was installed at the Rockville facility as part of the project, and he was also responsible for the security of the central computer system. During his tenure, he had full access to the computers and to a software system known as "WYLBUR" which resided within them. In June, 1975, Seidlitz resigned this job and returned to work at his own computer firm in Alexandria, Virginia.

William Coakley, a computer specialist employed by FEA, was assigned temporarily to the OSI facility. On December 30, 1975, in an attempt to locate a friend who might be using the OSI system, he had the computer display the initials of everyone who was then using the WYLBUR software. Among the initials displayed by the computer were those of his supervisor, who was standing nearby and who was not using the computer. Suspicious that an unauthorized "intruder" might be using these initials in order to gain access to the system, Coakley asked Mr. Ewing, an OSI employee, if Ewing could determine what was happening. He also asked Mr. Wack, an OSI supervisor, if he (Wack) could determine whether the mysterious user was at a remote terminal or at one of the terminals within the OSI complex which were directly wired to the computer and did not employ telephone circuits. Ewing instructed the computer to display for him the data it was about to transmit to the possible intruder, and it proved to be a portion of the "source code" of the WYLBUR software system. Using other data provided by the computer, Wack concluded that the connection was by telephone from outside the complex. At his request, the telephone company manually traced the call to the Alexandria office of the defendant.[7] Wack was told that the trace was successful, but the telephone company informed him that it could not divulge the results of the trace except in response to a legal subpoena.

The following day, OSI activated a special feature of the WYLBUR system known as the "Milten Spy Function," which automatically recorded, after they had been received by the machinery at Rockville, any requests made of the computer by the intruder. The "spy" also recorded, before they were sent out to the intruder over the telephone lines, the computer's responses to such requests. Mr. Wack again asked the telephone company to trace the line when it was suspected that the unauthorized person, employing the same initials, was using the computer to receive portions of the WYLBUR source code. This manual trace on December 31 led once more to the defendant's office in Virginia, although OSI was not so informed.

Advised by OSI of the events of December 30 and 31, the FBI on January 3, 1976, secured, but did not then execute, a warrant to search

---

user's personal initials, which were to be invalidated when he left OSI or FEA. This "access code" would be communicated to the central computers which, if they recognized the code as belonging to an authorized user, would proceed to perform the work the individual sent along.

7. A manual trace is accomplished without listening in on the line or breaking into the conversation. It entails a physical tracing of the telephone circuitry backward through the various switching points from the equipment which receives the call.

the defendant's Alexandria office. At the FBI's suggestion, the telephone company conducted two additional manual traces when alerted to incoming calls by OSI, but in each instance the calls were terminated before the traces had progressed beyond the telephone company's office in Lanham, Maryland, which served 10,000 subscribers. The phone company then installed "originating accounting identification equipment" in the Lanham office, the function of which was to automatically and quickly ascertain, without intercepting the contents of any communication, the telephone number of any of the 10,000 area telephones from which any subsequent calls to the OSI computers originated. Two such calls were made on the morning of January 9, and the equipment attributed both of them to a phone at the defendant's Lanham residence. That afternoon, the FBI executed the warrant to search Seidlitz' Alexandria office, seizing, among other items, a copy of the user's guide to the OSI system and some 40 rolls of computer paper upon which were printed the WYLBUR source code. A warrant was then issued to search the Seidlitz residence in Lanham, where officers found a portable communications terminal which contained a teleprinter for receiving written messages from the computer, as well as a notebook containing information relating to access codes previously assigned to authorized users of the OSI computers.

The indictment handed down on February 3, 1976, charged that the defendant had, on December 30 and 31, transmitted telephone calls in interstate commerce as part of a scheme to defraud OSI of property consisting of information from the computer system. A motion to suppress the evidence seized from the office and the residence was considered at a hearing on April 30, after which the district judge rendered an oral opinion rejecting the defendant's argument that the searches were invalidated by the use of illegal electronic surveillance to obtain the information contained in the affidavits supporting the warrants.

Over defense objection, much of the challenged evidence was admitted at trial, and the telephone traces, as well as the operation of the "Milten Spy," were described to the jury. In the face of this evidence, the defendant conceded that he had retrieved the information from the computers, but claimed to have acted only out of concern for the security of the OSI system. In negation of fraudulent intent, Seidlitz testified that he acquired the data with the sole intention of presenting the printouts to OSI officials to prove to them that the steps taken to prevent unauthorized use of the computers were inadequate. Additionally, it was his position at trial that the WYLBUR software was not a trade secret or other property interest of OSI sufficient to qualify as "property" within the meaning of the wire fraud statute. On appeal he * * * argues that the evidence before the jury was insufficient to establish either his fraudulent intent or that WYLBUR constituted "property."

Viewed in the light most favorable to the government, there was sufficient evidence from which the jury could find that the WYLBUR system was "property" as defined in the instruction given by the trial judge which is not contested on appeal. Even though software systems similar to OSI's WYLBUR were in use at non-OSI facilities, the evidence that OSI invested substantial sums to modify the system to suit its peculiar needs, that OSI enjoyed a multi-million dollar competitive advantage because of WYLBUR, and that OSI took steps to prevent persons other than clients and employees from using the system permitted a finding that the pilfered data was the property of OSI and not, as the defendant contends, property in the public domain subject to appropriation by persons such as himself. In a similar vein, the defendant disputes the sufficiency of the evidence to establish fraudulent intent, but in essence his argument is only that he feels the jury should not have discredited his own explanation of the purpose for which he acquired the WYLBUR data. It is of no consequence that Seidlitz was not shown by the government to have used the data retrieved from the OSI computers in his own business or to have attempted to sell it to others, and the circumstantial evidence in this case is ample to support a finding of the requisite intent.

Notes and Questions

1. WYLBUR was a text-editing program that allowed users to direct computers to perform particular tasks. In what sense was the WYLBUR software "property?" Scholars and judges have struggled to agree upon a simple definition of property. Consider the following definitions:

A. "That is property to which the following label can be attached. To the world: Keep off X unless you have my permission, which I may grant or withhold. Signed: private citizen. Endorsed: the state." Felix S. Cohen, *Dialogue on Private Property*, 9 Rutgers L. Rev. 357, 374 (1954).

B. "Give someone the right to exclude others from a valued resource, i.e., a resource that is scarce relative to the human demand for it, and you give them property. Deny someone the exclusion right and they do not have property." Thomas W. Merrill, Essay, *Property and the Right to Exclude*, 77 Neb. L. Rev. 730, 730 (1998).

C. "[Property] consists in the free use, enjoyment, and disposal of all his acquisitions, without any control or diminution, save only by the laws of the land." 1 William Blackstone, Commentaries on the Laws of England *138.

D. "[Property is] a euphonious collection of letters which serves as a general term for the miscellany of equities that persons hold in the commonwealth." Walter Hamilton, 11 Encyclopedia of the Social Sciences 528 (1937).

Under which of these definitions is the WYLBUR software property?

2. In Carpenter v. United States, 484 U.S. 19 (1987), an influential Wall Street Journal columnist conspired with others to buy and sell stocks in anticipation of the effect his newspaper column "Heard on the Street" would have on the stock prices of companies he discussed. The government charged the columnist and his co-conspirators with mail fraud and wire fraud on the theory that the conspiracy had defrauded the Wall Street Journal of its property. According to the government, the "property" was the confidential

information scheduled to appear in the newspaper. The Supreme Court agreed and affirmed the convictions:

> Here, the object of the scheme was to take the Journal's confidential business information–the publication schedule and contents of the "Heard" column–and its intangible nature does not make it any less "property" protected by the mail and wire fraud statutes. * * *

> Both courts below expressly referred to the Journal's interest in the confidentiality of the contents and timing of the "Heard" column as a property right, and we agree with that conclusion. Confidential business information has long been recognized as property. Confidential information acquired or compiled by a corporation in the course and conduct of its business is a species of property to which the corporation has the exclusive right and benefit, and which a court of equity will protect through the injunctive process or other appropriate remedy. The Journal had a property right in keeping confidential and making exclusive use, prior to publication, of the schedule and contents of the "Heard" column.

Id. at 25–26.

Why should confidential business information be considered property for the purposes of criminal fraud statutes? Does the information's market value automatically mean that it should be treated as property? Should confidential information that has no market value also be treated as property? What about publicly-known information? Is all information property?

For an argument that *Carpenter* reflects an overly broad conception of property that permits theft prosecutions for an improperly wide range of conduct, see John C. Coffee, Jr., Hush!: *The Criminal Status of Confidential Information After* McNally *and* Carpenter *and the Enduring Problem of Overcriminalization*, 26 Am. Crim. L. Rev. 121, 130–40 (1988).

3. Whatever conceptual problems may be raised by labeling information as property for the purpose of property crime statutes, courts have done so in a wide range of cases involving computers. Courts have concluded that computer usage was property, *see* United States v. Collins, 56 F.3d 1416, 1420 (D.C. Cir. 1995), that the data stored in a computer counted as property, *see* United States v. Girard, 601 F.2d 69, 71 (2d Cir. 1979), and even that the password that controlled access to a computer account was property, *see* People v. Johnson, 560 N.Y.S.2d 238, 241, 243–44 (N.Y. Crim. Ct. 1990).

4. Conviction under the federal wire fraud statute requires intent to defraud, which requires knowing conduct together with intent to deceive. *See* United States v. Keller, 14 F.3d 1051, 1056 (5th Cir. 1994). Who did Seidlitz deceive when he logged on to the OSI computer and instructed the computer to send him data? One answer might be the OSI computer itself: Seidlitz identified himself to the computer as William Coakley's supervisor, tricking the computer into giving him access. But is it possible to deceive a machine? Imagine that a car thief picks the lock on a car door, and then steals the car. Would the thief be guilty of fraud, on the theory that he tricked the car lock into opening by convincing the lock that he was the car's rightful owner?

STATE v. McGRAW

Supreme Court of Indiana, 1985.
480 N.E.2d 552.

PRENTICE, Justice.

Defendant was charged with nine counts of theft under Ind. Code § 35–43–4–2, by information alleging that he knowingly exerted "unauthorized control over the property of the City of Indianapolis, Indiana, to-wit: the use of computers and computer services with intent to deprive the City of Indianapolis." He was convicted upon two counts, following a trial by jury. The trial court, thereafter, granted his renewed motion to dismiss, citing, among other grounds, the insufficiency of the evidence. The Court of Appeals reversed the trial court and ordered the verdicts reinstated.

Defendant was employed by the City of Indianapolis, as a computer operator. The City leased computer services on a fixed charge or flat rate basis, hence the expense to it was not varied by the extent to which it was used. Defendant was provided with a terminal at his desk and was assigned a portion of the computer's information storage capacity, called a "private library," for his utilization in performing his duties. No other employees were authorized to use his terminal or his library.

Defendant became involved in a private sales venture and began soliciting his co-workers and using a small portion of his assigned library to maintain records associated with the venture. He was reprimanded several times for selling his products in the office and on "office time," and he was eventually discharged for unsatisfactory job performance and for continuing his personal business activities during office hours.

Defendant, at the time of his being hired by the City, received a handbook, as do all new employees, which discloses the general prohibition against the unauthorized use of city property. Other city employees sometimes used the computer for personal convenience or entertainment; and although Defendant's supervisor knew or suspected that Defendant was using the computer for his business records, he never investigated the matter or reprimanded Defendant in this regard, and such use of the computer was not cited as a basis for his discharge.

Defendant, following his discharge, applied for and received unemployment compensation benefits, over the protest of the City. He requested a former fellow employee to obtain a "print-out" of his business data and then to erase it from what had been his library. Instead, the "print-out" was turned over to Defendant's former supervisor and became the basis for the criminal charges.

Assuming that Defendant's use of the computer was unauthorized and that such use is a "property" under the theft statute, there remains an element of the offense missing under the evidence. The act provides: "A person who knowingly or intentionally exerts unauthorized control over property of another person with *intent* to deprive the other of any part of its value or use, commits theft, a class D felony." Ind. Code § 35–43–4–2. It is immediately apparent that the res of the statute, the harm sought to be prevented, is a deprivation to one of his property or its use–not a benefit to one which, although a windfall to him, harmed nobody.

The Court of Appeals focused upon Defendant's unauthorized use of the computer for monetary gain and upon the definition of "property" as used in the statute and as defined by Ind. Code § 35–41–1–2, which we may assume, arguendo, includes the "use" of a computer, although we think that it would be more accurate to say that the *information* derived by use of a computer is *property*. Having determined that Defendant's use was property, was unauthorized and was for his monetary benefit, it concluded that he committed a theft. Our question is, "Who was deprived of what?"

Not only was there no evidence that the City was ever deprived of any part of the value or the use of the computer by reason of Defendant's conduct, the uncontradicted evidence was to the contrary. The computer was utilized for City business by means of terminals assigned to various employee-operators, including Defendant. The computer processed the data from the various terminals simultaneously, and the limit of its capacity was never reached or likely to have been. The computer service was leased to the City at a fixed charge, and the tapes or discs upon which the imparted data was stored were erasable and reusable. Defendant's unauthorized use cost the City nothing and did not interfere with its use by others. He extracted from the system only such information as he had previously put into it. He did not, for his own benefit, withdraw City data intended for its exclusive use or for sale. Thus, Defendant did not deprive the City of the "use of computers and computer services" as the information alleged that he intended to do. We find no distinction between Defendant's use of the City's computer and the use, by a mechanic, of the employer's hammer or a stenographer's use of the employer's typewriter, for other than the employer's purposes. Under traditional concepts, the transgression is in the nature of a trespass, a civil matter–and a de minimis one, at that. Defendant has likened his conduct to the use of an employer's vacant bookshelf, for the temporary storage of one's personal items, and to the use of an employer's telephone facilities for toll-free calls. The analogies appear to us to be appropriate.

We have written innumerable times, that intent is a mental function and, absent an admission, it must be determined by courts and juries from a consideration of the conduct and natural and usual consequences of such conduct. It follows that when the natural and usual consequences of the conduct charged and proved are not such as would effect the wrong which the statute seeks to prevent, the intent to effect that wrong is not so inferrable. No deprivation to the City resulted from Defendant's use of the computer, and a deprivation to it was not a result to be expected from such use, hence not a natural and usual consequence. There was no evidence presented from which the intent to deprive, an essential element of the crime, could be inferred.

It is appropriate to note a companion statute to the theft statute is Ind. Code § 35–43–4–3, proscribing *conversion,* which is as follows:

"A person who knowingly or intentionally exerts unauthorized control over property of another person commits criminal conversion, a class A misdemeanor."

The only difference between the statutory definitions of theft and criminal conversion is that the definition for conversion omits the words "with intent to deprive the other of any part of its value or use." At most, the evidence in this case warranted a conviction for criminal conversion.

We find no error. The decision and opinion of the Court of Appeals are ordered vacated, and the judgment of the trial court is affirmed.

PIVARNIK, Justice, dissenting.

I must dissent from the majority opinion wherein the majority finds that Defendant did not take property of the City "with intent to deprive the owner of said property." In the first place, intent is clearly shown in that Defendant used the City computer system for his personal business, well knowing that he was doing so and well knowing that it was unauthorized. I think the Court of Appeals properly focused upon Defendant's unauthorized use of the computer for monetary gain and upon the definition of property as used in the statute and as defined by Ind. Code § 35–41–1–2. Time and use are at the very core of the value of a computer system. To say that only the information stored in the computer plus the tapes and discs and perhaps the machinery involved in the computer system, are the only elements that can be measured as the value or property feature of that system, is incorrect.

I think it is irrelevant that the computer processed the data from various terminals simultaneously and the limit of its capacity was never reached by any or all of the stations, including the defendant's. It is also irrelevant that the computer service was leased to the City at a fixed charge and that the tapes or discs upon which the imparted data was stored were erasable and reusable. The fact is the City owned the computer system of all the stations including the defendant's. The time and use of that equipment at that station belonged to the City. Thus, when the defendant used the computer system, putting on data from his private business and taking it out on printouts, he was taking that which was property of the City and converting it to his own use, thereby depriving the City of its use and value. The majority says: "Thus, Defendant did not deprive the City of the 'use of computers and computer services' as the information alleged that he intended to do." I disagree. I feel that is exactly what he did and I think the Court of Appeals properly found so.

Notes and Questions

1. The majority argues that McGraw's conduct did not deprive the City of its property. But did McGraw infringe upon the City's right to exclude others from using its valuable resources? If the City's computer resembles a limitless fountain of property, as the majority's opinion suggests, doesn't the City have a right to control who should receive its bounty?

On the other hand, do you think an employee should be prosecuted criminally for using his employer's computer for personal reasons when that use does not interfere with the employer's interests? Do you think this question influenced the court in *McGraw*?

2. In the case of physical property, depriving the owner of property transfers that property from its owner to the defendant. The victim's loss is the same as the defendant's gain, namely the property taken. In *McGraw*, by contrast, the defendant received a benefit but the victim did not suffer a loss. The owner retained the property allegedly "taken."

This also occurred in the *Seidlitz* case. Seidlitz obtained a copy of the WYLBUR software, which potentially harmed OSI by allowing Seidlitz or others to compete against OSI on a more equal footing. But OSI's loss did not equal Seidlitz's gain: OSI was not deprived of WYLBUR, but rather of the economic benefits flowing from the exclusive use of WYLBUR. *Seidlitz* held that the WYLBUR program was property, which seems plausible. But did Seidlitz have intent to deprive OSI of that property? Should it matter?

3. *Conversion.* The *McGraw* majority suggests that the doctrine of conversion might be used to prosecute an employee's computer misuse when the employee does not intend to deprive others of the use of the computer. Unlike theft, conversion does not generally require an intent to deprive the owner of the property.

This approach was tried in United States v. Collins, 56 F.3d 1416 (D.C. Cir. 1995). Collins, an employee of the Defense Intelligence Agency, used a highly classified government computer network to store hundreds of personal documents relating to his interest in ballroom dancing. He was charged with converting government property in violation of 18 U.S.C. § 641. The D.C. Circuit rejected the government's theory that Collins had converted government property by using the classified computer network for personal purposes:

> The cornerstone of conversion is the unauthorized exercise of control over property in such a manner that *serious interference* with ownership rights occurs. Section 228 of the Restatement (Second) of Torts states "[o]ne who is authorized to make a particular use of a chattel, and uses it in a manner exceeding the authorization, is subject to liability for conversion to another whose right to control the use of the chattel is thereby *seriously violated*." *Id.* (emphasis added). The interference is of such a magnitude that the converter must pay the rightful owner the full value of the property converted. Restatement (Second) of Torts § 222A.
>
> The court's decision in *United States v. Wilson*, 636 F.2d 225 (8th Cir. 1980), is illuminating on this point. Appellant was found guilty by a

jury of converting government property in violation of section 641. Specifically, appellant was charged with converting secretarial time by using a government secretary to type documents for his personal business. No evidence existed, however, that the work interfered with the secretary's official duties. The district court granted a motion for judgment of acquittal, and the appellate court affirmed this judgment. The court held there was no evidence that appellant's conduct seriously interfered with the rights of the government. The court focused on the fact that appellant and his secretary had little or no assigned work during the period in question. Consequently, appellant could not have seriously interfered with the government's ownership rights because the government was never deprived of the use or possession of its property. Thus, while appellant may have engaged in a breach of fiduciary duty, his conduct was not criminal.

Similarly, the government did not provide a shred of evidence in the case at bar that appellant seriously interfered with the government's ownership rights in its computer system. While appellant concedes he typed in data and stored information on the computer regarding his personal activities, no evidence exists that such conduct prevented him or others from performing their official duties on the computer. The government did not even attempt to show that appellant's use of the computer prevented agency personnel from accessing the computer or storing information. Thus, appellant's use of the government computer in no way seriously interfered with the government's ownership rights.

Id. at 1420–21.

Compare *Collins* with United States v. Girard, 601 F.2d 69 (2d Cir. 1979). In *Girard,* a corrupt Drug Enforcement Administration (DEA) agent used the DEA's computer to access and download files identifying undercover DEA agents that he then planned to sell to drug dealers. The defendant was charged with converting government property in violation of 18 U.S.C. § 641. The Second Circuit affirmed the conviction, announcing in a conclusory fashion that the defendant had converted the government's property.

How do you reconcile *Collins* and *Girard*? Is the difference that *Girard* had at best thwarted DEA investigations and at worst risked the lives of DEA undercover agents, but *Collins* had not caused any harm to his government employer?

Imagine that you are a defense attorney in a future § 641 case that involves less harm than the facts of *Girard* but more harm than the facts of *Collins.* How can you persuade the court that your case is more like *Collins* than *Girard*?

4. Does the law of theft provide a useful way of prohibiting computer misuse? Here is a critical perspective:

When computer misuse caused harm to a victim in some way, courts [applying theft law to computer misuse] generally concluded that property had in fact been taken and held the defendants liable. When no appreciable harm resulted, courts tended to find that no property was taken and hold that the defendants had committed no crime. To the extent that it was made explicit, the reasoning seemed to go something like this: When a person is harmed, the person loses something of value; when a person loses something of value, they are deprived of property. Therefore the infliction of harm triggers a theft. This reasoning allowed courts to reach reasonable results in particular cases, but followed no deeper principle than the courts' ex post assessments of whether particular instances of computer misuse had caused substantial harm.

Orin S. Kerr, *Cybercrime's Scope: Interpreting "Access" and "Authorization" in Computer Misuse Statutes,* 78 N.Y.U. L. Rev. 1596, 1611 (2003). If the use of theft law to punish computer misuse was result-oriented, is that a good thing or a bad thing?

5. *Arguments for and against computer crime statutes.* Starting in the late 1970s, dissatisfaction with the cases applying theft law to computer misuse led to a movement to adopt new computer misuse statutes. State computer crime prosecutor Donald Ingraham offered one rationale for such statutes in an early article. *See* Donald G. Ingraham, *On Charging Computer Crime,* 2 Computer/L.J. 429 (1980). Ingraham reasoned that computer crime statutes were needed for the same reason criminal codes prohibit burglary and trespass. It would be possible to repeal burglary and trespass laws and simply prosecute every property crime as a theft, Ingraham noted. But such an approach would be quite awkward:

> For example, attempted commercial burglary could be regarded as a usurpation of store floor space, and treated as a theft of the property interest in occupancy. Under such a statute, the victim would necessarily be compelled to calculate the value of the property invaded and the duration of the invasion. The prosecution would be for the theft of those values, and not for the intrusion as a crime complete in itself. It is precisely that absurdity–the requirement that the victim prepare evidence of an injury other than that with which he is really concerned—which the so-called computer crime bills have recognized and sought to redress.

Id. at 429–30.

Donn Parker, one of the leading proponents of the new computer misuse statutes, offered a less conceptual and more practical set of arguments in favor of enacting new statutes:

1. Specific, specialized statutes focus attention on the significant social and ethical problem of computer abuse. The potential size of single losses makes the problem significant and worthy of such attention.

2. Specific new laws confront technologists in high positions of trust with visible, direct deterrents from engaging in harmful acts in a new area of human endeavor where the harm of abusive acts has not been sufficiently perceived.

3. Computer crime laws encourage management to establish rules governing authorized and unauthorized computer-related activities of employees. This benefits organizations as well as employees because everybody then knows a consistent set of rules and where they stand.

4. Prosecution problems will be eased and litigation time can be reduced, thus reducing costs.

5. Specific laws will avoid the legal fictions of having to use other criminal statutes that weren't meant to apply to computer crime, and criminals can be convicted directly for their explicit acts.

6. Specific laws will provide a means to gather statistics on computer crime to determine the severity and characteristics of the problem.

7. A federal computer crime law will advance uniformity across other jurisdictions.

Donn B. Parker, Fighting Computer Crime 244 (1983).

More recently, other commentators have questioned whether the specific computer crime statutes are necessary. Consider this argument that traditional property laws are sufficient to deter and punish computer misuse:

> Legislators and others apprehensive about the misuse of technology too often have perceived a need to enact statutes to counteract "computer crimes" that are in fact already existing crimes accomplished with new techniques. To the extent that such statutes merely prohibit conduct that is already criminal, they are simply redundant. To the extent that they are drafted in "technology-specific" language, the pace of technological change and the ingenuity of computer-literate criminals guarantee that those statutes will be obsolete almost as soon as they are enacted. To the extent that they focus on technological means, rather than on the harm caused by a defendant's conduct, those statutes tend towards overbreadth by sweeping within their ambit anyone who uses the means regardless of result. To the extent that computer-specific statutes are enacted by legislators unfamiliar or uncomfortable with technology, such statutes tend to reflect a lack of clarity or understanding or, sometimes, simply fear. Thus, a "computer-specific" approach results, too often, in criminal statutes that are unnecessary, imprecise, clumsy, over-inclusive, or ineffective.

Joseph M. Olivenbaum, *Ctrl-Alt–Delete: Rethinking Federal Computer Crime Legislation*, 27 Seton Hall L. Rev. 574, 575–76 (1997).

In an article on the differences between physical crime and virtual crime, Professor Susan W. Brenner has also expressed some skepticism about the need for new laws:

> [T]he principles we have traditionally used to impose liability for crimes * * * can be extrapolated to encompass many, if not all, of the activities characterized as cybercrimes. The article argues for taking this approach rather than trying to devise new principles of criminal liability, a new law of cybercrimes, to address anti-social behavior occurring within or committed via cyberspace. At the same time, it concedes there may be reasons for devising a new law of cybercrimes, such as the greater harms that can be inflicted by cybercriminals and the advantages they enjoy in avoiding detection and prosecution. The article cautions, however, against taking hasty action in this regard, suggesting that we wait to see how crime in cyberspace evolves before committing ourselves to the adoption of cybercrime laws.

Susan W. Brenner, *Is There Such a Thing as "Virtual Crime?"* 4 Cal. Crim. L. Rev. 1, ¶ 129 (2001).

In contrast, Beryl Howell, former Chief Counsel to the Senate Judiciary Committee under Senator Patrick Leahy, has defended the computer-specific approach to prohibiting computer misuse against such criticisms:

> [S]pecific laws directed to specific problems are important for two main reasons. First, they serve to guide law enforcement as to how investigations may be conducted with appropriate respect for civil liberties and privacy. Second, specific laws make clear to people the boundary of legally permissible conduct.
>
> Does this require endless effort to update the laws to keep pace with technology? Yes, but Congress returns every year with the job of making new laws. Will the pace of legal changes always be behind technological developments? Yes, but in my view the correct pace is a slow one. By the time a proposal has gone through the legislative process, the problem it seeks to address will have become more defined. Policy-makers are better able to craft a narrow and circumscribed law to address a clearly defined problem, and thus, minimize the risk of an overly expansive law that could chill innovation and technological development.

Beryl A. Howell, *Real World Problems of Virtual Crime*, 7 Yale J. L. & Tech. 103, 104–105 (2004–2005).

When evaluating the need for computer crime statutes, it is worth noting that criminal codes contain many technology-specific statutes. For example, the United States Code includes statutes criminalizing the destruction of aircraft (18 U.S.C. § 32), use of aircraft or motor vehicles to hunt protected wild horses (18 U.S.C. § 47), sending a threatening communication through the postal mail (18 U.S.C. § 876), using a radio or television station to broadcast information about an unauthorized lottery (18 U.S.C. § 1304), broadcasting obscene language by radio (18 U.S.C. § 1464), carjacking (18 U.S.C. § 2119), transporting stolen vehicles (18 U.S.C. § 2312), selling or receiving stolen vehicles (18 U.S.C. § 2313), and engaging in telemarketing fraud (18 U.S.C. § 2326). In light of this list, do you think that a statute prohibiting computer misuse is really out of place? Are technology-specific criminal statutes the exception or the rule?

C. UNAUTHORIZED ACCESS STATUTES

1. INTRODUCTION TO UNAUTHORIZED ACCESS STATUTES

The perceived deficiencies of prosecuting computer misuse using theft laws led the federal government and all fifty states to enact statutes specifically prohibiting computer misuse. Florida passed the first state statute in 1978; the final state to enact a statute was Vermont in 1999. Congress enacted the first federal computer crime law in 1984, broadened it considerably in 1986, and then updated it in various ways in 1990, 1994, 1996, and 2001. No two of these statutory schemes are exactly alike, and many of the laws enumerate several distinct crimes in response to different types of misuse. *See generally* Susan W. Brenner, *State Cybercrime Legislation in the United States of America: A Survey*, 7 Rich. J.L. & Tech. 28 (2001). For a comprehensive review of all of the statutes, see A. Hugh Scott, Computer and Intellectual Property Crime: Federal and State Law (2001).

Despite the differences among the federal and state statutes, the statutory schemes share a number of basic features. The most important is the common building block of unauthorized access to a computer. Every state and the federal government has an unauthorized access statute. This basic offense is usually supplemented by other elements to create additional criminal prohibitions, such as statutes prohibiting computer fraud and computer damage.

To understand modern computer crime law, it is essential to understand the meaning of the basic prohibition on unauthorized access to a computer. The most helpful way to learn about unauthorized access statutes is to focus primarily on the influential federal statute, 18 U.S.C. § 1030.

Overview of 18 U.S.C. § 1030

18 U.S.C. § 1030 is the federal computer misuse statute, sometimes referred to as the Computer Fraud and Abuse Act or CFAA. Section 1030(a) lists seven distinct crimes, most of which are keyed to the basic unauthorized access prohibition. Oddly, the first of the seven crimes is the least important in practice: § 1030(a)(1) is an extremely narrow statute that prohibits accessing a computer without authorization or exceeding authorized access to obtain classified information to injure the United State or aid a foreign power. Although it is the first in the list of § 1030(a) crimes, it appears never to have been used.

In contrast, § 1030(a)(2) is the most frequently charged § 1030 crime. Section 1030(a)(2) prohibits accessing a computer without authorization or exceeding authorized access and obtaining information. Section 1030(a)(3) is only rarely used, and applies specifically to United States government computers. The statute prohibits accessing a United States government computer without authorization. Section 1030(a)(4) is the federal computer fraud statute: it combines the unauthorized access prohibition of § 1030(a)(2) with the basic workings of the wire fraud statute. Section 1030(a)(5) is the federal computer damage statute. It prohibits both unauthorized damage to a computer and also unauthorized access that results in damage. Section 1030(a)(6) prohibits computer password trafficking, and is based heavily on the federal credit card fraud statute, 18 U.S.C. § 1029. Finally, § 1030(a)(7) is an extortion statute, based largely on the federal interstate threat statute, 18 U.S.C. § 875. Section 1030(a)(7) prohibits extorting money or other property using threats to cause damage to computers.

The remaining sections of 18 U.S.C. § 1030 supplement the basic seven crimes in 18 U.S.C. § 1030(a). Section 1030(b) makes clear that attempts are covered by the statute; any attempt to engage in conduct that would be a violation of § 1030(a) if successful is considered a violation of § 1030(b). Section 1030(c) contains the statutory maximum punishments for all of the different §§ 1030(a) and (b) offenses. Section

1030(c) is quite detailed, as Congress chose to treat some § 1030 offenses as misdemeanors, others as felonies with 5–year maximum punishments, and others as more serious felonies. This subsection effectively adds elements to the different § 1030 crimes to trigger felony liability in some circumstances.

Sections 1030(d), 1040(f), and 1030(h) are mostly unimportant for our purposes. They concern jurisdiction, oversight, and create an exception for government investigations in some cases. In contrast, § 1030(e) and § 1030(g) are noteworthy. Section 1030(e) is critical from a doctrinal perspective because it contains statutory definitions of all of the key terms used elsewhere. Section 1030(g) is important at a conceptual level because it explains much of the shape of existing law. Section 1030(g) provides a civil remedy for some kinds of violations, permitting victims of computer misuse to sue in federal court. Thanks to § 1030(g), most of the published cases interpreting § 1030 arise in the civil context rather than the criminal context.

18 U.S.C. § 1030(a)(2)

The two provisions in § 1030 that embody the basic unauthorized access prohibition are 18 U.S.C. §§ 1030(a)(2) and (a)(3). Let's take a close look at them. Section 1030(a)(2) states that it is a crime if a person:

> intentionally accesses a computer without authorization or exceeds authorized access, and thereby obtains—
>
> (A) information contained in a financial record of a financial institution, or of a card issuer as defined in section 1602 (n) of title 15, or contained in a file of a consumer reporting agency on a consumer, as such terms are defined in the Fair Credit Reporting Act (15 U.S.C. 1681 et seq.);
>
> (B) information from any department or agency of the United States; or
>
> (C) information from any protected computer if the conduct involved an interstate or foreign communication.

The requirement that the defendant must obtain information required under (a)(2)(A), (B), or (C) may sound significant at first, but proves a surprisingly low hurdle. The Senate Report that accompanied the passage of § 1030(a)(2) contains the following discussion:

> The Department of Justice has expressed concerns that the term "obtains information" in 18 U.S.C. 1030(a)(2) makes that subsection more than an unauthorized access offense, i.e., that it might require the prosecution to prove asportation of the data in question. Because the premise of this subsection is privacy protection, the Committee wishes to make clear that "obtaining information" in this context includes mere observation of the data. Actual asportation, in the sense of physically removing the data from its original location or transcribing the data, need not be proved in order to establish a violation of this subsection.

S. Rep. No. 99–432 (1986), *reprinted in* 1986 U.S.C.C.A.N. 2479, 2484. It is unclear whether § 1030(a)(2) requires actual observation of the data, or whether merely coming into possession of the data is sufficient. In any event, the fact that most computer intruders will see information inside the victim network means that most computer hacking will end up violating 18 U.S.C. § 1030(a)(2).

The broad scope of § 1030(a)(2) is due largely to § 1030(a)(2)(C). Sections 1030(a)(2)(A) and (a)(2)(B) are comparatively narrow; the former covers financial records as defined in § 1030(e)(4)-(5), and the latter covers only information obtained from United States government computers as defined in § 1030(e)(7). In contrast, § 1030(a)(2)(C) has vast scope. Any information from any protected computer is sufficient so long as the conduct "involved an interstate or foreign communication," which presumably means that at least one communication that was part of the conduct must have crossed state or international boundaries.

The definition of "protected computer" is quite broad. Sections 1030(e)(1) and (e)(2) provide:

> (1) the term "computer" means an electronic, magnetic, optical, electrochemical, or other high speed data processing device performing logical, arithmetic, or storage functions, and includes any data storage facility or communications facility directly related to or operating in conjunction with such device, but such term does not include an automated typewriter or typesetter, a portable hand held calculator, or other similar device;

> (2) the term "protected computer" means a computer

> (A) exclusively for the use of a financial institution or the United States Government, or, in the case of a computer not exclusively for such use, used by or for a financial institution or the United States Government and the conduct constituting the offense affects that use by or for the financial institution or the Government; or

> (B) which is used in interstate or foreign commerce or communications, including a computer located outside the United States that is used in a manner that affects interstate or foreign commerce or communication of the United States[.]

Under this definition, it seems, any computer with an Internet connection is a "protected computer." As a result, "obtaining information" from a "protected computer" in § 1030(a)(2) can mean simply viewing data from a computer that is connected to the Internet.

The mens rea required under § 1030(a)(2) is intent. The Senate Report that accompanied a change of the mens rea from "knowingly" to "intentionally" in 1986 offered the following explanation for the change:

> First, intentional acts of unauthorized access—rather than mistaken, inadvertent, or careless ones—are precisely what the Committee intends to proscribe. Second, the Committee is concerned that the "knowingly" standard in the existing statute might be

inappropriate for cases involving computer technology. The Senate's Report on the Criminal Code states that a person is said to act knowingly if he is aware "that the result is practically certain to follow from his conduct, whatever his desire may be as to that result."

While appropriate to many criminal statutes, this standard might not be sufficient to preclude liability on the part of those who inadvertently "stumble into" someone else's computer file or computer data. This is particularly true in those cases where an individual is authorized to sign onto and use a particular computer, but subsequently exceeds his authorized access by mistakenly entering another computer file or data that happens to be accessible from the same terminal. Because the user had "knowingly" signed onto that terminal in the first place, the danger exists that he might incur liability for his mistaken access to another file. This is so because, while he may not have desired that result, i.e., the access of another file, it is possible that a trier of fact will infer that the user was "practically certain" such mistaken access could result from his initial decision to access the computer. The substitution of an "intentional" standard is designed to focus Federal criminal prosecutions on those whose conduct evinces a clear intent to enter, without proper authorization, computer files or data belonging to another. Again, this will comport with the Senate Report on the Criminal Code, which states that "intentional" means more than that one voluntarily engaged in conduct or caused a result. Such conduct or the causing of the result must have been the person's conscious objective.

S. Rep. No. 99–432, *reprinted in* 1986 U.S.C.C.A.N. 2479, 2483–84.

Violations of 18 U.S.C. § 1030(a)(2) can be either misdemeanors or felonies as determined by 18 U.S.C. § 1030(c)(2).[b] Violations of § 1030(a)(2) constitute misdemeanors unless the offense was committed "for purposes of commercial advantage or private financial gain," the offense was committed "in furtherance of any criminal or tortious act in violation of the Constitution or laws of the United States or of any State," or the value of the information obtained exceeds $5,000. In that case, the crime becomes a felony punishable by up to five years in prison. In addition, a § 1030(a)(2) offense becomes a felony punishable by up to 10 years in prison if the defendant has a prior conviction under § 1030(a) or 1030(b).

18 U.S.C. § 1030(a)(3)

Section 1030(a)(3) states that it is a crime if a person:

intentionally, without authorization to access any nonpublic computer of a department or agency of the United States, accesses such a

b. Federal law classifies misdemeanors as crimes punishable by a year or less of prison time. Felonies are crimes that allow the possibility of greater than a year of prison. *See* 18 U.S.C. § 3559(a).

computer of that department or agency that is exclusively for the use of the Government of the United States or, in the case of a computer not exclusively for such use, is used by or for the Government of the United States and such conduct affects that use by or for the Government of the United States.

Violations of § 1030(a)(3) are misdemeanors unless the defendant has a prior conviction under § 1030. If the defendant has a prior conviction, the crime is a felony punishable by up to ten years in prison.

Section 1030(a)(3) is different from § 1030(a)(2) in a number of ways. First, § 1030(a)(3) applies only to access into United States government computers. Second, it is a simple trespass statute; there is no requirement that any information be obtained by the defendant. Third, the basic prohibition is limited to "access without authorization," whereas § 1030(a)(2) includes both a defendant who "accessed without authorization" and a defendant who "exceeds authorized access." As we will see, the precise distinction between access without authorization and exceeding authorized access is quite difficult to follow, and it's not clear that a robust distinction exists. But the limitation of § (a)(3) reflects a design for the statute to reach only a limited class of cases.

The Senate Report that accompanied the enactment of the modern version of 18 U.S.C. § 1030(a)(3) included the following discussion of its scope:

> * * * [I]t applies to acts of simple trespass against computers belonging to, or being used by or for, the Federal Government. The Department of Justice and others have expressed concerns about whether the present subsection covers acts of mere trespass, i.e., unauthorized access, or whether it requires a further showing that the information perused was "used, modified, destroyed, or disclosed." To alleviate those concerns, the Committee wants to make clear that the new subsection will be a simple trespass offense, applicable to persons without authorized access to Federal computers.

> The Committee wishes to be very precise about who may be prosecuted under the new subsection (a)(3). The Committee was concerned that a Federal computer crime statute not be so broad as to create a risk that government employees and others who are authorized to use a Federal Government computer would face prosecution for acts of computer access and use that, while technically wrong, should not rise to the level of criminal conduct. At the same time, the Committee was required to balance its concern for Federal employees and other authorized users against the legitimate need to protect Government computers against abuse by "outsiders." The Committee struck that balance in the following manner.

> In the first place, the Committee has declined to criminalize acts in which the offending employee merely "exceeds authorized access" to computers in his own department. * * * It is not difficult to envision an employee or other individual who, while authorized to

use a particular computer in one department, briefly exceeds his authorized access and peruses data belonging to the department that he is not supposed to look at. This is especially true where the department in question lacks a clear method of delineating which individuals are authorized to access certain of its data. The Committee believes that administrative sanctions are more appropriate than criminal punishment in such a case. The Committee wishes to avoid the danger that every time an employee exceeds his authorized access to his department's computers–no matter how slightly–he could be prosecuted under this subsection. That danger will be prevented by not including "exceeds authorized access" as part of this subsection's offense.

In the second place, the Committee has distinguished between acts of unauthorized access that occur within a department and those that involve trespasses into computers belonging to another department. The former are not covered by subsection (a)(3); the latter are. Again, it is not difficult to envision an individual who, while authorized to use certain computers in one department, is not authorized to use them all. The danger existed that [the initial version of § 1030(a)(3)], might cover every employee who happens to sit down, within his department, at a computer terminal which he is not officially authorized to use. These acts can also be best handled by administrative sanctions, rather than by criminal punishment. To that end, the Committee has constructed its amended version of (a)(3) to prevent prosecution of those who, while authorized to use some computers in their department, use others for which they lack the proper authorization. By precluding liability in purely "insider" cases such as these, the Committee also seeks to alleviate concerns raised by Senators Mathias and Leahy that the existing statute casts a wide net over "whistleblowers," who disclose information they have gleaned from a government computer.

The Committee has thus limited 18 U.S.C. § 1030(a)(3) to cases where the offender is completely outside the Government, and has no authority to access a computer of any agency or department of the United States, or where the offender's act of trespass is interdepartmental in nature. The Committee does not intend to preclude prosecution under this subsection if, for example, a Labor Department employee authorized to use Labor's computers accesses without authorization an FBI computer. An employee who uses his department's computer and, without authorization, forages into data belonging to another department, is engaged in conduct directly analogous to an "outsider" tampering with Government computers. In both cases, the user is wholly lacking in authority to access or use that department's computer. The Committee believes criminal prosecution should be available in such cases.

The Committee acknowledges that in rare circumstances this may leave serious cases of intradepartmental trespass free from criminal prosecution under (a)(3). However, the Committee notes

that such serious acts may be subject to other criminal penalties....
The Committee believes this to be the best means of balancing the
legitimate need to protect the Government's computers against the
need to prevent unwarranted prosecutions of Federal employees and
others authorized to use Federal computers.

S. Rep. No. 99–432 (1986), *reprinted in* 1986 U.S.C.C.A.N. 2479, 2484–
87.

Note that the Senate Report reflects how computers were used in
the mid–1980s, when a government employee might use a terminal to
access a mainframe computer. How should these principles apply in the
case of a computer server connected to the Internet? When is a government computer a "public" computer versus a "nonpublic" computer?
Don't spend too much time pondering these questions: As a practical
matter, the broad scope of § 1030(a)(2) means that most cases charge-
able under § 1030(a)(3) can also be charged under § 1030(a)(2).

2. WHAT IS "ACCESS"?

Now that we have seen the basic framework of two unauthorized
access statutes, let's look in depth at the meaning of "access." The
prohibition on unauthorized access can be understood at a very general
level as a sort of computer trespass crime. The statute focuses on the
defendant's rights at the time he accesses the computer. Liability does
not hinge on whether we can artificially define some kind of property
interest, or whether the computer owner was deprived of some kind of
right. Instead, the law monitors the defendant's "access" to the victim
computer and then asks whether that access was authorized. But what is
"access" to a computer?

Obviously a computer user does not access a computer by
physically getting inside the computer. Some other principle must
govern. But what principle should that be? One approach would look
at computers from the standpoint of virtual reality, and try to draw
analogies between using a computer and entering real property. We
could say that access hinges on whether the user has made a virtual
entrance into the computer. For example, imagine a user tries to use
a password-protected computer network and is confronted by a
screen that requires a valid username and password to proceed. We
might say that this screen is akin to a lock on a front door, and that
entering a username and password is like using a key to open the
lock. This approach suggests that a user who enters a valid username and password has accessed the computer, but a user who
inputs an incorrect name or password has been denied access.

Similarly, we could say that visiting a publicly accessible website
is something like visiting an open store in the physical world.
Determining whether access has occurred then depends on whether
visiting an open store can be deemed "entering" in the physical
world. The correct answer is not obvious: Visiting a website could be
seen as equivalent to viewing a shop window from a public street

rather than actually entering the store. But at a conceptual level, the analogy to virtual space provides one heuristic to understand what it means to "access" a computer.

The virtual analogy does not provide the only tool, however. We can also look at the question of access from the standpoint of physical reality, in which we recognize that computers are simply machines that communicate with each other by sending and receiving information. For example, when a user visits a website, the user's computer sends requests to the computer that hosts the website asking the computer to send back computer files; when the files are returned to the user, the user's computer reassembles the files and presents them in the form of a website. If we focus on how computers operate, we can interpret access by looking to whether a user has sent communications that have physically entered the computer. For example, one standard could be that a user accesses a computer when she sends a command to that computer instructing the computer to perform a task, and the computer performs the request as instructed. Another standard could be that a user accesses a computer when the user sends a command requesting information in return and the computer responds by sending back information to the user. In this sense, accessing a computer is no different from simply using a computer.

Notably, physical-world standards and virtual-world standards can produce different outcomes. Imagine a user wishes to log on to a password-protected computer, and sends a request to the computer asking it to send back the page that prompts the user to enter a username and password. The computer complies, sending the page back to the user. This would not access the computer from a virtual perspective, as it would be something like walking up to a locked door but not yet trying the key. From a physical-world perspective, however, the request would be an access; the user sent a command to the computer and received the desired response. Similarly, consider whether sending an e-mail accesses the computers of the recipient's Internet service provider. From a virtual perspective, the answer would seem to be no; a user who sends an e-mail to the ISP does not understand herself to have "entered" the ISP. From a physical perspective, however, the answer seems to be yes; the user has in fact sent a communication to the ISP that its servers received and processed.

Which standard governs? The statutes themselves offer little guidance. Most computer crime statutes (including the federal statute) do not define access, and most statutes that do include a definition shed little light on these questions.

Orin S. Kerr, *Cybercrime's Scope: Interpreting "Access" and "Authorization" in Computer Misuse Statutes,* 78 N.Y.U. L. Rev. 1596, 1619–21 (2003). Consider these questions as you read the following case construing "access" in the context of a state unauthorized access statute.

STATE v. ALLEN

Supreme Court of Kansas, 1996.
260 Kan. 107, 917 P.2d 848.

LARSON, Justice.

In this first impression case, we are presented with the question of whether a person's telephonic connections that prompt a computer owner to change its security systems constitute felony computer crime in violation of K.S.A. 21–3755(b).

The charges against Anthony A. Allen arose from several telephonic connections he made with Southwestern Bell Telephone Company's computers in early 1995. After preliminary hearing, the trial court dismissed the complaint, finding no probable cause existed to believe Allen had committed any crime.

The State has appealed pursuant to K.S.A. 22–3602(b)(1). We affirm the trial court.

Because the result in this case must be limited to and driven by the facts presented at the preliminary hearing, we will summarize the evidence there presented in considerable detail.

Allen admitted to Detective Kent Willnauer that he had used his computer, equipped with a modem, to call various Southwestern Bell computer modems. The telephone numbers for the modems were obtained by random dialing. If one of Allen's calls were completed, his computer determined if it had been answered by voice or another computer. These were curiosity calls of short duration.

The State presented no evidence which showed that Allen ever had entered any Southwestern Bell computer system. Detective Willnauer was unable to state that Allen had altered any programs, added anything to the system, used it to perform any functions, or interfered with its operation. Willnauer specifically stated he had no evidence that the Southwestern Bell computer system had been damaged.

Ronald W. Knisley, Southwestern Bell's Regional Security Director, testified Allen had called two different types of Southwestern Bell computer equipment—SLC–96 system environmental controls and SMS–800 database systems.

The telephone numbers for the SLC–96 systems were thought to be known only to Southwestern Bell employees or agents on a need-to-know basis. Access to the SLC–96 systems required knowledge of a password. If one connected to the system it displayed "KEYWORD?" without any identification or warning. No evidence existed that Allen attempted to respond to the prompt.

Testimony confirmed Allen also called and connected 28 times with the SMS–800 systems at several different modem numbers. Each call but two was under 1 minute. Upon connection with this system, a person would see a log on request and a "banner." The banner identifies the system that has answered the incoming call and displays that it is Southwestern Bell property and that access is restricted. Entry into the system itself then requires both a user ID and a password which must agree with each other. No evidence indicated Allen went beyond this banner or even attempted to enter a user ID or password.

Knisley testified that if entry into an SMS–800 system were accomplished and proper commands were given, a PBX system could be located which would allow unlimited and nonchargeable long distance telephone calls. There was no evidence this occurred, nor was it shown that Allen had damaged, modified, destroyed, or copied any data.

James E. Robinson, Function Manager responsible for computer security, testified one call to an SMS–800 system lasted 6 minutes and 35 seconds. Although the system should have retained information about this call, it did not, leading to speculation the record-keeping system had been overridden. Robinson speculated Allen had gained entry into the system but admitted he had no evidence that Allen's computer had done anything more than sit idle for a few minutes after calling a Southwestern Bell modem number.

Robinson testified that Southwestern Bell was unable to document any damage to its computer equipment or software as a result of Allen's activities. However, as a result of its investigation, Southwestern Bell decided that prudence required it to upgrade its password security system to a more secure "token card" process. It was the cost of this investigation and upgrade that the State alleges comprises the damage caused by Allen's actions. Total investigative costs were estimated at $4,140. The cost of developing deterrents was estimated to be $1,656. The cost to distribute secure ID cards to employees totaled $18,000. Thus, the total estimated damage was $23,796.

In closing arguments, the State admitted Allen did not get into the computer system, nor did he modify, alter, destroy, copy, disclose, or take possession of anything. *See* K.S.A. 21–3755(b)(1). Instead, the State argued Allen's conduct in acquiring the unlisted numbers and calling them constituted an "approach" to the systems, within the meaning of K.S.A. 21–3755(a)(1), which questioned the integrity of the systems and resulted in the altered or added security precautions.

In its oral ruling, the trial court noted K.S.A. 21–3755 was unclear. The court then held the mere fact Allen made telephone calls, a legal activity, which resulted in the connection of two modems, was insufficient to prove he had "gained access" to Southwestern Bell's computer systems as the K.S.A. 21–3755(b)(1) charge required. * * *

The legal standard to be applied in a preliminary hearing is clear. If it appears from the evidence presented that a crime has been committed and there is probable cause to believe the defendant committed it, K.S.A. 22–2902(3) requires that the defendant be bound over for trial. If there is not sufficient evidence, the defendant must be discharged. From the evidence presented, the trial court must draw the inferences favorable to the prosecution, and the evidence need only establish probable cause. Probable cause at a preliminary hearing signifies evidence sufficient to cause a person of ordinary prudence and caution to conscientiously entertain a reasonable belief of the accused's guilt.

Allen was charged under K.S.A. 21–3755, which in applicable part provides:

(a) As used in this section, the following words and phrases shall have the meanings respectively ascribed thereto:

(1) "Access" means to approach, instruct, communicate with, store data in, retrieve data from, or otherwise make use of any resources of a computer, computer system or computer network.

* * *

(b) Computer crime is:

(1) Intentionally and without authorization gaining or attempting to gain access to and damaging, modifying, altering, destroying, copying, disclosing or taking possession of a computer, computer system, computer network or any other property;

* * *

(2) Computer crime which causes a loss of the value of at least $500 but less than $25,000 is a severity level 9, nonperson felony.

Allen was charged with a violation of K.S.A. 21–3755(b)(1), with the second amended complaint alleging that he "did then and there intentionally and without authorization gain access and damage a computer, computer system, computer network or other computer property which caused a loss of the value of at least $500.00 but less than $25,000.00, a severity level 9 non-person felony."

Felony computer crime as it is charged in this case under K.S.A. 21–3755(b)(1) required the State to prove three distinct elements: (1) intentional and unauthorized access to a computer, computer system, computer network, or any other property (as property is defined in K.S.A. 21–3755[a] [8]); (2) damage to a computer, computer system, computer network, or any other property; and (3) a loss in value as a result of such crime of at least $500 but less than $25,000. The trial court found that the State failed to show probable cause as to each of these elements.

After finding the evidence showed Allen had done nothing more than use his computer to call unlisted telephone numbers, the trial court ruled there was insufficient evidence to show Allen had gained access to the computer systems. Although a telephone connection had been established, the evidence showed Allen had done nothing more. The trial court reasoned that unless and until Allen produced a password that permitted him to interact with the data in the computer system, he had not "gained access" as the complaint required.

The State argues the trial court's construction of the statute ignores the fact that "access" is defined in the statute, K.S.A. 21–3755(a)(1), as "to approach, instruct, communicate with, store data in, retrieve data from, or otherwise make use of any resources of a computer, computer system or computer network." By this definition, the State would lead us to believe that any kind of an "approach" is criminal behavior sufficient to satisfy a charge that Allen did in fact "gain access" to a computer system.

The problem with the State's analysis is that K.S.A. 21–3755(b)(1) does not criminalize "accessing" (and, thus, "approaching") but rather "gaining or attempting to gain access." If we were to read "access" in this context as the equivalent of "approach," the statute would criminalize the behavior of "attempting to gain approach" to a computer or computer system. This phrase is lacking in any common meaning such that an ordinary person would have great difficulty discerning what conduct was prohibited, leading to an effective argument that the statute was void for vagueness.

The United States Department of Justice has commented about the use of "approach" in a definition of "access" in this context: "The use of the word 'approach' in the definition of 'access,' if taken literally, could mean that any unauthorized physical proximity to a computer could constitute a crime." National Institute of Justice, Computer Crime: Criminal Justice Resource Manual, p. 84 (2d ed.1989).

We read certain conduct as outside a statute's scope rather than as proscribed by the statute if including it within the statute would render the statute unconstitutionally vague. Consequently, although K.S.A. 21–3755 defines "access," the plain and ordinary meaning should apply rather than a tortured translation of the definition that is provided.

In addition, K.S.A. 21–3755 is certainly rendered ambiguous by the inclusion of the definition of "access" as a verb when its only use in the statute is as a noun. As a criminal statute, any ambiguity is to be resolved in favor of the accused.

Webster's defines "access" as "freedom or ability to obtain or make use of." Webster's New Collegiate Dictionary, p. 7 (1977). This is similar to the construction used by the trial court to find that no evidence showed that Allen had gained access to Southwestern Bell's computers. Until Allen proceeded beyond the initial banner and entered appropriate passwords, he could not be said to have had the ability to make use of Southwestern Bell's computers or obtain anything. Therefore, he cannot be said to have gained access to Southwestern Bell's computer systems as gaining access is commonly understood. The trial court did not err in determining the State had failed to present evidence showing probable cause that Allen had gained access to Southwestern Bell's computer system.

Notes and Questions

1. What would have been wrong with a literal reading of the definition of "access"? Is the problem that it would place too much weight on the

difficult question of when access is unauthorized? Or is the problem that the legislature defined access broadly in § 21–3755(a)(1), but then used it in a much narrower sense in § (b)(1)?

The broad statutory definition of "access" used by the Kansas statute at issue in *Allen* was copied from an early bill introduced in Congress in 1977, the Federal Computer Systems Protection Act introduced by Senator Ribicoff. S. 1766, 95th Cong. (1977). *See generally* Michael M. Krieger, *Current and Proposed Computer Crime Legislation*, 2 Computer/L.J. 721, 723 (1980) (compiling legislation). Senator Ribicoff's bill was never enacted by Congress, but it did influence a number of state computer crime statutes. Notably, Congress opted not to define "access" when it enacted 18 U.S.C. § 1030. Do you think it is wise for legislatures to try to define access, or should they leave it up to the courts to decide on a case-by-case basis?

2. *State v. Riley. Allen* suggests that a person accesses a computer only when she goes beyond the initial prompt and gains the ability to make use of the computer. Put another way, *Allen* requires actually getting "inside" the computer. Merely "knocking on the door" is not enough. This appears to be a virtual reality approach to access, in which access requires a kind of virtual entrance to the machine.

Compare *Allen* to State v. Riley, 846 P.2d 1365 (Wash. 1993) (en banc), which features facts similar to those of *Allen*. In *Riley*, however, the evidence showed that Riley had dialed up the phone company computers and entered in random numbers designed to enable him to place free long distance phone calls. There was no evidence that Riley had ever found the correct number or successfully placed a free call, but Riley had done more than simply dial up the computer and wait at the login prompt. The Supreme Court of Washington affirmed Riley's conviction for having accessed the phone company's computer without authorization:

> The term "access" is defined under RCW 9A.52.010(6) as "to approach ... or otherwise make use of any resources of a computer, directly or by electronic means." Riley's repeated attempts to discover access codes by sequentially entering random 6–digit numbers constitute "approach[ing]" or "otherwise mak[ing] use of any resources of a computer." The switch is a computer. Long distance calls are processed through the switch. Riley was approaching the switch each time he entered the general access number, followed by a random 6–digit number representing a customer access code, and a destination number. Therefore, Riley's conduct satisfied the statutory definition of "access" and so was properly treated as computer trespass.

Id. at 1373.

Is *Riley* consistent with *Allen*? Does it make sense that dialing up a computer and viewing the login prompt does not access a computer (*Allen*), but that viewing the login prompt and entering in nonfunctioning passwords does access it (*Riley*)?

Do you think either *Riley* or *Allen* accessed the phone company's computer? Or did they merely *attempt* to access the phone company's computer?

3. *Does sending an e-mail message "access" a computer?* While *Allen* suggests a virtual reality approach to access, other cases have suggested a physical reality approach. In America Online v. National Health Care Discount, Inc., 121 F. Supp. 2d 1255 (N.D. Iowa 2000), the Internet service provider America Online ("AOL") brought a civil case under 18 U.S.C. § 1030(g) against National Health Care Discount ("NHCD"), a company that sells discount health care plans, for hiring a spammer to send bulk e-mails about NHCD to AOL customers. AOL reasoned that by harvesting e-mail addresses and sending e-mail to AOL customers in violation of AOL's policies, the spammers had accessed AOL's computers without authorization. AOL moved for summary judgment, prompting the court to consider whether a computer user "accesses" another computer when he sends e-mail to that computer. The court answered in the affirmative, offering this expansive interpretation of "access":

> The CFAA does not define "access," but the general definition of the word, as a transitive verb, is to "gain access to." Merriam-Webster's Collegiate Dictionary 6 (10th ed.1994). As a noun, "access," in this context, means to exercise the "freedom or ability to ... make use of" something. The question here, therefore, is whether NHCD's e-mailers, by harvesting e-mail addresses of AOL members and then sending the members UBE messages, exercised the freedom or ability to make use of AOL's computers. The court finds they did. For purposes of the CFAA, when someone sends an e-mail message from his or her own computer, and the message then is transmitted through a number of other computers until it reaches its destination, the sender is making use of all of those computers, and is therefore "accessing" them. This is precisely what NHCD's e-mailers did with respect to AOL's computers.

Id. at 1272–1273. Note the inconsistency with *Allen, supra.* By dialing up the phone company computer and retrieving the login prompt, Allen had "exercised the freedom or ability to make use" of the phone company's computers, albeit in a limited way. While retrieving the login prompt doesn't access particularly private or valuable information, it does require making use of the target computer. Of course, this interpretation doesn't mean that Allen would be liable for violating the Kansas unauthorized access statute. Perhaps Allen "accessed" the phone company computer, but his apparent act of merely viewing the login prompt was not "without authorization."

4. *Do port scans "access" scanned computers?* Both computer hackers and security professionals regularly evaluate the security of networks by performing a series of well-known tests on the networks. One common test is a "port scan," which checks the targeted computer for open ports. Every computer connected to the Internet has 65,535 ports, which are akin to access doors by which a remote user can log into the computer. A port scan checks each port and reports back as to whether the port is open and listening, or whether it is closed. Port scanning is a common surveillance tool that often gives intruders important insights into how they can exploit weaknesses in a network. In a civil dispute between two computer security firms, a federal court concluded that port scans do not "access" the targeted computer under 18 U.S.C. § 1030. *See* Moulton v. VC3, No. 1:00CV434–TWT, 2000 WL 33310901, at *7 (N.D. Ga. 2000).

5.   In a world of computer networks, concepts of access have to consider not just one computer, but many. For example, imagine you are at home and you access the Internet from your home computer via your Internet service provider. You spend a few minutes surfing the web, and then you intentionally distribute a computer virus as an attachment to an e-mail. Did you "access" your home computer? Your ISP's server? Routers and mailservers that may have transferred your communications in the course of delivery? The webserver that stored the files you retrieved when you were surfing the web? The ISP of the person who received your e-mail? The ISPs of other people who eventually received the virus?

6.   Which is better, a virtual approach to access or a physical approach to access? Should access require a virtual entrance, or should the key question be whether communications physically enter the machine? It is difficult to assess this question without first understanding concepts of authorization. Given that the key prohibition is against access without authorization, access and authorization must work together.

At the same time, it is worth keeping in mind that scholars have disagreed on the best interpretation of access. The author of these materials has argued in favor of a physical approach to access:

> The problem with a narrow construction of access is that individual users interact with computers in countless ways for countless reasons, and it is difficult to carve out a type of interaction that should be exempted entirely from computer misuse laws. A typical computer user might log on to a network using a password, open files stored on a server, surf the web, and send e-mail. If any one of these activities does not constitute an access, then that entire category of activity may be exempted from laws that are designed broadly to prohibit exceeding privileges on a computer.

> Further, the distinctions between different types of use are sufficiently fluid, and the technology of the Internet changes so rapidly, that such distinctions would prove highly unstable and ultimately arbitrary. While a narrow meaning for access may have made sense in the 1970s, today's technologies cannot support it. * * *

> In light of the difficulty of drawing robust and sensible lines between different types of interactions with computers and limiting access to just some of them, the better approach is to allow access to refer broadly to any successful interaction with a computer, no matter how minor. The functional effect of this broad construction is to eliminate access as a limit on the scope of unauthorized access statutes, and to place major weight on the meaning of authorization.

Orin S. Kerr, *Cybercrime's Scope: Interpreting "Access" and "Authorization" in Computer Misuse Statutes,* 78 N.Y.U. L. Rev. 1596, 1647–48 (2003). In contrast, Patricia Bellia has argued in favor of a virtual reality approach to access, at least in the context of the federal unauthorized access statute:

> The narrower reading of "access" is in fact the more natural one. The provisions [of 18 U.S.C. § 1030] clearly contemplate conduct that involves obtaining information not generally available to the public, including national security information and financial and other records, or

conduct that involves access to computers that are nonpublic. Since the information is not available to the public, it is necessarily segregated by code–whether by a password or other technical measure, or by being placed on a system not generally accessible to the public.

Patricia L. Bellia, *Defending Cyberproperty*, 79 N.Y.U. L. Rev. 2164, 2254 (2004).

7.   Arguably, the government's problem in *Allen* was not that Allen did not access Southwestern Bell's computers, but that the government lacked proof that Allen had accessed the computers. Although most computer networks are configured to keep records of system use in what are known as log files, hackers routinely attempt to erase any logs files that might have recorded their unauthorized activities inside a network. If hackers can get "root" on a network, allowing them system administrator privileges, they can erase the log files and leave no trace of their unauthorized activities. *See, e.g.*, Eric J. Sinrod & William P. Reilly, *Cyber-Crimes: A Practical Approach to the Application of Federal Computer Crime Laws,* 16 Santa Clara Computer & High Tech. L.J. 177, 212 (2000). Do you think this happened in *Allen*? If Allen did in fact access Southwestern Bell's computer and simply erased the logs, how could the state have proved Allen's access? Alternatively, do you think the state could have shown that Allen attempted to access the computers?

8.   Do you think the meaning of "access" was a difficult issue in the 1980s, when the Computer Fraud and Abuse Act was passed? Is the problem that computer technologies are very different today as compared to what they were in the 1980s?

3.   WHAT IS AUTHORIZATION? THE CASE OF CODE–BASED RESTRICTIONS

Perhaps the most complex issues raised by computer misuse statutes concern authorization. Most computer misuse statutes criminalize unauthorized access to a computer, and some prohibit exceeding authorized access. In contrast, authorized access remains legal. This raises obvious questions. When is access unauthorized? Who can grant the authority to access a computer, and in what circumstances? Given that millions of computer users access millions of computers every day, finding the line between authorized and unauthorized access obviously is quite important. Specifically, deciding when an access is "without authorization" or "in excess of authorization" often determines the line between an act that is criminal and one that is not. But what exactly it means for access to be "without authorization" or "exceeding authorized access" turns out to be far from clear.

Imagine that a college student tasked with writing a research paper on the Ku Klux Klan decides to conduct her research using the Internet.[c] She logs on to her AOL account, which is governed by a Terms of Service agreement containing the following clause: "You may not use your AOL

c.   This material is taken from Orin S. Kerr, *Cybercrime's Scope: Interpreting "Access" and "Authorization" in Computer*   *Misuse Statutes,* 78 N.Y.U. L. Rev. 1596, 1622–24 (2003).

account to post, transmit, or promote any unlawful, harmful, threatening, abusive, harassing, defamatory, vulgar, hateful, racially, ethnically or otherwise objectionable content." Once connected to the Internet, she finds a web site hosted by a KKK chapter. The main page contains a click-through agreement: "Only white supremacists are authorized to access this site," the agreement states. "Access by people who are not white supremacists is unauthorized. By clicking 'I agree,' you agree that you are a white supremacist." Although she is not a white supremacist, she clicks "I Agree" and examines the site. The site contains links to other Klan-related sites, and when she clicks on one of the links, she is connected to a university-hosted site about the history of the Klan that asks her to enter a username and password. Although she does not have an account with the university, she guesses a username and password correctly, and the site grants her access to its contents. She then copies some of the information contained in the site, and e-mails it to her best friend, who previously has told her to stop e-mailing her information about her KKK research project.

Assuming that our student has "accessed" all four of the computers used in this example, which of these acts of access were "without authorization?" Did the student access AOL's computers without authorization because she used AOL to "transmit ... hateful ... or otherwise objectionable content" in violation of AOL's Terms of Service? Did she access the Klan's computers without authorization because she was not a white supremacist? Did she access the university's computer without authorization by guessing the username and password and then entering disguised as a legitimate user? Finally, did she access her friend's computer without authorization by sending her friend the e-mail after her friend had told her not to send it?

More broadly, who and what determines whether access is authorized, and under what circumstances? Can a computer owner set the scope of authorization by contractual language? Or do these standards derive from the social norms of Internet users? The statutes are silent on these questions. The phrase "without authorization" generally is left undefined.

To answer some of these questions, it may be useful to identify three basic ways in which access might be unauthorized. Every computer is configured to permit its users to enjoy a set of privileges, and there are three basic ways to set those privileges: by code, by contract, or by social norms. This means that a computer user can engage in computer misuse in three possible ways: by circumventing code-based restrictions, by breaching contract-based restrictions, or by breaching social norms on computer access.

When an owner regulates privileges by code, the owner or her agent designs and programs the computer's hardware and software so that the code limits each users' privileges. Perhaps every user must have an account, and access to that account is protected by a password. This regulates privileges by code because it limits the ability of others to access a particular person's account. For a user to exceed privileges imposed by code, the user must somehow "trick" the computer into giving the user greater privileges. The code creates a barrier designed to limit privileges.

Alternatively, a computer owner or operate may regulate computer privileges by contract. Access to the computer can be conditioned on the user's promise to abide by a set of terms such as Terms of Service for an e-mail account or Terms of Use for a website. Regulation by contract offers a significantly weaker form of regulation than regulation by code. Regulation by code enforces limits on privileges by actually blocking the user from performing the proscribed act, at least absent circumvention. In contrast, regulation by contract works by conditioning access based on a promise. To borrow a physical-world analogy, the difference between regulation by code and regulation by contract resembles the difference between trying to keep a stranger out by locking the front door, on one hand, and trying to keep a stranger out by putting a sign in front of the open door announcing that strangers may not enter.

Both types of regulatory approaches are familiar to every computer user. For example, imagine that you sign up for Internet service with a local Internet service provider and that the service comes with an e-mail account. Signing up for the service requires you to agree to the ISP's Terms of Service, and also requires you to select a username and password. If you use the account in a way that violates the Terms of Service, you will be breaching a contract-based restriction. You agreed to comply with the ISP's Terms of Service, but you accessed the ISP while violating that agreement. Now imagine that your friend Fred wants to read your e-mail, and successfully guesses your username and password and accesses your account without your permission. In that case, Fred has circumvented a code-based restriction. He has bypassed the password gate that was created to limit access to your account.

Third, computer use might be unauthorized if it violates a social norm on computer use. Social norms are widely shared attitudes that specify what behaviors an actor ought to exhibit. In the context of computer misuse, access might violate a social norm if most computer users would understand that you're not supposed to access the computer in that particular way even if it does not circumvent a code-based restriction or breach an explicit contract-based restriction. For example, perhaps it is understood that a user is not supposed to use an automated software program to send thousands of web queries in a short period of time to a particular web server, causing the server to slow down considerably. In such a case, social norms may set up an implicit contractual restriction; by accessing the computer in a way contrary to the expectations of most users, the access may be implicitly unauthorized. (This is arguably just a version of regulation by contract, but for our purposes it helps to treat it separately.)

Should circumvention of a code-based restriction make an access "without authorization" or in excess of authorization? How about breach of a contract-based restriction? How about breach of a social norm? The following materials consider these questions, beginning with the relatively straightforward case of code-based restrictions.

UNITED STATES v. MORRIS

United States Court of Appeals for the Second Circuit, 1991.
928 F.2d 504.

JON O. NEWMAN, Circuit Judge.

This appeal presents two narrow issues of statutory construction concerning a provision Congress recently adopted to strengthen protection against computer crimes. Section 2(d) of the Computer Fraud and Abuse Act of 1986, 18 U.S.C. § 1030(a)(5)(A) (1988), punishes anyone who intentionally accesses without authorization a category of computers known as "federal interest computers" and damages or prevents authorized use of information in such computers, causing loss of $1,000 or more. The issues raised are * * * what satisfies the statutory requirement of "access without authorization."

These questions are raised on an appeal by Robert Tappan Morris from the May 16, 1990, judgment of the District Court for the Northern District of New York convicting him, after a jury trial, of violating 18 U.S.C. § 1030(a)(5)(A). Morris released into INTERNET, a national computer network, a computer program known as a "worm"[2] that spread and multiplied, eventually causing computers at various educational institutions and military sites to "crash" or cease functioning.

We conclude * * * that there was sufficient evidence for the jury to conclude that Morris acted "without authorization" within the meaning of section 1030(a)(5)(A). We therefore affirm.

FACTS

In the fall of 1988, Morris was a first-year graduate student in Cornell University's computer science Ph.D. program. Through undergraduate work at Harvard and in various jobs he had acquired significant computer experience and expertise. When Morris entered Cornell, he was given an account on the computer at the Computer Science Division. This account gave him explicit authorization to use computers at Cornell. Morris engaged in various discussions with fellow graduate students about the security of computer networks and his ability to penetrate it.

In October 1988, Morris began work on a computer program, later known as the INTERNET "worm" or "virus." The goal of this program was to demonstrate the inadequacies of current security measures on

---

2. In the colorful argot of computers, a "worm" is a program that travels from one computer to another but does not attach itself to the operating system of the computer it "infects." It differs from a "virus," which is also a migrating program, but one that attaches itself to the operating system of any computer it enters and can infect any other computer that uses files from the infected computer.

computer networks by exploiting the security defects that Morris had discovered. The tactic he selected was release of a worm into network computers. Morris designed the program to spread across a national network of computers after being inserted at one computer location connected to the network. Morris released the worm into INTERNET, which is a group of national networks that connect university, governmental, and military computers around the country. The network permits communication and transfer of information between computers on the network.

Morris sought to program the INTERNET worm to spread widely without drawing attention to itself. The worm was supposed to occupy little computer operation time, and thus not interfere with normal use of the computers. Morris programmed the worm to make it difficult to detect and read, so that other programmers would not be able to "kill" the worm easily.

Morris also wanted to ensure that the worm did not copy itself onto a computer that already had a copy. Multiple copies of the worm on a computer would make the worm easier to detect and would bog down the system and ultimately cause the computer to crash. Therefore, Morris designed the worm to "ask" each computer whether it already had a copy of the worm. If it responded "no," then the worm would copy onto the computer; if it responded "yes," the worm would not duplicate. However, Morris was concerned that other programmers could kill the worm by programming their own computers to falsely respond "yes" to the question. To circumvent this protection, Morris programmed the worm to duplicate itself every seventh time it received a "yes" response. As it turned out, Morris underestimated the number of times a computer would be asked the question, and his one-out-of-seven ratio resulted in far more copying than he had anticipated. The worm was also designed so that it would be killed when a computer was shut down, an event that typically occurs once every week or two. This would have prevented the worm from accumulating on one computer, had Morris correctly estimated the likely rate of reinfection.

Morris identified four ways in which the worm could break into computers on the network:

(1) through a "hole" or "bug" (an error) in SEND MAIL, a computer program that transfers and receives electronic mail on a computer;

(2) through a bug in the "finger demon" program, a program that permits a person to obtain limited information about the users of another computer;

(3) through the "trusted hosts" feature, which permits a user with certain privileges on one computer to have equivalent privileges on another computer without using a password; and

(4) through a program of password guessing, whereby various combinations of letters are tried out in rapid sequence in the hope that

one will be an authorized user's password, which is entered to permit whatever level of activity that user is authorized to perform.

On November 2, 1988, Morris released the worm from a computer at the Massachusetts Institute of Technology. MIT was selected to disguise the fact that the worm came from Morris at Cornell. Morris soon discovered that the worm was replicating and reinfecting machines at a much faster rate than he had anticipated. Ultimately, many machines at locations around the country either crashed or became "catatonic." When Morris realized what was happening, he contacted a friend at Harvard to discuss a solution. Eventually, they sent an anonymous message from Harvard over the network, instructing programmers how to kill the worm and prevent reinfection. However, because the network route was clogged, this message did not get through until it was too late. Computers were affected at numerous installations, including leading universities, military sites, and medical research facilities. The estimated cost of dealing with the worm at each installation ranged from $200 to more than $53,000.

Morris was found guilty, following a jury trial, of violating 18 U.S.C. § 1030(a)(5)(A). He was sentenced to three years of probation, 400 hours of community service, a fine of $10,050, and the costs of his supervision.

DISCUSSION

Section 1030(a)(5)(A) penalizes the conduct of an individual who "intentionally accesses a Federal interest computer without authorization." Morris contends that his conduct constituted, at most, "exceeding authorized access" rather than the "unauthorized access" that the subsection punishes. Morris argues that there was insufficient evidence to convict him of "unauthorized access," and that even if the evidence sufficed, he was entitled to have the jury instructed on his "theory of defense."

We assess the sufficiency of the evidence under the traditional standard. Morris was authorized to use computers at Cornell, Harvard, and Berkeley, all of which were on INTERNET. As a result, Morris was authorized to communicate with other computers on the network to send electronic mail (SEND MAIL), and to find out certain information about the users of other computers (finger demon). The question is whether Morris's transmission of his worm constituted exceeding authorized access or accessing without authorization.

The Senate Report stated that section 1030(a)(5)(A), like the new section 1030(a)(3), would "be aimed at 'outsiders,' *i.e.,* those lacking authorization to access any Federal interest computer." Senate Report at 10, U.S. Code Cong. & Admin. News at 2488. But the Report also stated, in concluding its discussion on the scope of section 1030(a)(3), that it applies "where the offender is completely outside the Government, ... *or where the offender's act of trespass is interdepartmental in nature.*" *Id.* at 8, U.S. Code Cong. & Admin. News at 2486 (emphasis added).

Morris relies on the first quoted portion to argue that his actions can be characterized only as exceeding authorized access, since he had authorized access to a federal interest computer. However, the second quoted portion reveals that Congress was not drawing a bright line between those who have some access to any federal interest computer and those who have none. Congress contemplated that individuals with access to some federal interest computers would be subject to liability under the computer fraud provisions for gaining unauthorized access to other federal interest computers. *See, e.g., id.* (stating that a Labor Department employee who uses Labor's computers to access without authorization an FBI computer can be criminally prosecuted).

The evidence permitted the jury to conclude that Morris's use of the SEND MAIL and finger demon features constituted access without authorization. While a case might arise where the use of SEND MAIL or finger demon falls within a nebulous area in which the line between accessing without authorization and exceeding authorized access may not be clear, Morris's conduct here falls well within the area of unauthorized access. Morris did not use either of those features in any way related to their intended function. He did not send or read mail nor discover information about other users; instead he found holes in both programs that permitted him a special and unauthorized access route into other computers.

Moreover, the jury verdict need not be upheld solely on Morris's use of SEND MAIL and finger demon. As the District Court noted, in denying Morris' motion for acquittal,

> Although the evidence may have shown that defendant's initial insertion of the worm simply exceeded his authorized access, the evidence also demonstrated that the worm was designed to spread to other computers at which he had no account and no authority, express or implied, to unleash the worm program. Moreover, there was also evidence that the worm was designed to gain access to computers at which he had no account by guessing their passwords. Accordingly, the evidence did support the jury's conclusion that defendant accessed without authority as opposed to merely exceeding the scope of his authority.

In light of the reasonable conclusions that the jury could draw from Morris's use of SEND MAIL and finger demon, and from his use of the trusted hosts feature and password guessing, his challenge to the sufficiency of the evidence fails.

Morris endeavors to bolster his sufficiency argument by contending that his conduct was not punishable under subsection (a)(5) but was punishable under subsection (a)(3). That concession belies the validity of his claim that he only exceeded authorization rather than made unauthorized access. Neither subsection (a)(3) nor (a)(5) punishes conduct that exceeds authorization. Both punish a person who "accesses" "without authorization" certain computers. Subsection (a)(3) covers the computers of a department or agency of the United States; subsection (a)(5) more broadly covers any federal interest computers, defined to include, among other computers, those used exclusively by the United States, 18 U.S.C. § 1030(e)(2)(A), and adds the element of causing damage or loss of use of a value of $1,000 or more. If Morris violated subsection (a)(3), as he concedes, then his conduct in inserting the worm into the INTER-NET must have constituted "unauthorized access" under subsection (a)(5) to the computers of the federal departments the worm reached, for example, those of NASA and military bases.

To extricate himself from the consequence of conceding that he made "unauthorized access" within the meaning of subsection (a)(3), Morris subtly shifts his argument and contends that he is not within the reach of subsection (a)(5) at all. He argues that subsection (a)(5) covers only those who, unlike himself, lack access to *any* federal interest computer. It is true that a primary concern of Congress in drafting subsection (a)(5) was to reach those unauthorized to access any federal interest computer. The Senate Report stated, "[T]his subsection [(a)(5)] will be aimed at 'outsiders,' *i.e.,* those lacking authorization to access any Federal interest computer." Senate Report at 10, U.S.Code Cong. & Admin. News at 2488. But the fact that the subsection is "aimed" at such "outsiders" does not mean that its coverage is limited to them. Congress understandably thought that the group most likely to damage federal interest computers would be those who lack authorization to use any of them. But it surely did not mean to insulate from liability the person authorized to use computers at the State Department who causes damage to computers at the Defense Department. Congress created the misdemeanor offense of subsection (a)(3) to punish intentional trespass-es into computers for which one lacks authorized access; it added the felony offense of subsection (a)(5) to punish such a trespasser who also causes damage or loss in excess of $1,000, not only to computers of the United States but to any computer within the definition of federal interest computers. With both provisions, Congress was punishing those, like Morris, who, with access to some computers that enable them to communicate on a network linking other computers, gain access to other computers to which they lack authorization and either trespass, in violation of subsection (a)(3), or cause damage or loss of $1,000 or more, in violation of subsection (a)(5).

Morris also contends that the District Court should have instructed the jury on his theory that he was only exceeding authorized access. The District Court decided that it was unnecessary to provide the jury with a definition of "authorization." We agree. Since the word is of common usage, without any technical or ambiguous meaning, the Court was not obliged to instruct the jury on its meaning.

An instruction on "exceeding authorized access" would have risked misleading the jury into thinking that Morris could not be convicted if some of his conduct could be viewed as falling within this description. Yet, even if that phrase might have applied to some of his conduct, he could nonetheless be found liable for doing what the statute prohibited, gaining access where he was unauthorized and causing loss.

Additionally, the District Court properly refused to charge the jury with Morris's proposed jury instruction on access without authorization. That instruction stated, "To establish the element of lack of authorization, the government must prove beyond a reasonable doubt that Mr. Morris was an 'outsider,' that is, that he was not authorized to access any Federal interest computer in any manner." As the analysis of the legislative history reveals, Congress did not intend an individual's authorized access to one federal interest computer to protect him from prosecution, no matter what other federal interest computers he accesses.

Notes and Questions

1. The *Morris* opinion suggests two ways in which access to a computer could be "without authorization." The first is the "intended function" test. According to the court, Morris accessed federal interest computers without authorization because he did not use SENDMAIL and finger demon "in any way related to their intended function." Although the *Morris* court does not provide an elaborate explanation of the intended function test, it appears to derive largely from a sense of social norms in the community of computer users. Under these norms, software designers design programs to perform certain tasks, and network providers enable the programs to allow users to perform those tasks. Providers implicitly authorize users to use their computers to perform the intended functions, but implicitly do not authorize users to exploit weaknesses in the programs that allow them to perform unintended functions. When a user exploits weaknesses in a program and uses a function in an unintended way to access a computer, that access is "without authorization."

How can a court determine the "intended function" of a computer program or command? Should the court seek out its primary author and ask him what function he had in mind when he created it? How should a court determine the purpose of a computer command that is an open source project, such as the finger demon command at issue in *Morris*, and that has no one author?

What level of generality should a court apply to determine the intended function of a computer command? The meaning of the intended function test hinges on this question. For example, is the intended function of e-mail software to send communications generally? Or is its intended function to send communications in the form of e-mail messages, or to send communications in a way that complies with the network provider's Terms of Service? As the intended function of a command or program is described in increasingly specific ways, the scope of criminality that the intended function test creates will expand. Conversely, the more general the function, the narrower the scope of conduct that the intended function test prohibits.

2. The *Morris* opinion suggests that gaining access to a computer by correctly guessing or using a stolen password also can constitute access "without authorization." Another court has made a similar suggestion. *See* Sherman & Co. v. Salton Maxim Housewares, Inc., 94 F. Supp. 2d 817, 821 (E.D. Mich. 2000). This makes sense: Guessing a password is something like

picking a physical lock, and using a stolen password is something like making a copy of the key and using it without the owner's permission. Indeed, bypassing password gates using stolen or guessed passwords is a common way to "hack" into a computer.

At the same time, the addition of a third party raises interesting legal questions about when access to a computer using another person's password is "without authorization." In the case of access to a locked physical space using a lock pick or a stolen key, determining whether access was "without authorization" is easy in most cases. Only the legitimate keyholder who lives in or controls the place to be accessed can determine the scope of authorization; either the legitimate keyholder gave the defendant permission to access or he did not. Computer passwords are a bit different, at least in most cases. Usually there are two parties that have plausible claims to set authorization: the owner/operator of the computer, and the legitimate computer account holder. Which determines the scope of the defendant's authorization?

As an example, imagine that an ISP's Terms of Service state that subscribers are not permitted to distribute their passwords to other people, and that only access by the subscriber is permitted. Joe, a new subscriber, gives his password to Mary so Mary can check Joe's account for him while he is on a camping trip. Is Mary's access to the computer "without authorization?" It is authorized by Joe but not by the ISP. Which governs? Note that if you believe the ISP's Terms of Service should govern it does not necessarily mean that Mary's act of accessing Joe's account would violate an unauthorized access statute. Most unauthorized access statutes require that the mental state concerning lack of authorization must be intentional. If Mary accesses Joe's account and thinks that his permission is sufficient, Mary will not have intentionally accessed Joe's account without authorization.

3. *Outsiders and insiders.* The *Morris* opinion refers extensively to the legislative history of § 1030, and in particular to its discussion of liability for "insiders" and "outsiders." In the 1980s, drawing a line between the liability for "insiders" and "outsiders" made sense for a number of reasons. First, most computer network users used terminals to access a mainframe computer, and access to the mainframe computer generally required an account or privileges at another computer that was a trusted host. Second, the scope of § 1030 was very narrow: from 1986 until 1996, § 1030 applied only to "federal interest" computers, which were defined as a) computers used by financial institutions or the United States government in whole or in part or b) computers that were part of an interstate network if the offense was committed using computers in multiple states. In that environment, it made at least some sense to distinguish between users that had access privileges on some federal interest computers and those that did not.

The distinction is harder to understand today. Section 1030 now applies to "protected computers," and the definition is broad enough that every computer connected to the Internet is a protected computer. Anyone can sign up for an Internet account, and software applications such as the Web routinely grant access privileges to the public. In light of these changes, it is difficult (if not impossible) to classify computer users as "insiders" or "outsiders" in the abstract. A user may be an "insider" with respect to a group of machines and an "outsider" with respect to another group. Or, a user may be an "insider" with respect to some information stored on a server but an "outsider" with respect to other information.

A more profitable way to approach such questions is by asking whether the user circumvented a code-based restriction or breached a contract-based or norms-based restriction. A rough equivalence exists between the two sets of concepts. Those who circumvent code-based restrictions will often be considered outsiders, and those who merely breach contract-based or norms-based restrictions will often be considered insiders. At the same time, focusing on the means of gaining access to particular information provides a more precise and reliable tool for purposes of distinguishing among different types of authorization than the status-based distinction between outsiders and insiders.

4. Consider the following hypothetical criticism:

> The concept of unauthorized access to a computer is nonsensical. Access to a computer is always authorized. A user can access a computer only if the computer authorizes the user to access it. In fact, what we call computer hacking is really the art of convincing a computer to authorize you to access the computer. When you hack in to a computer, you gain the computer's authorization to access it. Accordingly, all access is authorized.

What does this assume about how authorization to access a computer is granted or denied? What does it assume about *who* has the authority to grant authorized access to a computer?

The High Court of Australia's opinion in Kennison v. Daire, 160 C.L.R. 129 (1986), may help you answer these questions. In *Daire*, a man withdrew $200 (AU) from an offline Automatic Teller Machine (ATM) using an expired card from a closed account. Bank employees had programmed their computers to dispense money whenever a person used an ATM card from that bank using a proper password. When the ATMs were offline, however, the machines were programmed to dispense money without checking whether there was money in the relevant account, or even if the account was still open. The defendant in *Daire* intentionally exploited this defect, took $200, and was charged and convicted of larceny. On appeal, he argued that he had not committed larceny because the bank, through the ATM, had consented to his taking the money. The High Court of Australia rejected the argument:

> The fact that the bank programmed the machine in a way that facilitated the commission of a fraud by a person holding a card did not mean that the bank consented to the withdrawal of money by a person who had no account with the bank. It is not suggested that any person, having the authority of the bank to consent to the particular transaction, did so. The machine could not give the bank's consent in fact and there is no principle of law that requires it to be treated as though it were a person with authority to decide and consent. The proper inference to be drawn from the facts is that the bank consented to the withdrawal of up to $200 by a card holder who presented his card and supplied his personal identification number, only if the card holder had an account which was current. It would be quite unreal to infer that the bank consented to the withdrawal by a card holder whose account had been closed.

Id. at 130. Do you agree? How do you know what "the bank" wanted? Who is "the bank," anyway? The person who programmed the bank's computer? The local branch manager? The bank's CEO?

4. WHAT IS AUTHORIZATION? THE CASE OF CONTRACT–BASED RESTRICTIONS

Does breaching an explicit condition on access to a computer make the access without authorization or in excess of authorization? Computer users encounter such conditions often in the form of Terms of Use and Terms of Service on Internet services, software, and websites. Employers routinely place restrictions on their employees, as well. Such restrictions can be clear or vague, broad or narrow. Should violating such restrictions be a crime?

EF CULTURAL TRAVEL BV v. EXPLORICA, INC.

United States Court of Appeals for the First Circuit, 2001.
274 F.3d 577.

COFFIN, Senior Circuit Judge.

Appellant Explorica, Inc. and several of its employees challenge a preliminary injunction issued against them for alleged violations of the Computer Fraud and Abuse Act, 18 U.S.C. § 1030. We affirm the district court's conclusion that appellees will likely succeed on the merits of their CFAA claim, but rest on a narrower basis than the court below.

BACKGROUND

Explorica was formed in 2000 to compete in the field of global tours for high school students. Several of Explorica's employees formerly were employed by appellee EF, which has been in business for more than thirty-five years. EF and its partners and subsidiaries make up the world's largest private student travel organization.

Shortly after the individual defendants left EF in the beginning of 2000, Explorica began competing in the teenage tour market. The company's vice president (and former vice president of information strategy at EF), Philip Gormley, envisioned that Explorica could gain a substantial advantage over all other student tour companies, and especially EF, by undercutting EF's already competitive prices on student tours. Gormley considered several ways to obtain and utilize EF's prices: by manually keying in the information from EF's brochures and other printed materials; by using a scanner to record that same information; or, by manually searching for each tour offered through EF's website. Ultimately, however, Gormley engaged Zefer, Explorica's Internet consultant, to design a computer program called a "scraper" to glean all of the necessary information from EF's website. Zefer designed the program in three days.

The scraper has been likened to a "robot," a tool that is extensively used on the Internet. Robots are used to gather information for countless purposes, ranging from compiling results for search engines such as Yahoo! to filtering for inappropriate content. The widespread deployment of robots enables global Internet users to find comprehensive information quickly and almost effortlessly.

Like a robot, the scraper sought information through the Internet. Unlike other robots, however, the scraper focused solely on EF's website, using information that other robots would not have. Specifically, Zefer utilized tour codes whose significance was not readily understandable to the public. With the tour codes, the scraper accessed EF's website repeatedly and easily obtained pricing information for those specific tours. The scraper sent more than 30,000 inquiries to EF's website and recorded the pricing information into a spreadsheet.[3]

Zefer ran the scraper program twice, first to retrieve the 2000 tour prices and then the 2001 prices. All told, the scraper downloaded 60,000 lines of data, the equivalent of eight telephone directories of information. Once Zefer "scraped" all of the prices, it sent a spreadsheet containing EF's pricing information to Explorica, which then systematically undercut EF's prices. Explorica thereafter printed its own brochures and began competing in EF's tour market.

The development and use of the scraper came to light about a year and a half later during state-court litigation regarding appellant Olsson's departure from appellee EFICE. EF then filed this action, alleging violations of the CFAA; the Copyright Act of 1976, 17 U.S.C. § 101; the Racketeer Influenced and Corrupt Organizations Act, 18 U.S.C. § 1961; and various related state laws. It sought a preliminary injunction barring Explorica and Zefer from using the scraper program and demanded the return of all materials generated through use of the scraper.

On May 30, 2001, the district court granted a preliminary injunction against Explorica based on the CFAA, which criminally and civilly prohibits certain access to computers. *See* 18 U.S.C. § 1030(a)(4). The court found that EF would likely prove that Explorica violated the CFAA when it used EF's website in a manner outside the "reasonable expectations" of both EF and its ordinary users. The court also concluded that EF could show that it suffered a loss, as required by the statute,

---

3. John Hawley, one of Zefer's senior technical associates, explained the technical progression of the scraper in an affidavit:

[a.] Open an Excel spreadsheet. The spreadsheet initially contains EFTours gateway and destination city codes, which are available on the EFTours web site.

[b.] Identify the first gateway and destination city codes [on the] Excel spreadsheet.

[c.] Create a [website address] request for the EFTours tour prices page based on a combination of gateway and destination city. Example: show me all the prices for a London trip leaving JFK.

[d.] View the requested web page which is retained in the random access memory of the requesting computer in the form of HTML [computer language] code. * * *

[e.] Search the HTML for the tour prices for each season, year, etc.

[f.] Store the prices into the Excel spreadsheet.

[g.] Identify the next gateway and city codes in the spreadsheet.

[h.] Repeat steps 3–7 for all gateway and destination city combinations.

consisting of reduced business, harm to its goodwill, and the cost of diagnostic measures it incurred to evaluate possible harm to EF's systems, although it could not show that Explorica's actions physically damaged its computers. In a supplemental opinion the district court further articulated its "reasonable expectations" standard and explained that copyright, contractual and technical restraints sufficiently notified Explorica that its use of a scraper would be unauthorized and thus would violate the CFAA.

The district court first relied on EF's use of a copyright symbol on one of the pages of its website and a link directing users with questions to contact the company, finding that "such a clear statement should have dispelled any notion a reasonable person may have had that the 'presumption of open access' applied to information on EF's website." The court next found that the manner by which Explorica accessed EF's website likely violated a confidentiality agreement between appellant Gormley and EF, because Gormley provided to Zefer technical instructions concerning the creation of the scraper. Finally, the district court noted without elaboration that the scraper bypassed technical restrictions embedded in the website to acquire the information. The court therefore let stand its earlier decision granting the preliminary injunction. Appellants contend that the district court erred in taking too narrow a view of what is authorized under the CFAA and similarly mistook the reach of the confidentiality agreement. Appellants also argue that the district court erred in finding that appellees suffered a "loss," as defined by the CFAA, and that the preliminary injunction violates the First Amendment.

THE COMPUTER FRAUD AND ABUSE ACT

Although appellees alleged violations of three provisions of the CFAA, the district court found that they were likely to succeed only under section 1030(a)(4). That section provides

> [Whoever] knowingly and with intent to defraud, accesses a protected computer without authorization, or exceeds authorized access, and by means of such conduct furthers the intended fraud and obtains anything of value . . . shall be punished.

18 U.S.C. § 1030(a)(4).

Appellees allege that the appellants knowingly and with intent to defraud accessed the server hosting EF's website more than 30,000 times to obtain proprietary pricing and tour information, and confidential information about appellees' technical abilities. At the heart of the parties' dispute is whether appellants' actions either were "without authorization" or "exceed[ed] authorized access" as defined by the CFAA. We conclude that because of the broad confidentiality agreement appellants' actions "exceed[ed] authorized access," and so we do not reach the more general arguments made about statutory meaning, including whether use of a scraper alone renders access unauthorized.[10]

---

10. Congress did not define the phrase "without authorization," perhaps assuming that the words speak for themselves. The meaning, however, has proven to be elusive.

Congress defined "exceeds authorized access," as accessing "a computer with authorization and [using] such access to obtain or alter information in the computer that the accesser is not entitled so to obtain or alter." 18 U.S.C. § 1030(e)(6). EF is likely to prove such excessive access based on the confidentiality agreement between Gormley and EF. Pertinently, that agreement provides:

> Employee agrees to maintain in strict confidence and not to disclose to any third party, either orally or in writing, any Confidential or Proprietary Information . . . and never to at any time (i) directly or indirectly publish, disseminate or otherwise disclose, deliver or make available to anybody any Confidential or Proprietary Information or (ii) use such Confidential or Proprietary Information for Employee's own benefit or for the benefit of any other person or business entity other than EF.

> As used in this Agreement, the term "Confidential or Proprietary Information" means (a) any trade or business secrets or confidential information of EF, whether or not reduced to writing; (b) any technical, business, or financial information, the use or disclosure of which might reasonably be construed to be contrary to the interests of EF.

The record contains at least two communications from Gormley to Zefer seeming to rely on information about EF to which he was privy only because of his employment there. First, in an email to Zefer employee Joseph Alt exploring the use of a scraper, Gormley wrote: "might one of the team be able to write a program to automatically extract prices? I could work with him/her on the specification." Gormley also sent the following email to Zefer employee John Hawley:

> Here is a link to the page where you can grab EF's prices. There are two important drop down menus on the right. With the lowest one you select one of about 150 tours. * * * You then select your origin gateway from a list of about 100 domestic gateways (middle drop down menu). When you select your origin gateway a page with a couple of tables comes up. One table has 1999–2000 prices and the other has 2000–2001 prices. * * * On a high speed connection it is possible to move quickly from one price table to the next by hitting backspace and then the down arrow.

This documentary evidence points to Gormley's heavy involvement in the conception of the scraper program. Furthermore, the voluminous

The district court applied what it termed the "default rule" that conduct is without authorization only if it is not "in line with the reasonable expectations" of the website owner and its users. Appellants argue that this is an overly broad reading that restricts access and is at odds with the Internet's intended purpose of providing the "open and free exchange of information." They urge us to adopt instead the Second Circuit's reasoning that computer use is "without authorization" only if the use is not "in any way related to [its] intended function," *United States v. Morris,* 928 F.2d 504, 510 (2d Cir. 1991). Appellees contend that the result would be the same under either test, but we need not resolve this dispute because we affirm the court's ruling based on the "exceeds authorized access" prong of § 1030(a)(4).

spreadsheet containing all of the scraped information includes the tour codes, which EF claims are proprietary information. Each page of the spreadsheet produced by Zefer includes the tour and gateway codes, the date of travel, and the price for the tour. An uninformed reader would regard the tour codes as nothing but gibberish.[11] Although the codes can be correlated to the actual tours and destination points, the codes standing alone need to be "translated" to be meaningful.

Explorica argues that none of the information Gormley provided Zefer was confidential and that the confidentiality agreement therefore is irrelevant. The case on which they rely, *Lanier Professional Services, Inc. v. Ricci,* 192 F.3d 1, 5 (1st Cir. 1999), focused almost exclusively on an employee's non-compete agreement. The opinion mentioned in passing that there was no actionable misuse of confidential information because the only evidence that the employee had taken protected information was a "practically worthless" affidavit from the employee's successor.

Here, on the other hand, there is ample evidence that Gormley provided Explorica proprietary information about the structure of the website and the tour codes. To be sure, gathering manually the various codes through repeated searching and deciphering of the URLs theoretically may be possible. Practically speaking, however, if proven, Explorica's wholesale use of EF's travel codes to facilitate gathering EF's prices from its website reeks of use—and, indeed, abuse—of proprietary information that goes beyond any authorized use of EF's website.

Gormley voluntarily entered a broad confidentiality agreement prohibiting his disclosure of any information "which might reasonably be construed to be contrary to the interests of EF." Appellants would face an uphill battle trying to argue that it was not against EF's interests for appellants to use the tour codes to mine EF's pricing data. If EF's allegations are proven, it will likely prove that whatever authorization Explorica had to navigate around EF's site (even in a competitive vein), it exceeded that authorization by providing proprietary information and know-how to Zefer to create the scraper. Accordingly, the district court's finding that Explorica likely violated the CFAA was not clearly erroneous.

Notes and Questions

1. *Explorica* is an odd opinion in some ways. For example, the argument that Explorica's access violated the confidentiality agreement seems rather convoluted. At the same time, the decision appears to stand for the proposition that using a computer in violation of a contractual agreement with the computer's owner constitutes exceeding authorized access to that computer. In other words, breaching a contract-based restriction constitutes exceeding authorized access.

11. An example of the website address including the tour information is *http://www.eftours.com/tours/PriceResult.asp?* Gate=GTF & TourID=LPM. In this address, the proprietary codes are "GTF" and "LPM."

As a matter of policy, do you agree with this approach? Does it depend on what the particular computer is used to do? On the nature of the data obtained? On the identity of the defendant? On what contractual restriction has been breached?

2. *Misuse of sensitive computers by government employees.* A number of criminal cases have followed reasoning similar to that in *Explorica* in the context of government employees who misused sensitive government computers. In these cases, the apparent test for whether the defendant had violated an unauthorized access statute was whether the defendant had violated workplace policies on computer access.

A. In United States v. Czubinski, 106 F.3d 1069 (1st Cir. 1997), an IRS employee browsed through an IRS database containing tax returns, and viewed the tax returns of various personal friends and enemies. IRS regulations made clear that employees "may not use any Service computer system for other than official purposes." Although the First Circuit reversed his convictions, the court did note in passing that Czubinski's conduct "unquestionably exceeded authorized access" to the IRS computer.

B. In Commonwealth v. McFadden, 850 A.2d 1290 (Pa. Super. Ct. 2004), a police officer sent a message over the police computer system from her squad car pretending to be a terrorist who had taken control of the car and was planning a terrorist attack. The officer was authorized to use the police computer system for official purposes only, and she was charged with and convicted of having accessed the police computer system "without authorization." The appellate court affirmed the conviction, reasoning that the defendant accessed the computer system "for purposes of typing a false threat message" rather than for official purposes.

C. In State v. Olson, 735 P.2d 1362 (Wash. Ct. App. 1987), a police officer used the police computer database to access and print out the driver's license photographs of female college students who attended a nearby university. The officer was charged and convicted at trial of having accessed the police computer database "without authorization." After carefully reviewing the workplace policies at the police department, the appellate court reversed the conviction. The workplace policies prohibited use of information obtained from the police computers, but not did not limit access to the computers conditioned on those uses. Because the defendant's access did not violate an explicit policy, it was not without authorization and the defendant was not liable.

Do you agree with these cases? If so, do you agree with them because you fear the consequences of government employee abuse of sensitive databases and computer systems? Or do you agree because you think that computer owners should have an absolute right to determine the scope of authorized access to their computers?

3. In State v. Schwartz, 21 P.3d 1128 (Or. Ct. App. 2001), an employee was convicted under Oregon's computer crime statute for using his employer's computer network in several ways that the employer had explicitly informed him were not authorized. The employee was charged with "unlawfully, knowingly and without authorization alter[ing] a computer and

computer network" in violation of ORS 164.377(3). On appeal following conviction, the defendant argued that the line between authorized and unauthorized access was so unclear that it was unconstitutionally vague. The court summarized the arguments for and against as follows:

> Defendant also contends that the phrase "without authorization" in ORS 164.377(3) is unconstitutionally vague. According to defendant, because that phrase does not identify what sort of authorization is required, or from what source it must come, it is vague. Defendant further suggests that ORS 164.377(3), as written, requires that any alteration be authorized and that such a construction is so broad as to allow ad hoc enforcement. The state responds that only substantial certainty is required. The state observes that ORS 164.377(3) criminalizes alteration of a computer only when a person *knows* that he or she is without authorization. The state further argues that we should read ORS 164.377(3) as a whole; as such, it is sufficiently clear that the source of the authorization must be the person in control of the computer.

Schwartz, 21 P.3d at 1133. The Court then rejected the defendant's argument:

> "[W]ithout authorization" in ORS 164.377(3) provides sufficiently definite notice of the prohibited conduct. In this case, defendant himself acknowledged that installing gate programs, [computer programs that allow users to obtain remote access to a computer network,] was against company policy. He did not argue that, despite company policy, he had obtained permission to install a gate program. Confronted with the phrase "without authorization," a potential violator of ORS 164.377(3) would be reasonably certain that he or she would run afoul of that prohibition by doing something to a computer in violation of the policy of the company that owned the computer without having sought permission for an exception to the policy.

Id. at 1135. In rejecting the defendant's vagueness claim, has the court provided a useful definition of the phrase "without authorization?" If so, how do we determine who the "owner" of a computer is, or what the owner's "policy" is?

4. Consider the policy implications of a rule that violating a contractual restriction on computer access renders that access without authorization or in excess of authorization. The cases involving government employee misuse of sensitive databases are at one end of the spectrum, as the information typically is sensitive and the public interest in the contractual restriction generally is clear. But most contractual restrictions arise in very different contexts. Anyone can own a computer, and computer owners can place an infinite range of different contractual restrictions on access. Should unauthorized access statutes permit all computer owners to rely on the criminal law to enforce all types of contractual restrictions on access? Or should the law protect only some types of computer owners, some types of sensitive data, and some types of reasonable restrictions?

Computer network users frequently agree to be bound to contracts that condition their use of a computer network on certain restrictions. For example, law students have access to free Westlaw and Lexis accounts, but may use the accounts only for specific reasons. Similarly, the Terms of Service (TOS) of many Internet service providers impose many conditions: for example, some TOS state that the user may not use the account to view offensive material. If a user uses the network in a way that violates those conditions, should access to the network be considered without authorization or in excess of authorization? If a law student uses Westlaw to read an article on a baseball game or research old newspaper stories about his favorite musician, is the student guilty of committing a federal crime? Does that depend on the precise wording of Westlaw's TOS? Should it?

No criminal cases have been brought that test the outer bounds of liability for breaching code-based restrictions. Prosecutors are sensibly wary about relying on such a broad theory. But if an aggressive prosecutor brought such a case, how should a court resolve it?

Consider America Online v. LCGM, Inc., 46 F. Supp. 2d 444 (E.D. Va. 1998). A sender of "spam," unsolicited commercial e-mail, used an America Online account to send thousands of e-mails. AOL sued the spammer in federal district court, and one of the causes of action was 18 U.S.C. § 1030. The court granted AOL's motion for summary judgment for several of the various causes of action, and offered the following very cursory analysis of whether the spammer had accessed AOL's computer without authorization or had exceeded authorized access:

> The facts before the Court establish that defendants violated 18 U.S.C. § 1030(a)(2)(c) of the Computer Fraud and Abuse Act, which prohibits individuals from "intentionally access[ing] a computer without authorization or exceed[ing] authorized access, and thereby obtain[ing] information from any protected computer if the conduct involved an interstate or foreign communication." Defendants' own admissions satisfy the Act's requirements. Defendants have admitted to maintaining an AOL membership and using that membership to harvest the e-mail addresses of AOL members. Defendants have stated that they acquired these e-mail addresses by using extractor software programs. Defendants' actions violated AOL's Terms of Service, and as such was unauthorized.

Id. at 450. If courts follow this approach in criminal cases, aren't all computer users criminals? Is it possible to surf the web without at some point violating a contractual restriction imposed by the owner of a computer that you access? Are most contractual restrictions clear enough that a typical computer user will know when she is violating the law?

5. Is criminal liability for breaching contract-based restrictions consistent with the theories of punishment? Is breaching a contractual restriction on access always or often a morally culpable act that demands punishment from a retributive perspective? Is it always or often a harmful act that the law should attempt to deter? Or does that depend on the nature of the restriction?

When you consider these questions, note that contract law generally is civil law. Breaching a contract ordinarily leads to liability to pay damages, but not criminal punishment. Does a contract-based approach to unauthorized access effectively criminalize contract law online? Moreover, does it do so in an environment in which users are unlikely to be aware of the contracts that they are entering into? If a computer owner can issue any arbitrary set of rules over how its network must be used, and those rules are backed by the sanction of criminal law, the criminal law will end up subjecting Internet users to a range of more or less arbitrary restrictions on their conduct. Is this desirable?

6. *Analogies to consent in criminal law.* One way of evaluating the merits of criminalizing the breach of contract-based restrictions on computer access is to draw analogies to how the criminal law deals with similar problems elsewhere. The prohibition on access without authorization and exceeding authorized access arguably resembles traditional prohibitions on conduct without the victim's consent found in doctrines such as trespass (entering or staying on a person's property without their consent) and rape (sexual intercourse without a person's consent). In both contexts, a body of law exists to determine whether trickery or fraud vitiates consent.

For example, a person might pose as a traveling salesman and gain access to a home when in fact he plans to commit a burglary inside. Does the trickery render the entrance to the home "without consent," such that entering the home is a trespass? In the context of rape law, a man posing as a doctor might invent a story that he must have sexual intercourse with a woman to cure her of a terrible disease. If the woman believes him and agrees, does the man's deception render the act of sexual intercourse "without consent" and therefore a sexual assault? *See* Boro v. People, 210 Cal.Rptr. 122 (Ct. App. 1985).

Although the comparison may seem odd at first, we might look at the legal consequences of code-based or contract-based restrictions on computer access as raising similar questions. For example, computer misuse laws prohibit access to a computer without authorization, whereas trespass laws prohibit entrance or continued presence in a home without permission. Speaking anthropomorphically for a moment, the computer is "tricked" into authorizing the defendant to access the computer in a way conceptually similar to how a homeowner might be tricked into allowing a person into their home. The question is, when does the trickery vitiate the computer's consent, such that access allowed by the computer is without authorization or in excess of authorization?

The traditional approach is to distinguish between "fraud in the factum" and "fraud in the inducement." *See generally* Rollin M. Perkins & Ronald N. Boyce, Criminal Law 1075–84 (3d ed. 1982). The overall question is, did the victim actually consent to the act that occurred, regardless of whether the victim consented in reliance on representations concerning collateral matters? If the answer is yes, then the trickery is only fraud in the inducement and the consent is valid. If the answer is no, and the victim was tricked as to the nature of the consent given, then the fraud is fraud in the factum and the consent is not valid. Of course, this framework does not answer everything: it requires courts to identify the nature of the act and distinguish it from mere collateral matters. At the same time, it provides a traditional doctrinal framework for understanding the scope of access without authorization and exceeding authorized access.

Judge Kozinski suggested that this approach might be the proper way to interpret unauthorized access statutes in Theofel v. Farey–Jones, 359 F.3d

1066 (9th Cir. 2004), a case arising under 18 U.S.C. § 2701. Section 2701 is part of the Stored Communications Act, a law explored in depth in Chapter Six. Section 2701 is an unauthorized access statute that applies specifically to Internet service providers, and prohibits both intentionally accessing an ISP's computer without authorization and intentionally exceeding an authorization to do so. In a civil case concerning an invalid subpoena served on a company that led to the disclosure of private information, Judge Kozinski offered the following framework for interpreting authorization in the context of § 2701, *id.* at 1073–74:

> We interpret federal statutes in light of the common law. Especially relevant here is the common law of trespass. Like the tort of trespass, the Stored Communications Act protects individuals' privacy and proprietary interests. The Act reflects Congress's judgment that users have a legitimate interest in the confidentiality of communications in electronic storage at a communications facility. Just as trespass protects those who rent space from a commercial storage facility to hold sensitive documents, *cf.* Prosser and Keeton on the Law of Torts § 13, at 78 (W. Page Keeton ed., 5th ed.1984), the Act protects users whose electronic communications are in electronic storage with an ISP or other electronic communications facility.

> A defendant is not liable for trespass if the plaintiff authorized his entry. *See* Prosser & Keeton § 13, at 70. But "an overt manifestation of assent or willingness would not be effective if the defendant knew, or probably if he ought to have known in the exercise of reasonable care, that the plaintiff was mistaken as to the nature and quality of the invasion intended." Id. § 18, at 119. Thus, the busybody who gets permission to come inside by posing as a meter reader is a trespasser. So too is the police officer who, invited into a home, conceals a recording device for the media.

> Not all deceit vitiates consent. "The mistake must extend to the essential character of the act itself, which is to say that which makes it harmful or offensive, rather than to some collateral matter which merely operates as an inducement." Prosser & Keeton § 18, at 120. In other words, it must be a "substantial mistake concerning the nature of the invasion or the extent of the harm." Restatement (Second) of Torts § 892B(2) cmt. g. Unlike the phony meter reader, the restaurant critic who poses as an ordinary customer is not liable for trespass, nor, unlike the wired cop, is the invitee who conceals only an intent to repeat what he hears. These results hold even if admission would have been refused had all the facts been known.

> These are fine and sometimes incoherent distinctions. But the theory is that some invited mistakes go to the essential nature of the invasion while others are merely collateral. Classification depends on the extent to which the intrusion trenches on the specific interests that the tort of trespass seeks to protect.

Assuming the framework is a valid one, does the law of trespass necessarily provide the right comparison to understand the scope of authorization in computer misuse statutes? Trespass is usually a civil offense, not a crime, and when it is a crime it tends to be a violation or at most a misdemeanor. Further, in order to protect the home, courts have been unusually willing to find that misrepresentation or bad faith triggers a trespass. *See, e.g.,* People v. Peeples, 616 N.E.2d 294 (Ill. 1993) (holding that the defendant's criminal actions undertaken inside another person's house vitiated the homeowner's consent to enter the house, rendering him guilty of trespass). Are computers different? Although a homeowner has a tremendous interest in protecting the privacy of his home, computers connected to computer networks generally are designed to be open. Networks can be used by thousands of people at the same time in countless different ways. A person can be in only one home at a time, while computer users can access dozens of computers at a time and thousands of computers in a day. Unauthorized access statutes are primarily criminal statutes, and often impose serious felony liability.

Given these differences, is trespass law a helpful standard? Is gaining entrance to a home by pretending to be a meter reader akin to visiting a website by pretending to be someone who will comply with the Terms of Use? Consider that in *Theofel*, Judge Kozinski reached the rather remarkable conclusion that serving an invalid subpoena on an ISP constituted an unauthorized access to that ISP in violation of 18 U.S.C. § 2701. According to Judge Kozinski, the fact that the subpoena was overly broad made the effort to obtain information unauthorized; serving the court order was deemed the legal equivalent of hacking into the computer. *See Theofel*, 359 F.3d at 1074. Do you agree? A narrower application of the same traditional principles of criminal law would reach very different outcomes. For example, if you define the purpose of access restrictions as confirming that the person accessing the user is the particular individual who is authorized to use it, then the traditional approach would prohibit circumventing code-based restrictions but not breaching contract-based restrictions.

5. WHAT IS AUTHORIZATION? THE CASE OF NORMS–BASED RESTRICTIONS

Should misuse of a computer render access to that computer unauthorized even if it neither circumvents a code-based restriction nor breaches an explicit contractual restriction? Are there some types of computer use that are simply understood as sufficiently out of bounds or contrary to the computer owner's interests that such access should be deemed "without authorization" or in excess of authorization? If so, it might be considered a norms-based approach to authorization. Access that violates generally understood social norms on normal or reasonable computer access might render that access without authorization or in excess of authorization.

Such issues arose in a follow-up to the *Explorica* case that considered the injunction at issue in *Explorica* with regard to a different defendant, Zefer Corp. As you may recall from the facts of *Explorica*, Zefer Corp. was the company hired to create the scraper program. Zefer filed a separate appeal asking the First Circuit to vacate the preliminary injunction with respect to Zefer, leading to the following opinion by Chief Judge Boudin.

EF CULTURAL TRAVEL BV v. ZEFER CORP.

United States Court of Appeals for the First Circuit, 2003.
318 F.3d 58.

BOUDIN, Chief Judge.

Defendant Zefer Corporation seeks review of a preliminary injunction prohibiting it from using a "scraper tool" to collect pricing information from the website of plaintiff EF Cultural Travel BV. This court earlier upheld the injunction against co-defendant Explorica, Inc. *EF Cultural Travel BV v. Explorica, Inc.*, 274 F.3d 577 (1st Cir. 2001) ("*EF I*"). The validity of the injunction as applied to Zefer was not addressed because Zefer's appeal was stayed when it filed for bankruptcy, but the stay has now been lifted.

On Zefer's re-activated appeal, the question presented is whether the preliminary injunction is proper as to Zefer. We conclude that it is proper even as to Zefer, which signed no confidentiality agreement, but on relatively narrow grounds. Given the prospect of further proceedings—this appeal is merely from a preliminary injunction—it is helpful to explain where and why our own reasoning differs from that of the district court. The principal issues are legal ones as to which our review is *de novo*.

EF argues at the outset that our decision in *EF I* is decisive as to Zefer. But the ground we adopted there in upholding the injunction as to the other defendants was that they had apparently used confidential information to facilitate the obtaining of the EF data. Explorica was created by former EF employees, some of whom were subject to confidentiality agreements. Zefer's position in that respect is quite different from that of Explorica or former EF employees. It signed no such agreement, and its prior knowledge as to the agreement is an open question.

EF suggests that Zefer must have known that information provided to it by Explorica had been improperly obtained. This is possible but not certain, and there are no express district court findings on this issue; indeed, given the district court's much broader basis for its injunction, it had no reason to make any detailed findings as to the role of the confidentiality agreement. What can be gleaned from the record as to Zefer's knowledge certainly does not permit us to make on appeal the finding urged by EF.

EF's alternative ground for affirmance is the rationale adopted by the district court for the preliminary injunction. That court relied on its "reasonable expectations" test as a gloss on the CFAA and then applied it to the facts of this case. Although we bypassed the issue in *EF I*, the district court's rationale would embrace Zefer as readily as Explorica itself. But the gloss presents a pure question of law to be reviewed *de novo* and, on this issue, we differ with the district court.

The CFAA provision relied upon by the district court states:

> Whoever ... knowingly and with intent to defraud, accesses a protected computer without authorization, or exceeds authorized access, and by means of such conduct furthers the intended fraud and obtains anything of value, unless the object of the fraud and the thing obtained consists only of the use of the computer and the value of such use is not more than $5,000 in any 1–year period ... shall be punished as provided in subsection (c) of this section.

18 U.S.C. § 1030(a)(4). The statute defines "exceeds authorized access" as "to access a computer with authorization and to use such access to obtain or alter information in the computer that the accesser is not entitled so to obtain or alter." *Id.* § 1030(e)(6). The CFAA furnishes a civil remedy for individuals who suffer damages or loss as a result of a violation of the above section. *Id.* § 1030(g).

The issue, then, is whether use of the scraper "exceed[ed] authorized access." A lack of authorization could be established by an explicit statement on the website restricting access. (Whether public policy might in turn limit certain restrictions is a separate issue.) Many webpages contain lengthy limiting conditions, including limitations on the use of scrapers.[3] However, at the time of Zefer's use of the scraper, EF had no such explicit prohibition in place, although it may well use one now.

The district court thought that a lack of authorization could also be inferred from the circumstances, using "reasonable expectations" as the test; and it said that three such circumstances comprised such a warning in this case: the copyright notice on EF's homepage with a link directing users to contact the company with questions; EF's provision to Zefer of confidential information obtained in breach of the employee confidentiality agreements; and the fact that the website was configured to allow ordinary visitors to the site to view only one page at a time.

We agree with the district court that lack of authorization may be implicit, rather than explicit. After all, password protection itself normally limits authorization by implication (and technology), even without express terms. But we think that in general a reasonable expectations test is not the proper gloss on subsection (a)(4) and we reject it. However useful a reasonable expectations test might be in other contexts where there may be a common understanding underpinning the notion, *cf. Terry v. Ohio*, 392 U.S. 1, 9 (1968) (Fourth Amendment), its use in this context is neither prescribed by the statute nor prudentially sound.

Our basis for this view is not, as some have urged, that there is a "presumption" of open access to Internet information. The CFAA, after

---

3. For example, the "legal notices" on one familiar website state that "you may print or download one copy of the materials or content on this site on any single computer for your personal, non-commercial use, provided you keep intact all copyright and other proprietary notices. Systematic retrieval of data or other content from this site to create or compile, directly or indirectly, a collection, compilation, database or directory without written permission from America Online is prohibited." AOL Anywhere Terms and Conditions of Use, *at* http:// www.aol.com/copyright.html (last visited Jan. 14, 2003).

all, is primarily a statute imposing limits on access and enhancing control by information providers. Instead, we think that the public website provider can easily spell out explicitly what is forbidden and, consonantly, that nothing justifies putting users at the mercy of a highly imprecise, litigation-spawning standard like "reasonable expectations." If EF wants to ban scrapers, let it say so on the webpage or a link clearly marked as containing restrictions.

This case itself illustrates the flaws in the "reasonable expectations" standard. Why should the copyright symbol, which arguably does not protect the substantive information anyway, or the provision of page-by-page access for that matter, be taken to suggest that downloading information at higher speed is forbidden. EF could easily include— indeed, by now probably has included—a sentence on its home page or in its terms of use stating that "no scrapers may be used," giving fair warning and avoiding time-consuming litigation about its private, albeit "reasonable," intentions.

Needless to say, Zefer can have been in no doubt that EF would dislike the use of the scraper to construct a database for Explorica to undercut EF's prices; but EF would equally have disliked the compilation of such a database manually without the use of a scraper tool. EF did not purport to exclude competitors from looking at its website and any such limitation would raise serious public policy concerns.

Although we conclude that the district court's rationale does not support an independent preliminary injunction against Zefer, there is no apparent reason to vacate the present injunction "as against Zefer." Despite being a party to the case, Zefer is not named in the ordering language of the injunction; it is merely precluded, like anyone else with notice, from acting in concert with, on behalf of, or at the direction of Explorica to use the scraper to access EF's information.

Under the applicable rules and case law, an injunction properly issued against a named party means that anyone else with notice is precluded from acting to assist the enjoined party from violating the decree or from doing so on behalf of that party. There is no reason why Zefer should be freer than any other third party who was never in this litigation to assist EF to violate the injunction against it or to do so on EF's behalf or at its direction. As we read the injunction, that is all that is forbidden.

It may still be of practical importance to Zefer to have clarified the limited basis on which we uphold the injunction. And nothing we have said would prevent EF, if it matters in continued litigation, from seeking to show that Zefer did use confidential information, aware that it was being supplied in violation of agreements made by former EF employees. It is also of some use for future litigation among other litigants in this circuit to indicate that, with rare exceptions, public website providers ought to say just what non-password protected access they purport to forbid.

Notes and Questions

1. Although dicta, the discussion in Judge Boudin's opinion rejects a norms-based approach to the scope of 18 U.S.C. § 1030 in the context of access to a public website. Under his approach, it seems, whether access to a website is without authorization or in excess of authorization hinges on the existence and circumvention of code-based or clear contract-based restrictions. Judge Boudin justifies this approach on the grounds of clarity and efficiency: website owners can easily impose clear contractual restrictions on access, whereas identifying the norms of computer users is more difficult. Is he right? Are contractual restrictions always clear, and were they clear in *Explorica*?

More broadly, does the rationale of *Zefer* apply beyond the narrow case of publicly accessible websites? Should it? Do you think Judge Boudin's aversion to a norms-based approach hinges on acceptance of the contract-based approach reflected in *Explorica*? If you are skeptical of permitting § 1030 to enforce contractual restrictions on access, should you be more willing to consider a norms-derived "reasonable expectations" approach to the scope of authorization? Do you think Judge Boudin would have been more willing to accept a norms-based approach if the issue had arisen in a criminal case rather than a civil case? Is it inconsistent to adopt the norms-derived "intended function" test of authorization from the *Morris* case but to reject a norms-derived "reasonable expectations" test for authorization in the context of a public website?

2. Imagine that an employee who is planning on leaving his job accesses his employer's computer and obtains work-related information that he plans to use in his next job to compete against his then-current employer. Should that access be deemed without authorization or in excess of authorization absent breach of a clear contractual restriction on access? Does the fact that the access was contrary to the employer's interests render it unauthorized? Courts that have considered this issue have reached inconsistent results.

In Sherman & Co. v. Salton Maxim Housewares, 94 F. Supp. 2d 817 (E.D. Mich. 2000), the court concluded that such employee misconduct does not constitute unauthorized access in the context of 18 U.S.C. § 2701, the narrow unauthorized access statute that appears in the Stored Communications Act. The court reasoned, *id.* at 821:

> [Section 2701's] prohibition on intentional exceeding of authorized access anticipates that a person with authorization to a computer database or certain public portions of a database is not thereby authorized to visit "private" zones of data in the system. *See* Raphael Winick, *Searches and Seizures of Computers and Computer Data*, 8 HARV.J.L. & TECH. 75, 98 (1994). Yet, for "intentional" access in excess of authorization to be a crime and actionable civilly, the offender must have obtained the access to private files without authorization (e.g., using a computer he was not to use, or obtaining and using someone else's password or code without authorization). At a minimum, there must be a clearer and more explicit restriction on the authorized access . * * * Here [the] access * * * was

in no way restricted by technical means or by any express limitation. Because § 2701 of the ECPA prohibits only unauthorized access and not the misappropriation or disclosure of information, there is no violation of § 2701 for a person with authorized access to the database no matter how malicious or larcenous his intended use of that access. Section 2701 outlaws illegal entry, not larceny.

In contrast, the court in Shurgard Storage Centers, Inc. v. Safeguard Self Storage, Inc., 119 F. Supp. 2d 1121 (W.D. Wash. 2000), held that such access does render the access "without authorization." The court interpreted the phrase "without authorization" in 18 U.S.C. § 1030 by looking to agency principles embodied in section 112 of the Restatement (Second) of Agency (1958). That section states that "[u]nless otherwise agreed, the authority of an agent terminates if, without knowledge of the principal, he acquires adverse interests or if he is otherwise guilty of a serious breach of loyalty to the principal." Applying the Restatement to employees who accessed their employer's computer to help a future employer, the court held that the purpose to aid the future employer made the access without authorization:

> Under this rule, the authority of the plaintiff's former employees ended when they allegedly became agents of the defendant. Therefore, for the purposes of this 12(b)(6) motion, they lost their authorization and were "without authorization" when they allegedly obtained and sent the proprietary information to the defendant via e-mail. The plaintiff has stated a claim under 18 U.S.C. § 1030(a)(2)(c).

Id. at 1125. *See also* International Airport Centers v. Citrin, 440 F.3d 418, 421 (7th Cir. 2006) (Posner, J.) (adopting the *Shurgard* approach in dicta).

Which approach makes more sense? Consider the fact that most employees use their employer's computers for personal reasons at least on occasion. If an employee accesses his network account at work in order to send a personal e-mail, has the employee committed an illegal unauthorized access to the employer's computer? What if the employee surfs the web in a search for a better job when he is on his lunch break? Does 18 U.S.C. § 1030 create an nationwide employee loyalty test, such that every time an employee accesses his employer's network for reasons not aligned with his employer's interest, the employee is committing a federal crime?

3. Many cases interpreting 18 U.S.C. § 1030 arise in a civil context, and this may have a significant effect on the law interpreting the prohibition on access without authorization and exceeding authorized access. The vague language of § 1030 and the civil remedy of § 1030(g) provide a tempting tool for businesses seeking to litigate against competitors. Because computers are integral to most businesses, a business can file a civil suit in federal court under § 1030(g) whenever there is a claim of potential foul play by a competitor. The theory will be that the foul play somehow involved accessing a computer, and it rendered the access without authorization or in excess of authorization. Judges faced with such claims in the civil context may be unaware that 18 U.S.C. § 1030 is primarily a criminal statute, and may adopt broad interpretations of authorization that make sense for injunctions sought in business disputes but make little sense in the context of a criminal prosecution against an individual. A sensible standard for stopping a compa-

ny from using a particular business practice may be much broader than the standard to put a person in jail.

This dynamic may explain cases such as Register.com v. Verio, 126 F. Supp. 2d 238 (S.D.N.Y. 2000). In *Verio*, the defendant company used an automated program to send queries to a database maintained by a business competitor, the plaintiff. The search robot gathered contact information about the plaintiff's customers, and the defendant's employees would then contact them and invite them to switch service providers from the plaintiff to the defendant. The plaintiff sued, and moved for a preliminary injunction against the use of the search robots on the ground (among others) that the defendant's use of the search robot constituted an unauthorized access to its database in violation of 18 U.S.C. § 1030. The district court agreed, holding that use of the search robot "represent an unauthorized access" because the plaintiff "objects to [the defendant]'s use of search robots." In effect, the fact that the computer owner had at some point decided to object to the defendant's use of its computer made any prior accesses to the computer "without authorization."

Can you imagine a court adopting *Verio*'s theory of authorization in a criminal case? Can you imagine a court adopting an agency approach in a criminal context? If not, should courts in criminal cases decline to follow broad interpretations of 18 U.S.C. § 1030 from civil cases? Courts generally use civil and criminal interpretations of federal statutes interchangeably absent an indication that Congress intended a contrary approach.

4. *"Access without authorization" versus "exceeds authorized access."* What is the difference between "access without authorization" and conduct that "exceeds authorized access"? Some statutes, such as 18 U.S.C. § 1030(a)(3), prohibit only the former, while other statutes, such as 18 U.S.C. § 1030(a)(2), prohibit both. What does the former prohibit that the latter does not? Section 1030 does not define "without authorization," but it does define "exceeds authorized access" in 18 U.S.C. § 1030(e)(6):

> the term "exceeds authorized access" means to access a computer with authorization and to use such access to obtain or alter information in the computer that the accesser is not entitled so to obtain or alter.

This isn't a particularly helpful definition, as it begs the question of how we measure what a user is "entitled" to do. In light of this ambiguity, several different schools of thought have emerged on the different meaning of "access without authorization" and "exceeds authorized access."

The first school of thought contends that the prohibition on "access without authorization" is limited to the circumvention of code-based restrictions, such as the facts of *Morris*. In contrast, the prohibition on exceeding authorized access extends beyond the circumvention of code-based restrictions, covering at least some kinds of contract-based and norms-based breaches. As the imprecise vernacular would put it, "without authorization" applies to outsiders but not insiders, while "exceeds authorized access" includes insiders. The legislative history cited in the *Morris* case suggests such a distinction, as does a Senate Report that accompanied 1996 amendments to Section 1030. *See* S. Rep. No. 104–357 (1996).

Perhaps the strongest statutory case for this understanding is the language Congress used in the first version of § 1030 enacted in 1984. In the 1984 version of § 1030, 18 U.S.C. §§ 1030(a)(1) and (a)(2) covered both whoever accessed a federal interest computer without authorization and also one who "having accessed a computer with authorization, uses the opportunity such access provides for purposes to which such authorization does not extend." The Computer Fraud and Abuse Act of 1986 amended this language, creating the phrase "exceeds authorized access" and defining that phrase in § 1030(e)(6). The accompanying Senate Report suggests that the change was designed only to simplify the "cumbersome phrase" in the 1984 version, not to change its meaning. S. Rep. 99–432, at 9 (1986), *reprinted in* 1986 U.S.C.C.A.N. 2479, 2486. The 1984 language arguably suggests a clearer distinction between access without authorization and exceeding authorized access: the former is focused on gaining access, which may suggest bypassing a code-based restriction, and the latter is focused on using access for inappropriate purposes, which may suggest breaching contract-based or code-based restrictions. *Cf.* Briggs v. State, 704 A.2d 904 (Md. Ct. App. 1998) (concluding that a system administrator who misused his employer's computer had not gained access without authorization, but suggesting that he may have exceeded his authorized access).

A second school of thought suggests that there is no difference between mere access without authorization and exceeding authorized access. The arguments for this position are as follows. First, despite the possible statutory clues discussed in the preceding paragraph, courts in fact often use the terms "access without authorization" and "exceeding authorized access" interchangeably. A number of courts have held that circumvention of contract-based or norms-based restrictions made the access "without authorization," and the existence of these cases makes it difficult to adopt a clear line between the two phrases. Second, under a broad construction of access it is hard to see how the definition of "exceeds authorizes access" differs from the meaning of "access without authorization." The definition of "exceeds authorized access" is textually meaningless; it states that a person exceeds authorized access when she does what she is not entitled to do, which simply restates the test for when access is without authorization. (If true, do you think this counsels in favor of a narrower interpretation of access?) Third, readings of "exceeding authorized access" as broadly prohibiting contract and norms-based breaches may raise constitutional problems, counseling against such an interpretation.

Judge Posner suggested a third approach in dicta found in International Airport Centers v. Citrin, 440 F.3d 418 (7th Cir. 2006). Ruminating about 18 U.S.C. § 1030, Judge Posner contended that "[t]he difference between 'without authorization' and 'exceeding authorized access' is paper thin, but not quite invisible." According to Judge Posner, EF Cultural Travel BV v. Explorica, Inc., 274 F.3d 577 (1st Cir. 2001), involved only exceeding authorized access:

> [T]he former employee of a travel agent, in violation of his confidentiality agreement with his former employer, used confidential information that he had obtained as an employee to create a program that enabled his new travel company to obtain information from his former employer's website that he could not have obtained as efficiently without the

use of that confidential information. The website was open to the public, so he was authorized to use it, but he exceeded his authorization by using confidential information to obtain better access than other members of the public.

440 F.3d at 420. In contrast, Posner suggested, the facts of *Citrin* satisfied the "access without authorization" standard. Citrin had been assigned a laptop by his company, and he decided to leave the company and start a competitor business. Citrin allegedly deleted the files on the laptop so his employer could not benefit from them when he returned the laptop. According to Judge Posner, "Citrin's breach of his duty of loyalty terminated his agency relationship (more precisely, terminated any rights he might have claimed as IAC's agent—he could not by unilaterally terminating any duties he owed his principal gain an advantage!) and with it his authority to access the laptop, because the only basis of his authority had been that relationship." *Id.* at 420–21.

Which of these approaches is the most persuasive?

5. In Fugarino v. State, 531 S.E.2d 187 (Ga. Ct. App. 2000), a system administrator became upset when his employer hired an additional system administrator. He announced to his boss that the company's network was "his product, that no one else was going to work on his code, that nobody was going to take his place and he was 'going to take his code with him.' " *Id.* at 188. He then deleted several important sections of code from the employer's computer. On appeal following his conviction, a Georgia state appellate court concluded that the defendant's accessing his employer's computer to delete the code was "without authority" because "[t]he owner of the company * * * did not give Fugarino authority or permission to delete portions of the company's program." *Id.* at 189. *See also* Briggs v. State, 704 A.2d 904 (Md. Ct. App. 1998) (concluding that a system administrator who encrypted files on his employer's computer to keep them from his employer had not gained access without authorization, but suggesting that likely he exceeded his authorized access).

6. The Michigan legislature has tried to clarify the line between authorized and unauthorized access to a computer by enacting the following "rebuttable presumption" in the Michigan computer crime statute:

It is a rebuttable presumption in a prosecution for [unauthorized access to computers] that the person did not have authorization from the owner, system operator, or other person who has authority from the owner or system operator to grant permission to access the computer program, computer, computer system, or computer network or has exceeded authorization unless 1 or more of the following circumstances existed at the time of access:

(a) Written or oral permission was granted by the owner, system operator, or other person who has authority from the owner or system operator to grant permission of the accessed computer program, computer, computer system, or computer network.

(b) The accessed computer program, computer, computer system, or computer network had a pre-programmed access procedure that would display a bulletin, command, or other message before access was achieved that a reasonable person would believe identified the computer program, computer, computer system, or computer network as within the public domain.

(c) Access was achieved without the use of a set of instructions, code, or computer program that bypasses, defrauds, or otherwise circumvents the pre-programmed access procedure for the computer program, computer, computer system, or computer network.

M.C.L.A. 752.797(6) (West 2001). Is this a useful solution to the problem of distinguishing authorized from unauthorized access? Note that the presumed lack of authorization may raise constitutional problems. *See* Sandstrom v. Montana, 442 U.S. 510, 524 (1979) (holding that a "presumption which, although not conclusive, had the effect of shifting the burden of persuasion to the defendant" in a criminal case violates the Due Process Clause).

7. *What is a "computer"?* 18 U.S.C. § 1030(e)(1) defines "computer" as:

an electronic, magnetic, optical, electrochemical, or other high speed data processing device performing logical, arithmetic, or storage functions, and includes any data storage facility or communications facility directly related to or operating in conjunction with such device, but such term does not include an automated typewriter or typesetter, a portable hand held calculator, or other similar device[.]

Does this definition include a cellular telephone? A Palm-type personal digital assistant (PDA)? A Blackberry? Does it include a thumb drive or floppy diskette? As a policy matter, should such devices be included in the statutory definition?

United States v. Mitra, 405 F.3d 492 (7th Cir. 2005), may shed some light on these questions. Mitra, a student at the University of Wisconsin, had figured out how to commandeer the radio system used by police, fire, ambulance, and other emergency workers in Madison, Wisconsin. The radio system was a Motorola Smartnet II, a sophisticated system that used a computer to host many different communications on a small number of radio frequencies. Mitra had learned how to control the system using a radio transmitter, and he used his transmitter to block the radio system to stop receiving signals. Mitra's conduct effectively blocked Madison emergency workers from being able to use their radio system and to coordinate emergency responses to incidents in the city.

Mitra was charged and convicted of violating 18 U.S.C. § 1030(a)(5), and appealed his convicted on the ground that the Madison radio system was not a "computer" covered by § 1030. In an opinion by Judge Easterbrook, the Seventh Circuit disagreed and affirmed the conviction:

Every cell phone and cell tower is a "computer" under this statute's definition; so is every iPod, every wireless base station in the corner coffee shop, and many another gadget. Reading § 1030 to cover all of these, and police radio too, would give the statute wide coverage, which by Mitra's lights means that Congress cannot have contemplated such breadth.

Well of course Congress did not contemplate or intend this particular application of the statute. * * * But although legislators may not know about [it], they *do* know that complexity is endemic in the modern world and that each passing year sees new developments. That's why they write general statutes rather than enacting a list of particular forbidden acts. And it is the statutes they enacted—not the thoughts they did or didn't have—that courts must apply.

Section 1030 is general. Exclusions show just *how* general. Subsection (e)(1) carves out automatic typewriters, typesetters, and handheld calculators; this shows that other devices with embedded processors and software are covered. As more devices come to have built-in intelligence, the effective scope of the statute grows. This might prompt Congress to amend the statute but does not authorize the judiciary to give the existing version less coverage than its language portends.

Id. at 495.

D. COMPUTER FRAUD STATUTES

Computer fraud statutes are hybrids between unauthorized access statutes and fraud statutes. The federal computer fraud statute is 18 U.S.C. § 1030(a)(4). It punishes whoever:

> knowingly and with intent to defraud, accesses a protected computer without authorization, or exceeds authorized access, and by means of such conduct furthers the intended fraud and obtains anything of value, unless the object of the fraud and the thing obtained consists only of the use of the computer and the value of such use is not more than $5,000 in any one-year period[.]

All § 1030(a)(4) crimes are felonies; the maximum punishment is 5 years for the first offense, and 10 years if the defendant has a prior § 1030 conviction. *See* 18 U.S.C. § 1030(c)(3).

The hybrid status of § 1030(a)(4) is readily apparent from its text. On one hand, it clearly is closely related to § 1030(a)(2). The basic prohibition on accessing a protected computer without authorization or exceeding authorized access is shared between the two. On the other hand, the prohibition is also similar to the wire fraud statute, 18 U.S.C. § 1343. The wire fraud statute punishes whoever,

> having devised or intending to devise any scheme or artifice to defraud, or for obtaining money or property by means of false or fraudulent pretenses, representations, or promises, transmits or causes to be transmitted by means of wire, radio, or television communication in interstate or foreign commerce, any writings, signs, signals, pictures, or sounds for the purpose of executing such scheme or artifice[.]

Section 1030(a)(4) puts the two basic concepts together. It combines the intent to defraud and obtaining of anything of value from the wire fraud statute and matches it with the *actus reus* of accessing a protected computer without authorization or exceeding authorized access from § 1030(a)(2). The hybrid status raises interesting questions about why

§ 1030(a)(4) exists. Just what does it punish that the combination of § 1030(a)(2) and the wire fraud statute does not?

The difference between unauthorized access statutes, wire fraud statutes, and computer fraud statutes was explored in the Senate Report that accompanied the enactment of § 1030(a)(4):

> The new subsection 1030(a)(4) to be created by this bill is designed to penalize thefts of property via computer that occur as part of a scheme to defraud. It will require a showing that the use of the computer or computers in question was integral to the intended fraud and was not merely incidental. It has been suggested that the Committee approach all computer fraud in a manner that directly tracks the existing mail fraud and wire fraud statutes. However, the Committee was concerned that such an approach might permit prosecution under this subsection of acts that do not deserve classification as "computer fraud."

> The Committee was concerned that computer usage that is wholly extraneous to an intended fraud might nevertheless be covered by this subsection if the subsection were patterned directly after the current mail fraud and wire fraud laws. If it were so patterned, the subsection might be construed as covering an individual who had devised a scheme or artifice to defraud solely because he used a computer to keep records or to add up his potential "take" from the crime. The Committee does not believe that a scheme or artifice to defraud should fall under the ambit of subsection (a)(4) merely because the offender signed onto a computer at some point near to the commission or execution of the fraud. While such a tenuous link might be covered under current law where the instrumentality used is the mails or the wires, the Committee does not consider that link sufficient with respect to computers. To be prosecuted under this subsection, the use of the computer must be more directly linked to the intended fraud. That is, it must be used by an offender without authorization or in excess of his authorization to obtain property of another, which property furthers the intended fraud. Likewise, this subsection may be triggered by conduct that can be shown to constitute an attempted offense.

> This approach is designed, in part, to help distinguish between acts of theft via computer and acts of computer trespass. In intentionally trespassing into someone else's computer files, the offender obtains at the very least information as to how to break into that computer system. If that is all he obtains, the offense should properly be treated as a simple trespass. But because the offender has obtained the small bit of information needed to get into the computer system, the danger exists that his and every other computer trespass could be treated as a theft, punishable as a felony under this subsection. * * *

> The Committee remains convinced that there must be a clear distinction between computer theft, punishable as a felony, and

computer trespass, punishable in the first instance as a misdemeanor. The element in the new paragraph (a)(4), requiring a showing of an intent to defraud, is meant to preserve that distinction, as is the requirement that the property wrongfully obtained via computer furthers the intended fraud.

S. Rep. No. 99–432, at 10 (1986), *reprinted in* 1986 U.S.C.C.A.N. 2479, 2488.

UNITED STATES v. CZUBINSKI

United States Court of Appeals for the First Circuit, 1997.
106 F.3d 1069.

TORRUELLA, Chief Judge.

Defendant-appellant Richard Czubinski appeals his jury conviction on nine counts of wire fraud, and four counts of computer fraud, 18 U.S.C. § 1030(a)(4). The wire fraud and computer fraud prosecution that led to the conviction survived serious challenges put forward by Czubinski in various pre-trial motions. Given the broad scope of the federal fraud statutes, motions charging insufficient pleadings or selective prosecution generally deserve careful consideration. We need not scrutinize the lower court's rejection of the defendant's arguments in favor of dismissing the indictment, however, because we reverse the conviction on the clearer ground that the trial evidence mustered by the government was insufficient to support a guilty verdict, and hold that the defendant's motion for judgment of acquittal should have been granted on all counts. Unauthorized browsing of taxpayer files, although certainly inappropriate conduct, cannot, without more, sustain this federal felony conviction.

BACKGROUND

For all periods relevant to the acts giving rise to his conviction, the defendant Czubinski was employed as a Contact Representative in the Boston office of the Taxpayer Services Division of the Internal Revenue Service. To perform his official duties, which mainly involved answering questions from taxpayers regarding their returns, Czubinski routinely accessed information from one of the IRS's computer systems known as the Integrated Data Retrieval System ("IDRS"). Using a valid password given to Contact Representatives, certain search codes, and taxpayer social security numbers, Czubinski was able to retrieve, to his terminal screen in Boston, income tax return information regarding virtually any taxpayer—information that is permanently stored in the IDRS "master file" located in Martinsburg, West Virginia. In the period of Czubinski's employ, IRS rules plainly stated that employees with passwords and access codes were not permitted to access files on IDRS outside of the course of their official duties.[1]

---

1. In 1987 Czubinski signed an acknowledgment of receipt of the IRS Rules of Conduct, which contained the following rule: Employees must make every effort to

In 1992, Czubinski carried out numerous unauthorized searches of IDRS files. He knowingly disregarded IRS rules by looking at confidential information obtained by performing computer searches that were outside of the scope of his duties as a Contact Representative, including, but not limited to, the searches listed in the indictment. Audit trails performed by internal IRS auditors establish that Czubinski frequently made unauthorized accesses on IDRS in 1992. For example, Czubinski accessed information regarding: the tax returns of two individuals involved in the David Duke presidential campaign; the joint tax return of an assistant district attorney (who had been prosecuting Czubinski's father on an unrelated felony offense) and his wife; the tax return of Boston City Counselor Jim Kelly's Campaign Committee (Kelly had defeated Czubinski in the previous election for the Counselor seat for District 2); the tax return of one of his brothers' instructors; the joint tax return of a Boston Housing Authority police officer, who was involved in a community organization with one of Czubinski's brothers, and the officer's wife; and the tax return of a woman Czubinski had dated a few times. Czubinski also accessed the files of various other social acquaintances by performing unauthorized searches.

Nothing in the record indicates that Czubinski did anything more than knowingly disregard IRS rules by observing the confidential information he accessed. No evidence suggests, nor does the government contend, that Czubinski disclosed the confidential information he accessed to any third parties. The government's only evidence demonstrating any intent to use the confidential information for nefarious ends was the trial testimony of William A. Murray, an acquaintance of Czubinski who briefly participated in Czubinski's local Invisible Knights of the Ku Klux Klan chapter and worked with him on the David Duke campaign. Murray testified that Czubinski had once stated at a social gathering in "early 1992" that "he intended to use some of that information to build dossiers on people" involved in "the white supremacist movement." There is, however, no evidence that Czubinski created dossiers, took steps toward making dossiers (such as by printing out or recording the information he browsed), or shared any of the information he accessed in the years following the single comment to Murray. No other witness testified to having any knowledge of Czubinski's alleged intent to create "dossiers" on KKK members.

The record shows that Czubinski did not perform any unauthorized searches after 1992. He continued to be employed as a Contact Representative until June 1995, when a grand jury returned an indictment against him on ten counts of federal wire fraud under 18 U.S.C. §§ 1343, 1346, and four counts of federal interest computer fraud under 18 U.S.C. § 1030(a)(4).

assure security and prevent unauthorized disclosure of protected information data in the use of Government owned or leased computers. In addition, employees may not use any Service computer system for other than official purposes.

In addition, Czubinski received separate rules regarding use of the IDRS, one of which states: Access only those accounts required to accomplish your official duties.

The portion of the indictment alleging wire fraud states that Czubinski defrauded the IRS of confidential property * * * by using his valid password to acquire confidential taxpayer information as part of a scheme to: 1) build "dossiers" on associates in the KKK; 2) seek information regarding an assistant district attorney who was then prosecuting Czubinski's father on an unrelated criminal charge; and 3) perform opposition research by inspecting the records of a political opponent in the race for a Boston City Councilor seat. The wire fraud indictment, therefore, articulated particular personal ends to which the unauthorized access to confidential information through interstate wires was allegedly a means.

The portion of the indictment setting forth the computer fraud charges stated that Czubinski obtained something of value, beyond the mere unauthorized use of a federal interest computer, by performing certain searches—searches representing a subset of those making up the mail fraud counts.

Discussion

I. The Wire Fraud Counts

To support a conviction for wire fraud, the government must prove two elements beyond a reasonable doubt: (1) the defendant's knowing and willing participation in a scheme or artifice to defraud with the specific intent to defraud, and (2) the use of interstate wire communications in furtherance of the scheme. Although defendant's motion for judgment of acquittal places emphasis on shortcomings in proof with regard to the second element, by arguing that the wire transmissions at issue were not proved to be interstate, we find the first element dispositive and hold that the government failed to prove beyond a reasonable doubt that the defendant willfully participated in a scheme to defraud within the meaning of the wire fraud statute.

The government correctly notes that confidential information may constitute intangible "property" and that its unauthorized dissemination or other use may deprive the owner of its property rights. *See Carpenter v. United States*, 484 U.S. 19, 26 (1987). Where such deprivation is effected through dishonest or deceitful means, a "scheme to defraud," within the meaning of the wire fraud statute, is shown. Thus, a necessary step toward satisfying the "scheme to defraud" element in this context is showing that the defendant intended to "deprive" another of their protected right.

The government, however, provides no case in support of its contention here that merely accessing confidential information, without doing, or clearly intending to do, more, is tantamount to a deprivation of IRS property under the wire fraud statute. In *Carpenter*, for example, the confidential information regarding the contents of a newspaper column was converted to the defendants's use to their substantial benefit. *See id.* at 27 (defendants participated in "ongoing scheme to share profit from trading in anticipation" of newspaper column). We do not think that

Czubinski's unauthorized browsing, even if done with the intent to deceive the IRS into thinking he was performing only authorized searches, constitutes a "deprivation" within the meaning of the federal fraud statutes.

Binding precedents, and good sense, support the conclusion that to "deprive" a person of their intangible property interest in confidential information under section 1343, either some articulable harm must befall the holder of the information as a result of the defendant's activities, or some gainful use must be intended by the person accessing the information, whether or not this use is profitable in the economic sense. Here, neither the taking of the IRS' right to "exclusive use" of the confidential information, nor Czubinski's gain from access to the information, can be shown absent evidence of his "use" of the information. Accordingly, without evidence that Czubinski used or intended to use the taxpayer information (beyond mere browsing), an intent to deprive cannot be proven, and, a fortiori, a scheme to defraud is not shown.

All of the cases cited by the government in support of their contention that the confidentiality breached by Czubinski's search in itself constitutes a deprivation of property in fact support our holding today, for they all involve, at a minimum, a finding of a further intended use of the confidential information accessed by the defendants. The government's best support comes from *United States v. Seidlitz*, 589 F.2d 152, 160 (4th Cir. 1978), in which a former employee of a computer systems firm secretly accessed its files, but never was shown to have sold or used the data he accessed, and was nevertheless convicted of wire fraud. The affirming Fourth Circuit held, however, that a jury could have reasonably found that, at the time the defendant raided a competitor's computer system, he intended to retrieve information that would be helpful for his own start-up, competing computer firm. In the instant case, Czubinski did indeed access confidential information through fraudulent pretenses—he appeared to be performing his duties when in fact he used IRS passwords to perform unauthorized searches. Nevertheless, it was not proven that he intended to deprive the IRS of their property interest through either disclosure or use of that information.

The resolution of the instant case is complex because it is well-established that to be convicted of mail or wire fraud, the defendant need not successfully carry out an intended scheme to defraud. The government does not contend either that Czubinski actually created dossiers or that he accomplished some other end through use of the information. It need not do so. All that the government was required to prove was the intent to follow through with a deprivation of the IRS's property and the use or foreseeable use of interstate wire transmissions pursuant to the accomplishment of the scheme to defraud. In the case at bar, the government failed to make even this showing.

The fatal flaw in the government's case is that it has not shown beyond a reasonable doubt that Czubinski intended to carry out a scheme to deprive the IRS of its property interest in confidential information. Had there been sufficient proof that Czubinski intended either to create dossiers for the sake of advancing personal causes or to disseminate confidential information to third parties, then his actions in searching files could arguably be said to be a step in furtherance of a scheme to deprive the IRS of its property interest in confidential information.

Mere browsing of the records of people about whom one might have a particular interest, although reprehensible, is not enough to sustain a wire fraud conviction on a "deprivation of intangible property" theory. Curiosity on the part of an IRS officer may lead to dismissal, but curiosity alone will not sustain a finding of participation in a felonious criminal scheme to deprive the IRS of its property.

II. *The Computer Fraud Counts*

Czubinski was convicted on all four of the computer fraud counts on which he was indicted; these counts arise out of unauthorized searches that also formed the basis of four of the ten wire fraud counts in the indictment. Specifically, he was convicted of violating 18 U.S.C. § 1030(a)(4), a provision enacted in the Computer Fraud and Abuse Act of 1986. Section 1030(a)(4) applies to:

> whoever ... knowingly and with intent to defraud, accesses a Federal interest computer without authorization, or exceeds authorized access, and by means of such conduct furthers the intended fraud and obtains anything of value, unless the object of the fraud and the thing obtained consists only of the use of the computer.

We have never before addressed section 1030(a)(4). Czubinski unquestionably exceeded authorized access to a Federal interest computer. On appeal he argues that he did not obtain "anything of value." We agree, finding that his searches of taxpayer return information did not satisfy the statutory requirement that he obtain "anything of value." The value of information is relative to one's needs and objectives; here, the government had to show that the information was valuable to Czubinski in light of a fraudulent scheme. The government failed, however, to prove that Czubinski intended anything more than to satisfy idle curiosity.

The plain language of section 1030(a)(4) emphasizes that more than mere unauthorized use is required: the "thing obtained" may not merely be the unauthorized use. It is the showing of some additional end—to which the unauthorized access is a means—that is lacking here. The evidence did not show that Czubinski's end was anything more than to satisfy his curiosity by viewing information about friends, acquaintances, and political rivals. No evidence suggests that he printed out, recorded, or used the information he browsed. No rational jury could conclude beyond a reasonable doubt that Czubinski intended to use or disclose that information, and merely viewing information cannot be deemed the same as obtaining something of value for the purposes of this statute.[15]

---

15. The district court, in denying a motion to dismiss the computer fraud counts in the indictment, found that the indictment sufficiently alleged that the confiden-

The legislative history further supports our reading of the term "anything of value." In the game of statutory interpretation, statutory language is the ultimate trump card, and the remarks of sponsors of legislation are authoritative only to the extent that they are compatible with the plain language of section 1030(a)(4). Here, a Senate co-sponsor's comments suggest that Congress intended section 1030(a)(4) to punish attempts to steal valuable data, and did not wish to punish mere unauthorized access:

> The acts of fraud we are addressing in proposed section 1030(a)(4) are essentially thefts in which someone uses a federal interest computer to wrongly obtain something of value from another.... Proposed section 1030(a)(4) is intended to reflect the distinction between the theft of information, a felony, and mere unauthorized access, a misdemeanor.

132 Cong. Rec. 7128, 7129, 99th Cong., 2d. Sess. (1986). The Senate Committee Report further underscores the fact that this section should apply to those who steal information through unauthorized access as part of an illegal scheme:

> The Committee remains convinced that there must be a clear distinction between computer theft, punishable as a felony [under section 1030(a)(4)], and computer trespass, punishable in the first instance as a misdemeanor [under a different provision]. The element in the new paragraph (a)(4), requiring a showing of an intent to defraud, is meant to preserve that distinction, as is the requirement that the property wrongfully obtained via computer furthers the intended fraud.

S. Rep. No. 432, 99th Cong., 2d Sess., *reprinted in* 1986 U.S.C.C.A.N. 2479, 2488. For the same reasons we deemed the trial evidence could not support a finding that Czubinski deprived the IRS of its property, *see* discussion of wire fraud under section 1343 *supra,* we find that Czubinski has not obtained valuable information in furtherance of a fraudulent scheme for the purposes of section 1030(a)(4).

CONCLUSION

We add a cautionary note. The broad language of the mail and wire fraud statutes are both their blessing and their curse. They can address new forms of serious crime that fail to fall within more specific legislation. On the other hand, they might be used to prosecute kinds of behavior that, albeit offensive to the morals or aesthetics of federal prosecutors, cannot reasonably be expected by the instigators to form the basis of a federal felony. The case at bar falls within the latter category.

tial taxpayer information was itself a "thing of value" to Czubinski, given his ends. The indictment, of course, alleged specific uses for the information, such as creating dossiers on KKK members, that were not proven at trial. In light of the trial evidence— which, as we have said, indicates that there was no recording, disclosure or further use of the confidential information—we find that Czubinski did not obtain "anything of value" through his unauthorized searches.

Also discomforting is the prosecution's insistence, before trial, on the admission of inflammatory evidence regarding the defendant's membership in white supremacist groups purportedly as a means to prove a scheme to defraud, when, on appeal, it argues that unauthorized access in itself is a sufficient ground for conviction on all counts. Finally, we caution that the wire fraud statute must not serve as a vehicle for prosecuting only those citizens whose views run against the tide, no matter how incorrect or uncivilized such views are.

Notes and Questions

1. *Comparing § 1030(a)(4) and § 1030(a)(2).* Consider the key differences between computer fraud and basic unauthorized access. *Czubinski* and the legislative history of § 1030 instruct that the most basic difference is that the unauthorized access and retrieval of information in a case of computer fraud is part of a broader scheme that harms the victim in an appreciable way. Absent such a broader scheme to harm the victim, the crime is mere trespass, a misdemeanor unauthorized access violation under § 1030(a)(2). Was Czubinski guilty of violating 18 U.S.C. § 1030(a)(2)(B)? If he was, why did the government charge Czubinski under § 1030(a)(4) instead?

Other slight differences exist between § 1030(a)(4) and § 1030(a)(2). For example, the mens rea of computer fraud is knowledge and intent to defraud, while the mens rea of unauthorized access is intentionally accessing without authorization. In addition, violations of § 1030(a)(2) typically require that the conduct involve a communication that traveled across state lines, while violations of § 1030(a)(4) do not.

With that said, the felony provisions of § 1030(a)(2) create a great deal of overlap with § 1030(a)(4). Felony liability under § 1030(a)(2) is triggered if the offense was committed "for purposes of commercial advantage or private financial gain," the offense was committed "in furtherance of any criminal or tortious act in violation of the Constitution or laws of the United States or of any State," or the value of the information obtained exceeds $5,000. 18 U.S.C. § 1030(c)(2). How different is this from *Czubinski*'s requirement of a broader scheme to harm the victim? To the extent there is a difference, which is a better approach?

2. *Comparing § 1030(a)(4) and § 1343.* Note the basic differences between the computer fraud statute and the wire fraud statute. The actus reus of computer fraud is accessing a computer without authorization or exceeding authorized access, while the actus reus of wire fraud is transmitting a wire, radio, or television communication across state or national boundaries. The computer fraud statute requires that the actus reus must further the fraud, while the wire fraud statute does not. Further, the computer fraud statute specifies that "use of the computer" cannot be the object of value fraudulently obtained if "the value of such use is not more than $5,000 in any one-year period," while the wire fraud statute contains no analogous limitation.

The limitation on use of a computer as an object obtained under the computer fraud statute is largely a leftover from the economics of computer usage in the 1980s. At that time, computers were rare and computer usage often had considerable economic value. Unauthorized access to a computer per se could impose costs on the computer's owner. The legislative history of § 1030(a)(4) suggests that the limitation on computer use as an object of value was designed to distinguish computer fraud from unauthorized access:

> [T]he mere use of a computer or computer service has a value all its own. Mere trespasses onto someone else's computer system can cost the system provider a "port" or access channel that he might otherwise be making available for a fee to an authorized user. At the same time, the Committee believes it is important to distinguish clearly between acts of fraud under (a)(4), punishable as felonies, and acts of simple trespass, punishable in the first instance as misdemeanors. That distinction would be wiped out were the Committee to treat every trespass as an attempt to defraud a service provider of computer time. One simply cannot trespass into another's computer without occupying a portion of the time that that computer service is available. Thus, that suggested approach would treat every act of unauthorized entry to a Federal interest computer—no matter how brief—as an act of fraud, punishable at the felony level. The Committee does not believe this is a proper approach to this problem. For that reason, the Committee has excluded from coverage under this subsection those instances where "the object of the fraud and the thing obtained consists only of the use of the computer."

S. Rep. No. 99–432, at 10 (1986), *reprinted in* 1986 U.S.C.C.A.N. 2479, 2488.

E.   COMPUTER DAMAGE STATUTES

Computer damage statutes are the third and final type of basic computer misuse statute. Computer damage statutes focus on the harm inflicted on the computer owner and attempt to impose criminal liability for conduct that caused a particular amount of harm. Computer damage statutes can be divided into two types. Some computer damage statutes are focused on conduct that exceeds privileges to use a computer. These statutes typically combine the basic prohibition on unauthorized access with an additional requirement that the conduct caused a particular amount of damage or harm.

Other statutes focus on conduct that denies privileges to other users. Such provisions do not require unauthorized access, but instead look to unauthorized acts of deleting, damaging, altering, or rendering inaccessible a set of files or programs on the victim computer. The line between the two types of computer damage statutes can be slippery in practice, in part because a user may exceed his privileges in the course of engaging in conduct that ultimately denies privileges to others. Indeed, many state statutes combine the two types into a single prohibition.

The federal computer damage statute is found in 18 U.S.C. § 1030(a)(5). In its current form, as modified considerably in 2001, it punishes whoever:

(A)(i) knowingly causes the transmission of a program, information, code, or command, and as a result of such conduct, intentionally causes damage without authorization, to a protected computer;

(ii) intentionally accesses a protected computer without authorization, and as a result of such conduct, recklessly causes damage; or

(iii) intentionally accesses a protected computer without authorization, and as a result of such conduct, causes damage; and

(B) by conduct described in clause (i), (ii), or (iii) of subparagraph (A), caused (or, in the case of an attempted offense, would, if completed, have caused)—

(i) loss to 1 or more persons during any 1–year period (and, for purposes of an investigation, prosecution, or other proceeding brought by the United States only, loss resulting from a related course of conduct affecting 1 or more other protected computers) aggregating at least $5,000 in value;

(ii) the modification or impairment, or potential modification or impairment, of the medical examination, diagnosis, treatment, or care of 1 or more individuals;

(iii) physical injury to any person;

(iv) a threat to public health or safety; or

(v) damage affecting a computer system used by or for a government entity in furtherance of the administration of justice, national defense, or national security[.]

Note that the statute rather clumsily breaks down the basic prohibition into three distinct offenses, found in 1030(a)(5)(A)(i)-(iii), and then requires that the relevant violations of 1030(a)(5)(A) must trigger a particular amount or type of harm as defined in 1030(a)(5)(B). In the argot of the American Law Institute's Model Penal Code, which divides each type of criminal offense element into conduct elements, result elements, and attendant circumstance elements, § 1030(a)(5)(A) contains the conduct element of the offense together with the first result element, while 1030(a)(5)(B) contains a second result element that must be caused by the conduct element.

There is considerable overlap among the three prohibitions of 18 U.S.C. § 1030(a)(5)(A). The first prohibition is a felony prohibition that targets conduct that denies privileges to other users, such as sending out computer viruses and launching denial-of-service attacks. 18 U.S.C. § 1030(a)(5)(A)(i) prohibits "knowingly caus[ing] the transmission of a program, information, code, or command, and as a result of such conduct, intentionally caus[ing] damage without authorization, to a protected computer." Note that the absence of authorization does not refer to the access, but rather to causing damage. Damage is defined in 18 U.S.C. § 1030(e)(8) as "any impairment to the integrity or availability of data, a program, a system, or information." While it may seem odd that the statute would require that the damage be unauthorized, authorized damage is possible. For example, an employee may be authorized to encrypt information belonging to an employer; the act of encrypting data constitutes damage because it impairs the availability of the encrypted information.

The second and third prohibitions in § 1030(a)(5)(A) are variations on unauthorized access statutes. 18 U.S.C. § 1030(a)(5)(A)(ii) prohibits "intentionally access[ing] a protected computer without authorization, and as a result of such conduct, recklessly caus[ing] damage." Note that the authorization requirement extends only to access "without authorization," and does not include exceeding authorized access. Here the conduct element is accessing a protected computer without authorization, and the result element that must be caused by the access is "damage," that is, "any impairment to the integrity or availability of data, a program, a system, or information." The third prohibition, 18 U.S.C. § 1030(a)(5)(A)(iii), is a misdemeanor version of the felony prohibition in 18 U.S.C. § 1030(a)(5)(A)(ii). The only difference between the felony and misdemeanor prohibition is the mens rea with respect to causing an impairment to the integrity or availability of data or information. The second prohibition is a felony prohibition and requires that the defendant must be reckless with respect to causing that impairment; the third prohibition is a misdemeanor and imposes strict liability with respect to causing the impairment.

The Senate Report that accompanied the enactment of these provisions explained Congress's decision to punish reckless and even entirely accidental damage:

> Although those who intentionally damage a system, without authority, should be punished regardless of whether they are authorized users, it is equally clear that anyone who knowingly invades a system without authority and causes significant loss to the victim should be punished as well, even when the damage caused is not intentional. In such cases, it is the intentional act of trespass that makes the conduct criminal. To provide otherwise is to openly invite hackers to break into computer systems, safe in the knowledge that no matter how much damage they cause, it is no crime unless that damage was either intentional or reckless. Rather than send such a dangerous message (and deny victims any relief), it is better to ensure that section 1030(a)(5) criminalizes all computer trespass, as well as intentional damage by insiders, albeit at different levels of severity.

S. Rep. 104–357, at 11 (1996).

18 U.S.C. § 1030(a)(5)(B) contains a second result element. It requires the government to show that the conduct in § 1030(a)(5)(A) caused one of the five specific forms of harm listed in § 1030(a)(5)(B). Of the five forms of harm, all but the first are efforts to identify particularly sensitive types of computers, computer data, and resulting harms. The

most commonly relevant form of harm is the first, however, and address-es monetary loss. It requires

> loss to 1 or more persons during any 1–year period (and, for purposes of an investigation, prosecution, or other proceeding brought by the United States only, loss resulting from a related course of conduct affecting 1 or more other protected computers) aggregating at least $5,000 in value[.]

Under this provision, a conviction under § 1030(a)(5) normally requires proof of at least $5,000 of dollars in loss. The parenthetical concerning cases brought by the United States is designed to limit § 1030(a)(5) civil claims in class action lawsuits while allowing aggrega-tion of losses from a course of conduct in criminal cases. Thus, in criminal cases, the loss is calculated by adding up the losses from the defendant's "course of conduct" over any 1–year period.

———

Prosecutions brought under § 1030(a)(5) generally raise two ques-tions. First, what is the methodology for calculating the $5,000 loss in 18 U.S.C. § 1030(a)(5)(B)(i), which turns out to be the most common way of establishing an element of § 1030(a)(5)(B)? And second, what mens rea applies with respect to each of the result elements? The following two cases consider these questions in turn. It is worth noting that both cases interpret earlier generations of § 1030(a)(5) that predate the current version enacted in 2001, and therefore use slightly different terminology and interpret slightly different text. It turns out that both cases remain highly relevant, however, as the existing text of § 1030(a)(5) was written in part to codify their holdings.

UNITED STATES v. MIDDLETON

United States Court of Appeals for the Ninth Circuit, 2000.
231 F.3d 1207.

GRABER, Circuit Judge.

Defendant Nicholas Middleton challenges his conviction for inten-tionally causing damage to a "protected computer" without authoriza-tion, in violation of 18 U.S.C. § 1030(a)(5)(A). Defendant * * * argues that the trial court incorrectly instructed the jury on the "damage" element of the offense and that the government presented insufficient evidence of the requisite amount of damage. We disagree with each of Defendant's contentions and, therefore, affirm the conviction.

FACTUAL AND PROCEDURAL BACKGROUND

Defendant worked as the personal computer administrator for Slip.net, an Internet service provider. His responsibilities included in-stalling software and hardware on the company's computers and provid-ing technical support to its employees. He had extensive knowledge of

Slip.net's internal systems, including employee and computer program passwords. Dissatisfied with his job, Defendant quit. He then began to write threatening e-mails to his former employer.

Slip.net had allowed Defendant to retain an e-mail account as a paying customer after he left the company's employ. Defendant used this account to commit his first unauthorized act. After logging in to Slip.net's system, Defendant used a computer program called "Switch User" to switch his account to that of a Slip.net receptionist, Valerie Wilson. This subterfuge allowed Defendant to take advantage of the benefits and privileges associated with that employee's account, such as creating and deleting accounts and adding features to existing accounts.

Ted Glenwright, Slip.net's president, discovered this unauthorized action while looking through a "Switch User log," which records all attempts to use the Switch User program. Glenwright cross-checked the information with the company's "Radius Log," which records an outside user's attempt to dial in to the company's modem banks. The information established that Defendant had connected to Slip.net.'s computers and had then switched to Wilson's account. Glenwright immediately terminated Defendant's e-mail account.

Nevertheless, Defendant was able to continue his activities. Three days later, he obtained access to Slip.net's computers by logging in to a computer that contained a test account and then using that test account to gain access to the company's main computers. Once in Slip.net's main system, Defendant accessed the account of a sales representative and created two new accounts, which he called "TERPID" and "SANTOS." Defendant used TERPID and SANTOS to obtain access to a different computer that the company had named "Lemming." Slip.net used Lemming to perform internal administrative functions and to host customers' websites. Lemming also contained the software for a new billing system. After gaining access to the Lemming computer, Defendant changed all the administrative passwords, altered the computer's registry, deleted the entire billing system (including programs that ran the billing software), and deleted two internal databases.

Glenwright discovered the damage the next morning. He immediately contacted the company's system administrator, Bruno Connelly. Glenwright and Connelly spent an entire weekend repairing the damage that Defendant had caused to Slip.net's computers, including restoring access to the computer system, assigning new passwords, reloading the billing software, and recreating the deleted databases. They also spent many hours investigating the source and the extent of the damage. Glenwright estimated that he spent 93 hours repairing the damage; Connelly estimated that he spent 28 hours; and other employees estimated that they spent a total of 33 hours. Additionally, Slip.net bought new software to replace software that Defendant had deleted, and the company hired an outside consultant for technical support.

Defendant was arrested and charged with a violation of 18 U.S.C. § 1030(a)(5)(A). He moved to dismiss the indictment, arguing that

Slip.net was not an "individual" within the meaning of the statute. The district court denied the motion, holding that "the statute encompasses damage sustained by a business entity as well as by a natural person." *United States v. Middleton,* 35 F. Supp. 2d 1189, 1192 (N. D. Cal. 1999).

The case was then tried to a jury. Defendant filed motions for acquittal, arguing that the government had failed to prove that Slip.net suffered at least $5,000 in damage. The district court denied the motions. Defendant requested a jury instruction on the meaning of "damage." This request, too, was denied, and the court gave a different instruction.

The jury convicted Defendant. The district court sentenced him to three years' probation, subject to the condition that he serve 180 days in community confinement. The court also ordered Defendant to pay $9,147 in restitution. This timely appeal ensued.

DISCUSSION

Congress originally enacted the Computer Fraud and Abuse Act in 1984. The 1990 version of § 1030(a)(5)(A) prohibited conduct that damages a "Federal interest computer" and "causes loss to one or more others of a value aggregating $1,000 or more." A "Federal interest computer" was defined as a computer owned or used by the United States Government or a financial institution, or "one of two or more computers used in committing the offense, not all of which are located in the same State." 18 U.S.C. § 1030(e)(2)(A) & (B) (1990). In 1994, Congress replaced the term "Federal interest computer" with the phrase "computer used in interstate commerce or communication" and changed the damage provision to read, "causes loss or damage to one or more other persons of value aggregating $1,000 or more." 18 U.S.C. § 1030(a)(5)(A)(ii)(II)(aa) (1995). Before the 1994 amendment, a hacker could escape the statute's prohibitions by containing activities within a single state. Congress' 1994 amendment attempted to broaden the statute's reach. Congress' 1994 amendments also added a private cause of action for victims of computer crime. 18 U.S.C. § 1030(g).

In 1996, Congress amended § 1030(a)(5) to its current form, using the term "protected computer" and concomitantly expanding the number of computers that the statute "protected." 18 U.S.C. § 1030(a)(5) & (e)(2). The 1996 amendments also altered the definition of damage to read, "loss aggregating at least $5,000 in value during any 1–year period to one or more individuals." 18 U.S.C. § 1030(e)(8)(A). We have found no explanation for this change. We do not believe, however, that this change evidences an intent to limit the statute's reach.

To the contrary, Congress has consciously broadened the statute consistently since its original enactment. The Senate Report on the 1996 amendments notes:

> As intended when the law was originally enacted, the Computer Fraud and Abuse statute facilitates addressing in a single statute the problem of computer crime.... *As computers continue to proli-*

ferate in businesses and homes, and new forms of computer crimes emerge, Congress must remain vigilant to ensure that the Computer Fraud and Abuse statute is up-to-date and provides law enforcement with the necessary legal framework to fight computer crime.

S.Rep. No. 104–357, pt. II (emphasis added). The report instructs that "the definition of 'damage' is amended to be sufficiently broad to encompass the types of harm against which people should be protected." The report notes that the interaction between § 1030(a)(5)(A) (the provision that prohibits conduct causing damage) and § 1030(e)(8) (the provision that defines damage) will prohibit a hacker from stealing passwords from an existing log-on program, when this conduct requires "all system users to change their passwords, and requires the system administrator to devote resources to resecuring the system.... If the loss to the victim meets the required monetary threshold, the conduct should be criminal, and the victim should be entitled to relief." * * *

Defendant * * * argues that the district court instructed the jury improperly on the definition of "damage." Defendant requested this instruction: "Damage does not include expenses relating to creating a better or making a more secure system than the one in existence prior to the impairment." The court refused the request and gave a different instruction. The court explained to the jury that "damage" is an impairment to Slip.net's computer system that caused a loss of at least $5,000. The court continued:

> The term "loss" means any monetary loss that Slip.net sustained as a result of any damage to Slip.net's computer data, program, system or information that you find occurred.
>
> And in considering whether the damage caused a loss less than or greater than $5,000, you may consider any loss that you find was a natural and foreseeable result of any damage that you find occurred.
>
> In determining the amount of losses, you may consider what measures were reasonably necessary to restore the data, program, system, or information that you find was damaged or what measures were reasonably necessary to resecure the data, program, system, or information from further damage.

In reviewing jury instructions, the relevant inquiry is whether the instructions as a whole are misleading or inadequate to guide the jury's deliberation. In this case, the district court's instructions on "damage" and "loss" correctly stated the applicable law. Defendant concedes that "damage" includes any loss that was a foreseeable consequence of his criminal conduct, including those costs necessary to "resecure" Slip.net's computers. He does not argue, therefore, that the court misstated the law.

Defendant contends instead that the court's instruction might have led the jury to believe that it could consider the cost of creating a better or more secure system and that his proposed additional instruction was needed to avoid that possibility. The district court's instruction, when read in its entirety, adequately presented Defendant's theory. The court instructed the jury that it could consider only those costs that were a "natural and foreseeable result" of Defendant's conduct, only those costs that were "reasonably necessary," and only those costs that would "resecure" the computer to avoid "further damage." That instruction logically excludes any costs that the jury believed were excessive, as well as any costs that would merely create an improved computer system unrelated to preventing further damage resulting from Defendant's conduct. In particular, the term "resecure" implies making the system as secure as it was before, not making it more secure than it was before. We presume that the jury followed the court's instructions.

Because the district court's instructions fairly and adequately covered the elements of the offense, we review the instruction's 'precise formulation' for an abuse of discretion. The district court in this case did not abuse its discretion in rejecting Defendant's "precise formulation" of the definition of "damage."

Defendant's final argument is that the government presented insufficient evidence of the requisite $5,000 in damage. The government computed the amount of damage that occurred by multiplying the number of hours that each employee spent in fixing the computer problems by their respective hourly rates (calculated using their annual salaries), then adding the cost of the consultant and the new software. The government estimated the total amount of damage to be $10,092. Defendant and the government agree that the cost of Glenwright's time made up the bulk of that total.

Defendant observes that Slip.net paid Glenwright a fixed salary and that Slip.net did not pay Glenwright anything extra to fix the problems caused by Defendant's conduct. There also is no evidence, says Defendant, that Glenwright was diverted from his other responsibilities or that such a diversion caused Slip.net a financial loss. Defendant argues that, unless Slip.net paid its salaried employees an extra $5,000 for the time spent fixing the computer system, or unless the company was prevented from making $5,000 that it otherwise would have made because of the employees' diversion, Slip.net has not suffered "damage" as defined in the statute. We disagree.

In *United States v. Sablan,* 92 F.3d 865, 869 (9th Cir. 1996), this court held that, under the Sentencing Guidelines for computer fraud, it was permissible for the district court to compute "loss" based on the hourly wage of the victim bank's employees. The court reasoned, in part, that the bank would have had to pay a similar amount had it hired an outside contractor to repair the damage. Analogous reasoning applies here. There is no basis to believe that Congress intended the element of "damage" to depend on a victim's choice whether to use hourly employees, outside contractors, or salaried employees to repair the same level of harm to a protected computer. Rather, whether the amount of time spent by the employees and their imputed hourly rates were reasonable for the repair tasks that they performed are questions to be answered by the trier of fact.

Our review of the record identifies sufficient evidence from which a rational trier of fact could have found that Slip.net suffered $5,000 or more in damage. Glenwright testified that he spent approximately 93 hours investigating and repairing the damage caused by Defendant. That total included 24 hours investigating the break-in, determining how to fix it, and taking temporary measures to prevent future break-ins. Glenwright testified that he spent 21 hours recreating deleted databases and 16 hours reloading and configuring the billing software and its related applications. Glenwright estimated that his time was worth $90 per hour, based on his salary of $180,000 per year. He also testified, among other things, that he did not hire an outside contractor to repair the damage because he believed that he, as a computer expert with a pre-existing knowledge of the customized features of his company's computers, could fix the problems more efficiently. It is worth noting that, because the jury had to find only $5,000 worth of damage, it could have discounted Glenwright's number of hours or his hourly rate considerably and still have found the requisite amount of damage.

Other Slip.net employees testified to the hours that they spent fixing the damage caused by Defendant, and to their respective salaries. The government then presented expert testimony from which a jury could determine that the time spent by the employees was reasonable. Defendant cross-examined the government's witnesses on these issues vigorously, and he presented contrary expert testimony. By the verdict, the jury found the government witnesses' testimony to be more credible, a finding that was within its power to make. We hold, on this record, that the conviction was not based on insufficient evidence.

Notes and Questions

1. The Uniting and Strengthening America by Providing Appropriate Tools Required to Intercept and Obstruct Terrorism Act of 2001, Pub. L. No. 107–56 (2001), generally known as the Patriot Act, restructured 18 U.S.C. § 1030(a)(5) and codified the holding of the *Middleton* case. Before the Patriot Act, the section prohibited causing damage, and defined damage as impairment to the availability or integrity of information causing at least $5,000 in loss. After the Patriot Act, damage has been redefined without the loss requirement, and the $5,000 requirement has been moved to 18 U.S.C. § 1030(a)(5)(B). In addition, "loss" has been defined in 18 U.S.C. § 1030(e)(11) to mean:

> any reasonable cost to any victim, including the cost of responding to an offense, conducting a damage assessment, and restoring the data, program, system, or information to its condition prior to the offense, and any revenue lost, cost incurred, or other consequential damages incurred because of interruption of service.

The Justice Department issued a Field Guide to the Patriot Act in late 2001 explaining that this amendment was designed to "codify the appropriately broad definition of loss adopted in Middleton." *See* Computer Crime and Intellectual Property Section (CCIPS), *Field Guidance on New Authorities that Relate to Computer Crime and Electronic Evidence Enacted in the USA Patriot Act of 2001, at* www.cybercrime.gov/PatriotAct.htm (last updated Nov. 5, 2001).

2. *Types of costs included in the loss definition.* The definition of loss in § 1030(e)(11) is quite broad. It refers to "any" reasonable cost, and includes what appears to be a non-exclusive list of costs taken largely from the *Middleton* case. What categories of costs can you imagine that are not expressly included in the list? A computer intrusion can incur monetary losses for the victim in a number of different ways. Imagine that an intruder gains unauthorized access to the servers of XYZ Corporation, an e-commerce company, and publicizes the intrusion. The following occurs as a consequence of the intrusion:

A. The company hires a security consultant to assess the damage and patch the vulnerability.

B. The company calls a meeting of the board of directors to discuss possible responses, and the meeting lasts a full day. An expensive lunch is served.

C. The company hires a very skillful public relations specialist to deal with press attention relating to the intrusion.

D. The company loses a stream of future business when the public hears that XYZ has poor computer security.

E. Rumors that XYZ has poor security pushes its publicly-traded stock down one dollar per share.

F. The company loses revenue when it has to take its website offline for one day.

G. The company loses a stream of future business when a client becomes so frustrated the website is down that he decides he will never work with XYZ again.

All of these events are associated with monetary losses, either directly or by occupying XYZ employees for a number of hours. Which of these losses are covered by 18 U.S.C. § 1030(e)(11)?

3. In United States v. Millot, 433 F.3d 1057 (8th Cir. 2006), a former employee of Aventis Pharmaceuticals hacked in to the Aventis network and deleted the account belonging to another employee. Aventis had outsourced its security functions to International Business Machines (IBM), and two IBM employees spent a total of 407 hours reconstructing the deleted account, investigating the intrusion, and performing a security audit to verify that all existing access accounts belonged to current employees. The contract between Aventis and IBM required both IBM employees to work full-time on Aventis security matters, although IBM normally billed its staff's services at $50 per hour. The government calculated damages at $20,350 ($50 per hour x 407 hours). The Eighth Circuit affirmed the conviction, rejecting the defendant's argument that the hours spent by the employees did not count because their costs were absorbed by the contract: "This argument neglects the fact that the hours spent ... addressing the issues caused by Millot's

unauthorized intrusion could have been spent on other duties under the contract." *Id.* at 1061.

4. In Nexans Wires S.A v. Sark–USA, Inc., 319 F. Supp. 2d 468 (S.D.N.Y. 2004), the plaintiff was a German company that kept the pricing schedules and manufacturing information for its line of advanced copper and optical fiber products in a password-protected area of a client's computer server in New York. According to the complaint, employees of the client company accessed that information and used it to start a competitor company to compete against the plaintiff company. The plaintiff company sued the competitor company, claiming that the defendants' unauthorized access to the plaintiff's data had triggered at least a $5,000 "loss" in two ways. First, the plaintiff had paid for its senior executives to take two trips from Germany to the client's headquarters in New York to discuss "the activities of [their] faithless employees" with the executives of the client. Second, it claimed it had lost two business opportunities taken by the defendant, which was now competing with the plaintiff.

The district court rejected the plaintiff's arguments that either could be considered losses under § 1030. The international trips could not be counted as losses because they were not related to computers, the court concluded:

> Nothing in either case law or legislative history suggests that something as far removed from a computer as the travel expenses of senior executives constitutes "loss." Therefore, the international travel expenses that plaintiffs' senior executives incurred to attend a meeting with their customer's senior executive, in which no computers are said to have been examined, and no computer consultant said to have been present cannot satisfy the $5,000 "loss" requirement of the statute.

Id. at 477. The court also rejected the plaintiff's argument that they had suffered "loss" when they had lost business to the competitor company given its used of the allegedly stolen data:

> [T]he "revenue lost" which constitutes "loss" under § 1030(e)(11) appears from the plain language of the statute to be revenue lost "because of [an] interruption of service." § 1030(e)(11). Therefore, if [the plaintiffs] had lost revenue because the computer systems of [the client] were down, that would seem to be the type of lost revenue contemplated by the statute. However, plaintiffs are not claiming to have lost money because the computers of [the client] were inoperable, but rather because of the way the information was later used by defendants.

Id. According to the court, this was insufficient: "revenue lost because the information was used by the defendant to unfairly compete after extraction from a computer does not appear to be the type of 'loss' contemplated by the statute." *See also* Civic Center Motors, Ltd. v. Mason Street Import Cars, Ltd., 387 F. Supp. 2d 378, 382 (S.D.N.Y. 2005) (same).

Is this reading of 18 U.S.C. § 1030(e)(11) persuasive? Do you think the phrase "because of interruption of service" is designed to modify only "other consequential damages," or is it also designed to modify "revenue lost" and "cost incurred?" If it is not, do you read the costs in § 1030(e)(11) as an exclusive list or a nonexclusive list?

5. *The reasonableness requirement.* The definition of loss that codifies the holding of *Middleton* requires that the relevant costs must be "reasonable." 18 U.S.C. § 1030(e)(11). As a textual matter, the definition does not make clear whether the enumerated examples are categories of loss that Congress deems reasonable per se, or whether costs involving those enumerated examples must be scrutinized for reasonableness. The *Middleton* opinion suggests the latter, as it approvingly noted that the jury instruction used at trial in that case "logically excludes any costs that the jury believed were excessive." Thus it seems likely that all costs must be scrutinized for reasonableness to count as "loss" for the purposes of 18 U.S.C. § 1030(a)(5)(B)(i).

Does that make sense? The legal question is whether the conduct prohibited in § 1030(a)(5)(A) "caused" the loss enumerated in § 1030(a)(5)(B)(i). Principles of causation in criminal law ordinarily do not ask whether the victim's suffering was reasonable. The question is only whether the conduct was the 'but for' and 'proximate' cause of the result. Under this approach, the defendant ordinarily must take the victim as he finds him. For example, if a man assaults an elderly lady, and the elderly lady dies from the shock to her frail system, a defendant cannot escape liability for the homicide on the ground that a younger woman would have been able to survive the assault. *See, e.g.*, People v. Brackett, 510 N.E.2d 877 (Ill. 1987). The victim's condition is relevant only if the victim engages in unforeseeable conduct that breaks the chain of causation, severing the link of culpability between the conduct and the result.

Is the reasonableness requirement in § 1030(e)(11) consistent with this principle? Under the existing definition, a hacker can raise the hypothetical question of whether a more careful victim would have suffered the specified harm (that is, the $5,000 loss). Whether the victim reasonably suffered $5,000 in loss becomes a question of fact for the jury, in effect putting the victim on trial.

Is this a sensible approach? The *Middleton* court seemed concerned that a victim should not be able to use a minor event as an excuse to upgrade its computer security, thus triggering $5,000 in loss and suddenly making the minor event a major felony. If a victim uses a minor event as an excuse to spend money on security, however, isn't the problem that the minor event did not actually *cause* the loss, rather than that the loss wasn't *reasonable*? Does the reasonableness requirement in § 1030(e)(11) erroneously incorporate questions of causation into the definition of loss?

6. Does *Middleton* turn 18 U.S.C. § 1030(a)(5) prosecutions into battles between dueling expert witnesses? The defense expert witness will testify that a reasonable victim would have been able to respond to the unauthorized activity by suffering less than $5,000 in loss, and the government expert witness will testify that a reasonable victim would have suffered more than $5,000 in loss. Does it make sense for computer hacking trials to be focused on the loss suffered by this hypothetical reasonable victim? How well do you think jurors can tell which expert witness is correct?

7. When a computer is restored following a hack, it is standard for the restorer to "patch" the security flaw (that is, correct the programming error or bug) that allowed the hacker to gain unauthorized access to the network.

Can the costs of patching the system be included in the loss? Doesn't patching the security flaw go beyond restoring the computer to its prior condition, and actually result in a more secure computer than existed previously? Or should a court assume that before the unauthorized activity the computer was secure, and that any costs that go towards bringing the computer back to the level of security that the computer network was believed to have is part of the reasonable loss?

8.   Recall State v. Allen, 917 P.2d 848 (Kan. 1996), from pages 36–39. Allen used his modem to dial up the computers of Southwestern Bell in an apparent effort to place unauthorized free long distance phone calls. Although Southwestern Bell could not establish that Allen had "accessed" their computers, Allen's conduct led Southwestern Bell to decide to invest $23,796 towards enhancing its computer security. The Supreme Court of Kansas rejected the prosecution's argument that Allen had "damaged" Southwestern Bell under the Kansas computer crime statute. According to the Court, "the State is essentially saying that a person looking at a no trespassing sign on a gate causes damage to the owner of the gate if the owner decides as a result to add a new lock." *Id.* at 853.

9.   Section 1030(a)(5) focuses primarily on punishing a defendant who damages a computer. But what does it mean to damage a computer? In the case of traditional physical property, damage occurs when the property is physically deformed or broken. The extent of the damage can be measured by the replacement cost or repair cost of the property. How should these principles apply in the case of a computer? Does the comparison shed light on the wisdom of the broad definition of loss in 18 U.S.C. § 1030(e)(11)?

10.   *Computer systems used in furtherance of the administration of justice, national defense, or national security.* 18 U.S.C. § 1030(a)(5)(B)(v) permits the government to show damage that "affect[s] a computer system used by or for a government entity in furtherance of the administration of justice, national defense, or national security" in lieu of proving $5,000 in loss to a protected computer. This provision was added as part of the USA Patriot Act of 2001. The Justice Department Field Guide to the Patriot Act offered the following argument in its favor:

> Section 1030 previously had no special provision that would enhance punishment for hackers who damage computers used in furtherance of the administration of justice, national defense, or national security. Thus, federal investigators and prosecutors did not have jurisdiction over efforts to damage criminal justice and military computers where the attack did not cause over $5,000 loss (or meet one of the other special requirements). Yet these systems serve critical functions and merit felony prosecutions even where the damage is relatively slight. Indeed, attacks on computers used in the national defense that occur during periods of active military engagement are particularly serious— even if they do not cause extensive damage or disrupt the war-fighting capabilities of the military—because they divert time and attention away from the military's proper objectives. Similarly, disruption of court computer systems and data could seriously impair the integrity of the criminal justice system.

Computer Crime and Intellectual Property Section (CCIPS), *Field Guidance on New Authorities that Relate to Computer Crime and Electronic Evidence Enacted in the USA Patriot Act of 2001, at* www.cybercrime.gov/PatriotAct.htm (last updated Nov. 5, 2001).

As a textual matter, what is a computer used in furtherance of the administration of justice? In furtherance of the national defense? In furtherance of national security? The only case to touch on this issue is United States v. Mitra, 405 F.3d 492 (7th Cir. 2005), which involved interference with a radio system used by local police, fire, ambulance, and other emergency workers in Madison, Wisconsin. The court noted with apparent approval the government's argument that interfering with messages sent over the system implicated 18 U.S.C. § 1030(a)(5)(B)(v) because the defendant had "hacked into a governmental safety-related communications system," and affirmed the conviction. *Id.* at 495.

11. *Impairment to the integrity or availability of data.* 18 U.S.C. § 1030(e)(8) defines damage as "any impairment to the integrity or availability of data, a program, a system, or information." The meaning of this phrase is found in technical authorities rather than legal ones, as the terms "integrity" and "availability" are well known in the field of computer security. Computer security specialists generally refer to the three foundational goals of computer security as protecting the confidentiality, integrity, and availability of data or information. *See, e.g.,* Matt Bishop, Introduction to Computer Security (2004).

Congress presumably intended availability and integrity to have the same meaning in § 1030 than they have in the computer security field. It seems likely that the third basic concept, confidentiality, was excluded from the damage definition because confidentiality is about exposure of information, a matter dealt with in § 1030(a)(2) rather than § 1030(a)(5).

Of the two concepts Congress did use, the availability of data or information is easier to understand. A denial-of-service attack impairs the availability of data or information, as does encrypting it, as does as any conduct that causes the computer be taken off-line for repairs. Conduct that interferes with the proper functioning of computers by denying other users their privileges impairs the availability of data, a program, a system, or information.

Impairing the "integrity" of information is somewhat more difficult to understand. As one treatise on computer security explains:

> Integrity refers to the trustworthiness of data or resources, and it is usually phrased in terms of preventing improper or unauthorized change. Integrity includes data integrity (the content of the information) and origin integrity (the source of the data, often called authentication). The source of the information may bear on its accuracy and credibility and on the trust that people place in the information . . . .

> Example: A newspaper may print information obtained from a leak at the White House but attribute it to the wrong source. The information is printed as received (preserving data integrity), but its source is incorrect (corrupting origin integrity).

Matt Bishop, Introduction to Computer Security 3 (2004).

This definition suggests that conduct impairs the integrity of information when it diminishes the trustworthiness of either the information's content or authenticity. Because "any" impairment of integrity constitutes damage, it seems that most or even all cases of unauthorized access trigger damage. The fact of the unauthorized access often leaves unclear whether the data accessed has been changed or altered in some way. *Compare* Shurgard Storage Centers, Inc. v. Safeguard Self Storage, Inc., 119 F. Supp. 2d 1121 (W.D. Wash. 2000) (finding than an unauthorized access impaired the integrity of the computer accessed) *with* Moulton v. VC3, No. 1:00CV434–TWT, 2000 WL 33310901 (N.D. Ga. 2000) (finding no impairment to integrity when "[d]efendant's network security was never actually compromised"). *See also* United States v. Mitra, 405 F.3d 492, 494 (7th Cir. 2005) (suggesting that a defendant who had hacked into a government computer and added a message to the end of every government communication had impaired the integrity of the communications).

12. *The transmission requirement.* 18 U.S.C. § 1030(a)(5)(A)(i) requires "knowingly caus[ing] the transmission of a program, information, code, or command." What exactly does this mean?

In International Airport Centers v. Citrin, 440 F.3d 418 (7th Cir. 2006), an employee of a real estate business decided to leave his company and go into business himself. The employee, Citrin, had been provided a laptop computer by his employer, IAC. The computer contained data Citrin had collected for IAC about potential real estate acquisitions. To ensure that IAC would be unable to access those files, Citrin obtained a "secure erase" software program that could permanently delete computer files from the laptop. Before returning the computer to IAC, Citrin deleted the files from the laptop.

IAC brought a civil suit against Citrin, claiming that he had violated 18 U.S.C. § 1030(a)(5)(A)(i). In an opinion by Judge Posner, the Seventh Circuit concluded that these facts were sufficient to establish "the transmission of a program, information, code, or command":

> Citrin argues that merely erasing a file from a computer is not a "transmission." Pressing a delete or erase key in fact transmits a command, but it might be stretching the statute too far (especially since it provides criminal as well as civil sanctions for its violation) to consider any typing on a computer keyboard to be a form of "transmission" just because it transmits a command to the computer.
>
> There is more here, however: the transmission of the secure-erasure program to the computer. We do not know whether the program was downloaded from the Internet or copied from a floppy disk (or the equivalent of a floppy disk, such as a CD) inserted into a disk drive that was either inside the computer or attached to it by a wire. Oddly, the complaint doesn't say; maybe IAC doesn't know–maybe all it knows is that when it got the computer back, the files in it had been erased. But we don't see what difference the precise mode of transmission can make. In either the Internet download or the disk insertion, a program intended to cause damage (not to the physical computer, of course, but to its files-but "damage" includes "any impairment to the integrity or availability of data, a program, a system, or information,"18 U.S.C.

§ 1030(e)(8)) is transmitted to the computer electronically. The only difference, so far as the mechanics of transmission are concerned, is that the disk is inserted manually before the program on it is transmitted electronically to the computer. The difference vanishes if the disk drive into which the disk is inserted is an external drive, connected to the computer by a wire, just as the computer is connected to the Internet by a telephone cable or a broadband cable or wirelessly.

There is the following contextual difference between the two modes of transmission, however: transmission via disk requires that the malefactor have physical access to the computer. By using the Internet, Citrin might have erased the laptop's files from afar by transmitting a virus. Such long-distance attacks can be more difficult to detect and thus to deter or punish than ones that can have been made only by someone with physical access, usually an employee. The inside attack, however, while easier to detect may also be easier to accomplish. Congress was concerned with both types of attack: attacks by virus and worm writers, on the one hand, which come mainly from the outside, and attacks by disgruntled programmers who decide to trash the employer's data system on the way out (or threaten to do so in order to extort payments), on the other. If the statute is to reach the disgruntled programmer, which Congress intended by providing that whoever "*intentionally* accesses a protected computer without authorization, and as a result of such conduct, recklessly causes damage" violates the Act, 18 U.S.C. § 1030(a)(5)(A)(ii) (emphasis added), it can't make any difference that the destructive program comes on a physical medium, such as a floppy disk or CD.

Id. at 419–20.

Does transmission include off-line transmission? In North Texas Preventive Imaging v. Eisenberg, No. SA CV 96–71AHS(EEX), 1996 WL 1359212 (C.D. Cal. 1996), the plaintiffs purchased a computer system from the defendants to perform advanced medical diagnostics. The plaintiffs became unsatisfied with the system and informed the defendants that they wished to cancel the purchase and have some of their money returned. The defendants then sent a floppy disk to the plaintiffs, apparently through the postal mail, that the defendants claimed would "update" the computer system. In fact, the floppy disk contained a program that at a future date would disable the software so the plaintiffs could no longer use it.

The plaintiffs installed the "update" not realizing that it would insert code that would eventually disable the network. After realizing that the "update" was a so-called "time bomb," the plaintiffs brought a civil action alleging that the defendants' conduct violated 18 U.S.C. § 1030(a)(5). Specifically, they claimed that sending the floppy disk that contained the harmful code constituted a "transmission of a program, information, code, or command." The district court agreed, *see id.* at *6:

By casting the net broadly to include many different "transmission" techniques, the 1994 amendment shifted the CFAA's focus from the act of unauthorized access to the intent of the defendant. The transmission of a disabling code by floppy computer disk may fall within the new language, if accompanied by the intent to cause harm.

The final set of questions concerning 18 U.S.C. § 1030(a)(5) address the required mens rea with respect to each element of the offense.

UNITED STATES v. SABLAN

United States Court of Appeals for the Ninth Circuit, 1996.
92 F.3d 865.

Hug, Chief Judge.

Bernadette H. Sablan appeals her conviction for computer fraud under 18 U.S.C. § 1030(a)(5) following a conditional guilty plea. Sablan argues that the district court wrongly interpreted the elements of the crime and, alternatively, that the statute is unconstitutional. We affirm Sablan's conviction and her sentence.

FACTS

In the early hours of August 15, 1992, Sablan, a former employee of the Bank of Hawaii's Agana, Guam branch, left a bar where she had been drinking with a friend. Sablan had recently been fired from the bank for circumventing security procedures in retrieving files. That morning, Sablan left the bar and entered the closed bank through an unlocked loading dock door. She went to her former work site (using a key she had kept) and used an old password to log into the bank's mainframe. Sablan contends that she then called up several computer files and logged off. The Government asserts that Sablan changed several of the files and deleted others. Under either version, Sablan's conduct severely damaged several bank files.

Sablan was charged with computer fraud in violation of 18 U.S.C. § 1030(a)(5). In a pretrial motion to dismiss, Sablan attacked the statute for its failure to require a *mens rea* for each of the essential elements of the offense. In the alternative, Sablan requested a jury instruction that required the Government to prove intent as to all elements of the crime. In particular, Sablan wanted the jury to be instructed that the Government needed to prove that she had the intent to damage bank files. The district court denied the motion and ruled that, as used in the computer fraud statute, the word "intentionally" applied only to the access element of the crime. Sablan then entered into a conditional plea agreement that preserved her right to appellate review of the issue raised in her motion.

DISCUSSION

Sablan contends on appeal that the computer fraud statute must have a *mens rea* requirement for all elements of the crime. She asserts that the indictment was defective because it did not allege the appropriate *mens rea* required by the statute. In the alternative, Sablan asserts that a jury instruction was required to inform the jurors that the state had to prove intent for every element of the crime.

Sablan was convicted under the version of the computer fraud statute in effect from 1986 to 1994. That statute stated:

> (a) Whoever-(5) intentionally accesses a Federal interest computer without authorization, and by means of one or more instances of such conduct alters, damages, or destroys information in any such Federal interest computer . . . and thereby-(A) causes loss to one or more others of a value aggregating $1,000 or more during any one year period; shall be punished as provided.

18 U.S.C. § 1030 (amended by Pub.L. No. 103–354). In order to have violated the statute, a defendant must have (1) accessed (2) a federal interest computer (3) without authorization and (4) have altered, damaged, or destroyed information (5) resulting in the loss to one or more others (6) of at least one thousand dollars. The district court held that the statute's *mens rea* requirement, "intentionally," applied only to the access element of the crime. We review questions of statutory interpretation *de novo*.

A.

We begin our analysis by noting that the statute is ambiguous as to its *mens rea* requirement. Although the statute explains that one must "intentionally access[ ] a Federal interest computer without authorization, and . . . destroy[ ] information in any such Federal interest computer," punctuation sets the "accesses" phrase off from the subsequent "damages" phrase. With some statutes punctuation has been used to indicate that a phrase set off by commas is independent of the language that followed. However, punctuation is not always decisive in construing statutes. In *Liparota v. United States,* 471 U.S. 419 (1985), and *United States v. X–Citement Video,* 513 U.S. 64 (1994), for example, the Supreme Court applied the mental state adjacent to initial words to later clauses without regard to intervening punctuation. In both cases, the Supreme Court resorted to legislative history to clarify the ambiguous language.

We conclude that the comma after "authorization" does not resolve the ambiguity. Allowing the *mens rea* requirement to reach subsequent elements of the crime would comport with general linguistic rules. Similarly, it is proper to read the statute without extending "intentionally" to the other clauses of the sentence. Therefore, we look to the statute's legislative history to clear up the textual ambiguity.

In *United States v. Morris,* 928 F.2d 504 (2d Cir. 1991), the Second Circuit examined the legislative history of the computer fraud statute and concluded that the "intentionally" standard applied only to the "accesses" element of the crime. The court focused on the fact that original version of the statute, passed in 1984, punished anyone who

> *knowingly* accesses a computer without authorization, or having accessed a computer with authorization, uses the opportunity such

access provides for purposes to which such authorization does not extend, and by means of such conduct *knowingly* uses, modifies, destroys, or discloses information in, or prevents authorized use of, such computer, if such computer is operated for or on behalf of the Government of United States and such conduct affects such operation.

Pub.L. No. 98–473, subsection (a)(3) (amended latest by Pub.L. No. 103–354) (emphasis added). When the statute was amended in 1986, the scienter requirement was changed from knowingly to intentionally and the second *mens rea* reference was eliminated. By contrast, other subsections of section 1030 retained the "dual-intent" language by placing the *mens rea* requirement at the beginning of both the "accesses" phrase and the "damages" phrase. *See, e.g.,* 18 U.S.C. § 1030(a)(1). The court concluded that the decision of Congress not to repeat the scienter requirement within this statute evidenced an intent not to require the Government to prove a defendant's intent to cause damage.

Sablan urges this court to reject the holding in *Morris,* contending that the 1986 bill was intended only to apply to those who intentionally damage computer data. She points to one line in a Senate report that evidenced a desire to retain the dual intent language: "The new subsection 1030(a)(5) to be created by the bill is designed to penalize those who intentionally alter, damage, or destroy certain computerized data belonging to another." 1986 U.S.C.C.A.N. at 2488. Thus, Sablan argues, the computer fraud statute has a *mens rea* requirement for the damages clause of the bill. We disagree.

As the *Morris* court concluded:

> Despite some isolated language in the legislative history that arguably suggests a scienter component for the "damages" phrase of section 1030(a)(5)(A), the wording, structure, and purpose of the subsection, examined in comparison with its departure from the format of its predecessor provision persuade us that the "intentionally" standard applies only to the "accesses" phrase of section 1030(a)(5)(A), and not to its "damages" phrase.

We adopt the reasoning of the *Morris* court and hold that the computer fraud statute does not require the Government to prove that the defendant intentionally damaged computer files.

B.

Sablan contends that if the computer fraud statute does not have a *mens rea* requirement for the damages element of the offense, the statute is unconstitutional. Relying on the Supreme Court's decision in *X-Citement Video,* Sablan states that a *mens rea* must be applied to all elements of an offense or due process standards are violated. We review *de novo* the district court's determination of federal constitutional law.

The Supreme Court has never ruled that *mens rea* is a constitutional requirement. However, in *X-Citement Video,* the Supreme Court stated that a statute without any scienter requirements "would raise serious constitutional doubts.'' Sablan contends that lack of a scienter requirement for the damages element of the offense renders the statute constitutionally infirm. In *X-Citement Video,* the Court construed the "knowingly" scienter requirement beyond the most proximate clause of 18 U.S.C. § 2252 to clarify that one charged with trafficking in child pornography must know that the material involves the use of a minor.

After reviewing the cases interpreting criminal statutes to include broadly applicable scienter requirements the Court held that the "presumption in favor of a scienter requirement should apply to each of the statutory elements which criminalize otherwise innocent conduct." However, the computer fraud statute does not criminalize otherwise innocent conduct. Under the statute, the Government must prove that the defendant intentionally accessed a federal interest computer without authorization. Thus, Sablan must have had a wrongful intent in accessing the computer in order to be convicted under the statute. This case does not present the prospect of a defendant being convicted without any wrongful intent as was the situation in *X-Citement Video.* Therefore, we hold that the computer fraud statute's *mens rea* requirement is sufficient to meet constitutional standards.

Notes and Questions

1. The *Sablan* decision sheds light on why the current text of 18 U.S.C. § 1030(a)(5) is clumsy and awkward. The division of the computer damage statute into § 1030(a)(5)(A) and § 1030(a)(5)(B) was undertaken to separate out the mens rea that applies to impairment from the mens rea that applies to the loss and its quantity. Computer Crime and Intellectual Property Section (CCIPS), *Field Guidance on New Authorities that Relate to Computer Crime and Electronic Evidence Enacted in the USA Patriot Act of 2001, at* www.cybercrime.gov/PatriotAct.htm (last updated Nov. 5, 2001). The existing text is complex, but the mens rea that attaches to each element is now fairly clear.

2. *Mens rea for the elements of § 1030(a)(5).* It is helpful to understand the mens rea that attaches to each of the statutory elements in § 1030(a)(5). Although federal law does not follow the Model Penal Code generally, the legislative history of § 1030 suggests that its drafters wished to incorporate the MPC's mens rea provisions. *See, e.g.,* S. Rep. 101–544, at 9 (1990 amendments) ("The standard for recklessness used in the bill is taken from the Model Penal Code."); S. Rep. No. 99–432, *reprinted in* 1986 U.S.C.C.A.N. 2479, 2483–84 (1986 amendments) (discussing intent using the key phrases of the MPC).

Under this framework, the primary mental states are intent, knowledge, and recklessness. *See* Model Penal Code § 2.02 (Official Draft 1962). The precise meaning of each mental state can vary depending on whether the element is a conduct element (describing the defendant's actions), a result element (describing a fact caused by the defendant's actions), or an attendant circumstances element (describing the state of the world surrounding the defendant's actions).

Specifically, a person acts intentionally when it is his conscious object to engage in conduct of that nature or to cause such a result; in the case of attendant circumstances, a person acts intentionally with respect to that element if he is aware of the element's existence, or he hopes or believes it will occur. *See* § 2.02(2)(a). A person acts knowingly if he is aware that his conduct is of that nature or that such circumstances exist; in the case of result elements, he acts knowingly if he is practically certain his conduct will cause such a result. *See* M.P.C. § 2.02(2)(b). Finally, a person acts recklessly if he consciously disregards a substantial and unjustifiable risk that the element exists or will result, and the disregard of the risk involves a gross deviation from the standard of a law-abiding person in the actor's situation considering the nature and purpose of the actor's conduct and the circumstances known to him. *See* M.P.C. § 2.02(2)(c).

Now consider the prohibition of § 1030(a)(5)(A)(i), which punishes whoever:

> knowingly causes the transmission of a program, information, code, or command, and as a result of such conduct, intentionally causes damage without authorization, to a protected computer ... and ... by [that] conduct ... caused (or, in the case of an attempted offense, would, if completed, have caused) ... loss to 1 or more persons during any 1–year period ... aggregating at least $5,000 in value[.]

The knowing mens rea attaches to the conduct element of "causes the transmission of a program, information, code, or command;" the intentional mens rea applies to the result element of causing damage and attendant circumstance element of lack of authorization;[d] and the result elements from 1030(a)(5)(B) are all strict liability elements that do not require proof of any mental state.

The only somewhat ambiguous element in this provision is the attendant circumstance element "protected computer." It is not entirely clear from the text of the statute whether it requires intent that the computer is a protected computer, which in this case would mean awareness that the computer is a government computer or a computer used in interstate or foreign commerce or communication. The definition of protected computer is sufficiently broad, however, that this question seems unlikely to arise very often.

The second prohibition, § 1030(a)(5)(A)(ii), punishes whoever:

> intentionally accesses a protected computer without authorization, and as a result of such conduct, recklessly causes damage ... and ... by [that] conduct ... caused (or, in the case of an attempted offense, would, if completed, have caused) ... loss to 1 or more persons during any 1–year period ... aggregating at least $5,000 in value[.]

Here the intentional mens rea applies to the conduct element of access as well as to the attendant circumstances elements of protected computer and without authorization; a reckless mens rea applies to the result element of damage; and the remaining result elements are strict liability.

---

d. Note that this standard does not require knowledge of or intent to satisfy the legal standards of damage or lack of authorization. Rather, it requires intent to impair the integrity or availability of data without authorization.

The misdemeanor prohibition found in § 1030(a)(5)(A)(iii) is similar to that in § 1030(a)(5)(A)(ii), but with one difference; the reckless mens rea used for the result element of damage is replaced by strict liability for that element. Given the statutory definition of damage, how likely is it that a typical computer intruder will satisfy the recklessness standard and therefore face felony liability?

3. Do the mental states that attach to the elements of § 1030(a)(5) make sense as a matter of policy? Or do they render the statute too broad? Section 1030(a)(5) requires that the defendant's conduct causes two distinct results: damage, defined as the impairment of the integrity or availability of information, and (in the usual case of monetary loss) loss totaling at least $5,000. The three provisions require different mental states with respect to causing damage: the first requires intent, the second recklessness, and the third (a misdemeanor provision) imposes strict liability. But all three prohibitions impose strict liability with respect to the monetary loss element.

Is this consistent with the theories of punishment? Does a defendant whose conduct accidentally or through freakish circumstances leads to greater harm deserve greater punishment? Should the law seek to deter such unlucky defendants? Or is the point that by punishing unlucky defendants, the law can deter other defendants from engaging in inherently risky conduct? To what extent should the difficulty of proving mens rea enter into the equation? How can the government prove intent to damage, or intent to cause a particular amount of damage?

Your answer to these questions may be guided by your sense of whether computer intrusions are inherently risky and harmful or usually innocent and sometimes even helpful. If you believe that hacking is inherently dangerous and likely to cause harm, then you may find it appropriate to punish those whose intrusions lead to additional harm. On the other hand, if you see most intrusions as generally harmless, you may conclude that the mens rea requirements of § 1030(a)(5) are far too broad. Consider the latter argument from a student author:

> [F]ew outside hackers intend to cause damage. In fact, most hackers break into systems to learn or to challenge themselves. Strict hacker ethics prohibit hackers from damaging the accessed systems. These types of hackers * * * should be punished less than those with the intent to damage. However, the 1996 Act includes not only hackers who truly intend to cause damage, but even the outsiders who accidentally cause damage. By punishing hackers who lack criminal intent in the same manner as those who possess criminal intent, Congress has overlooked the goal of retribution.

Haeji Hong, Note, *Hacking Through the Computer Fraud and Abuse Act*, 31 U.C. Davis L. Rev. 283, 303 (1997). Do you agree?

4. Consider the following hypothetical cases. Which of the two defendants deserves a greater punishment? What kinds of criminal liability are they likely to face under 18 U.S.C. § 1030?

A. *Discovered Versus Undiscovered Attacks.* On Monday, Hacker Bob hacks into the servers of the XYZ corporation and snoops around. On Tuesday, Hacker Joe hacks into the servers of the same company and also snoops around. On Wednesday, the system administrator at XYZ corporation finds evidence of Joe's attack and spends 50 hours over the next week (at a rate of $125 per hour) responding to the attack, conducting a damage assessment, and resecuring the server. The system administrator never notices Bob's attack.

B. *Differing Intents.* Two friends, Kate and Jane, don't like a large Internet service provider called Burns Online. Kate decides that she wants to destroy Burns Online by inflicting as much loss as she can upon it. Jane decides that she wants to cause only an infinitesimal amount of harm to Burns Online. Both Kate and Jane download a program that purports to allow the user to launch a denial-of-service attack. Jane configures the program so that it will disable Burns Online for only 1 second; Kate configures the program so that it will disable Burns Online indefinitely. At the second that Jane launches her one-second attack, a doctor who is a subscriber to Burns Online attempts to send an e-mail to one of his patients urging his patient to exercise more and maintain a balanced diet. Due to the one-second attack, he cannot send it, and decides to log off. Kate's attack takes Burns Online offline for ten minutes, until the system administrator at Burns Online comes up with a defense against it.

5. *Due process and the meaning of authorization.* The *Sablan* court concludes that requiring the government to prove intentional access without authorization is sufficient to satisfy any constitutional requirements of mens rea; the remaining elements can be strict liability elements without violating the Due Process clause. Although the Supreme Court has never expressly held that mens rea is a constitutional requirement, it has tended to read a mens rea requirement into criminal statutes when the conduct otherwise prohibited is innocent conduct. *See generally* Staples v. United States, 511 U.S. 600 (1994). The *Sablan* court concludes that no such construction of § 1030(a)(5) is needed because the Section "does not criminalize otherwise innocent conduct."

> Under the statute, the Government must prove that the defendant intentionally accessed a federal interest computer without authorization. Thus, [the defendant] must have had a wrongful intent in accessing the computer in order to be convicted under the statute.

Does this analysis hinge on a narrow definition of "without authorization"? If you adopt a broad contract-based or norms-based view of authorization, is § 1030(a)(5) unconstitutional?

6. *Offensive "self-help," a.k.a. hacking back.* Computer intrusions and denial-of-service attacks can cause a significant amount of economic and other damage to their victims. Should an owner/operator of a victim computer have a right to "hack back" against an intruder? If A launches an attack at B in violation of 18 U.S.C. § 1030(a)(5), can B launch a counterattack at A designed to stop A's attack? Does the counterattack violate § 1030 as well, or is it excused under principles of cyber-self-defense?

A number of scholars have advocated such a cyber-self-defense doctrine. For example, Michael O'Neill has argued that "just as settlers in the American West could not reliably count on the local sheriff to protect them, and instead kept a weapon handy to stymie potential aggressors, Internet users may need to protect themselves." Michael E. O'Neill, *Old Crimes in New Bottles: Sanctioning Cybercrime*, 9 Geo. Mason. L. Rev. 237, 277 (2000). According to Professor O'Neill, the threat of a counterstrike will deter attacks. "Just as a homeowner may defend his house, . . . computer companies ought to not only be permitted, but encouraged, to unleash their considerable talents to launch countermeasures against cyber-criminals." *Id.* at 280. Bruce Smith has also suggested that the law should recognize a hackback defense. *See* Bruce Smith, *Hacking, Poaching, and Counterattacking: Digital Counterstrikes and the Contours of Self–Help*, 1 J.L. Econ. & Pol'y 171, 191 (2005):

> A reasonably strong case can be made that counterstrikes against "hackers"—at least when such measures are proportionate to the threat posed—should be privileged. * * * Section 77 of the *Restatement (Second) of Torts* authorizes persons to use "reasonable force" to protect their property in instances where the intrusion is not "privileged," the property owner "reasonably believes that the intrusion can be prevented or terminated only by the force used," and the property owner "reasonably believes that a request will be useless or that substantial harm will be done before it can be made." And Section 84 permits the use of "devices" to accomplish these ends—merely adding the requirement that "the device [be] one customarily used for such a purpose, or reasonable care [be] taken to make its use known to probable intruders." Although it might well be the case that a party that "hacked back" against a network intruder might fall within the language of [18 U.S.C. § 1030] or other statutes, the party would seem to possess a colorable claim—at least under traditional tort principles—that a proportionate counterstrike against a hacker should not expose the counterattacker to either criminal or civil liability.

Other commentators have disagreed, noting that it is very easy to disguise your tracks online. As a result, victims often are unable to tell who exactly is attacking them, and often will accidentally launch counterattacks at innocent third-parties. Those innocent third-parties will in turn believe they are under attack, and will launch counterattacks as well. The result may be more computer misuse, not less. *See, e.g.,* Orin S. Kerr, *Virtual Crime, Virtual Deterrence: A Skeptical View of Self–Help, Architecture, and Civil Liability*, 1 J.L. Econ. & Pol'y 197, 204–06 (2005). Richard Epstein has noted that the high chances of error in a cyber-counterattack raises a number of difficult legal questions:

> What should be done if the program picks up the wrong target and wrecks the computer of an innocent party? What should be done if the attacked target is a zombie computer that has unwittingly transferred the offending material across cyberspace? Are there any limits of proportionality that are associated with these attacks? Should the self-help remedy be denied on the grounds that some form of civil liability could be imposed?

Richard Epstein, *The Theory and Practice of Self–Help*, 1 J.L. Econ. & Pol'y 1, 31 (2005). No defendant in a computer hacking case has attempted to invoke such a defense. State laws on the defense-of-property justification vary state-to-state, and federal law has recognized such a defense only intermittently. Do you think courts should recognize a right to cyber-self–defense right? And if so, what should it look like?

7. Are existing computer misuse statutes an effective response to the problem of computer misuse? Should we look for other answers? A number of scholars have suggested that the most effective methods for deterring computer misuse crimes look beyond criminal law. For example, some scholars have suggested imposing civil liability on ISPs for the criminal acts of their subscribers. The idea is that this will encourage ISPs to monitor and disable wrongdoers before significant harms occur. *See, e.g.,* Doug Lichtman & Eric Posner, *Holding Internet Service Providers Accountable*, in The Law and Economics of Cybersecurity (Mark Grady & Francesco Parisi eds., 2005). Others have suggested that computer owners should be subject to negligence suits if their poor computer security facilitates computer misuse offenses. *See, e.g.*, Stephen E. Henderson & Matthew E. Yarborough, *Suing the Insecure?: A Duty of Care in Cyberspace*, 32 N.M. L. Rev. 11 (2002).

Some scholars have looked to social norms instead of civil liability. Neal Katyal has suggested that computer crime can be deterred by redesigning the architecture of the on-line experience in a way that will encourage community monitoring and discourage vandalism. *See* Neal Kumar Katyal, Essay, *Digital Architecture as Crime Control*, 112 Yale L.J. 2261 (2003). In a similar vein, Brent Wible has argued that official "hack-in" contests for hackers challenging them to attack dummy networks can channel the urge to engage in unauthorized conduct and generate a respect for law that will deter computer crime. *See* Brent Wible, Note, *A Site Where Hackers Are Welcome: Using Hack-in Contests to Shape Preferences and Deter Computer Crime*, 112 Yale L.J. 1577 (2003).

Are these proposals realistic? Do they complement the need for computer misuse laws such as 18 U.S.C. § 1030, or could they replace such statutes? More broadly, what is the purpose of computer misuse laws? Is their purpose to punish culpable individuals? To deter criminal activity? To improve computer security? What kinds of laws beyond unauthorized access, computer fraud, and computer damage statutes are needed to address computer misuse crimes?

8. The scope of criminal liability for computer misuse is very broad. A critic of existing law might say that the legislature's basic approach is to criminalize everything and then rely on prosecutorial discretion to select appropriate cases for criminal punishment.

Is this criticism accurate? And if it is, do you think the legislature has acted wisely? Computer technologies and social practices change rapidly, and it may be difficult for the law to keep up. Is it sensible for legislatures to impose broad criminal liability ex ante, so that prosecutors are rarely or never in a position of being unable to charge a worthy case? Or should the legislature only impose liability narrowly, so that new computer technologies can evolve without the threat of criminal punishment? Do you trust prosecutors to charge only appropriate cases? Does the threat of criminal punishment have a significant chilling effect on legitimate computer use?

Chapter 3

TRADITIONAL CRIMES

There are many types of computer crimes beyond computer misuse offenses. Of course, not all crimes are relevant to a course in computer crime law. Computers are tools that transmit and store information, which means that crimes with no necessary link to transmitting information are not likely to arise often in computer-related cases.[a] At the same time, a number of traditional crimes do involve transmitting and storing information. These information-based crimes often find a natural home in the world of computers and the Internet. In some cases, the computer's ability to process and transmit information quickly and with relative anonymity has led entire subcultures of criminal activity to migrate from the physical world to a digital environment.

The purpose of this chapter is to study traditional crimes committed using computers. As with the previous chapter, the materials will focus primarily on federal law, with some coverage of state law. The chapter begins with laws concerning economic crimes, such as theft and copyright infringement, that exist primarily to protect economic interests. The materials turn next to crimes against persons, such as threats and harassment. The next subjects are vice crimes, such as Internet gambling and obscenity-related offenses. The chapter concludes with laws regarding child exploitation crimes such as offenses involving images of child pornography.

As you read these materials, consider whether criminal conduct changes when it shifts from the physical world to computer networks. Many of these crimes raise the issue of "old wine in new bottles," and ask us to adjust concepts and statutory language from an old set of facts to a new one. Should it matter whether a crime is committed using computer networks and the Internet? Does anything change when a traditional crime is committed using computers?

---

a. For example, it seems unnecessary to study offenses such as "murder by computer." *But see* Marc D. Goodman & Susan W. Brenner, *The Emerging Consensus on Criminal Conduct in Cyberspace*, 2002 UCLA J.L. & Tech. 3 at Sec. 2.a.7.

A. ECONOMIC CRIMES

Control of information can have considerable economic value. A file stored on a server may contain valuable secrets about a new product to go on the market. Alternatively, the file may be an expensive piece of software or a sought-after movie or sound recording. Whatever the source of the file's value, that value depends on information control. The more widely available information becomes, the less valuable it tends to be. You might pay for a stock tip from a private investment manager, but you won't pay if you can read the same stock tip in the newspaper for free. You might have exclusive rights to control access to a new piece of software, but fewer people are likely to purchase those rights if they can obtain illegal copies easily for free.

How should criminal law regulate control of information to protect these economic interests? Federal criminal law includes four types of information control statutes: general property crimes, such as theft and possession of stolen property; specific information-based crimes such as the Economic Espionage Act of 1996; statutes that govern authentication devices; and intellectual property laws such as the copyright statutes.

1. PROPERTY CRIMES

Property crimes were originally designed to protect interests in physical property. The basic idea is that physical property has an owner who enjoys the right to exclude others from accessing or using that property. Taking property away from the owner without his consent constitutes theft. Retaining the property, knowing it has been taken from its owner, constitutes possession of stolen property.

Can these principles be used to protect rights in information? Does information have an "owner"? What does it mean for information to be "stolen"? What does it mean to "possess" information?

PEOPLE v. JOHNSON

Criminal Court for the City of New York, 1990.
148 Misc.2d 103, 560 N.Y.S.2d 238.

Charles J. Heffernan, Jr., Judge.

This is another in a series of nearly identical fact patterns prosecuted in this jurisdiction with increasing frequency: a charge that use of an illegally possessed AT&T credit card number was unlawfully offered, for a fee, to travelers at the Port Authority terminal in Manhattan. Here, as in other cases, the People assert that the "service" was offered by a form of huckstering—in this case, that defendant's words were "you can call the whole world for $8.00." Such cases have engaged various legal issues, determined by the crimes charged in the respective prosecutions.

This case * * * [considers whether] charging criminal possession of stolen property in the fifth degree (P.L. § 165.40), should be dismissed for facial insufficiency on the ground that a telephone credit card number is not "property" under P.L. § 155.00(1).

The Facts

Deponent [a police officer who saw the alleged crime occur] states that he observed defendant at the above location saying to passersby "you can call the whole world for $8.00" and that deponent approached an unapprehended individual who said he was from Poland, and deponent then observed defendant pull a small scrap of paper from defendant's pocket and start dialing a number from the paper onto a phone.

Deponent further states that when defendant saw deponent approach, deponent observed defendant tear said scrap of paper and throw it to the ground.

Deponent states that he is informed by Tony Largo, of AT&T security that the number on said piece of paper had been used to make approximately 240 calls during the 2 hours before the defendant was arrested, and informant is the custodian of the phone computer code system and the credit card number and states that defendant had no permission or authority to access or attempt to access the phone computer code systems or to possess or use the said credit card number.

Deponent further states that defendant was apprehended in an area which had signs posted that said the area was for "Ticketed Passengers Only" and that deponent observed defendant had no bus ticket.

The Stolen Property Count

Defendant * * * moves to dismiss the third count of the information, charging the crime of criminal possession of stolen property in the fifth degree (P.L. § 165.40), also on the ground of facial insufficiency. Defendant rests his argument on the opinion in *People v. Molina,* 145 Misc.2d 612, 547 N.Y.S.2d 546 (Crim. Ct. Queens Co. 1989), where the court granted an identical motion on essentially identical facts. In both cases the allegation was that defendant possessed telephone credit card numbers belonging to AT & T, such numbers being written on a piece of paper that defendant possessed.

The court noted that

> the potentially unique 14 digit pattern and sequence of these numbers could support the People's assertion that they are unique AT&T credit card numbers. The identity of the nature of the numbers is not mere speculation. Adequate support for the conclusion that they are AT&T card numbers was provided by a representative of New York Telephone. It is also worth noting that defendant possessed three different patterns of numbers, and all were identified as having the necessary unique AT&T pattern. Any claims by defendant that these numbers had an independent significance goes towards challenging findings made by a trier of fact. This aspect of the complaint is sufficient.

Molina, supra, at 614, 615.

What troubled the *Molina* court, however, was the "property" element of the crime, the court finding that the defendant was not accused of holding the actual AT&T credit cards from which the numbers were presumably obtained. The court noted that the paper on which the numbers were written is the tangible personal property of the defendant, not of the credit card holders—a fact that would seemingly be undisputed. Nor would a reasonable person likely gainsay the *Molina* court's view that the credit card holders have no possessory interest in that paper.

The final step in the *Molina* analysis, however, is the point at which this court takes respectful departure from that holding: *i.e.,* that "the numbers in and of themselves are not tangible property." *Molina, supra,* at 615. It was the belief of that court that a more expansive reading would violate the rule that criminal statutes are to be strictly and narrowly construed.

Strict construction, however, need not ignore the clear import of facts and circumstances attending a criminal allegation implicating a technically-oriented charge. To do so would be unmindful of the ever-changing nature of American technology and its components.

P.L. § 155.00(1) defines "property" as meaning "any money, personal property, real property, computer data, computer program, thing in action, evidence of debt or contract, or any article, substance or thing of value, including any gas, steam, water or electricity, which is provided for a charge or compensation."

To rest the distinction between culpability and inculpability upon the type of physical material on which the credit card number is listed—or upon the absence of such material—would be to defeat the purpose underlying the statute at issue. The generic crime of criminal possession of stolen property is meant to proscribe knowing possession of property wrongfully taken from a lawful holder. On the facts before this court, there is little, if any, relevance to the form in which the telephone credit card number is possessed. Under the *Molina* rationale, a person who steals a telephone credit card would be criminally liable if he or she is found in possession of the card. The thief would escape liability, however, by either recording the card number on a piece of paper owned by the wrongdoer and then destroying the card, or by committing the number to memory after destroying the card. The lack of logic in that thesis is evidenced by the following question: is the number with the card of any more value to a person intent on placing phone calls without charge than is the number without the card? The number itself is what is crucial, and not who has the superior possessory interest in the paper on which the number is recorded, or whether the number is written as opposed to being memorized.

Such a number clearly has inherent value, apart from the card onto which the numbers are embossed. Most other credit cards require either that the card be presented for use or, as a pre-condition to its acceptance for use by telephone, that some verifying data as to the card or the party to whom it was issued be tendered. The use of a telephone credit card, on the other hand, is not encumbered by such constraints. Rather, a person in possession of a validly issued telephone credit card number can place a local, national or international call without immediate scrutiny simply by inputting the credit card number by dialing or pushing a button on the telephone instrument. Lawful bearers of that number will incur later cost for that service. Those who come into possession of those numbers without authorization, however, can place calls at no cost; the bill for those calls will, in due course, be sent to the lawful holder of the credit cards. It is, therefore, beyond quarrel that a telephone credit card number qualifies as a "thing of value."

More, however, is required in this analysis. While a telephone credit card number is a "thing of value," care must be taken to be sure that the number in question is indeed such a number. A court must be satisfied that the number possessed is not some innocuous number, innocently had by a defendant. Such a judgment can be made, of course, only in the context of attending circumstances. In the context of a motion to dismiss a count of an information for facial insufficiency, a court must look to the information itself.

The information before the court contains several factual assertions that are helpful in deciding whether the number in question was an AT&T credit card, as opposed to something else: (1) a security representative of AT&T, Tony Largo, states that he is the custodian of the phone computer system and the credit card number; (2) Mr. Largo also states that defendant had no permission to possess that number; (3) Detective Joseph Rullo of the Port Authority Police Department states that he saw defendant saying to passersby "you can call the whole world for $8.00"; (4) Detective Rullo further states that he saw defendant approach a person who said that he was from Poland, that defendant pulled a scrap of paper from defendant's pocket and began to dial a number from that paper onto a telephone; (5) Detective Rullo states that when defendant saw Detective Rullo approaching, defendant tore the scrap of paper and threw it to the ground; (6) Mr. Largo states that the number on the paper had been used to make approximately 240 calls during the 2 hours before defendant's apprehension.

The confluence of those factors persuades this court that the number that defendant is charged with possessing is, indeed, an AT&T credit card number, a "thing of value." That is, however, not the end of the inquiry on the question whether the telephone credit card number is "property" under P.L. § 155.00(1).

The statute couples "thing of value" with the modifying clause "which is provided for a charge or compensation." On the facts pled herein, there is no indication that the card was provided to the lawful owner in exchange for immediate charge or compensation. Nor need there be such an assertion. For the charge attaching to the credit card number is, of course, a subsequent charge, for calls that are placed by using that number. This is sufficient to meet the compensation or charge requirement of P.L. § 155.00(1).

Accordingly, this court does not concur with the sole challenge made by defendant to the facial sufficiency of the pleading of the count charging Criminal Possession of Stolen Property in the Fifth Degree: *i.e.,* that the number on the slip of paper in question is not "property" within the statutory definition. On the facts at bar, the AT&T telephone credit card number qualifies for inclusion within the statutory definition of "property."

Notes and Questions

1. The defendant in *Johnson* wrongfully obtained a calling card number that enabled him to place long-distance phone calls for free. The number was an access code—a password, a sort of intangible key—and its market value derived from the value of the service that could be accessed using the number.

Individuals use access codes every day. E-mail passwords and ATM PIN numbers are common examples. You can probably think of less high-tech examples as well. In high school, you probably had a locker that you protected with a combination lock. In grade school, you may have conditioned access to your neighborhood clubhouse on an entrant's knowledge of the "secret password." The combination for the lock and the secret password are both access codes. In the past, did you think of these access codes as your property? Does the fact that an access code can be used to obtain property mean that the access code is itself property? Why wasn't Johnson charged with fraud for placing the illegal calls, instead of possession of stolen property for knowing the card number?

2. What does it mean to "possess" a number? The legal concept of possession generally requires two elements: knowledge of the property and control over it. If you put a piece of paper in your wallet, you possess that paper because you know the paper exists and you control the contents of your pocket. Does it make sense to say that you also possess the intangible writing on the piece of paper, such as a number written on it? Can you control a number in the same way that you can control a physical object?

Arguably, the *Johnson* court evades this difficulty by simply eliminating the control requirement of possession and equating possession with knowledge. The court reasons that Johnson would be liable for possessing stolen property if he had merely seen the calling card numbers and then memorized them. Does that make sense?

Imagine a robber holds up a victim at gun point, demands that the victim tell him something valuable, and that the victim, afraid for his life, tells the robber his credit card number. If the robber memorizes the number, *Johnson* suggests, he would be guilty of possessing stolen property. What if the robber takes out an advertisement in the local newspaper that says, "Memorize this stolen credit card number!" and includes the number? Would anyone who reads the advertisement carefully be guilty of possessing stolen property, even if they have no intent to use the number fraudulently? What if the robber simply forgets the credit card number? Does he no longer possess the stolen property?

3.   Every Anglo–American crime must include a guilty act (in Latin, an *actus reus*). *See* Wayne R. LaFave, Criminal Law 206 (3d ed. 2000). According to this doctrine, the government cannot punish merely having a state of mind. If possession can be satisfied by knowledge alone, does the crime of possessing stolen property violate this principle? If you were the defense attorney in *Johnson*, what argument would you make on appeal to persuade a higher court that the trial court's construction is inconsistent with the *actus reus* requirement?

4.   If information can be property, what does it take for information to become "stolen" property? Physical property becomes stolen when someone intentionally takes it away from its owner. The same concept can apply to data: if Joe steals Jane's iPod, the data files stored in the iPod are stolen in exactly the same way as the physical iPod itself. But what if the information is divorced from physical storage media? If Joe copies Jane's computer data and Jane retains her copy, is that data stolen?

The facts of *Johnson* are instructive. AT&T issued a calling card to a legitimate customer, and Johnson found out the number and used it to place calls billed to that customer's account. Try to identify exactly what (if anything) made that number stolen. Was it stolen simply because Johnson possessed the number and was not an authorized account holder? This seems somewhat unlikely. Was the number stolen because Johnson did not have a legitimate business reason to possess the number? Was it stolen because Johnson had an intent to use the number to place calls but not pay for them?

Another possibility is that the word "stolen" expresses a result, not a legal status. Was the number stolen because Johnson deserves punishment for using AT&T's services without their permission?

5.   Under the New York law at issue in *Johnson*, property includes any "thing of value." Whether data has value is contextual, of course. Go back to the hypothetical in which a robber holds up a victim at gun point and demands that the victim tell him something valuable. The victim, afraid for his life, advises the robber to buy stock in General Motors. Is that advice a "thing of value"? Does it depend on whether General Motors' stock later goes up or down?

As these questions suggest, attempts to value a number generally measure the benefit of the use of that number in a specific context, rather than the value of the number as an abstract matter. Thus in *Johnson*, the court looked to the specific context in which Johnson had the number to determine whether he would use the number to obtain valuable services. The number was a thing of value because Johnson was using the number to obtain valuable services for free; in the court's terms, the number was not merely "some innocuous number, innocently had by a defendant."

Is this a helpful way to determine the value of information? What is the court really measuring?

UNITED STATES v. FARRAJ

United States District Court for the Southern District of New York, 2001.
142 F. Supp. 2d 484.

MARRERO, District Judge.

Defendants Said Farraj ("Said") and Yeazid Farraj ("Yeazid") are charged in a three-count indictment with * * * interstate transportation of stolen property in violation of 18 U.S.C. § 2314. Said now moves * * * to dismiss * * * on the ground that the allegedly stolen property does not fall within the scope of § 2314.

For the reasons discussed below, the motions are denied.

BACKGROUND

In summer of 2000, Said Farraj was a paralegal with the law firm of Orrick, Harrington & Sutcliffe LLP. At the time, Orrick represented plaintiffs in a class action tobacco case: *Falise v. American Tobacco Co.*, No. CV 99–7392(JBW) (E.D.N.Y.). In preparation for the *Falise* trial, the attorneys and paralegals at Orrick created a trial plan exceeding 400 pages and including, among other things, trial strategy, deposition excerpts and summaries, and references to anticipated trial exhibits. Only Orrick employees assigned to *Falise* were permitted access to the Trial Plan. The Indictment does not reveal whether Said was included among such employees.

The Government charges that Said, using the moniker "FlyGuy-NYt," e-mailed an 80–page excerpt of the Trial Plan to the *Falise* defendants' attorneys and offered to sell them the entire Plan. An FBI agent posing as one of the *Falise* defendants' attorneys negotiated with Said via e-mail and ultimately agreed to purchase the Trial Plan for $2 million. On July 21, 2000, Yeazid, Said's brother, met with a second undercover FBI agent at a McDonald's restaurant in lower Manhattan to receive payment. Yeazid was arrested then and gave a statement to the FBI implicating his brother in the conspiracy charged in the Indictment.

DISCUSSION

The Government charges in count two that by e-mailing the Trial Plan excerpt across state lines, Said violated 18 U.S.C. § 2314, which provides, in relevant part, that "whoever transports, transmits, or transfers in interstate or foreign commerce any goods, wares, merchandise, securities, or money, of the value of $5,000 or more, knowing the same to have been stolen, converted, or taken by fraud ... shall be fined under this title or imprisoned." Said moves to dismiss, arguing that § 2314 applies only to the physical asportation of tangible goods or currency, not to "information" stored and transmitted electronically, such as the Trial Plan excerpt e-mailed here. Neither the Supreme Court nor the Second Circuit has addressed this question directly, and this appears to be an issue of first impression in this District.

The Second Circuit has held that the phrase "goods, wares, or merchandise" is "a general and comprehensive designation of such personal property or chattels as are ordinarily a subject of commerce." *In re Vericker,* 446 F.2d 244, 248 (2d Cir. 1971) (Friendly, J.). Said, relying on *Vericker,* argues that the Second Circuit has at times determined that documents fall outside the scope of § 2314. At other times, however, the Second Circuit and other courts have held that documents may be considered "goods, wares, or merchandise" under § 2314. *See, e.g., United States v. Greenwald,* 479 F.2d 320 (6th Cir. 1973) (documents containing secret chemical formulae); *United States v. Bottone,* 365 F.2d 389 (2d Cir. 1966) (drug manufacturing processes); *United States v. Caparros,* No. 85 Cr. 990, 1987 WL 8653 (S.D.N.Y. March 25, 1987) (secret business plans).

The FBI documents at issue in *Vericker* detailed the criminal activity of certain individuals. Judge Friendly reasoned that the FBI documents were not "goods, wares, or merchandise" within the meaning of the statute because the substance contained in the documents was not ordinarily the subject of commerce. The Trial Plan at issue here, however, as is true for trial plans generally, was the work product of a business relationship between client and attorney, and may thus be viewed as an ordinary subject of commerce, created for a commercial purpose and carrying inherent commercial value at least as to the persons directly interested in the matter.

Said argues that even if trial plans generally may be viewed as goods under § 2314, he is accused of transmitting an "intangible," an electronic form of the document, and therefore that it was not a good, but merely "information."

The text of § 2314 makes no distinction between tangible and intangible property, or between electronic and other manner of transfer across state lines. Indeed, in 1988, Congress amended § 2314 to include the term "transmits" to reflect its agreement with the Second Circuit and other courts which had held that § 2314 applied to money wire transfers, where the only interstate transportation took place electronically and where there was no transportation of any physical item. In *United States v. Gilboe,* 684 F.2d 235 (2d Cir. 1982), the Second Circuit addressed the issue of electronic transfer for the first time and recognized that

> the manner in which funds were moved does not affect the ability to obtain tangible paper dollars or a bank check from the receiving account. Indeed, we suspect that actual dollars rarely move between banks, particularly in international transactions. The primary element of this offense, transportation, does not require proof that any specific means of transporting were used.

684 F.2d at 238.

The Second Circuit has also held that § 2314 was violated when the defendants stole documents containing some drug manufacturing process, copied and returned them, and then sent the copies abroad. *See*

Bottone, 365 F.2d at 391–92. The court noted that it did not matter that the item stolen was not the same as that transported. Rather, as observed by Judge Friendly,

> where the physical form of the stolen goods is secondary in every respect to the matter recorded in them, the transformation of the information in the stolen papers into a tangible object never possessed by the original owner should be deemed immaterial. It would offend common sense to hold that these defendants fall outside the statute simply because, in efforts to avoid detection, their confederates were at pains to restore the original papers to the employer and transport only copies or notes.

Id. at 394.

Relying in part on the Second Circuit's decisions in *Gilboe* and *Bottone,* the court in *United States v. Riggs,* 739 F. Supp. 414 (N.D. Ill. 1990) held that the defendant violated § 2314 when he downloaded a text file containing propriety information onto a home computer, transferred it over a computer network to his co-defendant in another state, who then uploaded it onto a computer bulletin board. The court reasoned that just because the defendant stored the information on a computer, rather than printing it on paper, his acts were not removed from the purview of the statute:

> In the instant case, if the information in Bell South's E911 text file had been affixed to a floppy disk, or printed out on a computer printer, then the defendant's transfer of that information across state lines would clearly constitute the transfer of "goods, wares, or merchandise" within the meaning of § 2314. This court sees no reason to hold differently simply because the defendant stored the information inside a computer instead of printing it out on paper. In either case, the information is in a transferrable, accessible, even salable form.

Id. at 421. The court noted that "reading a tangibility requirement into the definition of 'goods, wares, or merchandise' might unduly restrict the scope of § 2314, especially in this modern technological age," and recognized that although not tangible in a conventional sense, the stolen property was physically stored on a computer hard drive and could be viewed and printed out with the push of a button. "The accessibility of the information in readable form from a particular storage place also makes the information tangible, transferable, salable, and in this court's opinion, brings it within the definition of 'goods, wares, or merchandise' under § 2314."

The Supreme Court's decision in *Dowling v. United States,* 473 U.S. 207 (1985), relied on here by Said, was appropriately distinguished by the *Riggs* court. In *Dowling,* the Supreme Court held that where the victim holds only a copyright, distinct from the possessory interest of the owner of a simple good, and the only act charged involves an unauthorized infringement of that copyright, there is no violation of § 2314. The *Dowling* Court remarked that § 2314 contemplates "a physical identity between the items unlawfully obtained and those eventually transported." Said reads this statement to mean that the electronic transfer of a document falls without the statute.

The Tenth Circuit, relying on *Dowling,* has also taken the view that § 2314 requires the transfer of physical goods, wares, or merchandise. *See United States v. Brown,* 925 F.2d 1301, 1308 (10th Cir. 1991). The defendant in *Brown* crossed state lines with stolen computer code stored on a computer disk. The district court dismissed the indictment, stating that the material contained in the notebooks and on the hard drive was "not the type of property which is contemplated within the language of the statute, goods, wares or merchandise." The Tenth Circuit affirmed the dismissal, observing that "§ 2314 applies only to physical 'goods, wares or merchandise.' Purely intellectual property is not within this category. It can be represented physically, such as through writing on a page, but the underlying, intellectual property itself remains intangible." In this Court's view, the reasoning in *Brown* does not square with the Second Circuit's *Bottone* decision, and may be based on a misapplication of *Dowling.*

Lastly, Said turns to *United States v. Stafford,* 136 F.3d 1109 (7th Cir. 1998). In *Stafford,* the objects of the questioned transfers were "Comdata codes"—a sequence of numbers truckers use to acquire cash while on the road. The driver receives the code from his employer, writes them down on a "comcheck" and then cashes it like a check. The Seventh Circuit held that the codes were not "goods" but merely "information", and that therefore stealing them did not violate § 2314. Importantly, the Seventh Circuit does not reveal how the codes were transferred (presumably they were communicated over the telephone), and the court specifically declined to address whether § 2314 would be implicated if the perpetrator had written down the codes on a piece of paper and transported them across state lines. Consequently, the reasoning in *Stafford* sheds little light on the statute's application to the conduct charged against Said.

Weighing the scant authority at hand, the Court is persuaded that the view most closely analogous to Second Circuit doctrine is that which holds that the transfer of electronic documents via the Internet across state lines does fall within the purview of § 2314. The indictment is therefore upheld and the motion to dismiss count two is denied.

Notes and Questions

1. Farraj had access to the valuable Trial Plan in New York, and he e-mailed an excerpt from it to opposing counsel. Imagine other ways Farraj could have provided the excerpt to opposing counsel:

    A. He could have stolen a paper version of the Trial Plan and shipped it via postal mail to opposing counsel.

    B. He could have obtained a paper version of the Trial Plan, photocopied it, returned the original, and shipped the photocopied version to opposing counsel.

    C. He could have saved an electronic copy of the Trial Plan onto a floppy diskette, put the diskette in an envelope, and shipped the envelope to opposing counsel.

    D. He could have memorized the Trial Plan, traveled to the office of opposing counsel, and then written out a copy of the Trial Plan from memory.

Scenario A is a classic violation of 18 U.S.C. § 2314. But what about Scenarios B, C, and D? If you agree that Farraj violates § 2314 in Scenario B, must the same conclusion follow for Scenarios C and D? Note that Scenario B is the first to separate the physical item from the information it contains. Scenario C puts the data in electronic form, but transported via a physical storage device. The facts of *Farraj* put the data in electronic form, but transported electronically. Finally, the facts of Scenario D put the data in the neural networks of the human brain, transported by physically moving that brain (and the person below it, naturally) across state lines. Can you distinguish among these cases, or do they all involve basically the same thing?

    In United States v. Bottone, 365 F.2d 389 (2d Cir. 1966), Judge Henry Friendly offered a rationale to distinguish Scenario B from Scenario D. *Bottone* raised the basic facts of Scenario B: the defendants had stolen papers that contained the victim company's secret manufacturing processes, photocopied the papers, returned the originals, and sent the photocopies. As the *Farraj* court notes, Judge Friendly agreed with the government that the photocopies were 'goods' which had been 'stolen, converted or taken by fraud' pursuant to 18 U.S.C. § 2314. In a part of the opinion not discussed in *Farraj*, Judge Friendly distinguished this set of facts from those akin to Scenario D in the following way:

> To be sure, where no tangible objects were ever taken or transported, a court would be hard pressed to conclude that 'goods' had been stolen and transported within the meaning of 2314; the statute would presumably not extend to the case where a carefully guarded secret formula was memorized, carried away in the recesses of a thievish mind and placed in writing only after a boundary had been crossed. The situation, however, is quite different where tangible goods are stolen and transported and the only obstacle to condemnation is a clever intermediate transcription or use of a photocopy machine.

Bottone, 365 F.2d at 393. Are you convinced? How would Judge Friendly resolve the *Farraj* case? Is there a difference between memorizing information and crossing a state line and e-mailing that information across a state line?

    2. *Does sending an electronic signal "transport" property?* When property is tangible, it is possible to track its motion to establish that it has been transported across state lines. If property is merely electronic data, however, the only property being transported are the electrons that constitute the bits and bytes of the data. Does setting up a circuit that sends electrons across state lines "transport" property? In United States v. Gilboe, 684 F.2d 235 (2d Cir. 1982), discussed in *Farraj*, a defendant wired an electronic funds transfer to the Bahamas. The defendant argued that he did not actually

"transport" any property to the Bahamas. In an opinion by Judge Feinberg, the Second Circuit disagreed:

> Electronic signals in this context are the means by which funds are transported. The beginning of the transaction is money in one account and the ending is money in another. The manner in which the funds were moved does not affect the ability to obtain tangible paper dollars or a bank check from the receiving account. Indeed, we suspect that actual dollars rarely move between banks, particularly in international transactions. If anything, the means of transfer here were essential to the success of the fraudulent scheme. Defendant depended heavily on his ability to move funds rapidly out of reach of disgruntled shipowners who were to receive payment within days of loading the grain. And it was not until the funds, through a series of bank transfers, came to rest in the Bahamas that defendant's scheme was complete.

Id. at 238. Is the court right to focus not on the details of how the technology works, but rather on the net effect of the transaction?

3. *Property crimes and information misuse.* Cases such as *Johnson* and *Farraj* try to rework traditional property crimes to address information misuse. The cases assume that information is property that has an owner who sets the rules for its proper usage. When a wrongdoer obtains a copy of that information and misuses it in violation of those rules, the misuse renders that copy stolen property. Retaining the information constitutes possession of stolen property (*Johnson*), and sending that information can be considered transporting it (*Farraj*). Taken together, such cases create a theoretical framework for punishing misuse of information using general property crimes.

Is the effort a successful one? Both *Johnson* and *Farraj* involve individuals who deserved punishment for their harmful acts. *Johnson* obtained valuable services without paying, and *Farraj* attempted to sell a confidential litigation document so it could be used against his law firm's client. From a standpoint of criminal law theory, both men committed acts that deserve punishment and that the law should try to deter. But how close is the nexus between the defendants' wrongful acts and the theory of criminal liability applied by the courts? Is a general crime of information misuse derived from property law appropriate?

How similar is the crime of information misuse to the concepts of computer misuse described in Chapter Two? Both regimes imagine a proper usage of computers and/or information, and both punish deviations from that proper usage. In the case of computer misuse crimes, access at some point becomes unauthorized; in the case of information misuse crimes, information at some point becomes stolen. Does either regime feature a clear way to distinguish proper from improper conduct? Is the law here premised mostly on an intuition that at some point conduct becomes harmful enough that it should trigger criminal sanctions? If so, do some principles explain that intuition, or is it simply a moral judgment made on a case-by-case basis? From an ethical perspective, is it appropriate for prosecutors to make aggressive arguments about the scope of traditional criminal laws, or should they focus on prosecuting conduct that is clearly proscribed by existing statutes? Why am I asking so many questions? (Heh, just kidding.)

2. THE ECONOMIC ESPIONAGE ACT

One alternative to charging information misuse under general property crimes is for the legislature to enact new criminal statutes that punish information misuse in specific contexts. An example of this approach is the Economic Espionage Act of 1996 (EEA), Pub. L. No. 104–294, codified at 18 U.S.C. §§ 1831–39. The EEA was designed to punish and deter the theft of a specific type of information, namely trade secrets.

UNITED STATES v. GENOVESE

United States District Court for the Southern District of New York, 2005.
409 F. Supp. 2d 253.

PAULEY, J.

By Indictment dated January 3, 2005, the Government charged the defendant, William P. Genovese, Jr., with one count of unlawfully downloading and selling a trade secret in violation of 18 U.S.C. § 1832(a)(2). Genovese moves to dismiss the Indictment pursuant to Rule 12(b)(3)(B) of the Federal Rules of Criminal Procedure. Genovese contends that the statute criminalizing trade secret theft is facially overbroad in violation of the First Amendment and unconstitutionally vague as applied to him. For the reasons set forth below, Genovese's motion to dismiss the Indictment is denied.

BACKGROUND

In February 2004, portions of Microsoft Corporation's source code for two of its computer operating systems, Windows NT 4.0 and Windows 2000, appeared on the Internet.

The Indictment charges Genovese with downloading, copying, selling and attempting to sell Microsoft source code without authorization. Specifically, the Government contends that on February 12, 2004, Genovese posted a message on his website offering the code for sale: "win2000 source code jacked ... and illmob.org got a copy of it ... im sure if you look hard you can find it or if you wanna buy it ill give you a password to my ftp."

According to the Complaint, an investigator retained by Microsoft responded to the message later that month by sending Genovese an email that offered twenty dollars for the code. After Genovese accepted the offer, the investigator transferred twenty dollars to Genovese through an online payment service. Genovese then provided access to the source code through his FTP server. Microsoft alerted the FBI. In July 2004, an undercover Government agent contacted Genovese and purchased the Microsoft source code. Genovese was arrested and charged with violating 18 U.S.C. § 1832(a)(2).

DISCUSSION

Section 1832 was enacted as part of the Economic Espionage Act of 1996. In relevant part, the statute applies to anyone who, with intent to convert a trade secret, that is related to or included in a product that is produced for or placed in interstate or foreign commerce, to the economic benefit of anyone other than the owner thereof, and intending or knowing that the offense will, injure any owner of that trade secret, knowingly ... without authorization copies, duplicates, sketches, draws, photographs, downloads, uploads, alters, destroys, photocopies, replicates, transmits, delivers, sends, mails, communicates, or conveys such information.

18 U.S.C. § 1832(a)(2). "Trade secret," in turn, is defined to encompass all forms and types of financial, business, scientific, technical, economic, or engineering information, including patterns, plans, compilations, program devices, formulas, designs, prototypes, methods, techniques, processes, procedures, programs, or codes, whether tangible or intangible, and whether or how stored, compiled, or memorialized physically, electronically, graphically, photographically, or in writing if (A) the owner thereof has taken reasonable measures to keep such information secret; and (B) the information derives independent economic value, actual or potential, from not being generally known to, and not being readily ascertainable through proper means by, the public.

18 U.S.C. § 1839(3). The statute carries a ten-year maximum term of imprisonment. 18 U.S.C. § 1832(a).

Genovese argues that § 1832 violates the First Amendment because it restricts protected speech and sweeps more broadly than necessary. A statute is unconstitutionally overbroad if there exists "a substantial risk that application of the provision will lead to the suppression of speech." *Nat'l Endowment for the Arts v. Finley,* 524 U.S. 569, 580 (1998). When a litigant challenges a statute on its face as overly broad, the prudential limitations against third party standing are relaxed, and the litigant may assert the rights of individuals whose interests might be affected by the statute but who are not before the court.

While the First Amendment protects the formulation of source code and other types of trade secrets encompassed by the EEA, *see Universal City Studios, Inc. v. Corley,* 273 F.3d 429, 445–46 (2d Cir. 2001), the statute criminalizes their unauthorized copying, duplicating, downloading and uploading. 18 U.S.C. § 1832(a)(2). Moreover, the EEA limits its reach to such conduct that is done "with intent to convert a trade secret ... to the economic benefit of anyone other than the owner thereof." 18 U.S.C. § 1832(a)(2). Such conduct is not protected speech. *See United States v. Thompson,* 76 F.3d 442, 452 (2d Cir. 1996) ("A prohibition against corrupt acts is clearly limited to constitutionally unprotected and purportedly illicit activity."). Because § 1832 is specifically targeted toward illegal activity and does not reach protected speech, the statute is not unconstitutionally overbroad.

The void-for-vagueness doctrine requires that a statute define the criminal offense with sufficient precision "that ordinary people can understand what conduct is prohibited." *Kolender v. Lawson,* 461 U.S.

352, 357 (1983). Courts must also consider whether the law provides explicit standards for those who apply it. Vagueness challenges to statutes which do not involve First Amendment freedoms must be examined in the light of the facts of the case at hand.

Genovese does not contend that § 1832(a)(2) imprecisely describes the prohibited act (*i.e.,* that an individual is guilty if he "copies, duplicates, sketches, draws, photographs, downloads, uploads, alters, destroys, photocopies, replicates, transmits, delivers, sends, mails, communicates, or conveys" a trade secret). Rather, he maintains that Section 1839(3)'s definition of "trade secret" is unconstitutionally vague as applied to the facts of this case and does not afford due process. Specifically, Genovese argues that having found the source code on the Internet after it had been released to the general public by a third-party, he could not have known that it was "not . . . generally known to . . . the public" and that Microsoft had taken "reasonable measures" to safeguard it.

1. *"Not . . . generally known to . . . the public"*

Genovese maintains that "he had every reason to believe the code had become publicly available" when he found it on the Internet. However, a trade secret does not lose its protection under the EEA if it is temporarily, accidentally or illicitly released to the public, provided it does not become "generally known" or "readily ascertainable through proper means." 18 U.S.C. § 1839(3)(B). Genovese merges these two standards and, in so doing, elevates the standard for trade secret status to one of absolute secrecy. This formulation impermissibly writes the critical modifier "generally" out of the statutory definition and attempts to inject a vagueness otherwise absent from the facts of this case.

Indeed, a reasonable inference from Genovese's website posting is that he knew that the source code derived independent value because it was not "generally known." The Government alleges that he described the code as "jacked" and indicated that others would have to "look hard" to find it elsewhere. As such, Genovese was on notice that Microsoft had not publicly released the code and recognized its public scarcity. Moreover, because Genovese offered the code for sale and successfully sold it, he was on notice that it derived value from its relative obscurity, notwithstanding that it was available from other sources. *See United States v. Hsu,* 40 F. Supp. 2d 623, 630–31 (E.D. Pa. 1999) (rejecting a similar challenge to the definition of "trade secret" where the evidence showed that the defendant "knew (or at a minimum believed) that the information he was seeking to acquire was not generally known to or readily ascertainable through proper means by the public").

A statute may also be unconstitutionally vague if it "authorizes and even encourages arbitrary and discriminatory enforcement." *City of Chicago v. Morales,* 527 U.S. 41, 56 (1999). In this regard, Genovese argues that the statute provided no guidance to law enforcement officials to determine whether the source code constituted a trade secret. However, just as Genovese's announcement and conduct reflect his belief that the "jacked" source code was valuable because it was not generally known, it provided the FBI reason to believe that Genovese was trafficking in Microsoft's trade secret.

2.   *"Reasonable measures"*

With respect to the "reasonable measures" element of the EEA's "trade secret" definition, Genovese contends that he "was in no position to make a determination about whether Microsoft took any measures to protect the secrecy of its source code, let alone whether those measures were 'reasonable.'"

Once again, Genovese's website posting belies any claim that he was a casual Internet browser who happened upon the source code without knowledge of its owner or the manner in which the code entered the public domain. As discussed above, the posting reveals that Genovese knew that a third-party had "jacked" the source code from Microsoft. Having acknowledged both that the source code was proprietary to Microsoft and that someone else penetrated whatever safeguards Microsoft enlisted to protect it, Genovese cannot now argue that the statute was insufficient to put him on notice that the source code constituted a trade secret under the EEA. For Section 1839(3)'s "trade secret" definition to survive a vague-as-applied challenge, a "defendant need not have been aware of the particular security measures taken by" the trade secret's owner, as long as the "defendant knew the information was proprietary." *United States v. Krumrei,* 258 F.3d 535, 539 (6th Cir. 2001) (noting that the defendant "was aware that he was selling confidential information to which he had no claim"). In this case, one can infer that Genovese knew not only that the source code was proprietary, but that any protective measures by Microsoft had been circumvented. At a later stage in this proceeding, Genovese may choose to argue to this Court or to a jury that Microsoft's measures were not "reasonable," or that Genovese could not have known what, if any, measures Microsoft maintained. For purposes of his vagueness challenge, however, Genovese's knowledge that the source code belonged to Microsoft and that others had stolen it was sufficient for him to "reasonably understand" that the conduct alleged in the Indictment was proscribed by Section 1832(a)(2).

As such, Section 1839(3) defines "trade secret" with "sufficient definiteness" so that an ordinary person in Genovese's position could understand that trafficking in the Windows source code was prohibited by law. As applied to the facts of this case, the statute is not so vague that it violates the defendant's due process.

Notes and Questions

1.   Assuming the court is correct that prosecuting Genovese does not raise constitutional difficulties, do you think Genovese violated the Economic Espionage Act? Assume that Genovese found a copy of the source code online, copied it, and uploaded it to his ftp server. Assume from the facts that he knew the source code had been stolen from Microsoft and that

Microsoft did not want the code to be available to the public. To be liable, Genovese must have "intent to convert a trade secret," "to the economic benefit of anyone other than the owner thereof," "intending or knowing that the offense will, injure any owner of that trade secret," and must upload, download or copy it "knowingly ... without authorization." Has Genovese done so? Does it matter if the source code is widely available online? Did Genovese know that his conduct would injure Microsoft? Given that he found the copy online, is his conduct clearly "without authorization"? The legislative history of the EEA indicates that "authorization is the permission, approval, consent or sanction of the owner" to obtain, destroy or convey the trade secret. 142 Cong. Rec. S12202, S12212 (daily ed. Oct. 2, 1996).

2. How much narrower is the EEA compared to the general property approach seen in *Johnson* and *Farraj*? Which approach do you prefer?

3. Consider how the EEA handles the problem of identifying when information such as a trade secret becomes "stolen." The EEA punishes one who:

(1) steals, or without authorization appropriates, takes, carries away, or conceals, or by fraud, artifice, or deception obtains such information;

(2) without authorization copies, duplicates, sketches, draws, photographs, downloads, uploads, alters, destroys, photocopies, replicates, transmits, delivers, sends, mails, communicates, or conveys such information;

(3) receives, buys, or possesses such information, knowing the same to have been stolen or appropriated, obtained, or converted without authorization[.]

18 U.S.C. §§ 1831(a), 1832(a). Does this answer the question? Note that the definition of a trade secret may make it easier to determine when a trade secret is "stolen" or copied "without authorization." A trade secret exists only if it has an identifiable owner who has exercised his right to exclude others from his property by taking reasonable measures to keep it a secret. Reasonable measures generally include the imposition of clear rules governing when the secret can be copied, transmitted, and conveyed. In that context, then, copying or distributing the trade secret in violation of the rules needed to ensure that the secret remains a secret constitutes a copying or distributing "without authorization."

Does this shed light on the broader problem of identifying when information is "stolen"? Does it provide a reason to limit information misuse crimes to trade secrets?

4. Consider why Congress passed the EEA, and whether the law is necessary. Here is one perspective from a federal prosecutor:

By 1996, Congress recognized the serious economic risks created by the theft of trade secrets from American companies. A 1995 survey of 325 companies determined that nearly half of them had experienced a trade secret theft. S. Rep. No. 104–359 (1996). It was estimated that nearly $24 billion of corporate intellectual property was stolen every year. United States v. Hsu, 155 F.3d 189, 194 (3d Cir. 1998). The FBI suspected that more than twenty countries were actively trying to steal United States companies' trade secrets. Some warned that the end of the Cold War "sent government spies scurrying to the private sector to perform illicit work for businesses and corporations." Id. As the nation's workforce became more mobile, employees used their former employers' trade secrets for the benefit of their new employers, who had spent nothing to develop the information. Federal prosecutors often had difficulty fitting trade secret cases within the existing federal statutes. The National Stolen Property Act, 18 U.S.C. § 2314, did not apply to the theft of purely intellectual property. See Dowling v. United States, 473 U.S. 207, 216 (1985); United States v. Brown, 925 F.2d 1301, 1307–08 (10th Cir. 1991). Mail and wire fraud statutes did not always apply. The only federal statute explicitly targeting the theft of trade secrets was limited to government employees' unauthorized disclosure of trade secrets, and offenders were subject only to misdemeanor penalties. 18 U.S.C. § 1905. States lacked the resources to investigate these crimes, and faced substantial jurisdictional hurdles. While more than 40 states had enacted some form of the civil Uniform Trade Secret Act (UTSA), there was no effective criminal response to the problem.

George Dilworth, *The Economic Espionage Act of 1996: An Overview, available at* http://www.usdoj.gov/criminal/cybercrime/usamay2001_6.htm. Two defense attorneys, Joe Savage and Matthew Martel, offer a more skeptical perspective:

The congressional debates [over the EEA] contained dire accounts of foreign governments pilfering America's trade secrets. Simply put, the EEA was couched in terms of national security; the foreign espionage provisions were first proposed as an amendment to the National Security Act of 1947 * * * The outcry that "there oughta be a law" was hard to resist, especially since the lobby in support of foreign spying on America is fortunately limited and the FBI had claimed that it had investigations of economic espionage by at least 23 foreign governments. 142 Cong. Rec. H10,461 (daily ed. Sept. 17, 1996) (statements of Representative Hyde). Therefore, the EEA's foreign economic espionage provision breezed through Congress. Swept along with little notice was section 1832, prohibiting domestic trade secret theft.

Because of this original focus, one might surmise that the DOJ would immediately give priority to enforcement procedures involving foreign spies. Instead, not one prosecution has occurred enforcing the foreign espionage provisions of the EEA. Not a single one. The conclusion seems inescapable: The foreign economic espionage law either was not necessary or there is a real and ongoing problem that is not being addressed.

While the lack of section 1831 prosecutions suggests that the EEA is unnecessary, section 1832, the domestic trade secret theft provision, has been used 24 times [as of 2000], suggesting that the EEA is needed. Sixteen cases have resulted in convictions, seven are pending, and one has been dismissed. Yet, when actual prosecutions are examined, only about one-half of the cases involved solely EEA charges. And, of these, all but one involved plea bargains where another federal statute was violated. Thus, it seems the EEA is of little practical necessity. Nonetheless, defendants are more likely to face EEA charges and businesses are now exposed to prosecution for hiring practices, joint venture activity, or other routine trade secret disputes. At most, the law makes life easier for federal prosecutors, which might not be objectionable if it did not pose risks for everyone else.

Perhaps the necessity for the statute can be established by identifying theoretical gaps in existing law. Proponents cite the inadequacy of the fraud and stolen property statutes.

First, they say, theft of trade secrets is not reached by the mail or wire fraud statutes, 18 U.S.C. §§ 1341 and 1343, under circumstances where the theft does not involve a mailing or a wire transmission. And, second, the Interstate Transportation of Stolen Property Act (ITSP, but also commonly referred to as the NSPA), 18 U.S.C. § 2314, is limited to crimes including the theft of tangible property. United States v. Brown, 925 F.2d 1301 (10th Cir. 1991).

It is true that mail and wire fraud will not reach trade secret thefts that do not satisfy the jurisdictional requirement. 18 U.S.C. §§ 1341 and 1343. But the statutes also do not reach frauds that fail to meet the jurisdictional requirement. Why is theft sufficiently more significant than fraud, warranting a law removing jurisdictional prerequisites? Why not enact an equally broad Economic Fraud Act?

If the "tangible property" limitation of the NSPA creates a serious dilemma for law enforcement, it could be addressed by simple amendment, as Congress did with the mail and wire fraud statutes in 18 U.S.C. § 1346, to reach certain intangible property. Instead, the EEA includes intangible property but then eliminates the $5,000 minimum loss requirement in the NSPA.

Joseph F. Savage, Jr., Matthew A. Martel, and Marc J. Zwillinger, *Conflicting Views of the Economic Espionage Act*, Criminal Justice, Fall 2000, at 11–12.

5. Professor Geraldine Moohr has argued that the EEA probably does more harm than good in light of preexisting civil laws protecting trade secrets. *See* Geraldine Szott Moohr, *The Problematic Role of Criminal Law in Regulating Use of Information: The Case of the Economic Espionage Act*, 80 N.C. L. Rev. 853, 919 (2002).

According to Professor Moohr, the criminal provisions of the EEA are likely to have three negative consequences. First, the threat of criminal prosecution may scare some employees into staying at their companies instead of leaving for better jobs or starting new businesses. Moohr argues that employees with access to trade secrets at work may fear that legitimate efforts to start competitor businesses will lead to criminal prosecution for allegedly stealing trade secrets. Second, the combination of criminal punishments and the difficulty of identifying exactly what is a trade secret may overdeter competitors from using information in the public domain. Businesses will be extra careful, and decline to use information that can lead to better products out of a misplaced fear that they will end up being prosecuted under the EEA. Third, the EEA may overdeter individuals from disclosing trade secrets even when that disclosure would serve the public interest by placing ideas into the public domain.

Professor Moohr contends that civil remedies are likely to be a more effective way to regulate information misuse than criminal remedies:

> [C]ivil remedies appear to motivate adequately the creation of new products, while not over-compensating in a way that inhibits long-term innovation and economic growth. Civil remedies more effectively address the real harm that results when an information product is taken: the loss of value to its holder. When information is misappropriated, the original holder still possesses the information and may continue to use it. Because the owner has lost only exclusive use of the information, the loss is the diminished value that follows when others may use it. Civil remedies more precisely account for this harm because economic loss is a litigated issue. On the whole, civil law is more likely to produce a nuanced solution that takes into account the rights of others and the public policy of promoting efficient use of knowledge and information.

Id. at 919. Do you agree? What if the defendant is judgment-proof or the harm is irreversible? Do you think Microsoft could recover civil damages from Genovese that would "precisely account" for Microsoft's loss? Imagine a college student obtains the secret formula for Coca–Cola and posts it on the Web. Is a lawsuit against the student a viable option?

Another issue implicated by civil versus criminal remedies is the likelihood of legal action. Companies do not need anyone's permission to file a lawsuit against a business competitor; unsurprisingly, civil trade secret litigation between competitors is fairly common. In contrast, criminal prosecutions brought by federal prosecutors under the EEA remain quite rare. If civil trade secret lawsuits are common, but criminal trade secret prosecutions are rare, which is more likely to have the negative consequences that Professor Moohr predicts?

6. For a review of state criminal laws that address theft of trade secrets, see Eli Lederman, *Criminal Liability for Breach of Confidential Commercial Information*, 38 Emory L.J. 921, 947–65 (1989). For a discussion of the First Amendment implications of trade secret laws, see Eugene Volokh, *Freedom of Speech and Intellectual Property: Some Thoughts after Eldred, 44 Liquormart, and* Bartnicki, 40 Hous. L. Rev. 697, 739–48 (2003).

3. IDENTITY THEFT AND ACCESS DEVICE FRAUD

The federal criminal code contains two information misuse statutes that deal specifically with misuse of authentication and access device methods. 18 U.S.C. § 1028 is the federal identity theft statute, and prohibits fraud and misuse of identification documents such as driver's licenses and passports. 18 U.S.C. § 1029 is the federal access device fraud statute, and prohibits fraud and misuse of credit card numbers, computer passwords, and other information that controls account access. The basic thinking behind both statutes is the same: Access to information, property, and other rights may hinge on documents or data that are designed to authenticate individuals. The use of false or fraudulently obtained authentication methods can cause tremendous harms. Both

§ 1028 and § 1029 try to deter that use by prohibiting the possession, buying, selling, and making documents or data that provide false authentication. Both statutes attempt to punish and deter the harms associated with false identification by punishing misuse of identification information even if no access rights are fraudulently obtained.

UNITED STATES v. CABRERA

United States Court of Appeals for the First Circuit, 2000.
208 F.3d 309.

STAHL, Circuit Judge.

Defendant-appellant Vladimir Cabrera appeals his conviction for possession of a document-making implement under 18 U.S.C. § 1028. Specifically, he asserts that under a proper interpretation of § 1028, the prosecution presented insufficient evidence upon which to ground a conviction. * * * We affirm.

BACKGROUND

In early 1998, Cabrera and an accomplice, Joseph Medeiros, engaged in a scheme to produce counterfeit identification documents, including Massachusetts and Rhode Island driver's licenses, Massachusetts and Rhode Island state employee identification cards, Rhode Island and Puerto Rico birth certificates, U.S. Department of Health and Human Services Social Security cards, and U.S. Department of Justice Immigration and Naturalization Service Resident Alien cards. The government's evidence supported the conclusions that Cabrera employed a computer, a document scanner, a printer, and commercial software that together could be used to scan, alter, and reproduce documents. When used in conjunction with this hardware and software, computer files containing previously scanned official documents stripped of all identifying material served as digitized "templates" from which forgeries could easily be fabricated. First, using the aforementioned equipment, Cabrera scanned genuine documents into his computer, saved the images on his computer hard drive and on floppy disks, removed or altered the identifying information and photographs on the documents, and then printed the documents on photographic paper. Medeiros then inserted new identifying information onto the documents, trimmed the counterfeits, and laminated them as appropriate. Cabrera kept the computer equipment at his home, while the equipment Medeiros used was stored in a suitcase that the two owned jointly.

On June 10, 1998, U.S. Secret Service Agents searched Cabrera's apartment pursuant to a warrant. They found Cabrera's computer equipment, a board used for measuring and trimming documents, Microsoft's "Picture It!" software, which Cabrera apparently had used to create the counterfeit materials, the digitized templates, and sundry fake documents in various stages of completion.

Subsequently, on January 20, 1999, a federal grand jury in the District of Rhode Island returned a two-count indictment, charging, inter alia, that Cabrera possessed document-making implements with the intent that such implements be used in the production of false identification documents, in violation of 18 U.S.C. § 1028(a)(5). At the relevant time period, the statute defined "document-making implement" to mean "any implement or impression specially designed or primarily used for making an identification document, a false identification document, or another document-making implement." Count One—the only count relevant to this appeal—was based on Cabrera's possession of the computer, printer, and scanner.

During Cabrera's trial, Secret Service Agent James Mooney testified for the government regarding the templates found on Cabrera's hard drive and on the diskettes. Agent Mooney also described the software installed on Cabrera's computer and how it could be used for scanning, altering and reproducing documents. On cross-examination, Agent Mooney acknowledged that computers were available to the public and that they had uses aside from those of which Cabrera stood accused. But when Cabrera's counsel then attempted to further examine him regarding the general uses to which anyone could put computer equipment, the court intervened, and the following sidebar exchange regarding the meaning of § 1028's "primarily used" prong ensued:

THE COURT: Congress might have been a little bit more precise in their definition, but as I read that definition in the context of this statute, I read it as referring to the possession and the intent of the possessor in putting it to use. So I think that the general use that anyone might put a computer to—in this case, a computer to, is not relevant.

MR. McCORMICK [Cabrera's Counsel]: I wanted to ask generally if computer equipment was primarily used for the making of—

THE COURT: No, because that primarily refers to the possession of this individual, not the general public.

At the trial's close, the district court instructed the jury only that: "as used in these instructions, the term 'document making implement' means any implement or impression specially designed or primarily used for making an identification document, a false identification document or another document making implement."

The instructions did not specify any particular meaning for the terms "specially designed" or "primarily used." Although Cabrera's counsel did not object to these instructions, the government did object, stating that they did not adequately specify that the statute referred to Cabrera's primary use of the equipment rather than the general uses to which any computer user primarily would put such equipment.

Meanwhile, Cabrera had moved for judgment of acquittal on both counts, arguing that "on the evidence presented, it had not been shown that the computer, printer and scanner referred to in the indictment were document making implements." The district judge reserved judgment on the motion. On May 21, 1999, the jury convicted Cabrera on Count One, and the district judge denied his motion for a judgment of acquittal on that count. Cabrera appeals.

<h2 style="text-align:center">DISCUSSION</h2>

Cabrera argues first that his computer system was not proven to constitute a document-making implement within the meaning of the statute, because "there was no proof, either directly [sic] or by inference, that it was specially designed or generally used to produce identification documents, false identification documents or other document making implements." To determine the sufficiency of the evidence, we canvass the evidence (direct and circumstantial) in the light most agreeable to the prosecution and decide whether that evidence, including all plausible inferences extractable therefrom, enables a rational factfinder to conclude beyond a reasonable doubt that the defendant committed the charged crime.

A. "Specially Designed"

We first find that Cabrera's computer system was "specially designed" for the production of identification documents. As an initial matter, we hold that the statute's text is unambiguous. It does not exclude from its reach implements that could have legitimate other uses if not altered by the perpetrator's modifications. Cabrera suggests that the "specially designed" prong refers not to a defendant's specific implements, but to implements that as a class are uniquely configured to fabricate false identification documents. His interpretation is not tenable. Neither the statute nor Cabrera provides any basis upon which a court could determine the proper level of generality at which to define the class. Should we look to the class of "computers fitted with scanners, printers, document-altering software and digitized templates"? The class of all "computers"? All "electronic implements"? All "implements" of any sort? Nothing in § 1028 requires such arbitrary classification. Rather, the statute unambiguously asks the fact-finder to consider whether the item that the defendant is charged with possessing was "specially designed" for producing forgeries.

Asserting that the statute is ambiguous, Cabrera notes that courts may look to a statute's legislative history when its language itself is not conclusive and clear. But even if § 1028 were unclear (and we believe it is not) Cabrera's resort to its legislative history would be unavailing. The House Judiciary Committee's report on the False Identification Crime Control Act of 1982—in which the disputed "specially designed" language was first introduced—stated that "the committee intended to exclude implements such as office photocopying machines, which are designed for more general and legitimate purposes." H.R. Rep. No. 97–802, at 11 (1982), reprinted in 1982 U.S.C.C.A.N. 3519, 3530. This language might support an argument that standard computer equipment, bereft of any special-purpose hardware or software, would fall beyond the statute's reach. Perhaps an offender could, it would seem, have used an ordinary word processor and an ordinary printer with ordinary paper to produce false documents, just as an offender could have used an office photocopier to do so, without having violated former § 1028. But Cabrera's computer arrangement, unlike a standard office photocopier, was specifically designed to facilitate counterfeiting. A modern computer is not analogous to an "office photocopying machine" circa 1982, which in Congress's view likely could not be altered or specialized, but rather to a modern photocopier fitted with software and hardware that render it uniquely suited to produce illicit materials. We have no reason to believe that such a device would escape § 1028's reach simply because both it and its 1982 analogue were called "photocopiers." A photocopier configured with special-purpose hardware or software may be "specially designed" for the fabrication of identifying documents, and so may a similarly configured computer.

In fact, the more relevant portion of the legislative history is that which precedes the language quoted above. The House committee report noted that the term "document-making implement" would include "text in a distinctive type face and layout that when reproduced [is] part of an identification document." Id. This statement, of course, accurately describes the templates, which were merely computer files containing digital images of "text in a distinctive type face and layout." Alone, each template formed "part of an identification document" and together with the inserted data, each would constitute a complete document.

Cabrera contends that his system was not specially designed for the fabrication of false identification documents, emphasizing that the hardware at issue—namely, the computer, printer, and scanner—were not uniquely suited to such activity. However, the evidence adduced at trial permitted a jury to conclude that Cabrera's system also included software, such as the "Picture It!" program, which testimony indicated "could be used to accept scanned images and also to place those images onto computer-produced documents." Most tellingly, the system also included digitized templates of various official identification documents stored on Cabrera's hard drive and floppy disks. A jury viewing this paraphernalia as a whole could reasonably have deemed the system specially designed for making a false identification document.

B. "Primarily Used"

Cabrera urges that the "primarily used" prong of the "document-making implement" definition refers to an item's "general usage" rather than the particular use to which a defendant put it. The government acknowledges that if it was required to prove that as a general matter, computers, scanners, and printers are primarily used for making identification documents or false identification documents, Cabrera's conviction must be overturned because the court was presented with no evidence supporting that conclusion. The government contends, however, that the relevant inquiry focuses not on the uses of some hypothetical user, but on Cabrera's own primary use of the computer system. We share the government's view, and find that a jury reasonably could have found that Cabrera's equipment was "primarily used" for the fabrication of documents as that term is set forth in former § 1028.

First, as the government notes, Congress could have used a word such as "generally" in lieu of "primarily" if it intended the meaning that Cabrera proposes. Congress's choice not to use that term suggests that it did not intend the inquiry to focus on an item's typical use within society. Relatedly, the section's legislative history suggests that Congress fully expected § 1028 to cover implements that were "generally" used for purposes other than the fabrication of documents. The House Judiciary Committee report noted that "specialized paper or ink" could constitute document-making implements under the "primarily used" prong. H.R.Rep. No. 97–802, at 11, reprinted in 1982 U.S.C.C.A.N. at 3530. Paper and ink–even "specialized" paper and ink–are not "generally" used for the production of false identification documents, but could, in a given case, be "primarily used" in the service of such ends by a particular defendant. The committee's remarks, then, lend credence to the government's case-specific interpretation of the "primarily used" prong.

Moreover, the treatment which former § 1028 has been accorded by the courts suggests that "primarily used" refers to the defendant's primary use of the item in question. While no court appears to have analyzed the meaning of this prong, it has been found to encompass an assortment of paraphernalia not "generally" used for illicit purposes, including laminating machines, plastic laminating pouches, packets of rub-on letters, erasers, tape, scissors, and small photographs.

The evidence showed that Cabrera repeatedly used his computer, scanner, printer, software, and digitized templates to create false identification documents. This system was used in conjunction with laminates, Exacto blades, a supply of photographic-quality paper, and genuine identification documents. There was no evidence to demonstrate that Cabrera used his system for any other purpose. The jury thus reasonably could have found that this equipment was "primarily used" for Cabrera's document production.

Notes and Questions

1. The current language of 18 U.S.C. § 1028(d)(2) makes the statutory question in *Cabrera* somewhat different today, as it defines "document-making implement" as follows:

> any implement, impression, template, computer file, computer disc, electronic device, or computer hardware or software, that is specifically configured or primarily used for making an identification document, a false identification document, or another document-making implement.

What does it mean for a computer to be "specifically configured" to make an identification document? What software, hardware, or file does that require, and how (if at all) is that computer different from a typical personal computer purchased and loaded with standard software programs? 18 U.S.C. § 1028(a)(5) punishes one who knowingly possesses a document-making implement with intent that it will be used to make false identification documents. Does that just mean possessing a computer with intent to use it to make a false ID is a crime?

2. 18 U.S.C. § 1029 punishes a wide range of access device frauds, and is most often used to punish credit card fraud. An "access device" is broadly defined as:

> any card, plate, code, account number, electronic serial number, mobile identification number, personal identification number, or other telecommunications service, equipment, or instrument identifier, or other means of account access that can be used, alone or in conjunction with another access device, to obtain money, goods, services, or any other thing of value, or that can be used to initiate a transfer of funds (other than a transfer originated solely by paper instrument);

18 U.S.C. § 1029(e)(1). The statute also defines an "unauthorized access device" as "any access device that is lost, stolen, expired, revoked, canceled, or obtained with intent to defraud." 18 U.S.C. § 1029(e)(3). Among the acts prohibited by this statute are trafficking in and possessing unauthorized access devices with intent to defraud. *See* § 1029(a)(2)-(3).

Recall the facts of People v. Johnson, 560 N.Y.S.2d 238 (Crim. Ct. N.Y. 1990), from the beginning of this Chapter. Johnson possessed an AT&T credit card number on a slip of paper. The number was stolen and was being used by Johnson without the consent of the account holder. At the federal level, Johnson's criminal liability is clear. 18 U.S.C. § 1029(a)(6) punishes whoever, "without the authorization of the issuer of the access device, knowingly and with intent to defraud solicits a person for the purpose of . . . offering an access device . . . or selling information regarding . . . an access device." Isn't this exactly what Johnson did? Does it make more sense for Johnson to be punished under a specific access device fraud statute or a general property crime statute?

4. COPYRIGHT LAW

Copyright law is designed to provide economic incentives for authors to create new and original works such as stories, books, music, and movies. Digital technologies and the Internet have begun to revolutionize how such original works are made and distributed, raising a number of vital questions about the future of copyright law. At the same time, copyright law is overwhelmingly an area of civil law, not criminal law. The rights granted under the copyright laws generally are enforced by civil lawsuits brought by copyright owners, not criminal indictments obtained by federal prosecutors. The role of criminal law in the enforcement of copyright law traditionally has been much narrower than the role of civil law. As a result, few criminal copyright cases have been brought.

Should computer-facilitated copyright infringement change that traditional role? The Internet facilitates copyright infringement on a grand scale; it is now far easier and cheaper than ever before to copy and distribute copyrighted works in a relatively anonymous environment. Should criminal copyright laws be enforced to deter the digital reproduction and distribution of copyrighted materials? Can criminal prosecutions limit infringement in a way that civil penalties cannot? Or are criminal prosecutions too heavy-handed given that technology and social practice is in considerable flux?

A) *Introduction*

DAVID GOLDSTONE—PROSECUTING INTELLECTUAL PROPERTY CRIMES

Computer Crime and Intellectual Property Section
United States Department of Justice (2001).

The central precept of copyright law is:

For a limited time, an original work in fixed form may not be copied (or otherwise infringed) without permission.

Copyright law is intended to protect the creators of original expressive works. Copyright law protects the original expression of an idea or concept in tangible form (be it a novel, a song, a carpet design, or computer source code), but does not extend to protection of the idea or concept itself. Thus, copyright law protects interests distinct from those protected by the patent laws, which provide exclusive rights to inventors of new methods or processes, and the trademark laws, which protect the exclusive use of certain names and slogans in connection with certain goods or services.

A rich body of law has developed to give greater content to this edict, supported by an administrative scheme established and refined by Congress. For federal prosecutors, however, the critical aspects of copyright law can be distilled to a few basic questions: What is the legal basis for creating a property right in original intellectual property, such as a book, a movie, or computer software? What are the major developments in federal copyright protection? How does intellectual property become protected by copyright law? Does it need to be registered? How long does that protection last? What counts as "infringement" of a copy? Is infringement really a crime, and, if so, why? What if the infringer was not making any money?

What is the legal basis for creating a "property right" in original intellectual property, such as a book, a movie, or computer software? Since 1790, Congress has enacted numerous statutes developing and fine-tuning the copyright law, which is now codified primarily in Title 17 of the United States Code. The Constitution grants Congress both general authority to regulate interstate commerce, U.S. Const. art. I, § 8, cl. 3, and specific authority "to Promote the Progress of Science and Useful Arts, by securing for Limited Times to Authors and Inventors the exclusive Right to their respective Writings and Discoveries." U.S. Const. art. I, § 8, cl. 8.

What are the major developments in federal copyright protection?
Since 1790, Congress has enacted and repeatedly amended copyright
laws, with a trend of continually increased coverage and increased
remedies. Beginning in 1909, Congress also imposed criminal penalties
for certain types of copyright infringement. The major revision in 1976
was a watershed moment in copyright law; it revolutionized copyright
law by establishing federal pre-emption over state law. *See* 17 U.S.C.
§ 301. Other significant recent legislative developments include: (1) the
Computer Software Copyright Act of 1980 (codified at 17 U.S.C. §§ 101,
117), which clarified that computer software is entitled to copyright
protection; (2) expansion of criminal penalties for certain works in 1982
and for all works in 1992; *see* 17 U.S.C. § 506 and 18 U.S.C. § 2319; (3)
the creation of an exclusive right pertaining to digital audio transmission
of sound recordings by the Digital Performance Right in Sound Recordings Act of 1995 (1995); (4) the criminalization of large-scale copying
even in the absence of economic motivation by the No Electronic Theft
(NET) Act (1997); (5) the 1998 extension of the term of copyrights; *see*
Sonny Bono Copyright Term Extension Act (1998); and (6) the Digital
Millennium Copyright Act (codified at 17 U.S.C. §§ 1201–1205).

How does intellectual property become protected by copyright law?
Does it need to have been registered with the Copyright Office? Congress
has provided copyright protection to all "original works of authorship
fixed in any tangible medium of expression, now known or later developed, from which they can be perceived, reproduced, or otherwise communicated, either directly or with the aid of a machine or device." 17
U.S.C. § 102(a). This definition has two components, originality and
fixation, which set the outer limits of federal copyright protection. While
copyright protection exists from the time of the creation of a work, civil
infringement actions may be brought only with respect to those works
that have been registered with the Register of Copyrights. Similarly,
criminal prosecutions should be sought only after the infringed works
have been registered.

How long does copyright protection last? The term of copyright
protection for works created in 1978 or later is life of the author plus
seventy years. Pre–1978 works are protected for ninety-five years from
the date of creation. Corporate copyrights are treated similarly.

What constitutes "infringement" of a copyrighted work? Generally,
infringement is the violation of one of five exclusive rights granted to a
copyright owner by federal law. The five exclusive rights are: (1) reproduction, (2) distribution, (3) public display, or (4) public performance of
the copyrighted work, as well as '(5) preparation of derivative works
based upon the original copyrighted work. *See* 17 U.S.C. § 106(1)-(5). An
unlicensed use of the copyright is not an infringement unless it conflicts
with one of these specific exclusive rights conferred by the copyright
statute.

What makes copyright infringement a crime? Is it a felony? Copyright infringement is a crime where it is done willfully and either: (1) for

commercial advantage or private financial gain, 17 U.S.C. § 506(a)(1); or (2) by reproduction or distribution on a large scale (i.e., copying works with a total retail value of over $1,000), 17 U.S.C. § 506(a)(2). Felony punishment is provided only for reproduction or distribution of at least 10 copies during any 180 days of copyrighted works worth more than $2,500. 18 U.S.C. § 2319(b)-(c). The reason that copyright infringement is a crime is to punish and deter the misappropriation of intellectual property that an author—who may have no means to prevent copying—invested time, energy and money to create.

What other criminal laws protect copyrighted material besides 17 U.S.C. § 506(a) and 18 U.S.C. § 2319. A number of other federal laws specifically protect copyrighted works. 18 U.S.C. § 2318 prohibits the counterfeit labeling of copyrighted works. Further, in 1994, Congress created 18 U.S.C. § 2319A, which expressly covers the unauthorized "fixation" of and trafficking in recordings and musical videos of live musical performances. Systems of copyright management are protected by 17 U.S.C. § 1201 and § 1202. 17 U.S.C. § 506 also provides lesser criminal sanctions for conduct which does not constitute copyright infringement but which nonetheless undermines the integrity of the copyright system, such as for false representations in copyright applications.

There are four essential elements to a charge of felony copyright infringement. In order to obtain a felony conviction under 17 U.S.C. § 506(a) and 18 U.S.C. § 2319, the government must demonstrate that:

1. A copyright exists,

2. It was infringed by the defendant by reproduction or distribution of the copyrighted work,

3. The defendant acted willfully, and

4. The defendant infringed at least 10 copies of one or more copyrighted works with a total retail value of more than $2,500 within a 180–day period.

See 17 U.S.C. § 506(a)(2); 18 U.S.C. § 2319(a), (c)(1). The maximum punishment for this crime is 3 years imprisonment and $250,000.

Another element, if proven, enhances the maximum penalty: That the defendant acted "for purposes of commercial advantage or private financial gain." If it is proven, the statutory maximum prison sentence can rise to 5 years. *See* 17 U.S.C. § 506(a)(1); 18 U.S.C. § 2319(a), (b)(1) * * * * Moreover, a commercial motivation case will usually have better jury appeal than a case without commercial motivation. Indeed, if commercial motivation is not alleged, defendants may be more inclined to raise the affirmative defense of fair use, codified at 17 U.S.C. § 107, since fair use defenses are more plausible when defendants do not profit financially by their acts of infringement.

Notes and Questions

1. Many of the statutory elements of copyright liability are relatively clear-cut. Consider, for example, the requirement that the defendant's conduct infringed an existing copyright via reproduction or distribution. Downloading a copyrighted computer file constitutes reproducing it, and sending it to another counts as distribution. The primary legal issues raised in criminal copyright cases tend to be the willfulness requirement, fair use, and (if needed) the requirement of an intent to profit.

2. *Fair use.* Copying or distributing copyrighted works does not constitute infringement if it falls within the statutory fair use exception:

[T]he fair use of a copyrighted work * * * for purposes such as criticism, comment, news reporting, teaching (including multiple copies for classroom use), scholarship, or research, is not an infringement of copyright. In determining whether the use made of a work in any particular case is a fair use the factors to be considered shall include—

(1) the purpose and character of the use, including whether such use is of a commercial nature or is for nonprofit educational purposes;

(2) the nature of the copyrighted work;

(3) the amount and substantiality of the portion used in relation to the copyrighted work as a whole; and

(4) the effect of the use upon the potential market for or value of the copyrighted work.

17 U.S.C. § 107. The fair use doctrine requires applying this multi-factor test in light of the specific facts of the case.

The fair use defense arose in a civil case brought for downloading music over a peer-to-peer network in BMG Music v. Gonzalez, 430 F.3d 888 (7th Cir. 2005). The defendant, Cecilia Gonzalez, downloaded copyrighted music using the KaZaA file-sharing network. Judge Easterbrook held that the fair use defense did not apply to her conduct:

A "fair use" of copyrighted material is not infringement. Gonzalez insists that she was engaged in fair use under the terms of 17 U.S.C. § 107–or at least that a material dispute entitles her to a trial. It is undisputed, however, that she downloaded more than 1,370 copyrighted songs during a few weeks and kept them on her computer until she was caught. Her position is that she was just sampling music to determine what she liked enough to buy at retail. Because this suit was resolved on summary judgment, we must assume that Gonzalez is telling the truth when she says that she owned compact discs containing some of the songs before she downloaded them and that she purchased others later. She concedes, however, that she has never owned legitimate copies of 30 songs that she downloaded. (How many of the remainder she owned is disputed.)

Instead of erasing songs that she decided not to buy, she retained them. It is these 30 songs about which there is no dispute concerning ownership that formed the basis of the damages award. This is not a form of time-shifting, along the lines of *Sony Corp. of America v. Universal City Studios*, Inc., 464 U.S. 417 (1984) (*Betamax*). A copy downloaded, played, and retained on one's hard drive for future use is a direct substitute for a purchased copy-and without the benefit of the license fee paid to the broadcaster. The premise of *Betamax* is that the broadcast was licensed for one transmission and thus one viewing. *Betamax* held that shifting the time of this single viewing is fair use. The files that Gonzalez obtained, by contrast, were posted in violation of copyright law; there was no license covering a single transmission or hearing-and, to repeat, Gonzalez kept the copies. Time-shifting by an authorized recipient this is not. See William M. Landes & Richard A. Posner, *The Economic Structure of Intellectual Property Law* 117–22 (2003).

Section 107 provides that when considering a defense of fair use the court must take into account "(1) the purpose and character of the use, including whether such use is of a commercial nature or is for nonprofit educational purposes; (2) the nature of the copyrighted work; (3) the amount and substantiality of the portion used in relation to the copyrighted work as a whole; and (4) the effect of the use upon the potential market for or value of the copyrighted work." Gonzalez was not engaged in a nonprofit use; she downloaded (and kept) whole copyrighted songs (for which, as with poetry, copying of more than a couplet or two is deemed excessive); and she did this despite the fact that these works often are sold per song as well as per album. This leads her to concentrate on the fourth consideration: "the effect of the use upon the potential market for or value of the copyrighted work."

As she tells the tale, downloading on a try-before-you-buy basis is good advertising for copyright proprietors, expanding the value of their inventory. The Supreme Court thought otherwise in *Grokster*, with considerable empirical support. As file sharing has increased over the last four years, the sales of recorded music have dropped by approximately 30%. Perhaps other economic factors contributed, but the events likely are related. Music downloaded for free from the Internet is a close substitute for purchased music; many people are bound to keep the downloaded files without buying originals. That is exactly what Gonzalez did for at least 30 songs. It is no surprise, therefore, that the only appellate decision on point has held that downloading copyrighted songs cannot be defended as fair use, whether or not the recipient plans to buy songs she likes well enough to spring for. See *A & M Records, Inc. v. Napster, Inc.*, 239 F.3d 1004, 1014–19 (9th Cir. 2001).

Id. at 889–90.

For scholarly discussions of how the fair use doctrine does–and should– apply to copyright infringement online, *see* Ann Bartow, *Electrifying Copyright Norms and Making Cyberspace More Like a Book,* 48 Vill. L. Rev. 13 (2003); Niva Elkin–Koren, *Cyberlaw and Social Change: A Democratic Approach to Copyright Law in Cyberspace*, 14 Cardozo Arts & Ent. L.J. 215 (1996); Glynn S. Lunney, Jr., *The Death of Copyright: Digital Technology, Private Copying, and the Digital Millennium Copyright Act*, 87 Va. L. Rev.

813 (2001); Ruth Okediji, *Givers, Takers, and Other Kinds of Users: A Fair Use Doctrine for Cyberspace*, 53 Fla. L. Rev. 107 (2001).

3. Under 18 U.S.C. § 2319, the government must prove that the defendant "infringed at least 10 copies of one or more copyrighted works with a total retail value of more than $2,500 within a 180–day period." The House Report that accompanied the passage of this language contained the following explanation:

> The requirement that a requisite number of infringing copies or phonorecords be reproduced or distributed within a 180 day period serves a number of important purposes. First, it excludes from felony prosecution children making copies for friends as well as other incidental copying of copyrighted works having a relatively low retail value. Second, the requirement of reproducing or distributing at least 10 copies within a 180 day period removes the possibility that the increased penalties under the bill for computer program infringement can be used as a tool of harassment in business disputes over reverse engineering. Assuming arguendo that infringement due to unauthorized reverse engineering is established, and that the infringement was done with the requisite mens rea (which, as noted above, is unlikely), no felony liability should arise, since the Committee has been informed that reverse engineering does not require the reproduction of more than a handful of copies.

H.R. Rep. No. 102–997, at 6 (1992), *reprinted in* 1992 U.S.C.C.A.N. 3569, 3574. The Report continues:

> The phrase "of one or more copyrighted works" is intended to permit aggregation of different works of authorship to meet the required number of copies and retail value. For example, a defendant's reproduction of 5 copies of a copyrighted word processing computer program having a retail value of $1,300 and the reproduction of 5 copies of a copyrighted spreadsheet computer program also having a retail value of $1,300 would satisfy the requirement of reproducing 10 copies having a retail value of at least $2,500, if done within a 180 day period.

> The term "retail value" is deliberately undefined, since in most cases it will represent the price at which the work is sold through normal retail channels. At the same time, the Committee recognizes that copyrighted works are frequently infringed before a retail value has been established, and that in some cases, copyrighted works are not marketed through normal retail channels. Examples include motion pictures prints distributed only for theatrical release, and beta-test versions of computer programs. In such cases, the courts may look to the suggested retail price, the wholesale price, the replacement cost of the item, or financial injury caused to the copyright owner.

Id. at 3574–75.

B) The Willfulness Requirement

The willfulness requirement provides the most important line distinguishing civil from criminal copyright liability. Under current law, infringement cannot be a crime unless it is "willful." What does it mean to infringe a copyright willfully?

UNITED STATES v. MORAN

United States District Court for the District of Nebraska, 1991.
757 F. Supp. 1046.

RICHARD G. KOPF, United States Magistrate Judge.

The parties have consented to try this misdemeanor case before me. Trial was held on January 15, 1991, and briefs were received on January 23, 1991. I now find that the defendant is not guilty of the alleged willful infringement of a copyrighted video cassette in violation of 17 U.S.C. § 506(a).

FACTS

Dennis Moran, the defendant, is a full-time Omaha, Nebraska, police officer and the owner of a "mom-and-pop" movie rental business which rents video cassettes of copyrighted motion pictures to the public. On April 14, 1989, agents of the Federal Bureau of Investigation executed a court-ordered search warrant on the premises of Moran's business. The FBI seized various video cassettes appearing to be unauthorized copies of copyrighted motion pictures, including "Bat 21," "Big," "Crocodile Dundee II," "The Fourth Protocol," "Hell–Bound: Hellraiser II," and "Mystic Pizza." The parties have stipulated that these six motion pictures are validly copyrighted motion pictures. The parties have further stipulated that each of the six motion pictures was distributed to Moran, with the permission of the copyright holder, between February 1, 1989, and April 14, 1989. The parties have further stipulated that at least one of the movies identified was reproduced by Moran onto a video cassette, without the authorization of the copyright holder, placed into inventory for rental, and subsequently rented.

At the time the FBI executed the search warrant, Moran was fully cooperative. He told the FBI agents he put the "duped" copies out for rental and held the "originals" back because he feared the "original" motion pictures would be stolen or damaged. Moran told the FBI agents at the time they executed the warrant that he believed this practice was legal as long as he had purchased and was in possession of the "original" motion picture. Moran further advised the FBI agents that he would affix to the "duped" copies title labels for the copyrighted motion pictures and a copy of the FBI copyright warning label commonly found on video cassette tapes. Moran advised the FBI agents that he put the title labels and FBI warning on the tapes to stop customers from stealing or duplicating the tapes.

Moran testified at trial. He indicated that he had been employed as an Omaha, Nebraska, police officer for approximately twenty-two-and-a-half years, including service as a narcotics investigator and as a bodyguard to the mayor of the City of Omaha. Moran has a reputation for honesty among his associates.

Moran testified that he began to "insure" copyrighted video cassettes, meaning that he duplicated copyrighted video cassettes which he had validly purchased from distributors, when he realized copyrighted tapes were being vandalized. Moran testified he was under the impression that "insuring" tapes was legal whereas "pirating" tapes was not. For practical purposes, Moran defined "insuring" versus "pirating" as meaning that he could duplicate a copyrighted tape provided he had purchased the copyrighted tape and did not endeavor to rent both the copyrighted tape and the duplicate he had made. Moran testified that he formulated his belief about "insuring" versus "pirating" when talking with various colleagues in the business and from reading trade publications. However, Moran was not able to specifically identify the source of his information.

There was no persuasive evidence that Moran made multiple copies of each authorized version of the copyrighted material. The evidence indicates that Moran purchased more than one copyrighted tape of the same movie, but the persuasive evidence also reveals that Moran made only one copy of each copyrighted tape he purchased. There was no persuasive evidence that Moran endeavored to rent both the copyrighted tape and the duplicate. When Moran made the unauthorized copy, he put the unauthorized copy in a package made to resemble as closely as possible the package containing the original copyrighted motion picture Moran had purchased from an authorized distributor.

Law

Moran makes two arguments. First, Moran argues that the government must prove that he had the specific intent to violate the law, that is, he knew that what he was doing was illegal and he committed the act nevertheless. Secondly, Moran argues that he did not have the specific intent to violate the law and, as a consequence, should be found not guilty.

In pertinent part 17 U.S.C. § 506(a) punishes as a criminal any "person who infringes a copyright willfully and for purposes of commercial advantage or private financial gain." Pursuant to 17 U.S.C. § 106(3), the owner of a copyright has the exclusive right to "distribute copies ... of the copyrighted work to the public by sale or other transfer of ownership, or by rental, lease, or lending." The "exclusive right" of the owner of a copyright is subject to a variety of exceptions. *See* 17 U.S.C. §§ 107–118.

A.

It must first be determined whether the word "willfully," as used in 17 U.S.C. § 506(a), requires a showing of "bad purpose" or "evil motive" in the sense that there was an "intentional violation of a known legal duty." Adopting the research of the Motion Picture Association of America, the government argues that the term "willful" means only "an intent to copy and not to infringe." On the other hand, Moran argues that the use of the word "willful" implies the kind of specific intent required to be proven in federal tax cases, which is to say, a voluntary, intentional violation of a known legal duty.

The general rule is, of course, that ignorance of the law or mistake of the law is no defense to a criminal prosecution. However, when the term "willfully" is used in complex statutory schemes, such as federal criminal tax statutes, the term "willful" means a "voluntary, intentional violation of a known legal duty." *Cheek v. United States,* 498 U.S. 192 (1991) (holding in a criminal tax prosecution that a good faith misunderstanding of the law or a good faith belief that one is not violating the law negates willfulness, whether or not the claimed belief or misunderstanding is objectively reasonable). As the Court recognized in *Cheek,* in *United States v. Murdock,* 290 U.S. 389, 396 (1933), the Supreme Court said that:

> Congress did not intend that a person, by reason of a bona fide misunderstanding as to his liability for the tax, as to his duty to make a return, or as to the adequacy of the records he maintained, should become a criminal by his mere failure to measure up to the prescribed standard of conduct.

This was evidently so because "the proliferation of statutes and regulations has sometimes made it difficult for the average citizen to know and comprehend the extent of the duties and obligations imposed by the tax law."

Apparently no case has compared and analyzed the competing arguments, i.e., whether the word "willfully" requires either a showing of specific intent, as suggested by Moran, or the more generalized intent suggested by the government. Indeed, a leading text writer acknowledges that there are two divergent lines of cases, one of which requires specific intent and another which does not. 3 M. Nimmer & D. Nimmer, *Nimmer on Copyright,* § 15.01 at 15–5 n. 13 (1990) (hereinafter *Nimmer*). As pointed out by the government, some courts have suggested that "willful" only means an intent to copy, not to infringe. On the other hand, as suggested by Moran, other courts have seemingly required evidence of specific intent. At least two courts have specifically approved jury instructions essentially stating that an act of infringement done "willfully" means an act voluntarily and purposely done with specific intent to do that which the law forbids, that is to say, with bad purpose either to disobey or disregard the law. None of the cases recognize that there are divergent lines of cases on this point, and none of the cases endeavor to explain why one line of cases is more compelling than the other.

I am persuaded that under 17 U.S.C. § 506(a) "willfully" means that in order to be criminal the infringement must have been a "voluntary, intentional violation of a known legal duty." *Cheek,* 111 S.Ct. at 610. I am so persuaded because I believe that in using the word "willful" Congress intended to soften the impact of the common-law presumption that ignorance of the law or mistake of the law is no defense to a criminal prosecution by making specific intent to violate the law an element of federal criminal copyright offenses. I came to this conclusion after examining the use of the word "willful" in the civil copyright infringement context and applying that use to the criminal statute.

In the civil context there is "strict liability" for infringement, even where the infringement was "innocent." In this connection, a plaintiff in a civil case need not prove actual damages, but rather may seek what are called statutory damages. The term "willful" is used in the context of statutory damages, and it is instructive to compare the definition of the term "willful," as used in the civil context regarding statutory damages, with the definition of the term "willful" used in the criminal context.

In the statutory damage context, a civil plaintiff is generally entitled to recover no less than $250.00 nor more than $10,000.00 per act of infringement. 17 U.S.C. § 504(c)(1). But where the infringement is committed "willfully," the court in its discretion may increase the award of statutory damages up to a maximum of $50,000.00 per act of infringement. 17 U.S.C. § 504(c)(2). On the other hand, in the case of "innocent infringement," if the defendant sustains the burden of proving he/she was not aware, and had no reason to believe, that his/her acts constituted an infringement of the copyright, and the court so finds, the court may in its discretion reduce the applicable minimum to $100.00 per act of infringement. 17 U.S.C. § 504(c)(2).

As noted text writers have concluded, the meaning of the term "willful," used in 17 U.S.C. § 504, must mean that the infringement was with knowledge that the defendant's conduct constituted copyright infringement. *Nimmer, supra*, § 14.04[B][3] at 14–40.3–14–40.4 (citations omitted). Otherwise, there would be no point in providing specially for the reduction of awards to the $100.00 level in the case of "innocent" infringement since any infringement which was nonwillful would necessarily be innocent.

The circuit courts of appeal which have considered the issue have all adopted *Nimmer's* formulation with regard to the meaning of the word "willful" for purposes of 17 U.S.C. § 504(c)(2) and statutory civil damages. In other words, the term "willful," when used in the civil statutory damage statute, has consistently been interpreted to mean that the infringement must be "with knowledge that the defendant's conduct constitutes copyright infringement." *Nimmer, supra*, § 14.04[B][3] at 14–40.3–14–40.4.

There is nothing in the text of the criminal copyright statute, the overall scheme of the copyright laws, or the legislative history to suggest that Congress intended the word "willful," when used in the criminal statute, to mean simply, as the government suggests, an intent to copy. Rather, since Congress used "willful" in the civil damage copyright context to mean that the infringement must take place with the defendant being knowledgeable that his/her conduct constituted copyright infringement, there is no compelling reason to adopt a less stringent requirement in the criminal copyright context. Accordingly, I find that "willfully," when used in 17 U.S.C. § 506(a), means a "voluntary, intentional violation of a known legal duty."

B.

Having determined that the standard enunciated by the Supreme Court in *Cheek* applies, it is important to recognize that the rule does not require that a defendant's belief that his conduct is lawful be judged by an objective standard. Rather, the test is whether Moran truly believed that the copyright laws did not prohibit him from making one copy of a video cassette he had purchased in order to "insure" against vandalism. In other words, the test is not whether Moran's view was objectively reasonable, but rather, whether Moran truly believed that the law did not proscribe his conduct. Of course, the more unreasonable the asserted belief or misunderstanding, the more likely it is that the finder of fact will consider the asserted belief or misunderstanding to be nothing more than simple disagreement with known legal duties imposed by the law, and will find that the government has carried its burden of proving knowledge.

Most of the government's argument that it proved beyond a reasonable doubt that Moran violated the criminal copyright statute, even if the word "willfully" is defined as Moran suggests, is based upon the assumption that Moran's beliefs must be "objectively" reasonable. As indicated above, Moran's beliefs need not have been objectively reasonable; rather, if Moran truly believed that he was not subject to the copyright laws, then his subjective belief would defeat a finding that he "willfully" violated the statute.

First, I note that I had an opportunity to observe Moran when he testified. Moran struck me as an honest, albeit naive, person. I was left with the definite impression that Moran was befuddled and bewildered by the criminal prosecution.

Second, although Moran is a local police officer of long standing, there is nothing in his background to suggest any particular sophistication about business matters, and there is no evidence to suggest that he has any particular knowledge about the intricacies of the copyright laws. When confronted by FBI agents upon the execution of the search warrant, Moran was entirely cooperative. On the day the search warrant was executed, he told his story in the same way he now tells his story.

Third, Moran said he had heard from others and read in various publications that it was legally appropriate to engage in the practice he called "insuring." Moran could not cite the specific source of his information. In this regard, I note that the copyright laws permit libraries and archives to replace a copyrighted article that is damaged, deteriorated, lost, or stolen, if the library or archives have, after reasonable effort, determined that an unused replacement cannot be obtained at a fair price. 17 U.S.C. § 108(c). While Moran obviously did not operate his business as a library or archives, the government's assertion that the practice of "insuring" is patently unreasonable is belied by the recognition that under certain circumstances certain users of copyrighted materials may lawfully engage in copying activity which is similar to Moran's conduct.

Fourth, Moran testified that he made only one copy of the original motion picture purchased from the authorized distributor. The government doubts his testimony, but offers no persuasive evidence to contradict it. Moreover, Moran testified that he never rented both the original copyrighted version of the video cassette purchased from the authorized distributor and the copy he made. Instead, he testified that he always held back the original motion picture. Once again, the government doubts this testimony in its brief, but offers no persuasive evidence to the contrary. Furthermore, the evidence indicates that Moran purchased more than one authorized cassette of a particular motion picture, but made only one duplicate for each authorized cassette purchased.

This evidence suggests that Moran was not acting with a willful intention to violate the copyright laws because if he had such an intention it would make absolutely no sense to purchase multiple authorized video cassettes and then make only one duplicate of each authorized cassette. It would have been far simpler, and certainly more lucrative, for Moran to purchase one authorized cassette of a particular motion picture and make multiple copies from the authorized version. In this way Moran would have had to pay only one fee. The fact that Moran seems to have consistently followed the practice of buying an authorized version, but making only one copy of it, suggests that he was acting in accordance with his belief that to duplicate an authorized version in order to "insure it" was lawful so long as only one copy was made and the authorized version and copy were not both rented.

Fifth, the government argues that Moran must have known that what he was doing constituted a copyright infringement because he had before him the FBI warning label and in fact affixed such labels to the unauthorized copies he made. In pertinent part, the FBI warning states, "Federal law provides severe civil and criminal penalties for the *unauthorized* reproduction, distribution or exhibition of copyrighted motion pictures and video tapes" (emphasis added). Moran explained that he thought these warning labels applied to the renting public, not to him. The use of the word "unauthorized" on the warning label suggested to Moran that vendors who had purchased an authorized version were not subject to the legal restrictions expressed in the warning to the extent that the practice of "insuring" was legal. As Moran suggests, the FBI warning label does not specifically address the claim of legality professed by Moran. Accordingly, Moran's failure to heed the warning label is not determinative.

Sixth, the government further argues that Moran's effort to place the unauthorized copy into a video cassette package displaying a label on its spine and an FBI warning label suggests a sinister motivation. I disagree. Moran's testimony, as I understood it, indicated that when he made a copy he endeavored to make the duplicate look like the original in all respects. After all, the whole purpose of the practice of "insuring" was to use the unauthorized copy in lieu of the original when renting to the public. It was perfectly consistent with Moran's view of the law to make the unauthorized copy look as nearly as possible like the authorized version.

In summary, when Moran's actions were viewed from the totality of the circumstances, the government failed to convince me beyond a reasonable doubt that Moran acted willfully. Moran is a long-time street cop who was fully cooperative with law enforcement authorities. He is obviously not sophisticated and, at least from the record, his business operation of renting movies to the public was not large or sophisticated. Rather, Moran's business appears to have been of the "mom-and-pop" variety. Moran's practice of "insuring," while obviously shifting the risk of loss from Moran to the copyright holder, was conducted in such a way as not to maximize profits, which one assumes would have been his purpose if he had acted willfully. For example, Moran purchased multiple authorized copies of the same movie, but he made only one unauthorized copy for each authorized version purchased. This suggests that Moran truly believed that what he was doing was in fact legal. I therefore find Moran not guilty.

Notes and Questions

1. The willfulness requirement is designed to ensure that defendants are not held criminally liable when the law is murky. It is an exception to the usual rule that "ignorance of the law is no excuse." When Congress uses the willfulness standard, ignorance of the law *is* an excuse. Criminal liability is reserved for cases in which a defendant knew he acted wrongfully.

Does the willfulness requirement create a sensible line between civil and criminal copyright liability? A defendant can have an entirely unreasonable belief that his conduct was lawful. Under the willfulness standard as construed in *Cheek* and applied in *Moran*, however, no crime has occurred so long as the defendant actually believes that he has acted legally. How does a defendant know whether his conduct is illegal if there are so few cases addressing the scope of copyright liability online?

2. How can the government prove willfulness in court? In most criminal cases, the defendant will exercise his Fifth Amendment right not to testify. The government must collect other evidence of the defendant's state of mind with respect to the legality of his actions. Perhaps the defendant took steps to hide his conduct that are generally consistent with knowledge that particular conduct is illegal. Perhaps the defendant admitted to colleagues that he realized he was breaking the law. Defendants may also elect to waive their privilege and testify that they didn't know that what they did was illegal. The prosecution will then hinge on whether the factfinder believes the defendant.

3. Despite the clear holding of *Moran*, the exact meaning of willfulness in criminal copyright law is not necessarily settled:

> What it means to be "willful" in the context of copyright infringement is far from clear. Under the Copyright Act, willful infringement is used both as an element of criminal infringement and as a standard for increased statutory damages in a civil infringement suit. Yet what it

means to be a willful infringer is not defined in the Copyright Act. Perhaps due to this lack of definition, willfulness, as interpreted by the courts, seems to mean different things even within the Copyright Act itself.

The lack of a clear meaning for the term willful in the legislation is not surprising given that courts also have had great difficulty in defining the term. As the Supreme Court has recognized, "[t]he word 'willfully' is sometimes said to be 'a word of many meanings' whose construction is often dependent on the context in which it appears." Congressional failure to define willful leaves the task to the courts.

Lydia Pallas Loren, *Digitization, Commodification, Criminalization: The Evolution of Criminal Copyright Infringement and the Importance of the Willfulness Requirement*, 77 Wash. U. L.Q. 835, 872 (1999).

The differences in the various interpretations are generally minor ones, however. A majority of modern courts have adopted the *Cheek* approach applied in *Moran*. At least one court has suggested a different test: a decision by the Seventh Circuit concludes that a defendant acts willfully when he realizes "a high likelihood of being held by a court of competent jurisdiction to be [in] violation of a criminal statute." United States v. Heilman, 614 F.2d 1133, 1138 (7th Cir. 1980). It's worth wondering how different these standards are: What is the difference between knowing that you are violating the law and realizing a high likelihood of being held in violation of a criminal statute? *Cf.* Model Penal Code § 2.02(2)(b)(ii) (defining "knowingly" in the case of a conduct element as being "aware that it is practically certain that his conduct will cause such a result").

4. *Willfulness and the Digital Millennium Copyright Act.* The Digital Millennium Copyright Act (DMCA), Pub. L. No. 105–304 (1998), is an effort to maintain the effectiveness of technological restrictions that copyright owners may place on access to their copyrighted works to prevent unauthorized copying and distribution. In response to the tendency of digital technologies and the Internet to facilitate copyright infringement, some copyright owners have placed technological controls on their copyrighted works. Instead of hoping that users will follow the rules of copyright law, these copyright owners have used computer code to place the digital equivalent of "locks" around their copyrighted works to prevent unauthorized copying and distribution. Unsurprisingly, the presence of digital locks around copyrighted works has generated new digital lockpicking tools—computer programs that can be used to circumvent the technological restrictions on access and copying of copyrighted works.

The DMCA prohibits possession and distribution of digital lock-picking tools designed to circumvent technological restrictions on access to copyrighted works. By restricting access to digital lockpicking tools, the thinking goes, the DMCA will result in fewer picked locks. Fewer picked locks will mean more enforceable restrictions on copying and distributing copyrighted works, counterbalancing the Internet's ability to facilitate copyright infringement. Criminal liability under the DMCA resembles criminal liability for copyright law: it also contains a requirement that the infringement must be "willful." 17 U.S.C. § 1204(a).

The meaning of willfulness played an important role in the first criminal prosecution brought under the anticircumvention provisions of the DMCA. A Russian software company, ElcomSoft, created a program called the "Advanced eBook Processor" that cracked the protections on Adobe Systems' eBooks. The FBI arrested ElcomSoft employee Dmitry Sklyarov for his role in creating the Advanced eBook Processor, and Sklyarov eventually agreed to testify for the government against ElcomSoft. The two-week trial focused on ElcomSoft's state of mind in creating and distributing their product. Sklyarov and ElcomSoft President Alexander Katalov testified that they did not believe their software was illegal and had no intent for it to be used for illegal purposes.

The jury rendered a verdict of not guilty. According to press accounts, the jury acquitted because they did not believe the company acted willfully:

> Jury foreman Dennis Strader said the jurors agreed ElcomSoft's product was illegal but acquitted the company because they believed the company didn't mean to violate the law.
>
> "We didn't understand why a million-dollar company would put on their Web page an illegal thing that would ruin their whole business if they were caught," he said in an interview after the verdict. Strader added that the panel found the DMCA itself confusing, making it easy for jurors to believe that executives from Russia might not fully understand it.

Lisa M. Bowman, *Elcomsoft Verdict: Not Guilty*, CNET News.com, Dec. 17, 2002, http://news.com.com/2100–1023–978176.html.

C) Intent to Profit

Should copyright law require an intent to profit or achieve private financial gain before attaching criminal penalties? It did before 1997. In 1997, however, Congress passed the No Electronic Theft (NET) Act, Pub. L. No. 105–147 (1997), which eliminated the requirement. Under current law, intent to achieve commercial advantage or private financial gain is important for sentencing purposes but not liability. The NET Act is generally understood as a response to changing technology, and especially computers and the Internet. Was it a wise move? To evaluate this question, consider the facts from a fairly typical criminal copyright case from the early 1980s.

UNITED STATES v. SHABAZZ

United States Court of Appeals for the Eleventh Circuit, 1984.
724 F.2d 1536.

JONES, Senior Circuit Judge.

The appellant was engaged in the business of reproducing and distributing pirated eight track and cassette tapes. "Bootleg" or pirated tapes are the results of the illegal and unauthorized duplication of a sound recording without the permission of the copyright owners. Pirated tapes reproduce the sound but do not reproduce the tape cover or packaging of the legitimate tapes. The creation of a copyrighted tape begins with the studio master recording in the studio. One of the first duplicates of the studio master recording accompanies the copyright application. Another is sent to the Federal Bureau of Investigation for use in copyright infringement cases. A third duplicate is used for the production of legitimate copyrighted records and tapes.

The appellant purchased sophisticated audio equipment which was used for reproduction of audio tapes. He also purchased large quantities of unrecorded eight track and cassette tapes. He ordered eight track and cassette tape labels to be printed which listed the musicians and songs. He hired three employees to reproduce eight track and cassette tapes of copyrighted sound recordings of popular music. His employees, working in his home, would review work orders and reproduce selected music tapes by use of a high speed duplicator. The employees checked the tapes to insure music selection and sound quality. The tapes were individually wrapped in cellophane, placed in boxes and then sold.

An investigation lead to the issuance of a search warrant for the appellant's home and automobile. Federal agents seized blank and legitimate copyrighted tapes, duplicating equipment, blank and preprinted eight track and cassette labels, and various business records and materials. Ten legitimate copyrighted tapes and ten pirated copies were seized. The appellant was arrested for violating United States copyright laws under Title 17, §§ 106(1) and 506(a).

At the trial the government introduced ten copyright registrations, one for each tape alleged to be an infringement. Copyright owner representatives testified to the ownership of copyrights of the music recordings and to the absence of authorization for appellant to reproduce the legitimate copyrighted tapes. They also testified that it was a regular practice to send duplicates of such copyrighted recordings to the FBI for use in criminal copyright infringement cases. However, none of the copyright owner representatives had compared the duplicate sent to the FBI with either the studio master recording or the duplicate which accompanied the application to the United States copyright office.

Two FBI agents testified to examining the tapes seized from appellant's home. One agent testified that he listened to the seized legitimate copyrighted tapes and pirated copies to make sure the music listed on the tape label or box was contained on that particular tape. The second agent, an experienced aural examiner, was qualified by the district court as an expert witness. He acknowledged that the FBI received copyright owners duplicates to compare legitimate copyrighted tapes with pirated tapes. The expert compared the copyright owners duplicates with the legitimate copyrighted tapes and the pirated tapes seized from appellant's home and determined that the music on all three tapes had been produced from the same original source. The expert also testified that during the course of his examination of the pirated tapes, he listened to the entire tape and found that the tape labels and boxes accurately reflected the musical contents. The expert did not compare the copyright owners duplicates or the pirated tapes with the studio master recording or the duplicate which accompanied the application to the United States

Copyright Office. There was no evidence that the copyright owner duplicates were tampered with or altered in any way or contained anything other than the music indicated on the tape label or box. A jury returned a verdict of guilty to ten counts of copyright infringement.

The appellant asserts that the government failed to prove that any of the tapes introduced in evidence were made for commercial profit as required by the Statute. An employee identified specific tapes made in bulk under appellant's direction as reproduced for local and out of state sale. The appellant sold pirated tapes, solicited wholesale customers, and shipped large quantities of tapes out of state. This evidence is sufficient to show that the tapes produced were made with the intention to make a profit. It is not necessary that he actually made a profit. The only requirement is that he engaged in business "to hopefully or possibly make a profit."

Notes and Questions

1. Consider the economics of the operation in *Shabazz*. Shabazz created a considerable business enterprise to copy and distribute copyrighted materials. He had to purchase sophisticated equipment and pay several employees. The case for prohibiting conduct such as the operation in *Shabazz* is easy to make: Shabazz had created his own business that competed against the operations of the legitimate copyright owners. He was trying to line his pockets with money that should have gone to the copyright holders. Further, note the direct correlation between the scope of the operation and the intent to profit. Each bootleg cassette was costly for Shabazz to produce, and it seems unlikely that he would have been willing to engage in such widespread bootlegging without an economic incentive. In that environment, the statutory requirement of intent to profit makes sense. The requirement distinguishes a case like *Shabazz* from a case of small scale or personal copying.

Next consider how the picture changes when we shift to digital reproduction and distribution of copyrighted materials. Digital technologies bring the cost of copying and distributing files close to zero. A person can set up a server, connect it to the Internet, and make copyrighted files available to thousands of people at little or no cost to himself. How should the law respond, if at all?

2. *United States v. LaMacchia and the NET Act.* The traditional rationale of the intent-to-profit requirement caught up to the new facts of the Internet with the case of David LaMacchia. In 1994, LaMacchia was a 21 year-old college student at the Massachusetts Institute of Technology. LaMacchia set up an electronic bulletin board and encouraged visitors to share popular copyrighted software such as Excel and WordPerfect. Users could both upload software they possessed and download software they wanted, all for free and without the permission of the copyright holders. LaMacchia did not have an intent to profit from his efforts, which meant that he could not be prosecuted under the then-existing criminal copyright laws.

Prosecutors instead tried to prosecute LaMacchia under the wire fraud statute, 18 U.S.C. § 1343. Judge Stearns dismissed the indictment on the ground that trying to prosecute a copyright offense using the wire fraud statute ran afoul of Dowling v. United States, 473 U.S. 207 (1985). *See* United States v. LaMacchia, 871 F. Supp. 535 (D. Mass. 1994). In *Dowling*, prosecutors charged a defendant who had manufactured "bootleg" Elvis Presley records and distributed them in interstate commerce under the Interstate Transportation of Stolen Property Act, codified at 18 U.S.C. § 2314. In an opinion by Justice Blackmun, the Court held that the government could not use the ITSP Act to punish what amounted to a scheme of copyright infringement. Doing so would allow the government to circumvent Congress's design to have only narrow criminal liability for copyright infringement.

In the *LaMacchia* case, Judge Stearns held that the same rationale blocked the government from prosecuting LaMacchia under the wire fraud statute:

> While the government's objective is a laudable one, particularly when the facts alleged in this case are considered, its interpretation of the wire fraud statute would serve to criminalize the conduct of not only persons like LaMacchia, but also the myriad of home computer users who succumb to the temptation to copy even a single software program for private use. It is not clear that making criminals of a large number of consumers of computer software is a result that even the software industry would consider desirable.

> Accordingly, I rule that the decision of the Supreme Court in *Dowling v. United States* precludes LaMacchia's prosecution for criminal copyright infringement under the wire fraud statute.

> This is not, of course, to suggest that there is anything edifying about what LaMacchia is alleged to have done. If the indictment is to be believed, one might at best describe his actions as heedlessly irresponsible, and at worst as nihilistic, self-indulgent, and lacking in any fundamental sense of values. Criminal as well as civil penalties should probably attach to willful, multiple infringements of copyrighted software even absent a commercial motive on the part of the infringer. One can envision ways that the copyright law could be modified to permit such prosecution. But, it is the legislature, not the Court which is to define a crime, and ordain its punishment.

LaMacchia, 871 F. Supp. at 544.

Congress responded by passing the NET Act in 1997 to "reverse the practical consequences of United States v. LaMacchia." H.R. Rep. No. 105–339, at 3 (1997). Under the NET Act, individuals can receive criminal punishments for copyright infringement even if they do not have commercial motives. Any person who commits willful copyright infringement can be:

> imprisoned not more than 3 years, or fined in the amount set forth in this title, or both, if the offense consists of the reproduction or distribution of 10 or more copies or phonorecords of 1 or more copyrighted works, which have a total retail value of $2,500 or more;

18 U.S.C. § 2319(c)(1). If the government can show that the infringement took place "for purposes of commercial advantage or private financial gain," 17 U.S.C. § 506(a)(1), the maximum penalty is raised from three years to

five years. *See* 18 U.S.C. § 2319(b)(1). The NET Act also redefined the term "financial gain" so that it now "includes receipt, or expectation of receipt, of anything of value, including the receipt of other copyrighted works." 17 U.S.C. § 101.

3. Is the NET Act too broad? Lydia Pallas Loren, *Digitization, Commodification, Criminalization: The Evolution of Criminal Copyright Infringement and the Importance of the Willfulness Requirement*, 77 Wash. U. L.Q. 835, 871 (1999):

> Even if comfort is found in relying on prosecutorial discretion to curb the possible over-breadth of the NET Act, the mere threat of criminal prosecution will deter at least some lawful uses of copyrighted works. Unfortunately some of these lawful uses are precisely the types of conduct that the policies underlying copyright law seek to encourage, not discourage. While the NET Act was passed for the express purpose of deterring the sort of mass-scale infringement that occurred in the *LaMacchia* case, it may result in discouraging other types of lawful activity thereby hampering the ultimate aim of copyright which is to promote the progress of knowledge and learning.

4. The NET Act expands the scope of criminal liability to counter the effect of technological developments. But do those same technological developments alter the potential harms that follow from copyright infringement, and if so, what effect should that have on the scope of criminal liability?

> Technological change * * * suggests it is time to revisit [the need for criminal copyright law]. It may no longer be necessary to rely so heavily on law to provide an incentive to create. The tools of digitization, broadband capacity, and the Internet make low-cost distribution a reality that may stimulate creation. Although in its infant stages, Internet commerce allows authors, musicians, and others to sell their work directly to consumers. Avoiding the added costs imposed by distribution companies may decrease costs to consumers.

Geraldine Szott Moohr, *The Crime Of Copyright Infringement: An Inquiry Based On Morality, Harm, And Criminal Theory*, 83 B.U. L. Rev. 731, 758 (2003). Professor Moohr continues:

> Adding criminal penalties to enhanced civil protection similarly increases the possibility of a decline in innovation; the threat of criminal sanctions can influence law-abiding citizens to refrain from engaging in completely legal conduct. Fear of criminal penalties may inhibit second-generation creators from working with material they believe may be off-limits—even when such use is in fact lawful. Those who create new knowledge and information products inevitably build on the work of others, so chilling lawful use of copyrighted material could decrease rather than increase production of new work.

Id. at 759–60.

Is it likely that the additional threat of criminal penalties will have a marginal effect of deterring innovation relating to the use and distribution of copyrighted materials? Does your answer depend on the rarity of criminal copyright prosecutions?

5. *Private financial gain and the DMCA.* It is interesting to note, in light of *LaMacchia* and the NET Act, that the criminal provisions of the Digital Millennium Copyright Act apply only to willful conduct committed "for purposes of commercial advantage or private financial gain." 17 U.S.C. § 1204(a). In addition, the criminal prohibitions cannot apply to any "non-profit library, archives, educational institution, or public broadcasting entity." 17 U.S.C. § 1204(b). Why did Congress use a narrower criminal prohibition for the DMCA than for copyright law?

D) Prosecutorial Discretion

The broad scope of criminal copyright liability places a premium on prosecutorial discretion. The law permits prosecutors to charge a large number of infringers. Should they? Who should be targeted?

UNITED STATES DEPARTMENT OF JUSTICE— ILLEGAL "WAREZ" ORGANIZATIONS AND INTERNET PIRACY

http://www.cybercrime.gov/ob/OBorg&pr.htm

In the early 1990s, groups of individuals working in underground networks organized themselves into competitive gangs that obtained software, "cracked," or "ripped" it (i.e. removed various forms of copy protections) and posted it on the Internet for other members of the group. This network of individuals and groups, numbering in the thousands, evolved into what is today loosely called the "warez scene" or community.

At the top of the warez scene are a handful of "release" groups that specialize in being the first to obtain, crack (i.e., remove or circumvent copyright protections), and distribute or release the latest software, games, movies, or music to the warez scene. Frequently, these new "releases" reach the Internet days or weeks before the product is commercially available. Release groups compete against each other to attain a reputation as the fastest providers of the highest quality, free pirated software, including utility and application software, computer and console games, and movies.

As technology has advanced, the top warez groups have become more technologically sophisticated and security conscious to avoid detection by law enforcement. Many of the elite groups communicate about warez business only through private e-mail servers, sometimes using encryption, and in closed, invite-only IRC channels. Additionally, most members disguise their true IP addresses (and thus their true locations) when communicating in IRC by routing their communications through "virtual hosts" or bounce boxes. Finally, many warez groups protect their large FTP archive sites—which can contain tens of thousands of copies of software, games, music, and music for free downloading— through a combination of security measures that include bounce sites, automated programs for IP address and user password verification, and the use of non-standard ports for FTP traffic.

The specific reasons that an individual becomes and remains involved in the top warez "release" or "courier" organizations may vary. However, it is almost always the case that a primary motivator is the desire to gain access to a virtually unlimited amount of free software, game, movie, and/or music titles available on the huge file storage and transfer sites (FTP sites) maintained by, or offering user privileges to, these elite warez groups. These computer sites not only offer a tremendous variety of quality copyrighted works, but they also generally have extremely fast Internet connections for rapid, efficient download and uploading. Other possible motivators or enticements for warez group members may include: (1) the thrill and social comraderie they obtain through clandestine participation in illegal activity; (2) the improved personal reputation or fame in the warez scene that comes with membership in the "top" groups, and in helping to keep those groups on top; and (3) financial profit, as some involved in the larger warez organizations take the pirated products and sell them for commercial gain.

Today it is estimated that approximately 8–10 of the largest warez "release" groups in the world are responsible for the majority of the pirated software, games, and movies available on the Internet. These highly organized "release" groups specialize in being the first to release new pirated software, games, and movies to the warez community for unauthorized reproduction and further distribution worldwide. Individual groups generally specialize in "releasing" only certain types of copyrighted works; for instance, two of the oldest groups, DrinkOrDie and Razor1911, specialize in releasing application software and PC or console games, respectively. In addition to their release work, these warez groups also maintain large FTP archive (or "leech") sites for the benefit of their members and others engaged in Internet software piracy. An average FTP archive site may contain between 10,000 to 25,000 individual titles of software, games, movies, and music, all of which is made available for free downloading ("leeching") by group members and valued warez associates or contributors to the site.

The top-level release groups are highly structured organizations with defined roles and leadership hierarchy. These organizations generally have a Leader, who oversees and directs all aspects of the group; three Council members or Senior Staff, who direct and manage the day-to-day operations of the group; 10 to 15 Staff, who frequently are the most active and skilled contributors to the group's day to day "release" work; and finally, the general membership, whose functions and involvement in the group vary. Members generally only interact via the Internet and know each other only by their screen nicknames, such as "bandido," "hackrat," "erupt," or "doodad."

A pirated version of a software application, game or movie is frequently available worldwide even before it is made commercially available to the public. In many instances, warez groups illegally obtain advanced copies of copyrighted products from company or industry insiders, then crack the copyright protections before distributing the pirated versions on the Internet to an ever-expanding web of FTP sites worldwide. Within hours of first being posted on the Internet, a pirated version of a copyrighted product can be found on thousands of Internet sites worldwide. Eventually, these pirated versions find their way onto pay-for-access websites from China to the U.S., where users are charged monthly or per-purchase fees for downloading the unauthorized copies.

Additionally, these warez "releases" provide an unending supply of new product to counterfeit hard goods criminal organizations. For instance, almost every new PC and console game is "cracked" and available on warez sites either before or within 24 hours of their commercial release ("0–Day" releases). Hard good pirate syndicates in Asia and Russia (for example) will download a "warez" 0–Day game release and mass produce it at optical disc manufacturing facilities. These counterfeit hard goods are then illegally sold in foreign markets often weeks before the manufacturer ships the authentic goods for the official release date in those particular markets. This can cripple the market for the legitimate products.

The "Release" Process:

Speed and efficiency are essential to the process for preparing and packaging new pirated software for release and distribution to the warez community. The process generally has four stages and can occur within a matter of hours:

SUPPLY: First, a group member known as a supplier will post an original digital copy of new computer software to the group's Internet drop site, which is a computer where software is posted for retrieval by members of the group. Frequently, warez suppliers are company insiders who have access to final versions of the company's new software products before their public release date.

CRACK: Once the new supply is posted to the drop site, another group member, known as a cracker, retrieves the software and removes or circumvents all embedded copyright protection controls (e.g., serial numbers, tags, duplication controls, dongle protections, security locks).

TESTING and PACKING: Following a successful crack, the software must be tested to ensure that it is still fully operational. Following testing, the software is then "packed," or broken into file packets that are more easily distributed by other group members.

PRE–RELEASE/COURIER: After the software has been cracked, tested and packed, it is returned to the drop site, where individuals who will transfer or distribute the pirated copy across the Internet are waiting for new arrivals. Once picked up by the "preers," the illegal product is distributed to warez locations around the world in a matter of minutes. In each instance, the new "release" will include an information file (aka ".nfo file") which, among other things, proclaims and attributes credit for the release to the originating warez group. These messages allow groups and their members to get the credit they crave and develop not only their own reputations within the scene, but also that of the group.

Notes and Questions

1. Should members of warez groups be prosecuted? Would such prosecutions advance the goals of deterrence, retribution, or incapacitation?

2. Consider one prosecutor's perspective on selecting which intellectual property crimes should be prosecuted:

> What makes a given case attractive to federal prosecutors and law enforcement agents? Certainly the amount of the loss can be a significant factor. Because it is often difficult to measure the amount of foregone revenues that an infringement costs the true owner of goods, typically loss is measured by the value of the infringing or counterfeit goods. In addition to the amount of loss, prosecutors may also look at how blatant the piracy is, including whether the suspects had a license to produce the product, and whether they continued production greatly in excess of authorized quantities or after the license had expired.

> Prosecutors may also consider the adequacy of civil remedies. If an infringer has deep pockets and is not likely to flee a lawsuit, the substantial civil penalties available may suffice. On the other hand, if an infringer runs a fly-by-night operation with few ties to the community and little money to pay a judgment or has infringed the copyrights of a variety of victims, it may seem more appropriate for the government to file criminal charges to vindicate the rights of the victims.

> Finally, a case with novel or interesting facts often appeals to law enforcement entities hoping to deter other potential infringers in the community.

Kent Walker, *Federal Criminal Remedies for the Theft of Intellectual Property,* 16 Hastings Comm. & Ent. L.J. 681, 689 (1994).

3. *Copyright, criminal punishment, and the separation of powers.* Criminal copyright liability is broad in theory, but very few prosecutions are brought. Cases that are prosecuted tend to involve egregious facts far from the thresholds of liability.

The gap between the law and its enforcement owes largely to the different roles of legislators and prosecutors. Prosecutors tend to pick cases in which the defendant is morally culpable and societal losses are clear. The social norms surrounding copyright are unclear, however. Some people analogize infringement to theft, but others analogize it to sharing. In this environment, few prosecutors will be interested in prosecuting copyright cases. Indeed, the federal government has not brought *any* criminal prosecutions against individuals for using the Internet to obtain copyrighted materials without permission for their personal use. Copyright owners have brought civil lawsuits against users, and prosecutors have charged warez group members, but prosecutors have not charged mere users.

The legislative picture is quite different. Legislators decide what is a crime and what is not a crime. Legislators give prosecutors the tools to bring prosecutions when prosecutors wish to do so. When Congress wants to encourage more prosecutions, however, its options are limited. Members of Congress cannot order prosecutors to indict particular kinds of cases. Congress can fund task forces and provide money to hire prosecutors in particular areas, but even then it cannot determine what cases are brought. Legislators are also influenced by powerful lobbying groups, including those of copyright owners and their representatives. If Congress wants to "do something" to address copyright infringement, its primary option in the context of criminal law is to broaden the scope of criminality. Congress can expand the scope of what is criminal even if few if any prosecutors want to bring the cases that Congress has permitted them to bring.

This dynamic may explain the basic contour of criminal copyright law. The law is tremendously broad on paper, and penalties are harsh. But the law is actually used only very rarely. If you could design a regime of enforcing copyrights from scratch, would you propose something like the current system? Or would you favor less draconian laws combined with more enforcement?

4. *Peer-to-peer filesharing and criminal copyright infringement.* Starting in the late 1990s, peer-to-peer technologies such as Napster began to transform how individuals obtain copies of copyrighted works online. Peer-to-peer technologies have generated civil lawsuits against the owners and creators of the technologies. *See, e.g.,* A & M Records, Inc. v. Napster, Inc., 239 F.3d 1004 (9th Cir. 2001). These technologies have not led to criminal indictments, however. Why not? Is the barrier the willfulness requirement? Or is the reason that copyright owners can bring civil suits, and law enforcement intervention may not be necessary?

The design of different peer-to-peer technologies may also influence the role of criminal law. Napster's file-sharing technology was centralized. The Napster company ran centralized servers, providing a clear target for civil or criminal legal action. The next generation of file-sharing technologies is distributed. Programs such as Gnutella and Freenet allow users to make their own files available to others, as well as to access the files of others who use the software. No centralized database exists.

Do distributed file-sharing programs make it impossible for the government to enforce copyright laws? One option would be for prosecutors to use techniques modeled on the enforcement of speeding laws over the "distributed network" of public highways. Every state has laws that regulate the speed of cars driven on public roads. These laws are difficult to enforce, however, as the roads are decentralized and a single police officer can at most monitor one location on one road at any given time. However, the possibility (however low) that a driver will be ticketed for speeding does appear to impact the speed at which most people drive. Although most drivers speed, they presumably speed less often and less egregiously than they would if they knew that the government was not policing the roads. Should the government mirror this strategy to enforce copyright laws on the Internet? If so, how?

B. CRIMES AGAINST PERSONS

There are two major types of computer crimes that can be categorized as crimes against persons. The first type covers threats and harassment, and the second covers invasion of privacy crimes such as wiretapping. These crimes address harms to individuals that violate their sense of privacy and safety. They raise a difficult question: What kinds of online conduct violate an individual's sense of privacy and safety enough that it should be declared a crime? How can we draw lines between criminal and non-criminal conduct in light of the contingent and rapidly evolving norms of computer usage? Most of the materials focus on threats and harassment law. Invasion of privacy crimes will be covered briefly in this section, and a detailed discussion appears in Chapter 6.

1. THREATS AND HARASSMENT

Criminal laws that prohibit threats and harassment attempt to balance two policy concerns. On one hand, the laws try to deter and punish the social harms associated with threats and harassment. Those harms include both inducing fear that threats will be carried out and the harms that follow if they actually are. On the other hand, the First Amendment's protection of free speech sharply restricts the government's ability to punish threats and harassment. Threats can be a form of speech, and the Supreme Court has held that governments can only punish threats that amount to "true threats." In light of this balance, understanding threat and harassment law requires understanding two sources of law: the statutory laws that create the prohibitions and the constitutional doctrines that limit their application.

Three federal statutes address online threats and harassment. The most important is 18 U.S.C. § 875, and specifically 18 U.S.C. § 875(c). This section broadly prohibits interstate threats to harm a person:

> Whoever transmits in interstate or foreign commerce any communication containing any threat to kidnap any person or any threat to injure the person of another, shall be fined under this title or imprisoned not more than five years, or both.

Section 875(d) also covers extortionate threats to harm property, and is supplemented by the computer-specific extortionate threat prohibition found in 18 U.S.C. § 1030(a)(7).

A second statute that prohibits both threats and harassment is 47 U.S.C. § 223. Section 223 was originally enacted as a telephone misuse and harassment statute passed as part of the federal Communications Act of 1934. Over time, its scope has expanded from telephones to other communications devices. The statute in its current form is complex and quite long, and some of the sections are dormant due to obvious First Amendment difficulties. (The Supreme Court's decision in Reno v. ACLU, 521 U.S. 844 (1997), invalidated parts of § 223 that were amended by a part of the Telecommunications Act of 1996 known as the Communications Decency Act.) Two provisions in § 223 are occasionally used to prosecute Internet threats and harassment. These two provisions, 47 U.S.C. § 223(a)(1)(C) and § 223(a)(1)(E), punish whoever:

> (c) makes a telephone call or utilizes a telecommunications device, whether or not conversation or communication ensues, without disclosing his identity and with intent to annoy, abuse, threaten, or

harass any person at the called number or who receives the communications; * * * or

(E) makes repeated telephone calls or repeatedly initiates communication with a telecommunications device, during which conversation or communication ensues, solely to harass any person at the called number or who receives the communication[.]

The third federal statute relevant here is the federal stalking statute first enacted in 1996 codified at 18 U.S.C. § 2261A. The statute was expanded in 2000 specifically to address "cyberstalking," the use of computers and the Internet to engage in stalking activity. The most important part of the statute for our purposes is § 2261A(2)(B), which punishes one who,

with the intent * * * to place a person in another State or tribal jurisdiction, or within the special maritime and territorial jurisdiction of the United States, in reasonable fear of the death of, or serious bodily injury to—

(i) that person;

(ii) a member of the immediate family (as defined in section 115) of that person; or

(iii) a spouse or intimate partner of that person,

uses the mail or any facility of interstate or foreign commerce to engage in a course of conduct that places that person in reasonable fear of the death of, or serious bodily injury to, any of the persons described in clauses (i) through (iii).

Taken together, these three statutes offer relatively broad coverage of threats and harassing conduct that can occur via computers and the Internet. Of course, the fact that the statutes are relatively broad does not mean that they are limitless—or that the meaning of the various terms in the statutes are always clear. The following case considers one such limit, focusing on the meaning of the phrase "containing any threat" in 18 U.S.C. § 875(c).

UNITED STATES v. ALKHABAZ

United States Court of Appeals for the Sixth Circuit, 1997.
104 F.3d 1492.

BOYCE F. MARTIN, JR., Chief Judge.

Claiming that the district court erred in determining that certain electronic mail messages between Abraham Jacob Alkhabaz, a.k.a. Jake Baker, and Arthur Gonda did not constitute "true threats," the government appeals the dismissal of the indictment charging Baker with violations of 18 U.S.C. § 875(c).

From November 1994 until approximately January 1995, Baker and Gonda exchanged e-mail messages over the Internet, the content of which expressed a sexual interest in violence against women and girls. Baker sent and received messages through a computer in Ann Arbor, Michigan, while Gonda—whose true identity and whereabouts are still unknown—used a computer in Ontario, Canada.

Prior to this time, Baker had posted a number of fictional stories to "alt.sex.stories," a popular interactive Usenet news group. Using such shorthand references as "B & D," "snuff," "pedo," "mf," and "nc," Baker's fictional stories generally involved the abduction, rape, torture, mutilation, and murder of women and young girls. On January 9, Baker posted a story describing the torture, rape, and murder of a young woman who shared the name of one of Baker's classmates at the University of Michigan.

On February 9, Baker was arrested and appeared before a United States Magistrate Judge on a criminal complaint alleging violations of 18 U.S.C. § 875(c), which prohibits interstate communications containing threats to kidnap or injure another person. The government made the complaint based on an FBI agent's affidavit, which cited language from the story involving Baker's classmate. The Magistrate Judge ordered Baker detained as a danger to the community and a United States District Court affirmed his detention. Upon Baker's motion to be released on bond, this Court ordered a psychological evaluation. When the evaluation concluded that Baker posed no threat to the community, this Court ordered Baker's release.

On February 14, a federal grand jury returned a one-count indictment charging Baker with a violation of 18 U.S.C. § 875(c). On March 15, 1995, citing several e-mail messages between Gonda and Baker, a federal grand jury returned a superseding indictment, charging Baker and Gonda with five counts of violations of 18 U.S.C. § 875(c). The e-mail messages supporting the superseding indictment were not available in any publicly accessible portion of the Internet.

On April 15, Baker filed a Motion to Quash Indictment with the district court. In *United States v. Baker,* 890 F. Supp. 1375, 1381 (E.D. Mich. 1995), the district court dismissed the indictment against Baker, reasoning that the e-mail messages sent and received by Baker and Gonda did not constitute "true threats" under the First Amendment and, as such, were protected speech. The government argues that the district court erred in dismissing the indictment because the communications between Gonda and Baker do constitute "true threats" and, as such, do not implicate First Amendment free speech protections. In response, Baker urges this Court to adopt the reasoning of the district court and affirm the dismissal of the indictment against him.

Neither the district court's opinion, nor the parties' briefs contain any discussion regarding whether Baker's e-mail messages initially satisfy the requirements of Section 875(c). For the reasons stated below, we conclude that the indictment failed, as a matter of law, to allege violations of Section 875(c). Accordingly, we decline to address the First Amendment issues raised by the parties.

An indictment is sufficient if it sets forth the offense in the words of the statute itself, as long as those words fully, directly, and expressly set forth all the elements necessary to constitute the offense *intended* to be punished. Accordingly, in determining the sufficiency of the indictment against Baker, we must consider the elements of the offense that Congress intended to prohibit when it created Section 875(c). Because Congress's intent is essentially a question of statutory interpretation, we review the district court's decision *de novo.*

Title 18, United States Code, Section 875(c) states:

> Whoever transmits in interstate or foreign commerce any communication containing any threat to kidnap any person or any threat to injure the person of another, shall be fined under this title or imprisoned not more than five years, or both.

The government must allege and prove three elements to support a conviction under Section 875(c): (1) a transmission in interstate or foreign commerce; (2) a communication containing a threat; and (3) the threat must be a threat to injure or kidnap the person of another. In this case, the first and third elements cannot be seriously challenged by the defendant. However, the second element raises several issues that this Court must address. As this Court has recognized, it is one of the most fundamental postulates of our criminal justice system that conviction can result only from a violation of clearly defined standards of conduct. Indeed, our law does not punish bad purpose standing alone, however; instead we require that mens rea accompany the actus reus specifically proscribed by statute. As the Supreme Court has recognized, William Shakespeare's lines here illustrate sound legal doctrine.

> His acts did not o'ertake his bad intent;
> And must be buried but as an intent
> That perish'd by the way: thoughts are no subjects,
> Intents but merely thoughts.

United States v. Apfelbaum, 445 U.S. 115, 131 n. 13 (1980) (quoting William Shakespeare's Measure for Measure, Act V, Scene 1; G. Williams, Criminal Law, The General Part 1 (2d ed. 1961)).

Although its language does not specifically contain a mens rea element, this Court has interpreted Section 875(c) as requiring only general intent. Accordingly, Section 875(c) requires proof that a reasonable person would have taken the defendant's statement as "a serious expression of an intention to inflict bodily harm."

Additionally, Section 875(c) does not clearly define an actus reus. The language of Section 875(c) prohibits the transmission of "any communication containing any threat to kidnap any person or any threat to injure the person of another." However, in *United States v. Bellrichard,* 779 F. Supp. 454, 459 (D. Minn. 1991), *aff'd,* 994 F.2d 1318 (8th Cir. 1993), a Minnesota district court recognized the absurdity of a literal interpretation of this language in the context of Section 876, the companion statute of Section 875(c).

The statute should not be interpreted to cover every letter which, apart from its context, seems to threaten a person other than the addressee or letter recipient, as the government argues. For example, if a prosecutor mailed defendant's letters to another government official for analysis or review, that conduct could be covered by the statute—mailing a threat to injure the person of another. Similarly, if the court mails this opinion to West Publishing Company, having quoted verbatim the language used by defendant which is alleged to be threatening, that conduct could be covered by the statute. Also covered would be conduct of a member of the general public, who, attending this trial of widespread interest, took notes of defendant's statements and mailed them to a family member, law professor, or newspaper for their information.

The *Bellrichard* court concluded that such contingencies could be avoided by requiring that proscribable threats be communicated either to the threatened individual, or to a third party with "some connection" to the threatened individual.

We agree with the district court in *Bellrichard* that a literal interpretation of Section 875(c) would lead to absurd results not intended by Congress. However, instead of applying a test that requires "some connection," the unintended results noted in *Bellrichard* may be avoided simply by considering the type of offense that Congress intended to prohibit when it enacted Section 875(c).

To determine what type of action Congress intended to prohibit, it is necessary to consider the nature of a threat. At their core, threats are tools that are employed when one wishes to have some effect, or achieve some goal, through intimidation. This is true regardless of whether the goal is highly reprehensible or seemingly innocuous.

For example, the goal may be extortionate or coercive. In *United States v. Cox,* 957 F.2d 264 (6th Cir. 1992), a bank repossessed the defendant's vehicle, including several personal items. The defendant then telephoned the bank and threatened to "hurt people" at the bank, unless the bank returned his property. Similarly, in *United States v. Schroeder,* 902 F.2d 1469 (10th Cir. 1990), the defendant informed an Assistant United States Attorney that "people would get hurt" if the government did not give him money. In both cases, the defendant used a threat in an attempt to extort property from the threatened party.

Additionally, the goal, although not rising to the level of extortion, may be the furtherance of a political objective. For example, in *United States v. Kelner,* 534 F.2d 1020 (2d Cir. 1976), the defendant threatened to assassinate Yasser Arafat, leader of the Palestine Liberation Organization, during a news conference. Kelner claimed that his sole purpose in issuing the threat was to inform the PLO that "we (as Jews) would defend ourselves and protect ourselves." Although Kelner's threat was not extortionate, he apparently sought to further the political objectives of his organization by intimidating the PLO with warnings of violence.

Finally, a threat may be communicated for a seemingly innocuous purpose. For example, one may communicate a bomb threat, even if the bomb does not exist, for the sole purpose of creating a prank. However, such a communication would still constitute a threat because the threatening party is attempting to create levity (at least in his or her own mind) through the use of intimidation.

The above examples illustrate threats because they demonstrate a combination of the mens rea with the actus reus. Although it may offend our sensibilities, a communication objectively indicating a serious expression of an intention to inflict bodily harm cannot constitute a threat unless the communication also is conveyed for the purpose of furthering some goal through the use of intimidation.

Accordingly, to achieve the intent of Congress, we hold that, to constitute "a communication containing a threat" under Section 875(c), a communication must be such that a reasonable person (1) would take the statement as a serious expression of an intention to inflict bodily harm (the mens rea), and (2) would perceive such expression as being communicated to effect some change or achieve some goal through intimidation (the actus reus).

The dissent argues that Congress did not intend to include as an element of the crime the furthering of some goal through the use of intimidation. Emphasizing the term "any" in the language of the statute, the dissent maintains that Congress did not limit the scope of communications that constitutes criminal threats. While we agree that Congress chose inclusive language to identify the types of threats that it intended to prohibit, we cannot ignore the fact that Congress intended to forbid only those communications that in fact constitute a "threat." The conclusion that we reach here is one that the term "threat" necessarily implies. To emphasize the use of the term "any" without acknowledging the limitations imposed by the term "threat" ignores the intent of Congress and results in the absurd conclusions identified in *Bellrichard*, 779 F. Supp. at 459.

It is important to note that we are not expressing a subjective standard. This Court has held that the mens rea element of a Section 875(c) violation must be determined objectively. The rationale for applying an objective standard to establish the mens rea element of a Section 875(c) violation is equally as compelling with regard to establishing the actus reus element. Accordingly, * * * the actus reus element of a Section 875(c) violation must be determined objectively, from the perspective of the receiver.

Our interpretation of the actus reus requirement of Section 875(c) conforms not only to the nature of a threat, but also to the purpose of prohibiting threats. Several other circuits have recognized that statutes prohibiting threats are designed to protect the recipient's sense of personal safety and well being. If an otherwise threatening communication is not, from an objective standpoint, transmitted for the purpose of intimidation, then it is unlikely that the recipient will be intimidated or that the recipient's peace of mind will be disturbed.

For example, under a hypothetical expressed in *Bellrichard*, "if the court mails this opinion to West Publishing Company, having quoted verbatim the language used by defendant which is alleged to be threatening," it is unlikely that any reader's sense of personal safety and well being would be jeopardized. Likewise, if "a member of the general public, who, attending this trial of widespread interest, took notes of defendant's statements and mailed them to a family member, law professor, or newspaper for their information," such communication would not, from an objective standpoint, compromise the recipient's sense of personal safety. In both cases, the recipient's sense of well-being is not endangered because, from an objective standpoint, the sender has no desire to intimidate.

Applying our interpretation of the statute to the facts before us, we conclude that the communications between Baker and Gonda do not constitute "communications containing a threat" under Section 875(c). Even if a reasonable person would take the communications between Baker and Gonda as serious expressions of an intention to inflict bodily harm, no reasonable person would perceive such communications as being conveyed to effect some change or achieve some goal through intimidation. Quite the opposite, Baker and Gonda apparently sent e-mail messages to each other in an attempt to foster a friendship based on shared sexual fantasies.

Ultimately, the indictment against Baker fails to set forth all the elements necessary to constitute the offense intended to be punished and must be dismissed as a matter of law. We agree with the district court, that whatever Baker's faults, and he is to be faulted, he did not violate 18 U.S.C. § 875(c)

KRUPANSKY, Circuit Judge, dissenting.

The words in section 875(c) are simple, clear, concise, and unambiguous. The plain, expressed statutory language commands only that the alleged communication must contain *any threat* to kidnap or physically injure *any person,* made for *any reason* or no reason. Section 875(c) by its terms does *not* confine the scope of criminalized communications to those directed to identified individuals and intended to effect some particular change or goal.

The panel majority attempts to justify its improper fusion of an extra-legislative element re the "intent to intimidate some change or goal" upon section 875(c) by embracing an artificially narrow legal definition of the term "threat." The panel majority posits, "at their core, threats are tools that are employed when one wishes to have some effect, or achieve some goal, through intimidation." However, this interpretation does not comprise the *exclusive* ordinary or legal meaning of the word "threat." Undeniably, a simple, credible declaration of an intention to cause injury to some person, made for any reason, or for no reason whatsoever, may *also* constitute a "threat."

Although some reported threat convictions have embraced a form or degree of intimidation, this circuit has not previously adopted that element as an essential component of a prosecution under 18 U.S.C. § 875(c). To the contrary, controlling precedents clearly reflect the principle that a message is a "threat" *if a reasonable recipient would tend to believe that the originator of the message was serious about his words and intended to effect the violence or other harm forewarned,* regardless of the speaker's actual motive for issuing the communication.

The plain language of 18 U.S.C. § 875(c), together with its interpretive precedents, compels the conclusion that "threats" within the scope of the statute in controversy include all reasonably credible communications which express the speaker's objective intent to kidnap or physically injure another person. Whether the originator of the message intended to intimidate or coerce anyone thereby is irrelevant. Rather, the pertinent inquiry is whether a jury could find that a reasonable recipient of the communication would objectively tend to believe that the speaker was serious about his stated intention. There can be no doubt that a rational jury could find that some or all of the minacious communications charged in the superseding indictment against Baker constituted threats by the defendant to harm a female human being, which a reasonable objective recipient of the transmissions could find credible.

Notes and Questions

1. The *Alkhabaz* case received a tremendous amount of attention as an early "cyberlaw" case. The investigation began when Alkhabaz (using the pseudonym Jake Baker) posted a story on USENET, a public forum for posting messages on the Internet. The FBI began investigating the case, and investigators obtained the contents of Alkhabaz's e-mails with Gonda. The government's initial theory was that Alkhabaz and Gonda planned to act on their stories, and that a prosecution was needed to protect the young woman described in the stories. Somewhat oddly, however, the government based its case entirely on Alkhabaz's private e-mails with Gonda rather than his publicly posted messages; instead of claiming that Baker and Gonda had entered into a conspiracy to harm the young woman, the government argued that the communications themselves amounted to "threats." As a matter of law, isn't the *Alkhabaz* case an easy case for the defense?

2. If a defendant posts a threat online, should courts assume that victims will find them? Is the real harm that third parties will act on what they see posted online, or that the victim will find out about the threat and fear it will be carried out?

In People v. Munn, 688 N.Y.S.2d 384 (Crim. Ct. 1999), the defendant posted a message on an Internet newsgroup stating: "Please kill Police Lt. Steven Biegel, all other NYPD cops, and all of their adult relatives and friends...." The defendant was charged with violating New York state harassment law, which prohibits sending a communication by mechanical or electronic means with intent to harass, annoy, threaten or alarm another person. The court held that the law covered the defendant's conduct, and concluded:

Furthermore, the message was one directed at the complainant. The defendant's alleged posting of his message on an Internet "newsgroup" with the complainant's name included then transformed the communication to one not only intended for the general public, but specially generated to be communicated to the complainant. Indeed in this case, the complainant himself read the message on the computer screen, and became annoyed and alarmed.

Id. at 386.

3. While threats and harassment can be sent directly to their victims, the Internet also facilitates less direct forms of harassment. Consider the facts of People v. Kochanowski, 719 N.Y.S.2d 461, 462–63 (App. Term 2000):

[I]n late November 1998, defendant approached a younger co-worker who was more familiar with computers and asked if they could create an anonymous web site. Defendant's stated purpose was to negatively depict complainant, a woman with whom he had shared a prior relationship. Defendant said that complainant was falsely accusing and harassing him, that she had had him arrested and that he just wanted to strike back at her. The co-worker, who would later testify for the People at trial, agreed to set up the site. Defendant furnished suggestive photographs of complainant which the co-worker put on the Internet while trying to leave no trail. During the creation of the web site, the two chatted on AOL through a real time chat program. The co-worker typed in express references to intimate body parts and attributed to complainant an infatuation with sex. At one or two points within the web page, defendant asked him to include statements that complainant would drive out to meet people and that they should contact her. Defendant supplied complainant's address and telephone numbers for the web page, so that she could be reached at home, where she lived with her parents and younger sisters, or at her place of employment. Defendant subsequently asked the co-worker to create another anonymous E-mail account so that they could read what people were saying about the web site. In addition, defendant mentioned making the web site [known] to another witness who knew him and complainant.

The evidence also includes the testimony of complainant concerning her receipt of two calls at work in December 1998 and her reactions of crying and being frightened. She asked the first caller to send her the offensive material and she subsequently received copies of the three pages in the mail. The second caller gave her the address of the web site, and complainant, with the help of a friend's husband, obtained a print-out from a computer.

Should Kochanowski be any more or less liable for his conduct because he used the Internet? Would you feel differently about his conduct if he had placed an advertisement in the local newspaper instead of creating a web-site? What if he had placed a full-page advertisement in the *New York Times* and the *USA Today*?

4. In a report on the problem of "cyberstalking," the Justice Department has argued that stalking via the Internet differs from offline stalking in three ways:

- Offline stalking generally requires the perpetrator and the victim to be located in the same geographic area; cyberstalkers may be located across the street or across the country.

- Electronic communications technologies make it much easier for a cyberstalker to encourage third parties to harass and/or threaten a victim (e.g., impersonating the victim and posting inflammatory messages to bulletin boards and in chat rooms, causing viewers of that message to send threatening messages back to the victim "author.")

- Electronic communications technologies also lower the barriers to harassment and threats; a cyberstalker does need to physically confront the victim.

Cyberstalking: A New Challenge for Law Enforcement and Industry, A Report from the Attorney General to the Vice President (1999). Do you agree? Is "cyberstalking" something new, or is it merely another form of harassment via a new communications medium?

––––––

Although many criminal laws prohibit threats and harassment, they all must comply with the First Amendment and its "true threat" doctrine. The "true threat" doctrine teaches that the government cannot punish threats that in context are mere advocacy or political hyperbole, as these are protected speech under the First Amendment. The government can punish only "true threats."

The Supreme Court has never answered exactly how to measure whether a threat is a "true" threat. The lower courts have offered somewhat differing views. Some courts have held that a threat is a true threat when "a reasonable person would foresee that the statement would be interpreted by those to whom the maker communicates the statement as a serious expression of intent to harm or assault." United States v. Orozco–Santillan, 903 F.2d 1262, 1265 (9th Cir. 1990). Other courts have said that the critical question is whether an "ordinary, reasonable recipient who is familiar with the context of the [statement] would interpret it as a threat of injury." United States v. Maisonet, 484 F.2d 1356, 1358 (4th Cir. 1973). How should the true threat doctrine apply to threats that occur online? How can courts develop the context needed to identify true threats online?

The following case applies the true threat doctrine to a website operated by a defendant charged in a drug case. The government moved for a protective order that would have required the defendant to take down the website, and the district court considered whether the website was protected speech under the First Amendment's true threat doctrine.

UNITED STATES v. CARMICHAEL

United States District Court for the Middle District of Alabama, 2004.
326 F. Supp. 2d 1267.

MYRON H. THOMPSON, District Judge.

Carmichael was arrested in November 2003 in Montgomery, Alabama, after Gary Wayne George and Robert Patrick Denton—themselves under arrest for marijuana distribution—informed Drug Enforcement Administration (DEA) Task Force Agent R. David DeJohn that Carmichael had employed them to assist in his marijuana-distribution activities. On the day of his arrest, Denton told Agent DeJohn that Carmichael had been expecting a shipment of several hundred pounds of marijuana the previous day and that Carmichael had told him to assist Freddie Williams with re-packaging the marijuana. Denton's information led to a search of Williams's residence later that day; the search turned up eleven duffle bags filled with marijuana. Carmichael was arrested the same day by DEA Agent Thomas Halasz.

As stated, Carmichael is charged with one count of conspiracy to possess marijuana with the intent to distribute, and one count of conspiracy to commit money laundering. The conspiracy count alleges that, since 1993, Carmichael and others have conspired to possess with the intent to distribute 1000 kilograms or more of marijuana. Williams, Carmichael's co-defendant, is also named in the conspiracy count.

THE WEBSITE

The Internet website at issue in this case is www.carmichael-case.com. * * * The website first appeared in December 2003 and first came to the attention of law enforcement in January 2004. The site has gone through roughly three versions. The original version contained a picture of the Montgomery federal courthouse, and it stated that the media had misrepresented the case. The site allowed users to post comments about the case, and it contained links to articles about the case, including an article from a local weekly newspaper that identified Denton by name and listed his home address. The site also included a statement to the effect that Denton had been charged with six felonies.

Sometime in February 2004, the website was changed. The second version showed a picture of the scales of justice on the left side of the page below the words "we are under construction." On the right side of the page, the site displayed the statement, "Look for a new look at this very important case. We will have photos and information on all of the courtroom participants: Defendant, Defense Attorneys, U.S. Attorneys, DEA Agents, Informants." At some point prior to the end of February, this version of the site was amended to include a picture of Carmichael and the statement, "Only public records will be published on this site. This includes all participants, in this case, including their names, pictures, and statements."

Sometime around the beginning of April 2004, the website was changed to its current format. At the top of the site is the word "Wanted" in large, red letters, beneath which are the words "Information on these Informants and Agents." Underneath this header are eight boxes, each containing the name of a witness or agent involved in the case and, in parentheses, the word "Agent" or "Informants" listed are Denton, George, Sherry D. Pettis, and Walace Salery. The four "agents" listed are DeJohn, Halasz, Devin Whittle, and Robert Greenwood. As the site appeared on April 27, 2004, three of the eight boxes contained pictures of the named individuals; the individuals pictured were Denton, Pettis, and George. Currently, a fourth "informant"—Salery—is pictured as well. In the boxes without pictures, the words "Picture Coming" appear in parentheses.

Beneath the eight boxes, this statement appears: "If you have any information about these informants and agents, regardless of how insignificant you may feel it is, Please contact"; the statement is followed by a list of Carmichael's attorneys and their telephone numbers. At one point, only one of Carmichael's attorneys was listed. Currently, four of his attorneys are listed.

This latest version of the site was modified in the middle of April to include, at the bottom of the page, the following language:

> "This website, or any posters and advertisements concerning the Carmichael Case, is definitely not an attempt to intimidate or harass any informants or agents, but is simply an attempt to seek information. The Carmichael Case will not be a 'closed door' case.

> "Pictures (when available), names and testimonies of informants, agents and witnesses will be on television, on the web site, on the radio and published in newspapers. Carmichael maintains his innocence, and wants the public to know all the facts as well as the participants in this case."

This disclaimer was removed around the end of April. The current version of the website, however, now contains a similarly worded disclaimer.

Carmichael argues that the protective order sought by the government would infringe his free-speech rights under the First Amendment. The first question is whether Carmichael's website is protected speech. Because threats are not protected by the First Amendment, the court can issue a protective order shutting the site down or otherwise restricting it if the site is a 'true threat.' If the site is protected by the First Amendment, the court can issue the protective order sought by the government only if the government satisfies the constitutional rules for imposing prior restraints on the speech of trial participants.

As stated, true threats are not protected by the First Amendment. *Virginia v. Black*, 538 U.S. 343, 359 (2003); *Watts v. United States*, 394 U.S. 705, 707 (1969) (per curiam). True threats encompass those statements where the speaker means to communicate a serious expression of an intent to commit an act of unlawful violence to a particular individual or group of individuals. The prohibition on true threats protects individuals from the fear of violence and from the disruption that fear engenders, in addition to protecting people from the possibility that the threatened violence will occur.

Watts is the origin of the true threat doctrine. In *Watts*, the petitioner appealed his conviction for violating 18 U.S.C. § 871, which prohibits any person from knowingly and willfully making any threat to take the life of or to inflict bodily harm upon the President of the United States. The basis of petitioner's conviction was a statement he made during a 1966 anti-Vietnam War rally on the mall in Washington: "They always holler at us to get an education. And now I have already received my draft classification as 1–A and I have got to report for my physical this Monday coming. I am not going. If they ever make me carry a rifle the first man I want to get in my sights is L.B.J."

The Supreme Court, per curiam, reversed on the ground that petitioner's speech was not a threat. After noting that the government's valid, "even overwhelming," interest in the life of the President, the Court wrote: "Nevertheless, a statute such as this one, which makes criminal a form of pure speech, must be interpreted with the commands of the First Amendment clearly in mind. What is a threat must be distinguished from what is constitutionally protected speech."

"Against the background of a profound national commitment to the principle that debate on public issues should be uninhibited, robust, and wide open, and that it may well include vehement, caustic, and sometimes unpleasantly sharp attacks on government and public officials," the Court interpreted § 871 not to reach "the kind of political hyperbole indulged in by petitioner." The Court held that the petitioner's speech was not a true threat and was thus protected by the First Amendment.

The Supreme Court has not settled on a definition of a true threat, but the United States Court of Appeals for the Eleventh Circuit has:

"A communication is a threat when in its context it would have a reasonable tendency to create apprehension that its originator will act according to its tenor. In other words, the inquiry is whether there was sufficient evidence to prove beyond a reasonable doubt that the defendant intentionally made the statement under such circumstances that a reasonable person would construe them as a serious expression of an intention to inflict bodily harm. Thus, the offending remarks must be measured by an objective standard."

United States v. Alaboud, 347 F.3d 1293, 1296–97 (11th Cir. 2003). The Eleventh Circuit's objective approach accords with that taken by the majority of the United States Courts of Appeals.

A number of factors are relevant to determine whether speech is a threat proscribable under the First Amendment. First, the court must consider the language itself. Second, the court must look at the context in which the communication was made to determine if it would cause a reasonable person to construe it as a serious intention to inflict bodily harm. Third, testimony by the recipient of the communication is relevant to determining whether it is a threat or an act of intimidation.

a. The Website Itself

The language of Carmichael's website does not make out a threat. There is no explicit threat on the site, and neither the request for information nor the list of Carmichael's attorneys is threatening or intimidating. The statement that "Mr. Carmichael maintains his innocence and wants the public to know all the facts as well as all the participants in this case" is similarly unmenacing. Furthermore, the site actually disclaims any intent to threaten; the site includes the following statement at the bottom of the page: "This web site, or any posters, and advertisements concerning the Carmichael Case, is definitely not an attempt to intimidate or harass any informants or agents, but is simply an attempt to seek information." Indeed, these elements make the site appear to be just what Carmichael maintains it is: another way of gathering information to prepare his defense.

b. Context

The court must also consider the context in which the website operates in order to determine whether the reasonable viewer would see it as a threat. The importance of context is vividly illustrated by * * * cases arising under the Freedom of Access to Clinics Entrances Act (FACE), 18 U.S.C. § 248. FACE provides criminal penalties for

> "whoever by force or threat of force or by physical obstruction, intentionally injures, intimidates or interferes with or attempts to injure, intimidate or interfere with any person because that person is or has been, or in order to intimidate such person or any other person or any class of persons from, obtaining or providing reproductive health services."

18 U.S.C. § 248(a)(1). FACE also provides for a private right of action for "any person aggrieved by reason of the conduct prohibited by subsection (a)." 18 U.S.C. § 248(c)(1)(A). These * * * cases are helpful because they involve statements which surely lie at the outside edge of the definition of 'true threats.'

In *Planned Parenthood of the Columbia/Willamette, Inc. v. American Coalition of Life Activists*, 290 F.3d 1058 (9th Cir. 2002) (en banc), four doctors who provide abortions—Drs. Hern, Crist, Elizabeth Newhall, and James Newhall—and two abortion clinics brought a lawsuit under FACE's private cause-of-action provision against the American Coalition of Life Activists, Advocates of Life Ministries, and a number of individuals associated with these two groups. The plaintiffs' claim was that two posters and an Internet website produced by the defendants constituted "threats of force" under FACE. A jury found for the plaintiffs and awarded them substantial damages, including nearly $80 million in punitive damages. The trial court also permanently enjoined the defendants from publishing or distributing its posters and from providing material to the website. On appeal, the defendants argued that the posters and website were not 'true threats' and were thus protected by the First Amendment.

Like the www.carmichaelcase.com website, neither the posters nor the website in *Planned Parenthood* expressly threatened the plaintiffs. The first poster, published in January 1995, was captioned "GUILTY," beneath which were the words "OF CRIMES AGAINST HUMANITY." Under the heading "THE DEADLY DOZEN," the poster identified 13 doctors, including three of the plaintiffs, and listed their home addresses. At the bottom, the poster bore the legend "ABORTIONIST" in large, bold typeface. The second poster, released in August 1995, identified one of the plaintiff doctors and bore the word "GUILTY" in large bold letters at the top followed by the words "OF CRIMES AGAINST HUMANITY." The poster gave the doctor's home and work address, and it also bore the legend "ABORTIONIST" in large bold type at the bottom.

The website at issue was put up on the Internet in January 1997. It was called the "Nuremberg Files" in reference to the location of the post-World War II Nazi war crimes trial, and it listed information on abortion-providers, judges and politicians, and prominent abortion-rights supporters. The website listed the names of approximately 400 individuals and provided the following legend to interpret the font in which each name was listed: "Black font (working); Greyed-out Name (wounded); Strikethrough (fatality)." The names of three abortion providers who had been murdered between March 1993 and July 1994—Drs. Gunn, Patterson, and Britton—were struck through.

Applying roughly the same standard for determining when speech is a threat that the Eleventh Circuit applies, the United States Court of Appeals for the Ninth Circuit, sitting en banc, held that the two posters and the "Nuremberg Files" website constituted 'true threats' and affirmed the jury's verdict in favor of the plaintiffs. The court's reasoning was based on the history of violence directed against abortion-providers prior to the defendants' creation of the posters and the website. The court described how in the two years prior to January 1995, when the defendants produced the first poster, three abortion providers—Drs. Gunn, Patterson, and Britton—were killed after they appeared on similar posters which gave information about them and bore headings like "WANTED" and "unWANTED." The court described its reasoning this way:

> It is use of the 'wanted'-type format in the context of the poster pattern—poster followed by murder—that constitutes the threat. Because of the pattern, a 'wanted'-type poster naming a specific doctor who provides abortions was perceived by physicians, who are providers of reproductive health services, as a serious threat of death or bodily harm. After a 'WANTED' poster on Dr. David Gunn appeared, he was shot and killed. After a 'WANTED' poster on Dr. George Patterson appeared, he was shot and killed. After a 'WANT-

ED' poster on Dr. John Britton appeared, he was shot and killed. None of these 'WANTED' posters contained threatening language, either. Neither did they identify who would pull the trigger. But knowing this pattern, knowing that unlawful action had followed 'WANTED' posters on Gunn, Patterson and Britton, and knowing that 'wanted'-type posters were intimidating and caused fear of serious harm to those named on them, ACLA published a 'GUILTY' poster in essentially the same format on Dr. Crist and a Deadly Dozen 'GUILTY' poster in similar format naming Dr. Hern, Dr. Elizabeth Newhall and Dr. James Newhall because they perform abortions. Physicians could well believe that ACLA would make good on the threat. One of the other doctors on the Deadly Dozen poster had in fact been shot before the poster was published. In the context of the poster pattern, the posters were precise in their meaning to those in the relevant community of reproductive health service providers. They were a true threat.

Thus, even though the defendants were responsible neither for the earlier 'wanted posters' nor the earlier killings, the context created by those posters and killings gave the defendants' posters and website a threatening meaning.

The present case is obviously different because Carmichael's website was not put up in the context of a recent string of murders linked to similar publications. The crucial circumstance for the court in *Planned Parenthood* was the pattern of posters followed by murders that pre-dated the defendants' publication of their posters. The analogous situation in this case would be if there were a history of witnesses or government agents being threatened or killed after the release of 'wanted-style' posters on which they were pictured. Such a pattern does not exist here, so the case that www.carmichaelcase.com is a threat is not in any way as strong as that in *Planned Parenthood*.

This case is not totally dissimilar from *Planned Parenthood*, however. Just as the court in *Planned Parenthood* considered the history of violence against abortion providers, this court considers the history of violence committed against informants in drug-distribution cases generally. A brief search of recent reported decisions in the Federal Reporter reveals numerous cases involving the murder of informants in drug-conspiracy cases. This is the broad context in which Carmichael's site exists.

The facts of the present case are similar to those in the cases cited above. Carmichael is accused of heading a far-flung, long-running drug-distribution conspiracy. Denton and George—two of the 'informants' pictured on the site—have admitted to involvement in such a drug conspiracy, and marijuana and firearms have already been seized in this case.

Viewed in light of the general history of informants being killed in drug conspiracy cases and the evidence of a drug-conspiracy and other criminal activity in this case, www.carmichaelcase.com looks more like a threat. Indeed it may be that it is only this context that gives the site a threatening meaning. To illustrate how much of the website's threatening meaning is derived from the factual context of this case, imagine the same website put up by a defendant in a securities-fraud case. In the context of a white-collar crime prosecution, the same site might be an annoyance, but, absent other circumstances, it would be nearly impossible to conclude that it is a threat.

Nevertheless, it is important to recall that the inquiry here is whether a reasonable person would view Carmichael's website as "a serious expression of an intention to inflict bodily harm," *Alaboud*, 347 F.3d 1297, not whether the site calls to mind other cases in which harm has come to government informants, not whether it would be reasonable to think that Carmichael would threaten an informant, and not whether Carmichael himself is somehow threatening. Context can help explain the website's meaning, but it is the website that is the focus of the court's inquiry. Although the broad social context makes the case closer, the background facts described above are too general to make the Carmichael case site a 'true threat.'

The government's strongest argument based on context may not be that the Carmichael site is a direct threat that he will inflict harm on the 'informants' and 'agents,' but that the website is meant to encourage others to inflict harm on them. Agent Borland of the DEA suggested this interpretation when he testified that the website looked to him like a solicitation for others to inflict harm on the witnesses and agents.

The problem with this argument is that implicates the Supreme Court's stringent 'incitement' doctrine. *Brandenburg v. Ohio*, 395 U.S. 444, 447 (1969). *Brandenburg* stands for the proposition that, as a general rule, "the constitutional guarantees of free speech and free press do not permit a State to forbid or proscribe advocacy of the use of force or of law violation." To fall outside the First Amendment's protection, advocacy of violence must be "directed to inciting or producing imminent lawless action and [be] likely to incite or produce such action." There is no evidence that Carmichael's site meets the imminency requirement of *Brandenburg*. Indeed, in *Planned Parenthood*, Judge Kozinski in dissent noted that there was so little chance of proving that the posters and website in that case met the imminency requirement in *Brandenburg* that the plaintiffs did not even raise the argument. 290 F.3d at 1092 n. 5 (Kozinski, J., dissenting). Thus, the court cannot proscribe Carmichael's site as constitutionally unprotected advocacy of violence.

A final piece of 'context' evidence relevant to determining if the www.carmichaelcase.com website is a threat is the very fact that it is a website posted on the Internet. Courts and commentators have noted the unique features of the Internet, *see, e.g. Reno v. American Civil Liberties Union*, 521 U.S. 844, 851 (1997); Scott Hammack, *The Internet Loophole: Why Threatening Speech On–Line Requires a Modification of the Courts' Approach to True Threats and Incitement*, 36 Colum. J.L. & Soc. Probs. 65, 81–86 (2002), and a number of commentators have argued that these features make content posted on the Internet more likely to be threatening, *see, e.g.,* Hammack, *supra*; Jennifer L. Brenner, *True Threats—A More Appropriate Standard for Analyzing First Amendment Protection and Free Speech When Violence is Perpetrated Over the Internet,* 78 N.D. L. Rev. 753, 763–64 (2002). In fact, DEA Agent Borland testified at this court's hearing that one of his concerns about Carmichael's 'wanted poster' is that it is posted on the world-wide web.

That Carmichael's 'wanted poster' is on the Internet, however, is not enough to transform it into a true threat. First, notwithstanding the commentary cited above, the Supreme Court has held that speech on the Internet is subject to no greater or lesser constitutional protection than speech in more traditional media. Second, the general rule in the case law is that speech that is broadcast to a broad audience is less likely to be a true threat, not more. Thus, to the extent that the government's concern is that Carmichael's website will be seen by a lot of people, that fact makes the site look less like a true threat, not more.

Based on all of the above factors and the evidence presented, the court holds that Carmichael's website is not a true threat and is thus protected by the First Amendment.

Notes and Questions

1. The Eleventh Circuit uses an objective test to identify true threats. The question is whether a reasonable observer would construe the statements as a serious expression of an intent to inflict bodily harm. How does a reasonable observer determine whether a statement posted on a website is a serious expression of an intent to inflict bodily harm? Does it depend on the appearance of the page, which can vary depending on the browser used? Does it depend on the URL? On the other sites that link to the statement? On how much traffic the site receives? Is a reasonable observer a savvy Internet user or an Internet novice?

2. *The case of the anonymous blog.* Chris Langdell receives an anonymous e-mail one afternoon recommending that he take a look at http://langdellwilldie.blogspot.com. Langdell clicks on the link, and it takes him to an anonymous blog titled "CHRIS LANGDELL WILL DIE!!!" The blog has four posts, each of which claims that the anonymous author is planning to murder Chris Langdell. One post includes some personal details of Chris's life and states the following:

LANGDELL'S DAYS ARE NUMBERED:

[Posted by Anon. July 10, 2005 at 8:49pm] 0 Trackbacks

Chris, we know where you live. You live at 129 Main Street. You drive a silver Honda, too. Do you feel unsafe yet?

Langdell is terribly worried, and calls the police.

Is the blog a "true threat"? Why or why not? Does it matter how easy it is to set up such a blog? Does it matter how much it costs? Does it matter whether it is common to set up anonymous blogs? Does it matter how easy it is to trace the account and find out who set up the anonymous blog?

3. How can a court determine the immediacy of a threat posted on the Internet? In People v. Neuman, 2002 WL 800516 (Cal. App. 2002), a man was convicted of making criminal threats in violation of California state law for posting a webpage about a police officer who had given the defendant several traffic tickets and had impounded the defendant's car. The defendant added the page to his personal website that described his views about the illegitimacy of the government. The page stated:

> WANTED! Dead or Alive! (Reward) For Grand Theft Auto on 12/23/1998[.] J. Giles; Badge #233 VENTURA POLICE DEPARTMENT Height 6'3", Weight; approx. 280 lbs. Race: Aff. Amer. Last seen 12/29/1998 under HWY 101 Bridge/Johnston Rd. exit on a motorcycle. This Rogue Police Officer has been indicted and found guilty of Grand theft Auto. But has yet to be captured and brought to justice. THIS MAN IS ARMED AND DANGEROUS! USE EXTREME PREJUDICE IN APPREHENDING!

On appeal following his conviction, the defendant argued that the fact that he had posted this message on his website meant that it lacked the immediacy of a threat. According to the defendant, the message was "buried in an obscure web page, undelivered," and was therefore "too attenuated to convey a gravity of purpose and an immediate prospect of execution of the threat." *Id*. at *4. The state appellate court disagreed:

> We cannot agree that the "WANTED" notice was "buried" when it was prominently posted on a Web site accessible to millions of Internet users. The prosecution's computer expert testified that appellant's Web site had been indexed on three Internet search engines that would allow users to find it if they typed in key words such as "freedom" and "liberty."

Id. Doesn't this description apply to most things posted on the Web? Does this mean that every threat posted online is an immediate threat? What test would you devise for distinguishing immediate from non-immediate threats posted online?

4. *Brandenburg v. Ohio.* As the *Carmichael* court notes, the First Amendment framework that applies to incitement of illegal conduct—speech that encourages others to take action, rather than suggests an intent for the speaker to act—generally is governed by Brandenburg v. Ohio, 395 U.S. 444, 447 (1969) (per curiam). *Brandenburg* involved a KKK rally held by twelve hooded members of the Klan, in which one member of the Klan delivered a speech about the KKK that included the following warning:

> We're not a revengent organization, but if our President, our Congress, our Supreme Court, continues to suppress the white, Caucasian race, it's possible that there might have to be some revengeance taken.

The Supreme Court held that this warning of possible "revengeance" could not be punished under an Ohio law that punished advocating violence to achieve political goals. According to the Court, "the constitutional guarantees of free speech and free press do not permit a State to forbid or proscribe advocacy of the use of force or of law violation except where such advocacy is directed to inciting or producing imminent lawless action and is likely to incite or produce such action." *Id*. at 447–48.

A speech delivered in person may be likely to produce "imminent lawless action." Is an equivalent speech that appears posted on a website likely to do so? Will any efforts to use the Internet to urge others to engage in violence be likely to produce "imminent lawless action"? How does the imminence requirement apply to speech posted on a website? Who is the relevant audience, and how can a court measure when that audience is likely to be inspired into action?

5. Several commentators have argued that the First Amendment rules that apply to threats and incitement should be rethought for threats and incitement over the Internet. They reason that the basic facts of Internet threats and solicitations change when the architecture is shifted from the physical world to the Internet, and that the tests should change along with the changing architecture. Consider two such proposals:

- "A person makes a 'true threat' when the person makes a statement that, in context, a reasonable listener would interpret as communicating a serious expression of an intent to inflict or cause serious harm on or to the listener (objective); and the speaker intended that the statement be taken as a threat that would serve to place the listener in fear for his or her personal safety, regardless of whether the speaker actually intended to carry out the threat (subjective)." Scott Hammack, *The Internet Loophole: Why Threatening Speech On–Line Requires A Modification of the Courts' Approach to True Threats and Incitement*, 36 Colum. J.L. & Soc. Probs. 65, 97 (2002) (quoting Planned Parenthood of the Columbia/Willamette, Inc. v. American Coalition of Life Activists, 41 F. Supp. 2d 1130, 1155 n.1 (D. Or. 1999)).

- "The Internet incitement standard should consider four primary factors: (1) imminence from the perspective of the listener; (2) content of the message; (3) likely audience; and (4) nature of the issue involved." John P. Cronan, *The Next Challenge for the First Amendment: The Framework for an Internet Incitement Standard,* 51 Cath. U. L. Rev. 425, 455 (2002).

What test would you devise to determine when an online threat can be punished consistently with the First Amendment?

2. INVASION OF PRIVACY CRIMES

Congress has enacted three federal crimes to deter and punish personal invasions of privacy involving computers and the Internet. The offenses criminalize invasions of privacy involving a person's data online. The most important statute is the felony criminal prohibition found in the Wiretap Act, 18 U.S.C. § 2511, and the remaining two statutes are the misdemeanor criminal prohibitions found in the Stored Communications Act, 18 U.S.C. § 2701, and the Pen Register statute, 18 U.S.C. § 3121.

The Wiretap Act, Stored Communications Act, and Pen Register statute are complex surveillance statutes that were enacted to create a statutory form of the Fourth Amendment applicable to computer networks. The criminal prohibitions contained in these three statutes are best (and perhaps only) understood in the context of a broader study of surveillance law. Each of the statutes sets up both a regime of criminal procedure and a related criminal prohibition, and it helps to study the former to understand the latter. Chapter Six explores all three statutes in considerable detail, so a complete study of the three criminal offenses must await those materials.

For now, however, it is helpful to get just a flavor. The most important provision is the criminal prohibition contained in the Wiretap Act, codified at 18 U.S.C. § 2511. Section 2511(1)(a) penalizes one who "intentionally intercepts, endeavors to intercept, or procures any other person to intercept or endeavor to intercept, any wire, oral, or electronic communication." The statute defines "intercept" as "the aural or other acquisition of the contents of any wire, electronic, or oral communication through the use of any electronic, mechanical, or other device." 18 U.S.C. § 2510(4). The basic idea is that it is a crime to intentionally wiretap a private person's telephone or Internet communications. For example, a person who installs a "sniffer" Internet surveillance tool that reads an Internet user's e-mail in "real time" generally violates the Wiretap Act. If the person installs the sniffer intending to intercept a person's communications, he can be charged with criminal wiretapping. The Wiretap Act also contains criminal prohibitions against using and disclosing intercepted communications in a number of circumstances, but they are less often charged and also can raise First Amendment problems. *See* 18 U.S.C. § 2511(b)-(e); Bartnicki v. Vopper, 532 U.S. 514 (2001).

The prohibition contained in the Pen Register statute resembles that of the Wiretap Act. There are two key differences. First, violations of the Pen Register statute are only misdemeanors, *see* 18 U.S.C. § 3121(d), and are only very rarely prosecuted. Second, while violations of the Wiretap Act involve interception of the contents of information such as telephone calls and e-mail, the Pen Register statute is violated when a person obtains in real time the dialing, routing, addressing, and signaling information relating to an individual's telephone calls or Internet communications. The Pen Register statute's criminal prohibition appears in 18 U.S.C. § 3121(a) and (d), and states that one who knowingly "install[s] or use[s] a pen register or a trap and trace device without first obtaining a court order" can be prosecuted. The statute defines both pen registers and trap and trace devices in 18 U.S.C. § 3127(3)-(4), and defines those terms as devices that obtain dialing, routing, addressing, and signaling information relating to telephone and Internet communications. Put together, the statute prohibits knowingly using a device to obtain in real-time the dialing, routing, addressing, or signaling information relating to Internet communications of another person.

The criminal prohibition contained in the Stored Communications Act was discussed briefly in Chapter 2. The prohibition is a specific type of unauthorized access law, punishing one who "intentionally accesses without authorization a facility through which an electronic communication service is provided, [or] intentionally exceeds an authorization to access that facility; and thereby obtains, alters, or prevents authorized access to a wire or electronic communication while it is in electronic storage in such system." 18 U.S.C. § 2701(a). This prohibition is a close cousin of § 1030(a)(2). To be a bit imprecise, it is an unauthorized access law that applies specifically to Internet service providers. The statute is largely redundant in light of the broad scope of 18 U.S.C. § 1030(a)(2)(C).

C.   VICE CRIMES

Offenses involving pornography, narcotics, prostitution, and gambling are sometimes labeled "vice crimes." As a historical matter, such crimes exist because they are believed by many to relate to moral vices. Vice crimes can be controversial, as one person's upholding the moral fabric is another person's interfering with private affairs. As a general matter, however, vice crimes involve consensual transactions. The law seeks to block the defendant from engaging in a consensual transaction or conduct that a majority of the public finds harmful.

Computers often alter the ways in which vice crimes are committed. Traditionally, a person wishing to commit a vice crime needed to meet face-to-face with the person providing the sought-after goods or services. Some transactions could occur via postal mail (such as purchasing obscene books), and others could occur via the telephone (such as placing bets), but most vice crimes tended to occur face-to-face. Computers and the Internet change that. The transaction is no longer person-to-person; it is now person-to-computer. An individual sits at her computer, often in the comfort and privacy of her own home, and interacts with machines located hundreds or thousands of miles away.

The shift to digital vice crimes raises two difficult policy questions. The first is whether the new factual environment changes basic assumptions of the legal doctrine. Vice prohibition is often justified by its effect on the local physical environment. For example, a local prohibition on gambling may be a way to protect a neighborhood from illegal activities sometimes associated with gambling, such as organized crime and prostitution. The Internet brings new facts, and it is worth considering whether the new facts justify new law.

Second, the Internet may make it more difficult to enforce vice crime laws effectively. The enforcement of person-to-person vice crimes in the physical world focuses on particular places, which can help law enforcement allocate resources. Prostitutes may be known to walk a particular neighborhood or street; a particular park may be known for its narcotics market; an organized crime gang may run an illegal casino in a basement apartment. To commit a physical vice crime, a person must ordinarily go to a particular place in the physical world. The police can concentrate their enforcement efforts on those physical places.

In contrast, vice crimes online simply require a server, an Internet connection, and a user. The user and the server can be anywhere in the world. To investigate the offense, the police will have to conduct surveillance of the user or the server. Is this possible? Imagine that a defendant in Kansas likes to gamble online using a website that hosts its servers in the Cayman Islands. If you are a Kansas police officer, how can you gather sufficient evidence to charge the defendant in a Kansas court? Given your limited resources, are you likely to focus your efforts on investigating illegal online gambling happening in your state? Is it a coincidence that in the case of both Internet gambling and obscenity law, the legal prohibitions are broad but prosecutions remain quite rare?

1. INTERNET GAMBLING

RONALD J. RYCHLAK—LEGAL PROBLEMS WITH ON–LINE GAMBLING

Engage, May 2005, at 36.

INTRODUCTION

Not long ago, Nevada and Atlantic City, New Jersey stood out from the rest of the nation as jurisdictions where one could bet legally. With the emergence of Indian gaming, state lotteries, riverboat gambling, and other forms of legal wagering, today two states (Utah and Hawaii) stand alone as the only jurisdictions without some form of legalized gaming. In fact, today anyone with a computer and Internet access can go to a "virtual casino" and gamble on almost any casino-style game or place bets on professional and collegiate sporting events.

Online gaming is emerging as a major enterprise for the Internet, and a serious concern for lawmakers. There are presently more than 1,400 gambling sites on the web. With about 14.5 million patrons, it is estimated that global revenues for Internet gaming were about $4.2 billion in 2003. Many observers believe that Internet gaming is well on its way to becoming a $100 billion-a-year industry.

Despite its prevalence, Internet gambling is illegal in all fifty states. Several foreign nations, however, either sanction Internet gaming or do not enforce laws against it. Since web pages do not recognize international borders, a gaming site operated in any nation can attract gamblers from every other nation. Most Internet gamblers are from the United States, and that is a serious concern for American lawmakers.

Gambling, of course, has traditionally been seen as a vice, and in the United States it has a history associated with organized crime. As states have moved toward legalization, they have also instituted strict regulatory schemes designed to keep the games fair and the ownership honest. With Internet gaming, however, this may be impossible. One of the most heavily regulated industries in the world has crashed with full force into one of the most unregulated, and inherently unregulatable, phenomenon of modern times.

Several different concerns lead to the call for regulation or prohibition of Internet gambling:

- Concern about underage gamblers. Obviously, it is harder to verify age over the Internet than in person.

- Concern about fraud by Internet casino operators. Internet casino operators have already avoided paying their customers either by refusing to pay or by moving their website to another address and changing the name.

- Concern that video gambling (whose addictive nature has been compared to crack cocaine) from the privacy of one's own home will lead to an increase in gambling addiction.

- Concern that Internet casinos will negatively affect state tax revenues by taking business away from brick-and-mortar casinos that pay taxes.

These reasons for wanting to control Internet gaming, however, do not translate easily into action. When it comes to regulation or prohibition, there are two basic lines of thought. One line holds that Internet gambling cannot be entirely stopped, so it has to be regulated. The opposing argument is that it cannot be regulated, so it must be prohibited. Unfortunately, both groups are partially correct: Internet gaming is very difficult to regulate or to prohibit.

Since many of the Internet gaming web pages are sanctioned by some foreign government, one possibility would be simply to rely upon the regulatory authority provided by that nation. An obvious problem with that solution is that regulation in another nation is unlikely to protect American gamblers. More importantly, many (but not all) of the sanctioned virtual casinos are located in small, island nations that provide virtually no actual regulation; they just charge a fee. Consider:

> In Nevada and New Jersey the applicant for an unrestricted gaming license can expect the process to take one to two years. The applicant has the burden of proving to the licensing authorities that it is legitimate and has the necessary skills available to operate a casino in compliance with the law. The applicant must pay the costs of the independent investigation undertaken to test the accuracy and complete truthfulness of its responses to the myriad questions answered in filling out the application. These costs routinely amount to between $500,000 and $1,000,000. There are public hearings to delve into personal and business transgressions admitted in the application or turned up in the investigation. These amounts do not take into consideration the legal fees that each applicant incurs in getting help and advice in connection with the process.[14]

In contrast, most of the off-shore nations that license Internet casinos charge between $8,000 and $20,000, and the time to obtain the license is between one and five weeks. Obviously, these other nations do not devote as much time and effort to gaming regulation as is expected in

---

14. Chuck Humphrey, *Licensing Online Gambling by Foreign Countries*, Gambling–Law–US.com, http://www.gambling-law-us.com/Articles–Notes/online-licensing.htm (2003).

the United States. As such, reliance on the laws of other nations will not meet the needs of American lawmakers.

Since gambling has traditionally been a matter of state concern, some individual states have taken action to try to stop Internet gambling. In 2001, for instance, New Jersey's Attorney General filed civil suits against three offshore casinos. This is in line with similar actions taken by officials in New York, Minnesota, and Missouri. In Florida, the Attorney General distributed "cease and desist" letters to at least ten media companies providing publishing or broadcasting advertisements for offshore computer gambling sites.

The Attorney Generals of Indiana, Minnesota, and Texas have all issued opinions specifically declaring Internet gambling illegal under the laws of their respective states, and other states are putting new legislation in place. Legal actions, however, are very difficult to bring. The Internet casino operations are usually located beyond the state's jurisdictional limits, and even if the necessary evidence could be uncovered, prosecutors are unlikely to go after individual gamblers. As such, states have been unable to significantly impact online betting.

FINANCIAL TRANSACTIONS

Internet gaming relies on the use of credit cards and other means of transferring funds. As such, many legislators and commentators have identified financial institutions as a possible focus for Internet gaming regulation.

It is obvious that, in order for an Internet or related telephonic gambling operation to be commercially viable, money must flow from bettors to the operator and presumably in the opposite direction as well. The mechanisms for these transfers are the financial service providers, i.e. credit card companies, banks, and other entities that provide the means for fund transfers. Control of such financial service providers can therefore constitute a very potent and effective means of enforcing (albeit indirectly) a prohibition against illegal gambling activity.

In 2002, the New York Attorney General took action against online casinos by suing Citibank and PayPal for facilitating them. Citibank ultimately paid $100,000 in costs and $400,000 to groups providing counseling to recovering problem gamblers. It also agreed to block and decline authorizations for bankcard transactions consistent with and pursuant to, then-standard Visa and MasterCard rules and procedures for posting to bankcard accounts that are marketed to consumers in the United States.

The New York Attorney General also reached a settlement with the money transfer service, PayPal, Inc. This agreement provided that PayPal would stop "processing any payments for online gambling merchants, where such payments involved New York members." PayPal paid $200,000 in costs, penalties, and "disgorgement" of online gaming profits. There have also been attempts by losing gamblers to avoid payments to credit card companies for gambling debts (based on the Statute of Anne).

Because of legal actions like these, many leading credit card companies, including Bank of America, Fleet, Wells Fargo, MBNA, Chase Manhattan and others, now attempt to block Internet gaming transactions. It can be, however, difficult for financial institutions or government regulators to identify a particular business as being in the casino industry. This is particularly true if the business seeks to disguise itself by handling transactions through an ancillary "ghost" firm that shows up as a legitimate, non-gambling business. When that is done, it is extremely difficult for regulators [or financial institutions] to differentiate Internet gambling Web site data transfer and legal data transfer. Because of dodges like this, 85% of online casinos are able to report that they accept Visa and Mastercard, and about two-thirds report that they accept PayPal. So, like laws aimed at ISPs, federal laws aimed at financial institutions are not having much success in stopping online gambling.

INTERNATIONAL CONCERNS AND THE WTO

Recently, the World Trade Organization issued a preliminary ruling against the United States on Internet gaming. The island nations of Antigua and Barbuda contended that the United States ban on Internet gaming was an unfair trade practice in violation of the terms of its agreement with the WTO. Antigua and Barbuda complained that the United States through the various federal statutes in combination with state laws has created the effect of a complete and total prohibition of Internet gambling. Antigua also argued that the United States' ban on allowing its residents to use online wagering services based in Antigua harmed its ability to diversify Antigua's economy.

A panel from the WTO ruled that a United States ban on Internet gambling was indeed a violation of global trade rules. It held that United States was violating its commitments under the General Agreement on Trade Services (GATS) by not providing market access and/or national treatment under GATS to Internet gambling services provided by operators licensed by the governments of Antigua and Barbuda. The Bush Administration has vowed to vigorously appeal the decision.

Under international law, if the panel is upheld Antigua and Barbuda could impose trade sanctions (which would hurt their economies more than the United States), or the United States might elect to pay sanctions to the two nations. Obviously, neither of those outcomes is likely. The problem that may one day arise is that a more formidable nation with an economic interest in Internet gaming, such as England, may also challenge the United States laws and regulations. If that happens, the United States may be forced to take another look at how it treats Internet gambling.

CONCLUSION

In 2002, the United States General Accounting Office performed a survey of Internet gambling web sites. The findings showed that current federal statutes are not effective in controlling Internet gambling. Recent legislative proposals that have focused on ISPs or financial institutions also have difficulties. Must, then, American lawmakers resign themselves to permanent, unregulated Internet casinos? Maybe not.

Since Internet casinos cannot be stopped as long as they are legal in other nations, American lawmakers should focus on a certification process for online casinos. Those casinos that are already operating traditional gambling establishments within the United States could be given the opportunity to develop online casinos which would be accessible through a regulatory gateway page. These online casinos would face competition from unregulated virtual casinos, which might be able to operate at a lower cost than the regulated web pages. Gamblers wanting assurance of fair games, however, would presumably be interested in using the regulated pages, particularly when they are linked to well-established casino brand names. Regulators (and tax authorities) would have substantial control over these online casinos, because of the brick-and-mortar casinos over which they also have control. As such, reasonable regulations could be put in place to assure fair games, verify the age of gamblers, collect taxes, and minimize the risk to problem gamblers (to the extent that is possible). Unregulated online gaming would still exist, but if this regulation were done correctly, these officially sanctioned web pages should be able to capture a significant portion of the market. Consumers would have the choice of betting with casinos that are regulated and fair, or they could take their risks with other entities that are less secure but might offer better odds. In the end, the market could play a significant role in bringing online gaming under control.

Notes and Questions

1. Consider some of the ways Internet gambling is different from traditional forms of gambling. If you visit a casino, you first have to travel to it. You will subject yourself to the legal rules applicable in the jurisdiction where the casino is located; the casino will be a known business with physical assets and employees that can be audited and taxed; and the presence of the casino is likely to have spillover effects (whether negative or positive) on the physical neighborhood surrounding the casino. When you log on to a gambling website, however, you do not need to travel. You may not know what legal regime regulates the gambling transaction or where the company is located; you may not know anything about the gambling site; and the site will not have spillover effects in any physical neighborhood. Do these differences justify regulating Internet gambling differently than traditional forms of gambling?

2. Bruce P. Keller, *The Game's The Same: Why Gambling in Cyberspace Violates Federal Law*, 108 Yale L.J. 1569, 1591–92 (1999):

> The societal concerns that have led to the heavy regulation of brick-and-mortar casinos and other forms of gambling do not evaporate

online. In fact, because there is no strict governmental oversight of online gambling machinery and accounting procedures, the prospects for dishonest operations increase. Moreover, the anonymity of Internet gambling makes it easier to indulge in excessive gambling.

States that allow traditional casinos protect against these problems in a number of different ways:

- State gaming commissions require registration and licensing of all gambling operations.

- Inspections of all gambling machinery and gaming tables ensure the safety and honesty of the games themselves.

- Rigorous accounting standards and thorough inspections of account books ensure proper payouts, honest tax compliance, and minimal bribery and corruption.

- To curb gambling impulses, many states restrict how and where gambling operations can be advertised, and federal law forbids lottery ads from being broadcast in states where lotteries are illegal.

- Many states forbid gambling on credit.

- States allow casinos to forbid gambling by drunks, minors, and other problem gamblers.

Internet gambling eludes these safeguards. Because offshore gambling operations are beyond the reach of both state gambling laws and state regulatory laws, there is no way for regulators to ensure fair games and aboveboard accounting practices. Online gamblers already have complained that, although their losses are deducted immediately from their online accounts, their winnings often fail to appear. In most instances, the individual gambler does not know, or have the resources to determine, who exactly the Internet "house" is, further reducing the guarantee of a fair payout.

It also is easy to see how Internet gambling frustrates the state goals of preventing excessive gambling and gambling by addicts and minors. By enabling rampant advertising, it defeats advertising restrictions. By offering gambling in the home at any hour, it defies time and place restrictions. By allowing gambling by credit card, it allows people to bet, not just to the limit of their wallet or bank account, but to their credit limit. Additionally, Internet gambling operations have no way to screen out minors, drunks, or habituals, all of whom can easily bypass the primitive and pro forma safeguards that most sites have available. This raises the prospect of awestruck teenage techno-junkies or their gambling-addicted parents pounding the keyboard at unpoliced Internet gambling sites twenty-four hours a day.

3. If the federal government and state and local governments cannot enact an effective ban on Internet gambling, what should they do? Is there value to having a law on the books even if many violate that law? If state gambling laws are ineffective, why do all fifty states prohibit Internet gambling?

The following case involves one of the few prosecutions for operating an Internet gambling operation.

UNITED STATES v. COHEN

United States Court of Appeals for the Second Circuit, 2001.
260 F.3d 68.

KEENAN, District Judge.

In 1996, the Defendant, Jay Cohen was young, bright, and enjoyed a lucrative position at Group One, a San Francisco firm that traded in options and derivatives. That was not all to last, for by 1996 the Internet revolution was in the speed lane. Inspired by the new technology and its potential, Cohen decided to pursue the dream of owning his own e-business. By year's end he had left his job at Group One, moved to the Caribbean island of Antigua, and had become a bookmaker.

Cohen, as President, and his partners, all American citizens, dubbed their new venture the World Sports Exchange ("WSE"). WSE's sole business involved bookmaking on American sports events, and was purportedly patterned after New York's Off–Track Betting Corporation. WSE targeted customers in the United States, advertising its business throughout America by radio, newspaper, and television. Its advertisements invited customers to bet with WSE either by toll-free telephone or by Internet.

WSE operated an "account-wagering" system. It required that its new customers first open an account with WSE and wire at least $300 into that account in Antigua. A customer seeking to bet would then contact WSE either by telephone or Internet to request a particular bet. WSE would issue an immediate, automatic acceptance and confirmation of that bet, and would maintain the bet from that customer's account.

In one fifteen-month period, WSE collected approximately $5.3 million in funds wired from customers in the United States. In addition, WSE would typically retain a "vig" or commission of 10% on each bet. Cohen boasted that in its first year of operation, WSE had already attracted nearly 1,600 customers. By November 1998, WSE had received 60,000 phone calls from customers in the United States, including over 6,100 from New York.

In the course of an FBI investigation of offshore bookmakers, FBI agents in New York contacted WSE by telephone and Internet numerous times between October 1997 and March 1998 to open accounts and place bets. Cohen was arrested in March 1998 under an eight-count indictment charging him with conspiracy and substantive offenses in violation of 18 U.S.C. § 1084. That statute reads as follows:

(a) Whoever being engaged in the business of betting or wagering knowingly uses a wire communication facility for the transmission in interstate or foreign commerce of bets or wagers or information assisting in the placing of bets or wagers on any sporting event or contest, or for the transmission of a wire communication which entitles the recipient to receive money or credit as a result of bets or wagers, or for information assisting in the placing of bets or wagers, shall be fined under this title or imprisoned not more than two years, or both.

(b) Nothing in this section shall be construed to prevent the transmission in interstate or foreign commerce of information for use in news reporting of sporting events or contests, or for the transmission of information assisting in the placing of bets or wagers on a sporting event or contest from a State or foreign country where betting on that sporting event or contest is legal into a State or foreign country in which such betting is legal.

See § 1084(a)-(b). In the conspiracy count (Count One) and in five of the seven substantive counts (Counts Three through Six, and Eight), Cohen was charged with violating all three prohibitive clauses of § 1084(a)(1) transmission in interstate or foreign commerce of bets or wagers, (2) transmission of a wire communication which entitles the recipient to receive money or credit as a result of bets or wagers, (3) information assisting in the placement of bets or wagers). In two counts, Counts Two and Seven, he was charged only with transmitting "information assisting in the placing of bets or wagers."

Cohen was convicted on all eight counts on February 28, 2000 after a ten-day jury trial before Judge Thomas P. Griesa. The jury found in special interrogatories that Cohen had violated all three prohibitive clauses of § 1084(a) with respect to the five counts in which those violations were charged. Judge Griesa sentenced Cohen on August 10, 2000 to a term of twenty-one months' imprisonment. He has remained on bail pending the outcome of this appeal.

Cohen appeals the district court for instructing the jury to disregard the safe-harbor provision contained in § 1084(b). That subsection provides a safe harbor for transmissions that occur under both of the following two conditions: (1) betting is legal in both the place of origin and the destination of the transmission; and (2) the transmission is limited to mere information that assists in the placing of bets, as opposed to including the bets themselves. *See* § 1084(b).

The district court ruled as a matter of law that the safe-harbor provision did not apply because neither of the two conditions existed in the case of WSE's transmissions. Cohen disputes that ruling and argues that both conditions did, in fact, exist. He argues that betting is not only legal in Antigua, it is also "legal" in New York for the purposes of § 1084. He also argues that all of WSE's transmissions were limited to mere information assisting in the placing of bets. We agree with the district court's rulings on both issues.

A. "Legal" Betting

There can be no dispute that betting is illegal in New York. New York has expressly prohibited betting in both its Constitution, *see* N.Y.

Const. art. I, § 9 ("no ... bookmaking, or any other kind of gambling [with certain exceptions pertaining to lotteries and horseracing] shall hereafter be authorized or allowed within this state"), and its General Obligations Law, *see* N.Y. Gen. Oblig. L. § 5–401 ("All wagers, bets or stakes, made to depend on any race, or upon any gaming by lot or chance, or upon any lot, chance, casualty, or unknown or contingent event whatever, shall be unlawful"). Nevertheless, Cohen argues that Congress intended for the safe-harbor provision in § 1084(b) to exclude only those transmissions sent to or from jurisdictions in which betting was a crime. Cohen concludes that because the placing of bets is not a crime in New York, it is "legal" for the purposes of § 1084(b).

By its plain terms, the safe-harbor provision requires that betting be "legal," *i.e.*, permitted by law, in both jurisdictions. *See* § 1084(b); *see also* Black's Law Dictionary 902 (7th ed. 1999); Webster's 3d New Int'l Dictionary 1290 (1993). The plain meaning of a statute should be conclusive, except in the rare cases in which the literal application of a statute will produce a result demonstrably at odds with the intentions of its drafters. This is not the rare case.

Although, as Cohen notes, the First Circuit has stated that Congress "did not intend for § 1084 to criminalize acts that neither the affected states nor Congress itself deemed criminal in nature," it did not do so in the context of a § 1084 prosecution. *See Sterling Suffolk Racecourse Ltd. P'ship v. Burrillville Racing Ass'n,* 989 F.2d 1266, 1273 (1st Cir. 1993). Instead, that case involved a private bid for an injunction under RICO and the Interstate Horseracing Act ("IHA"). It does not stand for the proposition that § 1084 permits betting that is illegal as long as it is not criminal.

In *Sterling,* the defendant was an OTB office in Rhode Island that accepted bets on horse races from distant tracks and broadcasted the races. The office typically obtained the various consents required under the IHA, *i.e.*, from the host track, the host racing commission, and its own racing commission. However, it would often neglect to secure the consent of the plaintiff, a live horse-racing track located within the statutory sixty-mile radius from the OTB office. The plaintiff sought an injunction against the OTB office under RICO, alleging that it was engaged in a pattern of racketeering activity by violating § 1084 through its noncompliance with the IHA.

The *Sterling* court affirmed the district court's denial of the RICO injunction. It noted first that because the OTB office's business was legitimate under all applicable state laws, it fell under the safe-harbor provision in § 1084(b). Furthermore, the court held that in enacting the IHA, Congress had only created a private right of action for damages on the part of certain parties; it did not intend for any Government enforcement of the IHA. Consequently, the plaintiff could not use the IHA together with § 1084 to transform an otherwise legal OTB business into a criminal racketeering enterprise.

Neither *Sterling* nor the legislative history behind § 1084 demonstrates that Congress intended for § 1084(b) to mean anything other than what it says. Betting is illegal in New York, and thus the safeharbor provision in § 1084(b) cannot not apply in Cohen's case as a matter of law. As a result, the district court was not in error when it instructed the jury to disregard that provision.

B. TRANSMISSION OF A BET, PER SE

Cohen appeals the district court's instructions to the jury regarding what constitutes a bet *per se*. Cohen argues that under WSE's account-wagering system, the transmissions between WSE and its customers contained only information that enabled WSE itself to place bets entirely from customer accounts located in Antigua. He argues that this fact was precluded by the district court's instructions. We find no error in those instructions.

Judge Griesa repeatedly charged the jury as follows:

If there was a telephone call or an Internet transmission between New York and [WSE] in Antigua, and if a person in New York said or signaled that he or she wanted to place a specified bet, and if a person on an Internet device or a telephone said or signaled that the bet was accepted, this was the transmission of a bet within the meaning of Section 1084. Congress clearly did not intend to have this statute be made inapplicable because the party in a foreign gambling business deemed or construed the transmission as only starting with an employee in an Internet mechanism located on the premises in the foreign country.

Jury instructions are not improper simply because they resemble the conduct alleged to have occurred in a given case; nor were they improper in this case. It was the Government's burden in this case to prove that someone in New York signaled an offer to place a particular bet and that someone at WSE signaled an acceptance of that offer. The jury concluded that the Government had carried that burden.

Most of the cases that Cohen cites in support of the proposition that WSE did not transmit any bets involved problems pertaining either to proof of the acceptance of transmitted bets, or to proof of the locus of a betting business for taxation purposes.

No such problems existed in this case. This case was never about taxation, and there can be no dispute regarding WSE's acceptance of customers' bet requests. For example, a March 18, 1998 conversation between Spencer Hanson, a WSE employee, and a New York-based undercover FBI agent occurred as follows:

Agent: Can I place a bet right now?

Hanson: You can place a bet right now.

Agent: Alright, can you give me the line on the um Penn State/Georgia Tech game, it's the NIT Third Round game tonight.

Hanson: It's Georgia Tech minus 7 ½, total is 147.

Agent: Georgia Tech minus 7 1/2, umm I wanna take Georgia Tech. Can I take 'em for 50?

Hanson: Sure.

WSE could only book the bets that its customers requested and authorized it to book. By making those requests and having them accepted, WSE's customers were placing bets. So long as the customers' accounts were in good standing, WSE accepted those bets as a matter of course.

Moreover, the issue is immaterial in light of the fact that betting is illegal in New York. Section 1084(a) prohibits the transmission of information assisting in the placing of bets as well as the transmission of bets themselves. This issue, therefore, pertains only to the applicability of § 1084(b)'s safe-harbor provision. As we have noted, that safe harbor excludes not only the transmission of bets, but also the transmission of betting information to or from a jurisdiction in which betting is illegal. As a result, that provision is inapplicable here even if WSE had only ever transmitted betting information.

Notes and Questions

1. *The scope of the Wire Act.* Does the Wire Act forbid nonsports-related gambling such as online casinos, or does it only apply to sports-related gambling? The text of the Wire Act is ambiguous: it covers "bets or wagers or information assisting in the placing of bets or wagers on any sporting event or contest, or ... the transmission of a wire communication which entitles the recipient to receive money or credit as a result of bets or wagers, or ... information assisting in the placing of bets or wagers" 18 U.S.C. § 1084(a). Should the limitation "on any sporting event or contest" be read to apply to all of the clauses above, or only the first clause?

In a civil case brought by gamblers against credit card companies for facilitating their Internet gambling practices, the Fifth Circuit concluded that as a textual matter, the Wire Act only applies to gambling activity "related to a sporting event or contest" and does not prohibit the use of Internet casinos. In re Mastercard Int'l, 313 F.3d 257, 262 n.20 (5th Cir. 2002). As a result, online gambling that does not relate to sports does not currently violate federal law, at least in the Fifth Circuit (although it may violate state laws).

Is there a reason that federal law should address sports gambling but not other types of gambling?

2. The Wire Act applies only to those "engaged in the business of betting or wagering." What does that mean? Case law indicates that the phrase is designed to refer to bookmakers, also known as "bookies." *See, e.g.,* United States v. Tomeo, 459 F.2d 445, 447 (10th Cir. 1972). It can also refer to those who have a business relationship with bookmakers. For example, in United States v. Scavo, 593 F.2d 837 (8th Cir. 1979), the defendant established a working relationship with Dwight Mezo, who operated a substantial bookmaking business in the Minneapolis area. The defendant, Scavo, then a resident of Las Vegas, Nevada, provided Mezo with

"line" information. Line information refers to the odds or point spread established for various sporting events. The Eighth Circuit concluded that this was sufficient to make Scavo one who was "engaged in the business of betting or wagering":

> [The Wire Act] is not limited to persons who are exclusively engaged in the business of betting or wagering and the statute does not distinguish between persons engaged in such business on their own behalf and those engaged in the business on behalf of others.

> Although we reject appellant's blanket assertion that suppliers of line information are outside the scope of § 1084(a), we must nevertheless determine whether the government introduced evidence sufficient to show that appellant was "engaged in the business of betting and wagering." At trial, the government proceeded on the theory that appellant was part of Mezo's bookmaking business and on this aspect of the case the authorities relied upon by appellant are relevant to a prosecution under § 1084(a). They are not controlling, however, because the evidence adduced showed more than a mere occasional exchange of line information between appellant and Mezo.

> Viewed in the light most favorable to the government, the evidence showed that appellant furnished line information to Mezo on a regular basis; that Mezo relied on this information; that some sort of financial arrangement existed between appellant and Mezo; that appellant was fully aware of Mezo's bookmaking operation; and that accurate and up-to-date line information is of critical importance to any bookmaking operation.

Id. at 841–42.

3. *Aiding and abetting liability.* Federal criminal law contains a general prohibition creating accomplice liability codified at 18 U.S.C. § 2(a). The provision states that "[w]hoever commits an offense against the United States or aids, abets, counsels, commands, induces or procures its commission, is punishable as a principal." If Internet gambling is a crime, does this mean that promoting Internet gambling is also a crime? Consider:

> If you like to gamble, you might want to check out www.888.com, where you can play blackjack, poker, craps, slots and roulette. If you prefer sports betting, try www.betonsports.com.

> According to the U.S. Justice Department, I may have just committed a felony. Federal prosecutors say helping Americans find online casinos or sports betting operations could amount to "aiding and abetting" illegal gambling, a crime punishable by up to two years in prison.

> Last June, Deputy Assistant Attorney General John G. Malcolm sent a letter to media trade groups warning that their members could be breaking the law by accepting ads for gambling sites. Meanwhile, Raymond W. Gruender, the U.S. attorney for the Eastern District of Missouri, has convened a grand jury in St. Louis that is issuing subpoenas to companies that do business with the online gambling industry.

> This campaign of intimidation already has yielded results. Since last fall several media companies, including Infinity Broadcasting, Viacom

Outdoor, Discovery Networks, and Clear Channel Communications, have stopped running ads for online casinos and betting services.

This month Google and Yahoo!, two of the most widely used Web search engines, also caved. Although Google was vague about its motivation, Yahoo! said "a lack of clarity in the environment" makes gambling ads "too risky."

These companies have surrendered their First Amendment rights without a fight, allowing the government to silence speech it doesn't like by floating a legal theory that almost certainly would fail if it were tested in court. Their capitulation illustrates the chilling effect of vague laws in the hands of ambitious prosecutors.

Jacob Sullum, *Abetting Betting: Is Talking about Online Gambling Illegal?*, Reason Online, April 9, 2004. As a matter of law, do you think that online gambling advertisements encourage violations of the Wire Act? As a matter of policy, is it appropriate for the Justice Department to use the accomplice liability provision of federal law to discourage advertising relating to Internet gambling?

2. OBSCENITY

State and federal law has long punished the distribution and display of obscene materials with the goal of maintaining moral order. To oversimplify a very complex history, the thinking has been that there are some types of pornography and other types of displays and images that have no redeeming social value but that can corrupt and coarsen the moral fabric of society. To protect that social order and express society's disgust for the corrupting materials, the law prohibits the display and distribution of obscene materials.

Does obscenity law have a place in the Internet age? And if so, what should that place be? To understand the current state of the law, it is necessary to look at the Supreme Court decisions that have cut back on the definition of obscenity and the government's power to prosecute obscenity-related crimes. The starting point is Roth v. United States, 354 U.S. 476 (1957), an opinion by Justice Brennan that held that obscenity is categorically beyond First Amendment protection. Under *Roth*, the key question is defining the scope of what can be labeled "obscene" under the First Amendment. The definition of obscenity becomes a constitutional question for the Supreme Court; if an item falls within the definition of obscenity, the First Amendment does not apply. Over time, the Supreme Court has used a variety of different definitions to describe obscene materials. The present definition was announced in the following case.

MILLER v. CALIFORNIA

Supreme Court of the United States, 1973.
413 U.S. 15.

MR. CHIEF JUSTICE BURGER delivered the opinion of the Court.

This is one of a group of 'obscenity-pornography' cases being reviewed by the Court in a re-examination of standards enunciated in
earlier cases involving what Mr. Justice Harlan called 'the intractable
obscenity problem.'

Appellant conducted a mass mailing campaign to advertise the sale
of illustrated books, euphemistically called 'adult' material. After a jury
trial, he was convicted of violating California Penal Code § 311.2(a), a
misdemeanor, by knowingly distributing obscene matter, and the Appellate Department, Superior Court of California, County of Orange, summarily affirmed the judgment without opinion. Appellant's conviction
was specifically based on his conduct in causing five unsolicited advertising brochures to be sent through the mail in an envelope addressed to a
restaurant in Newport Beach, California. The envelope was opened by
the manager of the restaurant and his mother. They had not requested
the brochures; they complained to the police.

The brochures advertise four books entitled 'Intercourse,' 'Man–
Woman,' 'Sex Orgies Illustrated,' and 'An Illustrated History of Pornography,' and a film entitled 'Marital Intercourse.' While the brochures
contain some descriptive printed material, primarily they consist of
pictures and drawings very explicitly depicting men and women in
groups of two or more engaging in a variety of sexual activities, with
genitals often prominently displayed.

I

This case involves the application of a State's criminal obscenity
statute to a situation in which sexually explicit materials have been
thrust by aggressive sales action upon unwilling recipients who had in no
way indicated any desire to receive such materials. This Court has
recognized that the States have a legitimate interest in prohibiting
dissemination or exhibition of obscene material[15] when the mode of
dissemination carries with it a significant danger of offending the sensibilities of unwilling recipients or of exposure to juveniles. It is in this

---

15. This Court has defined 'obscene material' as 'material which deals with sex in a
manner appealing to prurient interest,'
Roth v. United States, supra, 354 U.S., at
487, but the Roth definition does not reflect
the precise meaning of 'obscene' as traditionally used in the English language. Derived from the Latin obscaenus, ob, to, plus
caenum, filth, 'obscene' is defined in the
Webster's Third New International Dictionary (Unabridged 1969) as '1a: disgusting
to the senses ... b: grossly repugnant to
the generally accepted notions of what is
appropriate ... 2: offensive or revolting as
countering or violating some ideal or principle.' The Oxford English Dictionary (1933
ed.) gives a similar definition, '(o)ffensive to
the senses, or to taste or refinement, disgusting, repulsive, filthy, foul, abominable,
loathsome.'

The material we are discussing in this
case is more accurately defined as 'pornography' or 'pornographic material.' 'Pornography' derives from the Greek (porne, harlot, and graphos, writing). The word now
means '1: a description of prostitutes or
prostitution 2: a depiction (as in writing or
painting) of licentiousness or lewdness: a a
portrayal of erotic behavior designed to
cause sexual excitement.' Webster's Third
New International Dictionary, supra. Pornographic material which is obscene forms
a subgroup of all 'obscene' expression, but
not the whole, at least as the word 'obscene'
is now used in our language. We note,
therefore, that the words 'obscene material,' as used in this case, have a specific
judicial meaning which derives from the
Roth case, i.e., obscene material 'which
deals with sex.'

context that we are called on to define the standards which must be used to identify obscene material that a State may regulate without infringing on the First Amendment as applicable to the States through the Fourteenth Amendment.

Since the Court now undertakes to formulate standards more concrete than those in the past, it is useful for us to focus on two of the landmark cases in the somewhat tortured history of the Court's obscenity decisions. In *Roth v. United States*, 354 U.S. 476 (1957), the Court sustained a conviction under a federal statute punishing the mailing of 'obscene, lewd, lascivious or filthy' materials. The key to that holding was the Court's rejection of the claim that obscene materials were protected by the First Amendment. Five Justices joined in the opinion stating:

> 'All ideas having even the slightest redeeming social importance— unorthodox ideas, controversial ideas, even ideas hateful to the prevailing climate of opinion—have the full protection of the (First Amendment) guaranties, unless excludable because they encroach upon the limited area of more important interests. But implicit in the history of the First Amendment is the rejection of obscenity as utterly without redeeming social importance.... This is the same judgment expressed by this Court in Chaplinsky v. New Hampshire, 315 U.S. 568, 571–572:

>> ' ... There are certain well-defined and narrowly limited classes of speech, the prevention and punishment of which have never been thought to raise any Constitutional problem. These include the lewd and obscene. *It has been well observed that such utterances are no essential part of any exposition of ideas, and are of such slight social value as a step to truth that any benefit that may be derived from them is clearly outweighed by the social interest in order and morality. ...*' (Emphasis by Court in *Roth* opinion.)

> 'We hold that obscenity is not within the area of constitutionally protected speech or press.'

Nine years later, in *Memoirs v. Massachusetts*, 383 U.S. 413 (1966), the Court veered sharply away from the *Roth* concept and, with only three Justices in the plurality opinion, articulated a new test of obscenity. The plurality held that under the *Roth* definition

> 'as elaborated in subsequent cases, three elements must coalesce: it must be established that (a) the dominant theme of the material taken as a whole appeals to a prurient interest in sex; (b) the material is patently offensive because if affronts contemporary community standards relating to the description or representation of sexual matters; and (c) the material is utterly without redeeming social value.'

While *Roth* presumed 'obscenity' to be 'utterly without redeeming social importance,' *Memoirs* required that to prove obscenity it must be affirmatively established that the material is 'utterly without redeeming social value.' Thus, even as they repeated the words of *Roth*, the *Memoirs* plurality produced a drastically altered test that called on the prosecution to prove a negative, i.e., that the material was 'utterly without redeeming social value'—a burden virtually impossible to discharge under our criminal standards of proof. Such considerations caused Mr. Justice Harlan to wonder if the 'utterly without redeeming social value' test had any meaning at all.

Apart from the initial formulation in the *Roth* case, no majority of the Court has at any given time been able to agree on a standard to determine what constitutes obscene, pornographic material subject to regulation under the States' police power. This is not remarkable, for in the area of freedom of speech and press the courts must always remain sensitive to any infringement on genuinely serious literary, artistic, political, or scientific expression. This is an area in which there are few eternal verities.

II

This much has been categorically settled by the Court, that obscene material is unprotected by the First Amendment. * * * We acknowledge, however, the inherent dangers of undertaking to regulate any form of expression. State statutes designed to regulate obscene materials must be carefully limited. As a result, we now confine the permissible scope of such regulation to works which depict or describe sexual conduct. That conduct must be specifically defined by the applicable state law, as written or authoritatively construed. A state offense must also be limited to works which, taken as a whole, appeal to the prurient interest in sex, which portray sexual conduct in a patently offensive way, and which, taken as a whole, do not have serious literary, artistic, political, or scientific value.

The basic guidelines for the trier of fact must be: (a) whether 'the average person, applying contemporary community standards' would find that the work, taken as a whole, appeals to the prurient interest; (b) whether the work depicts or describes, in a patently offensive way, sexual conduct specifically defined by the applicable state law; and (c) whether the work, taken as a whole, lacks serious literary, artistic, political, or scientific value. We do not adopt as a constitutional standard the 'utterly without redeeming social value' test of *Memoirs v. Massachusetts*, 383 U.S. at 419; that concept has never commanded the adherence of more than three Justices at one time. If a state law that regulates obscene material is thus limited, as written or construed, the First Amendment values applicable to the States through the Fourteenth Amendment are adequately protected by the ultimate power of appellate courts to conduct an independent review of constitutional claims when necessary.

We emphasize that it is not our function to propose regulatory schemes for the States. That must await their concrete legislative efforts. It is possible, however, to give a few plain examples of what a state statute could define for regulation under part (b) of the standard announced in this opinion, supra:

(a) Patently offensive representations or descriptions of ultimate sexual acts, normal or perverted, actual or simulated.

(b) Patently offensive representation or descriptions of masturbation, excretory functions, and lewd exhibition of the genitals.

Sex and nudity may not be exploited without limit by films or pictures exhibited or sold in places of public accommodation any more than live sex and nudity can be exhibited or sold without limit in such public places. At a minimum, prurient, patently offensive depiction or description of sexual conduct must have serious literary, artistic, political, or scientific value to merit First Amendment protection. For example, medical books for the education of physicians and related personnel necessarily use graphic illustrations and descriptions of human anatomy. In resolving the inevitably sensitive questions of fact and law, we must continue to rely on the jury system, accompanied by the safeguards that judges, rules of evidence, presumption of innocence, and other protective features provide, as we do with rape, murder, and a host of other offenses against society and its individual members.

Under the holdings announced today, no one will be subject to prosecution for the sale or exposure of obscene materials unless these materials depict or describe patently offensive 'hard core' sexual conduct specifically defined by the regulating state law, as written or construed. We are satisfied that these specific prerequisites will provide fair notice to a dealer in such materials that his public and commercial activities may bring prosecution. If the inability to define regulated materials with ultimate, god-like precision altogether removes the power of the States or the Congress to regulate, then 'hard core' pornography may be exposed without limit to the juvenile, the passerby, and the consenting adult alike, as, indeed, Mr. Justice Douglas contends. * * * In this belief, however, Mr. Justice Douglas now stands alone.

III

Under a National Constitution, fundamental First Amendment limitations on the powers of the States do not vary from community to community, but this does not mean that there are, or should or can be, fixed, uniform national standards of precisely what appeals to the 'prurient interest' or is 'patently offensive.' These are essentially questions of fact, and our Nation is simply too big and too diverse for this Court to reasonably expect that such standards could be articulated for all 50 States in a single formulation, even assuming the prerequisite consensus exists. When triers of fact are asked to decide whether 'the average person, applying contemporary community standards' would consider certain materials 'prurient,' it would be unrealistic to require that the answer be based on some abstract formulation. The adversary system, with lay jurors as the usual ultimate factfinders in criminal prosecutions, has historically permitted triers of fact to draw on the standards of their community, guided always by limiting instructions on the law. To require a State to structure obscenity proceedings around evidence of a national 'community standard' would be an exercise in futility.

As noted before, this case was tried on the theory that the California obscenity statute sought to incorporate the tripartite test of *Memoirs*. This, a 'national' standard of First Amendment protection enumerated by a plurality of this Court, was correctly regarded at the time of trial as limiting state prosecution under the controlling case law. The jury, however, was explicitly instructed that, in determining whether the 'dominant theme of the material as a whole . . . appeals to the prurient interest' and in determining whether the material 'goes substantially beyond customary limits of candor and affronts contemporary community standards of decency,' it was to apply 'contemporary community standards of the State of California.'

We conclude that neither the State's alleged failure to offer evidence of 'national standards,' nor the trial court's charge that the jury consider state community standards, were constitutional errors. Nothing in the First Amendment requires that a jury must consider hypothetical and unascertainable 'national standards' when attempting to determine whether certain materials are obscene as a matter of fact.

* * * It is neither realistic nor constitutionally sound to read the First Amendment as requiring that the people of Maine or Mississippi accept public depiction of conduct found tolerable in Las Vegas, or New York City. People in different States vary in their tastes and attitudes, and this diversity is not to be strangled by the absolutism of imposed uniformity. * * * [T]he primary concern with requiring a jury to apply the standard of 'the average person, applying contemporary community standards' is to be certain that, so far as material is not aimed at a deviant group, it will be judged by its impact on an average person, rather than a particularly susceptible or sensitive person—or indeed a totally insensitive one. We hold that the requirement that the jury evaluate the materials with reference to 'contemporary standards of the State of California' serves this protective purpose and is constitutionally adequate.

IV

The dissenting Justices sound the alarm of repression. But, in our view, to equate the free and robust exchange of ideas and political debate with commercial exploitation of obscene material demeans the grand conception of the First Amendment and its high purposes in the historic struggle for freedom. It is a misuse of the great guarantees of free speech and free press. The First Amendment protects works which, taken as a whole, have serious literary, artistic, political, or scientific value, regardless of whether the government or a majority of the people approve of the ideas these works represent. The protection given speech and press was fashioned to assure unfettered interchange of ideas for the bringing about of political and social changes desired by the people, but the public portrayal of hard-core sexual conduct for its own sake, and for the ensuing commercial gain, is a different matter.

MR. JUSTICE DOUGLAS, dissenting.

Today we leave open the way for California to send a man to prison for distributing brochures that advertise books and a movie under freshly written standards defining obscenity which until today's decision were never the part of any law.

Today the Court retreats from the earlier formulations of the constitutional test and undertakes to make new definitions. This effort, like the earlier ones, is earnest and well intentioned. The difficulty is that we do not deal with constitutional terms, since 'obscenity' is not mentioned in the Constitution or Bill of Rights. And the First Amendment makes no such exception from 'the press' which it undertakes to protect nor, as I have said on other occasions, is an exception necessarily implied, for there was no recognized exception to the free press at the time the Bill of Rights was adopted which treated 'obscene' publications differently from other types of papers, magazines, and books. So there are no constitutional guidelines for deciding what is and what is not 'obscene.' The Court is at large because we deal with tastes and standards of literature. What shocks me may be sustenance for my neighbor. What causes one person to boil up in rage over one pamphlet or movie may reflect only his neurosis, not shared by others. We deal here with a regime of censorship which, if adopted, should be done by constitutional amendment after full debate by the people.

While the right to know is the corollary of the right to speak or publish, no one can be forced by government to listen to disclosure that he finds offensive. * * * No one is being compelled to look or to listen. Those who enter newsstands or bookstalls may be offended by what they see. But they are not compelled by the State to frequent those places; and it is only state or governmental action against which the First Amendment, applicable to the States by virtue of the Fourteenth, raises a ban.

The idea that the First Amendment permits government to ban publications that are 'offensive' to some people puts an ominous gloss on freedom of the press. That test would make it possible to ban any paper or any journal or magazine in some benighted place. The First Amendment was designed to invite dispute, to induce a condition of unrest, to create dissatisfaction with conditions as they are, and even to stir people to anger. The idea that the First Amendment permits punishment for ideas that are 'offensive' to the particular judge or jury sitting in judgment is astounding. No greater leveler of speech or literature has ever been designed. To give the power to the censor, as we do today, is to make a sharp and radical break with the traditions of a free society.

Notes and Questions

1. Should the Supreme Court revisit *Miller v. California*? At the time *Miller* was decided, an adult could purchase pornography by buying a copy of *Playboy* at a local magazine store, but access to more hard-core pornography was often more difficult. The *Miller* test seems to target hard-core pornography that was relatively rare and difficult to find at the time. Today, however, anyone can access hard-core pornography via the Internet. Does the *Miller* test work in a world in which hard core pornography is readily available over the Internet? Has the Internet rendered *Miller* obsolete? Alternatively, does the ready availability of materials that would seem to be prohibited under the *Miller* test make obscenity prosecutions more important, not less?

2. The *Miller* obscenity standard assumes the existence of distinct local community standards. Residents of New York City will have one standard, residents of Utah will have another, and residents of Boston will have a third. The local standard test used in *Miller* is designed to ensure that persons in New York are not judged by the standards of Utah. Is this assumption sensible in an age when many individuals derive their standards from peers and the Internet? What effect has the Internet had on "community" standards? Has the global Internet reduced the local variation in community standards? And how could this be measured?

In a concurring opinion in Ashcroft v. American Civil Liberties Union, 535 U.S. 564, 590–91 (2002), Justice Breyer argued that Congress's use of the phrase "community standards" in the context of the Child Online Protection Act should be read to mean a national standard rather than a community standard. He offered the following argument in support of his approach:

> [T]his view of the statute avoids the need to examine the serious First Amendment problem that would otherwise exist. To read the statute as adopting the community standards of every locality in the United States would provide the most puritan of communities with a heckler's Internet veto affecting the rest of the Nation. The technical difficulties associated with efforts to confine Internet material to particular geographic areas make the problem particularly serious. And these special difficulties also potentially weaken the authority of prior cases in which they were not present. A nationally uniform adult-based standard * * * significantly alleviates any special need for First Amendment protection. Of course some regional variation may remain, but any such variations are inherent in a system that draws jurors from a local geographic area and they are not, from the perspective of the First Amendment, problematic.

Does a "community standard" based on the concept of a physical-world community make sense if allegedly obscene images are obtained and distributed online?

3. *Stanley v. Georgia*. The Supreme Court held that the government cannot criminalize mere private possession of obscenity in a pre-*Miller* case, Stanley v. Georgia, 394 U.S. 557 (1969). *Stanley* reasoned that the state had

no legitimate interest in controlling what people read in the confines of their own homes. Consider this excerpt from the Court's opinion:

> Whatever may be the justifications for other statutes regulating obscenity, we do not think they reach into the privacy of one's own home. If the First Amendment means anything, it means that a State has no business telling a man, sitting alone in his own house, what books he may read or what films he may watch. Our whole constitutional heritage rebels at the thought of giving government the power to control men's minds.
>
> And yet, in the face of these traditional notions of individual liberty, Georgia asserts the right to protect the individual's mind from the effects of obscenity. We are not certain that this argument amounts to anything more than the assertion that the State has the right to control the moral content of a person's thoughts. To some, this may be a noble purpose, but it is wholly inconsistent with the philosophy of the First Amendment. * * * Nor is it relevant that obscene materials in general, or the particular films before the Court, are arguably devoid of any ideological content. The line between the transmission of ideas and mere entertainment is much too elusive for this Court to draw, if indeed such a line can be drawn at all. Whatever the power of the state to control public dissemination of ideas inimical to the public morality, it cannot constitutionally premise legislation on the desirability of controlling a person's private thoughts.
>
> Perhaps recognizing this, Georgia asserts that exposure to obscene materials may lead to deviant sexual behavior or crimes of sexual violence. There appears to be little empirical basis for that assertion. But more important, if the State is only concerned about printed or filmed materials inducing antisocial conduct, we believe that in the context of private consumption of ideas and information we should adhere to the view that 'among free men, the deterrents ordinarily to be applied to prevent crime are education and punishment for violations of the law * * *.' Given the present state of knowledge, the State may no more prohibit mere possession of obscene matter on the ground that it may lead to antisocial conduct than it may prohibit possession of chemistry books on the ground that they may lead to the manufacture of homemade spirits.
>
> Finally, we are faced with the argument that prohibition of possession of obscene materials is a necessary incident to statutory schemes prohibiting distribution. That argument is based on alleged difficulties of proving an intent to distribute or in producing evidence of actual distribution. We are not convinced that such difficulties exist, but even if they did we do not think that they would justify infringement of the individual's right to read or observe what he pleases. Because that right is so fundamental to our scheme of individual liberty, its restriction may not be justified by the need to ease the administration of otherwise valid criminal laws.

Id. at 565–67. The Supreme Court has taken a very different path in the context of criminal laws that prohibit the *distribution* of obscene materials. In United States v. Reidel, 402 U.S. 351 (1971), decided soon after *Stanley*, the Court reaffirmed pre-*Stanley* law that the government could criminalize distributing obscene materials. The Court distinguished *Stanley* in the following way:

> The right Stanley asserted was "the right to read or observe what he pleases—the right to satisfy his intellectual and emotional needs in the privacy of his own home." The Court's response was that "a State has no business telling a man, sitting alone in his own house, what books he may read or what films he may watch. Our whole constitutional heritage rebels at the thought of giving government the power to control men's minds." The focus of this language was on freedom of mind and thought and on the privacy of one's home. It does not require that we fashion or recognize a constitutional right in people like Reidel to distribute or sell obscene materials. The personal constitutional rights of those like Stanley to possess and read obscenity in their homes and their freedom of mind and thought do not depend on whether the materials are obscene or whether obscenity is constitutionally protected. Their rights to have and view that material in private are independently saved by the Constitution.

> Reidel is in a wholly different position. He has no complaints about governmental violations of his private thoughts or fantasies, but stands squarely on a claimed First Amendment right to do business in obscenity and use the mails in the process. But Roth v. United States, 354 U.S. 476 (1957), has squarely placed obscenity and its distribution outside the reach of the First Amendment and they remain there today. *Stanley* did not overrule *Roth* and we decline to do so now.

402 U.S. at 355–56.

Is this rationale persuasive? Does it make sense for distribution to be a crime if the possession that follows from the distribution is constitutionally protected? One possible explanation for this otherwise puzzling result is that it channels law enforcement efforts by allowing the government to prosecute distributors but not users. Is that a desirable result?

4. In Lawrence v. Texas, 539 U.S. 558 (2003), the Supreme Court invalidated a Texas statute that criminalized consensual sodomy on the ground that it was inconsistent with the Due Process clause. In its briefs to the Court, Texas had attempted to justify the statute under rational basis scrutiny as an effort to advance and recognize societal mores relating to sexuality and decency. In ruling against Texas, Justice Kennedy's opinion for the Court agreed with Justice Stevens' dissenting position in Bowers v. Hardwick, 478 U.S. 186 (1986), that "the fact that the governing majority in a State has traditionally viewed a particular practice as immoral is not a sufficient reason for upholding a law prohibiting the practice." Writing in dissent in *Lawrence*, Justice Scalia argued that the Court's decision implicitly signaled that other legislation premised on "majoritarian sexual morality," including laws against obscenity, might also be unconstitutional:

> The Texas statute undeniably seeks to further the belief of its citizens that certain forms of sexual behavior are "immoral and unacceptable,"—the same interest furthered by criminal laws against fornication, bigamy, adultery, adult incest, bestiality, and obscenity. *Bowers* held that this *was* a legitimate state interest. The Court today reaches the

opposite conclusion. The Texas statute, it says, "furthers *no legitimate state interest* which can justify its intrusion into the personal and private life of the individual." The Court embraces instead Justice Stevens' declaration in his *Bowers* dissent, that "the fact that the governing majority in a State has traditionally viewed a particular practice as immoral is not a sufficient reason for upholding a law prohibiting the practice." This effectively decrees the end of all morals legislation. If, as the Court asserts, the promotion of majoritarian sexual morality is not even a *legitimate* state interest, none of the above-mentioned laws can survive rational-basis review.

Id. at 559 (Scalia, J., dissenting). Does *Lawrence* compel the invalidation of obscenity laws? *See* United States v. Extreme Assocs., Inc, 352 F. Supp. 2d 578 (W.D. Pa. 2005) (striking down federal obscenity laws under *Lawrence*), *reversed*, 431 F.3d 150 (3d Cir. 2005).

The federal obscenity statutes are codified at 18 U.S.C. §§ 1460–70. The statutes prohibit a range of offenses, ranging from selling obscene materials on federal land, 18 U.S.C. § 1460, to using a means of interstate commerce to transfer obscene materials to a minor, 18 U.S.C. § 1470. Owing to their pre-*Miller* heritage, the language of these statutes is quite archaic, and much broader than the modern first Amendment would allow. For example, many of the statutes refer to material that is not merely "obscene," but also "lewd, lascivious, or filthy." Only obscene materials can be prohibited under the First Amendment, however, so the statutes can be read as effectively being limited to obscene materials.

In the context of Internet-related crimes, the two key federal obscenity provisions are 18 U.S.C. § 1462 and 18 U.S.C. § 1465. Both sections prohibit a range of activities involving obscene materials that include using an "interactive computer service" to carry, receive, or transport obscene materials in interstate commerce. The phrase "interactive computer service" is defined in 47 U.S.C. § 230(f)(2):

> The term "interactive computer service" means any information service, system, or access software provider that provides or enables computer access by multiple users to a computer server, including specifically a service or system that provides access to the Internet and such systems operated or services offered by libraries or educational institutions.

This broad definition encompasses essentially all use of computer networks and the Internet. *See* Carafano v. Metrosplash.com, Inc., 339 F.3d 1119, 1123 (9th Cir. 2003).

UNITED STATES v. THOMAS

United States Court of Appeals for the Sixth Circuit, 1996.
74 F.3d 701.

EDMUNDS, District Judge.

Defendants Robert and Carleen Thomas appeal their convictions and sentences for violating 18 U.S.C. §§ 1462 and 1465, federal obscenity laws, in connection with their operation of an electronic bulletin board. For the following reasons, we affirm Robert and Carleen Thomas' convictions and sentences.

Robert Thomas and his wife Carleen Thomas began operating the Amateur Action Computer Bulletin Board System ("AABBS") from their home in Milpitas, California in February 1991. The AABBS was a computer bulletin board system that operated by using telephones, modems, and personal computers. Its features included e-mail, chat lines, public messages, and files that members could access, transfer, and download to their own computers and printers.

Information loaded onto the bulletin board was first converted into binary code, i.e., 0's and 1's, through the use of a scanning device. After purchasing sexually-explicit magazines from public adult book stores in California, Defendant Robert Thomas used an electronic device called a scanner to convert pictures from the magazines into computer files called Graphic Interchange Format files or "GIF" files. The AABBS contained approximately 14,000 GIF files. Mr. Thomas also purchased, sold, and delivered sexually-explicit videotapes to AABBS members. Customers ordered the tapes by sending Robert Thomas an e-mail message, and Thomas typically delivered them by use of the United Parcel Service.

Persons calling the AABBS without a password could view the introductory screens of the system which contained brief, sexually-explicit descriptions of the GIF files and adult videotapes that were offered for sale. Access to the GIF files, however, was limited to members who were given a password after they paid a membership fee and submitted a signed application form that Defendant Robert Thomas reviewed. The application form requested the applicant's age, address, and telephone number and required a signature.

Members accessed the GIF files by using a telephone, modem and personal computer. A modem located in the Defendants' home answered the calls. After they established membership by typing in a password, members could then select, retrieve, and instantly transport GIF files to their own computer. A caller could then view the GIF file on his computer screen and print the image out using his printer. The GIF files contained the AABBS name and access telephone number; many also had "Distribute Freely" printed on the image itself.

In July 1993, a United States Postal Inspector, Agent David Dirmeyer, received a complaint regarding the AABBS from an individual who resided in the Western District of Tennessee. Dirmeyer dialed the AABBS' telephone number. As a non-member, he viewed a screen that read "Welcome to AABBS, the Nastiest Place On Earth," and was able to select various "menus" and read graphic descriptions of the GIF files and videotapes that were offered for sale.

Subsequently, Dirmeyer used an assumed name and sent in $55 along with an executed application form to the AABBS. Defendant Robert Thomas called Dirmeyer at his undercover telephone number in

Memphis, Tennessee, acknowledged receipt of his application, and authorized him to log-on with his personal password. Thereafter, Dirmeyer dialed the AABBS's telephone number, logged-on and, using his computer/modem in Memphis, downloaded the GIF files listed in counts 2–7 of the Defendants' indictments. These GIF files depicted images of bestiality, oral sex, incest, sado-masochistic abuse, and sex scenes involving urination. Dirmeyer also ordered six sexually-explicit videotapes from the AABBS and received them via U.P.S. at a Memphis, Tennessee address. Dirmeyer also had several e-mail and chat-mode conversations with Defendant Robert Thomas.

On January 10, 1994, a search warrant was issued by a U.S. Magistrate Judge for the Northern District of California. The AABBS' location was subsequently searched, and the Defendants' computer system was seized.

On January 25, 1994, a federal grand jury for the Western District of Tennessee returned a twelve-count indictment charging Defendants Robert and Carleen Thomas with the following criminal violations: one count under 18 U.S.C. § 371 for conspiracy to violate federal obscenity laws—18 U.S.C. §§ 1462, 1465, six counts under 18 U.S.C. § 1465 for knowingly using and causing to be used a facility and means of interstate commerce—a combined computer/telephone system—for the purpose of transporting obscene, computer-generated materials (the GIF files) in interstate commerce, three counts under 18 U.S.C. § 1462 for shipping obscene videotapes via U.P.S., one count of causing the transportation of materials depicting minors engaged in sexually explicit conduct in violation of 18 U.S.C. § 2252(a)(1) as to Mr. Thomas only, and one count of forfeiture under 18 U.S.C. § 1467.

Both Defendants were represented by the same retained counsel, Mr. Richard Williams of San Jose, California. They appeared twice in federal district court for the Northern District of California, San Jose division, before being arraigned on March 15, 1994, in federal court in Memphis, Tennessee. They did not retain local counsel for the Tennessee criminal prosecution. Both Defendants were tried by a jury in July, 1994. Defendant Robert Thomas was found guilty on all counts except count 11 (child pornography). Defendant Carleen Thomas was found guilty on counts 1–10. The jury also found that the Defendants' interest in their computer system should be forfeited to the United States. Robert and Carleen Thomas were sentenced on December 2, 1994 to 37 and 30 months of incarceration, respectively.

Defendants * * * challenge venue in the Western District of Tennessee for [the counts relating to the transmission of GIF files to the Western District of Tennessee]. They argue that [these counts] should have been severed and transferred to California because Defendants did not cause the GIF files to be transmitted to the Western District of Tennessee. Rather, Defendants assert, it was Dirmeyer, a government agent, who, without their knowledge, accessed and downloaded the GIF files and caused them to enter Tennessee. We disagree. To establish a

Section 1465 violation, the Government must prove that a defendant knowingly used a facility or means of interstate commerce for the purpose of distributing obscene materials. Contrary to Defendants' position, Section 1465 does not require the Government to prove that Defendants had specific knowledge of the destination of each transmittal at the time it occurred.

Venue lies in any district in which the offense was committed, and the Government is required to establish venue by a preponderance of the evidence. This court examines the propriety of venue by taking into account a number of factors—the site of the defendant's acts, the elements and nature of the crime, the locus of the effect of the criminal conduct, and the suitability of each district for accurate fact finding.

Section 1465 is an obscenity statute, and federal obscenity laws, by virtue of their inherent nexus to interstate and foreign commerce, generally involve acts in more than one jurisdiction or state. Furthermore, it is well-established that "there is no constitutional impediment to the government's power to prosecute pornography dealers in any district into which the material is sent." *United States v. Bagnell,* 679 F.2d 826, 830 (11th Cir. 1982). Thus, the question of venue has become one of legislative intent.

The *Bagnell* court examined both §§ 1462 and 1465 and found that each statute established a continuing offense within the venue provisions of 18 U.S.C. § 3237(a) that occurs in every judicial district which the material touches. This court likewise recognized that venue for federal obscenity prosecutions lies in any district from, through, or into which the allegedly obscene material moves.

Substantial evidence introduced at trial demonstrated that the AABBS was set up so members located in other jurisdictions could access and order GIF files which would then be instantaneously transmitted in interstate commerce. Moreover, AABBS materials were distributed to an approved AABBS member known to reside in the Western District of Tennessee. Specifically, Defendant Robert Thomas knew of, approved, and had conversed with an AABBS member in that judicial district who had his permission to access and copy GIF files that ultimately ended up there. Some of these GIF files were clearly marked "Distribute Freely." In light of the above, the effects of the Defendants' criminal conduct reached the Western District of Tennessee, and that district was suitable for accurate fact-finding. Accordingly, we conclude venue was proper in that judicial district.

In *Miller v. California,* 413 U.S. 15 (1973), the Supreme Court set out a three-prong test for obscenity. It inquired whether (1) the average person applying contemporary community standards' would find that the work, taken as a whole appeals to the prurient interest; (2) it depicts or describes, in a patently offensive way, sexual conduct specifically defined by applicable state law; and (3) the work, taken as a whole, lacks serious literary, artistic, political, or scientific value.

Under the first prong of the *Miller* obscenity test, the jury is to apply "contemporary community standards." Defendants acknowledge the general principle that, in cases involving interstate transportation of obscene material, juries are properly instructed to apply the community standards of the geographic area where the materials are sent. Nonetheless, Defendants assert that this principle does not apply here for the same reasons they claim venue was improper. As demonstrated above, this argument cannot withstand scrutiny. The computer-generated images * * * were electronically transferred from Defendants' home in California to the Western District of Tennessee. Accordingly, the community standards of that judicial district were properly applied in this case.

Issues regarding which community's standards are to be applied are tied to those involving venue. It is well-established that:

> venue for federal obscenity prosecutions lies "in any district from, through, or into which" the allegedly obscene material moves, according to 18 U.S.C. § 3237. This may result in prosecutions of persons in a community to which they have sent materials which is obscene under that community's standards though the community from which it is sent would tolerate the same material.

United States v. Peraino, 645 F.2d 548, 551 (6th Cir. 1981).

Prosecutions may be brought either in the district of dispatch or the district of receipt, and obscenity is determined by the standards of the community where the trial takes place. Moreover, the federal courts have consistently recognized that it is not unconstitutional to subject interstate distributors of obscenity to varying community standards.

Defendants and *Amicus Curiae* appearing on their behalf argue that the computer technology used here requires a new definition of community, i.e., one that is based on the broad-ranging connections among people in cyberspace rather than the geographic locale of the federal judicial district of the criminal trial. Without a more flexible definition, they argue, there will be an impermissible chill on protected speech because BBS operators cannot select who gets the materials they make available on their bulletin boards. Therefore, they contend, BBS operators like Defendants will be forced to censor their materials so as not to run afoul of the standards of the community with the most restrictive standards.

Defendants' First Amendment issue, however, is not implicated by the facts of this case. This is not a situation where the bulletin board operator had no knowledge or control over the jurisdictions where materials were distributed for downloading or printing. Access to the Defendants' AABBS was limited. Membership was necessary and applications were submitted and screened before passwords were issued and materials were distributed. Thus, Defendants had in place methods to limit user access in jurisdictions where the risk of a finding of obscenity was greater than that in California. They knew they had a member in Memphis; the member's address and local phone number were provided on his application form. If Defendants did not wish to subject themselves to liability in jurisdictions with less tolerant standards for determining obscenity, they could have refused to give passwords to members in those districts, thus precluding the risk of liability.

This result is supported by the Supreme Court's decision in *Sable Communications v. FCC,* 492 U.S. 115, 125–26 (1989), where the Court rejected Sable's argument that it should not be compelled to tailor its dial-a-porn messages to the standards of the least tolerant community. The Court recognized that distributors of allegedly obscene materials may be subjected to the standards of the varying communities where they transmit their materials, citing *Hamling,* and further noted that Sable was "free to tailor its messages, on a selective basis, if it so chooses, to the communities it chooses to serve." The Court also found no constitutional impediment to forcing Sable to incur some costs in developing and implementing a method for screening a customer's location and providing messages compatible with community standards.

Thus, under the facts of this case, there is no need for this court to adopt a new definition of "community" for use in obscenity prosecutions involving electronic bulletin boards. This court's decision is guided by one of the cardinal rules governing the federal courts, i.e., never reach constitutional questions not squarely presented by the facts of a case.

Notes and Questions

1. The facts of *Thomas* rendered it an easy case, as the defendants intentionally sent the materials into Tennessee. Let's change the facts a bit. Imagine that Fred Felony uploads pornographic files to a website from Brooklyn, and an undercover police officer in Salt Lake City downloads the images. Assume that the files are obscene in Salt Lake City but not in Brooklyn. Has Fred Felony committed a federal crime? Can Fred Felony be indicted in Salt Lake City and measured by the community standards there? What if Fred Felony sets up a server in Antigua instead of Brooklyn, and he never enters the United States?

2. The Internet changes the regulation of obscenity by delinking the material to be regulated from physical location. Should that change trigger a rethinking of obscenity law?

> Any recognizable definition of a "local community" is quickly disappearing in the age of ubiquitous and homogenous media brought about by satellite and cable television, international news channels, and more recently, the Internet. Yet prosecutors, and to some extent the courts, have continued to cling to the archaic notion of "contemporary community standards" as measured by local geographic boundaries. As the United States, and indeed the world, becomes more transient, standardized, uniform, and homogenized, the ability of one community to isolate itself by erecting a fictitious legal barrier, designed to keep out certain categories of erotic speech, is quickly evaporating and the law must keep pace.

> * * *

If the obscenity test is to continue to embrace the concept of "community standards," recognition must be given the modern definition of "community." Where the test is applied to Internet transmissions accessible throughout the entire world, the courts must change the contours of the "community standards" test to recognize a mode of communication that nobody dreamed of when that concept was developed by the courts.

Ultimately, lawmakers and the courts will need to move to some form of regulation of the time, place, and manner of distribution of hard core erotic speech, as opposed to outright criminalization using obscenity laws based on the increasingly irrelevant concept of community standards. Restrictions that minimize the physical impact on the community, and the viewer's ability to shield himself or herself from accidental exposure to erotic speech, will take precedence over the limited modern utility of obscenity laws. Tomorrow's erotic content regulations will likely involve concepts such as labeling, filtering, warnings, and the like, instead of outright bans as have been used in the past. To the extent that state and federal governments have a legitimate interest in regulating the distribution of erotic materials in a given community, such regulation will only be successful in the Digital Age if it takes the form of valid time, place, and manner restrictions, as opposed to full content bans.

Lawrence G. Walters & Clyde DeWitt, *Obscenity in the Digital Age: The Reevaluation of Community Standards,* 10 NEXUS 59, 59, 69 (2005).

3. *Effective enforcement of obscenity laws.* Obscenity prosecutions are relatively rare. Would a switch to routine enforcement of obscenity laws make a difference in the accessibility of obscene materials given that obscene materials are increasingly obtained via the Internet? Professor Eugene Volokh has expressed doubts that a "crackdown" on obscenity could make a difference:

> As we know, there's lots of porn of all varieties out there on the Internet. I don't know how much of it is produced in the U.S.—but even if it's 75 percent, and every single U.S. producer is shut down, wouldn't foreign sites happily take up the slack?

> It's not like Americans have some great irreproducible national skills in smut-making, or like it takes a $100 million Hollywood budget to make a porn movie. Foreign porn will doubtless be quite an adequate substitute for the U.S. market. Plus the foreign distributors might even be able to make and distribute copies of the existing U.S.-produced stock—I doubt that the imprisoned copyright owners will be suing them for infringement[.] * * *

> And even if overall world production of porn somehow improbably falls by 75 percent [following criminal prosecutions for obscenity], will that seriously affect the typical porn consumer's diet? Does it matter whether you have, say, 100,000 porn titles (and live feeds) to choose from, or just 25,000?

Eugene Volokh, *Obscenity Crackdown—What Will the Next Step Be?*, Cato Institute TechKnowledge, April 12, 2004, http://www.cato.org/tech/tk/ 040412–tk.html.

4. *Online obscenity and Internet gambling compared.* In some ways, the regulation of Internet gambling and the regulation of online obscenity raise similar issues. The law has traditionally regulated a transaction that in the past occurred person-to-person, whether by meeting in person, through the mail, or by telephone. Computers and the Internet replace that with a person-to-computer transaction, and the computer need not be in the United States. In some ways, the relevance of the switch in fact patterns is similar. For example, policy arguments for preexisting law rooted in the community impact of the conduct regulated may be less powerful, and policy arguments rooted in the effects of the conduct on the individual in isolation may be strengthened. The law seems harder to enforce, and prosecutions are rare. Given these similarities, do you think the future of the law of Internet gambling and obscenity law will or should be the same? Or do the two present different problems?

5. *Minors, pornography, and the Internet.* One significant argument in favor of obscenity laws is that it allows legislatures to shield hard-core pornography from children. In the last decade, Congress has made several efforts to protect children online by enacting criminal laws that go beyond traditional obscenity laws. For example, the Communications Decency Act (CDA), Pub. L. No. 104–104, § 502 (1996), tried to limit the exposure of children to indecent materials online. The Supreme Court invalidated the CDA in Reno v. American Civil Liberties Union, 521 U.S. 844 (1997), on the ground that the law was not narrowly tailored to its compelling state interest of protecting children. Congress then tried again in the form of the Child Online Protection Act (COPA), Pub. L. No. 105–277, §§ 1401–06 (1998), codified at 47 U.S.C. § 231. COPA is considerably narrower than the CDA, but its constitutionality remains uncertain. *See* Ashcroft v. American Civil Liberties Union, 542 U.S. 656 (2004). Do you think Congress should be able to regulate how minors can access non-obscene pornography and other indecent materials via the Internet? Or does attempting to regulate when minors can access pornography inevitably place an impermissible burden on the rights of adults to access non-obscene pornography?

D. CHILD EXPLOITATION CRIMES

Tragically, child exploitation crimes are among the most common types of computer crimes. Such crimes fall into two basic categories. The first consists of offenses involving images of child pornography. These cases involve use of a computer to send, receive, and/or possess images of minors engaged in explicit sexual activity. The second category consists of offenses involving actual or attempted sexual contact with minors by adults. In these cases, the computer's role is facilitating the attempted or actual contact. The materials in this section begin with child pornography crimes and then turn to offenses involving attempted sexual contacts.

1. CHILD PORNOGRAPHY

A) Introduction

Child pornography is a term generally used to describe images of persons under the age of 18 engaged in sexually explicit conduct. Before the 1960s, such images were banned under the obscenity laws. Following *Miller v. California*, however, at least some images of child pornography fell outside the definition of obscenity. In the mid-to-late 1970s, many people believed that the loosening of obscenity standards both in the United States and in Europe had gone too far. They feared that the growing availability of sexualized images of minors facilitated widespread exploitation and abuse. *See generally* Philip Jenkins, Beyond Tolerance: Child Pornography on the Internet, 30–37 (2001); Amy Adler, *The Perverse Law of Child Pornography*, 101 Colum. L. Rev. 209 (2001). Legislatures responded by enacting laws specifically addressing child pornography. By 1982, the federal government and twenty states had enacted child pornography laws, although they varied in scope considerably. *See* New York v. Ferber, 458 U.S. 747, 749 (1982). Today, the federal government and every state has a child pornography law.

Although child pornography and obscenity both involve sexual imagery of some kind, they are prohibited for very different reasons. The distribution, receipt, and possession of child pornography is prohibited to protect children from sexual molestation and abuse. As the Supreme Court explained in *Ferber*, prohibiting child pornography can deter its creation. The creation of child pornography often involves sexual abuse, and distribution of the images inflicts a continuing harm on the child victim. Prohibiting the distribution, receipt, and possession of child pornography also can help "dry up the market" for such images, lowering demand for their creation. *See id.* at 757–61. In Osborne v. Ohio, 495 U.S. 103 (1990), the Supreme Court identified two more reasons for banning possession of child pornography images. First, a ban on possession can encourage those who possess such images to destroy them. Second, pedophiles use images of child pornography to show to potential victims to present child sexual activity as normal, a process sometimes referred to as 'grooming.' *See id.* at 111.

B) The Proxy Rationale

Another possible rationale for child pornography offenses—albeit a rationale not used to justify their constitutionality—is the perceived correlation between possession of images and acts of child molestation. This is a difficult argument to evaluate, in large part because little reliable empirical work exists on how strong the correlation may be.

Consider two competing perspectives. On one hand, some people believe that those who collect images of child pornography are likely to engage in actual acts of molestation. They reason that knowing possession of such images signals sexual attraction to children. Given the serious criminal liability that attaches to mere possession of the images, those who collect the images are also likely to attempt actual sexual contact with children. Possession thus indicates future dangerousness.

On the other hand, some people look at the problem very differently. They reason that interest in viewing images of child pornography is different from engaging in actual sexual contact. An interest in viewing violent movies is very different from engaging in actual acts of violence, they note, and the same distinction can be made in the context of child pornography.

The only empirical study on the correlation between child pornography and sexual molestation is an unpublished study by Dr. Andres Hernandez, director of the Sex Offender Treatment Program at the Federal Bureau of Prisons in Butner, North Carolina. *See* Andres E. Hernandez, *Self-Reported Contact Sexual Crimes of Federal Inmates Convicted of Child Pornography Crimes*, presented at the 19th Annual Research and Treatment Conference of the Association for the Treatment of Sexual Abusers (November 2000). This study involved 54 adult males in a voluntary sex offender treatment program at a medium-security federal prison. All of the participants were serving prison time for possessing or distributing child pornography. The sex offender treatment program encouraged participants to divulge their past sexual contacts with children as part of an intensive therapy program. The study then compared the total number of reported sexual contacts with the number of known sexual contacts at the time the defendants were sentenced for child pornography offenses.

Just over 50% of the participants in the study—29 out of 54—had no known sexual contacts with minors at the time of their sentencing. The remaining group, consisting of 25 participants, had been known to have contacted a collective total of 53 victims. Following therapy in the sex offender treatment program, however, the participants self-reported quite different histories. Participants in the program self-reported an average of 26.37 past victims each. Among the 29 participants with no known past sexual contacts with minors, 11 continued to report no past contacts. However, 18 of the 29 who had no known past contacts disclosed past contacts. This group self-reported an average of more than 12 victims each. Altogether, the percentage of participants with known past sexual contacts with minors went from 46% to 80%, and the known number of victims jumped from 53 to 1,371.

Does this study make a persuasive case for a link between possession of child pornography and actual acts of child molestation? Is the sample size sufficient to make a judgment? Do you think the results of a self-supported study are likely to be accurate? Are inmates who volunteered for treatment likely to be representative? For a skeptical view of the Hernandez study, see Joseph S. Fulda, *Internet Stings Directed at Pedophiles: A Study in Philosophy and Law*, 15 Widener L. J. 47, 67–72 (2005).

C) 18 U.S.C. § 2252

The primary federal statute addressing child pornography appears in 18 U.S.C. § 2252, and was originally enacted as part of the Protection of Children Against Sexual Exploitation Act, Pub. L. No. 95–225 (1978).

In its present form, it contains four distinct offenses in §§ 2252(a)(1)-(a)(4). The first, found at § 2252(a)(1), prohibits knowingly transporting or shipping in interstate or foreign commerce a visual depiction of a minor engaging in sexually explicit conduct. The second, § 2252(a)(2), prohibits receiving or distributing such depictions that have been sent in interstate or foreign commerce, or which contain materials which have been transported in interstate commerce, or reproducing such materials for distribution in interstate or foreign commerce.

The third and fourth prohibitions, §§ 2252(a)(3) and (a)(4), deal with possession-related crimes. Section 2252(a)(3) concerns selling or having possession with intent to sell, and § 2252(a)(4) concerns mere possession of such materials. Note that the jurisdictional hook for these two offenses is somewhat more complicated than for §§ 2251(a)(1)-(a)(2). In the case of a possession offense, the interstate and foreign commerce nexus is supplemented by an alternative jurisdictional path, namely possession occurring on federal property. Section 2252(a)(4) also permits defendants to raise an affirmative defense, albeit one that is invoked only rarely. If a defendant possesses only one or two "matters" containing child pornography, they can avoid criminal liability if they "promptly and in good faith, and without retaining or allowing any person, other than a law enforcement agency, to access any visual depiction or copy thereof ... took reasonable steps to destroy each such visual depiction; or ... reported the matter to a law enforcement agency and afforded that agency access to each such visual depiction." 18 U.S.C. § 2252(c).

Violations of §§ 2252(a)(1), (a)(2), or (a)(3) trigger a five-year mandatory minimum punishment, and can lead to higher punishments as well. *See* 18 U.S.C. § 2252(b)(1). Violations of § 2252(a)(4), the possession provision, do not trigger a mandatory minimum sentence, but permit a maximum punishment of up to ten years. *See* 18 U.S.C. § 2252(b)(2). In both cases, prior convictions will trigger higher punishments.

D) 18 U.S.C. § 2252A and 18 U.S.C. § 2256

Congress passed the Child Pornography Prevention Act, Pub. L. No. 104–208 (1996), in response to concerns that computer technologies were rendering existing child pornography laws out of date. Specifically, Congress was concerned that pedophiles could use computer software to create computer-generated child pornography, either by "morphing" a digital image of a real child's face to a computer-generated image of a child's body or by generating a life-like image entirely by computer. The CPPA was designed to expand the then-existing child pornography laws to encompass these new forms of child pornography.

Instead of amending 18 U.S.C. § 2252, Congress opted to create a new child pornography statute, 18 U.S.C. § 2252A and 18 U.S.C. § 2256. The decision to draft a new statute rather than amend the existing one was based largely on concerns that the new statute might be struck down in whole or in part under the First Amendment. If a court struck down the new statute and found that it was not severable from the preexisting language, the court's decision would leave no law on the books until Congress could act again. By creating a new statute, Congress preserved § 2252 and created new ground in 18 U.S.C. § 2252A and § 2256.

The text of 18 U.S.C. § 2252A is a modernized and expanded version of § 2252, with definitions of key terms appearing in 18 U.S.C. § 2256. Sections 2252A(a)(1), (a)(2), and (a)(3)(A) largely recreate the prohibitions in § 2252(a)(1) and (2). Sections 2252A(a)(4) and (a)(5) largely mirror § 2252(a)(3) and (a)(4); Section 2252A(d) mirrors the affirmative defense of § 2252(c). Sections 2252A(a)(3)(B) and 2252A(a)(6) are expansions beyond the traditional scope of child pornography laws; the former is addressed at advertising and soliciting images, and the latter at luring minors. Section 2256 provides definitions for key terms used in 2252A, most notably a definition of child pornography that goes beyond images of actual children to include morphed images of child pornography and virtual images of child pornography that are indistinguishable from real images. 18 U.S.C. § 2256(8) (2003).

E) Statutory Elements of 18 U.S.C. §§ 2252 and 2252A

When § 2252 was first enacted in 1978, materials containing images of child pornography typically appeared as physical books, magazines, and photographs. Existing law still reflects that assumption in some ways. The law prohibits conduct such as transporting, shipping, receiving, and possessing images, all conduct that is readily understood in the context of physical items. But what does it mean to "transport" or "possess" data?

UNITED STATES v. MOHRBACHER

United States Court of Appeals for the Ninth Circuit, 1999.
182 F.3d 1041.

REINHARDT, Circuit Judge:

Daniel Zane Mohrbacher appeals two counts of conviction under 18 U.S.C. § 2252(a)(1) for transporting visual depictions of minors engaged in sexually explicit conduct. He does not challenge his other two counts of conviction, one for receiving visual depictions of minors engaging in sexually explicit conduct under 18 U.S.C. § 2252(a)(2) and the other for possession of three or more items containing such depictions under § 2252(a)(4)(b). Mohrbacher's illegal conduct consisted of downloading images of child pornography from a foreign-based electronic bulletin board. As to the challenged counts, he argues that he was charged and convicted under the wrong section of the statute because while he may have *received* these images in violation of § 2252(a)(2) he did not *transport* or *ship* them in violation of § 2252(a)(1). We agree with his reading of the statute, and accordingly reverse these two counts of conviction.

I.

In March 1992, Danish police seized the business records of BAMSE, a computer bulletin board system based in Denmark that sold child pornography over the Internet. The records included information that Mohrbacher, who lived in Paradise, California, had downloaded two graphic interface format (GIF) images from BAMSE in January 1992.

In March 1993, police executed a search warrant at Mohrbacher's workplace and found, among other images, two files that had been downloaded from BAMSE, one of a nude girl and one of a girl engaged in a sex act with an adult; both girls were under twelve. During the execution of the warrant, Mohrbacher was cooperative, confessing that he had downloaded the two images from BAMSE, showing police where they could find the images that they were looking for on his computer, and providing telephone records that confirmed the dates of his Internet activity. Mohrbacher subsequently cooperated with the government's investigation of child pornography. He made monitored telephone calls to a number of electronic bulletin boards, provided the name of one bulletin board operator, and testified at a grand jury hearing. At that hearing, Mohrbacher again admitted that he had downloaded at least one of the two images.

In May 1996, Mohrbacher was indicted for one count of transporting visual depictions of minors engaged in sexually explicit conduct in violation of 18 U.S.C. § 2252(a)(1) and one count of possession of three or more items depicting sexually explicit conduct in violation of 18 U.S.C. § 2252(a)(4)(B).

Mohrbacher's trial began on September 30, 1997. On October 3, he made a Rule 29 motion for acquittal on the transporting counts, arguing that downloading images constituted *receiving,* rather than transporting or shipping, within the common sense meaning of the statute. The district court denied the motion, reasoning that downloading from a computer bulletin board was analogous to "the seller putting an item on his shelf and the buyer being the person who takes it off the shelf. Here, it was Mr. Mohrbacher who pushed the right buttons that caused the images to be sent from Denmark to California." The court also stated that Mohrbacher could be criminally liable for causing the images to be transported under 18 U.S.C. § 2,[3] commenting that "it was Mr. Mohrbacher who caused the images or visual depiction to be transported in foreign commerce."

At the trial, in addition to the witnesses who linked Mohrbacher directly to the images that were the subject of the criminal charges, the prosecution presented expert testimony about the operation of the bulletin board. The expert witness testified that "a computer bulletin board system is kind of like a store of sorts. There's the capability of sending

---

3. 18 U.S.C. § 2(b) provides: "whoever willfully causes an act to be done which if directly performed by him or another would be an offense against the United States, is punishable as a principal."

and receiving files and sending and receiving messages.'' Having studied BAMSE for two years, he provided the following description of it:

> BAMSE was a computerized bulletin board system. The bulletin board system is an automated system that runs 24 hours a day, seven days a week. That's a computer system that allows people to connect to it via computer and telephone modem. Once users connect to the BBS, they log in as a user name, they provide a password, and the BBS has a list of images available for download. Individuals would select pictures, then download them to their computer. The image files on the BAMSE BBS were GIF files, which stands for graphic interchange files. It's just a binary string of information. It's the computer's way of representing a visual image.

The expert described the process of downloading GIF image files, explaining that the bulletin board user selects an image and uses his own computer modem to download the image file through telephone lines. Once downloading has been completed, the image is contained in the user's own computer system. No human conduct is required at the bulletin board site in order to facilitate this file transfer. When asked whether a "store" analogy was appropriate, the expert agreed but then described one difference: when a customer purchases an item on the bulletin board, the supply is not depleted—rather, a copy of the original product is generated and sent. On cross-examination, he agreed that defense counsel's analogy to a mail order catalogue was fair, and the following exchange ensued in which Mohrbacher's attorney attempted to demonstrate how downloading would compare to calling in a mail order:

Q. I would call them on their catalog order number.

A. Okay.

Q. And I would either be connected with a human being or with, in your world—

A. Computer.

Q. Some computer. So the computer's just a substitute for the human being who initially we used to contact; isn't that right?

A. Sure.

Q. Just a way of doing business. Instead of the human being responding, the computer responds?

A. Sure. A lot of the sites have that with the Internet access right now.

Q. Sure. So what we're doing as the businessman that runs Penney's, I've substituted my computer system, which guys like you developed, for the human being I used to have to pay too much money?

A. Okay.

Q. Now the BBS is the same program; is it not? * * *

A. A systems operator is like a storekeeper or shopkeeper. He buys computer hardware, he buys BBS software, and he has his goods that he wants to sell. And he has to customize the BBS software to reflect what merchandise he wants to sell. He needs to create his catalog, if you will.

Q. Sure. So if he didn't have all this computer stuff, what he'd have is a room with a bunch of—like a wall with little compartments in it?

A. Sure.

Q. And you'd call him up, and he'd walk over, and he'd pull it out of the compartment, and he'd send it to you if you paid him for it?

A. Sure.

Q. So instead of having the sysop [systems operator] do the shipping, you've got the computer doing the shipping?

A. Correct.

During the presentation of the prosecution's case, Mohrbacher's attorney challenged and attempted to impeach some of the witnesses. However, after the government rested, Mohrbacher presented no witnesses, evidence or defense. His attorney's closing argument suggested the possibility that Mohrbacher might not have known the nature of the images that he was downloading or that someone else could have been responsible for downloading and storing the illegal material. The attorney also argued that downloading an image could constitute "receiving" but not "transporting" or "shipping." At the end of the trial, Mohrbacher renewed his Rule 29 motion and the district court again denied it. The jury convicted Mohrbacher on all counts.

II.

The facts relevant to Mohrbacher's motion for acquittal are not disputed. We therefore confront directly the legal question whether downloading images from a computer bulletin board constitutes shipping or transporting within the meaning of the terms as used in 18 U.S.C. § 2252(a)(1), a question of first impression. Mohrbacher argues that downloading is properly characterized as receiving images by computer, which is proscribed by § 2252(a)(2), rather than transporting or shipping images by computer as prohibited by § 2252(a)(1). If Mohrbacher is right, then with respect to the two challenged counts he was charged and convicted under the wrong statutory provision, and those convictions must be reversed.

Mohrbacher reasons that downloading is essentially an electronic request by one computer owner to another computer owner to deliver files or data electronically to the requesting owner's computer. He presents a definition of downloading in support: "To copy data from a main source to a peripheral device ... the process of copying a file from an online service or bulletin board service (BBS) to one's own Computer." Philip E. Margolis, Random House Personal Computer Dictionary at 156 (2d ed. 1996). This definition is in accord with the expert testimony that was presented by the prosecution at trial. As was discussed in greater detail earlier in this opinion, that expert testified that downloading is analogous to placing an order through a mail order catalogue except that a computer fills the order automatically and the inventory is not depleted because a new copy of the image is generated.

The question that we must resolve is whether, given what appears to be a noncontroversial definition of the term, Mohrbacher's "downloading" of two images constitutes a violation of § 2252(a)(1). Mohrbacher suggests an analogy for our consideration, an analogy that is consistent with that testified to by the government expert. Mohrbacher argues that his conduct was comparable to that of a customer who places a phone order requesting delivery of an item, the only difference being that the entity that was filling the order—the bulletin board—had a completely automated response and did not require any action by an individual at the time the order was filled. The government argues that the automated nature of the bulletin board's response makes *Mohrbacher* the one responsible for causing the visual images to move from one location to another and that an individual who causes transporting or shipping is guilty as a principal. At oral argument, when asked to clarify whether a computer bulletin board service operator could be liable for transporting or shipping images under its interpretation of the statute, the government answered in the negative. In the government's view, it is only the individual who downloads the image who has caused that image to be transported. Mohrbacher responds by pointing out that a request will not be filled unless the operator of the bulletin board has configured it to accept orders. Thus, he argues, it is the bulletin board operator who has transported or shipped the images, and the downloader has only received them. The disagreement is in essence over whether the government is correct that the automated nature of the process requires the conclusion that downloading is equivalent to transporting.

In interpreting a statute, we look first to the plain language of the statute, construing the provisions of the entire law, including its object and policy, to ascertain the intent of Congress. The statute at issue does not define the terms "transport," "ship" or "receive." *See* 18 U.S.C. § 2256 (1999). Where a statutory term is not defined in the statute, it is appropriate to accord the term its ordinary meaning. When there is no indication that Congress intended a specific legal meaning for the term, the court may look to sources such as dictionaries for a definition.

The first definition of "receive" in the Oxford English Dictionary is "to take into one's hand, or into one's possession (something held out or offered by another); to take delivery of (a thing) from another, either for oneself or for a third party." Oxford's English Dictionary 2d 314 (1989). An individual who downloads material takes possession or accepts delivery of the visual image; he has therefore certainly received it. In fact, guides to computer terminology often analogize downloading to receiving information and uploading to transmitting or sending. "To transmit a file from one computer to another. When conducting the session, download means receive, upload means transmit." Alan Freedman, Computer Words You Gotta Know! Essential Definitions for Survival in a High-tech World 49 (1993). "To download means to receive information, typically a file, from another computer to yours via your modem. The opposite term is upload, which means to send a file to another computer." Robin Williams, Jargon, An Informal Dictionary of Computer Terms 170–71 (1993).

However, it is also possible, employing dictionary definitions, to construe the terms "transport" and "ship" in a manner that encompasses a downloader's acts. "Transport" is defined as "to carry, convey, or remove from one place or person to another; to convey across." Oxford's English Dictionary 2d, *supra,* at 423. Shipping is usually defined as one manner of transporting. *See* Webster's Third, *supra,* at 2096 ("to cause to be transported" or "to move (something) from one place or position to another"). An individual who downloads an image to his own computer has indisputably received that image; however, he has also arguably moved that image from one place to another—from the bulletin board to his own computer. Of course, the downloader is only able to accomplish this task because another person has preconfigured the bulletin board to accept his order.[9] Given the role that another individual plays in uploading the images and configuring the bulletin board to send them upon request, and the fact that the process of downloading would seem to correspond much more closely with the term "receiving" than with "transporting" or "shipping," the dictionary definitions are not dispositive of the issue before us.

* * * [W]e conclude that Mohrbacher's interpretation of the statute is correct. An individual who downloads images from a computer bulletin board takes an action that is more analogous to ordering materials over the phone and receiving materials through the mail than to sending or shipping such materials. Those who are responsible for *providing* the images to a customer, by making them available on a computer bulletin board or by sending them via electronic mail, are properly charged with and convicted of shipping or transporting images under § 2252(a)(1). A customer who is simply on the receiving end—who downloads an image that has been made available through an automated, preconfigured process or that has been sent by another computer user—is guilty of receiving or possessing such materials under § 2252(a)(2) but not of shipping or transporting them.

We reject the argument that even if downloading itself is more analogous to receiving, Mohrbacher, by ordering the pornographic images, *caused* them to be transported and is therefore nonetheless criminally liable under § 2252(a)(1). Acceptance of this reasoning would allow any act of ordering, requesting, or indicating an interest in contraband to provide a basis for conviction of transporting or shipping such

9. The action of the bulletin board operator, on the other hand, cannot be properly characterized as receiving images but *only* as transporting or shipping—unless the operator's conduct does not violate *any* provision of the statute, as the government rather oddly suggested at oral argument. While of course more than one individual could be held responsible for transporting a given image, it is more difficult to claim that Mohrbacher himself *caused* the images to be transported when one considers that the bulletin board operator is in reality the individual who is primarily responsible for the images moving from the bulletin board to individuals' computers.

material, and would eliminate the distinction between purchasers and sellers or shippers and receivers. Because a request for drugs could be viewed as *causing* a drug sale to occur, any purchaser or receiver could be charged as a buyer or distributor at the prosecutor's discretion. For the reasons explained above, the distinctions between downloading an image and ordering an item from a human supplier—i.e., the facts that the response is automatic (because an individual has programmed it to be so) and that filling the order does not deplete the supply—provide no logical reason to limit the principle that would be established: any customer who requests or orders a product could be held liable for causing that product to be sent or sold.

The government's reliance upon 18 U.S.C. § 2(b) does not change our analysis. That provision does not eliminate the distinction between buyers and sellers, or between shippers and receivers. It serves a different purpose: it insures that an offender who utilizes an innocent agent to carry out a criminal act but may not be charged as a principal under § 2(a), the aiding and abetting provision, is not insulated from criminal liability. While the government relies upon *United States v. Thomas,* 893 F.2d 1066 (9th Cir. 1990), and *United States v. Michaels,* 796 F.2d 1112, 1117–18 (9th Cir. 1986), those cases both involve defendants who induced innocent parties to mail contraband on their behalf. They stand for the principle that a defendant may be convicted as a principal even if he uses another person as the agent to commit the crime. Such a concept is entirely different from the theory urged by the government in this case, which is essentially that, when a customer orders illegal materials from a producer or supplier, the ordering party has caused the supplying party's illegal act of filling the order. The government's interpretation of 18 U.S.C. § 2(b) would vest unconstrained discretion in prosecutors to decide how to charge a large number of crimes that involve actions by individuals who commit *different* offenses, and might unwittingly render many provisions of criminal statutes superfluous or duplicative.

For the above reasons, the district court's denial of Mohrbacher's motion for acquittal on counts one and two was in error, and we reverse as to those counts.

Notes and Questions

1. The holding of *Morhrbacher* is that "[t]hose who are responsible for providing the images to a customer, by making them available on a computer bulletin board or by sending them via electronic mail, are properly charged with and convicted of shipping or transporting images under § 2252(a)(1). A customer who is simply on the receiving end ... is guilty of receiving or possessing such materials under § 2252(a)(2) but not of shipping or transporting them."

Is this interpretation persuasive? Note that the *Mohrbacher* court overlooks an important fact about § 2252(a)(2). That section does not prohibit "receiving or possessing" images, as Judge Reinhardt says. Read the text again: it actually prohibits receiving or *distributing* images. Given that § 2252(a)(2) prohibits receiving or distributing images, how likely is it that Congress intended for § 2252(a)(1) to prohibit distributing images and for § 2252(a)(2) to prohibit receiving images? On the other hand, if Judge Reinhardt is wrong in *Mohrbacher*, what is the difference between § 2252(a)(1) and § 2252(a)(2)? Why would Congress prohibit shipping and transporting in § 2252(a)(1) and then prohibit distributing in § 2252(a)(2)? Isn't that redundant?

Two clues might explain this puzzle. First, note the jurisdictional difference between the two provisions. Section 2252(a)(1) requires shipping or transporting in interstate or foreign commerce, whereas § 2252(a)(2) prohibits receiving or distributing an image that has been shipped in interstate or foreign commerce. Second, consider the meaning of the term "distribute." In criminal law, distributing means delivering or transferring to another person. *See* Black's Law Dictionary 475 (6th ed. 1990). Receiving also implies the involvement of another person. For example, if you receive a birthday gift from a friend, the gift is transferred from your friend to you.

These clues suggest a different reading of the statute than that adopted in *Mohrbacher*. Perhaps § 2252(a)(1) prohibits moving images across state lines, whereas § 2252(a)(2) prohibits transfers of possession between two people. Under this reading, § 2252(a)(1) and § 2252(a)(2) will overlap in some cases but will be distinct in others. For example, an individual who has two e-mail addresses and e-mails the image from an account in one state to an account in another state has transported the image but has not distributed it. Conversely, a person who copies an image onto a CD and then hands the CD to a friend has distributed the image but has not transported it.

Which reading of the statute is more persuasive? If the interpretation offered in this comment is more persuasive than the one offered in the *Mohrbacher* case, is someone who downloads an image of child pornography guilty of violating § 2252(a)(1), § 2252(a)(2), or both?

2. *Problem.* You are an FBI agent investigating three individuals for possible child pornography offenses. Your investigation reveals that Suspect #1 posted images of child pornography to a password-protected website in California. Suspect #2 found out about the website, and downloaded the images to his personal computer in New York. When Suspect #3 learned of the images on Suspect #2's computer, he stole the computer and brought it from New York to New Jersey. Which of the suspects have violated § 2252(a)(1)? Which have violated § 2252(a)(2)?

3. The punishments for distributing images of child pornography are the same as the punishments for receiving those images. Does this make sense as a matter of policy?

4. *The receipt/possession distinction.* The receipt of child pornography is almost always accompanied by its possession. However, the penalties for receipt under § 2252(a)(2) are considerably more severe than the punishment for possession under § 2252(a)(4). If the conduct usually is the same, why did Congress impose two different levels of punishment?

In United States v. Richardson, 238 F.3d 837 (7th Cir. 2001), Judge Posner speculated about one possible reason:

The explanation may be that receivers increase the market for child pornography and hence the demand for children to pose as models for pornographic photographs; possessors, at least qua possessors, as distinct from receivers, though most of them are that too, do not. The possessor who creates his own pornography strictly for his personal use is not part of the interstate and international traffic in child pornography, a traffic that not only increases the demand for the production of such pornography but, by virtue of its far-flung scope, makes it extremely difficult to locate, let alone protect, the children exploited by it. Concern with the welfare of the children who are used to create pornography is part of the public concern over child pornography, and this makes the receiver a greater malefactor than the possessor.

Id. at 839.

The role of prosecutorial discretion may offer a more persuasive explanation. The statutory definition of child pornography arguably is quite broad, and it encompasses a number of different kinds of cases. The statutory overlap between receipt and possession crimes permits prosecutors to charge more severe cases differently than less severe cases. A prosecutor can inquire as to the nature of the images in the case and can choose whether to charge the defendant with the lesser offense of possession or the greater offense of receipt. The receipt/possession distinction may also give prosecutors an extra tool to pressure defendants to plead guilty. If the government's case is weak, a prosecutor may offer the defendant a choice between pleading guilty to possession or going to trial on more severe receipt charges.

Do any of these explanations justify the different treatment of receipt and possession?

4. Is the existing definition of child pornography too broad? Consider State v. Senters, 699 N.W.2d 810 (Neb. 2005). The defendant was a 28 year-old high school teacher who had a consensual sexual relationship with a 17 year-old student. The two decided to videotape themselves having intercourse, and the defendant kept the videotape in his apartment. The defendant's roommate later discovered the videotape and contacted the high school where he taught. Representatives of the school then contacted the police. The age of consent in Nebraska is sixteen, which meant that statutory rape charges could not be brought. Instead, state prosecutors charged the defendant with manufacturing child pornography. He was convicted and sentenced to two years of probation. The Nebraska Supreme Court affirmed the conviction, rejecting the defendant's claim that prosecuting him violated the Due Process and Equal Protection clauses. *See id.* at 817–18.

5. In United States v. X–Citement Video, Inc., 513 U.S. 64 (1994), the Supreme Court considered the mens rea that applies to the statutory element of the age of the person visually depicted contained in 18 U.S.C. §§ 2252(a)(1) and (a)(2). In an opinion by Chief Justice Rehnquist, the Court held that the "knowing" mens rea applied to the person's age. It is not enough that a defendant transported or received images that happen to contain child pornography; rather, the government must prove the defendant's knowledge that the person depicted in the image was under the age of

eighteen. The Court justified this holding on a number of factors, including the odd results that would follow from a contrary approach:

> If the term "knowingly" applies only to the relevant verbs in § 2252—transporting, shipping, receiving, distributing and reproducing—we would have to conclude that Congress wished to distinguish between someone who knowingly transported a particular package of film whose contents were unknown to him, and someone who unknowingly transported that package. It would seem odd, to say the least, that Congress distinguished between someone who inadvertently dropped an item into the mail without realizing it, and someone who consciously placed the same item in the mail, but was nonetheless unconcerned about whether the person had any knowledge of the prohibited contents of the package.

> Some applications of respondents' position would produce results that were not merely odd, but positively absurd. If we were to conclude that "knowingly" only modifies the relevant verbs in § 2252, we would sweep within the ambit of the statute actors who had no idea that they were even dealing with sexually explicit material. For instance, a retail druggist who returns an uninspected roll of developed film to a customer "knowingly distributes" a visual depiction and would be criminally liable if it were later discovered that the visual depiction contained images of children engaged in sexually explicit conduct. Or, a new resident of an apartment might receive mail for the prior resident and store the mail unopened. If the prior tenant had requested delivery of materials covered by § 2252, his residential successor could be prosecuted for "knowing receipt" of such materials. Similarly, a Federal Express courier who delivers a box in which the shipper has declared the contents to be "film" "knowingly transports" such film. We do not assume that Congress, in passing laws, intended such results.

Id. at 69.

6. According to a comprehensive study of the child pornography underworld, images of child pornography generally are distributed in ways that are different from ways of distributing obscenity. *See* Philip Jenkins, Beyond Tolerance (2001). Professor Jenkins explains that individuals interested in obtaining child pornography often mask their identity using proxy servers and anonymous accounts with foreign computers. The images themselves generally are not posted on public websites with fixed addresses. Such sites are discovered quickly, and the system administrators then contact law enforcement.

According to Professor Jenkins, individuals use bulletin board services, e-groups, and other relatively anonymous services to distribute information and materials. For example, an individual wanting to share images might open a free account with a website that permits users to post files anonymously, and then will upload encrypted images of child pornography from his collection. He will then post a message on one of several international bulletin boards informing readers that the images are posted to that site. In the hours before the site system administrator realizes that the site is hosting child pornography and shuts it down, hundreds of anonymous users will download the encrypted files. The individual then will send another message to the bulletin board posting the key to decrypt the files, permitting them to be viewed. For a more detailed account, see Jenkins, Ch. 3.

UNITED STATES v. TUCKER

United States District Court for the District of Utah, 2001.
150 F. Supp. 2d 1263, *aff'd* 305 F.3d 1193 (10th Cir. 2002).

CAMPBELL, District Judge.

Defendant Jeffrey Tucker is charged under 18 U.S.C. § 2252A(a)(5)(B) with knowing possession of child pornography. The court held a bench trial on this matter on January 4, 2001 and enters the following findings of fact, conclusions of law, and judgement.

FINDINGS OF FACT

At trial, evidence was presented that Tucker had participated in several Internet newsgroups that allowed him to receive images of child pornography. To gain access to these sites, Tucker paid a membership fee for which he received a password. Tucker visited these sites often, and posted several messages on them. The evidence demonstrated that Tucker frequently had visited these sights to view at least five thousand pictures of child pornography. In an interview with Detective Ryan Atack, Tucker admitted visiting pornographic websites on the Internet and seeking out those that featured pornographic depictions of children. When initially visiting one of these Internet sites, Tucker would view a series of "thumbnail" pictures (smaller pictorial versions which may be enlarged) of the child pornography available on the site. Tucker would enlarge any picture he wished so that he could view for as long as he liked and then move on to the next image. During these sessions Tucker had the ability to show the material to others; he could also manipulate the images by enlarging them, and make hard paper copies by printing them. The images Tucker viewed were automatically stored on Tucker's computer cache file, which would enable Tucker to load the picture more quickly if he sought to view an image again.[2]

In the interview where Agent Atack was present, Tucker also admitted that on June 11, 1998, he had been looking at pornographic images of children who were between the ages of ten and twelve through newsgroups entitled alt/sex/preteens and alt/sex/erotica/teens. He further admitted that he had deleted his computer cache file on June 11, 1998, because it was something that he always did when he "was done." He stated that he always deleted the images that he had viewed once he was finished with them because "it's like there's always new ones." Even though Tucker made a practice of deleting the images saved in his cache file after a session of viewing, at least one was saved on his computer's c-drive in a file folder called "Xmission." On another occasion Tucker

---

2. When a website is viewed on the Internet some of its contents are automatically stored to the computer's drive in the cache file so that future visits to that site can load more quickly. The information that is stored in the cache file retains images from the website that was visited.

either copied or attempted to copy two hundred and nine separate images to a floppy disk on his computer's a-drive. One of those images was then either copied on a disk in the a-drive or viewed by Tucker from a floppy disk on the a-drive. Tucker said that he did not save the images as a usual practice, but rather deleted them, because he could always access more.

Tucker's computer was seized pursuant to a parole search and was taken to the Salt Lake City Police Department and booked into evidence. Agent Dan Hooper from the Utah Department of Public Safety subsequently conducted a search and forensic examination of the computer. In this examination, Agent Hooper made an exact copy of Tucker's computer hard drive so as to preserve the original hard drive. In his investigation, Agent Hooper found numerous images of child pornography on the hard drive which depicted children engaged in sexually explicit conduct. These images were recovered from the Internet Explorer cache file and the Temporary Internet Files in the computer hard drive's recycle bin. Agent Hooper also found one image of child pornography, file 5–16–98, in the computer's c-drive—a location other than the cache file where images viewed from the Internet were stored by Tucker's computer.

CONCLUSIONS OF LAW

Tucker is charged with knowing possession of child pornography under the pre-amended version of 18 U.S.C. § 2252A(a)(5)(B), which imposes criminal liability on an individual who:

> knowingly possesses any book, magazine, periodical, film, videotape, computer disk, or any other material that contains 3 or more images of child pornography that has been mailed, or shipped or transported in interstate or foreign commerce by any means, including by computer, or that was produced using materials that have been mailed, or shipped or transported in interstate or foreign commerce by any means, including by computer, shall be punished as provided in subsection (b).

18 U.S.C. § 2252A(a)(5)(B) (1997).[3] The parties have both stipulated that the images Tucker viewed on the Internet were "mailed, or shipped or transported in interstate commerce." Tucker further does not contest the fact that he viewed a number of visual depictions of child pornography on his home computer. He does contend that he is not subject to criminal liability under the statute because he never "possessed" or "knowingly possessed" any child pornography. Because Tucker admits viewing the child pornography, and also concedes that the images viewed were "other material" constituting child pornography for the purposes of the statute, the only remaining questions to be resolved in this matter are: 1) whether Tucker had possession under 18 U.S.C. § 2252A(a)(5)(b)

---

3. The current version of the statute eliminates the "3 or more" requirement and would impose liability on possession of "any" child pornography. *See* 18 U.S.C. § 2252A(a)(5)(B).

such that he is subject to criminal liability; and 2) whether such possession was knowing possession.

I. Did Tucker "Possess" Child Pornography?

The word 'possess' means to own or to exert control over. The word 'possession' can take on several different, but related, meanings. The law recognizes two kinds of 'possession'—actual physical possession and constructive possession. A person who knowingly has *direct physical control over a thing* at a given time is then in actual possession of it. "The term 'possess' means to *exercise authority, dominion or control over*" a given thing. Devitt, Blackmar, and O'Malley, Federal Jury and Practice Instructions: Criminal § 36.12 (4th ed. 1992). As so defined, possession means actual physical possession, just as having the drugs or weapons in one's hand, in one's home or other place under one's exclusive control. Black's Law Dictionary defines natural possession as "the exercise of *physical detention* or *control* over a thing." Blacks Law Dictionary 1184 (7th ed. 1999). In order for an individual constructively to possess property, he must knowingly hold the power and ability to exercise dominion and control over it. Constructive possession may be established by circumstantial evidence. With regard to possession of contraband such as narcotics, the Tenth Circuit has also defined constructive possession as an appreciable *ability to guide the destiny* of the contraband.

Given this definition, Tucker had possession of the child pornography. Tucker had control over the images he viewed on his computer due to the fact that he could *detain* them on his monitor as long as he liked and *control* them by, among other things, enlarging and manipulating them. While the images that Tucker received were on his computer screen, he could control them in many ways: he could copy them had he chosen; he could print them had he chosen; he could enlarge them and "zoom-in" on the pictures as he chose; he could show them to others had he chosen; and he could copy them to other directories—as he attempted to do with the 5–16–98 files found on his c-drive, outside of his cache file. It is true that when Tucker viewed the images, the site and its images were automatically saved on Tucker's cache file, and that Tucker did not play any role in this automatic operation other than gaining access to the websites and viewing child pornography; yet Tucker also demonstrated ultimate dominion and control over these images because he was able to destroy them by deleting them from his hard drive. That Tucker had possession is not only evidenced by his showing and manipulation of the images, but also by the telling fact that he took the time to delete the image links from his computer cache file. Logically, one cannot destroy what one does not possess and control. Indeed, the ability to destroy is definitive evidence of control.

On the issue of destruction, defendant cites dicta from *United States v. Hall*, 142 F.3d 988 (7th Cir. 1998), for the proposition that deletion of computer files relieves one from criminal liability for possession under the statute. In *Hall,* the Defendant had purposefully downloaded and saved child pornography on his computer hard drive and was charged with possession under a different provision, 18 U.S.C. § 2252(a)(4)(B). At oral argument on appeal, the defendant argued that he merely viewed and did not possess child pornography, making an analogy between simply viewing television and viewing images on a computer accessing the Internet. The *Hall* court observed "that the Defendant's television analogy is incomplete in that one does not possess the images he views on a television screen. Hall had every opportunity to delete any computer files he did not wish to retain." The court then went on to find that the fact that Hall had downloaded the files containing child pornography surely evidenced possession. However, the dicta in *Hall* does not support defendant's contention; the *Hall* court specifically did not address what kinds of activity would constitute possession as it concluded that "since defendant did not raise this issue before the district judge or in his brief, we will not further consider it at this point." The *Hall* court therefore did not reach the issue of whether activities such as Tucker's constitutes possession under 18 U.S.C. § 2252A(a)(5)(b), and offered no other guidance regarding what types of activities would constitute possession under this statute.

Counsel for Tucker argued that: "Defendant's contention is that he cannot 'possess' something which he didn't down load, copy or intentionally store and that he cannot possess something he pro-actively deleted from his cache file immediately after *he regained control of his computer from the Internet*." (Def.'s Trial Br. at 4.) (emphasis added). This argument is faulty for at least two reasons. First, Tucker did not "regain control of his computer from the Internet." The Internet is not a nefarious force which "possessed" Tucker's computer; the Internet exercised no volition in this case. Tucker purposefully visited Internet sites for the express purpose of viewing child pornography. The "Internet" did not put these pictures on Tucker's computer monitor, Tucker did by entering the sites. The images would not have been saved to his cache file had Tucker not volitionally reached out for them. Second, there would have been no need for Tucker to delete the files containing child pornography had not his act of gaining access to the websites that offered access to child pornography caused the images to be stored on his cache file. Tucker's destruction of the images that were on his cache file—due to the fact that he purposefully visited websites to view them—does not evidence an absence of volition on his part; in fact, it suggests just the opposite. Just as a possessor of illegal narcotics is not able to escape criminal liability for possession by throwing drugs out a window, a person who possesses contraband such as child pornography cannot escape criminal liability by destroying it. Destruction of contraband does not logically lead to the conclusion that one never possessed it; indeed, it leads to the exact opposite.

Tellingly, Tucker's counsel further argued, when discussing the Government's reconstruction of Tucker's cache file for evidentiary purposes, that: "The government's created science, however technical and amazing, cannot be allowed to place contraband in a person's hands *even after the person thought that he had destroyed the contraband.''* (Def.'s Trial Br. at 25.) (emphasis added). This argument only strengthens the conclusion that Tucker possessed the images. Tucker could not rid himself of something that he did not possess—otherwise there would not have been the need to rid himself of it. It is also logically impossible to destroy contraband that one does not control. But for his act of reaching out for the child pornography, Tucker would not have found himself in the position of needing to destroy the contraband on his computer's cache file. The ability to control is the *sine qua non* of the ability to destroy. Tucker had control and dominion over the images he viewed and destroyed; he detained them for his pleasure and he guided their destiny when he destroyed them; Tucker therefore had possession of child pornography.

II.   *Did Tucker Possess Child Pornography Knowingly?*

18 U.S.C. § 2252A(a)(5)(B) mandates that criminal liability can only be found in cases where the accused ''knowingly possesses'' child pornography. Counsel for Tucker also argued that he never ''knowingly'' possessed child pornography because the images were automatically stored on his cache file and Tucker purposefully deleted them when he discovered this fact. While the scienter requirement of § 2252A(a)(5)(B) has not been addressed by any court, the Court in *United States v. X–Citement Video, Inc.,* 513 U.S. 64, 72 (1994), found that the scienter requirement extended to every element of The Protection of Children Against Sexual Exploitation Act of 1977 which dealt with distribution, shipping, reproducing and receiving child pornography. In *United States v. Lacy,* 119 F.3d 742, 747 (9th Cir. 1997), the Court of Appeals for the Ninth Circuit held that to satisfy the mens rea requirement of 18 U.S.C. § 2252A(a)(4)(B), ''the trial court had to instruct the jury that it must find that the defendant knew the depictions were on his disks and drive.'' For the purposes of criminal possession, ''knowingly'' means that the defendant was conscious and aware of his actions, realized what he was doing or what was happening around him, and did not act because of ignorance, mistake, or accident.

As discussed above, the Internet did not cause the images to be on Tucker's computer; Tucker volitionally reached out for them. This is not a case of ignorance, mistake or accident. Tucker paid a user fee to gain access to these sites and received a password that would give him access to them. Tucker admits that he knowingly visited the websites and manipulated the images on his computer. Moreover, Tucker knew that the images were stored on his computer drive. The fact that Tucker repeatedly deleted his cache files after his multiple visits to sites offering child pornography evidences his scienter; Tucker would not know to delete the files from his computer if he did not know that they were on his computer drive. Defense counsel asserted that: ''Absent knowledge by the Defendant that he was maintaining pornographic images on his computer, his mental state was innocent.'' (Def's Trial Br. at 36.) This is, indeed, true. Yet it is also the case that defendant ''maintained'' the images in his computer cache file from the time he viewed the images until the time he intentionally deleted them. He would not know to delete the files if he did not know that he possessed them. Tucker therefore knowingly possessed child pornography in violation of § 2252A(a)(5)(B).

Notes and Questions

1. Imagine Tucker had been a computer novice who did not understand how computers work. He searched for and viewed images of child pornography, but he did not realize that in viewing the images he was causing the images to be sent to his computer and stored in his browser cache. From his perspective, he was merely taking a look around cyberspace. In this hypothetical, is Tucker guilty of knowingly possessing child pornography? Is Tucker more culpable if he knows how computers work and therefore recognizes that the images are present and under his control? Does it make sense that liability should hinge on whether the individual understands how computers work?

2. In United States v. Romm, 455 F.3d 990 (9th Cir. 2006), the defendant used an Internet connection from a hotel room in Las Vegas to google for images of child pornography. Romm later told federal agents that when he visited a site that contained such images, he would "save" the pictures for a few minutes and then "delete" them. A subsequent search of Romm's computer revealed 42 images of child pornography stored in the browser cache. However, government investigators did not find images outside the browser cache. A government expert witness testified at trial that it was possible for a user to access the cache and control the images stored there. However, no evidence was presented that Romm knew how to access the cache.

On appeal, the Ninth Circuit rejected Romm's claim that that there was insufficient evidence he had knowingly possessed the images. The court agreed with the *Tucker* court that "to possess the images in the cache, the defendant must, at a minimum, know that the unlawful images are stored on a disk or other tangible material in his possession." *Id.* at 1000. The court concluded that Romm's conduct established sufficient control over the images:

> Romm exercised control over the cached images while they were contemporaneously saved to his cache and displayed on his screen. At that moment, as the expert testimony here established, Romm could print the images, enlarge them, copy them, or email them to others. No doubt, images could be saved to the cache when a defendant accidentally views the images, as through the occurrence of a "pop-up," for instance. But that is not the case here.

> By his own admission to [federal agents], Romm repeatedly sought out child pornography over the internet. When he found images he "liked," he would "view them, save them to his computer, look at them for about five minutes and then delete them." * * * He described his activities as the "saving" and "downloading" of the images. While the images were displayed on screen and simultaneously stored to his cache, Romm could print them, email them, or save them as copies elsewhere.

Romm could destroy the copy of the images that his browser stored to his cache. And according to [the government's expert witness], Romm did just that, either manually, or by instructing his browser to do so. Forensic evidence showed that Romm had enlarged several thumbnail images for better viewing. In short, given the indicia that Romm exercised control over the images in his cache, there was sufficient evidence for the jury to find that Romm committed the act of knowing possession.

* * * [A]s the record here indicates, Romm had access to, and control over, the images that were displayed on his screen and saved to his cache. He could copy the images, print them or email them to others, and did, in fact, enlarge several of the images. This control clearly differentiates Romm's conduct from that of a visitor to the Louvre who gazes on the Mona Lisa, even if we put aside the stringent museum rules against photographing or copying without museum permission.

In short, * * * given Romm's ability to control the images while they were displayed on screen, and the forensic and other evidence that he actually exercised this control over them, there was sufficient evidence to support the jury's finding that Romm possessed three or more images of child pornography. Coupled with Romm's conceded knowledge that the images were saved to his disk, the prosecution produced sufficient evidence to establish every element of knowingly possessing child pornography under 18 U.S.C. § 2252A.

Id. at 1000–01. Is this analysis persuasive? Does it depend on what Romm meant when he told the federal agents that he "saved" the images and later "deleted" them? Or does it depend on whether Romm knew how to access the browser cache?

3. In Commonwealth v. Simone, 2003 WL 22994245 (Va. Cir. Ct. 2003), the defendant used an Internet search engine to locate and view images of child pornography. The search terms he used included "lolitas," "pre-teens," and "pedophelia." Three images of child pornography were found in the cache of viewed images on his computer. However, there was no evidence that the defendant realized that the images he viewed had been saved to the cache. The court nonetheless found that there was sufficient evidence that the defendant had possessed the images. According to the court, the test for whether a defendant possessed contraband computer data should be whether he "reach[ed] out and control[led] the images at issue." The court reasoned that this test best captured how the concept of possession applies in the physical world:

If a person walks down the street and notices an item (such as child pornography or an illegal narcotic) whose possession is prohibited, has that person committed a criminal offense if they look at the item for a sufficient amount of time to know what it is and then walks away? The obvious answer seems to be "no." However, if the person looks at the item long enough to know what it is, then reaches out and picks it up, holding and viewing it and taking it with them to their home, that person has moved from merely viewing the item to knowingly possessing the item by reaching out for it and controlling it.

Id. at *7. Do you agree? Is searching for and viewing child pornography "in essence" the same as taking it home, or is it more like walking down the street, searching for contraband, and then looking at it when you find it? Does the court's approach redraft a statute that punishes knowingly possessing child pornography so that it prohibits intentionally viewing child pornography?

4. *The problem of accidental possession.* Imagine a computer user surfs the web and innocently clicks on a link that happens to bring up an image of child pornography. Clicking on the link causes the image of child pornography to travel across the network and store itself automatically in the user's browser cache. Is the user criminally liable for the accidental possession?

This hypothetical raises a potential error in the *Tucker* opinion. In *Tucker*, the court considered whether Tucker's retrieval of the image was accidental. The court concluded that Tucker had "reached out" for the images, and therefore that his possession was knowing. However, that would seem to be the wrong question in the context of a possession charge. Whether Tucker had obtained child pornography by mistake would be critical in a prosecution for knowingly *receiving* child pornography under § 2252(a)(2) or § 2252A(a)(2). If Tucker did not know that he was going to receive child pornography when he clicked on the link, then his receipt of the image could not be knowing.

The question of possession is different. A person knowingly possesses contraband when he has knowledge and control over the contraband, regardless of whether he initially wanted to have that control when he first came into possession of the substance. For example, imagine *A* hands *B* a jar of leafy substance with the label "oregano" across the jar. *B* believes the leafy substance is oregano. When he gets home, however, he opens the jar and realizes that the substance is marijuana. Under traditional principles of criminal law, *B* will be guilty of knowing possession as soon as he realizes that the substance is marijuana but does not take immediate steps to dispossess himself of the marijuana. Transferring that concept to digital images, it is presumably the case that a defendant has knowing possession of an accidentally downloaded image of child pornography when he realizes that the image contains child pornography and is stored in his computer but does not take immediate steps to dispossess himself of the image.

This dynamic may help explain why the safety valve clauses of 18 U.S.C. § 2252(c) and 18 U.S.C. § 2252A(d) are limited to possession, and do not cover distribution or receipt. A person who accidentally comes into possession of child pornography cannot be guilty of knowingly transporting or receiving child pornography, but he may be guilty of knowing possession. The affirmative defenses in § 2252(c) and § 2252A(d) are quite narrow, however. First, they only apply if a defendant possesses one or two "matters" containing child pornography, which presumably means one or two images. Second, the defendant must "promptly and in good faith, and without retaining or allowing any person, other than a law enforcement agency, to access any visual depiction or copy thereof," either take "reasonable steps to destroy each such visual depiction" or "report[] the matter to a law enforcement agency and afford[] that agency access to each such visual depiction."

5. For a useful discussion of how a person could unintentionally obtain a contraband digital image, see Matthew James Zappen, Comment, *How Well Do You Know Your Computer? The Level of Scienter in 18 U.S.C. § 1462*, 66 Alb. L. Rev. 1161, 1165–76 (2003). For more on the legal issues raised by prosecutions for possessing child pornography based on evidence found in the browser cache, see Ty E. Howard, *Don't Cache Out Your Case: Prosecuting Child Pornography Possession Laws Based on Images Located in Temporary Internet Files*, 19 Berkeley Tech. L.J. 1227 (2004).

6. Does copying a computer file containing images of child pornography constitute a separate crime beyond possession? Should it?

In People v. Hill, 715 N.W.2d 301 (Mich. Ct. App. 2006), a defendant downloaded images of child pornography from the Internet and then saved the images on a CD. Michigan law prohibits making, possessing, and distributing child pornography, but does not prohibit receiving it. The government charged the defendant with making child pornography (a 20-year felony) instead of merely possessing child pornography (a 4-year felony) on the theory that copying the digital images onto the CD literally "made" child pornography. The defendant argued that "making" child pornography referred only to recording actual acts of child molestation, not copying digital files. A Michigan intermediate appellate court agreed with the government:

The CD–Rs, as compiled by defendant, were defendant's own creations; he made child-pornography CD–Rs. The term "make" is defined as follows: "to bring into existence by shaping, changing, or combining material." Random House Webster's College Dictionary (2001). Defendant acquired child sexually abusive material via the Internet, and he shaped, formed, and combined the material through placement of various selected pictures, videos, and images onto specific CD–Rs, bringing into existence something that had not previously existed, i.e., distinctly created and compiled child-pornography CD–Rs.

Given the intricacies of computer and Internet technology, we think it helpful to present an analogy, viewing a simpler scenario in which an individual obtains a magazine containing photographs of children engaging in sexual acts from another person or source. Receipt and retention of the magazine would merely reflect evidence of possession, which would give rise to a four-year felony under MCL 750.145c(4). In this scenario, the amount of child pornography in our society is not increased by the act of transferring the magazine to another and the purchaser's mere possession of the magazine. If, however, the person in possession of the magazine makes copies and reproductions of the pornographic material, he has increased the amount of existing child pornography, or stated differently, he has engaged in acts leading to the proliferation of child pornography in our society. Under such circumstances, he would be guilty of a 20–year felony under the plain language of MCL 750.145c(2) as discussed above. This is essentially what occurred here, except it was accomplished through the use of a computer and CD–Rs.

Id. at 309–10. Under this approach, doesn't every effort to possess child pornography also involve "making" child pornography? Or is there a legal difference between a browser's making a temporary copy as a step toward permitting the user to view a file and a user's making a permanent copy by burning a CD? As a policy matter, should burning a CD of child pornography be a distinct crime beyond mere possession? Or does the prohibition against distributing images address this concern?

7. The first section of this Chapter explored how property crimes involving the possession and transportation of stolen property could be applied to economic crimes involving computers. One of the major questions was how the courts could apply concepts such as "transporting" and "possessing" stolen property to cases involving unauthorized uses of data. How do the child pornography laws approach these types of questions? Do the child pornography laws shed light on the use of stolen property laws to punish unauthorized uses of data, or vice versa?

F) Constitutional Issues

Child pornography laws raise a number of important First Amendment issues. The Constitution permits the government to criminalize possession of child pornography. Osborne v. Ohio, 495 U.S. 103 (1990). At the same time, the First Amendment places constitutional limits on the definition of child pornography much like Miller v. California, 413 U.S. 15 (1973), places limits on the definition of obscenity. Those limits were explored in the following case, which considered a constitutional challenge to aspects of the Child Pornography Prevention Act of 1996 that broadly regulated "virtual" child pornography.

ASHCROFT v. FREE SPEECH COALITION

Supreme Court of the United States, 2002.
535 U.S. 234.

JUSTICE KENNEDY delivered the opinion of the Court.

We consider in this case whether the Child Pornography Prevention Act of 1996 (CPPA), 18 U.S.C. § 2251 *et seq.,* abridges the freedom of speech. The CPPA extends the federal prohibition against child pornography to sexually explicit images that appear to depict minors but were produced without using any real children. The statute prohibits, in specific circumstances, possessing or distributing these images, which may be created by using adults who look like minors or by using computer imaging. The new technology, according to Congress, makes it possible to create realistic images of children who do not exist.

By prohibiting child pornography that does not depict an actual child, the statute goes beyond *New York v. Ferber,* 458 U.S. 747 (1982), which distinguished child pornography from other sexually explicit speech because of the State's interest in protecting the children exploited by the production process. As a general rule, pornography can be banned only if obscene, but under *Ferber,* pornography showing minors can be proscribed whether or not the images are obscene under the definition set forth in *Miller v. California,* 413 U.S. 15 (1973). *Ferber* recognized that the *Miller* standard, like all general definitions of what may be banned as obscene, does not reflect the State's particular and more compelling interest in prosecuting those who promote the sexual exploitation of children.

While we have not had occasion to consider the question, we may assume that the apparent age of persons engaged in sexual conduct is relevant to whether a depiction offends community standards. Pictures of young children engaged in certain acts might be obscene where similar depictions of adults, or perhaps even older adolescents, would not. The CPPA, however, is not directed at speech that is obscene; Congress has proscribed those materials through a separate statute. 18 U.S.C. §§ 1460–1466. Like the law in *Ferber,* the CPPA seeks to reach beyond obscenity, and it makes no attempt to conform to the *Miller* standard. For instance, the statute would reach visual depictions, such as movies, even if they have redeeming social value.

The principal question to be resolved, then, is whether the CPPA is constitutional where it proscribes a significant universe of speech that is neither obscene under *Miller* nor child pornography under *Ferber.*

I

Before 1996, Congress defined child pornography as the type of depictions at issue in *Ferber,* images made using actual minors. 18 U.S.C. § 2252 (1994 ed.). The CPPA retains that prohibition at 18 U.S.C. § 2256(8)(A) and adds three other prohibited categories of speech, of which the first, § 2256(8)(B), and the third, § 2256(8)(D), are at issue in this case. Section 2256(8)(B) prohibits "any visual depiction, including any photograph, film, video, picture, or computer or computer-generated image or picture" that "is, or appears to be, of a minor engaging in sexually explicit conduct." The prohibition on "any visual depiction" does not depend at all on how the image is produced. The section captures a range of depictions, sometimes called "virtual child pornography," which include computer-generated images, as well as images produced by more traditional means. For instance, the literal terms of the statute embrace a Renaissance painting depicting a scene from classical mythology, a "picture" that "appears to be, of a minor engaging in sexually explicit conduct." The statute also prohibits Hollywood movies, filmed without any child actors, if a jury believes an actor "appears to be" a minor engaging in "actual or simulated . . . sexual intercourse." § 2256(2).

These images do not involve, let alone harm, any children in the production process; but Congress decided the materials threaten children in other, less direct, ways. Pedophiles might use the materials to encourage children to participate in sexual activity. "A child who is reluctant to engage in sexual activity with an adult, or to pose for sexually explicit photographs, can sometimes be convinced by viewing depictions of other children 'having fun' participating in such activity." Congressional Finding note (3), notes following § 2251. Furthermore, pedophiles might "whet their own sexual appetites" with the pornographic images, "thereby increasing the creation and distribution of child pornography and the sexual abuse and exploitation of actual children." *Id.,* Findings

(4), (10)(B). Under these rationales, harm flows from the content of the images, not from the means of their production. In addition, Congress identified another problem created by computer-generated images: Their existence can make it harder to prosecute pornographers who do use real minors. See *id.,* Finding (6)(A). As imaging technology improves, Congress found, it becomes more difficult to prove that a particular picture was produced using actual children. To ensure that defendants possessing child pornography using real minors cannot evade prosecution, Congress extended the ban to virtual child pornography.

Section 2256(8)(C) prohibits a more common and lower tech means of creating virtual images, known as computer morphing. Rather than creating original images, pornographers can alter innocent pictures of real children so that the children appear to be engaged in sexual activity. Although morphed images may fall within the definition of virtual child pornography, they implicate the interests of real children and are in that sense closer to the images in *Ferber.* Respondents do not challenge this provision, and we do not consider it.

Respondents do challenge § 2256(8)(D). Like the text of the "appears to be" provision, the sweep of this provision is quite broad. Section 2256(8)(D) defines child pornography to include any sexually explicit image that was "advertised, promoted, presented, described, or distributed in such a manner that conveys the impression" it depicts "a minor engaging in sexually explicit conduct." One Committee Report identified the provision as directed at sexually explicit images pandered as child pornography. *See* S.Rep. No. 104–358, p. 22 (1996) ("This provision prevents child pornographers and pedophiles from exploiting prurient interests in child sexuality and sexual activity through the production or distribution of pornographic material which is intentionally pandered as child pornography"). The statute is not so limited in its reach, however, as it punishes even those possessors who took no part in pandering. Once a work has been described as child pornography, the taint remains on the speech in the hands of subsequent possessors, making possession unlawful even though the content otherwise would not be objectionable.

II

Congress may pass valid laws to protect children from abuse, and it has. *E.g.,* 18 U.S.C. §§ 2241, 2251. The prospect of crime, however, by itself does not justify laws suppressing protected speech. It is also well established that speech may not be prohibited because it concerns subjects offending our sensibilities.

As a general principle, the First Amendment bars the government from dictating what we see or read or speak or hear. The freedom of speech has its limits; it does not embrace certain categories of speech, including defamation, incitement, obscenity, and pornography produced with real children. While these categories may be prohibited without violating the First Amendment, none of them includes the speech prohibited by the CPPA. In his dissent from the opinion of the Court of Appeals, Judge Ferguson recognized this to be the law and proposed that virtual child pornography should be regarded as an additional category of unprotected speech. It would be necessary for us to take this step to uphold the statute.

The Government * * * argu[es] that speech prohibited by the CPPA is virtually indistinguishable from child pornography, which may be banned without regard to whether it depicts works of value. Where the images are themselves the product of child sexual abuse, *Ferber* recognized that the State had an interest in stamping it out without regard to any judgment about its content. The production of the work, not its content, was the target of the statute. The fact that a work contained serious literary, artistic, or other value did not excuse the harm it caused to its child participants. It was simply "unrealistic to equate a community's toleration for sexually oriented materials with the permissible scope of legislation aimed at protecting children from sexual exploitation."

Ferber upheld a prohibition on the distribution and sale of child pornography, as well as its production, because these acts were "intrinsically related" to the sexual abuse of children in two ways. First, as a permanent record of a child's abuse, the continued circulation itself would harm the child who had participated. Like a defamatory statement, each new publication of the speech would cause new injury to the child's reputation and emotional well-being. Second, because the traffic in child pornography was an economic motive for its production, the State had an interest in closing the distribution network. "The most expeditious if not the only practical method of law enforcement may be to dry up the market for this material by imposing severe criminal penalties on persons selling, advertising, or otherwise promoting the product." Under either rationale, the speech had what the Court in effect held was a proximate link to the crime from which it came.

Later, in *Osborne v. Ohio,* 495 U.S. 103 (1990), the Court ruled that these same interests justified a ban on the possession of pornography produced by using children. "Given the importance of the State's interest in protecting the victims of child pornography," the State was justified in "attempting to stamp out this vice at all levels in the distribution chain." *Osborne* also noted the State's interest in preventing child pornography from being used as an aid in the solicitation of minors. The Court, however, anchored its holding in the concern for the participants, those whom it called the "victims of child pornography." It did not suggest that, absent this concern, other governmental interests would suffice.

In contrast to the speech in *Ferber,* speech that itself is the record of sexual abuse, the CPPA prohibits speech that records no crime and creates no victims by its production. Virtual child pornography is not "intrinsically related" to the sexual abuse of children, as were the materials in *Ferber.* While the Government asserts that the images can lead to actual instances of child abuse, the causal link is contingent and indirect. The harm does not necessarily follow from the speech, but depends upon some unquantified potential for subsequent criminal acts.

The Government says these indirect harms are sufficient because, as *Ferber* acknowledged, child pornography rarely can be valuable speech. This argument, however, suffers from two flaws. First, *Ferber's* judgment about child pornography was based upon how it was made, not on what it communicated. The case reaffirmed that where the speech is neither obscene nor the product of sexual abuse, it does not fall outside the protection of the First Amendment.

The second flaw in the Government's position is that *Ferber* did not hold that child pornography is by definition without value. On the contrary, the Court recognized some works in this category might have significant value, but relied on virtual images—the very images prohibited by the CPPA—as an alternative and permissible means of expression: If it were necessary for literary or artistic value, a person over the statutory age who perhaps looked younger could be utilized. Simulation outside of the prohibition of the statute could provide another alternative. *Ferber,* then, not only referred to the distinction between actual and virtual child pornography, it relied on it as a reason supporting its holding. *Ferber* provides no support for a statute that eliminates the distinction and makes the alternative mode criminal as well.

III

Finally, the Government says that the possibility of producing images by using computer imaging makes it very difficult for it to prosecute those who produce pornography by using real children. Experts, we are told, may have difficulty in saying whether the pictures were made by using real children or by using computer imaging. The necessary solution, the argument runs, is to prohibit both kinds of images. The argument, in essence, is that protected speech may be banned as a means to ban unprotected speech. This analysis turns the First Amendment upside down.

The Government may not suppress lawful speech as the means to suppress unlawful speech. Protected speech does not become unprotected merely because it resembles the latter. The Constitution requires the reverse. The possible harm to society in permitting some unprotected speech to go unpunished is outweighed by the possibility that protected speech of others may be muted. The overbreadth doctrine prohibits the Government from banning unprotected speech if a substantial amount of protected speech is prohibited or chilled in the process.

In sum, § 2256(8)(B) covers materials beyond the categories recognized in *Ferber* and *Miller*, and the reasons the Government offers in support of limiting the freedom of speech have no justification in our precedents or in the law of the First Amendment. The provision abridges the freedom to engage in a substantial amount of lawful speech. For this reason, it is overbroad and unconstitutional.

JUSTICE THOMAS, concurring in the judgment.

In my view, the Government's most persuasive asserted interest in support of the Child Pornography Prevention Act of 1996 is the prosecution rationale—that persons who possess and disseminate pornographic images of real children may escape conviction by claiming that the images are computer generated, thereby raising a reasonable doubt as to their guilt. At this time, however, the Government asserts only that defendants *raise* such defenses, not that they have done so successfully. In fact, the Government points to no case in which a defendant has been acquitted based on a "computer-generated images" defense. While this speculative interest cannot support the broad reach of the CPPA, technology may evolve to the point where it becomes impossible to enforce actual child pornography laws because the Government cannot prove that certain pornographic images are of real children. In the event this occurs, the Government should not be foreclosed from enacting a regulation of virtual child pornography that contains an appropriate affirmative defense or some other narrowly drawn restriction.

The Court suggests that the Government's interest in enforcing prohibitions against real child pornography cannot justify prohibitions on virtual child pornography, because "this analysis turns the First Amendment upside down. The Government may not suppress lawful speech as the means to suppress unlawful speech." But if technological advances thwart prosecution of "unlawful speech," the Government may well have a compelling interest in barring or otherwise regulating some narrow category of "lawful speech" in order to enforce effectively laws against pornography made through the abuse of real children. The Court does leave open the possibility that a more complete affirmative defense could save a statute's constitutionality, implicitly accepting that some regulation of virtual child pornography might be constitutional. I would not prejudge, however, whether a more complete affirmative defense is the only way to narrowly tailor a criminal statute that prohibits the possession and dissemination of virtual child pornography. Thus, I concur in the judgment of the Court.

Notes and Questions

1. *Free Speech Coalition* holds that the government may not prohibit the possession of "virtual" child pornography, and that such images are protected by the First Amendment unless they fall within the definition of obscenity from *Miller v. California*. This leaves open the possibility that virtual child pornography can be prosecuted as obscenity if it meets the standard of *Miller*. As a result, one effect of *Free Speech Coalition* is a likely increase in the frequency of obscenity prosecutions. Is this a positive development?

2. Congress passed the PROTECT Act, Pub. L. No. 108–21 (2003), a year after the *Free Speech Coalition* decision. Section 502(a) of the PROTECT Act reworked the definition of 18 U.S.C. § 2256(8) so that it now defines "child pornography" for use in § 2252A as follows:

> any visual depiction, including any photograph, film, video, picture, or computer or computer-generated image or picture, whether made or produced by electronic, mechanical, or other means, of sexually explicit conduct, where—

(a) the production of such visual depiction involves the use of a minor engaging in sexually explicit conduct;

(b) such visual depiction is a digital image, computer image, or computer-generated image that is, or is indistinguishable from, that of a minor engaging in sexually explicit conduct; or

(c) such visual depiction has been created, adapted, or modified to appear that an identifiable minor is engaging in sexually explicit conduct.

Note that § 2256(8)(a), involving actual minors, and § 2256(8)(c), which involves so-called "morphed" images, both remain unchanged from the original 1996 Act. Section 2256(8)(d), struck down in *Free Speech Coalition*, has been repealed. Section 2256(8)(b), also invalidated in *Free Speech Coalition*, has been replaced with a much narrower version that applies only to virtual images "indistinguishable from" actual minors. Do you think that the PROTECT Act's narrow definition of virtual child pornography used in § 2256(8)(b) is constitutional?

3. In United States v. Bach, 400 F.3d 622 (8th Cir. 2005), the Eighth Circuit considered a constitutional challenge to punishment for receiving a "morphed" image of child pornography. The image in *Bach* was a morphed picture combining a headshot of a known and identifiable boy, referred to in the opinion as "AC," inserted onto a preexisting photograph of an unidentified nude boy. The effect was to create the impression that the image was a nude picture of AC. The Eighth Circuit concluded that punishing the receipt of this image did not violate the First Amendment:

> Although there is no contention that the nude body actually is that of AC or that he was involved in the production of the image, a lasting record has been created of AC, an identifiable minor child, seemingly engaged in sexually explicit activity. He is thus victimized every time the picture is displayed. Unlike the virtual pornography or the pornography using youthful looking adults which could be prosecuted under subsections (B) and (D), as discussed in *Free Speech Coalition*, this image created an identifiable child victim of sexual exploitation. In *Free Speech Coalition* the Supreme Court continued to recognize the government's compelling interest in protecting a minor's physical and psychological well being, building on its decision in *Ferber*, pointing out the harm arising from pornography which is "intrinsically related" to the sexual abuse of children.

> Although there may well be instances in which the application of § 2256(8)(c) violates the First Amendment, this is not such a case. The interests of real children are implicated in the image received by Bach showing a boy with the identifiable face of AC in a lascivious pose. This image involves the type of harm which can constitutionally be prosecuted under *Free Speech Coalition* and *Ferber*.

Id. at 632. Do you agree? Would you reach the same result if the real headshot of a known child had been inserted in a realistic way onto the body of an 18 year-old? What if the headshot of a known 18 year-old had been inserted in a realistic way onto the body of a child? What if the headshot had been inserted in a realistic way onto a computer-generated image of a child?

4. Perhaps the most important practical impact of *Free Speech Coalition* arises when it is combined with United States v. X–Citement Video, Inc., 513 U.S. 64 (1994). *X-Citement Video* construed the mens rea requirement of 18 U.S.C. §§ 2252(a)(1) and (a)(2) to require proof that the defendant knew the images were of a minor. Knowledge that an image is of a minor arguably presupposes knowledge that the image is of an actual child. A defendant with a good faith belief that an image is "virtual" child pornography presumably cannot act knowingly with respect to the factual element that the image is actual child pornography. Putting *Free Speech Coalition* and *X-Citement Video* together suggests that the government must not only prove that an image was of an actual child, but that the defendant *knew* the image was of an actual child. How can the government satisfy this burden? The following case explores these issues.

UNITED STATES v. MARCHAND

United States District Court for the District of New Jersey, 2004.
308 F. Supp. 2d 498.

HOCHBERG, District Judge.

The Defendant, Anthony Marchand, is accused of possessing Child Pornography, in violation of the Child Pornography Prevention Act, 18 U.S.C. § 2252A(a)(5)(B). The Defendant knowingly and voluntarily waived his right to a jury trial. Therefore, this Court is responsible for both findings of fact and conclusions of law. The issues for this Court are: 1) whether the images that the Defendant possessed depicted real minors and 2) whether the Defendant knew that the images he possessed depicted real minors.

I.   FINDINGS OF FACT

A. *Background*

Dr. Anthony Marchand was employed by Atlantic Health Systems ("AHS") as director of the pathology lab at Overlook Hospital in Summit, New Jersey. In October or November of 2000, the hospital experienced substantial problems with its computer network. During an investigation into the cause of these problems, a network engineer for the hospital noticed that Dr. Marchand's computer was accessing and downloading imagery from the Internet, resulting in massive re-transmissions on the network. These re-transmissions would cause the network to crash. In April 2001, new firewall software was installed, due to the problems the hospital had experienced with the network. In addition, AHS installed a sniffer[2] to monitor traffic through the AHS firewall in an effort to identify Internet use that violated AHS' policy.

Dr. Marchand used a computer designated OBE, with the password "amarchand" in his office at Overlook. Between April and August 2001, the OBE computer generated sniffer alerts several times a week while

---

2. A sniffer is a device that monitors Internet traffic across a firewall and gener- ates alerts based on packets of information or key words that cross the firewall.

being operated by Dr. Marchand. AHS then assigned a static IP address to Computer OBE to make it easier for the sniffer to trace information to and from Computer OBE and the Internet.[4] Monitoring of the sniffer revealed that Dr. Marchand accessed a variety of web sites that appeared to display child pornography. For example, the sniffer program indicated that the web sites accessed by the OBE computer contained information such as "free illegal site," "free illegal kds," "illegal ki()s porno video," "illegally shocking 3–11y.o," and "_real_illegal_lolitas archive."

AHS contacted the Federal Bureau of Investigation, and on March 14, 2002, pursuant to a search warrant, the Government conducted a search of Dr. Marchand's office and office computer. When Dr. Marchand was informed that a search warrant for child pornography was being executed in his office, he accompanied the FBI agents and hospital staff to another office where he answered questions. He also handed several computer disks to Special Agent William DeSa ("Agent DeSa"). Later in the interview, Agent DeSa stated that his use of the term child pornography referred to "actual kids engaging in sexual activity, either with children or with adults." During the interview at the hospital, Dr. Marchand stated that he had additional images at home, and that he thought he had approximately 500 images of child pornography. Dr. Marchand then accompanied Agent DeSa and Special Agent Tanya Lamb DeSa ("Agent Lamb") to his home, where he turned over several additional CDs and a computer. In total, the agents retrieved six CDs from Dr. Marchand's office and home as well as the central processing unit from Dr. Marchand's home computer. Dr. Marchand told Agent Lamb that collecting these images "was a hobby, that he didn't realize that it was illegal or improper for him to have for personal enjoyment." Dr. Marchand also explained to Agent Lamb "that some of the images on the CDs were images that he had morphed."

B. *The Images*

The Government introduced into evidence 35 images from the total number seized. The evidence depicts prepubescent children engaged in sexually explicit conduct. * * *

The children in each of the 35 images look real to the viewer. There is no indication in any of the pictures to alert the viewer that the image was created other than with the use of real children. The lighting in the images appears as it would in a photograph. The children's physical characteristics and their often highly expressive facial features are visible in great detail. A staple is visible in one of the images, indicating that the picture was taken from a compilation of multiple pages, such as a centerfold from a magazine. Some of the children are the subjects of a series of pictures. In each of the pictures within one series, the child

---

4. When a computer accesses another network, such as the Internet, it addresses a server which assigns the computer an IP address. That IP address normally changes each time the computer accesses the server. To make it easier to monitor the OBE computer, the firewall administrator made the server assign the same IP address each time the OBE computer accessed the Internet.

depicted has the same appearance, and other details of the images do not vary.

The children in the images range in age from three to fifteen. The Government's expert, Dr. Robert Johnson, estimated the age of the children by comparing the level of development of the children depicted in the images with the stages of sexual maturation designed by John Tanner ("the Tanner Scale"). The Tanner Scale shows pubic hair at specific stages and the age at which it is most likely to occur and the breast development in females and the genitalia, penis, and testicle development in males.

Eleven of the images introduced were earlier published as photographs in child pornography magazines that were printed prior to 1986, a date when computer technology to create realistic virtual images of human beings did not exist. Eight of the images introduced depict actual identified and named children from the United States, England, and Brazil, who had been the subject of investigations by law enforcement into the sexual abuse they suffered. Six of the images were part of two different series of photographs. Each of the images had a file name, and Dr. Marchand organized them into folders. He named the subdirectory containing these folders, "child."

C. Technology for Virtual Images

Defense Counsel maintained a thorough, creative, and vigorous defense, attacking the Government's case. The main thrust of the Defense was to show that technology exists to create realistic virtual images of child pornography that are indistinguishable from real images of child pornography, and that nothing in the bit structure of the digitized computer image would inform a diligent observer that the image was real rather than virtual. This defense was presented in order to rebut the Government's proofs that the images possessed by the Defendant were of real human children and to create reasonable doubt as to whether Dr. Marchand knew that the images were real rather than virtual from information available to him at the time he possessed the images.

Computer software such as POSER was presented by the Defense. POSER is a tool for artists to use in creating virtual images of people. Although the Defense did not submit any images that had been created using POSER, the Government introduced a limited number of virtual images of clothed adults as examples of what POSER can do. Two of these images were part of a recent contest held by POSER. No nude adults or children were adduced nor were any virtual images of sexually aroused body parts.

The degree to which the images created with POSER appear real and the accuracy of the details depend on the skill of the artist. For example, the software does not create details such as hair growth or vein visibility through skin, although POSER will adjust the size of each body part to be in proportion with the size of the overall human figure. Unlike images that are created by manipulating and "cutting and pasting" pre-existing images, images created with POSER will not contain internal inconsistencies in the background, known as artifacts, which indicate that the pictures are not real. However, when backgrounds other than those created by POSER are imported into the images, POSER will not automatically create proper lighting effects, leaving it to the artist to ensure that the lighting effects, such as shadows cast by one body upon an adjacent figure or upon the ground, appear realistic. The pictures that the Defendant's expert characterized as indicative of pictures created with POSER do not appear at all realistic to the viewer.

II. APPLICATION OF THE FACTS TO THE LAW

A. *The Charges Against the Defendant*

Dr. Marchand is charged with violating 18 U.S.C. § 2252A(a)(5)(B) by knowingly and willfully possessing six computer disks which contained at least three images of child pornography as defined in 18 U.S.C. § 2256(8)(A), which images were shipped and transported in interstate and foreign commerce and which were produced using materials that had been shipped and transported in interstate and foreign commerce.

B. *The Elements of the Crime of Possession*
of Child Pornography under the CPPA

The Government must prove: 1) that the Defendant possessed at least one image of a real minor engaged in sexually explicit conduct; and 2) that the Defendant knew that at least one of the images contained a picture of a real minor engaged in sexually explicit conduct.[14]

To prosecute a defendant under this section, the Government first must prove beyond a reasonable doubt that the image depicts a real child. Prior to the U.S. Supreme Court's decision in *Free Speech Coalition et al. v. Ashcroft,* 535 U.S. 234 (2002), the definition of child pornography included a visual depiction which appeared to be a minor engaging in sexually explicit conduct. 18 U.S.C. § 2256(8)(B). To the extent that this definition encompassed images that were generated entirely by computer, without the use of any actual minors, the Supreme Court held in *Free Speech Coalition* that, absent an obscenity charge, such material was protected by the First Amendment. Thus, the possession of virtual images of minors engaged in sexually explicit conduct is not a crime under the statute charged in this case.

The Government must also prove beyond a reasonable doubt that the Defendant knew that the images he possessed depicted real minors engaged in sexually explicit conduct. *United States v. X–Citement Video, Inc.,* 515 U.S. 64, 78 (1994). In *X-Citement Video,* the Court held that the

---

14. Possession of a single such image, with the knowledge that it depicts a real minor, is sufficient. Although there is an affirmative defense that may apply when the Defendant possesses less than three images, this defense is not applicable to this case because the number of images possessed was large and because the Defendant neither destroyed each image nor reported the matter to law enforcement, as the affirmative defense requires. 18 U.S.C. § 2252A(d).

term "knowingly" refers to the minority age of the persons depicted and the sexually explicit nature of the material. Thus, *Free Speech Coalition* and *X-Citement Video,* read together, require the Government to prove that the defendant knew the images he possessed depicted real children engaged in sexually explicit conduct.

C. *Proofs That the Images Depicted Real Minors*

The Government presented evidence that: 1) eleven of the images were taken from magazines created prior to the invention of computer technology that might make it possible to digitally create such images; 2) law enforcement agents from the U.S., England, and Brazil could positively identify by name the children in eight of the pictures as children whom they had met in person at a time not distant from the age that the child was when he or she was photographed; and 3) an opinion, from a qualified expert who reliably studied the images, that the physical development of the children depicted in the 35 images corresponds to the Tanner scale designed to show the level of physical development that children reach at different ages.

The Government linked the pre–1986 magazine photographs to the images that the Defendant downloaded from the Internet. The Government's computer expert testified that one of the ways to determine whether an image depicts real children is to compare the image to those in the FBI's Child Exploitation and Obscenity Reference File ("Reference File"). The Reference File contains approximately 10,000 images of scanned child pornography that were taken when computer technology was so primitive that a sound inference could be drawn that an image found in the Reference File depicts a real child. Eleven images possessed by Dr. Marchand matched the images in the Reference File and are found to be images of real minors engaged in sexually explicit conduct.

The Government also adduced proof in the form of direct witness identification of real children in eight of the images in evidence. These witnesses identified the children who appeared in the pictures, having met the children during law enforcement investigations into the abuse that these children had suffered.

Officer James Feehan of the Police Department in Peoria, Illinois positively identified the child in G122 as Melissa, who was between nine and ten years old when her father took pornographic pictures of her and distributed them over the Internet. During his investigation, Officer Feehan met Melissa when she was fifteen years old. He testified that Melissa looked nearly the same at that age as she had looked five or six years earlier when the pornographic pictures were taken. [Other children were identified through similar means.]

* * *

This evidence leaves no reasonable doubt that the images depict real children. Through direct identification of children, both by law enforcement and by comparison with the FBI Reference File, and through evidence of the appropriate level of development of each of the children depicted, the Government has proven beyond reasonable doubt that the files Dr. Marchand possessed contain pictures of real children.

D. The Defendant's State of Knowledge

The Court has reviewed evidence regarding: 1) the appearance of the images; 2) the number of images; 3) the number and identity of web sites the Defendant accessed; 4) the language used in the web sites; 5) the mode and manner by which the Defendant viewed and stored the images; 6) the Defendant's state of mind; and 7) the available computer technology and manual skill required to create realistic virtual images, including a small sample of such images posted on the Internet and created with the software most frequently discussed by the Defense. From this evidence, this Court must determine whether there is sufficient evidence from which an inference can be drawn beyond a reasonable doubt that the Defendant knew that the images he possessed were of real children engaged in sexually explicit conduct.

The knowledge element can be proven through direct and/or circumstantial evidence of actual knowledge and through a finding of willful blindness. A Defendant acts knowingly if the fact finder finds beyond reasonable doubt that the Defendant acted with deliberate disregard of the truth. The Government may prove that a person acted knowingly by proving beyond a reasonable doubt that that person deliberately closed his eyes to what otherwise would have been obvious to him. One cannot avoid responsibility for an offense by deliberately ignoring what is obvious. To find knowledge based on willful blindness, it is not enough that a reasonable person would have been aware of the high probability of the truth. The Defendant himself must have been aware of the high probability that the images depicted real children. The Defendant's stupidity or negligence in not knowing is not sufficient to support a finding of knowledge based on willful blindness.

* * * The crux of the issue in this case is whether the Government's evidence proved beyond a reasonable doubt that the Defendant knew that the pictures were of real children. Among other evidence, the Court considers: the details of each image, the staple that appeared in one of the images, a file name that includes the age of the child, the large number of images and the substantial number of separate web sites from which the pictures were downloaded, the fact that certain images showed the same child over and over again as part of a series, the very real facial expressions of the children (sometimes multiple children in the same image), the extremely detailed close-up * * * [of various sexual acts], and the background in the photographs depicting highly detailed furniture, rumpled bedding, general household clutter, and extremely realistic lighting effects.

The circumstantial evidence from which an inference of knowledge may be drawn includes the appearance and number of images which were proven to depict real children. *United States v. Pabon–Cruz,* 255 F. Supp. 2d 200, 207 (S.D.N.Y. 2003) (holding that jurors could determine from the appearance and number of images possessed that the defendant could not have believed they were all produced using digital technology rather than real children). The Government presented this Court with fewer images than it presented to the jury in *Pabon–Cruz.* However, *Pabon–Cruz* is still instructive regarding the type of evidence from which an inference of knowledge may be drawn. The appearance of the images and the number of them, once they are proven to depict real children, is appropriate circumstantial evidence that this Court may use to draw an inference of knowledge, including whether or not there is reasonable doubt that Dr. Marchand knew that at least one of the 35 images in evidence depicted a real child engaged in sexually explicit conduct.

This Court has viewed the images itself in considering whether reasonable doubt exists as to Dr. Marchand's knowledge that the children depicted in the images were real. All of the children in the 35 images look utterly real. The level of detail of the children's features in all of the images contrasts startlingly with the sample of POSER virtual images adduced as evidence of the best examples of what virtual-image technology can do. * * *

The multiplicity of images and the fact that the Defendant downloaded them from different web sites also supports a finding that Dr. Marchand knew that at least one of the images depicted a real child. The Court considers all of the evidence, including logical inferences therefrom, based on human experience. Could the Defendant have thought that each of the 35 images, downloaded from many unrelated web sites, was each digitally created by an artist who was skillful enough to complete the task so extraordinarily realistically? It is not as though Dr. Marchand confined himself to one web site which he believed was dedicated to virtual images. Is there reasonable doubt that this Defendant knew that in surfing the web for diverse child pornography sites, he would find at least one picture of a real child engaged in sexually explicit conduct?

In addition to the 35 images themselves, the Government also presented direct evidence regarding the Defendant's state of mind. Dr. Marchand defended himself in his interview with Agent Lamb by saying, *inter alia,* that he did not know it was illegal to possess the images and that some of the images were morphed (digitally manipulated using parts of different real children) on the CDs that he created. By distinguishing between pictures that were morphed and those that were not, the Defendant certainly implied that he believed that the "un-morphed" images depicted real children. Dr. Marchand attempted to exculpate his conduct by claiming that some images were morphed, but his effort at exculpation never claimed that some of the images were virtual. Moreover, the FBI agents told Dr. Marchand that they were interested in pictures of "actual kids engaging in sexual activity, either with children or with adults," and Dr. Marchand responded by saying that he had about 500 images of child pornography. This also sheds light on his state of mind. The Defendant's characterization of 500 of his images as child pornography, especially in light of his effort to distinguish between those that were morphed and those that were not, supports a strong inference that he knew that at least one depicted a real child.

In an effort to rebut the Government's proof as to the Defendant's state of mind, the Defendant points to evidence that he had labeled some of the disks that were seized "Yoda." Defendant argues that this indicates that he believed the children in the images were not real, just as Yoda, a fictional character from the movie Star Wars, is not a real person. This label does not shed light on Defendant's knowledge of the content of the pictures he downloaded, because Yoda was his pet name for the very large computer play station that he used to view the images, and bears no relationship to the images themselves.

The Defense did prove that software like POSER exists and can be used to create virtual images. In order to be persuaded by the Defendant's argument that the existence of POSER creates reasonable doubt, the fact finder must consider whether the Defendant believed that this virtual software was so widely used in 2002, with such consistent skill, that 35 different realistic action images of nude children and adults, including several in a single image, would appear on a wide range of child pornographic web sites. The Government introduced proof that POSER-created images do not look even remotely realistic. No POSER-created image was adduced of a single realistic-looking human, even fully clothed. No evidence of virtual, nude, sexually-aroused adults or virtual, nude, prepubescent children was adduced. No virtual action image was introduced. When asked whether the POSER images introduced into evidence were typical of the type of images that could be created using POSER, the Defendant's computer and Internet technology expert testified that the images were indicative, though not necessarily typical, of the kind of images that could be created using POSER. Not one looked like a real person. Yet, every picture that the Defendant possessed appears absolutely real. Even the lighting and the shadows in each of the pictures is perfectly consistent with the various backgrounds contained in the images, a highly difficult feat to accomplish virtually. Even the Defendant's computer expert, when asked to point out those images that did not look like real photographs, could only point to one image, G121, and no others. Moreover, the expert conceded that when he looked at the pictures, he thought they were real.

CONCLUSION

The Government has proved beyond a reasonable doubt each element of the crime of possession of child pornography by Dr. Marchand. While *Free Speech Coalition* now imposes a heavy burden on the Government in its proofs, in this case, that burden has been satisfied.

Notes and Questions

1. Proving that a defendant possessed at least one image that depicted a real child is not difficult for the government in most child pornography cases. Many images of child pornography are from collections that are well

known to collectors of child pornography as well as to law enforcement. Some images are known to have been created in a period before computer animation was well-established, often in the 1970s. *See* Philip Jenkins, Beyond Tolerance 80–83 (2001). Others involve known victims. In a case involving a collection of many images of child pornography, the government can search the defendant's computer and select a subset of the images known to involve a real child.

2. Proving a defendant knew that an image involved a real child presents a more difficult task. Imagine that a collector of child pornography reads *Marchand* and takes defensive action based on its teachings. He labels the real child pornography he receives "virtual1," "virtual2," "virtual3," etc.; adds the prefix "virtual" to everything he says or writes regarding pornography; and buys a book on computer-generated images and places it next to his computer. Imagine that the defendant is later arrested and he asserts his Fifth Amendment privilege. If you are the defense attorney, what are your chances of creating reasonable doubt that your client didn't know the images depicted real children? Alternatively, if you are the prosecutor, how might you try to prove beyond a reasonable doubt that the "virtual" defense is a sham?

Marchand offers a number of suggestions for prosecutors. To prove the elements of the offense, the government must present proof beyond a reasonable doubt that the defendant knew at least one of the images was of a real child. To do this, the government can base its case on a group of images that are particularly real-looking. The government may be able to retrieve information from the defendant's computer indicating the source of the images, and it may be able to show that the images saved as "virtual1" and "virtual2" were not retrieved with such filenames. Further, the government may be able to find evidence that the defendant planned a sham virtual defense. As with any such effort, an unintended inconsistency may expose the defendant's scheme.

Finally, imagine a person is interested in collecting only virtual child pornography. He makes an earnest attempt to collect only virtual images, all of which are protected under the First Amendment. Within the collection of mostly virtual images, however, the person ends up with a handful of images that (unbeknownst to him) depict real children. Assume that a prosecutor wrongly concludes that this is a "sham" virtual pornography case, and the prosecutor believes that the virtual collector has knowledge that the images depicted real children. He indicts the collector, and you are appointed to defend him against the charges. What is your trial strategy to show the jury that your client lacks the required mens rea?

3. Imagine that the government searches a suspect's computer hard drive and discovers 500 images of child pornography. The government selects twenty particularly real looking images and another twenty known images to offer as evidence of possession. Assume that there is some overlap between the two groups; some of the known images also look particularly real. Is it sufficient that the government can prove beyond a reasonable doubt that at least one of the images in the group was real and that the defendant believed one of the images in the group was real? Or must the government prove beyond a reasonable doubt that at least one of the images was both real and

believed to be real? If you are a defense attorney in such a case, do you want the trier of fact to be a judge or a jury?

4. As modified by the PROTECT Act of 2003, federal law prohibits the possession, receipt, and distribution of virtual child pornography if it is "indistinguishable" from images of actual children. *See* 18 U.S.C. §§ 2252A, 2256(8)(b) (2003). Assuming this law is constitutional, what must the government prove to establish a violation for possessing, distributing, or receiving virtual child pornography? Must the government prove that the image looks real, and that the defendant actually believed it was real? Or is it sufficient for the government to prove that the image looks real, and the defendant knew that it looked real? As a matter of statutory interpretation, does the combination of 18 U.S.C. §§ 2252A and 2256(8)(b) require proof of knowledge that the image involves a real child, or is the statute satisfied by knowledge that the image is virtual but indistinguishable from an image of a real child? If the latter, what exactly does it mean to know that a virtual image is indistinguishable from an image of a minor?

5. Compare the present state of technology (at least of the time of the writing of this casebook) with the likely situation several decades from now. E-frontier, Inc., the company that creates and sells the POSER software, has a number of images available on its website that purport to offer the most realistic pictures of individuals that can be generated by its software. In 2005, almost all of the examples were quite obviously computer-generated. By the summer of 2006, when this book was sent to the printer, a number of the images on the site looked quite real. *See* efrontier America, Inc. Galleries, http://www.e-frontier.com/article/archive/453/.

Assume this trend continues, and imagine the year is 2050. It is now easy to use a computer to generate a picture that looks real. There is no way to distinguish real photographs from computer-generated ones, and all photographs are presumed to be fake. In fact, one popular software program permits a user to scan in a set of photographs of a person, and the computer can then use those images to construct a computer-generated composite. The computer can output an endless series of entirely realistic images of that person, at any age, performing a wide range of acts as directed by the user.

If this future becomes reality, what will happen to child pornography laws?

2. TRAVELER CASES AND ENTRAPMENT

A second type of child exploitation offense involves so-called "traveler" cases. Traveler cases trace their lineage back to the White Slave Traffic Act, Pub. L. No. 61–277 (1910). This law is often referred to as the Mann Act, after its chief sponsor, Illinois Congressman James Mann.

The Mann Act was passed during a period of tremendous public concern that young girls, many of them recent immigrants, were being kidnaped and forced into lives of prostitution. Given the limits of federal court jurisdiction, especially at the time, Congress responded by passing a law that focused liability on the crossing of state lines with the purpose of engaging in illegal sexual activities. For example, the key provisions of the Act prohibited transporting women across interstate lines and enticing women and younger girls to cross state lines with the intent of having them engage in "prostitution or debauchery, or for any other immoral purpose."

The modern version of the Mann Act appears at 18 U.S.C. § 2421 *et seq.*, and contains a number of prohibitions that are often used in child exploitation cases involving the Internet. The statutes harness state law, and particular state statutory rape law, which generally prohibits sexual contact with a person under the age of consent as determined in that state. For example, 18 U.S.C. § 2422(b) prohibits using "the mail or any facility or means of interstate or foreign commerce" to entice a minor to engage in illegal sexual activity. The Internet obviously is such a means, which permits § 2422(b) to be used widely in cases involving the luring of children online. Similarly, 18 U.S.C. § 2423(a) prohibits enticing a minor to travel in interstate commerce to engage in "any sexual activity for which any person can be charged with a criminal offense," and § 2423(b) prohibits traveling in interstate commerce with the purpose of engaging in such an activity. This means that if an adult uses the Internet to contact a young girl, and then either travels across state lines to meet her or has her travel to meet him, the traveling or enticing violates § 2423.

The federal government prosecutes several hundred traveler cases every year. Many of the cases arise from undercover operations which begin with law enforcement officers posing as minors in Internet chat rooms. In many cases, the defendant contacts the undercover agent and asks to meet to engage in a sexual act. He then travels across state lines with the intent to meet the young victim. Upon crossing state lines, the defendant is arrested. In such cases, the elements of the offense are usually easy for the government to prove and difficult for a defense attorney to challenge. The traveling in interstate commerce is easy to show, and the government's case tends to focus on proving the defendant's intent to engage in sexual activity with a minor. Proving intent is straightforward in most cases. The combination of the chat room logs and items in the defendant's possession at the time of his arrest normally will establish the defendant's intent beyond a reasonable doubt.

The primary legal issue raised by traveler cases involves the defense of entrapment. Entrapment is not a constitutional defense, which means that federal and state standards for entrapment can and do vary. *See* Kevin A. Smith, *Psychology, Factfinding, and Entrapment*, 103 Mich. L. Rev. 759 (2005). The federal entrapment standard has two prongs: inducement and predisposition. The defendant must put forward evidence of both elements before being entitled to an instruction on entrapment. If some evidence is put forward by the defendant, then the government bears the burden of proving beyond a reasonable doubt that the defendant either was not induced to commit the crime or was predisposed to commit the offense.

UNITED STATES v. POEHLMAN

United States Court of Appeals for the Ninth Circuit, 2000.
217 F.3d 692.

KOZINSKI, CIRCUIT JUDGE.

Mark Poehlman, a cross-dresser and foot-fetishist, sought the company of like-minded adults on the Internet. What he found, instead, were federal agents looking to catch child molesters. We consider whether the government's actions amount to entrapment.

I

After graduating from high school, Mark Poehlman joined the Air Force, where he remained for nearly 17 years. Eventually, he got married and had two children. When Poehlman admitted to his wife that he couldn't control his compulsion to cross-dress, she divorced him. So did the Air Force, which forced him into early retirement, albeit with an honorable discharge.

These events left Poehlman lonely and depressed. He began trawling Internet "alternative lifestyle" discussion groups in an effort to find a suitable companion. Unfortunately, the women who frequented these groups were less accepting than he had hoped. After they learned of Poehlman's proclivities, several retorted with strong rebukes. One even recommended that Poehlman kill himself. Evidently, life in the HOV lane of the information superhighway is not as fast as one might have suspected.

Eventually, Poehlman got a positive reaction from a woman named Sharon. Poehlman started his correspondence with Sharon when he responded to an ad in which she indicated that she was looking for someone who understood her family's "unique needs" and preferred servicemen. Poehlman answered the ad and indicated that he "was looking for a long-term relationship leading to marriage," "didn't mind children," and "had unique needs too."

Sharon responded positively to Poehlman's e-mail. She said she had three children and was "looking for someone who understands us and does not let society's views stand in the way." She confessed that there were "some things I'm just not equipped to teach the children" and indicated that she wanted "someone to help with their special education." The full text of her first responsive e-mail is set out in the margin.[3]

---

3. Thanks for answering my posting. I got a lot of responses, but for some reason yours caught my eye.

I'll tell you a little about myself. I'm 30, divorced and have 3 children. We are a very close family. I'm looking for someone who understands us and does not let society's views stand in the way. I've had to be both mother and father to my sweethearts, but there are some things I'm just not equipped to teach them. I'm looking for someone to help with their special education.

If you have an interest, I'd love to hear your ideas, desires and experiences. If this doesn't interest you, I understand.

In his next e-mail, also set out in the margin,[4] Poehlman disclosed the specifics of his "unique needs." He also explained that he has strong family values and would treat Sharon's children as his own. Sharon's next e-mail focused on the children, explaining to Poehlman that she was looking for a "special man teacher" for them but not for herself. She closed her e-mail with the valediction, "If you understand and are interested, please write back. If you don't share my views I understand. Thanks again for your last letter."

Poehlman replied by expressing uncertainty as to what Sharon meant by special man teacher. He noted that he would teach the children "proper morals and give support to them where it is needed," and he reiterated his interest in Sharon.[5]

Sharon again rebuffed Poehlman's interest in her: "One thing I should make really clear though, is that there can't be anything between me and my sweethearts special teacher." She then asked Poehlman for a description of what he would teach her children as a first lesson, promising "not to get mad or upset at anything written. If I disagree with something I'll just say so. I do like to watch, though. I hope you don't think I'm too weird."

Appellant's Excerpts of Record at Tab 5 (July 27, 1995).

4. Hi There, talk about a pleasant surprise to see a answer from you, I too am divorced and have two boys not living with me they are 9 and 6. they live with their mother in upper N.Y. I don't get to see them very often matter of fact its been almost two years since last I saw them, I am planning a trip to see them now.

I am retired Air Force after 16.8 years I took the early retirement, decided it was time to get out and work for a living again.(g) I am extremely honest and straight forward type of guy I don't play head games and don't like to have them played against me. I tell you straight out and open that I am a in house tv, meaning I rather enjoy wearing hose and heels inside the house, not around small children of course but when mine are old enough to understand I will tell them that and the big foot fetish I have are about my only two major problems that need a open minded easy going woman, so as they say in the movies if you don't mind me wearing your hose and licking your toes then I am open for anything .. (g),, I also have a sense of humor. as far as your children are concerned I will treat them as my own (as I would treat my boys if I had them with me) I have huge family values and like kids and they seem to like me alright too. well now you know all about me, if you are still interested then please write back, if not and I would understand why you didn't then I wish you all the best in finding the person you are looking for. if you wish to call my number is xxx–xxx–xxxx, I am not home a lot due to work and school but there is an answering machine that only I listen to, have a nice day.

Mark

Appellant's Excerpt of Record at Tab 5 (July 31, 1995).

5. Hi Sharon,

so happy to finally learn your name, I am interested in being this special teacher, but in all honesty I really don't know exactly what you expect me to teach them other than proper morals and give support to them where it is needed. Can I ask how old your sweethearts are and if you don't mind telling me what kind of teachings do you expect me to give them? But I will tell you that I am interested in their mom too, you would be part of the picture with them right? this is why I tell you all about myself and what I like, cause I have to be honest and tell you I would hope you would support and enjoy me sexually as well as in company and hopefully love and the sexual relations that go with it.

Hope you are well and your sweethearts are well too, I truly hope to hear from you and hopefully some more information about what you are looking for .. till then Have a very nice day.

Mark

Appellant's Excerpts of Record at Tab 5 (Aug. 2, 1995).

Poehlman finally got the hint and expressed his willingness to play sex instructor to Sharon's children. In later e-mails, Poehlman graphically detailed his ideas to Sharon, usually at her prompting. Among these ideas were oral sex, anal sex and various acts too tasteless to mention. The correspondence blossomed to include a phone call from Sharon and hand written notes from one of her children. Poehlman made decorative belts for all the girls and shipped the gifts to them for Christmas.

Poehlman and Sharon eventually made plans for him to travel to California from his Florida home. After arriving in California, Poehlman proceeded to a hotel room where he met Sharon in person. She offered him some pornographic magazines featuring children, which he accepted and examined. He commented that he had always looked at little girls. Sharon also showed Poehlman photos of her children: Karen, aged 7, Bonnie, aged 10, and Abby, aged 12. She then directed Poehlman to the adjoining room, where he was to meet the children, presumably to give them their first lesson under their mother's protective supervision. Upon entering the room however, Poehlman was greeted by Naval Criminal Investigation Special Agents, FBI agents and Los Angeles County Sheriff's Deputies.

Poehlman was arrested and charged with attempted lewd acts with a minor in violation of California law. He was tried, convicted and sentenced to a year in state prison. Two years after his release, Poehlman was again arrested and charged with federal crimes arising from the same incident. A jury convicted him of crossing state lines for the purpose of engaging in sex acts with a minor in violation of 18 U.S.C. § 2423(b). He was sentenced to 121 months. Poehlman challenges the conviction on the grounds that it violates double jeopardy and that he was entrapped. Because we find there was entrapment, we need not address double jeopardy.

II

"In their zeal to enforce the law ... Government agents may not originate a criminal design, implant in an innocent person's mind the disposition to commit a criminal act, and then induce commission of the crime so that the Government may prosecute." *Jacobson v. United States,* 503 U.S. 540, 548 (1992). On the other hand, "the fact that officers or employees of the Government merely afford opportunity or facilities for the commission of the offense does not defeat the prosecution. Artifice and stratagem may be employed to catch those engaged in criminal enterprises." *Sorrells v. United States,* 287 U.S. 435, 441 (1932). The defense of entrapment seeks to reconcile these two, somewhat contradictory, principles.

When entrapment is properly raised, the trier of fact must answer two related questions: First, did government agents induce the defendant to commit the crime? And, second, was the defendant predisposed? We discuss inducement at greater length below, but at bottom the government induces a crime when it creates a special incentive for the defendant to commit the crime. This incentive can consist of anything that materially alters the balance of risks and rewards bearing on defendant's decision whether to commit the offense, so as to increase the likelihood that he will engage in the particular criminal conduct. Even if the government induces the crime, however, defendant can still be convicted if the trier of fact determines that he was predisposed to commit the offense. Predisposition, which we also discuss at length below, is the defendant's willingness to commit the offense *prior* to being contacted by government agents, coupled with the wherewithal to do so. While our cases treat inducement and predisposition as separate inquiries, the two are obviously related: If a defendant is predisposed to commit the offense, he will require little or no inducement to do so; conversely, if the government must work hard to induce a defendant to commit the offense, it is far less likely that he was predisposed.

To raise entrapment, defendant need only point to evidence from which a rational jury could find that he was induced to commit the crime but was not otherwise predisposed to do so. Defendant need not present the evidence himself; he can point to such evidence in the government's case-in-chief, or extract it from cross-examination of the government's witnesses. The burden then shifts to the government to prove beyond a reasonable doubt that defendant was *not* entrapped.

The district court properly determined that the government was required to prove that Poehlman was not entrapped and gave an appropriate instruction. The jury nonetheless convicted Poehlman, which means that either it did not find that the government induced him, or did find that Poehlman was predisposed to commit the crime. Poehlman argues that he was entrapped as a matter of law. To succeed, he must persuade us that, viewing the evidence in the light most favorable to the government, no reasonable jury could have found in favor of the government as to inducement or lack of predisposition.

INDUCEMENT

Inducement can be any government conduct creating a substantial risk that an otherwise law-abiding citizen would commit an offense, including persuasion, fraudulent representations, threats, coercive tactics, harassment, promises of reward, or pleas based on need, sympathy or friendship. Poehlman argues that he was induced by government agents who used friendship, sympathy and psychological pressure to "beguile him into committing crimes which he otherwise would not have attempted." *Sherman v. United States,* 356 U.S. 369, 376 (1958).

According to Poehlman, before he started corresponding with Sharon, he was harmlessly cruising the Internet looking for an adult relationship; the idea of sex with children had not entered his mind. When he answered Sharon's ad, he clearly expressed an interest in "a long-term relationship leading to marriage." His only reference to children was that he "didn't mind" them. Even after Sharon gave him an opening by hinting about "not letting society's views stand in the way," Poehlman continued to focus his sexual attentions on the mother and not the daughters: "If you don't mind me wearing your hose and licking your toes then I am open for anything."

It was Sharon who first suggested that Poehlman develop a relationship with her daughters: "I've had to be both mother and father to my sweethearts, but there are some things I'm just not equipped to teach them. I'm looking for someone to help with their special education." Poehlman's response to this ambiguous invitation was perfectly appropriate: "As far as your children are concerned I will treat them as my own (as I would treat my boys if I had them with me) I have huge family values and like kids and they seem to like me alright too." Even when Sharon, in her next e-mail, became more insistent about having Poehlman be a special man teacher to her daughters, he betrayed no interest in a sexual relationship with them: "I am interested in being this special teasher, but in all honesty I really don't know exactly what you expect me to teach them other than proper morals and give support to them where it is needed."

In the same e-mail, Poehlman expressed a continued interest in an adult relationship with Sharon: "I have to be honest and tell you I would hope you would support and enjoy me sexually as well as in company and hopefully love and the sexual relations that go with it." It was only after Sharon made it clear that agreeing to serve as sexual mentor to her daughters was a condition to any further communications between her and Poehlman that he agreed to play the role Sharon had in mind for him.

The government argues that it did not induce Poehlman because Sharon did not, in so many words, suggest he have sex with her daughters. But this is far too narrow a view of the matter. The clear implication of Sharon's messages is that this is precisely what she had in mind. Contributing to this impression is repeated use of the phrases "special teacher" and "man teacher," and her categorical rejection of Poehlman's suggestion that he would treat her daughters as his own children and teach them proper morals with a curt, "I don't think you understand."

In case the references to a special man teacher were insufficient to convey the idea that she was looking for a sexual mentor for her daughters, Sharon also salted her correspondence with details that clearly carried sexual innuendo. In her second e-mail to Poehlman, she explained that she had "discussed finding a special man teacher with my sweethearts and you should see the look of joy and excitement on their faces. They are very excited about the prospect of finding such a teacher." To round out the point, Sharon further explained that "I want my sweethearts to have the same special memories I have. I've told them about my special teacher and the memories I have. I still get goosebumps thinking about it." From Sharon's account, one does not get the impression that her own special teacher had given her lessons in basket weaving or croquet.

Sharon did not merely invite Poehlman to have a sexual relationship with her minor daughters, she made it a condition of her own continued interest in him. Sharon, moreover, pressured Poehlman to be explicit about his plans for teaching the girls: "Tell me more about how their first lesson will go. This will help me make my decision as to who their teacher will be." The implication is that unless Poehlman came up with lesson plans that were sufficiently creative, Sharon would discard Poehlman and select a different mentor for her daughters.

Sharon eventually drew Poehlman into a protracted e-mail exchange which became increasingly intimate and sexually explicit. Approximately three weeks into the correspondence, Poehlman started signing off as Nancy, the name he adopts when dressing in women's clothes. Sharon promptly started using that name, offering an important symbol of acceptance and friendship. In the same e-mail, Sharon complained that Poehlman had neglected to discuss the education of her two younger girls. "I thought it curious that you did not mention Bonnie or Karen. Are they too young to start their educations? I don't want them to feel left out, but at the same time If you aren't comfortable with them please say so."

Over six months and scores of e-mails, Sharon persistently urged Poehlman to articulate his fantasies concerning the girls. Meanwhile Poehlman continued his efforts to establish a relationship with Sharon. For example, Poehlman twice proposed marriage, but this drew a sharp rebuke from Sharon: "Nancy, I'm not interested in marriage or any type of relationship with my darlings' teacher. My quest as their mother is to find them the right teacher so that they get the same education I was fortunate enough to get at their ages. You need to understand this. This is not for me, but for them. I don't mean to sound harsh, but you can't imagine the number of people just looking for a wife or girlfriend online. I have to look past all this and concentrate on finding my darlings' special man teacher." Poehlman nevertheless continued to seek a familial relationship with Sharon and her daughters, expressing himself ready to quit his job and move across the country to be with them.

As Justice Frankfurter noted in his concurrence in *Sherman,*

> Of course in every case of this kind the intention that the particular crime be committed originates with the police, and without their inducement the crime would not have occurred. But it is perfectly clear that where the police in effect simply furnished the opportunity for the commission of the crime, that this is not enough to enable the defendant to escape conviction.

Sherman v. United States, 356 U.S. 369, 382 (1958) (Frankfurter, J., concurring). Whether the police did more than provide an opportunity— whether they actually induced the crime, as that term is used in our entrapment jurisprudence—depends on whether they employed some form of suasion that materially affected what Justice Frankfurter called the "self-struggle to resist ordinary temptations." *Id.* at 384 (Frankfurter, J., concurring).

Where government agents merely make themselves available to participate in a criminal transaction, such as standing ready to buy or sell illegal drugs, they do not induce commission of the crime. An improper inducement goes beyond providing an ordinary opportunity to commit a crime. An inducement consists of an opportunity *plus* something else—typically, excessive pressure by the government upon the defendant or the government's taking advantage of an alternative, non-criminal type of motive.

In *Jacobson,* the government conceded inducement based on the fact that the defendant there committed the offense after numerous contacts from the government spanning over two years, during the course of which government agents "waved the banner of individual rights and disparaged the legitimacy and constitutionality of efforts to restrict the availability of sexually explicit materials." *Jacobson,* 503 U.S. at 552. In doing so, "the Government not only excited petitioner's interest in sexually explicit materials banned by law but also exerted substantial pressure on petitioner to obtain and read such material as part of a fight against censorship and infringement of individual rights." *Jacobson* is consistent with prior cases such as *Sherman,* where the government played upon defendant's weakness as a drug user, and *Sorrells,* where the government agent called upon defendant's loyalty to a fellow war veteran to induce him to commit the offense.

Cases like *Jacobson, Sherman* and *Sorrells* demonstrate that even very subtle governmental pressure, if skillfully applied, can amount to inducement. In *Jacobson,* for example, the government merely advanced the view that the law in question was illegitimate and that, by ordering the prohibited materials, defendant would be joining in a fight against censorship and the infringement of individual rights. In *Sorrells,* the inducement consisted of repeated requests, made in an atmosphere of comradery among veterans. In *Sherman,* the inducement consisted of establishing a friendly relationship with the defendant, and then playing on his sympathy for the supposed suffering of a fellow drug user.

Measured against these precedents, there is no doubt that the government induced Poehlman to commit the crime here. Had Sharon merely responded enthusiastically to a hint from Poehlman that he wanted to serve as her daughters' sexual mentor, there certainly would have been no inducement. But Sharon did much more.

Through its aggressive intervention, the government materially affected the normal balance between risks and rewards from the commission of the crime, and thereby induced Poehlman to commit the offense.

PREDISPOSITION

The jury could, nevertheless, have found Poehlman guilty if it found that he was predisposed to commit the offense. Quite obviously, by the

time a defendant actually commits the crime, he will have become
disposed to do so. However, the relevant time frame for assessing a
defendant's disposition comes before he has any contact with government agents, which is doubtless why it's called *pre*disposition. *See
Jacobson*, 503 U.S. at 549 ("The prosecution must prove beyond a
reasonable doubt that the defendant was disposed to commit the criminal act prior to first being approached by Government agents.") In our
case, the question is whether there is evidence to support a finding that
Poehlman was disposed to have sex with minors prior to opening his
correspondence with Sharon.

The government argues that Poehlman was predisposed because he
jumped at the chance to cross state lines to sexually mentor Sharon's
children at the first opportunity available to him. But if willingness
alone were the test, *Jacobson* would have come out differently. The
defendant there had been contacted by government agents posing as
organizations espousing the view that child pornography should be made
legal, and asked a variety of questions about his interest in young boys.
Jacobson expressed such an interest and, in response to "surveys,"
expressed the view that such materials should be made legal. The
correspondence lasted two years, at the end of which the government
(posing as one of these organizations) offered to sell him some magazines
containing pictures of nude boys. Jacobson immediately placed an order
and was arrested after the materials were delivered.

Despite Jacobson's willingness to commit the offense at the first
opportunity offered to him, the Supreme Court held that the government
had failed to show predisposition because it had failed to show that he
would have been disposed to buy the materials before the government
started its correspondence with him. The fact that he was willing to
order illegal materials after he'd been harangued by the government for
over two years was not deemed sufficient to show predisposition. Jacobson's decision to order, the Court reasoned, could have been a consequence of the government's inducement.

By analogy, the fact that Poehlman willingly crossed state lines to
have sex with minors after his prolonged and steamy correspondence
with Sharon cannot, alone, support a finding of predisposition. It is
possible, after all, that it was the government's inducement that brought
Poehlman to the point where he became willing to break the law. As in
Jacobson, we must consider what evidence there is as to Poehlman's
state of mind *prior* to his contact with Sharon.

On this score, the record is sparse indeed; it is easier to say what the
record does not contain than what it does. The government produced no
e-mails or chat room postings where Poehlman expressed an interest in
sex with children, or even the view that sex with children should be
legalized. Nor did the government produce any notes, tapes, magazines,
photographs, letters or similar items which disclosed an interest in sex
with children, despite a thorough search of Poehlman's home. There was
no testimony from the playmates of Poehlman's children, his ex-wife or

anyone else indicating that Poehlman had behaved inappropriately toward children or otherwise manifested a sexual interest in them. Sharon's ad, to which Poehlman responded, does not clearly suggest that sex with children was to be the object of the relationship: "Divorced mother of 3 looking for someone who understands my family's unique needs. Servicemen preferred. Please E-mail me at Darlings3@aol.com." While one might presume that one or more of the children are minors, the phrase "unique needs" could, just as easily, connote children with physical disabilities, or merely the plight of a single mother of three.

Poehlman does not appear to have responded to her ad because it mentions children or their special needs. During the crucial first few exchanges, when Sharon focused Poehlman's attention on those special needs, he expressed confusion as to what she had in mind. Instead of exploiting the ambiguity in Sharon's messages to suggest the possibility of sex with her daughters, Poehlman pushed the conversation in the opposite direction, offering to act as a father figure to the girls and teach them "proper morals." While Poehlman's reluctance might have been borne of caution—the way a drug dealer might demur when he is unsure whether a prospective buyer is a government agent—the fact remains that Poehlman's earliest messages (which would be most indicative of his pre-existing state of mind) provide no support for the government's case on predisposition. To the contrary, Poehlman's reluctance forced Sharon to become more aggressive in her suggestions, augmenting the defendant's case for inducement.

The only indication in the record of any preexisting interest in children is Poehlman's statement in the hotel room that he has "always looked at little girls." But this is hardly an indication that he was prone to engage in sexual relations with minors. Having carefully combed the record for any evidence that Poehlman was predisposed to commit the offense of which he was convicted, we find none. To the extent the jury might have found that Poehlman was predisposed to commit the offense, that finding cannot be sustained.

CONCLUSION

"When the Government's quest for convictions leads to the apprehension of an otherwise law-abiding citizen who, if left to his own devices, likely would have never run afoul of the law, the courts should intervene." *Jacobson,* 503 U.S. at 553–54. So far as this record discloses, Poehlman is such a citizen. Prior to his unfortunate encounter with Sharon, he was on a quest for an adult relationship with a woman who would understand and accept his proclivities, which did not include sex with children. There is surely enough real crime in our society that it is unnecessary for our law enforcement officials to spend months luring an obviously lonely and confused individual to cross the line between fantasy and criminality.

THOMPSON, Circuit Judge, dissenting:

I respectfully dissent. Our task as an appellate court is not to reweigh the evidence but to uphold the jury's verdict so long as substantial evidence supports it. The fact that we would have decided the case differently is irrelevant.

Viewing the evidence in the light most favorable to the government, we may reverse the jury's verdict only if no reasonable jury could have concluded that Mark Poehlman was not legally entrapped. Because there was sufficient evidence for a reasonable jury to find that the government did not induce Poehlman to commit the crime, the jury's verdict should be upheld.

While the government sent Poehlman messages, it did not first suggest sexual relations with children nor propose any specific sexual acts. Moreover, the government's e-mails never forced Poehlman to respond and, in fact, offered Poehlman many opportunities to end the communications if he were interested in a relationship with Sharon and not the kids or if he were at all uncomfortable. The majority contends that the "clear implication of Sharon's messages" suggested that Poehlman have sex with the children, but, so long as ambiguous evidence requires inferences to be made, it is the role of the jury to draw such inferences.

A reasonable jury could also have found that Poehlman was predisposed to commit the crime. * * * While Poehlman claims that the government initiated the sexual conversation when Sharon wrote about the lessons for her children from a "special man teacher" and her desire to watch the lessons, Poehlman conceded at trial that Sharon "never came out and said that [he] have sex with the kids." Poehlman first introduced sexual remarks in his reply to the government's message stating Sharon's interest in finding a "special man teacher" for her children.

Although Poehlman's e-mail messages during the first two weeks of his communication with Sharon appeared free of sexual allusions directed toward her children, his communications for the next roughly 5½ months detailed sexual acts that he would perform with Sharon's three children, even asking Sharon to put the two older girls on birth control. Moreover, just prior to Poehlman's arrest, a female undercover agent, posing as Sharon, presented Poehlman with a child pornography magazine and pointed to a particular picture depicting a child in a sexual act. When the officer asked Poehlman whether he thought the children "will be ready for this," Poehlman responded, "God, I hope so." Poehlman also remarked that he has "always looked at little girls." Although Poehlman at trial stated that he meant women over the age of eighteen, a reasonable jury could have concluded that he revealed a predisposition toward having sexual relations with young children.

At trial, the government established that Poehlman first mentioned having sex with the children, and each proposed sexual act originated from him. Even though this case is not as clear cut as a case in which a defendant, for example, exemplifies predisposition by owning a library of explicit materials before the commencement of a sting operation, the jury heard enough evidence for it to reasonably conclude that Poehlman in fact had a predisposition to commit the crime.

As the majority acknowledges, the district court properly instructed the jury, and Poehlman does not contend otherwise. What we are left with is a case in which the jury followed the court's correct instructions, considered the evidence, and simply rejected the defense. I would affirm the conviction.

Notes and Questions

1. Poehlman was arrested and prosecuted by state officials, sent to prison, released, and then arrested and prosecuted a second time by federal officials. This appeal involves his second prosecution. Do you think that fact influenced the Ninth Circuit's resolution of Poehlman's appeal? It is also worth noting that the *Poehlman* case involves an appeal from a jury verdict based largely on e-mails submitted to the jury. E-mails can be notably ambiguous in their meaning. Would you construe the e-mails in a way that inculpates or exculpates Poehlman? What did the jury do? What did Judge Kozinski do?

2. You are a lawyer in the Office of the General Counsel at the Federal Bureau of Investigation, and you have just read the *Poehlman* case. What guidelines would you put in place to regulate FBI online undercover operations to avoid entrapment issues in future prosecutions for child exploitation crimes?

For example, would you permit your agents to place advertisements in online publications posing as young children? Would you permit them to post an undercover profile on myspace.com? To enter an Internet chatroom called "britneyspears" while using the screenname "sarah13"? How about an Internet chatroom called "oldermforyoungf"? If you permit agents to visit chatrooms posing as minors, would you let them contact individuals in the chatrooms, or would you require them to wait to be contacted by others?

3. Do the dynamics of online interactions indicate a need for changes in entrapment doctrine? Consider Dru Stevenson, *Entrapment by Numbers*, 16 U. Fla. J.L. & Pub. Pol'y 1, 69–70 (2005):

> There are * * * major problems with applying the traditional rules [to cases involving online entrapment], which have made the entrapment defense unworkable in these cases to the point of becoming nearly obsolete. First, "predisposition," usually the critical element under the subjective test, is a foregone conclusion in almost all of the cases because the defendants actively log onto certain chat rooms and engage in repeated, typed communications with their intended victims. Second, in states using the objective test, the conduct and conversations of the agents can be very difficult to trace or verify. There is less accountability for government where the enforcement method is cheap and relatively invisible when orchestrated. Traditional stings typically require a host of armed "backup" agents nearby in case the primary undercover operative encounters trouble. Catching pedophiles can be done mostly from a cubicle in an office. In addition, the Internet enables a single officer to

entrap multiple individuals at once, as through on-line bulletin board postings. This feature of on-line entrapment may not be undesirable from a policy perspective, but it is a significant change from the traditional arrangement that the entrapment defense contemplated. Third, the inexpensive, relatively invisible nature of such operations also permits private entrapment to become rampant, which is not the case in off-line settings or with other crimes. On-line vigilantism against pedophiles, in fact, has taken on unexpected proportions. Traditional entrapment rules do not allow consideration of "private entrapment." Individuals tempted, induced or set up by anyone besides a state agent cannot raise an entrapment defense to criminal charges. Historically this was not a problem because most individuals, even if they had the motivation to entrap others, did not have the resources to orchestrate a sting while protecting themselves from retaliation if caught. Private entrapment was therefore a rare occurrence. The Internet has changed this, for better or worse, at least for the crimes perpetrated partly on-line.

Do you agree that there is less police accountability online? If an agent turns on a logging function so that every word in a chat room or IM exchange is recorded, isn't there greater accountability online rather than less? Won't agents turn on that function to collect evidence against the defendant? And if there is more private entrapment online, is that "for better" or "for worse"?

For other perspectives on Internet entrapment, see Jennifer Gregg, Note, *Caught In The Web: Entrapment In Cyberspace*, 19 Hastings Comm. & Ent. L.J. 157 (1996); Jarrod S. Hanson, Comment, *Entrapment In Cyberspace: A Renewed Call For Reasonable Suspicion*, 1996 U. Chi. Legal F. 535 (1996).

4. Prosecutions under 18 U.S.C. § 2422 and § 2423(a) normally require a violation or attempted violation of state law. The statutes prohibit traveling or enticing with intent to engage in sexual activity "for which any person can be charged with a criminal offense," which generally requires an analysis of state sexual assault law. State sexual assault laws can vary, however, which may create issues as to whether particular conduct is prohibited by state law in that jurisdiction.

Consider the facts of United States v. Patten, 397 F.3d 1100 (8th Cir. 2005). A police officer in West Fargo, North Dakota, posed in an Internet chat room as a 16 year-old girl. The defendant, 26 year-old Casey Patten, visited the chat room from his home in nearby Moorhead, Minnesota. The officer persuaded Patten to come to a grocery store in West Fargo, where the defendant was arrested. The law of North Dakota and Minnesota differ in a critical respect: in Minnesota, consensual sexual conduct between a 26 year-old man and a 16 year-old girl is legal, whereas the same conduct is illegal in North Dakota.

The defendant argued that there was insufficient evidence that he had intended to engage in sexual activity in North Dakota, and therefore that he had not violated the federal statute. According to the defendant, he had planned to engage in the illegal activity in Minnesota, where it would have been legal. The Eighth Circuit affirmed the conviction, ruling that there was sufficient evidence from the facts of the case for a reasonable juror to conclude that the defendant intended to persuade the girl to engage in sexual activity in North Dakota. *See id.* at 1103–04.

5. *The impossibility defense.* Defendants in Internet undercover cases sometimes try to raise the impossibility defense. They argue that although they did try to meet a child to engage in sexual activity, they cannot be prosecuted because no actual child was involved. The offense was "impossible," the argument runs, because the child was actually an adult officer. Such defenses have been universally rejected, consistent with the modern trend away from recognizing an impossibility defense in other contexts. Courts have reasoned that the presence of a child is irrelevant because the liability is for attempt rather the substantive crime of engaging in sexual activities with a minor. *See, e.g.,* People v. Thousand, 631 N.W.2d 694 (Mich. 2002) (en banc).

Chapter 4

SENTENCING

When a defendant is convicted, a court must next impose a sentence. The law of criminal sentencing tends to focus on two issues. The first issue is whether to impose a prison term, and the length of any prison term imposed. The second issue is the conditions of any period of probation or post-incarceration supervised release.

The materials in this chapter consider sentencing law for computer crimes. The first part considers as a policy matter whether sentences for computer-related crimes should be different from sentences for equivalent physical crimes. The second part introduces the reader to the United States Sentencing Guidelines, and explores how the guidelines apply in child pornography cases. The third part considers how the Sentencing Guidelines apply in cases brought under 18 U.S.C. § 1030. The fourth section covers restrictions on computer use imposed in federal court as a condition of probation or supervised release.

A. ARE COMPUTER CRIMES DIFFERENT?

NEAL KUMAR KATYAL–CRIMINAL LAW IN CYBERSPACE

149 U. Pa. L. Rev. 1003, 1042–47, 1071–75 (2001).

Before computers, a criminal typically needed to work with other individuals to conduct serious criminal activity. Group crime arose for obvious reasons, from economies of scale to specialization of the labor pool. For example, it is nearly impossible for one person to rob a bank successfully. Several individuals are needed to carry weapons and provide firepower (economies of scale); someone needs to plan the operation (a form of specialization of labor); another must serve as a lookout (specialization again); and many people are needed to carry the money. Working together with others, whether in the criminal or corporate world, creates obvious efficiencies, as Ronald Coase explains in his pathbreaking article about why firms develop.

But computers change all this, and undermine the need for criminal conspiracy. * * * [A] cyberthief can, by herself, design a program to steal money from an electronic bank account or data from the Defense Department, rather than enlist a team to do so. A fraud artist can, by herself, send thousands of e-mails to unsuspecting recipients to create a Ponzi scheme. A child pornographer can create, store, and distribute images, and receive royalties or access fees without assistance. In these situations, a computer enables a single individual to launch a crime: No individual in realspace could break and enter a physical premise, and remove and steal the classified material without detection, perpetrate all the aspects of a Ponzi scheme, or run a child pornography ring. Cyberspace, however, is different. The electronic walls that secure money and data are pierced, not by additional thugs, but, rather, by additional computer power. In addition, cyberspace avoids the physical constraints of realspace (a burglar can only carry away a certain amount of loot and be in one place at a time).

If [the goal of criminal punishment is to deter harm], then it makes sense to punish the use of a computer to carry out a crime as if the computer were a quasi-conspirator. Doing so will deter the greater damage computer crime can incur per unit of investment in the enterprise. * * *

In sum, the law might develop penalties for using computers to aid a criminal offense. The case for criminalization proceeds from the fact that computers and co-conspirators are substitutes for each other. The solution proposed would not necessarily require treating computers as full co-conspirators, but it would require eliminating the law's current conceptualization of a computer as simply a method of crime, not a type of (or substitute for) a participant in crime.

A separate form of reduced costs to the criminal in cyberspace is the ease of escape. Because computer crime can be perpetrated by anyone, even someone who has never set foot near the target, the range of potential suspects is huge. This is unlike traditional crime, in which there is a high likelihood that a crime is committed by someone known to or seen by either the victim or the community in which the crime took place. A criminal in realspace has to be physically present to rob a bank, but a cybercriminal can be across the globe. This makes the crime easier to carry out, easier to conceal, and tougher to prosecute.

Despite some indications of the government's ability to trace criminal suspects online, the truth is that tracing is very difficult. A criminal may leave behind a trail of electronic footprints, but the footprints often end with a pseudonymous e-mail address from an ISP that possesses no subscriber information. Moreover, finding the footprints is often very difficult. Criminals can be sophisticated at weaving their footprints through computers based in several countries, which makes getting permission for real-time tracing very difficult. Unlike a criminal who needs to escape down a particular road, a criminal in cyberspace could be on any road, and these roads are not linked together in any meaningful fashion. The internet works by sending packets of data through whatever electronic pathway it finds most efficient at a given time. The protocol moves these packets a step closer to their destination, an electronic hop, without trying to map out a particular course for the next node to use when the packet arrives. Each hop ends in a host or router, which in turn sends the information on to the next host. What's more, sometimes large packets divide into smaller packets to be reassembled by the end-user when all the packets show up. Sometimes packets never arrive, due to network congestion and mistakes.

The upshot is that it is very difficult for law enforcement to find a criminal after an attack, particularly when the criminal can be on any road and evidence of her crime can be split into numerous subparcels, each of which is not itself incriminating. Even in those cases in which law enforcement has the technology and permission under applicable law to trace an attack, the investigators must be skilled at carrying out such a trace in order for it to be successful, and they must have knowledge about how to preserve the data trails in such a way that they will be admissible evidence in a criminal trial. Regular and frequent training of law enforcement is a necessity, as is up-to-date technological equipment. Government prosecutors and police must also be trained in the application of constitutional and statutory liberties in the internet context. Furthermore, the contraband and materials can be physically stored anywhere on the planet, making such evidence difficult to find and difficult to introduce in a court. Incriminating files of a criminal organization, such as the profits made from drug dealing, may be stored thousands of miles away. Alternatively, the evidence could reside in the United States but be moved abroad literally with a keystroke—whenever a person or an entity comes under criminal suspicion. Computers could also make it easier for criminals to disrupt law enforcement by spying on informants and sabotaging networks.

Because these factors lower the probability of successful enforcement, it may be appropriate to offset this lowered probability by increasing the magnitude of the criminal sanction.

Notes and Questions

1. Every technological tool has the capacity to facilitate criminal activity. When should using a tool to commit a crime lead to greater punishment? Imagine a man robs a bank while wearing a ski mask (to avoid being identified) and while carrying a gun (to encourage compliance with his demands). Should the defendant receive a higher punishment because he wore the ski mask? Should he receive a higher punishment because he carried the gun? Are the gun and ski mask "quasi-conspirators" in the bank robbery? What general principle explains our intuitions about when use of a tool to facilitate a crime should change the appropriate punishment? How do computers fit in to that picture?

2. Professor Katyal argues that higher punishments are needed for computer crimes to offset the ways computers facilitate crime. The thinking

is that defendants will know they are facing greater punishments for computer crimes, and the fear of greater punishment will deter criminal behavior.

Is this view of deterrence realistic? Consider the skeptical view offered in Paul H. Robinson & John M. Darley, *The Role of Deterrence in the Formulation of Criminal Law Rules: At Its Worst When Doing Its Best*, 91 Geo. L.J. 949, 954–55 (2003):

> The available studies suggest that most people do not know the law, that even career criminals who have a special incentive to know it do not, and that even when people think they know the law they frequently are wrong. Potential offenders typically do not read law books and their ability to learn the law, even indirectly through hearing or reading of particular cases, is limited by the fact that the legal rule is just one of hundreds of variables that influence a case disposition. To divine the operative liability rule, hidden as it is under the effects of all the other variables, would require both a higher number of reported cases than those to which potential offenders are exposed and a mind for complex calculation beyond that which is reasonable to expect.
>
> The possibilities of deterrent effect are further weakened by difficulties in establishing a punishment rate that would be meaningful to potential offenders, avoiding the delay in imposition of punishment that seriously erodes its deterrent effect, and establishing and modulating the amount of punishment imposed. First, establishing some base expectation of a meaningful chance for punishment is a necessary condition to any deterrent effect. Yet, the perceived probability of punishment is low to the point where the threatened punishment commonly is not thought to be relevant to the potential offender. Second, a delay between violation and punishment can dramatically reduce the perceived cost of the violation. Even if the punishment is certain, the more distant it is, the more its weight as a threat will be discounted. * * *
>
> Third, as to the amount of punishment, there is no question that any system that can impose punishment can produce a credible deterrent "bite." The challenge for a deterrence-based system is to modulate the threatened punishment bite as the program for optimum deterrence requires. Lawmakers assume they have the greatest control over this aspect of the cost-benefit calculus in that they can modulate the bite by simply altering the length of prison term. But, in reality, the studies suggest that this aspect of the cost-benefit balance is neither simple nor predictable.

If Robinson and Darley are correct, does it make sense to increase punishments for committing an offense using a computer?

3. Sentencing schemes usually factor in the amount of loss or damage caused by a particular criminal offense. If a crime causes greater damage, it leads to greater punishment regardless of how the crime was committed. This means that if computers help wrongdoers commit crimes on a broader scale than before, computer crimes will trigger higher punishment even without special rules for computer-related offenses. Does this make it unnecessary to have new rules for punishing computer crimes?

4. *Retribution and computer crime.* Deterrence is one goal of criminal punishment; retribution is another. What kinds of punishment are appropriate for computer crimes from a retributive perspective?

Retributivists might argue that a person who consciously confronts the wrongfulness of his conduct but continues with the offense is more culpable than one who does not fully appreciate the wrongfulness of his behavior. Computer-related crimes may seem more virtual, less harmful, and less real than their offline equivalents. From a retributive perspective, is someone who commits a computer-related crime likely to be *less* deserving of punishment than someone who commits an otherwise equivalent physical crime?

Imagine John breaks into a closed store at night and snoops around. That same night, Jane goes online and hacks into a server at an e-commerce site and looks through various files. It takes John two days to plan the physical crime and three hours to commit it; it takes Jane thirty minutes to plan and commit the digital version of the offense. To John, the offense is very real; to Jane, it feels like a computer game. Should Jane receive a higher sentence than John because computer crimes are easier to commit and harder to detect? Or should John receive a higher sentence because he fully appreciated the wrongfulness of his conduct?

If deterrence theory points in the direction of greater punishments for cybercrimes, and retributive theory points in the opposite direction, which theory should win out? Should we call it a tie?

5. It is widely believed that the relative anonymity of the Internet encourages unlawful behavior. But is it true? Researchers tried to answer this question using a decoy website. The goal was to determine how often Internet users searching for innocent material online would try to copy stolen software, obtain stolen passwords, and view hard-core pornography if given the chance. *See* Christina Demetriou & Andrew Silke, *A Criminological Internet "Sting": Experimental Evidence of Illegal and Deviant Visits to a Website Trap*, 43 Brit. J. Criminology 213 (2003).

The designers of the study set up a decoy website called "Cyber Magpie," and turned on logging functions that recorded every visit to the site. They advertised the site on newsgroups, promoting it as a legal source of "excellent freeware and shareware games." Upon entering the site, however, visitors were offered a choice of both legal and illegal materials. The site was configured to show visitors seven links: 1) a legal disclaimer, 2) shareware and freeware, 3) games (both free and hacked), 4) illegally obtained commercial software, 5) soft-core pornography, 6) hard-core pornography, and 7) stolen passwords that could be used to access pornographic sites. (The site did not actually distribute such materials; users who attempted to access them would encounter a message that the materials were unavailable.)

The Cyber Magpie site was available for 88 days, and during that time it logged 803 visitors. The researchers determined that 93% of the visitors initially accessed the site looking for legal shareware or freeware games. However, the most popular link turned out to be hard-core pornography: 60% of visitors to Cyber Magpie clicked on the link to try to view it. Further, 45% of users accessed the portion of the site that hosted soft-core pornography; 41% attempted to access the part of the site containing illegal copyrighted commercial software; and 38% accessed the portion of the site that claimed to have illegally hacked games. Roughly similar numbers accessed the parts of the website that featured the shareware and freeware games and other legally accessible software. Only 2% of visitors viewed the legal disclaimer.

Are you surprised by these results? The authors of the study comment, *id.* at 220:

> [T]he acts observed in this study * * * occurred in a situation of perceived anonymity for the perpetrators, and there were immediate personal rewards for the visitors to do what they did. Such a combination of factors creates a situation where deviant behavior is not simply common, it actually becomes the norm. Only a minority of visitors to Cyber Magpie avoided the illegal or pornographic sections. Such findings have disturbing implications with regard to how we think about–and respond to–crime and deviancy in cyberspace. As more and more people access and use the Internet on an increasingly regular basis, we can expect more people to become aware of, and exposed to, a range of opportunities to commit various illegal and socially questionable behaviours. Worryingly, this research suggests that a majority of Internet users will not resist temptation. The implications of this loom large for those charged with policing the Internet and with developing policy on how it should and can be governed.

Are the authors' concerns valid? Are Internet users who choose to visit a freeware site called "Cyber Magpie" representative of Internet users as a whole? On the other hand, if the authors are correct that "the majority of Internet users will not resist temptation" to engage in criminal activity online, how should the law respond?

6. In federal court, criminal sentences are imposed under the complex structure of the United States Sentencing Guidelines. Materials later in this chapter consider in detail how the Sentencing Guidelines apply to computer crimes. For now, however, it is worth noting that Congress and the Sentencing Commission have treated computer crimes differently from analogous physical crimes in a number of ways.

For example, provisions of the Sentencing Guidelines applicable to child pornography offenses provide for an enhanced sentence "[i]f the offense involved the use of a computer or an interactive computer service for the possession, transmission, receipt, or distribution of the material." U.S.S.G. § 2G2.2(b)(6). This enhancement was first enacted in 1995. The House Report accompanying the legislation that led to this enhancement explained the rationale:

> Distributing child pornography through computers is particularly harmful because it can reach an almost limitless audience. Because of its wide dissemination and instantaneous transmission, computer-assisted trafficking is also more difficult for law enforcement officials to investigate and prosecute. Additionally, the increasing use of computers to transmit child pornography substantially increases the likelihood that this material will be viewed by, and thus harm, children. Finally, the Committee notes with particular concern the fact that pedophiles may use a child's fascination with computer technology as a lure to drag children into

sexual relationships. In light of these significant harms, it is essential that those who are caught and convicted for this conduct be punished severely.

H.R. Rep. No. 104–90, at 3–4 (1995), *reprinted in* 1995 U.S.C.C.A.N. 759, 760–61. Do you agree? Most child pornography offenses prosecuted today involve computers. Does this make the case for an enhancement stronger or weaker today than in 1995, when Congress first enacted the enhancement?

7. *Use of a special skill.* The Sentencing Guidelines allow sentencing judges to increase the punishment when a defendant uses a special skill to facilitate the commission of an offense. The use of a special skill leads to an increase in the defendant's offense level, which, as we will see, corresponds to a higher sentence. The section, U.S.S.G. § 3B1.3, applies broadly across federal crimes:

> If the defendant abused a position of public or private trust, or used a special skill, in a manner that significantly facilitated the commission or concealment of the offense, increase by 2 levels. This adjustment may not be employed if an abuse of trust or skill is included in the base offense level or specific offense characteristic[.] * * *

Application Note 3 then explains that special skills "refers to a skill not possessed by members of the general public and usually requiring substantial education, training or licensing. Examples would include pilots, lawyers, doctors, accountants, chemists, and demolition experts."

When is using a computer in a crime "use of a special skill"? Are computer skills "special"? If a defendant commits a computer crime, does he necessarily deserve greater punishment?

UNITED STATES v. LEE

United States Court of Appeals for the Ninth Circuit, 2002.
296 F.3d 792.

KLEINFELD, Circuit Judge.

This case involves application of the special skills sentencing adjustment to the use of a computer.

FACTS

The Honolulu Marathon Association has a web site at "www.honolulu-marathon.org." During the relevant time, U.S. residents could use the site to register for the Honolulu Marathon and pay the registration fee online. Although many Japanese enter the race, the site did not permit online registration from Japan, but told Japanese entrants to register through an office in Japan.

The appellant, Kent Aoki Lee, lived in Honolulu, where he owned a video rental store. Lee came up with a scheme to sell marathon services to the marathon's Japanese market. Lee owned a computer server, which he kept on the premises of an internet service provider with whom he had a dial-up internet account. He registered the domain name "www.honolulu-marathon.com" and created a site almost identical to the official Honolulu Marathon site by copying its files onto his server. While the official site did not permit online registration from Japan, Lee's site contained an online registration form written in Japanese on which runners could enter personal information and credit card information. While the official registration fee was $65, Lee's site charged $165. The extra $100 over the registration fee covered a package including transportation to the race site, a meal, and a tour. Of course, none of this was legitimate, since Lee's web site and registration package were not authorized by the Honolulu Marathon Association. Seventeen people tried to register through Lee's site.

Lee's scheme was uncovered and he pleaded guilty to one count of wire fraud and one unrelated count of selling Viagra without a prescription. The main issue at sentencing was whether the district court could impose the special skills adjustment based on Lee's use of computer skills in creating his phony site.

Lee created his phony site by copying the legitimate site's files onto his computer server. Web sites consist of multiple web pages, which consist of individual computer files written in "hypertext markup language," or "HTML." The HTML files constituting a web site are located through a directory on a computer server. A computer directory is like a card in an old-fashioned library catalog, that tells where to find a book on a shelf. However a site's HTML files are referenced, they are linked together in the directory to create the whole web site. These links reflect the specific location of individual files within the server's structure of directories and subdirectories. The graphics on a web page are actually individual computer files to which that page's HTML file links, causing them to appear when the web page is displayed. An individual graphic file may be in the same directory as the HTML file to which it's linked, or in a subdirectory, or on another computer server altogether, and the link reflects that specific location. To copy a web site onto another computer server, it's not enough to copy the HTML file and the graphics for each web page. The copier must also recreate the directory structure of the original site or edit the links in the HTML files to reflect the different directory structure.

The creator of the genuine Honolulu Marathon site testified that Lee could have copied most of the site without knowing much about its directory structure, by using off-the-shelf software such as Microsoft's *FrontPage 98,* aided by a general circulation book such as *FrontPage 98 for Dummies.* She also testified that a program like *FrontPage* would have written a line of code into the fake site's HTML files, indicating that it had been used. There weren't any such lines of code in the HTML files on Lee's site, suggesting that he didn't use this easy approach to copying the site. The creator of the authorized web site also testified that Lee could have pirated the site, much more slowly and laboriously, by using a text editor to copy it page by page (there were 130 individual web pages) and recreating the original site's directory structure so that each web page would properly display graphics and link to the other pages on the site. The legitimate site had two features, databases containing entrants' registration information and a list of past race results, that Lee could not copy onto his phony site, so he linked to those features on the genuine site so that they would appear to be part of his fake web site.

Lee's phony site contained one feature that was not on the genuine site, the online entry form that allowed residents of Japan to sign up for the marathon and provide a credit card account number to be billed for payment of the entry fee. The information entered on this form was processed using a "script," which is a program written in "common gateway interface," or "CGI," a programming language. The CGI script used by Lee's phony site didn't directly charge credit cards. It just stored the credit card data in a file on Lee's server, so that Lee could manually charge the cards later. (This database file was password protected, which the government's witness testified would require some knowledge of the server's operating system.) An excerpt of *FrontPage 98 for Dummies* that was read into the record told readers that to do CGI scripts, they should get help from someone experienced with computer programming. The official site's creator testified that writing a CGI form-handling script from scratch would have required significant programming expertise, but that modifying an existing script would have been much easier. She also testified that CGI scripts could be downloaded from the internet, and that web sites could be found that advised how to modify scripts to suit particular online forms.

The district court did not make a finding as to whether Lee copied the web site the easy way, such as by using *FrontPage 98* and *FrontPage 98 for Dummies* (and perhaps deleting the software's identifying code using a text editor), or the hard way, using a text editor to copy the web site's HTML files page by page and figuring out the original site's directory structure. Nor did the court make a finding as to whether Lee downloaded the CGI script for his online form from the internet or made it himself from scratch, and if so, whether he had any expert assistance. Nor did the court make a finding as to whether Lee or his internet service provider maintained his server. The district court found that Lee "was skilled at accessing and manipulating computer systems" and imposed the special skills enhancement. The adjustment raised the guideline sentencing range from six to twelve months to ten to sixteen months. This increase deprived the district court of the sentencing option of imposing no imprisonment.

Although Lee pleaded guilty, he reserved his right to appeal if the district court imposed the two-level special skill adjustment under U.S.S.G. § 3B1.3. Serving of the sentence awaits disposition of this appeal.

ANALYSIS

The special skill adjustment provides for a two-level increase "[i]f the defendant abused a position of public or private trust, or used a special skill, in a manner that significantly facilitated the commission or concealment of the offense." The abuse of a position of trust part of the adjustment applies to positions "characterized by professional or managerial discretion," such as an attorney serving as a guardian who embezzles the client's money, a bank executive's fraudulent loan scheme, or a physician who sexually abuses a patient under the guise of an examination, but not to embezzlement by a bank teller or hotel clerk. The application note defining "special skill" says that it is "a skill not possessed by members of the general public and usually requiring substantial education, training, or licensing. Examples would include pilots, lawyers, doctors, accountants, chemists, and demolition experts."

The district court based its imposition of the adjustment on our decision in *United States v. Petersen,* 98 F.3d 502 (9th Cir. 1996). The issue in the case at bar is whether Lee was more like the defendant in *Petersen,* or more like the defendant in another of our special skills cases, going the other way, *United States v. Green,* 962 F.2d 938 (9th Cir. 1992). We conclude that the scope of discretion was not broad enough, in view of the limited findings, to treat this case like *Petersen,* and that it has to be put in the same class as *Green,* where we held that it was an abuse of discretion to impose the special skills adjustment. This conclusion keeps our circuit's law consistent with that of the Sixth Circuit, which held in *United States v. Godman,* 223 F.3d 320 (6th Cir. 2000), that a level of computer expertise like Lee's did not justify imposition of the adjustment.

The defendant in *United States v. Petersen,* which upheld the adjustment, was an expert hacker. He hacked into a national credit reporting agency's computer system and stole personal information that he used to order fraudulent credit cards. Then he hacked into a telephone company's computers, seized control of the telephone lines to a radio station, and arranged for himself and his confederates to be the callers who "won" two Porsches, $40,000, and two trips to Hawaii in a radio call-in contest. Then he hacked into a national commercial lender's computer and got it to wire $150,000 to him through two other banks. This goes far beyond the computer skills of a clever high school youth or even many people who earn their livings as computer technicians and software engineers. The district court found that Petersen had "extraordinary knowledge of how computers work and how information is stored, how information is retrieved, and how the security of those systems can be preserved or invaded" and imposed the special skill adjustment. We affirmed, holding that "despite Petersen's lack of formal training or licensing, his sophisticated computer skills reasonably can be equated to the skills possessed by pilots, lawyers, chemists, and demolition experts" for purposes of the special skills adjustment.

In a footnote, we went out of our way in *Petersen* to caution against routine application of the special skills enhancement to people with computer skills:

> We do not intend to suggest that the ability to use or access computers would support a special skill adjustment under all circumstances. Computer skills cover a wide spectrum of ability. Only where a defendant's computer skills are particularly sophisticated do

they correspond to the Sentencing Commission's examples of special skills—lawyer, doctor, pilot, etc. Courts should be particularly cautious in imposing special skills adjustments where substantial education, training, or licensing is not involved.

This footnote distinguishes *Petersen* from the case at bar, because Lee's skills are not "particularly sophisticated" like Petersen's, and unlike Petersen's, don't correspond to the Sentencing Commission's examples of special skills—lawyer, doctor, pilot, etc. As we said in *Petersen,* where substantial education, training or licensing is not involved, district courts must be especially cautious about imposing the adjustment.

Petersen distinguished *United States v. Green,* where we reversed a special skills adjustment. Green took graphic design classes, learned from an instructor about paper that could be used for currency and about how it could be properly cut, ordered the special paper from a paper company (which tipped off the Secret Service), and took numerous photographs of currency, in the course of his counterfeiting scheme. We held that the printing and photographic skills were not so special as to permit the district court to impose the adjustment, saying it's not enough that "the offense was difficult to commit or required a special skill to complete."

In *United States v. Godman,* the Sixth Circuit considered *Petersen* and quoted and followed our limiting footnote that we quote above. Like Green, Godman was a counterfeiter, but Godman used an off-the-shelf professional page publishing program, Adobe PageMaker, with a scanner and a color inkjet printer. He'd learned PageMaker in a week, and had specialized computer experience preparing and repeatedly updating a color catalog. Godman held that the special skills adjustment could not properly be imposed, because Godman's level of computer skills was not analogous to the level of skill possessed by the lawyers, doctors, pilots, etc. listed in the application note. The Sixth Circuit held that the district court erred by stressing "overmuch" that Godman's skills were not shared by the general public: "As the Application Note's reference to the substantial training of such professionals as doctors and accountants suggests, emphasis is better placed on the difficulty with which a particular skill is acquired." The Sixth Circuit emphasized that "such skills are acquired through months (or years) of training, or the equivalent in self-tutelage."

Our own cases have suggested factors that might make a skill "special" for purposes of this sentencing adjustment, including a "public trust" rationale, the level of sophistication, and special educational or licensing requirements. But this adjustment becomes open-ended to the point of meaninglessness if the phrase "special skill" is taken out of its context. There probably isn't an occupation on earth that doesn't involve some special skill not possessed by people outside it, and few of us who sit as judges would know how to do the work of most of the people who appear before us. So asking whether a skill is "special," in the sense of not being common among the adult population, like driving a car, doesn't get us very far toward deciding any cases.

And focusing much on the "specialness" of a skill is also hard to reconcile with our precedents. In *United States v. Harper,* 33 F.3d 1143 (9th Cir. 1994), the defendant's skills were very special indeed. The robber had worked for both a bank and an ATM service company, and used the knowledge gained in both occupations to come up with a unique scheme to rob an ATM. At just the right time for the last service call of the day, when the ATM service office would empty out while the robbery was going on, she made a withdrawal from an ATM but didn't take the money. She knew that leaving the cash would cause the ATM to shut itself down and generate a service call, which would put technicians on the site, and that they would open the machine so that she and her confederates could rob it. As skills go, Harper's were quite special, but we reversed the sentence because they weren't like those of pilots, lawyers, doctors, accountants, chemists and demolition experts.

Our cases are best reconciled, and this sentencing guideline is best read, as a two-part test. The test is not just whether the skill is "not possessed by members of the general public," but also, as a *sine qua non,* whether it is a skill "usually requiring substantial education, training, or licensing." The application note's reference to "pilots, lawyers, doctors, accountants, chemists, and demolition experts" requires reasoning by analogy, not just reference to dictionary definitions of "special" and "skill." The special skill adjustment falls within the same guideline as an adjustment for people who abuse a "position of public or private trust, or used a special skill." The application notes limit the position of trust adjustment to people with "professional or managerial discretion," analogous to attorneys who hold their clients' money in trust, physicians who treat patients, and "executives" (but not tellers) who manage a bank's loans. The application note for special skills parallels the application note for positions of trust in its reference to people trained or employed at a high level.

Lee was a video rental store operator who copied a web site. The findings don't establish whether he used off-the-shelf software or had to know more about programming, but it doesn't matter because either way, his level of sophistication was nothing like Petersen's. His skills were more like Green's or Godman's than Petersen's, and not in the class of "pilots, lawyers, doctors, accountants, chemists, and demolition experts." Thus, under our precedents and the guideline's application notes, the district court's imposition of the special skills adjustment was not supported by the findings. We therefore reverse and remand for resentencing.

Notes and Questions

1. In United States v. Mainard, 5 F.3d 404, 406 (9th Cir. 1993), the Ninth Circuit contended that the purpose of the special skills enhancement is "to add to the punishment of those who turn legitimate special skills to the perpetration of evil deeds":

In a sense, abuse of a special skill is a special kind of abuse of trust. It is a breach of the trust that society reposes in a person when it enables him to acquire and have a skill that other members of society do not possess. That special societal investment and encouragement allows a person to acquire skills that are then held in a kind of trust for all of us. When the person turns those skills to evil deeds, a special wrong is perpetrated upon society, just as other abuses of trust perpetrate a special wrong upon their victims.

Do you find this retributive rationale persuasive? How does it apply to computer skills?

2. What kinds of computer skills should count as special skills? In 1985, was reasonable proficiency in the use of a personal computer a special skill? How about today? Does the answer depend on the defendant's age? For example, an average set of computer skills among 18 year-olds might be exceptional among 75 year-olds. What standard should govern? Is the best answer a "reasonable person" standard at the time of the offense? Or should computer skills be categorically exempt from the special skills enhancement?

3. Technical skills may be needed to commit a particular crime. Can those skills also constitute "special skills" that justify a higher sentence following conviction?

In United States v. Young, 932 F.2d 1510 (D.C. Cir. 1991), the defendant was convicted of conspiring to manufacture and distribute 100 grams or more of pure phencyclidine ("PCP"). Manufacturing PCP requires following a complex chemical process, and the defendant had set up a laboratory to manufacture the drug. The government argued that the understanding of chemistry needed to manufacture PCP amounted to special skills justifying an enhancement. The D.C. Circuit disagreed, ruling that the defendant did not deserve the enhancement because he was not a trained chemist. Understanding chemistry just enough to commit the offense was insufficient:

> Section 3B1.3 provides a two-level enhancement if the defendant used a special skill, in a manner that significantly facilitated the commission or concealment of the offense. The use of the word "facilitate"—which means "to make easier," see Webster's New Collegiate Dictionary (1977)—is important in this context. It indicates to us that the Sentencing Commission assumed that the defendant knows how to commit the offense in the first place and that he uses a special skill to make it easier to commit the crime. Thus, the special skill necessary to justify a § 3B1.3 enhancement must be more than the mere ability to commit the offense; it must constitute an additional, pre-existing skill that the defendant uses to facilitate the commission or concealment of the offense.

> * * * Nothing in the commentary suggests that § 3B1.3 applies to a criminal who, like appellant, bones up on the tricks of his trade and becomes adept at committing a crime that the general public does not know how to commit. To the contrary, the commentary indicates that § 3B1.3 was intended to punish those who abuse their special skills by using them to facilitate criminal activity rather than legal, socially beneficial activity.

Id. at 1512–13.

How should this apply to computer crimes? Does it matter that most Americans have some computer skills, and that given the broad scope of 18 U.S.C. § 1030, most Americans are also capable of accessing a computer without authorization or exceeding authorized access? Does applying the special skills enhancement to a computer crime amount to double-counting?

4.   Imagine that *A* is a skilled programmer who creates a new and dangerous computer virus. *B* is *A*'s friend and a novice computer user. *A* shares the virus with *B*, and both *A* and *B*, acting individually, send out the virus in a series of e-mails. Is *A* more culpable than *B*, assuming that they have the same intent to cause damage? Would *A* receive the special skills enhancement under prevailing law?

B.   SENTENCING IN CHILD PORNOGRAPHY CASES

Criminal sentences imposed for federal crimes are determined under a framework set up by the United States Sentencing Guidelines. The Sentencing Guidelines are complicated, and studying how they apply in every detail would require a course of its own. For our purposes, however, we can quickly and profitably appreciate the basics of the Guidelines that arise in federal computer crime cases. This will let us see how courts determine the length of prison terms in most cases, even if it glosses over some of the details.

The Sentencing Guidelines are very important because substantive criminal law typically leaves open a wide range of criminal punishments that a court can impose following conviction. Every crime has a statutory maximum punishment, such as five years imprisonment or twenty years imprisonment. A small number of crimes also have mandatory minimum punishments that courts must impose regardless of the circumstances. In most cases, however, substantive statutory law leaves trial judges a great deal of sentencing discretion. For example, if a defendant is convicted of violating a crime with a ten-year statutory maximum punishment and no mandatory minimum punishment, the sentencing judge can in theory impose any prison sentence from zero days up to ten years.

The Sentencing Guidelines were enacted to limit this discretion and to ensure more uniform sentences. The basic idea is that factors relevant to sentencing are considered explicitly by the Guidelines, and this consideration leads sentencing judges to a very specific range of sentences that can be imposed in that particular case. For each case, the judge calculates the "offense level" for the case, calculates the defendant's criminal history category, and then matches up the offense level and criminal history category with a set range of prison time as measured in months. Under the Supreme Court's decision in United States v. Booker, 543 U.S. 220 (2005), Guidelines determinations are not binding on sentencing judges. Post-*Booker*, however, the Guidelines continue to be the primary authority used to determine the length of federal sentences.

Applying the Guidelines generally involves six steps:

1) Select the offense guideline.

The first step is to select the proper offense conduct guideline for the specific criminal offenses that the defendant violated. Chapter Two of the Guidelines contains the offense conduct guidelines that are applicable in different types of criminal offenses. Each offense conduct guideline explains how to calculate the offense level for that type of offense. For example, U.S.S.G. § 2A1.1 is the offense conduct guideline for first-degree murder cases, U.S.S.G. § 2A1.2 is for second-degree murder cases, and U.S.S.G. § 2A1.3 is for manslaughter cases. An appendix associated with the Guidelines contains a chart connecting most federal criminal statutes to their relevant offense conduct guidelines.

The Chapter Two offense guidelines that are most important in computer crime cases are U.S.S.G. § 2G2.2, applicable in child pornography offenses, and U.S.S.G. § 2B1.1, applicable in most economic crime cases including most computer misuse offenses. Because these are the two most important offense guidelines, the remainder of the material in this chapter will focus on their application.

2) Determine the offense level for the crime.

The next step is to determine the offense level for the crime by applying the relevant offense guideline from Chapter Two. To calculate this, start with the base offense level and then adjust that number by applying the special offense characteristics. This excerpt from § 2G2.2 provides the key guidance used to calculate sentences in most child pornography offenses:

(a) Base Offense Level:

    (1) 18, if the defendant is convicted of ... § 2252(a)(4), or § 2252A(a)(5).

    (2) 22, otherwise.

(b) Specific Offense Characteristics

    (1) If (A) subsection (a)(2) applies; (B) the defendant's conduct was limited to the receipt or solicitation of material involving the sexual exploitation of a minor; and (C) the defendant did not intend to traffic in, or distribute, such material, decrease by 2 levels.

    (2) If the material involved a prepubescent minor or a minor who had not attained the age of 12 years, increase by 2 levels.

    (3) (Apply the greatest) If the offense involved:

        (A) Distribution for pecuniary gain, increase by the number of levels from the table in § 2B1.1 (Theft, Property Destruction, and Fraud) corresponding to the retail value of the material, but by not less than 5 levels.

  (B) Distribution for the receipt, or expectation of receipt, of a thing of value, but not for pecuniary gain, increase by 5 levels.

  (C) Distribution to a minor, increase by 5 levels.

  (D) Distribution to a minor that was intended to persuade, induce, entice, or coerce the minor to engage in any illegal activity, other than illegal activity covered under subdivision (E), increase by 6 levels.

  (E) Distribution to a minor that was intended to persuade, induce, entice, coerce, or facilitate the travel of, the minor to engage in prohibited sexual conduct, increase by 7 levels.

  (F) Distribution other than distribution described in subdivisions (A) through (E), increase by 2 levels.

  (4) If the offense involved material that portrays sadistic or masochistic conduct or other depictions of violence, increase by 4 levels.

  (5) If the defendant engaged in a pattern of activity involving the sexual abuse or exploitation of a minor, increase by 5 levels.

  (6) If the offense involved the use of a computer or an interactive computer service for the possession, transmission, receipt, or distribution of the material, increase by 2 levels.

  (7) If the offense involved—

  (A) at least 10 images, but fewer than 150, increase by 2 levels;

  (B) at least 150 images, but fewer than 300, increase by 3 levels;

  (C) at least 300 images, but fewer than 600, increase by 4 levels; and

  (D) 600 or more images, increase by 5 levels.

Notably, the Sentencing Guidelines direct the sentencing court to include all "relevant conduct" in the court's calculations, even if that conduct was not charged in the indictment, admitted in a guilty plea, or proved at trial. *See* U.S.S.G. § 1B1.3. As a result, when considering what conduct the offense "involved," you should include all of the defendant's acts that relate to the crime, not just the specific facts that led to the conviction.

An example will help illustrate how these rules work in practice. Imagine an undercover agent is in an Internet chat room posing as a collector of child pornography, and that a suspect sends the agent one image of child pornography. The agent obtains the suspect's Internet records, finds out where he lives, and then searches his home to seize his computer. A search of the suspect's home computer reveals 200 images of child pornography. The suspect then pleads guilty to possessing child pornography. What offense level should be reached in the case? Begin with a base offense level of 18 under § 2G.2.2(a)(1) because the defendant pled guilty to possession instead of receipt or distribution. Second, increase two levels under § 2G2.2(b)(3)(F) because the relevant conduct included distributing the image to an undercover police officer. Next, increase two levels under § 2G.2.2(b)(6) because the crime involved a computer. Finally, increase another three levels under § 2G.2.2(b)(7)(B) because of the quantity of images. The resulting offense level should be 25.

3) Apply upward or downward adjustments.

Chapter Three of the Sentencing Guidelines contains adjustments to the offense level that a court can make to reflect the specific circumstances of the crime, the defendant, and the victim. These adjustments apply to all crimes, not just crimes covered in a specific offense conduct guideline. For example, a defendant who had a major role in a conspiracy can receive an increase in the offense level, *see* U.S.S.G. § 3B1.1, while a defendant who played only a minor role in a conspiracy can receive a decrease in the offense level, *see* U.S.S.G. § 3B1.2. As noted earlier, a defendant who used special skills in the commission of an offense can receive an increase in the offense level pursuant to U.S.S.G. § 3B1.3.

One downward adjustment that is applied in a majority of cases is the adjustment for acceptance of responsibility, U.S.S.G. § 3E1.1. This adjustment usually applies when a defendant elects to plead guilty rather than go to trial:

(a) If the defendant clearly demonstrates acceptance of responsibility for his offense, decrease the offense level by 2 levels.

(b) If the defendant qualifies for a decrease under subsection (a), the offense level determined prior to the operation of subsection (a) is level 16 or greater, and the defendant has assisted authorities in the investigation or prosecution of his own misconduct by taking one or more of the following steps: (1) timely providing complete information to the government concerning his own involvement in the offense; or (2) timely notifying authorities of his intention to enter a plea of guilty, thereby permitting the government to avoid preparing for trial and permitting the court to allocate its resources efficiently, decrease the offense level by 1 additional level.

Application Note 2 to this provision explains that "[t]his adjustment is not intended to apply to a defendant who puts the government to its burden of proof at trial by denying the essential factual elements of guilt, is convicted, and only then admits guilt and expresses remorse."

The Guidelines also include rules on grouping offenses when a defendant is convicted of multiple offenses. Such rules are necessary because a defendant may be convicted of multiple crimes, some of which are related to each other and others of which are not, and each crime will lead to its own offense level. The grouping rules appear in Chapter Three, Part D of the Guidelines, and explain how the different crimes and offense levels should be resolved to create a single offense level. The rules are quite complicated when considered in detail, but here is the basic approach:

(1) When the conduct involves fungible items, e.g., separate drug transactions or thefts of money, the amounts are added and the guidelines apply to the total amount.

(2) When nonfungible harms are involved, the offense level for the most serious count is increased (according to a somewhat diminishing scale) to reflect the existence of other counts of conviction.

United States Sentencing Commission, Guidelines Manual 6–7 (2005).

4) Determine the defendant's criminal history category.

Chapter Four of the Guidelines contains the rules for calculating a defendant's criminal history category. Criminal history categories range from I to VI, and are based on the number of criminal history "points" revealed by the defendant's record of past convictions. Criminal history is a very important part of criminal sentencing: If two defendants are convicted of the same crime, the defendant with a significant criminal history normally will receive a greater prison sentence than the defendant without such a history.

The general rule is that a defendant receives three points of criminal history for every past conviction that led to a sentence of greater than one year in prison; two points of criminal history for every past conviction that led to a sentence between sixty days and a year of prison; and one point for every other criminal conviction up to four points. *See* U.S.S.G. § 4A1.1. A defendant with zero or one criminal history points will have a criminal history category of I; a defendant with two or three points will have a criminal history category of II; four, five, or six points will be category III; and so forth.

5) Find the sentencing range from the sentencing table.

Chapter Five of the Guidelines contains a sentencing table that assigns a presumptive sentencing range based on the defendant's offense level and criminal history category. The table indicates the range of recommended sentences in months:

SENTENCING TABLE

(in months of imprisonment)

Offense Level	Criminal History Category (Criminal History Points)					
	I (0 or 1)	II (2 or 3)	III (4, 5, 6)	IV (7, 8, 9)	V (10, 11, 12)	VI (13 or more)
1	0–6	0–6	0–6	0–6	0–6	0–6
2	0–6	0–6	0–6	0–6	0–6	1–7
3	0–6	0–6	0–6	0–6	2–8	3–9
4	0–6	0–6	0–6	2–8	4–10	6–12
5	0–6	0–6	1–7	4–10	6–12	9–15
6	0–6	1–7	2–8	6–12	9–15	12–18

Offense Level	I (0 or 1)	II (2 or 3)	III (4, 5, 6)	IV (7, 8, 9)	V (10, 11, 12)	VI (13 or more)
7	0–6	2–8	4–10	8–14	12–18	15–21
8	0–6	4–10	6–12	10–16	15–21	18–24
9	4–10	6–12	8–14	12–18	18–24	21–27
10	6–12	8–14	10–16	15–21	21–27	24–30
11	8–14	10–16	12–18	18–24	24–30	27–33
12	10–16	12–18	15–21	21–27	27–33	30–37
13	12–18	15–21	18–24	24–30	30–37	33–41
14	15–21	18–24	21–27	27–33	33–41	37–46
15	18–24	21–27	24–30	30–37	37–46	41–51
16	21–27	24–30	27–33	33–41	41–51	46–57
17	24–30	27–33	30–37	37–46	46–57	51–63
18	27–33	30–37	33–41	41–51	51–63	57–71
19	30–37	33–41	37–46	46–57	57–71	63–78
20	33–41	37–46	41–51	51–63	63–78	70–87
21	37–46	41–51	46–57	57–71	70–87	77–96
22	41–51	46–57	51–63	63–78	77–96	84–105
23	46–57	51–63	57–71	70–87	84–105	92–115
24	51–63	57–71	63–78	77–96	92–115	100–125
25	57–71	63–78	70–87	84–105	100–125	110–137
26	63–78	70–87	78–97	92–115	110–137	120–150
27	70–87	78–97	87–108	100–125	120–150	130–162
28	78–97	87–108	97–121	110–137	130–162	140–175
29	87–108	97–121	108–135	121–151	140–175	151–188
30	97–121	108–135	121–151	135–168	151–188	168–210
31	108–135	121–151	135–168	151–188	168–210	188–235
32	121–151	135–168	151–188	168–210	188–235	210–262
33	135–168	151–188	168–210	188–235	210–262	235–293
34	151–188	168–210	188–235	210–262	235–293	262–327
35	168–210	188–235	210–262	235–293	262–327	292–365
36	188–235	210–262	235–293	262–327	292–365	324–405
37	210–262	235–293	262–327	292–365	324–405	360–life
38	235–293	262–327	292–365	324–405	360–life	360–life
39	262–327	292–365	324–405	360–life	360–life	360–life
40	292–365	324–405	360–life	360–life	360–life	360–life
41	324–405	360–life	360–life	360–life	360–life	360–life
42	360–life	360–life	360–life	360–life	360–life	360–life
43	life	life	life	life	life	life

6) Consider whether a non-guidelines sentence is appropriate.

The last step is to consider whether a non-guidelines sentence is appropriate. Chapter Five of the Guidelines contains provisions that permit a judge to depart from the Guidelines range in special circumstances. For example, a defendant who provided substantial assistance to the prosecution can receive a downward departure under U.S.S.G. § 5K1.1. More broadly, the Supreme Court's decision in United States v. Booker, 543 U.S. 220 (2005), permits sentencing judges to sentence defendants to prison terms outside the relevant Guidelines range so long as the departures from the Guidelines range are "reasonable." *Id.* at 261–62.

Notes and Questions

1.   The Sentencing Guidelines rely on the concept of a "heartland," a typical violation of a particular criminal offense. For example, in United States v. DeBeir, 186 F.3d 561 (4th Cir. 1999), the defendant was caught in an online undercover sting and charged with traveling in interstate commerce with the intent to engage in a sexual act with a minor in violation of 18 U.S.C. § 2423(b). The district judge sentenced the defendant to probation after departing downward under the "catch-all" provision of U.S.S.G. § 5K2.0, which permits judges to award sentences outside the Guidelines range of the facts of the case bring it outside the heartland of typical cases. The district court judge relied on a number of factors, including that the crime was "victimless" because it involved an Internet sting rather than an actual child. The Fourth Circuit reversed:

> The crux of the district court's * * * finding seems to be its conclusion that DeBeir is not the type of offender that the guideline is really aimed at targeting. We cannot agree. In fact, offenses of this nature are increasingly committed with the help of the internet, and in such cases the offender must necessarily have had access to and the skills to use a computer. Thus we find nothing extraordinary about the particular factual landscape of this case—*i.e.,* that DeBeir is an intelligent and well-educated adult, has a strong employment history, had no prior exposure to life in prison, is neither a chronic offender nor a pedophile, was caught in a sting operation, received coverage in the media, later attempted counseling, and experienced remorse—that brings it outside the heartland of cases sentenced under this guideline.

DeBeir, 186 F.3d at 573.

2.   What are the practical consequences of an extra offense level in terms of the jail time a defendant receives? The answer depends on whether the offense level is at the high end of the Guidelines or the low end, as well as the defendant's criminal record. Assuming a defendant has no criminal record, each added offense level generally translates to about two months of extra jail time at the low end of the Guidelines, but an extra seven or eight months at the high end. If the defendant has a significant criminal history, the impact of an extra offense level is substantially greater.

3.   Do you agree with the policy choices embodied in U.S.S.G. § 2G2.2? Under § 2G2.2, the length of the prison term depends on factors such as the types of images, the number of images, and what the defendant did with the images. For example, under § 2G2.2(b)(7), a defendant who possessed fifty images of child pornography will generally face a prison term about ten months longer than a defendant who possessed five images (that is, two extra levels); a defendant who possesses 200 images will face about five more

months in prison than one who possessed fifty images (one extra level); and a defendant who possessed 1,000 images will face about ten more months in prison than the defendant who possessed 200 images (two extra levels).

Do these numbers make sense? Are the punishments imposed by the Guidelines in child pornography cases too light, too heavy, or about right? Keep in mind that several child pornography offenses contain mandatory minimum punishments. If the Guidelines range is less than the statutory minimum, the statutory minimum trumps the guidelines range.

C. SENTENCING IN COMPUTER MISUSE CASES

The offense conduct guideline that applies in most computer misuse cases is U.S.S.G. § 2B1.1. This provision is known as the "economic crimes" guideline because it is broadly applicable in economic crime cases involving theft or fraud. *See generally* Frank O. Bowman, III, *The 2001 Federal Economic Crime Sentencing Reforms: An Analysis and Legislative History*, 35 Ind. L. Rev. 5 (2001).

The fact that computer misuse crimes are sentenced along with other economic crimes provides the answer to one basic question about how the Guidelines might apply. For the most part, computer misuse offenses are sentenced just like any other economic crime. At the same time, U.S.S.G. § 2B1.1 contains a number of special wrinkles that apply only in computer misuse cases.

Section 2B1.1 offenses start with a base offense level of 6. The loss chart contained in § 2B1.1(b)(1) adds to the base offense level depending on the dollar amount of the loss involved:

If the loss exceeded $5,000, increase the offense level as follows:

Loss (apply the greatest)	Increase in level
(A) $5,000 or less	no increase
(B) More than $5,000	add 2
(C) More than $10,000	add 4
(D) More than $30,000	add 6
(E) More than $70,000	add 8
(F) More than $120,000	add 10
(G) More than $200,000	add 12
(H) More than $400,000	add 14
(I) More than $1,000,000	add 16
(J) More than $2,500,000	add 18
(K) More than $7,000,000	add 20
(L) More than $20,000,000	add 22
(M) More than $50,000,000	add 24
(N) More than $100,000,000	add 26
(O) More than $200,000,000	add 28
(P) More than $400,000,000	add 30

As the loss chart suggests, the dollar value of loss is a critical factor used to determine the sentence in a computer misuse case. Application

Note 3(a) to U.S.S.G. § 2B1.1 provides specific guidance on calculating loss, including a special rule for § 1030 cases. According to the application note, "loss is the greater of actual loss or intended loss." Actual loss and intended loss are defined as follows:

>   (i) Actual Loss.—"Actual loss" means the reasonably foreseeable pecuniary harm that resulted from the offense.

>   (ii) Intended Loss.—"Intended loss" (I) means the pecuniary harm that was intended to result from the offense; and (II) includes intended pecuniary harm that would have been impossible or unlikely to occur (e.g., as in a government sting operation, or an insurance fraud in which the claim exceeded the insured value).

>   (iii) Pecuniary Harm.—"Pecuniary harm" means harm that is monetary or that otherwise is readily measurable in money. Accordingly, pecuniary harm does not include emotional distress, harm to reputation, or other non-economic harm.

>   (iv) Reasonably Foreseeable Pecuniary Harm.—For purposes of this guideline, "reasonably foreseeable pecuniary harm" means pecuniary harm that the defendant knew or, under the circumstances, reasonably should have known, was a potential result of the offense.

>   (v) Rules of Construction in Certain Cases.—In the cases described in subdivisions (I) through (III), reasonably foreseeable pecuniary harm shall be considered to include the pecuniary harm specified for those cases as follows:

> * * *

>   (III) Offenses Under 18 U.S.C. § 1030.—In the case of an offense under 18 U.S.C. § 1030, actual loss includes the following pecuniary harm, regardless of whether such pecuniary harm was reasonably foreseeable: Any reasonable cost to any victim, including the cost of responding to an offense, conducting a damage assessment, and restoring the data, program, system, or information to its condition prior to the offense, and any revenue lost, cost incurred, or other damages incurred because of interruption of service.

Note that the special rule of construction for offenses under 18 U.S.C. § 1030 defines "actual loss" using the statutory definition of loss from 18 U.S.C. § 1030(e)(11), which itself attempted to codify United States v. Middleton, 231 F.3d 1207 (9th Cir. 2000). As a result, the methodology used to measure the statutory $5,000 loss requirement for 18 U.S.C. § 1030(a)(5) cases is also used to calculate loss at sentencing, and is used even if the case was not charged under § 1030(a)(5). The loss need not have been reasonably foreseeable, unlike the loss used for other types of cases.

U.S.S.G. § 2B1.1(b)(14) also contains a special rule for enhancements in some types of § 1030 offenses:

>   (A) (Apply the greatest) If the defendant was convicted of an offense under:

    (i) 18 U.S.C. § 1030, and the offense involved (I) a computer system used to maintain or operate a critical infrastructure, or used by or for a government entity in furtherance of the administration of justice, national defense, or national security; or (II) an intent to obtain personal information, increase by 2 levels.

    (ii) 18 U.S.C. § 1030(a)(5)(A)(I), increase by 4 levels.

    (iii) 18 U.S.C. § 1030, and the offense caused a substantial disruption of a critical infrastructure, increase by 6 levels.

(B) If subdivision (A)(iii) applies, and the offense level is less than level 24, increase to level 24.

Application Note 13(A) to U.S.S.G. § 2B1.1 then provides more specific guidance on several of the terms used:

> "Critical infrastructure" means systems and assets vital to national defense, national security, economic security, public health or safety, or any combination of those matters. A critical infrastructure may be publicly or privately owned. Examples of critical infrastructures include gas and oil production, storage, and delivery systems, water supply systems, telecommunications networks, electrical power delivery systems, financing and banking systems, emergency services (including medical, police, fire, and rescue services), transportation systems and services (including highways, mass transit, airlines, and airports), and government operations that provide essential services to the public.

> "Government entity" has the meaning given that term in 18 U.S.C. § 1030(e)(9).

> "Personal information" means sensitive or private information (including such information in the possession of a third party), including (i) medical records; (ii) wills; (iii) diaries; (iv) private correspondence, including e-mail; (v) financial records; (vi) photographs of a sensitive or private nature; or (vii) similar information.

In general, the most important practical effect of U.S.S.G. § 2B1.1(b)(14) is that it increases the penalties when a defendant is convicted of 18 U.S.C. § 1030(a)(5)(A)(I). Under § 2B1.1(b)(14)(A)(ii), a conviction under 18 U.S.C. § 1030(a)(5)(A)(I) raises the offense level by four points, which on average will generally translate into an 8–12 month increase in the length of a prison term.

Finally, Application Note 19 to § 2B1.1 provides special guidance on when an upward departure may be needed to account for non-monetary harms. The guidance is general, but some of it relates specifically to 18 U.S.C. § 1030 offenses:

> There may be cases in which the offense level determined under this guideline substantially understates the seriousness of the offense.

> In such cases, an upward departure may be warranted. The following is a nonexhaustive list of factors that the court may consider in determining whether an upward departure is warranted:

>   * * *

(ii) The offense caused or risked substantial non-monetary harm. For example, the offense caused physical harm, psychological harm, or severe emotional trauma, or resulted in a substantial invasion of a privacy interest (through, for example, the theft of personal information such as medical, educational, or financial records). An upward departure would be warranted, for example, in an 18 U.S.C. § 1030 offense involving damage to a protected computer, if, as a result of that offense, death resulted. * * *

(v) In a case involving stolen information from a "protected computer", as defined in 18 U.S.C. § 1030(e)(2), the defendant sought the stolen information to further a broader criminal purpose.

This application note gives courts relatively wide discretion to fashion appropriate sentences to account for privacy harms in computer misuse cases.

Notes and Questions

1. Are sentences for federal computer misuse crimes too low, too high, or about right? How do sentences for typical 18 U.S.C. § 1030 offenses compare with sentences for typical child pornography offenses?

2. Why do you think the sentencing guidelines have special rules for calculating "actual loss" in 18 U.S.C. § 1030 cases? Why should unforeseeable pecuniary harms be included in § 1030 cases but not for any other type of criminal offense? Is the idea that any loss resulting from a § 1030 offense is actually foreseeable? If so, is it fair for a defendant to have his sentence increased under § 2B1.1 if he commits a § 1030 offense that leads to truly unforeseeable harms? Is the defendant more culpable in such cases? Is a defendant more responsible for unforeseeable harms in § 1030 cases than in other cases? Or is the idea to punish those who commit computer misuse crimes more harshly than those who commit other crimes because computer misuse crimes are more dangerous?

3. Are losses suffered in computer misuse cases similar to losses suffered in other economic crime cases? Consider the example of a garden-variety fraud case. For the most part, the victim's loss will equal the defendant's gain. If A defrauds B out of $50,000, B has lost the money and A has gained it. In all likelihood, A will have controlled the extent of the loss, and will benefit more and more as the losses increase.

In a computer misuse case, however, the victim's loss generally will not equal the defendant's gain. If A hacks into B's server, and B takes its computers offline and suffers $50,000 in loss from the interruption of service, A does not gain anything from B's $50,000 loss. In all likelihood, A will have little to no control over the extent of the loss, and will not benefit as the losses mount.

The guidelines do not distinguish between these two types of cases. The victim's loss in the former example is treated for sentencing purposes the same as the victim's loss in the latter example. Does that make sense?

4. *Problem*. Imagine that the Smith family has three brothers: Larry, Moe, and Curly. All three brothers are skilled computer hackers. One day,

each of the three brothers hacks into a server operated by a different local e-commerce company. Assume that all three intrusions are essentially the same, but that the responses of the system administrators in charge of the three victim networks are very different. The system administrator at the company targeted by Larry notices the attack but decides to ignore it. The system administrator at the company that Moe attacks takes the intrusion seriously, and his response to the offense racks up $50,000 in loss. The system administrator at the company that Curly hacks into also takes the intrusion extremely seriously, and responding to the offense racks up $250,000 in loss.

Assume that Larry, Moe, and Curly are all charged and convicted of violating § 1030. Based on the loss chart of § 2B1.1(b)(1), Moe's offense level will be six points higher than Larry's, and Curly's will be six offense levels higher than Moe's. This works out on average to about an extra year in prison for Moe, and an extra two years in prison for Curly, all based on the response of the system administrator. Is this a sensible result?

5. *Calculating loss in virus and worm cases.* How should courts calculate "actual loss" in cases involving computer viruses and worms? In such cases, the losses may be distributed among thousands or even tens of thousands of victims. It is presumably impractical to measure the losses from each individual victim. Application Note 3(c) to U.S.S.G. § 2B1.1 states that "[t]he court need only make a reasonable estimate of the loss. The sentencing judge is in a unique position to assess the evidence and estimate the loss based upon that evidence. For this reason, the court's loss determination is entitled to appropriate deference." The Application Note also states that the court may estimate the loss by considering "[t]he approximate number of victims multiplied by the average loss to each victim." *Id.* cmt. n.3(c)(iii).

What guidance does this provide in computer worm or virus cases? How can the court estimate the number of victims, and how can it determine the average loss to each victim? Do victims outside the United States count, or are only losses suffered inside the United States relevant?

The fact that the loss chart contained in U.S.S.G. § 2B1.1(b)(1) contemplates losses higher than $400 million dollars may be attributable to the particular needs of computer virus cases. In March 1999, David Smith launched the "Melissa" virus, a computer virus that spread as an e-mail attachment. The virus spread quickly, and shut down computers around the globe. At the time, the loss chart for U.S.S.G. § 2B1.1 maxed out when losses exceeded $80 million. The losses caused by the global Melissa virus were widely believed to dwarf this figure. Because the loss amounts exceeded $80 million by a wide margin, the guilty plea agreement between the government and the United States stipulated that the damage had been more than $80 million and gave Smith the full enhancement based on loss amount. *See Plea Agreement of David Smith* (Dec. 8, 1999), *available at* http://www.usdoj.gov/criminal/cybercrime/meliplea.htm.

D. SUPERVISED RELEASE AND PROBATION RE-STRICTIONS

The federal court system generally uses three different forms of punishment: prison time, fines, and probation or supervised release.

Probation and supervised release are similar: each permit a defendant to avoid prison time, contingent upon the defendant's compliance with terms of probation or supervised release. The difference between probation and supervised release primarily relates to timing: probation is in lieu of jail time, whereas supervised release follows jail time. For example, a defendant may be sentenced to a period of probation, or may be sentenced to a prison term followed by a period of supervised release. If a defendant violates the terms of probation or supervised release, the defendant may at the discretion of the trial judge be sent to prison to serve out the remaining period of the sentence.

Supervised release and probation raise a very interesting computer-related question: What kinds of restrictions on computer and Internet use can a court impose as a condition of probation or supervised release?

UNITED STATES v. PAUL

United States Court of Appeals for the Fifth Circuit, 2001.
274 F.3d 155.

KING, Chief Judge:

After pleading guilty to a charge of knowingly possessing child pornography in violation of 18 U.S.C. § 2252A, Defendant–Appellant Ronald Scott Paul was sentenced to five years of imprisonment and three years of supervised release pursuant to section 2G2.2 of the United States Sentencing Guidelines. Paul appeals to this court, challenging * * * the conditions of his supervised release * * *. For the following reasons, we affirm Paul's conviction and his sentencing determination, including the conditions of supervised release.

FACTUAL AND PROCEDURAL BACKGROUND

On May 8, 2000, Defendant–Appellant Ronald Scott Paul took his personal computer to Electronic Services and Repair, a small computer repair business in Port Isabel, Texas. While working on the computer, a technician discovered child pornography on the hard drive and contacted the Federal Bureau of Investigations. The FBI's background check on Paul revealed a 1986 offense involving child pornography. After Paul had retrieved his computer from the repair technician, FBI agents searched Paul's residence pursuant to a valid warrant. The agents seized the computer, which contained a large number of files with images of child pornography that had been downloaded from the Internet. The agents also seized assorted photographs of children, magazines with nude photographs of children and adults, books with pictures of nude prepubescent boys, videotapes of random children filmed in public settings, a large bag of children's clothes, and several children's swimsuits covered with sand.

Additionally, the agents seized a medical bag containing basic medical supplies and Spanish-language flyers advertising lice removal for children. In the flyers, Paul informed parents that he would spray their children with a product that kills lice. The flyers also stated that Paul would conduct a complete physical examination on each child for "overall health," which necessarily required the child to completely undress. The agents also found between ten and twenty personal cameras in Paul's residence.

Further review of Paul's computer revealed electronic mail communications discussing sources of child pornography, including websites, chat rooms, and newsgroups that allowed both receiving and sending of pornographic images. In one of these e-mails, Paul discussed how easy it was to find "young friends" by scouting single, dysfunctional parents through Alcoholics Anonymous or local welfare offices and winning their friendship, thereby securing access to their young sons.

On July 17, 2000, Paul pled guilty to one charge of knowingly possessing a computer hard drive with three or more images of child pornography that traveled through interstate commerce, in violation of the Child Pornography Prevention Act. *See* 18 U.S.C. § 2252A(a)(5)(B). The government offered four images as samples of the child pornography that Paul possessed. Paul admitted that these exhibits were images he received from the Internet and stored on his computer hard drive.

After Paul pled guilty to possession of child pornography and was rearraigned, the court ordered the probation office to prepare a presentence report ("PSR"). Applying section 2G2.2 of the Sentencing Guidelines, the PSR determined that Paul's total offense level was 35. *See* U.S. Sentencing Guidelines Manual § 2G2.2 (1998). The PSR then factored in Paul's criminal history category (category I), which resulted in an imprisonment range of 121 to 151 months. However, the PSR noted that the statutory maximum penalty was 60 months.

The district court imposed a number of special conditions on Paul's supervised release term. He must "undergo a complete psychological evaluation and/or participate in a sex offender/mental health program as deemed necessary and approved by the probation officer." Paul is also directed to avoid "direct and indirect contact with minors," as well as "places, establishments, and areas frequented by minors," and is prohibited from "engaging in any paid occupation or volunteer service which exposes him either directly or indirectly to minors." The conditions further provide that Paul "shall not have, possess or have access to computers, the Internet, photographic equipment, audio/video equipment, or any item capable of producing a visual image." Finally, Paul is instructed to "register with the sex offender registration in any state where he resides, is employed, carries on a vocation, or is a student, as directed by the probation officer and as required by law."

THE SPECIAL CONDITIONS OF SUPERVISED RELEASE

A district court has wide discretion in imposing terms and conditions of supervised release. However, this discretion is limited by 18 U.S.C. § 3583(d), which provides that a court may impose special conditions of supervised release only when the conditions meet certain criteria. First, special conditions of supervised release must be reasonably related to the factors set forth in § 3553(a)(1), (a)(2)(B), (a)(2)(C), and (a)(2)(D). *See* 18 U.S.C. § 3583(d). These factors include: (1) "the nature and circumstances of the offense and the history and characteristics of the defendant," (2) the need "to afford adequate deterrence to criminal conduct," (3) the need "to protect the public from further crimes of the defendant," and (4) the need "to provide the defendant with needed [training], medical care, or other correctional treatment in the most effective manner." 18 U.S.C. § 3553(a)(1)-(2). In addition, supervised release conditions cannot involve a greater deprivation of liberty than is reasonably necessary to achieve the latter three statutory goals. *See* 18 U.S.C. § 3583(d). We review the district court's determination of supervised release conditions for abuse of discretion.

Paul contends that a blanket prohibition on computer or Internet use is excessively broad and cannot be justified based solely on the fact that his offense involved a computer and the Internet. He points out that computers and Internet access have become indispensable communication tools in the modern world and that the restriction imposed by the district court would prohibit him from accessing computers and the Internet for legitimate purposes, such as word processing and research.

The government responds that the order prohibiting Paul from using a computer or the Internet is rationally related to his offense and that such an order is an appropriate public protection measure. The government points out that Paul's computer contained over 1200 images of child pornography and contained evidence that Paul had used the Internet to access child pornography chat rooms, bulletin boards, and newsgroups. According to the government, Paul also used his e-mail to advise fellow consumers of child pornography how to "scout" single, dysfunctional parents and gain access to their children and to solicit the participation of like-minded individuals in trips to "visit" children in Mexico. Under these circumstances, the government argues, restricting Paul's access to computers and the Internet is reasonably tailored to his offense and conviction and serves the dual purpose of deterrence and public protection.

The government correctly points out that a number of courts have upheld Internet and computer-use prohibitions as conditions of supervised release. *See, e.g., United States v. Crandon,* 173 F.3d 122, 127–28 (3d Cir. 1999) (upholding an Internet restriction as a condition of supervised release for a child pornography offender); *United States v. Mitnick,* 145 F.3d 1342 (unpublished table decision), *available at* 1998 WL 255343 (9th Cir. 1998) (determining that the district court did not abuse its discretion in prohibiting a defendant convicted of offenses related to computer "hacking" from accessing "computers, computer-related equipment, and certain telecommunications devices" during his probationary period without prior approval of his probation officer).

Most factually analogous to the instant case is *Crandon,* wherein a defendant convicted of receiving child pornography challenged the district court's imposition of a supervised release condition dictating that he could not "possess, procure, purchase, or otherwise obtain access to any form of computer network, bulletin board, Internet or exchange format involving computers unless specifically approved by the U.S. Probation Office." 173 F.3d at 125. The district court found that this restriction on the defendant's Internet access was "reasonably related to his criminal activities, to the goal of deterring him from engaging in further criminal conduct, and to protecting the public," in light of the fact that the defendant had once used the Internet as a means to develop an illegal sexual relationship with a young girl. The court was unpersuaded by the defendant's argument that the Internet prohibition was overly broad and would unnecessarily restrict his career opportunities and his freedoms of speech and expression. Noting that supervised release conditions restricting employment and First Amendment freedoms are permissible if the statutory tailoring requirements are satisfied, the court ultimately concluded that the restriction on the defendant was not overly broad despite its effects on his business opportunities and expressive activities.

As in *Crandon,* the supervised release condition at issue in the instant case is reasonably related to Paul's offense and to the need to prevent recidivism and protect the public. The record reveals that Paul has in the past used the Internet to encourage exploitation of children by seeking out fellow "boy lovers" and providing them with advice on how to find and obtain access to "young friends." Restricting his access to this communication medium clearly serves the dual statutory goals of protecting the public and preventing future criminal activity. While the condition at issue in the instant case is broader than the restriction at issue in *Crandon* because it prohibits access to both computers and the Internet and it contains no proviso permitting Paul to use these resources with the approval of his probation office, we cannot say that the district court abused its discretion in determining that an absolute ban on computer and Internet use was reasonably necessary to protect the public and to prevent recidivism.

In arguing that the district court's computer and Internet prohibition was an abuse of discretion, Paul points to the Tenth Circuit's decision in *United States v. White,* 244 F.3d 1199 (10th Cir. 2001). In *White,* the court of appeals remanded to the sentencing court a special condition of supervised release that was substantially similar to Paul's condition. While the Tenth Circuit was unclear about the scope of the restriction at issue in that case, it indicated that if the condition were read to absolutely ban all Internet and computer use, it would be "greater than necessary" to serve the goals of supervised release outlined in 18 U.S.C. § 3583(d). The Tenth Circuit reasoned that *Crandon* did not dictate a different result. While acknowledging that the Third Circuit did uphold an Internet restriction in *Crandon,* the *White* court noted that the *Crandon* court did not impose an absolute *ban* on computer or Internet access, despite the fact that the defendant in *Crandon* (unlike the defendant in *White*) had clearly used the Internet to "initiate and facilitate a pattern of criminal conduct and victimization that produced an immediate consequence and directly injured the victim" in that case.

We find the Tenth Circuit's reasoning in *White* unpersuasive. Initially, we note that there is some evidence that Paul did in fact use the Internet to "initiate and facilitate a pattern of criminal conduct and victimization," and thus that *White* can be distinguished on these grounds. More importantly, we reject the *White* court's implication that an absolute prohibition on accessing computers or the Internet is *per se* an unacceptable condition of supervised release, simply because such a prohibition might prevent a defendant from using a computer at the library to "get a weather forecast" or to "read a newspaper online" during the supervised release term. We find that such a supervised release condition can be acceptable if it is reasonably necessary to serve the statutory goals outlined in 18 U.S.C. § 3583(d). In the instant case, the district court had strong evidentiary support for its determination that a strict ban on computer and Internet use was reasonably necessary. Moreover, Paul has articulated no specific objections to the computer and Internet ban suggesting how his occupational affairs or his expressive activities will be adversely impacted by the fact that he will be unable to "use a computer or the Internet at a library, cybercafe or an airport" during the term of his supervised release. We conclude that the district court did not abuse its discretion in imposing this condition of supervised release.

UNITED STATES v. SOFSKY

United States Court of Appeals for the Second Circuit, 2002.
287 F.3d 122.

Jon O. Newman, Circuit Judge.

This opinion concerns only a challenge to a condition of supervised release included as part of the sentence of ten years and one month imposed on Gregory Sofsky by the District Court for the Eastern District of New York after Sofsky pled guilty to receiving child pornography in violation of 18 U.S.C. § 2252A(a)(2)(A). The condition prohibits Sofsky from using a computer or the Internet without the approval of his probation officer. We conclude that the condition exceeds even the broad discretion of the sentencing judge with respect to conditions of supervised release, and must be substantially modified.

Prior to the entry of a guilty plea on the third day of trial, the Government presented overwhelming evidence that Sofsky had received on his home computer via the Internet more than 1,000 images of child pornography in the form of both still and moving pictures. Some of the images had been transferred to CD–ROM disks. Sofsky had also used the Internet to exchange images of child pornography with other (apparently like-minded) individuals at their computers. There was no claim that

Sofsky had ever produced any of the images he received or exchanged with others.

At sentencing, Judge Ross, following the recommendation of the presentence report, determined that the adjusted offense level under the Sentencing Guidelines was 32. In Criminal History Category I, level 32 prescribes a sentence range of 121 to 151 months. Judge Ross imposed a sentence of 121 months to be followed by a three-year term of supervised release. In addition to the standard conditions of supervised release, the Court imposed four special conditions: (1) the defendant must participate in mental health treatment, including a program for sexual disorders, (2) the defendant must permit a search of his premises on reasonable suspicion that contraband or evidence of a violation of a condition of supervision may be found, (3) the defendant may not "access a computer, the Internet, or bulletin board systems at any time, unless approved by the probation officer," and (4) the defendant must not view, purchase, or possess child pornography materials. Only the third condition is challenged on this appeal.

A sentencing court may order a special condition of supervised release that is "reasonably related" to several of the statutory factors governing the selection of sentences, "involves no greater deprivation of liberty than is reasonably necessary" for several statutory purposes of sentencing, and is consistent with Sentencing Commission policy statements. 18 U.S.C. § 3583(d). Although the discretion thus conferred is broad, we have cautioned that we will carefully scrutinize unusual and severe conditions.

We previously considered a sentencing component that prohibited access to a computer or the Internet in *United States v. Peterson,* 248 F.3d 79, 82–84 (2d Cir. 2001). The restriction was imposed as a condition of probation for a defendant convicted of larceny because of the defendant's prior state conviction for incest and his accessing of adult pornography on his home computer. Noting that "computers and Internet access have become virtually indispensable in the modern world of communications and information gathering," *id.* at 83, we ruled the condition unreasonable. Appellate courts considering a similar restriction imposed upon defendants convicted of child pornography offenses have reached different conclusions. *Compare United States v. White,* 244 F.3d 1199, 1205–07 (10th Cir. 2001) (invalidating and requiring modification of restriction imposed on defendant who used Internet to receive child pornography), *with United States v. Paul,* 274 F.3d 155, 169 (5th Cir. 2001) (upholding restriction imposed on defendant who produced child pornography and used Internet to distribute it), *and United States v. Crandon,* 173 F.3d 122, 127–28 (3d Cir. 1999) (upholding restriction imposed on defendant who used Internet to contact 14-year-old girl with whom he had sexual relations and photographed such conduct).

We appreciate the Government's point that permitting Sofsky access to a computer and the Internet after serving his ten-year sentence can facilitate continuation of his electronic receipt of child pornography, but

we are more persuaded by the observation in *Peterson* that "although a defendant might use the telephone to commit fraud, this would not justify a condition of probation that includes an absolute bar on the use of telephones." *Peterson,* 248 F.3d at 83. The same could be said of a prohibition on the use of the mails imposed on a defendant convicted of mail fraud. A total ban on Internet access prevents use of e-mail, an increasingly widely used form of communication and, as the Tenth Circuit noted, prevents other common-place computer uses such as "doing any research, getting a weather forecast, or reading a newspaper online." *White,* 244 F.3d at 1206. Although the condition prohibiting Sofsky from accessing a computer or the Internet without his probation officer's approval is reasonably related to the purposes of his sentencing, in light of the nature of his offense, we hold that the condition inflicts a greater deprivation on Sofsky's liberty than is reasonably necessary.

The Government contended at oral argument that the restriction must be broad because a restriction limited to accessing pornography would be extremely difficult for the probation officer to enforce without constant monitoring of Sofsky's use of his computer. There are several responses. First, to the extent that even a broad restriction would be enforced by the probation officer, monitoring (presumably unannounced) of Sofsky would be required to check if he was using a computer at all. Second, a more focused restriction, limited to pornography sites and images, can be enforced by unannounced inspections of Sofsky's premises and examination of material stored on his hard drive or removable disks.[12] *Cf. United States v. Knights,* 534 U.S. 112 (2001) (rejecting Fourth Amendment challenge to search, on reasonable suspicion, of probationer's premises). Finally, the Government can check on Sofsky's Internet usage with a sting operation—surreptitiously inviting him to respond to Government placed Internet ads for pornography.

For all the above reasons, the condition of supervised release prohibiting all computer and Internet access is vacated, and the case is remanded for entry of a more restricted condition.

Notes and Questions

1.   Are judges well-equipped to determine what kinds of restrictions on computer and Internet use are likely to be effective? Are appellate judges better or worse equipped to resolve such questions than trial judges?

2.   If you were a probation officer, how would you respond to the court's guidance in *Sofsky?* According to one newspaper article, probation officers responded by installing monitoring software on several defendants' computers. The software let probation officers access the defendants' computers remotely and obtain records of Web surfing and other online activities. *See* Matt Richtel, *Courts Split on Internet Bans,* N.Y. Times, Jan. 21,

---

12. One of the standard conditions of supervised release imposed on Sofsky requires him to "permit a probation officer to visit him ... at any time at home or elsewhere." Judgment ¶ 11.

2003. How hard do you think it is for a defendant to circumvent this type of monitoring? Can't the defendant simply purchase another computer?

3.   In United States v. Scott, 316 F.3d 733, 736–37 (7th Cir. 2003), Judge Easterbrook offered the following response to the defendant's claim that limitations on Internet access could never be imposed as conditions of supervised release:

> That is not a tenable argument. Computers and the Internet may be used to commit crimes, of which child pornography and fraud are only two examples. Inveterate hackers who have used access to injure others may be ordered to give up the digital world. If full access posed an unacceptable risk of recidivism, yet all controls on access were forbidden, then a judge would have little alternative but to increase the term of imprisonment in order to incapacitate the offender. Few defendants would deem that a beneficial exchange; most would prefer the conditional freedom of supervised release, even with restrictions on using the Internet, to the more regimented life in prison.
>
> This is not to gainsay the point * * * that because the Internet is a medium of communication a total restriction rarely could be justified. The Internet is a vast repository, offering books, newspapers, magazines, and research tools along with smut. A judge who would not forbid [the defendant] to enter a video rental store (which may have an adult-video section) also should not forbid [him] to enter the Internet, even though Disney's web site coexists with others offering filthy pictures or audio files circulated in violation of the copyright laws. A judge who would not forbid a defendant to send or receive postal mail or use the telephone should not forbid that person to send or receive email or to order books at Amazon.com. [The defendant] does not have a record of extensive abuse of digital communications that could justify an outright ban.

Is forbidding the use of computers like forbidding the use of telephones? Or is it more like forbidding a person to drive a car, which is a common condition of probation in drunk driving cases? Or is it more like forbidding a person to leave his home?

4.   For more perspectives on restricting computer use as a condition of supervised release and probation, see Jessica Habib, Note, *Cyber Crime and Punishment: Filtering Out Internet Felons*, 14 Fordham Intell. Prop. Media & Ent. L.J. 1051 (2004); Brian W. McKay, Student Work, *Guardrails on the Information Superhighway: Supervising Computer Use of the Adjudicated Sex Offender*, 106 W. Va. L. Rev. 203 (2003); Christopher Wiest, Comment and Casenote, *The Netsurfing Split: Restrictions Imposed on Internet and Computer Usage by Those Convicted of a Crime Involving a Computer*, 72 U. Cin. L. Rev. 847 (2003); Doug Hyne, *Examining the Legal Challenges to the Restriction of Computer Access as a Term of Probation or Supervised Release*, 28 New Eng. J. on Crim. & Civ. Confinement 215 (2002); Christopher M.E. Painter, *Supervised Release and Probation Restrictions in Hacker Cases*, U.S.A. Bulletin (March 2001).

5.   When should sentencing courts decide on the terms of supervised release relating to a defendant's computer use? In United States v. Balon, 384 F.3d 38 (2d Cir. 2004), the defendant was sentenced to a five-year prison

term, followed by a period of supervised released. The terms of supervised release contained a number of restrictions involving computer and Internet use. In an opinion by Judge Winter, the court held that the defendant's challenge to the computer and Internet-related aspects of his supervised release was not yet ripe for review:

> The technology that holds the key to whether the special condition in this case involves a greater deprivation of liberty than reasonably necessary is constantly and rapidly changing. Because Balon will not begin his term of supervised release for three years, it is impossible to evaluate at this time whether one method or another, or a combination of methods, will occasion a greater deprivation of his liberty than necessary in light of the special needs of supervised release.

> We therefore dismiss this portion of the appeal but instruct the district court to reconsider * * * the special conditions regarding monitoring of Balon's computer at a time closer to Balon's term of supervised release.

Id. at 46–47. Is this a sensible approach? Should the law be changed so that terms of supervised release are set soon before the supervised released begins, rather than when the defendant is sentenced following conviction?

Chapter 5

THE FOURTH AMENDMENT

This chapter considers how the Fourth Amendment governs law enforcement investigations of computer crimes. It analyzes the constitutional limits on the government's ability to gather digital evidence, identify a suspect, and try to establish beyond a reasonable doubt that the defendant has committed the offense. The Fourth Amendment states:

> The right of the people to be secure in their persons, houses, papers, and effects, against unreasonable searches and seizures, shall not be violated, and no Warrants shall issue, but upon probable cause, supported by Oath or affirmation, and particularly describing the place to be searched, and the persons or things to be seized.

The overall framework of Fourth Amendment law is simple to state but difficult to apply. The Fourth Amendment prohibits unreasonable searches and seizures. To determine if government conduct violates the Fourth Amendment, one must first identify whether searches or seizures have occurred, and if so, whether they are reasonable or unreasonable. A search or seizure is reasonable if it was authorized by a valid search warrant, or if one of the exceptions to the warrant requirement applies. A search warrant is a judicial order authorizing the police to execute a search or seizure; a warrant is valid if it is based on probable cause and particularly describes the property to be searched and the items to be seized. The usual remedy for violations of the Fourth Amendment is suppression of evidence obtained in any subsequent criminal case. While there are many exceptions and caveats to this rule, the basic idea is that the government cannot use the "fruits" of illegal government searches and seizures.

The meaning of the Fourth Amendment is relatively well-established for investigations involving physical evidence. Entering a house or opening a person's private packages constitutes a "search" of that house or package. Taking physical property away "seizes" it. The Fourth Amendment thus requires the police to obtain a warrant or to satisfy an exception to the warrant requirement before they can enter private spaces or take away physical property. The exceptions to the warrant requirement include consent, exigent circumstances, searches incident to a valid arrest, and border searches. All of these exceptions permit investigators to search or seize private property without a warrant.

How should these rules apply to computers and digital evidence? When is action relating to computer data a governmental "search" or "seizure"? How do courts apply the exceptions to the warrant requirement in cases involving computers? The materials present these questions by first focusing on the stand-alone environment, when evidence of a crime is stored on a local computer. The materials then consider how the Fourth Amendment applies to information sent remotely over computer networks.

A. THE REQUIREMENT OF GOVERNMENT ACTION

The Fourth Amendment does not regulate all searches and seizures. As the Supreme Court stated in United States v. Jacobsen, 466 U.S. 109, 113 (1984), the Fourth Amendment is "wholly inapplicable to a search or seizure, even an unreasonable one, effected by a private individual not acting as an agent of the Government or with the participation or knowledge of any governmental official." Where is the line between private searches and government searches?

UNITED STATES v. JARRETT

United States Court of Appeals for the Fourth Circuit, 2003.
338 F.3d 339.

Diana Gribbon Motz, Circuit Judge.

In this case, the Government used information provided by an anonymous computer hacker to initiate a search which produced evidence that William Jarrett violated federal statutes prohibiting the manufacture and receipt of child pornography. The district court suppressed this evidence on the ground that the hacker acted as a Government agent, and so violated the Fourth Amendment, when he procured pornographic files from Jarrett's computer. The Government appeals. Because the Government did not know of, or in any way participate in, the hacker's search of Jarrett's computer at the time of that search, the hacker did not act as a Government agent. Accordingly, we reverse and remand for further proceedings.

I.

The parties do not dispute the underlying facts. Prior to his involvement in the case at hand, the hacker, referred to as Unknownuser, provided information through emails during July 2000 to the FBI and law enforcement agents in Alabama regarding a child pornographer, Dr. Bradley Steiger. In an early email, Unknownuser identified himself only as someone "from Istanbul, Turkey," who could not "afford an overseas phone call and cannot speak English fluently."

Employing the same method that he would later use to hack into Jarrett's computer, Unknownuser obtained access to Steiger's computer via a so-called Trojan Horse program that Unknownuser had attached to a picture he posted to a news group frequented by pornography enthusiasts. When Steiger downloaded the picture to his own computer, he inadvertently downloaded the Trojan Horse program, which then permitted Unknownuser to enter Steiger's computer undetected via the Internet. *See* United States v. Steiger, 318 F.3d 1039, 1044 (11th Cir. 2003). After searching Steiger's hard drive and finding evidence of child pornography, Unknownuser copied certain files and then emailed the information to the law enforcement officials who used it to identify and apprehend Steiger. A jury convicted Steiger of violating various federal statutes prohibiting the sexual exploitation of minors. He was sentenced to 210 months in prison.

Shortly after Steiger was indicted, in late November 2000, FBI Special Agent James Duffy, who served as Legal Attache for the FBI in Turkey, contacted Unknownuser via email and phone. In addition to informing Unknownuser that he would not be prosecuted for his assistance in apprehending Steiger, Duffy requested a meeting and posed a series of questions to Unknownuser, with the hope that Unknownuser would reveal his identity and perhaps agree to testify at Steiger's trial. Although Unknownuser was quite forthcoming in his responses, he refused to meet with Agent Duffy, stating emphatically that he would never allow himself to be identified. Agent Duffy closed this exchange (in an email dated December 4, 2000) by thanking Unknownuser for his assistance and stating that "If you want to bring other information forward, I am available."

Five months later, Agent Duffy contacted Unknownuser via email, informing him of a postponement in the Steiger trial, thanking him again for his assistance, and assuring him that he would not be prosecuted for his actions should he decide to serve as a witness in the Steiger trial. Unknownuser responded, repeating that he had no intention of revealing his identity.

The next contact between Unknownuser and law enforcement did not occur until December 3, 2001, almost seven months later, when Unknownuser sent an unsolicited email to his contact at the Montgomery, Alabama Police Department, Kevin Murphy, informing Murphy that he had "found another child molester from Richmond, VA" and requesting contact information for someone at the FBI dealing with these sorts of crimes. The alleged child molester referred to in the email was William Jarrett.

After contacting the FBI, Murphy informed Unknownuser that the FBI preferred that Unknownuser send the new information to Murphy's email address. On December 4, 2001, Unknownuser sent thirteen email messages to Murphy, including a ten-part series of emails with some forty-five attached files containing the "evidence" that Unknownuser had collected on Jarrett. Murphy forwarded the information to agents at the FBI, who initiated an investigation.

Based on the information provided by Unknownuser, the Government filed a criminal complaint and application for a search warrant against Jarrett on December 13, 2001. After receiving authorization from the district court, the FBI promptly executed the search warrant and arrested Jarrett.

Several days after Jarrett's arrest, on December 16, 2001, Agent Duffy sent Unknownuser an email informing him of Steiger's sentence and thanking Unknownuser for his assistance in the case. At the time, Duffy was unaware of the Jarrett investigation. The next day, Unknownuser replied, informing Duffy of his efforts to identify Jarrett and inquiring why he had heard nothing since he sent the Jarrett files to Murphy on December 4. Unknownuser sent a similar message the following day (December 18) indicating that he had read about Jarrett's arrest in the newspaper and asking Agent Duffy to have Agent Margaret Faulkner—a special agent based in Alabama who had been involved in the Steiger investigation—contact him. On December 19, 2001, Agent Duffy sent an email to Unknownuser thanking him again for his assistance, providing information on the Jarrett investigation and prosecution, and requesting that Unknownuser maintain email contact with Agent Faulkner via her personal email address.

Three weeks later, on January 9, 2002, a grand jury indicted Jarrett on one count of manufacturing child pornography in violation of 18 U.S.C.A. § 2251(a) and seven counts of receiving child pornography in violation of 18 U.S.C.A. § 2252A(a)(2)(A). Jarrett moved to suppress the evidence obtained through the execution of the search warrant on the ground that the Government violated his Fourth Amendment rights in using the information provided by Unknownuser to secure the search warrant. The district court denied the motion. Jarrett then entered a conditional guilty plea to a one-count criminal information charging him with manufacturing child pornography.

Prior to sentencing, however, Jarrett moved to reconsider his earlier motion to suppress on the basis of new evidence—a series of emails exchanged between Unknownuser and FBI agent Faulkner, beginning shortly after Jarrett's arrest and extending for almost two months. The Government did not disclose these emails until after Jarrett had entered his guilty plea.

In the initial email in this series, dated December 19, 2001, Agent Faulkner explicitly thanked Unknownuser for providing the information to law enforcement officials. She then engaged in what can only be characterized as the proverbial "wink and a nod":

> I can not ask you to search out cases such as the ones you have sent to us. That would make you an agent of the Federal Government and make how you obtain your information illegal and we could not use it against the men in the pictures you send. But if you should

happen across such pictures as the ones you have sent to us and wish us to look into the matter, please feel free to send them to us. We may have lots of questions and have to email you with the questions. But as long as you are not 'hacking' at our request, we can take the pictures and identify the men and take them to court. We also have no desire to charge you with hacking. You are not a U.S. citizen and are not bound by our laws.

Over the course of the next two months, Agent Faulkner sent at least four additional email messages, which constituted, in the words of the district court, a "pen-pal type correspondence" with Unknownuser. In addition to expressing gratitude and admiration for Unknownuser, Faulkner repeatedly sought to reassure Unknownuser that he was not a target of law enforcement for his hacking activities. For example, in an email dated January 29, 2002, she stated that

> the FACT still stands that you are not a citizen of the United States and are not bound by our laws. Our Federal attorneys have expressed NO desire to charge you with any CRIMINAL offense. You have not hacked into any computer at the request of the FBI or other law enforcement agency. You have not acted as an agent for the FBI or other law enforcement agency. Therefore, the information you have collected can be used in our criminal trials.

In his responses to Agent Faulkner, Unknownuser spoke freely of his "hacking adventures" and suggested in no uncertain terms that he would continue to search for child pornographers using the same methods employed to identify Steiger and Jarrett. As found by the district court, Agent Faulkner, despite her knowledge of Unknownuser's illegal hacking, never instructed Unknownuser that he should cease hacking.

Upon consideration of this series of emails, the district court reversed its earlier decision and suppressed the evidence obtained during the search of Jarrett's residence. At the same time, the court deemed Jarrett's motion to reconsider as a motion to withdraw his guilty plea, which it promptly granted. The court reasoned that the "totality of all the contact between law enforcement and Unknownuser encouraged Unknownuser to continue his behavior and to remain in contact with the FBI." The district court thus concluded that the Government and Unknownuser had "expressed their consent to an agency relationship," thereby rendering any evidence obtained on the basis of Unknownuser's hacking activities inadmissible on the ground that it was procured in violation of Jarrett's Fourth Amendment rights.

II.

The Fourth Amendment protects against unreasonable searches and seizures by Government officials and those private individuals acting as instruments or agents of the Government. *See* U.S. Const. amend. IV; Coolidge v. New Hampshire, 403 U.S. 443, 487 (1971). It does not provide protection against searches by private individuals acting in a private capacity. *See* United States v. Jacobsen, 466 U.S. 109, 113 (1984) (holding that the Fourth Amendment is "wholly inapplicable to a search or seizure, even an unreasonable one, effected by a private individual not acting as an agent of the Government or with the participation or knowledge of any governmental official"). Thus, evidence secured by private searches, even if illegal, need not be excluded from a criminal trial.

Determining whether the requisite agency relationship exists "necessarily turns on the degree of the Government's participation in the private party's activities, a question that can only be resolved in light of all the circumstances." Skinner v. Railway Labor Executives' Ass'n, 489 U.S. 602, 614–15 (1989) This is a fact-intensive inquiry that is guided by common law agency principles. The defendant bears the burden of proving that an agency relationship exists.

In order to run afoul of the Fourth Amendment, therefore, the Government must do more than passively accept or acquiesce in a private party's search efforts. Rather, there must be some degree of Government participation in the private search. In *Skinner*, for example, the Supreme Court found that private railroads, in performing drug tests on their employees in a manner expressly encouraged and authorized under Government regulations, acted as Government agents sufficient to implicate the Fourth Amendment. As the Court concluded, "specific features of the regulations combine to convince us that the Government did more than adopt a passive position toward the underlying private conduct."

Following the Supreme Court's pronouncements on the matter, the Courts of Appeals have identified two primary factors that should be considered in determining whether a search conducted by a private person constitutes a Government search triggering Fourth Amendment protections. These are: (1) whether the Government knew of and acquiesced in the private search; and (2) whether the private individual intended to assist law enforcement or had some other independent motivation. Although we have never articulated a specific "test," we too have embraced this two-factor approach. * * *

In this case, the Government concedes the existence of the second factor—that Unknownuser's motivation for conducting the illicit searches stemmed solely from his interest in assisting law enforcement authorities. Thus, the only question before us concerns the first factor— did the Government know of and acquiesce in Unknownuser's search in a manner sufficient to transform Unknownuser into an agent of the Government, and so render the search unconstitutional.

In seeking to give content to this factor, we have required evidence of more than mere knowledge and passive acquiescence by the Government before finding an agency relationship.

Viewed in the aggregate, * * * three major lessons emerge from the case law. First, courts should look to the facts and circumstances of each case in determining when a private search is in fact a Government search. Second, before a court will deem a private search a Government search, a defendant must demonstrate that the Government knew of and acquiesced in the private search and that the private individual intended to assist law enforcement authorities. Finally, simple acquiescence by the Government does not suffice to transform a private search into a Government search. Rather, there must be some evidence of Government participation in or affirmative encouragement of the private search before a court will hold it unconstitutional. Passive acceptance by the Government is not enough.

With these principles in mind, we turn to the case at hand.

III.

With respect to fact finding, the district court found the facts as we have recounted them above. The record adequately supports these findings; certainly they are not clearly erroneous.

The district court's conclusions of law, however, present problems. The court concluded that Unknownuser's extensive post-search email exchange with Agent Faulkner, together with the brief exchanges between Unknownuser and Agent Duffy in November and December 2000 (one year prior to the Jarrett search) and May 2001 (seven months prior to the Jarrett search), demonstrated that the Government had an "ongoing relationship" with Unknownuser sufficient to make Unknownuser an agent of the Government. Specifically, the court held that in light of the Government's collective efforts to praise Unknownuser for his assistance, its repeated requests for further assistance, its assurances that Unknownuser would not be prosecuted for his hacking activities, and its refusal to suggest that Unknownuser should cease hacking, "there was far more than mere knowledge on the government's part."

Although, as the Government conceded at oral argument, the Faulkner email exchange probably does constitute the sort of active Government participation sufficient to create an agency relationship going forward (absent other countervailing facts), the district court erred in relying on this exchange to find that the Government knew of and acquiesced in the Jarrett search. This is so because Unknownuser's email exchange with Faulkner took place after Unknownuser had hacked into Jarrett's computer, after the fruits of Unknownuser's hacking had been made available to the FBI, after Jarrett's home and computer had been searched, and after Jarrett himself had been arrested. Thus, Faulkner's knowledge and acquiescence was entirely post-search. Such after-the-fact conduct cannot serve to transform the prior relationship between Unknownuser and the Government into an agency relationship with respect to the search of Jarrett's computer.

Although the Government operated close to the line in this case, it did not (at least on the evidence before the district court) demonstrate the requisite level of knowledge and acquiescence sufficient to make Unknownuser a Government agent when he hacked into Jarrett's computer. When Unknownuser came forward with the Jarrett information, he had not been in contact with the Government for almost seven months, and nothing indicates that the Government had any intention of reestablishing contact with him. The only communications that could possibly be construed as signaling an agency relationship prior to the search of Jarrett's computer (the Duffy communications from November–December 2000 and May 2001) were simply too remote in time and too tenuous in substance to bring the Jarrett search within the scope of an agency relationship.

That the Government did not actively discourage Unknownuser from engaging in illicit hacking does not transform Unknownuser into a Government agent. Although the Government's behavior in this case is discomforting,[5] the Government was under no special obligation to affirmatively discourage Unknownuser from hacking.

At the end of the day, in order to bring Unknownuser within the grasp of an agency relationship, Jarrett would have to show that the Government made more explicit representations and assurances (as in the post-hoc Faulkner emails) that it was interested in furthering its relationship with Unknownuser and availing itself of the fruits of any information that Unknownuser obtained. Although evidence of such "encouragement" would not have to target a particular individual, it would have to signal affirmatively that the Government would be a ready and willing participant in an illegal search.

As the facts in this case make clear, no such relationship existed between Unknownuser and the Government when Unknownuser hacked into Jarrett's computer. Accordingly, we hold that the district court erred when it found that Unknownuser acted as an agent of the Government when he hacked into Jarrett's computer.

Notes and Questions

1. Do you believe that Unknownuser was a resident of Istanbul, Turkey? If Unknownuser had been a local Virginia police officer, would the FBI agents who investigated the case necessarily realize it?

2. Do private searches of computer data create a greater privacy threat than private searches of homes and other physical property? In the physical world, private searches are most often conducted by co-workers, spouses, and roommates. None are particularly likely to report the fruits of their searches to the police. Private searches by strangers are also relatively unlikely to be reported to the police. For example, a burglar is not likely to risk being caught by reporting evidence of crime that he finds inside a victim's home.

Are computer searches different? The anonymity of the Internet may make private searches by perfect strangers significantly more common, and may increase the odds that strangers will report discovered evidence to law enforcement. Any computer user located anywhere in the world can hack in

5. Notwithstanding the Government's assumptions, nothing in the record establishes that Unknownuser is a foreign national and, even if he is, of course, foreign nationals can, as the Government conceded, be prosecuted in the United States for sending and receiving child pornography. Unauthorized hacking also violates United States law.

to a person's computer when it is online, and can search the computer for evidence and share what he finds with the police without revealing his identity. *See, e.g.,* United States v. Kennedy, 81 F. Supp. 2d 1103, 1112 (D. Kan. 2000). One author comments:

> The consequences of enlisting private help in cyberspace are broader than enlisting such aid in the physical world in the form of neighborhood watch groups, tip hotlines, and informants. Electronic vigilantism may violate an individual's privacy to the same extent as a private party conducting a physical search. However, unlike invasions of privacy in the physical world—a nosy neighbor rummaging through your trash or a suspicious colleague snooping around your office—private party searches of computers connected to the internet require some form of technical expertise, can be performed much more systematically, reach a larger number of people, and leave no trace of intrusion.

> Moreover, the electronic search is more expansive in scope because a vigilante hacker can access all of an individual's files once he gains access to his computer. Also, it is more intrusive simply because the individual is unaware that his computer is being searched. Although his computer is connected to the internet, possibly at all times if he has a high-speed connection, he may not be aware that he is the target of an investigation. Perhaps this is a symptom of naivety or ignorance, but, nonetheless, individuals are more likely to place private information on their hard drives, thinking it is safer there than in a wastebasket or a file cabinet. Consequently, although an electronic search raises the same privacy concerns as a search in the physical world, the scope and intrusiveness of such a search is much more significant because the searcher victimizes a broader pool of people without their knowledge.

Monica R. Shah, Note, *The Case for a Statutory Suppression Remedy to Regulate Illegal Private Party Searches in Cyberspace*, 105 Colum. L. Rev. 250, 268–69 (2005). Should the private search doctrine be reworked so that the Fourth Amendment regulates computer searches conducted by anonymous hackers? Should the government have the burden of proving that an anonymous hacker was *not* a state actor?

3. A number of reported child pornography convictions followed searches by computer repairmen. In these cases, the defendant brought his personal computer to a local repairman because the computer was malfunctioning. In the course of diagnosing the problem, the repairman looked through the files on the computer, found child pornography, and contacted the police. Held: The repairman's search of the computer and discovery of contraband did not violate the Fourth Amendment because the repairman was a private actor. *See, e.g.,* United States v. Hall, 142 F.3d 988, 993 (7th Cir. 1998).

4. *Reenacting a private search.* According to United States v. Jacobsen, 466 U.S. 109 (1984), government agents who learn of evidence discovered by a private search can reenact the original private search without implicating the Fourth Amendment. The agents cannot "exceed the scope of the private search" without a warrant, *id.* at 115, but they can trace the steps of the prior search with the permission of the private party.

How does this apply to a computer search? If a private party searches a computer and opens a few files, finds evidence of crime, and gives the computer to the police, can the police search the entire computer without a warrant? Or does viewing more than the exact files that were opened by the private party "exceed the scope" of the private search under *Jacobsen*?

Courts are divided on this question. In United States v. Barth, 26 F. Supp. 2d 929 (W.D. Tex. 1998), the defendant gave his laptop computer to a computer repairman named Kellar. Kellar found contraband images on the computer, and then gave the computer to the Odessa Police Department (OPD). OPD officers searched the rest of the computer without a warrant. The court concluded that the police search of the computer beyond the specific images viewed by Kellar violated the Fourth Amendment: "Because the subsequent search in this case far exceeded Kellar's viewings, Defendant's Fourth Amendment rights were implicated during the OPD's subsequent viewing of his hard drive. . . . the OPD officers' viewing and copying of its entire contents exceeded the scope of Kellar's initial searches." *Id.* at 937.

A New York state court took a different approach in People v. Emerson, 766 N.Y.S.2d 482 (Sup. Ct. 2003). In *Emerson*, a computer repairman found a number of child pornography images in files located in two folders labeled "xxx" and "MPG." The repairman then brought the computer to the police, and showed them those files and several other files of child pornography located in the same two folders. The Court ruled that the repairman was a government actor when he conducted the search in front of the police to help them locate evidence, but that he did not exceed the scope of the initial private search because "the viewing of files on both dates concerned images of child pornography only, and * * * they were files contained in the only two computer file folders, denominated 'xxx' and 'MPG,' accessed during [the repairman's] private search." *Id.* at 487. Had the second search involved different folders, the Court suggested, the second search might have exceeded the scope of the initial private search. *See id.* at 487–88.

The Fifth Circuit adopted yet another approach in United States v. Runyan, 275 F.3d 449 (5th Cir. 2001). In *Runyan*, an estranged wife looked through some of her husband's computer disks and found contraband images. She turned over the entire set of disks to the police, and the police later conducted an extensive search of all of the disks without a warrant. The Fifth Circuit concluded that the police officers did not exceed the scope of the private search when they looked through the disks that the wife had accessed, even though the police viewed files that the wife had not seen. The governmental viewing had merely examined the disks "more thoroughly than did the private parties." *Id.* at 464. In contrast, the police could not search the disks that the wife had not accessed. Viewing files located on those disks exceeded the scope of the private search. *Id.*

Which case offers the most persuasive approach? *Barth, Emerson,* or *Runyan*?

B. DEFINING SEARCHES AND SEIZURES

1. SEARCHES

A Fourth Amendment "search" occurs when government action violates an individual's "reasonable expectation of privacy." *See* Smith v.

Maryland, 422 U.S. 735, 740 (1979) (citing Katz v. United States, 389 U.S. 347, 361 (1967) (Harlan, J., concurring)). Perhaps surprisingly, however, the Supreme Court has not provided a clear explanation of when a person enjoys a reasonable expectation of privacy in his property or information. Sometimes the Supreme Court suggests that a reasonable expectation of privacy is an expectation backed by a property right; sometimes it suggests that a reasonable expectation of privacy exists when a reasonable person would expect privacy in something; and sometimes it suggests that a reasonable expectation of privacy exists when Fourth Amendment protection in that property or information establishes a sufficient degree of privacy protection from government intrusion.

Given the uncertain explanations found in the case law, the best way to understand when a person has a reasonable expectation of privacy may be to reason by analogy. The Supreme Court has decided many cases involving Fourth Amendment rights in the contents of containers such as letters, packages, boxes, and trunks. The basic rule emerging from these cases is that individuals have a Fourth Amendment reasonable expectation of privacy in the contents of their sealed containers. *See, e.g.*, Robbins v. California, 453 U.S. 420, 427 (1981) (Stewart, J., plurality opinion). The same rule applies across a wide range of different types of containers:

> Even though such a distinction [among different containers] perhaps could evolve in a series of cases in which paper bags, locked trunks, lunch buckets, and orange crates were placed on one side of the line or the other, the central purpose of the Fourth Amendment forecloses such a distinction. For just as the most frail cottage in the kingdom is absolutely entitled to the same guarantees of privacy as the most majestic mansion, so also may a traveler who carries a toothbrush and a few articles of clothing in a paper bag or knotted scarf claim an equal right to conceal his possessions from official inspection as the sophisticated executive with the locked attache case.

United States v. Ross, 456 U.S. 798, 822 (1982). In contrast, "[w]hat a person knowingly exposes to the public, even in his own home or office, is not a subject of Fourth Amendment protection." Katz v. United States, 389 U.S. 347, 351 (1967). The following case considers how these principles apply to searches of computers.

UNITED STATES v. DAVID

United States District Court for the District of Nevada, 1991.
756 F. Supp. 1385.

LAWRENCE R. LEAVITT, United States Magistrate Judge.

On June 21, 1990, the federal grand jury returned a one-count Indictment charging the defendant, Artem Bautista David, with conspiracy to import more than 20 kilos of heroin into the United States.

An evidentiary hearing was conducted before the undersigned Magistrate Judge on September 12, 1990. The testimony established that in late April, 1990, David flew from Hong Kong to Las Vegas and was taken into custody by Customs agents on a charge of conspiracy to smuggle heroin into the United States. Government counsel engaged in discussions with David's then counsel, John R. Lusk, with a view toward enlisting David's cooperation in exchange for a favorable plea bargain. An agreement was reached whereby David, who would remain in custody under a detention order, would meet periodically with the agents in their office and make full disclosure of his knowledge of drug trafficking activities in an "off the record" proffer. * * * The agreement also provided that at the agents' direction, David would place consensually monitored telephone calls to his criminal associates. The telephone numbers of those associates were kept in David's computer memo book, access to which required the use of a password—"fortune"—which was known only to David.

During one such meeting in early May, 1990, which Lusk attended, David retrieved and disclosed certain information contained in the book. At the time, the agents were sitting across the table from him and were unable to see the password which David used or the information displayed on the book's screen. David did not volunteer the password to the agents, or offer to show them the book.

Jail regulations prohibited David from taking the book back to the jail at night. For the sake of convenience, Lusk permitted the agents to maintain custody of the book at the end of each session. Lusk did not, however, give them permission to access the book. Neither did David. Nor, as noted above, did the assistance agreement itself expressly permit the agents to gain access to the book or, for that matter, to any other property in David's possession.

At the next meeting on May 7, 1990, David met with Customs Special Agent Eric Peterson and DEA Special Agent Don Ware. Lusk did not attend this meeting. According to David's testimony, when he initially accessed the book at this meeting, Agent Peterson got up and stood directly behind him. David was aware that Peterson was looking over his shoulder, but did not feel that he could demand that Peterson move away. David did, however, try to position the book so as to minimize Peterson's view of it.

According to David's testimony, after he made two telephone calls for the agents, Peterson grabbed the book and accused David of deleting certain information. David demanded the book back, but Peterson refused. At the evidentiary hearing, David denied having deleted information from the book. Agent Peterson's version of what occurred at the meeting is a little different. Peterson testified that on May 7, 1990, he first requested the access code from David, but David was unresponsive. Peterson admitted that he then stood behind David and observed David use the password "fortune" to access the book. A little later, while Agent Ware was criticizing David for not cooperating fully during a consensually monitored phone call, Peterson, without requesting David's permission, used the password "fortune" and accessed the book himself. He then reviewed several of its entries. David saw Peterson doing this, but said nothing. Peterson came across an entry which read "1 = 12,000; 2 = 23,000," which, based on his experience as a Customs agent, he knew to be a heroin price list per kilo in Thailand. He then turned off the computer and returned it to David.

The Fourth Amendment provides that the "right of the people to be secure in their persons, houses, papers, and effects, against unreasonable searches and seizures, shall not be violated." The Supreme Court has defined a *search* as an infringement of "an expectation of privacy that society is prepared to consider reasonable." United States v. Jacobsen, 466 U.S. 109, 113 (1984). Hence, a law enforcement officer who looks at something has not engaged in a "search" within the meaning of the Fourth Amendment unless someone else has a right to expect that the thing which is seen will remain private.

In evaluating the factual scenario described above, we begin by identifying those events which may have Fourth Amendment implications. The *first* such event occurred when Agent Peterson deliberately looked over David's shoulder to see the password to the book. David himself voluntarily accessed the book at a time when the agents were in close proximity to him. Agent Peterson was not required to stay seated across the table from David. Nor did David have a reasonable expectation that Peterson would not walk behind him, or remain outside of some imaginary zone of privacy within the enclosed room. It was Peterson's office, and he could move about in it wherever he pleased. The Court therefore finds that under the circumstances David had no reasonable expectation of privacy in the display that appeared on the screen, and accordingly concludes that Peterson's act of looking over David's shoulder to see the password did not constitute a search within the meaning of the Fourth Amendment.

Peterson's act of accessing the book did constitute a search, however, if, under the circumstances, David had a reasonable expectation that when he turned the book off, its contents would remain private. For the purposes of this discussion, the book, in the Court's view, is indistinguishable from any other closed container, and is entitled to the same Fourth Amendment protection. *Robbins v. California,* 453 U.S. 420, 427 (1981); *United States v. Ross,* 456 U.S. 798 (1982). The Court does not question Agent Peterson's testimony that based on David's cooperation agreement with the government, Peterson had a good faith belief that he had the right to access the book. Peterson testified that in his mind the cooperation agreement implied that David would withhold nothing from the agents, including the contents of his memo book. But David's attempt to prevent Peterson from seeing the password, and his deletion of the heroin price list and attempted deletion of the firearms price list, clearly reflect that at the very least David did not *want* to share all of the contents of the book with the agents.

* * * Accordingly, the government should not be allowed to use as evidence the information which Agent Peterson obtained from the book when he accessed it without David's express consent.

Notes and Questions

1. A person ordinarily retains a reasonable expectation of privacy in the contents of his opaque containers when the containers are at home, in his possession, or are stored in a space that he legitimately controls. Opening such a container constitutes a Fourth Amendment search. Under the container analogy followed in *David*, an individual will retain a reasonable expectation of privacy in the contents of his computers in the same circumstances. When a government agent retrieves contents from the individual's computer, that retrieval is a Fourth Amendment search that ordinarily requires a warrant or a specific exception to the warrant requirement. Of course, if a computer is stored inside a private space such as a home or a car, entering the home or car is a separate search that also needs to be justified under the Fourth Amendment.

2. Is a computer just like any other container for the purposes of the Fourth Amendment? Professor Clancy argues that the container analogy is persuasive:

> [C]omputers are containers. As with all containers, they have the ability to hold physical evidence, including such items as wires, microchips, and hard drives. They also contain electronic evidence, that is, a series of digitally stored 0s and 1s that, when combined with a computer program, yield such items as images, words, and spreadsheets. Accordingly, the traditional standards of the Fourth Amendment regulate obtaining the evidence in containers that happen to be computers.

Thomas K. Clancy, *The Fourth Amendment Aspects of Computer Searches and Seizures: A Perspective and a Primer*, 75 Miss. L.J. 193, 196 (2005). On the other hand, Raphael Winick has suggested that the container analogy may be problematic:

> [A]nalogizing stored computer memory to a closed container presents several problems. The container model may make conceptual sense when discussing small electronic storage devices such as pagers or electronic address books, but the analogy becomes strained when applied to computers with larger storage capacities. For such systems, an analogy to a massive file cabinet, or even to an entire archive or record center, may be more appropriate.

Raphael Winick, *Searches and Seizures of Computers and Computer Data*, 8 Harv. J.L. & Tech. 75, 82 (1994).

Is this disagreement merely semantic? A "massive file cabinet" is really just a container of containers. Individuals retain a reasonable expectation of privacy in the contents of their file cabinets just as they do in the contents of their wallets or briefcases.

Perhaps the important question is not whether computers can be modeled as containers, but whether computers containing many files should be modeled as single containers or "containers of containers." Note that after the police search a container, they normally can examine it again without conducting a new Fourth Amendment "search." The first government search eliminates a reasonable expectation of privacy in the container, permitting subsequent searches. When a file on a computer has been viewed, however, what exactly has been searched? Is the computer a single container, such that viewing the file searched the entire computer? Is the computer a container of individual files, such that viewing the file searched just that one file? Consider Orin S. Kerr, *Searches and Seizures in a Digital World*, 119 Harv. L. Rev. 531, 556 (2005):

> A single physical storage device can store the private files of thousands of different users. It would be quite odd if looking at one file on a server meant that the entire server had been searched, and that the police could then analyze everything on the server, perhaps belonging to thousands of different people, without any restriction. Furthermore, a single file on a network may actually be stored in several physical boxes. Some computer storage devices may not be stored in any boxes at all. Over time, it should become increasingly clear that the Fourth Amendment should track the information, not the physical box.

See also Clancy, 75 Miss. L.J. at 240 ("[A] computer should be viewed as a physical container with a series of electronic "containers"—that is, directories, folders, and files that must be each separately opened. Each separate opening is the examination of a new container.") *See also* Note 4, pages [306–07].

3. Does a person retain a reasonable expectation of privacy in the contents of computers that they have stolen, or that they have obtained by fraud? In United States v. Caymen, 404 F.3d 1196 (9th Cir. 2005), a hotel desk clerk obtained the credit card of a hotel customer and used the account number to purchase a computer for his personal use without the customer's permission. The hotel customer complained about the $1,654 bill for a new computer on her credit card, and the investigation was traced back to the desk clerk, Nicolai Caymen. The police searched Caymen's apartment and found the computer in his bedroom. The police then searched the computer for evidence of criminal activity. When the fruits of the search led to criminal charges, Caymen challenged the search of the computer on Fourth Amendment grounds. The Ninth Circuit rejected the challenge on the ground that Caymen did not have a reasonable expectation of privacy in the computer:

> What matters is a reasonable expectation of privacy that society is prepared to accept as reasonable, and one who takes property by theft or fraud cannot reasonably expect to retain possession and exclude others from it once he is caught. Whatever expectation of privacy he might assert is not a legitimate expectation that society is prepared to honor. Because, as the district court found, Caymen obtained the laptop computer by fraud, he had no legitimate expectation of privacy in the contents of the hard drive.

Id. at 1201. Imagine Caymen had given the computer to a friend and did not tell his friend that the computer was obtained by fraud. Would Caymen's friend have a reasonable expectation of privacy in the computer even if Caymen did not?

4. The container analogy suggests that accessing information on a computer ordinarily constitutes a Fourth Amendment "search." But exactly when does the search occur? Does a "search" of data occur when a copy of the data is generated for the computer to use as input? When the computer processes the data? When the computer outputs the data to a monitor or printer? Or when a human being actually sees the output? Imagine a police officer performs a series of operations on computer data but never actually sees it. Has that data been "searched"?

Two Supreme Court cases shed light on this question. In Arizona v. Hicks, 480 U.S. 321 (1987), an officer was searching an apartment looking for evidence of a shooting. The officer came across expensive stereo equipment, and he picked up the equipment to look for the serial number so he could determine whether it was stolen. The Supreme Court held that the officer's act of moving the stereo equipment to expose the serial numbers constituted a search, *id.* at 327:

> Officer Nelson's moving of the equipment, however, did constitute a "search" separate and apart from the search for the shooter, victims, and weapons that was the lawful objective of his entry into the apartment. Merely inspecting those parts of the turntable that came into view during the latter search would not have constituted an independent search, because it would have produced no additional invasion of respondent's privacy interest. But taking action, unrelated to the objectives of the authorized intrusion, which exposed to view concealed portions of the apartment or its contents, did produce a new invasion of respondent's privacy unjustified by the exigent circumstance that validated the entry. * * * It matters not that the search uncovered nothing of any great personal value to respondent—serial numbers rather than (what might conceivably have been hidden behind or under the equipment) letters or photographs. A search is a search, even if it happens to disclose nothing but the bottom of a turntable.

Next consider United States v. Karo, 468 U.S. 705 (1984). Karo obtained cans of ether to extract cocaine as part of a narcotics conspiracy. Unbeknownst to him, however, investigators had replaced the ether in one of the cans with a radio transmitter that emitted a signal allowing the police to track the can's location. The Court of Appeals held that transferring the transmitter to Karo was a Fourth Amendment search because the transmitter had the potential to reveal invasive information. The Supreme Court disagreed, emphasizing that the key question was whether the use of the technology actually conveyed information to the police:

> We have never held that potential, as opposed to actual, invasions of privacy constitute searches for purposes of the Fourth Amendment. A holding to that effect would mean that a policeman walking down the street carrying a parabolic microphone capable of picking up conversations in nearby homes would be engaging in a search even if the microphone were not turned on. It is the exploitation of technological advances that implicates the Fourth Amendment, not their mere existence.

Id. at 712. Do *Hicks* and *Karo* pinpoint when a computer search occurs? *See generally* Kerr, *Digital World*, at 551–54.

5. In United States v. Gorshkov, 2001 WL 1024026 (W.D. Wash. 2001), undercover FBI agents lured a suspected hacker to a fake business, Invita, under the pretext of assessing the defendant's abilities as a computer security consultant. The undercover agents asked the suspect to show them his hacking skills using an Invita computer connected to the Internet. Unbeknownst to the suspect, the FBI had installed a monitoring program inside the computer that recorded his password when he logged on to his home account. The software collected the password, and FBI agents later used it to access the suspect's files and establish the suspect's guilt. The district court held that obtaining the suspect's password did not violate his reasonable expectation of privacy:

> The Court finds that Defendant could not have had an actual expectation of privacy in a private computer network belonging to a U.S. company. It was not his computer. When Defendant sat down at the networked computer at the Invita undercover site, he knew that the systems administrator could and likely would monitor his activities. Indeed, the undercover agents told Defendant that they wanted to watch in order to see what he was capable of doing. With the agents present in the room and frequently standing and looking over his shoulder, Defendant sat down at the networked computed and logged on to an account at a computer named "freebsd.tech net.ru." Therefore the Defendant had no expectation of privacy in his actions on the Invita computer. Even if Defendant could assert a subjective expectation of privacy, such an expectation would be unreasonable under these circumstances.

> This case is similar to that of United States v. David, 756 F.Supp. 1385 (D. Nev. 1991) In *David*, the defendant was cooperating with law enforcement and meeting with an agent in the agent's office when he accessed his "computer memo book" in the agent's presence. The agent, looking over David's shoulder, saw the password he entered. The court found that David had no reasonable expectation of privacy because of the agent's presence and monitoring[.]

> The circumstances in the present case even more thoroughly refute the notion that the Defendant had a reasonable expectation of privacy in his activities on the Invita computer, because it was not his computer and the entire purpose for his use of it was to demonstrate his hacking acumen for Invita personnel to review. Therefore, under the circumstances of this case, the FBI did not violate the Fourth Amendment by obtaining Defendant's password.

Id. at *2. Is the court's analysis persuasive? Why should looking over the defendant's shoulder remove constitutional protection for information that never appeared on the screen? Should it matter that it was not his computer?

6. In Illinois v. Caballes, 543 U.S. 405 (2005), the Supreme Court considered whether using a trained dog to sniff for narcotics constituted a Fourth Amendment search. During a traffic stop, officers dispatched a canine unit to the scene. An officer walked a dog around the trunk of the stopped car, and the dog alerted the officer to the presence of narcotics in the trunk. The officers interpreted the dog's alert as establishing probable cause to believe the trunk contained narcotics. A search of the car led to the

discovery of drugs inside the trunk. In an opinion by Justice Stevens, the Court held that the dog sniff was not a search:

> Official conduct that does not compromise any legitimate interest in privacy is not a search subject to the Fourth Amendment. We have held that any interest in possessing contraband cannot be deemed "legitimate," and thus, governmental conduct that only reveals the possession of contraband compromises no legitimate privacy interest. This is because the expectation that certain facts will not come to the attention of the authorities is not the same as an interest in privacy that society is prepared to consider reasonable. * * * Respondent * * * concedes that drug sniffs are designed, and if properly conducted are generally likely, to reveal only the presence of contraband. Although respondent argues that the error rates, particularly the existence of false positives, call into question the premise that drug-detection dogs alert only to contraband, the record contains no evidence or findings that support his argument. Moreover, respondent does not suggest that an erroneous alert, in and of itself, reveals any legitimate private information, and, in this case, the trial judge found that the dog sniff was sufficiently reliable to establish probable cause to conduct a full-blown search of the trunk.
>
> Accordingly, the use of a well-trained narcotics-detection dog—one that does not expose noncontraband items that otherwise would remain hidden from public view—during a lawful traffic stop, generally does not implicate legitimate privacy interests. In this case, the dog sniff was performed on the exterior of respondent's car while he was lawfully seized for a traffic violation. Any intrusion on respondent's privacy expectations does not rise to the level of a constitutionally cognizable infringement.

Id. at 408–09.

Does *Caballes* apply to retrieving evidence from a computer? Imagine a software tool scans a computer for evidence of child pornography and reports back if it identifies known contraband images. This can be done by means of a "hash," a scrambled set of data that can correspond to known files. The police can create a hash of all the files on a particular computer, and can program software to run an automated search for matches between the hashes of the files on the computer and hashes of known images of child pornography. A positive hit will establish that one of the known images of child pornography is stored on the hard drive; a negative hit will establish that it is not. No other information will be revealed. If the police use an automated tool to find images of child pornography on a target's computer, is this analogous to using a trained dog sniffing for narcotics in *Caballes*? Or is *Caballes* distinguishable?

> It would seem that *Caballes* would allow for the routine use by government of hash-based contraband detection in any search of a digital storage device, regardless of the scope of the search authority. But it may not be as simple as that. For hash-based examinations to work, the underlying known-file hash lists must contain hash values for images that are illegal to possess. It is one thing to conclude that child pornography is contraband; it is quite another to conclude that a particular image to be included in a hash set is child pornography.

The definition of child pornography cannot be set out as a chemical formula, unlike drug contraband, and no legislative body has declared particular images to be contraband, much less blessed a hash set. Instead, the definitions describe the attributes that make an image contraband. It would seem that populating a hash set requires exercise of discretion that is not required when teaching a dog to detect cocaine or developing a chemical test to react to particular narcotics.

Richard P. Salgado, *Fourth Amendment Search and the Power of the Hash*, 119 Harv. L. Rev. F. 38, 45–46 (2006), http://www.harvardlawreview.org/forum/issues/119/dec05/salgado.pdf.

Do you agree? If dozens of defendants have been convicted of possessing or distributing a particular image of child pornography, isn't that equivalent to a legal determination that the particular image is contraband? And aren't computers searching for known files much more accurate than trained dogs sniffing for narcotics?

On the other hand, is the idea that the government can search computers for contraband without a warrant simply too creepy to accept as a Fourth Amendment rule? Do computer search technologies pose more of a privacy threat than trained dogs?

For an early look at a some of these questions, see Michael Adler, Note, *Cyberspace, General Searches, and Digital Contraband: The Fourth Amendment and the Net–Wide Search*, 105 Yale L.J. 1093, 1109–10 (1996).

2. SEIZURES

The Supreme Court has defined a "seizure" of property as "some meaningful interference with an individual's possessory interest in [the individual's] property." United States v. Jacobsen, 466 U.S. 109, 113 (1984). Under this definition, a seizure occurs when the police take property away, block a person from being able to control her property in a meaningful way, or interfere with the path of property in transit. For example, if a package is sent through the mail, the police "seize" the package if they go to the mail room and take the package out of the stream of delivery. *See* United States v. Van Leeuwen, 397 U.S. 249 (1970). It is easy to apply these principles to computers in the case of physical storage devices. Under the container analogy, taking a computer away from its owner "seizes" it. This means that if the police want to take a person's computer away, they must ordinarily obtain a warrant to justify the seizure.

The legal question becomes more complicated when computer data is no longer linked to a physical container. For example, imagine that a police officer enters a coffee shop, orders a decaf latte, and sits down at a table. A patron at the table next to him has left his laptop computer on the table while he is away for a few minutes, and the officer sees what appears to be evidence of credit card fraud on the computer's monitor. If the officer writes down the text of what he sees, has he "seized" that data? What if the officer inserts a storage device into an input/output port in the back of the computer and copies the file that appears on the screen? Has he seized the file? Imagine the officer brings more sophisticated equipment and copies the entire computer hard drive. Does that copying seize the entire hard drive? More broadly, if a police officer copies data but does not otherwise interfere with the owner's possessory interest in the physical storage device, is that copying a "seizure"?

UNITED STATES v. GORSHKOV

United States District Court for the Western District of Washington, 2001.
2001 WL 1024026.

COUGHENOUR, J.

This matter comes before the Court on Defendant's Motion to Suppress Seized Computer Data. Defendant moves this Court for an order suppressing all computer data together with all derivative fruits therefrom seized by federal agents * * * from two computers located in Russia known as "tech.net.ru" and "freebsd.tech.net.ru."

Following an extensive national investigation of a series of computer hacker intrusions into the computer systems of businesses in the United States emanating from Russia, Alexey Ivanov was identified as one of the intruders. Around June, 2000, the FBI set up Invita, a "sting" computer security company in Seattle. On/about November 10, 2000 Mr Ivanov, along with his "business partner," Defendant Vasiliy Gorshkov, flew from Russia to [the Seattle–Tacoma International Airport].

In Seattle, the two men met with undercover FBI agents at the Invita office located in Seattle During the meeting and at the behest of the FBI, Defendant Gorshkov used an FBI IBM Thinkpad computer ostensibly to demonstrate his computer hacking and computer security skills and to access his computer system, "tech.net.ru," in Russia. After the meeting and demonstration, both Gorshkov and Ivanov were arrested.

Following the Defendants' arrest, without Defendant Gorshkov's knowledge or consent, the FBI searched and seized the IBM and all key strokes made by the Defendant while he used it, by means of a "sniffer" program which allowed the FBI to track and store the information. The FBI thereby obtained the Defendant's computer user name and password that he had used to access the Russian computer.

Armed with this information the FBI logged onto the subject computer(s) located in Russia. Faced with the possibility that a confederate of the defendant could destroy the files in the Russian computer, the FBI decided to download the file contents of the subject computer(s). This was done without reading same until after a search warrant was obtained. The FBI's downloading and copying of the downloaded data onto CD disk format took until November 21. The warrant was applied for and obtained on December 1, 2000. The delay between the downloading of the data and the procurement of the warrant was due to the slow process of obtaining approval and permission from FBI headquarters and the Department of Justice.

* * *

The agents' act of copying the data on the Russian computers was not a seizure under the Fourth Amendment because it did not interfere with Defendant's or anyone else's possessory interest in the data. The data remained intact and unaltered. It remained accessible to Defendant and any co-conspirators or partners with whom he had shared access. The copying of the data had absolutely no impact on his possessory rights.[1] Therefore it was not a seizure under the Fourth Amendment. *See* Arizona v. Hicks, 480 U.S. 321, 324 (1987) (recording of serial number on suspected stolen property was not seizure because it did not "meaningfully interfere" with respondent's possessory interest in either the serial number or the equipment); Bills v. Aseltine, 958 F.2d 697, 707 (6th Cir. 1992) (officer's photographic recording of visual images of scene was not seizure because it did not "meaningfully interfere" with any possessory interest).

Notes and Questions

1. The *Gorshkov* case relies on Arizona v. Hicks, 480 U.S. 321 (1987), for the view that copying data does not seize it. In *Hicks*, an officer came across stereo equipment that he believed was stolen. The officer wrote down the serial numbers he observed on the equipment, and then called in the numbers to the police station to confirm that the equipment was stolen. The Supreme Court held that the act of copying the numbers was not a seizure:

> We agree that the mere recording of the serial numbers did not constitute a seizure. To be sure, that was the first step in a process by which respondent was eventually deprived of the stereo equipment. In and of itself, however, it did not "meaningfully interfere" with respondent's possessory interest in either the serial numbers or the equipment, and therefore did not amount to a seizure.

Id. at 327. How should *Hicks* apply to computer data? Is creating a copy of data using electronic means different from manually writing down information that is visually observed? If so, why? Is the difference that the electronic copy is a perfect copy, indistinguishable from the original? Or is the difference that the electronic tool used to copy the data is not a person, and therefore the information has not been exposed to human observation? Or is there no appreciable difference at all?

2. Susan Brenner and Barbara Frederiksen have argued that *Hicks* can be distinguished from cases involving computer files:

> One critical difference between writing down serial numbers in *Hicks* and the act of copying computer files is the nature of the information. The officer did not record information that belonged to Hicks. Serial numbers are not property in the sense that the number belong to one person, but are more analogous to license plates or other public records. Serial numbers are assigned by the manufacturer of a product and are used to track and identify that product. Hicks had no

1. Defendant argues that the Government seized the data on the Russian computers because the tar command [used to copy the files] block's other users from accessing the data. After hearing the testimony on this subject, the Court is convinced that no authorized user is prevented from accessing the files that are being [copied].

interest in these serial numbers because the stereo equipment was stolen from its rightful owners. Hicks had no lawful possessory interest in the equipment or in the serial numbers on the equipment.

Unlike the serial numbers in *Hicks*, the information contained in computer files clearly belongs to the owner of the files. The ownership of information is similar to the contents of a private conversation in which the information belongs to the parties to the conversation. Copying computer data is analogous to recording a conversation in several ways. First, the object of both activities is the collection of information. The only difference is that the information is the data stored in the computer files while in a conversation the information is the content of the recorded conversation. Both use a collection process that duplicates the information at issue, the owner of the information is not deprived of possession or use of the information. Both activities result in the creation of a body of inchoate, yet unrealized, evidence. Officers cannot ascertain whether the copy of a computer file or the tape recording of a conversation actually contain relevant evidence until the officers access and search the contents of the file or tape. Therefore, copying computer files should be treated as a seizure.

Susan W. Brenner & Barbara A. Frederiksen, *Computer Searches And Seizures: Some Unresolved Issues*, 8 Mich Telecomm. & Tech. L. Rev. 39, 111–112 (2001–2002).

The usual rule is that observing private communications or property does not seize anything. Observing private facts may constitute a search if it violates an individual's reasonable expectation of privacy, but mere observation is not a seizure. Recall that in the *David* case, Agent Peterson observed David typing his password "fortune" into the computer memo book. The court considered whether this observation was a search, but did not ask whether it was a seizure.

Does copying digital evidence require a different rule? In Katz v. United States, 389 U.S. 347 (1967), the Supreme Court held that "electronically listening to and recording" a defendant's private conversation "constituted a 'search and seizure' within the meaning of the Fourth Amendment." *Katz* was not clear, however, on whether recording the conversation was considered a "search" of the conversation or a "seizure" of it (or both). Which do you think it should be? Also, how would you determine who has a possessory interest in information? Is the key question whether the defendant has a lawful ownership right in the physical property that contains the data, or does some other test provide a better guide?

3. In United States v. Thomas, 613 F.2d 787 (10th Cir. 1980), a package sent via UPS ripped open during sorting. The opening revealed obscene materials inside the package. UPS employees called the FBI, and an FBI agent made photocopies of the materials before resealing the package. The package was given back to UPS, although it was not delivered because apparently the address was improper. The FBI agents then requested a warrant to seize the package and attached the photocopies to the affidavit. The defendant challenged the FBI's conduct, claiming that photocopying the materials seized them. The Tenth Circuit disagreed: "The materials herein

remained in UPS's possession and their delivery was unaffected since they were undeliverable. The materials were searched but not seized." *Id.* at 789.

Similarly, in Bills v. Aseltine, 958 F.2d 697 (6th Cir. 1992), agents took photographs of the plaintiff's home while executing a search warrant there. The plaintiff sued, claiming that taking photographs had "seized" images of his home beyond the scope of the warrant. The Sixth Circuit disagreed, holding that taking photographs did not seize anything because it did not interfere with any possessory interest. *See id.* at 707.

4. In United States v. New York Telephone Co., 434 U.S. 159 (1977), the Supreme Court held that Federal Rule of Criminal Procedure 41 authorized the government to apply for a search warrant to install a monitoring device known as a pen register. Rule 41 is the statutory rule that authorizes federal investigators to obtain search warrants "to search for and seize" evidence of criminal activity; a pen register is a device that records the outgoing numbers dialed from a telephone. Although *New York Telephone* involved interpretation of a statutory rule, not the Fourth Amendment, the Court's language is suggestive. The Court ruled that Rule 41 "is broad enough to encompass a 'search' designed to ascertain the use which is being made of a telephone suspected of being employed as a means of facilitating a criminal venture and the 'seizure' of evidence which the 'search' of the telephone produces. * * * Rule 41 is sufficiently broad to include seizures of intangible items such as dial impulses recorded by pen registers as well as tangible items." *Id.* at 169–70. Does this language suggest that copying data "seizes" it?

Is copying computer data more like recording a number as in *Hicks* or recording a dialed impulse as in *New York Telephone*? Are these cases reconcilable?

5. If making a digital copy of data constitutes a seizure, does copying the copy also constitute a seizure? If the police make ten copies of a lawfully obtained file, has the file been seized ten times? Once? Never?

6. *The Fourth Amendment and the first stage of the computer forensics process.* When investigators retrieve evidence from a computer hard drive or other storage device, they generally follow a procedure known as the computer forensics process. *See generally* Bill Nelson et al., Guide to Computer Forensics and Investigations (2004). First, the officers seize the computer from the target's home or possession. They then bring the computer to the government's computer lab. Next, they use special equipment to generate a "bitstream copy" (also known as an "image") of the storage device onto a government computer. A bitstream copy is different from the kind of copy users normally make when copying individual files from one computer to another. A normal copy duplicates only the identified file, but a bitstream image copies every bit and byte on the target drive in exactly the order it appears on the original. The investigators then conduct their search on the bitstream copy instead of the original. This is necessary to ensure the evidentiary integrity of the original computer. Searching a computer for evidence can alter the evidence it contains, and executing the search on the image preserves the original for use and analysis at trial.

What are the Fourth Amendment implications of creating a bitstream copy and searching the copy? Does generating the copy seize the data? Does it seize the computer hardware on the ground that it occupies the machine while the copy is being made? Does creating the image search anything? Should the Fourth Amendment rules that regulate searching the bitstream copy be the same as the rules that govern searching the original, or can the police search the bitstream image on their own machine without restriction? Put in more practical terms, should the police ordinarily need a warrant to create the bitstream copy? Do they need a warrant to search the bitstream copy? For an analysis of these questions, see Orin S. Kerr, *Searches and Seizures in a Digital World,* 119 Harv. L. Rev. 531, 557–65 (2005).

7. In United States v. Triumph Capital Group, 211 F.R.D. 31 (D. Conn. 2002), an FBI agent made a bitstream copy of a seized hard drive to begin the forensic analysis of its contents. The defendant claimed that creating the copy was a "seizure" not authorized by the warrant. The court offered only the following cursory analysis:

> [The FBI agent] did not seize the entire hard drive when he created the image file, restored it to MOs [magneto-optical disks] for examination purposes or copied blocks of data to MOs and CDs. These were simply preliminary and reasonably necessary steps in the forensic examination, and did not require the magistrate judge's authorization.

Id. at 63–64. Does whether a step is "reasonably necessary" have anything to do with whether the step is a seizure? Or is the court saying that even if the step was a seizure, it wasn't an unreasonable seizure?

C. EXCEPTIONS TO THE WARRANT REQUIRE-MENT

If government action is a Fourth Amendment search or seizure, its legality hinges on whether the search or seizure is constitutionally "reasonable." Searches and seizures are reasonable if authorized by a valid warrant or an exception to the warrant requirement applies. The following materials consider the various exceptions to the warrant requirement.

1. EXIGENT CIRCUMSTANCES

The exigent circumstances exception permits the government to conduct searches or seizures when immediately necessary to protect public safety or preserve evidence. *See, e.g.,* Mincey v. Arizona, 437 U.S. 385 (1978). This long-established exception applies when circumstances "would cause a reasonable person to believe that entry ... was necessary to prevent physical harm to the officers or other persons, the destruction of relevant evidence, the escape of the suspect, or some other consequence improperly frustrating legitimate law enforcement efforts." United States v. McConney, 728 F.2d 1195, 1199 (9th Cir. 1984) (en banc). The Supreme Court has never articulated a clear test for exigent circumstances, and instead has applied a general balancing of interests to determine when and how broadly it applies. As a general matter, interests often include the degree of urgency involved, whether a warrant could have been obtained, the seriousness of the crime investigated, the possibility of danger, the likelihood evidence may be destroyed, and the availability of alternative means of obtaining or securing evidence or protecting public safety. Further, an exigent circumstances search must be "strictly circumscribed by the exigencies which justify its initiation." Terry v. Ohio, 392 U.S. 1, 25–36 (1968).

Early cases applying the exigent circumstances doctrine to computer storage devices often involved electronic pagers used in the narcotics trade. Each pager could store a handful of phone numbers that recorded incoming calls. Narcotics investigators would come across a suspect's pager, often immediately after arresting him for narcotics offenses, and would click through the pager and retrieve the phone numbers it contained. Several courts concluded that the search of the pagers was justified by exigent circumstances on the ground that the pagers could only store a few phone numbers. Any new number representing an incoming call would force the pager to delete a previous number, and the previous number could be useful evidence relevant to the offense. *See, e.g.,* United States v. Romero–Garcia, 991 F. Supp. 1223, 1225 (D. Or. 1997), *aff'd on other grounds,* 168 F.3d 502 (9th Cir. 1999). *But see* United States v. Reyes, 922 F. Supp. 818, 835–36 (S.D.N.Y. 1996) (concluding that when investigators found the suspect's pager turned off and turned it on themselves, they could not then rely on the exigent circumstances exception to search the pager).

The scope of the exigent circumstances exception also arose in United States v. David, 756 F. Supp. 1385 (D. Nev. 1991), parts of which appeared earlier in this chapter. At one point, the FBI agent investigating the case saw the defendant deleting files from his computer memo book. The FBI agent, Agent Peterson, quickly seized the computer from David to stop him from deleting evidence of his crimes. Peterson later searched the computer without a warrant. The court held that the seizure was justified but the search was not:

> When destruction of evidence is imminent, a warrantless seizure of that evidence is justified if there is probable cause to believe that the item seized constitutes evidence of criminal activity. Here, Agent Peterson saw David destroying evidence. David's use of the book in retrieving telephone numbers of criminal associates provided ample probable cause that the book contained information relative to criminal activity. Peterson therefore reasonably believed that prompt action was necessary to prevent further destruction of relevant evidence.

> * * * Although Peterson had the authority to seize and hold the book due to the exigency at hand, his authority to examine its contents is a different matter. The seizure of the book affected only David's possessory interests. It did not affect the privacy interests vested in the contents of the book.

> * * * Once he took the book from David the exigency which justified the seizure came to an end. Nevertheless, without seeking a warrant, Peterson conducted a complete search of the book's con-

tents. The seizure of the book did not justify the invasion of privacy involved in the subsequent search.

Id. at 1392–93. In a footnote, the court rejected the government's argument that exigent circumstances justified the search because the computer's batteries might have failed and its memory might have been lost:

> The government argues, lamely, that the exigency continued even after the seizure, because Agent Peterson did not know how much longer the book's batteries would live. It was therefore imperative, according to the government, that Peterson access the book before the batteries died and the information was erased. At the evidentiary hearing, however, no evidence was offered to substantiate this concern. In fact, Peterson testified that he successfully accessed the book at a later time without changing the batteries. The government bears a heavy burden of establishing exigent circumstances. Speculation is insufficient to carry that burden. The government has not met its burden here.

Id. at 1392 n.2.

2. CONSENT

The consent exception is a powerful exception to the warrant requirement. It encompasses two somewhat different types of consent: the consent of a suspect, and the consent of a third party with "common authority" over the property to be searched. The following excerpt from a Justice Department treatise on searching and seizing computers summarizes the law governing computer searches when consent is obtained directly from a suspect.

UNITED STATES DEPARTMENT OF JUSTICE— SEARCHING AND SEIZING COMPUTERS AND OBTAINING ELECTRONIC EVIDENCE IN CRIMINAL INVESTIGATIONS

(2002), available at www.cybercrime.gov/s&smanual2002.htm#_IC1_.

The scope of a consent to search is generally defined by its expressed object, and is limited by the breadth of the consent given. The standard for measuring the scope of consent under the Fourth Amendment is objective reasonableness: "What would the typical reasonable person have understood by the exchange between the [agent] and the [person granting consent]?" Florida v. Jimeno, 500 U.S. 248, 251 (1991). This requires a fact-intensive inquiry into whether it was reasonable for the agent to believe that the scope of consent included the items searched. Of course, when the limits of the consent are clearly given, either before or during the search, agents must respect these bounds.

Computer cases often raise the question of whether consent to search a location or item implicitly includes consent to access the memory of electronic storage devices encountered during the search. In such cases, courts look to whether the particular circumstances of the agents' request for consent implicitly or explicitly limited the scope of the search to a particular type, scope, or duration. Because this approach ultimately relies on fact-driven notions of common sense, results reached in published opinions have hinged upon subtle (if not entirely inscrutable) distinctions. Compare United States v. Reyes, 922 F. Supp. 818, 834 (S.D.N.Y. 1996) (holding that consent to "look inside" a car included consent to retrieve numbers stored inside pagers found in car's back seat) with United States v. Blas, 1990 WL 265179, at *20 (E.D. Wis. Dec. 4, 1990) (holding that consent to "look at" a pager did not include consent to activate pager and retrieve numbers, because looking at pager could be construed to mean "what the device is, or how small it is, or what brand of pager it may be"). *See also* United States v. Carey, 172 F.3d 1268, 1274 (10th Cir. 1999) (reading written consent form extremely narrowly, so that consent to seizure of "any property" under the defendant's control and to "a complete search of the premises and property" at the defendant's address merely permitted the agents to seize the defendant's computer from his apartment, not to search the computer off-site because it was no longer located at the defendant's address). Prosecutors can strengthen their argument that the scope of consent included consent to search electronic storage devices by relying on analogous cases involving closed containers. *See, e.g.,* United States v. Galante, 1995 WL 507249, at *3 (S.D.N.Y. Aug. 25, 1995) (holding that general consent to search car included consent to have officer access memory of cellular telephone found in the car, relying on circuit precedent involving closed containers).

Agents should be especially careful about relying on consent as the basis for a search of a computer when they obtain consent for one reason but then wish to conduct a search for another reason. In two recent cases, the Courts of Appeals suppressed images of child pornography found on computers after agents procured the defendant's consent to search his property for other evidence. In United States v. Turner, 169 F.3d 84 (1st Cir. 1999), detectives searching for physical evidence of an attempted sexual assault obtained written consent from the victim's neighbor to search the neighbor's "premises" and "personal property." Before the neighbor signed the consent form, the detectives discovered a large knife and blood stains in his apartment, and explained to him that they were looking for more evidence of the assault that the suspect might have left behind. While several agents searched for physical evidence, one detective searched the contents of the neighbor's personal computer and discovered stored images of child pornography. The neighbor was charged with possessing child pornography. On interlocutory appeal, the First Circuit held that the search of the computer exceeded the scope of consent and suppressed the evidence. According to the Court, the detectives' statements that they were looking for signs of the assault limited the scope of consent to the kind of physical evidence that an intruder might have left behind. By transforming the search for physical evidence into a search for computer files, the detective had exceeded the scope of consent. *See also* Carey, 172 F.3d at 1277 (Baldock, J., concurring) (concluding that agents exceeded scope of consent by searching computer after defendant signed broadly-worded written consent form, because agents told defendant that they were looking for drugs and drug-related items rather than computer files containing child pornography).

Notes and Questions

1.   The test for the scope of consent is what a "typical reasonable person" would have understood the consent to have included in light of the specific facts of the case. Would a "typical reasonable person" understand consent to search a place to include consent to search computers located in that place?

Imagine a police officer visits a home in response to a reported burglary. The officer asks the homeowner if he will let the officer "look around for evidence." The homeowner responds, "sure, officer, do whatever you want." Would a reasonable person understand this exchange to permit the officer to search any computers found inside the home? Does it matter whether the officer is searching for evidence of the burglary or evidence of some other crime?

Also consider how this test applies when a suspect consents to a search of a specific computer storage device. Does the consent ordinarily limit the type of evidence the officer may try to find? Does it limit the thoroughness of the search? If a target permits an officer to "look through" his computer, is the officer restricted in terms of what kind of search he can conduct? Or would a "typical reasonable person" understand that permitting an officer to search a computer permits the officer to look for any evidence using any technique?

2.   The consent doctrine extends to seizures as a well as searches. A person can consent to an on-site search of his computer, but not a seizure of it; a seizure and removal of the computer, but not a search of it; or a seizure *and* a subsequent search. If the terms of the consent are explicit, those terms govern. What should the default rule be if the terms are not explicit?

3.   *A consent brain teaser.* Officer Smith suspects that Fred Rowley is guilty of tax fraud, but he does not have probable cause needed to obtain a warrant to seize Rowley's computer and search it for evidence. Officer Smith visits Rowley at home and explains his suspicions, and Rowley emphatically denies his guilt. Smith asks Rowley if he would let Smith take his computer away and search it for evidence "just to make sure everything is on the up and up." Rowley doesn't want to arouse the officer's suspicion, so he agrees to let Officer Smith take the computer away and search it for evidence offsite.

The next day, Rowley has second thoughts and calls a lawyer for advice. The lawyer tells Rowley to call Officer Smith *immediately* and withdraw his consent. When Rowley calls Officer Smith and withdraws his permission to search the computer, Smith explains that he has just finished creating a bitstream copy of Rowley's computer and that he was just about to start searching the copy for evidence of tax fraud. Smith further explains that this is the standard process for searching computers: The police generate a perfect copy of the suspect's machine, and then search the copy to ensure the evidentiary integrity of the original. Smith agrees to return the original computer in light of Rowley's withdrawal of consent, but insists that he can search the copy made before Rowley's consent was withdrawn. Officer Smith searches the copy and discovers evidence that Rowley has engaged in a massive tax fraud scheme.

Has Officer Smith violated the Fourth Amendment by searching the copy after Rowley withdrew his consent to search the original? Would Smith violate the Fourth Amendment by retaining the copy, even if he does not search it? When Rowley withdraws his consent, does the Fourth Amendment require Officer Smith to delete the copy? Does it require Smith to give Rowley the government-owned computer that stores the copy?

As you ponder these questions, it may help you to sort through a number of preliminary issues. For example, does consent to take away the computer and search it implicitly permit the officer to generate a copy? Is generating the copy a search, a seizure, or neither? Should the scope of consent that applies to the original also apply to the copy, or is the copy the government's property that Rowley has no rights to control?

If you really want a challenge, consider two variations on the hypothetical. In the first variation, Officer Smith informs Rowley during his visit to Rowley's home that if Rowley consents, Smith will generate a bitstream copy of Smith's computer and return the original to Rowley. Rowley expressly consents to Smith's creating the copy. When Rowley calls Smith the next day to withdraw his consent, Smith has already generated the copy. Should this change the analysis?

In the second variation, Rowley calls Officer Smith when he is in the middle of generating the bitstream copy. (This is very possible, as the copying process can take several hours to complete.) Can Officer Smith complete the process of generating the copy, or must he unplug the machine as soon as consent is withdrawn? Can he search the portion of the copy that was created before consent was withdrawn?

———

Criminal investigators often seek consent to search a computer from an individual other than the suspect. In these cases, the government asks a third party to consent to the search for evidence of the suspect's offenses. If the individual who consents has common authority over the property, the consent is valid. United States v. Matlock, 415 U.S. 164, 171 (1974). In *Matlock*, the Supreme Court explained that common authority to establish third-party consent requires:

> mutual use of the property by persons generally having joint access or control for most purposes, so that it is reasonable to recognize that any of the co-inhabitants has the right to permit the inspection in his own right and that the others have assumed the risk that one of their number might permit the common area to be searched.

Id. at 171 n.7.

How does this apply to searches of computers? Does common authority refer to the physical space where the computer is stored, the computer itself, or the specific data the police wish to obtain?

STATE v. APPLEBY

Superior Court of Delaware, 2002.
2002 WL 1613716.

Keith Appleby has been indicted for crimes involving illegal interception of electronic communications, 11 Del. C. Sec. 2402, and unauthorized access to a computer system, 11 Del. C. Sec. 932. For now, the specific allegations against Appleby are unimportant. Basically, the State claims that Appleby hacked into the University of Delaware's computer system, where Appleby worked, in order to access and manipulate a co-worker's and a supervisor's computers.

This is the decision on Appleby's motion to suppress. Appleby is trying to prevent the State from using the contents of a personal computer's hard disk drive that was inoperative, but from which the police recovered incriminating evidence, and several diskettes. The police obtained the hard drive and diskettes from Appleby's then-estranged, now ex-, wife.

Appleby claims not only that his estranged wife did not have legal authority to turn in the hard drive, she had no authority to consent even to the slightest inspection of its contents. Appleby insists that he had a reasonable expectation of privacy to all the information in the hard drive.

I.

The evidentiary presentation at the suppression hearing was relatively detailed. In summary, Appleby and his wife married in 1999. They each brought a computer into their marital home. While they were together, they both had access to the machines and they even swapped parts, particularly hard drives. During the marriage's good times, the Applebys owned four hard drives. One hard drive failed and was discarded. A second hard drive, which was a Maxtor brand product, also failed. It was replaced, but not discarded. As the court understands the facts, the Maxtor originally was in "his" computer. Then it was moved to "her" computer. After it failed, the broken Maxtor was left lying around. The broken Maxtor is at this case's center.

As mentioned, during their marriage the Applebys had complete access to both computers and the Maxtor. The estranged wife told the police that before the Maxtor and their marriage broke, she actually made a point of rooting through Appleby's personal files. Both Applebys had user profiles on the Maxtor and, significantly, the police eventually found "several hundred" e-mails and other files of hers stored on it.

When the Applebys' marriage dramatically disintegrated in December 2000, Appleby abruptly left the marital home, leaving the Maxtor behind. It is unclear whether Appleby had an opportunity to take the Maxtor with him. But right after Appleby left, he was locked out and prevented by Family Court order from reentering. It was impossible for Appleby to recover any computer equipment, including the broken Maxtor. Important to his claim here, though unavailing, is the fact that between the time he swore-out divorce papers in December 2000, filed them in January 2001 and when he received the final decree on June 7, 2001, Appleby repeatedly tried to use lawful means to obtain possession of the computer equipment. As presented below, Appleby did not know that his wife turned the equipment over to their employer, the University of Delaware, only days after the couple separated.

Appleby's estranged wife gave the equipment, including the Maxtor, to the University's sociology department. Appleby implies in his argument that turning the hard drive over to the University violated a Family Court order prohibiting her from transferring marital property. The record is unclear whether she made her move before Appleby made his first demand for the equipment. It is clear, however, that she transferred the Maxtor in December. That was weeks before the divorce papers, including the standstill order, were served on her in January.

When the Applebys' domestic war broke out, Appleby resigned from the University. The resignation came after Appleby's supervisor accused him of hacking her computer. After he left, someone in the sociology department examined the computer in Appleby's former office and found highly suspicious material. Appleby allegedly had files and software supporting the belief that Appleby had been hacking into his co-workers' and supervisor's computers. In mid-February, the department's information technology person turned over to the police the equipment obtained from Appleby's estranged wife two months earlier. The police could not repair the Maxtor on the spot. Spare parts were ordered. Finally, on June 12, 2001, five days after the Applebys were divorced, a police specialist fixed the Maxtor and gained access to its electronic contents.

Meanwhile, on June 4, 2001, as part of an exchange of e-mail, Appleby told the police, "I only really wish to have my hard drive back." As far as the court can determine, Appleby's e-mail was the first notice to the police that Appleby was claiming the hard drive and, by implication, that he meant to deny his estranged wife's authority to consent to the hard drive's examination. For the reasons presented below, the court views Appleby's e-mail as too little and too late to undermine what the police eventually did with the hard drive on June 12.

Considering how important the point is and how much time was spent developing the record, it is unfortunate that the record is not crystal clear as to how the hard drive was organized and precisely how the incriminating data was stored. It appears, however, from the Affidavit of Probable Cause used to obtain the arrest warrant for Appleby and the search warrant for the Maxtor, that when the police got the Maxtor working, in its second partition, also known as the "D drive" or the "D: partition," which the court takes as all the same, the police found "several hundred" e-mails and other files with names linking them to Appleby's ex-wife by her nickname. A second directory, which the police did not look into, was in Appleby's name. The police found yet another directory labeled in the abbreviated name of Appleby's former employer. Inside that directory was a file labeled with an abbreviation for one of Appleby's co-worker's names. By then, the police already had reason to believe the co-worker had been victimized by a hacker, probably Appleby.

By their names alone, the police could not tell whether the directories with the abbreviated names were Appleby's, his ex-wife's or someone else's. But the police knew that possession of the hard drive had come from the ex-wife, that she had used the hard drive, that her personal files were on it, that both she and Appleby had worked for the agency named on the directory, and that she had given consent to search. So the police specialist correctly assumed that the police had valid consent and the expert opened the file. He then discovered what appeared to be an intercepted e-mail.

Based on the estranged wife's detailed accusations, other information from the University, including what was found on Appleby's office computer, and the directories and the intercepted e-mail in the Maxtor, the police computer specialist prepared an extensive affidavit. He then obtained a search warrant authorizing the police to examine the hard drive's entire contents and the diskettes.

II.

The State argues initially that Appleby only tried to retrieve the working equipment, not the broken Maxtor. Thus, Appleby abandoned the Maxtor. The State points to evidence supporting its position. There is stronger evidence, however, that Appleby wanted his computer and the broken hard drive. The thrust of Appleby's formal attempts to acquire the computer equipment was that he wanted possession of everything that was his. From his viewpoint that would have included the broken Maxtor. Under the circumstances, it is unproven that Appleby abandoned the Maxtor.

Having rejected the State's abandonment argument, the court now turns to consider the estranged wife's authority to give the broken hard drive to the University and to consent to the limited search of the hard drive. There is a distinction between the broken Maxtor as a piece of hardware and its contents. There is a further distinction between the hard drive's directory of folders and the folders' contents. A hard disk drive simply [i]s an electronic file cabinet. It has an electronic lock opened by a password acting like a key. It is organized by partitions, which are akin to drawers. Inside each partition are directories, which are somewhat analogous to folders stored inside an office filing cabinet. Each folder is identified by a name. Inside the folders there may be files containing documents.

By now, the computer age may have advanced to the point where describing a hard drive is unnecessary. Someday, however, the description here might serve as a reminder of what a filing cabinet was. Meanwhile, thinking of a hard drive as an old-fashioned filing cabinet is a way to put this case into a familiar perspective for Fourth Amendment purposes. The court accepts Appleby's analogizing a hard drive to a closed container, but a file cabinet is closer.

The Applebys had passwords for the Maxtor, but they did not use them. So the Maxtor was an unlocked file cabinet. The Maxtor was inoperative, but its contents remained intact. In that sense, the Maxtor was a filing cabinet, jammed shut. Inside the second partition, one of the filing cabinet's drawers, were several folders. As presented above, one folder appeared to be Appleby's, another appeared to be Appleby's ex-wife's and a third folder's name suggested that it was connected somehow with their employer. Inside that folder was a file bearing a suspicious name and an incriminating e-mail.

III.

The court concludes, as a mixed question of law and fact, that after the husband and wife co-mingled their computer hardware, using it freely as each saw fit, its ownership and possession were joint. Each spouse was entitled to the equipment as much as the other. Under the circumstances here, where the hard drive was left broken, uninstalled and in the estranged wife's possession and where the hard drive once was installed in the estranged wife's computer, she had complete access to it while it was working and hundreds of her personal documents remained on it, the hard drive was "theirs" in every sense.

Assuming it was "his" before the marriage, the Maxtor would not become "his" again until the Family Court declared it so. Appleby did not have unilateral authority to limit, much less deny, the Maxtor to his estranged wife. This is true, even though the Applebys' relationship had fallen apart and Appleby was trying to obtain sole possession of the equipment. Appleby's change of heart is understandable, but it did not negate his wife's claim to the hard drive. At the moment she turned it over to the authorities, the estranged wife had as much say over the broken Maxtor as Appleby. She controlled it no less than Appleby. In fact, she had more control over it than he because she possessed it.

Having received possession of the broken Maxtor lawfully from Appleby's estranged wife, by way of the University's sociology department, the police were entitled to inspect it and gain access to its contents as much as Appleby's ex-wife could. The authority of the police to examine the Maxtor was coextensive with the authority of the person consenting to its search.

The court concludes that when they separated, and especially after Appleby asked for the hard drive, Appleby's estranged wife no longer could poke through his personal files, much less give permission for someone else to do that. Thanks to the separation, Appleby regained his right to privacy over his personal files stored on the Maxtor. And the police needed a warrant to search them. The court assumes that but for the fact that Appleby's estranged wife also kept her personal files in the second partition, without a search warrant the police would have had no way to see what folders were stored in it.

But the Applebys' separation did not divest Appleby's estranged wife of her authority to look at her own files that were resident in the Maxtor, and to show them to others. Thus, she retained sufficient authority over the Maxtor not only to give it to the police as she did, but also to allow them basic access to the partition where her personal files were stored. It was while the police were looking in the partition containing her files, with her permission, that the potentially incriminating directories and the intercepted e-mail came to light. The police, therefore, were entitled to use that information as part of their application for a warrant to search and seize the hard drive's other contents as evidence.

In summary, even taking the Applebys' open hostility and Appleby's expressed desire to cut his ex-wife off from the Maxtor into account, she still had as much right as Appleby to possess the hard drive when she gave it to the police. And when the police, figuratively speaking, "opened" the hard drive and its "drawers," they did not look at anything that the ex-wife was not entitled to see for herself and let them see. That includes the suspiciously named directories, and the intercepted e-mail.

IV.

It is sad to see what can happen when a marriage fails. Here, an estranged wife incriminated her husband. Based on the event's timing, it is difficult to see her act as anything but spiteful and vindictive, as Appleby claims. But the Fourth Amendment and the exclusionary rule protect citizens from the government, not from their estranged spouses. If anyone behaved unreasonably it was not the police. Here, the police did not overreach. The police just capitalized on what human nature, albeit base human nature, provided.

Notes and Questions

1.   United States v. Matlock, 415 U.S. 164 (1974), permits a third party to consent if the third-party has "common authority over or other sufficient relationship to the premises or effects sought to be inspected." When the "premises or effects" are computers, should courts focus on common authority over the physical hardware or common authority over specific files? Put another way, should we model the computer from the standpoint of virtual reality or physical reality?

Applying law to computers often raises a choice between modeling facts from a virtual perspective or a physical perspective. The virtual perspective is the perspective of a user who sees the computer as a window to a virtual reality. In contrast, the physical perspective sees the machine as a physical device that sends, receives, and stores zeros and ones.[a]

The *Appleby* court adopts a virtual approach to construing the scope of consent. It assumes the perspective of a computer user, and analogizes the computer to a file cabinet and directories to physical folders. From this perspective, it is natural that different users have different authority to consent to searches of different files or folders on a single computer storage device.

From a physical perspective, however, distinguishing among files or folders may seem quite artificial. When government investigators search computers, they often search them at a physical level instead of a virtual level. From this perspective, the storage device is a magnetic platter or other device with zeros and ones mixed together rather than stored in distinct virtual "folders." Analysts working from a physical perspective may be unable to tell how access to a storage device would appear to a user from a virtual perspective. From the physical perspective, it seems unnatural to say that a user has common authority over some of the data on the device but not others.

If government investigators search computers at a physical level instead of a virtual one, does it make sense for courts to approach the scope of consent from a virtual perspective? Should investigators be required to reconstruct the search from a virtual perspective, and to limit the scope of consent based on what a user would observe?

2. In Georgia v. Randolph, ___ U.S. ___, 126 S.Ct. 1515 (2006), police officers answered a call reporting a domestic disturbance between a husband and wife. When the police arrived at the home, the wife volunteered to the police that her husband was a cocaine user and that he kept drug-related items inside the home. A police officer asked the husband for his consent to search the home, but he refused. The officer then asked the wife if she would consent to the search, and she readily agreed. The wife brought the officer to an upstairs bedroom where the officer found cocaine.

In a 5–3 decision, the Supreme Court held that the wife's consent to search the home was invalid because the husband was physically present and objected to the search. According to Justice Souter's majority opinion, the "common authority" test of *Matlock* must be interpreted in light of "widely shared social expectations." Individuals in society share a "commonly held understanding about the authority that co-inhabitants may exercise in ways that affect each other's interests," and those commonly held understandings determine the reasonableness of consent and therefore its constitutionality. *Id.* at 1526.

In *Randolph*, the Court found the husband's presence and objection to be critical. According to Justice Souter, a common understanding exists that consent is not valid if a co-inhabitant is present and refuses to permit the search. As a result, it was not reasonable for the police to rely on the wife's consent and the warrantless search violated the Fourth Amendment. On the other hand, if the husband had not been present, it would have been reasonable for the police to rely on the wife's consent because there is a

---

a. For more on the physical and virtual perspectives, see Orin S. Kerr, *The Problem* *of Perspective in Internet Law*, 91 Geo. L.J. 357 (2003).

commonly held understanding that co-inhabitants can consent to home searches absent an objection.

Does *Georgia v. Randolph* change the outcome of *State v. Appleby,* which was decided four years before *Randolph*? In *Appleby,* the husband was not present when the computer was seized, but he expressed his objection to the police before the computer was searched. The police searched the computer knowing that the husband objected to the search. Was the search invalid under *Randolph*? Do "widely shared social expectations" exist yet about who can consent to a computer search? If so, what are those expectations? *See* United States v. Hudspeth, ___ F.3d ___, 2006 WL 2456370 (8th Cir. 2006).

3. *Password protection.* In Trulock v. Freeh, 275 F.3d 391 (4th Cir. 2001), FBI agents were investigating alleged security breaches by Notra Trulock, a former Director of the Office of Intelligence at the U.S. Department of Energy. The agents obtained the consent of Trulock's girlfriend, Linda Conrad, to search a computer used jointly by Conrad and Trulock. According to the complaint filed in the case, an FBI computer specialist searched the computer for ninety minutes and looked at several of Trulock's files that were password-protected by him. Trulock filed a civil suit against the agents claiming that Conrad's consent was insufficient to permit a search of his password-protected files. The Fourth Circuit agreed that Conrad lacked the common authority to consent to the search:

> We conclude that, based on the facts in the complaint, Conrad lacked authority to consent to the search of Trulock's files. Conrad and Trulock both used a computer located in Conrad's bedroom and each had joint access to the hard drive. Conrad and Trulock, however, protected their personal files with passwords; Conrad did not have access to Trulock's passwords. Although Conrad had authority to consent to a general search of the computer, her authority did not extend to Trulock's password-protected files.
>
> In United States v. Block, 590 F.2d 535 (4th Cir. 1978), this Court held that the defendant's mother had authority to consent to a search of his room, which was located in the home they shared. The mother's authority did not extend to a search of a locked footlocker located within the room, however. We noted that authority to consent "cannot be thought automatically to extend to the interiors of every discrete enclosed space capable of search within the area . . . the rule has to be one of reason that assesses the critical circumstances indicating the presence or absence of a discrete expectation of privacy with respect to the particular object."
>
> Trulock's password-protected files are analogous to the locked footlocker inside the bedroom. By using a password, Trulock affirmatively intended to exclude Conrad and others from his personal files. Moreover, because he concealed his password from Conrad, it cannot be said that Trulock assumed the risk that Conrad would permit others to search his files. Thus, Trulock had a reasonable expectation of privacy in the password-protected computer files and Conrad's authority to consent to the search did not extend to them. Trulock, therefore, has alleged a violation of his Fourth Amendment rights.

Id. at 403. In contrast, a district court has held that when a man and woman who lived together both used the man's computer, and the man did not password-protect his files, the woman had common authority to consent to a search of his files. United States v. Smith, 27 F. Supp. 2d 1111, 1115–16 (C.D. Ill. 1998).

4. *The apparent authority doctrine.* The police may reasonably rely on a third party's claim to have common authority to consent to a search, only to find out later that the third party actually lacked that common authority. Is the search constitutional? In Illinois v. Rodriguez, 497 U.S. 177 (1990), the Supreme Court held that police can rely on a false claim of authority to consent if based on "the facts available to the officer at the moment, ... a man of reasonable caution ... [would believe] that the consenting party had authority" to consent to a search of the premises. *Id.* at 188–89. Under this so-called apparent authority doctrine, courts will not suppress evidence if the police reasonably but incorrectly rely on third-party consent to conduct a search.

5. In United States v. James, 353 F.3d 606 (8th Cir. 2003), the defendant was arrested on charges involving sexual misconduct with a minor. From jail, the defendant tried to smuggle out a letter to two friends asking them to contact a third man with instructions to destroy computer discs the defendant had left with him. Specifically, the letter provided instructions that Mr. Michael Laschober should "*destroy* and scratch ALL backup CD discs he has (BROWN envelope I just left) these are old and useless and one has a *virus* tell him to be sure to cut it up too." The letter ended up in the hands of a local prosecutor, and police approached Laschober to determine if he had the defendant's computer discs.

Laschober explained that he had known the defendant since childhood, and that the defendant had left a stack of computer discs with him in an envelope as storage for back-up purposes. The police asked Laschober if they could look at the discs, and Laschober gave them a sealed envelope that contained them. With Laschober's consent, an officer opened the envelope and found ten discs taped together. The top disc had a note attached that indicated the disc contained a dangerous virus as well as confidential and private information. Laschober consented to the police taking away the discs and searching them. Back at the police station, the officers attempted to view the top disc. The officers had some difficulty viewing the images on the disc—the court's opinion does not explain exactly why—but assistance from a computer specialist eventually allowed them to view the images on a special computer. The files on the disc included images of child pornography.

In an opinion by Judge Richard Arnold, the Eighth Circuit ruled that Laschober did not have common authority over the discs:

> We are firmly convinced that Mr. James did not give permission to Mr. Laschober to exercise control over the discs, or to consent to the searching of the discs. Instead, he gave the discs to Mr. Laschober for the sole purpose of storing them (except that, as the police knew, but Mr. Laschober did not, the defendant had given instructions that the discs be destroyed). The discs came to him in sealed envelopes. They were packaged within the envelope in tape. Mr. James never told Mr. Laschober "go ahead and look at these." Instead, he asked only that they be stored (and, as we have noted, that all of them be destroyed). Further, defendant marked the disc in question "confidential" and

"private," evidencing a desire that no one, including Mr. Laschober, view the contents of the disc. Similarly important, the disc could not be opened on just any computer. To get access to the disc, a special officer had to use an advanced computer. Taken as a whole, such demonstrations of intended privacy evidence Mr. James's expectation that Mr. Laschober not view the disc's contents.

Id. at 614. The court also held that Laschober did not have apparent authority to consent to searching the disk:

> [The officers] knew that the discs contained in the envelope belonged to defendant and not Mr. Laschober. They knew, once the envelope had been opened, that the top disc said "confidential," "personal," "private." They knew that it took an advanced computer to view the disc's contents. And they had a piece of information that Mr. Laschober did not. They knew that his actual authority had changed. They knew, because they had intercepted and read the letter * * *, that Mr. Laschober's only authority was to scratch and destroy the discs. This last fact is critical.

> It cannot be reasonable to rely on a certain theory of apparent authority, when the police themselves know what the consenting party's actual authority is—in this case, not to store the discs, but to destroy them. The standard of reasonableness is governed by what the law-enforcement officers know, not what the consenting party knows. Here the detectives knew too much about Mr. James's manifested desire to keep others, including Mr. Laschober, from seeing the contents of the disc to rely on Mr. Laschober's authority to consent.

Id. at 615. Is the relevant question the defendant's desire to keep others from seeing the contents of the disc or whether the defendant had given others authority over them? Did James give Laschober authority over the discs by sending a letter asking Laschober to destroy them?

3. SEARCH INCIDENT TO ARREST AND THE INVENTORY EXCEPTION

The Supreme Court has created two exceptions to the warrant requirement that are triggered by a suspect's arrest. The first involves searches incident to a lawful arrest, and the second involves inventory searches of seized property.

UNITED STATES DEPARTMENT OF JUSTICE— SEARCHING AND SEIZING COMPUTERS AND OBTAINING ELECTRONIC EVIDENCE IN CRIMINAL INVESTIGATIONS

(2002), available at www.cybercrime.gov/s&smanual2002.htm#_IC4_.

Search Incident to a Lawful Arrest

Pursuant to a lawful arrest, agents may conduct a "full search" of the arrested person, and a more limited search of his surrounding area, without a warrant. *See* United States v. Robinson, 414 U.S. 218, 235 (1973); Chimel v. California, 395 U.S. 752, 762–63 (1969). For example, in *Robinson*, a police officer conducting a patdown search incident to an arrest for a traffic offense discovered a crumpled cigarette package in the suspect's left breast pocket. Not knowing what the package contained, the officer opened the package and discovered fourteen capsules of heroin. The Supreme Court held that the search of the package was permissible, even though the officer had no articulable reason to open the package. In light of the general need to preserve evidence and prevent harm to the arresting officer, the Court reasoned, it was per se reasonable for an officer to conduct a "full search of the person" pursuant to a lawful arrest.

Due to the increasing use of handheld and portable computers and other electronic storage devices, agents often encounter computers when conducting searches incident to lawful arrests. Suspects may be carrying pagers, cellular telephones, Personal Digital assistants (such as Palm Pilots), or even laptop computers when they are arrested. Does the search-incident-to-arrest exception permit an agent to access the memory of an electronic storage device found on the arrestee's person during a warrantless search incident to arrest? In the case of electronic pagers, the answer clearly is "yes." Relying on *Robinson*, courts have uniformly permitted agents to access electronic pagers carried by the arrested person at the time of arrest. *See* United States v. Reyes, 922 F. Supp. 818, 833 (S.D.N.Y. 1996) (holding that accessing numbers in a pager found in bag attached to defendant's wheelchair within twenty minutes of arrest falls within search-incident-to-arrest exception); United States v. Chan, 830 F. Supp. 531, 535 (N.D. Cal. 1993); United States v. Lynch, 908 F. Supp. 284, 287 (D.V.I. 1995); Yu v. United States, 1997 WL 423070, at *2 (S.D.N.Y. Jul. 29, 1997); United States v. Thomas, 114 F.3d 403, 404 n.2 (3d Cir. 1997) (dicta).

Courts have not yet addressed whether *Robinson* will permit warrantless searches of electronic storage devices that contain more information than pagers. In the paper world, certainly, cases have allowed extensive searches of written materials discovered incident to lawful arrests. For example, courts have uniformly held that agents may inspect the entire contents of a suspect's wallet found on his person. See, e.g., United States v. Castro, 596 F.2d 674, 676 (5th Cir. 1979); United States v. Molinaro, 877 F.2d 1341, 1347 (7th Cir. 1989) (citing cases). Similarly, one court has held that agents could photocopy the entire contents of an address book found on the defendant's person during the arrest, *see* United States v. Rodriguez, 995 F.2d 776, 778 (7th Cir. 1993), and others have permitted the search of a defendant's briefcase that was at his side at the time of arrest. *See, e.g.*, United States v. Johnson, 846 F.2d 279, 283–84 (5th Cir. 1988); United States v. Lam Muk Chiu, 522 F.2d 330, 332 (2d Cir. 1975). If agents can examine the contents of wallets, address books, and briefcases without a warrant, it could be argued that they should be able to search their electronic counterparts (such as electronic organizers, floppy disks, and Palm Pilots) as well. *Cf.* United v. Tank, 200 F.3d 627, 632 (9th Cir. 2000) (holding that agents searching a car incident to a valid arrest properly seized a Zip disk found in the car, but failing to discuss whether the agents obtained a warrant before searching the disk for images of child pornography).

The limit on this argument is that any search incident to an arrest must be reasonable. While a search of physical items found on the arrestee's person may always be reasonable, more invasive searches in different circumstances may violate the Fourth Amendment. *See, e.g.* Mary Beth G. v. City of Chicago, 723 F.2d 1263, 1269–71 (7th Cir. 1983) (holding that *Robinson* does not permit strip searches incident to arrest because such searches are not reasonable in context). For example, the increasing storage capacity of handheld computers suggests that *Robinson's* bright line rule may not always apply in the case of electronic searches. When in doubt, agents should consider whether to obtain a search warrant before examining the contents of electronic storage devices that might contain large amounts of information.

Inventory Searches

Law enforcement officers routinely inventory the items they have seized. Such "inventory searches" are reasonable—and therefore fall under an exception to the warrant requirement—when two conditions are met. First, the search must serve a legitimate, non-investigatory purpose (e.g., to protect an owner's property while in custody; to insure against claims of lost, stolen, or vandalized property; or to guard the police from danger) that outweighs the intrusion on the individual's Fourth Amendment rights. *See* Illinois v. Lafayette, 462 U.S. 640, 644 (1983); South Dakota v. Opperman, 428 U.S. 364, 369–70 (1976). Second, the search must follow standardized procedures. *See* Colorado v. Bertine, 479 U.S. 367, 374 n.6 (1987); Florida v. Wells, 495 U.S. 1, 4–5 (1990).

It is unlikely that the inventory-search exception to the warrant requirement would support a search through seized computer files. *See* United States v. O'Razvi, 1998 WL 405048, at *6–7 (S.D.N.Y. July 17, 1998) (noting the difficulties of applying the inventory-search requirements to computer disks); *see also* United States v. Flores, 122 F. Supp. 2d 491, 493–95 (S.D.N.Y. 2000) (finding search of cellular telephone "purely investigatory" and thus not lawful inventory search). Even assuming that standard procedures authorized such a search, the legitimate purposes served by inventory searches in the physical world do not translate well into the intangible realm. Information does not generally need to be reviewed to be protected, and does not pose a risk of physical danger. Although an owner could claim that his computer files were altered or deleted while in police custody, examining the contents of the files would offer little protection from tampering. Accordingly, agents will generally need to obtain a search warrant in order to examine seized computer files held in custody.

Notes and Questions

1. A law student walking to class may carry a cell phone, an iPod, a PDA, and a laptop computer. If the student is arrested while walking to

class, should the search incident to arrest doctrine permit a warrantless search of the student's cell phone? The PDA? What about the iPod and the laptop? If courts impose limits on what searches can occur incident to a lawful arrest, what kinds of limits should they draw? Should the limits focus on the storage capacity of particular devices? Should courts permit searches that occur at the same time and place as the arrest, but disallow subsequent offsite searches or searches that take too much time?

2. Can you imagine any circumstances in which government agents could search a computer or data under the inventory search exception?

4. BORDER SEARCHES

The Supreme Court has created a special set of Fourth Amendment rules that apply at the international border "or its functional equivalents." United States v. Ortiz, 422 U.S. 891, 896 (1975). The following case considers how such rules apply to searches of computers.

UNITED STATES v. ICKES

United States Court of Appeals for the Fourth Circuit, 2005.
393 F.3d 501.

WILKINSON, Circuit Judge.

John Woodward Ickes, Jr., was attempting to enter the United States from Canada when U.S. Customs agents searched his van. The agents found several illegal items, most notably images of child pornography stored in photo albums and on Ickes's computer. Ickes was charged and convicted of transporting child pornography in violation of federal law. Prior to trial, the district court denied Ickes's motion to suppress the evidence obtained at the border.

We agree with the district court that the warrantless search of Ickes's van was permissible.

On August 4, 2000, John Ickes drove to the Canadian border with the United States, arriving at the Ambassador Bridge port of entry near Detroit, Michigan. At the primary inspection point, he told a U.S. Customs Inspector that he was returning from vacation. The inspector, however, was puzzled by this statement because Ickes's van appeared to contain "everything he owned."

Ickes was referred to a second inspector's station, where Agent Merchel Albanese began a routine inspection of the van. Initially, Agent Albanese was inclined to give Ickes's vehicle only a cursory search. However, his suspicions were raised after discovering a video camera containing a tape of a tennis match which focused excessively on a young ball boy. This led Albanese to enlist the help of a colleague and to search the van more thoroughly. The agents found marijuana seeds, marijuana pipes, and a copy of a Virginia warrant for Ickes's arrest. They also found several albums containing photographs of provocatively-posed prepubescent boys, most nude or semi-nude.

At this point, the agents placed Ickes under arrest and detained him. They ran his name through their computer and discovered that he was subject to two outstanding warrants—one from the Bureau of Alcohol, Tobacco, and Firearms, and one from Chesterfield County, Virginia.

While Ickes was in custody, but before he was interrogated, several agents continued to search the van. They confiscated a computer and approximately 75 disks * * *. [A warrantless search of the computer and disks revealed images of child pornography.]

Last term, the Supreme Court instructed that:

The Government's interest in preventing the entry of unwanted persons and effects is at its zenith at the international border. Time and again, we have stated that searches made at the border ... are reasonable simply by virtue of the fact that they occur at the border.

United States v. Flores–Montano, 541 U.S. 149 (2004) (holding that the government's authority to conduct border searches is broad enough to permit the removal, disassembly, and reassembly of a vehicle's fuel tank).

The border search doctrine is not a recent development in the law. The "longstanding recognition that searches at our borders without probable cause and without a warrant are nonetheless 'reasonable' has a history as old as the Fourth Amendment itself." *United States v. Ramsey,* 431 U.S. 606, 619 (1977). In fact, the same Congress which proposed the Fourth Amendment to state legislatures also enacted the first far-reaching customs statute in 1790. Thus, since the birth of our country, customs officials have wielded broad authority to search the belongings of would-be entrants without obtaining a warrant and without establishing probable cause.

This well-recognized exception to the safeguards of the Fourth Amendment comes with an equally well-established rationale. For it is axiomatic that the United States, as sovereign, has the inherent authority to protect, and a paramount interest in protecting, its territorial integrity. The government has an overriding interest in securing the safety of its citizens and to do this it must seek to prevent the introduction of contraband into this country.

Despite the Supreme Court's insistence that U.S. officials be given broad authority to conduct border searches, Ickes argues that the search of his computer was nonetheless invalid since it involved the search of expressive material. In essence, Ickes asks us to carve out a First Amendment exception to the border search doctrine.

However, the ramifications of accepting Ickes's First Amendment argument would be quite staggering. Ickes suggests that the border search doctrine does not apply when the item being searched is something "expressive." But this cannot be the case. The border search doctrine is justified by the longstanding right of the sovereign to protect itself. Particularly in today's world, national security interests may require uncovering terrorist communications, which are inherently "expressive." Following Ickes's logic would create a sanctuary at the border for all expressive material—even for terrorist plans. This would undermine the compelling reasons that lie at the very heart of the border search doctrine. Ickes's argument, at bottom, proves too much.

Ickes claims that our ruling is sweeping. He warns that "any person carrying a laptop computer on an international flight would be subject to a search of the files on the computer hard drive." This prediction seems far-fetched. Customs agents have neither the time nor the resources to search the contents of every computer.

As a practical matter, computer searches are most likely to occur where—as here—the traveler's conduct or the presence of other items in his possession suggest the need to search further. However, to state the probability that reasonable suspicions will give rise to more intrusive searches is a far cry from enthroning this notion as a matter of constitutional law. The essence of border search doctrine is a reliance upon the trained observations and judgments of customs officials, rather than upon constitutional requirements applied to the inapposite context of this sort of search.

Notes and Questions

1. *Ickes* suggests that "computer searches are most likely to occur where ... the traveler's conduct or the presence of other items in his possession suggest the need to search further." Is this true?

In United States v. Roberts, 86 F. Supp. 2d 678 (S.D. Tex. 2000), *aff'd on other grounds*, 274 F.3d 1007 (5th Cir. 2001), investigators suspected that a man named Roberts was carrying a computer containing images of child pornography on a trip from Houston, Texas to Paris, France. The investigators set up a customs inspection station on the jetway at the Houston airport with the sole purpose of harnessing the border search exception. When Roberts arrived at the inspection station, customs agents informed him that they were searching for "currency" and "high technology or other data" to ensure that it was not illegally exported. Of course, the real purpose of the inspection was to search Roberts' computer for child pornography. The agents searched his property and found a laptop computer and six Zip diskettes that together contained thousands of contraband images. The court applied the border search exception and approved the warrantless search because the runway was the "functional equivalent" of the border for an international flight.

Do you think that the agents should have been allowed to use the border exception to justify this search? Note that under Whren v. United States, 517 U.S. 806 (1996), an officer's motive for conducting a search or seizure is irrelevant to its constitutionality.

2. Does the border search exception apply to communications sent over the Internet, such as e-mails? Does the Fourth Amendment permit the government to install surveillance devices at the border and scan all Internet traffic passing into or out of the United States?

Consider United States v. Ramsey, 431 U.S. 606 (1977). In *Ramsey*, a postal inspector in New York was investigating a heroin importing conspiracy. In a search for evidence, the inspector opened a first-class international letter mailed from Thailand that was destined for an address in the Washington, D.C., area. The letter contained heroin, leading to criminal charges against the defendants. The defendants challenged the warrantless seizure and search of the envelope, but the Supreme Court rejected the challenge under the border search exception:

> The border-search exception is grounded in the recognized right of the sovereign to control, subject to substantive limitations imposed by the Constitution, who and what may enter the country. It is clear that there is nothing in the rationale behind the border-search exception which suggests that the mode of entry will be critical. It was conceded at oral argument that customs officials could search, without probable cause and without a warrant, envelopes carried by an entering traveler, whether in his luggage or on his person. Surely no different constitutional standard should apply simply because the envelopes were mailed, not carried. The critical fact is that the envelopes cross the border and enter this country, not that they are brought in by one mode of transportation rather than another. It is their entry into this country from without it that makes a resulting search "reasonable."

> Nor do we agree that, under the circumstances presented by this case, First Amendment considerations dictate a full panoply of Fourth Amendment rights prior to the border search of mailed letters. There is, again, no reason to distinguish between letters mailed into the country, and letters carried on the traveler's person. More fundamentally, however, the existing system of border searches has not been shown to invade protected First Amendment rights, and hence there is no reason to think that the potential presence of correspondence makes the otherwise constitutionally reasonable search "unreasonable."

Id. at 620, 623. Does *Ramsey* answer how the border search exception applies to international e-mail?

3. The National Security Agency is widely believed to attempt to collect all international telephone, fax, e-mail, and data transmissions. The program is often referred to by its alleged code name, ECHELON, and is coordinated with the governments of the United Kingdom, Canada, Australia, and New Zealand. *See generally* Lawrence D. Sloan, Note, *ECHELON and the Legal Restraints on Signals Intelligence: A Need for Reevaluation*, 50 Duke L.J. 1467 (2001).

Does ECHELON comply with the Fourth Amendment under the border search exception? What is the "functional equivalent of the border" for an e-mail or other Internet transmission? If the NSA installs a surveillance device at an ISP in the United States, and records all traffic either from abroad or to abroad (or both), does the border search exception permit the surveillance without a warrant?

5. GOVERNMENT WORKPLACE SEARCHES

Many people use computers at work. When a workplace computer is used to commit a crime, the rules that regulate government access to the computer depend on whether the employer is a private company or the government. The Fourth Amendment rules regulating access to private sector workplace computers is similar to the rules regulating access to computers stored in homes, with one major caveat: Employers almost always have common authority to provide third-party consent to a search. *Compare* Chapman v. United States, 365 U.S. 610 (1961) (holding that a landlord lacks authority to consent to search of premises used by his tenant) *with* United States v. Gargiso, 456 F.2d 584 (2d Cir. 1972) (holding that an employer can consent to a search of an employee's locked workspace). When investigators want to seize and analyze a computer in a private workplace, they ordinarily will obtain the employer's authorization and then rely on that consent to seize the computers without a warrant. If the employer does not consent, however, the police ordinarily will obtain a warrant.

Computer searches at government workplaces present a very different situation. In a government workplace, employers are by definition state actors covered by the Fourth Amendment. This sets up a puzzle: If government employers are state actors, does a supervisor violate the Fourth Amendment every time he enters an employee's office without a warrant or the employee's consent? Although they are state actors, government employers normally do not act in a law enforcement capacity at work. Given that, it would be rather odd to require them to obtain a warrant to do their job. Alternatively, it may seem equally troubling to say that government employees have no privacy rights at all in their workspaces. If that were the case, government employees would forfeit all Fourth Amendment rights upon arriving at work.

The Supreme Court has resolved this tension by creating a somewhat sui generis framework for analyzing government employee privacy. The key case is O'Connor v. Ortega, 480 U.S. 709 (1987), which was decided in a plurality opinion by Justice O'Connor combined with a concurrence by Justice Scalia. Under *O'Connor*, Fourth Amendment rights in government workplaces are determined by a two-step framework. First, the court must apply a rather unusual version of the reasonable expectation of privacy test. Unlike the traditional reasonable expectation of privacy test used in homes and private workplaces, the version of the test applied in government workplaces looks to (a) whether the defendant shared his space or property with others; and (b) whether legitimate workplace policies put the defendant on notice that he was denied otherwise existing Fourth Amendment rights. If a government employee shares his space with others, or legitimate workplace policies deny his privacy rights, he cannot have a reasonable expectation of privacy in the workplace.

If a government employee has a reasonable expectation of privacy under this test, the next question is whether the workplace search is "reasonable." In *O'Connor*, the Supreme Court held that this second question should be analyzed under the Supreme Court's "special needs" exception to the warrant requirement. The "special needs" exception permits state actors to dispense with the warrant requirement when acting in a non-law-enforcement capacity, such as the case of a school principal searching student lockers or mandatory drug testing by a government agency. The thinking is that the government interest beyond law enforcement must be balanced with the traditional Fourth Amendment rule, relaxing the warrant requirement when "the burden of obtaining a warrant is likely to frustrate the [non-law-enforcement] governmental purpose behind the search." Camara v. Municipal Court, 387 U.S. 523, 533 (1967). *O'Connor* brought government workplace searches within this category, permitting government employers to conduct reasonable warrantless searches even if the searches violated the employee's reasonable expectation of privacy. The employer must conduct the search for a work-related reason, rather than solely to obtain evidence in a criminal case, and the search must be justified at its inception and permissible in its scope.

LEVENTHAL v. KNAPEK

United States Court of Appeals for the Second Circuit, 2001.
266 F.3d 64.

SOTOMAYOR, Circuit Judge:

After receiving anonymous allegations that an employee reasonably suspected to be plaintiff-appellant Gary Leventhal was neglecting his duties in the Accounting Bureau of the New York State Department of Transportation, DOT investigators, without Leventhal's consent, printed out a list of the file names found on Leventhal's office computer. The list of file names contained evidence that certain non-standard software was loaded on Leventhal's computer. This led to additional searches confirming that Leventhal had a personal tax preparation program on his office computer and to disciplinary charges against Leventhal for misconduct. After settling the disciplinary charges, Leventhal sued defendants-appellees, challenging the legality of the searches * * * .

We affirm the district court's grant of summary judgment to defendants * * * . Even though, based on the particular facts of this case, Leventhal had some expectation of privacy in the contents of his computer, the searches were reasonable in light of the DOT's need to investigate the allegations of Leventhal's misconduct as balanced against the modest intrusion caused by the searches.

BACKGROUND

Leventhal began his career at the DOT in 1974. At the time of the searches in question, Leventhal had risen to the position of Principal Accountant in the Accounting Bureau of the DOT, a grade 27 position. In 1996, and for several previous years, Leventhal maintained a private tax practice while employed at the DOT. He received DOT approval to make up on weekends or after normal work hours any time he missed because of his outside employment. In order to receive approval for this arrangement, Leventhal declared that his outside employment would "not interfere with the complete and proper execution of my duties with the Department of Transportation."

The DOT had a written policy prohibiting theft. The policy broadly defined theft to include:

improper use of State equipment, material or vehicles. Examples include but are not limited to: conducting personal business on State time; using State equipment, material or vehicles for personal business; improper use of the mail, copiers, fax machines, personal computers, lincs codes or telephones and time spent on non-State business related activities during the workday.

The DOT also had an unwritten rule that only "standard" DOT software could be loaded on DOT computers. Although this rule was never officially promulgated as a DOT policy, Leventhal remarked during his interrogation that "the stated policy" was that employees were not to have personal software on a DOT computer "without permission." Nevertheless, it was known that the staff of the Accounting Bureau had loaded unlicensed copies of "non-standard" software on DOT computers and used the software to perform work-related activities due, at least in part, to the DOT's inability to purchase needed software for its employees. The DOT also had an official policy restricting office Internet access to DOT business.

In July 1996, the DOT circulated a memo from Ann Snow, the Network Administrator for the Budget and Finance Division, which stated that only original, licensed copies of software could be installed on DOT computers. Following the distribution of this memo, however, Leventhal's supervisors discussed their difficulties in complying with the memo because of the department's dependence upon the use of unlicensed software. Leventhal's immediate supervisor at the time, John Chevalier, instructed his subordinates, including Leventhal, that they could continue to use non-standard software for departmental business.

DOT computers were accessible, for certain limited purposes, by those other than their normal users. The computer support staff of the DOT engaged in troubleshooting and the upgrading of individual computers. During these maintenance operations, it was possible for the computer staff to observe whether non-standard DOT software had been loaded on an individual computer. DOT computers were also occasionally accessed without the user's knowledge to retrieve a needed document, sometimes bypassing a password prompt to obtain access. The computer staff of the DOT provided technical support for Leventhal's DOT computer upon his request three or four times between 1994 and 1996, and once, after hours, without his request, in order to change the name of the server.

On October 15, 1996, the New York State Office of the Inspector General referred to the DOT an anonymous letter it had received complaining of abuses at the DOT Accounting Bureau. This letter described specific employees by reference to their salary grades, genders, and job titles, without providing names. The letter made certain allegations concerning a grade 27 employee. Leventhal was the only grade 27 employee in the office at that time and, therefore, the DOT investigators inferred that the grade 27 employee described in the letter was Leventhal. The relevant portion of the letter states:

> The abuse of time and power is so far out of line with the intended functions of the bureau that to cite all specifics would be an endless task. The day to day operation of this bureau is a slap in the face to all good state workers. You have to see this place to believe it. I will cite a few examples. A grade 27 who is late everyday. The majority of his time is spent on non-DOT business related phone calls or talking to other personnel about personal computers. He is only in the office half the time he is either sick or on vacation.

Lawrence Knapek, the Assistant Commissioner of the DOT for the Office of Budget and Finance, met with John Samaniuk, the acting director of the Office of Internal Audit and Investigations, and Gary Cuyler, the chief investigator for that office, to discuss how to respond to the allegations made in the letter. They decided that the Office of Internal Audit and Investigation would conduct an investigation employing "such techniques as reviewing telephone records, reviewing computer records, Internet logs, that kind of thing." A "computer review" was ordered for all of the employees who could be identified from the letter. This involved printing out a list of file names found on these DOT computers to determine whether any contained non-standard software. After business hours on October 25, 1996, the investigators entered Leventhal's office through an open door, turned on his DOT computer, and reviewed the directories of files on the computer's hard drive. There was no power-on password to gain access to Leventhal's computer, but once the machine was turned on, some of the menu selections that appeared were password-protected. In order to perform their search, the investigators may have used a "boot-disk," a disk which allows the computer to start up without encountering the menus normally found there.

Having located the computer directories, the investigators printed out a list of the file names to enable the later identification of the programs loaded on Leventhal's computer without having to open each program. This included a printout of the names of the "hidden" files on Leventhal's computer. These "hidden" directories, the investigators found, contained "Morph," a type of drawing program and "PPU," a program suspected of containing tax software because of file names such as "TAX.FNT," and "CUSTTAX.DBF." On the non-"hidden" directories, the investigators found other non-standard software, including the programs Prodigy, Quicken, and Lotus Suite (although one part of Lotus Suite was standard DOT software at the time). * * *

In February 1997, DOT management and investigators met to examine the results from these searches. Assistant DOT Commissioner Knapek attended the meeting and, aware of Leventhal's private tax practice, was particularly interested in confirming the investigators' suspicion that Leventhal had loaded tax software on his DOT office computer. They decided to conduct a further search of Leventhal's computer to determine with greater certainty whether the "PPU" directory they had discovered during the first search was part of a tax preparation program. Investigators reexamined the computer in Leventhal's office once in February 1997 and twice in April 1997. During these subsequent searches, they copied the "Morph" and "PPU" directories onto a laptop computer, obtained additional printouts of the file directories, and opened a few files to examine their contents. In the first April search, an investigator noticed that some items had been added to the PPU directory since the previous search, indicating recent activity. The PPU directory was later identified as belonging to "Pencil Pushers," a tax preparation program.

On May 2, 1997, shortly after informing Leventhal that he was under investigation and that the computer in his office would be confiscated, the Director of the DOT Employee Relations Bureau observed Leventhal appearing to delete items from his computer directories. Leventhal was then interrogated. He admitted to belonging to a group that had jointly purchased a single copy of the Pencil Pushers software that was then copied onto his computer and the computers of other members of the group. Leventhal also admitted that he had printed out up to five personal income tax returns from the computer in his DOT office.

In September 1997, the DOT brought disciplinary charges against Leventhal under N.Y. Civ. Serv. Law § 75 charging six grounds of misconduct or incompetence. * * * Four days after he settled the DOT disciplinary charges, Leventhal filed this action in United States District Court for the Northern District of New York.

DISCUSSION

The Fourth Amendment protects individuals from unreasonable searches conducted by the Government, even when the Government acts as an employer. The "special needs" of public employers may, however, allow them to dispense with the probable cause and warrant requirements when conducting workplace searches related to investigations of work-related misconduct. *See O'Connor v. Ortega*, 480 U.S. 709, 719–26 (1987) (plurality opinion); *id.* at 732 (Scalia, J. concurring). In these situations, the Fourth Amendment's protection against "unreasonable" searches is enforced by "a careful balancing of governmental and private interests." *New Jersey v. T.L.O.*, 469 U.S. 325, 341 (1985). A public employer's search of an area in which an employee had a reasonable expectation of privacy is "reasonable" when "the measures adopted are reasonably related to the objectives of the search and not excessively intrusive in light of" its purpose. *O'Connor*, 480 U.S. at 726 (plurality opinion).

We begin by inquiring whether the conduct at issue infringed an expectation of privacy that society is prepared to consider reasonable. Without a reasonable expectation of privacy, a workplace search by a public employer will not violate the Fourth Amendment, regardless of the search's nature and scope. The workplace conditions can be such that an employee's expectation of privacy in a certain area is diminished. *See id.* at 717–18 (plurality opinion) (recognizing that offices that are "continually entered by fellow employees and other visitors during the workday for conferences, consultations, and other work-related visits," can be "so open to fellow employees or the public that no expectation of privacy is reasonable."). On the facts of *O'Connor*, the entire Court found a reasonable expectation of privacy with respect to the office desk and file cabinets in which the plaintiff had maintained his personal correspondence, medical files, correspondence from private patients unconnected with his employment, personal financial records, teaching aids and notes, and personal gifts and mementos. *Id.* at 718 (plurality opinion); *id.* at 731 (Scalia, J., concurring). In finding that the plaintiff had a reasonable expectation of privacy, the plurality noted that there was no evidence that the employer had "established a reasonable regulation or policy discouraging employees from storing personal papers and effects in their desks or file cabinets." *Id.* at 719 (plurality opinion).

We hold, based on the particular facts of this case, that Leventhal had a reasonable expectation of privacy in the contents of his office computer. We make this assessment in the context of the employment relation, after considering what access other employees or the public had to Leventhal's office.

Leventhal occupied a private office with a door. He had exclusive use of the desk, filing cabinet, and computer in his office. Leventhal did not share use of his computer with other employees in the Accounting Bureau nor was there evidence that visitors or the public had access to his computer.

We are aware that "public employees' expectations of privacy in their offices, desks, and file cabinets, like similar expectations of employees in the private sector, may be reduced by virtue of actual office practices and procedures, or by legitimate regulation." *Id.* Construing the evidence in favor of Leventhal, as we must in reviewing this grant of summary judgment against him, we do not find that the DOT either had a general practice of routinely conducting searches of office computers or had placed Leventhal on notice that he should have no expectation of privacy in the contents of his office computer.

Viewing the DOT anti-theft policy in the light most favorable to Leventhal, we find that it did not prohibit the mere storage of personal materials in his office computer. Rather, the anti-theft policy prohibited "using" state equipment "for personal business" without defining further these terms. John Samaniuk, acting director of the DOT's Office of Internal Audits and Investigations, testified at Leventhal's disciplinary hearing that an employee would not violate state policies by keeping a personal checkbook in an office drawer, even though it would take up space there. Under the circumstances presented here, we cannot say that the same anti-theft policy prohibited Leventhal from storing personal items in his office computer.

Although the DOT technical support staff had access to all computers in the DOT offices, their maintenance of these computers was normally announced and the one example in the record of an unannounced visit to Leventhal's computer was only to change the name of a server. DOT personnel might also need, at times, to search for a document in an unattended computer, but there was no evidence that these searches were frequent, widespread, or extensive enough to constitute an atmosphere "so open to fellow employees or the public that no expectation of privacy is reasonable." *Id.* at 718 (plurality opinion). This type of infrequent and selective search for maintenance purposes or to retrieve a needed document, justified by reference to the "special needs" of employers to pursue legitimate work-related objectives, does not destroy any underlying expectation of privacy that an employee could otherwise possess in the contents of an office computer.

Even though Leventhal had some expectation of privacy in the contents of his office computer, the investigatory searches by the DOT did not violate his Fourth Amendment rights. An investigatory search for evidence of suspected work-related employee misfeasance will be constitutionally "reasonable" if it is "justified at its inception" and of appropriate scope. *Id.* at 726 (plurality opinion). We agree with the district court that both of these requirements are satisfied here.

The initial consideration of the search's justification examines whether "there are reasonable grounds for suspecting that the search will turn up evidence that the employee is guilty of work-related misconduct." *O'Connor*, 480 U.S. at 726 (plurality opinion). Here, there were reasonable grounds to believe that the searches would uncover evidence of misconduct. The specific allegations against the grade 27 employee, who was reasonably assumed to be Leventhal, were that (1) he was "late everyday"; (2) he spent "the majority of his time on non-DOT business related phone calls or talking to other personnel about personal computers"; and that (3) "he is only in the office half the time; the other half he is either sick or on vacation." Probable cause is not necessary to conduct a search in this context, a plurality of the Court has explained, because "public employers have a direct and overriding interest in ensuring that the work of the agency is conducted in a proper and efficient manner." *Id.* at 724 (plurality opinion). The individualized suspicion of misconduct in this case justified the DOT's decision to instigate some type of search.

The scope of a search will be appropriate if reasonably related to the objectives of the search and not excessively intrusive in light of the nature of the misconduct. We conclude that the DOT search to identify whether Leventhal was using non-standard DOT software was reasonably related to the DOT's investigation of the allegations of Leventhal's workplace misconduct. Although the anonymous letter did not allege that the grade 27 employee was misusing DOT office computers, it did allege that the grade 27 employee was not attentive to his duties and spent a significant amount of work time discussing personal computers with other employees.

Leventhal argues that a search for non-standard software would be irrelevant to charges of misconduct because the DOT had, de facto, approved of the use of non-standard software needed to conduct DOT business. Even assuming that this were true, the investigation was more broadly aimed at uncovering evidence that Leventhal was using his office computer for non-DOT purposes. The searches accomplished this task by uncovering evidence that Leventhal had loaded a tax preparation program onto his office computer, a program that he later admitted he used to print out personal tax returns in his office.

We also find that the scope of the searches was not excessively intrusive in light of the nature of the misconduct. During the first search, the DOT investigators printed out a list of file names found on Leventhal's office computer. They did not run any program or open any files. The investigators entered Leventhal's office through an open door and found that Leventhal's computer had no power-on password although some menu selections were password protected. The investigators limited their search to viewing and printing file names that were reasonably related to the DOT's need to know whether Leventhal was misusing his office computer. The first search was permissible in scope.

Neither were the three subsequent searches "excessively intrusive." After the first search had established that files named "TAX.FNT" and "CUSTTAX.DBF" were loaded on Leventhal's computer, the investigators reasonably suspected that these files were part of a tax program. When DOT investigators and management met to discuss what they had found in the first search, Assistant Commissioner Knapek expressed a particular interest in confirming whether Leventhal had loaded tax preparation software on his DOT computer, aware that Leventhal had a private tax practice. Investigators reexamined the computer in Leventhal's office once in February 1997 and twice in April 1997. These searches were limited to copying onto a laptop computer the "PPU" directories that they later identified as referring to "Pencil Pushers," a tax preparation program, and the "Morph" directories, pertaining to a graphics program, to printing out additional copies of the file names, and to opening a few files to examine their contents. There is no evidence that the DOT opened and examined any computer files containing individual tax returns that may have been saved on Leventhal's computer, and, therefore, we need not address the permissibility of searching such materials. Considering that the first search yielded evidence upon which it was reasonable to suspect that a more thorough search would turn up additional proof that Leventhal had misused his DOT office computer, the DOT investigators were justified in returning to confirm the nature of the non-standard DOT programs loaded on Leventhal's computer by copying directories, printing file names, and opening selected files.

CONCLUSION

Because the DOT searches of Leventhal's office computer were not "unreasonable" under the Fourth Amendment, * * * we affirm the district court's grant of summary judgment to defendants.

Notes and Questions

1. *The first step of the* O'Connor *test.* The first step of the *O'Connor* test considers whether the employee shared his space with others and whether legitimate workplace policies put the defendant on notice that no privacy rights should be expected. In *Leventhal v. Knapek*, the court concludes that the workplace policies and practices at the DOT were insufficient to deny Leventhal Fourth Amendment rights. As a result, Leventhal enjoyed Fourth Amendment protection in his computer.

In many other cases, however, government employers have promulgated computer use policies that eliminate Fourth Amendment protection entirely. For example, in United States v. Thorn, 375 F.3d 679 (8th Cir. 2004), an employee of the Missouri Department of Social Services downloaded contraband images to his computer at work. When the employee had obtained computer access two years earlier, he had acknowledged a workplace policy that stated: "Employees *do not* have any personal privacy rights regarding their use of DSS information systems and technology. An employee's use of DSS information systems and technology indicates that the employee understands and *consents* to DSS's right to inspect and audit all such use as described in this policy." The Eighth Circuit held that the policy eliminated the employee's Fourth Amendment rights in his workplace computer. *Id.* at 683–84.

The powerful effect of workplace regulations under the first step of *O'Connor* encourages government employers to install network "banners" or enact Internet use policies. In the case of a banner, the employee is greeted with a privacy notice upon logging in to a workplace computer. In most cases, the notice explains that the user should have no reasonable expectation of privacy in his use of the network. Banners and Internet use policies are generally binding: if a notice says that a government employee has no privacy rights, the employee has no privacy rights. Should government employers be allowed to eliminate Fourth Amendment rights so easily?

2. *The second step of the* O'Connor *test.* At stage two of the *O'Connor* test, the court must determine whether the search was reasonable in its scope and justified by non-law-enforcement needs. *Leventhal v. Knapek* focuses on whether the employer search was reasonable in its scope, and concludes that the search in that case was indeed reasonable. Other cases have focused on the line between law enforcement searches and searches for non-law-enforcement reasons. The line may be difficult to draw because government employers often serve two roles at once. The head of a government office may want to end workplace misconduct and may also control criminal investigators who can build a case against employees who break the rules. In such situations, how should courts distinguish work-related searches from law enforcement searches?

In United States v. Simons, 206 F.3d 392 (4th Cir. 2000), an employee of the Foreign Bureau of Information Services (FBIS), a division of the CIA, used his computer at work to download child pornography. Two employees of the CIA Office of Inspector General, one of whom was a criminal investigator, were sent to search the employee's office for evidence. The Fourth Circuit held that this search fell within the *O'Connor* exception to the warrant requirement even though the dominant purpose of the search was to gather evidence:

> FBIS did not lose its special need for the efficient and proper operation of the workplace, merely because the evidence obtained was evidence of a crime. [The employee]'s violation of FBIS' Internet policy happened also to be a violation of criminal law; this does not mean that FBIS lost the capacity and interests of an employer. *See Gossmeyer v. McDonald*, 128 F.3d 481, 492–93 (7th Cir. 1997) (concluding that presence of law enforcement personnel at search of employee's office by government employer did not preclude application of *O'Connor*); *see also* 4 Wayne R. LaFave, *Search and Seizure* § 10.3(d), at 487–88 (3d ed.1996) (noting that conclusion that warrant requirement does not apply when employer is investigating work-related criminal conduct is consistent with reasoning of *O'Connor*).

Id. at 400.

3. *Computer searches involving probationers.* The special needs doctrine also applies to searches of individuals on probation. *See* Griffin v. Wisconsin, 483 U.S. 868 (1987). For example, in United States v. Lifshitz, 369 F.3d 173 (2d Cir. 2004), the defendant pled guilty to receiving images of child pornography using his computer. The district court imposed a sentence of probation that contained the following restriction, *id.* at 177 n.3:

> The defendant shall consent to the installation of systems that enable the probation officer or designee to monitor and filter computer use, on a regular or random basis, on any computer owned or controlled by the defendant. Upon reasonable suspicion, the probation office may make unannounced examinations of any computer equipment owned or controlled by the defendant, which may result in retrieval and copying of all data from the computer(s) and any internal or external peripherals, and may involve removal of such equipment for the purpose of conducting a more thorough inspection.

The Second Circuit held that the special needs exception permitted conditioning the defendant's probation on his agreement to computer monitoring. The court remanded the case back to the district court, however, on the ground that the district court needed to craft a narrower and more specific condition that would satisfy the reasonableness requirement of the special needs doctrine given the facts of that particular case. *See id.* at 193.

D. SEARCHING AND SEIZING COMPUTERS WITH A WARRANT

Searches and seizures are constitutional when authorized by a valid and properly executed search warrant. A search warrant is a court order signed by a judge that authorizes government agents to enter a place and seize property. The Fourth Amendment's requirement for issuing a search warrant is unusually clear from its text: "no Warrants shall issue, but upon probable cause, supported by Oath or affirmation, and particularly describing the place to be searched, and the persons or things to be seized." The Framers of the Fourth Amendment enacted these restrictions in reaction to the English and early Colonial experience with "general warrants," warrants that gave the King's officials wide discretion to execute searches as they believed necessary to enforce the law. The text of the Fourth Amendment forbids general warrants by ensuring that all warrants must be based on probable cause and must state with specificity where the police will go and what property they will seize.

The requirement that a warrant must be issued "upon probable cause" ordinarily is satisfied by a written affidavit submitted to the issuing judge. The affidavit explains the investigation and articulates the officer's probable cause that evidence of the crime will be located in the place to be searched. The proposed warrant itself is a one-page order containing the judge's authorization to enter the named place to be searched and to seize the property listed in the warrant. If the judge agrees that the affidavit establishes probable cause, and that the place to be searched and property to be seized are "particularly" described, then the judge will sign the warrant. The warrant then becomes a court order permitting the investigator or his agents to execute the search.

Both constitutional and statutory law regulate the process of obtaining and executing search warrants. Probable cause and the particularity requirement are obvious constitutional requirements governing what warrants may issue. The Fourth Amendment also imposes some restrictions on how investigators execute warrants and what property they may seize. Beyond the Fourth Amendment, statutes regulating the warrant process impose a number of nuts-and-bolts restrictions. At the federal level, for example, Federal Rule of Criminal Procedure 41 provides a relatively detailed set of instructions governing how and when warrants must be obtained and executed. Rule 41 requires agents to execute warrants within 10 days after the judge issues the warrant. It also requires agents to leave behind a copy of the warrant when it is executed, as well as to file a "return" of the warrant with the issuing judge listing the property investigators seized. Although the materials in this section will occasionally discuss Rule 41 and associated state statutory restrictions on computer warrants, they focus primarily on constitutional rules under the Fourth Amendment.

Searches and seizures of computers pursuant to warrants raise a number of challenging issues because they divide what is traditionally a one-step process into two steps. Warrants for physical property are executed in a single step. Investigators enter the place to be searched, seize the property named in the warrant, and then leave. When agents leave the place to be searched, the warrant has been executed and the government's work is done.

Computer searches usually work in a different way. Investigators ordinarily want to seize computers for the information they contain, not because they want the physical hardware for its own sake. This means that seized computers must be searched for evidence. The process of searching a seized computer is known as the computer forensics process, and can be tremendously time-consuming. Analyzing a single computer may take anywhere from a few hours to a few weeks, and often requires specialized tools and expert training. It is impractical to require agents to locate computers and search them onsite when the agents are executing the warrant. As a result, computer warrants normally are executed in a two-stage process. The investigators enter the place to be searched; seize the computer hardware; take the hardware into government custody offsite; and then later search the equipment for the data it contains that may be evidence of crime. Two searches occur instead of one: the physical search comes first and the electronic search comes second. *See generally* Orin S. Kerr, *Search Warrants In An Era of Digital Evidence*, 75 Miss. L.J. 85 (2005).

The bifurcation of the one-step search process into two steps raises a number of difficult questions. For example, should the probable cause required to seize a computer focus on probable cause to believe evidence is located in the physical place where the computer is located, or probable cause that evidence is located in a particular computer? Is the "place to be searched" the physical location of the physical search, the physical location of the electronic search, or the computer itself? What legal restrictions govern the execution of the electronic search stage?

The law governing this area presently is in a state of considerable uncertainty, owing largely to the novelty of the two-step search process. The overarching question is, how can the traditional rules governing warrant searches be applied to the new facts to retain the basic function of existing law? How can the law both deter general warrants and ensure that investigators have the ability to collect digital evidence to protect public safety?

1. PROBABLE CAUSE AND PARTICULARITY

Warrants must be based on probable cause and must particularly describe the property to be searched and the property to be seized. According to the Supreme Court, probable cause is "a fair probability that contraband or evidence of a crime will be found in a particular place." Illinois v. Gates, 462 U.S. 213, 238 (1983). No special rules determine when probable cause exists. The question is whether the affidavit submitted in support of the warrant establishes a fair probability in a practical, common-sense way based on the totality of the circumstances.

The Supreme Court explained the purpose of the particularity requirement in Maryland v. Garrison, 480 U.S. 79, 84 (1987):

The manifest purpose of this particularity requirement was to prevent general searches. By limiting the authorization to search to the specific areas and things for which there is probable cause to search, the requirement ensures that the search will be carefully tailored to its justifications, and will not take on the character of the wide-ranging exploratory searches the Framers intended to prohibit. Thus, the scope of a lawful search is defined by the object of the search and the places in which there is probable cause to believe that it may be found. Just as probable cause to believe that a stolen lawnmower may be found in a garage will not support a warrant to search an upstairs bedroom, probable cause to believe that undocumented aliens are being transported in a van will not justify a warrantless search of a suitcase.

As this excerpt suggests, the probable cause and particularly requirements work together. A warrant must specify a specific place in which specific evidence of the crime is probably located, and the affidavit must establish probable cause to believe that the evidence is located in the place to be searched.

Importantly, the remedy for violations of these two constitutional requirements is considerably narrower than the rights themselves. In United States v. Leon, 468 U.S. 897 (1984), the Supreme Court held that defects in search warrants should not lead to suppression of evidence if the government investigators have a reasonable good faith belief that the warrant satisfied the Fourth Amendment. The Court reasoned that an officer who has an objectively reasonable belief that the warrant was proper has not committed a wrong that courts must deter:

It is the magistrate's responsibility to determine whether the officer's allegations establish probable cause and, if so, to issue a warrant comporting in form with the requirements of the Fourth Amendment. In the ordinary case, an officer cannot be expected to question the magistrate's probable-cause determination or his judgment that the form of the warrant is technically sufficient. Once the warrant issues, there is literally nothing more the policeman can do in seeking to comply with the law. Penalizing the officer for the magistrate's error, rather than his own, cannot logically contribute to the deterrence of Fourth Amendment violation. * * * We conclude that the marginal or nonexistent benefits produced by suppressing evidence obtained in objectively reasonable reliance on a subsequently invalidated search warrant cannot justify the substantial costs of exclusion.

Id. at 920. In Malley v. Briggs, 475 U.S. 335, 344 (1986), the Supreme Court held that this "good faith" standard is the same as the qualified immunity standard that the courts have applied in civil suits for Fourth Amendment violations under Harlow v. Fitzgerald, 457 U.S. 800 (1982). This means that whether a Fourth Amendment challenge to a search warrant involves a civil suit or a motion to suppress, the standard is the same: a victim of a search pursuant to a defective warrant can obtain relief only if "it would be clear to a reasonable officer that his conduct was unlawful in the situation he confronted" at the time of the search. Saucier v. Katz, 533 U.S. 194, 202 (2001).

How do these requirements apply to warrants to search and seize computers?

UNITED STATES v. ADJANI

United States Court of Appeals for the Ninth Circuit, 2006.
452 F.3d 1140.

FISHER, Circuit Judge:

While executing a search warrant at the home of defendant Christopher Adjani to obtain evidence of his alleged extortion, agents from the Federal Bureau of Investigation seized Adjani's computer and external storage devices, which were later searched at an FBI computer lab. They also seized and subsequently searched a computer belonging to defendant Jana Reinhold, who lived with Adjani, even though she had not at that point been identified as a suspect and was not named as a target in the warrant. Some of the emails found on Reinhold's computer chronicled conversations between her and Adjani that implicated her in the extortion plot. Relying in part on the incriminating emails, the government charged both Adjani and Reinhold with conspiring to commit extortion in violation of 18 U.S.C. § 371 and transmitting a threatening communication with intent to extort in violation of 18 U.S.C. § 875(d).

The defendants brought motions to suppress the emails, arguing that the warrant did not authorize the seizure and search of Reinhold's computer and its contents; but if it did, the warrant was unconstitutionally overbroad or, alternatively, the emails fell outside the scope of the warrant. The district court granted the defendants' motion to suppress the email communications between Reinhold and Adjani, finding that the agents did not have sufficient probable cause to search Reinhold's computer, and that once they discovered information incriminating her, the agents should have obtained an additional search warrant. The government appeals this evidentiary ruling, but only with respect to three emails dated January 12, 2004.

We hold that the government had probable cause to search Reinhold's computer, the warrant satisfied our test for specificity and the seized e-mail communications fell within the scope of the properly issued warrant. Accordingly, we reverse the district court's order suppressing the January 12, 2004 email communications between Reinhold and Adjani.

I. BACKGROUND

A. The Extortion Scheme

Adjani was once employed by Paycom Billing Services Inc. (formerly Epoch), which facilitates payments from Internet users to its client websites. As a payment facilitator, Paycom receives and stores vast amounts of data containing credit card information. On January 8, 2004, a woman (later identified as Reinhold) delivered envelopes to three Paycom partners, Christopher Mallick, Clay Andrews and Joel Hall. Each envelope contained a letter from Adjani advising that he had purchased a copy of Paycom's database containing its clients' sensitive financial information. The letter threatened that Adjani would sell the Paycom database and master client control list if he did not receive $3 million. To prove his threats were real, Adjani included samples of the classified data. He directed the Paycom partners to sign an enclosed agreement attesting to the proposed quid pro quo and fax it back to him by January 12. The letter included Adjani's email address, cadjani@mac.com, and a fax number. Agents later learned that Adjani's email address was billed to Reinhold's account.

Evidence suggested that Adjani left Los Angeles on January 9, 2004, and ultimately ended up in Zurich, Switzerland. From Switzerland, Adjani sent an email on January 12 to Joel Hall to confirm that Hall and the others had received the envelopes. Adjani followed up on this email on January 13 by instructing Hall to contact him through AOL/Mac iChat instant messaging if he wanted to discuss the settlement agreement. With the FBI monitoring, Hall conversed several times with Adjani on the Internet and over the telephone. In spite of Adjani's insistence that he remain overseas, Hall convinced him to come to Los Angeles on January 26 to pick up $2.5 million in exchange for the database.

Adjani returned to Los Angeles on January 22, under FBI surveillance. Reinhold, driving in a car that the FBI had earlier identified as Adjani's, was observed leaving Adjani's residence in Venice, California, picking him up from the airport and returning to his residence. The FBI also observed Reinhold using an Apple computer, the same brand of computer Adjani used to email and chat with Paycom.

B. *Obtaining and Executing the Search Warrant*

On January 23, 2004, based on the facts recited above and attested to in FBI Agent Cloney's affidavit (which was affixed to the warrant), a federal magistrate judge granted the government an arrest warrant for Adjani and a search warrant covering Adjani's Venice residence, his vehicle, his person and the residence of the individual who had stolen the confidential information from Paycom. The warrant specifically sought "evidence of violations of 18 U.S.C. § 875(d): Transmitting Threatening Communications With Intent to Commit Extortion." Further, the warrant expressly authorized seizure of:

> 5g. Records, documents and materials containing Paycom's or Epoch's master client control documents, Paycom's or Epoch's email database, or other company information relating to Paycom or Epoch.

5h. Records, documents and materials which reflect communications with Christopher Mallick, Clay Andrews, Joel Hall or other employees or officers of Paycom or Epoch.

5i. Any and all evidence of travel, including hotel bills and receipts, gasoline receipts, plane tickets, bus tickets, train tickets, or any other documents related to travel from January 8, 2004 to the present.

. . . .

5k. Computer, hard drives, computer disks, CD's, and other computer storage devices.

With respect to the computer search, the warrant prescribed the process to be followed: "In searching the data, the computer personnel will examine all of the data contained in the computer equipment and storage devices to view their precise contents and determine whether the data falls within the items to be seized as set forth herein." Additionally, it noted that "in order to search for data that is capable of being read or intercepted by a computer, law enforcement personnel will need to seize and search any computer equipment and storage device capable of being used to commit, further, or store evidence of the offense listed above."

On January 26, 2004, agents observed Reinhold driving Adjani, in a car registered to him, to his meeting with Paycom. While Adjani went into a hotel, Reinhold slipped into the backseat of his car, placing curtains over the windows. at this point, agents proceeded to search Adjani's car. That same day, agents executed the search warrant for Adjani's Venice residence. There they found and seized various computers and hard drives, including Reinhold's computer, which were later sent to an FBI computer lab to be searched. During that search process, the hard drive from Reinhold's computer revealed certain email correspondence between Reinhold and Adjani, implicating Reinhold in the extortion plot and supporting a charge of conspiracy against both of them.

The defendants successfully sought suppression of these seized email communications in the district court. This appeal requires us to determine whether the agents permissibly searched Reinhold's computer; whether the warrant satisfied our specificity standards; and whether the emails seized fell within the scope of the otherwise properly issued warrant.

II. ANALYSIS

A. *Probable Cause*

The government principally argues that contrary to the district court's finding and the defendants' assertions, the search warrant affidavit established probable cause to search all instrumentalities that might contain "evidence of violations of" 18 U.S.C. § 875(d), including Reinhold's computer and emails. Reinhold counters that the affidavit may have generally established probable cause, but did not do so with respect to her computer, because "in the affidavit, Reinhold was not labeled as a target, suspect, or co-conspirator."

1. *Probable cause to issue the warrant*

A search warrant is issued upon a showing of probable cause to believe that the legitimate object of a search is located in a particular place, and therefore safeguards an individual's interest in the privacy of his home and possessions against the unjustified intrusion of the police. *Steagald v. United States*, 451 U.S. 204, 213 (1981). As the Supreme Court has explained, the "probable cause standard is a practical, non-technical conception." *Illinois v. Gates*, 462 U.S. 213, 231 (1983). Furthermore, "probable cause is a fluid concept—turning on the assessment of probabilities in particular factual contexts—not readily, or even usefully, reduced to a neat set of legal rules." *Id.* at 232. The warrant here was supported by probable cause, because the affidavit submitted to the magistrate judge established that "there was a fair probability that contraband or evidence of a crime would be found in" computers at Adjani's residence. *See Gates*, 462 U.S. at 238. The extensive 24–page supporting affidavit described the extortion scheme in detail, including that Adjani possessed a computer-generated database and communicated with Paycom over email, requiring the use of a computer. Furthermore, the agent's affidavit explained the need to search computers, in particular, for evidence of the extortion scheme: "I know that considerable planning is typically performed to construct and consummate an extortion. The plan can be documented in the form of a simple written note or more elaborate information stored on computer equipment."

Probable cause exists if it would be reasonable to seek the evidence in the place indicated in the affidavit. The crime contemplated by the warrant was transmitting a threatening communication with intent to extort. *See* 18 U.S.C. § 875(d). To find evidence of extortion, the government would have probable cause to search for and seize instrumentalities likely to have been used to facilitate the transmission. The magistrate judge could rightfully assume that there was a "fair probability" that such evidence could be contained on computers or storage devices found in Adjani's residence.

2. *Probable cause to search "Reinhold's computer"*

Having held that the affidavit supporting the warrant established probable cause to search for and seize instrumentalities of the extortion (including records, files and computers) in Adjani's residence, we turn to Reinhold's contention that the probable cause for the Adjani warrant did not extend so far as to permit a search of her property. We disagree. The agents, acting pursuant to a valid warrant to look for evidence of a computer-based crime, searched computers found in Adjani's residence and to which he had apparent access. That one of the computers actually belonged to Reinhold did not exempt it from being searched, especially given her association with Adjani and participation (however potentially innocuous) in some of his activities as documented in the agent's supporting affidavit. The officers therefore did not act unreasonably in searching Reinhold's computer as a source of the evidence targeted by the warrant.

Reinhold's argument that there was no probable cause to search her computer, a private and personal piece of property, because the warrant failed to list her as a "target, suspect, or co-conspirator" misunderstands Fourth Amendment jurisprudence. Although individuals undoubtedly have a high expectation of privacy in the files stored on their personal computers, we have never held that agents may establish probable cause to search only those items owned or possessed by the criminal suspect. The law is to the contrary. "The critical element in a reasonable search is not that the owner of the property is suspected of crime but that there is reasonable cause to believe that the specific 'things' to be searched for and seized are located on the property to which entry is sought." *Zurcher v. Stanford Daily*, 436 U.S. 547, 556 (1978).

In *United States v. Hay*, 231 F.3d 630 (9th Cir. 2000), the defendant made an argument similar to Reinhold's, challenging the district court's ruling allowing evidence of child pornography found on his computer to be used against him at trial. Hay claimed that the affidavit submitted by officers to obtain a warrant did not establish probable cause to engage in a search of Hay's computer because "there was no evidence that he fell within a class of persons likely to collect and traffic in child pornography because the affidavit does not indicate that he was a child molester, pedophile, or collector of child pornography and sets forth no evidence that he solicited, sold or transmitted child pornography." *Id.* at 635. We rejected Hay's challenge, holding that "it is well established that a location can be searched for evidence of a crime even if there is no probable cause to arrest the person at the location." *Id.*

Likewise, there was no need here for the agents expressly to claim in the affidavit that they wanted to arrest Reinhold, or even that Reinhold was suspected of any criminal activity. The government needed only to satisfy the magistrate judge that there was probable cause to believe that evidence of the crime in question—here extortion—could be found on computers accessible to Adjani in his home, including—as it developed— Reinhold's computer. By setting forth the details of the extortion scheme and the instrumentalities of the crime, augmented by descriptions of Reinhold's involvement with Adjani, the government satisfied its burden. The magistrate judge therefore properly approved the warrant, which in turn encompassed all the computers found at Adjani's residence.

B. *Specificity Requirement*

The defendants argue that if the warrant did authorize a search that properly included Reinhold's computer, the warrant was fatally over-broad, justifying the district court's exclusion of the Reinhold emails. The government counters that the warrant satisfied the particularity standards articulated by this court, so exclusion was improper.

The Fourth Amendment's specificity requirement prevents officers from engaging in general, exploratory searches by limiting their discretion and providing specific guidance as to what can and cannot be searched and seized. However, the level of detail necessary in a warrant is related to the particular circumstances and the nature of the evidence sought. *See United States v. Spilotro*, 800 F.2d 959, 963 (9th Cir. 1986). Warrants which describe generic categories of items are not necessarily invalid if a more precise description of the items subject to seizure is not possible.

In determining whether a warrant is sufficiently particular, we consider one or more of the following factors:

> (1) whether probable cause exists to seize all items of a particular type described in the warrant; (2) whether the warrant sets out objective standards by which executing officers can differentiate items subject to seizure from those which are not; and (3) whether the government was able to describe the items more particularly in light of the information available to it at the time the warrant was issued.

Id. at 963.

Spilotro involved a warrant issued against individuals suspected of loan sharking and gambling activities. The warrant authorized "the seizure of address books, notebooks, notes, documents, records, assets, photographs, and other items and paraphernalia evidencing violations of the multiple criminal statutes listed." *Id.* at 964. It failed, however, to state the "precise identity, type, or contents of the records sought." *Id.* Partly because of this reason, we held that the warrant was not sufficiently specific to pass muster under the Fourth Amendment. More could have been done to tie the documents sought to the crimes alleged by, for example, stating that the police were searching for "records relating to loan sharking and gambling, including pay and collection sheets, lists of loan customers, loan accounts and telephone numbers." *Id.*

In contrast to *Spilotro*, the warrant to search Adjani's residence satisfied our specificity criteria. First, we have already held that there was probable cause to search the computers. As to the second factor, the warrant objectively described the items to be searched and seized with adequate specificity and sufficiently restricted the discretion of agents executing the search. The warrant affidavit began by limiting the search for evidence of a specific crime—transmitting threatening communications with intent to commit extortion. *See id.* ("Reference to a specific illegal activity can, in appropriate cases, provide substantive guidance for the officer's exercise of discretion in executing the warrant."); *see also United States v. Wong*, 334 F.3d 831, 837–38 (9th Cir. 2003) ("The specificity of the items listed in the warrant combined with the language ... directing officers to 'obtain data as it relates to this case' from the computers is sufficiently specific to focus the officer's search."). Further, unlike in *Spilotro*, the Adjani warrant provided the "precise identity" and nature of the items to be seized. For example, paragraph 5h of the warrant instructed agents to search for documents reflecting communications with three individuals or other employees of a specific company.

Also, paragraph 5i authorized seizure of "any" evidence of travel but provided a specific, though not exhaustive, list of possible documents that fell within this category and temporally restricted the breadth of the search. Moreover, the extensive statement of probable cause in the affidavit detailed the alleged crime and Adjani's unlawful scheme.

With respect to the final *Spilotro* factor, we conclude that the government described the items to be searched and seized as particularly as could be reasonably expected given the nature of the crime and the evidence it then possessed. The Adjani warrant "described in great detail the items one commonly expects to find on premises used for the criminal activities in question" *Spilotro*, 800 F.2d at 964.

Center Art Galleries–Hawaii, Inc. v. United States, 875 F.2d 747 (9th Cir. 1989), the principal case defendants rely upon in making their overbreadth argument, is distinguishable. In that case, we held that a warrant providing for "the almost unrestricted seizure of items which are 'evidence of violations of federal criminal law' without describing the specific crimes suspected is constitutionally inadequate." *Id.* at 750. In contrast, the government here did describe at some length both the nature of and the means of committing the crime. Further, unlike in *Center Art Galleries*, the affidavit was expressly incorporated into the warrant. *Id.* ("An affidavit can cure the overbreadth of a warrant if the affidavit is 'attached to and incorporated by reference in' the warrant.")

We understand the heightened specificity concerns in the computer context, given the vast amount of data they can store. As the defendants urge, the warrant arguably might have provided for a "less invasive search of Adjani's email 'inbox' and 'outbox' for the addressees specifically cited in the warrant, as opposed to the wholesale search of the contents of all emails purportedly looking for evidence 'reflecting' communications with those individuals." Avoiding that kind of specificity and limitation was not unreasonable under the circumstances here, however. To require such a pinpointed computer search, restricting the search to an email program or to specific search terms, would likely have failed to cast a sufficiently wide net to capture the evidence sought. Moreover, agents are limited by the longstanding principle that a duly issued warrant, even one with a thorough affidavit, may not be used to engage in a general, exploratory search.

Computer files are easy to disguise or rename, and were we to limit the warrant to such a specific search protocol, much evidence could escape discovery simply because of Adjani's (or Reinhold's) labeling of the files documenting Adjani's criminal activity. The government should not be required to trust the suspect's self-labeling when executing a warrant.

C. Scope of the Warrant

Even assuming that the warrant was supported by probable cause and was adequately specific such that a search of Reinhold's computer and emails were permissible, Reinhold argues that the actual emails sought to be introduced into evidence were outside the scope of the warrant. Again, we disagree.

The three seized emails the government seeks to admit clearly fall within the scope of paragraph 5h of the warrant affidavit, authorizing seizure of "records, documents and materials which reflect communications with Christopher Mallick, Clay Andrews, Joel Hall or other employees or officers of Paycom or Epoch," which are relevant evidence of violations of 18 U.S.C. § 875(d). Each email specifically refers to communication with Joel Hall or one of the stated companies (identifying them by name).[8] Reinhold's argument that the term "reflect communications with" should be read narrowly to cover only those emails sent between one of the named Paycom employees and Adjani is nonsensical. The government already had the emails sent between the victims of the extortion and Adjani—obtained from the victims themselves. The purpose of the warrant was to obtain further and corroborating evidence of the extortion scheme and Adjani's criminal intent in communicating with the victims, and the three emails plainly "reflect" the relevant communications specified in paragraph 5h.

To the extent Reinhold argues that the emails were outside the scope of the warrant because they implicated her in the crime and supported a charge of conspiracy to commit extortion (a crime not specifically mentioned in the warrant), we reject the argument. There is no rule, and Reinhold points to no case law suggesting otherwise, that evidence turned up while officers are rightfully searching a location under a properly issued warrant must be excluded simply because the evidence found may support charges for a related crime (or against a suspect) not expressly contemplated in the warrant.

In *United States v. Beusch*, 596 F.2d 871 (9th Cir. 1979), the defendants argued that certain seized items, including two ledgers and a file, should be excluded because they contained information unrelated to the suspect identified in the warrant. The defendants claimed that the officers impermissibly engaged in a general search by not segregating out those items implicating a third individual in the crime. We rejected this proposition and refused to impose the burden of segregation on the police. In so doing we held,

> All three items admittedly contained information seizable under the terms of the warrant and they therefore met the particularity requirement of the Fourth Amendment. As long as an item appears, at the time of the search, to contain evidence reasonably related to the purposes of the search, there is no reason absent some other Fourth Amendment violation to suppress it. The fact that an item

---

8. The first email, sent from Adjani to Reinhold, states, in relevant part, "I sent Joel the message." The second, a reply from Reinhold, states, "I thought that you were going to wait until after today if they don't respond to send Joel an email?" The third, another email from Reinhold to Adjani, states, "I assume you have read Joel's fax by now. Funny or sucky thing is that I had ran out the door just 3 minutes before he sent that to go to a payphone to call Epoch.... A girl answered and I asked for Joel Hall."

seized happens to contain other incriminating information not covered by the terms of the warrant does not compel its suppression, either in whole or in part. In so holding we are careful to point out that we are discussing single files and single ledgers, i.e., single items which, though theoretically separable, in fact constitute one volume or file folder.

Id. at 877. *Beusch* is analogous to the situation at hand. The agents were rightfully searching Reinhold's computer for evidence of Adjani's crime of extortion. They were looking in Reinhold's email program when they came across information that was both related to the purposes of their search and implicated Reinhold in the crime. That the evidence could now support a new charge against a new (but already identified) person does not compel its suppression. On these facts, we disagree with the district court's conclusion that the officers should have obtained a new search warrant when they came across the incriminating emails. In so concluding, we are careful to note that in this case the evidence discovered was clearly related to the crime referred to in the warrant. We need not decide to what extent the government would be able to introduce evidence discovered that the police knew, at the time of discovery, was not related to the crime cited in the warrant.

III. CONCLUSION

The Fourth Amendment incorporates a great many specific protections against unreasonable searches and seizures. The contours of these protections in the context of computer searches pose difficult questions. Computers are simultaneously file cabinets (with millions of files) and locked desk drawers; they can be repositories of innocent and deeply personal information, but also of evidence of crimes. The former must be protected, the latter discovered. As society grows ever more reliant on computers as a means of storing data and communicating, courts will be called upon to analyze novel legal issues and develop new rules within our well established Fourth Amendment jurisprudence. The fact of an increasingly technological world is not lost upon us as we consider the proper balance to strike between protecting an individual's right to privacy and ensuring that the government is able to prosecute suspected criminals effectively. In this era of rapid change, we are mindful of Justice Brandeis's worry in *Olmstead v. United States*,

> Ways may some day be developed by which the Government, without removing papers from secret drawers, can reproduce them in court, and by which it will be enabled to expose to a jury the most intimate occurrences of the home. Can it be that the Constitution affords no protection against such invasions of individual security?

277 U.S. 438, 474 (1928) (Brandeis, J., dissenting).

We do not now have occasion to address the myriad complex issues raised in deciding when a court should exclude evidence found on a computer, but are satisfied that the agents in this case acted properly in searching Reinhold's computer and seizing the emails in question here.

The district court erred in excluding these emails. Therefore, the district court's ruling on the motion to suppress is reversed, and this matter is remanded for further proceedings consistent with this opinion.

Notes and Questions

1. *Particularity and computer search warrants.* Most computer warrants are executed in two stages. First, the computer hardware is taken away; second, the computers are searched for electronic evidence. The physical search comes first and the electronic search comes second. Should the particularly requirement focus on the physical search stage, the electronic search stage, or both? For example, imagine a warrant states with exquisite particularity exactly what kinds of computer hardware will be seized at the first stage but gives no guidance on the evidence the computer may contain. Alternatively, imagine a warrant names the exact computer file that agents will look for at the second stage, but it doesn't say anything about what computers the agents plan to remove at the place to be searched. Are either of these warrants sufficiently particular?

2. In United States v. Riccardi, 405 F.3d 852 (10th Cir. 2005), police executed a warrant to search for and seize computers in a child pornography investigation. The warrant authorized investigators to search the defendant's home and seize his computer as well as:

> all electronic and magnetic media stored therein, together with all storage devises [sic], internal or external to the computer or computer system, including but not limited to floppy disks, diskettes, hard disks, magnetic tapes, removable media drives, optical media such as CD–ROM, printers, modems, and any other electronic or magnetic devises used as a peripheral to the computer or computer system, and all electronic media stored within such devises.

The police executed the warrant, seized the defendant's home computer, and later searched it and found images of child pornography. In an opinion by Judge McConnell, the Tenth Circuit held that the warrant violated the Fourth Amendment because it was not sufficiently particular. According to the Judge McConnell, "warrants for computer searches must affirmatively limit the search to evidence of specific federal crimes or specific types of material." *Id.* at 862.

> The warrant in this case was not limited to any particular files, or to any particular federal crime. * * * By its terms, the warrant thus permitted the officers to search for anything–from child pornography to tax returns to private correspondence. It seemed to authorize precisely the kind of wide-ranging exploratory search that the Framers intended to prohibit.

Id. at 862–63.

Despite this defect, the court admitted the evidence because the officers had relied on the warrant in good faith:

> In determining whether the good-faith exception should apply in a particular case, the inquiry is confined to the objectively ascertainable question whether a reasonably well trained officer would have known

that the search was illegal despite the magistrate's authorization. In answering this question, the court should consider all of the circumstances and assume that the executing officers have a reasonable knowledge of what the law prohibits. Even if the court finds the warrant to be facially invalid—as was the case here—it must also review the text of the warrant and the circumstances of the search to ascertain whether the agents might have reasonably presumed it to be valid.

In this case, upon finding thumbnail files of child pornography on Mr. Riccardi's computer, Agent Finch suspended his search and asked Detective Dickey if they needed a more specific warrant. Detective Dickey consulted with a prosecutor who gave assurances that an additional warrant was not required. Detective Dickey then informed Agent Finch that it would "likely be okay" and that the warrant covered the child pornography found on the computer.

The district court noted the following factors in support of applying the *Leon* exception: (1) the affidavit limited the search to child pornography; (2) the officers executing the warrant were involved in the investigation throughout, and one of the executing officers actually wrote the affidavit to support the application; (3) Agent Finch stopped to ask if the warrant was sufficient and received assurances from Detective Dickey; (4) the search methodology was limited to finding child pornography; and (5) investigators seized only evidence relevant to the crimes identified in the affidavit.

These factors, combined with the fact that, at Agent Finch's request, Detective Dickey called the prosecutor for assurances, persuade us that the district court was correct in finding that the *Leon* exception to the exclusionary rule applied and that the evidence obtained from the hard drive need not have been suppressed. The officers remained within the terms of the warrant as well as the affidavit, and did not conduct a "fishing expedition" beyond the scope of the authorized investigation. They did not search for, or seize, any materials for which probable cause had not been shown. By consulting the prosecutor, they showed their good faith in compliance with constitutional requirements. Nor do we think the defect in the warrant was so flagrant or obvious that the executing officers could not reasonably presume it to be valid.

Id. at 863–64.

Judge McConnell's opinion in *Riccardi* suggests that naming the crimes or types of material sought can limit the scope of the subsequent electronic search. But will such limitations actually limit the scope of the search? Imagine that FBI agents seize a computer and obtain a warrant to search it for "evidence of violations of 18 U.S.C. § 1030." Does that limitation provide real guidance that will limit the scope of the electronic search? Does it stop investigators from conducting a sweeping, comprehensive search of a computer's hard drive? Does naming the crime or material sought limit the search at the initial physical search stage at all?

3. In Davis v. Gracey, 111 F.3d 1472 (10th Cir. 1997), agents conducting an obscenity investigation obtained a warrant permitting the seizure of "equipment pertaining to the distribution or display of pornographic material in violation of state obscenity laws." Investigators seized two computer

servers used to provide digital images and e-mail for about 2,000 subscribers; the servers stored about 150,000 e-mails and about 500 megabytes of software. The owner of the computer and several customers filed a civil suit, claiming that the warrant was insufficiently particular. The Tenth Circuit disagreed:

> The description given in the warrant was sufficient to provide a meaningful limitation on the search, and was far narrower than those we have found lacking sufficient particularity. * * * The warrant here was confined to that equipment pertaining to the distribution or display of pornographic material. This description included only that equipment directly connected to the suspected criminal activity, not a wide range of equipment used for purposes unrelated to the suspected criminal activity. Nor did it encompass all the equipment one might expect to find at a legitimate business. Furthermore, the criminal activity referenced in the warrant was very narrow, providing a ready guide to determine if a given item was one that might be the instrument or evidence of the criminal activity. The warrant was not overbroad.

Id. at 1479.

4. *Probable cause and digital evidence.* In United States v. Gourde, 440 F.3d 1065 (9th Cir. 2006) (en banc), an undercover FBI agent discovered a website called "Lolitagurls.com." According to the agent, the site contained images of nude and partially-dressed girls, some prepubescent, along with text promising pictures of young girls 12–17 to those who paid the subscription fee of $19.95 per month. The agent purchased a subscription and confirmed that the site hosted hundreds of images of child pornography. The FBI seized the server that hosted the website and obtained the list of e-mail addresses used by paid subscribers to the site. The FBI then obtained a list of customers associated with these e-mail addresses from Lancelot Security, a credit card processing company that handled credit card processing and access control for Lolitagurls.com.

The FBI later executed warrants at the homes of many of the subscribers. The sole basis for the warrants was the paid subscription with the website. Micah Gourde was a subscriber to Lolitagurls.com for several months, and a search of his home pursuant to a warrant led to the seizure of his computer and the discovery of images of child pornography inside it. Gourde challenged the warrant on the ground that his membership with the website did not establish probable cause to search his home. The en banc Ninth Circuit rejected this argument in an opinion by Judge McKeown:

> Gourde subscribed to Lolitagurls.com for over two months, from November 2001 to January 2002. As a paying member, Gourde had unlimited access to hundreds of illegal images. He clearly had the means to receive and possess images in violation of 18 U.S.C. § 2252. But more importantly, Gourde's status as a member manifested his intention and desire to obtain illegal images.

> Membership is both a small step and a giant leap. To become a member requires what are at first glance little, easy steps. It was easy for Gourde to submit his home address, email address and credit card data, and he consented to have $19.95 deducted from his credit card every month. But these steps, however easy, only could have been

intentional and were not insignificant. Gourde could not have become a member by accident or by a mere click of a button. This reality is perhaps easier to see by comparing Gourde to other archetypical visitors to the site. Gourde was not an accidental browser, such as a student who came across the site after "Googling" the term "Lolita" while research- ing the Internet for a term paper on Nabokov's book. Nor was Gourde someone who took advantage of the free tour but, after viewing the site, balked at taking the active steps necessary to become a member and gain unlimited access to images of child pornography. Gourde is differ- ent still from a person who actually mustered the money and nerve to become a member but, the next morning, suffered buyer's remorse or a belated fear of prosecution and cancelled his subscription. Instead, Gourde became a member and never looked back—his membership ended because the FBI shut down the site. The affidavit left little doubt that Gourde had paid to obtain unlimited access to images of child pornography knowingly and willingly, and not involuntary, unwittingly, or even passively. With evidence from Lancelot Security, the FBI linked the email user—"gilbert_95@yahoo.com," a known subscriber to Lolita- gurls.com—to Gourde and to his home address in Castle Rock, Washing- ton.

Having paid for multi-month access to a child pornography site, Gourde was also stuck with the near certainty that his computer would contain evidence of a crime had he received or downloaded images in violation of § 2252. Thanks to the long memory of computers, any evidence of a crime was almost certainly still on his computer, even if he had tried to delete the images. FBI computer experts, cited in the affidavit, stated that "even if graphic image files have been deleted these files can easily be restored." In other words, his computer would contain at least the digital footprint of the images. It was unlikely that evidence of a crime would have been stale or missing, as less than four months had elapsed between the closing of the Lolitagurls.com website and the execution of the search warrant.

Given this triad of solid facts—the site had illegal images, Gourde intended to have and wanted access to these images, and these images were almost certainly retrievable from his computer if he had ever received or downloaded them—the only inference the magistrate judge needed to make to find probable cause was that there was a "fair probability" Gourde had, in fact, received or downloaded images.

Here, the reasonable inference that Gourde had received or down- loaded images easily meets the "fair probability" test. It neither strains logic nor defies common sense to conclude, based on the totality of these circumstances, that someone who paid for access for two months to a website that actually purveyed child pornography probably had viewed or downloaded such images onto his computer. Together these facts form the basis of the totality-of-the-circumstances analysis that informs the probable cause determination. Employing the principles of *Gates*— practicality, common sense, a fluid and nontechnical conception of probable cause, and deference to the magistrate's determination—we conclude that the search warrant was supported by probable cause.

Id. at 1070–71. Judge Kleinfeld dissented:

> In my view, the majority errs in concluding that there was probable cause for a search because its inferences depend on unarticulated assumptions that do not make sense. The majority implicitly assumes that a person who likes something probably possesses it, even if possession is against the law.
>
> The importance of this case is considerable because, for most people, their computers are their most private spaces. People commonly talk about the bedroom as a very private space, yet when they have parties, all the guests—including perfect strangers—are invited to toss their coats on the bed. But if one of those guests is caught exploring the host's computer, that will be his last invitation.
>
> There are just too many secrets on people's computers, most legal, some embarrassing, and some potentially tragic in their implications, for loose liberality in allowing search warrants. Emails and history links may show that someone is ordering medication for a disease being kept secret even from family members. Or they may show that someone's child is being counseled by parents for a serious problem that is none of anyone else's business. Or a married mother of three may be carrying on a steamy email correspondence with an old high school boyfriend. Or an otherwise respectable, middle-aged gentleman may be looking at dirty pictures. Just as a conscientious public official may be hounded out of office because a party guest found a homosexual magazine when she went to the bathroom at his house, people's lives may be ruined because of legal but embarrassing materials found on their computers. And, in all but the largest metropolitan areas, it really does not matter whether any formal charges ensue—if the police or other visitors find the material, it will be all over town and hinted at in the newspaper within a few days.
>
> Nor are secrets the only problem. Warrants ordinarily direct seizure, not just search, and computers are often shared by family members. Seizure of a shared family computer may, though unrelated to the law enforcement purpose, effectively confiscate a professor's book, a student's almost completed Ph.D. thesis, or a business's accounts payable and receivable. People cannot get their legitimate work done if their computer is at the police station because of someone else's suspected child pornography downloads. Sex with children is so disgusting to most of us that we may be too liberal in allowing searches when the government investigates child pornography cases. The privacy of people's computers is too important to let it be eroded by sexual disgust.
>
>   * * *
>
> The reason [Gourde] could not be assumed to possess child pornography is that possession of child pornography is a very serious crime and the affidavit did not say he had downloaded any. He could use the site to look at child pornography without downloading it, a reasonable assumption in the absence of evidence that he had downloaded images. Common sense suggests that everyone, pervert or not, has the desire to stay out of jail. The ordinary desire to stay out of jail is a factor that must be considered in the totality of circumstances. It would be irrational to

assume that an individual is indifferent between subjecting himself to criminal sanctions and avoiding them, when he can attain his object while avoiding them. To commit the crime for which the warrant sought evidence, one has to do something more than look: he must ship, produce, or at the least knowingly possess. The two child pornography statutes at issue do not say that *viewing* child pornography is a crime. Congress could perhaps make it a crime to pay to view such images, but it did not.

Id. at 1077–79. Judge Kleinfeld's argument hinges on a purported distinction between viewing and possessing child pornography. Is Judge Kleinfeld interpreting the law correctly? Does the validity of the warrant in *Gourde* hinge on whether *United States v. Tucker* is correct about what it means to "possess" digital images?

More broadly, consider the inferences a court must draw before concluding that membership in a website or online group connected to child pornography creates probable cause to search a member's home for contraband images. Satisfying this burden requires an explicit or implicit assessment of the following questions:

A. How likely is it that the defendant is the one who controlled the account when it was used to join the group?

B. How likely is it that the defendant signed up for the service with the intent to obtain illegal images?

C. How likely is it that the defendant received the images?

D. How likely is it that the defendant initially received the images at home?

E. How likely is it that the images are currently present in the home?

Are judges well-equipped to answer these questions?

5. Investigators often try to establish probable cause to search a home for evidence of computer crimes by tracing Internet Protocol (IP) addresses. In many cases, the investigators collect evidence by linking IP addresses to accounts and then accounts to physical addresses.

The basic technology of the Internet makes IP addresses an essential tool for tracing Internet activity. Whenever a user connects to the Internet, the service provider that provides the connection will assign the user a series of numbers known as an IP address that serves as the unique identifying address of his computer for that session (and in some cases, for all of that user's sessions). As a general matter, communications sent by or to that user across the Internet will contain that IP address. This means that when investigators know the IP address used in a session of Internet activity that is linked to a crime, they will first identify the service provider known to control the block of IP addresses that includes that specific address.

When investigators know that a particular IP address was used in criminal activity, they can contact the owner/operator of the server that controls the address and try to find out more information. For example, if an IP address belongs to a specific ISP, the ISP system administrator may have business records that indicate what account controlled that address when it was used in criminal activity. If the account is associated with a physical address—in the case of a home user, for example, the home address used for billing purposes—investigators can then focus their suspicion on that physical location.

6. *Probable cause, wireless networks, and wardriving.* Can investigators reliably trace IP addresses to physical locations when individuals connect to the Internet over a wireless network? Many home users host wireless access points that are left unsecured. Any individual within range of the access point can hop on the Internet using the IP address assigned to the home user.

Unsecured wireless access provides an increasingly popular way to hide criminal activity. One technique is "wardriving," a term for traveling around by car in search of open access points. *See* Brendan I. Koerner, *License to Wardrive*, Legal Affairs, May/June 2005, at 68. A wrongdoer may drive around a neighborhood, find an unsecured wireless access point, and commit crimes ranging from hacking to wire fraud from the comfort of his car parked nearby. When he is done, he can drive away. Weeks or even months later, the police will trace the criminal activity to the account associated with the open wireless network. When they arrive to execute a warrant, however, they will find no evidence. All of the evidence will have vanished from the scene when the criminal drove away weeks before, and the police may end up executing the warrant at the home of an entirely innocent individual. *See* Seth Schiesel, *Growth of Wireless Internet Opens New Path for Thieves*, N.Y. Times, March 19, 2005; Alex Leary, *Wi-Fi Cloaks A New Brand of Intruder*, St. Petersburg Times, July 4, 2005.

The popularity of unsecured wireless networks raises two problems for investigators. The first is practical: How can investigators trace a crime back to its source when the wrongdoer has disguised his identity by using an unsecured wireless access point? The second is legal: How does the possibility that a criminal will have disguised his identity by using another person's wireless access point change what the government must show to establish probable cause to search a home for evidence of crime? When should agents consider the possibility that evidence of a crime that traces back to a home was really the work of a stranger who hopped on to the home's unsecured wireless Internet connection?

7. *Staleness.* One issue that often arises in computer crime cases is the "staleness" of the government's probable cause. Digital evidence may be present one day but erased, deleted, or removed by the next. To establish probable cause, the government must show probable cause to believe evidence of crime exists at the place to be searched at the time the warrant is issued, not just at the time the crime was committed. If too much time has elapsed after the relevant time period of the government's evidence, that evidence may become stale and may no longer satisfy the probable cause standard.

How should courts address staleness concerns in the context of digital evidence? In child pornography cases, several courts have taken judicial notice of the practices of child pornography collectors. Judge Munson offered the following summary in United States v. Lamb, 945 F. Supp. 441 (N.D.N.Y. 1996):

The observation that images of child pornography are likely to be hoarded by persons interested in those materials in the privacy of their homes is supported by common sense and the cases. Since the materials are illegal to distribute and possess, initial collection is difficult. Having succeeded in obtaining images, collectors are unlikely to quickly destroy them. Because of their illegality and the imprimatur of severe social stigma such images carry, collectors will want to secret them in secure places, like a private residence. This proposition is not novel in either state or federal court: pedophiles, preferential child molesters, and child pornography collectors maintain their materials for significant periods of time.

Id. at 460 (citations omitted). Judge Munson then added an important caveat:

Of course, before the presumption that pedophiles, preferential child molesters, or child pornography collectors hoard their materials for extended periods can be applied, the judicial officer scrutinizing the warrant application must have sufficient information from which it can be concluded that the target falls within these categories. The Ninth Circuit rejected the application of this presumption in United States v. Weber, 923 F.2d 1338 (9th Cir. 1990). In *Weber*, the facts alleged in the affidavit in support of the warrant were that the suspect made one order solicited by the government for child pornography which was never delivered, and the suspect had been sent advertising material that was described by the customs agent who intercepted it as "apparently child pornography" two years earlier. From this sparse information, the Ninth Circuit ruled that there was insufficient information to determine whether the target of the search was a pedophile, child molester, or child pornography collector. Without such information, the expert opinion that such people maintain large collections of the illegal materials in their homes was of little value in determining whether evidence of crime would be located at the suspect's home.

Id. at 460–61.

How should courts deal with staleness concerns in other types of computer crime cases? Imagine Sarah uses her home personal computer to hack into a sensitive government server, and that one year later the police develop reason to believe Sarah was the intruder. The police apply for a warrant to search Sarah's house. What are the chances that Sarah's computer will continue to store evidence of the crime a year after the intrusion? Does evidence stay on a computer forever?

2. EXECUTING THE WARRANT

After a warrant is issued, it must be executed. This section considers the Fourth Amendment rules governing how investigators execute a warrant to seize and search for digital evidence.

UNITED STATES v. SCARFO

United States District Court for the District of New Jersey, 2001.
180 F. Supp. 2d 572.

POLITAN, District Judge.

This matter comes before the Court on Defendant Nicodemo S. Scarfo's pretrial motion for discovery and suppression of evidence. The Court heard oral argument on July 30, 2001 and again on September 7, 2001. Co-defendant Frank Paolercio joined in the motion. For the following reasons, * * * the motion to suppress evidence is denied.

This case presents an interesting issue of first impression dealing with the ever-present tension between individual privacy and liberty rights and law enforcement's use of new and advanced technology to vigorously investigate criminal activity. It appears that no district court in the country has addressed a similar issue. Of course, the matter takes on added importance in light of recent events and potential national security implications.

The Court shall briefly recite the facts and procedural history of the case. Acting pursuant to federal search warrants, the FBI on January 15, 1999, entered Scarfo and Paolercio's business office, Merchant Services of Essex County, to search for evidence of an illegal gambling and loansharking operation. During their search of Merchant Services, the FBI came across a personal computer and attempted to access its various files. They were unable to gain entry to an encrypted file named "Factors."

Suspecting the "Factors" file contained evidence of an illegal gambling and loansharking operation, the FBI returned to the location and, pursuant to two search warrants, installed what is known as a Key Logger System ("KLS") on the computer and/or computer keyboard in order to decipher the passphrase to the encrypted file, thereby gaining entry to the file. The KLS records the keystrokes an individual enters on a personal computer's keyboard. The government utilized the KLS in order to "catch" Scarfo's passphrases to the encrypted file while he was entering them onto his keyboard. Scarfo's personal computer features a modem for communication over telephone lines and he possesses an America Online account. The FBI obtained the passphrase to the "Factors" file and retrieved what is alleged to be incriminating evidence.

On June 21, 2000, a federal grand jury returned a three-count indictment against the Defendants charging them with gambling and loansharking. The Defendant Scarfo then filed his motion for discovery and to suppress the evidence recovered from his computer. After oral argument was heard on July 30, 2001, the Court ordered additional briefing by the parties. * * * The Defendants contend that the KLS constituted an unlawful general warrant in violation of the Fourth Amendment to the Constitution.

Scarfo argues that since the government had the ability to capture and record only those keystrokes relevant to the "passphrase" to the encrypted file, and because it received an unnecessary over-collection of data, the warrants were written and executed as general warrants. This claim is without merit.

The Fourth Amendment states that "no Warrants shall issue, but upon probable cause, supported by Oath or affirmation, and particularly describing the place to be searched, and the persons or things to be seized." U.S. Const. amend. IV. Where a search warrant is obtained, the Fourth Amendment requires a certain modicum of particularity in the language of the warrant with respect to the area and items to be searched and/or seized. The particularity requirement exists so that law enforcement officers are constrained from undertaking a boundless and exploratory rummaging through one's personal property.

From a review of the two Court Orders authorizing the searches along with the accompanying Affidavits, it is clear that the Court Orders suffer from no constitutional infirmity with respect to particularity. Magistrate Judge Donald Haneke's May 8, 1999, Order permitting the search of Scarfo's computer clearly states that Judge Haneke found probable cause existed to believe that "Nicodemo S. Scarfo has committed and continues to commit offenses in violation of Title 18, U.S.C. §§ 371, 892–94, 1955 and § 1962." *See* Order at ¶ 1. That Order further stated that there was "probable cause to believe that Nicodemo S. Scarfo's computer, located in the TARGET LOCATION, is being used to store business records of Scarfo's illegal gambling business and loan-sharking operation, and that the above mentioned records have been encrypted." *See* Order at ¶ 3.

Because the encrypted file could not be accessed via traditional investigative means, Judge Haneke's Order permitted law enforcement officers to "install and leave behind software, firmware, and/or hardware equipment which will monitor the inputted data entered on Nicodemo S. Scarfo's computer in the TARGET LOCATION so that the FBI can capture the password necessary to decrypt computer files by recording the key related information as they are entered." *See* Order at pp. 4. The Order also allowed the FBI to

> search for and seize business records in whatever form they are kept (e.g., written, mechanically or computer maintained and any necessary computer hardware, including computers, computer hard drives, floppy disks or other storage disks or tapes as necessary to access such information, as well as, seizing the mirror hard drive to preserve configuration files, public keys, private keys, and other information that may be of assistance in interpreting the password)—including address and telephone books and electronic storage devices; ledgers and other accounting-type records; banking records and statements; travel records; correspondence; memoranda; notes; calendars; and diaries—that contain information about the identities and whereabouts of conspirators, betting customers and

victim debtors, and/or that otherwise reveal the origin, receipt, concealment or distribution of criminal proceeds relating to illegal gambling, loansharking and other racketeering offenses.

See Order at pp. 4–5.

On its face, the Order is very comprehensive and lists the items, including the evidence in the encrypted file, to be seized with more than sufficient specificity. One would be hardpressed to draft a more specified or detailed search warrant than the May 8, 1999 Order. Indeed, it could not be written with more particularity. It specifically identifies each piece of evidence the FBI sought which would be linked to the particular crimes the FBI had probable cause to believe were committed. Most importantly, Judge Haneke's Order clearly specifies the key piece of the puzzle the FBI sought—Scarfo's passphrase to the encrypted file.

That the KLS certainly recorded keystrokes typed into Scarfo's keyboard *other* than the searched-for passphrase is of no consequence. This does not, as Scarfo argues, convert the limited search for the passphrase into a general exploratory search. During many lawful searches, police officers may not know the exact nature of the incriminating evidence sought until they stumble upon it. Just like searches for incriminating documents in a closet or filing cabinet, it is true that during a search for a passphrase some innocuous items will be at least cursorily perused in order to determine whether they are among those items to be seized.

Hence, no tenet of the Fourth Amendment prohibits a search merely because it cannot be performed with surgical precision. Where proof of wrongdoing depends upon documents or computer passphrases whose precise nature cannot be known in advance, law enforcement officers must be afforded the leeway to wade through a potential morass of information in the target location to find the particular evidence which is properly specified in the warrant. As the Supreme Court stated in Andresen v. Maryland, 427 U.S. 463, 482 (1976), "the complexity of an illegal scheme may not be used as a shield to avoid detection when the [government] has demonstrated probable cause to believe that a crime has been committed and probable cause to believe that evidence of this crime is in the suspect's possession." Accordingly, Scarfo's claim that the warrants were written and executed as general warrants is rejected.

In this day and age, it appears that on a daily basis we are overwhelmed with new and exciting, technologically-advanced gadgetry. Indeed, the amazing capabilities bestowed upon us by science are at times mind-boggling. As a result, we must be ever vigilant against the evisceration of Constitutional rights at the hands of modern technology. Yet, at the same time, it is likewise true that modern-day criminals have also embraced technological advances and used them to further their felonious purposes. Each day, advanced computer technologies and the increased accessibility to the Internet means criminal behavior is becoming more sophisticated and complex. This includes the ability to find new ways to commit old crimes, as well as new crimes beyond the comprehension of courts. As a result of this surge in so-called "cyber crime," law enforcement's ability to vigorously pursue such rogues cannot be hindered where all Constitutional limitations are scrupulously observed.

Notes and Questions

1. The key logger device installed in *Scarfo* permitted real-time surveillance of the keystrokes Scarfo entered into his computer. Most computer search cases do not involve real-time surveillance; in most cases, the government retrieves information stored inside a storage device such as a computer hard drive. However, both situations present a needle-in-a-haystack problem. The government has a warrant that authorizes a search for specific evidence located somewhere in the haystack of evidence inside the computer, and investigators must try to find the evidentiary needle.

What rules should regulate this process? In *Scarfo*, Judge Politan concludes that "law enforcement officers must be afforded the leeway to wade through a potential morass of information in the target location to find the particular evidence which is properly specified in the warrant." But why? And how much leeway is too much? What rules should the courts impose to regulate the process of retrieving evidence from a computer pursuant to a warrant? Should the police be permitted to take whatever steps are necessary to find the needle in the electronic haystack?

2. In United States v. Ross, 456 U.S. 798, 820–21 (1982), the Supreme Court articulated the following standards for executing search warrants in the context of automobile searches:

> A lawful search of fixed premises generally extends to the entire area in which the object of the search may be found[.] * * * Thus, a warrant that authorizes an officer to search a home for illegal weapons also provides authority to open closets, chests, drawers, and containers in which the weapon might be found. A warrant to open a footlocker to search for marihuana would also authorize the opening of packages found inside. A warrant to search a vehicle would support a search of every part of the vehicle that might contain the object of the search. When a legitimate search is under way, and when its purpose and its limits have been precisely defined, nice distinctions between closets, drawers, and containers, in the case of a home, or between glove compartments, upholstered seats, trunks, and wrapped packages, in the case of a vehicle, must give way to the interest in the prompt and efficient completion of the task at hand.

Is *Scarfo* simply a routine application of *Ross*? Are searches of computers different from searches of cars?

3. The government needed Scarfo's passphrase to decrypt what investigators believed was an important computer file. The government collected the passphrase by obtaining a warrant and then installing a key logger surveillance system on Scarfo's personal computer. But was this necessary? Did the government have alternative ways of decrypting the seized file?

Investigators could have tried issuing a grand jury subpoena ordering Scarfo to disclose his passphrase to the grand jury. This raises two questions.

First, does Scarfo have a Fifth Amendment privilege that trumps the subpoena? And second, if he has no privilege, what are the chances that Scarfo would actually divulge the passphrase rather than claim to forget it? The answer to the second question (the odds are very low) presumably explains why there are no cases on the first question. However, a number of scholars have tackled the first question. *See, e.g.,* Phillip R. Reitinger, *Compelled Production of Plaintext and Keys,* 1996 U. Chi. Legal F. 171; Adam C. Bonin, *Protecting Protection: First and Fifth Amendment Challenges to Cryptography Regulation,* 1996 U. Chi. Legal F. 495, 503; Greg Sergienko, United States v. Hubbell: *Encryption and the Discovery of Documents,* 7 Rich. J.L. & Tech. 31 (2001).

Another way to bypass Scarfo's encryption would have been to guess the passphrase, either using a computer or by manually entering in possible phrases. In the Scarfo case, at least, the latter approach might have worked. According to press reports, Scarfo used his father's federal prison ID number as his passphrase. *See* Jim Smith, *Scarfo Jr. Jailed for Bookmaking,* Phila. Daily News, June 29, 2002.

4. *Seizing computers and offsite searches.* Searching a computer usually takes many hours and often requires special tools. In light of this practical concern, investigators normally seize computers first and search them offsite at a later date. Does the Fourth Amendment permit this seize-first, search-later approach? Or does it require the police to search the computer at the place to be searched when the warrant is initially executed?

The Supreme Court has never addressed this question. Lower courts have concluded that search warrants give the police broad authority to seize computers and search them later offsite. An early example is United States v. Schandl, 947 F.2d 462 (11th Cir. 1991). In *Schandl,* investigators seized paper documents and computer discs at the suspect's home and office as part of an investigation into tax evasion. The defendant later claimed that the Fourth Amendment required investigators to search through the documents and papers onsite rather than seize them and search them offsite. The Eleventh Circuit rejected the defendant's argument:

> It was inevitable that some irrelevant materials would be seized as agents searched through numerous documents for evidence of tax evasion and failure to file, crimes that are generally only detected through the careful analysis and synthesis of a large number of documents. Indeed, it might have been far more disruptive had the agents made a thorough search of each individual document and computer disc before removing it from Schandl's home and office. To insist on such a practice would substantially increase the time required to conduct the search, thereby aggravating the intrusiveness of the search.

Id. at 465–66.

Later courts have adopted a similar approach. For example, in United States v. Hill, ___ F.3d ___, 2006 WL 2328721 (9th Cir. 2006), a computer repairman came across child pornography stored in a personal computer. The computer's owner retrieved the computer from the repairman before the police could intervene, and state police then obtained a warrant to search the suspect's apartment for the computer and any computer storage devices. The officers executed the search but did not find the computer. However, the agents did find and seize several CD–ROMs, zip disks, and floppy diskettes from the defendant's bedroom, and a subsequent off-site search revealed that two of the zip disks contained child pornography. The Ninth Circuit held that the seizure of all of the storage devices was permissible:

> [I]s impossible to tell what a computer storage medium contains just by looking at it. Rather, one has to examine it electronically, using a computer that is running the appropriate operating system, hardware and software. The police had no assurance they would find such a computer at the scene—nor did they, for that matter—or that, if they found one, they could bypass any security measures and operate it.
>
> Defendant suggests that the police could have brought their own laptop computer: Having probable cause to seize only computer storage media that contained certain types of files, the police should have been required to bring with them the equipment necessary to separate the sheep from the goats. Defendant's argument raises an important question about how police must execute seizures pursuant to a warrant. Because seizable materials are seldom found neatly separated from their non-seizable counterparts, how much separating must police do at the scene to avoid taking items that are neither contraband nor evidence of criminal activity?
>
> As always under the Fourth Amendment, the standard is reasonableness. To take an extreme example, if police have probable cause to seize business records, the warrant could not authorize seizure of every piece of paper on the premises on the theory that the police conducting the search might not know how to read.
>
> The court concludes that the police were not required to bring with them equipment capable of reading computer storage media and an officer competent to operate it. Doing so would have posed significant technical problems and made the search more intrusive. To ensure that they could access any electronic storage medium they might find at the scene, police would have needed far more than an ordinary laptop computer. Because computers in common use run a variety of operating systems—various versions or flavors of Windows, Mac OS and Linux, to name only the most common—police would have had to bring with them a computer (or computers) equipped to read not only all of the major media types, but also files encoded by all major operating systems. Because operating systems, media types, file systems and file types are continually evolving, police departments would frequently have to modify their computers to keep them up-to-date. This would not be an insuperable obstacle for larger police departments and federal law enforcement agencies, but it would pose a significant burden on smaller agencies.
>
> Even if the police were to bring with them a properly equipped computer, and someone competent to operate it, using it would pose two significant problems. First, there is a serious risk that the police might damage the storage medium or compromise the integrity of the evidence by attempting to access the data at the scene. As everyone who has accidentally erased a computer file knows, it is fairly easy to make mistakes when operating computer equipment, especially equipment one is not intimately familiar with. The risk that the officer trying to read the suspect's storage medium on the police laptop will make a wrong

move and erase what is on the disk is not trivial. Even if the officer executes his task flawlessly, there might be a power failure or equipment malfunction that could affect the contents of the medium being searched. For that reason, experts will make a back-up copy of the medium before they start manipulating its contents. Various other technical problems might arise; without the necessary tools and expertise to deal with them, any effort to read computer files at the scene is fraught with difficulty and risk.

Second, the process of searching the files at the scene can take a long time. To be certain that the medium in question does *not* contain any seizable material, the officers would have to examine every one of what may be thousands of files on a disk—a process that could take many hours and perhaps days. Taking that much time to conduct the search would not only impose a significant and unjustified burden on police resources, it would also make the search more intrusive. Police would have to be present on the suspect's premises while the search was in progress, and this would necessarily interfere with the suspect's access to his home or business. If the search took hours or days, the intrusion would continue for that entire period, compromising the Fourth Amendment value of making police searches as brief and non-intrusive as possible.

Id. at *5–*6 (quoting United States v. Hill, 322 F.Supp.2d 1081, 1088–90 (C.D. Cal. 2004) (Kozinski, J.)).

Computer search warrant affidavits often articulate such practical concerns. The affidavits include an explanation of why investigators may need to seize the computers and take them offsite for review. Courts have relied on such explanations in the course of holding that offsite searches are permissible. *See, e.g.,* United States v. Upham, 168 F.3d 532, 535 (1st Cir. 1999) ("[I]t is no easy task to search a well-laden hard drive by going through all of the information it contains[.] The record shows that the mechanics of the search for images later performed off site could not readily have been done on the spot.").

In *United States v. Hill*, the Ninth Circuit took an additional step and held that such an explanation is a constitutional requirement if the government wants to seize computers first and then later search them offsite:

Although computer technology may in theory justify blanket seizures for the reasons discussed above, the government must still demonstrate to the magistrate *factually* why such a broad search and seizure authority is reasonable in the case at hand. There may well be situations where the government has no basis for believing that a computer search would involve the kind of technological problems that would make an immediate onsite search and selective removal of relevant evidence impracticable. Thus, there must be some threshold showing before the government may "seize the haystack to look for the needle."

We do not approve of issuing warrants authorizing blanket removal of all computer storage media for later examination when there is no affidavit giving a reasonable explanation * * * as to why a wholesale seizure is necessary. * * * For some people, computer files are the exclusive means of managing one's life—such as maintaining a calendar of appointments or paying bills. Thus, there may be significant collateral consequences resulting from a lengthy, indiscriminate seizure of all such files.

Hill, ___ F.3d ___, 2006 WL 2328721, at *7–*8, n.12. Notably, however, the *Hill* court further held that suppression is not an appropriate remedy when this requirement is violated. Although the court's opinion is not entirely clear on this point, it seems to suggest that courts should not suppress evidence on the grounds that the affidavit failed to justify a "seize-first, search-later" search procedure so long as the agents seized the computers because of practical concerns rather than a wish to conduct a 'fishing expedition.' *See id.* at *9. Should courts routinely permit investigators to seize computers and search them offsite? Should magistrate judges require a showing of need in the affidavit before they authorize an offsite seizure? If courts require such a showing, should form language be sufficient? Are your answers to these questions contingent on the technical realities of computer searches?

5. If a warrant does not expressly state that it permits the seizure of computers, should courts nonetheless allow investigators to seize computers they come across during the search if they believe the computers may contain evidence described in the warrant? Imagine investigators execute a search for particular "documents" or "papers," and during the search they come across a computer. Can the investigators seize the computer because it may contain the "documents" or "papers" in electronic form?

Courts have generally allowed the seizure of computers in such circumstances. For example, in People v. Gall, 30 P.3d 145 (Colo. 2001) (en banc), the police were investigating reports that a suspect planned to kill several people at work. Investigators obtained a warrant to search the suspect's home for a number of items, including "[a]ny and all written or printed material which shows an intent to do physical harm or physical damage against any person or building" and "[a]ny documents or materials that show the occupier or possessor of the premises." During the search, investigators came across and seized two desktop computers from the living room and five laptop computers found in individual carrying cases on the floor of one of the defendant's closet. The five laptop computers turned out to be stolen, and the defendant was charged with receiving stolen property (among other things). On appeal, the defendant argued that the seizure of the computers was impermissible because it was not authorized by the warrant. A 4–3 majority of the Colorado Supreme Court disagreed, concluding that the warrant could be construed to include the computers:

> In deciding whether items discovered during the execution of a search warrant are within the scope of the warrant, police officers are not obliged to interpret its terms narrowly. They may search the location authorized by the warrant, including any containers at that location that are reasonably likely to contain items described in the warrant. This container rationale is equally applicable to nontraditional, technological "containers" that are reasonably likely to hold information in less tangible forms. Similarly a warrant cannot be expected to anticipate every form an item or repository of information may take, and therefore courts have affirmed the seizure of things that are similar to, or the "functional equivalent" of, items enumerated in a warrant, as well as containers in which they are reasonably likely to be found.

Id. at 153. In dissent, Justice Martinez argued that courts should not permit computers to be seized unless the computers are expressly named in the warrant:

> In my view, the warrant here was insufficient to justify the seizure or search of the computers in this case because the warrant sought

writings, not computers. Computers are far more complex and versatile than mere writings and their purpose is significantly different from just a container storing writings. As such, the warrant authorizing the seizure of writings was not sufficiently particularized to include computers. We require a warrant to particularly describe the things to be seized in order to avoid the harm to privacy inherent in the seizure of items that are not the subject of a search. This purpose is not served if computers are seized when writings are sought.

Id. at 160 (Martinez, J., dissenting).

Which side is right—the majority or the dissent? Should warrants that permit the seizure of writings or documents automatically be construed to permit the seizure of any computer devices that may contain such writings or documents? Should computers be seized in every case? If not, how should courts determine when the seizure of a computer is necessary? How can judges or police officers know when a computer should be seized given that they normally will not know what evidence it contains until it is searched? And how are the answers to these questions changing as more and more devices and tools are becoming computerized?

6.   When a defendant moves to suppress evidence obtained pursuant to a facially valid warrant, the admissibility of the evidence usually depends on whether the evidence falls within the scope of the warrant. If the evidence is construed to fall beyond the scope of the warrant, the evidence is excluded unless it fits within the "plain view" exception (discussed in more detail shortly). If the evidence fits within the scope of the warrant, however, it will be admitted unless the warrant was executed in "flagrant disregard" of the warrant's terms.

The "flagrant disregard" standard is very hard for a defense attorney to satisfy. Agents execute a warrant in "flagrant disregard" of its terms only if the search so grossly exceeds what the warrant permits that the authorized search appears to be merely a pretext for a fishing expedition through the target's private property. *See, e.g.,* United States v. Shi Yan Liu, 239 F.3d 138, 140–42 (2d Cir. 2000). Is this burden too high? What kind of search through a computer would be in "flagrant disregard" of the warrant? Should courts regulate computer searches more closely than traditional physical searches, or is the traditional "flagrant disregard" standard appropriate?

7.   *The Privacy Protection Act and server searches.* Can the government obtain a warrant to search and seize the servers at an ISP to obtain account information relating to one of the ISP's subscribers? Put another way, if there is probable cause to believe an individual account contains evidence of a crime, can investigators obtain a warrant to seize the "haystack" of the ISP's servers just to search for the "needle" of the account?

As a practical matter, investigators will almost never physically seize servers used by a third party such as an ISP. The ISP will have no involvement with the offense, and its employees normally will be willing to share the evidence with law enforcement pursuant to proper court orders. (Almost all ISPs have employees tasked with complying with court orders served by criminal investigators. The next chapter explains the governing statutory law.)

As a matter of Fourth Amendment law, however, such searches are permissible. In Zurcher v. Stanford Daily, 436 U.S. 547 (1978), the Supreme

Court held that the Fourth Amendment permitted investigators to execute a search warrant at a newspaper for evidence of crime that the newspaper was believed to have gathered in the course of reporting the news. The Court reasoned that the Fourth Amendment's probable cause and particularity requirement already struck the proper balance, and that no new constitutional rules were needed in a case where the owner of the property searched was an innocent third-party publisher. The same rationale presumably permits searches of ISPs for evidence in individual accounts.

Although such a search may be permissible under the Fourth Amendment, it may violate a federal statute known as the Privacy Protection Act of 1980 (PPA), codified at 42 U.S.C. § 2000aa. The PPA is a complex law, and the details of the statute need not be explored here. In essence, the statute permits innocent third parties to bring a civil cause of action for damages against criminal investigators that search for and seize evidence from them relating to First Amendment activities. The statute was passed in response to *Zurcher,* and would have permitted the newspaper in that case to sue the police for damages. Because servers will often hold evidence relating to First Amendment activities of innocent third parties, searches and seizures of servers may raise difficult questions of civil liability under the PPA. *See, e.g.,* Steve Jackson Games, Inc. v. United States Secret Service, 816 F. Supp. 432 (W.D. Tex. 1993). For a thorough discussion of the PPA and its application to computer server searches, see http://www.cybercrime.gov/s&smanual2002.htm#_IIB2_.

3. PLAIN VIEW

The plain view doctrine is an exception to the general rule that the police can only seize evidence within the scope of a valid search warrant. Under this doctrine, investigators can seize evidence unrelated to the justification for the search if the incriminating nature of the evidence is immediately apparent and the search leading to its discovery was otherwise lawful.

The plain view exception often arises in computer cases because the computer forensic process is comprehensive, and computers can store an extraordinary amount of information. Investigators searching for evidence with a warrant for one kind of evidence often come across evidence of unrelated criminal activity. A great deal of unrelated evidence comes into plain view. When can that evidence be admitted in court?

UNITED STATES v. GRAY

United States District Court for the Eastern District of Virginia, 1999.
78 F. Supp. 2d 524.

ELLIS, District Judge.

This is a prosecution for (i) unlawfully accessing a government computer in violation of 18 U.S.C. § 1030(a)(2)(B) and (a)(2)(C), (ii) unlawfully accessing a government computer causing damage thereto, in violation of 18 U.S.C. § 1030(a)(5)(C), and (iii) possession of child pornography, in violation of 18 U.S.C. § 2252A(a)(5)(B). Pretrial motions *inter alia* raised * * * whether evidence of child pornography discovered during a search of defendant's computer files authorized by an unrelated warrant must be suppressed as beyond the scope of the warrant.

I.

On February 5, 1999, FBI agents executed a search warrant at defendant's home in Arlington, Virginia in connection with an investigation of unauthorized computer intrusions at the National Institute of Health's National Library of Medicine ("NLM"). Four computers belonging to defendant were seized and removed from defendant's home. At the FBI office, Special Agent Arthur Ehuan, of the Computer Analysis Response Team ("CART") made copies of the contents of the computers' electronic storage media, or hard drives. These copies, which Agent Ehuan made on magneto-optical disks, were in digital form. To translate the stored information into readable form, Agent Ehuan planned to make a series of CD–ROMs, so that the case agent, Special Agent Craig Sorum, could read and access defendant's files.

Prior to making the CD–ROMs. Agent Ehuan created, and gave to Agent Sorum, a separate CD–ROM containing a list of the directory structures of the hard drives on each of the four computers. Using this disc, Agent Sorum then performed a text string search of the file structures and identified which computers, of the four seized, appeared to contain the text strings most closely associated with the NLM items listed in the search warrant. Agent Sorum then asked Agent Ehuan to concentrate first on making readable CD–ROMs for this computer.

Before making the CD–ROMs, Agent Ehuan opened many of the directories and subdirectories on the targeted hard drive to determine the size of the files and to gauge how many directories would fit on a single CD–ROM, which can store only 650 megabytes, far less than the capacity of the magneto-optical disks. After determining which directories could be copied onto a particular CD–ROM, Agent Ehuan began the copying process. While information was being copied onto the CD–ROMs, a process that consumed approximately 45 minutes to an hour, Agent Ehuan, pursuant to CART routine practice, opened and looked briefly at each of the files contained in the directories and subdirectories being copied. CART agents routinely perform such preliminary reviews, opening files as they are being copied onto CD–ROMs to look for the materials listed in the search warrant in the hope that they might facilitate the case agent's search.[3]

Following this procedure, Agent Ehuan continued opening files and subdirectories until the copying process was completed, at which point he began storing information on the next CD–ROM. In this way, Agent Ehuan was able to open approximately 80% of the files from the targeted

3. Although he was not the case agent, Agent Ehuan knew what types of materials were the subject of the search, i.e., NLM documents and "hacker" materials, such as source code, and therefore he could focus his search accordingly. In the course of the evidentiary hearing, the term "hacker" was used in a manner consistent with its ordinary colloquial meaning to describe a person who breaks into computer systems.

hard drive. To open the directory files, Agent Ehuan used a program called CompuPic. When Agent Ehuan opened a file using CompuPic, thumbnail-sized images of all of the items contained within that file, pictures or text documents, would appear on the screen. This program enabled Agent Ehuan, upon opening a file, to see instantly the nature of the material contained within that file.

As Agent Ehuan was preparing to copy material onto the eighth CD–ROM, he opened a directory entitled "BBS," which is a common abbreviation for "Bulletin Board System/Service," in order to see the list of the individual files and subdirectories contained in that directory. He then selected which of the subdirectories and files from BBS could be transferred to the CD–ROM by estimating how many of them, added together, would aggregate to 650 megabytes of information. Next, he began transferring files to the CD–ROM. While this was underway, Agent Ehuan, pursuant to his normal practice, opened most of the files contained within the BBS directory, some of which contained adult pornography, some of which were text files. In the course of opening the files in the BBS directory, Agent Ehuan opened a subdirectory entitled "Teen," which contained several files with the suffix ".jpg," which commonly denotes a picture file.[5] Like a number of others, this subdirectory contained pornographic pictures, but these, Agent Ehuan thought, might also include images of minors in sexually explicit poses. Yet, he could not be certain, and, as the subdirectory did not contain any of the materials identified in the warrant, or other obvious evidence of a crime, Agent Ehuan continued his search of the BBS directory pursuant to the warrant. Thereafter, he saw a subdirectory entitled "Tiny Teen." The name of this subdirectory caused Agent Ehuan to wonder if the subdirectory contained child pornography. He testified, however, that he opened the "Tiny Teen" subdirectory not because he believed it might contain child pornography, but rather because it was the next subdirectory listed and he was opening all of the subdirectories as part of his routine search for the items listed in the warrant.

When he opened the "Tiny Teen" subdirectory, Agent Ehuan discovered yet another series of pornographic pictures, this time, however, he believed some of the pictures contained images of minors. He then asked another CART agent to view the pictures displayed on his computer screen. On doing so, this agent agreed the pictures appeared to be of minors. Agent Ehuan then notified Agent Sorum of his discovery, who after viewing the same images, also concluded that they contained child pornography. Agent Ehuan testified that, at that point, he may have returned to the subdirectory "Teen" to see if that directory indeed contained pornographic images of minors. After the brief return to the

---

5. The NLM files that were the subject of the search were believed likely to be text files. Agent Ehuan nonetheless opened files that were labeled as picture files because computer files can be misleadingly labeled, particularly if the owner of those files is trying to conceal illegal materials. Indeed, in the course of this search, Agent Ehuan discovered some text files that were, in fact, mixed in with picture files. Moreover, Agent Ehuan did not believe that the warrant foreclosed the possibility that the NLM materials might include pictures.

"Teen" subdirectory, however, Agent Ehuan ceased his search and he, based on what he had already discovered, obtained a second warrant authorizing a search of defendant's computer files for child pornography. This search disclosed additional images of child pornography, which, together with the images that triggered the application for the warrant, are the subject of defendant's motion to suppress.

II.

Defendant moves to suppress the evidence gained from Agent Ehuan's search of the "Teen" and "Tiny Teen" subdirectories on the ground that the search of these subdirectories was beyond the scope of the warrant authorizing a search for NLM documents and hacker materials.

The primary rules governing search warrants are too well-established to be disputed. The Fourth Amendment requires that a search warrant describe the things to be seized with sufficient particularity to prevent a general exploratory rummaging in a person's belongings. To prevent such rummaging, therefore, a warrant must enable the executing officer to ascertain and identify with reasonable certainty those items that the magistrate has authorized him to seize. In some searches, however, it is not immediately apparent whether or not an object is within the scope of a search warrant; in such cases, an officer must examine the object simply to determine whether or not it is one that he is authorized to seize. Searches of records or documents present a variant of this principle, as documents, unlike illegal drugs or other contraband, may not appear incriminating on their face. As a result, in any search for records or documents, "innocuous records must be examined to determine whether they fall into the category of those papers covered by the search warrant." United States v. Kufrovich, 997 F. Supp. 246, 264 (D. Conn.1997) (citing Andresen v. Maryland, 427 U.S. 463, 482 n. 11 (1976)). Although care must be taken to minimize the intrusion, records searches require that many, and often all, documents in the targeted location be searched because few people keep documents of their criminal transactions in a folder marked 'crime records.' Thus, agents authorized by warrant to search a home or office for documents containing certain specific information are entitled to examine all files located at the site to look for the specified information. So it is not surprising, then, that in the course of conducting a lawful search pursuant to a search warrant, law enforcement agents often discover evidence of criminal activity other than that which is the subject of the warrant. If an agent sees, in plain view, evidence of criminal activity other than that for which she is searching, this does not constitute an unreasonable search under the Fourth Amendment, for viewing an article that is already in plain view does not involve an invasion of privacy. Further, such evidence may be seized under the "plain view" exception to the warrant requirement, provided that (1) the officer is lawfully in a place from which the object may be plainly viewed; (2) the officer has a lawful right of access to the object itself; and (3) the object's incriminating character is immediately apparent. These principles applied in the context of a document or record search means that, if an agent searching files pursuant to a search warrant discovers a document that contains evidence of another crime, that document can be seized under the "plain view" exception to the warrant requirement.

These principles are also dispositive of the instant case, as searches of computer files present the same problem as document searches—the intermingling of relevant and irrelevant materials—but to a heightened degree because of the massive storage capacity of modern computers. Thus, although care must be taken to ensure a computer search is not overbroad, searches of computer records are no less constitutional than searches of physical records, where innocuous documents may be scanned to ascertain their relevancy.

It follows, then, that Agent Ehuan's search of the "Teen" and "Tiny Teen" subdirectories was not beyond the scope of the search warrant. In searching for the items listed in the warrant, Agent Ehuan was entitled to examine all of defendant's files to determine whether they contained items that fell within the scope of the warrant. In the course of doing so, he inadvertently discovered evidence of child pornography, which was clearly incriminating on its face. As Agent Ehuan was lawfully searching the "Teen" and "Tiny Teen" subdirectories pursuant to the first warrant when he saw the illegal pornography, viewing that evidence did not constitute an unreasonable search under the Fourth Amendment.

It is not persuasive to argue, as defendant does, that Agent Ehuan knew the two subdirectories did not contain NLM documents or hacker materials when he searched them because many of the files were tagged with the ".jpg" suffix, indicating a picture file, and none of the materials covered by the warrant were believed to be pictures. While the ".jpg" suffix generally denotes a picture file, there is no requirement that it do so, and, as a result, Agent Ehuan could not be certain that files with the ".jpg" suffix did not contain the materials for which he was authorized to search. Indeed, Agent Ehuan would have been remiss not to search files with a ".jpg" suffix simply because such files are generally pictures files, and he believed the NLM documents and hacker materials were more likely to be text files. He knew from his experience that computer hackers often intentionally mislabel files, or attempt to bury incriminating files within innocuously named directories. Indeed, in the course of his search of defendant's computer files, Agent Ehuan found some text files mixed in with picture files. This serves to underscore the soundness of the conclusion that Agent Ehuan was not required to accept as accurate any file name or suffix and limit his search accordingly.[8]

8. Defendant's proffered expert testimony does not change this result. The resolution of the motion to suppress does not turn on whether Agent Ehuan conducted the most technically advanced search possible, but on whether the search, as conducted was reasonable. *See Florida v. Jimeno,* 500 U.S. 248, 250 (1991). Even assuming that the CompuPic program could have been modified to allow the searching agent to determine, without viewing the file, whether it contained pictures or text, as the proffered testimony indicates, Agent Ehuan's search was reasonable under the Fourth

Defendant further argues that Agent Ehuan, having been alerted by the names of the "Teen" and "Tiny Teen" subdirectories, was looking for child pornography when he opened the two subdirectories. Agent Ehuan testified persuasively to the contrary; he stated that, while the names of the subdirectories were suspicious to him, he opened the "Teen" and "Tiny Teen" subdirectories in the course of a systematic search of the BBS directory. In other words, Agent Ehuan did not target those particular subdirectories because of their names, and, at all times, he was searching for the materials that were the subject of the search warrant.

The Tenth Circuit's recent decision in United States v. Carey, 172 F.3d 1268 (10th Cir. 1999), on which defendant chiefly relies, does not compel a different result; it is, in an important way, factually distinguishable, and ultimately supportive of the result reached here. In *Carey,* police accidentally discovered child pornography on the defendant's computer while conducting a search for evidence of drug transactions, and then, without obtaining another warrant, abandoned the search for drug trafficking evidence, and proceeded instead to download and view over 200 similarly labeled files in a search, successfully as it turns out, for further images of child pornography. The Tenth Circuit held that, while the first image of child pornography was discovered inadvertently, the officer had exceeded the scope of the search warrant because, after the accidental discovery of illegal pornography in the ".jpg" files, when the officer opened subsequent ".jpg" files, "he expected to find child pornography and not material related to drugs." As a result, the panel concluded that the officer had temporarily abandoned his search for drug trafficking evidence and intentionally commenced a search for more child pornography, which search was not authorized by the existing warrant.

The *Carey* court's reasoning actually confirms the result reached here. First, *Carey* held that the first illegal pornographic image, which was discovered inadvertently, was not subject to suppression because it was found in "plain view" in the course of the authorized search. Similarly, the child pornography images Agent Ehuan saw in the "Tiny Teen" subdirectory were discovered inadvertently during the course of a lawful search, and thus, consistent with *Carey,* are not subject to

Amendment. First, although the FBI believed the files for which they were searching were more likely to be text than pictures, it was certainly possible that the stolen NLM materials might contain pictures, and so it would have been reasonable for Agent Ehuan to examine files containing pictures. Second, there is no evidence that Agent Ehuan, or CART, was aware that the program could be used in this manner, which is significant because, as computer technology changes so rapidly, it would be unreasonable to require the FBI to know of, and use, only the most advanced computer searching techniques. Fi-

nally, because he was conducting a records search, Agent Ehuan was entitled to look at all of defendant's files to determine whether or not they fell within the scope of the search warrant. And, as this search targeted computer files, there was a large amount of material to review. Under these circumstances, it was reasonable, within the meaning of the Fourth Amendment, for Agent Ehuan, in his routine preliminary file review, to use a computer program that enabled him to see instantly, upon opening a file, the general nature of the material contained within that file.

suppression. Second, the *Carey* court suppressed all the remaining images because the officer there, unlike Agent Ehuan, testified that, when he thereafter searched the ".jpg" files, he was looking for more child pornography, and not drug-related material. By contrast, Agent Ehuan testified that at all times, he was looking for the NLM documents and hacker materials that were the subject of the warrant. Significantly, Agent Ehuan never abandoned his original search; he was not commencing a new search when he opened the "Teen" and "Tiny Teen" subdirectories, rather, he was continuing his systematic search of the BBS directory without regard to file names or suffixes because he was aware that the materials that were the subject of the warrant could be hidden anywhere in defendant's files.[11] In summary, the seized images of alleged child pornography may not be suppressed because the search was within the scope of the warrant, and reasonable under the Fourth Amendment.

Notes and Questions

1. The original purpose of the Fourth Amendment was to forbid the use of general warrants. General warrants generally did not name the place to be searched or the property to be seized, and as a result permitted a general rummaging through a suspect's property. The particularity requirement was designed to prevent such general rummaging. By limiting searches to a particular place for particular evidence, the requirement limited the government's powers to conduct dragnet searches.

Does the particularity requirement continue to serve this function in a world of digital evidence? Or do traditional Fourth Amendment rules make computer warrants that are particularized in theory general warrants in practice?

2. The *Gray* court focuses on the officer's subjective intent. Because the officer was looking for the evidence described in the warrant, the discovery of evidence beyond the scope of the warrant was permitted. If the officer had been looking for other evidence, as in *Carey*, its discovery would have violated the Fourth Amendment.

This subjective approach is in tension with how courts have applied the plain view doctrine in cases involving physical evidence. Under the traditional test, the officer's subjective intent is irrelevant and the standard is an objective one. *See* Horton v. California, 496 U.S. 128, 138–39 (1990) (eliminating the inadvertence requirement from the plain view exception on the ground that the particularity requirement can deter general searches and "evenhanded law enforcement is best achieved by the application of objective standards of conduct, rather than standards that depend upon the subjective state of mind of the officer").

---

11. Not presented here is what result would obtain had Agent Ehuan not stopped his search and obtained a warrant after the initial discovery of the child pornography. Arguably, Agent Ehuan could have continued his systematic search of defendant's computer files pursuant to the first search warrant, and, as long as he was searching for the items listed in the warrant, any child pornography discovered in the course of that search could have been seized under the "plain view" doctrine.

The switch from an objective standard for physical searches adopted by the Supreme Court in *Horton* to a subjective standard for digital evidence searches in *Gray* and *Carey* arguably reflects a more restrictive approach to the scope of plain view for digital evidence. In a traditional case, officers can intentionally look for evidence beyond the scope of the warrant so long as the search itself is reasonable. In a digital evidence case, they cannot.

Why have courts adopted a more restrictive approach in the context of digital evidence? Is the switch to a subjective approach designed to restore some of the functionality of the particularity requirement? Perhaps the courts are creating less flexible and more privacy-protective rules in the context of searching through computers to make up for the more flexible and less protective rules that courts have allowed for practical reasons to govern computer searches in other cases.

On the merits, do you think that district judges can accurately determine when a police officer was looking for evidence beyond the scope of the warrant? For a criticism of the subjective approach, see Jim Dowell, Note, *Criminal Procedure: Tenth Circuit Erroneously Allows Officers' Intentions to Define Reasonable Searches: United States v. Carey*, 54 Okla. L. Rev. 665, 676 (2001).

3. Most of the published cases involving the discovery of digital evidence beyond the scope of a warrant involve discovering child pornography. Child pornography offenses are very easy for the government to prove, and the penalties for such offenses are relatively severe. As a result, the discovery of child pornography during a computer search for other evidence may lead prosecutors to call off the initial investigation and bring charges under the child pornography statutes. Does this dynamic help explain why courts have used a subjective test when applying the plain view exception in computer search cases?

4. Under *Gray*, a government agent with a search warrant apparently can search anywhere in a computer so long as he looks for material described in the warrant. If the agent comes across evidence unrelated to the crime described in the warrant, the agent can copy the unrelated evidence for use in court. The agent can then continue to search for the evidence named in the warrant, and can continue to copy unrelated evidence he comes across during the search. Alternatively, the agent can use the discovery of the unrelated evidence as the basis for probable cause to obtain a second warrant to search the computer for more of the unrelated evidence. Either way, the unrelated evidence is admissible in court under prevailing Fourth Amendment law.

Do these rules impose sufficient limits on the search of seized computers? If not, should the plain view exception be abolished in computer cases so that any evidence beyond the scope of the warrant cannot be admitted in court?

> The dynamics of computer searches upset the basic assumptions underlying the plain view doctrine. More and more evidence comes into plain view, and the particularity requirement no longer functions effectively as a check on dragnet searches. In this new environment, a tightening of the plain view doctrine may be necessary to ensure that

computer warrants that are narrow in theory do not become broad in practice.

In time, abolishing the plain view exception may best balance the competing needs of privacy and law enforcement in light of developments in computer technology and the digital forensics process. Forensic analysis is an art, not a science; the process is contingent, technical, and difficult to reduce to rules. Eliminating the plain view exception in digital evidence cases would respect law enforcement interests by granting the police every power needed to identify and locate evidence within the scope of a warrant given the particular context-sensitive needs of the investigation. At the same time, the approach would protect privacy interests by barring the disclosure of any evidence beyond the scope of a valid warrant in most cases. It is an imperfect answer, to be sure, but it may be the best available rule. Although forensic practices may be invasive by technological necessity, a total suppression rule for evidence beyond the scope of a warrant would both remove any incentive for broad searches and neutralize the effect of broad searches that occur. It would regulate invasive practices by imposing use restrictions ex post rather than attempting to control searches ex ante, offering a long-term second-best approach to regulating the computer forensics process. In short, it would allow the police to conduct whatever search they needed to conduct (to ensure recovery) and then limit use of the evidence found (to deter abuses).

Orin S. Kerr, *Searches and Seizures in a Digital World*, 119 Harv. L. Rev. 531, 576–77, 583–84 (2005).

5.   The plain view exception allows law enforcement to seize evidence beyond the scope of a warrant only if the incriminating nature of that evidence is "immediately apparent." David Ziff argues that the plain view doctrine plays only a limited role in computer search cases because the incriminating nature of most digital evidence is not immediately apparent. *See* David J.S. Ziff, Note, *Fourth Amendment Limitations on the Execution of Computer Searches Conducted Pursuant to a Warrant*, 105 Colum. L. Rev. 841, 869 (2005):

> [A] file that is not particularly described in the warrant can be seized by officers only if the file's incriminating character becomes immediately apparent before it can be determined that the contents of the file are outside of the scope of the warrant. For the vast majority of computer files, this limitation will shield private information from inspection by officers. For example, suppose an officer is searching the contents of a computer for child pornography and opens a file labeled "letter to grandma.doc." Under the proposed standard, the officer is only allowed to open and view the file to the extent necessary to determine that it is not merely a mislabeled file concealing the object of the warrant. This limitation prohibits the officer from reading the contents of the letter. Any information in the letter, including information relating to other illegal activity, remains private. Even if an individual file appears suspicious to an officer but further investigation beyond what is necessary to determine that the file is outside the scope of the warrant is required to establish probable cause as to its association with criminal

activity, the item is not immediately incriminating and cannot be seized pursuant to the plain view doctrine.

Does this argument depend on how broadly the warrant is drafted? Computer warrants can be drafted in very broad ways that require agents to exercise considerable judgment as to whether a particular file is within the scope of the warrant. For example, imagine that the warrant in Ziff's hypothetical were not limited to actual images of child pornography, but instead encompassed "any documents, letters, memos, images, or other information concerning violations of child pornography crimes or child sex offenses." In that case, couldn't the officer read "letter to grandma.doc" to determine whether the letter contained any information relating to child sex offenses or child pornography? And if the letter contained discussions of unrelated crimes, couldn't the officer use the letter to prosecute the defendant for the unrelated crime under the plain view doctrine?

Also note that the "immediately apparent" limitation is only a limit on the seizure of evidence. Agents can view unrelated evidence that they come across in plain view, but can seize the evidence only if its incriminating nature is immediately apparent. This brings us back to a question considered earlier in the chapter: Does copying digital evidence for use in court constitute a Fourth Amendment seizure? If not, does the "immediately apparent" limitation even apply in digital evidence cases?

6. *Search protocols.* One way to limit the invasiveness of computer searches would be to require investigators to follow specific search protocols when a computer is searched. For example, a protocol might explain the search terms the investigators will use to locate evidence, or the specific steps investigators must follow when searching the hard drive. The idea is to restore the function of the particularity requirement for digital evidence by requiring the warrant to be executed in a particular way. *See generally* Raphael Winick, *Searches and Seizures of Computers and Computer Data*, 8 Harv. J. L. & Tech. 75, 106–08 (1994).

A few courts have imposed search protocol requirements to limit the scope of computer searches. For example, in the case of In re Search of 3817 W. West End, 321 F.Supp.2d 953 (N.D. Ill. 2004), investigators had probable cause to believe that a suspect was preparing and retaining fraudulent tax records in her home. Investigators applied for a warrant to search the suspect's home and seize her tax records, whether in paper or electronic form. The magistrate judge agreed that there was probable cause, and also agreed that the computer could be seized. The judge refused to permit investigators to search the computer, however, on the ground that investigators had not agreed to limit their search to a specific set of steps pre-approved by the judge. According to Magistrate Judge Schenkier, approval of a search protocol was necessary before the warrant could be issued:

> The purpose of review of warrant applications by "neutral, disinterested magistrates" is to ensure that the requirements of probable cause and particularity are met. When there are concerns about the particularity of a given search, as is the case here, it is both sensible and constitutionally required to address those concerns at the front end of the process,

and to resolve them in a way that avoids the later suppression of evidence. * * *

[A]s matters now stand, what the government seeks is a license to roam through everything in the computer without limitation and without standards. Such a request fails to satisfy the particularity requirement of the Fourth Amendment, and the Court therefore will not approve it.

Id. at 962.

Other courts have rejected a search protocol requirement for computer search warrants. For example, in United States v. Hill, ___ F.3d ___, 2006 WL 2328721 (9th Cir. 2006), a defendant charged with child pornography possession challenged the warrant used to search his computer on the ground that it did not include any search protocols. He claimed that search should have been limited to certain files that are more likely to be associated with child pornography, such as those with a ".jpg" suffix (which usually identifies files containing images) or those containing the word "sex" or other key words. The Ninth Circuit disagreed, noting that "we look favorably upon the inclusion of a search protocol; but its absence is not fatal." *Id.* at *10. The court concluded that the defendant's proposed search protocol was "unreasonable" in light of investigative realities:

> Computer records are extremely susceptible to tampering, hiding, or destruction, whether deliberate or inadvertent. Images can be hidden in all manner of files, even word processing documents and spreadsheets. Criminals will do all they can to conceal contraband, including the simple expedient of changing the names and extensions of files to disguise their content from the casual observer.

> Forcing police to limit their searches to files that the suspect has labeled in a particular way would be much like saying police may not seize a plastic bag containing a powdery white substance if it is labeled "flour" or "talcum powder." There is no way to know what is in a file without examining its contents, just as there is no sure way of separating talcum from cocaine except by testing it. The ease with which child pornography images can be disguised—whether by renaming sexyteenyboppersxxx.jpg as sundayschoollesson.doc, or something more sophisticated—forecloses defendant's proposed search methodology.

Id. at *10 (quoting United States v. Hill, 322 F.Supp.2d 1081, 1090–91 (C.D. Cal. 2004) (Kozinski, J.)).

The decision in *Hill* echoes United States v. Upham, 168 F.3d 532 (1st Cir. 1999). In *Upham*, the police recovered incriminating information by "undeleting" files stored on the defendant's personal computer. This was possible because information stored on a computer often continues to be present when the machine has been reformatted or a file "deleted." The First Circuit held that the warrant permitted investigators to find and recover the deleted files:

> The seizure of unlawful images is within the plain language of the warrant; their recovery, after attempted destruction, is no different than decoding a coded message lawfully seized or pasting together scraps of a torn-up ransom note. The * * * warrant did not prescribe methods of

recovery or tests to be performed, but warrants rarely do so. The warrant process is primarily concerned with identifying *what* may be searched or seized—not how—and *whether* there is sufficient cause for the invasion of privacy thus entailed.

Id. at 537. *See also* United States v. Brooks, 427 F.3d 1246, 1251–53 (10th Cir. 2005).

Finally, consider the U.S. Supreme Court's guidance in Dalia v. United States, 441 U.S. 238 (1979). The government obtained a warrant to conduct bugging surveillance, and investigators executed the warrant by covertly entering the place to install the bug. In an opinion by Justice Powell, the Court rejected the defendant's contention that the warrant had to state that it permitted covert entry:

> Nothing in the language of the Constitution or in this Court's decisions interpreting that language suggests that * * * search warrants also must include a specification of the precise manner in which they are to be executed. On the contrary, it is generally left to the discretion of the executing officers to determine the details of how best to proceed with the performance of a search authorized by warrant—subject of course to the general Fourth Amendment protection against unreasonable searches and seizures.

Id. at 257.

Do computer warrants merit a different approach? Does it depend on whether courts retain the traditional approach to the plain view doctrine in the context of digital evidence? Which is the better way to minimize the intrusiveness of computer searches: imposing ex ante restrictions through search protocols or altering standards ex post by narrowing or eliminating the plain view doctrine? Should courts embrace neither change? Or both?

7. After the police seize a computer pursuant to a warrant, the computer may be sent to a government forensic laboratory or kept at the police station for later analysis. The process of analyzing a computer can be very time-consuming. As a result, most agencies have a considerable backlog of computers awaiting analysis. Several months may pass before government computer experts begin the search. During that time, the computer's owner must wait for the government to start and then complete its analysis.

Existing statutory rules that regulate the warrant process do not impose many restrictions on when the government must search or return a seized computer. Most statutory warrant rules require the government to execute a search warrant within 7 or 10 days after the warrant is signed. *See, e.g.,* Fed. R. Crim. Pro. 41(e)(2) (stating that a federal search warrant "must command the officer to * * * execute the warrant within a specified time no longer than 10 days"). By forcing investigators to execute the warrant shortly after the magistrate has found probable cause, the time limits ensure that searches are executed before the probable cause has become stale. Courts have held, however, that these limitations apply only to the initial physical search of computers and not to the subsequent electronic search. *See, e.g.,* United States v. Gorrell, 360 F. Supp. 2d 48, 54 n.5. (D.D.C. 2004); United States v. Hernandez, 183 F. Supp. 2d 468, 480 (D.P.R. 2002) (stating that Rule 41 does not "provide[] for a specific time limit in which a computer may undergo a government forensic examination after it has been seized pursuant to a search warrant").

Some individual magistrate judges have imposed time limits on computer warrants on their own initiative. For example, in United States v. Brunette, 76 F. Supp. 2d 30 (D. Me. 1999), a magistrate judge signed a warrant allowing agents to seize the defendant's computers on the condition that the forensic analysis must occur "within 30 days." When agents failed to search the computer during the time window, the court suppressed the evidence discovered on the computer after the 30–day period had elapsed. *Id.* at 42. It is unclear, however, whether existing statutory rules give magistrate judges the authority to condition issuance of warrants on the search of the computer within a specific period of time.

Statutory warrant rules also permit individuals who have had property seized pursuant to a warrant to file a motion in court seeking a return of that property. *See, e.g.,* Fed. R. Crim. Pro. 41(g). The standards for return of property are not uniform among different jurisdictions. At the federal level, however, property ordinarily will be ordered returned only in rare case. As a general matter, the court must be convinced that the property owner would suffer "irreparable injury" unless the property is returned and the property owner's interest in the property must outweigh the government's interest in continued retention of it. *See, e.g.,* In re the Matter of the Search of Kitty's East, 905 F.2d 1367, 1370–71 (10th Cir. 1990); Ramsden v. United States, 2 F.3d 322, 325–26 (9th Cir. 1993).

Does the Fourth Amendment impose limits on when a seized computer must be searched? Courts have not recognized Fourth Amendment limitations on when the police must search seized documents. Nor have courts imposed Fourth Amendment limitations on when the police must conduct forensic analysis on other types of seized evidence such as guns or DNA samples. In a few recent cases, however, some courts have indicated that computers may be different. In United States v. Grimmett, 2004 WL 3171788 (D. Kan. 2004), police officers seized computers pursuant to a state warrant. Agents searched the computers several weeks later and found the evidence named in the warrant. The defendant claimed that the delay between the seizure and the search (which, all things considered, was actually a relatively brief period) rendered the search unreasonable and the evidence inadmissible as fruits of an unconstitutional search. The court rejected the claim, but did accept the basic idea that the timing of the computer search was governed by a reasonableness analysis:

> The conduct of law enforcement officers in executing a search warrant is governed by the Fourth Amendment's mandate of reasonableness. The Fourth Amendment does not provide a specific time in which a computer may be subjected to a government forensic examination after it has been seized pursuant to a search warrant. The court finds that the Fourth Amendment requires only that the subsequent search of the computer be made within a reasonable time. The court finds that the subsequent search was conducted within a reasonable time since it was concluded within a few weeks of the execution of the warrant.

Id. at *5. *See also* United States v. Syphers, 296 F. Supp. 2d 50 (D.N.H. 2003) (finding a seven month delay reasonable).

Do you agree that the Fourth Amendment requires agents to search a seized computer within a reasonable time? If so, how should a court determine whether a particular delay is reasonable? Is a case-by-case inquiry into reasonableness the best way to regulate the timing of computer searches? Should statutory rules require agents to search seized computers within a specific window of time, or to image seized computers and return the original within a particular period? For such a proposal, see Kerr, *Search Warrants in an Era of Digital Evidence*, 75 Miss L.J. at 129–32.

E. THE FOURTH AMENDMENT AND COMPUTER NETWORKS

The materials in this chapter have considered Fourth Amendment limitations on government access to computers and data under their owners' control. In many cases, however, data will not be stored with its owner. Computer users routinely send information over local, national, or even international computer networks. When computer networks are used to commit criminal acts, investigators may wish to collect evidence directly from those networks without approaching the suspect or his home. For example, local police trying to catch a fraud suspect might want to obtain account records and stored e-mail held by the suspect's Internet service provider. FBI agents pursuing a hacker might want to conduct real-time surveillance of his account from inside a victim network. Finally, undercover police officers trying to catch pedophiles might want to enter an Internet chat room posing as a child. In all of these cases, investigators will attempt to obtain information from a remote network rather than from the suspect's home computer.

This section considers how the Fourth Amendment applies to the collection of computer data sent over or stored on remote computers. To appreciate the difficult questions of Fourth Amendment law raised by network surveillance, it helps to review a few basic features about how computer networks (and specifically, today's Internet protocols) work. Individuals normally connect to networks and the Internet by having an account with a server that is connected to a broader network. For example, a home user may have an Internet service provider that serves as the user's contact point with the network. Every communication sent or received by the user is routed through the user's ISP.

Internet communications are sent across the network by being broken into "packets," individual chunks of data that contain about a page's worth of information. Internet packets are streams of data that act as the computer equivalent of letters between computers. Each packet begins with a IP (Internet protocol) header, a computer-generated envelope that contains the packet's originating and destination address along with information about the type and size of the information the packet carries. The IP header (also referred to as a packet header) is created when the communication is sent, and is used by the network to ensure delivery of the payload. The communication itself becomes the "payload" of the packet, and appears after the header. The header is automatically discarded by the receiving computer when the packet arrives at its destination. The receiving computer then reassembles the various packets into the original file that was sent.

Packet headers are not the only kind of addressing information generated by computers. Sending an e-mail generates an "e-mail header" that contains originating and destination e-mail addresses, as well as a brief history of where and when the e-mail was sent in the course of delivery. Many types of e-mail programs permit you to view the entire e-mail header of e-mails in your inbox; the header is akin to the envelope of a letter, complete with an electronic version of a postmark.

The existence of packet headers, e-mail headers, and other types of Internet communications means that the Fourth Amendment rules that govern network surveillance must consider a very wide range of different communications and surveillance techniques. Information relating to an individual's computer use may include the contents of e-mails, requests for web pages, e-mail headers, IP headers, and many other kinds of information. That information can be monitored in real-time or collected from storage from a wide range of places across the network.

When does a computer user have a reasonable expectation of privacy in such information, such that a particular surveillance technique triggers Fourth Amendment protection?

1. INTRODUCTION TO THE FOURTH AMENDMENT AND REMOTE TRANSMISSION

UNITED STATES v. HOROWITZ

United States Court of Appeals for the Fourth Circuit, 1986.
806 F.2d 1222.

DONALD RUSSELL, Circuit Judge.

The defendant, Richard I. Horowitz, appeals from the trial court's denial of his pre-trial motion to suppress evidence obtained by authorities pursuant to an authorized search of the premises of Electro–Methods, Inc. (EMI), a Connecticut corporation which contracted for defendant's services. The defendant was employed by Pratt & Whitney Aircraft (Pratt) as supervisor of pricing in its Government Products Division in North Palm Beach, Florida. In this role the defendant oversaw preparation of sealed bids which Pratt submitted to the Air Force for supplying spare parts for the F–100 jet engine. EMI was among several companies competing with Pratt for the Air Force contract.

In 1978, unbeknownst to Pratt, the defendant, while still employed by Pratt, established an independent consulting firm, Sandrich Associates, Inc., which was operated from his Florida home and which advised clients on government contracting and on pricing of aircraft parts. Two of these clients were Perry Oceanographics and Lenzar Optics. The defendant's primary client, however, was EMI, which was owned by Alfred Stanger. Stanger also owned Turbo Tech, Inc., which represented Fabrique Nationale and N.V. Philips in their efforts to compete with Pratt for the Air Force F–100 spare parts contracts. The defendant, until 1982, failed to report the existence of his consulting contracts to Pratt on the conflict of interest statements Pratt annually required of its employees.

In his role as "consultant" to EMI, the defendant sold to Alfred Stanger confidential Pratt pricing information which EMI used to underbid Pratt on the Air Force contracts. Stanger paid the defendant as much as $5,000 per month for his so-called "consulting services", reaching a total of $260,000. In 1982, Stanger installed a computer terminal and telephone modem in the defendant's Florida home to facilitate communication between the defendant and EMI's Connecticut office. The defendant transmitted the pricing information to EMI's computer terminal where the information was then stored on EMI's tapes.

On June 8, 1983, agents of the FBI executed a search warrant at EMI, having alleged in an affidavit probable cause to believe that Pratt pricing information was held by EMI on computer magnetic storage devices. The warrant authorized the agents to search a one-story industrial-commercial building housing EMI and to seize property listed on an attached schedule including computer magnetic storage devices, computer keypunch cards and computer print-outs containing Pratt pricing material. The agents, to prevent erasure of on-line tapes and discs (tapes), seized all of the tapes in EMI's computer room, including stored back-ups, and later examined them on outside compatible computer terminals with the aid of an expert. The contents of a tape could not be discerned from visual inspection but required specialized programming to review and record the information contained on the tapes. The agents looked specifically for a file designated RER which they believed contained the price data and for files containing messages between Stanger and the defendant.

In a subsequent proceeding brought by the government to suspend EMI from bidding on Air Force contracts, the defendant filed two sworn affidavits before the Air Force Debarment, Suspension and Review Board stating that he did not supply EMI with secret Pratt pricing information. Those affidavits conflicted with the evidence seized at EMI and the defendant was indicted on two counts of making false statements to the board in violation of 18 U.S.C. § 1001. Prior to trial, the defendant challenged the admissibility of the seized evidence on fourth amendment grounds. The trial judge denied his motion to suppress the evidence for lack of standing to contest the search and the defendant was convicted. On appeal the defendant challenges only the court's denial of his motion to suppress.

The defendant can contest the search and seizure on Fourth Amendment grounds only if "the disputed search and seizure has infringed an interest of the defendant which the Fourth Amendment was designed to protect."*Rakas v. Illinois,* 439 U.S. 128, 140 (1978). The Supreme Court has articulated the appropriate inquiry to be whether the individual had a reasonable expectation of privacy in the area searched, not merely in the items found, *Rawlings v. Kentucky,* 448 U.S. 98, 104–106 (1980), and the burden is upon the defendant to prove his reasonable expectation of privacy.

The defendant claims he had a reasonable expectation of privacy in the seized tapes storing the information he supplied to EMI. He alleges that for purposes of his Fourth Amendment challenge the search at issue was not the search of EMI's building, but was the search of the "intangible space where images and sounds are recorded in a computer memory disc or tape." Appellant's brief at 12. The defendant relies on Supreme Court decisions finding reasonable expectations of privacy in one's office, *Mancusi v. DeForte,* 392 U.S. 364 (1968), and in other areas beyond the home, *United States v. Chadwick,* 433 U.S. 1 (1977) (footlocker transported by rail), to support his novel argument that certain tapes seized on EMI's premises constituted his "electronic file cabinet," an extension of his private home office, and that the government agents violated his reasonable expectation of privacy in the tapes by playing them without obtaining a second search warrant. The government contends that the tapes were EMI's electronic records properly seized and later inspected pursuant to the search warrant. The government argues that the defendant had no reasonable and legitimate expectation of privacy in either the tapes or in EMI's premises.

The factors we must use to determine whether the defendant retained a reasonable expectation of privacy in the computer tapes can be stated generally as an analysis of the defendant's interest in and control of the area searched, his subjective expectation of privacy in the area as evidenced by his efforts to ensure that privacy, and society's willingness to recognize his expectation as reasonable. We agree with the trial court that the defendant had no reasonable expectation of privacy either in EMI's premises *or* in the tapes seized and played by the government.

The defendant claims that he had a privacy interest in the tapes storing the information he had transmitted to EMI because they constituted his workplace in that he maintained an ongoing relationship with EMI and a continuing interest in the material on the tapes, his work product. We disagree. The tapes may indeed have constituted an "electronic filing cabinet," but that filing cabinet belonged to EMI and was maintained by EMI for its own use. The defendant sold information to EMI and, once paid for, that information belonged to EMI, as did the tapes upon which the information was stored and the building in which the tapes were kept. Property rights, while not determinative, remain conceptually relevant to whether one's expectations are legitimate or 'reasonable.' And as the Supreme Court reiterated in *Rakas,* "a person who is aggrieved by an illegal search and seizure only through the introduction of damaging evidence secured by a search of a third person's premises or property has not had any of his Fourth Amendment rights infringed." The defendant has failed to show even a tenuous privacy interest in the tapes for he never owned or possessed them, was rarely if ever physically present at EMI, was assigned no office at EMI's headquarters, and was hundreds of miles away when the search and seizure took place.

The tapes merely stored for EMI's benefit, information transmitted by the defendant which, once recorded, could not be further manipulated by the defendant, albeit he could review the information from his home terminal. The defendant did not have an indelible privacy interest in the information. Having sold the information, the defendant lost any interest in it and EMI could use the information for any business purpose it pleased. Thus, the defendant's claim that the tapes were merely an electronic extension of his office fails because he cannot demonstrate a sufficient *nexus* between the area searched and his workplace in Florida.

Since the defendant has proved no interest in the tapes, the information recorded on them, or in the premises upon which the tapes were stored, for this reason alone the defendant's claim must fail. But the defendant has also failed to prove that he had any control over the tapes. Control is measured by physical presence in, or access to the area to be searched, and by the ability to exclude others. Although an individual need not maintain absolute personal control (exclusive use) over an area to support his expectation of privacy, occasional presence, without any right to exclude others, is not enough. The defendant lacked any ability to exclude others from the tapes; on the contrary, his own access was controlled by EMI. The defendant had no keys to either EMI's building or EMI's computer room. His only access to the RER file was by an electronic hookup through the use of a password. But employees of EMI could bar his access simply by removing the tapes from the computer or by changing the password. The defendant could not effectively exclude anyone from access to the tapes since any of several EMI employees knowing the password could give it to others and any employee with a key to the computer room could remove the tapes. Indeed, the defendant's very purpose in making the transmissions to EMI was to enable the employees of EMI to use the information in preparation of EMI's bids so that EMI could unfairly compete with Pratt, the defendant's employer. Thus, the information was necessarily disseminated to others within EMI and any security measures taken by EMI to restrict access primarily benefitted EMI and only incidentally the defendant.

Although the defendant may well have wished to conceal his egregious perfidy from his employer, as would any person wrongfully selling his employer's secrets, his willful disclosure to EMI vitiates any reasonable expectation of privacy he may have once had. Assurances by Stanger as to EMI's limited use of the information could not sustain a Fourth Amendment interest. *See United States v. Miller*, 425 U.S. 435, 443 (1973). "Legitimation of expectations of privacy by law must have a source outside of the Fourth Amendment, either by reference to concepts of real or personal property law or to understandings that are recognized and permitted by society." *Rakas*, 439 U.S. at 144, n. 12. The defendant has failed to show any source of legitimation in this case; therefore, we affirm the decision of the trial court.

Notes and Questions

1. *Horowitz* explores two distinct bases for determining whether the defendant had a reasonable expectation of privacy in the computer data he sent to EMI. The first focuses on the defendant's relationship to the data. The second examines his relationship to the physical storage device that contained the data. Which should be more important? If the relationship to the data is more important, how much of a relationship between an individual and the data should be sufficient to establish Fourth Amendment protection in it?

Imagine Horowitz had transmitted data to EMI not because he was selling the data to them, but because he wished to use EMI's computer as a remote storage facility for himself. Should this be enough of a relationship to trigger Fourth Amendment protection? Is the key question the defendant's hopes or goals when he transmitted the data? Are EMI's storage practices relevant? How important is EMI's contractual relationship with the defendant?

2. *Problem.* Arthur writes an e-mail to his best friend Bart describing his participation in a bank robbery. Bart receives the e-mail and forwards it on to his friend Chuck. An FBI agent investigating the bank robbery learns of the e-mail, and approaches the system administrator of Chuck's ISP. The agent asks the system administrator to copy the e-mail in Chuck's inbox, which Chuck has not yet viewed, and to send the copy to the FBI.

Who has a reasonable expectation of privacy in the copy of the e-mail message stored in Chuck's inbox? The owner/operator of the ISP will have Fourth Amendment rights because it owns the physical server. *See* Alderman v. United States, 394 U.S. 165, 176–77 (1969) (holding that a homeowner's Fourth Amendment rights are implicated by wiretapping of telephones in his home even though he did not participate in calls monitored). But does Chuck have Fourth Amendment rights in the data? Does Arthur? Does Bart?

3. The reasonable expectation of privacy test originated in Justice Harlan's concurrence in Katz v. United States, 389 U.S. 347 (1967). In *Katz,* FBI agents taped a microphone to the top of a public pay phone booth that Katz used to place illegal bets. When Katz entered the phone booth, agents turned on the microphone and recorded his half of the communication. Justice Stewart's majority opinion ruled that the warrantless surveillance of the phone booth was impermissible:

> One who occupies [a public phone booth], shuts the door behind him, and pays the toll that permits him to place a call is surely entitled to assume that the words he utters into the mouthpiece will not be broadcast to the world. To read the Constitution more narrowly is to ignore the vital role that the public telephone has come to play in private communication.

> The Government contends, however, that the activities of its agents in this case should not be tested by Fourth Amendment requirements, for the surveillance technique they employed involved no physical penetration of the telephone booth from which the petitioner placed his

calls. * * * But the premise that property interests control the right of the Government to search and seize has been discredited. * * * Once this much is acknowledged, and once it is recognized that the Fourth Amendment protects people—and not simply "areas"—against unreasonable searches and seizures, it becomes clear that the reach of that Amendment cannot turn upon the presence or absence of a physical intrusion into any given enclosure.

* * * The Government's activities in electronically listening to and recording the petitioner's words violated the privacy upon which he justifiably relied while using the telephone booth and thus constituted a "search and seizure" within the meaning of the Fourth Amendment. The fact that the electronic device employed to achieve that end did not happen to penetrate the wall of the booth can have no constitutional significance.

Id. at 352–53. Does the majority opinion in *Katz* shed light on how much protection the Fourth Amendment affords to computer networks and the Internet? Should courts construe the Fourth Amendment broadly to recognize the vital role that computer networks have come to play in private communication?

Justice Harlan's concurrence in *Katz* offered a somewhat narrower approach than Justice Stewart's majority opinion:

As the Court's opinion states, "the Fourth Amendment protects people, not places." The question, however, is what protection it affords to those people. Generally, as here, the answer to that question requires reference to a "place." My understanding of the rule that has emerged from prior decisions is that there is a twofold requirement, first that a person have exhibited an actual (subjective) expectation of privacy and, second, that the expectation be one that society is prepared to recognize as "reasonable." Thus a man's home is, for most purposes, a place where he expects privacy, but objects, activities, or statements that he exposes to the "plain view" of outsiders are not "protected" because no intention to keep them to himself has been exhibited. On the other hand, conversations in the open would not be protected against being overheard, for the expectation of privacy under the circumstances would be unreasonable.

The critical fact in this case is that "one who occupies [a telephone booth], shuts the door behind him, and pays the toll that permits him to place a call is surely entitled to assume" that his conversation is not being intercepted. The point is not that the booth is "accessible to the public" at other times, but that it is a temporarily private place whose momentary occupants' expectations of freedom from intrusion are recognized as reasonable.

Id. at 361 (Harlan, J., concurring).

Justice Harlan's concurrence suggests that Fourth Amendment protection generally requires reference to a "place." What is the "place" of a communication sent over the Internet? Is it cyberspace? Is it wherever the data is physically located? Does the concept of a "place" make sense when applied to Internet communications?

4. *"Understandings that are recognized and permitted by society."* In Rakas v. Illinois, 439 U.S. 128 (1978), then-Justice Rehnquist offered this explanation of when an expectation of privacy is constitutionally "reasonable" or "legitimate":

> [A] legitimate expectation of privacy by definition means more than a subjective expectation of not being discovered. A burglar plying his trade in a summer cabin during the off season may have a thoroughly justified subjective expectation of privacy, but it is not one which the law recognizes as legitimate. His presence * * * is wrongful; his expectation is not one that society is prepared to recognize as reasonable. And it would, of course, be merely tautological to fall back on the notion that those expectations of privacy which are legitimate depend primarily on cases deciding exclusionary-rule issues in criminal cases. Legitimation of expectations of privacy by law must have a source outside of the Fourth Amendment, either by reference to concepts of real or personal property law or to understandings that are recognized and permitted by society.

Id. at 144 n.12.

What source might legitimate an expectation of privacy in remote computer data? Can property law do it? Might statutory privacy laws create a legitimate expectation of privacy? What "understandings * * * are recognized and permitted by society" with regard to Internet privacy? In 1999, Sun Microsystems CEO Scott McNealy was reported to have told a gathering of reporters and analysts that consumers "have zero privacy anyway" and should "get over" concerns about privacy. Polly Sprenger, *Sun on Privacy: 'Get Over It'*, Wired News, January 26, 1999. If "understandings that are recognized and permitted by society" refers to social norms and expectations about computer privacy, can computer users ever have a reasonable expectation of privacy in remotely stored or transmitted data?

Two cases may be relevant to this question. In United States v. Butler, 151 F. Supp. 2d 82 (D. Me. 2001), a student at the University of Maine used computers in a university computer lab to engage in criminal activity. When visitors to the lab noticed the student's misconduct, the computers were searched and the evidence discovered. The student later argued that the warrantless search of the university computers violated his Fourth Amendment rights. The district court disagreed, holding that the student had no reasonable expectation of privacy in the university's computer:

> The defendant relies upon "a legitimate and reasonable expectation of privacy recognized by society in any work performed on, or documents and files produced on, computers he used while a student at the University of Maine." Pl.'s Mot. to Suppress at 3. Unlike the Supreme Court's treatment of generic payphone booths in 1967 in *Katz*, I conclude that in 2001 there is no generic expectation of privacy for shared usage on computers at large. Conditions of computer use and access still vary tremendously.

Id. at 84–85. If there was no "generic expectation of privacy for shared computer usage on computers at large" in 2001, is there such an expectation of privacy today? How can you tell?

Next consider United States v. Gines–Perez, 214 F. Supp. 2d 205 (D.P.R. 2002). The defendant managed a computer store and was also a suspect in a major heroin smuggling investigation. He had begun to set up a website for the computer store, and had posted a group portrait of all of the store's employees that included his own image. The officers who were investigating the smuggling operation found the picture and distributed it among themselves to help them recognize the defendant. The photograph helped the police identify the car the defendant was driving, which led to the discovery of 1.4 kilos of heroin and $5,000 in cash in the car. The defendant argued unsuccessfully that he had a subjective and objectively reasonable expectation of privacy in the photograph he posted on the web:

> The Court is convinced that placing information on the information superhighway necessarily makes said matter accessible to the public, no matter how many protectionist measures may be taken, or even when a web page is "under construction." While it is true that there is no case law on point regarding this issue, it strikes the Court as obvious that a claim to privacy is unavailable to someone who places information on an indisputably, public medium, such as the Internet, without taking any measures to protect the information.

> The defense may claim that the web site in controversy was not intended to be "public" or "commercial" in nature. But it is not the intention of the person who uses the Internet to communicate information which is important; it is the medium in which he or she places the information and the nature of the materials placed on the web which are important. A person who places information on the information superhighway clearly subjects said information to being accessed by every conceivable interested party. Simply expressed, if privacy is sought, then public communication mediums such as the Internet are not adequate forums without protective measures.

> * * * The Court finds that this society is simply not prepared to recognize as "reasonable" a claim that a picture on the Internet is "private" in nature, such that the Government cannot access it. In fact, the Court believes that our society would recognize the opposite; that a person who places a photograph on the Internet precisely intends to forsake and renounce all privacy rights to such imagery, particularly under circumstances such as here, where the Defendant did not employ protective measures or devices that would have controlled access to the Web page or the photograph itself.

Id. at 225. What kind of "protective measures" do you think should be sufficient to establish a reasonable expectation of privacy?

5. In Kyllo v. United States, 533 U.S. 27 (2001), the Supreme Court held that the warrantless use of an infrared camera directed at a home violates the Fourth Amendment by disclosing previously unknowable facts about the home, such as the temperature inside a room:

> While it may be difficult to refine *Katz* when the search of areas such as telephone booths, automobiles, or even the curtilage and uncovered portions of residences are at issue, in the case of the search of the interior of homes—the prototypical and hence most commonly litigated area of protected privacy—there is a ready criterion, with roots deep in

the common law, of the minimal expectation of privacy that *exists*, and that is acknowledged to be *reasonable*. To withdraw protection of this minimum expectation would be to permit police technology to erode the privacy guaranteed by the Fourth Amendment. We think that obtaining by sense-enhancing technology any information regarding the interior of the home that could not otherwise have been obtained without physical intrusion into a constitutionally protected area, constitutes a search—at least where (as here) the technology in question is not in general public use. This assures preservation of that degree of privacy against government that existed when the Fourth Amendment was adopted.

Id. at 28. The Internet did not exist when the Fourth Amendment was adopted. Does *Kyllo* have any application to computers and the Internet? Should the Fourth Amendment match the privacy we experience online to the privacy we experience in the physical world, and thus to the privacy the Framers experienced in their homes?

6. Encryption provides an extraordinarily powerful tool to create privacy in computer data. But can encryption create a reasonable expectation of privacy? The author of these materials has argued that encryption alone cannot create a reasonable expectation of privacy because the Fourth Amendment regulates access to information, not comprehension of data already accessed. A reasonable person can expect privacy in encrypted information, but that privacy derives from technology rather than the Fourth Amendment. *See* Orin S. Kerr, *The Fourth Amendment in Cyberspace: Can Encryption Create a "Reasonable Expectation of Privacy"?*, 33 Conn. L. Rev. 503 (2001).

According to this argument, the government may need a search warrant to obtain a file, but descrambling an encrypted file (transforming ciphertext into plaintext) cannot violate the file owner's reasonable expectation of privacy. This result may seem odd at first, but it parallels precedents involving shredded files and speech in foreign languages. Courts have held that the government can reassemble shredded paper documents and translate materials from a foreign language without implicating the Fourth Amendment. The fact that a reasonable person would expect that shredded documents or speech in a foreign tongue would remain secret does not mean that the government conduct violates a reasonable expectation of privacy.

Is this argument persuasive? Consider the following hypothetical. Renowned criminal Lex Luthor takes out a full page advertisement in *The Daily Planet* containing the following announcement:

> I am planning some colorful entertainment for Metropolis. The following encrypted message explains where and when the fun will take place. To obtain the key that will allow you to decrypt the secret message and learn of my diabolical plans, you must wire $100 million to my Swiss bank account by noon tomorrow. Here is the encrypted message:
>
> J XJMM CMPX VQ UIF UJNFT TRVBSF TVCXBZ
> TUBUJPO BU OPPO UPNPSSPX CZ MFBXJOH
> B CPNC JO B QBSLFE DIFWSPMFU UBYJDBC
> XJUI NPOUBOB MJDFOTF QMBUFT.
>
> Love, *Lex Luthor*

Imagine that an employee of the Metropolis police department sees Luthor's newspaper advertisement during breakfast that morning, and he spends a few minutes trying to decrypt the encoded message. He realizes that the key to Luthor's code is simple: It is the so-called "substitution cipher" that shifts every letter one space (turning A into B, B into C, C into D, etc.). Having generated the key to the encryption, the employee uses the key and unscrambles the message to find the following:

I WILL BLOW UP THE TIMES SQUARE SUBWAY
STATION AT NOON TOMORROW BY LEAVING
A BOMB IN A PARKED CHEVROLET TAXICAB
WITH MONTANA LICENSE PLATES.

The employee calls his supervisors at work and explains Luthor's plans. The police obtain a warrant to search the taxicab, seize a bomb in the trunk just before noon, trace the taxicab back to Luthor, and then charge Luthor with a range of felonies.

Now imagine that Luthor's counsel files a motion to suppress all of the evidence found in the cab. Does the Fourth Amendment require a court to grant Luthor's motion and dismiss the charges against him? It seems intuitively obvious that it does not. But why not? The author of this casebook has argued that decrypting Luthor's message does not implicate the Fourth Amendment because encryption cannot create a reasonable expectation of privacy. Luthor's message was public, and the Fourth Amendment does not regulate efforts to comprehend public information. If encryption creates a reasonable expectation of privacy, he contends, Luthor's motion to suppress must be granted:

> Luthor created a reasonable expectation of privacy in the contents of his message by encrypting the message. By using a "key" to decrypt the message, the police conducted a warrantless search of Luthor's communication in violation of Luthor's Fourth Amendment rights. As a result, the decrypted message must be suppressed, and the evidence found in the taxicab must be suppressed as fruits of the poisonous tree. Lex Luthor must go free.

Id. at 519–20. Do you agree? Or is it possible to believe that encryption can create Fourth Amendment protection while also agreeing that Luthor's motion to suppress should be denied? Stephen Henderson offers one such argument:

> Luthor's simple substitution cipher is akin to * * * a transparent bag, perhaps a Ziploc. In the words of the Court, "the Fourth Amendment provides protection to the owner of every container that conceals its contents from plain view." A Ziploc bag provides a wonderful seal, but it doesn't conceal its contents from an officer possessing ordinary eyesight. Likewise, a substitution cipher does not conceal a message from an officer possessing ordinary intelligence. In both instances the content is in "plain view."

Stephen E. Henderson, *Nothing New Under the Sun? A Technologically Rational Doctrine of Fourth Amendment Search*, 56 Mercer L. Rev. 507, 534

(2005). Is Professor Henderson applying the plain view doctrine, or something more like the "plain thought" doctrine? Are they the same? How complex must an encryption algorithm be before encrypted data is no longer in plain view?

A number of commentators have stated that encryption triggers Fourth Amendment protection because encryption "locks" information away until a "key" is used to decrypt it. *See, e.g.,* A. Michael Froomkin, *The Metaphor Is the Key: Cryptography, the Clipper Chip, and the Constitution,* 143 U. Pa. L. Rev. 709, 728–35 (1995); Sean J. Edgett, Comment, *Double-clicking on Fourth Amendment Protection: Encryption Creates a Reasonable Expectation of Privacy,* 30 Pepp. L. Rev. 339 (2003). Consider this counterargument:

> The lock that helps trigger a reasonable expectation of privacy in Fourth Amendment cases is a fastener that prevents or limits the movement of two or more surfaces relative to each other. Such a fastener helps create a reasonable expectation of privacy by preventing easy access to the contents of a container. The lock-and-key metaphor in encryption uses a second dictionary definition of "lock" that carries only a passing resemblance to the first one. Encryption "locks" a communication in the sense that it makes the communication inaccessible by making it incomprehensible. The code that translates ciphertext into plaintext is a "key" because it takes inaccessible ciphertext and helps translate it into understandable plaintext. Using this metaphorical definition of lock-and-key, we might say that a book explaining how the Internet works "provides the key to unlocking the secrets of the Internet." We would not mean that the Internet has a fastener on it that can be unfastened by reading the book; rather, we would mean that the Internet is hard to understand, and that the book can help aid the reader's cognitive understanding. In this sense, the philosophy of Hegel is locked to me, as is Arabic text and my physician's handwriting.

> * * * If the government needs a warrant to decrypt an encrypted communication, does it need a warrant before it can read a doctor's messy handwriting or understand Hegel? Does law enforcement need a warrant before it can figure out a criminal's clever scheme, on the ground that the scheme was so subtle that the criminal had a reasonable expectation that it would remain secret? If we decide that the Fourth Amendment can regulate law enforcement efforts to understand what it already has in its possession, it is hard to see where these strange questions can stop. If the Fourth Amendment regulates a state of mind, we have to answer when someone can expect others to think certain thoughts, which depends on who the others are and how much time they would have to think.

Kerr, *The Fourth Amendment in Cyberspace,* 33 Conn. L. Rev. at 522, 523–24. What do you think? Can encryption create a reasonable expectation of privacy?

2. ANALOGIES TO SPEECH, LETTERS, AND TELEPHONE CALLS

Reasoning by analogy is an important tool to help understand how the Fourth Amendment might apply to collecting information from computer networks. The courts have decided many cases applying the Fourth Amendment to earlier communications technologies such as the telephone network and the postal mail network. Perhaps we can best understand the Fourth Amendment in the context of computer networks by reasoning from analogy to these earlier technologies. In particular, consider three possible analogies: speech, postal letters, and telephone calls.

The Speech Analogy

Is sending computer data to a remote computer akin to speaking to that computer? When you send e-mail and surf the web, are you telling your ISP to send the information for you and then hearing from your ISP as to what information it received on your behalf? From this perspective, we might model computers as if they were people, and model transmission of information among computers as if it were an open sharing of information among them.

Is this analogy persuasive? If it is, sending data to a remote server likely eliminates a reasonable expectation of privacy in the data. The Supreme Court has consistently held that a person's Fourth Amendment rights are not violated if he reasonably but mistakenly tells another person his secrets and the person then relays that secret to the government.

For example, in Hoffa v. United States, 385 U.S. 293 (1966), James Hoffa admitted criminal activity to a confidant, Partin. Partin turned out to be a paid government informer, and he transmitted the information to the FBI. Hoffa objected, arguing that his Fourth Amendment rights had been violated when Partin shared Hoffa's private information with the police. The Court rejected this argument:

> Neither this Court nor any member of it has ever expressed the view that the Fourth Amendment protects a wrongdoer's misplaced belief that a person to whom he voluntarily confides his wrongdoing will not reveal it. * * * The risk of being overheard by an eavesdropper or betrayed by an informer or deceived as to the identity of one with whom one deals is probably inherent in the conditions of human society. It is the kind of risk we necessarily assume whenever we speak.

Id. at 302–03. Under *Hoffa*, a person assumes the risk that those within earshot of their speech will hear and understand the speech and will share it with the police. However unlikely it is, the person's Fourth Amendment rights are not violated if it happens.

This is true even if the person does not intend for others overhearing the speech to listen in or understand it. Consider the unpleasant surprise encountered by the Spanish-speaking members of the narcotics conspiracy in United States v. Longoria, 177 F.3d 1179 (10th Cir. 1999). Because the co-conspirators were the only individuals nearby who spoke or understood Spanish, they discussed their criminal activity to each other in Spanish in the presence of outsiders. One such outsider turned out to be a government informant who recorded the defendant's Spanish conversations using audio equipment. The informant did not understand Spanish, but government translators did. They translated the tapes into English and used the translations at trial. The Tenth Circuit rejected the notion that the co-conspirators had a reasonable expectation of privacy because they spoke in a foreign tongue that others present did not comprehend. "[O]ne exposing conversations to others must necessarily assume the risk his statements will be overheard and understood," the court reasoned. "[The defendant] exposed his statements by speaking in a manner clearly audible by the informant. His hope that the informant would not fully understand the contents of the conversation is not an expectation society is prepared to recognize as reasonable." *Id.* at 1182.

Courts have analogized Internet communications to speech in the context of online undercover operations. For example, in State v. Moller, 2002 WL 628634 (Ohio Ct. App. 2002), a police officer entered a chat room for older men posing as a 14 year–old girl. Defendant Moller contacted the officer and the two eventually arranged for Moller to drive 200 miles to meet the "girl" for sexual activities. Following his arrest, Moller argued that the officer's conduct violated his Fourth Amendment rights. The Court disagreed, relying on the rationale of *Hoffa*:

> Like Hoffa, Moller took the risk that the 14 year old he thought he was talking to, and planning to engage in sex with, was not who she seemed to be, but was in reality a police officer. This is a risk that anyone visiting a chat room necessarily takes when communicating with strangers. It is easy for anyone using the Internet to adopt a false persona, whether for purposes of law enforcement, or for other and nefarious purposes. It was unreasonable for Moller to assume that his unsuitable conversations would be kept private. Thus, in our view, his statements made in the chat room to a stranger are not entitled to protection under the Fourth Amendment.

Id. at *5.

The Letter or Package Analogy

Is sending computer data to a remote location like sending a document, letter or package? Existing Fourth Amendment law teaches that individuals who send letters and packages retain a reasonable expectation of privacy in the contents of their sealed containers but not in the exposed exteriors of those containers. Fourth Amendment protections track what is exposed and what is sealed away from view. For example, individuals do not retain a reasonable expectation of privacy in the outside of their letters or packages, or in documents disclosed to others. The police can observe the outside of packages, take pictures of envelopes, read postcards, and analyze disclosed documents all without implicating the Fourth Amendment. On the other hand, opening a sealed letter or package during transit to view its contents is a Fourth Amendment search that implicates the Fourth Amendment rights of the sender and receiver. It requires a warrant or an exception to the warrant requirement.

The Fourth Amendment's protection of postal letters dates back to dicta in Ex Parte Jackson, 96 U.S. (6 Otto) 727 (1877), a decision involving the power of Congress to regulate the postal system. Justice Field wrote the following about the privacy of items sent through the postal system, *id.* at 733:

> Letters and sealed packages * * * in the mail are as fully guarded from examination and inspection, except as to their outward form and weight, as if they were retained by the parties forwarding them in their own domiciles. The constitutional guaranty of the right of the people to be secure in their papers against unreasonable searches and seizures extends to their papers, thus closed against inspection, wherever they may be. Whilst in the mail, they can only be opened and examined under like warrant, issued upon similar oath or affirmation, particularly describing the thing to be seized, as is required when papers are subjected to search in one's own household. No law of Congress can place in the hands of officials connected with the postal service any authority to invade the secrecy of letters and such sealed packages in the mail; and all regulations adopted as to mail matter of this kind must be in subordination to the great principle embodied in the fourth amendment of the Constitution.

The basic principle of *Ex Parte Jackson* has been construed fairly broadly. Leaving a sealed package with a trustworthy bailee generally preserves the bailor's Fourth Amendment protections in the package's contents. For example, individuals have been held to retain a reasonable expectation of privacy in the contents of opaque packages when they send packages via private carriers, *see* Walter v. United States, 447 U.S. 649, 651 (1980); when they leave packages with store clerks, *see* United States v. Most, 876 F.2d 191, 197–98 (D.C. Cir. 1989); when they are stored with airport baggage counters, *see* United States v. Barry, 853 F.2d 1479, 1481–83 (8th Cir. 1988); and when they leave packages with their friends for safekeeping, *see* United States v. Presler, 610 F.2d 1206, 1213–14 (4th Cir. 1979). In all of these cases, governmental opening of the sealed package violates the owner's reasonable expectation of privacy.

However, there are two important limits on this principle. First, the sender's reasonable expectation of privacy in a sealed package or letter is eliminated when the package or letter reaches its destination. When the item is delivered and the letter becomes the property of the recipient, governmental access no longer implicates the sender's Fourth Amendment rights. For example, the search of a home that uncovers letters mailed to that address will not implicate the Fourth Amendment rights of the individuals who sent the letters. *See* United States v. King, 55 F.3d 1193, 1196 (6th Cir. 1995).

Second, the delivery of documents to a person who has some rights to access the documents may eliminate the sender's reasonable expectation of privacy. In United States v. Miller, 425 U.S. 435 (1976), federal agents investigating an illegal moonshine operation issued subpoenas to the suspect's banks for bank records relating to the suspect's accounts. The records included checks and deposit slips that had been filled out by the suspect, as well other account records. The Court held that the suspect had no legitimate expectation of privacy in the bank records:

> The checks are not confidential communications but negotiable instruments to be used in commercial transactions. All of the documents obtained, including financial statements and deposit slips, contain only information voluntarily conveyed to the banks and exposed to their employees in the ordinary course of business. The lack of any legitimate expectation of privacy concerning the information kept in bank records was assumed by Congress in enacting the Bank Secrecy Act, the expressed purpose of which is to require records to be maintained because they "have a high degree of usefulness in criminal tax, and regulatory investigations and proceedings." 12 U.S.C. § 829b(a)(1).
>
> The depositor takes the risk, in revealing his affairs to another, that the information will be conveyed by that person to the Government. This Court has held repeatedly that the Fourth Amendment does not prohibit the obtaining of information revealed to a third party and conveyed by him to Government authorities, even if the information is revealed on the assumption that it will be used only for a limited purpose and the confidence placed in the third party will not be betrayed.

Id. at 442–43.

This rule can even apply if the suspect retains ownership in the documents disclosed to a third party. For example, in Couch v. United States, 409 U.S. 322 (1973), the defendant was a business owner who provided bank statements, payroll records, and reports of sales and expenditures to her accountant so the accountant could prepare her income tax returns. The government subpoenaed the records from her accountant in an effort to determine if the defendant had committed tax offenses. In an opinion by Justice Powell, the Court held that the defendant had relinquished her reasonable expectation of privacy in the documents by disclosing them to her accountant. The reasoning of the opinion appears to hinge at least in part on the specific role of accountants; the Court held that "there can be little expectation of privacy where records are handed to an accountant, knowing that mandatory disclosure of much of the information therein is required in an income tax return. What information is not disclosed is largely in the accountant's discretion, not petitioner's." *Id.* at 335.

How should these principles apply to computer data sent remotely over at network? Is computer data "sealed" or "unsealed"? What is the "destination" of an e-mail or a request for a web page?

Imagine you send an e-mail from a law school account to a friend at another law school. The e-mail will be sent to your university's server, stored, copied, and sent on to the university server at your friend's school. Are these servers like the accountant in *Couch*, or more like bailees holding sealed packages? How do we choose which similarities or differences are most important for Fourth Amendment purposes?

The Telephone Analogy

Instead of analogizing computer network communications to speech or letters, we might try to analogize them to telephone calls. The Supreme Court's first decision on how the Fourth Amendment applies to telephone calls was Olmstead v. United States, 277 U.S. 438 (1928). Roy Olmstead was the leader of a massive Prohibition-era conspiracy to import illegal alcohol into the United States. Agents tapped the telephone lines to Olmstead's house and offices and then listened in on the calls to gather evidence against him. The Supreme Court ruled 5–4 that this wiretapping did not constitute a Fourth Amendment search. Writing for the majority, Chief Justice Taft rejected the letter analogy:

> The Fourth Amendment may have proper application to a sealed letter in the mail, because of the constitutional provision for the Postoffice Department and the relations between the government and those who pay to secure protection of their sealed letters. * * * It is plainly within the words of the amendment to say that the unlawful rifling by a government agent of a sealed letter is a search and seizure of the sender's papers of effects. The letter is a paper, an effect, and in the custody of a government that forbids carriage, except under its protection.

> The United States takes no such care of telegraph or telephone messages as of mailed sealed letters. The amendment does not forbid what was done here. There was no searching. There was no seizure. The evidence was secured by the use of the sense of hearing and that only. There was no entry of the houses or offices of the defendants.

> By the invention of the telephone 50 years ago, and its application for the purpose of extending communications, one can talk with another at a far distant place.

> The language of the amendment cannot be extended and expanded to include telephone wires, reaching to the whole world from the defendant's house or office. The intervening wires are not part of his house or office, any more than are the highways along which they are stretched.

Id. at 464–65. Chief Justice Taft construed telephone calls as more akin to human speech than letters:

> The reasonable view is that one who installs in his house a telephone instrument with connecting wires intends to project his voice to those quite outside, and that the wires beyond his house, and messages while passing over them, are not within the protection of the Fourth Amendment. Here those who intercepted the projected voices were not in the house of either party to the conversation.

Id. at 466.

In his famous dissent, Justice Louis Brandeis presented a very different picture of the Fourth Amendment and the role of wiretapping:

> When the Fourth and Fifth Amendments were adopted, the form that evil had theretofore taken had been necessarily simple. Force and violence were then the only means known to man by which a government could directly effect self-incrimination. It could compel the individual to testify—a compulsion effected, if need be, by torture. It could secure possession of his papers and other articles incident to his private life—a seizure effected, if need be, by breaking and entry. Protection against such invasion of the sanctities of a man's home and the privacies of life was provided in the Fourth and Fifth Amendments by specific language. But time works changes, brings into existence new conditions and purposes. Subtler and more far-reaching means of invading privacy have become available to the government. Discovery and invention have made it possible for the government, by means far more effective than stretching upon the rack, to obtain disclosure in court of what is whispered in the closet.

> Moreover, in the application of a Constitution, our contemplation cannot be only of what has been, but of what may be. The progress of science in furnishing the government with means of espionage is not likely to stop with wire tapping. Ways may some day be developed by which the government, without removing papers from secret drawers, can reproduce them in court, and by which it will be enabled to expose to a jury the most intimate occurrences of the home. Advances in the psychic and related sciences may bring means of exploring unexpressed beliefs, thoughts and emotions. 'That places the liberty of every man in the hands of every petty officer' was said by James Otis of much lesser intrusions than these. To Lord Camden a far slighter intrusion seemed 'subversive of all the comforts of society.' Can it be that the Constitution affords no protection against such invasions of individual security?

> In *Ex parte Jackson*, it was held that a sealed letter intrusted to the mail is protected by the amendments. The mail is a public service furnished by the government. The telephone is a public service furnished by its authority. There is, in essence, no difference between the sealed letter and the private telephone message. As Judge Rudkin said below: "True, the one is visible, the other invisible; the one is tangible, the other intangible; the one is sealed, and the other unsealed; but these are distinctions without a difference."

> The evil incident to invasion of the privacy of the telephone is far greater than that involved in tampering with the mails. Whenever a telephone line is tapped, the privacy of the persons at both ends of the line is invaded, and all conversations between them upon any subject, and although proper, confidential, and privileged, may be overheard. Moreover, the tapping of one man's telephone line in-

volves the tapping of the telephone of every other person whom he may call, or who may call him. As a means of espionage, writs of assistance and general warrants are but puny instruments of tyranny and oppression when compared with wire tapping.

* * * The makers of our Constitution undertook to secure conditions favorable to the pursuit of happiness. They recognized the significance of man's spiritual nature, of his feelings and of his intellect. They knew that only a part of the pain, pleasure and satisfactions of life are to be found in material things. They sought to protect Americans in their beliefs, their thoughts, their emotions and their sensations. They conferred, as against the government, the right to be let alone—the most comprehensive of rights and the right most valued by civilized men. To protect, that right, every unjustifiable intrusion by the government upon the privacy of the individual, whatever the means employed, must be deemed a violation of the Fourth Amendment.

Id. at 473–476, 478–79 (Brandeis, J., dissenting).

The Supreme Court effectively overruled *Olmstead* in two cases, Berger v. New York, 388 U.S. 41 (1967), and Katz v. United States, 389 U.S. 347 (1967). *Berger* invalidated a New York state wiretapping law on the ground that it did not provide sufficient Fourth Amendment safeguards. The majority opinion did not directly hold that the wiretapping violated the rights of the person whose phone was tapped. Instead, the opinion took the opportunity to articulate general Fourth Amendment requirements for wiretapping statutes. Unlike *Berger*, *Katz* was not a wiretapping case. *Katz* involved a microphone taped to a public phone booth, not the intercept of any calls. However, a passage in the majority opinion announced the end of the *Olmstead* regime:

It is true that the absence of [physical] penetration was at one time thought to foreclose further Fourth Amendment inquiry, for that Amendment was thought to limit only searches and seizures of tangible property. But the premise that property interests control the right of the Government to search and seize has been discredited. Thus, although a closely divided Court supposed in *Olmstead* that surveillance without any trespass and without the seizure of any material object fell outside the ambit of the Constitution, we have since departed from the narrow view on which that decision rested. Indeed, we have expressly held that the Fourth Amendment governs not only the seizure of tangible items, but extends as well to the recording of oral statements, over-heard without any technical trespass under local property law. Once this much is acknowledged, and once it is recognized that the Fourth Amendment protects people—and not simply "areas"—against unreasonable searches and seizures, it becomes clear that the reach of that Amendment cannot turn upon the presence or absence of a physical intrusion into any given enclosure.

We conclude that the underpinnings of *Olmstead* * * * have been so eroded by our subsequent decisions that the "trespass" doctrine there enunciated can no longer be regarded as controlling.

Katz, 389 U.S. at 352–53.

The combination of *Berger* and *Katz* indicates that wiretapping an individual's telephone calls normally amounts to a Fourth Amendment "search." An important limitation on this principle was made clear a decade later, when the Supreme Court handed down the following case.

SMITH v. MARYLAND

Supreme Court of the United States, 1979.
442 U.S. 735.

Mr. Justice Blackmun delivered the opinion of the Court.

This case presents the question whether the installation and use of a pen register[1] constitutes a "search" within the meaning of the Fourth Amendment, made applicable to the States through the Fourteenth Amendment.

I

On March 5, 1976, in Baltimore, Md., Patricia McDonough was robbed. She gave the police a description of the robber and of a 1975 Monte Carlo automobile she had observed near the scene of the crime. After the robbery, McDonough began receiving threatening and obscene phone calls from a man identifying himself as the robber. On one occasion, the caller asked that she step out on her front porch; she did so, and saw the 1975 Monte Carlo she had earlier described to police moving slowly past her home. On March 16, police spotted a man who met McDonough's description driving a 1975 Monte Carlo in her neighborhood. By tracing the license plate number, police learned that the car was registered in the name of petitioner, Michael Lee Smith.

The next day, the telephone company, at police request, installed a pen register at its central offices to record the numbers dialed from the telephone at petitioner's home. The police did not get a warrant or court order before having the pen register installed. The register revealed that on March 17 a call was placed from petitioner's home to McDonough's phone. On the basis of this and other evidence, the police obtained a warrant to search petitioner's residence. The search revealed that a page in petitioner's phone book was turned down to the name and number of Patricia McDonough; the phone book was seized. Petitioner was arrest-

---

1. "A pen register is a mechanical device that records the numbers dialed on a telephone by monitoring the electrical impulses caused when the dial on the telephone is released. It does not overhear oral communications and does not indicate whether calls are actually completed." *United States v. New York Tel. Co.,* 434 U.S. 159, 161 n. 1 (1977). A pen register is "usually installed at a central telephone facility [and] records on a paper tape all numbers dialed from [the] line" to which it is attached. *United States v. Giordano,* 416 U.S. 505, 549 n. 1 (1974) (opinion concurring in part and dissenting in part).

ed, and a six-man lineup was held on March 19. McDonough identified petitioner as the man who had robbed her.

Petitioner was indicted in the Criminal Court of Baltimore for robbery. By pretrial motion, he sought to suppress all fruits derived from the pen register on the ground that the police had failed to secure a warrant prior to its installation. The trial court denied the suppression motion, holding that the warrantless installation of the pen register did not violate the Fourth Amendment. Petitioner then waived a jury, and the case was submitted to the court on an agreed statement of facts. The pen register tape (evidencing the fact that a phone call had been made from petitioner's phone to McDonough's phone) and the phone book seized in the search of petitioner's residence were admitted into evidence against him. Petitioner was convicted, and was sentenced to six years. He appealed to the Maryland Court of Special Appeals, but the Court of Appeals of Maryland issued a writ of certiorari to the intermediate court in advance of its decision in order to consider whether the pen register evidence had been properly admitted at petitioner's trial.

II

A

The Fourth Amendment guarantees "the right of the people to be secure in their persons, houses, papers, and effects, against unreasonable searches and seizures." In determining whether a particular form of government-initiated electronic surveillance is a "search" within the meaning of the Fourth Amendment,[4] our lodestar is *Katz v. United States*, 389 U.S. 347 (1967). In *Katz*, Government agents had intercepted the contents of a telephone conversation by attaching an electronic listening device to the outside of a public phone booth. The Court rejected the argument that a "search" can occur only when there has been a "physical intrusion" into a "constitutionally protected area," noting that the Fourth Amendment "protects people, not places." Because the Government's monitoring of Katz' conversation "violated the privacy upon which he justifiably relied while using the telephone booth," the Court held that it constituted a search and seizure within the meaning of the Fourth Amendment.

Consistently with *Katz*, this Court uniformly has held that the application of the Fourth Amendment depends on whether the person invoking its protection can claim a "justifiable," a "reasonable," or a "legitimate expectation of privacy" that has been invaded by government action * * *. This inquiry, as Mr. Justice Harlan aptly noted in his *Katz* concurrence, normally embraces two discrete questions. The first is whether the individual, by his conduct, has exhibited an actual (subjec-

---

4. In this case, the pen register was installed, and the numbers dialed were recorded, by the telephone company. The telephone company, however, acted at police request. In view of this, respondent appears to concede that the company is to be deemed an "agent" of the police for purposes of this case, so as to render the installation and use of the pen register "state action" under the Fourth and Fourteenth Amendments. We may assume that "state action" was present here.

tive) expectation of privacy—whether, in the words of the *Katz* majority, the individual has shown that he seeks to preserve something as private. The second question is whether the individual's subjective expectation of privacy is one that society is prepared to recognize as reasonable—whether, in the words of the *Katz* majority, the individual's expectation, viewed objectively, is justifiable under the circumstances.[5]

B

In applying the *Katz* analysis to this case, it is important to begin by specifying precisely the nature of the state activity that is challenged. The activity here took the form of installing and using a pen register. Since the pen register was installed on telephone company property at the telephone company's central offices, petitioner obviously cannot claim that his property was invaded or that police intruded into a constitutionally protected area. Petitioner's claim, rather, is that, notwithstanding the absence of a trespass, the State, as did the Government in *Katz*, infringed a legitimate expectation of privacy that petitioner held. Yet a pen register differs significantly from the listening device employed in *Katz,* for pen registers do not acquire the *contents* of communications. This Court recently noted:

> "Indeed, a law enforcement official could not even determine from the use of a pen register whether a communication existed. These devices do not hear sound. They disclose only the telephone numbers that have been dialed—a means of establishing communication. Neither the purport of any communication between the caller and the recipient of the call, their identities, nor whether the call was even completed is disclosed by pen registers." *United States v. New York Tel. Co.,* 434 U.S. 159, 167 (1977).

Given a pen register's limited capabilities, therefore, petitioner's argument that its installation and use constituted a "search" necessarily rests upon a claim that he had a legitimate expectation of privacy regarding the numbers he dialed on his phone.

This claim must be rejected. First, we doubt that people in general entertain any actual expectation of privacy in the numbers they dial. All telephone users realize that they must "convey" phone numbers to the telephone company, since it is through telephone company switching

---

5. Situations can be imagined, of course, in which *Katz'* two-pronged inquiry would provide an inadequate index of Fourth Amendment protection. For example, if the Government were suddenly to announce on nationwide television that all homes henceforth would be subject to warrantless entry, individuals thereafter might not in fact entertain any actual expectation or privacy regarding their homes, papers, and effects. Similarly, if a refugee from a totalitarian country, unaware of this Nation's traditions, erroneously assumed that police were continuously monitoring his telephone conversations, a subjective expectation of privacy regarding the contents of his calls might be lacking as well. In such circumstances, where an individual's subjective expectations had been "conditioned" by influences alien to well-recognized Fourth Amendment freedoms, those subjective expectations obviously could play no meaningful role in ascertaining what the scope of Fourth Amendment protection was. In determining whether a "legitimate expectation of privacy" existed in such cases, a normative inquiry would be proper.

equipment that their calls are completed. All subscribers realize, moreover, that the phone company has facilities for making permanent records of the numbers they dial, for they see a list of their long-distance (toll) calls on their monthly bills. In fact, pen registers and similar devices are routinely used by telephone companies for the purposes of checking billing operations, detecting fraud and preventing violations of law. Electronic equipment is used not only to keep billing records of toll calls, but also to keep a record of all calls dialed from a telephone which is subject to a special rate structure. Pen registers are regularly employed to determine whether a home phone is being used to conduct a business, to check for a defective dial, or to check for overbilling. Although most people may be oblivious to a pen register's esoteric functions, they presumably have some awareness of one common use: to aid in the identification of persons making annoying or obscene calls. *See, e.g., Von Lusch v. C & P Telephone Co.,* 457 F. Supp. 814, 816 (Md. 1978); Claerhout, The Pen Register, 20 Drake L. Rev. 108, 110–111 (1970). Most phone books tell subscribers, on a page entitled "Consumer Information," that the company "can frequently help in identifying to the authorities the origin of unwelcome and troublesome calls." *E.g.,* Baltimore Telephone Directory 21 (1978); District of Columbia Telephone Directory 13 (1978). Telephone users, in sum, typically know that they must convey numerical information to the phone company; that the phone company has facilities for recording this information; and that the phone company does in fact record this information for a variety of legitimate business purposes. Although subjective expectations cannot be scientifically gauged, it is too much to believe that telephone subscribers, under these circumstances, harbor any general expectation that the numbers they dial will remain secret.

Petitioner argues, however, that, whatever the expectations of telephone users in general, he demonstrated an expectation of privacy by his own conduct here, since he "used the telephone *in his house* to the exclusion of all others." Brief for Petitioner 6 (emphasis added). But the site of the call is immaterial for purposes of analysis in this case. Although petitioner's conduct may have been calculated to keep the *contents* of his conversation private, his conduct was not and could not have been calculated to preserve the privacy of the number he dialed. Regardless of his location, petitioner had to convey that number to the telephone company in precisely the same way if he wished to complete his call. The fact that he dialed the number on his home phone rather than on some other phone could make no conceivable difference, nor could any subscriber rationally think that it would.

Second, even if petitioner did harbor some subjective expectation that the phone numbers he dialed would remain private, this expectation is not one that society is prepared to recognize as 'reasonable.' This Court consistently has held that a person has no legitimate expectation of privacy in information he voluntarily turns over to third parties. *E.g., United States v. Miller,* 425 U.S. 435, 442–4 (1976); *Hoffa v. United States,* 385 U.S. 293, 302 (1966). In *Miller,* for example, the Court held that a bank depositor has no legitimate expectation of privacy in financial information voluntarily conveyed to * * * banks and exposed to their employees in the ordinary course of business. The Court explained:

> The depositor takes the risk, in revealing his affairs to another, that the information will be conveyed by that person to the Government.... This Court has held repeatedly that the Fourth Amendment does not prohibit the obtaining of information revealed to a third party and conveyed by him to Government authorities, even if the information is revealed on the assumption that it will be used only for a limited purpose and the confidence placed in the third party will not be betrayed.

Id., at 443. Because the depositor "assumed the risk" of disclosure, the Court held that it would be unreasonable for him to expect his financial records to remain private.

This analysis dictates that petitioner can claim no legitimate expectation of privacy here. When he used his phone, petitioner voluntarily conveyed numerical information to the telephone company and "exposed" that information to its equipment in the ordinary course of business. In so doing, petitioner assumed the risk that the company would reveal to police the numbers he dialed. The switching equipment that processed those numbers is merely the modern counterpart of the operator who, in an earlier day, personally completed calls for the subscriber. Petitioner concedes that if he had placed his calls through an operator, he could claim no legitimate expectation of privacy. Tr. of Oral Arg. 3–5, 11–12, 32. We are not inclined to hold that a different constitutional result is required because the telephone company has decided to automate.

Petitioner argues, however, that automatic switching equipment differs from a live operator in one pertinent respect. An operator, in theory at least, is capable of remembering every number that is conveyed to him by callers. Electronic equipment, by contrast can "remember" only those numbers it is programmed to record, and telephone companies, in view of their present billing practices, usually do not record local calls. Since petitioner, in calling McDonough, was making a local call, his expectation of privacy as to her number, on this theory, would be "legitimate."

This argument does not withstand scrutiny. The fortuity of whether or not the phone company in fact elects to make a quasi-permanent record of a particular number dialed does not in our view, make any constitutional difference. Regardless of the phone company's election, petitioner voluntarily conveyed to it information that it had facilities for recording and that it was free to record. In these circumstances, petitioner assumed the risk that the information would be divulged to police. Under petitioner's theory, Fourth Amendment protection would exist, or not, depending on how the telephone company chose to define local-dialing zones, and depending on how it chose to bill its customers for local calls. Calls placed across town, or dialed directly, would be protected; calls placed across the river, or dialed with operator assistance, might not be. We are not inclined to make a crazy quilt of the Fourth Amendment, especially in circumstances where (as here) the pattern of protection would be dictated by billing practices of a private corporation.

We therefore conclude that petitioner in all probability entertained no actual expectation of privacy in the phone numbers he dialed, and that, even if he did, his expectation was not legitimate. The installation and use of a pen register, consequently, was not a "search," and no warrant was required.

Mr. Justice MARSHALL, with whom Mr. Justice BRENNAN joins, dissenting.

The crux of the Court's holding * * * is that whatever expectation of privacy petitioner may in fact have entertained regarding his calls, it is not one society is prepared to recognize as 'reasonable'. In so ruling, the Court determines that individuals who convey information to third parties have "assumed the risk" of disclosure to the government. This analysis is misconceived in two critical respects.

Implicit in the concept of assumption of risk is some notion of choice. At least in the third-party consensual surveillance cases, which first incorporated risk analysis into Fourth Amendment doctrine, the defendant presumably had exercised some discretion in deciding who should enjoy his confidential communications. By contrast here, unless a person is prepared to forgo use of what for many has become a personal or professional necessity, he cannot help but accept the risk of surveillance. It is idle to speak of "assuming" risks in contexts where, as a practical matter, individuals have no realistic alternative.

More fundamentally, to make risk analysis dispositive in assessing the reasonableness of privacy expectations would allow the government to define the scope of Fourth Amendment protections. For example, law enforcement officials, simply by announcing their intent to monitor the content of random samples of first-class mail or private phone conversations, could put the public on notice of the risks they would thereafter assume in such communications. *See* Amsterdam, Perspectives on the Fourth Amendment, 58 Minn. L. Rev. 349, 384, 407 (1974). Yet, although acknowledging this implication of its analysis, the Court is willing to concede only that, in some circumstances, a further "normative inquiry would be proper." No meaningful effort is made to explain what those circumstances might be, or why this case is not among them.

In my view, whether privacy expectations are legitimate within the meaning of *Katz* depends not on the risks an individual can be presumed to accept when imparting information to third parties, but on the risks he should be forced to assume in a free and open society. * * *

The use of pen registers, I believe, constitutes such an extensive intrusion. To hold otherwise ignores the vital role telephonic communication plays in our personal and professional relationships as well as the First and Fourth Amendment interests implicated by unfettered official surveillance. Privacy in placing calls is of value not only to those engaged in criminal activity. The prospect of unregulated governmental monitoring will undoubtedly prove disturbing even to those with nothing illicit to hide. Many individuals, including members of unpopular political organizations or journalists with confidential sources, may legitimately wish to avoid disclosure of their personal contacts. Permitting governmental access to telephone records on less than probable cause may thus impede certain forms of political affiliation and journalistic endeavor that are the hallmark of a truly free society. Particularly given the Government's previous reliance on warrantless telephonic surveillance to trace reporters' sources and monitor protected political activity, I am unwilling to insulate use of pen registers from independent judicial review.

Just as one who enters a public telephone booth is "entitled to assume that the words he utters into the mouthpiece will not be broadcast to the world," *Katz v. United States, supra,* 389 U.S. at 352, so too, he should be entitled to assume that the numbers he dials in the privacy of his home will be recorded, if at all, solely for the phone company's business purposes. Accordingly, I would require law enforcement officials to obtain a warrant before they enlist telephone companies to secure information otherwise beyond the government's reach.

Notes and Questions

1.   The majority opinion in *Smith* is somewhat hard to follow, in part because Justice Blackmun misapplies the subjective prong of the *Katz* test. The subjective prong of the expectation of privacy test is supposed to be, well, subjective. The question should be whether the individual actually expected privacy, regardless of how reasonable or unreasonable that belief may be. Justice Blackmun's discussion of the expectations of "people in general" as to telephone surveillance, culled from such sources as the DC phone book and law review articles, does not seem relevant to whether Michael Lee Smith expected that the numbers he dialed were being recorded. Similarly, footnote 5's discussion of a "normative" analysis of reasonable expectations is probably best understood as a discussion of when subjective expectations should be ignored (as Fourth Amendment opinions often do).

At the same time, the majority and dissenting opinions in *Smith v. Maryland* offer two significant competing approaches to applying the Fourth Amendment to a network. Justice Blackmun's majority opinion starts with the details of how the network works and then draws analogies to prior cases. Because the dialing of a telephone number constitutes a communication to the telephone company, and in particular, a request to direct the call to a particular number, monitoring by the phone company on behalf of the government is analogous to the use of an informant in *Hoffa*. In contrast, Justice Marshall's dissent focuses on whether permitting the installation of a pen register without Fourth Amendment restriction is consistent with "a free and open society." Under Justice Marshall's approach, the Justices should apply the Fourth Amendment by asking a policy question: Will a warrant requirement help create a free and open society in this particular context?

Consider which is the better approach. Do you prefer Blackmun's analogical reasoning based on the details of how the network works, or do you prefer Marshall's normative inquiry based on the needs of a free and open society? Does your answer depend on whether you have a normative policy preference for requiring warrants before the police can install pen registers? If you prefer Justice Marshall's approach, how can the judiciary determine the needs of a free and open society? Why not leave this up to Congress and state legislatures?

2. Try to reconcile *Smith v. Maryland* with *Katz* and *Berger*. Is the difference that the phone company was a recipient of the numbers dialed in *Smith*, but not a recipient of the contents of the call in *Katz* and *Berger*? Or is the difference that the contents of telephone calls merit greater privacy protection than mere information about such calls, such as the numbers dialed?

Imagine that instead of asking the phone company to install a pen register on Smith's phone, government agents had installed a pen register without the phone company's consent on the line just outside Smith's property. Under the reasoning of Justice Blackmun's majority opinion, would a warrant be necessary? Would the government need a warrant because it was intercepting the communication between Smith and the phone company, or would no warrant be needed because the pen register only recorded the numbers dialed?

3. In the 1980s, companies began offering cordless telephones for sale to the public. Cordless telephones work by broadcasting FM radio signals between the base of the phone and the handset. Each phone has two radio transmitters that work at the same time: the base transmits the incoming call signal to the handset, and the handset transmits the outgoing call signal to the base. Before the mid–1990s, cordless phones generally used analog FM signals that were easy to intercept. Government agents would occasionally use widely available FM radio scanners to listen in on the cordless telephone calls of suspects without a warrant.

In your view, should such surveillance be prohibited by *Katz v. United States* or permitted by *Smith v. Maryland*? Courts that have addressed this issue have relied on *Smith v. Maryland* to reject claims of Fourth Amendment protection in the contents of cordless telephone calls. Because cordless-phone intercepting devices merely pick up a signal that has been "broadcast over the radio waves to all who wish to overhear," the interception was held not to violate any reasonable expectation of privacy. McKamey v. Roach, 55 F.3d 1236, 1239–40 (6th Cir. 1995). *See also* Tyler v. Berodt, 877 F.2d 705, 707 (8th Cir. 1989); Price v. Turner, 260 F.3d 1144, 1149 (9th Cir. 2001). Courts reached the same result when the suspect was using a traditional landline telephone and happened to engage in conversation with someone who was using a cordless phone. *See* United States v. McNulty, 47 F.3d 100, 104–106 (4th Cir. 1995).

Are these cases correct under Justice Blackmun's method of analogical reasoning based on the functioning of the network? Are they correct using

Justice Marshall's normative inquiry into the needs of a free and open society?

Notably, the Fourth Amendment implications of intercepting cordless phone calls generally does not arise today. There are two reasons, one legal and the other technological. The legal reason is that the statutory Wiretap Act was amended in 1994 to prohibit the interception of cordless phone calls. The protections of the Wiretap Act tend to be broader than the Fourth Amendment, so any legal challenge to warrantless cordless phone surveillance ordinarily will be statutory rather than constitutional. *See generally* Adams v. City of Battle Creek, 250 F.3d 980, 986 (6th Cir. 2001). The technological reason is that modern cordless phones use digital signals. Digital signals are much more difficult to intercept successfully than analog signals.

Both factors also explain why there have been no cases involving warrantless government interception of cellular telephone calls. *But see* Bartnicki v. Vopper, 532 U.S. 514 (2001) (case involving private interception of a cell phone call).

4.   Network surveillance can be helpfully divided into two basic types: prospective surveillance and retrospective surveillance. Prospective surveillance refers to "real time" monitoring while communications are in transit. For example, wiretapping is prospective; it catches communications crossing the point being tapped. Similarly, the pen register used in *Smith v. Maryland* was prospective. It recorded numbers dialed as the calls were being placed. In contrast, retrospective surveillance refers to the collection of stored records generated by the network without government interference. For example, the telephone company may keep records of calls for billing purposes, and may keep a file for each account describing how that account was used. Government agents may approach the telephone service provider and ask (or order) it to divulge account records in its possession relating to a particular account.

As you might expect, the basic Fourth Amendment rules for the retrospective surveillance of a communication are the same as the rules for the prospective surveillance of that communication. For example, government agents can obtain account records relating to the past usage of a telephone account from the telephone company without implicating the telephone customer's Fourth Amendment rights. The same rule applies to other kinds of account records. *See, e.g.,* In re Grand Jury Proceedings, 827 F.2d 301, 302–03 (8th Cir. 1987) (Western Union account records). The one possible difference between how the Fourth Amendment treats prospective and retrospective surveillance was suggested in Berger v. New York, 388 U.S. 41 (1967). In *Berger*, the Court suggested that prospective surveillance raises heightened Fourth Amendment concerns because real-time wiretapping can permit a more invasive search over a long period of time as compared to a traditional search. *See id.* at 57. *See also id.* at 65 (Douglas, J., concurring). As a general rule, however, the Fourth Amendment rules for retrospective and prospective surveillance are the same.

5.   The majority opinion in *Smith v. Maryland* treats the telephone company's automated switching equipment as if it were a person:

The switching equipment that processed those numbers is merely the modern counterpart of the operator who, in an earlier day, personally completed calls for the subscriber. Petitioner concedes that if he had placed his calls through an operator, he could claim no legitimate expectation of privacy. Tr. of Oral Arg. 3–5, 11–12, 32. We are not inclined to hold that a different constitutional result is required because the telephone company has decided to automate.

Smith, 442 U.S. at 744–45. Was the Court's "disinclination" appropriate? How far can such an argument go? It could be argued that the telephone itself is "merely the modern counterpart" of the telegraph. In the old days, an individual would take his message to a local telegraph operator, who would read the message and transmit it using Morse code. A telegraph operator at the destination of the message would receive the Morse code signal and translate it back into the original message. Courts did not recognize Fourth Amendment protection in telegraph messages, which were viewed by telephone operators both on the sending end and receiving end. *See* Newfield v. Ryan, 91 F.2d 700, 702–05 (5th Cir. 1937).

Does it make sense that the Fourth Amendment does not protect the contents of telegraph messages but does protect the contents of telephone calls? Should it make a difference that the process is automated? How should these precedents apply to text messages sent via modern cellular phones?

6.   Consider whether precedents such as *Smith v. Maryland, United States v. Miller,* and *Couch v. United States* should be broadly applicable to computer network transmissions. Professor Deirdre Mulligan thinks that these precedents should be limited to their facts, and should not be expanded to computer networks. *See* Deirdre K. Mulligan, *Reasonable Expectations in Electronic Communications: A Critical Perspective on the Electronic Communications Privacy Act,* 72 Geo. Wash. L. Rev. 1557 (2004). Professor Mulligan offers three reasons. First, "[t]he records containing personal information sought by law enforcement in *Couch, Miller,* and *Smith* were records in which the business had an independent interest. . . . In these cases, the businesses did not merely act as conduits or storage facilities for the records; they acted upon the records independently." *Id.* at 1579. Second, "[i]n each of the business records cases, the individual intended to disclose the information at issue to the business." *Id.* at 1580. And third, the nature of the communications did not trigger strong privacy interests, whereas Internet communications often will. *Id.* at 1581. Do you agree that these cases are so easily limited? For an argument somewhat similar to Mulligan's, see Stephen E. Henderson, *Nothing New Under the Sun? A Technologically Rational Doctrine of Fourth Amendment Search,* 56 Mercer L. Rev. 507, 526–27 (2005).

3.   THE FOURTH AMENDMENT AND THE INTERNET

Enough with analogies; let's turn back to computers. Surprisingly few cases exist on how the Fourth Amendment applies to computer networks and the Internet. This is true for several reasons. First, *Smith v. Maryland* limits the Fourth Amendment protections that might apply to computer network surveillance. Second, Congress enacted a comprehensive set of statutory privacy laws in 1986 to regulate government access to computer network data. Statutory requirements have minimized the independent role of Fourth Amendment protections, leading to relatively few constitutional challenges to government practices. (The laws are covered in detail in the next chapter.) Third, computer technologies are new, and relatively few lawyers are sufficiently knowledgeable about them to raise creative challenges to government practices.

Whatever the reasons for the sparse case law today, more Fourth Amendment challenges to network surveillance practices are inevitable. How should the law evolve? Let's look at the current state of the law and then consider where it might go.

GUEST v. LEIS

United States Court of Appeals for the Sixth Circuit, 2001.
255 F.3d 325.

ALAN E. NORRIS, Circuit Judge.

In 1995, the Hamilton County, Ohio, Regional Electronic Computer Intelligence Task Force (RECI) was investigating on-line obscenity and seized two computer bulletin board systems. The first system seized was the Cincinnati Computer Connection Bulletin Board System (CCC BBS). Several users of the system filed a class action [referred to as the *Guest* case] on behalf of subscribers against RECI, the sheriff, and his department alleging violations of the First and Fourth Amendments * * *. The second system seized in the same general investigation was the Spanish Inquisition Bulletin Board System (SI BBS). The system's users, operator, and computer owner brought suit [referred to as the *O'Brien* case] against the same defendants alleging the same violations as in the CCC BBS Suit. The district court granted summary judgment for defendants in each case, and plaintiffs appeal. We affirm.

I. BACKGROUND

A. *Cincinnati Computer Connection Bulletin Board System*

In early 1995, there was a complaint lodged with the Hamilton County Sheriff's Department about on-line obscenity, and RECI, a division of the sheriff's department, began investigating several electronic bulletin board systems, including the CCC BBS. The CCC BBS computers were operated by Robert Emerson in Union Township, Ohio. The system, according to plaintiffs, included thousands of subscribers from the Greater Cincinnati area, the United States and even overseas. Users could, with a password, send e-mail to subscribers or to others on the Internet. They could also participate in chat room conversations, on-line games, and conferences, where they could post or read messages on many topics, and they could download files such as computer programs and pictures.

RECI officers assumed an undercover identity and obtained access to the adult part of the bulletin board system, where they downloaded sample images. A detective presented more than one hundred of these images to a Hamilton County municipal court judge, who determined that forty-five of them were obscene. RECI officers then prepared a search warrant, which identified the forty-five obscene images. The affidavit attached to the warrant listed the offenses in question as pandering obscenity and possessing criminal tools. RECI showed the warrant to attorneys in the Hamilton County prosecutor's office and edited it after this meeting. The revised warrant authorized the search and seizure of computer hardware, software, financial and computer records, and personal communications, limiting the items searched or seized to those that had been used in the offense. RECI officers then presented the warrant to a Clermont County municipal court judge, who signed the warrant, directing it to the police chief of Union Township, located in Clermont County.

On June 16, 1995, members of RECI and the Union Township Police Department went to the home of Robert Emerson to execute the warrant. The officers asked Emerson to locate the obscene images on his system so that they could seize only those files; Emerson denied knowledge of obscene images on the computer and placed a call to his lawyer. While everyone waited for the attorney to return the call, the Union Township officers left the house. Emerson eventually stated that he did not know where the images were on the computer. Several hours after the police's arrival, with still no word from the lawyer, the RECI officers began dismantling the computer system to take it away; Emerson then said that the images were on the large file server. The officers, skeptical of his statement, seized the large and small file servers and took them to the police station.

Deputy Sheriff Ausdenmoore explained the way the computer search proceeded at the station. He said that he used a computer program to locate the forty-five obscene files according to the file names listed in the warrant, and he also searched for unlicenced software. He testified that once he had located the image files, he did not review the rest of the seized property.

B. Spanish Inquisition Bulletin Board System

The SI BBS was a smaller bulletin board system than the CCC BBS, and it was run by a teenager on his father's home computer. Only one user could log on at a time, and the connection to the Internet was more rudimentary than the CCC BBS's connection. The SI BBS included a posted disclaimer on privacy:

> Pursuant to the Electronic and Communications Privacy Act of 1986, Title 18 U.S.Code 2510 and following, all users are hereby notified that there are NO provisions for private messages on this board. This is TRUE notwithstanding the fact that the system software indicates to the user that he or she may and can make a message "private." All messages may be read by the SysOp systems operator and his assigns.

O'Brien Joint Appendix at 655.

The SI BBS investigation began after a parent reported to police that his son and a friend were viewing child pornography. RECI officials interviewed several of the juveniles implicated and analyzed their computers, which disclosed child and adult pornography and files indicating unauthorized access to computer systems. RECI traced the latter files, called HPACV (hacker/phreaker/anarchy/cracking/virus) files, to the SI BBS, but the detectives were unable to gain access to the bulletin board system. They obtained a warrant on the basis of their interviews with the juveniles and examination of their computers, which indicated that the SI BBS was used to tap phone lines, recover debit card numbers, acquire pirated software, and download child pornography. The warrant borrowed the CCC BBS warrant language authorizing the seizure of all equipment, documentation, and personal communications that were used in the offenses listed. The supporting affidavit listed three offenses: illegal use of a minor in nudity-oriented material, unauthorized use of property, and possessing criminal tools. The warrant for a search of the owner's home in Butler County was issued by the Butler County Court of Common Pleas and directed to the Police Chief of Union Township.

On August 31, 1995, RECI executed the search warrant for the SI BBS. After unsuccessful attempts to contact the computer's owner, defendants removed computer equipment and disks. Union Township police accompanied RECI officials and remained present until RECI officials left the premises.

This lawsuit was filed on March 6, 1996, by four individual members of the SI BBS, the operator of the SI BBS, and [Michael O'Brien,] the owner of the computer that housed the system.

II.   FOURTH AMENDMENT

Defendants argue that plaintiffs do not have standing to assert Fourth Amendment claims in these cases. In order to challenge a search or seizure as a violation of the Fourth Amendment, a person must have had a subjective expectation of privacy in the place or property to be searched which was objectively reasonable. Minnesota v. Olson, 495 U.S. 91, 95–96 (1990). Home owners would of course have a reasonable expectation of privacy in their homes and in their belongings—including computers—inside the home. Bulletin board users would not share the same interest in someone else's house or computer, so they would not be able to challenge the search of the homes and the seizure of the computers as physical objects. Their interest in the computer content presents a different question and would depend on their expectations of privacy in the materials. In the *O'Brien* case, the SI BBS posted a disclaimer stating that personal communications were not private. This disclaimer defeats claims to an objectively reasonable expectation of privacy for the SI BBS users. *See* United States v. Simons, 206 F.3d 392, 398 (4th Cir. 2000) (finding no privacy interest in an employee's internet search records when an employer posted a privacy disclaimer regarding computer files). Accordingly, the *O'Brien* user-plaintiffs do not have standing to assert Fourth Amendment claims.

The *Guest* user-plaintiffs' standing would turn on the materials they had on the CCC BBS. Users would logically lack a legitimate expectation of privacy in the materials intended for publication or public posting. They would lose a legitimate expectation of privacy in an e-mail that had already reached its recipient; at this moment, the e-mailer would be analogous to a letter-writer, whose "expectation of privacy ordinarily terminates upon delivery" of the letter. United States v. King, 55 F.3d 1193, 1196 (6th Cir. 1995). Whether the users had more private material on the system that entitled them to standing is not a question we must reach since we conclude below that there was no Fourth Amendment violation in this case.

The warrant authorized the seizure of personal communications related to the offense. Although there were presumably communications on the computers that did not relate to the offenses, "a search does not become invalid merely because some items not covered by a warrant are seized." United States v. Henson, 848 F.2d 1374, 1383 (6th Cir. 1988). In *Henson*, a case affirming convictions involving false odometer statements, we rejected a Fourth Amendment challenge to the seizure of documents and computer files that were unrelated to the offenses because we concluded that it would have been unreasonable to require police to sort through extensive files in a suspect's office in order to separate out those items that were outside the warrant. In the instant cases, when the seizures occurred, defendants were unable to separate relevant files from unrelated files, so they took the computers to be able to sort out the documents off-site. Because of the technical difficulties of conducting a computer search in a suspect's home, the seizure of the computers, including their content, was reasonable in these cases to allow police to locate the offending files.

Plaintiffs argue that defendants violated the Fourth Amendment by accessing bulletin board subscriber information. These records include information such as subscribers' names, addresses, birthdates, and passwords. As we have noted above, a person must have a reasonable expectation of privacy in the matter searched in order to challenge a search under the Fourth Amendment. Individuals generally lose a reasonable expectation of privacy in their information once they reveal it to third parties. *See* United States v. Miller, 425 U.S. 435, 443 (1976). A bank customer, for instance, does not have a legitimate expectation of privacy in the information that he or she has conveyed to the bank; by placing the information under control of a third party, the customer assumes the risk that the bank will convey the information to the government. Courts have applied this principle to computer searches and seizures to conclude that computer users do not have a legitimate expectation of privacy in their subscriber information because they have conveyed it to another person—the system operator. *See* United States v. Hambrick, No. 99–4793, 2000 WL 1062039, at *4 (4th Cir. Aug. 3, 2000) (unpublished) (holding that defendant destroyed any privacy interest in his subscriber information when he conveyed it to an Internet service provider). We conclude that plaintiffs in these cases lack a Fourth

Amendment privacy interest in their subscriber information because they communicated it to the systems operators. In addition, in the *O'Brien* case, subscriber information would be that of the users, who do not have Fourth Amendment standing.

Notes and Questions

1. The opinion in *Guest v. Leis* is somewhat confusing, so it may be helpful to review what you just read. The Sixth Circuit's opinion consolidates two different lawsuits filed against law enforcement officers and groups for seizures of computers that hosted bulletin board services. Bulletin board services were popular before the World Wide Web came into widespread use in the mid-to-late 1990s: a BBS is something like a website that hosts various services for registered users, often including (as its name would suggest) an online message board. The first lawsuit in *Guest v. Leis* was filed by Guest and other users of the Cincinnati Computer Connection Bulletin Board System (CCC BBS). The second lawsuit was filed by O'Brien, his teenage son, and the users of the Spanish Inquisition Bulletin Board System (SI BBS). The named defendant, Leis, was the local Sheriff.

The court's analysis includes four steps. First, the court holds that O'Brien, the owner of the computer that hosted the SI BBS, has Fourth Amendment standing (that is, a reasonable expectation of privacy) needed to challenge the search and seizure of his computer. Second, the court holds that the users of the SI BBS do not have Fourth Amendment rights to challenge the seizure because the disclaimer defeats any claim to Fourth Amendment protection. Third, the court does not reach a conclusion about whether the users of the CCC BBS have rights to challenge the seizure of their personal communications, as it holds that the seizure of the communications was constitutional and the question of standing need not be decided. Finally, the court holds that users do not have a reasonable expectation of privacy in the basic subscriber information seized from either BBS under the disclosure rationale of *United States v. Miller*.

2. The court's conclusion that the owner of the SI BBS has standing to challenge the search seems difficult to dispute. Investigators forcibly entered his house and removed his computer: It must be right that the search and seizure violated his reasonable expectation of privacy.

3. *Fourth Amendment protection for basic subscriber information.* *Guest v. Leis* cites United States v. Hambrick, No. 99–4793, 2000 WL 1062039 (4th Cir. 2000), for the view that Internet users do not have a reasonable expectation of privacy in basic subscriber information stored with ISPs. In *Hambrick*, investigators served an invalid subpoena on MindSpring, a large commercial ISP, for basic subscriber information about a particular account. When compliance with the subpoena helped yield evidence of criminal activity, the account holder challenged the disclosure of his basic subscriber information on the ground that the invalidity of the subpoena rendered its use unconstitutional. The merits of this argument hinged on whether Hambrick had Fourth Amendment rights in the data to challenge its disclosure. The Fourth Circuit held that Hambrick had no reasonable expectation of privacy in his non-content information:

The subpoena at issue in this case requested that MindSpring produce "any records pertaining to the billing and/or user records documenting the subject using your services on March 14th, 1998 at 1210HRS (EST) using the Internet Protocol Number 207.69.169.92." This information was requested in order to determine the identity of the individual using [a particular] screen name * * * as this screen name is tied to the user's identity in all of MindSpring's business records. The information the government received from MindSpring consisted of Hambrick's subscriber information, which included his name; billing address; home, work, and fax phone numbers; and other billing information. When Hambrick entered into a service agreement with MindSpring, he knowingly revealed this information to MindSpring and its employees. The records that the government obtained from MindSpring had been available to MindSpring employees in the normal course of business. Once the government received this information, it was not later utilized to read Hambrick's e-mails or to attain any other content information.

While under certain circumstances, a person may have an expectation of privacy in content information, a person does not have an interest in the account information given to the ISP in order to establish the e-mail account, which is non-content information. Disclosure of this non-content information to a third party destroys the privacy expectation that might have existed previously. In this case, the government never utilized the non-content information retrieved from MindSpring to attain additional content information, such as the substance of Hambrick's e-mails. In this case, as in *Miller,* there is no legitimate expectation of privacy in information voluntarily conveyed to a third party and exposed to their employees in the ordinary course of business. The information subject to the motion to suppress is merely third-party business records, and therefore, Hambrick's Fourth Amendment claim cannot succeed.

Id. at *4.

How broadly should this principle extend? Should it apply only to basic subscriber information? To all non-content information? To both content and non-content information?

Imagine the faulty subpoena had ordered MindSpring to collect and disclose the following information about Hambrick's account, and that MindSpring had complied with the subpoena. In which of these cases does Hambrick have a reasonable expectation of privacy in the data such that compliance with the invalid subpoena violates Hambrick's Fourth Amendment rights?

A. Login records indicating when Hambrick was online during the month preceding March 14, 1998, the date of Hambrick's criminal activity.
B. A list of all of IP addresses assigned to Hambrick's account from January 1, 1998 to March 14, 1998, assuming that Mindspring assigned a new IP address to the account when the account owner logged in (so-called "dynamic" addressing).

    C.   Retrospective records, if any exist, of the URLs of any websites Hambrick visited using the account on March 14, 1998.

    D.   Prospective records listing all of the URLs of any websites that Hambrick will visit during the week following the receipt of the subpoena.

    E.   Records of the e-mail headers of any e-mails stored in Hambrick's account on the day the subpoena is received.

    F.   Prospective records of the e-mail headers from any e-mails that will arrive in Hambrick's account for the month after the subpoena is received.

    G.   The contents of any opened e-mail stored in Hambrick's inbox on the date the subpoena is received.

    H.   The contents of any outgoing e-mail stored in Hambrick's account on the date the subpoena is received.

    I.   The entire contents of Hambrick's account on the date the subpoena is received.

    J.   Prospective surveillance of every communication sent or received through Hambrick's account for a six-month period starting the day the subpoena is received.

    4. If the disclosure principle of *Smith v. Maryland* and *United States v. Miller* applies broadly to the Internet, covering both content and non-content information, what if any role will the Fourth Amendment play in the protection of Internet privacy? Consider Daniel Solove, *Digital Dossiers and the Dissipation of Fourth Amendment Privacy*, 75 S. Cal. L. Rev. 1083, 1086–87 (2002):

> The Court's current conception of privacy is as a form of total secrecy. As conceived by the Court, an individual's hidden world should be protected. It has expressed an interest in safeguarding the intimate information that individuals carefully conceal. Privacy is about protecting the skeletons that are meticulously hidden in the closet. Since information maintained by third parties is exposed to others, it is not private, and therefore not protected by the Fourth Amendment. This conception of privacy is not responsive to life in the modern Information Age, where most personal information exists in the record systems of hundreds of entities. The Court has turned its back on one of the most far-reaching and potentially dangerous law enforcement practices of our times.

If Solove is right, should we rethink Fourth Amendment protections? Or should we look to statutory privacy laws to fill in the gap left by constitutional decisions?

    5. *Content and non-content information.* Fourth Amendment precedents often distinguish between the contents of communications and non-content addressing information. The distinction between content and non-content addressing information is basic to any network. Non-content addressing information is needed to deliver the communication, while content information is the communication delivered. In the case of the postal network and the telephone network, these two types of information are

collected in different ways. Addressing information for a letter can be collected by examining the outside of the envelope, while obtaining content information requires actually opening the envelope and viewing the letter inside. Similarly, the phone company would traditionally install a pen register to obtain the numbers dialed by a phone, while it would need to tap the line to obtain call contents.

In contrast with letters and phone calls, Internet communications blend content and non-content information in a single stream of zeros and ones. The Internet works by combining content and non-content information into packets and sending them across networks. Computers that process the data can identify the zeros and ones that are content information only because distinctive patterns of zeros and ones indicate what data should be treated as contents and what data should be treated as non-content addressing information.

If computer communications blend content and non-content information together, does it make sense that the Fourth Amendment should provide a different level of protection for contents and addressing information? Does it make sense that some zeros and ones in a stream of data receive Fourth Amendment protection while others do not? If it doesn't make sense to treat content and non-content information differently, which standard should apply? Should the Fourth Amendment protect the entire stream of data or none of it?

To the extent courts distinguish between Fourth Amendment protection for contents and non-content information, it is worth flagging a question that will be considered in greater detail in the next chapter: Exactly what types of computer network communications count as contents? The distinction between content and non-content information is easy to apply in the case of human-to-human networks such as the postal network and the traditional telephone network. Letters and telephone calls are communications between human beings, and the contents of communications are the actual messages between human senders and human recipients. In contrast, computer networks permit the transmission of a much wider range of information than the postal or telephone network. Internet communications include human-to-computer communications such as website queries and computer-to-computer communications such as IP headers. When should human-to-computer communications count as contents? Can computer-to-computer communications ever count as contents?

6. *Should banners or Terms of Service define Fourth Amendment rights?* In *Guest*, the Sixth Circuit held that the users of the SI BBS had no reasonable expectation of privacy in the contents of the files stored with the BBS because of the disclaimer users encountered upon accessing the BBS. Recall that the disclaimer stated that "all users are hereby notified that there are NO provisions for private messages on this board." The Sixth Circuit concluded that this banner defeated any claim of Fourth Amendment protection, citing United States v. Simons, 206 F.3d 392, 398 (4th Cir.2000).

This may have been a simple error. *Simons* involved the Fourth Amendment rights of a government employee, and was decided under the unique framework of O'Connor v. Ortega, 480 U.S. 709 (1987). The *O'Connor* test for government employee privacy focuses on legitimate workplace regulations: if a government employer states that no privacy exists at work, then no privacy exists at work. But this rule is specific to government employment. The Sixth Circuit seems to miss this point in *Guest*; although its analysis is sparse, the court seems to read *Simons* as a computer privacy case instead of a government workplace privacy case.

With that said, should the *O'Connor v. Ortega* framework also apply in the case of a private bulletin board service or a commercial ISP? Does it make sense that a user's Fourth Amendment rights should hinge on banners and terms of service chosen by the provider?

Consider Freedman v. America Online, 412 F. Supp. 2d 174 (D. Conn. 2005). The plaintiff used an AOL account with a pseudonymous screenname to send a threatening e-mail to two supporters of a political opponent. The recipients of the e-mail filed a report with the local police, and the police filled out a search warrant form ordering AOL to disclose basic subscriber information for that account. The police neglected to have the warrant signed by a judge, however, and ended up faxing the unsigned warrant to AOL. AOL in turn disclosed the plaintiff's identity to the police. The plaintiff later sued AOL, claiming that its disclosure of his identity pursuant to an invalid warrant violated his Fourth Amendment rights. The plaintiff tried to distinguish his case from *Hambrick* using the terms of AOL's privacy policy. The court rejected the plaintiff's argument on at least the partial ground that AOL's privacy policy could be read to allow the disclosure: "AOL's promise was not absolute, as it had expressly informed Plaintiff that it may, in limited circumstances, reveal his subscriber information." *Id.* at 183.

Should the terms of AOL's privacy policy make a difference? Why should they be relevant?

7. *E-mail contents and the letter analogy.* United States v. Maxwell, 45 M.J. 406 (C.A.A.F. 1996), considered a Fourth Amendment challenge to a warrant used to compel America Online to disclose the contents of e-mails in a suspect's account. The U.S. Court of Appeals for the Armed Forces[b] relied on the letter analogy to conclude that contents of stored AOL e-mail should receive Fourth Amendment protection, *id.* at 417–19:

> E-mail transmissions are not unlike other forms of modern communication. We can draw parallels from these other mediums. For example, if a sender of first-class mail seals an envelope and addresses it to another person, the sender can reasonably expect the contents to remain private and free from the eyes of the police absent a search warrant founded upon probable cause. However, once the letter is received and opened, the destiny of the letter then lies in the control of the recipient of the letter, not the sender, absent some legal privilege.

> Drawing from these parallels, we can say that the transmitter of an e-mail message enjoys a reasonable expectation that police officials will not intercept the transmission without probable cause and a search

b. The U.S. Court of Appeals for the Armed Forces is an Article I court that reviews court-martial convictions of service members brought under the Uniform Code of Military Justice. Specifically, the Court reviews decisions of the four military intermediate appellate courts: the Army Court of Criminal Appeals, the Navy–Marine Corps Court of Criminal Appeals, the Air Force Court of Criminal Appeals, and the Coast Guard Court of Criminal Appeals.

warrant. However, once the transmissions are received by another person, the transmitter no longer controls its destiny. In a sense, e-mail is like a letter. It is sent and lies sealed in the computer until the recipient opens his or her computer and retrieves the transmission. The sender enjoys a reasonable expectation that the initial transmission will not be intercepted by the police. The fact that an unauthorized "hacker" might intercept an e-mail message does not diminish the legitimate expectation of privacy in any way.

There is, however, one major difference between an e-mail message which has been transmitted via a network such as AOL and a direct computer "real time" transmission. The former transmission is stored in a centralized computer until the recipient opens his or her network and retrieves the e-mail, while the latter is lost forever, unless one of the communicators chooses to download the conversation to a disk. This latter action would be much like clandestinely recording one's telephone conversation. Thus, while a user of an e-mail network may enjoy a reasonable expectation that his or her e-mail will not be revealed to police, there is the risk that an employee or other person with direct access to the network service will access the e-mail, despite any company promises to the contrary. One always bears the risk that a recipient of an e-mail message will redistribute the e-mail or an employee of the company will read e-mail against company policy. However, this is not the same as the police commanding an individual to intercept the message.

Also, in another context, the relationship of a computer network subscriber to the network is similar to that of a bank customer to a bank. So far as the company's records are concerned, there is no reasonable expectation that the records are private, and the customer has no control whatsoever over which employees may see the records.

The Government has argued that appellant forfeited any expectation of privacy in his e-mail messages through the e-mail forwarding process. If we accept this premise, any information forwarded would not be subject to Fourth Amendment protections. This argument parallels the rationale used by the Supreme Court in *Hoffa v. United States, supra.* In *Hoffa,* the Court decided that notorious labor leader, James "Jimmy" Hoffa, had no Fourth Amendment protection for a conversation overheard by a government informant who had been invited to be present. The Court reasoned that there is no protection under the Fourth Amendment for "a wrongdoer's misplaced belief that a person to whom he voluntarily confides his wrongdoing will not reveal it." Justice Stewart went on to say: "The risk of being overheard by an eavesdropper or betrayed by an informer or deceived as to the identity of one with whom one deals is probably inherent in the conditions of human society. It is the kind of risk we necessarily assume whenever we speak."

We agree to a limited extent with the Government. Expectations of privacy in e-mail transmissions depend in large part on the type of e-mail involved and the intended recipient. Messages sent to the public at large in the "chat room" or e-mail that is "forwarded" from correspondent to correspondent lose any semblance of privacy. Once these transmissions are sent out to more and more subscribers, the subsequent expectation of privacy incrementally diminishes. This loss of an expectation of privacy, however, only goes to these specific pieces of mail for which privacy interests were lessened and ultimately abandoned.

Maxwell states that "in a sense, e-mail is like a letter. It is sent and lies sealed in the computer until the recipient opens his or her computer and retrieves the transmission." Is that true? Are e-mails actually "sealed"? Are e-mails really more like e-postcards, and if so, should that impact whether they receive Fourth Amendment protection? Also, what does it mean for Fourth Amendment protections to "depend in large part on the type of e-mail involved"? And what does it mean for Fourth Amendment protection to "incrementally diminish"?

Contrast *Maxwell* with United States v. Geter, 2003 WL 21254249 (N.M. Ct. Crim. App. 2003) (unpublished), *vacated on other grounds*, 60 M.J. 344 (C.A.A.F. 2004). In *Geter*, a Marine used a government computer network account provided to him for official government business to send and receive personal e-mails, including e-mails relating to Geter's side business selling marijuana. At some point, a military system administrator decided to take a look at the unusually large storage space that Geter's account was occupying on the military server. The system administrator found the e-mails, and the e-mails were used against Geter when the military brought drug-related charges. Geter moved to suppress, arguing that the system administrator's warrantless search through Geter's e-mails on the military network violated his Fourth Amendment rights. The court concluded that Geter had no reasonable expectation of privacy in the contents of his remotely stored files, *id.* at *5:

> Appellant uses our superior Court's analogy to first-class mail, where a sender may enjoy a reasonable expectation of privacy to unopened mail in transit. * * * [T]he record does indicate that the e-mail messages in Appellant's account * * * were stored in archive on the U.S. Government's server. Additionally, when Appellant sent his individual e-mails, they were transmitted instantaneously, with a record of that message created and stored in the system's network server.

> Thus, even if Appellant's recipients had not read their e-mail messages, the system's server still contained a copy of Appellant's message accessible by network administrators, and his analogy to first-class mail fails.

Should it matter whether the e-mails were stored in archive and readily accessible by network administrators?

8.   Assuming individuals can have a reasonable expectation of privacy in the contents of their remotely stored files, what legal framework determines the reasonableness of collecting and searching through that data pursuant to a search warrant? Imagine a suspect has an account with an ISP, and government investigators obtain a search warrant permitting the seizure of the account files. Do the agents have to execute the warrant themselves, or can they just fax the warrant to the ISP and ask its employees to collect the files and send them to the agents? What standards determine whether the warrant is sufficiently particular? If agents fax a warrant to the ISP and receive a computer disk containing the files in

response, what constitutional rules must agents follow when searching through the disk?

Three cases shed light on these questions.

United States v. Bach, 310 F.3d 1063 (8th Cir. 2002), establishes that investigators can fax warrants to system administrators and have the system administrators execute the warrants on the government's behalf. In *Bach*, the government applied for and received a search warrant to obtain copies of materials in the defendant's Yahoo! e-mail account. The investigators faxed a copy of the warrant to Yahoo!, and employees at Yahoo! searched the servers, identified the materials named in the warrant, and sent the materials to the investigators. The defendant argued that this procedure was constitutionally "unreasonable" because the Fourth Amendment traditionally requires warrants to be executed by the police rather than by private individuals. The Eighth Circuit noted the uncertainty as to whether the defendant had a reasonable expectation of privacy in his content files, but held that, assuming he had such rights, the execution of the warrant by Yahoo! employees was constitutionally "reasonable" in light of the totality of the circumstances:

> We consider several factors in this case to determine whether the search and seizure of Bach's e-mail from Yahoo!'s server by Yahoo! technicians violated Bach's Fourth Amendment rights, including the fact that no warrant was physically "served," no persons or premises were searched in the traditional sense, and there was no confrontation between Yahoo! technicians and Bach. Other factors crucial to our decision include: (1) the actual physical presence of an officer would not have aided the search (in fact may have hindered it); (2) the technical expertise of Yahoo!'s technicians far outweighs that of the officers; (3) the items "seized" were located on Yahoo!'s property; (4) there was a warrant signed by a judge authorizing the search; and (5) the officers complied with the provisions of the Electronic Communications Privacy Act, 18 U.S.C. § 2701. All of these factors weigh in favor of the government and we therefore find that the search was constitutional under the Fourth Amendment's reasonableness standard.

Id. at 1067–68.

United States v. Lamb, 945 F. Supp. 441 (N.D.N.Y. 1996), considered how the particularity requirement applies to a search warrant for the contents of Internet accounts. In *Lamb*, investigators obtained a search warrant for 78 individual AOL accounts used by suspects that had traded images of child pornography using AOL services. The warrant requested all e-mails sent to or received by all 78 accounts as well as all stored files held by AOL relating to the 78 accounts. Judge Munson ruled that even this very broad warrant was sufficiently particular.

> Although the language does not limit investigators to seizing image files only or image files of child pornography only, the actual content of a computer file usually cannot be determined until it is opened with the appropriate application software on a computer. The agents who were tasked to obtain account records related to seventy-eight individuals were not obligated to identify the contents of computer files on AOL's premises. Because there was probable cause to believe that stored files

in the accounts of the suspects contained evidence of the crime, *viz.* the depictions of child pornography themselves, the warrant properly authorized the search and seizure of these particular items.

Id. at 458–59. In a footnote, the court added that "it is unreasonable to require the executing officers to identify which files actually contain child pornography and which do not in AOL's Virginia headquarters. That task may be more properly performed by a government computer technician at an FBI lab or office." *Id.* at 458 n.10.

Assuming it makes sense for AOL to send the entire contents of the account to the FBI and for FBI agents to search the files themselves, do you agree that the warrant in *Lamb* is sufficiently particular?

Finally, United States v. Maxwell, 45 M.J. 406 (C.A.A.F. 1996), applied the plain view doctrine to a search of an Internet account. In *Maxwell*, federal investigators informed employees at AOL that they planned to apply for a search warrant to obtain all e-mail associated with a list of AOL screennames. AOL employees collected the e-mails and waited for the warrant to arrive. When the warrant arrived, AOL employees released the e-mails to the investigators without scrutinizing the warrant. The employees failed to realize that the warrant actually obtained was substantially narrower than the one the agents had expected to obtain. The original list had included the screenname "Zirloc," but the signed warrant did not include this screenname on the list of accounts that could be seized. Investigators searched through Zirloc's e-mails, and learned that Zirloc was an Air Force member who questioned his sexual orientation. In litigation, the government defended the government search through Zirloc's files under the plain view exception. The Court of Appeals for the Armed Forces rejected this argument:

> The Supreme Court has recognized that if police are legitimately in a place where a citizen has a right of privacy, the police may seize contraband or other evidence of crime that is in "plain view." We decline, however, to hold the search of the "Zirloc" files was valid under a plain-view analysis. Because the warrant did not authorize the search of these files, the view was obtained as a result of the improper governmental "opening" of the files and not as a result of seeing what was legitimately in "plain view." The search here exceeded the scope of the search warrant; thus the "plain-view" exception does not apply.

Id. at 422.

9. *The role of statutory privacy laws.* Congress has passed a comprehensive statutory regime to protect the privacy of Internet communications. As a result, the rules governing Internet surveillance tend to be primarily statutory, not constitutional. How should the existence of statutory privacy laws impact interpretations of the Fourth Amendment?

Courts have suggested different answers to this question. Some courts have hinted that statutory protections might strengthen the case for Fourth Amendment protection. According to this rationale, the existence of statutory protection makes an expectation of privacy more reasonable. *See, e.g.,* In re John Doe Proceeding, 680 N.W.2d 792 (Wisc. 2004). Do you agree? If statutory protections are weaker than the potential constitutional protections, which they generally are, doesn't the fact that Congress opted for less protection undercut the argument that statutory law reflects a societal consensus that an expectation of privacy is reasonable? Or does the statutory half loaf make the full loaf "reasonable"?

Other courts have reached different conclusions. The *Hambrick* court suggested that the existence of statutory protections is irrelevant to the Fourth Amendment question. And at least one court has suggested that the existence of statutory privacy laws should actually *discourage* broad readings of the Fourth Amendment in new technologies. In United States v. McNulty, 47 F.3d 100 (4th Cir. 1995), the Fourth Circuit rejected a claim that the interception of a cordless phone call violated the Fourth Amendment. Judge Wilkinson's opinion suggested that the presence of the statutory Wiretap Act (also known as "Title III") bolstered the case against Fourth Amendment protections:

> In the fast-developing area of communications technology, courts should be cautious not to wield the amorphous "reasonable expectation of privacy" standard in a manner that nullifies the balance between privacy rights and law enforcement needs struck by Congress in Title III. Decisionmaking in this area demands a comprehension of complex technologies. Such understanding, however, requires precisely the type of expertise that courts are institutionally ill-equipped to acquire and to apply. As new technologies continue to appear in the marketplace and outpace existing surveillance law, the primary job of evaluating their impact on privacy rights and of updating the law must remain with the branch of government designed to make such policy choices, the legislature.

Id. at 105–06.

Should statutory protections lead courts to be expansive in their application of the Fourth Amendment to the Internet, or should it lead courts to be cautious? Do we need courts to determine when an expectation of privacy is "reasonable" if Congress is actively involved? *See generally* Orin S. Kerr, *The Fourth Amendment and New Technologies: Constitutional Myths and the Case for Caution*, 102 Mich. L. Rev. 801 (2004); Daniel Solove, *Fourth Amendment Codification and Professor Kerr's Misguided Call for Judicial Deference*, 74 Fordham L. Rev. 747 (2005).

10. Does Fourth Amendment protection depend in part on whether the government investigator is offline or online? Consider an example. Joe steals a computer file containing hundreds of credit card numbers. Wishing to store the file safely, Joe signs up for a free Yahoo e-mail account and e-mails himself the file so it will be stored permanently on Yahoo's servers. One month later, a police officer investigating the crime gets a tip that Joe may have left evidence of the crime in the Yahoo account. Instead of approaching Yahoo with a court order, the officer successfully guesses Joe's username and password and logs into Joe's account. The officer looks in Joe's inbox and sees an e-mail from Joe to himself mailed several hours after the credit card numbers were stolen. The subject line of the e-mail reads "stolen CC numbers," and the e-mail contains an attachment. The officer opens the e-mail and the attachment, and he sees that the attachment contains the stolen numbers.

Joe is arrested and charged with violations of 18 U.S.C. § 1030, and his lawyer moves to suppress the evidence collected against him. Specifically, he contends that the Fourth Amendment mandates the suppression of a) the fact that Joe had e-mailed himself a file on the day of the crime, b) the subject line of the e-mail, "stolen CC numbers," and c) the contents of the attachment.

How should a court rule? Consider the first question, whether the officer violated Joe's Fourth Amendment rights when he observed that Joe had e-mailed himself the file. Should the court apply *Smith v. Maryland,* and rule that non-content information about when a communication was received is not protected by the Fourth Amendment? Or should the court focus on how the officer obtained the information, and rule that "breaking in" to the suspect's account online is akin to "breaking in" to his virtual home (and thus a search)? When government investigators collect information by going online themselves, does Fourth Amendment law track the basic principles of 18 U.S.C. § 1030?

For a general discussion of Fourth Amendment standards in the case of online investigations, see Note, *Keeping Secrets in Cyberspace: Establishing Fourth Amendment Protection for Internet Communication*, 110 Harv. L. Rev. 1591 (1997).

11. The Fourth Amendment regulates the collection of information but not the use of information once collected. If information is collected in compliance with Fourth Amendment standards, the government can enter the data into a database, mine it for evidence, and manipulate it in any way.

Is this appropriate? Should the Fourth Amendment be rethought so that it limits the government's ability to manipulate data? Should the Fourth Amendment regulate datamining, or the aggregation of seized evidence into "digital dossiers" about individual suspects? If so, what standard should be used to determine when information is manipulated sufficiently to offend the Fourth Amendment? *See* Harold J. Krent, *Of Diaries and Data Banks: Use Restrictions Under the Fourth Amendment*, 74 Tex. L. Rev. 49 (1995); Daniel J. Solove, *Digital Dossiers and the Dissipation of Fourth Amendment Privacy*, 75 S. Cal. L. Rev. 1083 (2002).

4. THE SUBPOENA STANDARD

Subpoenas are legal orders that compel the recipient either to testify or else to produce materials in the recipient's possession. Whereas a search warrant authorizes the government to search property directly, a government subpoena compels the recipient to give property in his possession to the government within a specific period of time.

The law governing subpoenas is very different from the law governing search warrants. Most importantly, subpoenas do not require probable cause. As a general matter, the government can issue a grand jury subpoena when the evidence to be obtained is believed to be relevant to an investigation and compliance with the subpoena is not oppressive or overly burdensome. Warrants and subpoenas also differ in how and when they can be challenged in court. The recipient of a subpoena can challenge it (moving to "quash" the subpoena) before complying with it.

In contrast, warrants can only be challenged after the warrant is executed.

Subpoenas for evidence are primarily useful when a third party has evidence in its possession. Criminal suspects normally have a Fifth Amendment privilege not to comply with subpoenas for evidence, which means that the government normally cannot use a subpoena to collect evidence directly from suspects. In contrast, the Fifth Amendment privilege does not permit a third party to refuse to disclose evidence in its possession. *See* Fisher v. United States, 425 U.S. 391, 397 (1976) (holding that Fifth Amendment privilege does not immunize third-party agent from complying with subpoena directed to suspect's information in the agent's possession). Third parties can be subpoenaed and required to produce the property of others that happens to be in their possession, usually without notice to the person whose property is to be disclosed.

The role of subpoenas has obvious importance in the context of computer networks. Third parties such as ISPs and their system administrators often possess private information relating to hundreds or even thousands of individual users. If that information is not protected by a reasonable expectation of privacy, then individual users cannot challenge the subpoenas. The disclosure to a third party eliminates Fourth Amendment protection, so the court need not reach the standard that would apply if the record did retain Fourth Amendment protection. But imagine a government agent subpoenas user information from an ISP that *is* protected by the Fourth Amendment. What standard should govern? If the user challenges the subpoena, should the subpoena be upheld so long as it is relevant and compliance is not overly burdensome? Or should the subpoena be upheld only if it is based on probable cause?

UNITED STATES v. BARR

United States District Court for the Southern District of New York, 1985.
605 F. Supp. 114.

LASKER, District Judge.

Harold Barr moves to suppress evidence obtained from the Affiliated Answering Service. The issue presented is whether the circumstances surrounding the government's acquisition of mail through the use of a grand jury subpoena were such that they constituted a warrantless seizure in violation of the Fourth Amendment. We hold Barr's Fourth Amendment rights were not violated.

On June 1, 1984 Harold Barr was arrested for, among other things, conspiracy to violate federal narcotics laws. After his arrest he was incarcerated in the Metropolitan Correctional Center where he remains pending the outcome of his trial.

During the course of an investigation into the suspected narcotics and narcotics-related activities of Barr the government learned that Barr employed Affiliated to receive mail and telephone messages for him. On

June 4, 1984 a grand jury subpoena duces tecum was served on Affiliated. The subpoena requested production on June 12, 1984 of mail addressed to "Larry Freeman", an alleged alias for Harold Barr. Rather than bring the mail to the grand jury on that date, Affiliated complied with the subpoena immediately, that is, on June 4th. On June 11, 1984 the government secured a search warrant and opened the mail which had been delivered by Affiliated pursuant to the subpoena.

Barr argues that the mail should be suppressed because the government impermissibly used a subpoena duces tecum to obtain his mail in the first place, in circumvention of the warrant requirement. The government answers that "the subpoena duces tecum issued to Affiliated on June 1, 1984 was a wholly proper use of the subpoena process."

Although the Fourth Amendment prohibits the issuance of subpoenas duces tecum which are overbroad, *Hale v. Henkel,* 201 U.S. 43 (1906), a subpoena which compels production of evidence is generally not considered to be a "seizure" within the meaning of the Constitution, that is, a taking which cannot be undertaken without the authority of a warrant. *United States v. Dionisio,* 410 U.S. 1 (1973). In comparing the grand jury subpoena process with Fourth Amendment seizures the *Dionisio* Court relied upon the diminished compulsion attendant in grand jury subpoenas as the critical distinguishing factor.

The grand jury, as the sole instrument through which felony charges are constitutionally brought, has broad investigative powers. The power to subpoena witnesses to testify and to compel the production of documents is accepted as indispensable to the grand jury's exercise of its authority. Although "personal sacrifice" is incumbent in the duty to appear before the grand jury, *United States v. Dionisio,* 410 U.S. at 10, the obligation to furnish evidence is essential to the administration of justice. Accordingly, the benefits which an individual receives from performing his or her "civic obligation", i.e., a safer society, operate to lessen the compulsory nature of a subpoena.

The second distinction between the compulsion exerted by a subpoena and a seizure lies in the different nature of the two legal processes. Quoting with approval a decision of Judge Friendly, the *Dionisio* court stated:

> [A seizure] is abrupt, is effected with force or the threat of it and often in demeaning circumstances, and, in the case of arrest, results in a record involving stigma. A subpoena is served in the same manner as other legal process; it involves no stigma whatever; if the time for appearance is inconvenient, this can generally be altered; and it remains at all times under the control and supervision of a court.

Id., quoting *United States v. Doe (Schwartz),* 457 F.2d 895, 898 (2d Cir. 1972).

Despite the diminished compulsion of the subpoena process, however, a grand jury subpoena is not a talisman that dissolves all constitutional protections. Further, "the rule has long been established that a subpoena duces tecum may not be used in such a way as to impinge upon Fourth Amendment rights." *United States v. Re,* 313 F. Supp. 442, 448 (S.D.N.Y. 1970). The government devotes a substantial part of its brief to the argument that the subpoena duces tecum at issue in this case was not overly broad, an issue Barr does not seriously contest. However, even a subpoena duces tecum which is validly drawn and issued does not give the process server the right to seize the subpoenaed items. Accordingly, the question before us is whether the agents who obtained Barr's mail from Affiliated overstepped the subpoena's legal boundaries.

As a threshold showing, to invoke the Fourth Amendment successfully a defendant must demonstrate a reasonable expectation of privacy in the papers subpoenaed. *Katz v. United States,* 389 U.S. 347, 361 (1967) (Harlan, J., concurring). For example, a defendant's Fourth Amendment rights may be implicated where the items obtained are personal documents. On the other hand, an individual has no expectation of privacy in papers which are corporate records, or records required to be kept by law, *id.,* or, of course, papers in which the person has no possessory or proprietary interest.

The government asserts that the mail it obtained from Affiliated was "business and financial correspondence" and "junk mail" and not "personal correspondence." However, we do not interpret the decisions which hold that there is no reasonable expectation of privacy in corporate or other public records as precluding an individual's privacy interest in mail which relates to, for instance, his personal financial matters. Barr's personal mail is a type of property in which Barr ordinarily could have had a legitimate privacy expectation.

Beyond the determination of the simple proposition whether the property seized is of a nature which the Fourth Amendment generally protects, no bright line rule determines when a subpoena infringes upon Fourth Amendment rights. The evaluation must be made from the facts of each particular case. A review of the few relevant cases in this circuit demonstrates that, as in *Dionisio,* the focus of the inquiry relates to the level of compulsion present when the subpoena duces tecum is served.

In *United States v. Lartey,* 716 F.2d 955 (2d Cir. 1983), the defendant, a pharmacist, was suspected of unlawfully distributing certain prescription drugs. Forthwith subpoenas requiring production of records from the pharmacies out of which the defendant allegedly operated were served after the defendant had been arrested in connection with the crime. Acknowledging that forthwith subpoenas may "hamper the ability of one to contest its validity before a judicial officer" the court nevertheless declined to hold that such subpoenas were *per se* illegal, and upheld the subpoena in the case before it. Factors the court considered included the exigent circumstances presented by the substantiated belief that Lartey would attempt to tamper with the documents if warned of the imminent subpoena, the lack of Fourth or Fifth Amendment grounds upon which the defendant could have successfully moved to quash the subpoena and the lack of evidence that the agents coerced compliance with the subpoena, including the fact that the pharmacists upon which the subpoenas were served were allowed to communicate with an attorney as to how to respond to the subpoenas.

In *United States v. Re, supra,* the Res' accountant was served with a forthwith subpoena to hand over documents which Re had left in his possession. Despite the accountant's release of the records without challenging the subpoena and without first notifying the Res so that they could do so, the court held there was no seizure.

In contrast to the facts of *Lartey* and *Re,* the court in *In Re Nwamu,* 421 F. Supp. 1361, 1365–66 (S.D.N.Y. 1976), found the methods used in the subpoena process included "compelling instant surrender of the subpoenaed items to the agents, without court order, by threats of contempt and claim, or color, or authority." After evaluating the totality of the circumstances the court held "that compliance with the subpoenas would be unreasonable and oppressive; that neither movants nor their employees had voluntarily consented to surrender of the subpoenaed items; and that the government agents' taking of the subpoenaed items constituted an unreasonable and unlawful search and seizure." *Id.* at 1367. In so holding, the *Nwamu* court emphasized that the manner of service stripped the court of its authority to oversee the subpoena process and denied the defendant the opportunity to challenge its validity.

Although, as the decisions illustrate, the line between a permissible and an impermissible level of compulsion is not bright, guiding principles have evolved which aid in determining when a Fourth Amendment violation has occurred. Whether, and under what circumstances the person on whom process is served consents to the release of the items is a factor in evaluating the existence of a Fourth Amendment infraction. Clearly, a subpoena does not authorize the seizure of materials by the use of force or threats of violence, regardless of who has possession of the items or is charged with compliance.

A subpoena duces tecum may violate the Fourth Amendment if government agents improperly impinge on the defendant's right to contest the subpoena's validity or a court's authority to quash, alter or enforce it. Whether the defendant has notice of the subpoena is related to the opportunity to challenge the subpoena and is also a factor to be considered. Nonetheless, a mere lack of notice, standing alone, does not establish a violation. Indeed, the decisions indicate that the importance of notice as a factor diminishes when the defendant demonstrates an intent to tamper with or destroy documents, or when there are no grounds upon which to assert a successful motion to quash.

Further, as we interpret *United States v. Re, supra,* a decision we find persuasive, a defendant may be deemed to have constructive notice of the subpoena when he chooses to relinquish control of his property to another person if, when served with a subpoena, the person who has custody of the items can notify the defendant, consult an attorney or move to quash the subpoena.

Applying these principles to the case at hand we find Barr's Fourth Amendment rights not to have been violated. Barr does not argue, nor has he produced any evidence which indicates that Affiliated's compliance with the subpoena duces tecum was by other than voluntary consent. The agents who served the subpoena did not coerce compliance by force or threats or overstep their legal authority. Indeed, Affiliated chose to comply with the subpoena immediately although compliance was not called for until eight days after the date of service.

Although, because he was incarcerated when it was served, Barr did not have notice of the subpoena duces tecum, a motion to quash the subpoena on Fourth Amendment grounds would not have been successful in any event. The subpoena was not overly broad nor, as we have concluded, did the subpoena process in this case constitute an illegal seizure. Further, irrespective of any lack of notice at the time the subpoena was served, Barr has now had ample opportunity, which he is by this motion utilizing, to raise any alleged infirmities in the subpoena process which he would have challenged in a motion to quash. Moreover, Affiliated was free to consult counsel or move to quash the subpoena in Barr's absence.

The motion is denied.

Notes and Questions

1.   The Affiliated Answering Service held Barr's postal mail much like an ISP holds an Internet subscriber's e-mail. Does *Barr* indicate that the government can subpoena the contents of an e-mail account using a relevance standard, even if the e-mails are protected by a reasonable expectation of privacy? Or is *Barr* distinguishable? How much compulsion is associated with a subpoena for Internet account information?

Note that the government obtained a search warrant before opening Barr's sealed mail. Did investigators need a warrant to open the mail? Would it have needed a search warrant to read a postcard sent to Barr's mail box address?

2.   Should courts apply a probable cause requirement for subpoenas that implicate third-party Fourth Amendment rights? For such an argument, see Patricia L. Bellia, *Surveillance Law Through Cyberlaw's Lens*, 72 Geo. Wash. L. Rev. 1375, 1410–13 (2004). For more on the role of subpoenas, see Christopher Slobogin, *Subpoenas and Privacy*, 54 DePaul L. Rev. 805 (2005).

3.   Should subpoenas for Internet account information be served on third-party system administrators or on individual users? Consider United States v. Re, 313 F. Supp. 442, 451 (S.D.N.Y. 1970):

> Of course an owner of documents, while not actually in physical possession of the documents, may have such control over them as to be deemed to have constructive possession and in such cases the subpoena

should be served on the owner. In such cases the owner may properly assert his privilege against self-incrimination, and apparently the owner or the party in constructive possession on whom the subpoena should have been served may also challenge the service of the subpoena on the party in actual possession as an unlawful search and seizure.

Do Internet account holders have "constructive possession" of their files stored on remote servers? Of file contents? Of non-content account records?

4.   In the case of In re Amato, 2005 WL 1429743 (D. Me. 2005), the FBI obtained a warrant to search the office of a chiropractor. The chiropractor was suspected of committing health care fraud using two corporations he controlled. The agents executed the search at the office, but did not find all of the records that they wished to find. In an effort to find the rest of the records, the agents served two administrative subpoenas on the suspect ordering him to provide records relating to the corporations, as well as any computer equipment that had been used by the corporations. The suspect challenged the subpoenas on the ground that requesting computer equipment rather than specific information rendered the subpoena overbroad and therefore constitutionally unreasonable. The court agreed:

> While courts have been sensitive to the practical difficulties computer searches pose for law-enforcement agencies, inasmuch as appears most courts considering the issue (including this one) have deemed overbroad a warrant to seize all of a target's computer equipment in the absence of any further express limitation on the parameters of an off-site search and seizure. I discern no reason why, for purposes of overbreadth analysis, the off-site search of computer equipment obtained as a result of a subpoena should be treated differently from the off-site search of equipment seized pursuant to a search warrant.

> Inasmuch as * * * the Subpoenas in essence request[] the turnover of all computers (and related objects) of both corporations with no express safeguard against a subsequent rummaging through, and seizure of, irrelevant as well as relevant data, it cannot withstand Fourth Amendment reasonableness scrutiny.

Id. at *11–*12. Should a narrow subpoena to search a computer be permitted under the Fourth Amendment? What if the subpoena requests computers that contain evidence of a specific crime? Does it depend on whether the subpoena is supported by probable cause?

5.   In the case of In re John Doe Proceeding, 680 N.W.2d 792 (Wisc. 2004), the Dane County, Wisconsin, District Attorney opened a criminal investigation to investigate public corruption in the Wisconsin state government. The DA issued a subpoena to the state Legislative Technology Services Bureau (LTSB), a public agency in the Wisconsin government that stores back-up tapes of the contents of the servers used by the Wisconsin state government. Under Wisconsin law, the LTSB generates back-up tapes of the state legislature's 54 servers, and stores copies of those back-up tapes on what appears to be a permanent basis.

The subpoena issued by the DA was rather remarkably broad: it ordered the LTSB to produce the backup tapes made on a particular day for all 54 of the Wisconsin legislature's servers. Evidently, the DA wanted to reconstruct an exact copy of the entire legislature's computer system for a given day, and then access specific files relating to the investigation. The director of the LTSB moved to quash the subpoena on a range of theories, among them that the subpoena was overly broad under the Fourth Amendment.

The Supreme Court of Wisconsin agreed that the subpoena was overbroad in violation of the Fourth Amendment. In the course of reaching this conclusion, the Court discussed whether the data stored on the back-up tapes was protected by a reasonable expectation of privacy:

> Technology clearly has changed the ways in which we work and communicate with others. The federal government recognized that changing technology required changing laws, and to address those changes, it passed the Electronic Communications Privacy Act of 1986. The ECPA extended the privacy protections that have been given voice communications to electronic communications such as e-mail. This is a strong expression of society's expectation of privacy in electronic communications.

> Legislators use electronic technology to compose budgets, to prepare position papers, and to draft legislation; they communicate with each other, with their staff members and with their constituents via e-mail and instant messaging. According to the LTSB, the legislative e-mail system processes more than 60,000 transactions each day. Electronic assists to communication is the way in which the legislature does its work, and all of the data created is stored on the backup tapes at the LTSB.

> These circumstances—the way in which the legislature now does business; that the LTSB was created to serve legislators on "both sides of the aisle;" and the statutory directive of Wis. Stat. § 13.96 that requires that all data stored by the LTSB shall be kept confidential—support an objectively reasonable expectation of privacy by legislators in the data on the backup tapes. Therefore, we conclude that society has recognized a reasonable expectation of privacy in the electronically stored information on the backup tapes.

Id. at 806. Does it make sense that *all* of the data should be protected by a reasonable expectation of privacy? Or under *Smith v. Maryland* and *Guest v. Leis*, should the Fourth Amendment only protect the contents of communications? Who exactly has Fourth Amendment protection in the tapes, the legislators and their staff or the LTSB?

6. *Hybrid warrant/subpoenas.* In 1986, Congress enacted a statutory privacy law that requires the government to obtain a warrant to require a provider of computer network services to disclose the contents of certain kinds of communications. Such warrants are hybrids between subpoenas and traditional warrants, as they are obtained like warrants but served like subpoenas. Agents must have the warrant signed by a judge based on probable cause pursuant to the usual rules for obtaining search warrants, *see* 18 U.S.C. § 2703(a), but then they serve the warrant by sending it via mail or fax to the third party network provider and requesting a response within a specific window of time.

Are these hybrid orders subpoenas or warrants for Fourth Amendment purposes? In United States v. Bach, 310 F.3d 1063 (8th Cir. 2002), investigators applied for and received a search warrant to obtain copies of materials in the defendant's Yahoo e-mail account. The agents served the warrant on Yahoo by fax, and Yahoo complied with the warrant and sent the materials back to the agents. The Eighth Circuit specified that the constitutional reasonableness of the process should be analyzed under search warrant precedents rather than subpoena precedents:

> We analyze this case under the search warrant standard, not under the subpoena standard. While warrants for electronic data are often served like subpoenas (via fax), Congress called them warrants and we find that Congress intended them to be treated as warrants.

Id. at 1066 n.1. Professor Paul Ohm has suggested that this was an error:

> These "warrants" are not like the search warrants used in the physical world: they are "executed" when a law enforcement agent delivers (sometimes by fax) the warrant to the ISP. The ISP, not the agent, performs the "search"; the ISP "produces" the relevant material to the agent; the user associated with the inbox often never learns that his inbox has been "searched." In sum, these are not search warrants at all and to call them such confuses legal terminology. Congress should amend [the statute requiring a warrant, 18 U.S.C. § 2703(a),] to reflect what they really are, and I have a descriptive, if not particularly poetic, suggestion: "section 2703(a) probable cause orders."

Paul K. Ohm, *Parallel-Effect Statutes and E-mail "Warrants": Reframing the Internet Surveillance Debate*, 72 Geo. Wash. L. Rev. 1599, 1610–11 (2004).

Does the label matter? Should it? If it does, note the change in terminology when the *Bach* case was pending in the Eighth Circuit. From 1986 to 2001, the language referred to "a warrant issued under the Federal Rules of Criminal Procedure." 18 U.S.C. § 2703(a) (1986). This was the language at issue in *Bach*. In 2001, however, the statute was changed to read "a warrant issued using the procedures described in the Federal Rules of Criminal Procedure by a court with jurisdiction over the offense under investigation or equivalent State warrant." 18 U.S.C. § 2703(a) (2001). Does this change make a constitutional difference? *See* Sibron v. New York, 392 U.S. 40, 59 (1968) (noting that while the legislature is "free to develop its own law of search and seizure.... and in the process it may call the standards it employs by any names it may choose," what matters under the Fourth Amendment is not "the labels which [the legislature] attaches to such conduct," but rather "whether the search was reasonable under the Fourth Amendment").

Chapter 6

STATUTORY PRIVACY
PROTECTIONS

Fourth Amendment protections are fairly certain in the stand-alone computer environment, but they remain very hazy when investigators seek digital evidence transmitted across networks. Fortunately, Congress has stepped in and supplemented the Fourth Amendment with a set of statutory privacy laws that regulate the collection of digital evidence in the network context.

This chapter covers the three federal statutory privacy laws that regulate access to computer network communications in criminal investigations. The three laws are the Wiretap Act, 18 U.S.C. §§ 2510–22; the Pen Register statute, 18 U.S.C. §§ 3121–27; and the Stored Communications Act, 18 U.S.C. §§ 2701–11. These three laws work together to create what amounts to a statutory version of the Fourth Amendment for computer networks.

From an investigative standpoint, the material in this chapter usually is important at an earlier stage of investigations than the law covered in the previous chapter on Fourth Amendment protections. Most computer crime investigations begin in a network environment. A computer misuse investigation might begin when a system administrator realizes that his server has been attacked; a threat investigation might begin with the victim's receipt of an e-mail containing the threat; a child pornography case might begin when an undercover investigator is contacted in a chat room.

In all these cases, the first question is the same: Who is responsible for the criminal conduct? Investigators generally try to answer this question by collecting evidence from the network to trace the criminal conduct back to its source. A successful investigation might trace communications back to an Internet account being used from the suspect's home; a search of the suspect's home might then yield evidence establishing guilt beyond a reasonable doubt.

The major purpose of the statutory privacy laws is to regulate efforts by criminal investigators to collect evidence that can help them identify who is responsible for criminal conduct online. The Wiretap Act regulates efforts to collect evidence by intercepting the contents of Internet communications in real time; the Pen Register statute regulates collecting evidence by obtaining non-content information in real time; and the Stored Communications Act regulates access to stored content and non-content records held by ISPs.

Brief History of Statutory Privacy Laws

To understand the statutory privacy laws that regulate digital evidence collection, a page of history is worth a volume of logic. That history begins with the telephone network in the period following the Supreme Court's decision in Olmstead v. United States, 277 U.S. 438 (1928). *Olmstead* held that the Fourth Amendment did not regulate telephone wiretapping. The opinion for the Court expressly invited Congress to enact statutory prohibitions on wiretapping practices: "Congress may, of course, protect the secrecy of telephone messages by making them, when intercepted, inadmissible in evidence in federal criminal trials, by direct legislation." *Id.* at 465–66.

Congress responded in 1934 with the New Deal legislation known as the Communications Act. A provision of the Communications Act codified at 47 U.S.C. § 605 became the first federal wiretapping statute (with the exception of a temporary statute passed during World War I and repealed shortly after the war). In its original form, § 605 stated that "no person not being authorized by the sender shall intercept any communication and divulge or publish the existence, contents, substance, purport, effect, or meaning of such intercepted communication to any person." In Nardone v. United States, 302 U.S. 379, 384 (1937), the Supreme Court held that the remedy for violating this statute was suppression of any evidence unlawfully obtained.

It soon became clear that the Communications Act of 1934 was poorly suited to regulate telephone wiretapping. First, the statute did not provide an exception when the government had obtained a warrant. Second, the statute prohibited only the combination of "intercepting" and "divulging or publishing," which the Justice Department interpreted as permitting wiretapping so long as the information was never used in court. The combination made the statute both under-inclusive and over-inclusive: the FBI could wiretap without restriction so long as it didn't use the evidence in court, but the government could not obtain a warrant permitting admission of wiretapping evidence in court even in the most compelling case. Finally, the law only regulated the admissibility of wiretapping evidence in federal court. It had no application when state investigators sought to introduce wiretapping evidence in state court. *See* Schwartz v. Texas, 344 U.S. 199 (1952).

Congress revisited the law regulating telephone wiretapping in the late 1960s. Congress's goal was to replace the unsatisfactory Communications Act and regulate two distinct privacy-invading practices: bugging, the use of secret recording devices in a room or physical space; and wiretapping, the interception of private telephone calls. The statutory design was heavily influenced by the Supreme Court's pair of decisions in 1967 that explained the constitutional limitations on such practices. The first case, Berger v. New York, 388 U.S. 41 (1967), articulated constitutional requirements for wiretapping. The second case, Katz v. United States, 389 U.S. 347 (1967), articulated constitutional limits on bugging.

The law that Congress passed to regulate wiretapping is generally known either as the Wiretap Act or Title III,[a] and is codified at 18 U.S.C. §§ 2510–22. The statute regulates both government actors and private parties, and imposes strict limitations on the use of devices to intercept "oral communications" (that is, use of a bugging device to listen in on private conversations) or "wire communications" (that is, use of a wiretapping device to tap a telephone and listen in on private telephone conversations). It also allows the government to obtain court orders permitting interception when investigators have probable cause and can satisfy a number of additional requirements. The heightened requirements of Title III beyond the usual search warrant requirement have led some to describe Title III intercept orders as "super warrants."

The Wiretap Act effectively and comprehensively regulated government access to the contents of traditional telephone calls. In the 1980s, however, it became clear that additional privacy laws were necessary. This was true for two reasons. First, the Supreme Court's decision in Smith v. Maryland, 442 U.S. 735 (1979), indicated that the Fourth Amendment did not provide robust privacy protection in the network context. *Smith* made clear that the Fourth Amendment did not regulate the use of pen registers, and the opinion left uncertain how or even whether the Fourth Amendment would apply to computer networks. Second, the Wiretap Act was not equipped to protect computer network communications. The Wiretap Act applied only to "oral communications" and "wire communications," both of which were limited to communications containing the human voice. Further, the Wiretap Act applied only to the acquisition of communications "in transit," such as real-time wiretapping, and did not apply to accessing stored communications. This made sense for the traditional telephone network, as calls were never stored (or at least only rarely, as voicemail was in its infancy at the time). In contrast, computer communications were stored routinely, either in temporary storage pending transmission or after a communication had been delivered. *See* Office of Tech. Assessment, Federal Government Information Technology: Electronic Surveillance and Civil Liberties (1985).

In 1986, Congress passed the Electronic Communications Privacy Act, Pub. L. No. 99–508 (1986) ("ECPA"), to correct the gaps in existing

---

a. The Wiretap Act is often called "Title III" because the statute was passed as the third part (or "title") of the massive Omni-bus Crime Control and Safe Streets Act of 1968, Pub. L. No. 90–351 (1968).

legislation and respond to the new computer network technologies. ECPA included three basic parts. The first part expanded the Wiretap Act to include a new category of protected communications, "electronic communications," which broadly includes computer communications. The second part created a new statute to regulate access to stored electronic communications known as the Stored Communications Act, codified at 18 U.S.C. §§ 2701–11. Finally, the third part created a new statute, generally known as the Pen Register Statute, 18 U.S.C. §§ 3121–27, that responds to *Smith v. Maryland* and regulates the use of pen registers.[b]

The Basic Structure of the Statutory Privacy Laws

The basic framework created by ECPA remains in place today. The framework is premised on two major distinctions: the distinction between prospective surveillance and retrospective surveillance, and the distinction between the contents of communications and non-content information.

Prospective surveillance refers to obtaining communications still in the course of transmission, typically by installing a monitoring device at a particular point in the network and scanning the traffic as it passes by that point. The monitoring is prospective because the communication has not yet reached the place where the surveillance device is installed. For example, a traditional wiretapping device taps into the conversation while it is happening; any communication sent over the line will be tapped. Similarly, an Internet wiretapping program such as a "packet sniffer" scans packets of Internet traffic at a particular place in the network where the program is directed to function.

In contrast, retrospective surveillance refers to access to stored communications that may be kept in the ordinary course of business by a third-party provider. For example, if an FBI agent issues a subpoena ordering an ISP to disclose basic subscriber information about a particular Internet account, that access is a type of retrospective surveillance. The ISP will have generated that record at some time in the past in the ordinary course of its business; the subpoena seeks the disclosure of a stored record that already has been created.

The basic distinction between the contents of communications and non-content information was introduced in the previous chapter. Contents of communications are the substance of the message communicated from sender to receiver, while non-content information refers to the information used to deliver the communications from senders to receivers and other network-generated information about the communication. In the case of a telephone call, for example, a basic difference exists between the contents of the call itself (the conversation) and mere

b. Somewhat confusingly, cases and authorities refer to these statutes either by their individual names or as ECPA, the Act in which they were passed. These materials will refer to the individual names and refer to ECPA only to mean the 1986 Act as a whole.

information about the call (such as the phone numbers of the two parties and the duration of the call).

The three privacy statutes reflect these two distinctions. The Wiretap Act and the Pen Register statute regulate prospective surveillance, and the Stored Communications Act regulates retrospective surveillance. Within the category of prospective surveillance, the Wiretap Act handles access to the contents of communications, and the Pen Register regulates access to non-content information. The basic framework looks like this:

	Prospective	Retrospective
Contents	Wiretap Act 18 U.S.C. §§ 2510–22	Stored Communications Act 18 U.S.C. §§ 2701–11
Non-content	Pen Register Statute 18 U.S.C. §§ 3121–27	Stored Communications Act 18 U.S.C. §§ 2701–11

Remedies and A Note About Studying the Statutory Privacy Laws

One very unusual feature of the statutory privacy laws is the remedial scheme for statutory violations. The Fourth Amendment is enforced with an exclusionary rule, but the statutory privacy laws do not include a statutory suppression remedy in the computer context. Violations of the Wiretap Act, Pen Register statute, and Stored Communications Act can lead to criminal liability, as noted on pages 178–80. Violations of the Wiretap Act and the Stored Communications Act can also lead to civil liability, including attorney's fees awards and the possibility of punitive damages. However, suppression of evidence unlawfully obtained is not an available remedy in most computer-related cases. The only statutory suppression remedy is for violations of the Wiretap Act involving the interception of human voice communications. *See* 18 U.S.C. § 2515. Because computer communications normally do not include the human voice, no statutory suppression remedy exists for their unlawful interception.

The limited statutory suppression remedy dates back to 1986, when Congress first enacted ECPA. The rationale at the time was that computer communications implicated lesser privacy concerns than telephone calls and speech involving the human voice, so that the suppression remedy imposed by the Wiretap Act for violations relating to telephone calls did not need to be extended to cases involving computers. *See* Michael S. Leib, *E-mail and the Wiretap Laws: Why Congress Should Add Electronic Communication to Title III's Statutory Exclusionary Rule and Expressly Reject a "Good Faith" Exception*, 34 Harv. J. on Legis. 393 (1997).

It seems highly likely that Congress eventually will revisit this judgment. In 1986, it may have been rational to distinguish between voice transmissions and computer communications. Today it is not. Nonetheless, the law currently lacks a statutory suppression remedy for communications other than voice transmissions.

The narrow scope of the statutory exclusionary rule creates a special challenge for students attempting to understand the statutory privacy laws. Because no suppression remedy exists in most cases, defense lawyers in computer crime cases ordinarily have no incentive to file statutory challenges to government surveillance practices. The absence of challenges means that few judicial opinions explain how the statutory laws apply to computer technologies. *See generally* Orin S. Kerr, *Lifting the 'Fog' of Internet Surveillance: How a Suppression Remedy Would Change Computer Crime Law*, 54 Hastings L.J. 805 (2003). Learning how the statutes work requires careful study of statutory text and legislative history, drawing analogies from decisions involving telephone surveillance, and careful scrutiny of existing civil cases.

A. THE WIRETAP ACT

The Wiretap Act, 18 U.S.C. §§ 2510–22, is the first and probably the most important of the statutory privacy laws. It prohibits the real-time interception of telephone calls and computer communications unless an exception applies or investigators have a ''super warrant'' interception order. The statute applies whenever a surveillance device has been installed that acquires the contents of communications during transit. The exceptions to the statute articulate specific contexts in which the surveillance can occur without a court order.

The materials begin by exploring the basic framework of the statute and its prohibition on intercepting communications in transit. They then turn to the three most important exceptions to the statute: the consent exception, the provider exception, and the computer trespasser exception.

1. THE BASIC STRUCTURE

The basic structure of the Wiretap Act is surprisingly simple. The statute envisions that an individual is exchanging communications with another person or machine. The statute makes it a crime for someone who is not a party to the communication to use an intercepting device to intentionally access the private communications in ''real time.''

The following case shows how the framework works in practice. Although it is based on Florida law, the case interprets portions of the Florida statute that are identical to the federal Wiretap Act.

O'BRIEN v. O'BRIEN

District Court of Appeal of Florida, Fifth District, 2005.
899 So.2d 1133.

SAWAYA, C.J.

Emanating from a rather contentious divorce proceeding is an issue we must resolve regarding application of certain provisions of the Security of Communications Act found in Chapter 934, Florida Statutes (2003).

Specifically, we must determine whether the trial court properly concluded that pursuant to section 934.03(1), certain communications were inadmissible because they were illegally intercepted by the Wife who, unbeknownst to the Husband, had installed a spyware program on a computer used by the Husband that copied and stored electronic communications between the Husband and another woman.

When marital discord erupted between the Husband and the Wife, the Wife secretly installed a spyware program called Spector on the Husband's computer. It is undisputed that the Husband engaged in private on-line chats with another woman while playing Yahoo Dominoes on his computer. The Spector spyware secretly took snapshots of what appeared on the computer screen, and the frequency of these snapshots allowed Spector to capture and record all chat conversations, instant messages, e-mails sent and received, and the websites visited by the user of the computer. When the Husband discovered the Wife's clandestine attempt to monitor and record his conversations with his Dominoes partner, the Husband uninstalled the Spector software and filed a Motion for Temporary Injunction, which was subsequently granted, to prevent the Wife from disclosing the communications. Thereafter, the Husband requested and received a permanent injunction to prevent the Wife's disclosure of the communications and to prevent her from engaging in this activity in the future. The latter motion also requested that the trial court preclude introduction of the communications into evidence in the divorce proceeding. This request was also granted. The trial court, without considering the communications, entered a final judgment of dissolution of marriage. The Wife moved for rehearing, which was subsequently denied.

The Wife appeals the order granting the permanent injunction, the final judgment, and the order denying the Wife's motion for rehearing on the narrow issue of whether the trial court erred in refusing to admit evidence of the Husband's computer activities obtained through the spyware the Wife secretly installed on the computer. The Wife argues that the electronic communications do not fall under the umbra of the Act because these communications were retrieved from storage and, therefore, are not "intercepted communications" as defined by the Act. In opposition, the Husband contends that the Spector spyware installed on the computer acquired his electronic communications real-time as they were in transmission and, therefore, are intercepts illegally obtained under the Act.

The trial court found that the electronic communications were illegally obtained in violation of section 934.03(1)(a)-(e), and so we begin our analysis with the pertinent provisions of that statute, which subjects any person to criminal penalties who * * * :

> Intentionally intercepts, endeavors to intercept, or procures any other person to intercept or endeavor to intercept any wire, oral, or electronic communication;

§ 934.03(1)(a), Fla. Stat. (2003). Enactment of these prohibitions connotes a policy decision by the Florida legislature to allow each party to a conversation to have an expectation of privacy from interception by another party to the conversation. The purpose of the Act is to protect every person's right to privacy and to prevent the pernicious effect on all citizens who would otherwise feel insecure from intrusion into their private conversations and communications.

The clear intent of the Legislature in enacting section 934.03 was to make it illegal for a person to intercept wire, oral, or electronic communications. It is beyond doubt that what the trial court excluded from evidence are "electronic communications." The core of the issue lies in whether the electronic communications were intercepted. The term "intercept" is defined by the Act as "the aural or other acquisition of the contents of any wire, electronic, or oral communication through the use of any electronic, mechanical, or other device." § 934.02(3). We discern that there is a rather fine distinction between what is transmitted as an electronic communication subject to interception and the storage of what has been previously communicated. It is here that we tread upon new ground. Because we have found no precedent rendered by the Florida courts that considers this distinction, and in light of the fact that the Act was modeled after the Federal Wiretap Act, we advert to decisions by the federal courts that have addressed this issue for guidance.

The federal courts have consistently held that electronic communications, in order to be intercepted, must be acquired contemporaneously with transmission and that electronic communications are not intercepted within the meaning of the Federal Wiretap Act if they are retrieved from storage. *See Fraser v. Nationwide Mut. Ins. Co.*, 352 F.3d 107 (3d Cir. 2003); *Theofel v. Farey–Jones*, 359 F.3d 1066 (9th Cir. 2004); *United States v. Steiger*, 318 F.3d 1039 (11th Cir. 2003); *Konop v. Hawaiian Airlines, Inc.*, 302 F.3d 868 (9th Cir. 2002). * * * [T]he particular facts and circumstances of the instant case reveal that the electronic communications were intercepted contemporaneously with transmission.

The Spector spyware program that the Wife surreptitiously installed on the computer used by the Husband intercepted and copied the electronic communications as they were transmitted. We believe that particular method constitutes interception within the meaning of the Florida Act, and the decision in *Steiger* supports this conclusion. In *Steiger*, an individual was able to hack into the defendant's computer via a Trojan horse virus that allowed the hacker access to pornographic materials stored on the hard drive. The hacker was successful in transferring the pornographic material from that computer to the hacker's computer. The court held that because the Trojan horse virus simply copied information that had previously been stored on the computer's hard drive, the capture of the electronic communication was not an interception within the meaning of the Federal Wiretap Act. The court did indicate, however, that interception could occur if the virus or software intercepted the communication as it was being transmitted and copied it. The court stated:

There is only a narrow window during which an E-mail interception may occur—the seconds or milli-seconds before which a newly composed message is saved to any temporary location following a send command. Therefore, unless some type of automatic routing software is used (for example, a duplicate of all of an employee's messages are automatically sent to the employee's boss), interception of E-mail within the prohibition of the Wiretap Act is virtually impossible.

Steiger, 318 F.3d at 1050 (quoting Jarrod J. White, *E-Mail@Work.com: Employer Monitoring of Employee E-Mail*, 48 Ala. L. Rev. 1079, 1083 (1997)). Hence, a valid distinction exists between a spyware program similar to that in *Steiger*, which simply breaks into a computer and retrieves information already stored on the hard drive, and a spyware program similar to the one installed by the Wife in the instant case, which copies the communication as it is transmitted and routes the copy to a storage file in the computer.

The Wife argues that the communications were in fact stored before acquisition because once the text image became visible on the screen, the communication was no longer in transit and, therefore, not subject to intercept. We disagree. We do not believe that this evanescent time period is sufficient to transform acquisition of the communications from a contemporaneous interception to retrieval from electronic storage. We conclude that because the spyware installed by the Wife intercepted the electronic communication contemporaneously with transmission, copied it, and routed the copy to a file in the computer's hard drive, the electronic communications were intercepted in violation of the Florida Act.

We must next determine whether the improperly intercepted electronic communications may be excluded from evidence under the Act. The exclusionary provisions of the Act are found in section 934.06, Florida Statutes (2003), which provides that "whenever any wire or oral communication has been intercepted, no part of the contents of such communication and no evidence derived therefrom may be received in evidence." Conspicuously absent from the provisions of this statute is any reference to electronic communications. The federal courts, which interpreted an identical statute contained in the Federal Wiretap Act, have held that because provision is not made for exclusion of intercepted electronic communications, Congress intended that such communications not be excluded under the Federal Wiretap Act. We agree with this reasoning and conclude that the intercepted electronic communications in the instant case are not excludable under the Act. But this does not end the inquiry.

Although not specifically excludable under the Act, it is illegal and punishable as a crime under the Act to intercept electronic communications. § 934.03, Fla. Stat. (2003). The trial court found that the electronic communications were illegally intercepted in violation of the Act and ordered that they not be admitted in evidence. Generally, the admission of evidence is a matter within the sound discretion of the trial court. Because the evidence was illegally obtained, we conclude that the trial court did not abuse its discretion in refusing to admit it.

We affirm the orders and the final judgment under review in the instant case.

Notes and Questions

1. The *O'Brien* case interprets a Florida state law that mirrors the federal Wiretap Act, 18 U.S.C. §§ 2510–22. At this point it may be helpful to open your statutory supplement and carefully read the Wiretap Act to get an idea of its structure. Key terms used in the statute are defined in 18 U.S.C. § 2510, and § 2511(1) contains the basic prohibitions against intercepting oral, wire, and electronic communications. Section 2511(2) lists the most important exceptions to the statute, including the provider exception, § 2511(2)(a)(i), the consent exception, § 2511(2)(c)-(d), and the computer trespasser exception, § 2511(2)(i). Sections 2515 and 2518 create a statutory suppression remedy for violations involving oral and wire communications (although not violations involving electronic communications), and § 2516 lays out the requirements the government must follow to obtain Title III intercept "super warrants."

Notably, several sections of the statute are not directly relevant to our goal of understanding how the Wiretap Act works in computer crime cases. Just to give you a flavor of what you're missing, though, here is a rundown: 18 U.S.C. § 2512 prohibits possessing or distributing wiretapping devices in some circumstances; § 2513 involves the forfeiture of such devices; § 2514 has been repealed; § 2517 concerns the use and disclosure of the fruits of wiretapping; § 2519 requires the filing of annual reports on government wiretapping practices; § 2520 permits civil damages for unlawful wiretapping; § 2521 permits injunctions in civil cases; and § 2522 involves compliance with the Communications Assistance for Law Enforcement Act. It's all good stuff, but not material you need to worry about for this course.

2. *Oral, wire, and electronic communications.* The Wiretap Act covers three distinct types of communications: wire communications, electronic communications, and oral communications. Wire communications are communications that contain the human voice and that are sent over a wire. 18 U.S.C. § 2510(1); 18 U.S.C. § 2510(18). Oral communications are "in person" recordings of the human voice that can be picked up by a bugging device or microphone when the person recorded has a reasonable expectation of privacy. 18 U.S.C. § 2510(2). Electronic communications are communications that do not contain the human voice. 18 U.S.C. § 2510(12).

For our purposes, the two most important categories are wire communications and electronic communications. To simplify matters, telephone calls count as wire communications and almost all computer transmissions count as electronic communications. Computer communications can be wire communications in narrow situations; the most obvious examples are services that transfer the human voice using Internet protocols (so-called voice-over-Internet–Protocol, or VOIP). VOIP communications are "aural transfers" under 18 U.S.C. § 2510(18), as they contain the human voice at the point of origin and reception. This makes such communications "wire communications" under 18 U.S.C. § 2510(1).

3. *Prospective and retrospective surveillance.* The Wiretap Act only applies when a surveillance device is used to "intercept" a communication. 18 U.S.C. § 2510(4) defines intercept as "the aural or other acquisition of the contents of any wire, electronic, or oral communication through the use of any electronic, mechanical, or other device." As the *O'Brien* opinion indicates, the word "acquisition" generally has been understood to mean acquisition contemporaneously with transmission rather than when the communication has been stored. This explains why the Wiretap Act regulates prospective surveillance and not retrospective surveillance.

At the same time, the line between prospective surveillance and retrospective surveillance can become fuzzy. To see why, consider the facts of United States v. Councilman, 418 F.3d 67 (1st Cir. 2005) (en banc). Councilman was the Vice–President of Interloc, Inc., a book listing service that provided e-mail accounts for its customers. Councilman instructed an Interloc employee to design and install a computer program to scan all incoming e-mail sent to its customers at Interloc that originated from the bookseller Amazon.com. The program scanned incoming mail in the instant before delivery in the customer's inbox. The court explained the technology as follows:

> Data transmitted across the Internet are broken down into small "packets" that are forwarded from one computer to another until they reach their destination, where they are reconstituted. Each service on the Internet—e.g., e-mail, the World Wide Web, or instant messaging— has its own protocol for using packets of data to transmit information from one place to another. The e-mail protocol is known as Simple Mail Transfer Protocol ("SMTP").

> After a user composes a message in an e-mail client program, a program called a mail transfer agent ("MTA") formats that message and sends it to another program that "packetizes" it and sends the packets out to the Internet. Computers on the network then pass the packets from one to another; each computer along the route stores the packets in memory, retrieves the addresses of their final destinations, and then determines where to send them next. At various points the packets are reassembled to form the original e-mail message, copied, and then repacketized for the next leg of the journey. Sometimes messages cannot be transferred immediately and must be saved for later delivery. Even when delivery is immediate, intermediate computers often retain backup copies, which they delete later. This method of transmission is commonly called "store and forward" delivery.

> Once all the packets reach the recipient's mail server, they are reassembled to form the e-mail message. A mail delivery agent ("MDA") accepts the message from the MTA, determines which user should receive the message, and performs the actual delivery by placing the message in that user's mailbox. One popular MDA is "procmail," which is controlled by short programs or scripts called "recipe files." These recipe files can be used in various ways. For example, a procmail recipe can instruct the MDA to deposit mail addressed to one address into

another user's mailbox (e.g., to send mail addressed to "help" to the tech support department), to reject mail from certain addresses, or to make copies of certain messages.

Once the MDA has deposited a message into the recipient's mailbox, the recipient simply needs to use an e-mail client program to retrieve and read the message. While the journey from sender to recipient may seem rather involved, it usually takes just a few seconds, with each intermediate step taking well under a second.

* * * Councilman directed Interloc employees to intercept and copy all incoming communications to subscriber dealers from Amazon.com, an Internet retailer that sells books and other products. Interloc's systems administrator modified the server's procmail recipe so that, before delivering any message from Amazon.com to the recipient's mailbox, procmail would copy the message and place the copy in a separate mailbox that Councilman could access. Thus, procmail would intercept and copy all incoming messages from Amazon.com before they were delivered to the recipient's mailbox, and therefore, before the intended recipient could read the message. This diversion intercepted thousands of messages, and Councilman and other Interloc employees routinely read the e-mail messages sent to Interloc subscribers in the hope of gaining a commercial advantage.

Id. at 69–71. The First Circuit did not decide whether the use of the device "intercepted" the e-mails in question under the Wiretap Act, although the court suggested in dicta that it probably did. *Id.* at 80.

Do you think the use of the procmail recipe intercepted the customer e-mails in *Councilman*? If so, why? Is it because the e-mail was not yet delivered? Because it was collected in real-time? Because it was the functional equivalent of a wiretap, and the details of the technology shouldn't matter? Imagine that Councilman had instructed the system administrator to check the inboxes of customers with Interloc accounts once a week, and to read any e-mails from Amazon. Would checking the e-mail accounts and reading the e-mails constitute an "intercept" of those e-mails? Does it depend on whether the e-mails had been accessed by their recipients and had been read by them already? Does the situation change if the system administrator checks the e-mail inboxes once a day? How about once an hour? How about every minute, or every ten seconds?

4. *Contents and non-content information.* The Wiretap Act applies only to the acquisition of "contents." Contents are defined somewhat awkwardly based on what they include, rather than what they are. According to 18 U.S.C. § 2510(8), " 'contents', when used with respect to any wire, oral, or electronic communication, includes any information concerning the substance, purport, or meaning of that communication." The phrase "substance, purport, or meaning" derives largely from language originally used in the first wiretapping prohibition in the Communications Act of 1934. The 1934 statute stated that "no person not being authorized by the sender shall intercept any communication and divulge or publish the existence, contents, substance, purport, effect, or meaning of such intercepted communication to any person." The existing definition of "contents" retains the inclusion of

"substance, purport, or meaning," but drops the "existence" and "effect" of the communication.

The scope of "contents" under the Wiretap Act is clear in some cases. It includes e-mail messages and the subject lines of e-mails. *See* In re Application of United States for an Order Authorizing Use of A Pen Register, 396 F. Supp. 2d 45, 48 (D. Mass. 2005) (stating that e-mail subject lines are contents). It presumably includes the text of any attachments to e-mails, such as document files. As we will see when we study the Pen Register statute, it also excludes "dialing, routing, addressing, or signaling information," which presumably refers to IP headers and e-mail headers (other than subject lines). *See* 18 U.S.C. § 3127(3)-(4).

Other cases are less clear. Consider the status of "Uniform Resource Locators," also known as URLs, the address lines commonly used to retrieve information on the World Wide Web. Do you think a URL entered into a web browser contains contents?

Does it depend on the URL? For example, does the URL "http://www.cnn.com" contain contents? How about this URL:

http://www.cnn.com/2005/US/12/11/wikipedia.ap/index.html

Or how about this one:

http://www.google.com/search?hl=en & lr= & q=Ì+must+kill+the+queen

Do any of these URLs contain contents? Note that typing the first URL into a functioning browser will direct a visitor to the CNN.com homepage; entering the second will direct the user to a particular story; and entering the third will run a Google query and return matches for the quotation "I must kill the queen." *See generally* The Naked Gun (Paramount Pictures 1988).

Consider Orin S. Kerr, *Internet Surveillance Law After the USA Patriot Act: The Big Brother That Isn't*, 97 Nw. U. L. Rev. 607, 646, 646 n.190 (2003):

> When an Internet user surfs the web, he sends commands to his computer directing it to send commands to the host computer, asking the host to send back packets of data that will be assembled by his computer into a web page. We can look at the user's command in two ways: either the command is the "content" of the communication between the user and his computer or it is merely "addressing information" that the user entered into his computer to tell the computer where it should go and what it should do, much like the pen register information in *Smith v. Maryland*.

> This is a difficulty latent in *Smith* that has not yet fully been appreciated. In *Smith*, the Court analogized dialing a phone number to contacting an operator and asking the operator to connect the call. Because disclosing the number to an operator would eliminate the speaker's reasonable expectation of privacy in the information, so did disclosing the information to the phone company's computer. So far, so good. The difficulty is that if a speaker calls the operator and places that request, then that request constitutes the contents of the communica-

tion between the speaker and the operator. The contents of the conversation between the speaker and the operator becomes the addressing information for the ensuing conversation between the speaker and the person he wishes to call. As a result, it is difficult in the abstract to say whether that initial communication should be considered addressing information or contents.

See also In re Pharmatrak Privacy Litigation, 329 F.3d 9, 18 (1st Cir. 2003) (stating that the Wiretap Act's definition of contents "encompasses personally identifiable information such as a party's name, date of birth, and medical condition" entered into a web site and then included as a URL term); *In re Application*, 396 F. Supp. 2d at 49 (suggesting in dicta that search terms in URLs are contents, as they reveal the "substance" and meaning" of the user's search for information).

Imagine a computer hacker attempts to take over a remote server, and that the FBI is monitoring the hacker and intercepts the hacker's communications. Are those communications "contents," such that intercepting them implicates the Wiretap Act? *See* United States Telecom Ass'n v. FCC, 227 F.3d 450, 462 (D.C. Cir. 2000) ("Post-cut-through dialed digits [dialed on a telephone, such as with voicemail systems] can also represent call content. For example, subjects calling automated banking services enter account numbers. When calling voicemail systems, they enter passwords. When calling pagers, they dial digits that convey actual messages. And when calling pharmacies to renew prescriptions, they enter prescription numbers.").

5. *Packet sniffers and "Carnivore."* Many different kinds of tools can be used to intercept computer and Internet communications. One popular type of tool is known as a "packet sniffer." A packet sniffer scans the packets of network traffic passing by a particular point in the network, and it then copies the parts of the traffic that match whatever characteristics the sniffer has been programmed to copy. *See generally* David McPhie, *Almost Private: Pen Registers, Packet Sniffers, and Privacy at the Margin*, 2005 Stan. Tech. L. Rev. 1.

Packets themselves are actually just streams of zeros and ones of data, and specific patterns of zeros and ones represent specific alphanumeric symbols. For example, a packet sniffer looking for the e-mail address "bob@aol.com," will scan for the following sequence: 0110001001101111011000100100000001100001. If this particular sequence appears, the sniffer can then begin to record a particular number of digits representing the remainder of the packet. The fruits of the sniffer can then be copied to a file, and a user can access the file at a later time and reconstruct the packets into readable form.

Whether a packet sniffer intercepts the contents of communications depends on how it is programmed. A sniffer program must be programmed to scan for and record particular sequences of traffic. If a sniffer is programmed in a way such that the zeros and ones collected include parts of communications that are "contents," then the use of the sniffer implicates the Wiretap Act. On the other hand, if the sniffer is programmed such that it does not copy any data streams that represent contents, then the sniffer will not implicate the Wiretap Act.

In the late 1990s, a great deal of media attention focused on the FBI's "Carnivore" surveillance tool. Carnivore, later renamed "DCS–1000," was a packet sniffer with an unusually sophisticated filter designed specifically to comply with court orders. The Carnivore system presented the user with a graphic user interface set for "content" or "non-content" monitoring, and adjusted the filter automatically. The FBI developed Carnivore in the late 1990s because commercial packet sniffer software available at that time lacked a sophisticated filter, and the commercial software could accidentally collect some content information when the sniffer was programmed to intercept only non-content information. By 2003, improvements in commercial packet sniffer design led to a phase-out of Carnivore/DCS–1000.

For more on Carnivore, see Illinois Institute of Technology Research Institute, Independent Review of Carnivore System—Final Report (2000); Griffin S. Dunham, Note, *Carnivore, The FBI's E–Mail Surveillance System: Devouring Criminals, Not Privacy*, 54 Fed. Comm. L.J. 543 (2002).

6. *The beginning and end of the Wiretap Act.* In the case of a traditional telephone call, the beginning and end point of the Wiretap Act's protection is very clear. The Act applies from handset to handset. Information becomes a "wire communication" when the human voice is transferred into a signal, and ceases to be a wire communication when the signal is transferred back to a human voice. In the case of computer communications such as e-mails, however, the picture is more complicated. Computer data does not change form when that data is an "electronic communication," creating interesting issues about where and when the statute's protection begins and where and when it ends.

Consider an example. Suppose Jane turns on her computer at 9 am and begins to type up an e-mail that she plans to send to her boss Catherine. Jane completes the e-mail at 9:30 am, but decides not to send it immediately. Instead, she saves the e-mail as a draft. At 2 pm, Jane pulls up the draft, looks it over for a few minutes, and sends it. The e-mail arrives at Catherine's ISP at 2:15 pm. Catherine logs in to her e-mail account at 3:00 pm, downloads the file unopened to her laptop at 3:15 pm, and then reads the file from her laptop at 3:30 pm. Now imagine that the government believes that the e-mail from Jane to Catherine contains evidence of a crime, and that investigators want to obtain a copy. Does the Wiretap Act apply to efforts to obtain the email at 9:30 am? 2 pm? 3 pm? At any other time?

Two different sources of law regulate this question. First, the definition of intercept requires that the collection of evidence must be contemporaneous with transmission. Second, the Wiretap Act defines "electronic communication" in relevant part as "*any transfer* of signs, signals, writing, images, sounds, data, or intelligence of any nature *transmitted* in whole or in part by a wire, radio, electromagnetic, photoelectronic or photooptical system *that affects interstate or foreign commerce*". 18 U.S.C. § 2510(12) (emphasis added). This definition suggests that the Wiretap Act begins when data is first transferred over an interstate system, and that it ends when data reaches its destination and is no longer being transferred over an interstate system. A communication typed into a desktop computer that is not connected to the Internet should not be subject to the Wiretap Act, as the communication is not a transfer (at least yet).

Goldman v. United States, 316 U.S. 129 (1942), may provide additional insight. *Goldman* interpreted 47 U.S.C. § 605 of the 1934 Communications Act, the predecessor to the Wiretap Act that shares a number of principles with it. The *Goldman* defendants were attorneys engaged in a conspiracy relating to a bankruptcy scheme. Federal agents entered the room next door to one attorney's office, and used a type of microphone placed against the wall to amplify the sound from the adjacent room and record the defendant's speech while he was talking on the telephone. The defendant claimed that the use of the microphone from the next room had "intercepted" the "communication" of his telephone call. The Supreme Court disagreed:

> What is protected is the message itself throughout the course of its transmission by the instrumentality or agency of transmission. Words written by a person and intended ultimately to be carried as so written to a telegraph office do not constitute a communication within the terms of the Act until they are handed to an agent of the telegraph company. Words spoken in a room in the presence of another into a telephone receiver do not constitute a communication by wire within the meaning of the section. Letters deposited in the Post Office are protected from examination by federal statute, but it could not rightly be claimed that the office carbon of such letter, or indeed the letter itself before it has left the office of the sender, comes within the protection of the statute.

Id. at 133–34.

Did the *O'Brien* court apply these principles correctly? What is the electronic equivalent of handing a message to an agent of the telegraph company? In the case of e-mail, is it pressing "send"?

7. *Remedies*. The *O'Brien* court comes up with a rather creative way to impose a suppression remedy. The statute itself imposes no such remedy, and a federal court in analogous circumstances would not suppress the evidence. As a matter of policy, is a suppression remedy appropriate in this case? Note that the *O'Brien* case is a civil dispute: the Wife monitored the Husband, and she wanted to use the evidence against him in a divorce proceeding.

Should the Wiretap Act include a statutory suppression remedy, either for government violations, for private violations, or for both?

8. A number of provisions in the Wiretap Act seem rather odd today because they are artifacts from the telephone era of the 1950s and 1960s. For example, the definition of "intercept" in 18 U.S.C. § 2510(4) requires that a communication must be obtained "through the use of any electronic, mechanical, or other device." Section 2510(5) in turn broadly defines "electronic, mechanical, or other device" to mean "any device or apparatus which can be used to intercept a wire, oral, or electronic communication," with two notable exceptions:

(a) any telephone or telegraph instrument, equipment or facility, or any component thereof,

   (i) furnished to the subscriber or user by a provider of wire or electronic communication service in the ordinary course of its business and being used by the subscriber or user in the ordinary course of its business or furnished by such subscriber or user for connection to the facilities of such service and used in the ordinary course of its business; or

(ii) being used by a provider of wire or electronic communication service in the ordinary course of its business, or by an investigative or law enforcement officer in the ordinary course of his duties;

(b) a hearing aid or similar device being used to correct subnormal hearing to not better than normal.

This requirement and the two exceptions were designed to deal with the specific dynamics of the telephone. The requirement of a device made sense in the telephone-only era, when an eavesdropper could listen in to a call by being in the next room or hiding nearby. Excluding hearing aids was important before telephones had volume controls; hearing-impaired telephone users had to purchase amplifiers and attach them to the handset to increase volume.

The exclusion of telephones used "in the ordinary course of business" that appears in 18 U.S.C. § 2510(5)(a)(i) is generally known as the extension telephone exception. This exception was designed to permit businesses to use an "extension telephone" to monitor the performance of their employees when they spoke on the phone to customers. The exception establishes that when a phone company furnishes an employer with an extension telephone for a legitimate work-related purpose, employer monitoring of employees using the extension phone for legitimate work-related purposes does not violate the Wiretap Act. *See* Briggs v. American Air Filter Co., 630 F.2d 414, 418 (5th Cir. 1980).

Finally, the exemption of monitoring by police officers in 18 U.S.C. § 2510(5)(a)(ii) that involves the use of "any telephone" by "an investigative or law enforcement officer in the ordinary course of his duties" is easily misunderstood. Although the language appears broad, it has been interpreted to permit routine monitoring of calls to and from police stations and little else. *See, e.g.,* Amati v. City of Woodstock, 176 F.3d 952, 955 (7th Cir. 1999).

9. The Wiretap Act permits agents to intercept communications pursuant to a court order. *See* 18 U.S.C. §§ 2516, 2518. Obtaining a Title III "super warrant" order is quite burdensome, however, as the requirements extend far beyond probable cause and involve a great deal of paperwork. The Justice Department explains:

High-level Justice Department approval is required for federal Title III applications, by statute in the case of wire communications, and by Justice Department policy in the case of electronic communications (except for numeric pagers). When authorized by the Justice Department and signed by a United States District Court or Court of Appeals judge, a Title III order permits law enforcement to intercept communications for up to thirty days. *See* § 2518.

18 U.S.C. §§ 2516–2518 imposes several formidable requirements that must be satisfied before investigators can obtain a Title III order. Most importantly, the application for the order must show probable cause to believe that the interception will reveal evidence of a predicate felony offense listed in § 2516. *See* § 2518(3)(a)-(b). For federal agents,

the predicate felony offense must be one of the crimes specifically enumerated in § 2516(1)(a)-(r) to intercept wire communications, or any federal felony to intercept electronic communications. *See* 18 U.S.C. § 2516(3). The predicate crimes for state investigations are listed in 18 U.S.C. § 2516(2). The application for a Title III order also (1) must show that normal investigative procedures have been tried and failed, or that they reasonably appear to be unlikely to succeed or to be too dangerous, *see* § 2518(1)(c); (2) must establish probable cause that the communication facility is being used in a crime; and (3) must show that the surveillance will be conducted in a way that minimizes the interception of communications that do not provide evidence of a crime.

U.S. Department of Justice, Searching and Seizing Computers (2002), available at http://www.cybercrime.gov/s&smanual2002.htm#_IVD3a_.

The difficulty of obtaining a Title III order results in such orders being obtained only rarely. This is particularly true in computer-related cases. In 2004, investigators obtained Title III orders permitting real-time full-content computer monitoring in only 12 cases. *See* Administrative Office of the U.S. Courts, 2004 Wiretap Report 10 (2004). Granted, at least two of these cases involved surveillance on a massive scale:

The most active federal wiretap [in 2004] occurred in the District of New Jersey, where a counterfeiting investigation involving the interception of computer messages resulted in the interception of 206,444 messages over 30 days. The second most active federal intercept, also a computer wiretap, occurred in the Southern District of New York as part of a 30–day racketeering investigation and resulted in a total of 107,779 interceptions.

Id. at 9.

The very low number of Title III orders in computer cases should direct our attention to the three main exceptions applicable in computer wiretapping cases: the consent exception, § 2511(2)(c)-(d), the provider exception, § 2511(2)(a)(i), and the computer trespasser exception, § 2511(2)(i). In the great majority of cases, monitoring occurs pursuant to one of these three exceptions.

2. THE CONSENT EXCEPTION

Like the Fourth Amendment, the Wiretap Act has a consent exception. 18 U.S.C. § 2511(2)(c) and (d) state:

(c) It shall not be unlawful under this chapter for a person acting under color of law to intercept a wire, oral, or electronic communication, where such person is a party to the communication or one of the parties to the communication has given prior consent to such interception.

(d) It shall not be unlawful under this chapter for a person not acting under color of law to intercept a wire, oral, or electronic communication where such person is a party to the communication or where one of the parties to the communication has given prior consent to such interception unless such communication is intercepted for the purpose of committing any criminal or tortious act in violation of the Constitution or laws of the United States or of any State.

This exception permits "a party to the communication" to give "prior consent" to interception. If a party to the communication consents to the interception, the interception does not violate the Wiretap Act. For example, an undercover government agent can record a conversation between himself and a suspect or permit others to record the call. Similarly, if a private person records his own telephone conversations with others, his consent authorizes the interception unless the commission of a criminal, tortious, or other injurious act was a determinative factor in the person's motivation for intercepting the communication. *See* United States v. Cassiere, 4 F.3d 1006, 1021 (1st Cir. 1993).

GRIGGS–RYAN v. SMITH

United States Court of Appeals for the First Circuit, 1990.
904 F.2d 112.

SELYA, Circuit Judge.

Reaching out to touch someone, plaintiff-appellant Gerald Griggs–Ryan filed two related civil actions in the United States District Court for the District of Maine. Suing his landlady, Beulah Smith, plaintiff alleged that she unlawfully intercepted and disclosed the contents of a telephone conversation in which he participated.

I.

Plaintiff was a tenant at a campground which Smith operated in Wells. The individual units did not have telephones, but lodgers were allowed to use the landlady's telephone. During the summer of 1987, Smith was plagued by obscene calls. On the police department's advice, she began to record incoming calls through her answering machine. Because she suspected that plaintiff's friend, Paul Jackson, was responsible for the offensive overtures, Smith informed plaintiff on a number of occasions that all calls to her home were being recorded. She hoped, of course, that plaintiff would relay the message to Jackson.

On September 14, 1987, Smith answered the telephone in her bedroom. The caller identified himself as "Richard Kierstead" and asked to speak with plaintiff. Smith held the line open to maintain the connection while her daughter went to fetch plaintiff. When Griggs–Ryan picked up the office extension, Smith started to cradle her instrument. Overhearing the caller say, "Hi, it's Paul, she thinks its Kierstead," and believing the voice to be Paul Jackson's, Smith changed her mind. She did not hang up but instead listened to and recorded the ensuing discussion.

As a result of the eavesdropping, Smith came to suspect that the overheard conversation concerned a drug transaction. She immediately contacted the authorities. At police headquarters, she played the tape for defendant Connelly. Sharing Smith's suspicions, the detective revealed the conversation's contents to the district attorney and to a local magistrate. The magistrate issued a warrant to search plaintiff's abode and the Wells police executed it, seizing marijuana. Griggs–Ryan was arrested and charged with trafficking.

A suppression hearing was held in the state superior court. Smith testified about what she told Griggs–Ryan concerning her recording practice. The judge found that plaintiff was "unaware" that Smith was listening to, or recording, the September 14 conversation, and ruled that Smith's interception of the conversation was therefore inadmissible under Maine law. On September 28, 1989, the judge suppressed the fruits of the search.

In the meantime, plaintiff had begun the instant suits in federal court. For their part, defendants argued that plaintiff, by electing to talk to Jackson after Smith's warning that all incoming calls were being recorded, effectively acquiesced in the interception.

The district court concluded that the landlady's actions were not proscribed by federal law because Smith informed Plaintiff on more than one occasion that she was recording all incoming calls and that there was no evidence that Smith qualified her statements to Plaintiff on the matter. Thus, the district court held that Plaintiff's receiving of a telephone call inside of Smith's home, when considered in light of the warning he received, manifests implied consent sufficient to trigger the prior consent exception to Title III.

II.

Although plaintiff repeatedly declaims that wire communications are "protected absolutely from illegal interception," that rallying cry—like most sloganeering—overstates the proposition. Title III was intended to prohibit all interceptions except those specifically provided for in the Act. Congress, in its wisdom, chose to insert a myriad of exceptions and restrictive definitions into Title III, purposely leaving certain wire communications unprotected. Accordingly, there is little to be gained by pejorative declamations; the question is simply whether a particular intercept runs afoul of the statute's imperatives.

18 U.S.C. § 2511(2)(d) outlines a Title III exclusion applicable where one of the parties to the communication has given prior consent to such interception. We agree with the Second Circuit that "Congress intended the consent requirement to be construed broadly." United States v. Amen, 831 F.2d 373, 378 (2d Cir. 1987). In this spirit, we—and other courts—have held that Title III affords safe harbor not only for persons who intercept calls with the explicit consent of a conversant but also for those who do so after receiving implied consent. See United States v. Willoughby, 860 F.2d 15, 19 (2d Cir. 1988); Watkins v. L.M. Berry & Co., 704 F.2d 577, 581 (11th Cir. 1983); Campiti v. Walonis, 611 F.2d 387, 393 (1st Cir. 1979). Acknowledging the doctrinal vitality of implied consent, however, does not address its parameters—nor can we suggest any pat, all-purpose definition. In the Title III milieu as in other

settings, consent inheres where a person's behavior manifests acquiescence or a comparable voluntary diminution of his or her otherwise protected rights.

Of course, implied consent is not constructive consent. Rather, implied consent is "consent in fact" which is inferred from surrounding circumstances indicating that the party knowingly agreed to the surveillance. Thus, implied consent—or the absence of it—may be deduced from the circumstances prevailing in a given situation. The circumstances relevant to an implication of consent will vary from case to case, but the compendium will ordinarily include language or acts which tend to prove (or disprove) that a party knows of, or assents to, encroachments on the routine expectation that conversations are private. And the ultimate determination must proceed in light of the prophylactic purpose of Title III—a purpose which suggests that consent should not casually be inferred.

The salient facts are these. Prior to September 14, Griggs–Ryan had been repeatedly informed that all incoming calls were being monitored. Smith's affidavit in this respect stands uncontradicted and unimpeached:

> On several occasions during the course of the summer I spoke to Mr. Ryan and informed him that all incoming telephone calls to my home were being tape recorded. I had made it quite clear to Mr. Ryan by virtue of these several conversations that all of the incoming telephone calls to my home on my phones were being tape recorded.

There is no evidence that Smith, whatever her actual practice might have been, ever informed plaintiff that she would cease monitoring a call once she determined that it was not harassing. Indeed, the only record evidence speaking directly to this question is Smith's testimony at the state court suppression hearing, where the following colloquy occurred:

> Q. When you told Mr. Ryan that you were taping every phone call, did you tell him that you have stopped taping once you identified who the caller was?
>
> A. No.

* * * [W]e take as undisputed that (1) plaintiff was told unequivocally that all incoming calls would be recorded, and (2) Smith did not qualify the warning by telling him that she planned to listen only until she could ascertain whether the call was offensive.

It remains only for us to link applicable law to undisputed fact. The district court ruled that plaintiff, in taking the call from Jackson and conversing with him on Smith's telephone, impliedly consented to the interception. We think that this ruling was inevitable. Plaintiff had been unmistakably warned on a number of occasions that all incoming calls were being monitored. In light of so sweeping a warning, he continued to receive calls and talk unguardedly on Smith's personal line without the slightest hint of coercion or exigent circumstance. Plaintiff was free to use some other instrument; or since outgoing calls were not recorded, to return calls on Smith's telephone and thus avoid any unwanted eaves-dropping. Given the circumstances prevailing, it seems altogether clear that plaintiff knowingly agreed to the surveillance. His consent, albeit not explicit, was manifest. No more was required.

Smith's conduct on September 14 fell squarely within the parameters of what she had repeatedly told plaintiff to expect, and thus, fell squarely within the bounds of plaintiff's consent. Having persisted in using Smith's telephone to converse with callers in the face of unambiguous, unqualified notice that every incoming call would be monitored, plaintiff's consent necessarily encompassed every portion of every call he accepted on his landlady's line.

Plaintiff's final fizgig, centering on the upshot of the state court suppression hearing, is equally unimpressive. It is true that the state court found plaintiff "unaware" that the call in question was being recorded. Even assuming, however, that the finding has evidentiary significance in a federal civil case involving persons not parties to the state criminal proceedings—a matter on which we do not opine—it is beside the present point. Whether a person is cognizant that a particular call is being recorded does not answer, or fully respond to, the question of whether the scope of consent previously granted was sufficiently expansive to cover a generalized practice of recording.

Because plaintiff unqualifiedly consented to Smith's interception of all incoming calls, the latter's conduct was "not unlawful" within the meaning of 18 U.S.C. § 2511(2)(d). Consequently, no cause of action could be maintained against Smith under Title III.

Notes and Questions

1.   In what sense did Griggs–Ryan consent to Ryan's monitoring? He had been told a few times in the months leading up to the call that Ryan was recording calls made to her phone. But there was no evidence that he knew this particular call was recorded. Is the key question whether Griggs–Ryan proceeded after receiving notice, or whether he actually consented to being taped? Which court was right: the state court that ruled Griggs–Ryan had not consented, or the federal court that ruled he had?

Which is the better approach as a matter of policy? Should notice of monitoring be sufficient even if the person monitored did not realize the call was being monitored?

2.   Compare *Griggs-Ryan* with Deal v. Spears, 980 F.2d 1153 (8th Cir. 1992). In *Spears*, owners of a packaging store suspected that an employee was involved in an earlier burglary of the store. The employee often spent much of her day flirting on the store telephone with her boyfriend, and the store owners asked the employee to cut down on her personal calls and warned that they might start recording her calls to curtail abuses. The owners later decided to record all calls to and from the store in an effort to catch the employee making an unguarded admission of her involvement in the burglary. When the monitoring recorded the employee admitting petty wrongdoing at the store, the store owners fired her. The employee then

brought a wiretapping suit against the store owners. Held: The owners' warning that they "might" begin to monitor calls was insufficient to generate consent under the Wiretap Act. *See id.* at 1157.

3. Does a telephone or Internet user impliedly consent to monitoring if she did not receive notice but should have known that the communications would be monitored? Cases suggest that the answer is "no." For example, in United States v. Lanoue, 71 F.3d 966 (1st Cir. 1995), the defendant was a prisoner who was monitored while making calls from a detention center that did not notify prisoners of monitoring. The First Circuit articulated the following standard to determine whether consent exists absent sufficient formal notice:

> Deficient notice will almost always defeat a claim of implied consent. Keeping in mind that implied consent is not constructive consent but 'consent in fact,' consent might be implied in spite of deficient notice, but only in a rare case where the court can conclude with assurance from surrounding circumstances that the party knowingly agreed to the surveillance. We emphasize that consent should not casually be inferred, particularly in a case of deficient notice. The surrounding circumstances must convincingly show that the party knew about and consented to the interception in spite of the lack of formal notice or deficient formal notice.

Id. at 981. Similarly, in Jandak v. Village of Brookfield, 520 F. Supp. 815, 820 n. 5 (N.D. Ill. 1981), a police officer placed a personal call from the police station to another person. The call was secretly recorded, and the court rejected the notion that one of the parties consented because they should have known that a call from the police station would be recorded:

> [C]onsent may be implied in fact, from surrounding circumstances indicating that the party knowingly agreed to the surveillance. Defendants here are asking that the consent be implied in law, if the party reasonably should have known. This goes far beyond the language of the statute, or any indications in the legislative history, and the court declines to so expansively read the exception.

4. Computer owners sometimes install network banners to generate users' consent and permit monitoring. A banner is a message that greets computer users when they log on to a network; a typical banner informs users that their communications on the network may be monitored. After a user sees the banner and has knowledge of the monitoring, the computer can be monitored without violating the Wiretap Act under the consent theory of *Griggs–Ryan v. Smith*.

Banners are routinely used in government workplaces to regulate rights on government networks. In the context of government employment, computer network banners perform two functions at once. They generate consent to monitoring for purposes of Title III, and they also constitute a legitimate workplace policy that eliminates Fourth Amendment privacy rights in the network under O'Connor v. Ortega, 480 U.S. 709 (1987).

How clear must the wording of a banner be to generate a computer user's consent to monitoring? Should the banner require users to "click through" the notice? Is it sufficient if the notice of monitoring can be found somewhere in the Terms of Service or an employee manual? What if the computer user does not see the banner or does not understand it? What if the user is trying to avoid the banner and bypasses it to avoid actual notice?

5. *Problem.* A commercial ISP called Overcast requires its new subscribers to agree to Terms of Service as a condition of service. One of the terms states: "Overcast may wish to intercept your communications. By registering for an account with Overcast, you agree to allow Overcast to monitor your communications." A new subscriber named Hoover J. Edgar signs up with Overcast, and clicks "I Agree" to start his service contract. Like almost all subscribers, however, Edgar does not actually read the Terms of Service and has no idea what terms he has agreed to follow. Five years later, the FBI is conducting a terrorism investigation and suspects that Edgar may be involved with a terrorist plot. An FBI agent approaches an Overcast employee and asks Overcast to intercept all of Edgar's e-mails and send them to the FBI. Overcast agrees, relying on the Terms of Service, and begins to intercept Edgar's e-mails.

Does this monitoring violate the Wiretap Act, or is it permitted under the consent exception?

6. *Computers, victims, and intermediaries as parties to the communication.* In the case of telephone calls, a "party to the communication" is usually easy to identify. Any human participant in a telephone conversation is a party to the communication. The simple framework of a two-way communication between two parties may be more difficult to apply in the case of a computer network.

> When a hacker launches an attack against a computer network, for example, he may route the attack through a handful of compromised computer systems before directing the attack at a final victim. At the victim's computer, the hacker may direct the attack at a user's network account, at the system administrator's "root" account, or at common files. Finding a "person" who is a "party to the communication"—other than the hacker himself, of course—can be a difficult (if not entirely metaphysical) task.

U.S. Department of Justice, Searching and Seizing Computers (2002), available at www.cybercrime.gov/s&smanual2002.htm#_IVD3b_.

Can a computer be a party to the communication that can consent to monitoring under the Wiretap Act? Is the owner or system administrator a party to the communication? Recall the early case of United States v. Seidlitz, 589 F.2d 152 (4th Cir. 1978), first introduced in Chapter 2. Seidlitz used a stolen account to break into computers owned and operated by OSI. Employees at OSI monitored Seidlitz's unauthorized use of the OSI computer and used that monitoring to trace the attack back to Seidlitz. At trial, Seidlitz argued that the evidence of his conduct could not be used against him because the monitoring violated the Wiretap Act. The case was decided before the passage of ECPA, and the Fourth Circuit properly rejected the claim on the ground that the computer communication was not a "wire communication" protected by the 1968 statute. The Court then suggested this secondary rationale for its holding:

Title III specifically authorizes the interception of a wire communication by a party to the communication or by a person acting with the consent of a party to the communication. 18 U.S.C. § 2511(2)(c), (d). In our opinion OSI, which leased, housed, programmed, and maintained the computers and subscribed to the relevant telephone numbers, was for all intents and purposes a party to the communications initiated by the defendant, since in a very real sense the company used the computers solely as a medium for imparting to customers, via telephone lines, its own expertise. Insofar as OSI installed on its line a computer which was capable of recording the messages exchanged in the course of responding to a remote user's requests, we consider this case analogous to those which recognize that a party may, consistent with Title III, use a device to capture and record both sides of his telephone conversation with another party.

Id. at 158. Do you agree that OSI was a party to the communication in the *Seidlitz* case? If not, can OSI monitor intrusions into its network? As a matter of policy, what rights should the victim of a computer intrusion have to monitor attacks against it? *See also* United States v. Mullins, 992 F.2d 1472, 1478 (9th Cir. 1993) (suggesting in passing that the consent exception authorizes monitoring of computer system misuse because the owner of the victimized computer system is a party to the communication).

If you agree that OSI was a party to the communication in the *Seidlitz* case, do you reach the same conclusion with respect to intermediary computers that may be involved in computer intrusion cases? The question is very important in computer hacking investigations:

When the government investigates a computer hacking incident, investigators generally start at the victim that has reported the crime and trace back the attack to its origin. To avoid detection, hackers will not mount their attacks directly from their ISPs. Rather, they will route communications through a few victim computers along the way to throw the government off the trail. This can effectively disguise their location because computers only reveal the immediate source from which a user sent a communication. If a user routes a command from A to B to C to D, the computer at D will only know that the command came from C, and will not know that the command actually originated from A. To identify the intruder, the government must trace the communication step by step from D to C to B to A.

The rules that govern this tracing process depend heavily on whether the computers that the hacker has victimized count as parties to the communication under the Wiretap Act. Consider an example. Imagine that a computer hacker in New York plans to attack sensitive Defense Department computers in California, and starts off by accessing the Internet through his ISP in New Jersey. Rather than hack directly into the Defense Department computers in California, the hacker first breaks into a computer at a small company in Nebraska, and from that site in Nebraska he hacks into another computer belonging to a high school in Arizona. Finally, from the computer in Arizona he launches a computer attack against Defense Department computers in California that contain potentially sensitive information relating to national security. Defense

Department criminal investigators then begin an investigation into the attacks.

Orin S. Kerr, *Internet Surveillance Law After the USA Patriot Act: The Big Brother That Isn't*, 97 Nw. U. L. Rev. 607, 662–63 (2003). Do you think that the Defense Department computer in California is a party to the communication? How about the ISP in New Jersey? The small company in Nebraska? The high school in Arizona? Consider the stakes from the standpoint of privacy, focusing on whether the police would be able to monitor the hacker's activities at the school in Arizona with the consent of the school:

> [W]hether the police can conduct the monitoring with the school's consent depends on whether the school is a "party" to the hacker's communication. If the school is a party, the school can consent to law enforcement monitoring; if it is not a party, the school cannot consent to the monitoring without violating the Wiretap Act.

> Whether the school constitutes a party under the Wiretap Act then hinges upon how the hacker's attack is modeled. On one hand, if the hacker sent a communication to the school with instructions for the school's computer to launch attacks against the California victims, then the school itself is a party to the communication and can consent to the government's monitoring. This approach reflects a broad theory of the "party to the communication" exception. On the other hand, if we say that the hacker himself sent the communication to the California victim but merely routed the communication through the school, then the school is not a party and cannot consent. This approach applies a narrow conception of the "party to the communication" exception.

> What complicates this picture is that labeling the school a party to the communication may sound logical here because the school is a victim of crime, but ultimately would eviscerate the privacy protections of the Wiretap Act. Internet communications almost never travel directly from their point of origin to their destination: most travel from hop to hop as they traverse the network. If each hop is a party to the communication, as the broader approach to the exception would dictate, then any provider can monitor any communication within its network or can consent to monitoring by others.

Id. at 664–65.

If you write an e-mail to your best friend, is your ISP a party to the communication? Is your friend's ISP a party to the communication? Or are you and your friend the only parties to the communication?

A somewhat related issue came up in a case brought under 47 U.S.C. § 605, the predecessor to the Wiretap statute. In United States v. Dote, 371 F.2d 176 (7th Cir. 1966), the Illinois Bell Telephone company tipped off IRS agents that a particular telephone was being used in an illegal gambling ring. Acting at the request of IRS investigators, the company installed a pen register on the phone. The pen register led IRS investigators to the members of the gambling enterprise, who were then arrested and convicted of tax evasion. They appealed their convictions on the ground that the pen register violated 47 U.S.C. § 605. (Although the pen register did not collect contents, § 605 applied both to content and non-content information at that time.) The government defended its use of the pen register on the ground that the dial pulses of the numbers dialed from the telephone were communications to the phone company. In the parlance of the modern Wiretap Act, the government's claim was that the phone company could consent to monitoring because it was a party to the communication of the numbers dialed. The Seventh Circuit disagreed:

> We see no reason to indulge in a game of words, * * * [on] whether the telephone company as a legal entity is sufficiently embodied in the wires and devices of its system to be an intended recipient of the dial pulse signal. * * * [N]o person was the intended recipient of the dial pulses, but rather the communications system through which the pulses were to be relayed as a signal to activate the telephone of the intended recipient of a telephone call. * * * The dial telephone system does not generally require human intervention to connect two telephones. The telephone company was not therefore the intended recipient of the signal. The 'intended recipient' was the telephone of another subscriber, which would ring to notify the subscriber of a call. Ultimately, the intended human recipient of the signal was the subscriber called.

Id. at 180.

7. *All-party consent statutes.* The federal Wiretap Act is a one-party consent statute. That is, the consent of any one party to the communication permits monitoring of every other party. In contrast, some state wiretap statutes require every party to consent before the state consent exception applies. In the case of a telephone call, for example, each person on the call must authorize the monitoring.

How does an all-party consent approach apply to monitoring computer communications? In Commonwealth v. Proetto, 771 A.2d 823 (Pa. Super. Ct. 2001), *aff'd,* 837 A.2d 1163 (Pa. 2003), the defendant engaged in IRC and e-mail communications with an undercover police officer who was posing as a young girl. The police officer recorded all of the communications, and printouts of the exchanges were admitted at trial. Pennsylvania's state wiretap statute requires the consent of all parties, and the defendant argued that the officer had intercepted his communications unlawfully because the defendant had not consented to the officer recording his chat and e-mail exchanges. The Pennsylvania Superior Court rejected the claim, finding the defendant's consent implicit in his use of the technology:

> This situation is unlike one in which a party is engaging in a conversation over the telephone. While engaging in a conversation over the telephone, a party would have no reason to believe that the other party was taping the conversation. Any reasonably intelligent person, savvy enough to be using the Internet, however, would be aware of the fact that messages are received in a recorded format, by their very nature, and can be downloaded or printed by the party receiving the message. By the very act of sending a communication over the Internet, the party expressly consents to the recording of the message.

See id. at 830. Is this reasoning persuasive? Does an Internet user expressly (or impliedly) permit intended recipients of his communications to make copies of his communications?

3. THE PROVIDER EXCEPTION

The next exception to the Wiretap Act is the provider exception, 18 U.S.C. § 2511(2)(a)(i). The provider exception is particularly important in computer misuse cases, as it allows reasonable monitoring of computer misuse. The exception states in relevant part:

> an officer, employee, or agent of a provider of wire or electronic communication service, whose facilities are used in the transmission of a wire or electronic communication, [can] intercept, disclose, or use that communication in the normal course of his employment while engaged in any activity which is a necessary incident to the rendition of his service or to the protection of the rights or property of the provider of that service.

The provider exception recognizes that providers of network services may have legitimate business reasons to tap communications within their networks. Networks can be misused or abused, and providers may need to monitor the misuse to identify the wrongdoer and stop the misconduct. The provider exception thus gives providers a limited right to monitor communications to protect their property. The basic standard is reasonableness. *See* United States v. Harvey, 540 F.2d 1345, 1350 (8th Cir. 1976). Providers are permitted to conduct reasonable monitoring to protect their rights or property and can disclose the fruits of what they obtain to the government. However, they cannot take the monitoring or disclosure too far.

UNITED STATES v. AULER

United States Court of Appeals for the Seventh Circuit, 1976.
539 F.2d 642.

FAIRCHILD, Chief Judge.

In this appeal we are once again asked to consider the scope of the authority of a common carrier to intercept and disclose wire communications, 18 U.S.C. § 2511(2)(a)(i). The appellant, Raymond Auler, was convicted for violating the Wire Fraud Statute, 18 U.S.C. § 1343, and sentenced to six months imprisonment.

I

During June, 1973 a security supervisor for the Wisconsin Telephone Company, Bernard G. Schlimgen, attached a 2600 cycle detecting device to the telephone line serving Auler's residence in Milwaukee. Schlimgen believed that there was in use a device known as a "blue box" to fraudulently place toll-free long distance calls. The blue box is used to electronically bypass the telephone company's billing equipment. After engaging a wide area telephone service system (WATS), the blue box emits a 2600 cycle tone which allows the user to remain within the toll system after the WATS line has been disconnected. Subsequently, the user "key pulses" through the blue box a series of multifrequency tones, comparable to those normally generated by a long distance call. The telephone company's billing equipment only records the original toll-free call; consequently, the user is not charged for the call made with the blue box.

The 2600 cycle detector indicated that an out of state call was made by use of the blue box technique. Schlimgen informed Roger Davis, then a Special Agent for the F.B.I., of this suspected violation of the Wire Fraud Statute. Davis obtained a warrant, and accompanied by Schlimgen, searched Auler's residence. They did not find a blue box, but learned from Auler's daughter that Auler had been present earlier, but was moving to Wisconsin Dells.

On June 21, 1973, Schlimgen contacted Gary Mattila, a security agent for the General Telephone Company, the company which provides telephone service for the Wisconsin Dells area, concerning Auler's alleged use of the blue box. Mattila discovered that Auler had two telephone listings at a Wisconsin Dells residence. He further learned from another Wisconsin Telephone Company security agent that Auler was a suspected blue box user. This information was obtained by examining a computer printout list of all the toll-free calls placed in that area. On the basis of these reports, Mattila ordered on July 13, and 17, 1973 the installation of a 2600 cycle detector placed on both of Auler's Wisconsin Dells telephone lines.

After the detection of numerous 2600 cycle tones, Mattila, on July 27, 1973, ordered the attachment of magnetic tape recording devices to Auler's lines to monitor all multifrequency tones and conversations originating from Auler's residence. This taping was discontinued on one line on July 29, and on the other on July 30. General Telephone's logs indicate that the magnetic recorders also taped traffic over Auler's lines on August 2 through 3, and August 9 through 13.

On July 30 and 31, Mattila advised F.B.I. Agent Hunter that General Telephone had conducted an investigation regarding Raymond Auler, and that based on this investigation Auler was suspected of using a blue box. Hunter obtained a warrant on August 3 to search Auler's residence. Accompanied by Mattila, Hunter executed the warrant on August 10. Immediately preceding the search Mattila had been in contact with General Telephone agents who were monitoring Auler's lines. These agents informed Mattila that they had detected a 2600 cycle tone and had recorded Auler completing a call. During the search Hunter found and seized a blue box and other equipment. Auler was subsequently tried on stipulated facts and found guilty. Prior to trial Auler had unsuccessfully sought to suppress any evidence that was the product of General Telephone's interception of his telephone lines.

II

Section 2511(2)(a)(i) provides a telephone company with the power to protect its property through limited monitoring of the lines of suspected illegal users and the subsequent immunity to disclose necessary information to law enforcement agencies.

This authority of the telephone company to intercept and disclose wire communications is not unlimited. It may only intercept a communication which is a necessary incident to the rendition of service or for the protection of the company's rights or property. * * * Therefore, we think that any surveillance of a suspected blue box user must be restricted to a determination of (1) whether a blue box is being used; (2) the multifrequency tones of the number "dialed" by the blue box; (3) whether the call was completed; (4) the duration of the call; and (5) the identity of the caller. This information can be obtained through a 2600 cycle detector, or similar device, and a tape recording of the salutations at the beginning of the conversation. Therefore, section 2511(2)(a)(i) must reasonably be read to permit the telephone company to divulge, at least, the existence of the illegal calls and the fact that they were completed (the salutations) to law enforcement authorities. These authorized disclosures could properly be used to obtain a search warrant and would be admissible as evidence.

Auler points out that General Telephone's surveillance of his conversations extended beyond the scope of permissible interception just outlined. At oral argument, the Government conceded that during the approximately two week period of surveillance, General Telephone monitored and committed to tape all calls, whether made illicitly with a blue box or in compliance with the subscription agreement. This intrusive interception provided General Telephone with far more information than it needed to protect its interests.

However, General Telephone only disclosed to the F.B.I. the limited evidence which section 2511(2)(a)(i) reasonably permits. This consisted of edited tape recordings containing tones identified as those transmitted by a blue box, dialing signals, and salutations of the appellant. The interception of the material recorded on these tapes may be viewed apart from those more intrusive acts of surveillance which are not immunized by section 2511(2)(a)(i). The reasonable and necessary interceptions and disclosures need not be suppressed as the "fruits" of illegal surveillance. Neither the statute nor the Fourth Amendment, which does not prohibit unreasonable searches by private individuals. require lawful interceptions and disclosures to be excluded as evidence; only evidence obtained through surveillance beyond the authorization of section 2511(2)(a)(i) * * * must be suppressed. General Telephone provided no evidence stemming from excessive interception to the F.B.I., and the Government offered none at trial.[10] The edited tapes offered at trial were properly admitted. We do assume for the purpose of this discussion that General Telephone conducted excessive and therefore illegal surveillance. Any consequences to General Telephone in the context of the civil and criminal penalties imposed by [the Wiretap Act] would be the subject of an action to which General Telephone would be a party.

---

10. Evidence which is obtained through an unreasonably broad surveillance cannot be legally disclosed to the government, regardless whether it is offered at trial.

III

The appellant further argues that even if section 2511(2)(a)(i) permits limited telephone company surveillance, he is entitled to the protection provided by the Fourth Amendment. Auler asserts that the search warrant, executed by the F.B.I. was obtained as a result of illegal surveillance directed by Government agents. The tape recordings and the evidence secured as a result of the search of Auler's Wisconsin Dells residence should, he claims, therefore have been suppressed.

Auler relies on the principles that Government agents, state or federal, who engage in electronic eavesdropping must comply with the constitutional requirements of a reasonable search, *Katz v. United States,* 389 U.S. 347, 359 (1967), and that evidence, tangible or testimonial, which is seized without adherence to these constitutional safeguards must be excluded. *Weeks v. United States,* 232 U.S. 383, 391–92 (1914); *Wong Sun v. United States,* 371 U.S. 471, 485 (1963). Before we can apply these principles to the case before us, the appellant must demonstrate that the Government was directly or indirectly engaged in gathering the alleged illegal surveillance.

The district court found that the F.B.I. neither initiated nor directed the surveillance conducted by General Telephone. Our own search of the record supports this conclusion. Nor do we find that the F.B.I. participated in or tacitly approved of the interceptions made by General Telephone to the degree that they became a government search. Finally, we cannot agree with the circuitous reasoning that would label the surveillance permitted by section 2511(2)(a)(i) as governmental action, thereby requiring a warrant.

Auler further contends that the intimate collaboration between F.B.I. Agent Hunter and General Telephone employees Mattila and Nelson constituted a government wiretap, resulting in an illegally executed search warrant. The facts stipulated by both parties do indicate that on August 10, 1973 Nelson informed Mattila that the blue box was being used and that Auler had identified himself during the illegal call. Mattila received this information while he was in the company of Agent Hunter; both men were stationed outside Auler's residence. Upon receipt of this surveillance Hunter and Mattila executed the search warrant and found the blue box.

We are aware, as was the Government at oral argument, that Government agents must not rely on telephone company employees to act on their behalf without complying with the requirements of the Fourth Amendment. In no situation may the Government direct the telephone company to intercept wire communications in order to circumvent the warrant requirements of a reasonable search. The Government may not use their ears for what it cannot do. On the morning of August 10, 1973 General Telephone was engaged in surveillance permitted by section 2511(2)(a)(i). The interceptions recorded by Nelson were part of the continuing effort by General Telephone to gather evidence concerning Auler's illegal use of the telephone lines. The disclosure of this continuing illegal conduct was in furtherance of General Telephone's attempt to protect its equipment.

Based on information supplied by General Telephone, Agent Hunter had secured a valid search warrant. He had asked Mattila to accompany him to identify any illegal equipment found during the course of the search. Mattila's disclosure, just prior to execution of the warrant, that the blue box was being used, was a disclosure of information lawfully acquired through surveillance necessary to protect company rights and property. The surveillance had been conducted independently of any governmental direction. The search warrant had been obtained on the basis of legally intercepted and disclosed information. Consequently, the final disclosure by Mattila cannot transform authorized conduct into an illegal Government search. The trial record and the district court's analysis of these facts can bear no other interpretation.

For the reasons set forth above, the judgment appealed from is affirmed.

Notes and Questions

1. Imagine a system administrator has reason to believe that a computer hacker has intruded into his network from a particular IP address using a particular destination port.[c] The system administrator wants to take the following steps:

    A. Record every command from that IP address to that destination port for one week.

    B. Record every command from that IP address to any port for one week.

    C. Record every command to that port regardless of IP address for one week.

    D. Record every command into the network at every IP address and every port for 24 hours.

    E. Install intrusion detection software that will automatically record future intrusions that match known attack patterns common among computer hackers.

Which of these steps fall within the provider exception? Does it depend on the IP address, or how much traffic the network receives on that particular port? Does it depend on the intrusion detection software and how it is configured? Does it depend on what kind of communications the hacker routes through the victim network? What if the hacker sets up a private Internet chat channel from inside the network—can the system administrator monitor the Internet chat communications to identify the hacker?

c. Ports enable computers to classify different types of Internet traffic. Every computer server connected to the Internet makes its functions available to those connecting to the server by using specific numbered ports. Different port numbers translate into different services available on that server. For example, World Wide Web traffic typically is sent at port 80, and ftp (file transfer protocol) commands are sent at port 21. Most Internet packets are assigned a port number, and the port number tells the receiving computer what to do with the traffic when it arrives.

2. Unlike other Wiretap Act exceptions, the provider exception regulates both the interception and the disclosure of communications. If a provider wants to monitor communications and disclose them to the government under the provider exception, both steps must be independently justified. In contrast, exceptions such as the consent exception focus entirely on interception; when a communication has been intercepted permissibly under the consent exception, the Wiretap Act places no additional restrictions on its use or disclosure.

3. How broadly should courts interpret the "rights or property" of a provider? Are rights or property limited to delivering communications and protecting the network from attack, or do they extend to the broader purposes of the network and the interests of its owner?

Suppose a university provides Internet services to its undergraduate students living in on-campus dormitories. Can the university justify wiretapping student accounts under the provider exception to protect the safety of its students? May it do so to ensure that the students are not downloading copyrighted materials without permission? Can it monitor accounts to make sure no students are taking drugs? Is the university's interest limited to providing network services, or does it extend to taking care of students?

4. Does the existence of the provider exception shed new light on whether an intermediary computer should be a "party to the communication" for the purposes of the consent exception? The provider exception permits victims of unauthorized access to monitor unauthorized behavior to protect their "rights or property," 18 U.S.C. § 2511(2)(a)(i). In other words, victims can conduct monitoring without being parties to the communication under the consent exception. Does this suggest that a narrow approach to identifying a "party to the communication" is preferable to a broader approach?

5. *Fourth Amendment redux.* The *Auler* decision provides a helpful reminder of how statutory and constitutional issues can apply simultaneously in wiretapping investigations. Most network providers are private actors, and therefore are bound by the Wiretap Act but not the Fourth Amendment. As they collect evidence of wrongdoing, however, providers may wish to contact law enforcement investigators either to ask them for help or to forward on incriminating evidence. At some point, the private providers may become state actors under the Fourth Amendment.

Monitoring under the provider exception may raise interesting Fourth Amendment issues if a provider crosses the line and becomes a state actor. For example, does a computer hacker have a reasonable expectation of privacy against the monitoring of his communications inside the victim network? In Rakas v. Illinois, 439 U.S. 128, 143 n.12 (1978), the Supreme Court stated that: "[a] burglar plying his trade in a summer cabin during the off season may have a thoroughly justified subjective expectation of privacy, but it is not one which the law recognizes as 'legitimate.' His presence, * * * is wrongful; his expectation is not one that society is prepared to recognize as 'reasonable.' " For Fourth Amendment purposes, is a hacker just an electronic burglar?

Consider the dicta relevant to this issue in United States v. Seidlitz, 589 F.2d 152 (4th Cir. 1978). Recall that Seidlitz hacked into OSI, and employees at OSI installed a surveillance tool known as the Milten Spy to recorded the intrusion. After rejecting the defendant's argument that the monitoring violated his statutory privacy rights, the Fourth Circuit added this interesting aside:

> [W]e discern a certain speciousness which infects all of the illegal surveillance contentions made by the defendant with respect to the evidence which was obtained through use of the Milten Spy. Unlike the typical telephone user who employs the telephone merely as a convenience to converse with other persons over distances, Seidlitz used the telephone to tamper with and manipulate a machine which was owned by others, located on their premises, and obviously not intended for his use. * * * In this sense the use by the witnesses below of the term "intruder" to describe an unauthorized user of the computers is aptly applied to the defendant, since by telephonic signal he in fact intruded or trespassed upon the physical property of OSI as effectively as if he had broken into the Rockville facility and instructed the computers from one of the terminals directly wired to the machines. Under these circumstances, having been 'caught with his hand in the cookie jar', we seriously doubt that he is entitled to raise either statutory or constitutional objections to the evidence.

Id. at 160.

McCLELLAND v. McGRATH

United States District Court for the Northern District of Illinois, 1998.
31 F. Supp. 2d 616.

ASPEN, Chief Judge.

At first glance, it might seem the very definition of chutzpah for Michael McClelland to sue the City of Chicago and several of its police officers for asking a phone company to intercept a call he made on a cloned cellular phone. The user of a cloned cellular phone—a phone which has been rigged to imitate a legitimate cellular phone—is stealing from the phone company, and phone companies routinely investigate such theft.

The complication in this case is that the officers were investigating a kidnaping, not cellular service theft. Adalberto Valdavia had been abducted, and the officers asked Ameritech, the local telephone service provider, to trace the ransom calls. Ameritech determined that the calls were being made on a cellular line dedicated to Cellular One, and Cellular One informed Ameritech, who informed the officers, that the ransom calls had indeed been made on a cellular telephone and that other calls on the same line had been made almost simultaneously in another part of the state, where the cellular subscriber was located. From this Cellular One concluded that the ransom calls were being made on a cloned phone, and Cellular One indicated that it was able to monitor any conversations involving the cloned phone and to isolate its approximate location. The officers asked Cellular One to relay any information from those calls which might assist them in finding the kidnaper, and Cellular One agreed.

Late that afternoon, someone used the cloned phone to call a lifeguard station and informed the station that he would not be able to come to work that day. Cellular One intercepted the call and relayed the information to Ameritech, who informed the officers, who dispatched other officers to the lifeguard station. (No judge ever approved this intercept.) The officers learned that the caller was Michael McClelland, whom they arrested after securing Valdavia's release. McClelland was incarcerated pending trial on aggravated kidnaping charges, but for reasons unknown to us, his prosecution was terminated.

McClelland learned of the interception during his prosecution, and he filed a complaint with this Court alleging that the officers' failure to obtain judicial authorization for the interception constituted a violation of Title III of the Omnibus Crime Control and Safe Streets Act of 1968, which is codified at 18 U.S.C. §§ 2510–2520 and is popularly known as the "Wiretap Act." The defendants moved to dismiss the complaint on the ground that the Wiretap Act contains an exemption for interceptions by an employee of a phone company who intercepts, discloses, or uses that communication in the normal course of his employment while engaged in any activity which is a necessary incident to the protection of the rights or property of the provider of that service. They argued that since Cellular One intercepted the call and since Cellular one intercepts communications on cloned phones as a necessary incident to the protection of its rights or property, the interception of the call and the subsequent use of its contents was lawful * * *.

The defendants are of course correct that Cellular One is entitled to "intercept, disclose, and use," in the words of § 2511(2)(a)(ii), communications and their contents in order to protect its rights or property. McClelland does not dispute this point—in fact he did not even sue Cellular One. And obviously he would not have had a gripe with the officers had Cellular One intercepted his cloned phone calls on its own and then turned to the officers for assistance.

What the officers do not seem to understand, however, is that *they* are not free to ask or direct Cellular One to intercept *any* phone calls or disclose their contents, at least not without complying with the judicial authorization provisions of the Wiretap Act, *regardless* of whether Cellular One would have been entitled to intercept those calls on its own initiative. This is why the courts in [other cases] go to such lengths to determine whether the phone companies in those cases were acting at the request or direction of police officers.

This case is different, for here a jury could reasonably find that Cellular One was acting as an "instrument or agent" of the government. The officers, after being informed by Cellular One that it could monitor calls made on the cloned phone, asked that Cellular One relay the contents of those calls to them. This shows both that Cellular One acted at the government's request and (ergo) that the government knew of and agreed to Cellular One's actions, two important factors in the "instrument or agent" analysis. In addition, it seems clear that Cellular One was motivated by its desire to help the officers rather than to protect its own property, another important "instrument or agent" factor, *see id.,* as the content of the communication they passed along to the officers— that the caller wouldn't be at work that day—is irrelevant to a cloned phone investigation but is very useful to a kidnaping investigation. *Cf. United States v. Auler,* 539 F.2d 642, 646 (7th Cir. 1976) (telephone companies which intercept calls pursuant to § 2511(2)(a)(i) may forward to the police no more of the content of those calls than is necessary to protect telephone company rights).

It is easy to think that McClelland, the accused kidnaper and confessed cellular service thief, has no right to sue the officers whose jobs required that they find the kidnaper with all possible speed. But anyone who cannot shake this intuition would be wise to recall the sage words of Justices Holmes and Brandeis in an early wiretap case. The former thought it a lesser evil "that some criminals should escape than the government should play an ignoble part," and the latter wrote that "In a government of laws, existence of the government will be imperiled if it fails to observe the law scrupulously," since if "the government becomes a lawbreaker, it breeds contempt for law; it invites every man to become a law unto himself; it invites anarchy." *Olmstead v. United States,* 277 U.S. 438, 469, 485 (1928) (Holmes, J., and Brandeis, J., dissenting). They dissented that day, but their view has prevailed.

Notes and Questions

1. Imagine the facts had been different: Upon being contacted by the police, the provider decided to listen in on the call in an effort to combat cloned phone usage rather than to help the police find the kidnapper. Would the outcome of the case be different? What if the provider had decided on its own to monitor the calls to find the kidnapper, and it was never asked to do so by the police? Should the provider's intent matter? Should it matter whether the provider or the police came up with the idea of monitoring?

2. Did McClelland have Fourth Amendment rights in his telephone call? If not, does it make sense that he should have statutory rights against monitoring? Note that Wiretap Act protections do not hinge on judgements as to whether a particular telephone call implicates greater or lesser legitimate privacy interests. Every call receives full privacy protection, regardless of context.

3. Imagine that you set up a monitoring system on your home personal computer that records every communication sent from and received by your computer. You leave your computer logged on to an Internet connection 24 hours a day. One day, a burglar breaks into your apartment when you are away; after rifling through your valuables, the burglar decides to take a break and surf the web. He opens a web browser on your computer and visits a few blogs such as "How Appealing" and "The Volokh Conspiracy." He then gathers up your valuables, puts them in a large sack, and departs.

The next day, you return to your apartment and find that your valuables are missing.

Does your use of the monitoring system to record all of the burglar's communications violate the Wiretap Act? Can the burglar sue you under the Wiretap Act for violating his privacy? If not, what exception applies? *Hint:* Look carefully at the elements of 18 U.S.C. § 2511(1)(a).

4. Consider the practical impact of the *McGrath* case on computer intrusion investigations. Such investigations generally require investigators to track back the attack from the victim through intermediary computers and back to the intruder. If a hacker starts at computer *A*, routes communications through computer *B* and then attacks computer *C*, investigators must start at *C* and trace the attack back to *B* and then back to *A*.

What legal rules regulate this process? Imagine you are an FBI agent, and a system administrator at computer *C* contacts you and tells you that network *C* has been hacked. The sysadmin informs you that he has installed a "sniffer" device that is monitoring the intruder. The sysadmin seeks your advice: he wants to know how he should monitor the intruder to make sure that he has collected the evidence needed to prosecute the intruder when he is caught. After reading *McClelland v. McGrath*, what should you tell him?

Assume that you decline to give the system administrator advice on how to monitor the hacker. Instead, you tell the sysadmin that he is free to disclose the fruits of his wiretapping to you to the extent necessary to protect his "rights or property." (Note that such a limit isn't necessary if the victim is a "party to the communication," but is necessary otherwise under the provider exception.) The sysadmin tells you that the attacks are coming from a specific IP address hosted by computer *B*. You contact the system administrator at computer *B* and ask if he knows that his network is hosting an intruder. The sysadmin at *B* expresses surprise, but volunteers to help monitor the hacker; he indicates that he wants to be a "good citizen" and help the FBI catch the bad guy. Can you accept the offer of help under *McClelland v. McGrath*?

Assume you accept the offer of help, and the sysadmin at *B* starts monitoring the hacker's communications. The hacker is detected attacking through computer *A*, and the sysadmin calls you to tell you that the attacks are originating at *A*. Does this disclosure violate the Wiretap Act?

4. THE COMPUTER TRESPASSER EXCEPTION

The computer trespasser exception, 18 U.S.C. § 2511(2)(i), is the narrowest of the three exceptions to the Wiretap Act covered in this chapter. The consent exception applies in a very wide range of cases, and the provider exception ordinarily is used by providers outside of government investigations. In contrast, the computer trespasser exception deals with a very narrow and specific problem common in 18 U.S.C. § 1030 investigations.

At a general level, the trespasser exception responds to differences between the telephone network and the Internet. The Wiretap Act was originally designed to regulate telephone network privacy, and reflects the assumption that every telephone call deserves privacy. This is a fair assumption in the case of the telephone network: even cases such as *Auler* and *McClelland* involved interceptions of private calls. But computer communications reflect a much broader array of contents than telephone communications. Whereas telephone calls consist only of person-to-person speech, Internet communications include the full diversity of what users do online. Most of those communications deserve privacy, but some presumably do not. In particular, it seems plausible that computer users committing unauthorized accesses should not have privacy rights in their unauthorized behavior. The trespasser exception amends the Wiretap Act to ensure that the statute better reflects the full diversity of computer communications.

At a more specific level, the trespasser exception was designed to deal specifically with the dynamics of 18 U.S.C. § 1030 investigations. In particular, it deals with the critical question of authority to conduct monitoring in computer intrusion cases when the primary interest in monitoring comes from the government instead of the victim provider. In a sense, the exception responds to *McClelland v. McGrath*. Whereas *McGrath* held that the officers could not "hijack" provider monitoring, the trespasser exception permits such hijacking in a specific set of circumstances.

The exception provides:

It shall not be unlawful under this chapter for a person acting under color of law to intercept the wire or electronic communications of a computer trespasser transmitted to, through, or from the protected computer, if—

(I) the owner or operator of the protected computer authorizes the interception of the computer trespasser's communications on the protected computer;

(II) the person acting under color of law is lawfully engaged in an investigation;

(III) the person acting under color of law has reasonable grounds to believe that the contents of the computer trespasser's communications will be relevant to the investigation; and

(IV) such interception does not acquire communications other than those transmitted to or from the computer trespasser.

18 U.S.C. § 2511(2)(i). The phrase "computer trespasser" is defined in § 2510(21):

"computer trespasser"—

(A) means a person who accesses a protected computer without authorization and thus has no reasonable expectation of privacy in any communication transmitted to, through, or from the protected computer; and

(B) does not include a person known by the owner or operator of the protected computer to have an existing contractual relationship with the owner or operator of the protected computer for access to all or part of the protected computer.

Putting the two pieces together reveals how the trespasser exception works. For the exception to apply, an investigator must already be conducting an investigation, § 2511(2)(i)(II), and must have reasonable grounds to believe that intercepting an intruder's communication will further that investigation, § 2511(2)(i)(III), § 2510(21). The trespasser exception permits investigators to intercept the intruder's communications with the provider's consent, § 2511(2)(i)(II), although the exception does not justify any other monitoring, § 2511(2)(i)(IV). So long as the government is already conducting an investigation, the government can intercept the hacker's communications with the victim provider's permission.

The computer trespasser exception was enacted in 2001 as Section 217 of the USA Patriot Act. After the enactment of the Patriot Act, the Justice Department released the following guidance to the exception.

UNITED STATES DEPARTMENT OF JUSTICE— FIELD GUIDANCE ON NEW AUTHORITIES THAT RELATE TO COMPUTER CRIME AND ELECTRONIC EVIDENCE ENACTED IN THE USA PATRIOT ACT OF 2001

(2001), available at www.usdoj.gov/criminal/cybercrime/PatriotAct.htm.

Although the wiretap statute allows computer owners to monitor the activity on their machines to protect their rights and property, until Section 217 of the Act was enacted it was unclear whether computer owners could obtain the assistance of law enforcement in conducting such monitoring. This lack of clarity prevented law enforcement from assisting victims to take the natural and reasonable steps in their own defense that would be entirely legal in the physical world. In the physical world, burglary victims may invite the police into their homes to help them catch burglars in the act of committing their crimes. The wiretap statute should not block investigators from responding to similar requests in the computer context simply because the means of committing the burglary happen to fall within the definition of a "wire or electronic communication" according to the wiretap statute. Indeed, because providers often lack the expertise, equipment, or financial resources required to monitor attacks themselves, they commonly have no effective way to exercise their rights to protect themselves from unauthorized attackers. This anomaly in the law created * * * a bizarre result, in which a computer hacker's undeserved statutory privacy right trumps the legitimate privacy rights of the hacker's victims.

To correct this problem, the amendments in Section 217 of the Act allow victims of computer attacks to authorize persons "acting under color of law" to monitor trespassers on their computer systems. Under new section 2511(2)(i), law enforcement may intercept the communications of a computer trespasser transmitted to, through, or from a protected computer. Before monitoring can occur, however, four requirements must be met. First, section 2511(2)(i)(I) requires that the owner or operator of the protected computer must authorize the interception of the trespasser's communications. Second, section 2511(2)(i)(II) requires that the person who intercepts the communication be lawfully engaged in an ongoing investigation. Both criminal and intelligence investigations qualify, but the authority to intercept ceases at the conclusion of the investigation.

Third, section 2511(2)(i)(III) requires that the person acting under color of law have reasonable grounds to believe that the contents of the communication to be intercepted will be relevant to the ongoing investigation. Fourth, section 2511(2)(i)(IV) requires that investigators intercept only the communications sent or received by trespassers. Thus, this section would only apply where the configuration of the computer system allows the interception of communications to and from the trespasser, and not the interception of non-consenting users authorized to use the computer.

Finally, section 217 of the Act amends section 2510 of title 18 to create a definition of "computer trespasser." Such trespassers include any person who accesses a protected computer without authorization. In addition, the definition explicitly excludes any person "known by the owner or operator of the protected computer to have an existing contractual relationship with the owner or operator for access to all or part of the computer." 18 U.S.C. § 2510(21). For example, certain Internet service providers do not allow their customers to send bulk unsolicited e-mails (or "spam"). Customers who send spam would be in violation of the provider's terms of service, but would not qualify as trespassers–both because they are authorized users and because they have an existing contractual relationship with the provider.

Notes and Questions

1. *"A person acting under color of law."* The trespasser exception contemplates interceptions by persons "acting under color of law." The phrase "under color of law" has a long history, and ordinarily has been construed as equivalent to "state action" under the Fourteenth Amendment:

> Private persons, jointly engaged with state officials in the prohibited action, are acting 'under color' of law * * *. To act 'under color' of law does not require that the accused be an officer of the State. It is enough that he is a willful participant in joint activity with the State or its agents.

United States v. Price, 383 U.S. 787, 794 (1966).

Presumably, then, the trespasser exception permits monitoring either by government investigators or private individuals acting on their behalf. Note, however, that under §§ 2511(2)(i)(II)-(III) the person acting under color of law must be lawfully engaged in an investigation and must have reasonable grounds to believe that the contents of the intercepted communications must be relevant to that investigation. In a case where investigators ask a provider to monitor a hacker on the government's behalf, who is the "person acting under color of law" that must have these reasonable grounds: the investigators, or the owner/operator of the network?

2. The trespasser exception requires the owner or operator of the protected computer to authorize the interception of trespasser communications *See* 18 U.S.C. § 2511(2)(i)(I). What does it mean to "authorize" an interception? Is authorization different from consent under the consent exception?

3. *Defining "computer trespasser."* The definition of computer trespasser in § 2510(21) recalls materials covered in Chapter 2, and specifically the meaning of "access without authorization" and "exceeds authorized access" for the purposes of 18 U.S.C. § 1030. Under § 2510(21)(A), a computer trespasser is a person who has accessed a computer "without authorization."

The text of § 2510(21)(A) adds that such a person "thus has no reasonable expectation of privacy in any communication transmitted to, through, or from the protected computer." This is a rather puzzling addition. Congress does not normally add commentary explaining when it believes a person has Fourth Amendment protection, and the addition does not appear to have any other effect.

18 U.S.C. § 2510(21)(B) was added in response to concern about an early draft of the Patriot Act. Critics feared that uncertainty over the meaning of "without authorization" in 18 U.S.C. § 1030 would let the computer trespasser exception authorize the government to monitor Internet users who violated Terms of Service or Terms of Use. Section 2510(21)(B) clarifies that mere contractual breach cannot make a person a "computer trespasser."

Can you reconcile the definition of "computer trespasser" with the meaning of "access without authorization" and "exceeds authorized access" in § 1030? Does the definition of computer trespasser include those who breach code-based restrictions, but not those who circumvent contractual restrictions? Does the trespasser exception shed light on the meaning of § 1030?

4. The trespasser exception has interesting consequences for the scope of the consent exception, and in particular who can be a "party to a communication":

> Before the Patriot Act, it was unclear whether a pass-through intermediary computer could consent to monitoring, but at least two courts of appeals had suggested that they might. Such a reading would eviscerate the privacy protection offered by the Wiretap Act. The trespasser exception is the best argument against such a reading: the exception only makes sense if mere pass-through computers are not parties to communications. Otherwise, the trespasser exception would merely cover ground already covered by the consent exception. The existence of the trespasser exception sends a strong signal to the courts: to give effect to

the trespasser exception, courts should construe the consent exception narrowly.

Orin S. Kerr, *Internet Surveillance Law After the USA Patriot Act: The Big Brother That Isn't*, 97 Nw. U. L. Rev. 607, 670 (2003). Does the trespasser exception also suggest that hacker commands ordinarily will constitute "contents" of communications under 18 U.S.C. § 2510(8)?

5.   Let's return to a hypothetical we considered in the materials on the provider exception. This time, however, we can consider the role of the computer trespasser exception.

Suppose you are an FBI agent, and a system administrator at computer *C* contacts you and tells you that network *C* has been hacked. The sysadmin informs you that he has installed a "sniffer" device that is monitoring the intruder. The sysadmin seeks your advice: he wants to know how he should monitor the intruder to make sure that he has collected the evidence needed to prosecute the intruder when he is caught. What can you tell him?

Assume you tell the sysadmin to intercept all of the hacker's communications. The sysadmin does so, and the next day he intercepts communications indicating that the attacks are coming from a specific IP address hosted by computer *B*. You contact the system administrator at computer *B* and ask if he knows that his network is hosting an intruder. The sysadmin at *B* expresses surprise, but volunteers to help monitor the hacker; he indicates that he wants to be a "good citizen" and help the FBI catch the bad guy. Can you accept the offer of help?

Assume you accept the offer of help, and the sysadmin at *B* starts monitoring the hacker's communications. The hacker is detected attacking through computer *A*, and the sysadmin calls you to tell you that the attacks are originating at *A*. Does this disclosure violate the Wiretap Act?

6.   *Honey pots and the Wiretap Act.* Computer security professionals occasionally set up "honey pot" computer networks to test security efforts and understand hacker techniques. A "honey pot" is a decoy network connected to the Internet. To an intruder, the network looks like any other network. In truth, the network is a fake; it is set up with the sole purpose of being a target for anonymous attackers. When hackers try to break in, as some inevitably will, every aspect of the intrusion will be monitored, recorded, and later analyzed.

Does the use of honey pots by a computer security professional violate the Wiretap Act? Can you justify monitoring intrusions into the honey pot under the consent exception? Under the provider exception? Under the trespasser exception? Does the legal picture change if a criminal investigator wishes to set up a honey pot to identify intruders?

7.   Are the Wiretap Act's exceptions too broad? Too narrow? Just right? Given that the Act was originally drafted for the telephone, does it still work well in the context of Internet crime investigations? Or is the difference between monitoring phone calls and monitoring Internet communications too great for the same statute to regulate both contexts?

B. THE PEN REGISTER STATUTE

The Pen Registers and Trap and Trace Devices statute, commonly known as the Pen Register statute, is codified at 18 U.S.C. §§ 3121–27. At a very general level, the Pen Register statute can be understood as a non-content cousin of the Wiretap Act. Because it deals only with non-content information, however, the Pen Register statute generally receives substantially less attention than the Wiretap Act. Its prohibitions are weaker, its exceptions are broader, and penalties for violating the statute are modest.

The statute's history explains its rather odd structure. The Pen Register statute was designed as a legislative response to *Smith v. Maryland*, 442 U.S. 735 (1979). As enacted in 1986, the statute prohibited the installation of pen registers and trap and trace devices without a court order unless a statutory exception applied. In the technological era of the 1960s and 1970s, pen registers were devices that could be installed to record the numbers dialed from a telephone line, and "trap and trace" devices could be used to record the incoming numbers dialed into a phone line. (They were called "trap and trace" devices because collecting incoming numbers originally required the telephone company to trace the phone line using a tool known as a "terminating trap." *See* In re United States, 610 F.2d 1148, 1151 (3d Cir. 1979)). When first passed in 1986, the Pen Register statute regulated the use of the tools that were used to collect "to" and "from" information for telephone calls, namely pen registers and trap and trace devices.

The structure of the Pen Register statute makes sense in light of this history. Section 3121 contains the basic prohibition on the use of a pen register or trap and trace device, subject to exceptions in § 3121(b); § 3122 tells investigators how to apply for court orders authorizing the use of such devices; § 3123 instructs judges on what the orders should look like and what they should say; and § 3124 tells network providers how to comply with the orders. Finally, § 3125 concerns emergency court orders, § 3126 is a reporting requirement, and § 3127 contains definitions of key terms.

The trick to understanding the modern Pen Register statute is the definition of "pen register" and "trap and trace device" in §§ 3127(3)-(4). Section 216 of the USA Patriot Act replaced the telephone-focused language of the 1986 Act with more general language that covers non-content addressing information for both telephone calls and Internet communications. Specifically, a pen register is defined as "a device or process which records or decodes dialing, routing, addressing, or signaling information transmitted by an instrument or facility from which a wire or electronic communication is transmitted, provided, however, that such information shall not include the contents of any communication." 18 U.S.C. § 3127(3). A trap and trace device is defined as "a device or process which captures the incoming electronic or other impulses which identify the originating number or other dialing, routing, addressing, and signaling information reasonably likely to identify the source of a wire or electronic communication, provided, however, that such information shall not include the contents of any communication." 18 U.S.C. § 3127(4).

Putting the new definitions into the old statutory text yields a statute that regulates the collection of non-content "dialing, routing, addressing, or signaling information" for both telephone calls and Internet communications. For example, if investigators or providers install a sniffer device that collects only non-content addressing information such as IP headers, the sniffer device acts as both a pen register (when it collects "from" information) and a trap and trace device (when it collects "to" information). Because Internet communications normally combine "to" and "from" information, the two sides usually work together; the surveillance device becomes a "pen/trap," and the court order permitting the surveillance is often referred to as a "pen/trap order."

In practice, issues involving the Pen Register statute often arise at the same time as issues involving the Wiretap Act. Which statute applies depends on the filter setting of the particular surveillance tool. For example, a sniffer device that collects contents is a wiretap device implicating the Wiretap statute; a sniffer device that only collects non-content addressing information is a pen/trap that implicates the Pen Register statute. A sniffer device that collects both content and non-content information acts as both a wiretap device and a pen/trap, and must be used in compliance with both statutes.

Although the Pen Register statute is a non-content cousin of the Wiretap Act, Congress chose to regulate non-content acquisition very differently than content acquisition. The following case explores some of the differences between the Wiretap Act and the Pen Register statute.

IN RE APPLICATION OF THE UNITED STATES OF AMERICA

United States District Court for the Middle District of Florida, 1994.
846 F. Supp. 1555.

MERRYDAY, DISTRICT JUDGE.

The magistrate judge has twice denied the United States' application for an order authorizing the installation and use of a pen register and trap and trace device. The latter of the two applications, a somewhat supplemented edition of the earlier application, states in part that:

> Applicant certifies that the Federal Bureau of Investigation, United States Customs Service, County Sheriff's Office and * * * * Police Department are conducting a criminal investigation of * * * * *, owner/operator of * * * * * , located in * * * * *, Florida; employees of * * * * * located at * * * * *, and others known and unknown, in connection with possible violations of, inter alia, Title 21, United States Code, Sections 846 and 841(a)(1), occurring within the Middle District of Florida and elsewhere; that it is believed that the subjects of the investigation are using telephone number (* * *)

* * *-* * * *, listed in the name of * * * * * and located at * * * * *, in furtherance of the subject offenses; and that the information likely to be obtained from the pen register and trap and trace device, that is, a caller ID device, is relevant to the ongoing criminal investigation being conducted by the aforementioned law enforcement agencies in that it is believed that this information will concern the aforementioned offenses.

This Court has jurisdiction to issue an order authorizing the installation and use of the requested pen register and trap and trace device in that the actual pen register equipment and trap and trace device which will be used to monitor telephone number (* * *) * * *-* * * * [and] will be installed and used at the * * * * * County Sheriff's Office located in * * * * * County, within the Middle District of Florida.

Applicant knows that there are incoming telephone calls to telephone number (* * *) * * *-* * * * and believes the identification of the calling telephone facility will be relevant to the ongoing criminal investigation and that this information will concern the aforementioned offenses.[2]

The magistrate judge premised his denial on the failure of the United States to advance a factual demonstration that the pen register is likely to disclose information relevant to an ongoing criminal investigation that has a nexus to the Middle District of Florida. The magistrate judge determined that the statute governing the installation and use of pen registers requires a demonstration of qualifying facts sufficient to establish the correctness of both the United States' assertion of this court's jurisdiction and the pen register's purpose and probable results, i.e., the discovery of information beneficial to an investigation with a nexus to the Middle District of Florida. Asserting energetically that the pen register statute envisions only perfunctory judicial involvement, the United States appeals to the district court. The magistrate judge's order is reversed because the application of the United States satisfies the requirements of the applicable statute.

II.

In 1986, Congress enacted 18 U.S.C. §§ 3121–27, which governs pen registers. Section 3121(a) provides, with a few irrelevant exceptions, that "no person may install or use a pen register or a trap and trace device without first obtaining a court order under section 3123 of this title or under the Foreign Intelligence Surveillance Act of 1978 (50 U.S.C. 1801, *et seq.*)." Pursuant to Section 3121(c), the penalty for violation of the statute is imprisonment for not more than one year, a fine, or both.

Section 3122(a) authorizes an attorney for the United States to apply for an order, "in writing, under oath or equivalent affirmation, to a court of competent jurisdiction." First, Section 3122(b)(1) requires the

2. Because the original of this order is filed *in camera* and relates to an ongoing criminal investigation, any revealing and identifying words are replaced by asterisks.

application to include both the identity of the applying attorney and the identity of the law enforcement agency conducting the investigation. Second, Section 3122(b)(2) requires the application to include a certification by the attorney "that the information likely to be obtained is relevant to an ongoing criminal investigation being conducted by that agency."

Section 3123(a) states that, after a complying application:

[T]he court shall enter an ex parte order authorizing the installation and use of a pen register or a trap and trace device within the jurisdiction of the court if the court finds that the attorney for the Government ... has certified to the court that the information likely to be obtained by such installation and use is relevant to an ongoing criminal investigation.

Section 3124 requires that providers of telephone services and other persons, if the court so orders, must assist with the installation of the pen register. Section 3124(e) provides to any cooperating person a complete defense against either civil or criminal liability, if the person relies in good faith on a court order authorizing the pen register.

A review of these provisions demonstrates that Congress, absent Fourth Amendment concerns, intended to require an identified and presumably responsible official to attest the facts supporting the pen register application. The salient purpose of requiring the application to the court for an order is to affix personal responsibility for the veracity of the application (i.e., to ensure that the attesting United States Attorney is readily identifiable and legally qualified) and to confirm that the United States Attorney has sworn that the required investigation is in progress. Section 3122(b) requires only identification and certification by the official applying for the order. Section 3123(a) requires only confirmation by the court that identification and certification have occurred. No provision appears for independent judicial inquiry into the veracity of the attested facts. As a form of deterrence and as a guarantee of compliance, the statute provides instead for a term of imprisonment and a fine as punishment for a violation.

Requiring identification and certification, but nothing further, admittedly extends only minimal protection to whatever privacy expectations attend the dialing of a telephone number. On the other hand, prompt availability of pen registers usefully expedites law enforcement with no countervailing loss, the Supreme Court instructs, of the Fourth Amendment's protections against search and seizure. In other words, the statute's structure balances the need for accountability, the legitimate interest of law enforcement in advancing a criminal investigation, and the residual privacy interest of the public.

III.

A comparison of the statute governing wiretaps, 18 U.S.C. §§ 2510–21, with the statute governing pen registers demonstrates that Congress intended only minimal safeguards against the unwarranted use of a pen register. The procedure for obtaining authorization for a pen register is summary in nature and the requisite disclosure is perfunctory. In contrast, the wiretap statute provides formidable procedural protections and requires extensive and detailed information in the application. Perhaps most pertinent to this order is the presence of the following provision in Section 2518(2) of the wiretap statute:

> The judge may require the applicant to furnish additional testimony or documentary evidence in support of the application.

No similar provision for additional judicial inquiry appears in the pen register statute, indicating that Congress intended no focused judicial scrutiny of an application for a pen register (at least at the time of the application). The legislative history of the pen register statute contains a similar signal:

> To issue an order [authorizing a pen register], the court must first be satisfied that the information sought is relevant to an ongoing criminal investigation. This provision does not envision an independent judicial review of whether the application meets the relevance standard, rather the court needs only to review the completeness of the certification submitted.

S. Rep. No. 541, 99th Cong., 2d Sess. 47, *reprinted in* 1986 U.S.C.C.A.N. 3555, 3601.

Under Section 2518(1)(b) of the wiretap statute, an application must contain "a full and complete statement of the facts and circumstances relied upon by the applicant to justify his belief that an order should be issued," including details of the offense, the sites of the interception devices, the type of communication subject to interception, and the identity of the person whose communications are subject to interception. Section 2518(1)(c) requires that a wiretap application include "a full and complete statement as to whether or not other investigative procedures have been tried and failed or why they reasonably appear to be unlikely to succeed if tried or to be too dangerous." Section 2518(d) requires a prediction of the duration of the wiretap and Section 2518(e) requires a statement of the circumstances of any previous wiretap applications involving the same person or place. Section 2518(f) provides that, if the application extends a previous authorization, the application must contain "a statement setting forth the results thus far obtained from the interception, or a reasonable explanation of the failure to obtain such results."

By comparison, an application for a pen register includes only the identification and certification required by Section 3122(b). No requirement exists for a pen register applicant to unsuccessfully attempt other investigative techniques or to explain the failure to attempt other investigative techniques. Section 3123(c)(2) permits a pen register applicant to obtain an extension of an authorizing order by providing the same identification and certification required by the initial application. The statute excludes any requirement that an applicant for an extension set forth either the results previously obtained or an explanation for the failure to obtain results.

Other comparisons are similarly instructive. To authorize a wiretap, the court must find (1) probable cause to believe that an individual has committed, is committing, or imminently will commit an offense listed in the statute, (2) probable cause to believe that the intercepted communications will relate to the alleged offense, (3) probable cause to believe (with limited exceptions) that the communications facilities subject to the wiretap are being used in connection with the offense, and (4) that other investigative procedures have failed, are likely to fail, or will be too dangerous. To authorize a pen register, the court need not find any of these facts. The pen register statute contains no requirement for a finding of "probable cause," "reasonable suspicion," or the like.

Section 2518(6) of the wiretap statute permits the court to require periodic reports by the intercepting authorities of the progress of the wiretap. Sections 2518(8)(a) and (d) of the wiretap statute require that the intercepted communications be recorded and maintained both under seal and unedited and that an inventory of the intercepted communications be provided to the subjects after termination of the wiretap. Section 2518(9) of the wiretap statute bars the use of intercepted communications at trial without advance notice. Neither these provisions nor approximations of them appear in the pen register statute.

Section 2518(10)(a) of the wiretap statute provides for suppression of evidence obtained by wiretap [of wire communications] if the evidence was obtained in violation of the statute. The pen register statute contains no exclusionary remedy, and *United States v. Thompson*, 936 F.2d 1249 (11th Cir. 1991), declines to create a common law rule of exclusion.

As punishment for an unlawfully obtained wiretap, Section 2511(4)(a) of the wiretap statute provides a maximum penalty of imprisonment for five years and a fine. As noted already, Section 3121(c) provides that the maximum penalty for violation of the pen register statute is imprisonment for one year and a fine. Section 2520 of the wiretap statute also authorizes recovery of civil damages, including statutory damages of up to $10,000, punitive damages, equitable relief, and recovery of costs and attorney fees. The pen register statute contains no provision for recovery of civil damages.

The breadth and intricacy of the wiretap statute illustrate that Congress, when electing to do so, conceived and implemented formidable safeguards, including extensive judicial review, for the protection of electronic communications. Congress elected to provide only minimal regulation of the use of pen registers. Absent recognized constitutional considerations, the court should create and implement by decisional law no more extensive restrictions on the use of pen registers than Congress has provided explicitly in the governing statute after consideration in gross of all the pertinent factors, not the least of which is privacy.

IV.

No judicial imprimatur on pen registers is required, permitted, or implied under the pen register statute. The court is not asked to "approve" the application for a pen register in the sense that the court would vouch initially for the propriety of the use of a wiretap. Congress asks the court only to confirm that the approved safety measures are observed—that is, primarily, that the responsible persons are identified and accountable if any malfeasance or misprision comes to light and that the nature of that misconduct is readily provable. Undoubtedly, Congress knew that providing to a court false information about the nature of an investigation is an offense which, especially if committed by a United States Attorney, is due for a most unforgiving penalty.

Far from compromising the judiciary, the statutory procedure removes the court from unnecessary entanglement in decisions properly residing in the first instance in law enforcement and prosecuting authorities, yet subject to judicial inquiry at the end of the day. The judiciary is not the daily supervisor of the prosecutor. The judiciary should maintain a sanitary distance from law enforcement. The more the court is insinuated unduly into an *ex parte* inquiry conducted *in camera*, the more the independence of the judiciary is compromised. Serious Fourth Amendment concerns commend, in fact compel, a routinely undesirable, *ex parte* inquiry before the authorization of an arrest, a search, or a wiretap. But this is not so for the authorization of a mere pen register, which presents no privacy issue that rises to Fourth Amendment severity. On behalf of judicial independence, the court is better kept safely apart from the investigatory function unless some constitutional matter (or statutory, if Congress so declares) warrants intrusion. Only in this way is independence and integrity maintained.

The matter of judicial integrity and independence serves, on balance, to separate my conclusion from the magistrate judge's conclusion. He concludes that authorizing a pen register based on no more than the certification of a United States Attorney and without judicial scrutiny breeds suspicion and implies a compromise of independence. I conclude that undue entanglement with the prosecutor, if not required by constitutional matters, breeds suspicion and implies compromise. *Ex parte* and *in camera* hearings, I conclude, amplify those unsavory appearances, if they exist at all.

I conclude that the independence and integrity of the judiciary is best served by preserving, free of any undue entanglement and until a later stage, the oversight function of the court. This is the general rule. Exceptions appear for an arrest, a search, a wiretap, and for certain aspects of the grand jury's proceedings. However, at each stage for which an exception appears, the constitution appears also. Similarly, if no constitutional or statutory command appears, the courts must conform to the sharply constrained role assigned in pen register cases. To attempt after *Smith v. Maryland*, 442 U.S. 735 (1979), to raise a privacy consideration to sufficient dignity to overcome a direct Congressional limitation is to risk a form of judicial behavior likely to taint integrity more tellingly than the taint, if any, attendant to a mere application for a pen register.

V.

In the present case, the magistrate judge rejected the pen register application because the United States, in his view, failed to show that the pen register is "within the jurisdiction of the court" as required by Section 3123(a). The magistrate judge raised this concern because the pen register, which will be located in this district, will monitor a telephone located in the Southern District of Florida. The magistrate judge required "a factual demonstration that the pen register is likely to disclose information relevant to an ongoing criminal investigation that has a nexus to the Middle District of Florida." He determined that the United States failed to show the qualifying facts.

The court finds that the United States has met the requirements of the statute. The application contains the identification and certification required by Section 3122(b). In the certification, an assistant United States Attorney reports that local law enforcement agencies within this district and federal law enforcement agencies, acting in concert, are conducting within this district and within the Southern District an investigation of possible criminal offenses occurring within this district and elsewhere. Part of this investigation is prospectively a pen register installed in a county within the Middle District of Florida. This certification amply demonstrates that the pen register is "within the jurisdiction of the court." No further factual showing is necessary.

The order of the magistrate judge denying the application for a pen register is reversed. The application of the United States is granted.

Notes and Questions

1. As a matter of policy, are the standards for obtaining a pen register order too low? Professor Freiwald comments:

> [T]he language of the [pen register] court order requirement raises doubt as to its efficacy as a guard against fishing expeditions. The substantive standard in the court order requirement, "reasonable grounds to believe that the transaction records are relevant and material to an ongoing criminal investigation," pales in comparison to the requirements for access to the contents of communications. To acquire communication contents, a judge must have a particularized suspicion, rising to probable cause, that the targeted individual is guilty of criminal activity and that normal investigative procedures are inadequate. The relevance standard in the transaction records provision allows law enforcement agents to obtain records of people who may be tangentially involved in a crime, even as innocent victims.

> Moreover, * * * the procedural safeguards for access to transaction records lack rigor. Although the records must be relevant to an ongoing investigation, there remains no need to specify what crime is being

investigated, and no limit placed on the crimes that can form the predicate. Similarly, the new provisions do not redress the ECPA's other weak requirements for stored transaction records investigations, such as the failure to specify requirements for applications or court orders, and the lack of notice to subscribers. Again, these weaknesses contrast sharply with the protections for the contents of communications.

Susan Freiwald, *Uncertain Privacy: Communication Attributes After the Digital Telephony Act*, 69 S. Cal. L. Rev. 949, 1005–06 (1996).

Should the threshold for obtaining a pen register order be raised? If so, what should the new standard be? Should the law require reasonable suspicion? Should it require judicial review of the facts instead of certification by the applicant?

2. As amended by the Patriot Act, the Pen Register statute regulates the acquisition of "dialing, routing, addressing, or signaling information" relating to wire and electronic communications. But what exactly is "dialing, routing, addressing, or signaling information," a.k.a. DRAS? DRAS clearly includes IP addresses, as well as non-content information relating to e-mails. *See* In re Application of the United States, 396 F. Supp. 2d 45, 48 (D. Mass. 2005) (IP addresses); In re Application of the United States, 416 F. Supp. 2d 13 (D.D.C. 2006) (non-content information relating to e-mails).

But is all non-content information DRAS by default? Or does a category of information exist beyond contents and DRAS that is not covered either by the Wiretap Act or the Pen Register statute? If there is such a category, what treatment should it receive under the statutory privacy laws?

3. When a cellular telephone is turned on, the phone sends out regular communications to nearby cell towers letting the towers know that the phone is nearby. Such communications are an essential part of the cellular phone network; phones must be located before the network can route calls to them. If the phone company records the information, it will generate a log of the rough physical location of the phone when it is turned on. Criminal investigators sometimes seek access to such records in real time; because most people keep their cell phones with them, the telephone location information (called "cell site" data) can be used as a type of tracking device.

Can the government obtain a Pen Register order requiring the phone company to record cell-site information and give the log to the government? Does "dialing, routing, addressing, and signaling information" include cell-site data? Magistrate Judge Stephen Smith has concluded that the answer is "no":

> First, the Patriot Act's expansion of pen/trap definitions was intended only to reach electronic communications such as e-mail. The added term "dialing, routing, addressing, and signaling information," while not defined in the statute, was touted by the bill's proponents as a way to update the pen/trap statute to cover Internet traffic. *See* 147 Cong. Rec. S11006–07 (Oct. 25, 2001) (statement of Sen. Leahy); 147 Cong. Rec. H7197 (Oct. 23, 2001) (statement of Rep. Conyers). Nothing in the admittedly abbreviated legislative history of the Patriot Act suggests that this new definition would extend the reach of the Pen/Trap Statute to cell phone tracking. Contemporary summaries of the Patriot Act

prepared by knowledgeable commentators, including the DOJ itself, make no mention of expanding pen/traps to capture cell site data. Surely, even amidst the other important features of that broad-ranging statute, such an important change in electronic surveillance law would have been noticed by *someone*.

Nor is it certain that the new definition actually encompasses the cell site data now sought by the government. The traditional pen register was triggered only when the user dialed a telephone number; no information was recorded by the device unless the user attempted to make a call. The Patriot Act clarified that a pen register could also record "routing, addressing, and signaling information," as well as numbers dialed. But the expanded definition also indicates that this "routing, addressing, and signaling" information is generated by, and incidental to, the transmission of "a wire or electronic communication." 18 U.S.C. § 3127(3). In other words, today's pen register must still be tied to an actual or attempted phone call. As we have already seen, much cell site data is transmitted even when the user is not making or receiving a call, *i.e.*, when no wire or electronic communication is transmitted. In short, neither the text nor the legislative history of the Patriot Act offer much support for the government's contention that the cell site data it seeks is covered by the new pen/trap definitions.

In re Application for Pen Register and Trap/Trace Device with Cell Site Location Authority, 396 F. Supp. 2d 747, 761–62 (S.D. Tex. 2005). Are these arguments persuasive? In response to the latter argument, isn't the telephone's signal identifying itself to the cell tower an electronic communication?

If cell-site information is not DRAS, and it clearly is not content, then what is it?

4. Does the difference between contents and DRAS justify the very different protections of the Wiretap Act and the Pen Register statute? Daniel Solove contends that content and non-content addressing information raise equally strong privacy concerns and should be protected under the same statutory scheme:

> [T]he distinction between content and envelope information does not correlate well to the distinction between sensitive and innocuous information. Envelope information can be quite sensitive; content information can be quite innocuous. Admittedly, in many cases, people do not care very much about maintaining privacy over the identities of their friends and associates. But it is also true that in many cases, the contents of communications are not very revealing. Many e-mails are short messages which do not reveal any deep secrets, and even Kerr would agree that this should not lessen their protection under the law. This is because content information has the potential to be quite sensitive—but this is also the case with envelope information.

Daniel J. Solove, *Reconstructing Electronic Surveillance Law*, 72 Geo. Wash. L. Rev. 1264, 1288 (2004).

Do you agree? Should Congress come up with a new way to distinguish high-privacy communications from low-privacy communications? If so, what distinction would you propose? Should there be two categories, three categories, or more? *See generally* Susan Freiwald, *Online Surveillance: Remembering the Lessons of the Wiretap Act*, 56 Ala. L. Rev. 9, 69–74 (2004).

5. The Pen Register statute regulates prospective surveillance but not retrospective surveillance. The textual hook for this conclusion is the exclusion found in the definition of "pen register" in 18 U.S.C. § 3127(3). According to the definition, the term "pen register" does not include:

> any device or process used by a provider or customer of a wire or electronic communication service for billing, or recording as an incident to billing, for communications services provided by such provider or any device or process used by a provider or customer of a wire communication service for cost accounting or other like purposes in the ordinary course of its business.

Although this language is not a model of clarity, it has the effect of excluding retrospective surveillance from the scope of the Pen Register statute. If the government seeks records that were already made in the past and are stored by the provider, those records must have been made "in the ordinary course" of the provider's business for "cost accounting or other like purposes."

6. *Exceptions to the Pen Register statute.* The exceptions to the Pen Register statute appear in 18 U.S.C. § 3121(b):

> The prohibition of subsection (a) does not apply with respect to the use of a pen register or a trap and trace device by a provider of electronic or wire communication service—
>
> (1) relating to the operation, maintenance, and testing of a wire or electronic communication service or to the protection of the rights or property of such provider, or to the protection of users of that service from abuse of service or unlawful use of service; or
>
> (2) to record the fact that a wire or electronic communication was initiated or completed in order to protect such provider, another provider furnishing service toward the completion of the wire communication, or a user of that service, from fraudulent, unlawful or abusive use of service; or
>
> (3) where the consent of the user of that service has been obtained.

These exceptions are best understood in reference to the analogous exceptions of the Wiretap Act. Starting at the bottom, the consent exception in § 3121(b)(3) appears to mirror the Wiretap Act's consent exception in 18 U.S.C. § 2511(2)(c)-(d). Presumably the same standards apply. The consent exception in the Pen Register statute has a particularly important common-sense application: It makes sure that caller ID services are not illegal. *See, e.g.,* Wisconsin Professional Police Ass'n v. Public Service Commission, 555 N.W.2d 179 (Wisc. App. 1996).

The exceptions in § 3121(b)(1)-(2) appear to create an expanded version of the Wiretap Act's provider exception, 18 U.S.C. § 2511(2)(a)(i). The Pen Register statute's version starts with the common "rights or property" language, and then adds protection of users from abuse of service or unlawful service as well as protection of providers from fraudulent, unlawful, or abusive service. No cases explain how far these exceptions extend beyond the provider exception of the Wiretap Act, but it seems likely that courts would give such language the expansive reading the text suggests.

Although the statute is not explicit on this point, monitoring justified under the trespasser exception of the Wiretap Act for content data apparently would fall within 18 U.S.C. §§ 3121(b)(1)-(2) for non-content information. The trespasser exception requires that the trespasser must have engaged in access without authorization, and such access will always be unlawful and an abuse of the computer service under 18 U.S.C. §§ 3121(b)(1)-(2).

7.   United States v. Freeman, 524 F.2d 337 (7th Cir. 1975), also suggests that exceptions to the Pen Register statute should be construed broadly. In *Freeman*, the telephone company was investigating blue box fraud and installed a Hekimian Dialed Number Recorder (DNR) on the suspect telephone line. The DNR was a type of pen register; it registered outgoing calls made on a paper tape, and transcribed the time of a call, the date, and the number called. When the DNR would signal that a fraudulent phone call had been placed, the phone company would connect a wiretapping device that would record the first two minutes of the phone call. The government then used the device to convict the defendant Freeman of wire fraud.

On appeal, Freeman challenged the wiretapping of his phone calls, but the Seventh Circuit held that the wiretapping was in compliance with the provider exception, 18 U.S.C. § 2511(2)(a)(i). Freeman next challenged the use of the DNR under 47 U.S.C. § 605, a predecessor statute to the Wiretap Act that also covered some non-content information. The Seventh Circuit rejected the argument on policy grounds:

> An affirmative answer to this question would lead to an anomalous, if not absurd, result. To arrive at such an answer we would have to conclude that the paper taping operation, a lesser intrusion of privacy, compels suppression while the conversation recording, a greater intrusion, does not.

Freeman, 524 F.2d at 341. If the same reasoning applies to the Pen Register statute, its exceptions presumably are at least as broad as analogous exceptions to the Wiretap Act.

8.   *Problem.* Sam is the system administrator of a computer network at a small college. One day, a student named Kelly contacts him and reports that she suspects that someone has been breaking into her school web-based e-mail account. Kelly believes that her ex-boyfriend Charles may be the perpetrator, and that Charles guessed her password and is reading her mail. Sam agrees to help. The next day, he writes a software program that logs whenever anyone accesses Kelly's e-mail account: the software automatically records the time and IP address of the login. He then writes a program to record every IP address assigned to Charles' account. Over the course of the next 48 hours, Sam's program records 9 different logins to Kelly's account. In three of the cases, the IP address of the login matches the IP address used by Charles's account, indicating that Charles has in fact logged into Kelly's account.

Has Sam violated the Pen Register statute? Would he violate the Pen Register statute if he next began monitoring all non-content information sent to or from Charles's account? If he switched to full-content monitoring, would that surveillance violate the Wiretap Act?

9. Does the Pen Register statute permit wide-scale monitoring, or must the monitoring be limited to a single user or account? Imagine the FBI receives an anonymous tip that an AOL subscriber with the last name "Smith" is a narcotics dealer who frequently e-mails his sources in Mexico to arrange for more deliveries. Can the FBI obtain a pen register order requiring AOL to monitor all of the e-mails sent from all of the accounts owned by customers named Smith, and to collect the e-mail addresses and mail headers (minus the subject lines) for all of those e-mails? Can the FBI obtain a pen register order compelling AOL to collect the e-mail headers (minus subject lines) for every e-mail sent by a customer named Smith to one of the major ISPs in Mexico? See 18 U.S.C. §§ 3122–23.

10. *Intended and inadvertent collection.* When evaluating the legality of any prospective network surveillance, the first question should be whether the surveillance targets the collection of "contents" or "dialing, routing, addressing, or signaling information." If the surveillance targets contents, the Wiretap Act applies and the monitoring requires a Title III order or an applicable exception from 18 U.S.C. § 2511(2). If not, the Pen Register statute applies and the monitoring requires a Pen/Trap order or an exception from 18 U.S.C. § 3121(b).

What happens if surveillance targets DRAS, but due to technological limitations inadvertently collects contents? The inadvertent collection will not violate the Wiretap Act, as the Wiretap Act prohibits only intentional interception of contents. See 18 U.S.C. § 2511(1)(a). See also 18 U.S.C. § 3121(c) (requiring that pen register orders be implemented using technologies "reasonably available" to the government that "restrict[] the recording or decoding of electronic or other impulses to the dialing, routing, addressing, and signaling information utilized in the processing and transmitting of wire or electronic communications so as not to include the contents of any wire or electronic communications").

C. THE STORED COMMUNICATIONS ACT

The third and final statutory privacy law is the Stored Communications Act ("SCA"), codified at 18 U.S.C. §§ 2701–11. The SCA regulates the retrospective surveillance of telephone and Internet communications. More specifically, the SCA governs interactions between government investigators and system administrators in the case of stored content and non-content records.

The SCA shares common themes with the Wiretap Act and Pen Register statute, but it is also very different in two important ways. First, the SCA deals with retrospective surveillance instead of prospective surveillance. In other words, the SCA applies when investigators seek information already in a provider's possession rather than communications in transit. Second, the SCA is considerably more limited in its scope. Whereas the Wiretap Act and the Pen Register statute apply broadly to accessing communications in transit, the SCA only regulates records relating to legitimate customers and subscribers of two specific types of providers.

The heart of the SCA is found in § 2702 and § 2703. The former regulates voluntary disclosure and the latter regulates compelled disclosure. The other important sections for our purposes are the delayed notice provisions found in § 2705, the remedies limitation of § 2708, and the definitions of § 2711.[d]

1. THE BASIC STRUCTURE[e]

The SCA offers network account holders a range of statutory privacy rights against access to stored account information held by network service providers. The statute creates a set of Fourth Amendment-like privacy protections by statute, regulating the relationship between government investigators and service providers in possession of users' private information. It does this in two ways. First, the statute creates limits on the government's ability to compel providers to disclose information in their possession about their customers and subscribers. Although the Fourth Amendment may require no more than a subpoena to obtain e-mails, the statute confers greater privacy protection. Second, the statute places limits on the ability of ISPs to voluntarily disclose information about their customers and subscribers to the government. Although the private search doctrine of the Fourth Amendment allows private providers to make such disclosures, the SCA imposes limitations on the circumstances in which such a disclosure can occur.

Entities Regulated by the Stored Communications Act

The focal point of the SCA is the set of network service providers regulated by the statute. The statute creates rights held by "customers" and "subscribers" of network service providers in both content and noncontent information held by two particular types of providers. To know whether and how the SCA protects the privacy of a particular communication, you must start by classifying the provider to see whether it falls within the scope of the providers regulated by the statute—and if it does, which category of provider applies. If the provider fits within the two categories, the SCA protects the communication; otherwise, only Fourth Amendment protections apply.

The SCA provides privacy protection to communications held by two types of providers. As the 1986 Senate Report on the SCA explains, computer network account holders at that time generally used third-party network service providers in two ways. First, account holders used their accounts to send and receive communications such as e-mail. The

---

d. Other sections of the Act are less important for our purposes. Section 2701 is a rarely used criminal provision, covered briefly in Chapter 2. Section 2704 is almost never used; § 2706 involves reimbursement of costs for provider monitoring; § 2707 permits a civil remedy for violations; § 2709 involves intelligence national securi-

ty letters; and § 2710 regulates video rental privacy.

e. This discussion is adapted from Orin S. Kerr, *A User's Guide to the Stored Communications Act, and A Legislator's Guide to Amending It*, 72 Geo. Wash. L. Rev. 1208, 1212–23 (2004).

use of computer networks to communicate prompted privacy concerns because in the course of sending and retrieving messages, it was common for computers to copy the messages and store them temporarily pending delivery. The copies that these providers of "electronic communication service" created and placed in temporary "electronic storage" in the course of transmission sometimes stayed on a provider's computer for several months.

The second reason account holders used network service providers was to outsource computing tasks. For example, users paid to have remote computers store extra files or process large amounts of data. (This was in the era before spreadsheet programs, so users generally needed to outsource tasks to perform what by today's standards are simple number-crunching jobs.) When users hired such commercial "remote computing services" to perform tasks for them, they would send a copy of their private information to a third-party computing service, which retained the data for storage or processing. Remote computing services raised privacy concerns because the service providers often retained these copies of their customers' files for long periods of time.

The SCA adopts these two distinctions, freezing into the law the understandings of computer network use as of 1986. The text regulates two types of providers: providers of electronic communication service ("ECS") and providers of remote computing service ("RCS"). The statute defines ECS as "any service which provides to users thereof the ability to send or receive wire or electronic communications," and it defines "electronic storage" as "any temporary, intermediate storage of a wire or electronic communication incidental to the electronic transmission thereof," 18 U.S.C. § 2510(17)(A), plus any backup copies of files in such temporary storage. RCS is defined as "the provision to the public of computer storage or processing services by means of an electronic communications system." 18 U.S.C. § 2711(2). An "electronic communications system" is in turn defined as "any wire, radio, electromagnetic, photooptical or photoelectronic facilities for the transmission of electronic communications, and any computer facilities or related electronic equipment for the electronic storage of such communications." 18 U.S.C. § 2510(14).

The narrow scope of the SCA has two important implications. First, there are many problems of Internet privacy that the SCA does not address. The SCA is not a catch-all statute designed to protect the privacy of stored Internet communications; instead it is narrowly tailored to provide a set of Fourth Amendment-like protections for computer networks.

The second implication of the two distinctions adopted by the SCA is that we need to distinguish between providers of ECS, providers of RCS, and providers that provide neither ECS nor RCS. These distinctions are important because, as we will see shortly, the scope of privacy protections hinges on such distinctions. The distinction between providers of ECS and RCS is made somewhat confusing by the fact that most network service providers are multifunctional. They can act as providers of ECS in some contexts, providers of RCS in other contexts, and as neither in some contexts as well. In light of this, it is essential to recognize the functional nature of the definitions of ECS and RCS. The classifications of ECS and RCS are context sensitive: the key is the provider's role with respect to a particular copy of a particular communication, rather than the provider's status in the abstract. A provider can act as an RCS with respect to some communications, an ECS with respect to other communications, and neither an RCS nor an ECS with respect to other communications.

What does this mean in practice? Some cases are easy. For example, when an e-mail sits unopened on an ISP's server, the ISP is acting as a provider of ECS with respect to that e-mail. On the other hand, if I author a document and send it via ftp to a commercial long-term storage site for safekeeping, the storage site is acting as a provider of RCS with respect to that file. There are closer cases, however, and some of these closer cases are important ones. In particular, the proper treatment of opened e-mail is currently unclear. The traditional understanding has been that a copy of opened e-mail sitting on a server is protected by the RCS rules, not the ECS rules. The thinking is that when an e-mail customer leaves a copy of an already-accessed e-mail stored on a server, that copy is no longer "incident to transmission" nor a backup copy of a file that is incident to transmission: rather, it is just in remote storage like any other file held by an RCS.

An example can help explain how the rules fit together under this traditional understanding. Imagine that I send an e-mail to my friend Jane who has an account at a commercial ISP. When the message first arrives at the ISP, the ISP acts a provider of ECS with respect to the e-mail. The e-mail is in "electronic storage" awaiting Jane's retrieval of the message. Once Jane retrieves my e-mail, she can either delete the message from the ISP's server or leave the message stored on the ISP's server for safekeeping. If Jane chooses to store the e-mail with the ISP, the ISP now acts as a provider of RCS (and not ECS) with respect to that copy of the e-mail so long as the ISP is available to the public. The role of the ISP has changed from a transmitter of the e-mail to a storage facility available to the public, from an ECS to an RCS. If the ISP is not available to the public, then the ISP provides neither ECS nor RCS, and the remotely stored e-mail now is protected only under the Fourth Amendment. If Jane downloads a copy of the e-mail onto her personal computer, the ISP acts as neither a provider of ECS nor RCS with respect to the downloaded copy regardless of whether the ISP is available to the public. The ISP is not holding the downloaded copy either incident to transmission or for storage; in fact, the ISP does not hold that copy at all. As a result, only Fourth Amendment privacy protections apply.

Although this is the traditional understanding of how the ECS/RCS distinction applies to e-mail, a recent decision by the Ninth Circuit has taken a very different approach. In Theofel v. Farey–Jones, 359 F.3d

1066 (9th Cir. 2004), the Ninth Circuit concluded that all e-mails held by a server are protected under the ECS rules until "the underlying message has expired in the normal course," regardless of whether the e-mail has been accessed. This appears to be a fact-sensitive test: under *Theofel*, a server acts as a provider of ECS with respect to a message until both the user and the ISP no longer need the e-mail message.

The Privacy Protections of the Stored Communications Act

The privacy protections contained in 18 U.S.C. §§ 2702 and 2703 provide the heart of the SCA. Section 2703 provides the rules that the government must follow when it seeks to compel a provider to disclose information. Section 2702 provides the rules that govern whether a provider can disclose information to the government voluntarily.

A. Compelled Disclosure Rules in 18 U.S.C. § 2703

Section 2703 mandates different standards the government must satisfy to compel different types of communications. To compel a provider of ECS to disclose contents of communications in its possession that are in temporary "electronic storage" for 180 days or less, the government must obtain a search warrant. To compel a provider of ECS to disclose contents in electronic storage for greater than 180 days or to compel a provider of RCS to disclose contents, the government has three options. First, the government can obtain a search warrant. Alternatively, investigators can use less process than a warrant, as long as they combine that process with prior notice. Specifically, the government can use either a subpoena or a "specific and articulable facts" court order pursuant to 18 U.S.C. § 2703(d), combined with prior notice to the "subscriber or customer" (which can be delayed in some circumstances). The court order found in § 2703(d), often referred to as a "2703(d)" order or simply a "d" order, is something like a mix between a subpoena and a search warrant. To obtain the order, the government must provide "specific and articulable facts showing that there are reasonable grounds to believe" that the information to be compelled is "relevant and material to an ongoing criminal investigation." If the judge finds that the factual showing has been made, the judge signs the order. The order is then served like an ordinary subpoena; investigators bring or fax the order to the ISP, and the ISP complies by turning over the information to the investigators.

The rules governing compelled disclosure also cover noncontent records, such as logs maintained by a network server. The rules are the same for providers of ECS and RCS and give the government several ways to compel noncontent records. First, the government can obtain a 2703(d) order to compel such records. Alternatively, the government can obtain a search warrant instead. Investigators can also compel the disclosure of noncontent records if they obtain the consent of the customer or subscriber to such disclosure, and in the rare case that involves telemarketing fraud, they can obtain noncontent records merely by submitting a formal written request to the provider. Finally, the SCA has special rules for compelling a subset of noncontent records that Congress has deemed less private than other records. These records are sometimes known as "basic subscriber information" because they mostly involve information about the subscriber's identity. The government can obtain the basic subscriber information with a mere subpoena according to 18 U.S.C. § 2703(c)(2).

One interesting aspect of § 2703 is that it generally allows the government to obtain greater process when lesser process will do. If a provision of § 2703 allows government agents to compel information with a subpoena, it also allows them to obtain that information with a 2703(d) order; if it allows agents to obtain information with a 2703(d) order, then a search warrant is also acceptable. Why might the government want this option? The main reason is efficiency. Investigators may decide that they need to compel several types of information, some of which can be obtained with lesser process and some of which requires greater process. The "greater includes the lesser" rule in § 2703 allows the government to obtain only one court order—whatever process is greatest—and compel all of the information in one order all at once.

B. *Voluntary Disclosure Rules in 18 U.S.C. § 2702*

The rules regulating voluntary disclosure by providers of RCS and ECS appear in 18 U.S.C. § 2702. Importantly, § 2702 imposes restrictions only on providers of ECS and RCS that provide services "to the public." Nonpublic providers can voluntarily disclose information freely without violating the SCA. Among providers to the public, providers are also free to disclose noncontent information to nongovernment entities. For example, a company can disclose records about how its customers used its services to a marketing company. In contrast, § 2702(a) generally bans disclosure of contents by public providers, as well as the disclosure of noncontent records to any government entities. The statute then provides specific exceptions in which voluntary disclosure is allowed.

For mostly historical reasons that are of little importance today, § 2702 has slightly different exceptions depending on whether the information to be voluntarily disclosed consists of content or noncontent information.

Of the eight exceptions in § 2702(b), numbers one through four are common sense exceptions: a provider can divulge contents if it needs to do so in order to deliver the communication (§ 2702(b)(1), (4)), if otherwise authorized by law (§ 2702(b)(2)), or if the person whose rights are at stake consents (§ 2702(b)(3)). The remaining exceptions deal with specific circumstances in which an individual's privacy rights give way to other competing interests. A provider can disclose contents when disclosure is necessary given a dangerous emergency (§ 2702(b)(8)); when the provider inadvertently discovers the evidence and it relates to a crime (§ 2702(b)(7)); when such disclosure is needed to protect the provider, such as from unauthorized use of the network (§ 2702(b)(5)); and when a provider discovers images of child pornography that the provider must disclose to the police by federal law (§ 2702(b)(6)).

The exceptions for the disclosure of noncontent records in § 2702(c) are similar, but not quite identical, to those for contents.

Putting the Pieces Together

Although the rules found in § 2702 and § 2703 can seem maddeningly complicated at first, they prove surprisingly straightforward in practice. The rules for compelled disclosure operate like an upside-down pyramid. Because the SCA's rules allow greater process to include the lesser, different levels of process can compel different groups of information. The higher up the pyramid you go, the more information the government can obtain.

At the lowest threshold, only a simple subpoena is needed to compel basic subscriber information. Higher up the pyramid, a 2703(d) order compels all noncontent records. A simple subpoena combined with prior notice compels three categories of information: basic subscriber information, plus any opened e-mails or other permanently held files (covered by the RCS rules), plus any contents in temporary "electronic storage" such as unretrieved e-mails in storage for more than 180 days. A 2703(d) order plus prior notice is sufficient to compel all noncontent records, plus any opened e-mails or other permanently held files (covered by the RCS rules), plus any contents in temporary "electronic storage" such as unretrieved e-mails in storage for more than 180 days. Put another way, a 2703(d) order plus prior notice compels everything except contents in temporary "electronic storage" 180 days or less. Finally, a search warrant is needed to compel everything stored in an account.

The rules governing voluntary disclosure by providers are even simpler in practice. Nonpublic providers can disclose without restriction. Providers of ECS or RCS to the public ordinarily cannot disclose either content or noncontent information. Disclosure is allowed only when an exception applies: in the case of contents, the facts must fit within one of the eight exceptions found in § 2702(b); in the case of noncontent records, the facts must fit within one of the six exceptions found in § 2702(c).

This chart summarizes the basic rules of the SCA under both the traditional understanding and *Theofel v. Farey–Jones*. The first two columns on the left-hand side represent the categories of information under both the traditional understanding and *Theofel*. The columns in the center cover the voluntary disclosure rules for those categories, and the columns on the right-hand side cover the compelled disclosure rules.

Traditional Understanding	*Theofel v. Farey–Jones*	Voluntary Disclosure Allowed?		Mechanisms to Compel Disclosure	
		Public Provider	Non–Public Provider	Public Provider	Non–Public Provider
Unopened e-mail in storage 180 days or less	"Unexpired" e-mail in storage 180 days or less	No, unless § 2702(b) exception applies [§ 2702(a)(1)]	Yes [§ 2702(a)(1)]	Search warrant [§ 2703(a)]	Search warrant [§ 2703(a)]
Unopened e-mail in storage more than 180 days	"Unexpired" e-mail in storage more than 180 days	No, unless § 2702(b) exception applies [§ 2702(a)(1)]	Yes [§ 2702(a)(1)]	Subpoena with notice; 2703(d) order with notice; or search warrant [§ 2703(a,b)]	Subpoena with notice; 2703(d) order with notice; or search warrant [§ 2703(a,b)]
Opened e-mail, other content files being remotely stored or processed	Files not covered above being remotely stored or processed	No, unless § 2702(b) exception applies [§ 2702(a)(2)]	Yes [§ 2702(a)(2)]	Subpoena with notice; 2703(d) order with notice; or search warrant [§ 2703(b)]	SCA doesn't apply [§ 2711(2)]
Most non-content records	Most non-content records	No, unless § 2702(c) exception applies [§ 2702(a)(3)]	Yes [§ 2702(a)(3)]	2703(d) order or search warrant [§ 2703(c)(1)]	2703(d) order or search warrant § 2703(c)(1)]
Basic subscriber information, session logs, IP addresses	Basic subscriber information, session logs, IP addresses	No, unless § 2702(c) exception applies [§ 2702(a)(3)]	Yes [§ 2702(a)(3)]	Subpoena; 2703(d) order; or search warrant [§ 2703(c)(2)]	Subpoena; 2703(d) order; or search warrant [§ 2703(c)(2)]

Notes and Questions

1. Although the SCA is significantly more complicated than the Wiretap Act and the Pen Register statute, it borrows a number of their terms. The SCA borrows the terms "wire communication," "electronic communication," "provider," "consent," "necessarily incident to the rendition of the service or to the protection of the rights or property of the provider," and "contents" from the § 2510 of the Wiretap Act. *See* 18 U.S.C. § 2711(1). The SCA also borrows the term "court of competent jurisdiction" from § 3127 of the Pen Register statute. *See* 18 U.S.C. § 2711(3).

2. The most difficult aspect of the SCA is the scope of the two types of covered providers, providers of electronic communications service (ECS) and remote computing service (RCS). Before you spend time trying to master the difference, keep in mind that the meaning of these terms will matter only in two discrete ways. First, a threshold decision must be made in every SCA case as to whether the provider is a covered provider under the statute. Second, the difference between ECS and RCS becomes important primarily to determine the scope of protection for opened e-mails. The next two notes take a closer look at these two issues.

3. *Providers not covered by the SCA.* Computer network operators can be exempt from the SCA if they provide neither ECS nor RCS. Consider the facts of In re Jetblue Airways Corp. Privacy Litigation, 379 F. Supp. 2d 299

(E.D.N.Y. 2005). A nationwide class of airline customers sued the airline JetBlue under the SCA for disclosing customer data. The airline had disclosed data from the JetBlue Passenger Reservation System computer to a company that had contracted with the government to explore data mining techniques. The plaintiffs claimed that the disclosure of customer data violated the voluntary disclosure provisions of 18 U.S.C. § 2702. The district court correctly held that JetBlue did not violate the SCA because it was not a provider covered by the statute. First, JetBlue did not provide ECS:

> The term "electronic communication service," as defined, refers to a service that provides users with capacity to transmit electronic communications. Although JetBlue operates a website that receives and transmits data to and from its customers, it is undisputed that it is not the provider of the electronic communication service that allows such data to be transmitted over the Internet. Rather, JetBlue is more appropriately characterized as a provider of air travel services and a consumer of electronic communication services. The website that it operates, like a telephone, enables the company to communicate with its customers in the regular course of business. Mere operation of the website, however, does not transform JetBlue into a provider of internet access, just as the use of a telephone to accept telephone reservations does not transform the company into a provider of telephone service. Thus, a company such as JetBlue does not become an "electronic communication service" provider simply because it maintains a website that allows for the transmission of electronic communications between itself and its customers.

> This reading of the statute finds substantial support in the case law. Although the Second Circuit has not yet had occasion to construe the term "electronic communication service," a number of courts in this and other circuits have done so, some in cases factually similar to this case. The weight of this persuasive authority holds that companies that provide traditional products and services over the Internet, as opposed to Internet access itself, are not "electronic communication service" providers within the meaning of the ECPA.

Id. at 307. Next, the court held that JetBlue was not a provider of RCS:

> Plaintiffs have also failed to establish that JetBlue is a remote computing service. Plaintiffs simply make the allegation without providing any legal or factual support for such a claim. As discussed, the term "remote computing service" is defined in the ECPA as "the provision to the public of computer storage or processing services by means of an electronic communication system." 18 U.S.C. § 2711(2). The statute's legislative history explains that such services exist to provide sophisticated and convenient data processing services to subscribers and customers, such as hospitals and banks, from remote facilities. *See* S. Rep. No. 99–541 (1986), *reprinted in* 1986 U.S.C.C.A.N. 3555, 3564. By supplying the necessary equipment, remote computing services alleviate the need for users of computer technology to process data in-house. *See id.* Customers or subscribers may enter into time-sharing arrangements with the remote computing service, or data processing may be accomplished by the service provider on the basis of information supplied by the subscriber or customer. *Id.* at 3564–65. Although plaintiffs allege that JetBlue operates a website and computer servers, no facts alleged indicate that JetBlue provides either computer processing services or

computer storage to the public. As such, under the plain meaning of the statute, JetBlue is not a remote computing service.

Id. at 310.

4. *The surprisingly difficult case of opened e-mails.* Courts are presently divided on how the ECS/RCS distinction applies to opened e-mails. The source of the difficulty is the complex definition of "electronic storage" in 18 U.S.C. § 2510(17). This definition is critical because contents in "electronic storage" are the only types of contents held by providers of ECS. In other words, only contents in "electronic storage" receive ECS protections. As a result, the meaning of "electronic storage" defines whether particular contents receive ECS protections or RCS protections.

18 U.S.C. § 2510(17) defines "electronic storage" as:

(A) any temporary, intermediate storage of a wire or electronic communication incidental to the electronic transmission thereof; and

(B) any storage of such communication by an electronic communication service for purposes of backup protection of such communication[.]

Note that this is a counterintuitive definition. It refers only to a particular type of electronic storage rather than all electronic storage. Specifically, § 2510(17)(A) reflects the very specific function of ECS providers: servers may make temporary copies of e-mails in the course of transmission, and § 2510(17)(A) protects those temporary copies made pending transmission of communications. For example, unopened e-mail in a user's in-box is in "electronic storage," as it is awaiting the user's retrieval of the message.

The difficult question is how to interpret the text of the backup provision, § 2510(17)(B). Consider two possibilities. First, the backup provision may refer to backups made by the provider for the provider's purposes. It is common for system administrators to make backup copies of their files in the event of a system malfunction, and § 2510(17)(B) may simply ensure that the copies of e-mails generated as part of the backup process receive the same protections as originals.

An example shows the role of § 2510(17)(B) under this interpretation. Imagine an ISP makes backup copies of its entire server every night, and criminal investigators want a copy of an unopened e-mail in a particular customer's account. A day after the e-mail arrives, the ISP will have two copies of the opened e-mail, not one: it will have both the original copy in the account and the backup copy. Unlike the original, however, the backup copy is not a "temporary" or "intermediate" copy in storage "incidental" to transmission. It is a permanent copy made by the provider in the event of a system malfunction. Without § 2510(17)(B), the backup copy would not receive the same treatment as the original. Under this interpretation, the backup provision of the definition makes clear that the same legal rules govern access to the original and the backup copy.

Alternatively, the backup provision may refer to copies stored by the user for the user's purposes. After reading an e-mail, users often leave the e-mail on the ISP's server. At that point, the e-mail is no longer stored "incidental to the electronic transmission" of the communication. Users may think of their opened e-mails left with their ISP as "backups" of their messages. Under this approach, the purpose of § 2510(17)(B) is to ensure that opened and unopened e-mails receive the same protection. Opening an e-mail takes an e-mail from electronic storage in § 2510(17)(A) to electronic storage in § 2510(17)(B).

The difference between these two interpretations may seem very technical, but it has tremendous practical importance. Although there are no statistics on this question, it seems likely that most e-mail stored with ISPs is opened e-mail. Under the first approach, opened e-mails are no longer covered by the ECS rules because they are not in "electronic storage." Under the second approach, in contrast, opened e-mails are still in "electronic storage."

So which interpretation is correct? Right now, the answer is frustratingly unclear. The Justice Department and several district courts have endorsed the first approach. *See, e.g,* DOJ Search and Seizure Manual (2002), available at http://www.usdoj.gov/criminal/cybercrime/s&smanual 2002.- htm# _IIIB_; Fraser v. Nationwide Mut. Ins., 135 F. Supp. 2d 623 (E.D. Pa. 2001), *aff'd on other grounds*, 352 F.3d 107 (3d. Cir. 2003); In re Double-Click, Inc. Privacy Litig., 154 F. Supp. 2d 497, 511–12 (S.D.N.Y.2001). *See also* H.R. Rep. No. 99–647, at 64–65 (1986) (suggesting that opened e-mail should be covered by provisions relating to RCS rather than ECS).

In contrast, the Ninth Circuit endorsed the second approach in a case arising from rather unusual facts. *See* Theofel v. Farey–Jones, 359 F.3d 1066 (9th Cir. 2004). *Theofel* involved an abusive tactic in a civil discovery dispute. The defendants sent an overly broad subpoena to the plaintiffs' ISP; the subpoena asked for all of the plaintiffs' e-mails. The ISP responded to the subpoena by providing the defendants with all of the e-mails from the plaintiffs' accounts. Compliance with the subpoena presumably violated § 2703, but the plaintiffs did not sue under that statute. Instead, the plaintiffs sued under 18 U.S.C. § 2701, on the theory that issuing the overly broad subpoena had "accessed" the ISP "without authorization."

Surprisingly, Judge Kozinski agreed. Writing for the panel, Judge Kozinski held that the plaintiff's use of the overbroad subpoena to get information was an unauthorized access, the legal equivalent of hacking into the ISP. *See id.* at 1073–74. (Aside: Do you agree with this interpretation?) Notably, however, § 2701 applies only to contents in electronic storage held by providers of ECS. As a result, Judge Kozinski needed to conclude that the e-mails disclosed—most of which, presumably, had been opened and read— were in "electronic storage."

Judge Kozinski held that the e-mails in the accounts were in electronic storage regardless of whether they had been opened. According to Kozinski, the opened e-mails in the accounts were covered by the backup provisions of 18 U.S.C. § 2510(17)(B):

> An obvious purpose for storing a message on an ISP's server after delivery is to provide a second copy of the message in the event that the user needs to download it again—if, for example, the message is accidentally erased from the user's own computer. The ISP copy of the message functions as a "backup" for the user. Notably, nothing in the Act requires that the backup protection be for the benefit of the ISP rather than the user. Storage under these circumstances thus literally falls within the statutory definition. * * *

The United States, as *amicus curiae*, disputes our interpretation. It first argues that, because subsection (B) refers to "any storage of such communication," it applies only to backup copies of messages that are themselves in temporary, intermediate storage under subsection (A). The text of the statute, however, does not support this reading. Subsection (A) identifies a type of communication ("a wire or electronic communication") and a type of storage ("temporary, intermediate storage . . . incidental to the electronic transmission thereof"). The phrase "such communication" in subsection (B) does not, as a matter of grammar, reference attributes of the type of storage defined in subsection (A). The government's argument would be correct if subsection (B) referred to "a communication in such storage," or if subsection (A) referred to a communication in temporary, intermediate storage rather than temporary, intermediate storage of a communication. However, as the statute is written, "such communication" is nothing more than shorthand for "a wire or electronic communication."

The government's contrary interpretation * * * drains subsection (B) of independent content because virtually any backup of a subsection (A) message will itself qualify as a message in temporary, intermediate storage. The government counters that the statute requires only that the underlying message be temporary, not the backup. But the lifespan of a backup is necessarily tied to that of the underlying message. Where the underlying message has expired in the normal course, any copy is no longer performing any backup function. An ISP that kept permanent copies of temporary messages could not fairly be described as "backing up" those messages.

Id. at 1075–76.

Which interpretation do you think is most consistent with the text of the statute? Which interpretation is better from the standpoint of policy?

2. COMPELLED DISCLOSURE UNDER § 2703

Section 2703 contains the rules that govern compelled disclosure of stored records. Section 2703(a) covers the requirements for compelling contents from a provider of ECS; § 2703(b) addresses requirements for compelling contents from providers of RCS; and § 2703(c) turns to the rules that regulate non-content records.

UNITED STATES v. KENNEDY

United States District Court for the District of Kansas, 2000.
81 F. Supp. 2d 1103.

Belot, District Judge.

On August 25, 1999, Defendant Michael R. Kennedy was indicted for the intentional receipt of child pornography in violation of 18 U.S.C. § 2252(a)(2) and forfeiture under 18 U.S.C. § 2253. An evidentiary hearing was held December 2, 1999. For the following reasons, defendant's motion to suppress is denied.

Facts

On July 2, 1999, Steven Idelman was working as a customer support specialist for Road Runner, a high speed Internet service provider. At approximately 9:00 p.m., Idelman received an anonymous phone call from a still-unidentified male ("the caller"). The caller told Idelman that he was at a friend's house, scanning other computers through the Internet and had viewed images of child pornography on a computer the caller believed to be serviced by Road Runner. The caller told Idelman the IP address of the computer from which the images were viewed, 24.94.200.54, and the directory and file names in which the images were located.[4] The caller did not say that he was a law enforcement officer or that he was directed to view the computer's files by any law enforcement officer. The caller did not ask Idelman to call the police.

Shortly after the anonymous call, Idelman went to a computer and accessed the IP address given to him by the caller. His purpose was to determine if what the caller told him was correct. He located the computer with the IP address 24.94.200.54 and the directory tree and files mentioned by the caller. Idelman viewed two images located within those files. One of the images depicted two boys, whom Idelman estimated to be approximately eight or nine years old, posed in a sexual nature. Idelman then sent an e-mail to his supervisor, Anna Madden, describing the anonymous phone call and the results of his search of the computer with IP address 24.94.200.54.

On July 6, 1999, Kerry Jones, a network engineer for Road Runner, received an e-mail from Anna Madden asking him to research the owner of the Road Runner account connecting to the computer with the IP address 24.94.200.54. Jones was able to determine that the account was assigned to Rosemary D. Kennedy. Mr. Jones was able to determine that the account was assigned to the same IP address on July 2, 1999. Believing that the customer service agreement between Road Runner and the account holder authorized him to search a computer's files for offensive material, Jones then viewed the files on the computer's hard drive.[7] The files depicted images of boys, whom Jones estimated to be approximately 10 to 13 years old, engaged in sexual activity. Jones then printed out an image of the computer's directory tree in which the files with offensive material were located.

That same day, after consulting with Road Runner's corporate attorney, Scott Petrie, the manager of Road Runner, made the decision to contact law enforcement authorities. Kerry Jones contacted the Exploited Children's Unit of the Wichita Police Department, but his phone call was not returned. Road Runner then contacted Special Agent Leslie Earl of the FBI. Special Agent Earl was informed by Road Runner that the FBI would need to obtain a court order for it to be able to supply the FBI with any subscriber information.

---

4. The caller was able to view the computer's files because the computer with IP address 24.94.200.54 had its print and file sharing mechanism turned on, allowing other computers to view its files over the Internet.

7. Jones was able to do so because the computer's print and file sharing mechanism was still turned on.

The United States Attorney's Office then applied to a United States magistrate judge for an order directing Road Runner to disclose subscriber information related to IP address 24.94.200.54. In the application, the Assistant United States Attorney stated that:

> the Federal Bureau of Investigation is conducting a criminal investigation in connection with possible violation(s) of Tile 18, United States Code, Sections 2252 and 2252A; it is believed that the subject of the investigation used Road Runner's IP address 24.94.200.54 on July 2, 1999, at 11:48 p.m. in furtherance of the subject offenses; and that the information sought to be obtained is relevant to a legitimate law enforcement inquiry in that it is believed that this information will assist in the investigation relating to the aforementioned offenses.

The magistrate judge issued an order, which was presented to Road Runner personnel, who provided the FBI with the following information:

> The subscriber whose computer used I.P. address 24.94.200.54 on July 2, 1999, at 11:49 p.m. was Rosemay (sic) D. Kennedy of 9120 Harvest Court, Wichita, Kansas, telephone 316–722–6593. Two users were listed for that account: RKENNEDY@KSCable.COM and KENNEDYM@KSCable.Com. The account had been active since June 7, 1999.

Special Agent Earl next went to the house located at 9120 Harvest Court in Wichita, Kansas. He observed a Chrysler Sebring parked in the driveway. A records check with the Kansas Department of Motor Vehicles revealed that the car was registered to Michael R. Kennedy. Special Agent Earl then called the phone number given to the government by Road Runner. A person identifying himself as Michael Kennedy answered the phone.

In initiating the phone call, Special Agent Earl asked Kennedy if he was satisfied with his Road Runner cable modem Internet service.

> Kennedy confirmed that his address was 9120 Harvest Court, Wichita, Kansas, and he confirmed that he was the primary user of the Road Runner cable modem Internet service. Kennedy said he was satisfied with the service and especially liked the speed and quality of the e-mail service. Kennedy estimated he spent an average of two to three hours per night online. Kennedy noted that he always left his system on and connected to the Internet. Kennedy said he used his Internet access only for pleasure and his computer and modem were located in his home.

> Kennedy said his computer system was a Gateway 450 megahertz Pentium II with a 17 gigabyte hard drive. When asked if he had any concerns about the Road Runner service Kennedy said he thought the company should warn customers about the possibility of someone else trying to enter their computers through the Internet. Kennedy said he held Internet accounts through Netcom and AOL in the past. Kennedy left those services because they were too slow

and he could not use e-mail and Usenet news groups the way he wanted to. Kennedy noted that it took too long for him to download mail with pictures attached on those other services.

Affidavit in Support of Search Warrant at 14–15, Doc. 14, Ex. A. The government applied for and obtained a search warrant for property and evidence located at 9120 Harvest Court.

ANALYSIS

18 U.S.C. §§ 2701 *et seq.* regulates the disclosure of electronic communications and subscriber information. Section 2703(c)(1)(B) states that "[a] provider of electronic communication service ... shall disclose a record or other information pertaining to a subscriber to or customer of such service ... to a governmental entity only when the governmental entity ... (ii) obtains a court order for such disclosure under subsection (d) of this section." Subsection (d) sets forth the requirements of such a court order:

> A court order for disclosure under subsection (b) or (c) ... shall issue only if the governmental entity offers *specific and articulable facts* showing that there are reasonable grounds to believe that the contents of a wire or electronic communication, or the records or other information sought, are relevant and material to an ongoing criminal investigation.

18 U.S.C. § 2703(d) (emphasis added).

Defendant argues the government's application did not state specific and articulable facts, but mere conclusions. The government responds that at the time of the application, it did not know the identity of the subscriber, whether the subscriber was the person using the computer to store illegal material and how much child pornography was held by the computer. The government argues that the information it had at the time was minimal and the purpose of obtaining the order was to investigate the subscriber information completely.

The government's argument does not address the issue as to conclusory versus specific and articulable facts in regard to the information it *did* have. The government's application merely listed that the subscriber information connected to IP address 24.94.200.54 would possibly relate to an on-going criminal investigation.[8] In accordance with 18 U.S.C.

---

8. It appears as though the government's application would have satisfied the statute's requirements prior to the 1994 amendments to the ECPA. As the statute was originally enacted, the government's application for the court order sufficed by showing there was reason to believe the information sought was "relevant to a legitimate law enforcement inquiry." Electronic Communications Privacy Act, Pub. L. No. 99–508 § 201. In the early 1990's, a task force, assembled by Senator Patrick Leahy "questioned whether current restrictions on government access to transactional records generated in the course of electronic communications were adequate." H.R. Rep. No. 103–827, at 12 (1994), *reprinted in* 1994 U.S.C.A.A.N. 3489, 3492. In response, the statute was amended to its current version. *See* Communications Assistance for Law Enforcement Act, Pub. L. No. 103–414 § 207(2). The House Report reflects that

> [t]his section imposes an intermediate standard to protect on-line transactional records. It is a standard higher than a subpoena, but not a probable cause war-

§ 2703(d), the government should have articulated more specific facts such as how the government obtained the information it did have at the time and how this information lead the agents to believe that the attainment of the subscriber information of this particular IP address would assist in the investigation. The government's application for a section 2703(d) order did not meet the requirements of the statute.

Nonetheless, the government correctly points out that even if Road Runner divulged defendant's subscriber information pursuant to a court order based on an inadequate government application, suppression is not a remedy contemplated under the ECPA. The statute specifically allows for civil damages and criminal punishment for violations of the ECPA, *see* 18 U.S.C. §§ 2707, 2701(b), but speaks nothing about the suppression of information in a court proceeding. Instead, Congress clearly intended for suppression not to be an option for a defendant whose electronic communications have been intercepted in violation of the ECPA. The statute specifically states that "[t]he remedies and sanctions described in this chapter are the only judicial remedies and sanctions for nonconstitutional violations of this chapter." 18 U.S.C. § 2708.

Notes and Questions

1.   The prosecutor in the *Kennedy* case applied for the wrong order and then obtained it in the wrong way. The prosecutor applied for an § 2703(d) order under 18 U.S.C. § 2703(c)(1)(B), and requested "subscriber information" from the ISP. However, the prosecutor could have obtained that information from the ISP using a mere subpoena, without establishing "specific and articulable facts," under 18 U.S.C. § 2703(c)(2). The prosecutor then erred a second time by not establishing the "specific and articulable facts" required by § 2703(d).

2.   *Compelling non-content records.* The SCA has two sets of rules for compelling non-content records from covered providers. Basic subscriber information listed in 18 U.S.C. § 2703(c)(2) can be compelled with a subpoena. Compelling other non-content records requires a § 2703(d) order. As noted in the *Kennedy* case, the § 2703(d) standard requires "specific and articulable facts showing that there are reasonable grounds to believe" that the information sought is "relevant and material to an ongoing criminal investigation."

Congress apparently borrowed the "specific and articulable facts" language from Fourth Amendment law, and specifically the temporary stop standard articulated in Terry v. Ohio, 392 U.S. 1, 21 (1968) ("[I]n justifying the particular intrusion the police officer must be able to point to specific and articulable facts which, taken together with rational inferences from

rant. The intent of raising the standard for access to transactional data is to guard against "fishing expeditions" by law enforcement. Under the intermediate standard, the court must find, *based on law enforcement's showing of facts, that there are specific and articulable grounds*

to believe that the records are relevant and material to an ongoing criminal investigation.

H.R. Rep. No. 103–827, at 31–32 (1994), *reprinted in* 1994 U.S.C.A.A.N. 3489, 3511–12 (emphasis added).

those facts, reasonably warrant that intrusion."). Did the government have enough information to make such a showing in *Kennedy*?

3. The two-tiered approach to compelling non-content records was enacted as part of the Communications Assistance for Law Enforcement Act of 1994, Pub. L. No. 103–414 (1994) ("CALEA"). A Senate Report issued during work on S. 2375, a bill introduced on the way to the passage of CALEA, justified the change on the following grounds:

> In the 8 years since the enactment of ECPA, society's patterns of using electronic communications technology have changed dramatically. Millions of people now have electronic mail addresses. Business, non-profit organizations and political groups conduct their work over the Internet. Individuals maintain a wide range of relationships on-line. Transactional records documenting these activities and associations are generated by service providers. For those who increasingly use these services, this transactional data reveals a great deal about their private lives, all of it compiled in one place.

> Therefore, S. 2375 includes provisions, which FBI Director Freeh supported in his testimony, that add protections to the exercise of the Government's current surveillance authority. Specifically, the bill * * * [e]liminates the use of subpoenas to obtain E-mail addresses and other similar transactional data from electronic communications service providers. Currently, the Government can obtain transactional logs containing a person's entire on-line profile merely upon presentation of an administrative subpoena issued by an investigator without any judicial intervention. Under S. 2375, a court order would be required.

S. Rep. No. 103–402, at 17–18 (1994).

4. Note that the SCA requires "specific and articulable facts" for the retrospective surveillance of non-content transactional information, but the Pen Register statute only requires a certification of relevance for prospective surveillance of such information. In other words, government investigators can obtain non-content transactional information more easily prospectively than retrospectively. Does this make sense? Should the standards for prospective surveillance be lower than retrospective surveillance?

5. *Compelling content records.* The SCA's rules for compelling contents are also two-tiered. The top tier, required when the government seeks to compel contents from an ECS in electronic storage for 180 days or fewer, requires a probable cause search warrant. *See* 18 U.S.C. § 2703(a). The second tier, required when the government seeks to compel contents from an ECS in storage greater than 180 days or when it seeks to compel contents from an RCS, requires either a subpoena with prior notice, a § 2703(d) order with prior notice, or a search warrant. *See* 18 U.S.C. § 2703(b). Of course, what exactly this covers hinges on how you interpret the ECS/RCS distinction, as noted earlier in the discussion of *Theofel*.

6. Is the SCA's two-tiered approach to compelling contents desirable as a matter of policy? Should opened e-mail be treated differently than unopened e-mail? Should files stored with a remote storage facility be treated differently than unopened e-mails? Should unopened e-mail in storage for more than 180 days be treated differently than "fresh" e-mail, on the theory

that the former has been "abandoned" and should be protected less? Should privacy protections for e-mail hinge on whether the e-mails have "expired in the normal course"? Alternatively, should Congress create a broad warrant requirement for all contents, regardless of the circumstances?

7. Note that the SCA requires a standard search warrant for retrospective access to stored unopened e-mails, but the Wiretap Act requires a "super warrant" order for prospective interception of e-mail. In other words, government investigators can obtain content information more easily retrospectively than prospectively. Do you think this is appropriate? Or do you agree with Judge Boochever that "[a]n electronic communication in storage is no more or less private than an electronic communication in transmission," and that "[d]istinguishing between the two for purposes of protection from interception is irrational"? Konop v. Hawaiian Airlines, 236 F.3d 1035 (9th Cir. 2001), *withdrawn,* 262 F.3d 972 (9th Cir. 2001), *reargued,* 302 F.3d 868 (9th Cir. 2002), *cert. denied,* 537 U.S. 1193 (2003).

If the standards for retrospective and prospective content surveillance should be the same, which standard should Congress adopt? Should Congress use the standard search warrant requirement now used for retrospective surveillance or the "super warrant" standard currently reserved for prospective surveillance?

8. When investigators obtain court orders under 18 U.S.C. § 2703, the language of the court orders generally tracks the language of the statute. For example, a 2703(d) order might require the disclosure of contents in "electronic storage" for greater than 180 days, plus any contents held by the provider in its capacity as an RCS, plus any non-content records. The ISP must then comply, implicitly interpreting the requirements of the SCA along the way. If an ISP hands over information that exceeds the limits of the statute, is the ISP liable? Or are the investigators liable?

9. Does 18 U.S.C. § 2703 violate the Fourth Amendment, at least on an "as applied" basis? Does the answer hinge on whether you follow the traditional understanding of the statute or the Ninth Circuit's approach in *Theofel v. Farey–Jones?* Does the Fourth Amendment require a search warrant to compel an ISP to divulge opened e-mails, or e-mails that the user no longer wants to read?

10. *Notice requirements.* The statutory privacy laws put in place by ECPA require notice to the person monitored only in two contexts. First, the Wiretap Act requires that, within 90 days after an intercept order has expired, the persons named in the wiretap order and other parties to communications intercepted by the order "as the judge may determine in his discretion that is in the interest of justice" must receive notice of the dates and period of the monitoring. *See* 18 U.S.C. § 2518(8)(d).

Second, the SCA requires "prior notice from the governmental entity to the subscriber or customer" when investigators seek to compel contents of stored communications from covered providers with legal process lesser than a search warrant. 18 U.S.C. § 2703(b)(1)(B). Notably, however, the notice provisions of § 2703 are subject to the delayed notice provisions of § 2705. The delayed notice provisions permit a delay of notice up to 90 days "if there is reason to believe" that notice would trigger an "adverse result," defined as: "(A) endangering the life or physical safety of an individual; (B) flight from prosecution; (C) destruction of or tampering with evidence; (D) intimidation of potential witnesses; or (E) otherwise seriously jeopardizing an investigation or unduly delaying a trial." 18 U.S.C. § 2705(a)(2). The government may also obtain extensions beyond the initial delay period.

Are these notice provisions sufficient? How hard do you think it is to persuade a judge that there is "reason to believe" that notice might lead to an "adverse result"? How do the statutory notice requirements compare to notice requirements of the Fourth Amendment? *See generally* Brian D. Kaiser, Note, *Government Access to Transactional Information and the Lack of Subscriber Notice*, 8 B.U. J. Sci. & Tech. L. 648 (2002).

11. *Pre-disclosure challenges under § 2704.* 18 U.S.C. § 2704 permits the government to invite a pre-disclosure legal challenge to the compulsion of content with less process than a warrant. Under the statute, the government can order the ISP to make a backup of the contents to be disclosed, to provide notice to the customer or subscriber of the pending disclosure, and then to wait for 14 days. If the customer or subscriber does not challenge the order in that window, the provider can disclose the contents to the government. If the subscriber wishes to challenge the order, the provider will hold the backup copy and wait for the court to rule on the subscriber's motion to quash. Importantly, § 2704 is not mandatory. 18 U.S.C. § 2704(a)(1) states that the government "may" invite this challenge, not that it "must." Perhaps unsurprisingly, investigators and prosecutors invariably decline the invitation. Should § 2704 be amended to require such challenges when the government seeks contents without a search warrant?

12. *Preservation requests.* 18 U.S.C. § 2703(f) permits investigators to notify providers that they plan to seek a court order requiring the disclosure of particular records. Providers must then "take all necessary steps" to preserve those records. 18 U.S.C. § 2703(f)(1). As the Justice Department explains:

> Some providers retain records for months, others for hours, and others not at all. As a practical matter, this means that evidence may be destroyed or lost before law enforcement can obtain the appropriate legal order compelling disclosure. For example, agents may learn of a child pornography case on Day 1, begin work on a search warrant on Day 2, obtain the warrant on Day 5, and then learn that the network service provider deleted the records in the ordinary course of business on Day 3. To minimize this risk, ECPA permits the government to direct providers to "freeze" stored records and communications pursuant to 18 U.S.C. § 2703(f).

Searching and Seizing Computers (2002), available at www.cybercrime.gov/s&smanual2002.htm#_IIIG1_.

Importantly, the authority under § 2703(f) has no prospective effect. Providers must preserve records already generated in the ordinary course of business, but the authority does not permit investigators to request prospective monitoring.

13. Assume that an ISP retains the following information relating to an Internet account:

    A. name, address, home phone number, and credit card number

    B. login records for the last 30 days

    C. records of IP addresses assigned to that account for 20 days

    D. e-mail addresses associated with that account

    E. "buddy list" of other accounts belonging to friends of the subscriber

    F. opened e-mails received a year ago

    G. unopened e-mails received a year ago

    H. opened e-mails received the previous day

    I. unopened e-mails received the previous day

    J. copies of all outgoing e-mails for the last year

What legal process must the government use under the SCA to compel the ISP to disclose these records? In which cases does the answer hinge on whether you adopt the Justice Department's or the Ninth Circuit's approach to the ECS/RCS distinction?

3. VOLUNTARY DISCLOSURE UNDER § 2702

The SCA's rules that regulate voluntary disclosure by providers appear in 18 U.S.C. § 2702. As the following case demonstrates, the first important question under § 2702 is whether the provider provides services "to the public."

ANDERSEN CONSULTING LLP v. UOP

United States District Court for the Northern District of Illinois, 1998.
991 F. Supp. 1041.

BUCKLO, District Judge.

Plaintiff, Andersen Consulting LLP, brought an eight count complaint against the defendants, UOP and its counsel, the law firm of Bickel & Brewer. Andersen alleges that the defendants knowingly divulged, or caused to be divulged, the contents of Andersen's e-mail messages in violation of the Electronic Communications Privacy Act, 18 U.S.C. § 2701 *et seq.* For the reasons set forth below, the defendants' motion to dismiss is granted.

UOP hired Andersen to perform a systems integration project in 1992. During the project, Andersen employees had access to and used UOP's internal e-mail system to communicate with each other, with UOP, and with third parties.

Dissatisfied with Andersen's performance, UOP terminated the project in December 1993. Subsequently UOP hired Bickel and Brewer and brought suit in Connecticut state court charging Andersen with breach of contract, negligence, and fraud. Andersen countersued in two different suits for defamation.

While these three cases were pending, UOP and Bickel and Brewer divulged the contents of Andersen's e-mail messages on UOP's e-mail system to the *Wall Street Journal*. The *Journal* published an article on June 19, 1997 titled "E-Mail Trail Could Haunt Consultant in Court." The article excerpted some of Andersen's e-mail messages made during the course of its assignment at UOP. This disclosure of the e-mail messages and their subsequent publication is the basis of this suit.

18 U.S.C. § 2702(a)(1) states that "a person or entity providing an electronic communication service to the public shall not knowingly divulge to any person or entity the contents of a communication while in electronic storage by that service." Andersen claims that the defendants violated this section by knowingly divulging the contents of its e-mail message to the Wall Street Journal.

To be liable for the disclosure of Andersen's e-mail messages, UOP must fall under the purview of the Act: UOP must provide "electronic communication service to the public." 18 U.S.C. § 2702(a)(1). The statute defines "electronic communication service" as "any service which provides to users thereof the ability to send or receive wire or electronic communications." 18 U.S.C. § 2510(15). The statute does not define "public." The word "public," however, is unambiguous. Public means the "aggregate of the citizens" or "everybody" or "the people at large" or "the community at large." *Black's Law Dictionary* 1227 (6th ed.1990). Thus, the statute covers any entity that provides electronic communication service (e.g., e-mail) to the community at large.

Andersen attempts to render the phrase "to the public" superfluous by arguing that the statutory language indicates that the term "public" means something other than the community at large. It claims that if Congress wanted public to mean the community at large, it would have used the term "general public." However, the fact that Congress used both "public" and "general public" in the same statute does not lead to the conclusion that Congress intended public to have any other meaning than its commonly understood meaning. *Compare* 18 U.S.C. § 2511(2)(g) (using the term "general public") *with* §§ 2511(2)(a)(i), (3)(a), (3)(b), (4)(c)(ii) (using the term "public").

Andersen argues that the legislative history indicates that a provider of electronic communication services is subject to Section 2702 even if that provider maintains the system primarily for its own use and does not provide services to the general public. This legislative history argument is misguided. A court's starting point to determine the intent of Congress is the language of the statute itself. If the language is clear and unambiguous, the court must give effect to the plain meaning of the statute. Since the meaning of "public" is clear, there is no need to resort to legislative history.

Even if the language was somehow ambiguous, the legislative history does not support Andersen's interpretation. The legislative history indicates that there is a distinction between public and proprietary. In describing "electronic mail," the legislative history stated that "electronic mail systems may be available for public use or may be proprietary, such as systems operated by private companies for internal correspondence." S. Rep. No. 99–541, at 8 (1986), *reprinted in* 1986 U.S.C.C.A.N. 3555, 3562. Thus, Andersen must show that UOP's electronic mail system was available for public use.

In its complaint, Andersen alleges that UOP "is a general partnership which licenses process technologies and supplies catalysts, specialty chemicals, and other products to the petroleum refining, petrochemical, and gas processing industries." Complaint ¶ 3. UOP is not in the business of providing electronic communication services. It does, however, have an e-mail system for internal communication as e-mail is a necessary tool for almost any business today. *See State Wide Photocopy v. Tokai Fin. Servs., Inc.,* 909 F. Supp. 137, 145 (S.D.N.Y.1995) (finding that defendant was in the business of financing and that the mere use of fax machines and computers, as necessary tools of business, did not make it an electronic communication service provider).

UOP hired Andersen to provide services in connection with the integration of certain computer systems. As part of the project, "UOP provided an electronic communication service for Andersen to use. That electronic communication service could be used, and was used by Andersen and UOP personnel, to electronically communicate with (*i.e.,* send e-mail messages to, and receive e-mail messages from) other Andersen personnel, UOP personnel, third-party vendors and other third-parties both in and outside of Illinois." Complaint ¶ 10.

Based on these allegations, Andersen claims that UOP provides an electronic communication service to the public. However, giving Andersen access to its e-mail system is not equivalent to providing e-mail to the public. Andersen was hired by UOP to do a project and as such, was given access to UOP's e-mail system similar to UOP employees. Andersen was not any member of the community at large, but a hired contractor. Further, the fact that Andersen could communicate to third-parties over the internet and that third-parties could communicate with it did not mean that UOP provided an electronic communication service to the public. UOP's internal e-mail system is separate from the internet. UOP must purchase internet access from an electronic communication service provider like any other consumer; it does not independently provide internet services.

Notes and Questions

1. Why doesn't the SCA impose any restrictions on voluntary disclosure by non-public providers? Here is some speculation:

> Nonpublic accounts may exist more for the benefit of providers than for the benefit of users. For example, companies often provide e-mail accounts to employees for work-related purposes; the U.S. military often provides accounts to service members for official government business. These nonpublic providers generally have a legitimate interest in controlling and accessing the accounts they provide to users. Plus, their users tend to recognize that the providers will view those provider interests as more important than the privacy interests of users.

In contrast, an individual who contracts with a commercial ISP available to the public usually does so solely for his own benefit. The account belongs to the user, not the provider. As a result, the user may understandably rely more heavily on the privacy of the commercial account from the public provider rather than another account with a nonpublic provider. Many Internet users have experienced this dynamic. When an e-mail exchange using a work account turns to private matters, it is common for a user to move the discussion to a commercial account. "I don't want my boss to read this," a user might note, "I'll e-mail you from my personal account later." The law recognizes this distinction by drawing a line between accounts held with public and nonpublic providers. In practice, the public/nonpublic line often acts as a proxy for the distinction between a user's private account and one assigned to him by his employer.

A related explanation for this distinction is that private providers with a relationship to their users may approach their users' privacy differently than would commercial providers available to the public. To a commercial ISP, a particular customer is a source of revenue, no more and no less. In contrast, nonpublic providers may have a long-term, multifaceted relationship with their users, giving nonpublic providers unique incentives to protect the privacy of their users. The law may wish to protect privacy more heavily in the case of public providers because there is less incentive for public providers to protect their users' privacy. Alternatively, the law may take a more hands-off approach with respect to nonpublic providers in recognition of the different relationships that nonpublic providers may have with their users.

Orin S. Kerr, *A User's Guide to the Stored Communications Act, and A Legislator's Guide to Amending It*, 72 Geo. Wash. L. Rev. 1208, 1226–27 (2004).

Assuming this explanation is right as a descriptive matter, is the argument persuasive as a normative matter? Should § 2702 be amended to restrict disclosures by all providers? If an account exists for the provider's purposes rather than the user's, won't the provider obtain the user's consent to disclosure? Why not set a pro-privacy default and permit providers to contract around it?

2. Every law school issues e-mail accounts to students and faculty members, and many students and faculty members use those accounts as primary e-mail addresses. Does a university provide e-mail "to the public"? Can a university can disclose the contents of student e-mail accounts without restriction under the SCA? Does it matter whether the university is a state university or a private institution? Note that the disclosure may be prohibited by other laws, such as the Family Educational Rights and Privacy Act, codified at 20 U.S.C. § 1232g.

3. The SCA presupposes a sharp line between compelled disclosure (covered by § 2703) and voluntary disclosure (covered by § 2702). However, the line can be hazy in practice. For example, a police officer might ask a provider if he is interested in disclosing voluntarily; the sysadmin might agree only because he feels compelled to do so. Alternatively, a sysadmin may want to disclose voluntarily, but may ask for a subpoena to be served so

the ISP's lawyers have some legal process for their records. Should such cases be analyzed under § 2702, § 2703, or both?

The line between § 2702 and § 2703 was a central issue in Freedman v. America Online, 303 F. Supp. 2d 121 (D. Conn. 2004). In *Freedman*, two police officers were investigating a threatening AOL e-mail, and they wanted to know who had sent the e-mail. The officers filled out a state warrant application seeking the identity of the subscriber and faxed it to AOL without the warrant being signed by a judge. AOL complied with the warrant form and disclosed the plaintiff's identity. The plaintiff sued, contending that the use of an unsigned warrant violated § 2703. The officers first contended that they had not violated § 2703 because they had merely requested disclosure, not actually required it. The court disagreed:

> Defendants' argument that they merely requested but did not require AOL to disclose the information is disingenuous and does not absolve them from liability under the ECPA. The ECPA imposes an obligation on governmental entities to follow specific legal processes when seeking such information. 18 U.S.C. § 2703(c). Congress designed such procedures to both (1) protect personal privacy against unwarranted government searches and (2) preserve the legitimate needs of law enforcement. To conclude that Defendants did not act improperly upon merely requesting such information without following the ECPA procedural safeguards ignores the fact that a request accompanied by a court form has substantial resemblance to a compulsory court order. The deficiency would have excused AOL from complying. In what was submitted Young and Bensey clearly intended that AOL supply the information sought. That AOL responded was nothing less than what was intended and cannot be found to be otherwise. To hold that AOL was less than expected, i.e. required to respond, would erode Congress's intended protection in the ECPA and would undermine personal privacy rights. In soliciting the information from AOL, Defendants knew, or should have known, that AOL was requested to violate the ECPA. Even if AOL acted without lawful authority in disclosing the information, this does not absolve Defendants from unlawfully requesting or soliciting AOL's disclosure. Putting the burden and obligation on *both* the government and ISPs is consistent with Congress' intent to protect personal privacy. Violation by one does not excuse the other.

Id. at 127. The officers next claimed that AOL's disclosure did not violate the SCA because AOL may have disclosed the information on their own accord. The officers speculated that AOL employees may have realized that the threat under investigation was an emergency, and that they had acted voluntarily under § 2702(c)(4). Once again, the court disagreed:

> The government may not circumvent the legal process specified in the ECPA pursuant to the "emergency" exception on such a speculative basis. This is not a situation where, on its own initiative, AOL voluntarily disclosed Plaintiff's subscriber information to the government. Instead, the government's request, submitted with an invalid warrant, triggered AOL's response, six days later. The Court declines to speculate whether it would ever be appropriate, under exigent circumstances when it would not be feasible to get a signed warrant or comply with

other legal process, for the government to notify the ISP of an emergency and receive subscriber information without conforming with the ECPA.

Id. at 128. Do you think such emergency disclosures should fall under § 2702 or § 2703?

4. In McVeigh v. Cohen, 983 F. Supp. 215 (D.D.C. 1998), a Navy Lieutenant who was a member of the JAG Corps was investigating the sexual orientation of a Naval serviceman named McVeigh under the policy commonly known as "Don't Ask, Don't Tell." An AOL profile for the screenname "boysrch" indicated that the account holder for "boysrch" was gay, and the Lieutenant had reason to believe that McVeigh owned the "boyrsrch" account. The Lieutenant asked another serviceman to contact AOL and determine if the AOL screenname belonged to McVeigh. The serviceman called AOL's customer service number and falsely claimed to be a third party in receipt of a fax sheet who needed confirmation that the AOL profile belonged to McVeigh. The AOL representative fell for the serviceman's ruse and affirmatively identified McVeigh as the owner of "boysrch."

Did AOL's disclosure violate the SCA? If so, what section was violated, and who violated it?

5. Disclosure of customer-related records by public providers is forbidden under § 2702 unless one of the statutory exceptions applies. The exceptions appear in § 2702(b) for contents and § 2702(c) for non-content records. For the most part, these exceptions resemble analogous exceptions from the Wiretap Act and the Fourth Amendment.

Some of the § 2702 exceptions mirror analogous exceptions in the Wiretap Act. For example, the SCA has a consent exception, *see* § 2702(b)(3) (contents), § 2702(c)(2) (non-content records), and also has a provider exception, *see* § 2702(b)(5) (contents), § 2702(c)(3) (non-content records). Presumably these exceptions have the same meaning in the context of the SCA that they have in the context of the Wiretap Act.

18 U.S.C. § 2702 also has an emergency exception that is somewhat analogous to the exigent circumstances exception to the Fourth Amendment's warrant requirement. The emergency exception permits disclosure "to a governmental entity, if the provider, in good faith, believes that an emergency involving danger of death or serious physical injury to any person requires disclosure without delay of [communications or information] relating to the emergency." 18 U.S.C. § 2702(b)(8) (contents), § 2702(c)(4) (non-content records).

Section 2702(b)(7) contains an exception for contents that is roughly analogous to the Fourth Amendment's plain view exception. It states that the disclosure of contents is permitted "to a law enforcement agency ... if the contents (i) were inadvertently obtained by the service provider; and (ii) appear to pertain to the commission of a crime." 18 U.S.C. § 2702(b)(7).

Perhaps the most unique exceptions in § 2702 are the reporting requirements in § 2702(b)(6) and § 2702(c)(5) involving reports to the National Center for Missing and Exploited Children mandated by 47 U.S.C. § 13032. 47 U.S.C. § 13032 imposes a reporting requirement on public providers of

ECS and RCS for evidence relating to child exploitation and child pornography crimes:

> Whoever, while engaged in providing an electronic communication service or a remote computing service to the public, through a facility or means of interstate or foreign commerce, obtains knowledge of facts or circumstances from which a violation of section 2251, 2251A, 2252, 2252A, 2252B, or 2260 of Title 18, involving child pornography (as defined in section 2256 of that title), or a violation of section 1466A of that title, is apparent, shall, as soon as reasonably possible, make a report of such facts or circumstances to the Cyber Tip Line at the National Center for Missing and Exploited Children, which shall forward that report to a law enforcement agency or agencies designated by the Attorney General.

47 U.S.C. § 13032(b)(1).

6. Section 2702 does not prohibit the disclosure of non-content records when the disclosure is to a non-governmental entity. *See* 18 U.S.C. § 2702(a)(3). Why?

7. Imagine that a public ISP is hacked, and a system administrator at the ISP conducts warrantless monitoring of the intrusions under exceptions to the Wiretap Act and Pen Register statute. The ISP wishes to disclose the evidence to the FBI for criminal prosecution. Assuming that the monitoring and disclosure comply with the Pen Register statute and the Wiretap Act, does the disclosure automatically satisfy the SCA?

The proper answer is "no," although as a practical matter the SCA will bar disclosures in such cases only very rarely. The SCA will permit the disclosure in the great majority of cases for three possible reasons.

The first reason is that the disclosure prohibitions in § 2702 only regulate records that "pertain[] to a subscriber to or customer of such service." 18 U.S.C. § 2702(a)(3). That is, the SCA only limits the disclosure of information and communications belonging or referring to individual legitimate subscribers. In the case of a computer intrusion, the records an ISP might wish to disclose usually won't pertain to a legitimate subscriber, and thus § 2702 does not bar the disclosure. Hackers may have some rights against monitoring under the Wiretap Act and the Pen Register statute, but they have no rights against disclosure under § 2702 of the Stored Communications Act.

Second, if the ISP wishes to disclose records relating to a customer who is not implicated in the unlawful activity, the ISP can disclose the materials with the customer's consent. *See* 18 U.S.C. § 2702(b)(3) (contents), § 2702(c)(2) (non-content records). For example, if a hacker guesses Sarah's password and uses her account to engage in criminal activity, Sarah can consent to the disclosure of her account information to law enforcement.

Finally, § 2702 permits disclosure that is "necessarily incident ... to the rights or property" of the ISP, which will often permit the disclosure. *See* 18 U.S.C. § 2702(b)(5) (contents), § 2702(c)(5) (non-content records).

8. *Problem.* An anonymous person puts up a website purporting to be authored by you. The website contains a number of false and misleading statements about you. You contact the service provider that hosts the site,

and you ask the representative to tell you the name and contact information for the subscriber who set up and posted the site. Does 18 U.S.C. § 2702 apply, and if so, how? Can the service provider disclose the information to you voluntarily? What can you do to compel the host to disclose the information? As a matter of policy, what law should govern such situations?

9. The Stored Communications Act does not include a statutory suppression remedy. *See* 18 U.S.C. §§ 2707–08. What remedy should Congress impose for violations of 18 U.S.C. § 2702? When the provider errs instead of the government, is an exclusionary rule appropriate? If the only remedy is civil liability, who should be liable: the government or the providers? Should the answer be the same for § 2702 and § 2703 violations?

D. OVERVIEW AND PROBLEMS

Consider the following scholarly perspectives on the statutory privacy laws:

> The current statutory regime that has attempted to fill the void created by the judicial evisceration of the Fourth Amendment is inadequate because it results in the de facto watering down of the warrant and probable cause requirements of the Fourth Amendment. As warrants supported by probable cause are replaced by subpoenas and court orders supported by "articulable facts" that are "relevant" to an investigation, the role of the judge in the process is diminished to nothing more than a decorative seal of approval. In many circumstances, neither court orders nor subpoenas are required. The government can simply ask for the information. An individual's privacy is protected only by the vague and toothless privacy policies of the companies holding their information.

Daniel J. Solove, *Digital Dossiers and the Dissipation of Fourth Amendment Privacy*, 75 S. Cal. L. Rev. 1083, 1150–51 (2002).

> [T]he SCA offers far less protection for electronic communications than we might expect. The narrow definition of "electronic storage" drastically limits both the communications covered by the prohibition on private acquisition and the communications given the most robust protection against government acquisition. Some communications–such as opened communications held by nonpublic providers–fall entirely outside of the SCA. The outdated "remote computing service" concept may or may not capture some communications that fall outside of the "electronic storage" category, but the protections offered against governmental acquisition are so low as to raise constitutional questions. Even if the SCA did not raise constitutional questions, however, it raises significant policy questions, in that it attaches tremendous legal significance to seemingly trivial choices about how to construct and use an e-mail system.

Patricia L. Bellia, *Surveillance Law Through Cyberlaw's Lens*, 72 Geo. Wash. L. Rev. 1375, 1427 (2004).

Whether or not servers can be accused of being prone to gossip, there is no doubt that they will cooperate with government authorities when those authorities come calling, warrant or not, unless laws protective of privacy have been put in place before the knock at the door. Fortunately, such laws are, in most respects, already in place for U.S. citizens, ensuring a broad scope of constitutional and statutory safeguards that almost provide us with a truly reasonable expectation of privacy. The trouble, of course, with the notion of "almost private" is that * * * sometimes almost-privacy is as bad as no privacy at all.

What to do at the margin? Congress should revisit its pen register statutes, clarifying its language to eliminate perilous ambiguities, and providing additional substantive protections so as to limit the ease with which the government can obtain sensitive information. The Supreme Court should rethink the reasoning of the *Smith* decision, especially in light of the capabilities of modern surveillance technologies. Finally, as citizens, we should demand clear lines that will unambiguously protect privacy rights[.]

David McPhie, *Almost Private: Pen Registers, Packet Sniffers, and Privacy at the Margin*, 2005 Stan. Tech. L. Rev. 1, 69–70.

Whenever I tell a layperson, or even a lawyer unfamiliar with electronic privacy laws, that the protections for e-mail vary depending upon the duration and location of its storage and whether it has been opened, and that the statutory protections afforded their remotely stored private Web diary or calendar falls short of Fourth Amendment protections, they look at me with disbelief. While clearly not a rigorous assessment, I believe their disbelief is indicative of a major gap between society's expectation of privacy and the privacy provided by current statutory law.

One reason for the current disconnect between privacy expectations and the statutory protections of the ECPA is that Congress was drafting legislation in the early stages of a technology that has fundamentally changed the way we communicate, store, and use information. E-mail links to commercial mail carriers, such as MCI Mail and Compuserve, would not be available until 1989. The first commercial provider of Internet dial-up access would not emerge until 1990. The World Wide Web and Web browsing functionality was released in 1991. The first cyberbank came online in 1994, at the same time electronic commerce sites began to appear. Private companies would not fully host the Internet backbone until 1995. Congress, with good reason, did not envision the pervasive role communications technology would come to play in our daily lives.

Deirdre K. Mulligan, *Reasonable Expectations in Electronic Communications: A Critical Perspective on the Electronic Communications Privacy Act*, 72 Geo. Wash. L. Rev. 1557, 1571–72 (2004).

I would give the current SCA a "B." On the positive side, the statute's basic mechanisms are sound. The statute creates a set of

Fourth Amendment-like rules in light of the uncertain application of Fourth Amendment protections to stored Internet files. It is a complex statute, but it is complex in part for the same reason that Fourth Amendment doctrine is complex: any effort to give a rule for every circumstance in which the government may obtain evidence must consider a wide range of facts, and the law should provide a context-sensitive rule to be followed for each set of facts. The SCA's distinctions and dichotomies try to recognize the important facts and set rules accordingly; in effect, the statute reflects an effort to codify the notion of Fourth Amendment reasonableness in the context of ISP interactions with law enforcement without the baggage of existing Fourth Amendment doctrine. It is a particularly remarkable achievement given that its enactment dates back to 1986. The SCA has weathered intervening technological advances surprisingly well.

At the same time, the SCA suffers from several flaws. It is more complicated than it needs to be. It has sections that are redundant and merely add confusion. The absence of a statutory suppression remedy has created significant uncertainty about how the statute works. The SCA also offers surprisingly low privacy protections when the government seeks to compel contents other than unretrieved communications held pending transmission for 180 days or less. The SCA needs significant legislative attention to bring its grade up from a "B" to an "A."

Orin S. Kerr, *A User's Guide to the Stored Communications Act, and A Legislator's Guide to Amending It*, 72 Geo. Wash. L. Rev. 1208, 1242–43 (2004).

The current legal framework for online surveillance ignores the lessons learned in the context of the Wiretap Act [as enacted in 1968]. Namely, the allure of electronic surveillance to law enforcement and its threat to privacy requires a comprehensive and workable framework that strictly limits government's ability to surveil and that affords myriad opportunities for oversight by members of the judiciary, Congress, and the public. As interpreted, and particularly as advocated by the Justice Department, the ECPA reduces to almost zero the number of investigations that will be accorded wiretap-like restrictions. Even then, victims of unlawful online surveillance lack a statutory suppression remedy. Most online surveillance proceeds without the involvement of the judiciary, and without meaningful remedies for abuse. The statutory framework persists in an outdated and nearly incomprehensible form. It leaves significant questions unanswered about the scope of governmental powers to surveil, even after the USA PATRIOT Act.

Unless we are convinced that there should be no privacy on the Internet, or that there should be no privacy in our modern era, the system of online surveillance law warrants revision. The similarities among online surveillance, video surveillance, and traditional electronic surveillance suggest that the legal framework that protects the privacy of telephones and private spaces should be extended to protect the privacy of the Internet.

Susan Freiwald, *Online Surveillance: Remembering the Lessons of the Wiretap Act*, 56 Ala. L. Rev. 9, 83–84 (2004).

These comments prompt a number of important questions about the basic structure of the computer crime laws. Are the existing statutory privacy laws adequate? If not, is the answer to tweak existing law or to start from scratch?

If you could design a regime of statutory privacy laws to protect Internet communications, what would your regime look like? Would you distinguish content from non-content information? Would you treat prospective and retrospective surveillance under separate statutes? What thresholds would be required for the government to obtain court orders? Would providers be permitted to disclose information they had obtained? Should a suppression remedy exist for violations? How similar would your ideal regime be to existing statutory law?

It is also worthwhile to ask if Congress is up to the task of generating statutory privacy laws. Does the technology move too quickly for Congress to keep up? Should Congress get out of the way and let the Supreme Court create a regime of Internet surveillance law under the Fourth Amendment? If the courts should take over, what principles should guide them? If Congress continues to function as the primary expositor of Internet surveillance law, how might Congress restructure the law in the future?

Should the rules regulating online surveillance be similar to or different from the traditional rules regulating offline surveillance? Should the goal be to create new rules that mirror off-line privacy law, such that the statutory laws amount to a "virtual" Fourth Amendment? Alternatively, should the rules regulate Internet surveillance more strictly than Fourth Amendment law restricts physical searches? Should the rules provide less protection to the Internet than people receive in their homes?

Finally, how do existing statutory privacy laws measure up to traditional Fourth Amendment protections? Are traditional investigations governed by the Fourth Amendment likely to have greater or lesser judicial oversight than computer crime investigations? Are investigations involving digital evidence easier, harder, or about the same for investigators compared to traditional investigations involving physical evidence?

––––––

In each of the following problems, consider whether the investigation violated any of the statutory privacy laws or the Fourth Amendment.

Problem One

You are a law student at Kennedy University. You find out that someone is using your Hotmail e-mail account without your permission and is sending out all sorts of e-mails in your name. You suspect that this "someone" is fellow law student Fred Rowley, your arch enemy, who uses an e-mail account frowley@law.kennedy.edu.

You contact the FBI for help. An FBI agent calls both Hotmail and the computer center at Kennedy University asking for their help to catch Fred. Both are eager to help. The contact at Hotmail agrees to send the FBI all of the stored e-mails and account records relating to your account, and the system administrator at Kennedy University agrees to do the same with Fred's stored e-mails and account records.

The system administrator at Kennedy University also agrees to monitor Rowley's account prospectively, albeit in a limited way. He writes a program that logs the IP address of every login to Rowley's account and sends the results to the FBI every few days to keep the FBI informed of Rowley's whereabouts.

When all the e-mails and records are in, however, it turns out that Rowley is not the individual who is using your account.

Problem Two

John Jefferson is a system administrator for an online auction site, www.better-than-ebay.com. One day, Jefferson notices that the server is acting strangely, and he suspects that the site may have been accessed by an intruder. Jefferson pulls up the server logs and quickly sees that yes, a hacker coming in from the IP address 152.163.159.233 had connected to the network a few hours earlier. Jefferson knows that this IP address is controlled by the ISP MindThink, and concludes that someone using a MindThink account hacked into his network.

Jefferson is terribly worried. He decides that he will try to catch the intruder in the act the next time and watch his every move. Jefferson installs a sniffer on his network and configures it to record all incoming information originating from any IP address belonging to MindThink. Whenever any MindThink user connects to www.better-than-ebay.com, the sniffer will record everything.

Over the course of the next few days, the sniffer collects a tremendous amount of data unrelated to the hacking, including thousands of requests for webpages and hundreds of messages sent to www.better-than-ebay.com by MindThink subscribers who are legitimate users of the auction site. The sniffer also picks up the hacker re-entering the auction site server. The sniffer records the commands that the hacker entered, enabling Jefferson to reconstruct that the hacker broke in to the network, looked around, and then read opened and unopened e-mail of the auction site employees who have work e-mail accounts stored on the auction site server.

Jefferson contacts the FBI, and speaks with FBI Special Agent Mary Markley. Jefferson tells Markley what happened and volunteers to send

Markley copies of all of the documents he has collected. Markley agrees and opens a criminal investigation into the computer intrsion incident. Jefferson sends Markley copies of all of the logs, the entire output of the sniffer, and the employee e-mails stored on the server belonging to www.better-than-ebay.com.

Problem Three

FBI Special Agent Free Louis is undercover in an America Online chatroom called "helikesthemyoung," using the screenname "britney14f." An individual in the chat room who uses the screenname "FunTimeinCA" sends an instant message to "britney14f" asking if she "likes to party with older men."

Special Agent Louis suspects that the person who controls "FunTimein-CA" is a pedophile in possession of child pornography. To confirm his suspicions, Louis serves a subpoena on AOL ordering AOL to disclose a) the name and billing address on file associated with the screenname "FunTimeinCA," b) any additional screennames associated with the account, and c) any images of child pornography stored as an attachment in any e-mail sent from or to that account that is stored with AOL.

An AOL employee receives the subpoena and attempts to comply with it. First, he accesses AOL's computer and prints out a page containing all of the basic subscriber information listed in 18 U.S.C. § 2703(c)(2) relating to the "FunTimeinCA" account. The page includes the alternative screennames associated with the "FunTimeinCA" account.

The AOL employee then looks through the stored e-mail in the account. The AOL employee finds nine images of what appear to be child pornography. He sends a fax to Special Agent Louis containing the page of basic subscriber information and the nine images.

Chapter 7

JURISDICTION

Traditional crimes usually occur in a single jurisdiction. The evidence is collected locally, and charges are brought under state criminal codes. Computer crimes are different. The borderless Internet makes jurisdictional issues routine. In most computer crime cases, the defendant, intermediaries, and the victim are located in different states—and sometimes in different countries. The Internet is borderless but the law is not, resulting in complex questions of both substantive and procedural law.

This chapter considers the jurisdictional questions that arise frequently in computer crime cases. The first part of the chapter considers the role of federal law. Does the borderless nature of the Internet make all computer crime law federal computer crime law? What are the limits on federal power to regulate computer crimes?

The second part turns to the role of the states in the enforcement of computer crime law. What powers do states have to prohibit interstate computer crimes? How are state authorities governing the collection of digital evidence different from analogous federal authorities? How can state investigators collect digital evidence located beyond state borders?

The third part of the chapter turns to international computer crimes. When is an international computer crime a violation of United States law? Procedurally, what laws govern the collection of evidence outside the United States needed for computer crime prosecutions inside the United States? What laws govern the collection of evidence inside the United States for prosecutions abroad?

As you read these materials, consider the role of uniformity. The borderless Internet exerts strong pressures toward uniform computer crime laws. Uniform laws simplify both the investigation and prosecution of criminal activity. Is uniformity desirable? What are the alternatives?

A. FEDERAL POWER

This book has focused largely on federal law; the materials in this section will help explain why. Congress has almost limitless power to regulate computer crimes, and statutory jurisdictional hurdles usually are easy to meet. This section considers the limits of federal criminal law in domestic computer crime investigations. It analyzes three questions: First, what constitutional limits exist on the ability of Congress to punish computer crimes in the United States? Second, what evidence is required to establish statutory jurisdictional hooks, such as interstate commerce requirements? Third, what procedural limits exist on how federal investigators can gather digital evidence located in different states?

1. CONSTITUTIONAL LIMITS

Most federal computer crimes have been enacted under the Congressional power "[t]o regulate Commerce ... among the several States" granted by Article I, Section 8, Clause 3 of the United States Constitution. The Supreme Court has construed the Commerce Clause power very broadly. United States v. Lopez, 514 U.S. 549, 558–59 (1995), explains the three basic types of conduct that can be regulated under the Commerce Clause:

> First, Congress may regulate the use of the channels of interstate commerce. Second, Congress is empowered to regulate and protect the instrumentalities of interstate commerce, or persons or things in interstate commerce, even though the threat may come only from intrastate activities. Finally, Congress' commerce authority includes the power to regulate those activities having a substantial relation to interstate commerce, i.e., those activities that substantially affect interstate commerce.

Federal statutes that regulate the telephone network and the Internet are generally covered by the first and second categories, as interstate communications networks are considered both channels and instrumentalities of interstate commerce. As the Eleventh Circuit emphasized in United States v. Hornaday, 392 F.3d 1306, 1311 (11th Cir. 2004):

> The Internet is an instrumentality of interstate commerce. Congress clearly has the power to regulate the Internet, as it does other instrumentalities and channels of interstate commerce, and to prohibit its use for harmful or immoral purposes regardless of whether those purposes would have a primarily intrastate impact.

See also United States v. Gilbert, 181 F.3d 152 (1st Cir. 1999) (holding that the telephone network is an instrumentality of interstate commerce, even when a specific call in question is intrastate); United States v. Carnes, 309 F.3d 950 (6th Cir. 2002) (upholding the Wiretap Act as a valid regulation of interstate commerce because "telecommunications are both channels and instrumentalities of interstate commerce"); United States v. Mitra, 405 F.3d 492, 496 (7th Cir. 2005) ("Section 1030 is within the national power as applied to computer-based channel-switching communications systems."). Such broad readings of the Commerce Clause give Congress broad and unquestioned authority to regulate interstate computer networks and the Internet.

The harder questions arise in cases that involve stand-alone computers. For example, the child pornography laws prohibit producing or possessing child pornography images within one state when the images are "produced using materials that have been mailed, or shipped or transported" in interstate commerce. 18 U.S.C. § 2252(a)(4)(B), § 2252A(a)(5)(B), § 2251(a). The law does not require that the images have been transported in interstate commerce, or that they have been distributed or received over the Internet. Rather, it generally prohibits the storage of images on the ground that the materials used to produce the materials have themselves been transported in interstate commerce. Is this prohibition within the scope of Congressional power?

UNITED STATES v. JERONIMO–BAUTISTA

United States Court of Appeals for the Tenth Circuit, 2005.
425 F.3d 1266.

SEYMOUR, Circuit Judge.

Virgilio Jeronimo–Bautista was indicted, in part, for coercing a minor to engage in sexually explicit conduct "for the purpose of producing visual depictions of such conduct using materials that have been transported in interstate and foreign commerce," in violation of 18 U.S.C. § 2251(a). The district court dismissed the charge, concluding that as applied to Mr. Jeronimo–Bautista, § 2251(a) exceeded Congress' authority under the Commerce Clause. The government appeals, and we reverse.

I

While Mr. Jeronimo–Bautista asserts he is actually innocent, for the purposes of our review * * * we make all factual inferences in favor of the government, assuming it could prove the facts alleged against Mr. Jeronimo–Bautista at a trial. Accordingly, for the purposes of this appeal only, we assume the following facts.

On January 29, 2004, Mr. Jeronimo–Bautista and two other men, while in the company of a thirteen year-old girl, entered a vacant residence in Magna, Utah. At some point the girl became unconscious, possibly after ingesting an intoxicating substance. After she lost consciousness, the three men removed her clothing, sexually assaulted her, and took photographs of their actions. The camera used to take the photographs was not manufactured in the state of Utah.

One of the men took the film to a one-hour photo lab for processing. In the course of developing the film, staff at the lab noticed images that appeared to depict the sexual assault of a minor female. The manager of the lab called the police, who viewed the photographs and then initiated an investigation resulting in the arrest and indictment of Mr. Jeronimo–

Bautista. As noted by the district court, it was undisputed that Mr. Jeronimo–Bautista was a citizen of Mexico and resided in the State of Utah. The victim was born in Utah and was not transported across state lines in connection with the acts charged in the indictment. Moreover, the photos were never disseminated, were not stored or transmitted electronically via the Internet, the United States Postal Service, nor by any other method across state lines or internationally.

The indictment charged that Mr. Jeronimo–Bautista, along with the two other men, did knowingly employ, use, persuade, induce, entice, and coerce a minor to engage in sexually explicit conduct for the purpose of producing visual depictions of such conduct, which visual depictions were produced using materials that have been mailed, shipped, and transported in interstate and foreign commerce, and did aid and abet each other therein, thereby violating § 2251(a) (production of child pornography) and 18 U.S.C. § 2 (aiding and abetting). Mr. Jeronimo–Bautista moved to dismiss the indictment on the ground that the district court did not have subject matter jurisdiction over the acts charged against him, contending § 2251(a) violated the Commerce Clause as applied to him. The district court agreed, concluding that Mr. Jeronimo–Bautista's charged activity "was not of a type demonstrated to be substantially connected or related to interstate commerce." This case is now before us on the government's appeal.

II

The United States Constitution grants to Congress the power to regulate Commerce among the several States. U.S. Const. art I, § 8, cl. 3. As relevant here, "Congress' commerce authority includes the power to regulate those activities having a substantial relation to interstate commerce, i.e., those activities that substantially affect interstate commerce." *United States v. Lopez*, 514 U.S. 549, 558–59 (1995). Hence we must determine whether Mr. Jeronimo–Bautista's local production of pornographic images of a child substantially affects interstate commerce.

In addressing Mr. Jeronimo–Bautista's as applied challenge to the statute, the district court noted the four factors delineated by the Supreme Court in *United States v. Morrison*, 529 U.S. 598 (2000), and in *Lopez* for consideration in addressing the constitutionality of a statute based upon Commerce Clause authority. The court accurately described those factors as (1) whether the prohibited activity is commercial or economic in nature; (2) whether the statute's reach was limited by an express jurisdictional element; (3) whether Congress made findings about the effects of the prohibited conduct on interstate commerce; and (4) whether there exists a link between the prohibited conduct and the effect on interstate commerce.

Working its way through the *Lopez/Morrison* factors, the district court first rejected the argument that Mr. Jeronimo–Bautista's activity was economic in nature and, in doing so, rejected the assertion that Mr. Jeronimo–Bautista's intrastate activities could, in the aggregate, affect interstate commerce. Second, the court determined § 2251(a)'s express jurisdictional element failed to place any meaningful restrictions on federal jurisdiction and failed to establish the link between the violation and interstate commerce. Third, the court was not convinced the existence of Congressional findings regarding the child pornography industry was sufficient, by itself, to sustain the constitutionality of Commerce Clause legislation as applied to the facts of this case. Finally, referring back to its determination that Mr. Jeronimo–Bautista's activity could not be deemed economic in nature, the court also rejected the use of an aggregation theory to support the argument that there existed something more than only a tenuous link between Mr. Jeronimo–Bautista's prohibited activity and interstate commerce. The court dismissed the indictment against Mr. Jeronimo–Bautista on the grounds that as applied to the specific facts of his case, § 2251(a) violated the Commerce Clause.

Pending this appeal, the Supreme Court decided *Gonzales v. Raich*, 125 S. Ct. 2195 (2005), in which it rejected an as applied challenge to the Controlled Substances Act (CSA), 21 U.S.C. § 801 *et seq.*, and held that Congress could regulate the purely local production, possession, and use of marijuana for personal medical purposes. As we discuss in more detail below, the Court's reasoning in *Raich*, coupled with the standard four factor *Lopez/Morrison* analysis, supports our conclusion that the district court erred in concluding § 2251(a) violates the Commerce Clause as applied to Mr. Jeronimo–Bautista.

We begin by examining the findings accompanying the comprehensive scheme developed by Congress to eliminate the production, possession, and dissemination of child pornography. When Congress first passed the Protection of Children Against Sexual Exploitation Act of 1977, it noted "that child pornography has become a highly organized, multimillion dollar industry that operates on a nationwide scale and that the sale and distribution of such pornographic materials are carried on to a substantial extent through the mails and other instrumentalities of interstate and foreign commerce." S. Rep. No. 95–438, at 5 (1977), *reprinted in* 1978 U.S.C.C.A.N. 40, 42–43. Findings supporting the 1977 Act also noted that

> since the production, distribution and sale of child pornography is often a clandestine operation, it is extremely difficult to determine its full extent. At present, however, a wide variety of child pornography is available in most areas of the country. Moreover, because of the vast potential profits involved, it would appear that this sordid enterprise is growing at a rapid rate.

Id. at 43.

Amendments to the Act in 1984 eliminated the requirement that the production, receipt, transportation, or distribution of child pornography be for a pecuniary profit. The purpose of this amendment was to eliminate an enforcement gap in the statute: "Many of the individuals who distribute materials covered by the statute do so by gift or exchange without any commercial motive and thus remain outside the coverage of this provision." H.R. Rep. No. 98–536, at 2 (1983), *reprinted in* 1984 U.S.C.C.A.N. 492, 493. Likewise, in 1984, in support of § 2251, Congress echoed its findings supporting the original 1977 legislation, stating in part that "child pornography has developed into a highly organized, multi-million-dollar industry which operates on a nationwide scale." H.R. 3635, 98th Cong. (2nd Sess. 1984).

In 1996, Congress further amended the Act regarding the electronic creation of child pornography. The findings supporting those amend- ments noted that "the existence of child pornographic images inflames the desires of child molesters, pedophiles, and child pornographers who prey on children, thereby increasing the creation and distribution of child pornography." S. Rep. No. 104–358, at 2 (1996). Congress also stated that "prohibiting the possession and viewing of child pornography will encourage the possessors of such material to rid themselves of or destroy the material, thereby helping to protect the victims of child pornography and to eliminate the market for the sexual exploitative use of children." *Id.* at 3. Finally, in a 1998 amendment to the Act, a jurisdictional element was added to cover child pornography created "using materials that have been mailed, shipped, or transported in interstate or foreign commerce by any means." § 2251(a). This addition reflected Congress' concern about federal law enforcement's current inability to prosecute 'a number of cases where the defendant produced the child pornography but did not intend to transport the images in interstate commerce.

In reviewing this history, we acknowledge that Congress may not have engaged in specific fact finding regarding how the intrastate production of child pornography substantially affects the larger inter- state pornography market. But the Supreme Court noted in *Raich*, 125 S. Ct. at 2208, that it has "never required Congress to make particular- ized findings in order to legislate." Moreover, we agree with our col- leagues on the First Circuit that Congress' explicit findings regarding the extensive national market in child pornography and the need to diminish that national market support the contention that prohibiting the production of child pornography at the local level helps to further the Congressional goal.

The decision in *Raich* also supports the conclusion that Mr. Jeroni- mo–Bautista's production of the images in this case is economic in nature. "Economics refers to the production, distribution, and consump- tion of commodities." *Raich*, 125 S. Ct. at 2211. The Court held that the Controlled Substances Act "is a statute that regulates the production, distribution, and consumption of commodities for which there is an established, and lucrative, interstate market. Prohibiting the intrastate possession or manufacture of an article of commerce is a rational (and commonly utilized) means of regulating commerce in that product." *Id.* The same reasoning is applicable to the intrastate production of child pornography. Like the CSA, the child pornography statutes regulate the production, distribution, and consumption of commodities for which there is an established, and lucrative, interstate market. Congress' prohibition against the intrastate possession or manufacture of child pornography is a rational (and commonly utilized) means of regulating commerce in that product.

In holding that a sufficient link existed between the local production and use of marijuana and its effect on interstate commerce, the Court in *Raich* relied extensively on *Wickard v. Filburn*, 317 U.S. 111 (1942). In *Wickard*, the Court upheld the Agriculture Adjustment Act of 1938, 52 Stat. 31, which permitted congressional regulation of a farmer's wholly intrastate production and consumption of wheat on his farm. *Wickard* "establishes that Congress can regulate purely intrastate activity that is not itself 'commercial,' in that it is not produced for sale, if it concludes that failure to regulate that class of activity would undercut the regulation of the interstate market in that commodity." *Raich*, 125 S.Ct. at 2006. The Court noted that

> in *Wickard*, we had no difficulty concluding that Congress had a rational basis for believing that, when viewed in the aggregate, leaving home-consumed wheat outside the regulatory scheme would have a substantial influence on price and market conditions. Here too, Congress had a rational basis for concluding that leaving home-consumed marijuana outside federal control would similarly affect price and market conditions.

Id. at 2207. It viewed its task as not to determine whether respondents' activities, taken in the aggregate, substantially affect interstate commerce in fact, but only whether a 'rational basis' exists for so concluding.

Dismissing arguments that regulation of locally cultivated and possessed marijuana was beyond the "outer limits" of Congress' Commerce Clause authority, the Court observed:

> one need not have a degree in economics to understand why a nationwide exemption for the vast quantity of marijuana (or other drugs) locally cultivated for personal use (which presumably would include use by friends, neighbors, and family members) may have a substantial impact on the interstate market for this extraordinarily popular substance. The congressional judgment that an exemption for such a significant segment of the total market would undermine the orderly enforcement of the entire regulatory scheme is entitled to a strong presumption of validity.

Id. Finally, noting the "findings in the CSA and the undisputed magnitude of the commercial market for marijuana, the decisions in *Wickard v. Filburn* and the later cases endorsing its reasoning," the Court concluded Congress could regulate the "intrastate, noncommercial cultivation, possession and use of marijuana." *Id.* at 2215.

This reasoning applies to the child pornography statute at issue here. Under the aggregation theory espoused in *Wickard* and in *Raich*, the intrastate production of child pornography could, in the aggregate, have a substantial effect on the interstate market for such materials. In *Raich*, the respondents were "cultivating, for home consumption, a fungible commodity for which there was an established, albeit illegal, interstate market." *Id.* at 2206. Child pornography is equally fungible and there is no question an established market exists for its sale and exchange. The Court in *Raich* reasoned that where there is a high demand in the interstate market for a product, the exemption from regulation of materials produced intrastate "tends to frustrate the federal interest in eliminating commercial transactions in the interstate market in their entirety." *Id.* at 2207. For the same reasons, § 2251(a) is squarely within Congress' commerce power because production of the commodity meant for home consumption, be it wheat, marijuana, or child pornography has a substantial effect on supply and demand in the national market for the commodity.

Mr. Jeronimo–Bautista is challenging the statute's constitutionality as applied to him. The Court in *Raich* held the plaintiffs' as applied challenges to the CSA failed because the Court had no difficulty concluding that Congress acted rationally in determining that the intrastate, noncommercial, cultivation, possession, and use of marijuana for personal medical uses, whether viewed individually or in the aggregate, did not compel an exemption from the CSA. * * * So too in Mr. Jeronimo–Bautista's case. Congress' decision to deem illegal Mr. Jeronimo–Bautista's local production of child pornography represents a rational determination that such local activities constitute an essential part of the interstate market for child pornography that is well within Congress' power to regulate.

Notes and Questions

1. Can you distinguish the market in marijuana at issue in *Gonzales v. Raich* from the market for child pornography images at issue in this case?

2. Federal child pornography laws prohibit producing or possessing child pornography images within one state when the images are "produced using materials that have been mailed, or shipped or transported" in interstate commerce. 18 U.S.C. § 2252(a)(4)(B), § 2252A(a)(5)(B), § 2251(a). Is this jurisdictional hook constitutionally required? Under *Gonzales v. Raich*, as interpreted in *Jeronimo–Bautista*, could Congress remove this requirement and simply prohibit possessing images of child pornography?

3. Is any computer crime beyond the Commerce Clause power? Can you envision any criminal activity involving any kind of computer that cannot be regulated by the federal government?

2. SUBSTANTIVE STATUTORY LIMITS

As the preceding materials suggest, Congress has virtually plenary authority to punish computer-related activity in the United States. Most statutes do not go this far, of course. Federal computer crime statutes ordinarily impose some kind of statutory interstate requirement that the government must satisfy in each prosecution.

UNITED STATES v. KAMMERSELL

United States Court of Appeals for the Tenth Circuit, 1999.
196 F.3d 1137.

PAUL KELLY, JR., Circuit Judge.

Defendant–Appellant Matthew Joseph Kammersell entered a conditional guilty plea to a charge of transmitting a threatening communication in interstate commerce, in violation of 18 U.S.C. § 875(c). Upon recommendation of the magistrate judge, the district court rejected Mr. Kammersell's contention that federal jurisdiction did not exist because both he and the recipient of the threat were located in the same state when the transmission occurred. He was sentenced to four months imprisonment, and twenty-four months supervised release. Our jurisdiction arises under 28 U.S.C. § 1291 and we affirm.

BACKGROUND

The facts in this case are undisputed. On January 16, 1997, Mr. Kammersell, then nineteen years old, logged on to the Internet service provider America OnLine from his home computer in Riverdale, Utah. Mr. Kammersell's girlfriend was employed at AOL's service center in Ogden, Utah. He sent a bomb threat to her computer terminal via instant message, hoping that the threat would enable her to leave work early so they could go on a date.

When he sent the bomb threat, it was automatically transmitted through interstate telephone lines from his computer in Utah to the AOL server in Virginia and then back to Utah to his girlfriend's terminal at the Ogden service center. Every message sent via AOL automatically goes from the state of origin to AOL's main server in Virginia before going on to its final destination. This pattern of transmission is the same whether the communication is an electronic mail message or an instant message.

Mr. Kammersell does not contest that the threat traveled out of Utah to Virginia before returning to Utah. Nor does he contest that his message constituted a sufficient "threat" to trigger § 875(c). His only claim is that the jurisdictional element of § 875(c) cannot be met if based solely on the route of the transmission, where the sender and recipient are both in the same state.

DISCUSSION

The district court's refusal to dismiss the case on jurisdictional grounds was based upon its interpretation of § 875(c), therefore, its conclusion is reviewed de novo. Section 875(c) provides:

> Whoever transmits in interstate or foreign commerce any communication containing any threat to kidnap any person or any threat to injure the person of another, shall be fined under this title or imprisoned not more than five years, or both.

This provision was enacted in 1934, and its last significant amendment was in 1939. At that time, the telegraph was still the primary mode of interstate communication.

Mr. Kammersell argues that the statute must be interpreted in light of the sweeping changes in technology over the past 60 years and with reference to Congressional intent. The government urges the court to adhere to the plain meaning of the statute; because Mr. Kamersell's threat was transmitted from Utah to Virginia to Utah, it was "transmitted in interstate commerce." Because so many local telephone calls and locally-sent Internet messages are routed out of state, under the government's interpretation, federal jurisdiction would exist to cover almost any communication made by telephone or modem, no matter how much it would otherwise appear to be intrastate in nature. Mr. Kammersell argues that such an interpretation will immeasurably broaden federal criminal jurisdiction without any discussion by Congress of the matter, and it would be wrong to view sixty years of Congressional inaction on the statute as clear intent.

This may be a compelling argument that Congress should re-examine the statute, but it cannot remove Mr. Kammersell from the reach of the current statute. A federal court must give effect to the will of Congress, and where its will has been expressed in reasonably plain terms, that language must ordinarily be regarded as conclusive. As long as the statutory scheme is coherent and consistent, there generally is no need for a court to inquire beyond the plain language of the statute. A threat that was unquestionably transmitted over interstate telephone lines falls within the literal scope of the statute and gives rise to federal jurisdiction.

Mr. Kammersell argues that the threat should not be considered as transmitted interstate because only the recipient could have viewed this instant message. An instant message can only be sent if the recipient is online at the time of transmission, whereas an e-mail may be held in a holding center until it is retrieved. According to Mr. Kammersell, this distinction is crucial because it means that no one outside of the State of Utah could have seen the threat. The distinction, even if correct, is immaterial. No requirement exists under § 875(c) that the threat actually be received or seen by anyone out of state. The gravamen of the crime is the threat itself.

The "instant message" distinction does enable Kammersell to distinguish the primary case upon which the Government relies, but in the end this does not help him either. Because this is a case of first impression, both sides must rely on analogies. The Government relies upon *United States v. Kelner,* 534 F.2d 1020 (2d Cir. 1976). There, the defendant was convicted under § 875(c) for threatening to assassinate Yasser Arafat during a television interview that was broadcast over three states. Both the defendant and Arafat were in New York at the time the threat was made. Like Mr. Kammersell, Kelner argued that the nexus of his activity was predominantly local, and that the statute should not be read literally to reach into spheres of primarily local concern. In upholding Kelner's conviction, the court noted:

> However much we might agree as a matter of principle that the congressional reach should not be overextended or that prosecutorial discretion might be exercised more frequently to permit essentially local crimes to be prosecuted locally, we do not feel that Congress is powerless to regulate matters in commerce when the interstate features of the activity represent a relatively small, or in a sense unimportant, portion of the overall criminal scheme. Our problem is not whether the nexus of the activity is "local" or "interstate"; rather, under the standards which we are to apply, so long as the crime involves a necessary interstate element, the statute must be treated as valid.

Id at 1024. While *Kelner* can be distinguished on the ground that it involved a transmission that was seen by people in more than one state, the Second Circuit's logic remains just as cogent when applied to the current case.

Finally, Mr. Kammersell contends that, based on the spirit of the Supreme Court's decision in *United States v. Lopez*, 514 U.S. 549 (1995), federal jurisdiction is inappropriate in this case. "*Lopez* stands for the proposition that Congress may not limitlessly expand the federal criminal jurisdiction based on the commerce clause," and "after *Lopez* the constitutionality of assertions of federal jurisdiction over what are essentially local crimes must be closely scrutinized." Aplt. Br. at 34. Yet, we cannot overlook plain language in favor of the "spirit" of *Lopez*, particularly given the difference between the deficient statute in *Lopez*, 18 U.S.C. § 922(q)(1)(A), and § 875(c). The deficient statute in *Lopez* did not require an interstate jurisdictional nexus. *See Lopez*, 514 U.S. at 561 (noting that statute does not contain a requirement that would ensure that the firearm possession in question would affect interstate commerce). Because § 875(c) requires the use of a channel of interstate commerce, it is not subject to the same limiting interpretation as *Lopez*.

Notes and Questions

1. The federal interstate threat statute is phrased in general terms. It covers "any communication" transmitted in interstate or foreign commerce. Under *Kammersell*, this means that the scope of the statute depends on the technical details of the network. If AOL configured its networks so that the instant message stayed inside Utah, the federal statute apparently would not apply. But AOL's technical decision to route all IMs through Virginia seems to ensure that all IMs are covered by the federal statute (except those from one person in Virginia to another person in Virginia). Does this make sense? Should the communication's physical path make a difference?

2. Should it matter whether Matthew Kammersell knew that the instant message he sent traveled out of Utah in the course of delivery? According to one news report, Kammersell was a former employee of AOL.

The prosecutor in the case argued that Kammersell presumably knew that his threat traveled to Virginia and back in the course of delivery. *See* Sheila R. McCann, *'Net Threat A Federal Offense?; Prosecutors Argue It Crossed State Lines*, Salt Lake Trib. Oct. 14, 1997, at A1. In other cases, however, the defendant may have no idea that his communication is going to travel interstate. Should the defendant's awareness of the interstate nexus make a difference?

The general rule is that when a federal criminal statute is based on the Commerce Clause power, knowledge of an interstate nexus is not required as matter of statutory law. *See* United States v. Darby, 37 F.3d 1059, 1067 (4th Cir. 1994); United States v. Blackmon, 839 F.2d 900, 907 (2d Cir. 1988). Cases involving telephone calls illustrate the principle. In United States v. Francis, 975 F. Supp. 288 (S.D.N.Y. 1997), *rev'd on other grounds*, 164 F.3d 120 (2d Cir. 1999), the defendant placed several telephone calls from Santa Cruz, California, to San Francisco, California. The victim did not pick up the call, and the defendant left threatening messages for the victim on his voicemail. Unbeknownst to the defendant, the defendant had implemented a "call forwarding" feature on his telephone, and the messages were automatically routed to New York instead of to San Francisco. The district court held that the calls satisfied the jurisdictional nexus because they had been sent from California and were received in New York. *See id.* at 291–92.

An unpublished decision, United States v. Veliz, 2004 WL 964005 (S.D.N.Y. 2004), reflects a similar dynamic. Veliz called Arreaga's cell phone from New York and threatened to kill him. Although Arreaga's cell phone was registered to a New York-area number, Arreaga answered the call when he was in Palm Beach, Florida. The Court refused to dismiss the indictment on jurisdictional grounds, noting that the call had originated in New York and had been received in Florida.

3. Assuming Kammersell's conduct fell within the federal threat statute, we are still left with the interesting question of why he was prosecuted. The full text of the bomb threat is unknown, as is the reaction of AOL to the threat. One news clip on Kammersell's arrest makes the threat seem fairly innocuous. According to that report, the threat included the following:

> You should really check out those new keyboards, if you know what I mean, . . . We are sick of your censorship and bad service. You can kiss your assess [sic] goodbye.

High-Tech Bomb Scare, Salt Lake Trib, March 8, 1997, at B2.

Following his conviction and sentencing to four months in prison, Kammersell was interviewed by a reporter and had the following comment:

> I do recognize what I did was wrong . . . I just think this is going too far for a prank. It's like putting me in front of a firing squad for throwing an apple.

Ray Rivera, *Cyber-Prank Earns Prison Term*, Salt Lake Trib., October 16, 1998, at D6. Why do you think Kammersell was prosecuted?

4. *The scope of 18 U.S.C. § 1030.* 18 U.S.C. § 1030(e)(2)(B) states that a "protected computer" includes a computer:

which is used in interstate or foreign commerce or communication, including a computer located outside the United States that is used in a manner that affects interstate or foreign commerce or communication of the United States[.]

Does the word "used" in this definition mean used regularly? Used occasionally? Or does it require use in interstate or foreign commerce or communication *in the particular offense?*

Imagine you are sitting with your laptop computer at a coffee shop. Your computer has wireless capabilities that are enabled to let you surf the web using the coffee shop's wireless network. If a person comes up to your computer and starts viewing your files, is your computer a "protected computer"? Does it depend on whether you have connected to the coffee shop's network at that particular time? What if you disable your wireless network card? Is your computer still "used in interstate or foreign commerce or communication"?

5. The federalization of computer crime law partially reflects broader trends. Consider Edwin Meese, *Big Brother on the Beat: The Expanding Federalization of Crime*, 1 Tex. Rev. L. & Pol. 1, 2–4 (1997):

> "We federalize everything that walks, talks, and moves," said Senator Joseph R. Biden, Jr., Chairman of the Senate Judiciary Committee from 1986–1994. Unfortunately, this is not much of an exaggeration; there are well over 3,000 federal crimes today. And this number does not include the 10,000 regulatory requirements that carry criminal penalties. Few crimes, no matter how local in nature, are beyond the reach of the federal criminal jurisdiction. For example, the following is a representative sample of serious, but purely local, crimes that have been duplicated in the federal code: virtually all drug crimes, carjacking, blocking an abortion clinic, failure to pay child support, drive-by shootings, possession of a handgun near a school, possession of a handgun by a juvenile, embezzlement from an insurance company, and murder of a state official assisting a federal law enforcement agent. While most of these crimes pose real threats to public safety, they are outlawed by the states already and need not be duplicated in the federal criminal code.
>
> The federalization of crime also includes trivial crimes that further clog the federal code. The following is a sampling of actual federal crimes: damaging a livestock facility, unauthorized reproduction of the "Smokey the Bear" image, transporting artificial teeth into a state without permission, theft of a major artwork, writing checks for less than a dollar, and falsely impersonating a 4–H member. Unfortunately, the federalization of criminal offenses is on the rise.

See also Sara Sun Beale, *The Many Faces of Overcriminalization: From Morals and Mattress Tags to Overfederalization*, 54 Am. U. L. Rev. 747, 753–56 (2005).

UNITED STATES v. HENRIQUES

United States Court of Appeals for the Fifth Circuit, 2000.
234 F.3d 263.

DONALD C. POGUE, Judge.

Defendant-appellant Bart Henriques appeals his conviction on one count of possession of child pornography in violation of 18 U.S.C. § 2252A(a)(5)(B). The district court sentenced Henriques to 42 months imprisonment, followed by three years of supervised release. Henriques appeals on several grounds. The outcome of the case turns on one issue: whether the evidence is sufficient to support a finding that the images were transported in interstate commerce. We agree with Henriques that the evidence does not support such a finding. We, therefore, reverse the conviction.

FACTS AND PRIOR PROCEEDINGS

In February 1998, Warren County's Sheriff's Department was contacted about a runaway teenage girl named Gabrielle Phillips. The Sheriff's Department discovered Phillips at Henriques' apartment. In the process of searching for Phillips, the Sheriff's Department learned of several other children who visited Henriques' apartment and that Henriques often used his computer to view both child and adult pornography in the youths' presence. After Phillips' removal from Henriques' apartment, Henriques was called into the Office of Internal Affairs at the Vicksburg Police Department. There, at the Department's request, he voluntarily consented to a search of his apartment, putting his consent in writing. The police then searched Henriques' apartment during which time Henriques' computer was seized and taken into custody.

In March 1998, FBI Special Agent Jeffrey Artis took the computer into FBI custody and transported it for examination by a bureau computer expert. At this time, without turning on the computer, a "mirror" copy of the computer's hard drive was made. Upon review of this copy, several files containing pornography, all organized into subdirectories, were found on the computer.

At trial approximately seventeen images found on Henriques' computer were put into evidence. The jury concluded that three images, Exhibits G–11, G–20, and G–21, fell within the behavior prohibited by 18 U.S.C. § 2252A. As a result of the jury's finding, Henriques was convicted.

SUFFICIENCY OF EVIDENCE

The statute mandates that at least three of the images in the defendant's possession traveled in interstate commerce. This includes any image "that has been mailed, or shipped or transported in interstate or foreign commerce by any means, including by computer." 18 U.S.C. § 2252A(a)(5)(B)(1997). Transport of the goods through interstate commerce is an element of the crime which the government must prove to obtain a conviction. Henriques contends that the government failed to prove this element.

The requirement in 18 U.S.C. § 2252A that child pornography be transported in interstate commerce raises two issues. First, to what extent must the government prove that the image came from the Internet. Second, does proof that a picture was downloaded from the Internet satisfy the jurisdictional nexus of "interstate commerce."

Although this court has not previously addressed the extent of the government's burden in connecting the specific images to the Internet, the Tenth Circuit has already developed a test to ensure that the government satisfies its burden. The Tenth Circuit requires the government to independently link all the images upon which a conviction is based to the Internet. *See United States v. Wilson*, 182 F.3d 737, 744 (10th Cir. 1999) (holding evidence linking one diskette to interstate commerce was not sufficient to allow an inference that the other two diskettes were similarly linked). This standard limits the government's ability to build a case on inferences, e.g., by analogizing that since one image was downloaded from the Internet, the rest of the images must also be connected to the Internet.

The transport of images through interstate commerce, as an element of the crime, must be proved beyond a reasonable doubt. Requiring the government to independently link each image to interstate commerce is therefore necessary and appropriate in order that the government satisfies its burden. If we did not require the government to independently link each image to interstate commerce, we would allow the government to obtain a conviction without proving beyond a reasonable doubt each element of the crime. Therefore, we adopt the Tenth Circuit's position.

In this case, the government presented little evidence connecting all the images to the Internet independently. Indeed, as to one of the images, the government presented no evidence connecting it to the Internet. It is not disputed that the evidence supports a finding that Henriques accessed the Internet. Nor is it disputed that Henriques' computer contained pornographic material. The required jurisdictional nexus between the images and interstate commerce, however, was not established.

The government established that Henriques owned a computer and subscribed to an Internet Service Provider. Through this service, Henriques was able to access and view images on the Internet. His computer also contained pornographic images, which were located on his hard drive. These images were stored in separate folders on his computer. The evidence clearly supports a finding that these folders were consciously created. Also, since Henriques owned the computer, the computer was found in his apartment, and he was the only adult living in the apartment, the jury could reasonably conclude that the evidence establishes that Henriques was the individual responsible for the images found on the hard drive.

Despite this evidence, at trial, no evidence was introduced by the government to establish whether the images came from a website, were downloaded from a floppy disk, or came from some other source, such as another hard drive. Rather, Agent Artis, in his trial testimony, argued that if images of nude children were on the hard drive, and that computer was connected to the Internet, somebody had to use the Internet to put them there.

In order to prove the connection between the images found on Henriques' hard drive and the Internet, the government relied on the testimony of one witness and internal evidence on some of the images. Witness testimony was introduced to prove that Henriques viewed pornographic images on the Internet.[1] This testimony, however, was only applicable for a few of the images, while the government introduced approximately seventeen images for deliberation by the jury. The attorney for the government also argued that the interstate commerce element of the statute was satisfied because website addresses were embedded on some of the images.

The government attorney, however, never discussed how the connection to the Internet can be made for the photographs with no internal evidence or without testimony connecting the images to the Internet. Rather, the government attempted to prove the Internet connection mainly through inferences. This, however, leaves a gap in the evidence.

Phillips, the girl found at Henriques' apartment, testified that Henriques used the Internet to view pornographic images in her presence. She identified a model in G–11 as one she saw Henriques view on the Internet. The government relied on Phillips' testimony to prove a connection between the images and the Internet. Although Phillips' testimony connects one image, G–11, to the Internet, her testimony cannot be used to infer that the other two images upon which Henriques' conviction is based, were also obtained from the Internet.

Of the other two images, one, G–21, contains a world-wide web address embedded on the image. Although, it is possible for this "internal evidence" to support a connection to the Internet for G–21, the government is still required to independently connect G–20 to the Internet. The third image, G–20, does not contain internal evidence. There was also no testimony introduced to connect this specific image to the Internet. Since there is no evidence to connect this last image, G–20, to the Internet, we find that there is not independent evidence connecting all three images to the Internet.[10]

Although the evidence clearly established Henriques use of the Internet, since the government did not attempt to prove the nexus to the

1. Phillips identified some of the images as ones she witnessed Henriques view on the Internet.

10. The failure of the government to meet its burden for all three images, ren-

ders it unnecessary to decide the issue of whether downloading an image from the Internet satisfies "interstate commerce."

Internet for the three images independently, Henriques' conviction must be reversed.

Notes and Questions

1.   *Henriques* assumes without deciding that a connection to the Internet satisfies the interstate commerce requirement. The court then reverses the conviction because the prosecution failed to prove a connection to the Internet for each of the three images. The Fifth Circuit clarified the holding of *Henriques* in a subsequent case, United States v. Runyan, 290 F.3d 223, 242 (5th Cir. 2002):

> *Henriques* establishes that the Government must provide some evidence linking the specific images supporting the conviction to the Internet in order to establish an interstate commerce connection under § 2252A. Thus, as we indicated in *Henriques*, it is not enough for the Government merely to introduce evidence indicating that the defendant had Internet access and that the defendant, at some point in time, accessed or downloaded images from pornography websites or newsgroups. Rather, the Government must make a specific connection between the images introduced at trial and the Internet to provide the requisite jurisdictional nexus. We did not suggest in *Henriques* that circumstantial evidence would be insufficient to establish such a link. Indeed, *Henriques* implicitly supports the notion that circumstantial evidence linking a particular image to the Internet (such as the presence of a website address embedded on the image) can be sufficient evidence of interstate transportation to support a conviction under § 2252A.

2.   The law charged in *Henriques* was amended in October 1998. *See* Pub. L. No. 105–314 (1998). The amendment reduced the number of images a defendant must possess from three to one. The conduct at issue in *Henriques* occurred several months before the law was changed, however, so the government was required to show possession and an interstate commerce nexus for all three images. If the same issue came up today, the government would be required to show only that a single image traveled in interstate commerce.

3.   The *Henriques* court does not resolve whether transporting an image via the Internet necessarily means the image was transported in interstate commerce. How should courts answer this question? Is the Internet inherently interstate?

In United States v. Carroll, 105 F.3d 740 (1st Cir. 1997), the defendant had taken sexually explicit photographs of a young woman. She later testified that the defendant had told her of his plans to distribute the images on the Internet. In dicta, the First Circuit suggested that this fact alone could establish the interstate commerce requirement, *id.* at 742:

> This testimony, if believed, proved the government's point. Transmission of photographs by means of the Internet is tantamount to moving photographs across state lines and thus constitutes transportation in interstate commerce.

In what sense is transmission by means of the Internet "tantamount" to transportation across state lines?

4. In United States v. MacEwan, 445 F.3d 237 (3d Cir. 2006), the defendant downloaded images of child pornography from the Web to his computer at home in West Chester, Pennsylvania. MacEwan's ISP was located in Pennsylvania, and the government did not identify the source of the images he had downloaded. MacEwan argued that the government failed to prove the images were transported in interstate commerce because it did not prove the images crossed state lines. The Third Circuit disagreed, holding that the images were transported in interstate commerce even if they never crossed state lines. According to the court, the fact that the images had been received using an Internet connection was sufficient:

> MacEwan is conflating "interstate commerce" with "interstate transmission" and confusing the nature of the jurisdictional basis for his charged offense. Nowhere in the statute does it state that the child pornography images must have crossed state lines; rather, it states solely that they must have been "transported in interstate commerce by any means, including by computer."

> * * * [I]t is almost impossible to know the exact route taken by an Internet user's website connection request, such as MacEwan's requests to connect with various child pornography websites. Because of fluctuations in the volume of Internet traffic and determinations by the systems as to what line constitutes the "Shortest Path First," a website connection request can travel entirely intrastate or partially interstate.

> Regardless of the route taken, however, we conclude that because of the very interstate nature of the Internet, once a user submits a connection request to a website server or an image is transmitted from the website server back to user, the data has traveled in interstate commerce. Here, once the images of child pornography left the website server and entered the complex global data transmission system that is the Internet, the images were being transmitted in interstate commerce.

Id. at 244. Is this a persuasive interpretation as a matter of statutory construction? Or is the court construing the requirement of transportation "in" interstate commerce as if it were a requirement of transportation "using a means" of interstate commerce? *Compare* 18 U.S.C. § 2252 *with* 18 U.S.C. § 2422(b).

5. In United States v. Mitra, 405 F.3d 492 (7th Cir. 2005), the defendant had commandeered a radio broadcast system used by police and emergency workers in Madison, Wisconsin. The radio system used frequencies allocated by the Federal Communications Commission for police, fire, and other public health services. The defendant argued that the radio system was not a "protected computer" under 18 U.S.C. § 1030(e)(2), which requires that the computer be "used in interstate or foreign commerce or communication." In an opinion by Judge Easterbrook, the Court held that the radio system was a "protected computer" because the system operated on spectrum licensed by the FCC:

> It met the statutory definition because the interference affected "communication." Mitra observes that his interference did not affect any

radio system on the other side of a state line, yet this is true of many cell-phone calls, all of which are part of interstate commerce because the electromagnetic spectrum is securely within the federal regulatory domain.

Id. at 496. Why should it matter that the computer used a frequency regulated by the FCC?

6. A number of federal crimes regulate conduct within "the special maritime and territorial jurisdiction of the United States." *See, e.g.,* 18 U.S.C. § 2252(a)(3)(A), § 2252(a)(4)(A). This phrase is defined in 18 U.S.C. § 7, and it mostly refers to places owned by the United States government such as United States military bases and federal parks.

The meaning of "special maritime and territorial jurisdiction" has particular importance under the Assimilative Crimes Act, 18 U.S.C. § 13. The Assimilative Crimes Act makes it a federal crime to violate a state criminal law within "the special maritime and territorial jurisdiction of the United States." As the name of the Act suggests, the statute assimilates state law, in effect federalizing the law of the home state. Here is the relevant text:

> Whoever within or upon any of the places now existing or hereafter reserved or acquired as provided in [18 U.S.C. § 7] * * * is guilty of any act or omission which, although not made punishable by any enactment of Congress, would be punishable if committed or omitted within the jurisdiction of the State, Territory, Possession, or District in which such place is situated, by the laws thereof in force at the time of such act or omission, shall be guilty of a like offense and subject to a like punishment.

18 U.S.C. § 13(a).

The Assimilative Crimes Act can be used in computer crime cases when a state's computer crime laws are broader than federal law. For example, if a person on a United States military base commits a computer-related offense that violates state law, the person can be charged in federal court under the federal Assimilated Crimes Act based on the state law violation. *Cf.* United States v. Smith, 47 M.J. 588 (N.M. Ct. Crim. App. 1997) (charging defendant on a military base in North Carolina with violations of the Assimilative Crimes Act for showing another person images of child pornography in violation of North Carolina state law).

3. PROCEDURAL STATUTORY LIMITS

Statutory limits on the scope of federal power can also impact the investigatory powers of federal agents. This can occur in two ways. First, the scope of statutory prohibitions can exclude some intrastate conduct by federal officials. Second, statutory limits can determine where federal officials must obtain court orders needed to collect digital evidence.

A) Statutory Privacy Laws

Although the Fourth Amendment regulates federal investigators at all times, statutory laws that contain an interstate commerce requirement can have a more limited scope. When a federal statute regulates criminal investigations and includes an interstate requirement, intra-state conduct by federal officials may not trigger the statute's prohibitions.

The interstate requirements of statutory privacy laws have arisen in a number of cases involving the Wiretap Act. In United States v. Scarfo, 180 F. Supp. 2d 572 (D.N.J. 2001), FBI investigators secretly placed a Key Logger System (KLS) inside the defendant's computer. To avoid implicating the Wiretap Act, the KLS was programmed to record the defendant's keystrokes only when the computer was not connected to the Internet. After the KLS recorded the defendant's passphrase, leading to proof of the defendant's criminal activity, the defendant argued that the evidence could not be used against him because it was obtained without a wiretap order. The Court rejected the defendant's argument on the ground that the design of the KLS placed it outside the scope of the Wiretap Act:

> [T]he Court finds that the KLS technique * * * did not intercept any wire communications and therefore did not violate the wiretap statute, Title III, 18 U.S.C. § 2510. I am satisfied the KLS did not operate during any period of time in which the computer's modem was activated.
>
> * * * Recognizing that Scarfo's computer had a modem and thus was capable of transmitting electronic communications via the modem, the F.B.I. configured the KLS to avoid intercepting electronic communications typed on the keyboard and simultaneously transmitted in real time via the communication ports. * * * Hence, when the modem was operating, the KLS did not record keystrokes. It was designed to prohibit the capture of keyboard keystrokes whenever the modem operated. Since Scarfo's computer possessed no other means of communicating with another computer save for the modem, the KLS did not intercept any wire communications. Accordingly, the Defendants' motion to suppress evidence for violation of Title III is denied.

Id. at 581–82.[a]

The jurisdictional scope of the Wiretap Act also arose in United States v. Ropp, 347 F. Supp. 2d 831 (C.D. Cal. 2004). Ropp installed a keystroke monitoring device called a "KeyKatcher" on the workplace computer of Karen Beck. The KeyKatcher was connected to the cable between Beck's keyboard and computer, and recorded all of Beck's keystrokes, including messages typed as part of e-mails she sent. Ropp was indicted for violating the Wiretap Act, but Judge Feess dismissed the indictment on the ground that the keystroke monitoring device had merely recorded impulses inside Beck's computer:

a. Note that the defendant's argument also should have failed because Title III does not include a suppression remedy for the interception of electronic communications.

[T]he Court concludes that the communication in question is not an "electronic communication" within the meaning of the statute because it is not transmitted by a system that affects interstate or foreign commerce. The "system" involved consists of the local computer's hardware—the Central Processing Unit, hard drive and peripherals (including the keyboard)—and one or more software programs including the computer's operating system (most likely some version of Microsoft Windows although other possibilities exist), and either an e-mail or other communications program being used to compose messages. Although this system is connected to a larger system—the network—which affects interstate or foreign commerce, the transmission in issue did not involve that system. The network connection is irrelevant to the transmissions, which could have been made on a stand-alone computer that had no link at all to the internet or any other external network. Thus, although defendant engaged in a gross invasion of privacy by his installation of the KeyKatcher on Ms. Beck's computer, his conduct did not violate the Wiretap Act.

Id. at 837–38.

Ropp suggests that the government would not need a Wiretap order to install a similar device; a standard probable cause warrant under the Fourth Amendment would suffice. On the other hand, was *Ropp* correctly decided? The definition of "electronic communication" covers "any transfer * * * transmitted in whole or in part by a wire, radio, electromagnetic, photoelectronic or photooptical system that affects interstate or foreign commerce." 18 U.S.C. § 2510(12). If a computer is connected to a network, isn't the "system" the network as a whole rather than the individual computer?

B) National Versus Local Orders

A second limit on the scope of federal power concerns the enforcement of federal orders that cross state or district lines. When federal investigators wish to obtain a court order, must they obtain the order in the district where the evidence is stored? Or can they obtain an order in one state permitting the collection of evidence in another state?

Most federal statutes permit the federal government to obtain a court order in one state or district for evidence in another state or district. For example, federal subpoenas are nationwide in scope. *See generally* Weinberg v. United States, 126 F.2d 1004, 1008 (2d Cir. 1942) (citing American Lithographic Co. v. Werckmeister, 221 U.S. 603 (1911)). As a result, a federal prosecutor in state *A* can serve a subpoena on an ISP in state *B*, and the ISP must comply with the out-of-state federal subpoena.

Court orders obtained under the Pen Register statute and 18 U.S.C. § 2703(d) of the Stored Communications Act also are nationwide in scope. 18 U.S.C. § 3121(a) of the Pen Register statute states that pen/trap orders "authoriz[e] the installation and use of a pen register or trap and trace device anywhere within the United States." Similarly, the text of § 2703(d) provides that "any court that is a court of competent jurisdiction" may issue the order, and 18 U.S.C. § 2711(3) establishes that this includes "any Federal court * * * without geographic limitation."

Federal search warrants present a somewhat different picture. Search warrants for physical evidence ordinarily must be obtained in the district where the physical evidence is located. Some exceptions exist. Federal Rule of Criminal Procedure 41(b) states:

(1) a magistrate judge with authority in the district—or if none is reasonably available, a judge of a state court of record in the district—has authority to issue a warrant to search for and seize a person or property located within the district;

(2) a magistrate judge with authority in the district has authority to issue a warrant for a person or property outside the district if the person or property is located within the district when the warrant is issued but might move or be moved outside the district before the warrant is executed; and

(3) a magistrate judge—in an investigation of domestic terrorism or international terrorism (as defined in 18 U.S.C. § 2331)—having authority in any district in which activities related to the terrorism may have occurred, may issue a warrant for a person or property within or outside that district.

Search warrants for electronic evidence obtained to satisfy 18 U.S.C. § 2703(a) can be nationwide in scope. Prior to the passage of the USA Patriot Act in 2001, Section 2703(a) required warrants to be obtained in the district where the evidence was located. Section 220 of the USA Patriot Act, titled "Nationwide Service of Search Warrants for Electronic Evidence," amended 18 U.S.C. § 2703(a) to specify that search warrants obtained to satisfy that section must be obtained "using the procedures described in the Federal Rules of Criminal Procedure by a court with jurisdiction over the offense." The Justice Department intended this amendment to permit nationwide warrants obtained under 18 U.S.C. § 2703(a). Any court with an open investigation into the offense has "jurisdiction over the offense," and federal courts in those districts should be able to issue § 2703(a) warrants "using the procedures described" in Rule 41.

Finally, Title III intercept orders obtained under 18 U.S.C. § 2518 can be obtained in the state where the tap is placed or where the investigators who will review the collected evidence are located. While the statute authorizes a district judge to approve "interception within the territorial jurisdiction of the court in which the judge is sitting," 18 U.S.C. § 2518(3), courts have held that the situs of an interception is where it is first heard and understood by human ears. *See, e.g.,* United States v. Rodriguez, 968 F.2d 130, 136 (2d Cir. 1992). As a result, use of a monitoring device in state *A* that pipes data to officials located in state *B* is an intercept in state *B* for purposes of the statute, and officers can obtain a Wiretap order in state *B* even though the device is installed in state *A*.

B. STATE POWER

Congress has virtually plenary power to regulate computer-related crimes, and most federal court orders can be obtained with nationwide effect. State powers are quite different. State officials face considerable substantive and procedural barriers to the successful investigation and prosecution of computer crimes. The materials that follow start with substantive law, and in particular the limits imposed on state efforts to regulate interstate computer crimes imposed by the so-called "dormant" Commerce Clause. The materials then turn to procedural laws, and study the procedural hurdles faced by state computer crime investigators. As you read these materials, keep this question in mind: What role can states play in the enforcement of computer crime laws?

1. SUBSTANTIVE LIMITS

AMERICAN LIBRARY ASSOCIATION v. PATAKI

United States District Court for the Southern District of New York, 1997.
969 F. Supp. 160.

Preska, District Judge.

The plaintiffs in the present case filed this action challenging New York Penal Law § 235.21(3). Plaintiffs contend that the Act is unconstitutional * * * because it unduly burdens interstate commerce in violation of the Commerce Clause. For the reasons that follow, the motion for a preliminary injunction is granted.

The Act in question amended N.Y. Penal Law § 235.21 by adding a new subdivision. The amendment makes it a crime for an individual:

> Knowing the character and content of the communication which, in whole or in part, depicts actual or simulated nudity, sexual conduct or sado-masochistic abuse, and which is harmful to minors, to intentionally use any computer communication system allowing the input, output, examination or transfer, of computer data or computer programs from one computer to another, to initiate or engage in such communication with a person who is a minor.

Violation of the Act is a Class E felony, punishable by one to four years of incarceration. The Act applies to both commercial and non-commercial disseminations of material.

Section 235.20(6) defines "harmful to minors" as:

> that quality of any description or representation, in whatever form, of nudity, sexual conduct, sexual excitement, or sado-masochistic abuse, when it:
>
> (a) Considered as a whole, appeals to the prurient interest in sex of minors; and

(b) Is patently offensive to prevailing standards in the adult community as a whole with respect to what is suitable material for minors; and

(c) Considered as a whole, lacks serious literary, artistic, political and scientific value for minors.

N.Y. Penal Law § 235.20(6). The statute provides six defenses to liability. First, Section 235.15(1) provides the following affirmative defense to prosecution under § 235.21(3):

> In any prosecution for obscenity, or disseminating indecent material to minors in the second degree in violation of subdivision three of section 235.21 of this article, it is an affirmative defense that the persons to whom the allegedly obscene or indecent material was disseminated, or the audience to an allegedly obscene performance, consisted of persons or institutions having scientific, educational, governmental or other similar justification for possessing, disseminating or viewing the same.

The statute further provides four regular defenses to prosecution:

(a) The defendant made a reasonable effort to ascertain the true age of the minor and was unable to do so as a result of the actions taken by the minor; or

(b) The defendant has taken, in good faith, reasonable, effective and appropriate actions under the circumstances to restrict or prevent access by minors to materials specified in such subdivision, which may involve any appropriate measures to restrict minors from access to such communications, including any method which is feasible under available technology; or

(c) The defendant has restricted access to such materials by requiring use of a verified credit card, debit account, adult access code or adult personal identification number; or

(d) The defendant has in good faith established a mechanism such that the labeling, segregation or other mechanism enables such material to be automatically blocked or screened by software or other capabilities reasonably available to responsible adults wishing to effect such blocking or screening and the defendant has not otherwise solicited minors not subject to such screening or blocking capabilities to access that material or circumvent any such screening or blocking.

N.Y. Penal Law § 235.23(3). And, finally, Section 235.24 provides that no individual shall be held liable:

> solely for providing access or connection to or from a facility, system, or network not under that person's control, including transmission, downloading, intermediate storage, access software, or other related capabilities that are incidental to providing such access or connection that do not include the creation of the content of the communication.

N.Y. Penal Law § 235.24.

The borderless world of the Internet raises profound questions concerning the relationship among the several states and the relationship of the federal government to each state, questions that go to the heart of "our federalism."

The unique nature of the Internet highlights the likelihood that a single actor might be subject to haphazard, uncoordinated, and even outright inconsistent regulation by states that the actor never intended to reach and possibly was unaware were being accessed. Typically, states' jurisdictional limits are related to geography; geography, however, is a virtually meaningless construct on the Internet. The menace of inconsistent state regulation invites analysis under the Commerce Clause of the Constitution, because that clause represented the framers' reaction to overreaching by the individual states that might jeopardize the growth of the nation—and in particular, the national infrastructure of communications and trade—as a whole.

The Commerce Clause is more than an affirmative grant of power to Congress. As long ago as 1824, Justice Johnson in his concurring opinion in *Gibbons v. Ogden,* 9 Wheat. 1, 231–32 (1824), recognized that the Commerce Clause has a negative sweep as well. In what commentators have come to term its negative or "dormant" aspect, the Commerce Clause restricts the individual states' interference with the flow of interstate commerce in two ways. The Clause prohibits discrimination aimed directly at interstate commerce, and bars state regulations that, although facially nondiscriminatory, unduly burden interstate commerce. Moreover, courts have long held that state regulation of those aspects of commerce that by their unique nature demand cohesive national treatment is offensive to the Commerce Clause.

Thus, as will be discussed in more detail below, the New York Act is concerned with interstate commerce and contravenes the Commerce Clause for three reasons. First, the Act represents an unconstitutional projection of New York law into conduct that occurs wholly outside New York. Second, the Act is invalid because although protecting children from indecent material is a legitimate and indisputably worthy subject of state legislation, the burdens on interstate commerce resulting from the Act clearly exceed any local benefit derived from it. Finally, the Internet is one of those areas of commerce that must be marked off as a national preserve to protect users from inconsistent legislation that, taken to its most extreme, could paralyze development of the Internet altogether. Thus, the Commerce Clause ordains that only Congress can legislate in this area, subject, of course, to whatever limitations other provisions of the Constitution (such as the First Amendment) may require.

A. The Act Concerns Interstate Commerce

At oral argument, the defendants advanced the theory that the Act is aimed solely at intrastate conduct. This argument is unsupportable in light of the text of the statute itself, its legislative history, and the reality of Internet communications. The section in question contains no such limitation; it reads:

A person is guilty of disseminating indecent material to minors in the second degree when: * * *

(3) Knowing the character and content of the communication which, in whole or in part, depicts actual or simulated nudity, sexual conduct or sado-masochistic abuse, and which is harmful to minors, he intentionally uses any computer communication system allowing the input, output, examination or transfer, of computer data or computer programs from one computer to another, to initiate or engage in such communication with a person who is a minor.

N.Y. Penal Law § 235.21(3). Section 235.20, which contains the definitions applicable to the challenged portion of the Act, does not import any restriction that the criminal communication must take place entirely within the State of New York. By its terms, the Act applies to any communication, intrastate or interstate, that fits within the prohibition and over which New York has the capacity to exercise criminal jurisdiction.

The conclusion that the Act must apply to interstate as well as intrastate communications receives perhaps its strongest support from the nature of the Internet itself. The Internet is wholly insensitive to geographic distinctions. In almost every case, users of the Internet neither know nor care about the physical location of the Internet resources they access. Internet protocols were designed to ignore rather than document geographic location; while computers on the network do have "addresses," they are logical addresses on the network rather than geographic addresses in real space.

Moreover, no aspect of the Internet can feasibly be closed off to users from another state. An internet user who posts a Web page cannot prevent New Yorkers or Oklahomans or Iowans from accessing that page and will not even know from what state visitors to that site hail. Nor can a participant in a chat room prevent other participants from a particular state from joining the conversation. Someone who uses a mail exploder is similarly unaware of the precise contours of the mailing list that will ultimately determine the recipients of his or her message, because users can add or remove their names from a mailing list automatically. Thus, a person could choose a list believed not to include any New Yorkers, but an after-added New Yorker would still receive the message.

The New York Act, therefore, cannot effectively be limited to purely intrastate communications over the Internet because no such communications exist. No user could reliably restrict her communications only to New York recipients. Moreover, no user could avoid liability under the New York Act simply by directing his or her communications elsewhere, given that there is no feasible way to preclude New Yorkers from accessing a Web site, receiving a mail exploder message or a newsgroup posting, or participating in a chat room. Similarly, a user has no way to ensure that an e-mail does not pass through New York even if the ultimate recipient is not located there, or that a message never leaves New York even if both sender and recipient are located there.

The courts have long recognized that railroads, trucks, and highways are themselves "instruments of commerce," because they serve as conduits for the transport of products and services. The Internet is more than a means of communication; it also serves as a conduit for transporting digitized goods, including software, data, music, graphics, and videos which can be downloaded from the provider's site to the Internet user's computer.

The inescapable conclusion is that the Internet represents an instrument of interstate commerce, albeit an innovative one; the novelty of the technology should not obscure the fact that regulation of the Internet impels traditional Commerce Clause considerations. The New York Act is therefore closely concerned with interstate commerce, and scrutiny of the Act under the Commerce Clause is entirely appropriate. As discussed in the following sections, the Act cannot survive such scrutiny, because it places an undue burden on interstate traffic, whether that traffic be in goods, services, or ideas.

B. New York Has Overreached by Enacting a Law That Seeks to Regulate Conduct Occurring Outside its Borders

The interdiction against direct interference with interstate commerce by state legislative overreaching is apparent in a number of the Supreme Court's decisions. In *Baldwin v. G.A.F. Seelig, Inc.,* 294 U.S. 511, 521 (1935), for example, Justice Cardozo authored an opinion enjoining enforcement of a law that prohibited a dealer from selling within New York milk purchased from the producer in Vermont at less than the minimum price fixed for milk produced in New York. Justice Cardozo sternly admonished, "New York has no power to project its legislation into Vermont by regulating the price to be paid in that state for milk," finding that "such a power, if exerted, would set a barrier to traffic between one state and another as effective as if customs duties, equal to the price differential, had been laid upon the thing transported." *Id.*

In the present case, a number of witnesses testified to the chill that they felt as a result of the enactment of the New York statute; these witnesses refrained from engaging in particular types of interstate commerce. In particular, I note the testimony of Rudolf Kinsky, an artist with a virtual studio on Art on the Net's Website. Mr. Kinsky testified that he removed several images from his virtual studio because he feared prosecution under the New York Act. As described above, no Web siteholder is able to close his site to New Yorkers. Thus, even if Mr. Kinsky were located in California and wanted to display his work to a prospective purchaser in Oregon, he could not employ his virtual studio to do so without risking prosecution under the New York law.

The nature of the Internet makes it impossible to restrict the effects of the New York Act to conduct occurring within New York. An Internet user may not intend that a message be accessible to New Yorkers, but lacks the ability to prevent New Yorkers from visiting a particular Website or viewing a particular newsgroup posting or receiving a particular mail exploder. Thus, conduct that may be legal in the state in which the user acts can subject the user to prosecution in New York and thus subordinate the user's home state's policy—perhaps favoring freedom of expression over a more protective stance—to New York's local concerns. New York has deliberately imposed its legislation on the Internet and, by doing so, projected its law into other states whose citizens use the Net. This encroachment upon the authority which the Constitution specifically confers upon the federal government and upon the sovereignty of New York's sister states is per se violative of the Commerce Clause.

C. The Burdens the Act Imposes on Interstate Commerce Exceed Any Local Benefit

Even if the Act were not a per se violation of the Commerce Clause by virtue of its extraterritorial effects, the Act would nonetheless be an invalid indirect regulation of interstate commerce, because the burdens it imposes on interstate commerce are excessive in relation to the local benefits it confers. The Supreme Court set forth the balancing test applicable to indirect regulations of interstate commerce in *Pike v. Bruce Church,* 397 U.S. 137, 142 (1970). *Pike* requires a two-fold inquiry. The first level of examination is directed at the legitimacy of the state's interest. The next, and more difficult, determination weighs the burden on interstate commerce in light of the local benefit derived from the statute.

In the present case, I accept that the protection of children against pedophilia is a quintessentially legitimate state objective—a proposition with which I believe even the plaintiffs have expressed no quarrel. The defendants spent considerable time in their Memorandum and at argument asserting the legitimacy of the state's interest. Even with the fullest recognition that the protection of children from sexual exploitation is an indisputably valid state goal, however, the present statute cannot survive even the lesser scrutiny to which indirect regulations of interstate commerce are subject under the Constitution. * * *

The local benefits likely to result from the New York Act are not overwhelming. The Act can have no effect on communications originating outside the United States. Further, in the present case, New York's prosecution of parties from out of state who have allegedly violated the Act, but whose only contact with New York occurs via the Internet, is beset with practical difficulties, even if New York is able to exercise criminal jurisdiction over such parties. The prospect of New York bounty hunters dragging pedophiles from the other 49 states into New York is not consistent with traditional concepts of comity.

The Act is, of course, not the only law in New York's statute books designed to protect children against sexual exploitation. The State is able to protect children through vigorous enforcement of the existing laws criminalizing obscenity and child pornography. Moreover, plaintiffs do not challenge the sections of the statute that criminalize the sale of obscene materials to children, over the Internet or otherwise, and prohibit adults from luring children into sexual contact by communicating with them via the Internet. *See* N.Y. Penal Law § 235.21(1); N.Y. Penal Law § 235.22(2). The local benefit to be derived from the challenged section of the statute is therefore confined to that narrow class of cases that does not fit within the parameters of any other law. The efficacy of the statute is further limited, as discussed above, to those cases which New York is realistically able to prosecute.

Balanced against the limited local benefits resulting from the Act is an extreme burden on interstate commerce. The New York Act casts its net worldwide; moreover, the chilling effect that it produces is bound to exceed the actual cases that are likely to be prosecuted, as Internet users will steer clear of the Act by significant margin. At oral argument, the State asserted that only a small percentage of Internet communications are "harmful to minors" and would fall within the proscriptions of the statute; therefore, the State argued, the burden on interstate commerce is small. On the record before me, I conclude that the range of Internet communications potentially affected by the Act is far broader than the State suggests. I note that in the past, various communities within the United States have found works including *I Know Why the Caged Bird Sings* by Maya Angelou, *Funhouse* by Dean Koontz, *The Adventures of Huckleberry Finn* by Mark Twain, and *The Color Purple* by Alice Walker to be indecent.

D. The Act Unconstitutionally Subjects Interstate Use of the Internet to Inconsistent Regulations

Finally, a third mode of Commerce Clause analysis further confirms that the plaintiffs are likely to succeed on the merits of their claim that the New York Act is unconstitutional. The courts have long recognized that certain types of commerce demand consistent treatment and are therefore susceptible to regulation only on a national level. The Internet represents one of those areas; effective regulation will require national, and more likely global, cooperation. Regulation by any single state can only result in chaos, because at least some states will likely enact laws subjecting Internet users to conflicting obligations. Without the limitation's imposed by the Commerce Clause, these inconsistent regulatory schemes could paralyze the development of the Internet altogether.

The Internet * * * requires a cohesive national scheme of regulation so that users are reasonably able to determine their obligations. Regulation on a local level, by contrast, will leave users lost in a welter of inconsistent laws, imposed by different states with different priorities. New York is not the only state to enact a law purporting to regulate the content of communications on the Internet. Already Oklahoma and Georgia have enacted laws designed to protect minors from indecent communications over the Internet; as might be expected, the states have selected different methods to accomplish their aims. Georgia has made it a crime to communicate anonymously over the Internet, while Oklahoma, like New York, has prohibited the online transmission of material deemed harmful to minors. *See* Ga. Code Ann. § 16–19–93.1 (1996); Okla. Stat. tit. 21, § 1040.76 (1996).

Moreover, the regulation of communications that may be "harmful to minors" taking place over the Internet poses particular difficulties. New York has defined "harmful to minors" as including:

> that quality of any description or representation, in whatever form, of nudity, sexual conduct, sexual excitement, or sado-masochistic abuse, when it:
>
> (a) Considered as a whole, appeals to the prurient interest in sex of minors; and
>
> (b) Is patently offensive to prevailing standards in the adult community as a whole with respect to what is suitable material for minors; and
>
> (c) Considered as a whole, lacks serious literary, artistic, political and scientific value for minors.

N.Y. Penal Law § 235.20(6). Courts have long recognized, however, that there is no single "prevailing community standard" in the United States. Thus, even were all 50 states to enact laws that were verbatim copies of the New York Act, Internet users would still be subject to discordant responsibilities.

As discussed at length above, an Internet user cannot foreclose access to her work from certain states or send differing versions of her communication to different jurisdictions. In this sense, the Internet user is in a worse position than the truck driver or train engineer who can steer around Illinois or Arizona, or change the mudguard or train configuration at the state line; the Internet user has no ability to bypass any particular state. The user must thus comply with the regulation imposed by the state with the most stringent standard or forego Internet communication of the message that might or might not subject her to prosecution.

Further development of the Internet requires that users be able to predict the results of their Internet use with some degree of assurance. Haphazard and uncoordinated state regulation can only frustrate the growth of cyberspace. The need for uniformity in this unique sphere of commerce requires that New York's law be stricken as a violation of the Commerce Clause.

Notes and Questions

1. Other courts have agreed with the approach of the *Pataki* decision, and have enjoined similar statutes enacted in other states. *See, e.g.,* American Booksellers Foundation v. Dean, 342 F.3d 96 (2d Cir. 2003) (enjoining a Vermont law); American Civil Liberties Union v. Johnson, 194 F.3d 1149 (10th Cir. 1999) (enjoining a New Mexico law); PSINet, Inc. v. Chapman, 362 F.3d 227 (4th Cir. 2004) (Virginia statute).

2. Does the dormant Commerce Clause require exclusively federal regulation of the Internet? Consider American Booksellers Foundation v. Dean, 342 F.3d 96, 103–04 (2d Cir. 2003), commenting on a Vermont statute similar to the one struck down in *Pataki*:

> Even if a website is never visited by people in Vermont, it is available to them in a way that a beer purchase in New York or Massachusetts is plainly not. Vermont's interest in out-of-state internet activity is thus more significant than a state's interest in the price of out-of-state beer sales. However, internet regulation of the sort at issue here still runs afoul of the dormant Commerce Clause because the Clause protects against inconsistent legislation arising from the projection of one state regulatory regime into the jurisdiction of another State. Thus, at the same time that the internet's geographic reach increases Vermont's interest in regulating out-of-state conduct, it makes state regulation impracticable. We think it likely that the internet will soon be seen as falling within the class of subjects that are protected from State regulation because they imperatively demand a single uniform rule.

For a critical perspective on this "common wisdom," and an argument that the dormant Commerce Clause permits vigorous state regulation of the Internet, see Jack L. Goldsmith & Alan O. Sykes, *The Internet and the Dormant Commerce Clause*, 110 Yale L.J. 785 (2001).

3. *Online solicitation*. In People v. Hsu, 82 Cal. App. 4th 976 (2000), a man in California e-mailed pornographic pictures to a 14 year-old boy in California in an effort to convince the boy to meet him for sexual activities. The defendant was charged with violating California Penal Code § 288.2(b), which prohibits knowingly sending "harmful matter" to a minor with the intent of seducing that minor. A state court rejected the defendant's argument that the statute violated the dormant Commerce Clause:

> Under the *Pike* test, section 288.2, subdivision (b) does not violate the commerce clause. Statutes affecting public safety carry a strong presumption of validity, and the definition and enforcement of criminal laws lie primarily with states. States have a compelling interest in protecting minors from harm generally and certainly from being seduced to engage in sexual activities. Conversely, it is difficult to conceive of any legitimate commerce that would be burdened by penalizing the transmission of harmful sexual material to known minors in order to seduce them. To the extent section 288.2, subdivision (b) may affect interstate commerce, its effect is incidental at best and far outweighed by the state's abiding interest in preventing harm to minors.

Id. at 983–84. The court distinguished *Pataki* as follows, *id.* at 984–85:

> The knowledge and intent elements missing from the New York statute but present in section 288.2, subdivision (b) significantly distinguish the two statutes. The New York statute broadly banned the communication of harmful material to minors via the Internet. The scope of section 288.2, subdivision (b) is much narrower. Only when the material is disseminated to a *known* minor with the *intent* to arouse the prurient interest of the sender and/or minor and with the *intent* to seduce the minor does the dissemination become a criminal act. The proscription against Internet use for these specifically defined and

limited purposes does not burden interstate commerce by subjecting Internet users to inconsistent regulations. As *Pataki* itself observed,* * * New York could realistically prosecute violations of New York Penal Law section 235.22(2), which, like section 288.2, subdivision (b), prohibits adults from luring minors into sexual contact via Internet communication of harmful material, without violating the commerce clause.

When section 288.2, subdivision (b) is harmonized with the entire California penal scheme, it does not effectively regulate activities beyond California. California prosecutes only those criminal acts that occur wholly or partially within the state. Statutes must be construed in the light of the general principle that, ordinarily, a state does not impose punishment for acts done outside its territory. Section 288.2, subdivision (b) makes no reference to place of performance, so courts must assume the Legislature did not intend to regulate conduct taking place outside the state. Given the historical and statutory limitations on California's ability to prosecute, section 288.2, subdivision (b) cannot be enforced beyond what is jurisdictionally allowed. Consequently, such enforcement would not burden interstate commerce.

4. *State anti-spam statutes.* Several states prohibit the distribution of spam, unsolicited commercial e-mail. Most states have upheld such statutes against Commerce Clause challenges. For example, in State v. Heckel, 24 P.3d 404 (Wash. 2001), the Washington Supreme Court upheld a state law that prohibited using false or misleading subject lines in commercial e-mail sent in or to residents of Washington. The Court held that the truthfulness requirement satisfied the *Pike* balancing test, as it protected ISPs and consumers without placing any burden on commerce.

The permissible scope of state anti-spam statutes is also limited by the preemption provision in the federal anti-spam statute, the Controlling the Assault of Non–Solicited Pornography and Marketing (CAN–SPAM) Act of 2003, Pub. L. No. 108–187 (2003). Section 8(b)(1) of the Act states:

> This Act supersedes any statute, regulation, or rule of a State or political subdivision of a State that expressly regulates the use of electronic mail to send commercial messages, except to the extent that any such statute, regulation, or rule prohibits falsity or deception in any portion of a commercial electronic mail message or information attached thereto.

15 U.S.C.A. § 7707(b)(1). For a discussion of how this provision applies to state anti-spam statutes, see Roger Allan Ford, *Preemption of State Spam Laws By The Federal CAN–SPAM Act*, 72 U. Chi. L. Rev. 355, 370–79 (2005).

5. In 2002, Pennsylvania enacted the Internet Child Pornography Act, codified at 18 Pa. Cons. Stat. §§ 7621–30, in an effort to block the availability of Internet child pornography in Pennsylvania. The statute permits law enforcement officials in Pennsylvania to seek an ex parte court order ordering an ISP located anywhere in the United States to "remove or disable items residing on or accessible through" an ISP's service upon a showing of probable cause that the item constitutes child pornography and is available in Pennsylvania. The apparent thinking behind the statute is that states

have no power to block the distribution of out-of-state child pornography, but they may be able to require ISPs to block such information and thus make it unavailable from inside the state. When challenged in court, however, a district court invalidated the Pennsylvania law on dormant Commerce Clause grounds (among other rationales):

> [T]he burdens imposed by the Act are clearly excessive in relation to the local benefits. Defendant claims the Act is justified by reducing the sexual abuse of children. However, as discussed, defendant did not produce any evidence that the Act effectuates this goal. To the contrary, there have been no prosecutions of child pornographers and the evidence shows that individuals interested in obtaining or providing child pornography can evade blocking efforts using a number of different methods.
>
> Moreover, there is evidence that this Act places a substantial burden on interstate commerce. Defendant argues that the Act only burdens child pornography, which is not a legitimate form of commerce. To the contrary, the evidence demonstrates that implementation of the Act has impacted a number of entities involved in the commerce of the Internet—ISPs, web publishers, and users of the Internet. To comply with the Act, ISPs have used two types of filtering—IP filtering and DNS filtering—to disable access to alleged child pornography. This filtering resulted in the suppression of 376 web sites containing child pornography, certainly a local benefit. However, the filtering used by the ISPs also resulted in the suppression of in excess of 1,190,000 web sites not targeted by defendant and, as demonstrated at trial, a number of these web sites, probably most of them, do not contain child pornography. The overblocking harms web publishers which seek wide distribution for their web sites and Internet users who want access to the broadest range of content possible. For example, as a result of a block implemented by AOL in response to an Informal Notice, Ms. Goldwater, a self employed documentary film maker, was unable to access a web site selling movie posters.
>
> This Act [also] has the practical effect of exporting Pennsylvania's domestic policies. As an example, a WorldCom witness testified that a customer in Minnesota would not be able to access a web site hosted in Georgia if an IP Address was blocked by a Pennsylvania order. The Act is even more burdensome than the legislation examined in *Pataki* because Pennsylvania has suppressed speech that was not targeted by the Act. Thus, a Minnesotan would be prevented from accessing a Georgia web site that is not even alleged to contain child pornography.

Center For Democracy & Technology v. Pappert, 337 F. Supp. 2d 606, 661–63 (E.D. Pa. 2004). Should the result be the same if the Pennsylvania law only applies to ISPs based in Pennsylvania? Would such a law be effective? For a critique of the Pennsylvania law, see Jonathan Zittrain, *Internet Points of Control*, 44 B.C. L. Rev. 653, 674–88 (2003).

2. PROCEDURAL LIMITS

State investigators confront a number of procedural hurdles to the collection of digital evidence that their federal counterparts do not encounter. Like federal investigators, state officers are bound by the

Fourth Amendment and federal privacy laws. Unlike federal investigators, however, state investigators are also bound by four additional limits:

(1) federal privacy laws that expressly regulate the states,

(2) state statutory laws that extend beyond federal statutory laws,

(3) state constitutional protections that extend beyond the federal Fourth Amendment, and

(4) limits on the ability of state subpoena and search warrant authorities to demand evidence out-of-state.

Let's start with the first case, federal privacy laws that expressly regulate the states. Each of the federal statutory privacy laws has special rules that apply to state investigations, and that determine when and how state officials can obtain court orders. For example, the Wiretap Act places significant federal limits on state wiretapping laws. 18 U.S.C. § 2516(2) provides that state investigators can only obtain wiretapping orders "when such interception may provide or has provided evidence of the commission of the offense of murder, kidnapping, gambling, robbery, bribery, extortion, or dealing in narcotic drugs, marihuana or other dangerous drugs, or other crime dangerous to life, limb, or property, and punishable by imprisonment for more than one year." Further, a state investigator can only obtain a wiretapping order if the state legislature has decided to enact a wiretapping statute. If the state has chosen not to pass a wiretapping law, state investigators cannot obtain wiretap orders. *But see* 18 U.S.C. § 2703(d) (explaining when state courts can issue SCA orders); 18 U.S.C. § 3122(a)(2) (permitting state courts to issue pen register orders).

Second, state statutory privacy laws can impose greater restrictions than federal law. Such restrictions are binding only on state investigators: Under the Supremacy Clause, federal officials acting in the course of their official duties are not bound by state statutory privacy laws. However, states may choose to limit state investigators more than federal law requires. States may impose higher thresholds than federal law, or may carve out narrower exceptions. For example, a number of states require the consent of all parties to satisfy the consent exception of state wiretap statutes. If state undercover investigators wish to record telephone calls or Internet communications, state law may require the consent of the monitored parties even if federal law does not. For a useful summary of the state statutes that regulate wiretapping, pen registers, and access to stored communications, see Charles H. Kennedy & Peter P. Swire, *State Wiretaps and Electronic Surveillance After September 11*, 54 Hastings L.J. 971, 987–1162 (2003).

Even if a state enacts statutory surveillance laws that match federal standards, state courts are free to construe state constitutions in ways that impose greater restrictions than those imposed by the Fourth Amendment.

COMMONWEALTH v. BEAUFORD

Superior Court of Pennsylvania, 1984.
475 A.2d 783.

CIRILLO, JUDGE.

These consolidated, direct appeals raise an issue of first impression in this Commonwealth: whether the utilization by law enforcement agencies of pen registers or dialed number recorders (DNRs) requires a judicial order based upon probable cause. We hold that such an order is required, and reverse the judgments of sentence.

Each of the six appellants was arrested in March of 1981 after searches of their individual residences revealed various illegal gambling paraphernalia and, as to certain appellants, controlled substances. After separate non-jury trials, each appellant was convicted of lotteries and gambling.

Viewing the evidence in the light most favorable to the verdict winner, the record discloses that an investigation into alleged illegal gambling activities in Delaware County during January of 1981 revealed that Cynthia O. Forcino was operating an illegal numbers operation from her residence in Drexel Hill. On February 10, 1981, the police submitted an application to the trial court for an order permitting the installation of a DNR on Forcino's telephone line to monitor the numbers dialed from that unit. The trial court granted the application on the same day.

On February 11, 1981 a confidential informant contacted the police with information concerning Forcino's numbers operation. The informant told of personally witnessing Forcino taking bets by telephone in her residence. The informant gave a description of Forcino, her address, telephone number, and the vehicles she drove and also stated that Forcino had eight to ten numbers writers with whom she kept in contact by telephone. Through subsequent checks the police substantially corroborated the informant's tips.

Thereafter, an order was secured from the trial court for DNR monitoring of the telephone number registered to appellant Karin Guinn, as police had subsequently received information from the same informant stating that Forcino would be forwarding her incoming calls to that number.

On February 27 and March 2, 1981 the confidential informant spoke with police and informed them that Forcino had told him that she was moving her gambling operation telephone number. On each occasion the informant gave police the new number. Checks of the new telephone numbers by police revealed the names and addresses of the parties to whom these numbers were registered. Subsequent police surveillance also confirmed the presence of one of Forcino's vehicles parked outside those addresses. The authorities then secured orders for the installation of DNRs for those telephone numbers received from the informant.

As a result of monitoring the various DNRs, the evidence revealed substantial numbers of outgoing and incoming calls of short duration (one minute or less) between the hours of noon and 7:00 p.m., Monday through Saturday among the various telephone lines used by Forcino and Guinn. The remaining four appellants were implicated by evidence of frequent calls made during the monitored time period from the Forcino and Guinn monitored telephones, to numbers registered to appellants.

Separate search warrants for each appellant were secured and executed on March 6, 1981, resulting in each appellant's arrest and the confiscation of gambling materials and, in the case of Forcino and Hayes, controlled substances. Each appellant subsequently filed motions to suppress, which were denied.

Appellants raise various challenges to the searches and seizures conducted in this case, but the issue which most concerns us is the legality of the DNR monitoring which later led to the searches of appellants' residences. Appellants contend the monitoring was both constitutionally and statutorily unlawful.

Before explaining why we accept appellants' constitutional argument, we review the statutory argument to lay the groundwork for our holding.

I

Appellants argue that under the Wiretapping and Electronic Surveillance Control Act, 18 Pa. C.S. §§ 5701–5726, the police were required to obtain authorization from a Superior Court judge before installing DNRs. The argument turns on a distinction drawn between "pen registers" and DNRs.

The Act, in general, makes criminal the willful interception of any wire or oral communication. The Act provides conditions under which law enforcement authorities may obtain legal authorization to intercept wire or oral communications. In brief, the Act provides that such authorization may issue only from a Superior Court judge upon application from the Attorney General or a district attorney or their designees. The requirements for such an application and order are detailed at *id.,* §§ 5708–5710, 5712.

Section 5704 of the Act enumerates certain activities which it holds not to be unlawful. Specifically, section 5704(5) states that it shall not be unlawful for "any investigative or law enforcement officer to use a pen register."

II

Appellants' constitutional claim is that, notwithstanding the Act, neither a pen register nor a DNR may be installed by law enforcement authorities without a judicial order based on probable cause. Since the court orders authorizing installation of the DNRs in this case indisputably were not based on records establishing probable cause, appellants argue that the evidence gathered through use of the DNRs was unconstitutionally obtained.

The right upon which appellants rely is recognized in both the Fourth Amendment to the federal constitution and article 1, § 8 of the Pennsylvania Constitution, which states:

> The people shall be secure in their persons, houses, papers and possessions from unreasonable searches and seizures, and no warrant to search any place or seize any person or things shall issue without describing them as nearly as may be, nor without probable cause, supported by oath or affirmation subscribed to by the affiant.

The Commonwealth's position is that it has already been conclusively decided that the information obtainable through use of a pen register—that is, information concerning the numbers dialed from a particular telephone—is outside the constitutionally protected sphere of privacy. In *Smith v. Maryland,* 442 U.S. 735 (1979), a 5–3 majority of the United States Supreme Court held that use of a pen register is not a "search" under the Fourth Amendment to the United States Constitution, thus affirming the decision of a divided Maryland Court of Appeals that the Fourth and Fourteenth Amendments did not preclude Maryland authorities from installing pen registers without probable cause.

The *Smith* majority found that a telephone caller could entertain no legitimate expectation of privacy in the numbers he dialed because the telephone company and its employees as a matter of course had access to this information. Finding that a caller voluntarily conveyed this information to the telephone company, the Court determined that the Constitution imposed no restriction on third-party access to the information.

The fallacy in the Commonwealth's reliance on *Smith* is the implicit assumption that our *state* constitution provides no greater protection against the installation and use of pen registers than the *federal* constitution provides. Although *Smith* conclusively decides the extent of the Fourth Amendment guarantee in this area, appellants have also asserted their rights under article 1, § 8 of the Pennsylvania Constitution. We turn now to the state constitutional claim.

Preliminarily, it cannot be doubted that this state has the constitutional power to guard individual rights, including the right to be free from unreasonable searches and seizures, more zealously than the federal government does under the United States Constitution. "The present function of state constitutions is as a second line of defense for those rights protected by the federal constitution *and as an independent source of supplemental rights unrecognized by federal law.*" Note, *The Interpretation of State Constitutional Rights,* 95 Harv. L. Rev. 1324, 1367 (1982) (emphasis added). Commentators urge state governments to reflect deeply before deciding whether state constitutional provisions affecting individual liberties conform to similar provisions in the federal constitution. W. Brennan, *State Constitutions and the Protection of Individual Rights,* 90 Harv. L. Rev. 489, 501 (1977).

In our effort to delineate the protection afforded to privacy interests under our state constitution, we have a particularly instructive precedent in *Commonwealth v. DeJohn,* 403 A.2d 1283 (1979). There our own Supreme Court expressly rejected the reasoning in *Miller* and held that police can gain access to banking records only through a warrant based on probable cause. Our state high court thus extended more privacy protection to banking records under article 1, § 8, than the United States Supreme Court provides under the federal constitution.

We must question whether, under our state constitution, there is a valid distinction between privacy interests in telephone records and privacy interests in banking records—a distinction the *Smith* Court rejected in Fourth Amendment analysis. * * *

Having considered * * * the jealousness with which the right to privacy in telephonic communications traditionally has been guarded in Pennsylvania, we strongly believe we should reject the *Smith* reasoning and extend the *DeJohn* holding to information obtainable through use of a pen register.

According to the *Smith* majority a caller who dials a telephone in our society should expect that the police will have complete access to the numbers dialed because he provides them to the telephone company. The logic of this position escapes us. For all practical purposes an individual in America today has very little choice about whether the telephone company will have access to the numbers he dials and the frequency of times he dials them. The company has a virtual monopoly over vital communications media, and the individual must accept that this information will be collected by the company for billing purposes. It is quite another thing to suggest that the telephone caller should therefore expect that the company will turn this information over to a third party without legal process for a purpose unrelated to providing telephone service.

We thus appraise *Smith* as manifestly unpersuasive.

Moreover, our constitutional interpretation derives independent support from Pennsylvania's long history of affording special protection to the privacy interest inherent in a telephone call. For most of this century the legislature absolutely prohibited wiretapping by law enforcement authorities, and imposed both civil and criminal liability for violations. Justice Roberts commented on this absolute ban:

> Hence, the Legislature has determined as a matter of state public policy that the rights of any caller to the privacy of his conversation is of greater societal value than the interest served by permitting eavesdropping and wiretapping.

Commonwealth v. Papszychi, 275 A.2d 28, 30 (1971).

This state's prohibition on investigative wiretapping of any sort continued in force until the provisions of the 1972 act were replaced by the Wiretapping and Electronic Surveillance Control Act of Oct. 4, 1978, 18 Pa. C.S. §§ 5701–5726. The new act for the first time allows wiretapping for police investigative purposes, but only after a strict showing of need by the attorney general or a district attorney before a Superior Court judge. The remarks of Mr. Rhodes, who reported the proposed act out of the House Judiciary Committee, reflect the caution with which the General Assembly approached this sensitive area. * * * The legislature further evidenced its intention to "start modestly in this area of eavesdropping and wiretapping" by attaching an automatic five-year repealer to the act.

Although it is true the use of pen registers by law enforcement authorities is exempted from the strict requirements of the Act, 18 Pa. C.S. §§ 5704(5), we do not consider this to be an expression of opinion by the legislature that use of pen registers is free from constitutional restraints as well. The far-reaching consequences of such a position would fly directly in the face of the legislative intent to forge a modest start in electronic surveillance. If any law enforcement officer could, with or without probable cause or even reasonable suspicion, use a pen register on his own authority to record every number dialed by any citizen in Pennsylvania from a residential, business, or government phone, the pen register clearly could become a powerful weapon threatening invasion not only of the individual's intimate privacy, but also his political liberty, including his rights to associate, to express his views, and even to think in freedom.

We hold that the installation and use of pen registers and DNRs by law enforcement authorities is limited to those situations in which an order issues upon probable cause. Our holding is in accord with well-reasoned decisions in our sister states where the state constitutional right to be free from unreasonable searches and seizures precludes the government from without probable cause using pen registers to record telephone numbers dialed in privacy. *People v. Blair,* 159 Cal. Rptr. 818 (1979); *People v. Sporleder,* 666 P.2d 135 (Colo.1983); *State v. Hunt,* 450 A.2d 952 (N.J. 1982) (applied to toll billing records); *see also* Dissenting Opinions by Stewart and Marshall, JJ., in *Smith v. Maryland, supra.*

Notes and Questions

1. How might the rationale of *Beauford* apply to the Internet? Under the Pennsylvania constitution, what kind of digital evidence can Pennsylvania police officers collect without a search warrant? Can the police install an Internet pen/trap device? Can they obtain logs from an ISP with only a 18 U.S.C. § 2703(d) order? Can they subpoena basic subscriber information from an ISP? Or does every interaction with an ISP require a search warrant?

2. Imagine that you are a Pennsylvania state police officer charged with investigating computer crimes in Pennsylvania. How easy is it to investigate computer hacking crimes in Pennsylvania? Internet threats? Child pornography offenses? What types of computer crimes can you investigate without a warrant? How does a broad warrant requirement change what crimes you can successfully investigate?

3. According to Stephen Henderson, Pennsylvania is one of eleven states in which courts have rejected the third-party disclosure principle underlying *Smith v. Maryland* as a matter of state constitutional law. In those eleven states, state investigators must obtain a probable cause search warrant to install a pen register. In contrast, courts in eighteen states either have explicitly adopted *Smith v. Maryland* as a matter of state constitutional law or else have strongly suggested they would do so if the question were directly raised. The remaining states have not addressed the question. *See* Stephen E. Henderson, *Learning From All Fifty States: How to Apply the Fourth Amendment and its State Analogs to Protect Third Party Information From Unreasonable Search*, 55 Cath. U. L. Rev. 373, 395–412 (2006).

Computer crime investigations often cross state lines, which means that police in one state may need to collect digital evidence located in another state. What powers do state investigators have to obtain digital evidence located outside state borders?

STATE v. SIGNORE

Superior Court of Connecticut, 2001.
31 Conn. L. Rptr. 91.

KAVANEWSKY, J.

The defendant has filed a motion to suppress "tangible evidence," more particularly evidence obtained from America Online following the production of a search and seizure warrant to it for account or subscriber information relating to the defendant.

* * * [T]he Greenwich police applied for a search and seizure warrant for AOL account information relating to the defendant. A court found probable cause and signed the warrant. The Greenwich police then faxed the warrant to AOL headquarters in Dulles, Virginia. They obtained the requested information.

The sole issue now before the court is whether, on federal and state constitutional grounds, evidence obtained as the result of the AOL search and seizure warrant, and any derivative evidence, should be suppressed. The defendant contends that the Court had no jurisdiction over the property outside of this state, and the Greenwich Police officers had no authority to act outside of the Town of Greenwich.

The court believes that the authority of the Greenwich police to carry out the search and seizure order derives from the provisions of 18 U.S.C. § 2701 et seq.

The language of 18 U.S.C. § 2703 is plain and unambiguous. It requires that the service provider disclose the subject information only when the governmental entity "obtains" the warrant. While it may not be entirely self-executing, any question as to how service of the warrant may be made can be considered against the backdrop of Connecticut's own legislation concerning search and seizure warrants.

The case of State v. Stevens, 224 Conn. 730 (1993), while not on point, is at least instructive. There, a Connecticut police officer performed field sobriety tests and gathered consensual blood samples from a defendant at a hospital in Rhode Island to which she had been transported by emergency medical personnel for treatment of her injuries following a car accident and her arrest. The defendant challenged the admission of evidence of the sobriety tests and * * * the analysis of the blood samples. She claimed that the officer had no authority to act as a police officer outside his territorial jurisdiction for purposes of that statute. The Supreme Court rejected that claim. "Although bereft of some of his statutory and common law authority outside of Connecticut and the municipality that employed him, the officer did not cease to be a Connecticut police officer for purposes of § 14–227b(b)." *Stevens*, 224 Conn. at 742–43. "In similar circumstances, courts of other states have held that the fact that evidence had been gathered outside an officer's territorial jurisdiction does not require suppression of the evidence." *Id.* at 741.

The defendant's motion to suppress seeks, in practice and effect, to apply the exclusionary rule to the information obtained under the AOL warrant. The facts of this case do not justify this sanction. The exclusionary rule is a judicially created remedy for protecting citizens' Fourth Amendment rights from overzealous law enforcement officials. The law enforcement officials here, having obtained a warrant supported by a neutral and detached Magistrate's determination of probable cause, can hardly be accused of overzealous behavior. The circumstances do not warrant application of the exclusionary rule.

Notes and Questions

1. In *Signore*, the police faxed a Connecticut state warrant to AOL in Virginia. AOL complied with the warrant and sent the information back to Connecticut under 18 U.S.C. § 2703. But was AOL required to respond? The text of § 2703 states that a "governmental entity" may require a provider to disclose evidence "only pursuant to a warrant issued using the procedures described in the Federal Rules of Criminal Procedure by a court with jurisdiction over the offense under investigation or equivalent State warrant." This language has generally been understood as a limit on when ISPs can disclose evidence rather than an affirmative requirement that ISPs must comply with all federal and state warrants.

2. When a state court order attempts to compel the collection of evidence outside the state, individuals and officials outside the state may opt to comply with the order. However, the fact that state authorities can *allow* extraterritorial enforcement does not mean that they can *compel* it. As a general rule, state court orders issued in one state are not enforceable outside the state. A state subpoena or warrant issued in state *A* for evidence in state *B* does not have binding force in state *B*. See, e.g., Ex parte Dillon,

29 S.W.2d 236, 238 (Mo. Ct. App. 1930) (holding that Full Faith and Credit clause does not require states to recognize court orders from other states); National Institute of Justice, Electronic Crime Needs Assessment for State and Local Law Enforcement 25 (2001).

3. If you are a criminal investigator in one state, and you need digital evidence located in another state, how can you ensure that you can collect the out-of-state evidence? One way for a state to collect out-of-state evidence is to persuade law enforcement officials in the other state to open an investigation and obtain court orders locally. Some state law enforcement offices set aside resources to provide this service for investigators in sister states as a matter of comity. A good example is the sheriff's office in Loudoun County, Virginia, home to the ISP America Online. In 2000, AOL had 23 million customers. State criminal investigators sought warrants to compel AOL to disclose account information several hundred times per year. To assist state officials outside Virginia, the sheriff's office assigned Detective Ron Horak the task of opening Virginia investigations and obtaining Virginia warrants to serve on AOL. When contacted by state investigators from outside Virginia, Horak would open a local investigation, obtain the local warrant, serve it on AOL, and then forward the information sent to him from AOL to the investigators outside Virginia. *See* Maria Glod, *Loudoun's AOL Detective Finds Clues in E–Mail*, Wash. Post, Aug. 28, 2000, at A1.

If you are a state computer crime investigator, can you rely on such arrangements to collect evidence outside your state? What if you need evidence from a small ISP in Rhode Island rather than AOL?

4. In response to the perceived inadequacy of relying on voluntary assistance to enforce court orders extraterritorially, a few states have passed laws requiring ISPs to comply with out-of-state legal process. Terry Berg explains:

> In order to address the problem of gathering evidence from out-of-state service providers, some states have adopted, or are considering adopting, a state statute requiring ISP's doing business within the state to accept and comply with the legal process from other state courts, and further requiring the resident agent of any out-of-state ISP registered to do business within the state to comply with process from forum state courts upon service of the resident agent. This approach is relatively new and remains untested in the courts, but it clearly addresses lowering the hurdles that state courts currently face when needing to obtain records from an out-of-state service provider.

Terrence Berg, *WWW.WILDWEST.GOV: The Impact of the Internet on State Power to Enforce the Law*, 2000 BYU L. Rev. 1305, 1355.

An example of such a law is Cal. Penal Code 1524.2. Under this law, ISPs incorporated in California must comply with out-of-state warrants:

> A California corporation that provides electronic communication services or remote computing services to the general public, when served with a warrant issued by another state to produce records that would reveal the identity of the customers using those services, data stored by, or on behalf of, the customer, the customer's usage of those services, the

recipient or destination of communications sent to or from those customers, or the content of those communications, shall produce those records as if that warrant had been issued by a California court.

Cal. Penal Code § 1524.2(c). Further, ISPs that do business in California must comply with California state warrants:

> The following provisions shall apply to any search warrant issued pursuant to this chapter allowing a search for records that are in the actual or constructive possession of a foreign corporation that provides electronic communication services or remote computing services to the general public, where those records would reveal the identity of the customers using those services, data stored by, or on behalf of, the customer, the customer's usage of those services, the recipient or destination of communications sent to or from those customers, or the content of those communications.

> * * * When properly served with a search warrant issued by the California court, a foreign corporation subject to this section shall provide to the applicant, all records sought pursuant to that warrant within five business days of receipt, including those records maintained or located outside this state.

Cal. Penal Code § 1524.2(b)-(b)(1).

5. A government-funded research report on state and local cybercrime law summarized the problem of extraterritorial evidence collection in the following way:

> Currently there is no formal legal mechanism to allow for the enforcement of State subpoenas in other States. Cooperation can be achieved when one State attorney general's office voluntarily assists a sister State authority in either serving an out-of-State subpoena or seeking an in-State court order to enforce the out-of-State subpoena. However, the reliability and consistency of this procedure is not uniform, and the ability to secure enforcement of an out-of-State subpoena on a recalcitrant party is questionable at best.

> To enhance the authority of State and local law enforcement to investigate cybercrimes that are too small to justify the investment of Federal resources but nevertheless require interstate process, more effective tools are required for enforcing State subpoenas in other jurisdictions. There are at least two possible models for creating these tools. One model is to develop an interstate compact that would establish procedures for signatory States to follow in enforcing out-of-State subpoenas. The Uniform Act to Secure the Attendance of Witnesses from Without a State in Criminal Proceedings is a comparable legal regime that has been adopted in the 50 States, the District of Columbia, Puerto Rico, and the Virgin Islands.

> A second model involves a Federal statute empowering the Federal courts to issue "full faith and credit" orders enforcing out-of-State criminal subpoenas. This alternative might avoid the complexities of developing and adopting an interstate agreement, but it could possibly raise federalism concerns. Whichever type of approach is pursued, action is necessary in this area to ensure that victims of Internet crime have an

effective recourse to which they can turn for protection and enforcement.

National Institute of Justice, Electronic Crime Needs Assessment for State and Local Law Enforcement 25–26 (2001).

Professor Brenner has explained one important effort to draft a federal statute. Susan W. Brenner, *Need for Reciprocal Enforcement of Warrants and Subpoenas in Cybercrime Cases*, 37 Prosecutor 29, 30 (2003):

> The National Institute of Justice's Electronic Crime Partnership Initiative has had a working group investigating these issues. After researching the law and surveying prosecutors around the country, the working group concluded that a full faith and credit statute is the best alternative for achieving reciprocity in this area.

The working group prepared the following draft statute:

18 U.S. Code § ___

(a) Full Faith and Credit—Any production order issued that is consistent with subsection (b) of this section by the court of another State (the issuing State) shall be accorded full faith and credit by the court of another State (the enforcing State) and enforced as if it were the order of the enforcing state.

(b) Production Order—A production order issued by a State court is consistent with this subsection if—(1) The order is pursuant to the investigation or prosecution of a crime of the issuing state; (2) The order was issued in accordance with the law of the issuing state; and (3) Such court had jurisdiction over the criminal investigation or prosecution under the law of the issuing state.

(c) "Production Order" means any order, warrant, or subpoena for the production of records, issued by a court of competent jurisdiction.

(d) "Records" includes those items in whatever form created or stored.

Professor Brenner explains:

> The draft statute is limited to orders for the production of records for at least two reasons. One is that the working group focused on the problems encountered in cybercrime investigations, which typically involve efforts to obtain records from another jurisdiction. The other reason is that members of the working group were concerned about the possibility of providing for reciprocal enforcement of all warrants, subpoenas and orders. They concluded that it was not advisable—at least not at this point in our history—to create a statute that would require full faith and credit to be given to, say, all search warrants, including those that require intrusions into the home or other private areas.

6. How important is it for state computer crime investigators to have the legal tools necessary to collect digital evidence nationwide? Is voluntary compliance adequate? Are model state statutes needed? Or is a federal statute the best solution? If a federal solution is needed, should the federal statute focus specifically on ISPs and computer crime cases or should it be more general in scope? Alternatively, is it appropriate in our federal system that state investigators cannot compel evidence nationwide?

C. INTERNATIONAL COMPUTER CRIMES

Computer crimes can cross national boundaries just as easily as they can cross state lines. As a result, federal investigators routinely face international jurisdictional issues analogous to those confronted by state investigators. Investigators might want to prosecute a defendant for committing a computer crime that originated domestically but targeted computers outside its borders, or they might want to punish a crime originating abroad that targets a computer inside the United States. Evidence might need to be collected outside the United States for an otherwise domestic investigation. Foreign governments face the same questions from the other side, as well: law enforcement officials from other countries may wish to punish computer crimes originating in the United States directed at computers in their home countries, or they may need to collect evidence in the United States to help domestic investigations. The following materials consider the law regulating international computer crime cases.

1. UNITED STATES SUBSTANTIVE LAW

Do computer crime laws in the United States apply to conduct either originating from outside the United States or targeting computers located outside the United States?

UNITED STATES v. IVANOV

United States District Court for the District of Connecticut, 2001.
175 F. Supp. 2d 367.

THOMPSON, DISTRICT JUDGE.

Defendant Aleksey Vladimirovich Ivanov has been indicted, in a superseding indictment, on charges of conspiracy, computer fraud and related activity, extortion and possession of unauthorized access devices. Ivanov has moved to dismiss the indictment on the grounds that the court lacks subject matter jurisdiction. Ivanov argues that because it is alleged that he was physically located in Russia when the offenses were committed, he can not be charged with violations of United States law. For the reasons set forth below, the defendant's motion is being denied.

I. BACKGROUND

Online Information Bureau, Inc. ("OIB"), the alleged victim in this case, is a Connecticut corporation based in Vernon, Connecticut. It is an "e-commerce" business which assists retail and Internet merchants by, among other things, hosting their websites and processing their credit card data and other financial transactions. In this capacity, OIB acts as a financial transaction "clearinghouse," by aggregating and assisting in the debiting or crediting of funds against each account for thousands of retail and Internet purchasers and vendors. In doing so, OIB collects and maintains customer credit card information, merchant account numbers, and related financial data from credit card companies and other financial institutions.

The government alleges that Ivanov hacked into OIB's computer system and obtained the key passwords to control OIB's entire network. The government contends that in late January and early February 2000, OIB received from Ivanov a series of unsolicited e-mails indicating that the defendant had obtained the "root" passwords for certain computer systems operated by OIB. A "root" password grants its user access to and control over an entire computer system, including the ability to manipulate, extract, and delete any and all data. Such passwords are generally reserved for use by the system administrator only.

The government claims that Ivanov then threatened OIB with the destruction of its computer systems (including its merchant account database) and demanded approximately $10,000 for his assistance in making those systems secure. It claims, for example, that on February 3, 2000, after his initial solicitations had been rebuffed, Ivanov sent the following e-mail to an employee of OIB:

> [name redacted], now imagine please Somebody hack you network (and not notify you about this), he download Atomic software with more than 300 merchants, transfer money, and after this did 'rm-rf/' and after this you company be ruined. I don't want this, and because this I notify you about possible hack in you network, if you want you can hire me and im allways be check security in you network. What you think about this?[1]

The government contends that Ivanov's extortionate communications originated from an e-mail account at Lightrealm.com, an Internet Service Provider based in Kirkland, Washington. It contends that while he was in Russia, Ivanov gained access to the Lightrealm computer network and that he used that system to communicate with OIB, also while he was in Russia. Thus, each e-mail sent by Ivanov was allegedly transmitted from a Lightrealm.com computer in Kirkland, Washington through the Internet to an OIB computer in Vernon, Connecticut, where the e-mail was opened by an OIB employee.

The parties agree that the defendant was physically located in Russia (or one of the other former Soviet Bloc countries) when, it is alleged, he committed the offenses set forth in the superseding indictment.

The superseding indictment comprises eight counts. Count One charges that beginning in or about December 1999, or earlier, the defendant and others conspired to commit the substantive offenses charged in Counts Two through Eight of the indictment, in violation of 18 U.S.C. § 371. Count Two charges that the defendant, knowingly and with intent to defraud, accessed protected computers owned by OIB and by means of this conduct furthered a fraud and obtained something of

---

1. An individual with "root access" who inputs the UNIX command "rm-rf/" will delete all files on the network server, including all operating system software.

value, in violation of 18 U.S.C. §§ 2, 1030(a)(4) and 1030(c)(3)(A). Count Three charges that the defendant intentionally accessed protected computers owned by OIB and thereby obtained information, which conduct involved interstate and foreign communications and was engaged in for purposes of financial gain and in furtherance of a criminal act, in violation of 18 U.S.C. §§ 2, 1030(a)(2)(c) and 1030(c)(2)(B).

Count Six charges that the defendant transmitted in interstate and foreign commerce communications containing a threat to cause damage to protected computers owned by OIB, in violation of 18 U.S.C. §§ 1030(a)(7) and 1030(c)(3)(A). Count Seven charges that the defendant obstructed, delayed and affected commerce, and attempted to obstruct, delay and affect commerce, by means of extortion by attempting to obtain property from OIB with OIB's consent, inducing such consent by means of threats to damage OIB and its business unless OIB paid the defendant money and hired the defendant as a security consultant, in violation of 18 U.S.C. § 1951(a). Count Eight charges that the defendant, knowingly and with intent to defraud, possessed unauthorized access devices, which conduct affected interstate and foreign commerce, in violation of 18 U.S.C. §§ 1029(a)(3).

II. DISCUSSION

The defendant and the government agree that when Ivanov allegedly engaged in the conduct charged in the superseding indictment, he was physically present in Russia and using a computer there at all relevant times. Ivanov contends that for this reason, charging him under the Hobbs Act, 18 U.S.C. § 1951, under the Computer Fraud and Abuse Act, 18 U.S.C. § 1030, and under the access device statute, 18 U.S.C. § 1029, would in each case require extraterritorial application of that law and such application is impermissible. The court concludes that it has jurisdiction, first, because the intended and actual detrimental effects of Ivanov's actions in Russia occurred within the United States, and second, because each of the statutes under which Ivanov was charged with a substantive offense was intended by Congress to apply extraterritorially.

A. The Intended and Actual Detrimental Effects of the Charged Offenses Occurred Within the United States

As noted by the court in *United States v. Muench,* 694 F.2d 28 (2d Cir. 1982), the intent to cause effects within the United States makes it reasonable to apply to persons outside United States territory a statute which is not expressly extraterritorial in scope. It has long been a commonplace of criminal liability that a person may be charged in the place where the evil results, though he is beyond the jurisdiction when he starts the train of events of which that evil is the fruit. The Government may punish a defendant in the same manner as if he were present in the jurisdiction when the detrimental effects occurred.

The Supreme Court has quoted with approval the following language from Moore's International Law Digest:

The principle that a man, who outside of a country willfully puts in motion a force to take effect in it, is answerable at the place where the evil is done, is recognized in the criminal jurisprudence of all countries. And the methods which modern invention has furnished for the performance of criminal acts in that manner has made this principle one of constantly growing importance and of increasing frequency of application.

Moreover, the court noted in *Marc Rich & Co. v. United States,* 707 F.2d 663 (2d Cir. 1983) that:

It is certain that the courts of many countries, even of countries which have given their criminal legislation a strictly territorial character, interpret criminal law in the sense that offences, the authors of which at the moment of commission are in the territory of another State, are nevertheless to be regarded as having been committed in the national territory, if one of the constituent elements of the offence, and more especially its effects, have taken place there.

Id. at 666.

Here, all of the intended and actual detrimental effects of the substantive offenses Ivanov is charged with in the indictment occurred within the United States. In Counts Two and Three, the defendant is charged with accessing OIB's computers. Those computers were located in Vernon, Connecticut. The fact that the computers were accessed by means of a complex process initiated and controlled from a remote location does not alter the fact that the accessing of the computers, i.e. part of the detrimental effect prohibited by the statute, occurred at the place where the computers were physically located, namely OIB's place of business in Vernon, Connecticut.

Count Two charges further that Ivanov obtained something of value when he accessed OIB's computers, that "something of value" being the data obtained from OIB's computers. In order for Ivanov to violate § 1030(a)(4), it was necessary that he do more than merely access OIB's computers and view the data. *See United States v. Czubinski,* 106 F.3d 1069, 1078 (1st Cir. 1997) ("Merely viewing information cannot be deemed the same as obtaining something of value for purposes of this statute. This section should apply to those who steal information through unauthorized access."). The indictment charges that Ivanov did more than merely gain unauthorized access and view the data. Ivanov allegedly obtained root access to the OIB computers located in Vernon, Connecticut. Once Ivanov had root access to the computers, he was able to control the data, e.g., credit card numbers and merchant account numbers, stored in the OIB computers; Ivanov could copy, sell, transfer, alter, or destroy that data. That data is intangible property of OIB. In determining where, in the case of intangibles, possession resides, the measure of control exercised is the deciding factor.

At the point Ivanov gained root access to OIB's computers, he had complete control over that data, and consequently, had possession of it.

That data was in OIB's computers. Since Ivanov possessed that data while it was in OIB's computers in Vernon, Connecticut, the court concludes that he obtained it, for purposes of § 1030(a)(4), in Vernon, Connecticut. The fact that Ivanov is charged with obtaining OIB's valuable data by means of a complex process initiated and controlled from a remote location, and that he subsequently moved that data to a computer located in Russia, does not alter the fact that at the point when Ivanov first possessed that data, it was on OIB's computers in Vernon, Connecticut.

Count Three charges further that when he accessed OIB's computers, Ivanov obtained information from protected computers. The analysis as to the location at which Ivanov obtained the information referenced in this count is the same as the analysis as to the location at which he obtained the "something of value" referenced in Count Two. Thus, as to both Counts Two and Three, it is charged that the balance of the detrimental effect prohibited by the pertinent statute, i.e., Ivanov's obtaining something of value or obtaining information, also occurred within the United States.

Count Six charges that Ivanov transmitted a threat to cause damage to protected computers. The detrimental effect prohibited by § 1030(a)(7), namely the receipt by an individual or entity of a threat to cause damage to a protected computer, occurred in Vernon, Connecticut because that is where OIB was located, where it received the threat, and where the protected computers were located. The analysis is the same as to Count Seven, the charge under the Hobbs Act.

Count Eight charges that Ivanov knowingly and with intent to defraud possessed over ten thousand unauthorized access devices, i.e., credit card numbers and merchant account numbers. For the reasons discussed above, although it is charged that Ivanov later transferred this intangible property to Russia, he first possessed it while it was on OIB's computers in Vernon, Connecticut. Had he not possessed it here, he would not have been able to transfer it to his computer in Russia. Thus, the detrimental effect prohibited by the statute occurred within the United States.

Finally, Count One charges that Ivanov and others conspired to commit each of the substantive offenses charged in the indictment. The Second Circuit has stated that "the jurisdictional element should be viewed for purposes of the conspiracy count exactly as we view it for purposes of the substantive offense." *United States v. Blackmon,* 839 F.2d 900, 910 (2d Cir. 1988). Federal jurisdiction over a conspiracy charge is established by proof that the accused planned to commit a substantive offense which, if attainable, would have violated a federal statute, and that at least one overt act has been committed in furtherance of the conspiracy. Here, Ivanov is charged with planning to commit substantive offenses in violation of federal statutes, and it is charged that at least one overt act was committed in furtherance of the conspiracy. As discussed above, the court has jurisdiction over the underlying substantive charges. Therefore, the court has jurisdiction over the conspiracy charge, at a minimum, to the extent it relates to Counts Two, Three, Six, Seven or Eight.

Accordingly, the court concludes that it has subject matter jurisdiction over each of the charges against Ivanov, whether or not the statutes under which the substantive offenses are charged are intended by Congress to apply extraterritorially, because the intended and actual detrimental effects of the substantive offenses Ivanov is charged with in the indictment occurred within the United States.

B. *Intended Extraterritorial Application*

The defendant's motion should also be denied because, as to each of the statutes under which the defendant has been indicted for a substantive offense, there is clear evidence that the statute was intended by Congress to apply extraterritorially. This fact is evidenced by both the plain language and the legislative history of each of these statutes.

There is a presumption that Congress intends its acts to apply only within the United States, and not extraterritorially. However, this presumption against extraterritoriality may be overcome by showing clear evidence of congressional intent to apply a statute beyond our borders. Congress has the authority to enforce its laws beyond the territorial boundaries of the United States. Whether Congress has in fact exercised that authority in a particular case is a matter of statutory construction.

The Computer Fraud and Abuse Act was amended in 1996 by Pub. L. No. 104–294, 110 Stat. 3491, 3508. The 1996 amendments made several changes that are relevant to the issue of extraterritoriality, including a change in the definition of "protected computer" so that it included any computer "which is used in interstate *or foreign* commerce or communication." 18 U.S.C. § 1030(e)(2)(B) (emphasis added). The 1996 amendments also added subsections (a)(2)(c) and (a)(7), which explicitly address "interstate or foreign commerce," and subsection (e)(9), which added to the definition of "government entity" the clause "any foreign country, and any state, province, municipality or other political subdivision of a foreign country."

The plain language of the statute, as amended, is clear. Congress intended the CFAA to apply to computers used "in interstate or foreign commerce or communication." The defendant argues that this language is ambiguous. The court disagrees. The Supreme Court has often stated that "a statute ought, upon the whole, to be so construed that, if it can be prevented, no clause, sentence, or word shall be superfluous, void, or insignificant." *Regions Hosp. v. Shalala,* 522 U.S. 448, 467 (1998). In order for the word "foreign" to have meaning, and not be superfluous, it must mean something other than "interstate." In other words, "foreign" in this context must mean international. Thus, Congress has clearly manifested its intent to apply § 1030 to computers used either in interstate or in foreign commerce.

The legislative history of the CFAA supports this reading of the plain language of the statute. The Senate Judiciary Committee issued a report explaining its reasons for adopting the 1996 amendments. S. Rep. No. 357, 104th Congr., 2d Sess. (1996). In that report, the Committee specifically noted its concern that the statute as it existed prior to the 1996 amendments did not cover "computers used in foreign communications or commerce, despite the fact that hackers are often foreign-based." *Id.* at 4. The Committee cited two specific cases in which foreign-based hackers had infiltrated computer systems in the United States, as examples of the kind of situation the amendments were intended to address:

> For example, the 1994 intrusion into the Rome Laboratory at Grifess Air Force Base in New York, was perpetrated by a 16 year-old hacker in the United Kingdom. More recently, in March 1996, the Justice Department tracked down a young Argentinean man who had broken into Harvard University's computers from Buenos Aires and used those computers as a staging ground to hack into many other computer sites, including the Defense Department and NASA.

Id. at 4–5. Congress has the power to apply its statutes extraterritorially, and in the case of 18 U.S.C. § 1030, it has clearly manifested its intention to do so.

Notes and Questions

1. As a matter of policy, should it be a federal crime for a person located abroad to hack into or damage a computer located in the United States? Why not let officials in the other country handle the case? Is it likely that Russian authorities would prosecute Ivanov for his unauthorized access into United States computers?

2. Should it be a federal crime for a person located in the United States to hack into or damage a computer located in a foreign country? Imagine that a person in the United States dislikes the government of China, and he decides to launch a denial-of-service attack against computers owned by the Chinese government located in China. Does the attack violate United States law? As a matter of policy, should it?

3. *The scope of § 1030 and international investigations.* The USA Patriot Act of 2001 amended the definition of "protected computer" in 18 U.S.C. § 1030(e)(2) so that it now explicitly includes computers located outside of the United States. Before the Patriot Act, the term "protected computer" was defined (as in the *Ivanov* case) as including a computer "which is used in interstate or foreign commerce or communication." 18 U.S.C. § 1030(e)(2) (1996). The new definition of "protected computer" amends this definition, adding the phrase "including a computer located outside the United States that is used in a manner that affects interstate or foreign commerce or communication of the United States." The Justice Department has offered the following explanation for the amendment:

Because of the interdependency and availability of global computer networks, hackers from within the United States are increasingly targeting systems located entirely outside of this country. The statute did not explicitly allow for prosecution of such hackers. In addition, individuals in foreign countries frequently route communications through the United States, even as they hack from one foreign country to another. In such cases, their hope may be that the lack of any U.S. victim would either prevent or discourage U.S. law enforcement agencies from assisting in any foreign investigation or prosecution.

Section 814 of the Act amends the definition of "protected computer" to make clear that this term includes computers outside of the United States so long as they affect "interstate or foreign commerce or communication of the United States." 18 U.S.C. § 1030(e)(2)(B). By clarifying the fact that a domestic offense exists, the United States can now use speedier domestic procedures to join in international hacker investigations. As these crimes often involve investigators and victims in more than one country, fostering international law enforcement cooperation is essential.

In addition, the amendment creates the option, where appropriate, of prosecuting such criminals in the United States. Since the U.S. is urging other countries to ensure that they can vindicate the interests of U.S. victims for computer crimes that originate in their nations, this provision will allow the U.S. to provide reciprocal coverage.

Computer Crime and Intellectual Property Section (CCIPS), Field Guidance on New Authorities that Relate to Computer Crime and Electronic Evidence Enacted in the USA Patriot Act of 2001 (2001), *available at* www.cybercrime.gov/PatriotAct.htm.

Note that the Justice Department mostly justifies the expansion of 18 U.S.C. § 1030 based on its impact on international investigations. According to DOJ, "the United States can now use speedier domestic procedures to join in international hacker investigations." When an international computer crime does not violate U.S. law, officials must follow fairly complicated and time-consuming evidence-collecting procedures (described later in this chapter). On the other hand, if an international computer crime violates 18 U.S.C. § 1030, U.S. law enforcement officials can open a *domestic* investigation into the violation. They can then use statutes such as the Electronic Communications Privacy Act to collect digital evidence in the United States and forward their findings on to counterparts abroad. As a result, a change in the substantive law of 18 U.S.C. § 1030 can have important procedural implications for international computer crime cases.

We observed a similar dynamic in the context of state criminal investigations that cross state lines. Recall that if investigators in state *A* need electronic evidence in state *B*, law enforcement officials in state *B* can open an investigation in that state, obtain the evidence, and then send it to officials in state *A*. Opening a second investigation in the jurisdiction where the evidence is located circumvents the hurdle of extraterritorial evidence collection, at least if the officials in the second jurisdiction are willing to help. The Patriot Act's amendment to § 1030(e)(2)(B) permits United States officials to perform the same role for foreign authorities investigating international computer crimes.

Is this a good idea? One commentator has argued that this expansion of 18 U.S.C. § 1030 goes too far:

> Where the affect on U.S. computer networks is slight—to the point of non-existence—the U.S. should not impose its law on the activity.
>
> The new statute requires no threshold of damage or even effect on U.S. computers to trigger U.S. sovereignty. The vast majority of Internet traffic travels through the United States, with more than half of the traffic traveling through Northern Virginia alone. The mere fact that packets relating to the criminal activity travel through the United States should not be enough to trigger U.S. jurisdiction, even though such traffic would "affect" international commerce, albeit infinitesimally.

Mark Rasch, *Ashcroft's Global Internet Power–Grab* (Nov. 25, 2001), http://www.security focus.com/columnists/39. Should Congress change the law back to the 1996 version?

4. In May, 2000, the Internet was hit by an e-mail-based computer virus known as the "I Love You" virus. The virus was believed to have been sent by Onel A. de Guzman, a 23 year-old computer programmer from the Phillipines. The virus quickly infected millions of machines. Although the precise way in which the virus was unleashed remains unknown, let's assume that it began when de Guzman sent an e-mail using an account in the Phillipines to various individuals with e-mail accounts in the Phillipines. The virus then spread outside the Phillipines and infected computers all around the world.

Assuming these facts are accurate, did Onel de Guzman violate 18 U.S.C. § 1030? Does the answer depend on whether the definition of "protected computer" is the 1996 definition or the current definition enacted by the Patriot Act? Does the answer depend on de Guzman's *mens rea* with respect to whether the virus would damage computers located in the United States?

5. Ellen S. Podgor, *International Computer Fraud: A Paradigm for Limiting National Jurisdiction*, 35 U.C. Davis L. Rev. 267, 269–70, 317 (2002):

> Computers present a new issue for consideration in determining the extraterritorial application of United States criminal laws. At first blush, the universal speed and accessibility of computers would seem to make computer-related crimes appropriate for broad extraterritorial jurisdiction. After all, a touch of a mouse by a person in one country can be destructive and criminal in another country. As stated by former Attorney General Janet Reno, "a hacker needs no passport and passes no checkpoints." Criminal computer conduct that occurs outside the United States can easily affect those within the United States. When this happens, some might argue that the United States should be able to exercise extraterritorial jurisdiction over the perpetrator.
>
> Further reflection, however, reveals problems with having such a broad exercise of extraterritorial jurisdiction. Should the United States

acquire jurisdiction of all criminal activity when the medium for the crime involves the use of a computer, and the activity has an effect in this country? Should every "I Love You" type worm or virus that invades the United States be the source of a criminal prosecution within this country? When computers are involved in the criminal activity, the issue of extraterritorial application is not simplistic. Whether one standard should apply to all computer crimes, whether the focus should be on the criminal act as opposed to the medium used to commit the act, and whether the location of the alleged perpetrator or victims should control, are just some of the many issues for consideration.

* * * U.S. law enforcement should tread carefully in imposing its jurisdiction throughout the world. It is one thing to lead the charge in prosecuting international computer fraud crimes; it is another, however, to take charge. Until sufficient international measures are operational, it is important for the United States to remind itself that it is not the world's police, prosecutor and court.

6. *Internet gambling and international law.* Recall that in United States v. Cohen, 260 F.3d 68 (2d Cir. 2001), discussed in Chapter 3, the defendant was convicted in New York for operating an Internet sports betting site from Antigua. Given that the computer was operated from Antigua, what was the basis for prosecuting Cohen in New York?

More broadly, can the United States government prevent foreign gambling sites from being available inside the United States without making them unavailable outside the United States? If the United States wants to ban such sites, but other countries do not, which side should win? And who should decide? The World Trade Organization considered a case brought by Antigua and Barbuda alleging that the United States ban on Internet gambling violated the General Agreement on Trade Services (GATS). *See* Jonathan Schwartz, Essay, *Click the Mouse and Bet the House: The United States' Internet Gambling Restrictions Before the World Trade Organization,* 2005 U. Ill. J.L. Tech. & Pol'y 125. Is the WTO the proper forum for resolving the legality of Internet gambling?

2. UNITED STATES PROCEDURAL LAW

When a computer crime occurs entirely in the United States, federal investigators must comply with the Fourth Amendment, the Wiretap Act, the Pen Register Statute, and the Stored Communications Act. But what laws govern investigations when the collection of evidence occurs in part or in whole outside the United States?

The case of statutory law is relatively easy. Several courts have held that the Wiretap Act applies only to interception inside the United States. Any interception of wire or electronic communications outside the United States is not covered by the Act. *See, e.g.,* United States v. Cotroni, 527 F.2d 708, 711 (2d Cir. 1975). As a district court has explained:

> Congress intended Title III to protect the integrity of United States communications systems against unauthorized interceptions taking place in the United States. If Congress had meant to require law

enforcement agencies to satisfy Title III for interceptions conducted outside the United States, it would have provided some mechanism by which agents could obtain such approval. Congress did not do so.

United States v. Angulo–Hurtado, 165 F. Supp. 2d 1363, 1369 (N.D. Ga. 2001).

Although courts have not addressed the question, it seems likely that the Stored Communications Act and the Pen Register statute have the same territorial limit. Both statutes share common roots with the Wiretap Act, as well as many statutory terms, so it seems probable that they share the Wiretap Act's territorial scope. As a result, acquisition of digital evidence outside the United States does not require compliance with the statutory surveillance laws.

Fourth Amendment limits on the acquisition of digital evidence outside the United States are much more complicated. Existing caselaw remains sparse, but the framework appears to hinge on two key questions: first, who is being monitored, and second, who is doing the monitoring. The next case introduces the framework.

UNITED STATES v. BARONA

United States Court of Appeals for the Ninth Circuit, 1995.
56 F.3d 1087.

WALLACE, CHIEF JUDGE.

Following extensive investigation, including wiretaps in foreign countries, the appellants were indicted and convicted of drug-related crimes.

I

The issues we discuss arose in the context of a criminal prosecution of six individuals for an ongoing conspiracy to distribute cocaine. Mario Ernesto Villabona–Alvarado and Brian Bennett organized and supervised the operation. Cocaine from Colombia entered the United States through a source named "Oscar." The cocaine was then delivered by Maria Barona and Luz Janneth Martinez to Michael McCarver and Michael Harris for further distribution.

Several events led to the identification of this conspiracy and its participants. Between 1985 and 1987, the Drug Enforcement Administration and the Los Angeles Police Department conducted a money-laundering investigation code-named "Operation Pisces." The result of this investigation was the arrest of Leonardo Gomez in Villabona's residence. Then in December 1987, Villabona and Bennett traveled to Copenhagen, Denmark, and registered at the Savoy Hotel. On December 7, 1987, Villabona, his wife (Helle Nielsen), and Bennett traveled to Aalborg, Denmark, to stay with Nielsen's parents. While in Aalborg, Villabona placed calls from the Nielsen residence and from a public telephone. On December 8, 1987, Villabona and Bennett returned to Copenhagen and stayed at the Hotel Sara–Dan. From Copenhagen,

Villabona and Bennett flew to Milan, Italy, and registered at the Hilton International Hotel on December 9, 1987. In late March 1988, Villabona returned to Aalborg, Denmark, and again used the same public telephone. In each of these locations, the telephone calls made by Villabona were monitored by the Danish (or in one case, Italian) authorities. Tapes of these wiretaps were played for the jury and were relied on at least in part to convict Villabona, Bennett, Martinez, Barona, Harris, and McCarver.

Between March and November 1988, Bennett asked Stanley McCarns to transport 502 kilograms of cocaine from Los Angeles to Detroit and to return with millions of dollars. Stanley McCarns then arranged for Willie Childress and his cousin, James McCarns, to transport the cocaine. Childress and James McCarns were stopped en route on November 6, 1988, and a Missouri state trooper seized the cocaine. On November 11, 1988, domestic wiretaps commenced on two cellular telephones used by Villabona. These taps also resulted in the interception of several incriminating conversations.

II

The district court ruled on the motion to suppress the Denmark wiretap evidence as follows:

> The Court agrees with the Defense, that other than the Milan Wiretap, that these were wiretaps which were engaged in as a joint venture by the United States and Denmark. The Court finds that the order issued by the Danish Court was lawful and in accordance with their law. The Court finds that the United States authorities reasonably relied upon the representations of the Danish officials with respect to the wiretaps, and therefore they were acting—in the Court's opinion—in good faith.

The question of whether the wiretaps were a joint venture requires the district court to scrutinize the attendant facts. Therefore, we will not disturb such a finding unless it is clearly erroneous. We review de novo, however, the finding that the wiretaps were conducted in accordance with foreign law, *United States v. Peterson,* 812 F.2d 486, 490 (9th Cir. 1987), as well as the question of whether United States agents reasonably relied in good faith upon the foreign officials' representations that the wiretaps were legal under foreign law.

A.

When determining the validity of a foreign wiretap, we start with two general and undisputed propositions. The first is that Title III of the Omnibus Crime Control and Safe Streets Act of 1968, 18 U.S.C. §§ 2510–21, "has no extraterritorial force." *Peterson,* 812 F.2d at 492. Our analysis, then, is guided only by the applicable principles of constitutional law. The second proposition is that neither our Fourth Amendment nor the judicially created exclusionary rule applies to acts of foreign officials.

Two very limited exceptions apply. One exception, clearly inapplicable here, occurs if the circumstances of the foreign search and seizure are so extreme that they shock the judicial conscience, so that a federal appellate court in the exercise of its supervisory powers can require exclusion of the evidence. This type of exclusion is not based on our Fourth Amendment jurisprudence, but rather on the recognition that we may employ our supervisory powers when absolutely necessary to preserve the integrity of the criminal justice system. The wiretaps at issue cannot be said to shock the conscience. Even when no authorization for a foreign wiretap was secured in violation of the foreign law itself, we have not excluded the evidence under this rationale, nor should we. Here, the foreign courts were involved and purported to authorize the wiretaps. The conduct here, therefore, does not come close to requiring the invocation of this exception.

The second exception to the inapplicability of the exclusionary rule applies when United States agents' participation in the investigation is so substantial that the action is a joint venture between United States and foreign officials. If a joint venture is found to have existed, the law of the foreign country must be consulted at the outset as part of the determination whether or not the search was reasonable. If foreign law was not complied with, the good faith exception to the exclusionary rule becomes part of the analysis. The good faith exception is grounded in the realization that the exclusionary rule does not function as a deterrent in cases in which the law enforcement officers acted on a reasonable belief that their conduct was legal.

It is this exception that the appellants invoke, asking us to conclude (1) that the United States and foreign officials were engaged in a joint venture, (2) that a violation of foreign law occurred making the search unreasonable, and (3) that the United States did not rely in good faith upon the foreign officials' representations that their law was being complied with.

B.

Because this exception is based solely on the Fourth Amendment, the appellants must first show that they are among the class of persons that the Fourth Amendment was meant to protect. In this case, three appellants, Martinez, Barona, and Villabona, are not United States citizens.

The Supreme Court has said, with regard to foreign searches involving aliens with "no voluntary connection" to the United States, that the Fourth Amendment is simply inapplicable. *See United States v. Verdugo–Urquidez*, 494 U.S. 259, 274–75 (1990). *Verdugo* reversed a decision of this circuit in which the panel majority found the Fourth Amendment applicable to a search of a Mexican citizen's Mexicali residence. *See United States v. Verdugo–Urquidez*, 856 F.2d 1214 (9th Cir. 1988), *rev'd*, 494 U.S. 259 (1990). The Supreme Court rejected this court's "global view of the Fourth Amendment's applicability which would plunge us into a sea of uncertainty as to what might be reasonable in the way of searches and seizures conducted abroad." *Verdugo,* 494 U.S. at 274.

Unlike the Due Process Clause of the Fifth Amendment, which protects all "persons," the Fourth Amendment protects only "the People of the United States." *Id.* at 265 (explaining that the term "people" used in the Fourth Amendment was a term of art employed in selected parts of the Constitution to refer to "the People of the United States"). This term "refers to a class of persons who are part of a national community or who have otherwise developed sufficient connection with this country to be considered part of that community." *Id.* The Fourth Amendment therefore protects a much narrower class of individuals than the Fifth Amendment.

Because our constitutional theory is premised in large measure on the conception that our Constitution is a "social contract," *Verdugo-Urquidez,* 856 F.2d at 1231–33, the scope of an alien's rights depends intimately on the extent to which he has chosen to shoulder the burdens that citizens must bear. Not until an alien has assumed the complete range of obligations that we impose on the citizenry may he be considered one of 'the people of the United States' entitled to the full panoply of rights guaranteed by our Constitution.

The term "People of the United States" includes "American citizens at home and abroad" and lawful resident aliens within the borders of the United States "who are victims of actions taken *in the United States* by American officials." *Verdugo–Urquidez,* 856 F.2d at 1234 (Wallace, J., dissenting) (emphasis in original). It is yet to be decided, however, whether a resident alien has undertaken sufficient obligations of citizenship or has otherwise developed sufficient connection with this country to be considered one of "the People of the United States" even when he or she steps outside the territorial borders of the United States.

It is not clear, therefore, that Villabona or the other non-citizen defendants in this case are entitled to receive any Fourth Amendment protection whatsoever. Any entitlement that they may have to invoke the Fourth Amendment in the context of an *extraterritorial* search is by no means clear. We could hold, therefore, that Barona, Martinez, and Villabona have failed to demonstrate that, at the time of the extraterritorial search, they were "People of the United States" entitled to receive the full panoply of rights guaranteed by our Constitution. We choose, however, not to reach the question because even if they were entitled to invoke the Fourth Amendment, their effort would be unsuccessful.

C.

Bennett, Harris, and McCarver are all United States citizens, and thus can invoke the protection of the Fourth Amendment generally. Our cases establishing the exception as to when the Fourth Amendment can be invoked in an extraterritorial search control our analysis.

First, the district court did not clearly err in finding that the four Danish wiretaps at issue were "joint ventures." In *Peterson,* we gave weight to the fact that the DEA "was involved daily in translating and decoding intercepted transmissions as well as advising the foreign authorities of their relevance." 812 F.2d at 490. Similarly here, the American Embassy was interested in the movement of Villabona and Bennett, American agents requested the wiretaps, information obtained was immediately forwarded to them, and throughout the surveillance a Spanish to English interpreter was provided by the United States.

Because there was a joint venture, we must decide whether the search was reasonable. In determining whether the search was reasonable, we must first consult the law of the relevant foreign countries. The relevant provisions of Danish law are: (1) section 191 of the Danish Criminal Code (Code) and (2) sections 780–791 of the Danish Administration of Justice Act (Justice Act).

Justice Act § 781(1) authorizes the intervention of secret communications, including the wiretapping of telephonic communications, if: (1) "weighty reasons" exist to assume messages are being conveyed via the medium in question, (2) the intervention is of decisive importance to the investigation, and (3) the investigation concerns an offense punishable by six or more years or is one of several other specifically enumerated offenses. Under Code § 191(1), the drug offenses at issue here are punishable by six or more years, thus satisfying section 781(1)(3).

In addition to these three requirements under Justice Act § 781(1), Danish law is somewhat more strict when it comes to monitoring conversations by use of a listening device or "bug" rather than by the tapping of telephone lines. Justice Act § 781(4) allows the use of such devices to intercept communications only if the suspected offense involves "danger to the lives or welfare of human beings or considerable social assets." This latter section was relevant to the Danish Court in two of the surveillances because the government sought to use both a listening device and wiretaps. The section is not relevant to us, however, because it appears that no surveillance evidence, other than wiretap evidence, was used at trial. Even if such evidence were admitted, however, section 781(4) was followed.

Justice Act § 783 outlines procedures to acquire a wiretap, section 784 provides for an attorney to be appointed for the target party, and section 788 provides for notification of the wiretap to the target party, unless the court omits or postpones such notification under section 788(4). After carefully reviewing the record, we are satisfied that Danish law was followed.

The first monitoring of communications occurred at the Savoy Hotel, Copenhagen, from December 4 to 7, 1987. The Danish police monitored communications both by tapping the hotel telephone lines, and by installing an electronic listening device in Villabona's room. In accordance with Danish law, the court held a hearing on December 5, 1987, at 10:00 a.m. to determine whether the wiretap and electronic eavesdropping, begun on December 4, 1987, was to be maintained. Justice Act § 783(3) allows police to make the necessary intervention subject to court approval within 24 hours. The Danish court gave its approval based on information that Villabona, Nielsen (who is not a party in this appeal), and Bennett (the occupants of the room) were suspected of violations of Code § 191, that they had transferred large amounts of money to Danish bank accounts, and that within a few days they had spent thousands of dollars on telephone calls. The Danish court concluded: "According to the available information, including, especially the transfers of money and the extent of the telephone bills, definite reasons exist to believe that the said telephone is being used to give information to, or from, a person suspected of violation of Penal Code § 191." These findings satisfied Justice Act §§ 781(1), (3), and the Danish court satisfied Justice Act § 781(2) by determining that the monitoring was of definite importance to the investigation. The targeted parties had been appointed counsel according to Justice Act § 784(1)(1)-(3). The court authorized the monitoring until December 11, 1987.

The second wiretaps were of the Nielsen residence and the public telephone, Aalborg, from December 7 to 9, 1987. On December 7, 1987, the court was notified that Villabona, Bennett, and Nielsen had made plans to travel to Aalborg. The Danish police then requested permission to monitor the telephone at Nielsen's residence in Aalborg, as well as authorization to install an electronic eavesdropping device in any hotel rooms they might move to, and to monitor any telephone calls from any such hotel rooms. The court granted the requested authorization until December 11, 1987.

After investigators observed Villabona making calls from the public telephone in Aalborg, Danish officials requested that the public telephone calls also be monitored. The Aalborg court allowed the monitoring of the public telephone calls until December 11, 1987. Again, the provisions of the Justice Act were followed. On December 18, 1987, the court, in accordance with Justice Act § 788 found that Nielsen and the owner of the public telephone "should not be informed about the phone bugging undertaken, as disclosure would be damaging to the investigation of the case."

The third wiretap involved the Hotel Sara–Dan, Copenhagen, from December 8 to 9, 1987. On December 9, 1987, the Copenhagen Municipal Court was told that on December 8 a tap was placed on a telephone at the Hotel Sara–Dan. Villabona and Bennett had returned from Aalborg to Copenhagen so that they could fly to Milan on December 9, 1987. The court, in accordance with Justice Act § 781, found that "definite reasons" existed to believe that the monitored communications contained information concerning suspected violations of Penal Code § 191, and that the monitoring "must be considered of decisive importance for the investigation." The monitoring stopped on December 9 because Villabona, Bennett, and Nielsen left the hotel. As in the previous episodes, the court waived the "duty to notify" the targets in accordance with Justice Act § 788(4).

The fourth tap involved the Nielsen residence and the public telephone, Aalborg, from March 28 to April 16, 1988. The Aalborg court was informed that Villabona and Nielsen were to return to Aalborg on March 28. Permission to tap the telephone at Nielsen's residence and the public telephone were sought. The Aalborg court found that based on Villabona's and Nielsen's last visit and telephone use, the tap was justified under the Justice Act. The tap was to expire on April 22, 1988, "with the provision that monitoring must be discontinued immediately if the defendants move."

A fifth wiretap occurred in Milan, Italy. On December 9, 1987, Villabona and Bennett arrived in Milan from Copenhagen. The day before, the Danish police notified a United States special agent of this planned trip. He, in turn, telephoned a United States special agent in Milan and requested physical surveillance. The latter agent contacted Major Rabiti of the Guardia Di Finanza and requested a watch on Villabona and Bennett. Rabiti obtained authorization to wiretap their hotel room.

The district court found that this wiretap was not the product of a joint venture between United States and Italian authorities. That a United States agent told Rabiti about Villabona and Bennett did not create a "joint venture" between the United States and Italy regarding this wiretap. We hold that the district court did not clearly err when it found no joint investigation surrounding the Milan wiretap, and, therefore, that Fourth Amendment principles do not apply. Because the wiretap was conducted by foreign officials without substantial United States involvement, the results are admissible.

In summary, the finding that the Milan wiretap was not a joint venture is not clearly erroneous. The finding that the Danish wiretaps were conducted pursuant to a joint venture is also not clearly erroneous, but Danish law was complied with for each Danish wiretap. None of the evidence from the wiretaps is therefore subject to exclusion under the Fourth Amendment.

REINHARDT, CIRCUIT JUDGE, dissenting.

Here, in a few, short, deceptively simple paragraphs, the majority has taken another substantial step toward the elimination of what was once a firmly established constitutional right—the right of American citizens to be free from unreasonable searches conducted by their own government.

This time, the majority holds that for all practical purposes the Fourth Amendment's protections do not extend beyond our borders, and that the only limitations on searches of Americans abroad are those imposed by foreign governments, *even when our government initiates and participates in the search.* Oddly, the majority reaches this erroneous and unfortunate result by first acknowledging what it must—that the Fourth Amendment *is* applicable to such searches. However, it then strips this important principle of all significance by holding that we must look exclusively to *foreign law* when determining whether the search violates the Fourth Amendment. According to the majority, our government's decision to initiate the search of an American citizen satisfies the requirements of that once powerful Amendment so long as the foreign officials who conduct the search comply with their own laws. Thus, the majority opinion stands for the paradoxical rule that the Fourth Amendment applies to searches of American citizens in which United States agents play a substantial role but that probable cause, the most basic requirement of the Fourth Amendment, does not—except in the unlikely circumstance that the foreign land in which the search is conducted happens to have the identical requirements that our Constitution imposes.

The practical consequences of the majority's opinion can be simply stated. Without the probable cause requirement, the Fourth Amendment is without any real force. Searches of American citizens abroad can be instigated at the will of government agents. Any American traveling outside our nation's boundaries on vacation, business, or just visiting his family, is now fair game for wiretapping, surreptitious searches, and other invasions of privacy *whenever* members of the CIA, the DEA, the FBI, or who knows how many other alphabet law enforcement agencies, so desire.

Put simply, what the majority holds is that the only Fourth Amendment protections United States citizens who travel abroad enjoy vis-a-vis the United States government are those safeguards, if any, afforded by the laws of the foreign nations they visit. Under the majority's holding, the Fourth Amendment's requirements are wholly redundant since they provide nothing more than is already provided by foreign law. In fact, under the majority's rule, the Fourth Amendment provides even less protection than foreign law since, according to the principal case on which the majority relies, the Constitution does not even require foreign officials to comply with their own law; all that is required is that American officials have a good faith belief that they did so. Thus, even though the majority concedes that the Fourth Amendment applies to joint-venture searches like the one before us, it holds that when Americans enter Iraq, Iran, Singapore, Kuwait, China, or other similarly inclined foreign lands, they can be treated by the United States government exactly the way those foreign nations treat their own citizens—at least for Fourth Amendment purposes.

Notes and Questions

1. *The first question: Who is being monitored?* As the *Barona* case explains, the threshold Fourth Amendment question in a case involving extraterritorial evidence collection is the identity of the person subject to surveillance.

The key case is United States v. Verdugo–Urquidez, 494 U.S. 259 (1990), which considered a search of Mexican residences belonging to a suspected drug kingpin who was a citizen of Mexico. The defendant was arrested in Mexico by Mexico authorities, and he was turned over to the United States to face criminal charges in the United States. United States agents arranged a search of the defendant's home as part of a joint operation between United States and Mexico law enforcement agencies. A search of Verdugo–Urquidez's residence in Mexicali, Mexico, uncovered a "tally sheet" that investigators believed reflected quantities of marijuana smuggled into the United States. When charges were filed against Verdugo–Urquidez in the United States, his attorney moved to suppress the tally sheet on the ground that the search of the defendant's Mexicali home violated the Fourth Amendment.

In a majority opinion by Chief Justice Rehnquist, the Supreme Court concluded that the defendant had no Fourth Amendment rights because he lacked sufficient voluntary contacts with the United States to be among "the People" covered by the Fourth Amendment:

> What we know of the history of the drafting of the Fourth Amendment * * * suggests that its purpose was to restrict searches and seizures which might be conducted by the United States in domestic matters. * * * The available historical data show * * * that the purpose of the Fourth Amendment was to protect the people of the United States against arbitrary action by their own Government; it was never suggested that the provision was intended to restrain the actions of the Federal Government against aliens outside of the United States territory.

> We think that the text of the Fourth Amendment, its history, and our cases discussing the application of the Constitution to aliens and extraterritorially require rejection of respondent's claim. At the time of the search, he was a citizen and resident of Mexico with no voluntary attachment to the United States, and the place searched was located in Mexico. Under these circumstances, the Fourth Amendment has no application.

> For better or for worse, we live in a world of nation-states in which our Government must be able to function effectively in the company of sovereign nations. Some who violate our laws may live outside our borders under a regime quite different from that which obtains in this country. Situations threatening to important American interests may arise half-way around the globe, situations which in the view of the political branches of our Government require an American response with armed force. If there are to be restrictions on searches and seizures which occur incident to such American action, they must be imposed by the political branches through diplomatic understanding, treaty, or legislation.

Id. at 266, 274–75.

Justice Kennedy provided the fifth vote for the *Verdugo–Urquidez* majority opinion, but he also wrote a concurring opinion suggesting a different approach. Justice Kennedy rejected Chief Justice Rehnquist's focus on the original meaning of "the People," and instead focused on the practical difficulty of applying a warrant requirement overseas:

> I cannot place any weight on the reference to "the people" in the Fourth Amendment as a source of restricting its protections. With respect, I submit these words do not detract from its force or its reach. Given the history of our Nation's concern over warrantless and unrea-

sonable searches, explicit recognition of "the right of the people" to Fourth Amendment protection may be interpreted to underscore the importance of the right, rather than to restrict the category of persons who may assert it. The restrictions that the United States must observe with reference to aliens beyond its territory or jurisdiction depend, as a consequence, on general principles of interpretation, not on an inquiry as to who formed the Constitution or a construction that some rights are mentioned as being those of "the people."

The conditions and considerations of this case would make adherence to the Fourth Amendment's warrant requirement impracticable and anomalous. * * * [T]he Constitution does not require United States agents to obtain a warrant when searching the foreign home of a nonresident alien. If the search had occurred in a residence within the United States, I have little doubt that the full protections of the Fourth Amendment would apply. But that is not this case. The absence of local judges or magistrates available to issue warrants, the differing and perhaps unascertainable conceptions of reasonableness and privacy that prevail abroad, and the need to cooperate with foreign officials all indicate that the Fourth Amendment's warrant requirement should not apply in Mexico as it does in this country. For this reason, in addition to the other persuasive justifications stated by the Court, I agree that no violation of the Fourth Amendment has occurred in the case before us.

Id. at 276, 278 (Kennedy, J., concurring). Justice Brennan dissented, joined by Justice Marshall:

[T]he majority ignores * * * the most obvious connection between Verdugo–Urquidez and the United States: he was investigated and is being prosecuted for violations of United States law and may well spend the rest of his life in a United States prison. The "sufficient connection" is supplied not by Verdugo–Urquidez, but by the Government. Respondent is entitled to the protections of the Fourth Amendment because our Government, by investigating him and attempting to hold him accountable under United States criminal laws, has treated him as a member of our community for purposes of enforcing our laws. He has become, quite literally, one of the governed. Fundamental fairness and the ideals underlying our Bill of Rights compel the conclusion that when we impose societal obligations such as the obligation to comply with our criminal laws, on foreign nationals, we in turn are obliged to respect certain correlative rights, among them the Fourth Amendment.

Id. at 283–84 (Brennan, J., dissenting).

The *Barona* majority opinion suggests that Barona, Martinez, and Villabona might have no Fourth Amendment rights under *Verdugo–Urquidez.* Do you agree? What facts would you want to know to answer this question?

2. *The second question: Who is doing the monitoring?* Assuming that a defendant has Fourth Amendment rights under *Verdugo–Urquidez,* the next question considers who is doing the monitoring. There are three categories to consider: 1) investigations conducted by foreign governments, 2) joint investigations by U.S. officials and foreign government investigators, and 3) investigations conducted exclusively by U.S. officials.

As the *Barona* case indicates, the Fourth Amendment does not apply to investigations by foreign governments. This makes sense: The Fourth Amendment does not regulate conduct by private actors, and officials from foreign governments are the equivalent of private actors from a constitutional standpoint. At the same time, some courts have suggested that there are limits on the admissibility of evidence from searches and seizures by foreign governments. The *Barona* case articulates the standard that has been recited a number of times in the Ninth Circuit: the test is whether the search and seizure by the foreign government "shocks the judicial conscience." If it does, the court can require exclusion of the evidence "in the exercise of its supervisory powers." *But see* United States v. Mount, 757 F.2d 1315, 1320 (D.C. Cir. 1985) (Bork, J., concurring) (arguing that lower courts lack supervisory powers to impose an exclusionary rule for searches by foreign governments).

The Fourth Amendment does apply to searches and seizures undertaken as part of a joint investigation by U.S. officials and foreign government investigators. The governing law here is rather murky, as the Supreme Court has never directly addressed the relevant legal standard. In the Ninth Circuit, however, the general Fourth Amendment command is reasonableness; specifically, it is reasonableness measured by reference to the law in the country where the search occurred. If investigators in the United States ask French investigators to wiretap an e-mail account in France, for example, the constitutional reasonableness of the surveillance is measured by reference to French law. This standard requires judges to apply foreign law and determine if the monitoring was legal where it occurred. If it was legal, the thinking goes, it was constitutionally reasonable. *See* United States v. Peterson, 812 F.2d 486, 490 (9th Cir. 1987) (Kennedy, J.).

The Fourth Amendment also applies to searches abroad conducted exclusively by United States officials. As a practical matter, such searches are rare. United States officials normally will work with governments abroad, triggering the "joint investigation" standards. As a result of the rarity of such unilateral searches, the law here is particularly unclear. However, you can see some of the difficult legal questions these searches raise. For example, United States law presently does not permit officials to obtain a search warrant to conduct a search outside the United States. If the Fourth Amendment requires a warrant but statutory law does not permit one to be obtained, does the exclusionary rule apply?

Related issues arose in United States v. Bin Laden, 126 F. Supp. 2d 264 (S.D.N.Y. 2000), a criminal prosecution against several members of Al–Qaeda for taking part in a conspiracy that included the bombings of United States embassies in Tanzania and Kenya in 1998. (Bin Laden himself was indicted, but was not located and therefore was not tried along with the defendants who were present.) The evidence against the defendants included recordings of telephone calls made by several of the defendants from an Al–Qaeda operation in Kenya that had been monitored by U.S. intelligence agencies starting in 1996. One of the defendants, El–Hage, was a United States citizen, and argued that the warrantless monitoring violated his Fourth Amendment rights. The district court agreed with El–Hage that the Fourth Amendment applied fully to the monitoring of his telephone calls in Kenya.

However, the court held that in light of the unusual circumstances of the case, the exclusionary rule did not apply. *See id.* at 282–85.

3. In the *Barona* case, Judge Wallace and Judge Reinhardt disagree on the Fourth Amendment framework that should apply to "joint investigations" outside the United States. Judge Wallace measures reasonableness based on compliance with the law where the search occurs, whereas Judge Reinhardt apparently would analyze joint searches outside the United States using the same Fourth Amendment rules that apply inside the United States to searches conducted exclusively by United States investigators.

Which approach makes more sense? Let's break down the possibilities. If the Fourth Amendment and foreign search and seizure law happen to be identical, then it makes no difference which approach is followed. If foreign law is more privacy-protective than the Fourth Amendment, however, Judge Wallace's approach will hold investigators to a higher standard than will Judge Reinhardt's standard. For example, if surveillance law in Freedonia does not have a consent exception, a joint investigation that listens in on a telephone call of a United States citizen vacationing in Freedonia with the other party's consent would violate the Fourth Amendment even if the same surveillance technique would not violate the Fourth Amendment if it occurred inside the United States. On the other hand, if foreign law is less protective than the Fourth Amendment, Judge Wallace's approach will hold investigators to a lower standard than Judge Reinhardt's standard. For example, if surveillance law in Freedonia lets the police obtain a wiretap order based only on reasonable suspicion (that is, without probable cause), a joint investigation that taps a phone in Freedonia would not violate the Fourth Amendment even if the same technique would violate the Fourth Amendment if it occurred inside the United States.

Does it make sense that the Fourth Amendment rights of United States citizens fluctuates based on the domestic law of the country where they are physically present? Does your answer depend on whether foreign law only determines the reasonableness of searches, as compared to compliance with the Fourth Amendment more broadly? The difference may be important. For example, suppose the Freedonia Constitution requires a probable cause search warrant to install a pen register. Does this mean that the warrantless use of a pen register in Freedonia to monitor a United States citizen violates the Fourth Amendment? Or does *Smith v. Maryland* apply to the question of what is a search, with the *Barona* inquiry into foreign law used only to determine whether a search or seizure is reasonable?

Finally, consider how Judge Reinhardt's approach might work (or not work) in practice. If United States investigators must follow the same Fourth Amendment rules abroad that they follow in the United States, they may need to obtain court orders or follow procedures that local law does not have or even flatly forbids. For example, one pillar of Fourth Amendment law is that warrants must be issued by a detached and neutral magistrate. *See* Johnson v. United States 333 U.S. 10, 13–14 (1948). Foreign judges may not qualify under this standard, as not every country follows the tripartite scheme of separation of powers found in the United States. Does this mean that foreign search warrants may not satisfy the Fourth Amendment, even if they require probable cause and particularity? If so, how can United States investigators collect evidence without violating the Fourth Amendment?

4. *Foreign law and the exclusionary rule.* In his *Barona* dissent, Judge Reinhardt claims that "[u]nder the majority's holding, the Fourth Amendment's requirements are wholly redundant since they provide nothing more than is already provided by foreign law." Is this accurate? Fourth Amendment protection adds something critically important: the remedy of a constitutional exclusionary rule. The exclusionary rule is very rare outside the United States, and where it applies it is optional rather than mandatory. *See* Craig M. Bradley, *The Emerging International Consensus as to Criminal Procedure Rule*, 14 Mich. J. Int'l L. 171, 174 (1993).

5. *Cross-border searches.* In United States v. Gorshkov, 2001 WL 1024026 (W.D. Wash. 2001), a computer hacker from Russia who had hacked into several United States computers was lured to the United States by an FBI undercover operation. The hacker believed that he was interviewing for a computer security job at an American company called "Invita." Working from Invita's office, he used his username and password to access an Internet account in Russia. FBI agents copied the username and password, and they later used them to remotely access and download the defendant's files stored on the Russian server. The district court held that accessing and downloading the file did not violate the Fourth Amendment under *Verdugo–Urquidez*:

> The use of the password to access the Russian computers and download the data did not constitute a Fourth Amendment violation. The Fourth Amendment does not apply to the agents' extraterritorial access to computers in Russia and their copying of data contained thereon. * * * [T]he Russian computers are not protected by the Fourth Amendment because they are property of a non-resident and located outside the territory of the United States. Under *United States v. Verdugo–Urquidez,* 494 U.S. 259 (1990), the Fourth Amendment does not apply to a search or seizure of a non-resident alien's property outside the territory of the United States. In this case, the computers accessed by the agents were located in Russia, as was the data contained on those computers that the agents copied. Until the copied data was transmitted to the United States, it was outside the territory of this country and not subject to the protections of the Fourth Amendment.

> Defendant attempts to distinguish *Verdugo* by first noting that the defendant in that case was found not to have significant contacts with the United States because he involuntarily entered the country after his arrest, while in this case Defendant Gorshkov voluntarily entered the country. The Court finds, however, that a single entry into the United States that is made for a criminal purpose is hardly the sort of voluntary association with this country that should qualify Defendant as part of our national community for purposes of the Fourth Amendment. Defendant also attempts to distinguish *Verdugo* by noting that the search in *Verdugo* was effected by a joint effort made lawfully pursuant to Mexican law, with the consent and authorization of Mexican officials, while in this case the search was done by FBI fiat. Nothing in the opinion, however, indicates that the reach of the Fourth Amendment

turns on this issue. Therefore, the search of the Russian computers was not protected by the Fourth Amendment.

Id. at *3. Is this argument persuasive? Did the defendant really enter the United States "for a criminal purpose"? Wasn't his purpose to obtain legitimate employment as a computer security consultant?

More broadly, what legal framework should govern so-called "cross-border searches," remote searches from one country of data located in another country?

Assume FBI agents are conducting an investigation of a United States citizen located abroad. What Fourth Amendment rules regulate access to that person's remotely stored files? Should the location of the person under investigation make any difference? Should the legality of such searches consider the law where the data is located?

What factors are relevant to determining a "reasonable expectation of privacy" abroad? If an FBI agent in the United States accesses an account in France belonging to an American citizen, should the FBI agent need to obtain a warrant? Where can he obtain the warrant—in the United States or in France? What if the FBI agent is located in France?

For more on cross-border searches, see Stewart M. Young, Comment, *Verdugo in Cyberspace: Boundaries of Fourth Amendment Rights for Foreign Nationals in Cybercrime Cases*, 10 Mich. Telecomm. & Tech. L. Rev. 139 (2003); Jack L. Goldsmith, *The Internet and the Legitimacy of Remote Cross-Border Searches*, 2001 U. Chi. Legal. F. 103; Patricia L. Bellia, *Chasing Bits Across Borders*, 2001 U. Chi. Legal. F. 35.

3. MUTUAL LEGAL ASSISTANCE AND INTERNATIONAL TREATIES

In most computer crime cases, digital evidence located abroad is collected by agents of foreign governments under laws that govern mutual legal assistance. These laws regulate both the collection of evidence in the United States by United States officials at the behest of foreign governments and the collection of evidence outside of the United States by foreign governments at the behest of the United States.

BRUCE ZAGARIS—UNCLE SAM EXTENDS REACH FOR EVIDENCE WORLDWIDE

15 Crim. Just. 4 (Winter 2001).

As the world grows smaller, the United States has substantially increased its reach in transnational criminal cases. Its most significant accomplishment has been extending its treaty network and the practical arrangements for gathering evidence admissible for the investigation and prosecution of criminal cases. These new mechanisms enable the United States and other countries to send and receive evidence in a form that is admissible for prosecuting crimes ranging from murder to white collar cases in which some of the evidence (e.g., witnesses, bank accounts, weapons, documents, and proceeds of crime) is in another country.

This article traces the developments of evidence gathering through unilateral means, letters rogatory, mutual assistance in criminal matters treaties (MLATs), and mini-MLATs.

Letters rogatory

The letter rogatory is one of the most often used methods to obtain evidence through a compulsory process in the United States. Letter rogatory refers to the judicial procedures whereby one country requests judicial assistance from another. Under 28 U.S.C. § 1782, any tribunal, foreign or U.S., can obtain evidence in foreign criminal proceedings. The term "tribunal" includes magistrates in civil law countries who conduct investigations to determine whether criminal charges should be brought against individuals.

A tribunal or an interested person may initiate a letter rogatory or other request for judicial assistance in a criminal matter. In its discretion, a U.S. district court can grant or refuse an order and may impose conditions on such assistance, which may include obtaining witness testimony, business records, forensic evidence, and tangible documents. Usually, if it grants assistance, a U.S. district court will appoint a person, referred to as a commissioner, to supervise the taking of testimony. If the foreign court does not prescribe the procedure to be used in executing the request, § 1782 requires application of the Federal Rules of Civil Procedure. A person who testifies pursuant to a U.S. court order may assert any legally applicable privilege under the laws of the United States or the country in which the relevant proceeding is pending.

U.S. jurisprudence has allowed prosecutors in common-law countries to compel the testimony of witnesses in the United States even though no proceeding is pending before a foreign court, provided that an actual criminal investigation exists in connection with the requested testimony; the testimony is requested for use in a proceeding before a court in the requesting state, if criminal charges are brought, and criminal proceedings are imminent or very likely.

U.S. federal and state courts regularly use the letters rogatory procedure to obtain evidence from abroad. A state court that issues a letter rogatory in a criminal case can ask the U.S. State Department to help transmit it to the requested country, or the court may transmit it through other channels, e.g., through the U.S. Department of Justice, which may result in more timely execution.

The letters rogatory process is clearly inferior to the procedures of a MLAT. Letters rogatory cannot be used prior to the grand jury stage of a criminal investigation since a U.S. court can issue a letter rogatory only if a judicial proceeding is pending before it. An investigator cannot always persuade an assistant U.S. attorney to spend the time necessary to start a grand jury investigation. Not all countries, especially common-law countries, will allow the use of letters rogatory at the grand jury stage. Because letters rogatory are normally not transmitted directly (usually it's done through the State Department or its foreign counterpart), substantial delays ensue. The lack of proper supervision and monitoring of the transmission and implementation of letters rogatory results in other problems in their execution as well. The execution of letters rogatory is discretionary, but the execution of a MLAT is mandatory—as is the method of implementing the request.

Mutual legal assistance treaties

Recently, the United States concluded a series of MLATs. They have proven to be more effective and efficient than letters rogatory when a compulsory process is required to obtain evidence in a requested state or when specific procedures must be complied with for the requested evidence to be admissible at a criminal trial in the requesting state.

On September 12, 2000, the U.S. Senate's Committee on Foreign Relations approved proposed criminal cooperation treaties, including the Inter–American MLAT and Related Optional Protocol, as well as bilateral treaties with Cyprus, Egypt, France, Greece, Nigeria, Romania, Russia, South Africa, and Ukraine.

Bruce C. Swartz, Deputy Assistant Attorney General of the U.S. Department of Justice, testified in support of ratification. Swartz explained that the nine bilateral MLATs would join 36 other existing MLATs. He noted that in 1999 the U.S. Department of Justice's Office of International Affairs made close to 500 requests for international assistance on behalf of state and federal prosecutors, and received more than 1,000 requests for assistance from abroad. Prior to the MLATs, there were far fewer requests and the results were less positive. Swartz pointed out that MLATs are important because they make assistance obligatory as a matter of international law, whereas letters rogatory are executed solely on the basis of comity. He noted that, under the MLATs, a request for assistance cannot be refused unless refusal is specifically allowed by the terms of the treaty, and the grounds for refusal of assistance under MLATs are quite limited. For instance, MLATs provide that before a country can refuse to execute a request under the treaty, the state must determine whether conditions are present that would make rendering assistance possible. If the requesting state accepts the assistance, subject to such conditions, it must comply with them. For example, a state that has been asked to furnish information could provide it on the condition that it be used only in the routine criminal case and not for any ancillary situation, e.g., administrative or civil case or legislative oversight proceeding. It could also agree to furnish information after redacting the portion of a document that might reveal confidential information affecting national security.

The United States, with its adversarial system of jurisprudence, has complex and stringent evidentiary rules, including hearsay rules and constitutional confrontation rights. Those evidentiary rules may not have any analogue in countries with an inquisitorial judicial system. MLATs provide an opportunity to develop procedures for obtaining foreign evidence in a form admissible in U.S. courts. The MLATs are especially helpful in providing a framework for cooperation in tracing, seizure, and forfeiture of criminal assets. The MLATs can provide a predictable and effective regime for obtaining evidence in criminal cases and can help federal, state, and local prosecutors pursue international cases in nine foreign countries.

There are also multilateral MLATs. Until now, the United States had only bilateral MLATs, although it is a member of multilateral treaties that have mutual assistance requirements, e.g., the 1988 U.N. Convention against the Trafficking of Illicit Narcotic and Psychotropic Substances. The Inter–American MLAT, when ratified, will constitute the first multilateral convention between the United States and other members of the Organization of American States (OAS) in the field of international judicial cooperation in criminal matters. It will provide a means for the United States to extend its mutual assistance treaty relationships in the Western hemisphere to countries where there might not be a sufficient basis to justify the resources needed to conclude separate bilateral treaties. For instance, upon ratification, the OAS–MLAT will create an immediate treaty relationship between the United States and Peru, where no bilateral MLAT now exists.

Notes and Questions

1. The Justice Department provides the following guidance to federal prosecutors on the process of obtaining letters rogatory in criminal cases:

> Letters rogatory are the customary method of obtaining assistance from abroad in the absence of a treaty or executive agreement. A letter rogatory is a request from a judge in the United States to the judiciary of a foreign country requesting the performance of an act which, if done without the sanction of the foreign court, would constitute a violation of that country's sovereignty. Prosecutors should assume that the process will take a year or more. Letters rogatory are customarily transmitted via the diplomatic channel, a time-consuming means of transmission. The time involved may be shortened by transmitting a copy of the request through Interpol, or through some other more direct route, but even in urgent cases the request may take over a month to execute.

> The form of a letter rogatory depends on the country to which it is addressed and the assistance sought. Some countries have statutory guidelines for granting assistance. Assistant United States Attorneys should seek specific guidance from the Office of International Affairs (OIA) before drafting a letter rogatory.

> Letters rogatory generally include: (1) background (who is investigating whom and for what charge); (2) the facts (enough information about the case for the foreign judge to conclude that a crime has been committed and to see the relevance of the evidence that is being sought); (3) assistance requested (be specific but include an elastic clause to allow subsequent expansion of the request without filing an additional letter rogatory); (4) the text of the statutes alleged to have been violated; and (5) a promise of reciprocity.

Letters rogatory must be signed by a judge and, normally, authenticated by (1) an apostille, (2) an exemplification certificate, (3) a chain certificate of authentication, or (4) as directed by OIA. If the requested state has ratified the Hague Convention Abolishing the Requirement of Legalization of Foreign Public Documents, it is preferable to use an apostille. The chain certification is a cumbersome process involving authentication by the Department of Justice, the Department of State, and the embassy of the foreign country to which the letter rogatory is directed.

U.S. Attorney's Manual, Criminal Resource Manual § 275 (1997).

2. *Letters rogatory by state officials.* State law enforcement officials can obtain letters rogatory to collect evidence abroad much like federal officials can. *See* Susan W. Brenner & Joseph J. Schwerha IV, *Transnational Evidence Gathering and Local Prosecution of International Cybercrime*, 20 J. Marshall J. Computer & Info. L. 347, 384–85 (2002).

3. *Letters rogatory by the defense.* After a defendant is charged, counsel for the defendant can obtain letters rogatory for use at trial. The defendant must ask the trial court for the authority to issue the letter, and must satisfy any other legal requirements for the request. *See, e.g.*, United States v. Korogodsky, 4 F. Supp. 2d 262 (S.D.N.Y. 1998). *See also* Ellen S. Podgor, Understanding International Criminal Law 89 (2004).

4. Henry H. Perritt, Jr., *Jurisdiction in Cyberspace*, 41 Vill. L. Rev. 1, 84–85 (1996):

[L]etters rogatory have serious limitations as a means of criminal investigation and discovery. Civil law systems typically will not accept letters rogatory from prosecutors because of the tradition in those systems that judges, called examining magistrates, conduct criminal investigation and discovery. Thus, letters rogatory are of little use when the requesting state is a common law jurisdiction, in which the prosecutor is in charge of investigation rather than a judicial official, and when the requested state is a civil law jurisdiction, which works in reverse.

MLATs are therefore of greater value. Each treaty to which the U.S. is a party contains a provision obligating a requested country to conduct searches and seizures on behalf of a requesting country if the request includes information justifying such action under the laws of the requested country. Although the treaties require that allegations of treaty violation be presented only to the executive authority of the requesting country and not to its courts, persons adversely affected by warrant equivalents or subpoenas do have recourse to the courts of the requested country to the extent that those courts are involved in obtaining the information. Because many other treaty partners lack a process equivalent to a subpoena duces tecum, the standards applicable to warrants are used for such countries.

5. *Challenging international legal process.* Imagine you are a defense attorney and you have just accepted a new case. Your client is a German citizen who lives in Germany and has been charged in federal court in the United States. According to the indictment, your client set up a fake website that looked just like the website for the Bank of America. Dozens of Bank of

America customers were tricked by the fake site, which was hosted on a server in California, and they entered their account information without realizing that the website was phony. Your client collected the information, accessed the customers' accounts online, and wired money to various accounts he controlled in African banks.

You contact the lead prosecutor, and he tells you that your client was caught after investigators conducted extensive surveillance both in the United States and in Germany. After the victims reported their lost funds, the FBI began monitoring all communications to and from the server in California. When communications traced back to Germany, the FBI requested mutual legal assistance pursuant to the MLAT between the United States and Germany. German investigators conducted extensive monitoring of your client's Internet and telephone use from his home in Munich. When your client took a vacation and traveled to the United States, he was arrested at the airport by the FBI.

Assume you believe that the investigation was conducted in violation of both United States and German wiretapping law, and you believe the proper forms were not filled out to comply with the terms of the mutual legal assistance treaty. What arguments can you make in court to challenge the legality of the investigation? Importantly, it seems that your only suppression remedy derives from the Fourth Amendment. Errors in the mutual legal assistance process ordinarily do not lead to suppression, unless perhaps a successful evidentiary argument can be made on authentication grounds. *See* United States v. Phillips, 1979 WL 1505 (M.D. Fla. 1979). German wiretapping law has a narrow exclusionary rule, *see* Paul Schwartz, *German and U.S. Telecommunications Privacy Law: Legal Regulation of Domestic Law Enforcement Surveillance*, 54 Hastings L.J. 751, 794 (2003), but it is unenforceable in a United States court. From your perspective, then, you are forced to try to assert Fourth Amendment arguments.

As a policy matter, is this appropriate? What remedies should defense counsel have to challenge international evidence collection and mutual legal assistance procedures?

MICHAEL A. SUSSMANN—THE CRITICAL CHALLENGES FROM INTERNATIONAL HIGH–TECH AND COMPUTER–RELATED CRIME AT THE MILLENNIUM

9 Duke J. Comp. & Int'l L. 451, 453–84 (1999).

Imagine this scene out of tomorrow's headlines: A hacker, going online through the Internet, breaks into computers that the Federal Aviation Administration uses for air traffic control. He disrupts a regional air traffic network, and the disruption causes the crash of a DC–10 in the Rocky Mountains, killing all aboard. The FAA and the FBI know there has been a hacker intrusion, originating through the Internet, but nothing else. Since anyone can access the Internet from anywhere in the world, the FBI has no idea where the hacker may be located. Moreover, they do not know the motive of the attack or the identity of the attackers. Is it a terrorist group, targeting the United States and likely to strike again at any time, or is it a fourteen-year-old hacker whose prank has spun tragically out of control?

Let us follow this scenario a bit further. Within thirty minutes of the plane crash, the FBI tracks the source of the attack to an Internet Service Provider in Germany. Assuming the worst, another attack could occur at any time, and hundreds of planes in flight over the United States are at risk. The next investigative step is to determine whether the ISP in Germany is a mere conduit, or whether the attack actually originated with a subscriber to that service. In either case, the FBI needs the assistance of the German ISP to help identify the source of the attack, but it is now 3:00 a.m. in Germany.

- Does the FBI dare wait until morning in Europe to seek formal legal assistance from Germany or permission from the German government to continue its investigation within their borders?

- Does the Department of Justice authorize the FBI's computer experts to conduct a search, without German consent, on the German ISP from their terminals in Washington?

- Does the FBI agent need a U.S. court order to access private information overseas? What would be the reach of such an order?

- If the FBI agent plows forward and accesses information from computers in Germany, will the German government be sympathetic to the U.S. plight, will the violation of German sovereignty be condemned, or both?

- What are the diplomatic and foreign policy implications of the United States remotely (and without advance notice) conducting a search that may intrude into German sovereignty?

The legal and policy implications of possible "transborder searches," such as the one contemplated in this scenario, are quickly becoming a concern for law enforcement agencies around the globe as they grapple with new challenges posed by networked communications and new technologies. Traditional investigative procedures—and particularly the often cumbersome procedures that govern investigations at the international level—may not be adequate to meet the need in computer crime cases for immediate law enforcement action reaching beyond national borders. The globalization of criminal activity has created vexing problems that, in some cases, defy simple solutions.

Needed: Sufficient Laws to Punish Computer Crimes

When Country A criminalizes certain conduct and Country B does not, a bridge for cooperation in solving a crime committed in Country A may not be possible. The United States has entered into bilateral treaties of extradition with over 100 countries. These treaties are either "list treaties," containing a list of offenses for which extradition is available, or they require dual criminality (i.e., require that the conduct under investigation is a crime in both the requesting and requested countries and is punishable by at least one year in prison). With regard to treaties for international legal assistance such as those involving the issuance of subpoenas, interviewing of witnesses, or production of documents, some treaties permit assistance as long as the conduct under investigation is a crime in the requesting state. The United States strongly favors this approach. Other treaties permit assistance only if dual criminality exits and if the offense is extraditable. Therefore, if one country does not criminalize computer misuse (or provide for sufficient punishment), extradition and the collection of certain evidence may be prohibited. Consider the following two examples.

In 1992, hackers from Switzerland attacked the San Diego Super-computer Center. The United States sought help from the Swiss, but the investigation was stymied due to lack of dual criminality (i.e., the two nations did not have similar laws banning the conduct), which became an impediment to official cooperation. Eventually, local police in Zurich did render informal assistance, and they prepared a list of questions for U.S. authorities to answer, transmitted through official channels, so the case could be properly pursued. After the United States answered those questions, but before follow-up questions could be answered through official channels, the hacking stopped, the trail went cold, and the case had to be closed.

Several years later a similar problem arose, when the United States found itself unable to reach a criminal in order to bring him to justice. From August 1995 until February 1996, the Naval Criminal Investigative Service and the FBI investigated a hacker who was stealing password files and altering log files in military, university, and other private computer systems. Many of these systems contained sensitive research on satellites, radiation, and energy-related engineering. U.S. authorities tracked the hacker to Argentina and notified a local Argentine telecommunications carrier. The carrier contacted local law enforcement, which began its own investigation. Subsequently, an Argentine judge authorized the search of the hacker's apartment and the seizure of his computer equipment based on potential violations of Argentine law. Unfortunately, the treaty between Argentina and the United States did not authorize the extradition of individuals for "computer crimes" (although it does for more traditional crimes). The U.S. Attorney's Office in Boston charged the perpetrator with several criminal violations, but it was unclear whether or not the case would ever be resolved due to the absence of uniformity between U.S. and Argentine laws. Fortunately, the hacker agreed to a plea bargain wherein he waived extradition and agreed to plead guilty in the United States.

These cases demonstrate how inadequate laws can allow criminals to go unpunished in one country, while they thwart the efforts of other countries to vindicate the rights of the state and protect its citizens. While the United States has amended its criminal code to specifically penalize a wide variety of computer crimes, other countries have been slower to do so. At a meeting of senior law enforcement officials from the G–8 countries in January 1997, Attorney General Reno stated:

[U]ntil recently, computer crime has not received the emphasis that other international crimes have engendered. Even now, not all affected nations recognize the threat it poses to public safety or the need for international cooperation to effectively respond to the problem. Consequently, many countries have weak laws, or no laws, against computer hacking—a major obstacle to solving and to prosecuting computer crimes.

The solution to this problem is simple to state: countries need to reach a consensus as to which computer and technology-related activities should be criminalized, and then commit to taking appropriate domestic actions. But it is not as easy to implement. An international consensus concerning the activities that universally should be criminalized may take time to develop. Meanwhile, individual countries that lack this kind of legislation will each have to pass new laws, an often cumbersome and time-consuming process. In the United States, for example, action by both the Congress and the President is required for new legislation.

Needed: Experts Available on a Twenty–Four Hour Basis.

A unique feature of high-tech and computer-related crime is that it requires immediate action to locate and identify perpetrators. Due to a general lack of historical communications data, the trail of a criminal may be impossible to trace once a communication link is terminated. This lack of data is due, in part, to the fact that businesses no longer bill their customers by individual telephone call or Internet connection but, instead, by bulk billing (e.g., a single rate for one month of usage). When bulk billing is employed, there is no longer a business need to record the transmission information (i.e., connection times or source and destination) for individual connections; therefore, traffic data may not be available at a later date. Thus, investigators and prosecutors with expertise in this field must be available twenty-four hours a day, at home and by pager, so that appropriate steps can be taken in a fast-breaking high-tech case.

Needed: Effective Means for Obtaining Evidence Internationally

Even if all countries have adequate computer crime laws, possess dedicated, well-trained and well-equipped experts who are available twenty-four hours a day, and have the ability to locate and identify criminals who use networked communications, there remains a significant hurdle to overcome. How does law enforcement collect electronic evidence that may be scattered across several different countries, can be deleted or altered with one click of a mouse, may be encrypted, and will ultimately need to be authenticated in another country's court? Again, these are areas where the challenges have been recognized but solutions either may not be apparent or may be difficult to implement.

1. Protected Seizures or "Quick Freeze/Quick Thaw." One characteristic of electronic evidence is that it can be altered, transferred or destroyed almost instantaneously, and from remote locations, often with little more than a single keystroke. These changes to evidence may result from a criminal trying to cover his tracks, or a system administrator routinely clearing old e-mails or other data from a company's servers. Whatever the case, critical evidence can be lost–long before an international request for assistance is ever transmitted. Traditional methods of obtaining evidence from foreign governments can include lengthy delays, as foreign legal processes, translations, and diplomacy slowly proceed. Old modalities may not always be practical when considering new technologies.

Therefore, when electronic evidence is sought, there may be a need for mechanisms such as a "preservation of evidence request" or "protected seizure," which would work as follows. Where there is a particularized concern about the loss of electronic evidence, a country would make an informal international request that the data immediately be preserved. This could be accomplished in a number of ways, from having a telecommunications carrier or ISP copy and store a customer's data, to actually seizing a criminal's computer and securing, but not searching, it for a short period of time. Once data is protected from loss, expedited processes would provide the foreign country with formal documentation to authorize the issuance of a domestic search warrant or similar process.

2. Transborder Search and Seizure. Since paper documents must be within close proximity to be of use, they are usually located in the same country as the person being investigated. By contrast, electronic documents are often stored remotely on computers, sometimes thousands of miles away from their author. This may be done because of the structure of a particular business (where data is maintained at company headquarters) or the architecture of the network. At other times, data may be purposely stored in another country to keep it beyond the reach of law enforcement.

A transborder search occurs when a law enforcement agent in his or her own country accesses a computer in another country to obtain electronic evidence, perhaps in furtherance of the execution of a domestic warrant. * * * Because searches made under exigent circumstances (including those where it is believed evidence will be destroyed if not seized) and inadvertent searches across borders are likely to occur, it may be wise for countries to consider developing rules and/or guidelines to govern a transborder search (e.g., regarding notice to the searched country).

Governments have three potential solutions at this juncture. First, governments could decide to forego the development of principles, allowing each country to decide for itself whether transborder searches constitute an acceptable law enforcement practice. Second, governments could limit transborder searches to cases where production of the data could otherwise be compelled through legal processes. This approach expedites the gathering of certain critical evidence while allowing data outside the traditional reach of a country to remain so. The third solution involves creating principles permitting law enforcement agents to conduct transborder searches under clearly defined circumstances that are more broad than those above. Support for this approach may rest on a consensus that the need for effective law enforcement outweighs concerns over protecting data stored in a particular country.

What Is Being Done by Multi-lateral Organizations?

To date, three multilateral organizations (i.e., groups with multiple-nation membership) are doing the bulk of the international policy work on high-tech and computer-related crime: the Council of Europe, the European Union and its related institutions, and the G–8. To a lesser degree, some work in this area has been done by the Organization for Economic Cooperation and Development, and the United Nations.

Of the three main groups, the G–8 has been particularly effective in making progress on several fronts. While the EU and COE have large European memberships, the G–8 has broader representation, with members from Europe, Russia, North America, and Japan. Because networked communications traverse every continent, and because leading communications and computer technology is developed in areas besides Europe (such as Asia and North America), regional efforts to solve universal crime problems will inevitably be either slower or less effective than similar efforts by policy-making bodies with a broad geographic base.

The heads of state of the G–8 countries meet annually. At their 1998 Summit, they adopted a comprehensive plan to fight high-tech and computer-related crime. While the COE started addressing computer crime at the technical level in 1988, its heads of state have only met twice since 1949 when the COE was created, and have never addressed computer crime. While EU heads of state called for a study of the subject and development of relevant policies, the heads of state from its member countries have not settled on a specific plan of action to combat computer crime. Finally, unlike the COE and EU, the G–8 is neither governed by international convention nor constrained by a convention-created bureaucracy. It can therefore move faster and address new and emerging areas as the will of its leaders dictates.

A.   The Council of Europe

The Council of Europe is an international organization based in Strasbourg, France. It was established by ten Western European countries in the wake of the Second World War, with the signing of its founding treaty, known as the Statute of the Council of Europe, in 1949. Today, it has a pan-European membership of forty countries, which include the Baltic states, Russia and Turkey. It defines its main role as strengthening democracy, human rights, and the rule of law throughout its member states. In the area of criminal law, twenty conventions and over eighty recommendations have been adopted, as well as a number of reports on crime issues.

In 1989, the Committee of Ministers adopted a recommendation and report on computer-related crime, Recommendation No. R. (89) 9. The recommendation called on member states to consider computer crimes when either reviewing or proposing domestic legislation, and the report contained guidelines in this area for legislators. In 1995, the Committee adopted Recommendation No. R. (95) 13, which provided procedures for implementing Recommendation (89) 9, and contained principles "concerning problems of criminal procedure law connected with information technology" on such topics as search and seizure, technical surveillance, electronic evidence, encryption, and international cooperation.

In February 1997, a Committee of Experts on Crime in Cyber-space (PC-CY) was formed to examine computer crime and related problems in criminal procedure law. Its work is aimed at drafting a binding legal instrument (i.e., a "Cybercrime Convention") which defines cybercrime offenses, and addresses such topics as jurisdiction, international cooperation, search and seizure, data protection, and liability of ISPs. * * * After approval by the Committee of Ministers, the Convention will be open for signature by COE members and non-member states which participated in its drafting.

B.   The European Union

The European Union has its roots in three organizations formed in the 1950s by Belgium, West Germany, France, Italy, Luxembourg, and the Netherlands: the European Coal and Steel Community (ECSC); the European Atomic Energy Community (Euratom); and the European Economic Community (EEC). These three communities are still at the heart of the EU, and the treaties which founded them have since been revised and extended. The Treaty on European Union, generally called the Maastricht Treaty, gives a single legal framework to the three European Communities.

The EU now has fifteen member states, and its own flag, anthem and currency (the Euro). The EU's objective is to "promote economic and social progress which is balanced and sustainable, assert the European identity on the international scene, and introduce a European citizenship for the nationals of the Member States."

In the area of high-tech crime, the EU has issued several texts. In 1995, it promulgated a directive which established certain rights and protections for citizens concerning electronically processed data. For example, the directive establishes the right of a citizen to know what electronic data a corporation maintains on that person, and provides protection against personal data being transferred to a non-EU country if that country has inadequate privacy protections. Member states are required to establish mechanisms to enforce these rights. In 1997, the EU issued a directive designed to ensure privacy relating to telecommunications data. That directive requires telecommunications carriers to delete traffic data at the end of each transmission (with exceptions for billing purposes and for law enforcement and national security needs). In light of these Directives, it is imperative that government policy decisions concerning electronic commerce and privacy be made in concert with decisions concerning public safety.

In 1997, the European Council endorsed an action plan to combat organized crime, and assembled a Multidisciplinary Group on Organized Crime (MDG) to implement the action plan. Recommendation Five of the action plan calls for a study on high-tech crime, and development of a policy addressing public safety which provides law enforcement and judicial authorities with the means to prevent and combat the misuse of new technologies. Since its inception, the MDG has adopted the study of Dr. Ulrich Sieber on legal aspects of computer related crime, and it is exploring what role Europol might play in combating computer crime.

C. The G–8

1. Background. The present G–8 (or "Group of Eight") leading industrialized democracies originated in 1975 at an Economic Summit convened by President Valery Giscard d'Estaing of France and attended by leaders from Germany, Japan, the United Kingdom and the United States. President Giscard and Chancellor Schmidt of Germany wanted to establish an informal forum for world leaders to discuss world economic issues. Italy and Canada joined this original "Group of Five" in 1976–77 and the configuration became known as the Group of Seven, or "G–7." G–7 meetings followed a limited agenda of economic issues, and were intended to provide an informal consultation forum. In the 1980s, these annual meetings became more formalized, with an agreed statement, or communique, issued by the leaders at the conclusion of each summit. Leaders such as President Reagan, French President Mitterand, German Chancellor Kohl, and British Prime Minister Thatcher brought increasingly broader agendas to the table. At the end of the cold war, as democratic and economic reform got underway in Russia, Russian leaders were gradually integrated into the G–7. In 1998, the group's name was formally changed to the "G–8," and the first full G–8 Summit was held in Birmingham in June of that year.

In its current configuration, the G–8's membership includes the majority of the world's most powerful democracies—countries that are global leaders economically, technologically, legally, and politically. This small but powerful membership gives the G–8 certain advantages over more bureaucratic or cumbersome multilateral organizations.

2. Focus on High-tech Crime. After the 1995 Summit in Halifax, Nova Scotia, a group of experts was brought together to look for better ways to fight international crime. In 1996 this group (which became known as the "Lyon Group") produced forty recommendations to combat international crime that were endorsed by the G–8 heads of state at the Lyon Summit in June 1996. Recommendation Sixteen, in part, called for countries to "review their laws in order to ensure that abuses of modern technology that are deserving of criminal sanctions are criminalized and that problems with respect to jurisdiction, enforcement powers, investigation, training, crime prevention and international cooperation in respect of such abuses are effectively addressed."

To implement Recommendation Sixteen and otherwise enhance the abilities of law enforcement in combating high-tech and computer-related crime, a subgroup of the Lyon Group was formed in January 1997 ("G–8 Subgroup on High-tech Crime"), and it held its first five meetings during that year. In December 1997, Attorney General Reno hosted the first-ever meeting of her counterparts from the G–8 countries, and the meeting centered on computer crime. At the conclusion of the meeting, the Ministers adopted ten Principles and a ten-point Action Plan to combat high-tech crime, and issued a Communique. At the 1998 G–8 Summit in Birmingham, England, the Heads of State endorsed and agreed to implement their Ministers' Principles and Action Plan. Essentially an international template for fighting high-tech crime, the Principles and Action Plan have been adopted by President Clinton, British Prime Minister Tony Blair, French President Jacques Chirac, Russian President Boris Yeltsin, and the other G–8 leaders. This is quite significant. It is the first time a group of powerful world leaders have jointly adopted a detailed plan for fighting computer crime. Additionally, instead of referring the plan back to member countries for individual action, a subgroup of G–8 experts meets regularly to work cooperatively toward implementation of the Action Plan.

3. High-tech Crime Subgroup. As of May 1999, the G–8 Subgroup on High-tech Crime had met fourteen times. Its focus has been on enhancing the abilities of law enforcement to investigate and prosecute high-tech and computer-related crime. The Subgroup's progress and accomplishments include * * * high-tech points of contact. In March 1998, a network of high-tech points of contact for law enforcement in each of the G–8 countries was established. These contacts are available twenty-four hours a day to respond to urgent requests for assistance in international high-tech crime investigations or cases involving electronic evidence. Recruitment and education efforts are currently underway to expand this network to include many more Internet-connected countries. The hope is that in the near future, international investigations in this area will not be delayed because of the inability to locate the proper computer crime expert or because of differences in time zones.

Notes and Questions

1. Recall the case of the "I Love You" virus allegedly sent by a student from the Philippines in 2000. The student was not charged with a crime after authorities in the Philippines concluded that his conduct was not criminal under domestic law. The Philippines did not have a computer misuse statute at the time. The fact that the student's conduct was not criminal according to local law meant that he could not be extradited to the United States to face prosecution under 18 U.S.C. § 1030.

How should United States policymakers respond to such situations? Should they: (a) resign themselves to the fact that they cannot prosecute all international computer crimes, (b) encourage other countries to enact computer crime statutes that resemble U.S. computer crime laws, or (c) try to negotiate extradition treaties that do not require mutual criminality?

2. A study of computer crime laws conducted after the "I Love You" virus case found that only about 20% of countries have adequate computer

crime laws. Many countries have no computer crime laws at all. *See* McConnell International, Cyber Crime ... and Punishment? Archaic Laws Threaten Global Information (2000).

3. *Uniformity versus diversity and the problem of reciprocity.* In recent years, the United States government has encouraged other countries to synchronize their substantive and procedural computer crime laws to avoid problems such as the one that surfaced in the "I Love You" virus case. Is this inevitable? Is it desirable? Should the entire world adopt a single model approach to computer crime laws, or are local differences desirable? How much of the substantive criminal law covered in Chapters 2 and 3 is normatively desirable at the global level? How much of the procedural law covered in Chapters 5 and 6 is normatively desirable at the global level?

Is it possible to resolve the tension between the need for uniform laws to enforce computer crime statutes and the need for regional variation based on local preferences? Consider the case of child pornography. Imagine the government of Freedonia decides that it should be legal to possess or distribute images of child pornography in Freedonia, including on servers located in Freedonia that are connected to the Internet. Will such a decision have a significant impact on the enforcement of child pornography laws worldwide? Can an individual simply post images from Freedonia and escape liability (or at least capture)? Does the popularity of Internet gambling sites based in countries like Antigua provide empirical support for the answer?

Alternatively, consider foreign criminal laws prohibiting racist speech, the sale of Nazi memorabilia, or the distribution of virtual child pornography. In the United States, First Amendment protection renders such laws unenforceable. Should the United States be allowed to "opt out" of assisting other countries in their efforts to prosecute violations of these laws? Is there an argument that the United States should be able to opt out of helping foreign governments with investigations that violate the First Amendment, but that Freedonia should not be allowed to opt out of assisting other countries with child pornography prosecutions?

For more on the process of synchronizing computer crime laws, see Abraham D. Sofaer & Seymour E. Goodman, Eds., The Transnational Dimension of Cyber Crime and Terrorism (2001).

4. *The Council of Europe Convention on Cybercrime.* The most important effort to synchronize computer crime laws to date is the Council of Europe Convention on Cybercrime completed in 2001. The Convention articulates a set of principles that member states agree to adopt in their domestic law. The United States is not a member of the Council of Europe, but representatives of the United States Department of Justice, State, and Commerce were "observers" and active participants in the negotiating and drafting of the convention. The United States was one of the thirty countries that signed the convention in 2001, and the United States Senate ratified the Convention in August 2006. Here are the key portions of the text:

COUNCIL OF EUROPE—CONVENTION ON CYBERCRIME

http://conventions.coe.int/Treaty/en/Treaties/Html/185.htm (2001).

Section 1—Substantive criminal law

Article 2—Illegal access

Each Party shall adopt such legislative and other measures as may be necessary to establish as criminal offences under its domestic law, when committed intentionally, the access to the whole or any part of a computer system without right. A Party may require that the offence be committed by infringing security measures, with the intent of obtaining computer data or other dishonest intent, or in relation to a computer system that is connected to another computer system.

Article 3—Illegal interception

Each Party shall adopt such legislative and other measures as may be necessary to establish as criminal offences under its domestic law, when committed intentionally, the interception without right, made by technical means, of non-public transmissions of computer data to, from or within a computer system, including electromagnetic emissions from a computer system carrying such computer data. A Party may require that the offence be committed with dishonest intent, or in relation to a computer system that is connected to another computer system.

Article 4—Data interference

1. Each Party shall adopt such legislative and other measures as may be necessary to establish as criminal offences under its domestic law, when committed intentionally, the damaging, deletion, deterioration, alteration or suppression of computer data without right.

2. A Party may reserve the right to require that the conduct described in paragraph 1 result in serious harm.

Article 7—Computer-related forgery

Each Party shall adopt such legislative and other measures as may be necessary to establish as criminal offences under its domestic law, when committed intentionally and without right, the input, alteration, deletion, or suppression of computer data, resulting in inauthentic data with the intent that it be considered or acted upon for legal purposes as if it were authentic, regardless whether or not the data is directly readable and intelligible. A Party may require an intent to defraud, or similar dishonest intent, before criminal liability attaches.

Article 8—Computer-related fraud

Each Party shall adopt such legislative and other measures as may be necessary to establish as criminal offences under its domestic law, when committed intentionally and without right, the causing of a loss of property to another by:

a. any input, alteration, deletion or suppression of computer data,

    b.   any interference with the functioning of a computer system,

with fraudulent or dishonest intent of procuring, without right, an economic benefit for oneself or for another.

Article 9—Offences related to child pornography

Each Party shall adopt such legislative and other measures as may be necessary to establish as criminal offences under its domestic law, when committed intentionally and without right, the following conduct:

    a.   producing child pornography for the purpose of its distribution through a computer system;

    b.   offering or making available child pornography through a computer system;

    c.   distributing or transmitting child pornography through a computer system;

    d.   procuring child pornography through a computer system for oneself or for another;

    e.   possessing child pornography in a computer system or on a computer-data storage medium.

Article 10—Offences related to infringements of copyright and related rights

Each Party shall adopt such legislative and other measures as may be necessary to establish as criminal offences under its domestic law the infringement of copyright, as defined under the law of that Party pursuant to the obligations it has undertaken under the Paris Act of 24 July 1971 of the Bern Convention for the Protection of Literary and Artistic Works, the Agreement on Trade–Related Aspects of Intellectual Property Rights and the WIPO Copyright Treaty, with the exception of any moral rights conferred by such Conventions, where such acts are committed wilfully, on a commercial scale and by means of a computer system.

Section 2–Procedural law

Article 14—Scope of procedural provisions

Each Party shall adopt such legislative and other measures as may be necessary to establish the powers and procedures provided for in this Section for the purpose of specific criminal investigations or proceedings.

Article 15—Conditions and safeguards

Each Party shall ensure that the establishment, implementation and application of the powers and procedures provided for in this Section are subject to conditions and safeguards provided for under its domestic law, which shall provide for the adequate protection of human rights and liberties, including rights arising pursuant to obligations it has undertaken under the 1950 Council of Europe Convention for the Protection of Human Rights and Fundamental Freedoms, the 1966 United Nations International Covenant on Civil and Political Rights, and other applicable international human rights instruments, and which shall incorporate the principle of proportionality.

Article 16—Expedited preservation of stored computer data

Each Party shall adopt such legislative and other measures as may be necessary to enable its competent authorities to order or similarly obtain the expeditious preservation of specified computer data, including traffic data, that has been stored by means of a computer system, in particular where there are grounds to believe that the computer data is particularly vulnerable to loss or modification.

Article 18—Production order

1. Each Party shall adopt such legislative and other measures as may be necessary to empower its competent authorities to order:

   a. a person in its territory to submit specified computer data in that person's possession or control, which is stored in a computer system or a computer-data storage medium; and

   b. a service provider offering its services in the territory of the Party to submit subscriber information relating to such services in that service provider's possession or control;

3. For the purpose of this article, "subscriber information" means any information, contained in the form of computer data or any other form, that is held by a service provider, relating to subscribers of its services, other than traffic or content data, by which can be established:

   a. the type of the communication service used, the technical provisions taken thereto and the period of service;

   b. the subscriber's identity, postal or geographic address, telephone and other access number, billing and payment information, available on the basis of the service agreement or arrangement;

   c. any other information on the site of the installation of communication equipment available on the basis of the service agreement or arrangement.

Article 19—Search and seizure of stored computer data

1. Each Party shall adopt such legislative and other measures as may be necessary to empower its competent authorities to search or similarly access:

   a. a computer system or part of it and computer data stored therein; and

   b. computer-data storage medium in which computer data may be stored in its territory.

2. Each Party shall adopt such legislative and other measures as may be necessary to ensure that where its authorities search or similarly access a specific computer system or part of it, pursuant to paragraph 1(a), and have grounds to believe that the data sought is stored in another computer system or part of it in its territory, and such data is lawfully accessible from or available to the initial system, such authori-

ties shall be able to expeditiously extend the search or similar accessing to the other system.

3. Each Party shall adopt such legislative and other measures as may be necessary to empower its competent authorities to seize or similarly secure computer data accessed according to paragraphs 1 or 2. These measures shall include the power to:

a. seize or similarly secure a computer system or part of it or a computer-data storage medium;

b. make and retain a copy of those computer data;

c. maintain the integrity of the relevant stored computer data; and

d. render inaccessible or remove those computer data in the accessed computer system.

Article 20—Real-time collection of traffic data

Each Party shall adopt such legislative and other measures as may be necessary to empower its competent authorities to:

a. collect or record through application of technical means on the territory of that Party, and

b. compel a service provider, within its existing technical capability, to:

i. collect or record through application of technical means on the territory of that Party, or ii. co-operate and assist the competent authorities in the collection or recording of, traffic data, in real-time, associated with specified communications in its territory transmitted by means of a computer system.

Article 21—Interception of content data

Each Party shall adopt such legislative and other measures as may be necessary, in relation to a range of serious offences to be determined by domestic law, to empower its competent authorities to:

a. collect or record through application of technical means on the territory of that Party, and

b. compel a service provider, within its existing technical capability, to:

i. collect or record through application of technical means on the territory of that Party, or ii. co-operate and assist the competent authorities in the collection or recording of, content data, in real-time, of specified communications in its territory transmitted by means of a computer system.

Chapter III–International co-operation

Article 23—General principles relating to international co-operation

The Parties shall co-operate with each other, in accordance with the provisions of this chapter, and through the application of relevant international instruments on international co-operation in criminal matters, arrangements agreed on the basis of uniform or reciprocal legislation, and domestic laws, to the widest extent possible for the purposes of investigations or proceedings concerning criminal offences related to computer systems and data, or for the collection of evidence in electronic form of a criminal offence.

Article 24—Extradition

1. This article applies to extradition between Parties for the criminal offences established in accordance with Articles 2 through 11 of this Convention, provided that they are punishable under the laws of both Parties concerned by deprivation of liberty for a maximum period of at least one year, or by a more severe penalty.

2. The criminal offences described in paragraph 1 of this article shall be deemed to be included as extraditable offences in any extradition treaty existing between or among the Parties. The Parties undertake to include such offences as extraditable offences in any extradition treaty to be concluded between or among them.

Article 25—General principles relating to mutual assistance

The Parties shall afford one another mutual assistance to the widest extent possible for the purpose of investigations or proceedings concerning criminal offences related to computer systems and data, or for the collection of evidence in electronic form of a criminal offence.

Article 27—Procedures pertaining to mutual assistance requests in the absence of applicable international agreements

Where there is no mutual assistance treaty or arrangement on the basis of uniform or reciprocal legislation in force between the requesting and requested Parties, the provisions of paragraphs 2 through 9 of this article shall apply. The provisions of this article shall not apply where such treaty, arrangement or legislation exists, unless the Parties concerned agree to apply any or all of the remainder of this article in lieu thereof.

Article 31—Mutual assistance regarding accessing of stored computer data

A Party may request another Party to search or similarly access, seize or similarly secure, and disclose data stored by means of a computer system located within the territory of the requested Party.

Article 32—Trans-border access to stored computer data with consent or where publicly available

A Party may, without the authorisation of another Party:

a. access publicly available (open source) stored computer data, regardless of where the data is located geographically; or

b. access or receive, through a computer system in its territory, stored computer data located in another Party, if the Party obtains the lawful and voluntary consent of the person who has the lawful authority to disclose the data to the Party through that computer system.

Article 33—Mutual assistance regarding the real-time collection of traffic data

1. The Parties shall provide mutual assistance to each other in the real-time collection of traffic data associated with specified communications in their territory transmitted by means of a computer system. Subject to the provisions of paragraph 2, this assistance shall be governed by the conditions and procedures provided for under domestic law.

2. Each Party shall provide such assistance at least with respect to criminal offences for which real-time collection of traffic data would be available in a similar domestic case.

Article 34—Mutual assistance regarding the interception of content data

The Parties shall provide mutual assistance to each other in the real-time collection or recording of content data of specified communications transmitted by means of a computer system to the extent permitted under their applicable treaties and domestic laws.

Article 35—24/7 Network

Each Party shall designate a point of contact available on a twenty-four hour, seven-day-a-week basis, in order to ensure the provision of immediate assistance for the purpose of investigations or proceedings concerning criminal offences related to computer systems and data, or for the collection of evidence in electronic form of a criminal offence. Such assistance shall include facilitating, or, if permitted by its domestic law and practice, directly carrying out the following measures:

a. the provision of technical advice;

b. the preservation of data pursuant to Articles 29 and 30;

c. the collection of evidence, the provision of legal information, and locating of suspects.

Notes and Questions

1. Are any provisions of the COE convention inconsistent with United States law? Or are the terms of the convention a restatement of the basic elements of United States computer crime law? *See generally* Richard W. Downing, *Shoring up the Weakest Link: What Lawmakers Around the World Need to Consider in Developing Comprehensive Laws to Combat Cybercrime*, 43 Colum. J. Transnat'l L. 705 (2005).

2. *The additional protocol on "racist and xenophobic" acts.* In 2002, at the request of the French government, the Council of Europe added an additional protocol "concerning the criminalisation of acts of a racist and xenophobic nature committed through computer systems." The protocol requires each country that signs it to criminalize a number of acts, including: distributing racist and xenophobic material to the public through a

computer system; sending an Internet threat solely because of a person's race, national origin or religion; insulting a person through a computer communication on the basis of the person's race, national origin or religion; and denying, grossly minimizing, or justifying atrocities or crimes against humanity. *See generally* Christopher D. Van Blarcum, Note, *Internet Hate Speech: The European Framework and the Emerging American Haven*, 62 Wash. & Lee L. Rev. 781, 787–802 (2005).

A number of countries have signed the additional protocol, which acts as a separate agreement in addition to the cybercrime convention. Of course, the United States has not signed the protocol. Government officials have indicated that the United States cannot agree to the protocol because its provisions would violate the First Amendment. *See* Declan McCullagh, *U.S. Won't Support Net "Hate Speech" Ban*, C–Net News, Nov. 15, 2002. As a result, the requirements of the additional protocol have no effect on United States policy.

3. The COE cybercrime convention has been controversial less for what it does than for what it does not do. Privacy advocates and civil liberties groups note that the convention focuses on law enforcement powers but does not address privacy protections beyond the general statement in Article 15. The convention empowers governments without limiting how they might exercise those new powers. Consider the perspective offered by one group, the Center for Democracy and Technology:

> The treaty is fundamentally imbalanced: it includes very detailed and sweeping powers of computer search and seizure and government surveillance of voice, email and data communications, but no correspondingly detailed standards to protect privacy and limit government use of such powers, despite the fact that privacy is the #1 concern of Internet users worldwide who see an increase, not a decrease, in the surveillance capabilities of governments brought on by the digital revolution.

> While the treaty's express terms do not require companies to modify their equipment or business practices, the treaty must be viewed as part of the ongoing government efforts nationally and internationally to require telephone companies, Internet service providers, web site operators, and computer hardware and software manufacturers to design their systems, their record-keeping procedures and their very business models to guarantee the practical effectiveness of such surveillance authorities.

> The treaty also raises concerns over the definition of criminal conduct online. The computer crime provisions of the treaty are drafted in very broad terms that could cover a wide range of common behavior. Consequently, the provisions may not achieve the "harmonization" that is the treaty's goal, but rather may subject U.S. corporations and Internet users to criminal liability from Europe. Also, the treaty has been expanded to include matters such as fraud and copyright infringement that are not computer crimes per se, but offline crimes sometimes committed through computer systems. There have been efforts to further add "content" offenses such as hate speech that would translate cultural norms into transborder criminal offenses.

In making specific suggestions about the text and intent of the draft, we remain skeptical that a treaty of this scope is needed to achieve the desirable goal of improved international cooperation on computer crime. Moreover, we remain deeply concerned that the treaty, with its current emphasis on government powers over privacy protection, will lend international support, no matter what its precise language, to government demands to control communications services.

Comments of the Center for Democracy and Technology on the Council of Europe Draft "Convention on Cyber-crime," *available at* http://www.cdt.org/international/cybercrime/010206cdt.shtml.

Should the COE convention mandate privacy protections as well as law enforcement powers? If so, what should those protections look like? Should the convention require every country to impose a probable cause warrant requirement for wiretapping or government access to stored e-mail? Should the requirements track current United States law, or should they be more (or less) protective? Does an international consensus exist on standards for Internet privacy law? If not, who should decide what the standard will be?

4. Another criticism of the COE convention is that its requirements are too general. The convention's broad language requires general categories of legislation instead of specific statutes. Are general categories sufficient to achieve the uniformity that the convention's drafters had in mind? If one country enacts a narrow statute and another enacts a broad one, will the laws be sufficiently uniform to facilitate international evidence collection and extradition? Should the convention itself contain the precise statutory text of the criminal prohibitions and procedural laws that signatories must enact? For such a suggestion, see Shannon Hopkins, *Cybercrime Convention: A Positive Beginning to a Long Road Ahead*, 2 J. High Tech. L. 101, 104–07 (2003).

Imagine COE countries decided to adopt this suggestion. What would the model law look like? Suppose the COE convention were amended so that every country was required to copy United States computer crime law as it exists today in every detail. Would this be a good idea? Is existing United States law an appropriate model?

Of course, it is highly unlikely that the United States could persuade COE member countries to adopt existing United States law as a universal model. Different countries have very different traditions, legal systems, and constitutional requirements. If it were possible reach an agreement on the specific text for a uniform set of computer crime laws, it seems likely that the language chosen would involve a major re-writing of existing United States law. United States negotiators would have some influence over this process, but would be only one voice among many.

Further, such an agreement would block individual countries from attempting to improve their own computer crime statutes unilaterally. To change United States computer crime law without violating the convention, United States officials would be required to renegotiate the cybercrime convention first. The new language agreed to by the members of the Council of Europe would then be submitted for Senate approval, requiring a vote on the very specific language negotiated abroad. Is this desirable?

Finally, some variation in the law is inevitable because different courts will construe the same language differently. Imagine every country adopted a uniform computer crime law that prohibited "access without authorization," "unreasonable searches and seizures," and "interception of the contents of communications without the consent of a party." What are the chances that the United States Supreme Court, the English House of Lords, the French Cour de Cassation, and the German Bundesgerichtsh would interpret these phrases in exactly (or even roughly) the same way?

4. FOREIGN COMPUTER CRIME LAW

Although the materials in this book focus on United States computer crime law, the preceding materials point out the role of foreign computer crime laws even for domestic investigations. For example, if a defendant located in a foreign country damages a computer in the United States, and the United States wishes to bring a criminal prosecution, the outcome may hinge on (a) whether the offense is a substantive criminal offense under the law of the country where the defendant is located (for extradition purposes), and (b) whether the other country has procedural laws in place allowing investigators in that country to investigate the crime and share the evidence with investigators in the United States. The next case considers the interpretation of a computer misuse law in the United Kingdom for purposes of an extradition proceeding brought at the request of the United States.

REX v. BOW STREET MAGISTRATES' COURT

House of Lords, [1999] 4 All ER 1.

Lord Hobhouse of Woodborough

My Lords,

On 18 March 1997, Mr. Allison was arrested upon a provisional warrant issued under the Extradition Act 1989 at the request of the Government of the United States. It alleged that he had between 1 January 1996 and 18 June 1996 within the jurisdiction of the United States of America conspired with Joan Ojomo and others (1) to secure unauthorised access to the American Express computer system with intent to commit theft, (2) to secure unauthorised access to the American Express computer system with intent to commit forgery, and (3) to cause unauthorised modification to the contents of the American Express computer system.

On 11 June 1997 the Bow Street Magistrate committed Mr. Allison on the third charge but declined to commit him on the first and second of the proposed charges. Mr. Allison brought *Habeas Corpus* proceedings challenging the view that any of the offences alleged were "extradition crimes" under the Act of 1989 and the United States of America (Extradition) Order 1976, SI 1976 No. 2144. The Government brought judicial review proceedings challenging the decision in law of the magistrate that the evidence did not disclose a *prima facie* case that there had been a conspiracy to commit offences falling within section 2 of the

Computer Misuse Act 1990 as alleged in the first and second charges in the warrant.

Joan Ojomo was an employee of American Express. She was assigned to the credit section of the Company's office in Plantation, Florida, as a credit analyst. In her daily work it was possible for her to access all customers' accounts but she was only authorised to access those accounts that were assigned to her. However she accessed various other accounts and files which had not been assigned to her and which she had not been given authority to work on. Having accessed those accounts and files without authority, she gave confidential information obtained from those accounts and files to, among others, Mr. Allison. The information she gave to him and to others was then used to encode other credit cards and supply PIN numbers which could then be fraudulently used to obtain large sums of money from automatic teller machines.

The evidence concerning Joan Ojomo's authority to access the material data showed that she did not have authority to access the data she used for this purpose. At no time did she have any blanket authorisation to access any account or file not specifically assigned to her to work on. Any access by her to an account which she was not authorised to be working on would be considered a breach of company policy and ethics and would be considered an unauthorised access by the Company. The computer records showed that she accessed 189 accounts that did not fall within the scope of her duties. Her accessing of these accounts was unauthorised.

Using these methods, she and her fellow conspirators defrauded American Express of approximately $1,000,000. Mr. Allison was arrested with forged American Express cards in his possession and was photographed using one such card to obtain money from an automatic teller machine in London.

The proposed charges against Mr. Allison therefore involved his alleged conspiracy with Joan Ojomo for her to secure unauthorised access to data on the American Express computer with the intent to commit the further offences of forging cards and stealing from that Company. It is Joan Ojomo's alleged lack of authority which is an essential element in the offences charged.

The [Extradition] Act of 1989 was enacted following reports of the English and Scottish Law Commissions recommending revisions of the law of extradition. The Act consolidated the previous law with amendments to give effect to those recommendations. The Extradition Act 1870 was among those repealed by the Act of 1989. The Act of 1870 included a definition of "extradition crime" as meaning "a crime which, if committed in England, would be one of the crimes described in the first schedule" to the Act. The schedule, as would be expected having regard to its date, consisted of a relatively short list. Between 1870 and 1989 the list was extensively added to by later Acts. But none of these statutes included a reference to computer crime such as that made criminal by the Computer Misuse Act 1990.

The relevant Order in Council governing extradition to the United States of America * * * gives effect to and schedules the Extradition Treaty between the respective Governments of the United Kingdom and the United States. Article III of the Treaty provides:

(1) Extradition shall be granted for an act or omission the facts of which disclose an offence within any of the descriptions listed in the Schedule annexed to this Treaty, which is an integral part of the Treaty, or any other offence, if:

(a) the offence is punishable under the laws of both Parties by imprisonment or other form of detention for more than one year or by the death penalty;

(b) the offence is extraditable under the relevant law, being the law of the United Kingdom or other territory to which this Treaty applies by virtue of sub-paragraph (1)(a) of Article II; and

(c) the offence constitutes a felony under the law of the United States of America.

(2) Extradition shall also be granted for any attempt or conspiracy to commit an offence within paragraph (1) of this Article if such attempt or conspiracy is one for which extradition may be granted under the laws of both Parties and is punishable under the laws of both Parties by imprisonment or other form of detention for more than one year or by the death penalty.

The schedule annexed to the Treaty does not include any reference to computer crime. Therefore if an offence under the Computer Misuse Act 1990 is to come within the terms of the Treaty it will have to be as some "other offence." There is no dispute in the present case that an offence under § 2 of the Act of 1990 comes within (1)(a) being punishable by imprisonment for more than one year. Similarly it is not disputed that the conduct charged would constitute felonies under the law of the United States, (1)(c). The question which has been raised by Mr. Allison on his *Habeas Corpus* application is whether the offences alleged are extraditable under the law of the United Kingdom, (1)(b), and therefore as conspiracies come within paragraph (2) of the Article.

In September 1989 there was no provision of the law of the United Kingdom which made computer crime extraditable; indeed, there was no such provision which made it (as such) criminal at all. At that time such conduct fell outside the scope of the criminal law of the United Kingdom and accordingly outside the scope of the Extradition Treaty.

The Treaty and the Order in Council have not been amended. The provision which has been relied upon by the Government of the United States as bringing offences under the Computer Misuse Act 1990 within the terms of the Treaty is § 15 of that Act which provides—

The offences to which an Order in Council under § 2 of the Extradition Act 1870 can apply shall include—(a) offences under § 2 or 3 above; (b) any conspiracy to commit such an offence; and (c) any attempt to commit an offence under § 3 above.

The Computer Misuse Act 1990 does not purport to alter the Treaty or the Order nor does it need to; they include not only the offences listed in the schedule annexed to the Treaty but also "any other offence." All that is needed is some provision of the law of the United Kingdom which provides, supplementing the provisions of the 1989 and earlier Acts, that computer crime shall both become an offence and be extraditable under the law of the United Kingdom; the 1990 Act contains provisions that meet this need.

Sections 1 and 2 of the [Computer Misuse Act of 1990] provide:

1(1) A person is guilty of an offence if—

   (a) he causes a computer to perform any function with intent to secure access to any program or data held in any computer;

   (b) the access he intends to secure is unauthorised; and

   (c) he knows at the time when he causes the computer to perform the function that that is the case.

(2) The intent a person has to have to commit an offence under this section need not be directed at—

   (a) any particular program or data;

   (b) a program or data of any particular kind; or

   (c) a program or data held in any particular computer....

2(1) A person is guilty of an offence under this section if he commits an offence under section 1 above ("the unauthorised access offence") with intent (a) to commit an offence to which this section applies; or (b) to facilitate the commission of such an offence (whether by himself or by any other person).

Section 2 is thus dependent on § 1.

On the evidence before the magistrate, the conduct of Joan Ojomo came fairly and squarely within the provisions of § 1(1). She intentionally caused a computer to give her access to data which she knew she was not authorised to access. The reason why the magistrate did not commit Mr. Allison on charges 1 and 2 was that he felt constrained by the provisions of § 17 * * *. The relevant subsections of § 17 reads—

   (1) The following provisions of this section apply for the interpretation of this Act.

   (2) A person secures access to any program or data held in a computer if by causing a computer to perform any function he—

      (a) alters or erases the program or data;

(b) copies or moves it to any storage medium other than that in which it is held or to a different location in the storage medium in which it is held;

(c) uses it; or

(d) has it output from the computer in which it is held (whether by having it displayed or in any other manner); and references to access to a program or data (and to an intent to secure such access) shall be read accordingly.

(5) Access of any kind by any person to any program or data held in a computer is unauthorised if—(a) he is not himself entitled to control access of the kind in question to the program or data; and (b) he does not have consent to access by him of the kind in question to the program or data from any person who is so entitled.

Section 17 is an interpretation section. Subsection (2) defines what is meant by access and securing access to any programme or data. It lists four ways in which this may occur or be achieved. Its purpose is clearly to give a specific meaning to the phrase "to secure access." Subsection (5) is to be read with subsection (2). It deals with the relationship between the widened definition of securing access and the scope of the authority which the relevant person may hold. That is why the subsection refers to "access of any kind" and "access of the kind in question." Authority to view data may not extend to authority to copy or alter that data. The refinement of the concept of access requires a refinement of the concept of authorisation. The authorisation must be authority to secure access of the kind in question. As part of this refinement, the subsection lays down two cumulative requirements of lack of authority. The first is the requirement that the relevant person be not the person entitled to control the relevant kind of access. The word "control" in this context clearly means authorise and forbid. If the relevant person is so entitled, then it would be unrealistic to treat his access as being unauthorised. The second is that the relevant person does not have the consent to secure the relevant kind of access from a person entitled to control, *i.e.* authorise, that access.

Subsection (5) therefore has a plain meaning subsidiary to the other provisions of the Act. It simply identifies the two ways in which authority may be acquired—by being oneself the person entitled to authorise and by being a person who has been authorised by a person entitled to authorise. It also makes clear that the authority must relate not simply to the data or programme but also to the actual kind of access secured.

My Lords, what I have already said serves to identify the points upon which the Divisional Court fell into error. The certified question refers to "authority to access data of the kind in question". The use of the phrase "data of the kind in question" seems to derive from a simple mis-reading of § 17(5) and a confusion between kinds of access and kinds of data. Nor is § 1 of the Act concerned with authority to access kinds of data. It is concerned with authority to access the actual data involved. Because § 1(1) creates an offence which can be committed as a result of having an intent to secure unauthorised access without in fact actually succeeding in accessing any data, § 1(2) does not require that the relevant intent relate to any specific data. But that does not mean that access to the data in question does not have to be authorised.

* * * [The lower court judge] treats the phrase "entitlement to control" as if it related to the control of the computer as opposed to the entitlement to authorise operators to access to programs and data. He adopts the extraneous idea of an authorised level of access without considering whether, on the facts of the case, it corresponds to the relevant person's authority to access the data in fact accessed. He confines § 1 of the Act to the "hacking" of computer systems as opposed to the use of a computer to secure unauthorised access to programs or data. Upon a misreading of § 17(5), he fails to give effect to the plain words of § 1. The meaning of the statute is clear and unambiguous. But it is right that I should briefly say something about the argument based upon the Working Party Paper and Report of the Law Commission which (together with the Report of the Scottish Law Commission) led to the passing of the Act of 1990. * * * The Respondent quoted passages from the Paper and the Report to the effect:

> It should be made clear that 'unauthorised' refers to the obtaining of access to a computer system. Our preliminary view is that it would be undesirable for a hacking offence to extend to an authorised user who is using the computer system for an unauthorised purpose.

> If an employee deliberately seeks to enter part of his employer's system from which he is clearly debarred his conduct is of the same type as the outside hacker, and our proposed offence will apply to him as much as it applies to the outside hacker.

> If the hacking offence is to be aimed at protecting the integrity of the computer (and our view is that it should), then there is no justification for exempting employees who threaten that integrity.

Read as a whole, the Report makes it clear that the term "hacking" is used conveniently to refer to all forms of unauthorised access whether by insiders or outsiders and that the problem of misuse by insiders is as serious as that by outsiders. The offence should cover a person who causes the computer to perform a function when he "should know that *that* access is unauthorised." An employee should only be guilty of an offence if his employer has clearly defined the limits of the employee's authority to access a program or data.

The consideration of the mischief which the Act was designed to meet confirms and does not contradict the clear meaning of § 1 of the Act and the equally clear purpose of § 17(2) and (5).

The decision of the Divisional Court in the present case was erroneous and the appeal fell to be allowed.

Notes and Questions

1. This case involves one piece of an international fraud scheme.[b] Two American Express employees, Joan Ojomo and Blessing Egbarin, obtained secret information from American Express computers in violation of American Express workplace rules. The information permitted individuals to create counterfeit credit cards or file fraudulent applications for new cards. Ojomo sold the information to a number of street dealers both inside and outside the United States. American Express suffered millions of dollars in losses from the scheme.

In 1996, Ojomo and 12 co-conspirators were indicted in the United States. Ojomo pled guilty and agreed to assist the government in its efforts to prosecute the remaining co-conspirators. Defendant Allison was indicted in the United States but was found in the United Kingdom. Although at least two other defendants in the case were charged in the United Kingdom under UK law, the United States government sought Allison's extradition so Allison could face charges in the United States.

2. How different is the computer misuse statute in the United Kingdom from 18 U.S.C. § 1030 in the United States? Is the legal issue raised in the case you just read one that also arises under § 1030? If the issues are similar, is that because the nature of computer misuse demands that courts in different countries confront the same questions? Or is it because the two statutes use the same basic principles?

3. According to a 2002 study performed by Judge Stein Schjolberg of Norway, 44 countries have enacted some form of "unauthorized access" statutes modeled after 18 U.S.C. § 1030. *See* Stein Schjolberg, Unauthorized Access to Computer Systems: Penal Legislation in 44 Countries 2 (2002).

4. *Alternatives to extradition: The Ardita case.* In one unusual case in the mid–1990s, an Argentinian computer hacker named Julio Ardita hacked into about two hundred government and university computers in the United States from his location in Argentina. United States investigators traced the attack back to Buenos Aires, and Ardita was located with the help of Argentine authorities. The United States government sought extradition, but Ardita persuaded an Argentinian count that extradition was improper because his offense was not illegal under the law of Argentina (and thus the dual criminality requirement was not met).

The case did not end there, however. Although Ardita did not face the threat of extradition to the United States from Argentina, he faced a risk of extradition if he traveled to a country that had an extradition treaty with the United States in which his acts would have violated the domestic law of that country. Rather than face that risk, Ardita reached an agreement with United States officials: he agreed to waive extradition and plead guilty to reduced charges in the United States. Ardita was fined $5,000 and sentenced to three years of probation. *See* Russell G. Smith, Peter Grabosky, & Gregor Urbas, Cyber Criminals on Trial 56 (2004).

---

b. This summary draws from the briefs and decisions in two related cases, United Kingdom v. United States, 238 F.3d 1312 (11th Cir. 2001) and United States v. Ojomo, 149 F.3d 1195 (11th Cir. 1998) (unpublished).

5. The materials in this chapter suggest that the legal issues raised by computer-related crime are not merely questions for the legal system in the United States. Most industrialized countries are facing the same issues, and all are being called on to adjust their domestic regimes of criminal law and criminal procedure in response to the new dynamics of computer crimes.

In light of the materials you have read in this book, do you think governments face a major challenge? Does computer crime require a fundamental rethinking of domestic and international approaches to criminal investigations and prosecutions? Will computer crimes "change everything"? Or do the new crimes simply require a slight tweaking of the old principles, or even no adjustment at all?

Are computers and the Internet the kind of transformative technologies that are likely to have a profound effect on criminal law doctrine? Some legal historians have argued that the invention of the railroad had a profound effect on tort law principles a century ago. Will computers and the Internet have a similar impact on criminal law and procedure in the next century?

Chapter 8

NATIONAL SECURITY

On the morning of September 11, 2001, members of the Al Qaeda terrorist network hijacked four planes and crashed them into the World Trade Center towers, the Pentagon, and a field in southwest Pennsylvania. The attacks caused approximately 3,000 American deaths. Following the attacks, American intelligence agencies quickly mobilized efforts to uncover any additional terrorist plots. The monitoring included surveillance of e-mail and other Internet transactions on a massive scale, both in the United States and abroad. Although terrorist plots would obviously violate criminal law, the surveillance efforts were not designed to collect evidence that could prove a criminal case beyond a reasonable doubt. Rather, the purpose of the surveillance was to collect information that could thwart a future terrorist attack.

The wide-scale Internet surveillance that followed the September 11th attacks is one example of national security intelligence surveillance. The purpose of such surveillance is to gather information about threats to the United States and the status of foreign governments with the hope that United States government officials can use the information to protect the United States and further its interests in world affairs. Essentially all governments engage in such surveillance, and United States intelligence efforts are particularly vast. The United States intelligence budget is classified, but just one agency, the National Security Agency, has been estimated to employ about 38,000 individuals full time. *See* James Bamford, Body of Secrets 482 (2001).

National security surveillance plays no role in most computer crime cases, but it can play an essential role in a few particularly important investigations. A great deal of intelligence surveillance involves e-mail and other Internet communications, and individuals subject to intelligence monitoring eventually may be charged criminally. In such cases, digital evidence collected under national security authorities may be essential to the government's case.

The use of digital evidence collected for national security reasons raises three important questions. First, how does the Fourth Amendment apply to the collection of digital evidence for national security purposes? Second, how does the Foreign Intelligence Surveillance Act (FISA) regulate the collection of digital evidence for such purposes? And third, when can digital evidence collected under FISA be admitted in criminal prosecutions?

A. THE FOURTH AMENDMENT

In the decades before Katz v. United States, 389 U.S. 347 (1967), government officials conducted warrantless wiretapping for national security purposes with little or no legal restriction. The Fourth Amendment did not apply to wiretapping under Olmstead v. United States, 277 U.S. 438 (1928). The Communications Act of 1934 prohibited "intercepting" and "disclosing" wire communications, but the Justice Department construed this to prohibit only the combination of wiretapping and publicly disclosing the fruits of the monitoring. Because national security wiretapping did not require public disclosure, government agents could tap telephone and telegraph lines unhindered by statutory or constitutional regulation.

Katz changed the legal picture considerably, although it settled very little. The *Katz* court certainly was aware of the special constitutional questions raised by national security monitoring. However, Justice Stewart's majority opinion expressly declined to take a position on these issues. *See Katz,* 389 U.S. at 358 n.23 ("Whether safeguards other than prior authorization by a magistrate would satisfy the Fourth Amendment in a situation involving the national security is a question not presented by this case."). Justice White's solo concurrence was more explicit, and expressed the following opinion:

> Wiretapping to protect the security of the Nation has been authorized by successive Presidents. The present Administration would apparently save national security cases from restrictions against wiretapping. We should not require the warrant procedure and the magistrate's judgment if the President of the United States or his chief legal officer, the Attorney General, has considered the requirements of national security and authorized electronic surveillance as reasonable.

Id. at 363 (White, J., concurring).

Congress took a hands-off approach to national security surveillance when it passed the Wiretap Act in 1968, a year after *Katz.* In the original version of the Wiretap Act, Congress carved out an exception to the statute for national security monitoring. When the President deemed it necessary to use his constitutional power to conduct national security monitoring, such monitoring was exempt from the statutory prohibition of the Wiretap Act. *See* 18 U.S.C. § 2511(3) (1968). This approach left open the constitutional question of the President's authority to conduct such monitoring in light of the *Katz*-era Fourth Amendment. The following case was the first (and so far, the only) Supreme Court case to help answer this question.

UNITED STATES v. UNITED STATES DISTRICT COURT

Supreme Court of the United States, 1972.
407 U.S. 297.

MR. JUSTICE POWELL delivered the opinion of the Court.

The issue before us is an important one for the people of our country and their Government. It involves the delicate question of the President's power, acting through the Attorney General, to authorize electronic surveillance in internal security matters without prior judicial approval. Successive Presidents for more than one-quarter of a century have authorized such surveillance in varying degrees, without guidance from the Congress or a definitive decision of this Court. This case brings the issue here for the first time. Its resolution is a matter of national concern, requiring sensitivity both to the Government's right to protect itself from unlawful subversion and attack and to the citizen's right to be secure in his privacy against unreasonable Government intrusion.

This case arises from a criminal proceeding in the United States District Court for the Eastern District of Michigan, in which the United States charged three defendants with conspiracy to destroy Government property in violation of 18 U.S.C. § 371. One of the defendants, Plamondon, was charged with the dynamite bombing of an office of the Central Intelligence Agency in Ann Arbor, Michigan.

During pretrial proceedings, the defendants moved to compel the United States to disclose certain electronic surveillance information and to conduct a hearing to determine whether this information "tainted" the evidence on which the indictment was based or which the Government intended to offer at trial. In response, the Government filed an affidavit of the Attorney General, acknowledging that its agents had overheard conversations in which Plamondon had participated. The affidavit also stated that the Attorney General approved the wiretaps "to gather intelligence information deemed necessary to protect the nation from attempts of domestic organizations to attack and subvert the existing structure of the Government." The logs of the surveillance were filed in a sealed exhibit for *in camera* inspection by the District Court.

On the basis of the Attorney General's affidavit and the sealed exhibit, the Government asserted that the surveillance was lawful, though conducted without prior judicial approval, as a reasonable exercise of the President's power (exercised through the Attorney General) to protect the national security. The District Court held that the surveillance violated the Fourth Amendment, and ordered the Government to make full disclosure to Plamondon of his overheard conversations.

The Government then filed in the Court of Appeals for the Sixth Circuit a petition for a writ of mandamus to set aside the District Court order, which was stayed pending final disposition of the case. After concluding that it had jurisdiction, that court held that the surveillance was unlawful and that the District Court had properly required disclosure of the overheard conversations. We granted certiorari.

I

Title III of the Omnibus Crime Control and Safe Streets Act, 18 U.S.C. §§ 2510–20, authorizes the use of electronic surveillance for classes of crimes carefully specified in 18 U.S.C. § 2516. Such surveillance is subject to prior court order. Section 2518 sets forth the detailed and particularized application necessary to obtain such an order as well as carefully circumscribed conditions for its use. The Act represents a comprehensive attempt by Congress to promote more effective control of crime while protecting the privacy of individual thought and expression. Much of Title III was drawn to meet the constitutional requirements for electronic surveillance enunciated by this Court in Berger v. New York, 388 U.S. 41 (1967), and Katz v. United States, 389 U.S. 347 (1967).

Together with the elaborate surveillance requirements in Title III, there is the following proviso, 18 U.S.C. § 2511(3):

> Nothing contained in this chapter or in section 605 of the Communications Act of 1934 shall limit the constitutional power of the President to take such measures as he deems necessary to protect the Nation against actual or potential attack or other hostile acts of a foreign power, to obtain foreign intelligence information deemed essential to the security of the United States, or to protect national security information against foreign intelligence activities. *Nor shall anything contained in this chapter be deemed to limit the constitutional power of the President to take such measures as he deems necessary to protect the United States against the overthrow of the Government by force or other unlawful means, or against any other clear and present danger to the structure or existence of the Government.* The contents of any wire or oral communication intercepted by authority of the President in the exercise of the foregoing powers may be received in evidence in any trial hearing, or other proceeding only where such interception was reasonable, and shall not be otherwise used or disclosed except as is necessary to implement that power. (Emphasis supplied.)

The Government relies on § 2511(3). It argues that "in excepting national security surveillances from the Act's warrant requirement Congress recognized the President's authority to conduct such surveillances without prior judicial approval." Brief for United States 7, 28. The section thus is viewed as a recognition or affirmance of a constitutional authority in the President to conduct warrantless domestic security surveillance such as that involved in this case.

We think the language of § 2511(3), as well as the legislative history of the statute, refutes this interpretation. The relevant language is that: "Nothing contained in this chapter . . . shall limit the constitutional power of the President to take such measures as he deems necessary to protect" against the dangers specified. At most, this is an implicit recognition that the President does have certain powers in the specified areas. Few would doubt this, as the section refers—among other things—to protection "against actual or potential attack or other hostile acts of a foreign power." But so far as the use of the President's electronic surveillance power is concerned, the language is essentially neutral.

Section 2511(3) certainly confers no power, as the language is wholly inappropriate for such a purpose. It merely provides that the Act shall not be interpreted to limit or disturb such power as the President may have under the Constitution. In short, Congress simply left presidential powers where it found them.

* * * [N]othing in § 2511(3) was intended to *expand* or to *contract* or to *define* whatever presidential surveillance powers existed in matters affecting the national security. If we could accept the Government's characterization of § 2511(3) as a congressionally prescribed exception to the general requirement of a warrant, it would be necessary to consider the question of whether the surveillance in this case came within the exception and, if so, whether the statutory exception was itself constitutionally valid. But viewing § 2511(3) as a congressional disclaimer and expression of neutrality, we hold that the statute is not the measure of the executive authority asserted in this case. Rather, we must look to the constitutional powers of the President.

II

It is important at the outset to emphasize the limited nature of the question before the Court. This case raises no constitutional challenge to electronic surveillance as specifically authorized by Title III of the Omnibus Crime Control and Safe Streets Act of 1968. Nor is there any question or doubt as to the necessity of obtaining a warrant in the surveillance of crimes unrelated to the national security interest. Katz v. United States, 389 U.S. 347 (1967); Berger v. New York, 388 U.S. 41 (1967). Further, the instant case requires no judgment on the scope of the President's surveillance power with respect to the activities of foreign powers, within or without this country. The Attorney General's affidavit in this case states that the surveillances were "deemed necessary to protect the nation from attempts of *domestic organizations* to attack and subvert the existing structure of Government" (emphasis supplied). There is no evidence of any involvement, directly or indirectly, of a foreign power.[1]

Our present inquiry, though important, is therefore a narrow one. * * * The determination of this question requires the essential Fourth

---

1. Although we attempt no precise definition, we use the term "domestic organization" in this opinion to mean a group or organization (whether formally or informally constituted) composed of citizens of the United States and which has no significant connection with a foreign power, its agents or agencies. No doubt there are cases where it will be difficult to distinguish between "domestic" and "foreign" unlawful activities directed against the Government of the United States where there is collaboration in varying degrees between domestic groups or organizations and agents or agencies of foreign powers. But this is not such a case.

Amendment inquiry into the "reasonableness" of the search and seizure in question, and the way in which that "reasonableness" derives content and meaning through reference to the warrant clause.

We begin the inquiry by noting that the President of the United States has the fundamental duty, under Art. II, § 1, of the Constitution, to "preserve, protect and defend the Constitution of the United States." Implicit in that duty is the power to protect our Government against those who would subvert or overthrow it by unlawful means. In the discharge of this duty, the President—through the Attorney General—may find it necessary to employ electronic surveillance to obtain intelligence information on the plans of those who plot unlawful acts against the Government. The use of such surveillance in internal security cases has been sanctioned more or less continuously by various Presidents and Attorneys General since July 1946. Herbert Brownell, Attorney General under President Eisenhower, urged the use of electronic surveillance both in internal and international security matters on the grounds that those acting against the Government

> "turn to the telephone to carry on their intrigue. The success of their plans frequently rests upon piecing together shreds of information received from many sources and many nests. The participants in the conspiracy are often dispersed and stationed in various strategic positions in government and industry throughout the country."[11]

Though the Government and respondents debate their seriousness and magnitude, threats and acts of sabotage against the Government exist in sufficient number to justify investigative powers with respect to them. The covertness and complexity of potential unlawful conduct against the Government and the necessary dependency of many conspirators upon the telephone make electronic surveillance an effective investigatory instrument in certain circumstances. The marked acceleration in technological developments and sophistication in their use have resulted in new techniques for the planning, commission, and concealment of criminal activities. It would be contrary to the public interest for Government to deny to itself the prudent and lawful employment of those very techniques which are employed against the Government and its law-abiding citizens.

It has been said that the most basic function of any government is to provide for the security of the individual and of his property. And unless Government safeguards its own capacity to function and to preserve the security of its people, society itself could become so disordered that all rights and liberties would be endangered.

But a recognition of these elementary truths does not make the employment by Government of electronic surveillance a welcome development—even when employed with restraint and under judicial supervi-

---

11. Brownell, The Public Security and Wire Tapping, 39 Cornell L.Q. 195, 202 (1954).

sion. There is, understandably, a deep-seated uneasiness and apprehension that this capability will be used to intrude upon cherished privacy of law-abiding citizens. We look to the Bill of Rights to safeguard this privacy. Though physical entry of the home is the chief evil against which the wording of the Fourth Amendment is directed, its broader spirit now shields private speech from unreasonable surveillance. Our decision in *Katz* refused to lock the Fourth Amendment into instances of actual physical trespass. Rather, the Amendment governs "not only the seizure of tangible items, but extends as well to the recording of oral statements without any 'technical trespass under local property law.' " *Katz, supra,* 389 U.S., at 353. That decision implicitly recognized that the broad and unsuspected governmental incursions into conversational privacy which electronic surveillance entails necessitate the application of Fourth Amendment safeguards.

National security cases, moreover, often reflect a convergence of First and Fourth Amendment values not present in cases of "ordinary" crime. Though the investigative duty of the executive may be stronger in such cases, so also is there greater jeopardy to constitutionally protected speech. * * * History abundantly documents the tendency of Government—however benevolent and benign its motives—to view with suspicion those who most fervently dispute its policies. Fourth Amendment protections become the more necessary when the targets of official surveillance may be those suspected of unorthodoxy in their political beliefs. The danger to political dissent is acute where the Government attempts to act under so vague a concept as the power to protect "domestic security." Given the difficulty of defining the domestic security interest, the danger of abuse in acting to protect that interest becomes apparent. * * * The price of lawful public dissent must not be a dread of subjection to an unchecked surveillance power. Nor must the fear of unauthorized official eavesdropping deter vigorous citizen dissent and discussion of Government action in private conversation. For private dissent, no less than open public discourse, is essential to our free society.

III

As the Fourth Amendment is not absolute in its terms, our task is to examine and balance the basic values at stake in this case: the duty of Government to protect the domestic security, and the potential danger posed by unreasonable surveillance to individual privacy and free expression. If the legitimate need of Government to safeguard domestic security requires the use of electronic surveillance, the question is whether the needs of citizens for privacy and free expression may not be better protected by requiring a warrant before such surveillance is undertaken. We must also ask whether a warrant requirement would unduly frustrate the efforts of Government to protect itself from acts of subversion and overthrow directed against it.

Over two centuries ago, Lord Mansfield held that common-law principles prohibited warrants that ordered the arrest of unnamed individuals who the *officer* might conclude were guilty of seditious libel. "It is not fit," said Mansfield, "that the receiving or judging of the information should be left to the discretion of the officer. The magistrate ought to judge; and should give certain directions to the officer." Leach v. Three of the King's Messengers, 19 How. St. Tr. 1001, 1027 (1765).

Lord Mansfield's formulation touches the very heart of the Fourth Amendment directive: that, where practical, a governmental search and seizure should represent both the efforts of the officer to gather evidence of wrongful acts and the judgment of the magistrate that the collected evidence is sufficient to justify invasion of a citizen's private premises or conversation. Inherent in the concept of a warrant is its issuance by a "neutral and detached magistrate." * * * The Fourth Amendment does not contemplate the executive officers of Government as neutral and disinterested magistrates. Their duty and responsibility are to enforce the laws, to investigate, and to prosecute. But those charged with this investigative and prosecutorial duty should not be the sole judges of when to utilize constitutionally sensitive means in pursuing their tasks. The historical judgment, which the Fourth Amendment accepts, is that unreviewed executive discretion may yield too readily to pressures to obtain incriminating evidence and overlook potential invasions of privacy and protected speech.

It is true that there have been some exceptions to the warrant requirement. But those exceptions are few in number and carefully delineated; in general, they serve the legitimate needs of law enforcement officers to protect their own well-being and preserve evidence from destruction. Even while carving out those exceptions, the Court has reaffirmed the principle that the police must, whenever practicable, obtain advance judicial approval of searches and seizures through the warrant procedure.

The Government argues that the special circumstances applicable to domestic security surveillances necessitate a further exception to the warrant requirement. It is urged that the requirement of prior judicial review would obstruct the President in the discharge of his constitutional duty to protect domestic security. We are told further that these surveillances are directed primarily to the collecting and maintaining of intelligence with respect to subversive forces, and are not an attempt to gather evidence for specific criminal prosecutions. It is said that this type of surveillance should not be subject to traditional warrant requirements which were established to govern investigation of criminal activity, not ongoing intelligence gathering.

The Government further insists that courts as a practical matter would have neither the knowledge nor the techniques necessary to determine whether there was probable cause to believe that surveillance was necessary to protect national security. These security problems, the Government contends, involve a large number of complex and subtle factors beyond the competence of courts to evaluate.

* * * There is, no doubt, pragmatic force to the Government's position.* * * But we do not think a case has been made for the requested departure from Fourth Amendment standards. The circumstances described do not justify complete exemption of domestic security surveillance from prior judicial scrutiny. Official surveillance, whether its purpose be criminal investigation or ongoing intelligence gathering, risks infringement of constitutionally protected privacy of speech. Security surveillances are especially sensitive because of the inherent vagueness of the domestic security concept, the necessarily broad and continuing nature of intelligence gathering, and the temptation to utilize such surveillances to oversee political dissent. We recognize, as we have before, the constitutional basis of the President's domestic security role, but we think it must be exercised in a manner compatible with the Fourth Amendment. In this case we hold that this requires an appropriate prior warrant procedure.

We cannot accept the Government's argument that internal security matters are too subtle and complex for judicial evaluation. Courts regularly deal with the most difficult issues of our society. There is no reason to believe that federal judges will be insensitive to or uncomprehending of the issues involved in domestic security cases. Certainly courts can recognize that domestic security surveillance involves different considerations from the surveillance of "ordinary crime." If the threat is too subtle or complex for our senior law enforcement officers to convey its significance to a court, one may question whether there is probable cause for surveillance.

Thus, we conclude that the Government's concerns do not justify departure in this case from the customary Fourth Amendment requirement of judicial approval prior to initiation of a search or surveillance. Although some added burden will be imposed upon the Attorney General, this inconvenience is justified in a free society to protect constitutional values. Nor do we think the Government's domestic surveillance powers will be impaired to any significant degree. A prior warrant establishes presumptive validity of the surveillance and will minimize the burden of justification in post-surveillance judicial review. By no means of least importance will be the reassurance of the public generally that indiscriminate wiretapping and bugging of law-abiding citizens cannot occur.

IV

We emphasize, before concluding this opinion, the scope of our decision. As stated at the outset, this case involves only the domestic aspects of national security. We have not addressed, and express no opinion as to, the issues which may be involved with respect to activities of foreign powers or their agents. Nor does our decision rest on the language of § 2511(3) or any other section of Title III of the Omnibus Crime Control and Safe Streets Act of 1968. That Act does not attempt to define or delineate the powers of the President to meet domestic threats to the national security.

Moreover, we do not hold that the same type of standards and procedures prescribed by Title III are necessarily applicable to this case. We recognize that domestic security surveillance may involve different policy and practical considerations from the surveillance of "ordinary crime." The gathering of security intelligence is often long range and involves the interrelation of various sources and types of information. The exact targets of such surveillance may be more difficult to identify than in surveillance operations against many types of crime specified in Title III. Often, too, the emphasis of domestic intelligence gathering is on the prevention of unlawful activity or the enhancement of the Government's preparedness for some possible future crisis or emergency. Thus, the focus of domestic surveillance may be less precise than that directed against more conventional types of crime.

Given those potential distinctions between Title III criminal surveillances and those involving the domestic security, Congress may wish to consider protective standards for the latter which differ from those already prescribed for specified crimes in Title III. Different standards may be compatible with the Fourth Amendment if they are reasonable both in relation to the legitimate need of Government for intelligence information and the protected rights of our citizens. For the warrant application may vary according to the governmental interest to be enforced and the nature of citizen rights deserving protection. As the Court said in Camara v. Municipal Court, 387 U.S. 523, 534–535 (1967):

> In cases in which the Fourth Amendment requires that a warrant to search be obtained, 'probable cause' is the standard by which a particular decision to search is tested against the constitutional mandate of reasonableness. In determining whether a particular inspection is reasonable—and thus in determining whether there is probable cause to issue a warrant for that inspection—the need for the inspection must be weighed in terms of these reasonable goals of code enforcement.

It may be that Congress, for example, would judge that the application and affidavit showing probable cause need not follow the exact requirements of § 2518 but should allege other circumstances more appropriate to domestic security cases; that the request for prior court authorization could, in sensitive cases, be made to any member of a specially designated court (e.g., the District Court for the District of Columbia or the Court of Appeals for the District of Columbia Circuit); and that the time and reporting requirements need not be so strict as those in § 2518.

The above paragraph does not, of course, attempt to guide the congressional judgment but rather to delineate the present scope of our own opinion. We do not attempt to detail the precise standards for domestic security warrants any more than our decision in *Katz* sought to set the refined requirements for the specified criminal surveillances which now constitute Title III. We do hold, however, that prior judicial approval is required for the type of domestic security surveillance involved in this case and that such approval may be made in accordance with such reasonable standards as the Congress may prescribe.

Notes and Questions

1. *United States v. United States District Court* is generally known as "the *Keith* case" because the district court judge in the case was Judge Damon Keith. The case has an unusual procedural history that explains its unusual name. The defendants were accused of bombing a CIA office in Michigan, and they claimed that the government had conducted warrantless interception of their telephone calls in violation of the Fourth Amendment. The government agreed that it had monitored the defendants, but argued that the warrantless monitoring was legal.

At the trial level, Judge Keith agreed with the defendants that the monitoring violated the Fourth Amendment. Under Alderman v. United States, 394 U.S. 165 (1969), the proper procedure for addressing the scope of the taint from illegal wiretapping was disclosure to the defendants of all of the wiretapping evidence against them so they could litigate the scope of the suppression remedy under the "fruit of the poisonous tree" doctrine. Judge Keith applied *Alderman*, ordered the government to turn over the wiretapping evidence to the defense, and announced that he would hold a suppression hearing to determine the scope of the remedy. *See* United States v. Sinclair, 321 F. Supp. 1074 (E.D. Mich. 1971).

The government then filed a petition for a writ of mandamus in the court of appeals seeking to overturn Judge Keith's order. The legality of the government's surveillance was the central issue in the *Keith* case because *Alderman*'s disclosure requirement applied only if the wiretapping was illegal. If the monitoring was lawful, there was no need for a hearing to determine the scope of the suppression remedy and no need for the government to turn over the evidence to the defense.

The unusual case name derives from the government's choice of writ. The government's petition was styled as a petition for a writ of mandamus, which is a request for an order from the higher court ordering the lower court to take a specific action. For historical reasons, such petitions are styled as lawsuits by the petitioner against the lower court. In the *Keith* case, the United States government wanted the Supreme Court to order Judge Keith of the United States District Court to rescind the disclosure order. Thus the strange case title, *United States v. United States District Court*.

2. Justice Powell's opinion in the *Keith* case is quintessentially pragmatic. Justice Powell views the constitutional question as a balance between government and individual interests in the context of domestic security surveillance cases. The key language appears at the beginning of Part III:

> [O]ur task is to examine and balance the basic values at stake in this case: the duty of Government to protect the domestic security, and the potential danger posed by unreasonable surveillance to individual privacy and free expression. If the legitimate need of Government to safeguard domestic security requires the use of electronic surveillance, the question is whether the needs of citizens for privacy and free expression

may not be better protected by requiring a warrant before such surveillance is undertaken. We must also ask whether a warrant requirement would unduly frustrate the efforts of Government to protect itself from acts of subversion and overthrow directed against it.

Justice Powell concludes that the balance favors a warrant requirement: in his view, the requirement would better protect the needs of citizens and would not unduly frustrate the efforts of the government.

At the same time, the warrant requirement Justice Powell has in mind is no ordinary warrant requirement. Part IV of the opinion explains that Congress is free to enact a new type of warrant procedure and a new type of warrant that is tailored to the needs of domestic security investigations. The new procedures simply need to be "reasonable both in relation to the legitimate need of Government for intelligence information and the protected rights of our citizens." Once again, the standard is reasonableness. Putting Part III and Part IV of the *Keith* opinion together, a warrant is required in domestic security cases because some kind of reasonable warrant requirement would be a reasonable limitation on government surveillance practices.

3. *Domestic security versus foreign intelligence.* The *Keith* opinion considers legal standards for domestic security surveillance, but it explicitly excludes foreign intelligence surveillance. What's the difference?

Although the opinion does not elaborate extensively on the two categories, it seems that domestic security surveillance refers to the monitoring of threats to the nation from United States citizens operating in the United States, while foreign intelligence surveillance refers to gathering intelligence concerning foreign nations, governments, and their agents. The two categories may not seem intuitive today. The idea that the Nation would face threats to its existence from its own citizenry may seem puzzling, as does the notion that foreign threats are limited to threats from foreign governments and their agents. At the time of the *Keith* case, however, these two categories seemed more natural. Domestic intelligence referred to monitoring of American citizens who were believed to be communists, fascists, or members of radical groups committed to overthrowing the United States government. Foreign intelligence referred to the monitoring of foreign governments and their agents, such as Soviet spies and employees of foreign embassies.

Today the most important goal of national security monitoring is to identify and disrupt terror attacks planned by groups such as the Al Qaeda network. Does monitoring designed to disrupt such attacks count as foreign intelligence, domestic intelligence, or something else? *See* 50 U.S.C. § 1801(a)(4) (defining "foreign power" to include "a group engaged in international terrorism or activities in preparation therefor").

4. *Fourth Amendment standards for foreign intelligence surveillance.* The Supreme Court has never addressed whether and when foreign intelligence surveillance requires a search warrant, or what kind of warrant it may require. However, the Court's opinions in related areas narrow the inquiry. For example, a great deal of foreign intelligence surveillance does not trigger Fourth Amendment protections under United States v. Verdugo–Urquidez, 494 U.S. 259 (1990). *See* pages 593–95. Under *Verdugo*, foreign nationals located outside the United States normally have no Fourth Amendment

rights. *Verdugo* thus permits a great deal of monitoring by United States intelligence authorities abroad.

Second, the border search exception to the Fourth Amendment as interpreted in cases like United States v. Ramsey, 431 U.S. 606 (1977), probably permits intelligence agencies to monitor computer traffic entering and exiting the United States. *See* page 341. Finally, in both the domestic and foreign intelligence surveillance context, Fourth Amendment protections exist only to the extent a user has a reasonable expectation of privacy in remote data.

Let's assume that none of these doctrines eliminate Fourth Amendment protection, and that a computer user normally has a reasonable expectation of privacy in the contents of his communications online. According to the *Keith* case, the government normally must obtain a warrant to monitor that individual's communications if the government is engaging in domestic intelligence surveillance. But does the warrant requirement apply if the government is conducting *foreign* intelligence surveillance?

Two court of appeals cases shed light on this question. United States v. Butenko, 494 F.2d 593 (3d Cir. 1974) (en banc), involved the prosecution of a Soviet national and an American citizen for transmitting defense information to the Soviet Union. The Soviet national, Igor Ivanov, sought disclosure of the fruits of warrantless wiretapping against him on the ground that the monitoring was illegal. In an opinion by Judge Adams, the Third Circuit concluded that the Fourth Amendment did not require a warrant before the government conducted foreign intelligence surveillance:

> [F]oreign intelligence gathering is a clandestine and highly unstructured activity, and the need for electronic surveillance often cannot be anticipated in advance. Certainly occasions arise when officers, acting under the President's authority, are seeking foreign intelligence information, where exigent circumstances would excuse a warrant. To demand that such officers be so sensitive to the nuances of complex situations that they must interrupt their activities and rush to the nearest available magistrate to seek a warrant would seriously fetter the Executive in the performance of his foreign affairs duties.

Id. at 605. According to the Third Circuit, the Fourth Amendment merely required that foreign intelligence surveillance must be reasonable:

> The government interest here—to acquire the information necessary to exercise an informed judgment in foreign affairs—is surely weighty. Moreover, officers conceivably undertake certain electronic surveillance with no suspicion that a criminal activity may be discovered. Thus, a demand that they show that before engaging in such surveillance they had a reasonable belief that criminal activity would be unearthed would be to ignore the overriding object of the intrusions. Since the primary purpose of these searches is to secure foreign intelligence information, a judge, when reviewing a particular search must, above all, be assured that this was in fact its primary purpose and that the accumulation of evidence of criminal activity was incidental. If the court, for example, finds that members of a domestic political organization were the subjects of wiretaps or that the agents were looking for evidence of criminal conduct unrelated to the foreign affairs needs of a President, then he

would undoubtedly hold the surveillances to be illegal and take appropriate measures.

Id. at 606.

The Fourth Circuit reached a similar conclusion in United States v. Truong Dinh Hung, 629 F.2d 908 (4th Cir. 1980). A Vietnamese citizen was convicted of espionage for passing classified diplomatic cables and sensitive strategic plans to the government of the Socialist Republic of Vietnam. The defendant's home telephone was tapped for 268 consecutive days without a warrant, and the evidence was used against him at trial. The defendant challenged the surveillance under the Fourth Amendment, but the Fourth Circuit held that the monitoring was legal:

[T]he needs of the executive are so compelling in the area of foreign intelligence, unlike the area of domestic security, that a uniform warrant requirement would, following *Keith*, "unduly frustrate" the President in carrying out his foreign affairs responsibilities. First of all, attempts to counter foreign threats to the national security require the utmost stealth, speed, and secrecy. A warrant requirement would add a procedural hurdle that would reduce the flexibility of executive foreign intelligence initiatives, in some cases delay executive response to foreign intelligence threats, and increase the chance of leaks regarding sensitive executive operations.

More importantly, the executive possesses unparalleled expertise to make the decision whether to conduct foreign intelligence surveillance, whereas the judiciary is largely inexperienced in making the delicate and complex decisions that lie behind foreign intelligence surveillance. The executive branch, containing the State Department, the intelligence agencies, and the military, is constantly aware of the nation's security needs and the magnitude of external threats posed by a panoply of foreign nations and organizations. On the other hand, while the courts possess expertise in making the probable cause determination involved in surveillance of suspected criminals, the courts are unschooled in diplomacy and military affairs, a mastery of which would be essential to passing upon an executive branch request that a foreign intelligence wiretap be authorized. Few, if any, district courts would be truly competent to judge the importance of particular information to the security of the United States or the "probable cause" to demonstrate that the government in fact needs to recover that information from one particular source.

Perhaps most crucially, the executive branch not only has superior expertise in the area of foreign intelligence, it is also constitutionally designated as the pre-eminent authority in foreign affairs. The President and his deputies are charged by the constitution with the conduct of the foreign policy of the United States in times of war and peace. Just as the separation of powers in *Keith* forced the executive to recognize a judicial role when the President conducts domestic security surveillance, so the separation of powers requires us to acknowledge the principal responsibility of the President for foreign affairs and concomitantly for foreign intelligence surveillance.

Id. at 913–14. The Court limited this holding to contexts in which two requirements were met. "First, the government should be relieved of seeking a warrant only when the object of the search or the surveillance is a foreign power, its agent or collaborators." *Id.* at 915. Second, "the executive should be excused from securing a warrant only when the surveillance is conducted primarily for foreign intelligence reasons." *Id.* The court explained:

> [O]nce surveillance becomes primarily a criminal investigation, the courts are entirely competent to make the usual probable cause determination, and * * * individual privacy interests come to the fore and government foreign policy concerns recede when the government is primarily attempting to form the basis for a criminal prosecution. We thus reject the government's assertion that, if surveillance is to any degree directed at gathering foreign intelligence, the executive may ignore the warrant requirement of the Fourth Amendment.

Id. In those contexts, warrantless surveillance was permissible so long as it was "reasonable."

5. In 2005, *The New York Times* disclosed that the National Security Agency was tapping telecommunications switches in the United States to intercept international telephone calls and Internet communications without first obtaining a warrant. The alleged program focuses mostly on communications among individuals outside the United States that happen to be routed inside the United States in the course of delivery, but includes some communications between United States citizens and permanent residents in the United States and others outside the United States. *See generally* James Risen, State of War 39–60 (2006). According to one report, the program works by generating copies of millions and millions of e-mails and telephone calls being sent through individual communications switches—mostly communications among those inside the United States—and scanning the communications for particular e-mail addresses or keywords believed to relate to members of Al Qaeda or allied organizations. Communications that register with the filters are then reviewed by individuals at the NSA for further action. *See* James Bamford, *Big Brother is Listening*, The Atlantic Monthly, April 2006, at 65–70.

The Justice Department has defended the constitutionality of this program under the "special needs" exception to the Fourth Amendment, which is arguably the same doctrinal box applied in the *Keith* case. Here is the argument:

> With respect to the individual privacy interests at stake, there can be no doubt that, as a general matter, interception of telephone communications implicates a significant privacy interest of the individual whose conversation is intercepted. The Supreme Court has made clear at least since Katz v. United States, 389 U.S. 347 (1967), that individuals have a substantial and constitutionally protected reasonable expectation of privacy that their telephone conversations will not be subject to governmental eavesdropping. Although the individual privacy interests at stake may be substantial, it is well recognized that a variety of governmental interests—including routine law enforcement and foreign-intelligence gathering—can overcome those interests.

On the other side of the scale here, the Government's interest in engaging in the NSA activities is the most compelling interest possible— securing the Nation from foreign attack in the midst of an armed conflict. One attack already has taken thousands of lives and placed the Nation in state of armed conflict. Defending the Nation from attack is perhaps the most important function of the federal Government—and one of the few express obligations of the federal Government enshrined in the Constitution. As the Supreme Court has declared, "[i]t is 'obvious and unarguable' that no governmental interest is more compelling than the security of the Nation." Haig v. Agee, 453 U.S. 280, 307 (1981). The Government's overwhelming interest in detecting and thwarting further al Qaeda attacks is easily sufficient to make reasonable the intrusion into privacy involved in intercepting one-end foreign communications where there is "a reasonable basis to conclude that one party to the communication is a member of al Qaeda, affiliated with al Qaeda, or a member of an organization affiliated with al Qaeda."

Of course, because the magnitude of the Government's interest here depends in part upon the threat posed by al Qaeda, it might be possible for the weight that interest carries in the balance to change over time. It is thus significant for the reasonableness of the NSA activities that the President has established a system under which he authorizes the surveillance only for a limited period, typically for 45 days. This process of reauthorization ensures a periodic review to evaluate whether the threat from al Qaeda remains sufficiently strong that the Government's interest in protecting the Nation and its citizens from foreign attack continues to outweigh the individual privacy interests at stake.

United States Department of Justice, Legal Authorities Supporting the Activities of the National Security Agency Described by the President 39–40 (Jan. 19, 2006).

Is this defense persuasive? Does it depend on the magnitude of the Al Qaeda threat, or on the technical details of the surveillance program?

6. *Reasonable warrants under the USA Patriot Act.* The *Keith* case establishes that warrants are required for domestic security surveillance, and advises that such warrants must be "reasonable both in relation to the legitimate need of Government for intelligence information and the protected rights of our citizens." What does this mean? What types of warrants can Congress authorize in intelligence cases that will satisfy this test?

This issue arose in In re Sealed Case, 310 F.3d 717 (Foreign Intel. Surv. Ct. Rev. 2002), which considered the constitutionality of amendments to the Foreign Intelligence Surveillance Act (FISA) put in place by the USA Patriot Act of 2001. Before the Patriot Act, FISA conditioned the issuance of national security warrants on the absence of intent to collect evidence for possible criminal prosecution. Specifically, FISA required investigators seeking a national security warrant to establish probable cause that the person monitored was an agent of a foreign power and that "the purpose of the surveillance is to obtain foreign intelligence information."

The Patriot Act changed the standard to permit intelligence officials to share information collected under FISA with criminal investigators. The new standard requires the government to establish probable cause that the person monitored is the agent of a foreign power, and that "a significant purpose" of surveillance is to obtain foreign intelligence information. 50 U.S.C. § 1804(a)(7)(B). It also adds a provision allowing "Federal officers who conduct electronic surveillance to acquire foreign intelligence information" to "consult with Federal law enforcement officers to coordinate efforts to investigate or protect against" attack or other grave hostile acts, sabotage or international terrorism, or clandestine intelligence activities, by foreign powers or their agents. 50 U.S.C. § 1806(k)(1).

The Foreign Intelligence Surveillance Court of Review, a special court of three federal appellate judges, ruled that this statutory framework satisfies the *Keith* reasonableness standard:

> FISA's general programmatic purpose, to protect the nation against terrorists and espionage threats directed by foreign powers, has from its outset been distinguishable from "ordinary crime control." After the events of September 11, 2001, though, it is hard to imagine greater emergencies facing Americans than those experienced on that date.

> Although * * * the threat to society is not dispositive in determining whether a search or seizure is reasonable, it certainly remains a crucial factor. Our case may well involve the most serious threat our country faces. Even without taking into account the President's inherent constitutional authority to conduct warrantless foreign intelligence surveillance, we think the procedures and government showings required under FISA, if they do not meet the minimum Fourth Amendment warrant standards, certainly come close. We, therefore, believe firmly, applying the balancing test drawn from *Keith,* that FISA as amended is constitutional because the surveillances it authorizes are reasonable.

In re Sealed Case, 310 F.3d at 746.

B. THE FOREIGN INTELLIGENCE SURVEILLANCE ACT

The *Keith* case pointed to the need for statutory regulation of national security surveillance. That need became particularly clear in the mid 1970s during hearings into intelligence collection abuses held by the United States Senate Select Committee to Study Governmental Operations with Respect to Intelligence Activities, presided over by Senator Frank Church. The so-called "Church Committee" published 14 reports in 1975 and 1976 detailing the intelligence practices of several government agencies, and the reports led to calls for a new statute to regulate intelligence surveillance. *See generally* Peter P. Swire, *The System of Foreign Intelligence Surveillance Law*, 72 Geo. Wash. L. Rev. 1306, 1315–20 (2004).

Congress responded by enacting the Foreign Intelligence Surveillance Act (FISA), Pub. L. 95–511 (1978). FISA replaced the reservation clause of 18 U.S.C. § 2511(3) (1968), and imposed direct regulation of Executive Branch intelligence activities. *See* 18 U.S.C. § 2511(2)(f). Under FISA, if the government seeks evidence of domestic security violations, it must follow the usual criminal law authorities. If the President wishes to conduct foreign intelligence surveillance, the President must comply with the requirements of the FISA statute, which acts as a cousin of the criminal-law statutory privacy laws covered in Chapter 6.

FISA requires the Executive Branch to apply for and obtain court orders to conduct foreign intelligence surveillance from the Foreign Intelligence Surveillance Court. Eleven United States District Court judges are appointed to the court by the Chief Justice of the United States. *See* 50 U.S.C. § 1803. When the government needs a FISA order signed, it submits an application to one of the eleven judges assigned to the Court.

FISA's Equivalent of the Wiretap Act

The FISA equivalent of the Wiretap Act is codified at 50 U.S.C. §§ 1801–11. In lieu of regulating the interception of contents of wire and electronic communications, FISA regulates engaging in "electronic surveillance." "Electronic surveillance" is defined in a fairly complicated way by 50 U.S.C. § 1801(f):

(1) the acquisition by an electronic, mechanical, or other surveillance device of the contents of any wire or radio communication sent by or intended to be received by a particular, known United States person who is in the United States, if the contents are acquired by intentionally targeting that United States person, under circumstances in which a person has a reasonable expectation of privacy and a warrant would be required for law enforcement purposes;

(2) the acquisition by an electronic, mechanical, or other surveillance device of the contents of any wire communication to or from a person in the United States, without the consent of any party thereto, if such acquisition occurs in the United States, but does not include the acquisition of those communications of computer trespassers that would be permissible under section 2511(2)(i) of title 18;

(3) the intentional acquisition by an electronic, mechanical, or other surveillance device of the contents of any radio communication, under circumstances in which a person has a reasonable expectation of privacy and a warrant would be required for law enforcement purposes, and if both the sender and all intended recipients are located within the United States; or

(4) the installation or use of an electronic, mechanical, or other surveillance device in the United States for monitoring to acquire information, other than from a wire or radio communication, under circumstances in which a person has a reasonable expectation of privacy and a warrant would be required for law enforcement purposes.

It is important to note that FISA's version of the Wiretap Act contains definitions that differ from the same terms used in the Wiretap

Act. For example, "contents" are defined more broadly in FISA than in the Wiretap Act. According to 50 U.S.C. § 1801(n), "contents" as used in FISA "includes any information concerning the identity of the parties to such communication or the existence, substance, purport, or meaning of that communication." Similarly, "wire communication" in FISA does not mean a call containing the human voice, but rather means "any communication while it is being carried by a wire, cable, or other like connection furnished or operated by any person engaged as a common carrier in providing or operating such facilities for the transmission of interstate or foreign communications." *Id.* § 1801(l). FISA also occasionally hinges rules on whether the subject of monitoring is a "United States person," which essentially means a United States citizen or permanent resident alien. *See id.* § 1801(i).

FISA prohibits intentionally conducting electronic surveillance "except as authorized by statute," *id.* § 1809(a)(1), and provides a statutory authority for obtaining FISA wiretap orders. *See* 50 U.S.C. § 1804. The government's application to the FISC must be personally reviewed by the Attorney General, and must include the following, *id.* § 1804(a):

(1) the identity of the Federal officer making the application;

(2) the authority conferred on the Attorney General by the President of the United States and the approval of the Attorney General to make the application;

(3) the identity, if known, or a description of the target of the electronic surveillance;

(4) a statement of the facts and circumstances relied upon by the applicant to justify his belief that—

    (A) the target of the electronic surveillance is a foreign power or an agent of a foreign power; and

    (B) each of the facilities or places at which the electronic surveillance is directed is being used, or is about to be used, by a foreign power or an agent of a foreign power;

(5) a statement of the proposed minimization procedures;

(6) a detailed description of the nature of the information sought and the type of communications or activities to be subjected to the surveillance;

(7) a certification or certifications by the Assistant to the President for National Security Affairs or an executive branch official or officials designated by the President from among those executive officers employed in the area of national security or defense and appointed by the President with the advice and consent of the Senate—

    (A) that the certifying official deems the information sought to be foreign intelligence information;

    (B) that a significant purpose of the surveillance is to obtain foreign intelligence information;

(C) that such information cannot reasonably be obtained by normal investigative techniques;

(D) that designates the type of foreign intelligence information being sought according to the categories described in section 1801 (e) of this title; and

(E) including a statement of the basis for the certification that—(i) the information sought is the type of foreign intelligence information designated; and (ii) such information cannot reasonably be obtained by normal investigative techniques;

(8) a statement of the means by which the surveillance will be effected and a statement whether physical entry is required to effect the surveillance;

(9) a statement of the facts concerning all previous applications that have been made to any judge under this subchapter involving any of the persons, facilities, or places specified in the application, and the action taken on each previous application;

(10) a statement of the period of time for which the electronic surveillance is required to be maintained, and if the nature of the intelligence gathering is such that the approval of the use of electronic surveillance under this subchapter should not automatically terminate when the described type of information has first been obtained, a description of facts supporting the belief that additional information of the same type will be obtained thereafter; and

(11) whenever more than one electronic, mechanical or other surveillance device is to be used with respect to a particular proposed electronic surveillance, the coverage of the devices involved and what minimization procedures apply to information acquired by each device.

The reviewing judge must then issue the order if the statutory requirements are met and "there is probable cause to believe that . . . the target of the electronic surveillance is a foreign power or an agent of a foreign power," provided that "no United States person may be considered a foreign power or an agent of a foreign power solely upon the basis of activities protected by the first amendment to the Constitution of the United States." 50 U.S.C. § 1805(a)(3).

FISA's Equivalent of the Pen Register Statute

The FISA equivalent of the Pen Register statute is codified at 50 U.S.C. §§ 1841–46. Pen registers and trap and trace devices are defined under FISA using the definitions in the Pen Register statute. *See* 50 U.S.C. § 1841(2). FISA states that a pen/trap order can be obtained if investigators submit:

a certification by the applicant that the information likely to be obtained is foreign intelligence information not concerning a United States person or is relevant to an ongoing investigation to protect against international terrorism or clandestine intelligence activities, provided that such investigation of a United States person is not conducted solely upon the basis of activities protected by the first amendment to the Constitution.

50 U.S.C. § 1842(c)(2).

FISA's Equivalent of the Stored Communications Act

FISA's equivalent of the Stored Communications Act is found among several different statutes. When FBI investigators seek to compel non-content information from ISPs for intelligence cases, they use 18 U.S.C. § 2709. Section 2709 is a "National Security Letter" provision in the SCA itself. The National Security Letter provision in § 2709 is something like an administrative subpoena authority, as it does not require an order signed by a judge or issued by a court. Instead, high-ranking FBI officials can request information from ISPs via written letters. According to § 2709, a "wire or electronic communication service provider shall comply with a request for subscriber information and toll billing records information, or electronic communication transactional records in its custody or possession" made by appropriate authorities within the FBI. 18 U.S.C. § 2709(a). The records sought must be "relevant to an authorized investigation to protect against international terrorism or clandestine intelligence activities, provided that such an investigation of a United States person is not conducted solely on the basis of activities protected by the first amendment to the Constitution of the United States." *Id.* § 2709(b).

Intelligence investigators normally compel the contents of communications held by ISPs using the authorities in 50 U.S.C. §§ 1821–29. These provisions regulate "physical searches," defined as "any physical intrusion within the United States into premises or property (including examination of the interior of property by technical means) that is intended to result in a seizure, reproduction, inspection, or alteration of information, material, or property, under circumstances in which a person has a reasonable expectation of privacy and a warrant would be required for law enforcement purposes." 50 U.S.C. § 1821(5). Although the scope of this authority is somewhat unclear in the case of Internet investigations, it seems that intelligence investigators generally have interpreted this provision as the required statutory framework that applies to the compelled disclosure of contents of communications from ISPs. The statute requires the government to establish probable cause that:

(A) the target of the physical search is a foreign power or an agent of a foreign power, except that no United States person may be considered an agent of a foreign power solely upon the basis of activities protected by the first amendment to the Constitution of the United States; and

(B) the premises or property to be searched is owned, used, possessed by, or is in transit to or from an agent of a foreign power or a foreign power[.]

50 U.S.C. § 1824(a)(3). In the case of Internet communications, the "premises or property" presumably would be the account and its contents rather than the physical ISP.

Intelligence investigators also can compel information from ISPs using Section 215 orders. *See* 50 U.S.C. §§ 1861–62. Section 215 orders are the national security equivalent of grand jury subpoenas, and are so-named because the authority was expanded under Section 215 of the USA Patriot Act. The Section 215 authority has been the subject of particular controversy in recent years in light of concerns that the authority might be used at libraries to compel library records. The Section 215 authority permits high-level FBI officials to apply for a FISA order requiring the recipient to produce "any tangible things (including books, records, papers, documents, and other items) for an investigation to obtain foreign intelligence information not concerning a United States person or to protect against international terrorism or clandestine intelligence activities, provided that such investigation of a United States person is not conducted solely upon the basis of activities protected by the first amendment to the Constitution." 50 U.S.C. § 1861(a)(1). As amended in 2006, the statute requires the government's application to establish:

> reasonable grounds to believe that the tangible things sought are relevant to an authorized investigation * * * to obtain foreign intelligence information not concerning a United States person or to protect against international terrorism or clandestine intelligence activities, such things being presumptively relevant to an authorized investigation if the applicant shows in the statement of the facts that they pertain to—
>
> (i) a foreign power or an agent of a foreign power;
>
> (ii) the activities of a suspected agent of a foreign power who is the subject of such authorized investigation; or
>
> (iii) an individual in contact with, or known to, a suspected agent of a foreign power who is the subject of such authorized investigation[.]

Id. § 1861(b)(2)(A).

The scope of Section 215 orders remains unclear. There is some evidence that the FBI interprets Section 215 orders as permitting only the disclosure of non-content transactional information. The former chief of the FBI's National Security Law Unit has stated: "Given that § 215 was clearly part of a set of parallel revisions to all FBI counterintelligence authorities for access to transactional information (national security letters, pen register/trap and trace, and business records), it seems reasonable to conclude that Congress saw § 215 as applying only to transactional information that is not subject to constitutional protections." Michael J. Woods, *Counterintelligence and Access to Transactional Records: A Practical History of USA Patriot Act Section 215*, 1 J. Nat'l Security L. & Pol'y 37, 59 (2005). To the extent that this interpretation is correct, Section 215 is a general parallel authority to the specific authority in 18 U.S.C. § 2709.

Voluntary disclosure by ISPs in national security cases is governed by 18 U.S.C. § 2702, just as in criminal investigations. Note that the emergency disclosure provisions in § 2702 are phrased in general terms: they permit disclosure to "a governmental entity," not just to law enforcement officials. 18 U.S.C. §§ 2702(b)(8), 2702(c)(4).

Notes and Questions

1. How do the surveillance standards for foreign intelligence investigations compare to the standards for criminal investigations? Are they lower? Higher? Or are they just different? Consider the Foreign Intelligence Surveillance Court of Review's comparison of the wiretapping authorities in Title III and FISA:

> With limited exceptions not at issue here, both Title III and FISA require prior judicial scrutiny of an application for an order authorizing electronic surveillance.

> The statutes differ to some extent in their probable cause showings. Title III allows a court to enter an ex parte order authorizing electronic surveillance if it determines on the basis of the facts submitted in the government's application that there is probable cause for belief that an individual is committing, has committed, or is about to commit a specified predicate offense. FISA by contrast requires a showing of probable cause that the target is a foreign power or an agent of a foreign power. * * * FISA applies only to certain carefully delineated, and particularly serious, foreign threats to national security.

> Turning then to the first of the particularity requirements, while Title III requires probable cause to believe that particular communications concerning the specified crime will be obtained through the interception, FISA instead requires an official to designate the type of foreign intelligence information being sought, and to certify that the information sought is foreign intelligence information. When the target is a U.S. person, the FISA judge reviews the certification for clear error, but this standard of review is not, of course, comparable to a probable cause finding by the judge. Nevertheless, FISA provides additional protections to ensure that only pertinent information is sought. The certification must be made by a national security officer—typically the FBI Director—and must be approved by the Attorney General or the Attorney General's Deputy. Congress recognized that this certification would assure written accountability within the Executive Branch and provide an internal check on Executive Branch arbitrariness.

> With respect to the second element of particularity, although Title III generally requires probable cause to believe that the facilities subject to surveillance are being used or are about to be used in connection with the commission of a crime or are leased to, listed in the name of, or used by the individual committing the crime, FISA requires probable cause to believe that each of the facilities or places at which the surveillance is directed is being used, or is about to be used, by a foreign power or

agent. In cases where the targeted facilities are not leased to, listed in the name of, or used by the individual committing the crime, Title III requires the government to show a nexus between the facilities and communications regarding the criminal offense. The government does not have to show, however, anything about the target of the surveillance; it is enough that "an individual"—not necessarily the target—is committing a crime. On the other hand, FISA requires probable cause to believe the target is an agent of a foreign power (that is, the individual committing a foreign intelligence crime) who uses or is about to use the targeted facility. Simply put, FISA requires less of a nexus between the facility and the pertinent communications than Title III, but more of a nexus between the target and the pertinent communications.

* * * Both statutes have a "necessity" provision, which requires the court to find that the information sought is not available through normal investigative procedures. Although the court's clearly erroneous review under FISA is more limited than under Title III, this greater deference must be viewed in light of FISA's additional requirement that the certification of necessity come from an upper level Executive Branch official. The statutes also have duration provisions; Title III orders may last up to 30 days, while FISA orders may last up to 90 days for U.S. persons. This difference is based on the nature of national security surveillance, which is "often long range and involves the interrelation of various sources and types of information." *Keith*, 407 U.S. at 322. Moreover, the longer surveillance period is balanced by continuing FISA court oversight of minimization procedures during that period. And where Title III requires minimization of what is acquired, as we have discussed, for U.S. persons, FISA requires minimization of what is acquired, retained, and disseminated. The FISA court notes, however, that in practice FISA surveillance devices are normally left on continuously, and the minimization occurs in the process of indexing and logging the pertinent communications. The reasonableness of this approach depends on the facts and circumstances of each case. Less minimization in the acquisition stage may well be justified to the extent the intercepted communications are ambiguous in nature or apparently involve guarded or coded language, or the investigation is focusing on what is thought to be a widespread conspiracy where more extensive surveillance may be justified in an attempt to determine the precise scope of the enterprise. Given the targets of FISA surveillance, it will often be the case that intercepted communications will be in code or a foreign language for which there is no contemporaneously available translator, and the activities of foreign agents will involve multiple actors and complex plots.

Based on the foregoing, it should be evident that while Title III contains some protections that are not in FISA, in many significant respects the two statutes are equivalent, and in some, FISA contains additional protections.

In re Sealed Case, 310 F.3d 717, 738–41 (Foreign Intel. Surv. Ct. of Rev. 2002). Do you agree? How do the standards compare when investigators seek to install a pen register or to compel content or non-content information stored with ISPs?

Some commentators argue that FISA standards are considerably lower than ECPA standards used in criminal investigations, and have expressed concern that criminal investigators may use the lower standards under FISA to conduct investigations with far fewer checks and balances than exist in the criminal law context. They argue that criminal investigators can use FISA authorities to conduct surveillance even in cases where the investigators do not have a *bona fide* purpose to collect foreign intelligence information. The ACLU has offered the following perspective:

> Under [FISA as modified by] the Patriot Act, the FBI can secretly conduct a physical search or wiretap on American citizens to obtain evidence of crime without proving probable cause, as the Fourth Amendment explicitly requires.

> A 1978 law called the Foreign Intelligence Surveillance Act created an exception to the Fourth Amendment's requirement for probable cause when the purpose of a wiretap or search was to gather foreign intelligence. The rationale was that since the search was not conducted for the purpose of gathering evidence to put someone on trial, the standards could be loosened. In a stark demonstration of why it can be dangerous to create exceptions to fundamental rights, however, the Patriot Act expanded this once-narrow exception to cover wiretaps and searches that *do* collect evidence for regular domestic criminal cases. FISA previously allowed searches only if the primary purpose was to gather foreign intelligence. But the Patriot Act changes the law to allow searches when "a significant purpose" is intelligence. That lets the government circumvent the Constitution's probable cause requirement even when its main goal is ordinary law enforcement.

Surveillance Under the USA PATRIOT Act (Apr. 3, 2003), *available at* http://www.aclu.org/safefree/general/17326res20030403.html.

Is the ACLU's description accurate? How likely is it that criminal investigators will obtain court orders under FISA instead of obtaining orders under the Wiretap Act, the Pen Register statute, and the Stored Communications Act?

2. *Is the FISA Court a "rubber stamp"?* The Justice Department publishes a one-page report every year indicating the number of applications the FISA Court received and the number of applications that were approved (in whole or in part) under FISA's authorities relating to wiretapping and physical searches. Consider the statistics for the number of applications and approvals from 1998 to 2005:

Year	Applications	Approvals
2005	2,074	2,072
2004	1,758	1,754
2003	1,727	1,724
2002	1,228	1,228
2001	932	932
2000	1,005	1,005
1999	886	886
1998	796	796

Do these numbers suggest that the FISA Court acts as a "rubber stamp" that approves almost every application? Or do you think the Justice Department is overly cautious, submitting an application for wiretapping or physical searches to the FISA Court judges only when the legal standard clearly has been met? How do the answers to these questions influence your understanding of whether the FISA regime is effective?

3. *Intelligence monitoring outside of FISA.* FISA's prohibition on wiretapping states that an individual cannot "engage[] in electronic surveillance under color of law except as authorized by statute." 50 U.S.C. § 1809(a)(1). 18 U.S.C. § 2511(2)(f) also imposes a limitation on wiretapping; it states that "procedures in [the Wiretap Act] or [the Stored Communications Act] and the Foreign Intelligence Surveillance Act of 1978 shall be the exclusive means by which electronic surveillance, as defined in [50 U.S.C. § 1801], and the interception of domestic wire, oral, and electronic communications may be conducted."

A week after the September 11, 2001, attacks, Congress passed the Authorization for Use of Military Force (AUMF), Pub. L. No. 107–40 (2001). It states in relevant part:

> [T]he President is authorized to use all necessary and appropriate force against those nations, organizations, or persons he determines planned, authorized, committed, or aided the terrorist attacks that occurred on September 11, 2001, or harbored such organizations or persons, in order to prevent any future acts of international terrorism against the United States by such nations, organizations or persons.

Id. § 2(a). Should the AUMF be read to grant the Executive Branch the statutory authorization to conduct national security wiretapping without complying with FISA? *Cf.* Hamdi v. Rumsfeld, 542 U.S. 507 (2004). Alternatively, is FISA unconstitutional to the extent it attempts to limit the Executive's authority to monitor foreign threats under the Commander-in-Chief power? *See In re Sealed Case*, 310 F.3d at 742.

C. USE OF FISA EVIDENCE IN CRIMINAL CASES

Evidence collected under FISA can be used in criminal cases subject to the Fourth Amendment's exclusionary rule and the procedures and statutory suppression remedies found in 50 U.S.C. § 1806 (electronic surveillance), § 1825 (physical searches), and § 1845 (pen/trap). The procedures are designed to permit judicial review without the disclosure of sensitive national security information.

The statutory procedures are essentially the same under the different authorities. The government must first notify the court and the defendant that it seeks to use evidence either collected under FISA or derived from such evidence. *See* 50 U.S.C. § 1806(c). The defendant can then file a motion to suppress electronic surveillance or its fruits on the ground that (1) the information was unlawfully acquired; or (2) the surveillance was not made in conformity with an order of authorization or approval. *See id.* § 1806(e). Next, the Attorney General ordinarily will file an affidavit under oath taking the position that disclosure of how the evidence was obtained or an adversary hearing addressing that question would harm the national security of the United States. *See id.* § 1806(f). If such an application is filed, the district court must:

> review in camera and ex parte the application, order, and such other materials relating to the surveillance as may be necessary to determine whether the surveillance of the aggrieved person was lawfully authorized and conducted. In making this determination, the court may disclose to the aggrieved person, under appropriate security procedures and protective orders, portions of the application, order, or other materials relating to the surveillance only where such disclosure is necessary to make an accurate determination of the legality of the surveillance.

Id. If the court concludes that disclosure of materials relating to the surveillance is not necessary for the court to make an accurate determination of the legality of the surveillance, the court will not disclose the materials to the defendant. Instead, the court will make the determination in chambers without an adversary hearing.

UNITED STATES v. SQUILLACOTE

United States Court of Appeals for the Fourth Circuit, 2000.
221 F.3d 542.

TRAXLER, Circuit Judge.

Appellants Theresa Squillacote and her husband Kurt Stand appeal from their convictions on various espionage-related charges. We affirm.

I.

Viewed in the light most favorable to the government, the evidence presented at trial established the following. Kurt Stand's parents fled to the United States from Germany during Hitler's reign. After the war, his family maintained contact with friends in the German Democratic Republic ("East Germany"). When Stand was approximately 18, his father introduced him to Lothar Ziemer, an officer with the Ministerium fur Staatssicherheit ("MfS"), East Germany's intelligence agency. The "HVA" was the foreign intelligence arm of the MfS, and Ziemer was in charge of Section 3 of the HVA's Department XI. The "primary mission" of Department XI was the operational reconnaissance of North America. Its purpose was to "acquire data of significance to the German Democratic Republic that could not be acquired by legal means." In the early 1970s, Stand began working for Ziemer as an HVA agent.

Stand's HVA activities consisted primarily of recruiting other agents. In 1976, Stand invited James Michael Clark, a college friend, to travel with him to Germany. Stand introduced Clark to an HVA operative, who introduced him to Ziemer. Ziemer invited Clark to join his organization, which he described as performing intelligence work on behalf of East Germany and other socialist countries, as well as "liberation movements" in Asia, Latin America, and Africa. Clark agreed.

Sometime between 1979 and 1981, Stand brought his wife Theresa Squillacote into the fold, and she too became what Ziemer described as an "informal collaborator." At some point, Squillacote's relationship with Ziemer became more than professional, and they had an affair that lasted until 1996.

The HVA devoted substantial resources to the training of Stand, Squillacote, and Clark. They traveled to many countries, including East Germany and Mexico, to meet with their "handlers." They received training on detecting and avoiding surveillance, receiving and decoding messages sent by shortwave radio from Cuba, mailing and receiving packages through the use of "accommodation" addresses, using codewords and phrases, using a miniature camera to photograph documents, and removing classified markings from documents. HVA records indicate that the three conspirators were together paid more than $40,000 between 1985 and 1989, primarily as reimbursement for travel expenses.

As part of his "operational plan" devised with Ziemer, Clark moved to Washington, D.C., and obtained a master's degree in Russian. For a time Clark worked for a private company in a position that required him to obtain a security clearance. He later obtained a position with the United States Army, in its environmental law division, which also required a security clearance. Clark had friends who worked for the State Department, and through them he obtained numerous classified documents that he turned over to the HVA.

Squillacote and Stand also moved to Washington, D.C., and she went to law school at the HVA's suggestion. Squillacote first followed in her father's footsteps by becoming an attorney for the National Labor Relations Board. When she realized that she had taken a career path that was not "in the best direction," she began trying to move her professional work more in line with the commitments that she had made. To that end, Squillacote used her father's connections to obtain an unprecedented temporary detail from the NLRB to the House Armed Services Committee. In 1991, Squillacote obtained a permanent job as an attorney in the Department of Defense, eventually becoming the Director of Legislative Affairs in the Office of the Undersecretary of Defense (Acquisition Reform), a position that required a security clearance and provided access to valuable information. During her tenure with the federal government, Squillacote applied for numerous government jobs, including positions with the Central Intelligence Agency, the National Security Agency, United States Army, Navy, and Air Force, and the Departments of State, Commerce, Energy, and Treasury. Apparently it was not until she began working for the Department of Defense that Squillacote gained access to the kind of information sought by her handlers. However, by that time, East Germany had collapsed.

After the fall of the Berlin Wall, Ziemer began working with the KGB, the Soviet Union's intelligence agency. Ziemer maintained his relationships with Stand, Squillacote, and Clark during this time, and they, too, became involved with the KGB. Stand, Squillacote, and Clark each traveled overseas to meet with Ziemer during the period after the collapse of East Germany. Ziemer instructed the conspirators to purchase Casio digital diaries with interchangeable memory cards. The conspirators, Ziemer, and their KGB contacts communicated with each other by exchanging memory cards.

In April 1992, Ziemer and another former HVA official were arrested and ultimately convicted for their post-unification intelligence activities with the KGB. Stand, Squillacote, and Clark became understandably concerned about their personal safety after Ziemer's arrest. They knew that "western services" were looking for two men and one woman operating out of Washington, D.C., and that the western services were aware of code names they had used. However, they believed that Ziemer and other former HVA officials would not compromise their identities. When Ziemer was released from prison in September 1992, Stand, Squillacote, and Clark re-established a system of communication with him, one purpose of which was to keep everyone informed about any threats to their safety.

From the beginning of their involvement with the HVA, Stand, Squillacote, and Clark operated independently of each other and generally were unaware of the others' activities. After Ziemer's arrest in 1992, however, the three began talking in detail about their activities and precautions needed to maintain their security. They began discussing the possibility of future intelligence work, perhaps for Vietnam or Cuba. Squillacote also talked to Clark about her interest in South Africa's Communist Party.

In 1994, Squillacote, as part of her search for "another connection," went to Amsterdam to speak to David Truong, whom she had met in college. Truong, who had been convicted of espionage on behalf of North Vietnam, was intrigued, but took no further action.

In 1995, Squillacote went to great lengths to obtain a post office box under the name of "Lisa Martin." In June 1995, Squillacote, as Lisa Martin, sent a letter to Ronnie Kasrils, the Deputy Defense Minister of South Africa. Kasrils was a Communist party official, and had received training in East Germany, the Soviet Union, and Cuba. The letter, which took Squillacote months to write, was primarily devoted to Squillacote's explanation for the collapse of socialism that began with the fall of the Berlin Wall, and her views on how the communist movement should proceed in the future. The letter was an attempt by Squillacote to make a connection with Kasrils, whom Squillacote hoped would "read between the lines." Stand and Clark were aware of the letter, but Clark apparently doubted its effectiveness.

In February 1996, Squillacote received a Christmas card from Kasrils addressed to L. Martin. In the card, Kasrils thanked "Lisa" for "the best letter" he had received in 1995. Stand and Squillacote were thrilled they received the note, and they began to think that perhaps a connection could be made. In September 1996, Squillacote found another letter from Kasrils in her Lisa Martin post office box. The letter stated that "you may have the interest and vision to assist in our struggle," and invited Squillacote to a meeting in New York City with a representative of "our special components."

Squillacote and Stand, however, were unaware that, for many years, they had been the subjects of an intense FBI investigation. As part of its investigation, the FBI in January 1996 obtained authorization to conduct clandestine electronic surveillance, which included the monitoring of all conversations in the Appellants' home, as well as calls made to and from their home and Squillacote's office. Through its investigation, the FBI had learned of Squillacote's letter to Kasrils and the Appellants' response to the February 1996 note from Kasrils. The September 1996 Kasrils letter in fact was written by the FBI as part of a "false flag" operation intended to uncover information about the prior espionage activities of Stand, Squillacote, and Clark.

When designing the false flag operation, the FBI's Behavioral Analysis Program Team prepared a report to examine the personality of Squillacote, and based on this examination, to provide suggestions that could be used * * * to obtain evidence regarding the subject's espionage activity. The report (the "BAP report") was based on information the FBI had learned during its extensive investigation and surveillance of the Appellants.

The BAP report traced Squillacote's family background, including the suicide of her older sister and her mother's history of depression. The report stated that Squillacote was suffering from depression and listed the anti-depressant medications she was taking. The primary focus of the BAP report, however, was Squillacote's emotional makeup and how to tailor the approach to her emotional characteristics. * * * The BAP report also made very specific recommendations about how the false flag operation should be designed:

> The following scenario has been developed upon an analysis of the subject's personality, and includes suggestions designed to exploit her narcissistic and histrionic characteristics. It is believed that Squillacote will be susceptible to an approach through her mail drop based on her recent rejection by her long-term German handler, and her thrill at receiving a Christmas card from the South African official.

J.A.2064.

The false flag letter received by Squillacote in September 1996 served its intended purpose. Unaware of any FBI involvement, Squillacote and Stand were thrilled about the letter, and Squillacote began enthusiastically making plans for a trip to New York City to meet the South African emissary.

In October 1996, Squillacote met with an undercover FBI agent posing as a South African intelligence officer. She had face-to-face meetings with the agent a total of four times, including one meeting where she brought Stand and her two children. Several letters were also exchanged, including a letter that Squillacote wrote at the request of the undercover agent describing her previous activities with Ziemer. In these meetings and letters, Squillacote expressed her enthusiasm for her new South African connection and her hope for a productive collaboration.

Throughout her association with the undercover agent, Squillacote discussed the possibility of bringing Ziemer and other former East German contacts into the operation. In December 1996, she contacted Ziemer to see if he was interested in the operation. According to Squillacote, Ziemer's response was "yes, yes, yes, yes, yes!"

At the second meeting with the undercover agent on January 5, 1997, Squillacote presented the agent with four classified documents she had obtained from the Department of Defense. Although the agent had never requested any documents or classified information from Squillacote, she explained that one day when she and her secretary were alone in her office, she decided to "score what she could score."

Squillacote and Stand were convicted of conspiracy to transmit information relating to the national defense, *see* 18 U.S.C. § 794(a) and (c); attempted transmission of national defense information, *see* 18 U.S.C. § 794(a); and obtaining national defense information, *see* 18 U.S.C. § 793(b).

II.

The government conducted 550 consecutive days of clandestine surveillance of the Appellants, surveillance that was authorized under the Foreign Intelligence Surveillance Act of 1978, 50 U.S.C. § 1801–1811. FISA was enacted to put to rest a troubling constitutional issue regarding the President's "inherent power to conduct warrantless electronic surveillance in order to gather foreign intelligence in the interests of national security," *ACLU Found. of Southern California v. Barr*, 952 F.2d 457, 460 (D.C. Cir. 1991), a question that had not been definitively answered by the Supreme Court. FISA thus created a secure framework by which the Executive Branch may conduct legitimate electronic surveillance for foreign intelligence purposes within the context of this Nation's commitment to privacy and individual rights.

Prior to trial, the Appellants sought to suppress the fruits of the FISA surveillance. They attacked the validity of the surveillance on several grounds, all of which were rejected by the district court. On appeal, however, the Appellants press only one FISA-related issue: They contend that the surveillance was improper because there was no probable cause to believe that Squillacote or Stand were agents of a foreign power. We disagree.

Under FISA, an agent of a foreign power is any person who "knowingly engages in clandestine intelligence gathering activities for or on behalf of a foreign power, which activities involve or may involve a violation of the criminal statutes of the United States." 50 U.S.C. § 1801(b)(2)(A). One who knowingly aids and abets another engaging in such clandestine intelligence activities, or one who knowingly conspires with another to engage in the clandestine intelligence activities, is also considered an agent of a foreign power. *See* 50 U.S.C. § 1801(b)(2)(D). A "United States person" may not be determined to be an agent of a foreign power "solely upon the basis of activities protected by the first amendment to the Constitution of the United States." 50 U.S.C. § 1805(a)(3)(A).

FISA provides that the district court must review *in camera* and *ex parte* the FISA application and other materials necessary to rule upon a defendant's suppression motion "if the Attorney General files an affidavit under oath that disclosure or an adversary hearing would harm the national security of the United States." 50 U.S.C. § 1806(f). Because the Attorney General filed such an affidavit in this case, the district court reviewed the applications and other materials *in camera*, and the documents were not disclosed to counsel for the Appellants. *See* 50 U.S.C. § 1806(f) (The district court "may disclose to the aggrieved person, under appropriate security procedures and protective orders, portions of the application, order, or other materials relating to the surveillance only where such disclosure is necessary to make an accurate determination of the legality of the surveillance.").

After reviewing the applications, the district court concluded that each of the more than 20 FISA applications established probable cause to believe that the Appellants were agents of a foreign power. We have reviewed de novo the relevant materials, and likewise conclude that each FISA application established probable cause to believe that Squillacote and Stand were agents of a foreign power at the time the applications were granted, notwithstanding the fact that East Germany was no longer in existence when the applications were granted. *See* 50 U.S.C. § 1801(a) (defining "foreign power"); 50 U.S.C. § 1801(b) (defining "agent of a foreign power"). We are also satisfied that the Appellants were not targeted solely because of any protected First Amendment activities in which they may have engaged. Given the sensitive nature of the information upon which we have relied in making this determination and the Attorney General's conclusion that disclosure of the underlying information would harm the national security, it would be improper to elaborate further.

Notes and Questions

1. The FISA Court issued more than 20 orders permitting 550 days of consecutive monitoring. On one hand, the facts described in the opinion clearly indicate that the appellants were agents of a foreign power at some point. On the other hand, the opinion does not tell us enough to establish probable cause that the appellants were agents of a foreign power each time the orders were granted. As a result, the opinion does not establish that the evidence used against the appellants was collected using properly obtained FISA orders. Instead, the court recites public facts and the relevant legal standard, and then announces that the court is satisfied that the legal standards were met and that "it would be improper to elaborate further."

Is this a satisfying resolution of the appellants' case? Are you confident that the court was correct? On the other hand, what are the alternatives? If the basis for the court's conclusion involves national security secrets, disclosing that basis would disclose the secret. Are there alternatives to this approach that can better balance interests in judicial review with interests in secrecy? Or is this the best that can be done?

2. *The Classified Information Procedures Act.* Shortly after the passage of FISA, Congress enacted the Classified Information Procedures Act (CIPA), Pub. L. 96–456 (1980), codified at 18 U.S.C. app. §§ 1–16. CIPA regulates the discovery and use of classified information in criminal trials. The statute authorizes judges to control the disclosure of classified information using *ex parte, in camera* proceedings. Under CIPA, the presiding judge serves a gatekeeping function, hearing all claims concerning the discovery of and disclosure of classified information pre-trial. The gatekeeping serves a number of functions, including limiting a defendant's ability to avoid prosecution by threatening to disclose secrets if prosecuted (a practice known as "greymail"). *See generally* Saul M. Pilchen & Benjamin B. Klubes, *Using the Classified Information Procedures Act in Criminal Cases: A Primer for Defense Counsel*, 31 Am. Crim. L. Rev. 191 (1994).

The requirements of CIPA arose in United States v. Scarfo, 180 F. Supp. 2d 572 (D.N.J. 2001), discussed pages 372–375, a case involving a Key Logger System installed on a mob boss's computer to collect his passphrase and decrypt his seized files. When Scarfo sought discovery of the details of the Key Logger System (KLS) to argue his motion to suppress, the United States objected on the ground that the workings of the KLS were classified. Judge Politan resolved the discovery dispute under CIPA as follows:

In light of the government's grave concern over the national security implications such a revelation might raise, the Court permitted the United States to submit any additional evidence which would provide particular and specific reasons how and why disclosure of the KLS would jeopardize both ongoing and future domestic criminal investigations and national security interests.

The United States responded by filing a request for modification of this Court's August 7, 2001, Letter Opinion and Order so as to comply with the procedures set forth in the Classified Information Procedures Act, Title 18, United States Code, Appendix III, § 1 et seq. ("CIPA"). * * * Defendant Scarfo objected to the government's request, alleging that the United States did not make a sufficient showing that the information concerning the KLS had been properly classified.

In response to Scarfo's objection, the United States submitted the affidavit of Neil J. Gallagher, Assistant Director, Federal Bureau of Investigation, dated September 6, 2001. In his affidavit, Mr. Gallagher stated that the characteristics and/or functional components of the KLS were previously classified and marked "SECRET" at or around November 1997.

The Court heard oral argument on September 7, 2001, to explore whether the government may invoke CIPA and, specifically, whether the government had classified the KLS. Although the defense conceded that the KLS was classified for purposes of CIPA, the Court reserved on that question and ordered the government to provide written submissions to the Court. The government then filed an *ex parte, in camera* motion for the Court's inspection of the classified material.

On September 26, 2001, the Court held an *in camera, ex parte hearing* with several high-ranking officials from the United States Attorney General's office and the F.B.I. Because of the sensitive nature of the material presented, all CIPA regulations were followed and only those persons with top-secret clearance were permitted to attend. Pursuant to CIPA's regulations, the United States presented the Court with detailed and top-secret, classified information regarding the KLS, including how it operates in connection with a modem. The government also demonstrated to the Court how the KLS affects national security.

After reviewing the classified material, I issued a Protective Order pursuant [to] CIPA on October 2, 2001, wherein I found that the government could properly invoke CIPA and that the government made a sufficient showing to warrant the issuance of an order protecting against disclosure of the classified information. The October 2, 2001, Protective Order also directed that the government's proposed unclassified summary of information relating to the KLS under Section 4 of CIPA would be sufficient to allow the defense to effectively argue the motion to suppress. Accordingly, the Protective Order permitted the government to provide Scarfo with the unclassified summary statement in lieu of the classified information regarding the KLS. Pursuant to Section 6(d) of CIPA, the Court also sealed the transcript of the September 26th ex parte, in camera hearing and the government's supporting Affidavits. The government filed with the Court and served on Scarfo the unclassified summary on October 5, 2001, in the form of an October 4, 2001, Affidavit of Randall S. Murch, Supervisory Special Agent of the Federal Bureau of Investigation, Laboratory Division (the "Murch Affidavit").

Pursuant to CIPA, the United States requested a hearing in order to block the disclosure of supposedly classified information concerning the KLS technique. The Court held an *in camera, ex parte* hearing on September 26, 2001, to assess the classified nature of the KLS and the sufficiency of the unclassified summary proposed by the government. Prior to the September 26th *in camera, ex parte* hearing, and as expressed during the September 7th hearing, the Court was not satisfied that the KLS was properly classified as defined by CIPA. Nor was the Court at the time content with the United States' conclusory and generalized expressions of concern that revelation of the KLS would compromise the national security of the United States.

However, as a result of the September 26th *in camera, ex parte hearing*, the Court is now satisfied that the KLS was in fact classified as defined by CIPA. The Court also concludes that under Section 4 and 6(c) of CIPA the government met its burden in showing that the information sought by the Defendants constitutes classified information touching upon national security concerns as defined in CIPA. Moreover, it is the opinion of the Court that as a result of the September 26th hearing, the government presented to the Court's satisfaction proof that disclosure of the classified KLS information would cause identifiable damage to the national security of the United States. The Court is precluded from discussing this information in detail since it remains classified.

Further, upon comparing the specific classified information sought and the government's proposed unclassified summary, the Court finds that the United States met its burden in showing that the summary in the form of the Murch Affidavit would provide Scarfo with substantially the same ability to make his defense as would disclosure of the specific classified information regarding the KLS technique. The Murch Affidavit explains, to a reasonable and sufficient degree of specificity without disclosing the highly sensitive and classified information, the operating features of the KLS. The Murch Affidavit is more than sufficient and has provided ample information for the Defendants to litigate this motion. Therefore, no further discovery with regard to the KLS technique is necessary.

Id. at 575–76, 580–81. For more on CIPA, see Richard P. Salgado, Note, *Government Secrets, Fair Trials, and the Classified Information Procedures Act*, 98 Yale L.J. 427 (1988); Brian Z. Tamanaha, *A Critical Review of the Classified Information Procedures Act*, 13 Am. J. Crim. L. 277 (1986).

3. *Information warfare.* If the law of intelligence surveillance is the national security analog of criminal procedure, the law of information warfare is the national security analog of computer misuse law. United States government networks can come under attack by agents of foreign governments engaging in "information warfare." Such attacks raise a number of questions. For example, when should a computer intrusion be treated as an act of war instead of as a simple criminal act? What rights do United States government officials have to launch counterattacks to defend the United States?

Consider Richard W. Aldrich, *How Do You Know You Are at War in the Information Age?*, 22 Hous. J. Int'l L. 223, 224–26 (2000):

In earlier times the question, "How do you know you are at war?" would have seemed disingenuous. When the boulders came catapulting over the fortress wall, one could be fairly certain one was at war. Battering rams punching in the king's fortifications, rows of redcoats firing muskets in unison, and incoming cannonballs were all fairly clear indicators of war. Wars, at one time, were even formally declared, which of course took much of the guesswork out of it. But in recent times war has * * * become more difficult to define, and information warfare (IW) seems likely to be the most elusive yet. Part of the reason is that IW can take place in an entirely new realm, that ethereal place some call "cyberspace" and others call the "infosphere." Another reason is that many of the weapons used can be bought in any computer store and look exactly like the tools used to produce term papers and generate spreadsheets. The weapons' effects may not be to produce immediate death and destruction of property, but to innocuously manipulate bits of data, changing ones to zeros and vice versa, to deleterious effect nonetheless. Finally, the objects of the attack are less likely to be traditional military targets, and more likely to be a nation's "commercial and industrial underpinnings," its telecommunications companies, power companies, financial centers, and the like. Many believe that an "electronic Pearl Harbor" is inevitable. This all requires a serious reevaluation of what constitutes an illegal use of force in the Information Age.

The importance of delineating what constitutes a "use of force" in the age of IW is twofold. First, it assists in determining when the United States may be entitled to exercise self-defense or some lesser form of sanctions against one who uses certain infowar techniques against the United States. Second, it puts the United States on notice as to when its own conduct may legitimately be described as a use of force, thereby entitling other nations to take self-defense or other appropriate measures. Currently there is a dearth of guidance on the issue. Indeed, one prominent practitioner has opined, "Currently, we are unable to reliably forecast what kinds of electronic attack would be considered by a target country or by the international community to be an 'act of war'."

See also Michael N. Schmitt, *Computer Network Attack and the Use of Force in International Law: Thoughts on a Normative Framework*, 37 Colum. J. Transnat'l L. 885 (1999); Eric Talbot Jensen, *Computer Attacks on Critical National Infrastructure: A Use of Force Invoking the Right of Self–Defense*, 38 Stan. J. Int'l L. 207 (2002). *Cf.* 18 U.S.C. § 1030(f) ("This section does not prohibit any lawfully authorized investigative, protective, or intelligence activity of a law enforcement agency of the United States, a State, or a political subdivision of a State, or of an intelligence agency of the United States.").

Appendix

STATUTORY SUPPLEMENT

18 U.S.C. § 2. PRINCIPALS

(a) Whoever commits an offense against the United States or aids, abets, counsels, commands, induces or procures its commission, is punishable as a principal.

(b) Whoever willfully causes an act to be done which if directly performed by him or another would be an offense against the United States, is punishable as a principal.

18 U.S.C. § 641. PUBLIC MONEY, PROPERTY OR RECORDS

Whoever embezzles, steals, purloins, or knowingly converts to his use or the use of another, or without authority, sells, conveys or disposes of any record, voucher, money, or thing of value of the United States or of any department or agency thereof, or any property made or being made under contract for the United States or any department or agency thereof; or

Whoever receives, conceals, or retains the same with intent to convert it to his use or gain, knowing it to have been embezzled, stolen, purloined or converted—

Shall be fined under this title or imprisoned not more than ten years, or both; but if the value of such property in the aggregate, combining amounts from all the counts for which the defendant is convicted in a single case, does not exceed the sum of $1,000, he shall be fined under this title or imprisoned not more than one year, or both.

The word "value" means face, par, or market value, or cost price, either wholesale or retail, whichever is greater.

18 U.S.C. § 875. INTERSTATE COMMUNICATIONS

(a) Whoever transmits in interstate or foreign commerce any communication containing any demand or request for a ransom or reward for the release of any kidnapped person, shall be fined under this title or imprisoned not more than twenty years, or both.

(b) Whoever, with intent to extort from any person, firm, association, or corporation, any money or other thing of value, transmits in interstate or foreign commerce any communication containing any threat to kidnap any person or any threat to injure the person of another, shall be fined under this title or imprisoned not more than twenty years, or both.

(c) Whoever transmits in interstate or foreign commerce any communication containing any threat to kidnap any person or any threat to injure the person of another, shall be fined under this title or imprisoned not more than five years, or both.

(d) Whoever, with intent to extort from any person, firm, association, or corporation, any money or other thing of value, transmits in interstate or foreign commerce any communication containing any threat to injure the property or reputation of the addressee or of another or the reputation of a deceased person or any threat to accuse the addressee or any other person of a crime, shall be fined under this title or imprisoned not more than two years, or both.

18 U.S.C. § 1028. FRAUD AND RELATED ACTIVITY IN CONNECTION WITH IDENTIFICATION DOCUMENTS, AUTHENTICATION FEATURES, AND INFORMATION

(a) Whoever, in a circumstance described in subsection (c) of this section—

(1) knowingly and without lawful authority produces an identification document, authentication feature, or a false identification document;

(2) knowingly transfers an identification document, authentication feature, or a false identification document knowing that such document or feature was stolen or produced without lawful authority;

(3) knowingly possesses with intent to use unlawfully or transfer unlawfully five or more identification documents (other than those issued lawfully for the use of the possessor), authentication features, or false identification documents;

(4) knowingly possesses an identification document (other than one issued lawfully for the use of the possessor), authentication feature, or a false identification document, with the intent such document or feature be used to defraud the United States;

(5) knowingly produces, transfers, or possesses a document-making implement or authentication feature with the intent such document-making implement or authentication feature will be used in the production of a false identification document or another document-making implement or authentication feature which will be so used;

(6) knowingly possesses an identification document or authentication feature that is or appears to be an identification document or

authentication feature of the United States or a sponsoring entity of an event designated as a special event of national significance which is stolen or produced without lawful authority knowing that such document or feature was stolen or produced without such authority;

(7) knowingly transfers, possesses, or uses, without lawful authority, a means of identification of another person with the intent to commit, or to aid or abet, or in connection with, any unlawful activity that constitutes a violation of Federal law, or that constitutes a felony under any applicable State or local law; or

(8) knowingly traffics in false or actual authentication features for use in false identification documents, document-making implements, or means of identification;

shall be punished * * * .

* * *

(c) The circumstance referred to in subsection (a) of this section is that—

(1) the identification document, authentication feature, or false identification document is or appears to be issued by or under the authority of the United States or a sponsoring entity of an event designated as a special event of national significance or the document-making implement is designed or suited for making such an identification document, authentication feature, or false identification document;

(2) the offense is an offense under subsection (a)(4) of this section; or

(3) either—

(A) the production, transfer, possession, or use prohibited by this section is in or affects interstate or foreign commerce, including the transfer of a document by electronic means; or

(B) the means of identification, identification document, false identification document, or document-making implement is transported in the mail in the course of the production, transfer, possession, or use prohibited by this section.

(d) In this section and section 1028A—

(1) the term "authentication feature" means any hologram, watermark, certification, symbol, code, image, sequence of numbers or letters, or other feature that either individually or in combination with another feature is used by the issuing authority on an identification document, document-making implement, or means of identification to determine if the document is counterfeit, altered, or otherwise falsified;

(2) the term "document-making implement" means any implement, impression, template, computer file, computer disc, electronic device, or computer hardware or software, that is specifically configured or primarily used for making an identification document, a

false identification document, or another document-making implement;

(3) the term "identification document" means a document made or issued by or under the authority of the United States Government, a State, political subdivision of a State, a sponsoring entity of an event designated as a special event of national significance, a foreign government, political subdivision of a foreign government, an international governmental or an international quasi-governmental organization which, when completed with information concerning a particular individual, is of a type intended or commonly accepted for the purpose of identification of individuals;

(4) the term "false identification document" means a document of a type intended or commonly accepted for the purposes of identification of individuals that—

(A) is not issued by or under the authority of a governmental entity or was issued under the authority of a governmental entity but was subsequently altered for purposes of deceit; and

(B) appears to be issued by or under the authority of the United States Government, a State, a political subdivision of a State, a sponsoring entity of an event designated by the President as a special event of national significance, a foreign government, a political subdivision of a foreign government, or an international governmental or quasi-governmental organization;

(5) the term "false authentication feature" means an authentication feature that—

(A) is genuine in origin, but, without the authorization of the issuing authority, has been tampered with or altered for purposes of deceit;

(B) is genuine, but has been distributed, or is intended for distribution, without the authorization of the issuing authority and not in connection with a lawfully made identification document, document-making implement, or means of identification to which such authentication feature is intended to be affixed or embedded by the respective issuing authority; or

(C) appears to be genuine, but is not;

(6) the term "issuing authority"—

(A) means any governmental entity or agency that is authorized to issue identification documents, means of identification, or authentication features; and

(B) includes the United States Government, a State, a political subdivision of a State, a sponsoring entity of an event designated by the President as a special event of national significance, a foreign government, a political subdivision of a foreign government, or an international government or quasi-governmental organization;

(7) the term "means of identification" means any name or number that may be used, alone or in conjunction with any other information, to identify a specific individual, including any—

(A) name, social security number, date of birth, official State or government issued driver's license or identification number, alien registration number, government passport number, employer or taxpayer identification number;

(B) unique biometric data, such as fingerprint, voice print, retina or iris image, or other unique physical representation;

(C) unique electronic identification number, address, or routing code; or

(D) telecommunication identifying information or access device (as defined in section 1029(e));

(8) the term "personal identification card" means an identification document issued by a State or local government solely for the purpose of identification;

(9) the term "produce" includes alter, authenticate, or assemble;

(10) the term "transfer" includes selecting an identification document, false identification document, or document-making implement and placing or directing the placement of such identification document, false identification document, or document-making implement on an online location where it is available to others;

(11) the term "State" includes any State of the United States, the District of Columbia, the Commonwealth of Puerto Rico, and any other commonwealth, possession, or territory of the United States; and

(12) the term "traffic" means—

(A) to transport, transfer, or otherwise dispose of, to another, as consideration for anything of value; or

(B) to make or obtain control of with intent to so transport, transfer, or otherwise dispose of.

(e) This section does not prohibit any lawfully authorized investigative, protective, or intelligence activity of a law enforcement agency of the United States, a State, or a political subdivision of a State, or of an intelligence agency of the United States, or any activity authorized under chapter 224 of this title et seq.].

(f) **Attempt and conspiracy**. Any person who attempts or conspires to commit any offense under this section shall be subject to the same penalties as those prescribed for the offense, the commission of which was the object of the attempt or conspiracy.

18 U.S.C. § 1029. FRAUD AND RELATED ACTIVITY IN CONNECTION WITH ACCESS DEVICES

(a) Whoever—

(1) knowingly and with intent to defraud produces, uses, or traffics in one or more counterfeit access devices;

(2) knowingly and with intent to defraud traffics in or uses one or more unauthorized access devises during any one-year period, and by such conduct obtains anything of value aggregating $1,000 or more during that period;

(3) knowingly and with intent to defraud possesses fifteen or more devices which are counterfeit or unauthorized access devices;

(4) knowingly, and with intent to defraud, produces, traffics in, has control or custody of, or possesses device-making equipment;

(5) knowingly and with intent to defraud effects transactions, with 1 or more access devices issued to another person or persons, to receive payment or any other thing of value during any 1–year period the aggregate value of which is equal to or greater than $1,000;

(6) without the authorization of the issuer of the access device, knowingly and with intent to defraud solicits a person for the purpose of—

(A) offering an access device; or

(B) selling information regarding or an application to obtain an access device;

(7) knowingly and with intent to defraud uses, produces, traffics in, has control or custody of, or possesses a telecommunications instrument that has been modified or altered to obtain unauthorized use of telecommunications services;

(8) knowingly and with intent to defraud uses, produces, traffics in, has control or custody of, or possesses a scanning receiver;

(9) knowingly uses, produces, traffics in, has control or custody of, or possesses hardware or software, knowing it has been configured to insert or modify telecommunication identifying information associated with or contained in a telecommunications instrument so that such instrument may be used to obtain telecommunications service without authorization; or

(10) without the authorization of the credit card system member or its agent, knowingly and with intent to defraud causes or arranges for another person to present to the member or its agent, for payment, 1 or more evidences or records of transactions made by an access device;

shall, if the offense affects interstate or foreign commerce, be punished as provided in subsection (c) of this section.

(b) (1) Whoever attempts to commit an offense under subsection (a) of this section shall be subject to the same penalties as those prescribed for the offense attempted.

(2) Whoever is a party to a conspiracy of two or more persons to commit an offense under subsection (a) of this section, if any of the parties engages in any conduct in furtherance of such offense, shall be fined an amount not greater than the amount provided as the maximum fine for such offense under subsection (c) of this section or imprisoned not longer than one-half the period provided as the maximum imprisonment for such offense under subsection (c) of this section, or both.

* * *

(e) As used in this section—

(1) the term "access device" means any card, plate, code, account number, electronic serial number, mobile identification number, personal identification number, or other telecommunications service, equipment, or instrument identifier, or other means of account access that can be used, alone or in conjunction with another access device, to obtain money, goods, services, or any other thing of value, or that can be used to initiate a transfer of funds (other than a transfer originated solely by paper instrument);

(2) the term "counterfeit access device" means any access device that is counterfeit, fictitious, altered, or forged, or an identifiable component of an access device or a counterfeit access device;

(3) the term "unauthorized access device" means any access device that is lost, stolen, expired, revoked, canceled, or obtained with intent to defraud;

(4) the term "produce" includes design, alter, authenticate, duplicate, or assemble;

(5) the term "traffic" means transfer, or otherwise dispose of, to another, or obtain control of with intent to transfer or dispose of;

(6) the term "device-making equipment" means any equipment, mechanism, or impression designed or primarily used for making an access device or a counterfeit access device;

(7) the term "credit card system member" means a financial institution or other entity that is a member of a credit card system, including an entity, whether affiliated with or identical to the credit card issuer, that is the sole member of a credit card system;

(8) the term "scanning receiver" means a device or apparatus that can be used to intercept a wire or electronic communication in violation of chapter 119 or to intercept an electronic serial number, mobile identification number, or other identifier of any telecommunications service, equipment, or instrument;

(9) the term "telecommunications service" has the meaning given such term in section 3 of title I of the Communications Act of 1934 (47 U.S.C. § 153);

(10) the term "facilities-based carrier" means an entity that owns communications transmission facilities, is responsible for the operation and maintenance of those facilities, and holds an operat-

ing license issued by the Federal Communications Commission under the authority of title III of the Communications Act of 1934; and

(11) the term "telecommunication identifying information" means electronic serial number or any other number or signal that identifies a specific telecommunications instrument or account, or a specific communication transmitted from a telecommunications instrument.

(f) This section does not prohibit any lawfully authorized investigative, protective, or intelligence activity of a law enforcement agency of the United States, a State, or a political subdivision of a State, or of an intelligence agency of the United States, or any activity authorized under chapter 224 of this title. For purposes of this subsection, the term "State" includes a State of the United States, the District of Columbia, and any commonwealth, territory, or possession of the United States.

(g) (1) It is not a violation of subsection (a)(9) for an officer, employee, or agent of, or a person engaged in business with, a facilities-based carrier, to engage in conduct (other than trafficking) otherwise prohibited by that subsection for the purpose of protecting the property or legal rights of that carrier, unless such conduct is for the purpose of obtaining telecommunications service provided by another facilities-based carrier without the authorization of such carrier.

(2) In a prosecution for a violation of subsection (a)(9), (other than a violation consisting of producing or trafficking) it is an affirmative defense (which the defendant must establish by a preponderance of the evidence) that the conduct charged was engaged in for research or development in connection with a lawful purpose.

(h) Any person who, outside the jurisdiction of the United States, engages in any act that, if committed within the jurisdiction of the United States, would constitute an offense under subsection (a) or (b) of this section, shall be subject to the fines, penalties, imprisonment, and forfeiture provided in this title if—

(1) the offense involves an access device issued, owned, managed, or controlled by a financial institution, account issuer, credit card system member, or other entity within the jurisdiction of the United States; and

(2) the person transports, delivers, conveys, transfers to or through, or otherwise stores, secrets, or holds within the jurisdiction of the United States, any article used to assist in the commission of the offense or the proceeds of such offense or property derived therefrom.

18 U.S.C. § 1030. FRAUD AND RELATED ACTIVITY IN CONNECTION WITH COMPUTERS

(a) Whoever—

(1) having knowingly accessed a computer without authorization or exceeding authorized access, and by means of such conduct having

obtained information that has been determined by the United States Government pursuant to an Executive order or statute to require protection against unauthorized disclosure for reasons of national defense or foreign relations, or any restricted data, as defined in paragraph y of section 11 of the Atomic Energy Act of 1954, with reason to believe that such information so obtained could be used to the injury of the United States, or to the advantage of any foreign nation willfully communicates, delivers, transmits, or causes to be communicated, delivered, or transmitted, or attempts to communicate, deliver, transmit or cause to be communicated, delivered, or transmitted the same to any person not entitled to receive it, or willfully retains the same and fails to deliver it to the officer or employee of the United States entitled to receive it;

(2) intentionally accesses a computer without authorization or exceeds authorized access, and thereby obtains—

(A) information contained in a financial record of a financial institution, or of a card issuer as defined in section 1602(n) of title 15, or contained in a file of a consumer reporting agency on a consumer, as such terms are defined in the Fair Credit Reporting Act (15 U.S.C. § 1681 et seq.);

(B) information from any department or agency of the United States; or

(C) information from any protected computer if the conduct involved an interstate or foreign communication;

(3) intentionally, without authorization to access any nonpublic computer of a department or agency of the United States, accesses such a computer of that department or agency that is exclusively for the use of the Government of the United States or, in the case of a computer not exclusively for such use, is used by or for the Government of the United States and such conduct affects that use by or for the Government of the United States;

(4) knowingly and with intent to defraud, accesses a protected computer without authorization, or exceeds authorized access, and by means of such conduct furthers the intended fraud and obtains anything of value, unless the object of the fraud and the thing obtained consists only of the use of the computer and the value of such use is not more than $5,000 in any 1–year period;

(5) (A) (i) knowingly causes the transmission of a program, information, code, or command, and as a result of such conduct, intentionally causes damage without authorization, to a protected computer;

(ii) intentionally accesses a protected computer without authorization, and as a result of such conduct, recklessly causes damage; or

(iii) intentionally accesses a protected computer without authorization, and as a result of such conduct, causes damage; and

(B) by conduct described in clause (i), (ii), or (iii) of subparagraph (A), caused (or, in the case of an attempted offense, would, if completed, have caused)—

(i) loss to 1 or more persons during any 1–year period (and, for purposes of an investigation, prosecution, or other proceeding brought by the United States only, loss resulting from a related course of conduct affecting 1 or more other protected computers) aggregating at least $5,000 in value;

(ii) the modification or impairment, or potential modification or impairment, of the medical examination, diagnosis, treatment, or care of 1 or more individuals;

(iii) physical injury to any person;

(iv) a threat to public health or safety; or

(v) damage affecting a computer system used by or for a government entity in furtherance of the administration of justice, national defense, or national security;

(6) knowingly and with intent to defraud traffics (as defined in section 1029) in any password or similar information through which a computer may be accessed without authorization, if—

(A) such trafficking affects interstate or foreign commerce; or

(B) such computer is used by or for the Government of the United States;

(7) with intent to extort from any person any money or other thing of value, transmits in interstate or foreign commerce any communication containing any threat to cause damage to a protected computer;

shall be punished as provided in subsection (c) of this section.

(b) Whoever attempts to commit an offense under subsection (a) of this section shall be punished as provided in subsection (c) of this section.

(c) The punishment for an offense under subsection (a) or (b) of this section is—

(1) (A) a fine under this title or imprisonment for not more than ten years, or both, in the case of an offense under subsection (a)(1) of this section which does not occur after a conviction for another offense under this section, or an attempt to commit an offense punishable under this subparagraph; and

(B) a fine under this title or imprisonment for not more than twenty years, or both, in the case of an offense under subsection (a)(1) of this section which occurs after a conviction for another offense under this section; or an attempt to commit an offense punishable under this subparagraph;

(2) (A) except as provided in subparagraph (B), a fine under this title or imprisonment for not more than one year, or both, in the case of an offense under subsection (a)(2), (a)(3), (a)(5)(A)(iii), or (a)(6) of this section which does not occur after a conviction for another offense under this section, or an attempt to commit an offense punishable under this subparagraph;

(B) a fine under this title or imprisonment for not more than 5 years, or both, in the case of an offense under subsection (a)(2), or an attempt to commit an offense punishable under this subparagraph, if—

(i) the offense was committed for purposes of commercial advantage or private financial gain;

(ii) the offense was committed in furtherance of any criminal or tortious act in violation of the Constitution or laws of the United States or of any State; or

(iii) the value of the information obtained exceeds $5,000; and

(C) a fine under this title or imprisonment for not more than ten years, or both, in the case of an offense under subsection (a)(2), (a)(3) or (a)(6) of this section which occurs after a conviction for another offense under this section, or an attempt to commit an offense punishable under this subparagraph;

(3) (A) a fine under this title or imprisonment for not more than five years, or both, in the case of an offense under subsection (a)(4) or (a)(7) of this section which does not occur after a conviction for another offense under this section, or an attempt to commit an offense punishable under this subparagraph; and

(B) a fine under this title or imprisonment for not more than ten years, or both, in the case of an offense under subsection (a)(4), (a)(5)(A)(iii), or (a)(7) of this section which occurs after a conviction for another offense under this section, or an attempt to commit an offense punishable under this section;

(4) (A) except as provided in paragraph (5), a fine under this title, imprisonment for not more than 10 years, or both, in the case of an offense under subsection (a)(5)(A)(i), or an attempt to commit an offense punishable under that subsection;

(B) a fine under this title, imprisonment for not more than 5 years, or both, in the case of an offense under subsection (a)(5)(A)(ii), or an attempt to commit an offense punishable under that subsection;

(C) except as provided in paragraph (5), a fine under this title, imprisonment for not more than 20 years, or both, in the case of an offense under subsection (a)(5)(A)(i) or (a)(5)(A)(ii), or an attempt to commit an offense punishable under either subsection, that occurs after a conviction for another offense under this section; and

(5) (A) if the offender knowingly or recklessly causes or attempts to cause serious bodily injury from conduct in violation of subsection (a)(5)(A)(i), a fine under this title or imprisonment for not more than 20 years, or both; and

(B) if the offender knowingly or recklessly causes or attempts to cause death from conduct in violation of subsection (a)(5)(A)(i), a fine under this title or imprisonment for any term of years or for life, or both.

(d) (1) The United States Secret Service shall, in addition to any other agency having such authority, have the authority to investigate offenses under this section.

(2) The Federal Bureau of Investigation shall have primary authority to investigate offenses under subsection (a)(1) for any cases involving espionage, foreign counterintelligence, information protected against unauthorized disclosure for reasons of national defense or foreign relations, or Restricted Data (as that term is defined in section 11y of the Atomic Energy Act of 1954 (42 U.S.C. § 2014(y)), except for offenses affecting the duties of the United States Secret Service pursuant to section 3056(a) of this title.

(3) Such authority shall be exercised in accordance with an agreement which shall be entered into by the Secretary of the Treasury and the Attorney General.

(e) As used in this section—

(1) the term "computer" means an electronic, magnetic, optical, electrochemical, or other high speed data processing device performing logical, arithmetic, or storage functions, and includes any data storage facility or communications facility directly related to or operating in conjunction with such device, but such term does not include an automated typewriter or typesetter, a portable hand held calculator, or other similar device;

(2) the term "protected computer" means a computer—

(A) exclusively for the use of a financial institution or the United States Government, or, in the case of a computer not exclusively for such use, used by or for a financial institution or the United States Government and the conduct constituting the offense affects that use by or for the financial institution or the Government; or

(B) which is used in interstate or foreign commerce or communication, including a computer located outside the United States that is used in a manner that affects interstate or foreign commerce or communication of the United States;

(3) the term "State" includes the District of Columbia, the Commonwealth of Puerto Rico, and any other commonwealth, possession or territory of the United States;

(4) the term "financial institution" means—

(A) an institution, with deposits insured by the Federal Deposit Insurance Corporation;

(B) the Federal Reserve or a member of the Federal Reserve including any Federal Reserve Bank;

(C) a credit union with accounts insured by the National Credit Union Administration;

(D) a member of the Federal home loan bank system and any home loan bank;

(E) any institution of the Farm Credit System under the Farm Credit Act of 1971;

(F) a broker-dealer registered with the Securities and Exchange Commission pursuant to section 15 of the Securities Exchange Act of 1934;

(G) the Securities Investor Protection Corporation;

(H) a branch or agency of a foreign bank (as such terms are defined in paragraphs (1) and (3) of section 1(b) of the International Banking Act of 1978); and

(I) an organization operating under section 25 or section 25(a) of the Federal Reserve Act;

(5) the term "financial record" means information derived from any record held by a financial institution pertaining to a customer's relationship with the financial institution;

(6) the term "exceeds authorized access" means to access a computer with authorization and to use such access to obtain or alter information in the computer that the accesser is not entitled so to obtain or alter;

(7) the term "department of the United States" means the legislative or judicial branch of the Government or one of the executive department enumerated in section 101 of title 5;

(8) the term "damage" means any impairment to the integrity or availability of data, a program, a system, or information;

(9) the term "government entity" includes the Government of the United States, any State or political subdivision of the United States, any foreign country, and any state, province, municipality, or other political subdivision of a foreign country;

(10) the term "conviction" shall include a conviction under the law of any State for a crime punishable by imprisonment for more than 1

year, an element of which is unauthorized access, or exceeding authorized access, to a computer;

(11) the term "loss" means any reasonable cost to any victim, including the cost of responding to an offense, conducting a damage assessment, and restoring the data, program, system, or information to its condition prior to the offense, and any revenue lost, cost incurred, or other consequential damages incurred because of interruption of service; and

(12) the term "person" means any individual, firm, corporation, educational institution, financial institution, governmental entity, or legal or other entity.

(f) This section does not prohibit any lawfully authorized investigative, protective, or intelligence activity of a law enforcement agency of the United States, a State, or a political subdivision of a State, or of an intelligence agency of the United States.

(g) Any person who suffers damage or loss by reason of a violation of this section may maintain a civil action against the violator to obtain compensatory damages and injunctive relief or other equitable relief. A civil action for a violation of this section may be brought only if the conduct involves 1 of the factors set forth in clause (i), (ii), (iii), (iv), or (v) of subsection (a)(5)(B). Damages for a violation involving only conduct described in subsection (a)(5)(B)(i) are limited to economic damages. No action may be brought under this subsection unless such action is begun within 2 years of the date of the act complained of or the date of the discovery of the damage. No action may be brought under this subsection for the negligent design or manufacture of computer hardware, computer software, or firmware.

(h) The Attorney General and the Secretary of the Treasury shall report to the Congress annually, during the first 3 years following the date of the enactment of this subsection, concerning investigations and prosecutions under subsection (a)(5).

18 U.S.C. § 1084. TRANSMISSION OF WAGERING INFORMATION; PENALTIES

(a) Whoever being engaged in the business of betting or wagering knowingly uses a wire communication facility for the transmission in interstate or foreign commerce of bets or wagers or information assisting in the placing of bets or wagers on any sporting event or contest, or for the transmission of a wire communication which entitles the recipient to receive money or credit as a result of bets or wagers, or for information assisting in the placing of bets or wagers, shall be fined under this title or imprisoned not more than two years, or both.

(b) Nothing in this section shall be construed to prevent the transmission in interstate or foreign commerce of information for use in news reporting of sporting events or contests, or for the transmission of information assisting in the placing of bets or wagers on a sporting event or contest from a State or foreign country where betting on that sporting event or contest is legal into a State or foreign country in which such betting is legal.

(c) Nothing contained in this section shall create immunity from criminal prosecution under any laws of any State.

18 U.S.C. § 1343. FRAUD BY WIRE, RADIO, OR TELEVISION

Whoever, having devised or intending to devise any scheme or artifice to defraud, or for obtaining money or property by means of false or fraudulent pretenses, representations, or promises, transmits or causes to be transmitted by means of wire, radio, or television communication in interstate or foreign commerce, any writings, signs, signals, pictures, or sounds for the purpose of executing such scheme or artifice, shall be fined under this title or imprisoned not more than 20 years, or both. If the violation affects a financial institution, such person shall be fined not more than $1,000,000 or imprisoned not more than 30 years, or both.

18 U.S.C. § 1462. IMPORTATION OR TRANSPORTATION OF OBSCENE MATTERS

Whoever brings into the United States, or any place subject to the jurisdiction thereof, or knowingly uses any express company or other common carrier or interactive computer service (as defined in section 230(e)(2) of the Communications Act of 1934), for carriage in interstate or foreign commerce—

(a) any obscene, lewd, lascivious, or filthy book, pamphlet, picture, motion-picture film, paper, letter, writing, print, or other matter of indecent character; or

(b) any obscene, lewd, lascivious, or filthy phonograph recording, electrical transcription, or other article or thing capable of producing sound; or

(c) any drug, medicine, article, or thing designed, adapted, or intended for producing abortion, or for any indecent or immoral use; or any written or printed card, letter, circular, book, pamphlet, advertisement, or notice of any kind giving information, directly or indirectly, where, how, or of whom, or by what means any of such mentioned articles, matters, or things may be obtained or made; or

Whoever knowingly takes or receives, from such express company or other common carrier or interactive computer service (as defined in section 230(e)(2) of the Communications Act of 1934) any matter or thing the carriage or importation of which is herein made unlawful

Shall be fined under this title or imprisoned not more than five years, or both, for the first such offense and shall be fined under this title or imprisoned not more than ten years, or both, for each such offense thereafter.

18 U.S.C. § 1465. TRANSPORTATION OF OBSCENE MATTERS FOR SALE OR DISTRIBUTION

Whoever knowingly transports or travels in, or uses a facility or means of, interstate or foreign commerce or an interactive computer service (as defined in section 230(e)(2) of the Communications Act of 1934) in or affecting such commerce for the purpose of sale or distribution of any obscene, lewd, lascivious, or filthy book, pamphlet, picture, film, paper, letter, writing, print, silhouette, drawing, figure, image, cast, phonograph recording, electrical transcription or other article capable of producing sound or any other matter of indecent or immoral character, shall be fined under this title or imprisoned not more than five years, or both.

The transportation as aforesaid of two or more copies of any publication or two or more of any article of the character described above, or a combined total of five such publications and articles, shall create a presumption that such publications or articles are intended for sale or distribution, but such presumption shall be rebuttable.

18 U.S.C. § 1831. ECONOMIC ESPIONAGE

(a) **In general**. Whoever, intending or knowing that the offense will benefit any foreign government, foreign instrumentality, or foreign agent, knowingly—

(1) steals, or without authorization appropriates, takes, carries away, or conceals, or by fraud, artifice, or deception obtains a trade secret;

(2) without authorization copies, duplicates, sketches, draws, photographs, downloads, uploads, alters, destroys, photocopies, replicates, transmits, delivers, sends, mails, communicates, or conveys a trade secret;

(3) receives, buys, or possesses a trade secret, knowing the same to have been stolen or appropriated, obtained, or converted without authorization;

(4) attempts to commit any offense described in any of paragraphs (1) through (3); or

(5) conspires with one or more other persons to commit any offense described in any of paragraphs (1) through (3), and one or more of such persons do any act to effect the object of the conspiracy,

shall, except as provided in subsection (b), be fined not more than $500,000 or imprisoned not more than 15 years, or both.

(b) **Organizations**. Any organization that commits any offense described in subsection (a) shall be fined not more than $10,000,000.

18 U.S.C. § 1832. THEFT OF TRADE SECRETS

(a) Whoever, with intent to convert a trade secret, that is related to or included in a product that is produced for or placed in interstate or foreign commerce, to the economic benefit of anyone other than the owner thereof, and intending or knowing that the offense will, injure any owner of that trade secret, knowingly—

(1) steals, or without authorization appropriates, takes, carries away, or conceals, or by fraud, artifice, or deception obtains such information;

(2) without authorization copies, duplicates, sketches, draws, photographs, downloads, uploads, alters, destroys, photocopies, replicates, transmits, delivers, sends, mails, communicates, or conveys such information;

(3) receives, buys, or possesses such information, knowing the same to have been stolen or appropriated, obtained, or converted without authorization;

(4) attempts to commit any offense described in paragraphs (1) through (3); or

(5) conspires with one or more other persons to commit any offense described in paragraphs (1) through (3), and one or more of such persons do any act to effect the object of the conspiracy,

shall, except as provided in subsection (b), be fined under this title or imprisoned not more than 10 years, or both.

(b) Any organization that commits any offense described in subsection (a) shall be fined not more than $5,000,000.

18 U.S.C. § 1839. DEFINITIONS

As used in this chapter—

(1) the term "foreign instrumentality" means any agency, bureau, ministry, component, institution, association, or any legal, commercial, or business organization, corporation, firm, or entity that is substantially owned, controlled, sponsored, commanded, managed, or dominated by a foreign government;

(2) the term "foreign agent" means any officer, employee, proxy, servant, delegate, or representative of a foreign government;

(3) the term "trade secret" means all forms and types of financial, business, scientific, technical, economic, or engineering information, including patterns, plans, compilations, program devices, formulas, designs, prototypes, methods, techniques, processes, procedures, programs, or codes, whether tangible or intangible, and whether or how stored, compiled, or memorialized physically, electronically, graphically, photographically, or in writing if—

(A) the owner thereof has taken reasonable measures to keep such information secret; and

(B) the information derives independent economic value, actual or potential, from not being generally known to, and not being readily ascertainable through proper means by, the public; and

(4) the term "owner", with respect to a trade secret, means the person or entity in whom or in which rightful legal or equitable title to, or license in, the trade secret is reposed.

18 U.S.C. § 2252. CERTAIN ACTIVITIES RELATING TO MATERIAL INVOLVING THE SEXUAL EXPLOITATION OF MINORS

(a) Any person who—

(1) knowingly transports or ships in interstate or foreign commerce by any means including by computer or mails, any visual depiction, if—

(A) the producing of such visual depiction involves the use of a minor engaging in sexually explicit conduct; and

(B) such visual depiction is of such conduct;

(2) knowingly receives, or distributes any visual depiction that has been mailed, or has been shipped or transported in interstate or foreign commerce, or which contains materials which have been mailed or so shipped or transported, by any means including by computer, or knowingly reproduces any visual depiction for distribution in interstate or foreign commerce by any means including by computer or through the mails, if—

(A) the producing of such visual depiction involves the use of a minor engaging in sexually explicit conduct; and

(B) such visual depiction is of such conduct;

(3) either—

(A) in the special maritime and territorial jurisdiction of the United States, or on any land or building owned by, leased to, or otherwise used by or under the control of the Government of the United States, or in the Indian country as defined in section 1151 of this title, knowingly sells or possesses with intent to sell any visual depiction; or

(B) knowingly sells or possesses with intent to sell any visual depiction that has been mailed, or has been shipped or transported in interstate or foreign commerce, or which was produced using materials which have been mailed or so shipped or transported, by any means, including by computer, if—

(i) the producing of such visual depiction involves the use of a minor engaging in sexually explicit conduct; and

(ii) such visual depiction is of such conduct; or

(4) either—

(A) in the special maritime and territorial jurisdiction of the United States, or on any land or building owned by, leased to, or otherwise used by or under the control of the Government of the United States, or in the Indian country as defined in section 1151 of this title, knowingly possesses 1 or more books, magazines, periodicals, films, video tapes, or other matter which contain any visual depiction; or

(B) knowingly possesses 1 or more books, magazines, periodicals, films, video tapes, or other matter which contain any visual depiction that has been mailed, or has been shipped or transported in interstate or foreign commerce, or which was produced using materials which have been mailed or so shipped or transported, by any means including by computer, if—

(i) the producing of such visual depiction involves the use of a minor engaging in sexually explicit conduct; and

(ii) such visual depiction is of such conduct;

shall be punished as provided in subsection (b) of this section.

(b) (1) Whoever violates, or attempts or conspires to violate, paragraphs (1), (2), or (3) of subsection (a) shall be fined under this title and imprisoned not less than 5 years and not more than 20 years, but if such person has a prior conviction under this chapter, chapter 71, chapter 109A, or chapter 117, or under section 920 of title 10 (article 120 of the Uniform Code of Military Justice), or under the laws of any State relating to aggravated sexual abuse, sexual abuse, or abusive sexual conduct involving a minor or ward, or the production, possession, receipt, mailing, sale, distribution, shipment, or transportation of child pornography, such person shall be fined under this title and imprisoned for not less than 15 years nor more than 40 years.

(2) Whoever violates, or attempts or conspires to violate, paragraph (4) of subsection (a) shall be fined under this title or imprisoned not more than 10 years, or both, but if such person has a prior conviction under this chapter, chapter 71, chapter 109A, or chapter 117, or under section 920 of title 10 (article 120 of the Uniform Code of Military Justice), or under the laws of any State relating to aggravated sexual abuse, sexual abuse, or abusive sexual conduct involving a minor or ward, or the production, possession, receipt, mailing, sale, distribution, shipment, or transportation of child pornography, such person shall be fined under this title and imprisoned for not less than 10 years nor more than 20 years.

(c) Affirmative defense. It shall be an affirmative defense to a charge of violating paragraph (4) of subsection (a) that the defendant—

(1) possessed less than three matters containing any visual depiction proscribed by that paragraph; and

(2) promptly and in good faith, and without retaining or allowing any person, other than a law enforcement agency, to access any visual depiction or copy thereof—

(A) took reasonable steps to destroy each such visual depiction; or

(B) reported the matter to a law enforcement agency and afforded that agency access to each such visual depiction.

18 U.S.C. § 2252A. CERTAIN ACTIVITIES RELATING TO MATERIAL CONSTITUTING OR CONTAINING CHILD PORNOGRAPHY

(a) Any person who—

(1) knowingly mails, or transports or ships in interstate or foreign commerce by any means, including by computer, any child pornography;

(2) knowingly receives or distributes—

(A) any child pornography that has been mailed, or shipped or transported in interstate or foreign commerce by any means, including by computer; or

(B) any material that contains child pornography that has been mailed, or shipped or transported in interstate or foreign commerce by any means, including by computer;

(3) knowingly—

(A) reproduces any child pornography for distribution through the mails, or in interstate or foreign commerce by any means, including by computer; or

(B) advertises, promotes, presents, distributes, or solicits through the mails, or in interstate or foreign commerce by any means, including by computer, any material or purported material in a manner that reflects the belief, or that is intended to cause another to believe, that the material or purported material is, or contains—

(i) an obscene visual depiction of a minor engaging in sexually explicit conduct; or

(ii) a visual depiction of an actual minor engaging in sexually explicit conduct;

(4) either—

(A) in the special maritime and territorial jurisdiction of the United States, or on any land or building owned by, leased to, or otherwise used by or under the control of the United States Government, or in the Indian country (as defined in section 1151), knowingly sells or possesses with the intent to sell any child pornography; or

(B) knowingly sells or possesses with the intent to sell any child pornography that has been mailed, or shipped or transported in interstate or foreign commerce by any means, including by computer, or that was produced using materials that have been mailed, or shipped or transported in interstate or foreign commerce by any means, including by computer;

(5) either—

(A) in the special maritime and territorial jurisdiction of the United States, or on any land or building owned by, leased to, or otherwise used by or under the control of the United States Government, or in the Indian country (as defined in section 1151), knowingly possesses any book, magazine, periodical, film, videotape, computer disk, or any other material that contains an image of child pornography; or

(B) knowingly possesses any book, magazine, periodical, film, videotape, computer disk, or any other material that contains an image of child pornography that has been mailed, or shipped or transported in interstate or foreign commerce by any means, including by computer, or that was produced using materials that have been mailed, or shipped or transported in interstate or foreign commerce by any means, including by computer; or

(6) knowingly distributes, offers, sends, or provides to a minor any visual depiction, including any photograph, film, video, picture, or computer generated image or picture, whether made or produced by electronic, mechanical, or other means, where such visual depiction is, or appears to be, of a minor engaging in sexually explicit conduct—

(A) that has been mailed, shipped, or transported in interstate or foreign commerce by any means, including by computer;

(B) that was produced using materials that have been mailed, shipped, or transported in interstate or foreign commerce by any means, including by computer; or

(C) which distribution, offer, sending, or provision is accomplished using the mails or by transmitting or causing to be transmitted any wire communication in interstate or foreign commerce, including by computer,

for purposes of inducing or persuading a minor to participate in any activity that is illegal.

shall be punished as provided in subsection (b); or

(b) (1) Whoever violates, or attempts or conspires to violate, paragraph (1), (2), (3), (4), or (6) of subsection (a) shall be fined under this title and imprisoned not less than 5 years and not more than 20 years, but, if such person has a prior conviction under this chapter, chapter 71, chapter 109A, or chapter 117, or under section 920 of title 10 (article 120 of the Uniform Code of Military Justice), or under the laws of any State relating to aggravated sexual abuse, sexual abuse, or abusive sexual conduct involving a minor or ward, or the production, possession, receipt, mailing, sale, distribution, shipment, or transportation of child pornography, such person shall be fined under this title and imprisoned for not less than 15 years nor more than 40 years.

(2) Whoever violates, or attempts or conspires to violate, subsection (a)(5) shall be fined under this title or imprisoned not more than 10 years, or both, but, if such person has a prior conviction

under this chapter, chapter 71, chapter 109A, or chapter 117, or under section 920 of title 10 (article 120 of the Uniform Code of Military Justice), or under the laws of any State relating to aggravated sexual abuse, sexual abuse, or abusive sexual conduct involving a minor or ward, or the production, possession, receipt, mailing, sale, distribution, shipment, or transportation of child pornography, such person shall be fined under this title and imprisoned for not less than 10 years nor more than 20 years.

(c) It shall be an affirmative defense to a charge of violating paragraph (1), (2), (3)(A), (4), or (5) of subsection (a) that—

(1) (A) the alleged child pornography was produced using an actual person or persons engaging in sexually explicit conduct; and

(B) each such person was an adult at the time the material was produced; or

(2) the alleged child pornography was not produced using any actual minor or minors.

No affirmative defense under subsection (c)(2) shall be available in any prosecution that involves child pornography as described in section 2256(8)(C). A defendant may not assert an affirmative defense to a charge of violating paragraph (1), (2), (3)(A), (4), or (5) of subsection (a) unless, within the time provided for filing pretrial motions or at such time prior to trial as the judge may direct, but in no event later than 10 days before the commencement of the trial, the defendant provides the court and the United States with notice of the intent to assert such defense and the substance of any expert or other specialized testimony or evidence upon which the defendant intends to rely. If the defendant fails to comply with this subsection, the court shall, absent a finding of extraordinary circumstances that prevented timely compliance, prohibit the defendant from asserting such defense to a charge of violating paragraph (1), (2), (3)(A), (4), or (5) of subsection (a) or presenting any evidence for which the defendant has failed to provide proper and timely notice.

(d) **Affirmative defense**. It shall be an affirmative defense to a charge of violating subsection (a)(5) that the defendant—

(1) possessed less than three images of child pornography; and

(2) promptly and in good faith, and without retaining or allowing any person, other than a law enforcement agency, to access any image or copy thereof—

(A) took reasonable steps to destroy each such image; or

(B) reported the matter to a law enforcement agency and afforded that agency access to each such image.

(e) **Admissibility of evidence**. On motion of the government, in any prosecution under this chapter or section 1466A, except for good cause shown, the name, address, social security number, or other non-physical identifying information, other than the age or approximate age, of any minor who is depicted in any child pornography shall not be admissible and may be redacted from any otherwise admissible evidence, and the jury shall be instructed, upon request of the United States, that it can draw no inference from the absence of such evidence in deciding whether the child pornography depicts an actual minor.

(f) **Civil remedies.**—

(1) *In general.* Any person aggrieved by reason of the conduct prohibited under subsection (a) or (b) or section 1466A may commence a civil action for the relief set forth in paragraph (2).

(2) *Relief.* In any action commenced in accordance with paragraph (1), the court may award appropriate relief, including—

(A) temporary, preliminary, or permanent injunctive relief;

(B) compensatory and punitive damages; and

(C) the costs of the civil action and reasonable fees for attorneys and expert witnesses.

18 U.S.C. § 2256. DEFINITIONS FOR CHAPTER

For the purposes of this chapter, the term—

(1) "minor" means any person under the age of eighteen years;

(2) (A) Except as provided in subparagraph (B), "sexually explicit conduct" means actual or simulated—

(i) sexual intercourse, including genital-genital, oral-genital, anal-genital, or oral-anal, whether between persons of the same or opposite sex;

(ii) bestiality;

(iii) masturbation;

(iv) sadistic or masochistic abuse; or

(v) lascivious exhibition of the genitals or pubic area of any person;

(B) For purposes of subsection 8(B) of this section, "sexually explicit conduct" means—

(i) graphic sexual intercourse, including genital-genital, oral-genital, anal-genital, or oral-anal, whether between persons of the same or opposite sex, or lascivious simulated sexual intercourse where the genitals, breast, or pubic area of any person is exhibited;

(ii) graphic or lascivious simulated;

(I) bestiality;

(II) masturbation; or

(III) sadistic or masochistic abuse; or

(iii) graphic or simulated lascivious exhibition of the genitals or pubic area of any person;

(3) "producing" means producing, directing, manufacturing, issuing, publishing, or advertising;

(4) "organization" means a person other than an individual;

(5) "visual depiction" includes undeveloped film and videotape, and data stored on computer disk or by electronic means which is capable of conversion into a visual image;

(6) "computer" has the meaning given that term in section 1030 of this title;

(7) "custody or control" includes temporary supervision over or responsibility for a minor whether legally or illegally obtained;

(8) "child pornography" means any visual depiction, including any photograph, film, video, picture, or computer or computer-generated image or picture, whether made or produced by electronic, mechanical, or other means, of sexually explicit conduct, where—

(A) the production of such visual depiction involves the use of a minor engaging in sexually explicit conduct;

(B) such visual depiction is a digital image, computer image, or computer-generated image that is, or is indistinguishable from, that of a minor engaging in sexually explicit conduct; or

(C) such visual depiction has been created, adapted, or modified to appear that an identifiable minor is engaging in sexually explicit conduct.

(9) "identifiable minor"—

(A) means a person—

(i) (I) who was a minor at the time the visual depiction was created, adapted, or modified; or

(II) whose image as a minor was used in creating, adapting, or modifying the visual depiction; and

(ii) who is recognizable as an actual person by the person's face, likeness, or other distinguishing characteristic, such as a unique birthmark or other recognizable feature; and

(B) shall not be construed to require proof of the actual identity of the identifiable minor.

(10) "graphic", when used with respect to a depiction of sexually explicit conduct, means that a viewer can observe any part of the genitals or pubic area of any depicted person or animal during any part of the time that the sexually explicit conduct is being depicted; and

(11) the term "indistinguishable" used with respect to a depiction, means virtually indistinguishable, in that the depiction is

such that an ordinary person viewing the depiction would conclude that the depiction is of an actual minor engaged in sexually explicit conduct. This definition does not apply to depictions that are drawings, cartoons, sculptures, or paintings depicting minors or adults.

18 U.S.C. § 2261A. STALKING

Whoever—

(1) travels in interstate or foreign commerce or within the special maritime and territorial jurisdiction of the United States, or enters or leaves Indian country, with the intent to kill, injure, harass, or place under surveillance with intent to kill, injure, harass, or intimidate another person, and in the course of, or as a result of, such travel places that person in reasonable fear of the death of, or serious bodily injury to, or causes substantial emotional distress to that person, a member of the immediate family (as defined in section 115) of that person, or the spouse or intimate partner of that person; or

(2) with the intent—

(A) to kill, injure, harass, or place under surveillance with intent to kill, injure, harass, or intimidate, or cause substantial emotional distress to a person in another State or tribal jurisdiction or within the special maritime and territorial jurisdiction of the United States; or

(B) to place a person in another State or tribal jurisdiction, or within the special maritime and territorial jurisdiction of the United States, in reasonable fear of the death of, or serious bodily injury to

(i) that person;

(ii) a member of the immediate family (as defined in section 115 of that person; or

(iii) a spouse or intimate partner of that person;

uses the mail, any interactive computer service, or any facility of interstate or foreign commerce to engage in a course of conduct that causes substantial emotional distress to that person or places that person in reasonable fear of the death of, or serious bodily injury to, any of the persons described in clauses (i) through (iii) of subparagraph (B);

shall be punished as provided in section 2261(b) of this title.

18 U.S.C. § 2314. TRANSPORTATION OF STOLEN GOODS, SECURITIES, MONEYS, FRAUDULENT STATE TAX STAMPS, OR ARTICLES USED IN COUNTERFEITING

Whoever transports, transmits, or transfers in interstate or foreign commerce any goods, wares, merchandise, securities or money, of the value of $5,000 or more, knowing the same to have been stolen, converted or taken by fraud; or

Whoever, having devised or intending to devise any scheme or artifice to defraud, or for obtaining money or property by means of false or fraudulent pretenses, representations, or promises, transports or causes to be transported, or induces any person or persons to travel in, or to be transported in interstate or foreign commerce in the execution or concealment of a scheme or artifice to defraud that person or those persons of money or property having a value of $5,000 or more; or

Whoever, with unlawful or fraudulent intent, transports in interstate or foreign commerce any falsely made, forged, altered, or counterfeited securities or tax stamps, knowing the same to have been falsely made, forged, altered, or counterfeited; or

Whoever, with unlawful or fraudulent intent, transports in interstate or foreign commerce any traveler's check bearing a forged countersignature; or

Whoever, with unlawful or fraudulent intent, transports in interstate or foreign commerce, any tool, implement, or thing used or fitted to be used in falsely making, forging, altering, or counterfeiting any security or tax stamps, or any part thereof

Shall be fined under this title or imprisoned not more than ten years, or both.

This section shall not apply to any falsely made, forged, altered, counterfeited or spurious representation of an obligation or other security of the United States, or of an obligation, bond, certificate, security, treasury note, bill, promise to pay or bank note issued by any foreign government. This section also shall not apply to any falsely made, forged, altered, counterfeited, or spurious representation of any bank note or bill issued by a bank or corporation of any foreign country which is intended by the laws or usage of such country to circulate as money.

18 U.S.C. § 2319. CRIMINAL INFRINGEMENT OF A COPYRIGHT

(a) Any person who violates section 506(a) (relating to criminal offenses) of title 17 shall be punished as provided in subsections (b), (c), and (d) and such penalties shall be in addition to any other provisions of title 17 or any other law.

(b) Any person who commits an offense under section 506(a)(1)(A) of title 17—

(1) shall be imprisoned not more than 5 years, or fined in the amount set forth in this title, or both, if the offense consists of the reproduction or distribution, including by electronic means, during any 180–day period, of at least 10 copies or phonorecords, of 1 or more copyrighted works, which have a total retail value of more than $2,500;

(2) shall be imprisoned not more than 10 years, or fined in the amount set forth in this title, or both, if the offense is a second or subsequent offense under paragraph (1); and

(3) shall be imprisoned not more than 1 year, or fined in the amount set forth in this title, or both, in any other case.

(c) Any person who commits an offense under section 506(a)(1)(B) of title 17—

(1) shall be imprisoned not more than 3 years, or fined in the amount set forth in this title, or both, if the offense consists of the reproduction or distribution of 10 or more copies or phonorecords of 1 or more copyrighted works, which have a total retail value of $2,500 or more;

(2) shall be imprisoned not more than 6 years, or fined in the amount set forth in this title, or both, if the offense is a second or subsequent offense under paragraph (1); and

(3) shall be imprisoned not more than 1 year, or fined in the amount set forth in this title, or both, if the offense consists of the reproduction or distribution of 1 or more copies or phonorecords of 1 or more copyrighted works, which have a total retail value of more than $1,000.

(d) Any person who commits an offense under section 506(a)(1)(C) of title 17—

(1) shall be imprisoned not more than 3 years, fined under this title, or both;

(2) shall be imprisoned not more than 5 years, fined under this title, or both, if the offense was committed for purposes of commercial advantage or private financial gain;

(3) shall be imprisoned not more than 6 years, fined under this title, or both, if the offense is a second or subsequent offense; and

(4) shall be imprisoned not more than 10 years, fined under this title, or both, if the offense is a second or subsequent offense under paragraph (2).

(e) (1) During preparation of the presentence report pursuant to Rule 32(c) of the Federal Rules of Criminal Procedure, victims of the offense shall be permitted to submit, and the probation officer shall receive, a victim impact statement that identifies the victim of the offense and the extent and scope of the injury and loss suffered by the victim, including the estimated economic impact of the offense on that victim.

(2) Persons permitted to submit victim impact statements shall include—

(A) producers and sellers of legitimate works affected by conduct involved in the offense;

(B) holders of intellectual property rights in such works; and

(C) the legal representatives of such producers, sellers, and holders.

(f) As used in this section—

(1) the terms "phonorecord" and "copies" have, respectively, the meanings set forth in section 101 (relating to definitions) of title 17;

(2) the terms "reproduction" and "distribution" refer to the exclusive rights of a copyright owner under clauses (1) and (3) respectively of section 106 (relating to exclusive rights in copyrighted works), as limited by sections 107 through 122, of title 17;

(3) the term "financial gain" has the meaning given the term in section 101 of title 17; and

(4) the term "work being prepared for commercial distribution" has the meaning given the term in section 506(a) of title 17.

17 U.S.C. § 506. Criminal Offenses

(a) Criminal infringement.

(1) *In general.* Any person who willfully infringes a copyright shall be punished as provided under section 2319 of title 18, if the infringement was committed—

(A) for purposes of commercial advantage or private financial gain;

(B) by the reproduction or distribution, including by electronic means, during any 180–day period, of 1 or more copies or phonorecords of 1 or more copyrighted works, which have a total retail value of more than $1,000; or

(C) by the distribution of a work being prepared for commercial distribution, by making it available on a computer network accessible to members of the public, if such person knew or should have known that the work was intended for commercial distribution.

(2) *Evidence.* For purposes of this subsection, evidence of reproduction or distribution of a copyrighted work, by itself, shall not be sufficient to establish willful infringement of a copyright.

(3) *Definition.* In this subsection, the term "work being prepared for commercial distribution" means—

(A) a computer program, a musical work, a motion picture or other audiovisual work, or a sound recording, if, at the time of unauthorized distribution—

(i) the copyright owner has a reasonable expectation of commercial distribution; and

(ii) the copies or phonorecords of the work have not been commercially distributed;

(B) a motion picture, if, at the time of unauthorized distribution, the motion picture—

(i) has been made available for viewing in a motion picture exhibition facility; and

(ii) has not been made available in copies for sale to the general public in the United States in a format intended to permit viewing outside a motion picture exhibition facility.

(b) **Forfeiture and destruction**. When any person is convicted of any violation of subsection (a), the court in its judgment of conviction shall, in addition to the penalty therein prescribed, order the forfeiture and destruction or other disposition of all infringing copies or phonorecords and all implements, devices, or equipment used in the manufacture of such infringing copies or phonorecords.

(c) **Fraudulent copyright notice**. Any person who, with fraudulent intent, places on any article a notice of copyright or words of the same purport that such person knows to be false, or who, with fraudulent intent, publicly distributes or imports for public distribution any article bearing such notice or words that such person knows to be false, shall be fined not more than $2,500.

(d) **Fraudulent removal of copyright notice**. Any person who, with fraudulent intent, removes or alters any notice of copyright appearing on a copy of a copyrighted work shall be fined not more than $2,500.

(e) **False representation**. Any person who knowingly makes a false representation of a material fact in the application for copyright registration provided for by section 409, or in any written statement filed in connection with the application, shall be fined not more than $2,500.

(f) **Rights of attribution and integrity**. Nothing in this section applies to infringement of the rights conferred by section 106A(a).

18 U.S.C. § 2422. Coercion and Enticement

(a) Whoever knowingly persuades, induces, entices, or coerces any individual to travel in interstate or foreign commerce, or in any Territory or Possession of the United States, to engage in prostitution, or in any sexual activity for which any person can be charged with a criminal offense, or attempts to do so, shall be fined under this title or imprisoned not more than 20 years, or both.

(b) Whoever, using the mail or any facility or means of interstate or foreign commerce, or within the special maritime and territorial jurisdiction of the United States knowingly persuades, induces, entices, or coerces any individual who has not attained the age of 18 years, to engage in prostitution or any sexual activity for which any person can be charged with a criminal offense, or attempts to do so, shall be fined under this title and imprisoned not less than 5 years and not more than 30 years.

18 U.S.C. § 2423. Transportation of Minors

(a) **Transportation with intent to engage in criminal sexual activity**. A person who knowingly transports an individual who has not attained the age of 18 years in interstate or foreign commerce, or in any commonwealth, territory or possession of the United States, with intent that the individual engage in prostitution, or in any sexual activity for which any person can be charged with a criminal offense, shall be fined under this title and imprisoned not less than 5 years and not more than 30 years.

(b) **Travel with intent to engage in illicit sexual conduct**. A person who travels in interstate commerce or travels into the United States, or a United States citizen or an alien admitted for permanent residence in the United States who travels in foreign commerce, for the purpose of engaging in any illicit sexual conduct with another person shall be fined under this title or imprisoned not more than 30 years, or both.

(c) **Engaging in illicit sexual conduct in foreign places**. Any United States citizen or alien admitted for permanent residence who travels in foreign commerce, and engages in any illicit sexual conduct with another person shall be fined under this title or imprisoned not more than 30 years, or both.

(d) **Ancillary offenses**. Whoever, for the purpose of commercial advantage or private financial gain, arranges, induces, procures, or facilitates the travel of a person knowing that such a person is traveling in interstate commerce or foreign commerce for the purpose of engaging in illicit sexual conduct shall be fined under this title, imprisoned not more than 30 years, or both.

(e) **Attempt and conspiracy**. Whoever attempts or conspires to violate subsection (a), (b), (c), or (d) shall be punishable in the same manner as a completed violation of that subsection.

(f) **Definition**. As used in this section, the term "illicit sexual conduct" means (1) a sexual act (as defined in section 2246) with a person under 18 years of age that would be in violation of chapter 109A if the sexual act occurred in the special maritime and territorial jurisdiction of the United States; or (2) any commercial sex act (as defined in section 1591) with a person under 18 years of age.

(g) **Defense**. In a prosecution under this section based on illicit sexual conduct as defined in subsection (f)(2), it is a defense, which the defendant must establish by a preponderance of the evidence, that the defendant reasonably believed that the person with whom the defendant engaged in the commercial sex act had attained the age of 18 years.

18 U.S.C. § 2510. Definitions

As used in this chapter—

(1) "wire communication" means any aural transfer made in whole or in part through the use of facilities for the transmission of

communications by the aid of wire, cable, or other like connection between the point of origin and the point of reception (including the use of such connection in a switching station) furnished or operated by any person engaged in providing or operating such facilities for the transmission of interstate or foreign communications or communications affecting interstate or foreign commerce;

(2) "oral communication" means any oral communication uttered by a person exhibiting an expectation that such communication is not subject to interception under circumstances justifying such expectation, but such term does not include any electronic communication;

(3) "State" means any State of the United States, the District of Columbia, the Commonwealth of Puerto Rico, and any territory or possession of the United States;

(4) "intercept" means the aural or other acquisition of the contents of any wire, electronic, or oral communication through the use of any electronic, mechanical, or other device.

(5) "electronic, mechanical, or other device" means any device or apparatus which can be used to intercept a wire, oral, or electronic communication other than—

    (a) any telephone or telegraph instrument, equipment or facility, or any component thereof, (i) furnished to the subscriber or user by a provider of wire or electronic communication service in the ordinary course of its business and being used by the subscriber or user in the ordinary course of its business or furnished by such subscriber or user for connection to the facilities of such service and used in the ordinary course of its business; or (ii) being used by a provider of wire or electronic communication service in the ordinary course of its business, or by an investigative or law enforcement officer in the ordinary course of his duties;

    (b) a hearing aid or similar device being used to correct subnormal hearing to not better than normal;

(6) "person" means any employee, or agent of the United States or any State or political subdivision thereof, and any individual, partnership, association, joint stock company, trust, or corporation;

(7) "Investigative or law enforcement officer" means any officer of the United States or of a State or political subdivision thereof, who is empowered by law to conduct investigations of or to make arrests for offenses enumerated in this chapter, and any attorney authorized by law to prosecute or participate in the prosecution of such offenses;

(8) "contents", when used with respect to any wire, oral, or electronic communication, includes any information concerning the substance, purport, or meaning of that communication;

(9) "Judge of competent jurisdiction" means—

(a) a judge of a United States district court or a United States court of appeals; and

(b) a judge of any court of general criminal jurisdiction of a State who is authorized by a statute of that State to enter orders authorizing interceptions of wire, oral, or electronic communications;

(10) "communication common carrier" has the meaning given that term in section 3 of the Communications Act of 1934;

(11) "aggrieved person" means a person who was a party to any intercepted wire, oral, or electronic communication or a person against whom the interception was directed;

(12) "electronic communication" means any transfer of signs, signals, writing, images, sounds, data, or intelligence of any nature transmitted in whole or in part by a wire, radio, electromagnetic, photoelectronic or photooptical system that affects interstate or foreign commerce, but does not include—

(A) any wire or oral communication;

(B) any communication made through a tone-only paging device;

(C) any communication from a tracking device (as defined in section 3117 of this title); or

(D) electronic funds transfer information stored by a financial institution in a communications system used for the electronic storage and transfer of funds;

(13) "user" means any person or entity who—

(A) uses an electronic communication service; and

(B) is duly authorized by the provider of such service to engage in such use;

(14) "electronic communications system" means any wire, radio, electromagnetic, photooptical or photoelectronic facilities for the transmission of wire or electronic communications, and any computer facilities or related electronic equipment for the electronic storage of such communications;

(15) "electronic communication service" means any service which provides to users thereof the ability to send or receive wire or electronic communications;

(16) "readily accessible to the general public" means, with respect to a radio communication, that such communication is not—

(A) scrambled or encrypted;

(B) transmitted using modulation techniques whose essential parameters have been withheld from the public with the intention of preserving the privacy of such communication;

(C) carried on a subcarrier or other signal subsidiary to a radio transmission;

(D) transmitted over a communication system provided by a common carrier, unless the communication is a tone only paging system communication; or

(E) transmitted on frequencies allocated under part 25, subpart D, E, or F of part 74, or part 94 of the Rules of the Federal Communications Commission, unless, in the case of a communication transmitted on a frequency allocated under part 74 that is not exclusively allocated to broadcast auxiliary services, the communication is a two-way voice communication by radio;

(17) "electronic storage" means—

(A) any temporary, intermediate storage of a wire or electronic communication incidental to the electronic transmission thereof; and

(B) any storage of such communication by an electronic communication service for purposes of backup protection of such communication;

(18) "aural transfer" means a transfer containing the human voice at any point between and including the point of origin and the point of reception;

(19) "foreign intelligence information", for purposes of section 2517(6) of this title, means—

(A) information, whether or not concerning a United States person, that relates to the ability of the United States to protect against—

(i) actual or potential attack or other grave hostile acts of a foreign power or an agent of a foreign power;

(ii) sabotage or international terrorism by a foreign power or an agent of a foreign power; or

(iii) clandestine intelligence activities by an intelligence service or network of a foreign power or by an agent of a foreign power; or

(B) information, whether or not concerning a United States person, with respect to a foreign power or foreign territory that relates to—

(i) the national defense or the security of the United States; or

(ii) the conduct of the foreign affairs of the United States;

(20) "protected computer" has the meaning set forth in section 1030; and

(21) "computer trespasser"—

(A) means a person who accesses a protected computer without authorization and thus has no reasonable expectation of privacy in any communication transmitted to, through, or from the protected computer; and

(B) does not include a person known by the owner or operator of the protected computer to have an existing contractual relationship with the owner or operator of the protected computer for access to all or part of the protected computer.

18 U.S.C. § 2511. Interception and Disclosure of Wire, Oral, or Electronic Communications Prohibited

(1) Except as otherwise specifically provided in this chapter any person who—

(a) intentionally intercepts, endeavors to intercept, or procures any other person to intercept or endeavor to intercept, any wire, oral, or electronic communication;

(b) intentionally uses, endeavors to use, or procures any other person to use or endeavor to use any electronic, mechanical, or other device to intercept any oral communication when—

(i) such device is affixed to, or otherwise transmits a signal through, a wire, cable, or other like connection used in wire communication; or

(ii) such device transmits communications by radio, or interferes with the transmission of such communication; or

(iii) such person knows, or has reason to know, that such device or any component thereof has been sent through the mail or transported in interstate or foreign commerce; or

(iv) such use or endeavor to use (A) takes place on the premises of any business or other commercial establishment the operations of which affect interstate or foreign commerce; or (B) obtains or is for the purpose of obtaining information relating to the operations of any business or other commercial establishment the operations of which affect interstate or foreign commerce; or

(v) such person acts in the District of Columbia, the Commonwealth of Puerto Rico, or any territory or possession of the United States;

(c) intentionally discloses, or endeavors to disclose, to any other person the contents of any wire, oral, or electronic communication, knowing or having reason to know that the information was obtained through the interception of a wire, oral, or electronic communication in violation of this subsection;

(d) intentionally uses, or endeavors to use, the contents of any wire, oral, or electronic communication, knowing or having reason to know that the information was obtained through the interception of a wire, oral, or electronic communication in violation of this subsection; or

(e) (i) intentionally discloses, or endeavors to disclose, to any other person the contents of any wire, oral, or electronic communication, intercepted by means authorized by sections 2511(2)(a)(ii), 2511(2)(b)-(c), 2511(2)(e), 2516, and 2518 of this chapter, (ii) knowing or having reason to know that the information was obtained through the interception of such a communication in connection with a criminal investigation, (iii) having obtained or received the information in connection with a criminal investigation, and (iv) with intent to improperly obstruct, impede, or interfere with a duly authorized criminal investigation,

shall be punished as provided in subsection (4) or shall be subject to suit as provided in subsection (5).

(2) (a) (i) It shall not be unlawful under this chapter for an operator of a switchboard, or an officer, employee, or agent of a provider of wire or electronic communication service, whose facilities are used in the transmission of a wire or electronic communication, to intercept, disclose, or use that communication in the normal course of his employment while engaged in any activity which is a necessary incident to the rendition of his service or to the protection of the rights or property of the provider of that service, except that a provider of wire communication service to the public shall not utilize service observing or random monitoring except for mechanical or service quality control checks.

(ii) Notwithstanding any other law, providers of wire or electronic communication service, their officers, employees, and agents, landlords, custodians, or other persons, are authorized to provide information, facilities, or technical assistance to persons authorized by law to intercept wire, oral, or electronic communications or to conduct electronic surveillance, as defined in section 101 of the Foreign Intelligence Surveillance Act of 1978 if such provider, its officers, employees, or agents, landlord, custodian, or other specified person, has been provided with—

(A) a court order directing such assistance signed by the authorizing judge, or

(B) a certification in writing by a person specified in section 2518(7) of this title or the Attorney General of the United States that no warrant or court order is required by law, that all statutory requirements have been met, and that the specified assistance is required, setting forth the period of time during which the provision of the information, facilities, or technical assistance is authorized and specifying the information, facilities, or technical assistance required. No provider of wire or electronic communication service, officer, employee, or agent thereof, or landlord, custodian, or other specified person shall disclose the existence of any interception or surveillance or the device used to accomplish the interception or surveillance with respect to which the person has been furnished an order or certification under this subparagraph, except as may otherwise be required by legal process and then only after prior notification to the Attorney General or to the principal prosecuting attorney of a State or any political subdivision of a State, as may be appropriate. Any such disclosure, shall render such person liable for the civil damages provided for in section 2520. No cause of action shall lie in any court against any provider of wire or electronic communication service, its officers, employees, or agents, landlord, custodian, or other specified person for providing information, facilities, or assistance in accordance with the terms of a court order, statutory authorization, or certification under this chapter.

(b) It shall not be unlawful under this chapter for an officer, employee, or agent of the Federal Communications Commission, in the normal course of his employment and in discharge of the monitoring responsibilities exercised by the Commission in the enforcement of chapter 5 of title 47 of the United States Code, to intercept a wire or electronic communication, or oral communication transmitted by radio, or to disclose or use the information thereby obtained.

(c) It shall not be unlawful under this chapter for a person acting under color of law to intercept a wire, oral, or electronic communication, where such person is a party to the communication or one of the parties to the communication has given prior consent to such interception.

(d) It shall not be unlawful under this chapter for a person not acting under color of law to intercept a wire, oral, or electronic communication where such person is a party to the communication or where one of the parties to the communication has given prior consent to such interception unless such communication is intercepted for the purpose of committing any criminal or tortious act in violation of the Constitution or laws of the United States or of any State.

(e) Notwithstanding any other provision of this title or section 705 or 706 of the Communications Act of 1934, it shall not be unlawful for an officer, employee, or agent of the United States in the normal course of his official duty to conduct electronic surveillance, as defined in section 101 of the Foreign Intelligence Surveillance Act of 1978, as authorized by that Act.

(f) Nothing contained in this chapter or chapter 121 or 206 of this title, or section 705 of the Communications Act of 1934, shall be deemed to affect the acquisition by the United States Government of foreign intelligence information from international or foreign communications, or foreign intelligence activities conducted in accordance with otherwise applicable Federal law involving a foreign electronic communications system, utilizing a means other than electronic surveillance as defined in section 101 of the Foreign Intelligence Surveillance Act of 1978, and procedures in this chapter or chapter 121 or 206 of this title and the Foreign Intelligence Surveillance Act of 1978 shall be the exclusive means by which electronic surveillance, as defined in section 101 of such Act, and the interception of domestic wire, oral, and electronic communications may be conducted.

(g) It shall not be unlawful under this chapter or chapter 121 of this title for any person—

(i) to intercept or access an electronic communication made through an electronic communication system that is configured so that such electronic communication is readily accessible to the general public;

(ii) to intercept any radio communication which is transmitted—

(I) by any station for the use of the general public, or that relates to ships, aircraft, vehicles, or persons in distress;

(II) by any governmental, law enforcement, civil defense, private land mobile, or public safety communications system, including police and fire, readily accessible to the general public;

(III) by a station operating on an authorized frequency within the bands allocated to the amateur, citizens band, or general mobile radio services; or

(IV) by any marine or aeronautical communications system;

(iii) to engage in any conduct which—

(I) is prohibited by section 633 of the Communications Act of 1934; or

(II) is excepted from the application of section 705(a) of the Communications Act of 1934 by section 705(b) of that Act;

(iv) to intercept any wire or electronic communication the transmission of which is causing harmful interference to any lawfully operating station or consumer electronic equipment, to the extent necessary to identify the source of such interference; or

(v) for other users of the same frequency to intercept any radio communication made through a system that utilizes frequencies monitored by individuals engaged in the provision or the use of such system, if such communication is not scrambled or encrypted.

(h) It shall not be unlawful under this chapter—

(i) to use a pen register or a trap and trace device (as those terms are defined for the purposes of chapter 206 (relating to pen registers and trap and trace devices) of this title); or

(ii) for a provider of electronic communication service to record the fact that a wire or electronic communication was initiated or completed in order to protect such provider, another provider furnishing service toward the completion of the wire or electronic communication, or a user of that service, from fraudulent, unlawful or abusive use of such service.

(i) It shall not be unlawful under this chapter for a person acting under color of law to intercept the wire or electronic communications of a computer trespasser transmitted to, through, or from the protected computer, if—

(I) the owner or operator of the protected computer authorizes the interception of the computer trespasser's communications on the protected computer;

(II) the person acting under color of law is lawfully engaged in an investigation;

(III) the person acting under color of law has reasonable grounds to believe that the contents of the computer trespasser's communications will be relevant to the investigation; and

(IV) such interception does not acquire communications other than those transmitted to or from the computer trespasser.

(3) (a) Except as provided in paragraph (b) of this subection, a person or entity providing an electronic communication service to the public shall not intentionally divulge the contents of any communication (other than one to such person or entity, or an agent thereof) while in transmission on that service to any person or entity other than an addressee or intended recipient of such communication or an agent of such addressee or intended recipient.

(b) A person or entity providing electronic communication service to the public may divulge the contents of any such communication—

(i) as otherwise authorized in section 2511(2)(a) or 2517 of this title;

(ii) with the lawful consent of the originator or any addressee or intended recipient of such communication;

(iii) to a person employed or authorized, or whose facilities are used, to forward such communication to its destination; or

(iv) which were inadvertently obtained by the service provider and which appear to pertain to the commission of a crime, if such divulgence is made to a law enforcement agency.

(4) (a) Except as provided in paragraph (b) of this subsection or in subsection (5), whoever violates subsection (1) of this section shall be fined under this title or imprisoned not more than five years, or both.

(b) Conduct otherwise an offense under this subsection that consists of or relates to the interception of a satellite transmission that is not encrypted or scrambled and that is transmitted—

(i) to a broadcasting station for purposes of retransmission to the general public; or

(ii) as an audio subcarrier intended for redistribution to facilities open to the public, but not including data transmissions or telephone calls,

is not an offense under this subsection unless the conduct is for the purposes of direct or indirect commercial advantage or private financial gain.

(5) (a) (i) If the communication is—

(A) a private satellite video communication that is not scrambled or encrypted and the conduct in violation of this chapter is the private viewing of that communication and is not for a tortious or illegal purpose or for purposes of direct or indirect commercial advantage or private commercial gain; or

(B) a radio communication that is transmitted on frequencies allocated under subpart D of part 74 of the rules of the Federal Communications Commission that is not scrambled or encrypted and the conduct in violation of this chapter is not for a tortious or illegal purpose or for purposes of direct or indirect commercial advantage or private commercial gain,

then the person who engages in such conduct shall be subject to suit by the Federal Government in a court of competent jurisdiction.

(ii) In an action under this subsection—

(A) if the violation of this chapter is a first offense for the person under paragraph (a) of subsection (4) and such person has not been found liable in a civil action under section 2520 of this title, the Federal Government shall be entitled to appropriate injunctive relief; and

(B) if the violation of this chapter is a second or subsequent offense under paragraph (a) of subsection (4) or such person has been found liable in any prior civil action under section 2520, the person shall be subject to a mandatory $500 civil fine.

(b) The court may use any means within its authority to enforce an injunction issued under paragraph (ii)(A), and shall impose a civil fine of not less than $500 for each violation of such an injunction.

18 U.S.C. § 2512. MANUFACTURE, DISTRIBUTION, POSSESSION, AND ADVERTISING OF WIRE, ORAL, OR ELECTRONIC COMMUNICATION INTERCEPTING DEVICES PROHIBITED

(1) Except as otherwise specifically provided in this chapter, any person who intentionally—

(a) sends through the mail, or sends or carries in interstate or foreign commerce, any electronic, mechanical, or other device, knowing or having reason to know that the design of such device renders it primarily useful for the purpose of the surreptitious interception of wire, oral, or electronic communications;

(b) manufactures, assembles, possesses, or sells any electronic, mechanical, or other device, knowing or having reason to know that the design of such device renders it primarily useful for the purpose of the surreptitious interception of wire, oral, or electronic communications, and that such device or any component thereof has been or will be sent through the mail or transported in interstate or foreign commerce; or

(c) places in any newspaper, magazine, handbill, or other publication or disseminates by electronic means any advertisement of—

(i) any electronic, mechanical, or other device knowing or having reason to know that the design of such device renders it primarily useful for the purpose of the surreptitious interception of wire, oral, or electronic communications; or

(ii) any other electronic, mechanical, or other device, where such advertisement promotes the use of such device for the purpose of the surreptitious interception of wire, oral, or electronic communications,

knowing the content of the advertisement and knowing or having reason to know that such advertisement will be sent through the mail or transported in interstate or foreign commerce,

shall be fined under this title or imprisoned not more than five years, or both.

(2) It shall not be unlawful under this section for—

(a) a provider of wire or electronic communication service or an officer, agent, or employee of, or a person under contract with, such a provider, in the normal course of the business of providing that wire or electronic communication service, or

(b) an officer, agent, or employee of, or a person under contract with, the United States, a State, or a political subdivision thereof, in the normal course of the activities of the United States, a State, or a political subdivision thereof,

to send through the mail, send or carry in interstate or foreign commerce, or manufacture, assemble, possess, or sell any electronic, mechanical, or other device knowing or having reason to know that the design of such device renders it primarily useful for the purpose of the surreptitious interception of wire, oral, or electronic communications.

(3) It shall not be unlawful under this section to advertise for sale a device described in subsection (1) of this section if the advertisement is mailed, sent, or carried in interstate or foreign commerce solely to a domestic provider of wire or electronic communication service or to an agency of the United States, a State, or a political subdivision thereof which is duly authorized to use such device.

18 U.S.C. § 2513. CONFISCATION OF WIRE, ORAL, OR ELECTRONIC COMMUNICATION INTERCEPTING DEVICES

Any electronic, mechanical, or other device used, sent, carried, manufactured, assembled, possessed, sold, or advertised in violation of section 2511 or section 2512 of this chapter may be seized and forfeited to the United States. All provisions of law relating to (1) the seizure, summary and judicial forfeiture, and condemnation of vessels, vehicles, merchandise, and baggage for violations of the customs laws contained in title 19 of the United States Code, (2) the disposition of such vessels, vehicles, merchandise, and baggage or the proceeds from the sale thereof, (3) the remission or mitigation of such forfeiture, (4) the compromise of claims, and (5) the award of compensation to informers in respect of such forfeitures, shall apply to seizures and forfeitures incurred, or alleged to have been incurred, under the provisions of this section, insofar as applicable and not inconsistent with the provisions of this section; except that such duties as are imposed upon the collector of customs or any other person with respect to the seizure and forfeiture of vessels, vehicles, merchandise, and baggage under the provisions of the customs laws contained in title 19 of the United States Code shall be performed with respect to seizure and forfeiture of electronic, mechanical, or other intercepting devices under this section by such officers, agents, or other persons as may be authorized or designated for that purpose by the Attorney General.

18 U.S.C. § 2515. PROHIBITION OF USE AS EVIDENCE OF INTERCEPTED WIRE OR ORAL COMMUNICATIONS

Whenever any wire or oral communication has been intercepted, no part of the contents of such communication and no evidence derived therefrom may be received in evidence in any trial, hearing, or other proceeding in or before any court, grand jury, department, officer, agency, regulatory body, legislative committee, or other authority of the United States, a State, or a political subdivision thereof if the disclosure of that information would be in violation of this chapter.

18 U.S.C. § 2516. AUTHORIZATION FOR INTERCEPTION OF WIRE, ORAL, OR ELECTRONIC COMMUNICATIONS

(1) The Attorney General, Deputy Attorney General, Associate Attorney General, or any Assistant Attorney General, any acting Assistant Attorney General, or any Deputy Assistant Attorney General or acting Deputy Assistant Attorney General in the Criminal Division or National Security Division specially designated by the Attorney General, may authorize an application to a Federal judge of competent jurisdiction for, and such judge may grant in conformity with section 2518 of this chapter an order authorizing or approving the interception of wire or oral communications by the Federal Bureau of Investigation, or a Federal agency having responsibility for the investigation of the offense as to which the application is made, when such interception may provide or has provided evidence of—

(a) any offense punishable by death or by imprisonment for more than one year under sections 2122 and 2274 through 2277 of title 42 of the United States Code (relating to the enforcement of the Atomic Energy Act of 1954), section 2284 of title 42 of the United States Code (relating to sabotage of nuclear facilities or fuel), or under the following chapters of this title: chapter 10 (relating to biological weapons), chapter 37 (relating to espionage), chapter 55 (relating to kidnapping), chapter 90 (relating to protection of trade secrets), chapter 105 (relating to sabotage), chapter 115 (relating to treason), chapter 102 (relating to riots), chapter 65 (relating to malicious mischief), chapter 111 (relating to destruction of vessels), or chapter 81 (relating to piracy);

(b) a violation of section 186 or section 501(c) of title 29, United States Code (dealing with restrictions on payments and loans to labor organizations), or any offense which involves murder, kidnapping, robbery, or extortion, and which is punishable under this title;

(c) any offense which is punishable under the following sections of this title: section 37 (relating to violence at international airports), section 43 (relating to animal enterprise terrorism), section 81 (arson within special maritime and territorial jurisdiction), section 201 (bribery of public officials and witnesses), section 215 (relating to bribery of bank officials), section 224 (bribery in sporting contests), subsection (d), (e), (f), (g), (h), or (i) of section 844 (unlawful use of explosives), section 1032 (relating to concealment of assets), section 1084 (transmission of wagering information), section 751 (relating to escape), section 832 (relating to nuclear and weapons of mass destruction threats), section 842 (relating to explosive materials), section 930 (relating to possession of weapons in Federal facilities), section 1014 (relating to loans and credit applications generally; renewals and discounts), section 1114 (relating to officers and employees of the United States), section 1116 (relating to protection of foreign officials), sections 1503, 1512, and 1513 (influencing or injuring an officer, juror, or witness generally), section 1510 (obstruction of criminal investigations), section 1511 (obstruction of State or local law enforcement), section 1591 (sex trafficking of children by force, fraud, or coercion), section 1751 (Presidential and Presidential staff assassination, kidnapping, and assault), section 1951 (interference with commerce by threats or violence), section 1952 (interstate and foreign travel or transportation in aid of racketeering enterprises), section 1958 (relating to use of interstate commerce facilities in the commission of murder for hire), section 1959 (relating to violent crimes in aid of racketeering activity), section 1954 (offer, acceptance, or solicitation to influence operations of employee benefit plan), section 1955 (prohibition of business enterprises of gambling), section 1956 (laundering of monetary instruments), section 1957 (relating to engaging in monetary transactions in property derived from specified unlawful activity), section 659 (theft from interstate shipment), section 664 (embezzlement from pension and welfare funds), section 1343 (fraud by wire, radio, or television), section 1344 (relating to bank fraud), section 1992 (relating to terrorist attacks against mass transportation), sections 2251 and 2252 (sexual exploitation of children), section 2251A (selling or buying of children), section 2252A (relating to material constituting or containing child pornography), section 1466A (relating to child obscenity), section 2260 (production of sexually explicit depictions of a minor for importation into the United States), sections 2421, 2422, 2423, and 2425 (relating to transportation for illegal sexual activity and related crimes), sections 2312, 2313, 2314, and 2315 (interstate transportation of stolen property), section 2321 (relating to trafficking in certain motor vehicles or motor vehicle parts), section 2340A (relating to torture), section 1203 (relating to hostage taking), section 1029 (relating to fraud and related activity in connection with access devices), section 3146 (relating to penalty for failure to appear), section 3521(b)(3) (relating to witness relocation and assistance), section 32 (relating to destruction of aircraft or aircraft facilities), section 38 (relating to aircraft parts fraud), section 1963 (violations with respect to racketeer influenced and corrupt organizations), section 115 (relating to threatening or retaliating against a Federal official), section 1341 (relating to mail fraud), a felony violation of section 1030 (relating to computer fraud and abuse), section 351 (violations with respect to congressional, Cabinet, or Supreme Court assassinations, kidnapping, and assault), section 831 (relating to prohibited transactions involving nuclear materials), section 33 (relating to destruction of motor vehicles or motor vehicle facilities), section 175 (relating to biological weapons), section 175c (relating to variola virus), section 956 (conspiracy to harm persons or property overseas), section 1992 (relating to wrecking trains), a felony violation of section 1028 (relating to production of false identification documentation), section 1425 (relating to the procurement of citizenship or nationalization unlawfully), section 1426 (relating to the reproduction of naturalization or citizenship papers), section 1427 (relating to the sale of naturalization or citizenship papers), section 1541 (relating to passport issuance without authority), section 1542 (relating to false statements in passport applications), section 1543 (relating to forgery or false use of passports), section 1544 (relating to misuse of passports), or section 1546 (relating to fraud and misuse of visas, permits, and other documents);

(d) any offense involving counterfeiting punishable under section 471, 472, or 473 of this title;

(e) any offense involving fraud connected with a case under title 11 or the manufacture, importation, receiving, concealment, buying, selling, or otherwise dealing in narcotic drugs, marihuana, or other dangerous drugs, punishable under any law of the United States;

(f) any offense including extortionate credit transactions under sections 892, 893, or 894 of this title;

(g) a violation of section 5322 of title 31, United States Code (dealing with the reporting of currency transactions), or section 5324 of title 31, United States Code (relating to structuring transactions to evade reporting requirement prohibited);

(h) any felony violation of sections 2511 and 2512 (relating to interception and disclosure of certain communications and to certain intercepting devices) of this title;

(i) any felony violation of chapter 71 (relating to obscenity) of this title;

(j) any violation of section 60123(b) (relating to destruction of a natural gas pipeline), 46502 (relating to aircraft piracy), the second sentence of section 46504 (relating to assault on a flight crew with dangerous weapon), or section 46505(b)(3) or (c) (relating to explosive or incendiary devices, or endangerment of human life, by means of weapons on aircraft) of title 49;

(k) any criminal violation of section 2778 of title 22 (relating to the Arms Export Control Act);

(l) the location of any fugitive from justice from an offense described in this section;

(m) a violation of section 274, 277, or 278 of the Immigration and Nationality Act (8 U.S.C. 1324, 1327, or 1328) (relating to the smuggling of aliens);

(n) any felony violation of sections 922 and 924 of title 18, United States Code (relating to firearms);

(o) any violation of section 5861 of the Internal Revenue Code of 1986 (relating to firearms); or

(p) a felony violation of section 1028 (relating to production of false identification documents), section 1542 (relating to false statements in passport applications), section 1546 (relating to fraud and misuse of visas, permits, and other documents), section 1028A (relating to aggravated identity theft) of this title or a violation of section 274, 277, or 278 of the Immigration and Nationality Act (relating to the smuggling of aliens); or

(q) any criminal violation of section 229 (relating to chemical weapons) or section 2332, 2332a, 2332b, 2332d, 2332f, 2332g, 2332h, 2339, 2339A, 2339B, 2339C, or 2339D of this title (relating to terrorism);

(r) any criminal violation of section 1 (relating to illegal restraints of trade or commerce), 2 (relating to illegal monopolizing of trade or commerce), or 3 (relating to illegal restraints of trade or commerce in territories or the District of Columbia) of the Sherman Act (15 U.S.C. 1, 2, 3); or

(s) any conspiracy to commit any offense described in any subparagraph of this paragraph.

(2) The principal prosecuting attorney of any State, or the principal prosecuting attorney of any political subdivision thereof, if such attorney is authorized by a statute of that State to make application to a State court judge of competent jurisdiction for an order authorizing or approving the interception of wire, oral, or electronic communications, may apply to such judge for, and such judge may grant in conformity with section 2518 of this chapter and with the applicable State statute an order authorizing, or approving the interception of wire, oral or electronic communications by investigative or law enforcement officers having responsibility for the investigation of the offense as to which the application is made, when such interception may provide or has provided evidence of the commission of the offense of murder, kidnapping, gambling, robbery, bribery, extortion, or dealing in narcotic drugs, marihuana or other dangerous drugs, or other crime dangerous to life, limb, or property, and punishable by imprisonment for more than one year, designated in any applicable State statute authorizing such interception, or any conspiracy to commit any of the foregoing offenses.

(3) Any attorney for the Government (as such term is defined for the purposes of the Federal Rules of Criminal Procedure) may authorize an application to a Federal judge of competent jurisdiction for, and such judge may grant, in conformity with section 2518 of this title, an order authorizing or approving the interception of electronic communications by an investigative or law enforcement officer having responsibility for the investigation of the offense as to which the application is made, when such interception may provide or has provided evidence of any Federal felony.

18 U.S.C. § 2517. AUTHORIZATION FOR DISCLOSURE AND USE OF INTERCEPTED WIRE, ORAL, OR ELECTRONIC COMMUNICATIONS

(1) Any investigative or law enforcement officer who, by any means authorized by this chapter, has obtained knowledge of the contents of

any wire, oral, or electronic communication, or evidence derived therefrom, may disclose such contents to another investigative or law enforcement officer to the extent that such disclosure is appropriate to the proper performance of the official duties of the officer making or receiving the disclosure.

(2) Any investigative or law enforcement officer who, by any means authorized by this chapter, has obtained knowledge of the contents of any wire, oral, or electronic communication or evidence derived therefrom may use such contents to the extent such use is appropriate to the proper performance of his official duties.

(3) Any person who has received, by any means authorized by this chapter, any information concerning a wire, oral, or electronic communication, or evidence derived therefrom intercepted in accordance with the provisions of this chapter may disclose the contents of that communication or such derivative evidence while giving testimony under oath or affirmation in any proceeding held under the authority of the United States or of any State or political subdivision thereof.

(4) No otherwise privileged wire, oral, or electronic communication intercepted in accordance with, or in violation of, the provisions of this chapter shall lose its privileged character.

(5) When an investigative or law enforcement officer, while engaged in intercepting wire, oral, or electronic communications in the manner authorized herein, intercepts wire, oral, or electronic communications relating to offenses other than those specified in the order of authorization or approval, the contents thereof, and evidence derived therefrom, may be disclosed or used as provided in subsections (1) and (2) of this section. Such contents and any evidence derived therefrom may be used under subsection (3) of this section when authorized or approved by a judge of competent jurisdiction where such judge finds on subsequent application that the contents were otherwise intercepted in accordance with the provisions of this chapter. Such application shall be made as soon as practicable.

(6) Any investigative or law enforcement officer, or attorney for the Government, who by any means authorized by this chapter, has obtained knowledge of the contents of any wire, oral, or electronic communication, or evidence derived therefrom, may disclose such contents to any other Federal law enforcement, intelligence, protective, immigration, national defense, or national security official to the extent that such contents include foreign intelligence or counterintelligence (as defined in section 3 of the National Security Act of 1947 (50 U.S.C. 401a)), or foreign intelligence information (as defined in subsection (19) of section 2510 of this title), to assist the official who is to receive that information in the performance of his official duties. Any Federal official who receives information pursuant to this provision may use that information only as necessary in the conduct of that person's official duties subject to any limitations on the unauthorized disclosure of such information.

(7) Any investigative or law enforcement officer, or other Federal official in carrying out official duties as such Federal official, who by any means authorized by this chapter, has obtained knowledge of the contents of any wire, oral, or electronic communication, or evidence derived therefrom, may disclose such contents or derivative evidence to a foreign investigative or law enforcement officer to the extent that such disclosure is appropriate to the proper performance of the official duties of the officer making or receiving the disclosure, and foreign investigative or law enforcement officers may use or disclose such contents or derivative evidence to the extent such use or disclosure is appropriate to the proper performance of their official duties.

(8) Any investigative or law enforcement officer, or other Federal official in carrying out official duties as such Federal official, who by any means authorized by this chapter, has obtained knowledge of the contents of any wire, oral, or electronic communication, or evidence derived therefrom, may disclose such contents or derivative evidence to any appropriate Federal, State, local, or foreign government official to the extent that such contents or derivative evidence reveals a threat of actual or potential attack or other grave hostile acts of a foreign power or an agent of a foreign power, domestic or international sabotage, domestic or international terrorism, or clandestine intelligence gathering activities by an intelligence service or network of a foreign power or by an agent of a foreign power, within the United States or elsewhere, for the purpose of preventing or responding to such a threat. Any official who receives information pursuant to this provision may use that information only as necessary in the conduct of that person's official duties subject to any limitations on the unauthorized disclosure of such information, and any State, local, or foreign official who receives information pursuant to this provision may use that information only consistent with such guidelines as the Attorney General and Director of Central Intelligence shall jointly issue.

18 U.S.C. § 2518. PROCEDURE FOR INTERCEPTION OF WIRE, ORAL, OR ELECTRONIC COMMUNICATIONS

(1) Each application for an order authorizing or approving the interception of a wire, oral, or electronic communication under this chapter shall be made in writing upon oath or affirmation to a judge of competent jurisdiction and shall state the applicant's authority to make such application. Each application shall include the following information:

(a) the identity of the investigative or law enforcement officer making the application, and the officer authorizing the application;

(b) a full and complete statement of the facts and circumstances relied upon by the applicant, to justify his belief that an order should be issued, including (i) details as to the particular offense that has been, is being, or is about to be committed, (ii) except as provided in subsection (11), a particular description of the nature and location of the facilities from which or the place where the communication is to be intercepted, (iii) a particular description of the type of communications sought to be intercepted, (iv) the identity of the person, if known, committing the offense and whose communications are to be intercepted;

(c) a full and complete statement as to whether or not other investigative procedures have been tried and failed or why they reasonably appear to be unlikely to succeed if tried or to be too dangerous;

(d) a statement of the period of time for which the interception is required to be maintained. If the nature of the investigation is such that the authorization for interception should not automatically terminate when the described type of communication has been first obtained, a particular description of facts establishing probable cause to believe that additional communications of the same type will occur thereafter;

(e) a full and complete statement of the facts concerning all previous applications known to the individual authorizing and making the application, made to any judge for authorization to intercept, or for approval of interceptions of, wire, oral, or electronic communications involving any of the same persons, facilities or places specified in the application, and the action taken by the judge on each such application; and

(f) where the application is for the extension of an order, a statement setting forth the results thus far obtained from the interception, or a reasonable explanation of the failure to obtain such results.

(2) The judge may require the applicant to furnish additional testimony or documentary evidence in support of the application.

(3) Upon such application the judge may enter an ex parte order, as requested or as modified, authorizing or approving interception of wire, oral, or electronic communications within the territorial jurisdiction of the court in which the judge is sitting (and outside that jurisdiction but within the United States in the case of a mobile interception device authorized by a Federal court within such jurisdiction), if the judge determines on the basis of the facts submitted by the applicant that—

(a) there is probable cause for belief that an individual is committing, has committed, or is about to commit a particular offense enumerated in section 2516 of this chapter;

(b) there is probable cause for belief that particular communications concerning that offense will be obtained through such interception;

(c) normal investigative procedures have been tried and have failed or reasonably appear to be unlikely to succeed if tried or to be too dangerous;

(d) except as provided in subsection (11), there is probable cause for belief that the facilities from which, or the place where, the wire, oral, or electronic communications are to be intercepted are being used, or are about to be used, in connection with the commission of such offense, or are leased to, listed in the name of, or commonly used by such person.

(4) Each order authorizing or approving the interception of any wire, oral, or electronic communication under this chapter shall specify—

(a) the identity of the person, if known, whose communications are to be intercepted;

(b) the nature and location of the communications facilities as to which, or the place where, authority to intercept is granted;

(c) a particular description of the type of communication sought to be intercepted, and a statement of the particular offense to which it relates;

(d) the identity of the agency authorized to intercept the communications, and of the person authorizing the application; and

(e) the period of time during which such interception is authorized, including a statement as to whether or not the interception shall automatically terminate when the described communication has been first obtained.

An order authorizing the interception of a wire, oral, or electronic communication under this chapter shall, upon request of the applicant, direct that a provider of wire or electronic communication service, landlord, custodian or other person shall furnish the applicant forthwith all information, facilities, and technical assistance necessary to accomplish the interception unobtrusively and with a minimum of interference with the services that such service provider, landlord, custodian, or person is according the person whose communications are to be intercepted. Any provider of wire or electronic communication service, landlord, custodian or other person furnishing such facilities or technical assistance shall be compensated therefor by the applicant for reasonable expenses incurred in providing such facilities or assistance. Pursuant to section 2522 of this chapter, an order may also be issued to enforce the assistance capability and capacity requirements under the Communications Assistance for Law Enforcement Act.

(5) No order entered under this section may authorize or approve the interception of any wire, oral, or electronic communication for any period longer than is necessary to achieve the objective of the authorization, nor in any event longer than thirty days. Such thirty-day period begins on the earlier of the day on which the investigative or law enforcement officer first begins to conduct an interception under the order or ten days after the order is entered. Extensions of an order may be granted, but only upon application for an extension made in accordance with subsection (1) of this section and the court making the

findings required by subsection (3) of this section. The period of extension shall be no longer than the authorizing judge deems necessary to achieve the purposes for which it was granted and in no event for longer than thirty days. Every order and extension thereof shall contain a provision that the authorization to intercept shall be executed as soon as practicable, shall be conducted in such a way as to minimize the interception of communications not otherwise subject to interception under this chapter, and must terminate upon attainment of the authorized objective, or in any event in thirty days. In the event the intercepted communication is in a code or foreign language, and an expert in that foreign language or code is not reasonably available during the interception period, minimization may be accomplished as soon as practicable after such interception. An interception under this chapter may be conducted in whole or in part by Government personnel, or by an individual operating under a contract with the Government, acting under the supervision of an investigative or law enforcement officer authorized to conduct the interception.

(6) Whenever an order authorizing interception is entered pursuant to this chapter, the order may require reports to be made to the judge who issued the order showing what progress has been made toward achievement of the authorized objective and the need for continued interception. Such reports shall be made at such intervals as the judge may require.

(7) Notwithstanding any other provision of this chapter, any investigative or law enforcement officer, specially designated by the Attorney General, the Deputy Attorney General, the Associate Attorney General, or by the principal prosecuting attorney of any State or subdivision thereof acting pursuant to a statute of that State, who reasonably determines that—

(a) an emergency situation exists that involves—

(i) immediate danger of death or serious physical injury to any person,

(ii) conspiratorial activities threatening the national security interest, or

(iii) conspiratorial activities characteristic of organized crime,

that requires a wire, oral, or electronic communication to be intercepted before an order authorizing such interception can, with due diligence, be obtained, and

(b) there are grounds upon which an order could be entered under this chapter to authorize such interception,

may intercept such wire, oral, or electronic communication if an application for an order approving the interception is made in accordance with this section within forty-eight hours after the interception has occurred, or begins to occur. In the absence of an order, such interception shall immediately terminate when the communication sought is obtained or when the application for the order is denied, whichever is earlier. In the event such application for approval is denied, or in any other case where the interception is terminated without an order having been issued, the contents of any wire, oral, or electronic communication intercepted shall be treated as having been obtained in violation of this chapter, and an inventory shall be served as provided for in subsection (d) of this section on the person named in the application.

(8) (a) The contents of any wire, oral, or electronic communication intercepted by any means authorized by this chapter shall, if possible, be recorded on tape or wire or other comparable device. The recording of the contents of any wire, oral, or electronic communication under this subsection shall be done in such way as will protect the recording from editing or other alterations. Immediately upon the expiration of the period of the order, or extensions thereof, such recordings shall be made available to the judge issuing such order and sealed under his directions. Custody of the recordings shall be wherever the judge orders. They shall not be destroyed except upon an order of the issuing or denying judge and in any event shall be kept for ten years. Duplicate recordings may be made for use or disclosure pursuant to the provisions of subsections (1) and (2) of section 2517 of this chapter for investigations. The presence of the seal provided for by this subsection, or a satisfactory explanation for the absence thereof, shall be a prerequisite for the use or disclosure of the contents of any wire, oral, or electronic communication or evidence derived therefrom under subsection (3) of section 2517.

(b) Applications made and orders granted under this chapter shall be sealed by the judge. Custody of the applications and orders shall be wherever the judge directs. Such applications and orders shall be disclosed only upon a showing of good cause before a judge of competent jurisdiction and shall not be destroyed except on order of the issuing or denying judge, and in any event shall be kept for ten years.

(c) Any violation of the provisions of this subsection may be punished as contempt of the issuing or denying judge.

(d) Within a reasonable time but not later than ninety days after the filing of an application for an order of approval under section 2518(7)(b) which is denied or the termination of the period of an order or extensions thereof, the issuing or denying judge shall cause to be served, on the persons named in the order or the application, and such other parties to intercepted communications as the judge may determine in his discretion that is in the interest of justice, an inventory which shall include notice of—

(1) the fact of the entry of the order or the application;

(2) the date of the entry and the period of authorized, approved or disapproved interception, or the denial of the application; and

(3) the fact that during the period wire, oral, or electronic communications were or were not intercepted.

The judge, upon the filing of a motion, may in his discretion make available to such person or his counsel for inspection such portions of the intercepted communications, applications and orders as the judge determines to be in the interest of justice. On an ex parte showing of good cause to a judge of competent jurisdiction the serving of the inventory required by this subsection may be postponed.

(9) The contents of any wire, oral, or electronic communication intercepted pursuant to this chapter or evidence derived therefrom shall not be received in evidence or otherwise disclosed in any trial, hearing, or other proceeding in a Federal or State court unless each party, not less than ten days before the trial, hearing, or proceeding, has been furnished with a copy of the court order, and accompanying application, under which the interception was authorized or approved. This ten-day period may be waived by the judge if he finds that it was not possible to furnish the party with the above information ten days before the trial, hearing, or proceeding and that the party will not be prejudiced by the delay in receiving such information.

(10) (a) Any aggrieved person in any trial, hearing, or proceeding in or before any court, department, officer, agency, regulatory body, or other authority of the United States, a State, or a political subdivision thereof, may move to suppress the contents of any wire or oral communication intercepted pursuant to this chapter, or evidence derived therefrom, on the grounds that—

(i) the communication was unlawfully intercepted;

(ii) the order of authorization or approval under which it was intercepted is insufficient on its face; or

(iii) the interception was not made in conformity with the order of authorization or approval.

Such motion shall be made before the trial, hearing, or proceeding unless there was no opportunity to make such motion or the person was not aware of the grounds of the motion. If the motion is granted, the contents of the intercepted wire or oral communication, or evidence derived therefrom, shall be treated as having been obtained in violation of this chapter. The judge, upon the filing of such motion by the aggrieved person, may in his discretion make available to the aggrieved person or his counsel for inspection such portions of the intercepted communication or evidence derived therefrom as the judge determines to be in the interests of justice.

(b) In addition to any other right to appeal, the United States shall have the right to appeal from an order granting a motion to suppress made under paragraph (a) of this subsection, or the denial of an application for an order of approval, if the United States attorney shall certify to the judge or other official granting such motion or denying such application that the appeal is not taken for purposes of delay. Such appeal shall be taken within thirty days after the date the order was entered and shall be diligently prosecuted.

(c) The remedies and sanctions described in this chapter with respect to the interception of electronic communications are the only judicial remedies and sanctions for nonconstitutional violations of this chapter involving such communications.

(11) The requirements of subsections (1)(b)(ii) and (3)(d) of this section relating to the specification of the facilities from which, or the place where, the communication is to be intercepted do not apply if—

(a) in the case of an application with respect to the interception of an oral communication—

(i) the application is by a Federal investigative or law enforcement officer and is approved by the Attorney General, the Deputy Attorney General, the Associate Attorney General, an Assistant Attorney General, or an acting Assistant Attorney General;

(ii) the application contains a full and complete statement as to why such specification is not practical and identifies the person committing the offense and whose communications are to be intercepted; and

(iii) the judge finds that such specification is not practical; and

(b) in the case of an application with respect to a wire or electronic communication—

(i) the application is by a Federal investigative or law enforcement officer and is approved by the Attorney General, the Deputy Attorney General, the Associate Attorney General, an Assistant Attorney General, or an acting Assistant Attorney General;

(ii) the application identifies the person believed to be committing the offense and whose communications are to be intercepted and the applicant makes a showing that there is probable cause to believe that the person's actions could have the effect of thwarting interception from a specified facility;

(iii) the judge finds that such showing has been adequately made; and

(iv) the order authorizing or approving the interception is limited to interception only for such time as it is reasonable to presume that the person identified in the application is or was reasonably proximate to the instrument through which such communication will be or was transmitted.

(12) An interception of a communication under an order with respect to which the requirements of subsections (1)(b)(ii) and (3)(d) of

this section do not apply by reason of subsection (11)(a) shall not begin until the place where the communication is to be intercepted is ascertained by the person implementing the interception order. A provider of wire or electronic communications service that has received an order as provided for in subsection (11)(b) may move the court to modify or quash the order on the ground that its assistance with respect to the interception cannot be performed in a timely or reasonable fashion. The court, upon notice to the government, shall decide such a motion expeditiously.

18 U.S.C. § 2519. REPORTS CONCERNING INTERCEPTED WIRE, ORAL, OR ELECTRONIC COMMUNICATIONS

(1) Within thirty days after the expiration of an order (or each extension thereof) entered under section 2518, or the denial of an order approving an interception, the issuing or denying judge shall report to the Administrative Office of the United States Courts—

(a) the fact that an order or extension was applied for;

(b) the kind of order or extension applied for (including whether or not the order was an order with respect to which the requirements of sections 2518(1)(b)(ii) and 2518(3)(d) of this title did not apply by reason of section 2518(11) of this title);

(c) the fact that the order or extension was granted as applied for, was modified, or was denied;

(d) the period of interceptions authorized by the order, and the number and duration of any extensions of the order;

(e) the offense specified in the order or application, or extension of an order;

(f) the identity of the applying investigative or law enforcement officer and agency making the application and the person authorizing the application; and

(g) the nature of the facilities from which or the place where communications were to be intercepted.

(2) In January of each year the Attorney General, an Assistant Attorney General specially designated by the Attorney General, or the principal prosecuting attorney of a State, or the principal prosecuting attorney for any political subdivision of a State, shall report to the Administrative Office of the United States Courts—

(a) the information required by paragraphs (a) through (g) of subsection (1) of this section with respect to each application for an order or extension made during the preceding calendar year;

(b) a general description of the interceptions made under such order or extension, including (i) the approximate nature and frequency of incriminating communications intercepted, (ii) the approximate nature and frequency of other communications intercepted, (iii) the approximate number of persons whose communications were intercepted, (iv) the number of orders in which encryption was encountered and whether such encryption prevented law enforcement from obtaining the plain text of communications intercepted pursuant to such order, and (v) the approximate nature, amount, and cost of the manpower and other resources used in the interceptions;

(c) the number of arrests resulting from interceptions made under such order or extension, and the offenses for which arrests were made;

(d) the number of trials resulting from such interceptions;

(e) the number of motions to suppress made with respect to such interceptions, and the number granted or denied;

(f) the number of convictions resulting from such interceptions and the offenses for which the convictions were obtained and a general assessment of the importance of the interceptions; and

(g) the information required by paragraphs (b) through (f) of this subsection with respect to orders or extensions obtained in a preceding calendar year.

(3) In April of each year the Director of the Administrative Office of the United States Courts shall transmit to the Congress a full and complete report concerning the number of applications for orders authorizing or approving the interception of wire, oral, or electronic communications pursuant to this chapter and the number of orders and extensions granted or denied pursuant to this chapter during the preceding calendar year. Such report shall include a summary and analysis of the data required to be filed with the Administrative Office by subsections (1) and (2) of this section. The Director of the Administrative Office of the United States Courts is authorized to issue binding regulations dealing with the content and form of the reports required to be filed by subsections (1) and (2) of this section.

18 U.S.C. § 2520. RECOVERY OF CIVIL DAMAGES AUTHORIZED

(a) **In general**. Except as provided in section 2511(2)(a)(ii), any person whose wire, oral, or electronic communication is intercepted, disclosed, or intentionally used in violation of this chapter may in a civil action recover from the person or entity, other than the United States, which engaged in that violation such relief as may be appropriate.

(b) **Relief**. In an action under this section, appropriate relief includes—

(1) such preliminary and other equitable or declaratory relief as may be appropriate;

(2) damages under subsection (c) and punitive damages in appropriate cases; and

(3) a reasonable attorney's fee and other litigation costs reasonably incurred.

(c) **Computation of damages**.

(1) In an action under this section, if the conduct in violation of this chapter, is the private viewing of a private satellite video communication that is not scrambled or encrypted or if the communication is a radio communication that is transmitted on frequencies allocated under subpart D of part 74 of the rules of the Federal Communications Commission that is not scrambled or encrypted and the conduct is not for a tortious or illegal purpose or for purposes of direct or indirect commercial advantage or private commercial gain, then the court shall assess damages as follows:

(A) If the person who engaged in that conduct has not previously been enjoined under section 2511(5) and has not been found liable in a prior civil action under this section, the court shall assess the greater of the sum of actual damages suffered by the plaintiff, or statutory damages of not less than $50 and not more than $500.

(B) If, on one prior occasion, the person who engaged in that conduct has been enjoined under section 2511(5) or has been found liable in a civil action under this section, the court shall assess the greater of the sum of actual damages suffered by the plaintiff, or statutory damages of not less than $100 and not more than $1000.

(2) In any other action under this section, the court may assess as damages whichever is the greater of—

(A) the sum of the actual damages suffered by the plaintiff and any profits made by the violator as a result of the violation; or

(B) statutory damages of whichever is the greater of $100 a day for each day of violation or $10,000.

(d) **Defense**. A good faith reliance on—

(1) a court warrant or order, a grand jury subpoena, a legislative authorization, or a statutory authorization;

(2) a request of an investigative or law enforcement officer under section 2518(7) of this title; or

(3) a good faith determination that section 2511(3) or 2511(2)(i) of this title permitted the conduct complained of;

is a complete defense against any civil or criminal action brought under this chapter or any other law.

(e) **Limitation**. A civil action under this section may not be commenced later than two years after the date upon which the claimant first has a reasonable opportunity to discover the violation.

(f) **Administrative discipline**. If a court or appropriate department or agency determines that the United States or any of its departments or agencies has violated any provision of this chapter, and the court or appropriate department or agency finds that the circumstances surrounding the violation raise serious questions about whether or not an officer or employee of the United States acted willfully or intentionally with respect to the violation, the department or agency shall, upon receipt of a true and correct copy of the decision and findings of the court or appropriate department or agency promptly initiate a proceeding to determine whether disciplinary action against the officer or employee is warranted. If the head of the department or agency involved determines that disciplinary action is not warranted, he or she shall notify the Inspector General with jurisdiction over the department or agency concerned and shall provide the Inspector General with the reasons for such determination.

(g) **Improper disclosure is violation**. Any willful disclosure or use by an investigative or law enforcement officer or governmental entity of information beyond the extent permitted by section 2517 is a violation of this chapter for purposes of section 2520(a).

18 U.S.C. § 2521. INJUNCTION AGAINST ILLEGAL INTERCEPTION

Whenever it shall appear that any person is engaged or is about to engage in any act which constitutes or will constitute a felony violation of this chapter, the Attorney General may initiate a civil action in a district court of the United States to enjoin such violation. The court shall proceed as soon as practicable to the hearing and determination of such an action, and may, at any time before final determination, enter such a restraining order or prohibition, or take such other action, as is warranted to prevent a continuing and substantial injury to the United States or to any person or class of persons for whose protection the action is brought. A proceeding under this section is governed by the Federal Rules of Civil Procedure, except that, if an indictment has been returned against the respondent, discovery is governed by the Federal Rules of Criminal Procedure.

18 U.S.C. § 2522. ENFORCEMENT OF THE COMMUNICATIONS ASSISTANCE FOR LAW ENFORCEMENT ACT

(a) **Enforcement by court issuing surveillance order**. If a court authorizing an interception under this chapter, a State statute, or the Foreign Intelligence Surveillance Act of 1978 (50 U.S.C. 1801 et seq.) or authorizing use of a pen register or a trap and trace device under chapter 206 or a State statute finds that a telecommunications carrier has failed to comply with the requirements of the Communications Assistance for Law Enforcement Act, the court may, in accordance with section 108 of such Act, direct that the carrier comply forthwith and may direct that a provider of support services to the carrier or the manufacturer of the carrier's transmission or switching equipment furnish forthwith modifications necessary for the carrier to comply.

(b) **Enforcement upon application by Attorney General**. The Attorney General may, in a civil action in the appropriate United States district court, obtain an order, in accordance with section 108 of the Communications Assistance for Law Enforcement Act, directing that a telecommunications carrier, a manufacturer of telecommunications transmission or switching equipment, or a provider of telecommunications support services comply with such Act.

(c) **Civil penalty**.

(1) *In general*. A court issuing an order under this section against a telecommunications carrier, a manufacturer of telecommunications transmission or switching equipment, or a provider of telecommunications support services may impose a civil penalty of up to $10,000 per day for each day in violation after the issuance of the order or after such future date as the court may specify.

(2) *Considerations*. In determining whether to impose a civil penalty and in determining its amount, the court shall take into account—

(A) the nature, circumstances, and extent of the violation;

(B) the violator's ability to pay, the violator's good faith efforts to comply in a timely manner, any effect on the violator's ability to continue to do business, the degree of culpability, and the length of any delay in undertaking efforts to comply; and

(C) such other matters as justice may require.

(d) **Definitions**. As used in this section, the terms defined in section 102 of the Communications Assistance for Law Enforcement Act have the meanings provided, respectively, in such section.

18 U.S.C. § 2701. Unlawful Access to Stored Communications

(a) **Offense**. Except as provided in subsection (c) of this section whoever—

(1) intentionally accesses without authorization a facility through which an electronic communication service is provided; or

(2) intentionally exceeds an authorization to access that facility; and thereby obtains, alters, or prevents authorized access to a wire or electronic communication while it is in electronic storage in such system shall be punished as provided in subsection (b) of this section.

(b) **Punishment**. The punishment for an offense under subsection (a) of this section is—

(1) if the offense is committed for purposes of commercial advantage, malicious destruction or damage, or private commercial gain, or in furtherance of any criminal or tortious act in violation of the Constitution or laws of the United States or any State—

(A) a fine under this title or imprisonment for not more than 5 years, or both, in the case of a first offense under this subparagraph; and

(B) a fine under this title or imprisonment for not more than 10 years, or both, for any subsequent offense under this subparagraph; and

(2) in any other case—

(A) a fine under this title or imprisonment for not more than 1 year or both, in the case of a first offense under this paragraph; and

(B) a fine under this title or imprisonment for not more than 5 years, or both, in the case of an offense under this subparagraph that occurs after a conviction of another offense under this section.

(c) **Exceptions**. Subsection (a) of this section does not apply with respect to conduct authorized—

(1) by the person or entity providing a wire or electronic communications service;

(2) by a user of that service with respect to a communication of or intended for that user; or

(3) in section 2703, 2704 or 2518 of this title.

18 U.S.C. § 2702. VOLUNTARY DISCLOSURE OF CUSTOMER COMMUNICATIONS OR RECORDS

(a) **Prohibitions**. Except as provided in subsection (b) or (c)—

(1) a person or entity providing an electronic communication service to the public shall not knowingly divulge to any person or entity the contents of a communication while in electronic storage by that service; and

(2) a person or entity providing remote computing service to the public shall not knowingly divulge to any person or entity the contents of any communication which is carried or maintained on that service—

(A) on behalf of, and received by means of electronic transmission from (or created by means of computer processing of communications received by means of electronic transmission from), a subscriber or customer of such service;

(B) solely for the purpose of providing storage or computer processing services to such subscriber or customer, if the provider is not authorized to access the contents of any such communications for purposes of providing any services other than storage or computer processing; and

(3) a provider of remote computing service or electronic communication service to the public shall not knowingly divulge a record or other information pertaining to a subscriber to or customer of such service (not including the contents of communications covered by paragraph (1) or (2)) to any governmental entity.

(b) **Exceptions for disclosure of communications**. A provider described in subsection (a) may divulge the contents of a communication—

(1) to an addressee or intended recipient of such communication or an agent of such addressee or intended recipient;

(2) as otherwise authorized in section 2517, 2511(2)(a), or 2703 of this title;

(3) with the lawful consent of the originator or an addressee or intended recipient of such communication, or the subscriber in the case of remote computing service;

(4) to a person employed or authorized or whose facilities are used to forward such communication to its destination;

(5) as may be necessarily incident to the rendition of the service or to the protection of the rights or property of the provider of that service;

(6) to the National Center for Missing and Exploited Children, in connection with a report submitted thereto under section 227 of the Victims of Child Abuse Act of 1990 (42 U.S.C. 13032);

(7) to a law enforcement agency—

(A) if the contents—

(i) were inadvertently obtained by the service provider; and

(ii) appear to pertain to the commission of a crime; or

(B) [Deleted]

(8) to a governmental entity, if the provider, in good faith, believes that an emergency involving danger of death or serious physical injury to any person requires disclosure without delay of communications relating to the emergency.

(c) **Exceptions for disclosure of customer records**. A provider described in subsection (a) may divulge a record or other information pertaining to a subscriber to or customer of such service (not including the contents of communications covered by subsection (a)(1) or (a)(2))—

(1) as otherwise authorized in section 2703;

(2) with the lawful consent of the customer or subscriber;

(3) as may be necessarily incident to the rendition of the service or to the protection of the rights or property of the provider of that service;

(4) to a governmental entity, if the provider, in good faith, believes that an emergency involving danger of death or serious physical injury to any person requires disclosure without delay of information relating to the emergency;

(5) to the National Center for Missing and Exploited Children, in connection with a report submitted thereto under section 227 of the Victims of Child Abuse Act of 1990 (42 U.S.C. 13032); or

(6) to any person other than a governmental entity.

(d) **Reporting of Emergency Disclosures.**—On an annual basis, the Attorney General shall submit to the Committee on the Judiciary of the House of Representatives and the Committee on the Judiciary of the Senate a report containing—

(1) the number of accounts from which the Department of Justice has received voluntary disclosures under subsection (b)(8); and

(2) a summary of the basis for disclosure in those instances where—

(A) voluntary disclosures under subsection (b)(8) were made to the Department of Justice; and

(B) the investigation pertaining to those disclosures was closed without the filing of criminal charges.

18 U.S.C. § 2703. REQUIRED DISCLOSURE OF CUSTOMER COMMUNICATIONS OR RECORDS

(a) **Contents of wire or electronic communications in electronic storage.** A governmental entity may require the disclosure by a provider of electronic communication service of the contents of a wire or electronic communication, that is in electronic storage in an electronic communications system for one hundred and eighty days or less, only pursuant to a warrant issued using the procedures described in the Federal Rules of Criminal Procedure by a court with jurisdiction over the offense under investigation or equivalent State warrant. A governmental entity may require the disclosure by a provider of electronic communications services of the contents of a wire or electronic communication that has been in electronic storage in an electronic communications system for more than one hundred and eighty days by the means available under subsection (b) of this section.

(b) **Contents of wire or electronic communications in a remote computing service.**

(1) A governmental entity may require a provider of remote computing service to disclose the contents of any wire or electronic communication to which this paragraph is made applicable by paragraph (2) of this subsection—

(A) without required notice to the subscriber or customer, if the governmental entity obtains a warrant issued using the procedures described in the Federal Rules of Criminal Procedure by a court with jurisdiction over the offense under investigation or equivalent State warrant; or

(B) with prior notice from the governmental entity to the subscriber or customer if the governmental entity—

(i) uses an administrative subpoena authorized by a Federal or State statute or a Federal or State grand jury or trial subpoena; or

(ii) obtains a court order for such disclosure under subsection (d) of this section; except that delayed notice may be given pursuant to section 2705 of this title.

(2) Paragraph (1) is applicable with respect to any wire or electronic communication that is held or maintained on that service—

(A) on behalf of, and received by means of electronic transmission from (or created by means of computer processing of communications received by means of electronic transmission from), a subscriber or customer of such remote computing service; and

(B) solely for the purpose of providing storage or computer processing services to such subscriber or customer, if the provider is not authorized to access the contents of any such communications for purposes of providing any services other than storage or computer processing.

(c) **Records concerning electronic communication service or remote computing service**.

(1) A governmental entity may require a provider of electronic communication service or remote computing service to disclose a record or other information pertaining to a subscriber to or customer of such service (not including the contents of communications) only when the governmental entity—

(A) obtains a warrant issued using the procedures described in the Federal Rules of Criminal Procedure by a court with jurisdiction over the offense under investigation or equivalent State warrant;

(B) obtains a court order for such disclosure under subsection (d) of this section;

(C) has the consent of the subscriber or customer to such disclosure;

(D) submits a formal written request relevant to a law enforcement investigation concerning telemarketing fraud for the name, address, and place of business of a subscriber or customer of such provider, which subscriber or customer is engaged in telemarketing (as such term is defined in section 2325 of this title); or

(E) seeks information under paragraph (2).

(2) A provider of electronic communication service or remote computing service shall disclose to a governmental entity the—

(A) name;

(B) address;

(C) local and long distance telephone connection records, or records of session times and durations;

(D) length of service (including start date) and types of service utilized;

(E) telephone or instrument number or other subscriber number or identity, including any temporarily assigned network address; and

(F) means and source of payment for such service (including any credit card or bank account number),

of a subscriber to or customer of such service when the governmental entity uses an administrative subpoena authorized by a Federal or State statute or a Federal or State grand jury or trial subpoena or any means available under paragraph (1).

(3) A governmental entity receiving records or information under this subsection is not required to provide notice to a subscriber or customer.

(d) **Requirements for court order**. A court order for disclosure under subsection (b) or (c) may be issued by any court that is a court of competent jurisdiction and shall issue only if the governmental entity offers specific and articulable facts showing that there are reasonable grounds to believe that the contents of a wire or electronic communication, or the records or other information sought, are relevant and material to an ongoing criminal investigation. In the case of a State governmental authority, such a court order shall not issue if prohibited by the law of such State. A court issuing an order pursuant to this section, on a motion made promptly by the service provider, may quash or modify such order, if the information or records requested are unusually voluminous in nature or compliance with such order otherwise would cause an undue burden on such provider.

(e) **No cause of action against a provider disclosing information under this chapter**. No cause of action shall lie in any court against any provider of wire or electronic communication service, its officers, employees, agents, or other specified persons for providing information, facilities, or assistance in accordance with the terms of a court order, warrant, subpoena, statutory authorization, or certification under this chapter.

(f) **Requirement to preserve evidence**.

(1) *In general*. A provider of wire or electronic communication services or a remote computing service, upon the request of a governmental entity, shall take all necessary steps to preserve records and other evidence in its possession pending the issuance of a court order or other process.

(2) Period of retention. Records referred to in paragraph (1) shall be retained for a period of 90 days, which shall be extended for an additional 90–day period upon a renewed request by the governmental entity.

(g) **Presence of officer not required**. Notwithstanding section 3105 of this title, the presence of an officer shall not be required for service or execution of a search warrant issued in accordance with this chapter requiring disclosure by a provider of electronic communications service or remote computing service of the contents of communications or records or other information pertaining to a subscriber to or customer of such service.

SECTION 2704. BACKUP PRESERVATION

(a) **Backup preservation**.

(1) A governmental entity acting under section 2703(b)(2) may include in its subpoena or court order a requirement that the service provider to whom the request is directed create a backup copy of the contents of the electronic communications sought in order to preserve those communications. Without notifying the subscriber or customer of such subpoena or court order, such service provider shall create such backup copy as soon as practicable consistent with its regular business practices and shall confirm to the governmental entity that such backup copy has been made. Such backup copy shall be created within two business days after receipt by the service provider of the subpoena or court order.

(2) Notice to the subscriber or customer shall be made by the governmental entity within three days after receipt of such confirmation, unless such notice is delayed pursuant to section 2705(a).

(3) The service provider shall not destroy such backup copy until the later of—

(A) the delivery of the information; or

(B) the resolution of any proceedings (including appeals of any proceeding) concerning the government's subpoena or court order.

(4) The service provider shall release such backup copy to the requesting governmental entity no sooner than fourteen days after the governmental entity's notice to the subscriber or customer if such service provider—

(A) has not received notice from the subscriber or customer that the subscriber or customer has challenged the governmental entity's request; and

(B) has not initiated proceedings to challenge the request of the governmental entity.

(5) A governmental entity may seek to require the creation of a backup copy under subsection (a)(1) of this section if in its sole discretion such entity determines that there is reason to believe that notification under section 2703 of this title of the existence of the subpoena or court order may result in destruction of or tampering with evidence. This determination is not subject to challenge by the subscriber or customer or service provider.

(b) **Customer challenges**.

(1) Within fourteen days after notice by the governmental entity to the subscriber or customer under subsection (a)(2) of this section, such subscriber or customer may file a motion to quash such subpoena or vacate such court order, with copies served upon the governmental entity and with written notice of such challenge to the service provider. A motion to vacate a court order shall be filed in the court which issued such order. A motion to quash a subpoena shall be filed in the appropriate United States district court or State court. Such motion or application shall contain an affidavit or sworn statement—

(A) stating that the applicant is a customer or subscriber to the service from which the contents of electronic communications maintained for him have been sought; and

(B) stating the applicant's reasons for believing that the records sought are not relevant to a legitimate law enforcement inquiry or that there has not been substantial compliance with the provisions of this chapter in some other respect.

(2) Service shall be made under this section upon a governmental entity by delivering or mailing by registered or certified mail a copy of the papers to the person, office, or department specified in the notice which the customer has received pursuant to this chapter. For the purposes of this section, the term "delivery" has the meaning given that term in the Federal Rules of Civil Procedure.

(3) If the court finds that the customer has complied with paragraphs (1) and (2) of this subsection, the court shall order the governmental entity to file a sworn response, which may be filed in camera if the governmental entity includes in its response the reasons which make in camera review appropriate. If the court is unable to determine the motion or application on the basis of the parties' initial allegations and response, the court may conduct such additional proceedings as it deems appropriate. All such proceedings shall be completed and the motion or application decided as soon as practicable after the filing of the governmental entity's response.

(4) If the court finds that the applicant is not the subscriber or customer for whom the communications sought by the governmental entity are maintained, or that there is a reason to believe that the law enforcement inquiry is legitimate and that the communications sought are relevant to that inquiry, it shall deny the motion or application and order such process enforced. If the court finds that the applicant is the subscriber or customer for whom the communications sought by the governmental entity are maintained, and that there is not a reason to believe that the communications sought are relevant to a legitimate law enforcement inquiry, or that there has not been substantial compliance with the provisions of this chapter, it shall order the process quashed.

(5) A court order denying a motion or application under this section shall not be deemed a final order and no interlocutory appeal may be taken therefrom by the customer.

18 U.S.C. § 2705. DELAYED NOTICE

(a) **Delay of notification**.

(1) A governmental entity acting under section 2703(b) of this title may—

(A) where a court order is sought, include in the application a request, which the court shall grant, for an order delaying the notification required under section 2703(b) of this title for a period not to exceed ninety days, if the court determines that there is reason to believe that notification of the existence of the court order may have an adverse result described in paragraph (2) of this subsection; or

(B) where an administrative subpoena authorized by a Federal or State statute or a Federal or State grand jury subpoena is obtained, delay the notification required under section 2703(b) of this title for a period not to exceed ninety days upon the execution of a written certification of a supervisory official that there is reason to believe that notification of the existence of the subpoena may have an adverse result described in paragraph (2) of this subsection.

(2) An adverse result for the purposes of paragraph (1) of this subsection is—

(A) endangering the life or physical safety of an individual;

(B) flight from prosecution;

(C) destruction of or tampering with evidence;

(D) intimidation of potential witnesses; or

(E) otherwise seriously jeopardizing an investigation or unduly delaying a trial.

(3) The governmental entity shall maintain a true copy of certification under paragraph (1)(B).

(4) Extensions of the delay of notification provided in section 2703 of up to ninety days each may be granted by the court upon application, or by certification by a governmental entity, but only in accordance with subsection (b) of this section.

(5) Upon expiration of the period of delay of notification under paragraph (1) or (4) of this subsection, the governmental entity shall serve upon, or deliver by registered or first-class mail to, the customer or subscriber a copy of the process or request together with notice that—

(A) states with reasonable specificity the nature of the law enforcement inquiry; and

(B) informs such customer or subscriber—

(i) that information maintained for such customer or subscriber by the service provider named in such process or request was supplied to or requested by that governmental authority and the date on which the supplying or request took place;

(ii) that notification of such customer or subscriber was delayed;

(iii) what governmental entity or court made the certification or determination pursuant to which that delay was made; and

(iv) which provision of this chapter allowed such delay.

(6) As used in this subsection, the term "supervisory official" means the investigative agent in charge or assistant investigative agent in charge or an equivalent of an investigating agency's headquarters or regional office, or the chief prosecuting attorney or the first assistant prosecuting attorney or an equivalent of a prosecuting attorney's headquarters or regional office.

(b) **Preclusion of notice to subject of governmental access**. A governmental entity acting under section 2703, when it is not required to notify the subscriber or customer under section 2703(b)(1), or to the extent that it may delay such notice pursuant to subsection (a) of this section, may apply to a court for an order commanding a provider of electronic communications service or remote computing service to whom a warrant, subpoena, or court order is directed, for such period as the court deems appropriate, not to notify any other person of the existence of the warrant, subpoena, or court order. The court shall enter such an order if it determines that there is reason to believe that notification of the existence of the warrant, subpoena, or court order will result in—

(1) endangering the life or physical safety of an individual;

(2) flight from prosecution;

(3) destruction of or tampering with evidence;

(4) intimidation of potential witnesses; or

(5) otherwise seriously jeopardizing an investigation or unduly delaying a trial.

18 U.S.C. § 2706. Cost Reimbursement

(a) **Payment**. Except as otherwise provided in subsection (c), a governmental entity obtaining the contents of communications, records, or other information under section 2702, 2703, or 2704 of this title shall pay to the person or entity assembling or providing such information a fee for reimbursement for such costs as are reasonably necessary and which have been directly incurred in searching for, assembling, reproducing, or otherwise providing such information. Such reimbursable costs shall include any costs due to necessary disruption of normal operations of any electronic communication service or remote computing service in which such information may be stored.

(b) **Amount**. The amount of the fee provided by subsection (a) shall be as mutually agreed by the governmental entity and the person or entity providing the information, or, in the absence of agreement, shall be as determined by the court which issued the order for production of such information (or the court before which a criminal prosecution relating to such information would be brought, if no court order was issued for production of the information).

(c) **Exception**. The requirement of subsection (a) of this section does not apply with respect to records or other information maintained by a communications common carrier that relate to telephone toll records and telephone listings obtained under section 2703 of this title. The court may, however, order a payment as described in subsection (a) if the court determines the information required is unusually voluminous in nature or otherwise caused an undue burden on the provider.

18 U.S.C. § 2707. CIVIL ACTION

(a) **Cause of action**. Except as provided in section 2703(e), any provider of electronic communication service, subscriber, or other person aggrieved by any violation of this chapter in which the conduct constituting the violation is engaged in with a knowing or intentional state of mind may, in a civil action, recover from the person or entity, other than the United States, which engaged in that violation such relief as may be appropriate.

(b) **Relief**. In a civil action under this section, appropriate relief includes—

(1) such preliminary and other equitable or declaratory relief as may be appropriate;

(2) damages under subsection (c); and

(3) a reasonable attorney's fee and other litigation costs reasonably incurred.

(c) **Damages**. The court may assess as damages in a civil action under this section the sum of the actual damages suffered by the plaintiff and any profits made by the violator as a result of the violation, but in no case shall a person entitled to recover receive less than the sum of $1,000. If the violation is willful or intentional, the court may assess punitive damages. In the case of a successful action to enforce liability under this section, the court may assess the costs of the action, together with reasonable attorney fees determined by the court.

(d) **Administrative discipline**. If a court or appropriate department or agency determines that the United States or any of its departments or agencies has violated any provision of this chapter, and the court or appropriate department or agency finds that the circumstances surrounding the violation raise serious questions about whether or not an officer or employee of the United States acted willfully or intentionally with respect to the violation, the department or agency shall, upon receipt of a true and correct copy of the decision and findings of the court or appropriate department or agency promptly initiate a proceeding to determine whether disciplinary action against the officer or employee is warranted. If the head of the department or agency involved determines that disciplinary action is not warranted, he or she shall notify the Inspector General with jurisdiction over the department or agency concerned and shall provide the Inspector General with the reasons for such determination.

(e) **Defense**. A good faith reliance on—

(1) a court warrant or order, a grand jury subpoena, a legislative authorization, or a statutory authorization (including a request of a governmental entity under section 2703(f) of this title;

(2) a request of an investigative or law enforcement officer under section 2518(7) of this title; or

(3) a good faith determination that section 2511(3) of this title permitted the conduct complained of; is a complete defense to any civil or criminal action brought under this chapter or any other law.

(f) **Limitation**. A civil action under this section may not be commenced later than two years after the date upon which the claimant first discovered or had a reasonable opportunity to discover the violation.

(g) **Improper disclosure**. Any willful disclosure of a "record", as that term is defined in section 552a(a) of title 5, United States Code, obtained by an investigative or law enforcement officer, or a governmental entity, pursuant to section 2703 of this title, or from a device installed pursuant to section 3123 or 3125 of this title, that is not a disclosure made in the proper performance of the official functions of the officer or governmental entity making the disclosure, is a violation of this chapter. This provision shall not apply to information previously lawfully disclosed (prior to the commencement of any civil or administrative proceeding under this chapter) to the public by a Federal, State, or local governmental entity or by the plaintiff in a civil action under this chapter.

18 U.S.C. § 2708. Exclusivity of Remedies

The remedies and sanctions described in this chapter are the only judicial remedies and sanctions for nonconstitutional violations of this chapter.

18 U.S.C. § 2711. Definitions for Chapter

As used in this chapter—

(1) the terms defined in section 2510 of this title have, respectively, the definitions given such terms in that section;

(2) the term "remote computing service" means the provision to the public of computer storage or processing services by means of an electronic communications system;

(3) the term "court of competent jurisdiction" has the meaning assigned by section 3127, and includes any Federal court within that definition, without geographic limitation; and

(4) the term "governmental entity" means a department or agency of the United States or any State or political subdivision thereof.

18 U.S.C. § 3121. GENERAL PROHIBITION ON PEN REGISTER AND TRAP AND TRACE DEVICE USE; EXCEPTION

(a) **In general**. Except as provided in this section, no person may install or use a pen register or a trap and trace device without first obtaining a court order under section 3123 of this title or under the Foreign Intelligence Surveillance Act of 1978 (50 U.S.C. 1801 et seq.).

(b) **Exception**. The prohibition of subsection (a) does not apply with respect to the use of a pen register or a trap and trace device by a provider of electronic or wire communication service—

(1) relating to the operation, maintenance, and testing of a wire or electronic communication service or to the protection of the rights or property of such provider, or to the protection of users of that service from abuse of service or unlawful use of service; or

(2) to record the fact that a wire or electronic communication was initiated or completed in order to protect such provider, another provider furnishing service toward the completion of the wire communication, or a user of that service, from fraudulent, unlawful or abusive use of service; or

(3) where the consent of the user of that service has been obtained.

(c) **Limitation**. A government agency authorized to install and use a pen register or trap and trace device under this chapter or under State law shall use technology reasonably available to it that restricts the recording or decoding of electronic or other impulses to the dialing, routing, addressing, and signaling information utilized in the processing and transmitting of wire or electronic communications so as not to include the contents of any wire or electronic communications.

(d) **Penalty**. Whoever knowingly violates subsection (a) shall be fined under this title or imprisoned not more than one year, or both.

18 U.S.C. § 3122. APPLICATION FOR AN ORDER FOR A PEN REGISTER OR A TRAP AND TRACE DEVICE

(a) **Application**.

(1) An attorney for the Government may make application for an order or an extension of an order under section 3123 of this title authorizing or approving the installation and use of a pen register or a trap and trace device under this chapter, in writing under oath or equivalent affirmation, to a court of competent jurisdiction.

(2) Unless prohibited by State law, a State investigative or law enforcement officer may make application for an order or an extension of an order under section 3123 of this title authorizing or approving the installation and use of a pen register or a trap and trace device under this chapter, in writing under oath or equivalent affirmation, to a court of competent jurisdiction of such State.

(b) **Contents of application**. An application under subsection (a) of this section shall include—

(1) the identity of the attorney for the Government or the State law enforcement or investigative officer making the application and the identity of the law enforcement agency conducting the investigation; and

(2) a certification by the applicant that the information likely to be obtained is relevant to an ongoing criminal investigation being conducted by that agency.

SECTION 3123. ISSUANCE OF AN ORDER FOR A PEN REGISTER OR A TRAP AND TRACE DEVICE

(a) **In general**.

(1) *Attorney for the Government*. Upon an application made under section 3122(a)(1), the court shall enter an ex parte order authorizing the installation and use of a pen register or trap and trace device anywhere within the United States, if the court finds that the attorney for the Government has certified to the court that the information likely to be obtained by such installation and use is relevant to an ongoing criminal investigation. The order, upon service of that order, shall apply to any person or entity providing wire or electronic communication service in the United States whose assistance may facilitate the execution of the order. Whenever such an order is served on any person or entity not specifically named in the order, upon request of such person or entity, the attorney for the Government or law enforcement or investigative officer that is serving the order shall provide written or electronic certification that the order applies to the person or entity being served.

(2) *State investigative or law enforcement officer*. Upon an application made under section 3122(a)(2), the court shall enter an ex parte order authorizing the installation and use of a pen register or trap and trace device within the jurisdiction of the court, if the court finds that the State law enforcement or investigative officer has certified to the court that the information likely to be obtained by such installation and use is relevant to an ongoing criminal investigation.

(3) (A) Where the law enforcement agency implementing an ex parte order under this subsection seeks to do so by installing and using its own pen register or trap and trace device on a packet-switched data network of a provider of electronic com-

munication service to the public, the agency shall ensure that a record will be maintained which will identify—

(i) any officer or officers who installed the device and any officer or officers who accessed the device to obtain information from the network;

(ii) the date and time the device was installed, the date and time the device was uninstalled, and the date, time, and duration of each time the device is accessed to obtain information;

(iii) the configuration of the device at the time of its installation and any subsequent modification thereof; and

(iv) any information which has been collected by the device.

To the extent that the pen register or trap and trace device can be set automatically to record this information electronically, the record shall be maintained electronically throughout the installation and use of such device.

(B) The record maintained under subparagraph (A) shall be provided ex parte and under seal to the court which entered the ex parte order authorizing the installation and use of the device within 30 days after termination of the order (including any extensions thereof).

(b) **Contents of order.** An order issued under this section—

(1) shall specify—

(A) the identity, if known, of the person to whom is leased or in whose name is listed the telephone line or other facility to which the pen register or trap and trace device is to be attached or applied;

(B) the identity, if known, of the person who is the subject of the criminal investigation;

(C) the attributes of the communications to which the order applies, including the number or other identifier and, if known, the location of the telephone line or other facility to which the pen register or trap and trace device is to be attached or applied, and, in the case of an order authorizing installation and use of a trap and trace device under subsection (a)(2), the geographic limits of the order; and

(D) a statement of the offense to which the information likely to be obtained by the pen register or trap and trace device relates; and

(2) shall direct, upon the request of the applicant, the furnishing of information, facilities, and technical assistance necessary to accomplish the installation of the pen register or trap and trace device under section 3124 of this title.

(c) **Time period and extensions**.

(1) An order issued under this section shall authorize the installation and use of a pen register or a trap and trace device for a period not to exceed sixty days.

(2) Extensions of such an order may be granted, but only upon an application for an order under section 3122 of this title and upon the judicial finding required by subsection (a) of this section. The period of extension shall be for a period not to exceed sixty days.

(d) **Nondisclosure of existence of pen register or a trap and trace device**. An order authorizing or approving the installation and use of a pen register or a trap and trace device shall direct that

(1) the order be sealed until otherwise ordered by the court; and

(2) the person owning or leasing the line or other facility to which the pen register or a trap and trace device is attached, or applied, or who is obligated by the order to provide assistance to the applicant, not disclose the existence of the pen register or trap and trace device or the existence of the investigation to the listed subscriber, or to any other person, unless or until otherwise ordered by the court.

18 U.S.C. § 3124. Assistance in Installation and Use of a Pen Register or a Trap and Trace Device

(a) **Pen registers**. Upon the request of an attorney for the government or an officer of a law enforcement agency authorized to install and use a pen register under this chapter, a provider of wire or electronic communication service, landlord, custodian, or other person shall furnish such investigative or law enforcement officer forthwith all information, facilities, and technical assistance necessary to accomplish the installation of the pen register unobtrusively and with a minimum of interference with the services that the person so ordered by the court accords the party with respect to whom the installation and use is to take place, if such assistance is directed by a court order as provided in section 3123(b)(2) of this title.

(b) **Trap and trace device**. Upon the request of an attorney for the Government or an officer of a law enforcement agency authorized to receive the results of a trap and trace device under this chapter, a provider of a wire or electronic communication service, landlord, custodian, or other person shall install such device forthwith on the appropriate line or other facility and shall furnish such investigative or law enforcement officer all additional information, facilities and technical assistance including installation and operation of the device unobtrusively and with a minimum of interference with the services that the person so ordered by the court accords the party with respect to whom the installation and use is to take place, if such installation and assistance is directed by a court order as provided in section 3123(b)(2) of this title. Unless otherwise ordered by the court, the results of the trap and trace device shall be furnished, pursuant to section 3123(b) or section 3125 of this title, to the officer of a law enforcement agency, designated in the court order, at reasonable intervals during regular business hours for the duration of the order.

(c) **Compensation**. A provider of a wire or electronic communication service, landlord, custodian, or other person who furnishes facilities or technical assistance pursuant to this section shall be reasonably compensated for such reasonable expenses incurred in providing such facilities and assistance.

(d) **No cause of action against a provider disclosing information under this chapter**. No cause of action shall lie in any court against any provider of a wire or electronic communication service, its officers, employees, agents, or other specified persons for providing information, facilities, or assistance in accordance with a court order under this chapter or request pursuant to section 3125 of this title.

(e) **Defense**. A good faith reliance on a court order under this chapter, a request pursuant to section 3125 of this title, a legislative authorization, or a statutory authorization is a complete defense against any civil or criminal action brought under this chapter or any other law.

(f) **Communications assistance enforcement orders**. Pursuant to section 2522, an order may be issued to enforce the assistance capability and capacity requirements under the Communications Assistance for Law Enforcement Act.

SECTION 3125. EMERGENCY PEN REGISTER AND TRAP AND TRACE DEVICE INSTALLATION

(a) Notwithstanding any other provision of this chapter, any investigative or law enforcement officer, specially designated by the Attorney General, the Deputy Attorney General, the Associate Attorney General, any Assistant Attorney General, any acting Assistant Attorney General, or any Deputy Assistant Attorney General, or by the principal prosecuting attorney of any State or subdivision thereof acting pursuant to a statute of that State, who reasonably determines that—

(1) an emergency situation exists that involves—

(A) immediate danger of death or serious bodily injury to any person;

(B) conspiratorial activities characteristic of organized crime;

(C) an immediate threat to a national security interest; or

(D) an ongoing attack on a protected computer (as defined in section 1030 that constitutes a crime punishable by a term of imprisonment greater than one year;

that requires the installation and use of a pen register or a trap and trace device before an order authorizing such installation and use can, with due diligence, be obtained, and

(2) there are grounds upon which an order could be entered under this chapter to authorize such installation and use;

may have installed and use a pen register or trap and trace device if, within forty-eight hours after the installation has occurred, or begins to occur, an order approving the installation or use is issued in accordance with section 3123 of this title.

(b) In the absence of an authorizing order, such use shall immediately terminate when the information sought is obtained, when the application for the order is denied or when forty-eight hours have lapsed since the installation of the pen register or trap and trace device, whichever is earlier.

(c) The knowing installation or use by any investigative or law enforcement officer of a pen register or trap and trace device pursuant to subsection (a) without application for the authorizing order within forty-eight hours of the installation shall constitute a violation of this chapter.

(d) A provider of a wire or electronic service, landlord, custodian, or other person who furnished facilities or technical assistance pursuant to this section shall be reasonably compensated for such reasonable expenses incurred in providing such facilities and assistance.

18 U.S.C. § 3126. REPORTS CONCERNING PEN REGISTERS AND TRAP AND TRACE DEVICES

The Attorney General shall annually report to Congress on the number of pen register orders and orders for trap and trace devices applied for by law enforcement agencies of the Department of Justice, which report shall include information concerning—

(1) the period of interceptions authorized by the order, and the number and duration of any extensions of the order;

(2) the offense specified in the order or application, or extension of an order;

(3) the number of investigations involved;

(4) the number and nature of the facilities affected; and

(5) the identity, including district, of the applying investigative or law enforcement agency making the application and the person authorizing the order.

18 U.S.C. § 3127. DEFINITIONS FOR CHAPTER

As used in this chapter—

(1) the terms "wire communication", "electronic communication", "electronic communication service", and "contents" have the meanings set forth for such terms in section 2510 of this title;

(2) the term "court of competent jurisdiction" means—

(A) any district court of the United States (including a magistrate judge of such a court) or any United States court of appeals having jurisdiction over the offense being investigated; or

(B) a court of general criminal jurisdiction of a State authorized by the law of that State to enter orders authorizing the use of a pen register or a trap and trace device;

(3) the term "pen register" means a device or process which records or decodes dialing, routing, addressing, or signaling information transmitted by an instrument or facility from which a wire or electronic communication is transmitted, provided, however, that such information shall not include the contents of any communication, but such term does not include any device or process used by a provider or customer of a wire or electronic communication service for billing, or recording as an incident to billing, for communications services provided by such provider or any device or process used by a provider or customer of a wire communication service for cost accounting or other like purposes in the ordinary course of its business;

(4) the term "trap and trace device" means a device or process which captures the incoming electronic or other impulses which identify the originating number or other dialing, routing, addressing, and signaling information reasonably likely to identify the source of a wire or electronic communication, provided, however, that such information shall not include the contents of any communication;

(5) the term "attorney for the Government" has the meaning given such term for the purposes of the Federal Rules of Criminal Procedure; and

(6) the term "State" means a State, the District of Columbia, Puerto Rico, and any other possession or territory of the United States.

47 U.S.C. § 223. Obscene or Harassing Telephone Calls in the District of Columbia or in Interstate or Foreign Communications

(a) **Prohibited acts generally**. Whoever—

(1) in interstate or foreign communications—

(A) by means of a telecommunications device knowingly—

(i) makes, creates, or solicits, and

(ii) initiates the transmission of,

any comment, request, suggestion, proposal, image, or other communication which is obscene or child pornography, with intent to annoy, abuse, threaten, or harass another person;

(B) by means of a telecommunications device knowingly—

(i) makes, creates, or solicits, and

(ii) initiates the transmission of,

any comment, request, suggestion, proposal, image, or other communication which is obscene or child pornography, knowing that the recipient of the communication is under 18 years of age, regardless of whether the maker of such communication placed the call or initiated the communication;

(C) makes a telephone call or utilizes a telecommunications device, whether or not conversation or communication ensues, without disclosing his identity and with intent to annoy, abuse, threaten, or harass any person at the called number or who receives the communications;

(D) makes or causes the telephone of another repeatedly or continuously to ring, with intent to harass any person at the called number; or

(E) makes repeated telephone calls or repeatedly initiates communication with a telecommunications device, during which conversation or communication ensues, solely to harass any person at the called number or who receives the communication; or

(2) knowingly permits any telecommunications facility under his control to be used for any activity prohibited by paragraph (1) with the intent that it be used for such activity,

shall be fined under title 18, United States Code, or imprisoned not more than two years, or both.

(b) **Prohibited acts for commercial purposes; defense to prosecution**.

(1) Whoever knowingly—

(A) within the United States, by means of telephone, makes (directly or by recording device) any obscene communication for commercial purposes to any person, regardless of whether the maker of such communication placed the call; or

(B) permits any telephone facility under such person's control to be used for an activity prohibited by subparagraph (A), shall be fined in accordance with title 18, United States Code, or imprisoned not more than two years, or both.

(2) Whoever knowingly—

(A) within the United States, by means of telephone, makes (directly or by recording device) any indecent communication for commercial purposes which is available to any person under 18 years of age or to any other person without that person's consent, regardless of whether the maker of such communication placed the call; or

(B) permits any telephone facility under such person's control to be used for an activity prohibited by subparagraph (A), shall be fined not more than $50,000 or imprisoned not more than six months, or both.

(3) It is a defense to prosecution under paragraph (2) of this subsection that the defendant restricted access to the prohibited communication to persons 18 years of age or older in accordance with subsection (c) of this section and with such procedures as the Commission may prescribe by regulation.

(4) In addition to the penalties under paragraph (1), whoever, within the United States, intentionally violates paragraph (1) or (2) shall be subject to a fine of not more than $50,000 for each violation. For purposes of this paragraph, each day of violation shall constitute a separate violation.

(5) (A) In addition to the penalties under paragraphs (1), (2), and (5), whoever, within the United States, violates paragraph (1) or (2) shall be subject to a civil fine of not more than $50,000 for each violation. For purposes of this paragraph, each day of violation shall constitute a separate violation.

(B) A fine under this paragraph may be assessed either—

(i) by a court, pursuant to civil action by the Commission or any attorney employed by the Commission who is designated by the Commission for such purposes, or

(ii) by the Commission after appropriate administrative proceedings.

(6) The Attorney General may bring a suit in the appropriate district court of the United States to enjoin any act or practice which violates paragraph (1) or (2). An injunction may be granted in accordance with the Federal Rules of Civil Procedure.

(c) **Restriction on access to subscribers by common carriers; judicial remedies respecting restrictions**.

(1) A common carrier within the District of Columbia or within any State, or in interstate or foreign commerce, shall not, to the extent technically feasible, provide access to a communication specified in subsection (b) from the telephone of any subscriber who has not previously requested in writing the carrier to provide access to such communication if the carrier collects from subscribers an identifiable charge for such communication that the carrier remits, in whole or in part, to the provider of such communication.

(2) Except as provided in paragraph (3), no cause of action may be brought in any court or administrative agency against any common carrier, or any of its affiliates, including their officers, directors, employees, agents, or authorized representatives on account of—

(A) any action which the carrier demonstrates was taken in good faith to restrict access pursuant to paragraph (1) of this subsection; or

(B) any access permitted—

(i) in good faith reliance upon the lack of any representation by a provider of communications that communications provided by that provider are communications specified in subsection (b), or

(ii) because a specific representation by the provider did not allow the carrier, acting in good faith, a sufficient period to restrict access to communications described in subsection (b).

(3) Notwithstanding paragraph (2) of this subsection, a provider of communications services to which subscribers are denied access pursuant to paragraph (1) of this subsection may bring an action for a declaratory judgment or similar action in a court. Any such action shall be limited to the question of whether the communications which the provider seeks to provide fall within the category of communications to which the carrier will provide access only to subscribers who have previously requested such access.

(d) **Sending or displaying offensive material to persons under 18**. Whoever—

(1) in interstate or foreign communications knowingly—

(A) uses an interactive computer service to send to a specific person or persons under 18 years of age, or

(B) uses any interactive computer service to display in a manner available to a person under 18 years of age,

any comment, request, suggestion, proposal, image, or other communication that is obscene or child pornography, regardless of whether the user of such service placed the call or initiated the communication; or

(2) knowingly permits any telecommunications facility under such person's control to be used for an activity prohibited by paragraph (1) with the intent that it be used for such activity,

shall be fined under title 18, United States Code, or imprisoned not more than two years, or both.

(e) **Defenses**. In addition to any other defenses available by law:

(1) No person shall be held to have violated subsection (a) or (d) solely for providing access or connection to or from a facility, system, or network not under that person's control, including transmission, downloading, intermediate storage, access software, or other related capabilities that are incidental to providing such access or connection that does not include the creation of the content of the communication.

(2) The defenses provided by paragraph (1) of this subsection shall not be applicable to a person who is a conspirator with an entity actively involved in the creation or knowing distribution of communications that violate this section, or who knowingly advertises the availability of such communications.

(3) The defenses provided in paragraph (1) of this subsection shall not be applicable to a person who provides access or connection to a facility, system, or network engaged in the violation of this section that is owned or controlled by such person.

(4) No employer shall be held liable under this section for the actions of an employee or agent unless the employee's or agent's conduct is within the scope of his or her employment or agency and the employer (A) having knowledge of such conduct, authorizes or ratifies such conduct, or (B) recklessly disregards such conduct.

(5) It is a defense to a prosecution under subsection (a)(1)(B) or (d), or under subsection (a)(2) with respect to the use of a facility for an activity under subsection (a)(1)(B) that a person—

(A) has taken, in good faith, reasonable, effective, and appropriate actions under the circumstances to restrict or prevent access by minors to a communication specified in such subsections, which may involve any appropriate measures to restrict minors from such communications, including any method which is feasible under available technology; or

(B) has restricted access to such communication by requiring use of a verified credit card, debit account, adult access code, or adult personal identification number.

(6) The Commission may describe measures which are reasonable, effective, and appropriate to restrict access to prohibited communications under subsection (d). Nothing in this section authorizes the Commission to enforce, or is intended to provide the Commission with the authority to approve, sanction, or permit, the use of such measures. The Commission shall have no enforcement authority over the failure to utilize such measures. The Commission shall not endorse specific products relating to such measures. The use of such measures shall be admitted as evidence of good faith efforts for purposes of paragraph (5) in any action arising under subsection (d). Nothing in this section shall be construed to treat interactive computer services as common carriers or telecommunications carriers.

(f) **Violations of law required; commercial entities, nonprofit libraries, or institutions of higher education**.

(1) No cause of action may be brought in any court or administrative agency against any person on account of any activity that is not in violation of any law punishable by criminal or civil penalty, and that the person has taken in good faith to implement a defense authorized under this section or otherwise to restrict or prevent the transmission of, or access to, a communication specified in this section.

(2) No State or local government may impose any liability for commercial activities or actions by commercial entities, nonprofit libraries, or institutions of higher education in connection with an

activity or action described in subsection (a)(2) or (d) that is inconsistent with the treatment of those activities or actions under this section: *Provided, however,* That nothing herein shall preclude any State or local government from enacting and enforcing complementary oversight, liability, and regulatory systems, procedures, and requirements, so long as such systems, procedures, and requirements govern only intrastate services and do not result in the imposition of inconsistent rights, duties or obligations on the provision of interstate services. Nothing in this subsection shall preclude any State or local government from governing conduct not covered by this section.

(g) **Application and enforcement of other Federal law**. Nothing in subsection (a), (d), (e), or (f) or in the defenses to prosecution under subsection (a) or (d) shall be construed to affect or limit the application or enforcement of any other Federal law.

(h) **Definitions**. For purposes of this section

(1) The use of the term "telecommunications device" in this section—

(A) shall not impose new obligations on broadcasting station licensees and cable operators covered by obscenity and indecency provisions elsewhere in this Act;

(B) does not include an interactive computer service; and

(C) in the case of subparagraph (C) of subsection (a)(1), includes any device or software that can be used to originate telecommunications or other types of communications that are transmitted, in whole or in part, by the Internet (as such term is defined in section 1104 of the Internet Tax Freedom Act (47 U.S.C. § 151 note)).

(2) The term "interactive computer service" has the meaning provided in section 230(f)(2).

(3) The term "access software" means software (including client or server software) or enabling tools that do not create or provide the content of the communication but that allow a user to do any one or more of the following:

(A) filter, screen, allow, or disallow content;

(B) pick, choose, analyze, or digest content; or

(C) transmit, receive, display, forward, cache, search, subset, organize, reorganize, or translate content.

(4) The term "institution of higher education" has the meaning provided in section 101 of the Higher Education Act of 1965.

(5) The term "library" means a library eligible for participation in State-based plans for funds under title III of the Library Services and Construction Act (20 U.S.C. § 335e et seq.).

FEDERAL RULE OF CRIMINAL PROCEDURE 41

SEARCH AND SEIZURE

(a) **Scope and Definitions**.

(1) *Scope.* This rule does not modify any statute regulating search or seizure, or the issuance and execution of a search warrant in special circumstances.

(2) *Definitions.* The following definitions apply under this rule:

(A) "Property" includes documents, books, papers, any other tangible objects, and information.

(B) "Daytime" means the hours between 6:00 a.m. and 10:00 p.m. according to local time.

(C) "Federal law enforcement officer" means a government agent (other than an attorney for the government) who is engaged in enforcing the criminal laws and is within any category of officers authorized by the Attorney General to request a search warrant.

(b) **Authority to Issue a Warrant**. At the request of a federal law enforcement officer or an attorney for the government:

(1) a magistrate judge with authority in the district—or if none is reasonably available, a judge of a state court of record in the district—has authority to issue a warrant to search for and seize a person or property located within the district;

(2) a magistrate judge with authority in the district has authority to issue a warrant for a person or property outside the district if the person or property is located within the district when the warrant is issued but might move or be moved outside the district before the warrant is executed; and

(3) a magistrate judge—in an investigation of domestic terrorism or international terrorism (as defined in 18 U.S.C. § 2331)—having authority in any district in which activities related to the terrorism may have occurred, may issue a warrant for a person or property within or outside that district.

(c) **Persons or Property Subject to Search or Seizure**. A warrant may be issued for any of the following:

(1) evidence of a crime;

(2) contraband, fruits of crime, or other items illegally possessed;

(3) property designed for use, intended for use, or used in committing a crime; or

(4) a person to be arrested or a person who is unlawfully restrained.

(d) **Obtaining a Warrant**.

(1) *Probable Cause.* After receiving an affidavit or other information, a magistrate judge or a judge of a state court of record must issue the warrant if there is probable cause to search for and seize a person or property under Rule 41(c).

(2) *Requesting a Warrant in the Presence of a Judge.*

(A) *Warrant on an Affidavit.* When a federal law enforcement officer or an attorney for the government presents an affidavit in support of a warrant, the judge may require the affiant to appear personally and may examine under oath the affiant and any witness the affiant produces.

(B) *Warrant on Sworn Testimony.* The judge may wholly or partially dispense with a written affidavit and base a warrant on sworn testimony if doing so is reasonable under the circumstances.

(C) *Recording Testimony.* Testimony taken in support of a warrant must be recorded by a court reporter or by a suitable recording device, and the judge must file the transcript or recording with the clerk, along with any affidavit.

(3) *Requesting a Warrant by Telephonic or Other Means.*

(A) *In General.* A magistrate judge may issue a warrant based on information communicated by telephone or other appropriate means, including facsimile transmission.

(B) *Recording Testimony.* Upon learning that an applicant is requesting a warrant, a magistrate judge must:

(i) place under oath the applicant and any person on whose testimony the application is based; and

(ii) make a verbatim record of the conversation with a suitable recording device, if available, or by a court reporter, or in writing.

(C) *Certifying Testimony.* The magistrate judge must have any recording or court reporter's notes transcribed, certify the transcription's accuracy, and file a copy of the record and the transcription with the clerk. Any written verbatim record must be signed by the magistrate judge and filed with the clerk.

(D) *Suppression Limited.* Absent a finding of bad faith, evidence obtained from a warrant issued under Rule 41(d)(3)(A) is not subject to suppression on the ground that issuing the warrant in that manner was unreasonable under the circumstances.

(e) **Issuing the Warrant**.

(1) *In General.* The magistrate judge or a judge of a state court of record must issue the warrant to an officer authorized to execute it.

(2) *Contents of the Warrant.* The warrant must identify the person or property to be searched, identify any person or property to be seized, and designate the magistrate judge to whom it must be returned. The warrant must command the officer to:

    (A) execute the warrant within a specified time no longer than 10 days;

    (B) execute the warrant during the daytime, unless the judge for good cause expressly authorizes execution at another time; and

    (C) return the warrant to the magistrate judge designated in the warrant.

(3) *Warrant by Telephonic or Other Means.* If a magistrate judge decides to proceed under Rule 41(d)(3)(A), the following additional procedures apply:

    (A) *Preparing a Proposed Duplicate Original Warrant.* The applicant must prepare a "proposed duplicate original warrant" and must read or otherwise transmit the contents of that document verbatim to the magistrate judge.

    (B) *Preparing an Original Warrant.* The magistrate judge must enter the contents of the proposed duplicate original warrant into an original warrant.

    (C) *Modifications.* The magistrate judge may direct the applicant to modify the proposed duplicate original warrant. In that case, the judge must also modify the original warrant.

    (D) *Signing the Original Warrant and the Duplicate Original Warrant.* Upon determining to issue the warrant, the magistrate judge must immediately sign the original warrant, enter on its face the exact time it is issued, and direct the applicant to sign the judge's name on the duplicate original warrant.

(f) **Executing and Returning the Warrant**.

(1) *Noting the Time.* The officer executing the warrant must enter on its face the exact date and time it is executed.

(2) *Inventory.* An officer present during the execution of the warrant must prepare and verify an inventory of any property seized. The officer must do so in the presence of another officer and the person from whom, or from whose premises, the property was taken. If either one is not present, the officer must prepare and verify the inventory in the presence of at least one other credible person.

(3) *Receipt.* The officer executing the warrant must:

    (A) give a copy of the warrant and a receipt for the property taken to the person from whom, or from whose premises, the property was taken; or

(B) leave a copy of the warrant and receipt at the place where the officer took the property.

(4) *Return.* The officer executing the warrant must promptly return it together with a copy of the inventory to the magistrate judge designated on the warrant. The judge must, on request, give a copy of the inventory to the person from whom, or from whose premises, the property was taken and to the applicant for the warrant.

(g) **Motion to Return Property**. A person aggrieved by an unlawful search and seizure of property or by the deprivation of property may move for the property's return. The motion must be filed in the district where the property was seized. The court must receive evidence on any factual issue necessary to decide the motion. If it grants the motion, the court must return the property to the movant, but may impose reasonable conditions to protect access to the property and its use in later proceedings.

(h) **Motion to Suppress**. A defendant may move to suppress evidence in the court where the trial will occur, as Rule 12 provides.

(i) **Forwarding Papers to the Clerk**. The magistrate judge to whom the warrant is returned must attach to the warrant a copy of the return, of the inventory, and of all other related papers and must deliver them to the clerk in the district where the property was seized.

*

Index

References are to Pages

753

†